Lincoln Christian College

9789027918697

LANGUAGE IN RELATION TO A UNIFIED THEORY
OF THE STRUCTURE OF HUMAN BEHAVIOR

JANUA LINGUARUM

STUDIA MEMORIAE
NICOLAI VAN WIJK DEDICATA

edenda curat

C. H. VAN SCHOONEVELD
STANFORD UNIVERSITY

SERIES MAIOR
XXIV

1967
MOUTON & CO.
THE HAGUE · PARIS

LANGUAGE IN RELATION TO A UNIFIED THEORY OF THE STRUCTURE OF HUMAN BEHAVIOR

by

KENNETH L. PIKE

UNIVERSITY OF MICHIGAN

Second, Revised Edition

1967
MOUTON & CO.
THE HAGUE · PARIS

© Copyright 1967, Mouton & Co., Publishers, The Hague, The Netherlands.

No part of this book may be translated or reproduced in any form, by print, photoprint, microfilm, or any other means, without written permission from the publishers.

Printed in The Netherlands by Mouton & Co., Printers, The Hague.

DEDICATED TO THE MEMORY OF

PROFESSOR EDWARD SAPIR (1834-1939)

Photo taken by the author in the summer of 1937, at Ann Arbor, Michigan

TRAIL BLAZER IN THE STUDY OF SOUNDS
WITH REFERENCE TO "THE INNER CONFIGURATION
OF THE SOUND *SYSTEM* OF A LANGUAGE, THE INTUITIVE 'PLACING'
OF THE SOUNDS WITH REFERENCE TO ONE ANOTHER",
AND PIONEER IN THE STATING OF THE RELATION OF LANGUAGE
TO OTHER CULTURAL PATTERNS OF MAN

PREFACE TO THE PRELIMINARY EDITION

The theoretical phases of the conceptual framework which we set out to provide some years ago for showing the relationship between the structure of verbal and nonverbal behavior is finished, in preliminary form, with Part III (chapters 11-17) of this work. Pedagogical material for teaching tagmemic methodology, not included here, is being prepared by Pickett, Elson, and Longacre.

The total work arose from a struggle to describe empirical data, especially the Mixtec and Mazatec languages of Mexico. Attention to hierarchical structure stems from an article on Taxemes and Immediate Constituents (1943b), a theoretical article written after unsuccessful attempts to find in the current literature a satisfactory basis for Mixtec grammatical analysis. Emphasis upon position (slot function) as over against construction reflects a positive attempt to describe some of the resistant problems of Mixtec grammatical analysis (1944). In the last article I first struggled with the extensive disconformities which occur there in reference to borders and units of the phonological versus grammatical hierarchies. The attempt to find internal organization of high-level phonological units was the result of an attempt to describe (with Eunice Pike) the immediate constituents of Mazatec syllables (1947). Constant reference to substitution frames as theoretically relevant was expanded from analytical techniques developed to determine the number of tones in tone languages (1938, 1948), while my study of the interplay of intonation, stress, quantity, and voice quality developed from publications in 1942, 1945.

In 1948, weary of studying phonology, I decided to turn attention to grammar — and to see if some correlate of the phoneme (other than the morpheme) might be found for grammar. I tentatively labelled such a unit 'grameme' (for unit of grammar) and started to search. I reasoned that as the phoneme was reflected in practical orthographical work for millennia before being "found" by the scientists (whose "X-ray eyes" could find cells but not faces), so some unit of grammar might be present in the work and thought of practical language teachers which was not adequately reflected in current theory of linguistic structure. Various kinds of subjects, predicates, and modifiers seemed to meet the specifications. Extensive, deep-seated changes in language theory were necessary before these units could be worked into a conceptual framework which would (a) allow them to fit a place in theory analogous to that of the phoneme, (b) fit the etic-emic requirements of our view, and (c) be subject to treatment in pedagogical materials for analysis of language structures and for preparation of language-learning texts.

In the process, it proved necessary to make certain generalizations which were of such a high level of abstraction that it became clear that — if useful at all in linguistics — they must in theory be applicable also to some phases of nonlanguage behavior. It was at this point that the theoretical view broadened to set up an approach of a scope wider than linguistics. Thus Chapters 3-5 included the structuring of the behavior at church services, football games, and breakfast scenes. Now in Chapter 17 the implications are seen as including the structuring of the acting groups themselves in addition to their behavior.

The essentials of the linguistic tagmemic unit were largely in view by 1949, when I began to write this material. (The term grameme, meanwhile, 1958a, has been replaced with 'tagmeme' for etymological reasons — and see discussion, § 11.74). Extension of the framework to include nonlanguage material and to tidy up the general trimodal framework brought delays until the academic year of 1952-53. During that year, aided by a grant from the Rockefeller Foundation which allowed me to devote time to writing, all three parts were drafted. Revision of the material, however, took several years longer than I had hoped — so that the chapters have appeared in separate volumes rather than as a single unit.

In the meantime, on the basis of the first parts, various studies have been testing the linguistic concepts with field work. Note, in the bibliography, grammatical items by Cox, Shell, Mayers, Hart, Waterhouse, Pickett, Longacre; and phonological items by Pike (1957c) and Crawford. Various other works by Peeke, Wise, Delgaty, Ellis, and others are in manuscript and should appear in due season. The ethnological implications have yet to be tested in field situations.

I am quite aware that our attempt is an ambitious one — to revise the conceptual framework for language study into etic versus emic views (§ 2) with a grammatical tagmeme unit added to phonological phoneme and lexical morpheme units (§§ 7, 11), with a trimodal set of interlocking hierarchies (§§ 3, 15), with approaches via particle, wave, and field overlapping and supplementing one another (§ 12.1, and 1959). I am also aware of the dangers of leaving one's own discipline and attempting to build a bridge across to another, as I have tried to show analogies between linguistic structure and the structure of society (§ 17) and of nonverbal behavior (§§ 1-5).

Nevertheless I have ventured, because some of us need to explore this trail. We should profit if we can find in theoretical structure some components which will contribute toward binding us into departmental unity — linguists, archeologists, ethnologists, physical anthropologists, sociologists, and students of personality structure. The fact that we all study man is no longer enough to satisfy all of us — or some of our students.

In principle, the attempt might equally well have been made by someone coming from the opposite direction, building on ethnological theory and seeking analogies in linguistics. In practice, however, the recent formal studies in the linguistic area seem to have provided a base which at the moment is easier to build on.

Of course, serious errors can be made — undoubtedly have been here — in such an endeavor. In my opinion, however, the excitement of the chase is worth it. One may at least *aim* at avoiding the epitaph written on a recent book by its reviewer (Orlans, 1958): 'His claims are modest, his subject is narrow, and the presentation brief; failure is thereby precluded but success is slight.'

Readers of Part III who have not studied the earlier parts might prefer to by-pass the argument in the early sections of Chapter 11. If so, they may find it possible to read immediately the commentary on Tables 1-3. Chapter 12 on Models and Chapters 16 and 17 on Meaning and on Society are somewhat independent of the others and can in large measure be read without extensive study of earlier sections.

I am indebted to Miss Ruth Brend for helping in the many details of preparation and proofing of the manuscript of this third part.

Ann Arbor, Michigan   KENNETH L. PIKE
November, 1959

PREFACE TO THE SECOND EDITION

Ten years full of linguistic development have passed since the first part (1954, Chapters 1-7) of the Preliminary Edition appeared, setting up the basic form of tagmemic theory, and nine since the phonological data were published (1955, Chapters 8-9). In the United States, transformational attention to generative grammar, and in Britain a development of prosodic views into wider categorical concepts have changed the context into which any book now fits.

The basic difference between the first and second editions of this book represents an attempt to show how tagmemic theory relates to these and other recent views. The original biliographical sections (retained here for historical orientation) seem to read as if coming out of another age, so fast have battle grounds shifted. I have added to these sections, however, several hundreds of references to the newer materials of the decade.[1] Dr. Ruth Brend has been responsible for trying to catch my inaccuracies in these and the earlier references.

The attention which tagmemic theory earlier directed to the nature of units-in-general, however, seems even more needed now than in 1954. The explicit conventional phoneme has in many areas disappeared from view; the morpheme — though few sense it yet — is similarly threatened; grammatical units such as 'subject' are politely and helpfully introduced as labels — only to be brusquely bowed out as theory.[2] The tagmemic theory of this book, on the contrary, has tried to specify characteristics of units (contrast, variation, distribution — cf. feature mode, manifestation mode, distribution mode) as related to a three-way hierarchical relationship

---

[1] Yet even before this manuscript can get into print, scores of relevant articles and books are appearing which cannot be listed; one must, after all, stop somewhere on the continuum. Three bibliographical items, however, are of special interest:

Hymes (1964) includes not only many reprints of articles on language in culture, and an extensive general bibliography, but dozens of special sub-bibliographies (index on his page 760).

For tagmemics and its related developments in matrix theory, an annotated bibliography, including references which reached me after the completion of this revised manuscript, will be included in *Current Trends in Linguistics: American Linguistics* (T. A. Sebeok, Ed., to appear).

For a full listing of the reviews of the three volumes of the first edition of this work (1954, 1955, 1960) see *Bibliography of the Summer Institute of Linguistics* (Santa Ana, Calif., 1964).

[2] The sentence remains temporarily immune from attack only because it is taken (in a regularized form) as an axiomatic starting point. When its broader setting is allowed to come into focus, the deep problem of identity of unit-against-ground will assert itself here, also.

(lexicon, phonology, grammar). Insistence on three hierarchies which are partially independent while also partially interlocking continues to be necessary in the present climate of opinion, as over against a two-hierarchy arrangement (of phonology versus lexico-grammar) or as a corrective to an attempt to generate all phenomena as a monistic system. Here, again, the contribution of the book is as much needed as in 1954.

In addition, our theoretical emphasis upon the integration of linguistic structure into a view which accommodates without jar the larger structures of humans-while-behaving-nonverbally (with the relation of language-behavior-in-context to the form-meaning composites of language), and the structures of people in societal groups, continues to be needed. The work of this book will not have been finished until some such over-view stimulates more fruit in an extensive, integrated approach (in descriptive fact, as it does here in tentative conceptual framework) to all varieties of human mental and physical behavior, organization, and production.

In the meantime, however, tagmemic principles are already being applied to the analysis of scores of languages (including a large number of the more than 350 currently being studied by the Summer Institute of Linguistics); publication in many of these is available. Pedagogical material on linguistic — but not nonverbal — tagmemics is available for some of the beginning concepts in Elson and Pickett (1962), and on a more advanced level in Longacre (1964a). The latter publications have made it unnecessary for me to add the chapters on pedagogy which were earlier announced for this present book.

Tagmemic theory has broadened its scope since the 1954–1960 volumes, rather than retreating; confrontation with a wide variety of natural-language data has shown its usefulness, and stimulated the making explicit of peripheral concepts earlier left weakly developed. Perhaps the stronger attention to *complementary perspective* through particle, wave, and field (Pike, 1959) represents the most important of these. The preliminary volumes placed attention on units — that is, on particles or elements viewed in some sense as whole entities set apart from others — with minor attention to the slurring and to the nuclear-marginal characteristics of units as waves. The phonological-wave characteristics of sound segments, earlier discussed (in Pike, 1943a:107-13, 44, 48-53), were amplified in Part II (1955, §§ 8.42, 9.236, 9.241, 9.311-312, see below); but more extensive and systematic treatment is now available for phonological waves (Pike, 1962b), with initial mention of wave characteristics of grammatical constructions in Pickett (1960:91-92; — and compare, also, Pittman, 1948b, and Longacre, 1964a).

Much more extensive since 1960, however, has been further development of the concept of grammatical field. Starting from an attempt to find grammatical analogies for the traditionally-fruitful (and, for us, theoretically-relevant — see § 8.623) phonetic chart, dimensional (matrix) analyses of clausal systems began to appear. These proved so helpful in illuminating a perspective arising from the field structure, that the approach is being intensively exploited.

In each instance in the present revision where the new researches on field might be brought to bear on the particle-unit emphasis, I have attempted to supply the reader, in footnotes, with the relevant references. (Most of these footnote numbers on matrix are also gathered into a list in a note to § 11.225.) The attempt to highlight matrix theory with its ramifications, however (e.g., in poetry, Pike, 1964b, 1965a), must wait for other books. This one is already long.

When points of view in the text have been modified by these or later articles or chapters, however, the reader is warned in footnotes about the nature of these changes. Bibliographical additions are usually inserted in older sections, but occasionally a new bibliographical section is added. Otherwise the description is substantially unchanged apart from minor stylistic revision, updating of terminology (grameme to tagmeme), and abbreviation and clarification of Chapter 2 where it was puzzling some nonlinguistic readers.

The relevance of the human observer — not a testing by a physical or mathematical machine — dominates this book. The complicated observer resists being dissected into logical parts — and ultimately resists even more strongly being forced into a single logically-coherent Procrustian view or set of one-dimensional rules: he demands the right of multiple perspective, the recognition of his parallel, *simultaneous* reaction to criss-crossing, intersecting vectors of experience, mental tools, values, and psychological pre-sets. Who is sufficient to deal with such a system? The relaxed comfort of some scholars just a decade ago (at the very time our Part I appeared — cf. Hoijer: "few if any major methodological problems remain today", 1954:11) meets with upheaval in confronting modern interdisciplinary complexity which one must nevertheless act in.

I end this preface, as the former one, with a quotation — but one vigorous in despair: "It is impossible that a layman should not make blunders, some of them perhaps serious. I am under no illusion in this respect, but simply had to take the risk" (Urban, 1939:13). The thrill of illumination has justified it.

Ann Arbor, Michigan
May 29, 1964

KENNETH L. PIKE

TABLE OF CONTENTS

Preface to the Preliminary Edition 5

Preface to the Second Edition 8

1. Language as Behavior 25
   1.1 An Illustration of the Need for a Unified Theory 25
   1.2 Language Behavior and Non-Language Behavior Fused in Single Events 26
      1.21 Nonlanguage Reports Which Need a Language Supplement . . 27
      1.22 Language Reports Which Need a Nonlanguage Supplement . . 28
   1.3 Verbal and Nonverbal Elements Substituting for One Another in Function 30
   1.4 Bibliographical Comments on Chapter 1. 32

2. Etic and Emic Standpoints for the Description of Behavior. 37
   2.1 Characteristics of the Two Standpoints 37
      2.11 Cross-Cultural Versus Specific 37
      2.12 Physical Nature, Response, and Distribution 39
      2.13 Value of Standpoints 40
      2.14 Caution — Not a Dichotomy. 41
   2.2 Illustrations of Purposive Emic Differences Within a Culture 42
   2.3 Variants of Emic Units 44
   2.4 Differences in Etic Observers. 46
   2.5 Organization of Similar Etic Units Within Distinct Emic Systems. . . 47
   2.6 Predictability of Difficulties in Learning to React Emically to an Alien Emic System. 51
   2.7 Bibliographical Comments on Chapter 2. 53
      2.71 On Etic versus Emic Viewpoints 53
      2.72 On the Nature of Structure 55
      2.73 On Extralinguistic Cultural Distribution as Relevant to Emic Analysis. 59

2.74 On Clash between Systems as a Source of Evidence or Assumptions Relevant to the Emic Analysis of Language 64
2.75 On Theory Formation and the Philosophy of Science 68

3. The Structure of Behavior Illustrated 73

   3.1 Glimpses of a Church Service 73

   3.2 Segments and Waves of Activity 74
      3.21 Nuclei of Segments 74
      3.22 Borders of Etic Segments 75
      3.23 Etic Segments as Waves of Activity 76
      3.24 Markers of Emic Segments 76
      3.25 Indeterminacy of Segment Borders 77

   3.3 Focus and the Whole 78
      3.31 Hierarchical Structure 79
      3.32 Focus and Participants 79
      3.33 Lower Limits to Focus 80
      3.34 Indeterminacy of Focus 80
      3.35 Criteria for Closure 81

   3.4 Slots and Classes 82
      3.41 Functional Slots in Larger Wholes 82
      3.42 Segment Classes 83
      3.43 Indeterminacy of Class 84

   3.5 Modes of Units 84
      3.51 Distribution Mode 86
      3.52 Manifestation Mode 87
      3.53 Feature Mode 89
      3.54 Indeterminacy of Modes 92
      3.55 Modal Formula Symbolizing Units 92
      3.56 Manifestation of Each Mode as the Manifestation of the Whole 92

   3.6 Bibliographical Comments on Chapter 3 94
      3.61 On Segmenting a Continuum 94
      3.62 On Hierarchical Structure 95
      3.63 On Units 96

4. Focus Illustrated 98

   4.1 A Football Game in Focus 98
      4.11 The Length of the Game 98
      4.12 The Spectacle 99

4.13	The Season	100
4.14	Miscellaneous Overlapping Hierarchies	101
4.15	Abstraction Focus (Hypostasis)	102
4.16	Periods in the Official Game	103
4.17	Plays, Play Sequences, and Closure	103
4.18	Plays in Slots with Choice and Variants	104
4.19	Wholes Smaller than Plays	105
4.1.10	Homomorphic Activity and Indeterminacy	105
4.2	Height of Focus	106
4.21	Predominant Focus	106
4.22	Exponents in Formulas	106
4.23	Hypostasis Formulas and Types	107
4.24	Modal Elements in Focus Formulas	108
4.25	Diagram of Changes of Focus Height	109
4.3	Depth of Focus	109
4.31	Shallow and Deep Focus	109
4.32	Thresholds, With Lower and Upper Limits to Height of Focus	111
4.4	Breadth of Focus	112
4.41	Focusing Processes	112
4.42	Wide versus Narrow Focus	114
4.43	Relevance in Reference to Composites	114
4.44	Segmental Borders of Composites	116
4.45	Segments as Simultaneously Members of Separate Intersecting Hierarchies	117
4.46	Composites in a Setting	117
4.5	Bibliographical Comments on Chapter 4	118
5. The Behavioreme (Including the Sentence)		120
5.1	The Behavioreme Defined or Described	121
5.2	The Behavioreme Illustrated by a Breakfast Unit	122
5.3	Included Behavioremes, Minimum Behavioremes, and Thresholds	128
5.4	Systems of Behavioremes	131
5.5	The Uttereme (The Sentence Syntagmeme) and the Etics of Utterances	133
5.51	Segmentation of a Continuum into Utterances and Hyper-Utterances	133
5.52	Etic Classificatory Criteria for Utterance Types	135
5.53	Etic Utterance Types	138
5.54	Utterance Distribution Classes	139

       5.55 Emic Procedure in the Analysis of Utterances and Hyper-Utterances 141
  5.6 Bibliographical Comments on Chapter 5. 144
       5.61 On Behavioremes 144
       5.62 An Etic Classification in Anthropology 145
       5.63 On Linguistic Units Larger than Sentences 145
       5.64 On Meaning in Definitions of Sentence Types 148

6. The Minimum Unit of the Feature Mode of the Behavioreme (Including the Morpheme) 150

  6.1 Definition of the Emic Motif 150
  6.2 The Emic Motif Partially Illustrated 151
  6.3 The Emic Motif Contrasted with the Behavioreme 153
  6.4 The Feature Mode of the Morpheme 154
       6.41 Minimum Purposive Units in Reference to Hypostasis in a Componential System 154
       6.42 Sources of Analytical Knowledge of Purposes and Meanings. . 155
       6.43 Conceptualized Hypostasis in Participant Awareness of Purpose and Meaning 156
       6.44 Indeterminacy and Margin of Error in Analyzing Purpose and Meaning. 158
       6.45 Morphemes Without Lexical Meaning 160
       6.46 Contrastive-Identificational and Meaningful-Formal Characteristics of a Morpheme 162
  6.5 The Manifestation Mode of the Morpheme 163
       6.51 Identical Manifestations 163
       6.52 Free Variants of a Morpheme 164
       6.53 Locally-Conditioned Variants of a Morpheme 164
       6.54 Morphetically-Complex Variants of a Morpheme 166
       6.55 Fused versus Clearly-Segmented Variants of Morphemes . . 168
       6.56 Locally-Free but Systemically-Conditioned Variants of Morphemes 168
  6.6 The Distribution Mode of the Morpheme 169
       6.61 Activeness of Morphemes 169
       6.62 Parasitic (Latent) Morphs, and Differences in Participants. . . 172
       6.63 Morphemic-Class Membership and Potential-Distribution as Components of the Distribution Mode of a Morpheme . . . 173
       6.64 The Internal Structure of a Morpheme. 175
       6.65 An Occuring Allomorph Viewed as Constituting an Occurring Morpheme 176

6.66 Border Limits of Morphemes in Reference to Tagmemes	177
6.7 Systems of Morphemes as Composed of Emic Classes of Morphemes	178
6.8 Morphetics	179
6.81 Segmentation of a Continuum into Morphs	179
6.82 Etic Classificatory Criteria for Morph Types	180
6.83 Etic Classificatory Criteria for Morphs in Relation to their Distribution Classes	181
6.84 Summary of the Relation of Morphs to Morphemes	181
6.9 Bibliographical Comments on Chapter 6.	182
6.91 On Morpheme Definition	183
6.92 On Active Elements	190
6.93 On Indeterminacy in Morphemic Analysis	191
6.94 On Etic Classifications.	192

7. The Minimum Unit of the Distribution Mode of the Behavioreme (Including the Tagmeme) 194

    7.1 Definition of Motifemic-Slot-Class-Correlative 194

    7.2 The Motifemic-Slot-Class Correlative Partially Illustrated within the Breakfast Unit 195

    7.3 The Feature Mode of the Tagmeme 196
        7.31 Distribution Classes of Morphemes as Tagmemic Components 196
            7.311 Choice in Relation to Classes of Morphemes. 197
            7.312 A Class of Morphemes as a Tagmemic Clue 198
            7.313 Etic Classes of Morphemes versus Emic Trimodally-Structured Classes of Morphemes 198
                7.313(1) The Feature Mode of an Emic Class of Morphemes 198
                7.313(2) The Distribution Mode of an Emic Morpheme Class 201
                7.313(3) The Manifestation Mode of an Emic Class of Morphemes 204
                7.313(4) Lexical Sets and Systems of Morpheme Classes 208
        7.32 Tagmemic Slot, Proportion, and Structural Meaning as Tagmemic Components. 217
            7.321 Tagmatic versus Tagmemic Slots 218
            7.322 Recognition of Proportion 222
            7.323 Tagmemic Meaning in Relation to Morphemic Meaning 226
            7.324 Tagmemic Meaning in Relation to Morphemic-Distribution-Class Meaning 227

7.4	The Manifestation Mode of the Tagmeme.	228
	7.41 Identical Manifestations of a Tagmeme	228
	7.42 Free Variants of a Tagmeme	229
	7.43 Locally-Conditioned Manifested Variants of a Tagmeme . .	229
	7.44 Morphemically-Complex Manifested Variants of a Tagmeme .	232
	7.45 Fused versus Clearly-Segmented Variants of Tagmemes . . .	235
	7.46 Systematically-Conditioned Variants of Tagmemes	235
7.5	The Distribution Mode of the Tagmeme	236
	7.51 Activeness of Tagmemes	236
	7.52 The Tagmemic-Class Membership and the Potential Occurrence of a Tagmeme as a Component of Its Distribution Mode . . .	238
	7.53 Potential for the Correlation of the Manifestations of One Tagmeme with the Manifestations of Another Tagmeme	239
	7.54 The Internal Structure of the Tagmeme	240
	7.55 An Occurring Tagmemic Manifestation Viewed as an Occurring Tagmeme	241
	7.56 Border Limits of Tagmemes in Reference to Morphemes and Hypermorphemes	242
7.6	Systems of Tagmemes as Composed of Emic Classes of Tagmemes .	245
7.7	Tagmatics	251
	7.71 Segmentation of a Continuum into Tagmas	251
	7.72 Etic Classificatory Criteria for Tagma Types	252
	7.73 Etic Classificatory Criteria for Tagmas in Reference to Their Distribution Classes	254
	7.74 Utteremic-Tagmemic Formulas Following Tagmatic Analysis .	254
	7.741 Summary of the Relation of Tagmas to Tagmemes . .	254
	7.742 Utteremic-Tagmemic Formulas for Languagette A . .	255
	7.743 Utteremic-Tagmemic Formulas for Languagette B . .	258
	7.744 Utteremic-Tagmemic Formulas for Languagette A' . .	258
	7.745 Utteremic-Tagmemic Formulas for Languagette B' . .	259
	7.746 Utteremic-Tagmemic Formulas for Languagette C . .	261
	7.75 Languagettes for Student Analysis	265
7.8	Bibliographical Comments on Chapter 7	270
	7.81 On Classes of Morphemes	272
	7.82 On Slot or Position	275
	7.83 On Proportion, Positional Meaning, and Substitutability . . .	276
	7.84 On Potential and Prediction	280
	7.85 On Morphemic Slot-Class Correlatives versus Constructions or Relationships	282

7.86 On the Etics of Relationships 285
7.87 On the Initial Development of Tagmemic Theory 286
7.88 On Tagmemic Method 289

8. The Minimum Unit of the Manifestation Mode of the Behavioreme (Including the Phoneme) 290

   8.1 Definition of the Acteme 290

   8.2 The Acteme Partially Illustrated Within the Breakfast Unit 291
      8.21 Nonverbal Actemes (Kinemes) Illustrated 291
      8.22 Verbal Actemes (Phonemes) Illustrated 293

   8.3 The Feature Mode of the Phoneme 294
      8.31 Simultaneous, Sequential, and Contrastive-Identificational Features 294
      8.32 Units versus Relationships or Poles of Contrast 297
      8.33 Relativity of Features and Phonetic Overlap 298
      8.34 Fused Ranges of Features with Intermediate Phonetic Manifestations 300
      8.35 The Possibility of Contrastive-Identificational Features of Phonemes as Emes 302

   8.4 The Manifestation Mode of the Phoneme 306
      8.41 Movement as Basic to Phonemic Manifestation 306
      8.42 Waves of Activity in Phonemic Manifestation 307
      8.43 Participant Type in Relation to Phonemic Movement 309
      8.44 Variants of Phonemes 311
          8.441 Systemically-Conditioned but Topologically-Same Variants of the Phoneme 311
          8.442 Phonemically- and Hyperphonemically-Conditioned Variants of the Phoneme 312
          8.443 The Possibility of Grammatically-Conditioned Variants of the Phoneme 313
          8.444 Free (Nonconditioned) Variants of the Phoneme . . . 316
          8.445 Phonetically-Complex Variants of the Phoneme . . . 317
          8.446 Fused versus Clearly-Segmented Variants of the Phoneme 317

   8.5 The Distribution Mode of the Phoneme 318
      8.51 Actual and Potential Distribution of the Phoneme in Hyperphonemes 318
      8.52 Actual and Potential Distribution of the Phoneme in Grammatical Units and in the Behavioreme 320

8.53 The Internal Structure of the Phoneme and its Active Membership in a Class of Phonemes 322
8.54 An Occurring Allophone Viewed as Constituting an Occurring Phoneme 323

8.6 Systems of Phonemes 323
    8.61 Congruent Systems of Phonemes in a Hypercongruent System 323
    8.62 Trimodally-Structured Classes of Phonemes 325
        8.621 The Distribution Mode of an Emic Class of Phonemes 325
        8.622 The Manifestation Mode of an Emic Class of Phonemes 326
        8.623 The Feature Mode of an Emic Class of Phonemes . . 328
    8.63 An English Illustration of Emic Classes of Phonemes 331
    8.64 A Hierarchy of English Classes of Phonemes 338
    8.65 Phonemically-Complex Members of an Emic Class of Phonemes 339
    8.66 Emic Slot-Class Units in Phonology 340
    8.67 Order or Relationship as a Conceptualized Hypostasis. . . . 341

8.7 Phonetics 341
    8.71 Segmentation of a Continuum into Phones 341
    8.72 Etic Classificatory Criteria for Phone Types 342
    8.73 Etic Criteria for Phones in Relation to their Distribution Classes 343
    8.74 Summary of the Relation of Phones to Phonemes 343

8.8 Bibliographical Comments on Chapter 8. 344
    8.81 The History of Phonemics and of Articulatory Phonetics . . . 344
        8.811 On Early Phonemics 344
        8.812 On Phonemics in the United States 345
        8.813 On Articulatory and Acoustic Phonetics 346
        8.814 On the Validity of the Phonemic Principle 349
        8.815 On Psycholinguistics 351
    8.82 On Substance 354
    8.83 On Phonetic Similarity 355
    8.84 On Feature versus Opposition, and Identification versus Contrast. 357
    8.85 On Neutralization, Overlap, Archiphoneme, Intersection, and Related Matters 359
    8.86 On Emic Classes of Phonemes 360
    8.87 On the Relation of Grammar to Phonemic Analysis 361

9. Higher-Layered Units of the Manifestation Mode of the Uttereme (Including the Syllable, Stress Group, and Juncture) 364
    9.1 Hyperphonemes 364
    9.2 The Emic Syllable 365

9.21 Definition of the Emic Syllable 365
9.22 The Feature Mode of the Emic Syllable 365
    9.221 The Chest Pulse 365
    9.222 Releasing and Arresting Margins of the Syllable . . . 370
    9.223 The Syllabic and the Syllable Nucleus 371
    9.224 The Phonemic Content of Emic Syllables 373
    9.225 The Emic Syllable as a Potential Carrier of a Unit of Pitch, Stress, Length, or Morpheme Shape Type . . . 373
9.23 The Manifestation Mode of the Emic Syllable 377
    9.231 Systematically-Conditioned but Topologically-Same Variants of the Emic Syllable 378
    9.232 Phonemically- and Hyperphonemically-Conditioned Variants of the Emic Syllable 378
    9.233 The Possibility of Grammatically-Conditioned Variants of the Emic Syllable 379
    9.234 Free (Unconditioned) Variants of the Emic Syllable . 379
    9.235 Etically-Complex Variants of the Emic Syllable . . . 379
    9.236 Fused versus Clearly-Segmented Variants of Emic Syllables 380
    9.237 Abbreviated Forms in Reference to Variants, Complexes, and Fusion 383
9.24 The Distribution Mode of the Emic Syllable 384
    9.241 Distribution of the Emic Syllable in Larger Hyperphonemes 384
    9.242 Distribution of the Emic Syllable in Grammatical Units 385
    9.243 Immediate Constituents of the Emic Syllable 386
    9.244 Emic Classes of Emic Syllables 389
    9.245 Emic Hyperclasses of Emic Syllables 390
9.25 The Etics of Syllable Structure 391

9.3 The Emic Stress Group 392
    9.31 The Feature Mode of the Emic Stress Group 392
        9.311 The Abdominal Pulse 392
        9.312 Nucleus and Margins of the Stress Group 395
    9.32 The Manifestation Mode of the Emic Stress Group 397
    9.33 The Distribution Mode of the Emic Stress Group 399

9.4 The Emic Pause Group 402

9.5 Further Hyperphonemes 403

9.6 The Possibility of Contrastive-Identificational Features of Hyperphonemes as Themselves Emes 405

       9.61 Juncture and Peak Emes: Solution A   405
       9.62 Terminal and Peak Emes: Solution B   407
       9.63 Contrastive-Identificational Features of Hyperphonemes: Solution C.   408

   9.7 Bibliographical Comments on Chapter 9.   409
       9.71 On Pyramiding from Phoneme to Syllable versus to Morpheme   409
       9.72 On the Nature of the Syllable   410
       9.73 On the Structure of the Syllable   413
       9.74 On the Nature of the Stress Group and Juncture   417
       9.75 On Breath Groups and Pauses   419
       9.76 On the Possibility of Languages without Syllables or Stress Groups—or Vowels   419

10. Higher-Layered Units of the Feature Mode of the Uttereme   424

   10.1 Hypermorpheme Definition and Types   424
   10.2 The Feature Mode of the Hypermorpheme   426
   10.3 The Manifestation Mode of the Hypermorpheme.   427
   10.4 The Distribution Mode of the Hypermorpheme   428
   10.5 Bibliographical Comments on Chapter 10   429
       10.51 On Phonological Characteristics of Hypermorphemes   429
       10.52 On Hypermorphemic Meanings   430

11. Higher-Layered Units of the Distribution Mode of the Syntagmeme . . .   432

   11.1 The Term OC-Hypertagmeme Tentatively Applied to Obligatorily-Complex Units.   432
       11.11 Definition of Tentative Obligatorily-Complex Hypertagmeme .   433
       11.12 Disadvantages and Advantages of the Definition of OC-Hypertagmeme as Obligatorily Complex.   434
       11.13 An Obligatorily-Complex Structure Re-Analyzed as a Special Kind of Emic Class of Hypermorphemes   435
   11.2 The Terms RL-Hypertagmeme and RL-Tagmeme Tentatively Applied Relativistically to Levels of Focus   436
       11.21 Definition of Relativistic RL-Tagmeme and RL-Hypertagmeme   436
       11.22 Levels of Structure   437
           11.221 Word Level   437
           11.222 Phrase Level and Portmanteau Levels.   439
           11.223 Clause Level.   441
           11.224 Sentence Level.   441
           11.225 Monologue, Utterance-Response, Conversation, and Intra-Word Levels   442

	11.23 Advantages and Disadvantages of a Relativistic RL-Hypertagmeme	443
11.3	The Terms AL-Hypertagmeme and AL-Tagmeme Tentatively Applied in Reference to Levels as Absolute	446
	11.31 Advantages of the AL-Hypertagmeme	447
	11.32 Disadvantages of the AL-Hypertagmeme	447
11.4	The Term Hypertagmeme (or SC-Hypertagmeme) Applied to Slot-Plus-Class Correlative on Nonminimum Levels of Structure	448
	11.41 Implications of Reworking the Hypertagmeme into a Slot-Plus-Class Correlative in Reference to Levels	448
	11.42 Advantages and Disadvantages of the Hypertagmeme as Slot-Plus-Class Correlative on Higher Levels	451
	11.43 Illustrations of Hypermorpheme Constructions (Syntagmemes) and of Slot-Plus-Class Hypertagmemes	452
	11.44 Trimodal Structuring of Hypertagmeme as Slot-Plus-Class Correlative	459
11.5	Etics and Emics of Hypertagmemes and of Hypermorpheme Types	467
	11.51 Segmentation of Hypertagmemes and of Hypermorpheme Structures	467
	11.52 Etics of Hypertagmemes and of Syntagmemes	469
	11.53 Summary of Relation of Hypertagmas to Hypertagmemes and of Etic to Emic Classes of Hypermorphemes	471
11.6	Tagmemic System in Reference to Kernel Matrix and Transforms	472
11.7	Bibliographical Comments on Chapter 11	473
	11.71 On Hierarchical versus Combinatorial Grammar	474
	11.711 On Item-in-Slot versus Construction	476
	11.712 On Immediate Constituents as End Products of Analysis Rather than as Starting Points	477
	11.72 On Emic Levels of Grammatical Structure	479
	11.721 On Words and Morphology versus Syntax	481
	11.722 On Portmanteau Levels	483
	11.723 On Sentences in Relation to Higher-Level Units	484
	11.724 On Clause versus Phrase	486
	11.73 On Parts of Speech	488
	11.74 On Tagmemes née Gramemes	490
	11.75 On Discovery versus Presentation	492
	11.76 On Transform Grammar and Tagmemics	495
	11.761 On Sources of Transformational Grammar	497
	11.762 On Some Problems in Description	498
	11.763 On Intuition and Meaning	499
	11.764 On Transformation as Process	501

	11.765 On Derivational History and Tagmeme Units	503
	11.77 On Halliday's Prosodic Approach to Grammar	506

12. Trimodal Restrictions on Setting up Emic Units. 510
    12.1 Restrictions Imposed by the Trimodal View of Language as Particle, Wave, and Field 510
    12.2 The Restriction Imposed by the Retention of Simultaneous Modes. . 513
    12.3 "Spectrum" Restrictions on Emic Progression 515
    12.4 Restrictions in Solving for Modal Components 518
    12.5 Modifications Imposed by a Model which Includes Phonotagmemes 520

13. Mode-Like Emic Units and Systems. 522
    13.1 Background of the Suprasegmental Problem 522
    13.2 Segmental Phonemes as Analogous to the Manifestation Mode . . . 524
    13.3 Suprasegmental Phonemes as Analogous to the Feature Mode . . . 524
    13.4 Subsegmental Phonemes (Voice Quality) as Analogous to the Distribution Mode. 525
    13.5 Componential Systems of Mode-Like Emic Units. 527
    13.6 Larger but Incomplete Modal Analogies 532
    13.7 Overlapping Hierarchies of Mode-Like Emic Units 533
    13.8 Bibliographical Comments on Chapter 13 535
        13.81 On Voice Quality, La Langue and La Parole 536
        13.82 On Suprasegmental Phonemes 538
        13.83 On Intonation 539
        13.84 On Tone. 541
        13.85 On Communication with Abstracted Components 543

14. Fused Units 545
    14.1 The Item-and-Arrangement (Particle) and Item-and-Process (Wave) Views of Sequence 545
        14.11 The Modal Analogy. 545
        14.12 Summary of Some Fusion Types 548
    14.2 Distortion Introduced by Arbitrary Cuts and by Reconstructed Bases 550
    14.3 The Hyper-Unit (Field) View of Sequence 553
    14.4 Distortion Introduced by Incomplete Segmentation 555
    14.5 Bibliographical Comments on Chapter 14 556
        14.51 On Item-and-Arrangement versus Item-and-Process 556
        14.52 On Arbitrary Cuts and Hyper-Units. 558
        14.53 On Zero. 561

15. Interlocking Hierarchies and Systems 565
    15.1 Interlocking Between Hierarchies. 566
        15.11 Interlocking Between the Lexical and Phonological Hierarchies 567

    15.12 Interlocking Between the Phonological and Grammatical Hierarchies 569
    15.13 Interlocking Between the Lexical and Grammatical Hierarchies 573
 15.2 Interlocking Between Systems 580
 15.3 Bibliographical Comments on Chapter 15 586
    15.31 On Simplicity, Elegance, and Levels of Analysis. 586
    15.32 On Mixing, Skipping, and Mashing Levels and Hierarchies. . 589
    15.33 On Systems 592
        15.331 On Over-All Pattern 592
        15.332 On Bilingualism 593
        15.333 On Dialects 593
        15.334 On Coexistent Systems 593
        15.335 On Style 595
        15.336 On Field and Matrix 596

16. Meaning 598
 16.1 Meanings of Units of the Lexical Hierarchy 598
    16.11 Semantic Variants of Morphemes 599
    16.12 Central Meanings of the Hierarchy 600
    16.13 Metaphorical Meanings of the Hierarchy 602
    16.14 Collocational Meanings of the Hierarchy 605
    16.15 Class Meanings within the Lexical Hierarchy 606
 16.2 Meanings of the Phonological Hierarchy 606
 16.3 Meanings of the Grammatical Hierarchy 607
 16.4 Meanings of Componential Systems 608
 16.5 Meaning of the Total Structure and Semantic Segmentation 608
 16.6 Segmental versus Subsegmental Meanings 610
 16.7 Hypermeanings—Concepts and Ideas 612
 16.8 Bibliographical Comments on Chapter 16 616
    16.81 On the Definition or Nature of Meaning 616
    16.82 On Meaning in Relation to Structure 620
        16.821 On Sememes 620
        16.822 On Synonymy 621
        16.823 On Variants and Universals 623
        16.824 On Forms of Perception 625
        16.825 On Componential and Hierarchical Analysis of Meaning 626
    16.83 On Phonological Meaning 628
    16.84 On Grammatical Meaning 630
    16.85 On Meanings of the Lexical Hierarchy 630
    16.86 On Concept Formation 633
    16.87 On Subsegmental Meanings and Preverbal Mental Activity . . 638
    16.88 On Translation 640

17. The Context of Behavior 641
    17.1 A Society as a Whole 643
    17.2 An S-Sentence-Type within Society 649
        17.21 Feature Mode of the Football S-Syntagmeme 649
        17.22 Manifestation Mode of the Football S-Syntagmeme 650
        17.23 Distribution Mode of Football S-Syntagmeme 652
    17.3 An S-Syllable within Society (the Family) 653
    17.4 The Individual 655
    17.5 Things 658
    17.6 The Struggle to Understand 663
    17.7 Bibliographical Comments on Chapter 17 665
        17.71 On the "Grammar" of Society 665
        17.72 On Society Requisites 668
        17.73 On Role as S-Tagmemic 670
        17.74 On Personality and the Individual 674
        17.75 On Things 676

References 679

Index 730

CHAPTER 1

LANGUAGE AS BEHAVIOR

1.1 *An Illustration of the Need for a Unified Theory*

In a certain party game people start by singing a stanza which begins *Under the spreading chestnut tree...* Then they repeat the stanza to the same tune but replace the word *spreading* with a quick gesture in which the arms are extended rapidly outward, leaving a vocal silence during the length of time which would otherwise have been filled by singing. On the next repetition the word *spreading* gives place to the gesture, as before, and in addition the syllable *chest* is omitted and the gap is filled with a gesture of thumping the chest. On the succeeding repetition the head is slapped instead of the syllable *nut* being uttered. In another round the arms may be extended upward as a gesture to replace *tree*. Finally, after further repetitions and replacements, there may be left only a few connecting words like *the*, and a sequence of gestures performed in unison to the original timing of the song.

This gesture song constitutes a single complex unit, a total experience which is perceived by the participants as beginning, as ending, and as constituting a unified whole — a single game. After it is finished a different unit of the party — the next game — may begin. Certainly the gesture-song game is in some way a single unit of activity, an event which must be studied as a cohesive set of actions.

Yet the structural analysis of the event as a single unit may be difficult or impossible under a fractionated approach to the analysis of behavior. If a language analyst has set up his tape recorder and captured the sounds emitted during the game he can make good progress on analyzing and describing the first verse; it resolves itself into sentences, clauses, words, stems, affixes, vocal sounds, and so on. But for the second verse the language analyst, as such, is unable to 'make sense' out of the data. Since language analysis by itself contains no techniques which provide ways of analyzing and describing bodily actions other than the articulating movements of the vocal apparatus, nor ways of symbolizing the relevant length of time elapsed during the gesture, nor a unified theory to allow for or to explain the structural replacement of words by non-vocal movements, it cannot handle such data. By the time the language analyst comes to the last verse, he is able to find no organization — scattered words are spaced far apart, unconnected, unstructured.

Persons using theories and field techniques adequate for describing nonlinguistic behavior, but discontinuous with linguistic theory and practice, would, on the other hand, face problems complementary to those just described for the linguist. Starting with a moving-picture record of the game, with supporting data, the sociologist or anthropologist could give an over-all description of the social situation in which the game occurred and could in detail describe the gestures. Yet except for the general statements of the kind given in the first paragraph of this chapter, it would be difficult or impossible for him to give for the total event, as a unit, a unified description which — with no change of outlook or procedure — would simultaneously analyze and describe the nonlinguistic behavior as well as the smallest and most intricate elements of linguistic structure.

A musician, similarly, might give an adequate account of the musical elements of the first verse, and even record satisfactorily the first gap or two, but by the time he had reached the almost total lack of vocalization at the end of the game his record would be unsatisfactory. If, furthermore, he did in some way manage to record the words, gestures, timing, and tune whenever present, these might be reported in reference to a theory which had not been correlated in detail with those linguistic concepts necessary to analyze the structure of the sentences as the linguist has come to see that structure; in addition, these verbal and nonverbal elements probably would be labelled by terms which are different from and not correlated with those of linguistics.

In this chapter, therefore, it is suggested (1) that there is needed a theory which will not be discontinuous, and which will not cause a severe jar as one passes from nonverbal to verbal activity. There is needed a unified theory, a unified set of terms, and a unified methodology which can start from any kind of complex human activity with various sub-types of activity included, and analyze it without sharp theoretical or methodological discontinuities.

It is concluded (2) that language is behavior, i.e., a phase of human activity which must not be treated in essence as structurally divorced from the structure of nonverbal human activity. The activity of man constitutes a structural whole, in such a way that it cannot be subdivided into neat 'parts' or 'levels' or 'compartments' with language in a behavioral compartment insulated in character, content, and organization from other behavior. Verbal and nonverbal activity is a unified whole, and theory and methodology should be organized or created to treat it as such.

Succeeding chapters in this book outline an initial attempt at the development of such a theory and procedure. First, however, the balance of this chapter illustrates further the fact that language must be treated as human behavior, as a phase of an integrated whole, by showing (1) that language behavior and nonlanguage behavior are fused in single events, and (2) that verbal and nonverbal elements may at times substitute structurally for one another in function.

1.2 *Language Behavior and Non-Language Behavior Fused in Single Events*

Since means of communication and description of events for archives are largely handled through the printed word, we tend to feel that, somehow, language stands apart from and outside of behavior and that the two go on simultaneously but independently. Such an impression may be heightened by experiences with radio (not television), where speech without visual contact with the actors may appear fairly adequate for giving a report of sports, news events, or for presenting a play. Silent movies of the old type, and current wordless cartoons, may heighten this impression. Yet in many events the visual record is by itself meaningless, and the auditory record is likewise unintelligible by itself; in such instances an analysis must embrace simultaneously both vocal and nonvocal activity.

1.21 *Nonlanguage Reports Which Need a Language Supplement*

Let us suppose, for example, that we are watching a moving-picture record of an American wedding, and studying all of the movements of the participants except the movements involved in speech. Could we say that the description was significant, or relevant? Probably the participants, at least, would want to know that the clergyman had uttered in some legal way the phrase *I pronounce you man and wife*. The wedding record must include this verbal component of the behavior. Similarly, if a pseudo-baptism ceremony were performed in such a way as to include all the normal activity except the verbal formula which says *I baptise thee in the name of the Father, Son, and Holy Spirit*, the event would presumably be without validity in a Baptist community — meaningless in terms of the normal expected response of that community to the regular ceremony. On the other hand, I have observed such a ceremony in a river out in the country, with no audience, where the proper words by the acceptable clergyman gave the immersion full community sanction.

Recently I attended a farewell banquet given to a class of departing students. Here, again, a report of that occasion would completely distort the function and structure of the event if it were described without reference to the fact that speeches were given. The banquet was not merely a dinner, but an occasion for certain kinds of things to be said within the setting of a formal meal.

Many other occasions can be observed on which a report of nonverbal actions is meaningless unless it is accompanied by a report of some of the concomitant verbal activity. For example, play-by-play reports of a game would be inadequate without a report as to any decisions of the umpire which were verbally expressed (and not otherwise signalled to the officials or to the audience), as to who is 'out', or who is ruled to have gone out of bounds (possibly in direct contradiction to the evidence that a moving picture record might give), or who has 'scored a touchdown' or has 'made a point' or, even, who has 'won'. Pronouncements as to such decisions must somehow be reflected in any adequate report. Similarly, one interested in foreign cultures would want to have information on the existence and nature of any incantations considered by the participants as essential, say, at planting or harvest time; or the presence and meaning of 'boos' and 'catcalls' or 'whistles' (meaning approval in USA, the opposite, I am told, in some European areas) following a vocal number during a concert; or the presence and meaning of a 'wolf whistle' in a street scene, and so on.

This last instance leads to the mention of an elaborate cultural situation in the Mazatec language of Mexico, where conversation, buying, selling, and bargaining is sometimes carried on entirely by means of whistles. Here there are no known limits to the length or type of conversation which can be carried on by whistles without words (Cowan, 1948). Conversations may begin at a distance with whistles (rather than with shouts, as in our culture), and may be continued in words as the participants come closer together; or boys may be carrying on a conversation in quiet whistles so as not to disturb their elders who are having a regular conversation in the same room. The whistling would not ordinarily be called speech, so presumably in a fractionated approach to behavior it would have to be analyzed by nonlinguistic techniques. Such an approach would be impossible without overlapping on language matters, however, since the 'tune' whistled comprises the abstracted tones which are normally a part of the words of the language and which would have been used had the conversation been spoken instead of being whistled. Mazatec is a "tone language" with four pitch levels (high or low relative to the norm of the voice of the speaker at that moment), one of which accompanies each syllable of the spoken sentence, and these same pitches are retained without the consonants and vowels in the whistle speech. Hence in the analysis of the whistle speech the description of the structure of the pitch sequences must often parallel the analysis of the sequences of words in spoken speech — yet this is impossible if the theory and techniques of analyzing speech are discontinuous with the analysis of whistles.

1.22 *Language Reports Which Need a Nonlanguage Supplement*

Just as nonlanguage reports must often have language reports added, if they are to have significance and if they are to be analyzable, so language reports must often have nonlanguage reports given, or they too will be unintelligible.

If, for example, one has a tape recording of the word *No!*, with silence for a long period on either side, the incident in which it occurred would not be structurally significant; one needs to know, as well, through a moving picture or a verbal report about the incident, that a child has just reached for a fragile article on a table and his mother has called *No!* to him. Similarly, a tape recording of the phrase *Why, Mommie?* needs an accompanying verbal or pictographic record of the mother gesturing for the child to come, before the incident emerges as a significant behavioral entity.

Recently I heard two people talking, and during the conversation one of them said quietly, *No thank you*. This phrase did not fit culturally into the rest of the conversation. The total conversation as a unit therefore is meaningless — culturally unanalyzable in any way which would treat this bit of vocal material as an integrated part of the remainder — unless one is also told that I was listening to these two people while they were eating, and that the phrase *No thank you* was uttered as an aside to a waitress who, without a word, had held a plate of cakes over the shoulder of the man then talking.

Some time ago I was playing water polo. A tape recorder set at the pool would have recorded calls for attention, shouted directions, and cries of various kinds. That record, as a document of organized behavior, would fail to contain the data from which a significant record of the game as a coherent unit of behavior could be described. For that, the tape recorder would have needed supplementation by a movie camera as well. Similarly, a record at a basketball game would simultaneously, in hopeless confusion, have registered cheering, calls from the crowd, calls from one player to another, reports of the scorer, and the umpires' decisions. Only a simultaneous visual report, and structural data allowing the various speakers to be sorted out in terms of their function as spectators, officials, players, members of a cheering section, etc., would allow the unit as such to be described usefully for purposes of understanding the nature of that kind of game or the progress of that particular match.

A decade ago I recorded the following: *I see a hat. See it Ted? May I have your attention, please* — whistling — *It is a great honor to welcome...* The sequence was part of utterances by various speakers during a brief street program welcoming a celebrity who was passing through the town. Only in the light of the nonlinguistic facts would the verbal report make sense. Craning of necks, with comments and exclamations by the students; cheers and clapping upon the appearance of the University president; groans at continued presentation of speakers other than the guest of honor; *Thank you* from the guest's wife, as she received a corsage; interruption of the guest's speech by the striking of the big clock in the tower — and the modification of his speech to accommodate to that interruption; reference to a neighboring school and its football teams; ominous reference to the *third world war* in which university men were *now engaged* — these, and other vocal and nonvocal items, became intelligible only against the background of the whole behavioral incident and of a larger and more inclusive outlook than that of any unit of mere verbal behavior heard on that occasion.

Analysis of the linguistic phase of events, like the description of such a phase following its analysis, is also seen to be heavily and essentially dependent upon its relation to nonlanguage behavior. Probably at no time, for example, does the interdependence of language and nonlanguage behavior appear more strikingly to be interlocked than when one is trying to analyze a language which one does not understand, and to do so without written or translated documents and without an interpreter (i.e., with a 'monolingual approach'). Under these circumstances the analyst is compelled to correlate particular sequences of sounds (words, or sequences of words of unknown meaning) with the particular environment in which they are uttered and with the particular nonlanguage activity which is then going on. Often (twice by necessity, for the lack of interpreters, and many more times in public and under laboratory conditions for demonstration purposes or to test the validity of my operational methods, in an environment where bias from translation by the informant is eliminated) I have taken the first steps in the analysis of various languages of Asia, Africa, Australia, New Guinea, Europe, and North America, by such a monolingual gesture approach without any translation help. In order to find the meanings of words or expressions without an interpreter it is certain that some of the nonverbal activity must also be observed — whether it be the gestures of pointing and the like, in special learning situations, or the common daily activity accompanying common speech activity in the community. One never completely outgrows this analytical necessity; no matter how long one studies a language, many of the meanings of new words which he meets (e.g., in a culture with a vocabulary being rapidly enlarged by new names for new technical processes) can only be determined by watching the new processes being named, or by obtaining directly or indirectly a report from some other person who has done so.

1.3 *Verbal and Nonverbal Elements Substituting for One Another in Function*

The preceding section has illustrated the concomitance and interdependence of language behavior with nonlanguage behavior in single events, but their interrelations are structurally much more intimate than such a statement can show. Language behavior and nonlanguage behavior are structurally so analogous that on some occasions certain of their parts are interchangeable, as we have already seen in the illustration introducing this chapter — a game in which a sung word is replaced by a gesture. Now we wish to give a further illustration which will show that such incidents are part of everyday living and to emphasize that such substitutability must be interpreted as evidence that language behavior and nonlanguage behavior must be comprised of structures which are partly alike, in principle, in order to allow for this interchangeability of parts. Here, indeed, there must be no discontinuity of analysis.

Let us assume that we observe successively the following four incidents:
Incident A:
John, walking down the street, sees Bill standing on the other side. He calls out: *Howdy, come along with me?*
Bill replies: *No.*
John says: *Bye!*
Incident B:
John, walking down the street, sees Bill standing on the other side. He calls out: *Howdy, come along with me?*
Bill says nothing, but shakes his head negatively.
John says: *Bye!*
Incident C:
John meets Bill, as in A and B. He waves a greeting, with elbow flexed up in the air, and open hand pivoting slightly at the wrist, but with no word uttered. He then

'crooks a finger' (forearm extended, palm upward, three fingers and thumb clasped lightly together, index finger extended and then bent, at the two end joints, toward the palm of the hand) to urge Bill to come with him.

Bill replies: *No.*

John then waves goodbye (arm extended, slightly bent at the elbow, forearm slightly raised, palm downward, fingers loosely extended, hand moves up and down with flexible wrist).

Incident D:

John meets Bill as in A, B, C. He waves a greeting and signals Bill to come, as in C.

Bill silently shakes his head negatively (rotating it slowly from side to side through a small arc).

John waves goodbye.

In each of these incidents there are several important parts: greeting, request, reply, sign off. These parts occur at FUNCTIONAL SLOTS crucial to the understanding of these particular incidents. Numerous options exist for filling these particular functional slots. For the greeting there might have been used: *Howdy!; Hi!; Hello!; Look who's here!;* or others. For the request there might have occurred: *Come; Listen; What are you doing there?; You ought to have been with us last night;* and innumerable others. For the response there are: *Yes; No; Tomorrow;* and so on. For leave taking there are: *Be seeing you; So long; Be good; Take care of yourself;* and many more, all appropriate to the setting.

Bills' gesture of response in incident B, it should be noticed, becomes one of the CLASS OF ACTIVITIES APPROPRIATE to that functional slot, and as such the nonvocal response is integrated into the vocal system. The implications of such integration must not be ignored, nor must the integrations be treated as "exceptions," nor be by-passed by assuming that gesture is here just "functioning as language". The implications go much deeper, pointing the way toward a unified theory of structure for all types of human behavior, in each of which there are crucial functional slots filled by their corresponding classes of activities.

In the last of the incidents, no vocalization was heard. Such an exchange is common in our culture between people who know each other intimately, either when they need to exchange semi-private signals in the presence of others (*Investigate that noise and see what the children are up to. Shall I bring in the tea now? Hand me that hammer*), or in solitude (a squeeze of the hand and a directed glance of the eyes: *Look at and enjoy silently with me that gorgeous sunset*).

In some other cultures, such gesture communication seems to be used between strangers more often than it is with us. One of my colleagues observed the following incident in a large Latin-American city: A poorly dressed man had been standing a long time in a queue at a post office window. Just as he got up to the window the official closed it and then came out of a door near the window. The man turned toward him, threw his hands out sideways, rotating the palms upward, while tossing the head back and up, with lifted eyebrows (i.e., *How come, what now?*). The official, also without a word, raised his hand, thumb downward, thumb and forefinger extended slightly apart, as if measuring half an inch (i.e., *Just a little while, patience!*).

In situations in which only one person is involved such substitutions may also occur. A man who hits his fingernail with a hammer or hurts himself in some other way, for example, may on occasion either silently, with a grimace, throw the hammer, or he may vocally exclaim, or he may merely draw in his breath sharply to produce a culturally specified kind of hissing sound without more violent reaction.

In thinking through a mechanical problem, one can use trial and error by actually placing two pieces together to see if they belong thus, or the action can be omitted and the person can, as he looks at them, say aloud to himself (or silently): *Now let's see, if I put this piece there, and that one here, they would not fit*.

Even the analysis of thinking, therefore, cannot in this broad structural sense be handled discontinuously from the analysis of the mechanical movements of problem solving: mechanical movements and thinking are *structurally* mixed together in events, not haphazardly so. To use a chemical figure of speech, they form compound molecules which can be analyzed as structured; they are not mere physical mixtures.

From this point of view, we see that it is not enough that language behavior and overt physical activity be handled by one approach. All psychological processes, all internal structured responses to sensations, all of thinking and feeling, must also be considered as parts of human behavior which will become structurally intelligible only when a theory, a set of terms, and an analytical procedure are provided which deal simultaneously and without sharp discontinuities with all human overt and covert activity. Language is but one structured phase of that activity.

1.4 *Bibliographical Comments on Chapter 1*

One of the points of view suggested by this chapter — that language events and non-language events may constitute structurally equivalent members of classes of events which may constitute interchangeable parts within larger unit events — has been anticipated by Sapir, without development of its structural implications: "If one says to me 'Lend me a dollar', I may hand over the money without a word or I may give it with an accompanying 'Here it is' or I may say 'I haven't got it' or 'I'll give it to you tomorrow'. Each of these responses is structurally equivalent, if one thinks of the larger behavior patterns" (1933, in his Selected Writings: 12; see also Hjelmslev, 1953: 66).

Sapir early suggested that linguistics might help in "the interpretation of human conduct in general" (in his Selected Writings, 1949 [1929]:166).

He also treated language itself as behavior, though more specifically 'purely linguistic facts may be seen as specialized forms of symbolic behavior' (1929, in his Selected Writings: 163). For Kluckhohn 'language is just one kind of cultural behavior' (1949:148); similar opinions of various other authors are to be found in Kroeber and

Kluckhohn (1952:115-24); and in Levi-Strauss and others (1953:27-32). Compare also Zipf, "speech is but a form of human behavior" (1935:7); and Malinowski, "Language, in its primitive function, [is] to be regarded as a *mode of action*, rather than as a *countersign of thought*" (1948 [1923]:296; cf. also Weber, 1947 — a translation of earlier works — 88, 94). For a somewhat different approach to language, note Morris, "*a language is a system of comsign-families*" (1946:36), with the prior statement that "A sign which has the same signification to the organism which produces it that it has to other organisms stimulated by it will be called a *comsign*" (33). Some other writers emphasize, as I have done here, the close relation of language to nonlanguage behavior. Thus Malinowski shows such interdependence in situations of the hunt, or of planting, fishing, and the like. Malinowski insists on the importance of "*context of situation*" in the relationship between speech and activities such as hunting, fishing, planting (1948[1923]:306-316); J. R. Firth also emphasizes context of situation, but differs from Malinowski by pointing out that "'context of situation' is, however, more often used to refer to a scheme of general categories" (1952:7), or to the 'actual verbal context' (1935a:51n) so that "For linguistics, the pivotal or 'focal' term of the context of situation is the actual verbal context" (1935a:51n; see also 1950:42-43); so that, for Robins, "the cardinal principle of linguistics, at least in Great Britain, [is] that language must always, and in every analysis, be studied as a part of social process and social activity, and every utterance must be considered and understood within its context of situation. ...and it is contextual function alone that constitutes and guarantees linguistic meaning" (1951:91-92; see also (89), language as a 'part of social action').

For language as 'patterned activity' see also Halliday (1961:250), and compare Firth (1937:19).

Ethnolinguistic discussion has treated some aspects of the relation of language to behavior. See, for brief early bibliography, Olmstead (1950); see also Goodell (1964); and very extensive bibliography and reprinted articles in Hymes (1964). See also §§ 16.8 and 17.7 below. Skinner includes in the definition of verbal behavior the component of a listener responding in "ways which have been conditioned *precisely in order to reinforce the behavior of the speaker*" (1957:225). Carroll (1953:106) suggests that language description might provide a way of dealing with units of other kinds of behavior. He implies a hierarchical structuring for 'behavior in general' suggested by psycholinguistics (1953:111).

In spite of the intimate linking of language and nonlanguage behavior in many large units of human activity, however, some workers have maintained "that the line between linguistics and non-linguistics could be clearly drawn" (Voegelin, and Ray, in Levi-Strauss and others, 1953:30).

Attempts to show pattern similarities between language and nonlanguage behavior, however, have so far [i.e., as of 1954] been disappointing. Thus Kroeber and Kluckhohn say: "What the 'cultural' equivalent of phonemes, or the linguistic equivalent of 'cultural traits,' may be has not yet become apparent" (1952:124). In the same year, for example, Voegelin and Harris seemed to imply that the attempt to find such equivalents was hopeless, since linguistic approaches were unique to language: "It became clear that anthropologists and others working with languages had in their hands a tool [i.e. phonemics] which simplified the description of languages, and proved to be uniquely fitted to language [i.e., not applicable to nonlanguage activity], since all attempts to extend this phonemic tool to the analysis of culture have been in vain." And: "Like the phonemic method, so also the combinatorial method [i.e., descriptive techniques, such as morphemics, applied to grammatical analysis] proved to be uniquely fitted to the data of language, rather than to culture in general" (1952:325).

Nevertheless, in that same year, also, two widely different studies appeared which made some progress in this direction. Birdwhistell, building on a considerable tradition of the study and symbolization of gesture and of other bodily movements, carried forward these studies and, under stimulus from Trager and Smith, pointed out numerous parallels in theory and technique between the study of such motions and the principles of linguistics, even though it stopped short of an integrated theory of the type for which we have felt the need. (A later study by E. T. Hall and Trager, 1953, is excessively compartmentalized, with an attempt at an a priori classification of systems of behavior, but actual behavior events — with all their integrated complexities — receive little attention. See now, however, E. T. Hall's extensive and elegant studies on the structuring of space — proxemics — 1963.)

The second study was one by Fries, on the English sentence; it was developed purely as a linguistic analysis of a body of mechanically recorded utterances, but as a matter of fact it made, in addition, a most important contribution to the study of the relationship between verbal structure and nonverbal events, by founding a classification of basic sentence types on linguistic data combined with nonverbal data — the kinds of responses, which included 'action' responses (characteristic of type II) in contradistinction to 'oral' responses (characteristic of type I) (1952:53). Compare, also, Hoijer: "Language may no longer be viewed as something entirely distinct from other cultural systems but must rather be viewed as part of the whole and functionally related to it" (in Kroeber, 1953:554).

Robins, on the contrary, has stated that he considers my suggestion of structural inter-relations of language and behavior as being 'intrinsically improbable' (1959b:2); and for an extensive discussion which insists on 'an initial sharp separation' between verbal and nonverbal units, and so is 'exactly contrary' to Pike's, see M. Harris (1964:136).

My own attitude toward the relation of language to nonlanguage behavior grew out of three kinds of experience: (1) When I was first learning Mixtec, of Mexico, by a monolingual approach (i.e., without an interpreter), I was forced in 1935 to consider language and other activity together. The next year at the Summer Institute of Linguistics I developed a method for demonstrating to students — many of whom could not be certain of finding interpreters in the areas to which they were heading — the way in which they could learn a language by gesture, that is, by demonstrating a monolingual approach. Under such conditions, language, or "propositions," without reference to other activity became operationally meaningless. (2) In 1948 I began to devote all my research to a study of basic units of language structure in preparation for this present volume. Early in 1949 it appeared that a useful definition of each of these units had to include information concerning the distribution of these units in larger organized units. When, however, I dealt with the largest language units under attention, this principle necessitated the postulation of their distribution within similarly organized but larger units, units of a nonlanguage type, if the elsewhere useful insistence on mentioning the distributional characteristics of the units was to be preserved. This at first seemed outside of my range of investigation until I suddenly noticed that in describing the formal characteristics of a certain document — a business letter — I had actually left the area of vocal matters which I had been studying, and was in something quite different, but an area in which the principles developed for vocal utterance were already serving adequately without my having noticed the change from the one area to the other. From this point onward I kept in view nonvocal activity in the development of the theory. (3) It was not until there came to my attention certain instances where language behavior and nonlanguage behavior were structurally interchangeable (§§ 1.1, 1.3, above), however, that I was fully convinced that a satisfactory theory of language must assuredly contain some reference to the structuring of nonvocal activity and to units composed of vocal and nonvocal activity in single composite events.

Since this chapter first appeared (1954) the outlook for the integration of verbal and nonverbal studies has become much brighter. Lounsbury (1956) and Goodenough (1956) have independently shown how kinship structures can be analyzed, starting, as Goodenough states (195), from "the methods of componential analysis as they have been developed for analyzing linguistic forms". Conklin (1955, and in Householder and Saporta, 1962) and Frake (1961, 1962) have shown hierarchic treatment of cultural terms.

Frake wishes to "tap the cognitive world of one's informants" in order to make the analog of a grammar which will make it possible to "generate new acts which will be considered appropriate responses" (1962:54). See also below, § 16.825. E. T. Hall has attempted extensive finding out of relations between verbal and nonverbal materials as "a map of culture" (see 1959:224).

For Bock "the stimulus as well as some of the concepts and procedures employed have been derived from descriptive (structural) linguistics" (1962:154); he treated the analysis of social roles and their interrelationships in terms of their relation to social tagmemes and social matrices. (See further discussion of Bock in § 17.73.)

Interest in the study of gesture has increased. Its integration with speech and culture has been studied by E. T. Hall (1959, 1963). Bibliography on the use of gestures can be found in Hayes (1957), and Birdwhistell (1959).

For report of an elaborate communication without sound, note Morris (1946:191). For speech surrogates, see below, § 13.85.

Illustrations of gestures replacing language do not need to be confined to special situations such as party games of § 1.1. They become regular parts of language in normal discourse. In Papago, for example, Dean Saxton, of the Summer Institute of Linguistics tells me that he has recorded čʔab hab aš ʔi (nodding gesture) with the meaning 'and they are just dropping off to sleep'; also k gamhu (gesture of going) huḍunk 'and over there (going in the evening)'. Similarly, in Mazatec an object slot can be filled either by a verbal element or by a nonverbal event in immediate context. See Gudschinsky (1959a: 85, fn. 14).

The relevance of contrastive culture studies in reference to language study has also come to the fore (Lado, 1957; Marckwardt, 1961:153). Hymes (1962) has discussed many details of the relationship of speech to its cultural setting.

Interest in animal communication in reference to linguistic concepts has also increased; see Sebeok (1963a) for bibliography. Chandola discusses commands of man to animals in reference to the linguistic slots of human discourse into which they fit (1963).

Finally, note for our thesis here that language is a variety of behavior. Goodenough: "Theory and method applicable to the one [language or culture] must have implications for the other" since the relation "is that of part to whole" (1957:169). And compare the supporting connection of Gross, Mason, and McEachern, that "There is a great need for concepts in social science that can be played 'across the board, that is, concepts whose utility is not limited to a single discipline but which can be used by students of the several social science disciplines in conceptual formulations of certain of their strategic problems" (1958:325).

CHAPTER 2

ETIC AND EMIC STANDPOINTS FOR THE DESCRIPTION OF BEHAVIOR

It proves convenient — though partially arbitrary — to describe behavior from two different standpoints, which lead to results which shade into one another. The etic viewpoint studies behavior as from outside of a particular system, and as an essential initial approach to an alien system. The emic viewpoint results from studying behavior as from inside the system. (I coined the words etic and emic from the words phonetic and phonemic, following the conventional linguistic usage of these latter terms. The short terms are used in an analogous manner, but for more general purposes.)

2.1 *Characteristics of the Two Standpoints*

The principal differences between the etic and emic approaches to language and culture can be summarized as follows:

2.11 *Cross-cultural versus specific*

The etic approach treats all cultures or languages — or a selected group of them — at one time. It might well be called 'comparative' in the anthropological sense (cf. M. Mead, 1952:344) were it not for the fact that the phrase 'comparative linguistics' has a quite different usage already current in linguistic circles, in reference to comparing related languages with a view to reconstructing parent forms. The emic approach is, on the contrary, culturally specific, applied to one language or culture at a time.

Units available in advance, versus determined during analysis: Etic units and classifications, based on prior broad sampling or surveys (and studied in training courses) may be available before one begins the analysis of a further particular language or culture. Regardless of how much training one has however, emic units of a language must be determined during the analysis of that language; they must be discovered, not predicted — even though the range of kinds of components of language has restrictions placed upon it by the physiology of the human organism, and these restrictions are to some degree reflected in the events of the observed range of language phenomena.

Creation versus discovery of a system: The etic organization of a world-wide cross-cultural scheme may be created by the analyst. The emic structure of a particular system must, I hold, be discovered. (But here I am assuming a philosophy of science which grants that in the universe some structures occur other than in the mind of the analyst himself. If one adopts a view that no structure of language or culture is present in the universe, except as a theoretical construct created by the analyst, then the paragraph must be restated in a different way, to preserve its usefulness in such a context. Specifically, the linguist who denies structure to a naïve sentence or to a sonnet must settle for having his own statements, descriptions, or rules about these phenomena as also being without a publicly available structure or ordering. Linguistic statement comprises a subvariety of language utterance, and hence can have no structure if language has no structure. See §§ 2.72 and 2.75 for bibliographical references to these matters.)

External versus internal view: Descriptions or analyses from the etic standpoint are "alien" in view, with criteria external to the system. Emic descriptions provide an internal view, with criteria chosen from within the system. They represent to us the view of one familiar with the system and who knows how to function within it himself.

External versus internal plan: An etic system may be set up by criteria or 'logical' plan whose relevance is external to the system being studied. The discovery or setting up of the emic system requires the inclusion of criteria relevant to the internal functioning of the system itself.

Absolute versus relative criteria: The etic criteria may often be considered absolute, or measurable directly. Emic criteria are relative to the internal characteristics of the system, and can be usefully described or measured relative to each other.

Non-integration versus integration: The etic view does not require that every unit be viewed as part of a larger setting. The emic view, however, insists that every unit be seen as somehow distributed and functioning within a larger structural unit or setting, in a hierarchy of units and hierarchy of settings as units.

Sameness and difference as measured versus systemic: Two units are different etically when instrumental measurements can show them to be so. Units are different emically only when they elicit different responses from people acting within the system.

Partial versus total data: Etic data are obtainable early in analysis with partial information. In principle, on the contrary, emic criteria require a knowledge of the total system to which they are relative and from which they ultimately draw their significance.

Preliminary versus final presentation: Hence, etic data provide access into the system — the starting point of analysis. They give tentative results, tentative units. The final analysis or presentation, however, would be in emic units. In the total analysis, the initial etic description gradually is refined, and is ultimately — in principle, but probably never in practice — replaced by one which is totally emic.

If, furthermore, it is desired to present the emic — structural — units not only as algebraic points relative to a system, but also as elements physically described, the emic notation must be supplemented by etic, physical description.

The penalty for ignoring the etic-emic distinction, and of attempting to utilize (without knowing it) an etic description when an emic one is needed, is best stated in the words of Sapir, who anticipated this position years ago:

It is impossible to say what an individual is doing unless we have tacitly accepted the essentially arbitrary modes of interpretation that social tradition is constantly suggesting to us from the very moment of our birth. Let anyone who doubts this try the experiment of making a painstaking report [i.e. an etic one] of the actions of a group of natives engaged in some activity, say religious, to which he has not the cultural key [i.e. a knowledge of the emic system]. If he is a skilful writer, he may succeed in giving a picturesque account of what he sees and hears, or thinks he sees and hears, but the chances of his being able to give a relation of what happens, in terms that would be intelligible and acceptable to the natives themselves, are practically nil. He will be guilty of all manner of distortion; his emphasis will be constantly askew. He will find interesting what the natives take for granted as a casual kind of behavior worthy of no particular comment, and he will utterly fail to observe the crucial turning points in the course of action that give formal significance to the whole in the minds of those who do possess the key to its understanding (1927, in his Selected Writings: 546-547).

An illustration remote from human behavior may be helpful: in an emic approach, the analyst might describe the structural functioning of a particular car as a whole, and might include charts showing the parts of the whole car as they function in relation one to another; in an etic approach he might describe the elements one at a time as they are found in a stock room, where bolts, screws, rims, fenders and complex parts, such as generators and motors from various models and makes of cars, have been systematically 'filed' according to general criteria.

2.12 *Physical Nature, Response, and Distribution*

Certain physical events must be kept in mind for an emic analysis of verbal materials. They include at least two types, neither of which, in the view presented here, can be ignored at any level of language structure without ultimate loss of some relevant data, or distortion of the system being studied. These two types of events are (a) linguistic — i.e., verbal, and (b) extralinguistic — i.e., nonverbal. Every emic unit of language behavior must be studied in reference to its distribution — distribution in reference to verbal behavior, and distribution in reference to nonverbal cultural behavior. Within the study of the distribution of language units in nonverbal contexts is included the consideration of the nonverbal responses of individuals to speech addressed to them. Just as the verbal replies of a speaker help one determine meanings of elements of communication, so the nonverbal ones do likewise. To attempt to analyze or describe language without reference to its function in eliciting responses — verbal and nonverbal — is to ignore one of the crucial kinds of evidence which is essential if the emic structure of language is to be determined, whether one is dealing with the larger units of that structure, such as the sentence, or smaller ones, such as some of the emic units of the sound system.

This analytical dependence can be in part ignored at the presentation of the material after the language structure has been analyzed. But this theory maintains that in the analytical process there is tacit or explicit reference to cultural distribution, nonverbal as well as verbal. If one is working through a second language, by interpretation, it is easy to succumb to the illusion that there is no such dependence, since one may appear to be using 'words', only, to get data and to determine its function and structure. With a monolingual approach (cf. § 1.4), the direct dependence upon nonverbal contexts is more easily seen. In either case, once the analyst notes his ultimate reliance upon cultural distribution of nonverbal as well as verbal types, he is ready to appreciate, in further detail, the insistence of Chapter 1 that a theory of language is needed which is not discontinuous with a theory of other phases of human activity.

2.13 *Value of Standpoints*

Both etic and emic approaches are of great value for special phases of behavioral analysis. The etic approach to behavior is of especial value, first, in giving to a beginning student a broad training as to the kinds of behavior occurring around the world, so that he may be the more prepared to recognize quickly the different kinds of events observed, and to help him see slight differences between similar events. Second, during this process he may obtain a technique and symbolism (say a phonetic alphabet) for recording the events of a culture. Third, even the specialist, coming from one culture to a sharply different one, has no other way to begin its analysis than by starting with a rough, tentative (and inaccurate) etic description of it. No matter how skilful an emicist he may be, he can complete his emic description only after the analysis is complete — not before — and that analysis must be begun by recording data etically in terms of his prior experience (systematic training, or unclassified knowledge gained in terms of his own culture). Fourth, in studies of the geographical occurrence or diffusion of single kinds of activity, or of a pre-selected list of activities within an area, the analyst may not choose (because of financial limitations, pressure of time, and so on), to make a complete emic study of each local culture or dialect; under such circumstances an etic comparison may be used — or, better, a widespread etic sampling of many local areas with additional intensive emic studies of a few strategically located areas.

The value of emic study is, first, that it leads to an understanding of the way in which a language or culture is constructed, not as a series of miscellaneous parts, but as a working whole. Second, it helps one to appreciate not only the culture or language as an ordered whole, but it helps one to understand the individual actors in such a life drama — their attitudes, motives, interests, responses, conflicts, and personality development. In addition, it provides the only basis upon which a predictive science of behavior can be expected to make some of its greatest progress, since even statistical predictive studies will in many instances ultimately prove invalid, except as they reflect samplings and classifications which are homogeneous — but homogeneity in behavior must for many of these purposes be emically defined. Later in the chapter (§ 2.6) we shall return to one phase of predictability of behavior.

2.14 *Caution — Not a Dichotomy*

A caution needs to be given at this point: in many instances, an etic and an emic description may appear to be almost alike — so much so, in fact, that the unwary reader may say that there is 'no difference', say, between the phonetic and phonemic descriptions of the system of sounds of a language, or that the difference is so slight as not to warrant the extra effort an emic description requires.

To be sure, much of the data is the same, and the general content looks much alike. Yet this is also true of the two separate pictures which go into a stereoscopic viewer; an untrained person usually sees them as identical, but the three-dimensional effect evoked by seeing simultaneously through the stereoscope the two views of the same scene — taken at the same time, under the same lighting conditions, but with viewpoints scant inches apart — makes this added perception startling indeed. And so it can be with the two viewpoints of etics and emics. Through the etic 'lens' the analyst views the data in tacit reference to a perspective oriented to all comparable events (whether sounds, ceremonies, activities), of all peoples, of all parts of the earth; through the other lens, the emic one, he views the same events, at the same time, in the same context, in reference to a perspective oriented to the particular function of those particular events in that particular culture, as it and it alone is structured. The result is a kind of 'tri-dimensional understanding' of human behavior instead of a 'flat' etic one.

It must be further emphasized that etic and emic data do not constitute a rigid dichotomy of bits of data, but often present the same data from two points of view. Specifically, for example, the emic units of a language, once discovered by emic procedures, may be listed for comparative purposes with the similar emic units from other languages so studied. The moment that this has been done, however, the emic units have changed into etic units, since they are divorced from the context of the structure of the language from which they have come, and are viewed as generalized instances of abstract stereotypes, rather than as living parts of an actual sequence of behavior events within a particular culture. Similarly, if a person working in one dialect moves to a very similar neighboring dialect, his first transcription is an etic one, perforce, because he is alien to that dialect, but it may actually be very close to the final emic transcription which he will produce; many of his tentative etic units will turn out to be emic units as well.

We turn, now, to illustrations of differences in outlook on particular events where a camera recording of the physical event would not be enough — but where other data must also be used.

2.2 *Illustrations of Purposive Emic Differences Within a Culture*

Within a particular culture there are many events which on the surface appear to be similar or identical, but which function very differently. This difference often consists in the different purpose of the actors. This purpose is frequently obvious to the outside observer or other participants; at other times it is obscure both to the outside observer and to the participant. When the difference of purpose is easily seen, it is detected in terms of the kind of observable larger sequence of events within which the smaller event occurs (i.e., its distribution) — and in terms of the response which it immediately receives. When the purpose is temporarily hidden from the other participants, the choice of alternate responses may be delayed until after other events have made the purposive difference clear, or a response may be given which the participants may later judge to have been inappropriate.

In the United States Senate a camera and recorder on different occasions might register two speeches which were physically similar. The first, let us say, is intended to affect the attitude of listeners, such as to convince them of the necessity of the course of action being presented. The second is discussing the same course of action, with the same words, but without any such purpose. It is a filibuster designed not to affect that irrelevant issue which happens to provide the words, but is calculated so to delay the course of business as to force the speaker's opponents to give up the attempt to pass a measure unpalatable to him. Some of the immediate reactions to a filibuster (such as inattention by the audience) may be quite different from that of the same data given as part of a different address.

A partial small-scale parallel with such an instance would be the speaking of any pair of homophones such as *pare, pair; rite, write; seal* (animal, noun), *seal* (of wax, noun), *seal* (verb). Here, too, the outward visible form may be the same, whereas the words as a whole must be considered different because of the responses which they elicit from the hearers, and the kind of verbal sequences into which they enter.

Units of size intermediate between a filibuster and single words may occur which must be similarly differentiated. Note such items as mimicry, where a child is trying to learn to speak by repeating sentences after adults; the homonymous repeated sentence is often inappropriate to normal conversation since the child may fail, for example, to change *you* to *I*, or to replace question with answer. A lie is homophonous with a parallel normal sentence, but they must be considered different emically, in spite of the identity of their internal structures. Even the immediate responses — and hence their apparent meanings — may be the same. In order to detect the essential difference between them, the observer must be prepared to notice reactions (say, a spanking) delayed for a much longer time. In lying, therefore, we have an illustration of an emic difference, where the natives themselves cannot immediately detect that difference — or it may go permanently undetected by the hearers. Here, then, there is some temporary or permanent indeterminacy of meaning.

Irony brings us a different type of homophony which includes, usually, the intention of having at least part of the audience to so detect it; if that purpose fails, the irony will be "lost on" the receiver of it — though it may cause the amusement of on-lookers. Mimicry of the lisping character of someone's speech is similar to such irony — and quite different from the mimicry of an adult by a child learning to talk. An adult in learning a foreign language may be badly inhibited from adequate mimicry by reacting to his own learning process as if it were the kind of socially inacceptable mimicry rather than the other.

Nonverbal mimicry shows a similar patterning: a child utilizes small-scale implements to *do like Daddy*, in raking the lawn, digging a hole, or fishing. With his father gone from the scene, and the mimicry purpose removed, the child may not finish raking the lawn.

On an adult scale, the working activity may be quite similar, whether the regular workers or strike breakers are performing it, but the reaction to the first is one of normal community relations, whereas reaction to the second may include violent attempts by the strikers to interrupt the work of the strike breakers. The killing of a single fly by a Western adult might be an act of cleanliness, but by a Hindu might have implications of profound religious significance, because of their beliefs concerning the possibility of the reincarnation of human souls into animal bodies. Tea drinking at 4:30 p.m. in some parts of the U.S.A. would imply a somewhat formal social gathering; in Australia it often means little more than quenching one's thirst. In meetings of the United Nations, the circumstances (i.e. distribution) and purpose of activities affect the reaction of people — to seeing one of, e.g., the participants 'walk out' as a political measure to indicate disapproval (rather than to go to the toilet).

In our culture there are, furthermore, specific legal procedures which are used in an attempt to differentiate between events which are physically similar but emically different, with sharply different cultural penalties: Was the man carrying a pistol when he robbed the house? Did the driver run through a red light when he hit the man? Was the violence premeditated or the result of sudden anger? Was the author of it insane or was he deliberately cruel? Was the prisoner really trying to escape, or did the guard misunderstand, or pretend to do so, or even stage the event under orders? Nonlegal activity similarly attempts to apply criteria to determine such matters: Is this explanation the real reason, or is it just an excuse to mask laziness or irresponsibility or viciousness? Was the plate really cracked?

In nonverbal activity as in verbal activity there may be temporary ambiguities which can only be resolved by a study of a larger context. For example: Do the people of Country X know the issues which lead to their activity and choose that activity deliberately, or are they following the lead of someone else blindly or under compulsion?

Perhaps the illustration of such emic differences best known to linguistic circles is one given by Sapir (1925, in his Selected Writings, 34). A candle-blowing *wh*, though physically similar to the *wh* of *which, why* in some dialects of English is, nevertheless, 'entirely distinct' from it in the series of kinds of events to which it belongs. For both of them the lips are puckered up, and air is blown out of the mouth with a slight friction sound. In the first, the purpose is to blow out a candle, and the event is part of a series, such as 'going to bed'; in the second, the sound becomes part of a word, and the word becomes part of a sentence, and the sentence becomes part of a conversation.

An emic approach would treat as significantly different the preceding pairs of events. One kind of etic approach — one which ignored meaning or purpose — might treat them as nearly identical pairs. In between these two approaches would be a different etic classification of these emic types, listing them in relation to differential purpose, meaning, or response, but not in relation to the full systems from which they were abstracted.

2.3 *Variants of Emic Units*

Sapir says that

Every typical human action has a certain range of variation and, properly speaking, no such reaction can be understood except as a series of variants distributed about a norm or type. (1925, in his Selected Writings, 34).

In the preceding section we illustrated events which were physically same, or approximately so, but emically different. Now we show how events may be physically different but emically same.

It proves impossible for a person to repeat any movement so that it is *exactly* duplicated. Delicate measuring instruments will show some variation, a 'scatter' or 'spread' of slight differences when a person tries to do so. Whether it be shaking the head to signal *no*, or moving the lips, tongue, and vocal cords to say *no*, or jumping out of the way to refuse to catch a ball — none of these movement types can be repeated without deviation; minor differences are certain to appear.

There will be such minor physical variants of any unit of purposeful activity. Etically, each repetition of such a unit may be considered to be distinct, within that variety of etic study which is looking for absolute physical differences. Emically, such a scatter of variation would be irrelevant.

Often, however, the physical variation between repetitions of the same emic event is much greater than the physiological characteristics of man impose on his activity. Although, in some instances, the variation may be so small that the eye cannot see it — nor the ear hear the resultant acoustic differences, for speech — the variation in other instances may be large enough for trained alien observers to notice it very clearly and easily, even while untrained native participants do not ordinarily notice it at all, or may fail to see it or hear it even when one attempts to point it out to them. Following the last sound in the phrase, *Here is a cup*, spoken in a matter-of-fact manner, for example, the lips sometimes remain closed; at other times they open slightly, allowing a puff of breath to escape. Such pronunciations of English are etically (here, absolutely) different but emically the same.

Any other kind of activity may have comparable variants. In hopscotch, for example, it is irrelevant to the progress of the game whether a child hops high on one foot, with the other wildly swinging, or whether the hop is low, with relatively steady opposite foot; relevant — emic — factors are rather the success in reaching the next square without stepping on a line or letting both feet touch ground, and so on.

Etic, non-emic differences occur elsewhere than in sheer repetition of emically same events: the variants may be caused by inevitable, minimal changes of movement accompanying the slurring of one emic movement into a following (or preceding) movement. Every movement is so modified. The movements of the tongue in forming *s* differ etically in *missile* from what the movements can be in forming *s* in *task;* starting from a position during the pronunciation of the *i* of *missile*, the tongue glides by degrees into movements which in part constitute *s*. The border between *i* and *s* cannot, in fact, be determined — but that problem must await discussion in § 8. The first part of the *s* is inevitably modified by the movements which produce the last part of the *i;* similarly, in *task*, the first part of *s* is modified by the end of *a;* likewise, *s* differs before *l* and *k*. To some extent, no matter how small (even if below the threshold of perception), every sound differs etically according to the sequences of comparable movements within which it occurs.

Every movement, including nonvocal ones, is so affected. The movements of the first hop of a child playing hopscotch differ considerably from the others. The first hop starts from a standing position, whereas the middle ones may have movements slurred together from the momentum of earlier movements, and the last hop into the center must (lest the child receive a penalty) have the movements checked from going too far and throwing the child off balance.

As with repeated movements, however, so with those in sequence, the observed difference between emically same movements may be considerably greater than is necessitated by the physiological mechanisms involved. Like the repeated types, also, the etic difference may be so great as to be easily noted by an alien observer even while the native actor, reacting emically, fails to see any difference between them. I clearly remember, for example, the surprise — almost incredulity — with which I first received the information that the two *p* sounds in *paper* were not the same — that a puff of breath followed the first one, but no breath, or a weak puff only, followed the second; it was probably two years before I heard the difference easily.

These types of etic differences occur simultaneously in sequences. Thus, every repetition of *missle* by itself finds the *s* different each time, and every repetition of *past* has each *s* different. This scatter of differences in repetition is in addition to the etic differences caused by (or accompanying) the differences in environment when, say, *s* slurs from or to *i*, *l*, *a* or *k*.

It should also be observed that the first *p* of *paper* differs not only in movement type but in movement sequence from the second. Whereas, perceptually, the second seems etically to be a 'single' sound, the first may seem etically to be two — the *p* plus the puff.

The type of variant seen in sheer repetition may be called FREE; that resultant from or accompanying a slur into or from neighboring movements, CONDITIONED; that from a sequence of movements acting in some way as a single unit, COMPLEX. Free, conditioned, and complex variants occur in all general types of behavior; the analyst must be prepared to find them at any stage in the analysis.

In addition to being simple or complex, variants may also be fused, such that a single etic segment is a fused composite of two emic segments; these types of variants will be discussed later (see, especially, Chapter 14 on fusion).

2.4 *Differences in Etic Observers*

In the alien reporting of observations, the human element brings in great differences. One observer may have much more etic training than another; one may have keener hearing of pitch differences, or of intensity, duration, rhythm, or timbre; or one may have a longer memory span than the other. The one observer may fix his attention on one set of etic details through accident, or intention, or training, and hence 'see' and record them; the other may not notice these details, though watching the same event. Likewise, the one observer may be interested temporarily or permanently in one component of behavior and fail to report other components.

Each observer will also have some bias in terms of the behavior events most familiar to him — those which are emic in his own activity. These he tends to take as his point of departure, as his norms, so that cultural background may affect an etic report.

Adequate etic training lessens these differences a great deal, so that individual phonetic reports of the sounds of a language tend to be similar. Nevertheless, the differences in the etic reports of different observers frequently cause confusion.

In order to refer to certain etic types we may label as an INSTRUMENTAL etic report one which records details as absolute, i.e., as accurately as some particular measuring machine is capable of recording. A THRESHOLD etic report will be one which attempts to give differentiations as fine as the physiological limits of a particular individual — or, the average of a group of such individuals — permits. A PERCEPTUAL etic report would be the report of a particular observer at a particular time, reflecting within it the variables and idiosyncrasies of individual ability, training, and momentary focus of attention.

Emic reports of a particular phase or component of behavior of a particular culture should be much more uniform than etic ones, however, since the emic procedures are specifically designed to help *any* observer report the data from an internal structured standpoint.

2.5 *Organization of Similar Etic Units Within Distinct Emic Systems*

In § 2.2 illustrations were given to show that items apparently (etically) alike could be structurally (emically) different, and in § 2.3 it was pointed out that items apparently different could be structurally alike. Now we wish to carry one step further the insistence that structural likeness or difference is determined by and should be analytically related to an emically structured whole, a SYSTEM. The nature of the intricate convolutions of such a system will not emerge until later chapters; it is only the fact of such a relationship that is now to be demonstrated.

We will assume that a game constitutes a small cultural system or sub-system — somewhat analogous to a small dialect, or special style, or some language. Two games — say two card games — may be similar, so that an untutored onlooker may not know which game is being played, even though he is vaguely aware that two such games are played in his community. The cards of the two games may look alike; the players may have similar seating arrangements; they may hold a similar number of cards in a similar fashion in their hands; they may in rotation put cards face down on the table; they may pick up groups of these cards after a certain number are down; a scorer may record some number at intervals; the cards may be re-dealt to the individuals periodically — these items and many others may all be etically very similar. Yet one game as a whole differs from the other, and any particular act in one of the games attains its significance only in relation to the total sequence of events constituting that game.

Recently I observed, as an alien, my first cricket match. In it there were many events to remind me of baseball. A pitcher (called a "bowler") hurled the ball; the batsman on occasion swung his bat at the ball, and sometimes hit it, and if he hit it he sometimes ran; fielders caught the ball in the air, or picked it from the ground, and returned it quickly to one of the players near the path of the runner; the players were organized into teams which changed places during the middle and end of an inning.

There were, to be sure, some differences in these activities: the bowler ran upwards of five to twenty steps before throwing the ball, and then did so with a full overhand sweep of the arm, and a stiff elbow, instead of pitching with a snap of elbow and wrist; usually (all but once, on this occasion) he threw the ball on the ground, so that it reached the batter only on the bounce, instead of pitching it entirely through the air; the batsman stood relaxed, often making little attempt to hit the ball forward or with any swing — but frequently just put his bat limply in front of the ball, so it glanced or bounced off it in any direction an enormous (from my alien viewpoint) number of times. An outfielder on one occasion threw the ball at the 'stumps' (i.e. 'home base', made of three sticks stuck vertically into the ground, with 'bails' — two small sticks — lying horizontally on top of them) instead of to the catcher; the innings were long — such that the last half of the last inning lasted four hours, even though only two thirds of the complement of ten players were out, instead of an entire game lasting two to three hours as in baseball; and so on.

Yet these visible differences fail to show, in themselves, the basic differences in strategy and sequence of events into which the particular events fitted. At the beginning of the game the fastest bowlers (upwards of eighty miles per hour) hurled the balls violently onto the playing field (called the 'pitch') in front of the batsmen, in part of a deliberate attempt to injure its surface and the surface of the ball (as well as to get the ball past the batsman); this, in turn, was designed (so my hosts told me) to prepare for the slow bowlers, who would then hurl a spinning ball into the resultant depressions[1] in the turf, which would impart to the ball an unpredictable bounce in addition to a curve imparted by the air as the roughened surface of the ball traveled through it; this in turn was designed to get the ball past the batsman so that it would bump the stumps, knock off the bails, and put the batsman out. Unlike baseball, with its relatively few tries allowed the batter, the cricket batsman can keep at his task indefinitely — say an entire day of a several day game. Thus in one inning of the particular match to which I have referred, two of the men made over one hundred runs each, since they did not have to hit the ball unless they felt it endangered their 'wicket' (stumps plus bails), nor were they required to run even if they hit the ball; they ran only when they felt — after hitting the ball or letting it go past them from one to twenty times — it was safe to do so. In fact, the desire of the first batsman in a game is not so much to make runs as to maintain calm, and to spoil so many bowls that the bowlers will tire, lose control or speed, and allow later sharpshooting batsman to hit safely for runs. All this, in turn, contributes to the deliberate relaxed stance of a man setting himself for a grueling period of many minutes of constant attention to trick bounces, spins, and speed — in contrast to the baseball batter who has a much shorter period of opportunity, with fewer variables to consider (for example, the atmospheric condition, short of rain, in baseball, is seldom likely to have enough effect on the flight of the ball through the air to allow the baseball pitcher to utilize

---

[1] Evidently my earlier informant here was inadequate. David Abercrombie — both linguist and cricketer — tells me that the fast bowlers hit the ground farther from the batsmen than do the slow bowlers. In addition, he mentioned that the opening bowler tries to keep a shine on one side of the ball, roughing up the other. The unevenness of the two sides, combined with its single large seam, allow the ball to be thrown with the seam especially directed to help produce the desired curve or wobble.

atmospheric changes sufficiently to interest the fans in their effect on the batter — but the contrary is true in cricket).

As the activity of the batsman 'makes sense' only in relation to the whole system of the game, so a consonant, or a vowel sound, is relevant to communication only as it is related to the whole system of sounds of which it is a part. Within two languages, a pair of sounds which are so similar as to seem the same to an alien observer may nevertheless have entirely different places in the functional system in the respective languages in which they occur. It is conceivable, for example, that two languages might etically be composed of lists of sounds which were perceptually almost identical, but with the sounds organized into emic systems which were very different. Let us suppose, for example, that language A and language B each contain the following list of consonants. (This material reflects one kind of illustration used in Sapir's "Sound Patterns in Language" [1925, reprinted in his *Selected Writings*, pp. 35-40] and is the pioneer in such a point of view. The serious student is urged to consult this article, which, in my opinion, has never been equalled for clarity of presentation of some of these emic matters):

p	t	k	K
p^h	t^h	k^h	
b	d	g	G
f	s		
v	z		

The first row of symbols here represents sounds characterized in their production by vocal movements which (among other things) close the oral cavity; during *p* the lips perform this movement; for *t* the tongue tip does so; for *k* this is accomplished by the top part of the tongue, and for *K* the closure is made by a part of the tongue farther back in the mouth. The p^h, t^h, k^h are the same as *p*, *t*, *k* with a slight audible puff of breath after the closure is released. The *b*, *d*, *g*, and *G* are also the same as the first row, except that the vocal cords are vibrating during their production. In *f* and *s*, movements are made in the same general direction in the mouth (except that for *f* the lower lip touches the upper teeth instead of the upper lip) and by the same parts of the mouth as for *p* and *t* respectively, but without quite fully stopping the air stream; *v* and *z* add vocal-cord vibration to *f* and *s*.

Now in language A the p^h is a member of the same emic sound unit as *p*; the p^h is an etic variant restricted to occurrence at the end of phrases; similarly t^h is a variant of *t*, and k^h of *k*. No words in A can ever differ by these sounds alone. In language B, however, the two series are emically distinct. In language A, furthermore, the *K* is an etic variant of the emic unit which contains *k*; the back variety, *K*, occurs only preceding back vowels such as *a* and *o* (whereas the *k* precedes the front vowels *i* and *e* or precedes another consonant, or comes at the end of words); the *G* must be considered part of the emic sound unit which contains *g*, for a similar reason. In language B, on the contrary, the k and K constitute separate emes, with many distinct words differing only by the occurrence of one or the other of them.

In language A, p is a distinct unit from b, t from d, k from g. In B, however, the voiceless-voiced pairs unite into single phonemes, with the voiced member restricted in occurrence to a place between vowels, where the voiceless members are not found.

In language A, the f, s, v, and z are all distinct emic sound units, but in language B the f and v are members of a single unit as are also s and z, since v and z are etic distributional variants which occur only between vowels, where f and s do not so occur.

The list of emic units for language A, then, follows, with one symbol representing each such unit:

Language A, ten emic units:

p	t	k
b	d	g
v	z	
f	s	

Language B, nine emic units:

p^h	t^h	k^h	
p	t	k	K
f	s		

If the etic variants with restricted distribution were added to these lists, but placed in parentheses close to the symbols which represent the units as a whole, the two systems would appear thus:

Language A

p	t	k(K)
(p^h)	(t^h)	(k^h)
b	d	g(G)
f	s	
v	z	

Language B

p^h	t^h	k^h	
p	t	k	K
(b)	(d)	(g)	(G)
f	s		
(v)	(z)		

Of incalculable importance to the analysis of international and personal misunderstandings is the appreciation of the fact that not only sounds, grammar, games and overt activity can contain similar etic inventories of events arranged in different emic systems, but that thinking processes also may be similarly different in so far as these processes utilize words whose meanings are subject to a comparable kind of structuring, and in so far as basic epistemological attitudes, emotional outlook and moral character is also so structured. People of one nation (or class of society, etc.) may sometimes appear to another to be 'illogical' or 'stupid' or 'incomprehensible' simply because the observer is over a long period of time taking an alien standpoint from which to view their activity, instead of seeking to learn their emic patterns of overt and covert behavior.

The same theory must deal with certain problems of individual communication or of child education. Each person to some extent constitutes a separate sub-culture, with his own emic organization. For a common emic structure a common experience is prerequisite, both verbal and nonverbal, in a unified whole. Since this never occurs for any two people, there are always problems of understanding.

After long married life together a well-adjusted couple does learn to communicate many emic attitudes with the faintest of etic hints. Between people who have less in common, or between disciplines in science, the achievement of mutual understanding becomes more difficult. In this book, for example, the term 'morphology' will refer to a phase of the structure of grammar — not to the structure of plants (biology) or of topographic features (geology).

We shall turn again to the structuring of meaning in a later chapter (16), after we have laid the groundwork by setting forth other phases of emic structure.

2.6 *Predictability of Difficulties in Learning to React Emically to an Alien Emic System*

Now that we have briefly discussed (§ 2.3) variants within emic units, and the relation of units to the whole system, we are in a position to turn to the possibility of predicting certain kinds of behavior.

Before I had seen cricket played — and before I knew anything about its rules — I attempted to teach baseball to persons who had played the former but not the latter. There were moments of frustration. What, for example, is there to be said in the heat of the game when the new batter hits ahead into the field but nonchalantly stands and is put out? An urgent *Run, run, RUN!* for some time continued to get only blank looks — or even a protest, *Do I HAVE to run?* to which one is tempted to reply, none too gently, *Yes, run (that is what the game is made for, isn't it)!*

Had I known cricket, however, the failure of the beginners to run on a short infield hit would not only have brought no surprise, but it would have been expected. In view of the fact that in cricket the competent batsman would normally wait for a safe hit before trying to run at all, I would have predicted that they would meet some difficulty in learning that for baseball they must run, since they would be given no other chance to try again before being put out, and that this slim chance of success at reaching first base was the only chance they had.

It should follow, too, that a course designed to teach baseball to cricketers should be drastically different, for best effect, from one designed to teach it to people who had played only chess. The skills learned by the cricketer in catching the ball, in throwing it in from the field (as distinct from the "bowling"), in shifting position in the field to meet the threat of different kinds of batsmen, or the shift under different pitchers — these and many other skills should be utilized and built on immediately. It would be folly to waste the time of such a man by making him undergo, in the same detail and in the same way, many of the first months of work in ball handling which the chess player would need. Of the etics of ball handling, and of watching the ball curve as it came toward him, he would already know a great deal — perhaps much more, in particular instances, than his baseball teacher.

On the other hand he would need specific training to prevent certain activities (such as throwing to hit home plate instead of to the catcher at the plate) and to dissociate certain activities, to break up certain sequences he had trained for in cricket, and to replace them with baseball sequences (e.g., hitting the ball to the infield, dropping the bat, and running). Much of this training is an emic re-training — teaching what *not* to do, the breaking up of old patterns and substituting new ones.

The reader is now in a position to see why it is that Fries (1945) insists that for *every language situation*, a newly designed textbook is necessary. A single 'model', with translation for a variety of languages, will not do. A speaker of Spanish learning English needs one textbook; the Chinese speaker of English needs a very different textbook. Many of the specific details — the etics — of English, Spanish, and Chinese sounds, grammar, and vocabulary differ, so they may need to be taught as items. But, in addition (and, for language, this is perhaps even more difficult), the ways in which these items are grouped into emic units and sequences of emic units vary enough to necessitate separate treatment.

Nor is this all. Just as the cricketer needs, for most rapid training, special instruction on some points of baseball, so the baseball player needs special training on the way to play cricket — but the rules are not necessarily reciprocal. Thus a textbook for teaching English to Spanish speakers may need to be quite different from one designed for teaching Spanish to English speakers.

The more one knows about two comparable but different systems of activity the easier it is to predict the kinds of difficulties which will face a learner. Where game A is complex, and game B simple, one can in general predict that it is easier to pass in one direction — toward the simple — than the other; the same is true for systems of activity, whether they be games or languages. More specifically, if two languages contain like emic units of sound, with like variants similarly distributed, there is relatively little difficulty in learning to pronounce those items intelligibly. If, however, in language A there are two emically separate sound units but in language B these same etic sounds are variants of a single emic unit, the speakers of B will have great difficulty in speaking A intelligibly at that point, but the reverse is not true. In English, for example, the first *p* of *paper* and the second are variants of a single emic sound unit, but differ etically in that the first is followed by a slight puff of breath, as we have stated before. English speakers, therefore, have considerable difficulty in learning to pronounce correctly the sounds of languages in which this difference is emic; note, for example, an illustration from Pame (of Mexico): *lakèdnʔ* 'he will pull' in which no puff of breath follows k, but *lakhèdnʔ* 'they will pull'. (Data from Lorna Gibson, Summer Institute of Linguistics).

One may also predict that a native member of a culture will have various kinds of difficulties in analyzing his own behavior — in learning to notice free or conditioned variants in the physical form of an emic unit of his own speech, for example. (See Fries, 1948:13.)

2.7 Bibliographical Comments on Chapter 2

2.71 *On Etic versus Emic Viewpoints*

By an earlier quotation (§ 2.1) and discussion we indicated that Sapir had anticipated the basic viewpoint of this chapter, that etic and emic viewpoints must be distinguished, and had specifically indicated for phonological systems the manner in which two languages might have identical etic systems but different emic ones (§ 2.5). I consider this latter study the source of the basic understanding in the linguistic field of the systematic relation of emic units, and of the nature of emic systems as such, although other authors had earlier reached some understanding of phonemic units, without the same depth of understanding of their relationship to a total emic system. (See Chapter 8 for further references to some of these other authors; and in § 8.815 note reference to Chomsky for a different view of Sapir's contribution.)

Two further quotations from Sapir may be of interest:

External observations on the adjustment processes of individuals are often highly misleading as to their psychological significance. The usual treatment, for instance, of behavior tendencies known as radical and conservative must leave the genuine psychiatrist cold because he best realizes that the same types of behavior, judged externally, may have entirely distinct, even contradictory, meanings for different individuals' (Sapir, 1932, in his Selected Writings: 520). [And] It is as though an observer from Mars, knowing nothing of the custom we call war, were intuitively led to confound a punishable murder with a throughly legal and noble act of killing in the course of battle (Sapir, 1927, in his Selected Writings: 556; see, for a related theme developed in more detail, Pike, 1952b: 618).

Compare Kluckhohn, "Two cultures could have almost identical inventories and still be extremely different" (1949, p. 34), and "the first responsibility of the anthropologist is to set down events as seen by the people he is studying" (299-300). For some examples where the same or approximately the same custom is functionally different in two cultures, see Benedict (1946: Chapter 4: 78-82).

The development of the relationship between phonetics and phonemics, especially since Sapir's important article appeared (1925 now in his Selected writings), has been carried on by many workers in numerous parts of the world. Similarly, the study of morphemics has grown rapidly, with the principal stimulus, after Bloomfield (1933a), being an article by Z. Harris (1942a). Further references to such matters will appear in following chapters.

For my own understanding of the phonemic principle I am indebted principally to Sapir (1925), Bloomfield (1933a), Swadesh (1934, 1935a, 1937a) and — to much lesser extent — Trubetzkoy (1935). From Sapir, at a luncheon conference in Ann Arbor in 1937, I first heard language compared to a game — tennis. My own reasons for moving from language matters into the etic-emic cultural parallels of the present theory, however, came independently, from problems met in linguistic theory, in the manner indicated in Chapter 1; it was not until the present theory was well advanced that I came across the anticipating quotations from Sapir which were given earlier in the present chapter. The emphasis on the necessity of separate textbooks for each situation in which a student is transferring from one emic language structure to another, on the other hand, comes from Fries (see especially 1945; it is also interesting to note that Fries has used a game — baseball — as an effective source of linguistic illustrations, 1952).

For the suffix *-eme* as productive in English, see R. A. Hall (1950b:72).

For an etic continuum as a "cline" see Halliday (1961:249, 258); as "delicacy" (287, 272).

Some recent insistance on generality in treatments of the theory of language (see § 11.52n) can be rephrased as the requirement of an etic handling of elements for language as a whole, for application to particular language. The problem of universal grammar[2] can, in my view, be stated partly in etic-emic terms. Our prior classification based on general experience, and the prior setting up of the components of such classification, are etic. Dealing with analysis of the specific languages brings in emic units. For a problem of language universals, see Greenberg (1957:86-91). Typological classifications are etic ones. For phonological typology see Hockett (1955); for etics of grammar, see below, §§ 5.5, 6.8, 7.7, 8.7, and 11.5.

For emics and etics treated from a viewpoint which objects to giving much weight to native reaction, see M. Harris (1964:133-50).

Lasswell and Kaplan use the term behavior for acts related to the culture, but the term conduct when acts conform to the culture (1950:48). An act is by them called an operation when it is viewed apart from significance [compare etic units], but a practice when it is in the perspective of significance [compare emic units] (10, 25).

---

[2] Now I would suggest further that an over-all etic system for language in general is one built by taking the emic systems of all languages of the world, and conflating them so as to preserve all observed contrasts. An etic universal system, therefore, becomes the representation of the contrastive features of all known systems, conflated into a single matrix. (For conflated matrices see Pike and Erickson, 1964.)

Mäder contrasts languages of freedom with languages of communism and nazism (1962:92-95-97); for discussion of democracy note Lasswell and Kaplan (1950:239); and compare my discussion — omitted here — in the 1954 edition of § 2.5. Compare C. Morris who suggests that the speaker changes denotation of some terms while continuing their appraisive and prescriptive features (1946:149).

For the etic-emic concept applied to folk tales, see Dundes (1962b, 1963); compare Armstrong (in de Sola Pool, 1959:155) for units relative to context. For the application of emic concepts to social structure note Bock, who says that he has 'tried to adopt what Pike (1954:8) calls an *emic* approach' (1962:155; and see below, § 17.73). For etics of human societies, procedures and terms which are cross-culturally applicable, see Oliver (1958:807-11). For emic units as grid, note Pike (1957-58:146-54). For extensive etic descriptions of plants and their usage in a primitive culture, see Robbins, Harrington, and Freire-Marreco (1916). For approaching study of culture from the point of view of the actor, see Nadel, in reference to Parsons (1951:33); see also Parsons (1951:20, 21). For etic marks in reference to archeological artifacts, note Gardin (1958).

For earlier concepts which have some relationship to our etic-emic approach note Lewin, who compares Aristotle's treatment of perceptible appearance with the biologist's concept of phenotype, while he implies that Aristotle's treatment of properties that determine an object's dynamic relations may be comparable to a genotype with its conditional-genetic relations (1935:11); thus a falling stone, orbiting planet, and oscillating pendulum represent different phenotypes but the same genotype.

The general problem can be summed up in the words of Goodenough, who affirms that "The great problem for a science of man is how to get from the objective world of materiality, with its infinite variability [an etic view of the world], to the subjective world of form as it exists in... the minds of our fellow men" [through the discovery of their emic units] (1957:173). (Our view would insist, however, that every emic unit has a physically manifested component, so that physical characteristics are tied to function ones in a form-meaning composite; see §§ 2.2, 6.46, and Index. For psycholinguistic discussion, see § 8.815.)

2.72 *On the Nature of Structure*

As regards the nature of emic units, and the nature of the systems containing them, the present volume is written from the point of view that emic systems and emic units of these systems are in some sense to be discovered by the analyst, not created by him (cf. Pike, 1947c, 64n). Etic systems, on the other hand, are assumed to be classifications created by the analyst — constructs for the handling of the comparative data, or for the handling of data before its emic ordering can be ascertained. Etic units, within this point of view, would vary: insofar as they approached the emic system and emic units of a system, they would be discovered within that data but to the extent that distortion occurred, they would be only provisional constructs of the analyst. In addition, it should be carefully noted that the etic-emic approach is useful — and necessary — whether or not one adopts this attitude toward the data. Practically, the conviction that there is an emic system to be discovered serves as a stimulus to refuse to accept too readily, as definitive description of a particular set of data, any pair of analyses which appear to be equally valid but contradictory. In such a situation the outlook given here would insist that, before accepting such a result, we try to find a third analysis which does violence to neither of the first two, but merges both analyses in a synthesis at a higher level — possibly by bringing in kinds of data or other levels of data which each of the earlier partial analyses rejected as nonrelevant to the immediate problem, but which now appear relevant.

For an approach based on the tacit assumption that language has structure and that we must find the structures, see Haugen (1951:222); compare also Trager and Smith (1951:8).

This viewpoint specifically does not rule out alternate descriptions of a single system (especially if these purport to be partial descriptions, only) — descriptions differing as to starting point, order of presentation of the relevant materials, and the like. Nor does it rule out alternate ways of symbolizing such a system, as a means of such alternate descriptions. It is precisely here that a much referred to (e.g., Haugen, 1949b:57; Harris, 1951:2) article by Chao (1934:363, 391) had a major impact on American thinking. For the problem of non-unique solutions, compare Sinclair (1951: 23-25, 171); and Whitehead (1925:4, 13). Compare, also, Harris:

It therefore does not matter for basic descriptive method whether the system for a particular language is so *devised* as to have the least number of elements (e.g., phonemes), or the least number of statements about them, or the greatest over-all compactness, etc. These different formulations differ *not linguistically but logically*. They differ not in validity but in their usefulness for one purpose or another (e.g. for teaching the language, for describing its structure, for comparing it with genetically related languages) (1951:9n, italics added; see Hockett's criticism of this viewpoint, 1952a:98).

Later, Harris asks the question "Does the structure really exist in the language?" — to which he replies: "The answer is yes, as much as any scientific structure really obtains in the data which it describes: the scientific structure states a network of relations, and these relations really hold in the data investigated" (1954a:149). For a related network view of culture, see Radcliffe-Brown (1952:190); see, also, § 15.33.

For the viewpoint of another linguist who, like Harris, assumes that emic units are abstracted constructs, only, compare Firth: "Our schematic constructs ...have no ontological status and we do not project them as having being or existence. They are neither immanent nor transcendent, but just language turned back on itself" (1950:42). And, he later states "For me a *fact* must be technically stated and find a place in a system of related statements, all of them arising from a theory and found applicable in renewal of connection in experience. It is probably true that even in mathematics the possibilities of complete axiomatization have been over-estimated" (1956:94).

W. S. Allen has "systems as set up by linguists ... not inherent in language" (1953b: 90; 1956:164; 1957 — the linguist makes the facts, quoted in Zgusta, 1960). Robins, likewise, has linguistic structures as "the product of the linguist" (1957b:3). Zgusta, however, in reviewing Allen, shows lack of sympathy with the view (1960:327).

Chomsky makes a distinction between fact and data: a fact is "a specific set of factual claims" (1961b:220), so that some discussions are said to deal with "linguistic data and not with the facts of language".

Compare Twaddell "A phoneme, accordingly, does not occur; it 'exists' in the somewhat peculiar sense of existence that a brother, *qua* brother, 'exists' — as a term of a relation" (1935:49), and the term 'fiction' applied to it describes "a relational, abstractional class, the sum of terms of differences" (1936a:297). Note also Robins — "The grammarian must discover, but not impose, regularity in the structure of a language" (1951:52). For a discussion of contrasting viewpoints of this type, labelled the 'God's truth' and the 'hocus-pocus' positions, see Householder (1952:260).

For certain abstracted emic components — as against emic units — which within this theory are treated as created constructs rather than as discovered behavioral units, see §§ 7.321, 6.43.

An intermediate viewpoint is that of Hockett, who insists that "a language is what it is, it has the structure it has, whether studied and analyzed by a linguist or not" (1948a:271), and "His purpose in analyzing a language is not to create structure, but to determine the structure actually created by the speakers of the language" (270); but who elsewhere indicates that "The 'phonemic structure' of a language is not to be equated to any [one] such phonemicization; rather it is the 'least common denominator' of every possible sufficient phonemization" (1949a:38; also, more recently, Hockett, 1953:165; compare Haugen, 1951:222, versus Pike, 1947c:61b). Compare, also, Hjelmslev, "It is the aim of linguistic theory to test, on what seems a particularly inviting object, the thesis that there is a system underlying the process — a constant underlying the fluctuation" (1953:5); it "searches for the specific structure of language" (4), with the 'correct' solution identified by various criteria (10-11); compare Hjelmslev: "If it is true that language is a social institution, existing outside of and independently of the individuals..." 1936:49.

For an anthropologist's view, note Honigman, who affirms that patterns "do not exist in nature but are constructed by the observer" (1954). Compare Buettner-Janusch, who labels as 'antiscientific' Boas' concept of scientific law as found by the investigator in nature (1957:322).

For psychology, compare Bruner: "Alas, too, principles are not discovered in nature ...they are *invented* and tested against data" (1951:312).

For an epistemologist's view of the problems of order and system, see Sinclair (1951:38-46, 60-61, 75). For him, in "the independently real which is common to us all, if such can be intelligibly referred to, there is neither a political situation nor no political situation. A political situation exists only within the situation which each man experiences by... selecting and grouping in attention" (246).

Quine states that: "As Fraenkel has put it, logicism holds that classes are discovered while intuitionism holds that they are invented — a fair statement indeed of the old opposition between realism and conceptualism" (1953:14); the "two competing conceptual schemes ...phenomenalistic and physicalistic... "Each has its advantages" and each... deserves to be developed" (17), since "the one is epistemologically, the other physically fundamental", even though the question as to the ontology to adopt "still stands open" (1953:19). Compare discussion in Braithwaite (1953:367-68). For indeterminacy as a prerequisite to structure, see Garner (1962:339).

As I look back on this problem after a decade, it seems to me that a theological component may sometimes enter my thinking here. If one starts — as I do — with belief in an ultimate Designer of nature, the choice of a philosophy of science which allows one to *search* for pattern in science (or to represent pattern in art) appears normal, as does the *creating* of pattern in art (or of constructs in science). Compare Walter: "Broadly speaking one may say that sciences derive from pattern-seeking, the arts from pattern-making" (1953:69).

The creative work of either the scientist or the artist can in turn be analyzed for the presence of pattern. If I have succeeded in understanding Sinclair (1951:41) at this point, then the underlying reason why I was empirically forced to adapt the theory to allow for the emic analysis by one analyst of the etic or emic activity of a second analyst was to avoid one variety of 'the epistemologist's fallacy'.

The traditional problem of 'realism' versus 'nominalism' is reflected here. Compare, with a structure-in-date view, Hempel's summary: "A real definition is conceived of as a statement of the 'essential characteristics' of some entity, as when a man is defined as a rational animal or a chair as a separate movable seat for one person" (1952:2); for structure-created-by-analyst, compare his statement that "A nominal definition ...is a convention which merely introduces an alternative... notation for a given linguistic expression in the manner of stipulation... Let the word 'tiglon' be short [for] (i.e., synonymous with) the phrase 'offspring of a male tiger and a female lion'" (1952:2) or "Let the expression E_2 be synonymous with the expression E_1."

My view of structure, by insisting on differentiation of etic versus emic analysis and description, seems to me to leave room for the most important contributions of all of these approaches. On the one hand, it grants the need for creating constructs (cf. § 2.75) — this book is one; and insists that an observer component enters into all ability to discover, understand, emically report on or act as a member of a community in reference to facts (cf. § 17.5) — which implies relevance of the study of native reaction to situations (§§ 2.74, 6.65, 7.322, 8.54, 8.815). But, on the other hand, it specifies that within human behavior emic structure is present — and at least in part describable by successive approximations. Our theory makes no statements or claims whatsoever — whether positive or negative — about situations in which an observer is not involved.

For further bibliography on the nature of structure see Pike and Pike (1960:1-3).

Note, also, discussion concerning theory formation, in § 2.75. For concept formation see also § 16.86.

2.73. *On Extralinguistic Cultural Distribution as Relevant to Emic Analysis*

We have already given references in § 1.4 for the relevance of 'context of situation' to language study. The point would not need to be discussed further, here, were it not for the fact that some linguists in this country have tried to eliminate or to reduce to a minimum such cultural references in certain phases of linguistic analysis. While insisting on the validity, in general, of distributional studies in the analysis of linguistic units in verbal contexts, and even making it a key to their entire outlook, they fail to see that distribution of verbal elements in *cultural* but *nonverbal* contexts — and hence their analysis in reference to their distribution in relation to meaningful units whose meanings are in part determined by such cultural distribution — can also be structurally valid and procedurally essential at every level of the emic analysis. This oversight seems to be due to an assumption that rigid water-tight compartments or levels are esthetically satisfying, and provide the only valid scientific conclusions. It is precisely at this point that certain residues of data, not fitting into such a compartmentalization, have forced the development of the present theory and the rejection of such an overly-compartmentalized outlook. The implications of this integrated approach will not appear clearly in detail until later sections — e.g., Chapter 15; but in the meantime we indicate certain of the sources of our conclusions cited earlier in this paragraph, even though the integration of some of these elements with the balance of the volume will have to be kept in abeyance until later chapters. Lest we be misunderstood, however, it should be mentioned that we have no objection to an 'as if' procedure, in which the analyst temporarily and deliberately ignores data except that which comes into a chosen area of study — provided that he does not then forget the fact that this was an 'as if' analysis and that the description is limited in validity by that initial selection, and provided that he does not then insist that such a particular limited selection of data is the only 'respectable' or 'scientific' one, as over against a different selection which allows for a wider view of relevent materials, and a synthesis of knowledge on a broader base.

For separation of phonological from grammatical levels of structure, note: "I believe that the phonemes of a language should be analyzed without reference to syntax or morphology" (Moulton, 1947:225n); also Hockett (1942:20, 1955); for a discussion of these and other items by Bloch, Smith, Trager, Wells, and Welmers, see Pike, 1947a, and 1952a. For emphasis on levels: "Hill said that the history of linguistics has been characterized by sharper and sharper divisions of levels, each stage marking an advance" (in Levi-Strauss and others, 1953:29); also Trager and Smith (1951:81); or, more recently, E. T. Hall and Trager: "we have emphasized... [also, that] culture *integrates* at various levels of complexity, and only by taking into account the nature of these levels, and keeping them *strictly apart*, can the analyst of culture hope to arrive at a clear picture of what he is dealing with" (1953:57; italics added to point up the conflict between the ideas of integration, on the one hand, and elements strictly apart, on the other; this conflict between empirical interlocking and theoretical compartmentalization I am trying to resolve by treating with systems but with provision in the theory for their overlapping, interpenetration, etc., at various points).

Note, in addition, Z. Harris (1951): "The main research of descriptive linguistics, and the only relation which will be accepted as relevant in the present survey, is the distribution or arrangement within the flow of speech of some parts or features relatively to others. The present survey is thus explicitly limited to questions of distribution, i.e. of the freedom of occurrence of portions of an utterance relatively *to each other*. All terms and statements will be relative to this criterion" (5; italics added, to point out that Harris' use of the term 'distribution' is in reference to verbal distribution, as in contrast to my usage of cultural, nonverbal distribution and of verbal distribution as well). Later (7) in a footnote, the basic inadequacy of Harris' position is seen in the necessity for the word *if* in the following quotation: "However, this differentiation of *life* and *rife* on the basis of meaning is only the linguist's and the layman's shortcut to a distributional differentiation. In principle, meaning need be involved only to the extent of determining what is repetition. If we know that *life* and *rife* are not entirely repetitions of each other, we will then discover that they differ in distribution (and hence in 'meaning')". The difficulty here is the fact that the evidence that two utterances are or are not repetitions may in some instances come from cultural distribution, not from the verbal context, in any adequate test case — i.e., in a situation in which a monolingual approach is used, so that there can be no ultimate use of cultural, nonverbal distribution, disguised as verbal, through the use of an intermediate language known by both investigator and native speaker. In such a situation, the fact that there may be "data about a hearer accepting an utterance or part of an utterance as a repetition" (Harris, 20), is likely to be nonverbal, and the use of this nonverbal element, like Harris' verbal affirmation, "seems inescapable" (Harris, 20), and "in addition to the data concerning sounds *we require data about the hearer's response*" (Harris, 20; italics added). The necessity for the rejection of Harris' basic assumption, then, becomes apparent on the evidence of his own procedures which are "inescapable", not just a "shortcut". For a similar unsuccessful attempt to reject the implications of one's own procedures in using meaning and cultural distribution, by labelling them as a shortcut, see Trager and Smith (1951:54; for analysis of this material, see Pike 1952a:116). For a further protest against Harris' rejection of extralinguistic cultural data, see McQuown (1952:496-97, 501, 503, 504). For a very careful argument that, by a rigid application of his techniques, Harris cannot obtain his first morpheme as a starting point, see Fowler (1952:505-08). Bloch, in a similar attempt to set up "basic assumptions that underlie phonemics, ...without any mention of mind or meaning" (1948:5), accomplishes that goal, it seems to me, by the expedient of using a synonym for that word. Thus, in setting up his Postulate 2, with a corollary which states that "Some utterances contain auditory fractions that are the same" (7), he admits that this corollary is 'crucial' — but then states that "While we grant that this sameness is no doubt ultimately a matter of biosocial equivalence, we prefer to account for it here simply in terms of recurrent auditory fractions that are (by assumption) the same" (8). Since the phrase 'biosocial equivalence' is footnoted to refer to an article by Hockett, and Hockett defines the phrase such that "Two speech acts are BIOSOCIALLY EQUIVALENT if they are produced under similar conditions and act similarly as biosocial stimuli" (Hockett, 1942:6), I can conclude only that the phrase is equivalent to or at least overlaps with the phrase "have the same meaning" — and that Bloch, in admitting that 'ultimately' this is the basis of sameness has in fact by-passed the mention of meaning without by-passing the use of meaning. This conclusion is supported, in addition, by the statement that "meaning, at least, is so obviously useful as a shortcut in the investigation of phonemic structure — one might almost say, so inescapable..." (5).

If one attempts to take a compromise position between the use of no extralinguistic data (or the use of no meaning), and the use of a great deal of such extralinguistic data, one may try to restrict oneself to the use of a formula such that he will use just enough linguistic or extralinguistic informant reaction to establish whether elements are the 'same' or 'different', or are 'repetitions' (see references to Harris, above). For example: "MICROLINGUISTIC analysis proceeds without recourse to meaning except as DIFFERENTIAL MEANING. The informant is asked only whether items under consideration on various levels of analysis, from phones through sentences, are the same or different", but "the consideration of WHO IS TALKING TO WHOM AND HOW THEY ARE INTERACTING (AND REACTING) IN TERMS OF THEIR COMMON CULTURAL EXPERIENCE... constitutes the METALINGUISTIC MEANING (or META-MEANING or, more simply, the MEANING[)] of the material", and this is "left for the consideration of the analyst only after the linguistic system has been completely described" (Smith, in Report of the Third Annual Round Table..., 1952:59). This point of view seems to be a later development than the position in Trager and Smith (1951:68), where in respect to phonemic transcription, establishing of words, constructions, intonation patterns etc., the authors state that "It is emphasized that all this is done without the use of 'meaning'" (a position evaluated in Pike 1952a:116).

From the point of view of the theory of the present volume, several objections to Smith's statement (which can earlier be seen in Trager, 1949) should by now be easily seen by the reader: it over-compartmentalizes; it rejects the interaction and reacting of informants as legitimate data even while the 'same or different' test is specifically one kind of such response; it assumes a bilingual analytical situation, whereas a test of the assumption in a monolingual environment or by a monolingual analytical procedure would have forced extralinguistic gestures — reactions and re-enactments of scenes — to be used in addition to those data purportedly to be admitted as legitimate; it implies that the linguist as such is not interested in language as it functions, i.e., as a communicating device, and cannot analyze the communication process as such — i.e., the content of the communication, as an integrated, interlocking part of the larger cultural patterns of the community. Two much more subtle difficulties, however, should also be pointed out.

The first of these difficulties is that the reaction of 'same' or 'different' by an informant is an exceedingly complex process (e.g., cf. §§ 7.321-22) — not the simple choice of a 'yes' or 'no'. Specifically, we ask: How does the informant know what level he is supposed to be responding to? Surely other linguists have received responses such as I have, where an informant would on occasion insist that homonyms such as English *seal* (e.g., on an envelope) and *seal* (animal) were 'different' — which is precisely the response the linguist is after, when dealing with morphemes, but wrong, when dealing with significant sounds. Yet even more complex is the situation if one asks: Are the three sentences *The seal is over there*,[3] *The seal is over there*, and *The dog is over there*, the same? When we are dealing with classes of words, and the structure of sentences, it is important that the informant state that all three of these are the 'same' (cf. Fries, 1952:74n), but that in reference to the earlier goals mentioned, the *seal* and *seal* in one instance are the 'same' and in another are 'different'. Smith, who in the quotation given above mentions levels of analysis, does not appear to give sufficient weight to the fact that, in order to operate with the procedure mentioned, he must be able either to use elaborate nonlinguistic gestures, in a monolingual test, or else be able to help the informant identify the level on which the analyst is working, by an elaborate gestural situation, or by some degree of specific linguistic training, either of which destroys the apparent simplicity of the procedure. This is a far cry from avoiding encroachment on the innate linguistic naïveté of the informant recommended by Bloomfield (1942), and from Bloomfield's insistence on the use of meaning in linguistic analysis (1943:102, quoted in Pike, 1952a:116n). For a sharp rejection of the criterion of 'same' or 'different', starting from an argument such as this one, see Bloch and Trager, 1942:38 and 40, but compare Hockett (1952a:96), Chao (1934:379).

The second of the special difficulties with this attempt to avoid meaning while analyzing the grammatical units is that it commits the linguistic analyst to a dualistic view of language. If the linguist can in fact analyze the word *man* without any tacit reliance on the fact that it has, in relationship to the total language system, a specific meaning — more than just a differential one — then he has demonstrated that there is a dichotomy between form and meaning which is innate, deep, and far reaching in its implications. I suspect that carried to its logical extreme it would result in a variety of a mentalistic view of meaning which the authors would themselves repudiate if they saw its end point. In ordinary speech, like every one else, however, I frequently utilize statements based upon such an outlook. Nevertheless, in the present theory I am attempting to develop a point of view within which form and meaning must not be

---

[3] Philip Bock has now presented me with a match holder on which was a company $seal_1$, plus the wording $seal_2$ *of perfection* partially encircling the picture of a $seal_3$ (animal).

separated in theory; there are rather form-meaning composites (see §§ 6.52, 5.64, and Index).[4]

For convenience, one may on occasion discuss the form and meaning aspects *as if* they were separate, while taking pains to indicate that such an expedient is a distortion which must be corrected at proper intervals and in the relevant places in the discussion (cf. for example, conceptualized hypostasis in §§ 6.43, 7.321). For the same reason, therefore, we reject the theory of signs of de Saussure (1931), and of Hjelmslev — who says that "A 'sign' functions, designates, denotes; a 'sign', in contradistinction to a nonsign, is the bearer of a meaning" (1953:27); our present theory would not allow us to say — when we are on guard, or consistent — that a linguistic item "is the bearer of a meaning", since there would be no available linguistic units to 'bear' meanings, in view of the fact that there are only form-meaning composites. Compare, also, Bloomfield who states that "In language, forms cannot be separated from their meanings" (1943:102); compare also his "*fundamental assumption of linguistics*" that "*In certain communities (speech-communities) some speech-utterances are alike as to form and meaning*" (1933a: 144; but compare an outdated form of this assumption — from a work in 1926 — without direct mention of meaning as such, utilized by Bloch, 1948: 7-8). For a theoretical rejection of form-meaning dualisms, see J. R. Firth, 1952:5-6; for an empirical demonstration of the necessity and usefulness of a composite linguistic-extralinguistic approach, see Fries, 1952:42-53, who makes his basic dichotomies of sentence types based in part on extralinguistic distribution. Note, further, that a dualism of form versus meaning is correlated with a dualism of verbal versus nonverbal behavior; and it is toward a unified theory of language and behavior which avoids such a dualism that this present volume is in part directed, as we stated in Chapter 1.

For language treated as a sign system, however, see Greenberg (1957:1); and compare Fries for whom (1962:99-100) learning a language code "is learning the signals by which meanings or messages are sent or received" (1962:103). For language rejected as code, see Halliday (1961:280). For discussion of distribution as an analytical tool, without reference to meaning see now Harris (1955), Diderichsen (in Proceedings of the Eighth... 1958) and Henning Spang-Hanssen (in Preprints..., 1962).

For emphasis upon studying observed native reaction of native behaviors, in analysis of linguistic or nonlinguistic material, note Riffaterre who notes a secondary response — a subjective judgment of a behavior — as itself an effective fact to be studied (1959:163). Compare my insistence on the objective nature of *observed* native reaction (1947c:160n): "...our establishment of phonetic principles and procedures must ultimately rest upon our observations of native reactions to the phonetic data." Compare Harris (1951:20, 29n, 30-31, 38, 76-77, 173, 187, 218, 363, 372).

See also Nadel's quotation of Parsons in which the cardinal point that is social action has reference to "the point of view of the actor" (1951:33n). In cultural situa-

---

[4] The form and meaning do not have to be in a one-to-one relationship, even though requirement of both is still preserved. See Pike (1963d) and Pike and Erickson (1964).

tions, note a similar emphasis by Goodenough that relevant data include the way in which Trukese 'react' to data — an observable fact (1951:11). Compare Bruner, Goodnow and Austin in reference to legal action determining further action (1956:32) in the face of initial indeterminacies.

Chomsky has attempted to show how a pair test can be non-semantic — such that the speaker's action in identifying sames on a tape recorder can be used as behavioral criteria for phonemic analysis without reference to specific meanings (1955). Nevertheless, he elsewhere insists on finding "a basis for intuitive judgments" such that "it is pointless to refuse to make use of such data in evaluating the success of a particular attempt to formulate the rules of some grammar" (1961b:225); (but he combines this view with a rejection of the level of conventional phonemics — see below, § 8.815).

Native reaction in its relation to linguistics (i.e., psycholinguistics) is further discussed in §§ 2.74, 8.815.

2.74 *On Clash between Systems as a Source of Evidence or Assumptions Relevant to the Emic Analysis of Language*

In physics, a great deal of information about the invisible structure of particles is obtained by bombarding them with other particles; changes in the target particles, in the bombarding particles, or in the production of new particles all contribute to a fuller understanding of the nature of these particles — and in some instances prove that the target particles do have a structure, though prior to the bombardment this fact may not have been known. This procedure in physics may serve as a useful analogy to help the reader see how it is that the coming together of two linguistic systems, or elements thereof, may give an observer an opportunity to learn something about both of their structures. The utilization of the data obtained by seeing language systems 'clash' as speakers of one language come into contact with speakers of a second language, is just as legitimate a source of data for the linguist as nuclear bombardment is for the physicist. It is this kind of material which served as the basis for the discussion of baseball versus cricket, and of the prediction of difficulties in language learning (§ 2.6).

For an excellent discussion of specific difficulties in pronunciation, in reference to language systems, see Polivanov (1931) — Japanese versus Russian, Northern Chinese versus Russian, Russian versus Northern Chinese. For brief comments, note Rowe (1950:140, English versus Inca), Sapir (1925, in his Selected Writings, 44, Nootka versus English), Swadesh (1934:118), Marckwardt (1946:109,111, Spanish versus English), Fries (1945:16), Fries and Pike (1949:36-37), Nida (1950:110), Jones (1950: 36, 37, 38, 138), Harris (1951:30n); a number of these emphasize that a person coming from one language to another will have difficulty if the second language has two somewhat similar phonemes in its system where the first has only one. Note also discussion of the general problem in Lado (1957). Various contrastive studies appear from time to time in journals such as *Language Learning* showing further detail of these problems.

The most extensive studies of interferences from languages in contact are found in Weinreich (1953a) and Haugen (1953); see also below, § 15.33.

The difficulties of a student in a phonetics class room are, in some respects, similar to those which he faces in learning a second language: He is confronted with sounds which are 'emically distinct' — but their emic nature is established relative to the phonetic system being dictated at that moment by the teacher, and by the teacher's arbitrary norms, rather than being established relative to a natural language. In principle, however, the clash of systems is in part the same (though the extralinguistic distribution is artificial, and limited to utilization of the sounds in the classroom, and the linguistic distribution is artificially limited to the drills, etc.). To whatever extent they can be adequately observed and controlled, these classroom data are as valid, in linguistics, as data obtained from the artificial bombardment of a target with fast-moving particles (and in the 'artificial' disintegration of atomic nuclei) are valid in relation to the data obtained by natural radioactivity. Difficulties encountered by students in the phonetic classroom have been used in some of my previous writings as essential elements in establishing the necessity for assuming that a language has a phonemic structure; I still know of no way to demonstrate this fact more effectively. Note Pike, 1947c:64-65 (and 160n), in reference to the difficulty in hearing the difference between the two stop sounds in *paper*, etc., as the source of a premise concerning conditioned variants. Note, also, a reaffirmation and amplification of this point of view in Fries and Pike (1949:50), "Evidence for the phonemic structure of a language is of two kinds: (1) phonetic and distributional data of the traditional kind; and (2) the observable reactions of native speakers as they attempt to write or analyze their own language or to speak a foreign language. If, as we believe, the second kind of evidence is actually the foundation on which postulates concerning the first kind must be built, then the two kinds should lead to similar or identical results, provided the phonemic system of the language is uniform." Note also, Pike (1947b:151-53, in reference to English diphthongs), Welmers (1950b:494); and see §§ 2.73, 8.815.

The problem of learning to write one's own language may in part be considered a clash of systems (if the orthography is nonphonemic), or a clash in phonetics (to the extent that one is learning to equate symbols and sounds). It should be seen, then, that the utilization of objective observations carefully made of persons learning to write must also be considered data which should receive the attention of the linguist — the more so when one realizes that this was the basic source from which Sapir got his whole outlook as to the fact that a language has a system of sounds, and from which basis he pioneered in showing that languages have contrastive patterns of sound, not merely different sounds. For the first reference to his discovery, see Sapir, (1921:58); for the pattern theory based on it, see Sapir, 1925 (in his Selected Writings, 33-45); for a detailed account of the earlier experience, see (1933; in his Selected Writings, 46-60). For other arguments based on observable native reaction as they attempted to write their own languages, or other languages, see Pike (1947b:152), and Fries and Pike (1949:30-31, 34), Gudshinsky (1958b).

In spite of these reasons, which seem to me very weighty, linguists often reject evidence from such sources. Twaddell denies the validity of Sapir's orthographical data on the ground that it is merely evidence for eliciting "a uniform response to different stimuli" (1935:11-13). William Smith objects to "Pike's persistent use of non-phonetic criteria in phonemics" on the ground that it is "unprovable speculation" (1950:8). Hockett rejects "Pike's non-phonetic criteria" in reference to phonemics, but suggests that they "belong somewhere in the total task of linguistic analysis" (1950b:55). Bloch rejects "non-phonetic evidence" (1950:122), and states that "no phonemic description is valid... if these [phonetic] qualities are not the sole basis on which it is built" (1950:92). Hjelmslev states that "no phoneme can be correctly defined except by linguistic criteria, i.e. by means of its function in the language. No extra-lingual criteria can be relevant" (1936:49), and Fischer-Jørgensen states that "the glossematic approach... does not take native reactions into account" (1949:105).

Informant reaction is not uniform in some situations. Out of, say, ten speakers of a particular language, possibly eight or nine of them will act as one's predictions indicate, but one or two of them may diverge from that expected course. This lack of consistency gives to the evidence an appearance of non-objectivity, of "private," subjective techniques of the analyst which cannot be checked by other observers, and casts doubt on the validity of the data. It is quite possible, however, to set up experiments objectively, so they can be duplicated by other observers; Marckwardt (1944, 1946) has made a start in this direction, in the problems of Spanish speakers using English nasals and sibilants. If we had a large mass of data of this type, carefully documented and experimentally controlled, the objectivity of this kind of data would be more apparent. The results may need to be expressed in statistical terms, or in terms of probability, to allow room for deviant responses (cf. Fries and Pike, 1949:37).

The use of observable native reaction to clashing systems, and the like, is unacceptable to a number of workers because it appears to them to be an unwarranted intrusion of psychology or of a 'mentalistic' approach into linguistics. D. Jones, for example, rejects the "mentalistic view" "that a phoneme is a single 'abstract sound' or 'sound image', which the speaker is capable of bringing to mind at will" (1950:212). Trnka, however, uses 'linguistic consciousness' to confirm conclusions (1939:23-24), and, in regard to English, states that "We must point out that [British] English speakers feel unmistakably the three long vowels to correspond to the short ones and this feeling of correspondence entitles us to the assumption that the correlation of quantity *is* represented in English" (1935:187). Note, further, Sapir's use of such matters: "In most languages, what is felt by the speakers to be the 'same' sound has perceptibly different forms as these conditions vary" (1925, in his Selected Writings, 37). Compare also Bazell, the phrase, "...without appeal to native linguistic instinct, the ultimate basis of our working hypotheses" (1948b:287, and compare 279).

Twaddell, in commenting on various definitions of the phoneme, objects to explaining behavior in terms of 'mind' since "The linguistic processes of the 'mind' as such are quite simply unobservable; and introspection about linguistic processes is notoriously a fire in a wooden stove" (1935:9). Bloch and Trager state that "The native speaker's feeling about sounds or about anything else is inaccessible to investigation by the techniques of linguistic science, and any appeal to it is a plain evasion of the linguist's proper function. The linguist is concerned solely with the facts of speech. The psychological correlates of these facts are undoubtedly important; but the linguist has no means — as a linguist — of analyzing them" (1942:40). Chao, on the other hand, has suggested giving the feeling of native speaker "due consideration" (1934: 384).

It is important to note clearly the difference between an appeal to a 'feeling'[5] which is inaccessible to direct observation, as over against observable, testable, independently verifiable abilities or objective responses of language speakers. One must not reject the utilization of observable objective evidence just because attention to it may historically have developed in a 'mentalistic' context. Much of the objective data can be utilized as evidence of structure while avoiding many of the kinds of statements which in the past have proved to be inadequate. Even so, however, there occasionally may appear, in certain contexts, useful statements implying a structuring of some type within the speaker. Compare, for example, Bloch's statement in 1950 in reference to a "cultural correlate of the linguistic structure" that "The Japanese speaker's 'feeling' for the number of syllables in a phrase is no doubt partly due to his knowledge of how the phrase is written in the native syllabary; but the syllabary, in turn, must reflect the speakers' naïve structural analysis of their language" (92); compare Haugen, "Its [the syllable's] reality to the native speaker is pragmatically undeniable, at least in the languages with which I am familiar" (1949a:280-81). Compare Twaddell's discussion of the degree of competence necessary for the native speaker to be able to count syllables, versus phonemes (1946:106-07). Compare, also, the way in which an informant with 'linguistic intelligence' was a help to Freeland (1951:iv); or the manner in which Welmers and Harris utilized the informant's "reports that the words are foreign" (1942:322), or a similar comment by Oftedal (1949:267); Nida's use of informant reaction in reference to word division (1947b:140); or Sapir, with grammar "defined as the sum total of formal economies intuitively recognized by the speakers of a language" (1933, in his Selected Writings, 9); or Trager and Smith, "The remark that someone speaks 'well' or 'crudely' or 'with a Brooklyn accent' is a datum" (1951:83); or even the implications of psychological structuring in testing for mutual intelligibility between dialects (Hickerson, Turner, and Hickerson, 1952); or Preston and Voegelin, with the informant signalling at a halting place in text (1949:23-24); or Hockett, that "ALL morphemic analysis is in a sense folk-analysis" (1950a:84); or Bloomfield, in reference to native reaction to immediate constituents (1933a:161).

In sum, then, we may say that the linguist wishes to discover[6] the structure of

---

[5] In more recent linguistic discussion one is more likely to find the word 'intuition' (cf. §§ 8.815, 11.75 11.763) but applied, now, more frequently to grammatical than to phonological structures.
[6] For relation of discovery of structure to theory formation, however, see §§ 2.75, 2.73, 11.75.

language behavior, but that since this behavior is a part of total human behavior, and obtains its structuring *only* in reference to that larger behavior field, and relative to the structural units of that larger field, the linguist must on occasion refer to that larger field in order to get access to that frame of reference within which the linguistic units obtain part of their definition. The linguist, then, should not hesitate to utilize *any* observable data which will help him discover the emic units of the language — whether that data be extralinguistic, in actions simultaneous with speech, or resulting from speech, or eliciting speech; and he should be prepared to utilize any observable data of a verbal type, whether it be speech of the informants in normal cultural settings, or in special cultural settings which are abnormal due to intrusion of the linguist himself; or whether they consist of comments about his own speech (taken, of course, as data needing weighing and analysis, and not as a substitute for hard work or analysis by the linguist — see Pike, 1947c:160n, and Fries and Pike, 1949:30); or about the speech of his neighbors of that same speech community; or about the speech of persons with a language foreign to him; or may include errors, successes, and comments in the process of trying to learn to speak a foreign language or phonetics in the classroom, and the like.

Z. Harris, however, would claim that "All such predictions [of difficulty of speakers of one language in pronouncing the sounds of another] are outside the techniques and scope of descriptive linguistics" (1951:21n).

For a similar type of problem in reference to the analysis of nonverbal materials, note Nadel: "Radcliffe-Brown, Malinowski, and many others have emphasized that we must not expect correct answers when questioning the people about the reason for or the meaning of some cultural activity. But their answers are not altogether without value; though they are sources of error in one sense, in another they are themselves significant social facts, data in their own right, and so sources of knowledge" (1951:37, and cf. 39, 68).

2.75 *On Theory Formation and the Philosophy of Science*

In § 2.72 we gave references to structure treated as discovered in nature or as created by the analyst. The analysis of theory formation contains related problems.

A theory may be viewed rather broadly as a statement purporting to describe, or to explain, or to help one to understand a phenomenon. More narrowly, a theory may present a claim of truth, or assert the presence of relationships between phenomena, or predict the occurrence of phenomena.

One approach to theory, influenced by logic, (a) sets up axiomatic affirmations and develops systematic statements coherent with these axioms, (b) presents a mechanical device — for example a known mathematics — which can be brought to bear on this system so as to predict some — but not all — of the phenomena of the real world, and

(c) tests for adequate relationships between this prediction and (possibly a few) observed data as a justification for the larger theoretical system. Compare the extensive attempt of Goodman "to use the technique and example of modern logic in the investigation of problems of philosophy" (1951:xiii); and cf. Braithwaite who is interested in "the straight logical problems of the internal structure of scientific systems and of the role played in such systems by the formal truths of logic and mathematics" (1953:21). Hempel summarizes this kind of view: "A theoretical system may then be conceived as an uninterpreted theory in axiomatic form", characterized also by its primitive terms and by its postulates which may also be called primitive or basic hypotheses (1952:33).

Carnap insists that it "is true a theory must not be a 'mere calculus' but possesses an interpretation, on the basis of which it can be applied to facts of nature" (1955[1939]: 210). But, indeed, the "calculus is first constructed floating in the air, so to speak; the construction begins at the top" adds lower levels, and is finally "by the semantical rules" at the lowest level "anchored at the solid ground of the observable facts" (207); and in the theory the "abstract terms are taken as primitive" (207).

See also Cohen and Nagel (1934, in Feigl and Brodbeck 1953:129-47). That, under such an approach, some items and propositions must be taken as clear and believed, is affirmed both by Goodman (1955:37) and Braithwaite (1953:5).

Growing out of the approach through logic is an attitude toward the relation of science to proof, language, and meaning. Thus Carnap says that "a *syntactical system* or *calculus* (sometimes also called a formal deductive system or a formal system) is a system of formal rules which determine certain formal properties and relations of sentences, especially for the purpose of formal deduction" (1939:17); and "the logic of science... without referring to anything outside of language... is called *formal*" (1938, in Feigl and Sellars 1949:409); within such a system "a definition is the simplest form of a reduction statement" [i.e., a substitute statement, representing conditions under which it can be applied] ([1939] 1955:50).

The goal of tight, logical linkage from assumption through a mathematics to data leads to an algorithmic view of the theory of grammar. Thus Bar-Hillel and Shamir refer to "certain devices variously called 'grammars', 'automata' and 'machines'" (1960:156).

The choice, here, of a philosophy of generative theory leads to a machine goal — but to a generating machine rather than to an analyzing machine. Hopes for the adequacy of such generating machines, for language, seem to be based on an artificial ceiling imposed on the largest formal arrangement to be treated, and to be used as a starting point for the axioms of the system. If, instead of taking sentence as the top — see §§ 5.63, 11.723 — one accepts larger units, then the need for the mechanical generation of Paradise Lost — and comparable language units — may be seen as involving further problems. Generativeness is in turn related to the need for 'interpretive connections' between axiom and phenomena, and to lead to 'empirical content' for "the primitives of the theory and to render its basic hypotheses capable of test"

(Hempel, 1952:36, 35). Yet a rigid operationism is insufficient; judgment as to systematic or theoretical import of the theory is also essential (Hempel:1952, 46-49; versus Bridgeman, 41).

In a pragmatic view of the philosophy of science a theory is a tool. A dentist drill and a steam shovel are both used for excavation — but at different places. So the value of a theory is determined by one's purpose and goals. I find it helpful, also, to think of theories as windows with types differing as they do in a house, a ship, a telescope. A theory as an instrument, according to Frank, must "be helpful in predicting future observable facts". It "should also be helpful in the contribution of devices which can save us time and labor", and it should give us a "world picture and support a philosophy which, in turn, supports a desirable way of life" (1957:356). Such a view of the philosophy of science includes sociological and historical elements not treated directly by an approach through logic alone. It notes, for example, that a theory unacceptable at one time may later be acceptable because of further available data, mathematics, or other developments. All approaches to theory include some reference to simplicity (see, for example, Goodman, 1951:60, 64-85; for further references to simplicity, see below, § 15.31). Frank, however, points out that the "mathematical simplicity of a theory depends on the state of science at a certain period" — as the mathematics needed for corpuscular (versus wave) theory was at first simpler than that for wave treatment; but "If we investigate which theories have actually been preferred because of their simplicity, we find that the decisive reason for acceptance has been neither economic nor aesthetic, but... that the theory was preferred that proved to make science more 'dynamic', *i.e.*, more fit to expand into unknown territory" (1957:351-52). Thus "From... the Ptolemaic system... to the Copernican system... men have had to accept these succeeding theories because they yielded practical results, even though it meant the breakdown of their intelligible principles" (1957:33). Frank concludes, therefore, that "the acceptance of a scientific theory is not essentially different from the acceptance of an airplane" (1957:357); with compromise necessary between demands of simplicity, the facts, and common sense (353).

Limits must be placed on the degree to which simplicity or economy can be helpful in a theory. The logician Quine affirms that "elegance, conceptual economy, is secondary" to efficacy in communication and prediction; the latter carry the ultimate duty of language, science, and philosophy. And "it is in relation to that duty that a conceptual scheme has finally to be appraised" (1953:79). Bar-Hillel illustrates how a "gain in 'economy'" may be offset "by a certain loss of intuitiveness" — e.g., a rectangle being defined in reference to three right angles instead of four "might be a useful [less redundant] thing to do for certain axiomatic purposes", but "it is regarded as pointless by most mathematicians" (1957:328).

Goodman shows that the "mere counting of primitives is plainly unsatisfactory" since unenlightening but "maximum economy could quickly be achieved in most systems simply by compounding all the predicates into one having many places" (1951:60; and 64-85 for logical problems in connection with simplicity). There counting of symbols would seem to have other but comparable flaws. (See Chao's comment (1934) on Liu Fu's numerical code for Peiping syllables, in which [kuaŋ] would be 312241, with 31 for [k], 224 for [uaŋ], 1 for first tone — a system symmetrical and economical of symbols, but not useful for a transcription.)

The nature of similarity raises further problems for a theory. George Kelly seems to feel that a construct "is the *way* in which two or more elements are judged to be alike and, by the same token, different from one or more elements" (1955:305) with judgments of difference as "just as pertinent" as likeness (105).

Braithwaite points to classification of items as an early stage of the development of a science, with more generalized laws coming later (1953:1). Hempel shows in detail how traditional definition in terms of genus and class fails to cover such relational concepts as length (1952:29-30), and certain specific circumstances where a class is the sum of elements (6) rather than the "logical product (the intersection)" of two classes (5). Nevertheless a concept may be "a nonlinguistic entity such as a property, a class, a relation, a function, or the like" named by a nominal definition (4; and cf. above, end of § 2.72).

For further discussion of "the status of scientific concepts" note Bruner, for whom categories such as tomatoes, lions, snobs, atoms and mammalia "exist as inventions, not as discoveries" (1956:7 in Bruner, Goodnow, and Austin); Campbell (1920, in Feigl and Brodbeck, 1953:290).

For epistemological conditions on knowing, see Sinclair (1951:239, with relation to theory replacement), and Montague (1925).

An anthropologist's view of theory which is akin to our emic approach is seen in Goodenough. He wishes a "theory of the conceptual models" represented by artefacts which are community behavior, and tested by its ability to help us "interpret and predict what goes on in the community as measured by the interpretations and predictions of its members, our informants" (1957:167-68). Furthermore, it is tested by our ability 'to behave' in such a way as to elicit expected responses from the community, inasmuch as "a society's culture consists of whatever it is one has to know or believe in order to operate in a manner acceptable to its members, and to do so in any role that they accept for any one of themselves" (167).

Linguistic reaction to the nature of theory formation is varied. For Firth, "General linguistic theory is invented for application in the description of particular languages and in dealing with specific language problems. It is not a theory of universals for general linguistic description" (1958:6). For Chomsky, on the other hand "a theory of linguistic structure is an hypothesis about linguistic universals" (1961b:219; see also 1962:sec. 2, for emphasis upon explanatory adequacy). Halliday emphasizes the importance of distinguishing "between calculus (description) and theory; also between description and the set of generalizations and hypotheses by which the theory was arrived at in the first place" (1961:243 fn. 7). For Olmstead one means, by theory a set of statements consisting of ... postulates, definitions, transformation rules, and theorems (1954:106). Peterson and Fillmore hold that the "problem of constructing a scientific theory is thus basically that of finding the relevant mathematical system and of specifying appropriate relations or correspondences between the scientific observations or data and the mathematical system" (1962:477). Emeneau, however, held that "epistemological matters are to be left to the epistemologists and that we can talk about language without raising those matters" (1950:200).

Saporta says that "If one maintains that the constructs are in the meta-language" then one does not look for behavioral correlates or psychological reality, but that one only demands that "the rules of conversion ... to the object language be made explicit" (1958:328). Householder discusses the conditions (recoverability, nonviolation of universals, sociological probability) under which "linguistic coding or mapping is acceptable" (1962a:183). Halle justifies theory by "insightfulness, generality, and simplicity" of its consequences in "representation of specific phonetic facts" (1959a:19).

An alternative to discussing linguistic structures in terms of theory has been to treat them in terms of models. See, for example, Harris, for whom the model becomes a theory of the structure of something when it is interpreted or when particular values are given to its parameters (1959:27); and see Voegelin (1959:11, 13, 20-23).

For an extensive bibliography on the philosophy of science, see Feigl and Brodbeck (1953:783-99).

We would now like to be able to present a careful point-by-point development of the theory with which we hope to meet the need, to some degree, for a unified theory of verbal and nonverbal human behavior. We meet a practical difficulty in attempting to do so, however: The theory postulates a system of behavior in which each element in part defines every other element so that no one element can be defined before the whole is vaguely seen, nor can the whole be seen before many components are partially known.

In order to get past this difficulty, it seems wisest to delay the more formal matters until Chapter 5, and in the meantime to immerse the reader in a discussion of some large unit of activity which can be viewed as a whole, and yet serve as an illustration of the way in which smaller parts of a unit are related to that total unit. For this purpose, we need an activity which combines as essential, prominent features both verbal and nonverbal elements, which is long enough and complex enough to include many of the most perplexing analytical problems, which is short enough to be observed on numerous occasions and to be discussed as to its broad outlines and some of its details within the limits of a chapter, and which is sufficiently rigid in form or ceremonial to be repeatable in general type with recognizable recurring elements. As meeting these specifications we have chosen a church service for discussion in Chapter 3.

CHAPTER 3

THE STRUCTURE OF BEHAVIOR ILLUSTRATED

3.1 *Glimpses of a Church Service*

A few days ago[1] I attended the morning service of a young independent church of a rather informal evangelical type — a church which I had attended on numerous previous occasions. Each week as the congregation begins to arrive, the people entering the front door are met by one of the men of the church stationed there, are given a word of greeting, a handshake, and a partially printed, partially mimeographed program containing a schedule of the activities for the week.

The early comers enter the auditorium, sit quietly in some pew, or talk to friends in tones low enough as not to disturb any Bible School class whose teacher may have held it too long.

With the start of the organ prelude a few minutes later, talking quiets down, or ceases. A song leader, standing by the pulpit, raises his arms to signal to people to rise as he leads them in singing the doxology to the accompaniment of the small pipe organ and (sometimes) the simultaneous playing of a piano. The doxology is followed by a brief prayer from the pastor, and a couple of hymns.

On this particular day, however, doxology and invocation were omitted, and an opening hymn followed immediately after the prelude, with the hymn, in turn, followed by a prayer and two further hymns. This last hymn was introduced: *Now for another old hymn ... more familiar*. After all its verses had been sung, the chairman of the executive board of the church gave the announcements — in the absence of the pastor, — emphasizing certain items printed in the bulletin, and mentioning the number of people (children or adults) who had attended the Bible School classes during the preceding hour. He then announced the collection; the ushers came forward; he led in brief prayer; the ushers took up the offering, with a collection plate sent in from the outside aisle toward the receiving usher in the middle aisle past the people in the pew who put in their money or envelopes containing it; at the same time the middle-aisle usher started another plate, one row further back, toward the outside usher; and so on. While this was being done the organist was playing a hymn (*Tell me more*, by Randolph).

---

[1] October, 1952.

The program for that meeting had so far listed *Hymn #14, Prayer, Hymn #3, Hymn #81, Announcements, Offering,* and *Choir;* but this time — a quite infrequent occurrence — no choir was present in spite of the listing, and the next item, *Hymn #131,* was announced, with mention of the fact that no choir number could be sung that day because of so many choir members being ill.

A visiting speaker then preached the sermon. He requested — and received — considerable cooperative activity from the audience, as many of them turned to their Bibles to look up numerous references to which he referred in sequence. On the other hand, there was some simultaneous activity not directly related to the service or sermon — scattered coughs in the audience; a yawn; someone fidgeting with collar, glasses, ear, or hair; holding chin in hand; wetting of finger to turn a page; reading a Bible School paper; — and, muffled in the distance, but nevertheless intelligible during the quieter moments in the auditorium (during the first prayer, for example), the singing of children for Junior Church in a neighboring part of the building (*Hear Christ Calling Come unto Me*).

At the conclusion of the sermon the song leader led in *When I Survey the Wondrous Cross* — a hymn chosen so as to carry on something of the theme of the sermon. The speaker then pronounced a benediction. The "Choir Response", listed in the bulletin as following Sermon and Hymn, was by-passed, and the audience stood up to speak to friends or strangers and to leave the church, while the organist played a postlude, consisting of a repetition of the music of the last song sung.

3.2 *Segments and Waves of Activity*

Within this church service there were crucial parts; the service, though a single continuum of constant physical activity, nevertheless was divided into significant major chunks of activity. Such a service is by no means describable, emically, by the single smooth curve of a graph. Rather there are SEGMENTS of the sequence during which the purpose of the service is being vigorously forwarded by activity, and separated by moments where one type of significant activity slurs into the next segment of activity.

3.21 *Nuclei of Segments*

The sermon constituted the nucleus of one such segment (bordered at its beginning — on this particular day — by the introduction of the visiting speaker and at its end by his turning to the song leader to have him take over the direction of the service). Each hymn, likewise, was a segment (introduced by the song leader and closed by his gesture). The prayers, offering, and period of announcements similarly constituted major segments of the service.

Within the larger segments which divide the service into its major parts, smaller segments may be observed. Within a hymn, for example, there are stanzas; within the sermon there are usually an introduction, three or four principal sections, and a conclusion; within the period of announcements, each announcement constitutes a smaller segment. Then, noting smaller segments still, there are within an announcement sentences, within the sentences are words, while within words are segments constituted of the sounds. Within the general activity of singing a hymn, there is for the individual singer the segment composed of picking the hymnal from the rack off the back of the pew, the segment of opening the hymnal to the proper number, of standing up, of singing, of closing the book, of sitting down — and many more.

The nucleus of a movement sequence may often be identified as the point at which that movement reaches its culmination — its most rapid movement, or most extensive movement. In single sounds, for example, this may be seen as a peak or trough of movement, when the moving part of the mouth comes closest to closure (as at [i] in the sound sequence [aia]), or when it reaches its wides extension (at [a] in the sequence [iai]).

3.22 *Borders of Etic Segments*

One segment ends, and another begins, whenever there is an appreciable CHANGE in activity. The most apparent changes are seen when the actors differ. For the prelude it was the organist who was the prominent one advancing the emic course of the service — although an alien observer might have noticed, rather, people taking their seats in the pews, and have failed to see the activity of the organist, who was partly hidden behind the console. When the song leader stood up, and the congregation with him, a new segment (simultaneously etic and emic) began; when they sat down and the board chairman stood, a further segment got under way; the action of the ushers started the taking up of the offering; and the visiting preacher, taking his place behind the pulpit, initiated the sermon.

The change in a sequence of motions from one moving part of an actor to another moving part of his body likewise causes a break between segments, though these segments are usually small ones within the large segments. For pronouncing *Samuel*, for example, the front part of the tongue moves toward the upper gum while air forced out of the mouth from the lungs makes the noise [s]; when the vocal cords begin to vibrate and the tongue drops, a different segment, a vowel, is heard; when the lips close as the nasal passage is opened, a third segment — [m] — is produced.

A change in the direction of movement of some body part will also institute a new segment, usually a small one. When the song leader moved his arm up, it indicated the crucial part of a beat; when he started it down and up again, that produced a further segment. Similarly there are small action segments as each of the people turn the pages of their hymnals, stand, sit down, look up, and so on, or sing [ai] (in which the tongue is low in the mouth for [a] and rises toward the top of the mouth for [i] at the end of the word).

3.23 *Etic Segments as Waves of Activity*

It is this process of changing actions and actors which gives to a behavior sequence a character of pulsations of activity. The nucleus of a new type of activity acts as the peak of a WAVE OF MOTION — and segments within segments are pulses within pulses which added together form complex waves of activity (analogous to the manner in which ripples can be superimposed upon a larger water wave).

The song leader's arm motion, for example, becomes part of a larger complex of activity which includes the motion of his eyes (to follow the book, the audience, and choir), of his head (to help emphasize important stresses, or turning to look at book, audience, choir), of his leg movements (in standing), of his lip movements (for [m,] [b], [p], [o]), tongue movements for [s], [t], [l], [i]); and of audience movements for looking, standing, vocalization; of pipe organist movements (of fingers, arms, feet, ankles, head, eyes); of ushers' movements (seating latecomers — or looking, walking, gesturing); and so on.

3.24 *Markers of Emic Segments*

Those segments which constitute significant, emic units in the service are often marked at either beginning or end — or both — by special forms of activity which signal to the participants (1) that crucial changes are coming, and (2) the nature of the next segment.

Most obvious of these markers are vocal activity. In one such service there were, (among others) the following[2]: 5/7 *Let's begin this morning by singing the Doxology — we will stand.* 5/8 *Our heavenly Father, we come to Thee this morning...* 5/10 *...in Jesus' name, Amen.* 5/13.9 *Turn now to number fifty-two.* 5/16 *Several announcements I would like to bring to your attention.* 5/18.8 *Now as you give of your offerings this morning...* 5/24 *Now at this time we'll hear from Brother F—.* 5/24 *It's a real joy to be with you this morning...* 5/25 *I want to read one verse of scripture this morning...* 5/2/27 *Shall we bow our heads; ...suggest a four-fold outline...; Finally we come back...; Next...; First of all...; ...to ...for our closing thought; In closing I'd like to suggest; That's the message for us today...; Shall we pray; We'll sing the first and the last verse; ...Amen.*

In addition, certain nonverbal activities without verbal activity signalled some of these changes: the playing of the prelude; the gesture to stand; the raising of the arm

---

[2] Taken from recorded event no. 10; other numbers in the key refer to time and place in the mechanical recording.

ready to start people on the first note of a song; the passing of the offering plates as a signal to make individual offerings; the gesture to the choir to rise.

3.25 *Indeterminacy of Segment Borders*

In spite of the indication of segmental borders by change of activity or by verbal or nonverbal special signals, it is impossible to state exactly where one segment leaves off and another begins. The first reason for this indeterminacy is that the physical movements of a particular moving body part glide or slur from one to another, so that often at no one instant could one cut the continuum and say that the preceding segment ended and the following one began exactly at that point. In beating time, for example, the arm and hand movements often end in a loop perceptible to the eye, and not in a very sharp point. Similarly, there is no sharp physical line of demarcation between the first sound of [ai] (the [a]), and the second (the [i]).

Secondly, when the motion of two body parts produces a sequence of two segments, the motion of the first body part may not be finished before the second begins. This results in an overlap of segments, as when the movement of the lips, rounding for the first vowel of *today*, has begun before the tongue-tip releases from its position for the first [t] — or, at the notes of the organ, when the congregation begins to rise before the leader has finished his gesture to them. Anticipation of action, then, may be relevant to two motions of a single person or to overlapping motions of different people.

Thirdly, segmentation is often not sharp cut at its borders because, when numerous activities are going on simultaneously, they may be loosely integrated or integrated only in a much larger whole, or into units of different lengths. The actions of the organist's feet and fingers are designed to be in time with (i.e., to be segmentally integrated with) the gestures of the song leader — as are the vocal movements of the audience. Yet if the audience is 'dragging', its singing motions are 'out of phase' with those arm movements of the leader — they begin too late to be simultaneous with his, so that the border of any one complex segment is fuzzy.

Much less integrated are those movements of the audience which have no direct relation to the emic course of the service — their motions constituting whispering, fidgeting, looking around at neighbors, and the like.

Those vocal movements registered as the distant singing of junior church have no immediate emic integration with the regular service. Their movements must first be described in reference to the structure of the junior service but treated as 'noise' (the result of activity nonemic to the segments under immediate attention) insofar as senior service is concerned. Yet, in reference to the entire activity of the church as a whole, they would be highly relevant (emic) as components of the junior-senior systems coexisting at that moment. On this high level of focus, there is a very specific integration of segmental borders — junior church must not end more than a moment before senior church does, lest nondirected loud activity of the children constitute noise sufficient to disturb the senior service.

Highly integrated into the senior service was the choir number on another Sunday. Yet for certain phrases one melody was sung by some of the choir members, but a different melody with different timing by other members. Although the sequences of words were the same, and the members ended the song together, there were times when the two groups were — from the point of view of the verbal segments — out of phase, and hence it was not possible to show a single series of significant internal word segments simultaneously applicable to the choir number as a whole. Here, however, the lack of phase was deliberate, for artistic effect.

3.3 *Focus and the Whole*

Although the preceding paragraphs were not specifically designed to show that behavior structure is built like "wheels within wheels", very little can be said about the details of any complex behavior pattern without this fact being implicit in the description. The church service includes the singing of a hymn, the hymn a stanza, the stanza a line (or phrase), the line a word, the word a sound, and the sound is sung by a composite of articulatory movements; or the song leader attends the service, he leads the singing throughout, stands, gestures and sings for a particular song, lifts his arm for a particular note; his small motions are part of a larger series of motions which is part of a larger one, and so on.

Even the church service itself is a segment in a larger series. For the individual it is part of a series of activities of that particular day of worship, and of a weekly cycle of church activities. The *Bulletin*, itself, indicates this clearly: the bulletin for the day first referred to in this chapter has sections entitled *Today*, *This Week*, and *Coming* i.e., a view beyond the immediate cycle, which would ultimately lead to a yearly one with regularly celebrated special days such as Easter. The section on *This Week* includes items for every evening — though the announced participants vary from choir members (rehearsal), to members of a committee (missionary program), to members of the church (business meeting). The section *Today* includes four simultaneous services for different age groups during church time, and a later jail service, youth groups, and prayer service.

Considered as a total single segment, the church service has fuzzy borders as its parts do. Whereas the song leader on one occasion stated, after the prelude, *We will start our service by singing number...*, and the audience was not completely quiet until then, there is printed on a number of the bulletins, just before the prelude, the injunction: *Let the first note of the organ be a call to worship the Lord in quietness and reverence*. Similarly, after the choir finishes singing a response following the benediction, people start moving and talking to their neighbors (in part as a deliberate attempt to be friendly to strangers); this shows that the service is finished — even though the organ postlude is being played during this time and in another sense is part of the service.

3.31 *Hierarchical Structure*

The indeterminacy of borders leaves impossible of solution the question: Exactly where does such and such a segment begin and end? — and forces us to set up theory and techniques that allow us to identify the nuclei of segments without prequisite rigid delineation of their end points. We assume that such etic segment centers will be constituted of the 'peaks' or 'troughs' of waves of activity.

Nevertheless, etic segmental identification leaves unsolved the question: What segments or segment sequences shall we consider to be wholes, from an emic point of view? Is the church service a whole? If so, how can the preaching of the sermon which is part of the whole service be itself a whole (even though it may seem obvious that it is such)? Or what if a sonnet is quoted in a sermon — is the sonnet not a whole? If, as a point of departure for a study, one decides as I do that sonnet, sermon, and church service are each in some way wholes, then one must conclude that there is in behavior a HIERARCHICAL STRUCTURE (which we referred to as wheels within wheels) in which smaller emic wholes may be viewed as parts of larger emic wholes, which in turn are parts of still larger ones — somewhat in the way in which on an old-type Dutch Cleanser can is a picture of a Dutch maiden holding in her hand a Dutch Cleanser can on which is a picture of a Dutch maiden holding in her hand a can on which...

3.32 *Focus and Participants*

Now a person contemplating a church service or participating in it may find that his attention varies a great deal. One kind of participant may be somewhat drowsy and be uninterested in the details, on which he does not focus with clear concentration at any point. When he has gone home after the service he has 'gone to church' — but can give no coherent report on the songs sung, or the content of the sermon, or other detail — except possibly details not emic to the service itself, such as that Mr. X winked at him. For him, the service began and ended (perhaps to his relief), and was a vague whole.

A second participant — possibly the parent of the first — may have been highly attentive to the entire service, following carefully all its parts, and yet end the service with an appreciation of the service as a whole. He might even be heard to say, afterwards, *Wasn't that an inspiring service, everything fitted so beautifully together and was helpful.*

Later, however, the second participant might be discussing with a third the sermon heard that day — its content, purpose and effectiveness. Under these circumstances he has lowered focus, by considering a shorter sequence of activity; his attention, in retrospect, has changed so that he is now considering the sermon as a unit. For him, at this point, the sermon is a whole.

The boundaries of the top level of FOCUS at any one time constitute in this way the essence of the boundaries of a whole. Focus can shift up (to include a larger time span) or down (to include a shorter one), and the 'whole' shifts with it. This shift, for the second kind of participant mentioned, may occur during the service many times: At the beginning this focus is on the entire span of the service in anticipation of the whole; during it, his attention may lower, to focus on the singing of the choir number; he may temporarily shift focus up again, to feel, that the 'preliminaries' are over, as he settles down for the sermon; and so on; then, after lowering focus to the sermon — or to a poem in the sermon — he may at the end raise focus to the whole service again, 'picking up' the whole, to finish in fact that which he earlier felt by anticipation.

3.33 *Lower Limits to Focus*

There are lower limits beyond which the ordinary participant in a church service does not normally go in changing focus. If he does so, he has become an analyst, rather than a worshiper — or 'critical' rather than 'enjoying it'. Possibly most observers will not react to many units of structure in the sermon as wholes other than the entire sermon itself; the chief exceptions are likely to be sporadic illustrations (especially an illustrative joke, which one may later recall as a unit without being able to specify the context — the larger immediate whole — from which it was drawn or the point it was intended to illustrate). Other observers, especially those who do some speaking themselves, may look for major structural breaks, the young preacher's rule-of-thumb, 'introduction, conclusion, and three points well illustrated'. Others may have private 'pet dislikes', and notice, as wholes, an occasional grammatical infelicity, or noncurrent pronuciation.

3.34 *Indeterminacy of Focus*

The analysis of the structural wholes in behavior is therefore complicated by individual differences. What can be done, in the face of this indeterminacy of focus, to find 'the' essential wholes within the behavior patterns of the church service?

In part we can never be certain, since any particular person may be acting analytically rather than participating in the purposes for which the service is intended — and this difference of purpose results in a different set of emic units, as the filibuster differed from a persuading talk in Chapter 1.

3.35 *Criteria for Closure*

If, however, we assume that in order to demonstrate that a segment is emically a 'whole' we need to do so only in reference to persons acting as actual participants — not in reference to critics, or pseudo-participants — then a usable though not precise criterion can be found.

This criterion consists of clues observable in the actions of the participants. These are clues which in some way, whether by nonverbal action or by direct statement, indicate that the church goers (as worshipers or in their capacity as regular attendants) consider that a large unit or a small one has begun, or has ended, or is in process. This, to be sure, still leaves room for great fluctuation in individual or group attention, but there is no avoiding this complication since a denial of such focus changes would be a rejection of vast amounts of the empirical data itself, which indicates that such variation actually occurs. In spite of such focus changes, however, cultural units of activity can be found; they begin (though fuzzily) and end (also fuzzily), but are nevertheless part of our experience.

That the church goers consider the church service to be a unit is seen, then, in the following kinds of stray remarks heard preceding, following, or during the service: *Hurry, we'll be late to church. Has church begun yet? No, you're still on time. Shh! church has started. We will open our service by... Stop whispering, tell me after church is over. In closing... Did you go to church yesterday?*

Even a young child sometimes recognizes these units. My young (three years old when this paragraph was written) son, two days ago, as he danced a little jig outside said: *Church is ALL OVER.* Once in a while, he has detected the ending of a church service with amazing skill; he will have been quiet, with not a word aloud throughout an hour's service, and then, less than a half second following the final prayer (so close that I can hear no pause whatever between the preacher's voice and his — and before more staid members of the congregation have 'shifted gears' for the next behavior pattern), he will have started to speak aloud in delighted tones about something irrelevant to the service.

Similarly, the non-coordinated activity of the congregation after church is dismissed — the lack of integration and lack of co-terminal etic segments in the action of members, choir, preacher, and song leader — let the observer see when 'church is out'. On the other hand, the relevant, joint, integrated activity shows that church is in progress.

Within the service, similar clues give evidence that the worshipers recognize sub-wholes: *Our choir number this morning... Mr. ... will lead in prayer. Shh* (whispered) *listen, son, the lady's going to sing.* Likewise, nonverbal activity plays its part — the getting adjusted for listening to the sermon — feet shuffled, books arranged, shoulders twitched, hair adjusted, throat cleared, or a half-hundred other individual mannerisms signalling the relaxing of the audience as its most active 'preliminary' units are now ended; and either the alert focusing of attention to listen for encouragement, and inspiration, or else the setting of the mind in neutral so it can idly dream of things while the ear registers word by word, but with no connected thought while the eye stares vacantly in space, — all these things at times mark the change to the sermon, and most of them are observable to an alien analyst — or to any competent preacher, who attempts to lead all minds to focus on the message instead of on the window panes, ceiling, neighbor's hat, or a letter that needs to be written.

Specifically, then, such wholes are culturally marked as having beginning and ending; they may be said to have CLOSURE, so that one feels them to be satisfactorily ended, and would miss any deletion in the same way that all would be unsatisfied if the choir left the last two notes off the anthem. Just a month ago, a university colleague told me that he might attend the church I have been describing except for one thing — he missed the *Amen* at the end of each hymn; he had been brought up to expect it — but here, he said, they *just stopped!* For him, this informal service failed to mark the hymn with the signal requisite for acceptable closure of that type of emic unit.

3.4 *Slots and Classes*

3.41 *Functional Slots in Larger Wholes*

For this particular service we have already indicated that a strange thing happened: The song leader referred to an event which in one respect was part of the service, but in another respect was not part of the service — the choir number, which was to be omitted. How could something be omitted which was never present? And why was it listed in the bulletin if it was not part of the service?

The answer: There is an optional SLOT (cf. § 1.3) in the behavior unit 'morning-service-of-church-X' for a choir number or other special musical selection; it is expected, planned for, counted on by pulpit, pew, and choir loft. The particular number cannot be predicted by the congregation, but the fact that there will be such a number is probable. The pressure to fill the pattern slot is so strong that even in its absence a short verbal substitute (i.e., an explanation for the absence) was given. This incident was not a mere 'change of program' such as might occur at a concert, as evidenced by the fact that the church secretary seems to have included in the bulletin a mention of the slot, even without an advanced listing of the specific number expected to fill it; and the lack of special music would also have been noticed and regretted by many worshipers even if there had been no bulletin whatever. (On two recent occasions, similarly, I have noted that a hymn was sung in the place in the service for which a hymn was listed, but for which the particular number was changed: here the functional slot was preserved, and only the particular segment filling that slot was replaced).

With this in mind it is possible, now, to see more clearly the manner in which the church bulletin served us: It listed for that service the principal slots to be filled; by number it mentioned, in addition, the particular hymns to fill the hymn slots; it also named the preacher, i.e., the actor for the sermon behavior, but did not give the title of his sermon for that week. On various other Sundays the title of the particular sermon has been listed, and as such corresponds structurally to the number or name of the hymn. Further, the church service is seen listed as filling a slot in the activity of the time unit *Today*, while it is also related by implication to a larger time unit, *This Week*.

It is evident, then, that focus comes into play in reference to slots as it did in the consideration of segments — a large whole (say the service) may contain slots into which fall smaller wholes, such as the singing of a hymn. If focus is lowered to the hymn as a new whole, then within it one finds slots filled by stanzas, while stanzas as wholes have slots filled by particular lines (or phrases), and lines as wholes may have slots for rime at their ends. And so one continues analysis to the lower limit of immediate (cultural or analytical) relevance.

3.42 *Segment Classes*

The musical number sung in the slot just before the sermon was a hymn. It was Number 181, chosen from the hymn book and entitled *My Hope is Built*. Almost any of the songs in the book would have been appropriate for use in that slot — but not quite all of them. I have never heard — nor do those participants I have consulted ever expect to hear — Number 392, *Gloria Patri* sung there, nor Number 395, a chant called *Nunc Dimittis;* and it is only slightly less improbable that the short chorus, Number 385, *Shine Just Where You Are* would occur there in senior church, even though in primary church it would not be startling.

That is to say, for each kind of slot there is a CLASS (§ 1.3) of segments APROPRIATE to that slot, and actually or potentially observed there. It is their occurrence in this and similar slots which, from this point of view, makes hymns constitute a class. *Sweet Adeline* and *Jingle Bells* would not occur in this slot. Participants would know this fact (could make the negative prediction with a very high degree of certainty) since they react consciously or unconsciously to other characteristics observed to belong to members of the class, characteristics which serve as a yardstick to determine, for example, whether or not *Sweet Adeline* is a hymn.

If the normal worshiper from this church were to attend a service somewhere and hear *Sweet Adeline* in a pre-sermon slot, or if he were to hear *My Hope is Built* used as the theme song of a beer advertisement, he would consider both activities sacrilegious.

At each level of focus in the church service, classes of segments occur and are determined by the slots they fill: There are classes, so defined, of organ preludes, of invocations, of announcements, sermons, and benedictions; of junior, senior, and primary services; of morning and evening service types; of musical introductions to the hymns; of types of arm movements for leading the singing; movements of the congregation standing, sitting, bowing the head; of words or phrases to serve as subjects of sentences, words to serve as modifiers of subjects; consonants in prevocalic position in the syllable, and so on. On these other levels, too, segments inappropriate to a slot but occurring in it may get reactions as sacrilege: whispering instead of listening; or children's misbehavior during the service.

3.43 *Indeterminacy of Class*

Individual and group usage varies enough that it is not always clear to the participants what the behavior appropriate to a particular occasion would be. Hesitant people are likely to get help from someone who has observed more of the kind of activity involved than they have: Parents instruct their children when to stand up in church; old timers often help visitors find the proper place in a hymnal; future clergymen are taught in school how many major slots can occur in a typical sermon and still have it effective.

Change may also occur over a period of time; the tempo and structure of some of the newer church songs has changed sufficiently to cause some uncertainty as to their appropriateness for particular kinds of services. This in turn leads to differences in selection by different leaders, and to some indeterminacy of class. An evening service in this church, for example, would frequently contain songs or choruses inappropriate to the somewhat more conventional morning service.

3.5 *Modes of Units*

Thus far we have looked principally at emic units as total chunks (or segments) of activity. To be sure, we have here and there indicated that some behavior was irrelevant to a particular emic unit (distant singing of children during the senior service), but the balance was divided up into segmental parts (although with fuzzy borders where components of the behavior segments did not all end at the same time).

Now, however, we are ready to see that on any level of focus each such emic unit, each chunk, even one for which the borders seem relatively clear cut, is divided structurally into three specific kinds of complex overlapping components which I shall call MODES.

We have already discussed numerous components of the three modes, without an attempt to indicate the relationship of these components to trimodal structuring as such. In this section we shall make a start at doing so, and the next few chapters will carry this process further.

For those linguistic readers who would like at this point a crude 'rule-of-thumb' to aid in understanding our approach to the analysis of the modes,[3] even though, like other rules-of-thumb, this one is only a helpful approximation, the following may be of interest:

(1) The *feature mode* of an emic unit of activity will in general be viewed as composed of simultaneously occurring identificational-contrastive components, with its internal segmentation analyzed with special reference to stimulus-response features (including purpose or lexical meaning, where relevant). Example: the voicing, bilabiality, and occlusion of /b/ contrasted with the voicelessness, alveolarity, and continuant sibilant nature of /s/; in addition, the components serve to identify /b/ in the absence of /s/ in immediate contrastive environments. The morpheme *cat* has the sound sequence as one contrastive component, and its meaning of 'feline' as another.

(2) The *manifestation mode* of an emic unit of activity will often be viewed as composed of nonsimultaneuosly occurring physical variants (or nonsimultaneous components), with its internal segmentation analyzed with special reference to the hierarchy of the mechanisms of its physical production. Phonological example: The /t/ at the beginning of *tatter* is followed by a characteristic puff of breath, whereas the one in the middle, for American English, has a light flip of the tongue. Morphological example: The phonological component of the plural morpheme in *tubs* and in *houses* differs.

(3) The *distribution mode* of an emic unit of activity will be seen as composed of relational components, including its class membership and its function in a slot of a hierarchically-ordered larger construction (its external distribution), and its internal segmentation (its internal distribution),[4] especially in reference to the

---

[3] In more recent publications I have tried to help readers follow this kind of discussion more easily by a change in choice of terms. For feature mode one can in general read CONTRAST (contrastive-identificational components); for manifestation mode VARIATION (range of free, conditioned, or complex variants with physical component obligatory); for distribution mode DISTRIBUTION (occurrence in a class as member of that class, in a sequence of segments organized hierarchically, and in cells of a matrix made up of intersecting dimensions). See Pike (1962a: 241-42; 1963b: 218 n. 6).

We use three modes, not two, because we have not been able to handle the data with two alone (and two distort the picture by leading to a system of separable parts additive rather than to a system of overlapping, simultaneously occurring elements). We use three rather than four or more since by a repeated application of the three we seem to be able to take care of the empirical data (and do not wish to add more than are empirically necessary). The choice of three, therefore, has been strictly an empirical one. Any philosophical elements which seem to be implied by this fact come as a result of the empirical decision, not vice versa. (Although I personally find the three simultaneous modes philosophically congenial, this factor has been irrelevant to my development of the theory itself, insofar as I can trace its development in fact.) I have the suspicion — which I am not equipped to check adequately — that results presented logically are likely to be dichotomous or binary; but that life processes must somehow operate in a three-modal system. To whatever degree this hunch is valid, it would help to explain both the desire for binary presentation, on the one hand, and trimodal analysis on the other.

[4] This term has not appeared frequently in recent tagmemic writings. The included sequence of tagmemes characterizing a construction has by Crawford (see § 11.44) been referred to the feature mode. I am attempting to follow him in this, but the implications are not yet clear enough to allow full revision here.

hierarchy of mechanisms of its physical production. Example: The sound /b/ is a member of a class of consonants, which occur in the pre-syllabic slot of a syllable. The morpheme *boy* is a member of a class of animate nouns; may occur in subject, object, and other positions in the clause, and internally is made up of a characteristic sequence of sounds comprising a syllable.

Each of these modes covers the same physical data, however, with a *simultaneous structuring* in these respective ways. Each of the modes, in turn, can be discovered only in reference to a system which embraces all three, such that the units of each enter into a network of units characterized by and discoverable by their *relationship to the entire system* of modes and units of modes of which they are a part.

3.51 *Distribution Mode*

The chief complex of components of the distribution mode is its SLOT-CLASS CORRELATION: the distribution mode of the church service, as described above, includes within its structuring not only the fact that the church service fills a slot within a larger behavior unit (the complex of religious activities of the week) and has within itself interior slots filled by smaller units of activity, but it also includes the fact that a class of emic units of behavior may fill that slot — the class composed of variants of the regular church service on the one hand, and of special types such as a Christmas program or Children's Day program on the other. Since, however, most of our attention has been focused here on the church service as our top focus, it is simpler to lower our analytical attention to review these matters in reference to a smaller unit included within that service — e.g., the singing of the pre-sermon hymn, Number 181, *My Hope is Built*.

The activity consisting of singing the hymn Number 181 has, as part of its distribution mode, a number of important characteristics. One of these is precisely the fact that it can — and here does — fill the pre-sermon slot; secondly, that as such it is a member of a class of activities (composed of the singing of various other hymns) which can similarly so occur. Thirdly, however, this hymn — and the class of which it is a member — may appropriately have occurred in the other hymn slots of this service, and this slot-class POTENTIAL for so occurring is an important component of its distribution mode, just as its immediate occurrence and its class membership are such components. This potential, furthermore, may be re-expressed as a set of positive and negative predictions as to future occurrence, based upon the slot in which it is at present occurring, and those slots in which it may be discovered to have occurred in the past. Thus the distribution mode includes a relationship to past and present occurrence and future probability[5] of occurrence acceptable to the actors within a certain emic slot or set of emic slots. (Cf. §§ 7.52, 6.63.)

[5] Some scholars might now prefer to speak of potential, prediction, and of probability for future occurrence or the like as the generative power of the structure. See discussion of transformational grammar in Chapter 11. See also § 7.52.

As a fourth characteristic of the hymn's distribution mode we note that it also has an internal structuring, with slots internal to it. In the singing of this hymn, for example, there are four major slots filled by the singing of one stanza for each of these slots, alternating with a further slot filled by a chorus repeated after each stanza.[6]

The slot-filling nature of a third stanza outside of a series of more than three can occasionally be observed, furthermore, as when the leader states: *We will sing the third stanza as the last* (in my data for a different hymn, two weeks later, at an evening service), in which the 'last' slot is filled by a stanza used there, but not structurally last in the hymn as fully used on other occasions. Within each stanza are four rhythmic slots of one line each, whereas the chorus has only three such lines. Each line of each stanza and chorus has six slots filled with stressed syllables, with the second and fifth followed by slots filled with unstressed syllables. (An unstressed syllable and its preceding stressed syllable together are equal in timing to one of the other stressed syllables.) In each syllable is at least one slot filled by a vowel, and sometimes other slots filled by consonants. Simultaneously, the stanzas as sung are composed of sentences with subject, action, and modifying slots, and so on, filled with appropriate nouns, verbs and other classes of linguistic elements.

The DISTRIBUTION MODE of that hymn-singing activity is a composite of all these distributional characteristics: its potential for occurrence in various slots and classes in this service or elsewhere in other kinds of religious meetings, its actual occurrence in this particular slot and class on this particular day, and its internal slots and classes on lower internal focus levels.

3.52 *Manifestation Mode*

The activity of singing Hymn 181 is a unit, an emic one (Chapter 2). If the hymn had been repeated immediately by choir and congregation the vocal movements would not have been exactly the same (§ 2.3). An infinite number of slight etic differences would have occurred; none of the thousands of individual tongue and lip movements could have been quite duplicated; timing of individual pronunciations of consonants and vowels, arm movements of the song leader (one of these leaders beats upwards, another downwards), finger movements of the accompanying organist, — all would have varied freely (§ 2.3), sometimes imperceptibly and at some points perceptibly.

The emic unit composed of the activity of 'singing Hymn 181 in a church service' is not limited to just the one occurrence of the singing of that hymn but is a composite[7] of all such occurrences. The particular, single, physical event, the bodily and singing activity at a particular time and place in a particular slot, is just one single

---

[6] But see, now, § 3.5(3).
[7] Compare the problem of determining what is 'the' poem, with or without various oral readings of it.

manifestation of that emic unit. Repeated occurrences of that singing would result in further manifestations of that emic unit, just as the word *turn* repeated fifty times contains fifty manifestations of the one emic unit /t/.

Suppose, however, that Hymn 181 is now sung in junior church. Is that activity a manifestation of the same emic unit of activity as the singing of the same hymn by senior church? In spite of a different audience, a different leader, a piano instead of organ (or organ plus piano), a slightly different tempo, different voice quality (resultant from different age of singers), we consider them the same emically. The differences in the two manifestations are, in part, conditioned variants (§ 2.3) with differences in the manifestation as a result of their differences in distribution.

Let us suppose, again, that the senior church sings Hymn 181 the next week, but that this time it omits the third stanza; — is it, or is it not, emically the same activity as before but with a different manifestation in which one slot is unfilled? We consider it to be the same emic unit; the audience would still report: *We sang Hymn Number 181* or *We sang two verses of Number 181*. (Compare, for example, the sentence *Turn again to Number 443;* if now we also hear *Turn to Number 443*, the two sentences differ, in that one potential slot on a low-level focus is unfilled in the second, since the place where *again* occurred has no word there, but from the point of view of high-level focus, its basic arrangement in terms of slots is similar). This, then, is a kind of free variation in which potential slots internally on a low-level focus need not be filled in every manifestation of the same emic unit of activity. On a still lower-focus level, *I'm here* is the same sentence as *I am here*. Possibly, too, we could see in such variation an analogy with complex variants (§ 2.3) such as the sub-emic variation between [p] and [pʰ] at the end of the English sentence *Let us stand up*.

Differences in manifestation occur on every focus level. On a level higher than that of the hymn, the entire service may be repeated in considerable detail an hour later for an overflow audience, as I have seen done frequently in a certain Southern Baptist church; or regular senior 'Morning service' as a whole,[8] as a slot in the religious activities of the week and year may be considered on this high focus level as a single unit of emic activity, with manifestations radically different each week — i.e., with different hymns, different choir number, different sermon, but with the same major slots.

A complete description of the MANIFESTATION MODE of an emic unit would include a statement of all actual and potential variants in the unit at its top-focus layer and internal lower-focus layers as well. Since, however, such potential variants are infinite in number, the descriptive task is made manageable by treating subperceptual variants in special studies only, which can concentrate, for example, on the minute acoustic detail of a relatively small amount of data — or by dealing with classes of units; by limiting attention, for certain purposes, to high-focus levels of activity

---

[8] It is not clear, in this discussion, where an emic unit differs from an emic class (cf. § 7.313) of units. If the single morning service is an emic unit then the composite of a number of them would be an emic class of such services.

where the perceptible variants are fewer; and by accepting sample occurrences of an emic unit as representative of the total variation of its manifestation mode.

In addition to placing attention on the variants of an emic unit as alternate non-simultaneous manifestations of that unit, a study of its manifestation mode must include attention addressed to the physical characteristics, as such, of the activity constituting each of these variants. These elements have already been mentioned, and need only brief reference here: the movements of tongue, lips, jaw, etc. (which lead to the vocal noises), organized into movements producing syllables, stress groups, etc.; the accompanying movements of organist and song leader; etc. All such physical elements are components of the manifestation of the emic unit of that hymn-singing activity. We never, in my view, completely 'abstract' a behavioral emic unit out of and away from the actual physical action which constitutes the specific manifested substance of behavior. (Compare Hill: "Since items enter into manipulable combinations, they must have some substance or body" (1962:347).

3.53 Feature Mode

The morning senior church service as a whole is related to the junior service, but with a number of differences which should allow a domestic onlooker to recognize which was which. One of my principal informants for junior church, one who has helped plan and execute its programs on occasion, suggests that the chief difference is that the junior service has "less rigidity in form"; the leaders will "drop anything at any time" and switch to other activities according as it may be necessary to keep interest.

There are numerous specific differences also: There is a worship section analogous to senior service, with "as much worship as one can get in" but also there is a "work shop approach" for the remainder of the time — say two thirds, if the types are not woven in together. There is more singing, beginning with lively short choruses often repeated once or twice (for pleasure, and interest, and to take a longer period of time since a short chorus is over so quickly) leading into the quieter worship section and songs. The 'sermon' (i.e., the filling of the slot analogous to the sermon in senior service) is often composed of activity by the children themselves — identification of the author of a Scripture passage, or quoting it from memory — or the adult leader may tell a story, illustrated at times with paper figures placed on a flannel background. In the workshop section some of the same may occur, with contests among the children — for example, to see who can most rapidly locate certain places in the Bible. Another informant said — after a service in which Bible stories were acted out in pantomime: "The chief problem is to have a varied program with them all doing something".

Such elements serve to show the difference between the two emic units, the senior and junior church services; they are therefore CONTRASTIVE features (or distinctive features). Yet, from a slightly different analytical point of view, these items likewise allow the identification of the units, so they are equally IDENTIFICATIONAL features of the unit under attention.

Identificational-contrastive features are present within every emic unit of behavior, on every focus level; they are components of these units. The segmental parts of the service are segmental or sequence components, whereas elements present together at any one time are simultaneous components. The regular sermon is a sequence component of senior church; the playing of a musical number during the taking up of the offering is one simultaneous component of the offering segment; the ushers' activity of passing the offering plates is a simultaneous component of that same offering segment.

On a lower level of focus, say for the *m* in *my*, the components at first appear to be much simpler — the closing of the lips would be one component, the opening of the nasal passage would be another simultaneous one, the vibration of the vocal cords would be a third. Actually these, too, are exceedingly complex and appear simple only because as students of language behavior we so seldom lower our focus to smaller elements. The physiologists would not find the closing of lips so simple, but would find complexity in simultaneous or sequential muscle movements. The biological chemist on a still lower level of analytical focus would see components of atomic and molecular activity of enormous complexity within the muscles and nerves. The physicist might go to a lower focus and analyze sub-atomic components of activity within these molecules.

Among the identificational-contrastive features are some which are elusive and difficult to identify objectively in spite of their emic importance. These features are the ones which relate to meaning and purpose in human activity, and give data allowing the significant segmentation of human activity. Such an element as the purpose of the singing of the hymn is obviously not a chunk of activity which can be photographed or recorded directly on a tape. If the analyst utilizes as evidence the claims of the participants, the evidence will vary, since some of the people may be inarticulate, most of those in the pew will not know the preacher's purposes, nor would most of them know the historical sources of activity (at which time the purposes of the participants who founded the ceremony might be quite different from the purposes of those people now in the pew).

The language analyst frequently asks his informants for the meaning of words, and utilizes this evidence. Yet he must do so with caution because speakers of the language may be misinformed on technical vocabulary outside their experience (compare the naming of woodworking tools and of colors by a carpenter and his seamstress wife); or they may merely be unable to express in words the meanings and purposes to which they react; or they may be deliberately deceptive.

The analyst, therefore, supplements such inquiry with a much more objective tool than informant definitions of meaning and purpose. He studies the kinds of slots in which activity occurs. He sees that, by and large, the particular activity (e.g., the speaking of a particular word in a particular context, or the singing of a hymn in a particular slot in a church service) tends to be followed by a response, or sequel, of some type, such that the first has something of the nature of cause and the second of effect. He notices, further, that these word-activities and ceremony activities are found frequently in certain slots, adjacent to specific items in adjacent slots (as *the merrier* frequently follows *the more*); etc. By such a study of contexts a partial objective study of meanings and purposes can be made (§ 6.42).

In this respect a meaning or purpose component is analogous to the character of the distribution mode of a unit. The distribution mode of a unit could only be described in reference to the slot in the higher-focus unit in which it then occurred, with reference also to its potential and past occurrence in other slots (and in reference to its internal slots and their contents).[9] Meaning, or purpose, as a feature component of an emic segment, must similarly be detected by reference to elements beyond the chunk as a whole. Thus the purpose of an offertory prayer can be seen in that it immediately precedes (or, in some churches immediately follows) the activity of the ushers in taking up the offering. (It includes references to the gifts; it usually includes special references of gratefulness to God for supplies, with further relation of this offering to an expression of thanks; and it is paralleled by physical activity such as the bowing of heads and closing of eyes.) All these things together would lead the analyst to conclude, even without being told, that this was a prayer of thanksgiving by pastor and congregation — or would lead him to do so subject to further consideration of the slot which the church service activity as a whole played in the more extensive daily life of each individual (i.e., if he found that one of the members cheated consistently in business, he might conclude in retrospect that the bowing of the head for offertory prayer in church was a physical feature of the manifestation of a unit of formal ceremony — without worship content — for purposes of establishing business contacts, rather than a feature of physical activity which was part of the manifestation mode of an emic unit of genuine worship activity).

Internal segmentation of the feature mode of a large emic unit of behavior is specifically oriented toward the purposeful or meaningful character of the unit as a whole, and the purposeful or meaningful character of its parts. On the contrary, the internal segmentation of its manifestation mode, in reference to large physical units of activity, may or may not coincide with such meaningful units. The units of physical activity such as an abdominal pulse producing a stress group, for example, may or may not begin and end with the beginning and ending of a grammatical phrase — as, in the singing of a hymn, the end of a musical phrase does not always coincide with the end of a grammatical one. (This skewness of boundaries of modal units will in § 15.12 be seen as one of the compelling bits of evidence forcing us to some kind of modal theory.)

---

[9] See fn. to § 3.5(3).

3.54 *Indeterminacy of Modes*

Sometimes it is impossible to separate clearly the modal components of a unit. Take, for example, a certain Congregational service in which without exception, so far as I can recall, the prelude is always followed by the singing of the Doxology (*Praise God from whom all blessings flow*) to the tune of Old Hundred. Here the slot for the Doxology is always filled by the same manifestation of that slot, the Doxology itself: no member of any class of items can substitute for the Doxology. If the Doxology were never to be sung elsewhere by members of that church, but were reserved exclusively for this slot, then the purpose or meaning or function of the slot, and the purpose or meaning or function of the Doxology, would be inseparable. There would be an indeterminacy in isolating the purposive component of the slot itself from the purposive component of the slot-filling activity.

Similar problems arise in the analysis of single words or even a small group of words which come only in one slot in a sentence — words like *not* (in *I did not talk to him at all*); or a group like *if, since, when;* or a suffix like *-s* (plural). Here, too, it is difficult or impossible to separate the purposive or meaning component of the slot from that of the single word or word group which may fill the slot.

3.55 *Modal Formula Symbolizing Units*

If we symbolize an emic unit of activity as U, the feature mode as F, the manifestation mode as M, and the distribution mode as D, then any emic unit of any type on any level of focus is symbolized as: $U = F, M, D$.

This formula applies not only to emic units which are chunks of activity, but also to all special kinds of emic units such as emic classes. It is this fact which — the theory suggests — lies at the heart of the structure of behavior.

3.56 *Manifestation of Each Mode as the Manifestation of the Whole*

A basic misunderstanding can easily arise at this point. The reader may assume that the emic unit on any focus level — say the singing of Hymn 181 — is a tripartite unit constituted of three separate physical things added one to another — of features *plus* formal manifestation *plus* distribution. Such an outlook vitiates the structural theory presented here.

The variant forms of the singing of the hymn include the total manifestation of the hymn unit activity, not just one third of that form. There is no substance left over.

Similarly, the features which identify the singing of Hymn 181 and separate it distinctly from the singing of other specific songs embrace the entire substance of the hymn — the same substance as seen in the manifestation mode itself. The feature mode then is also from this point of view, the whole.

Finally, the slot which the hymn fills and the slots which it contains can ultimately be known as slots only through the substance filling or manifesting those structural slots. The distribution mode is not a system of empty slots within empty slots, but a system of FILLED SLOTS, in which the substance filling the slot — the particular item occurring at the time — is part of the distribution mode. It, too, engulfs the entire substance.

The reason for labelling contrastive-identificational features, formal manifestation, and distributional character as 'modes' rather than 'fragments' or 'parts' is now clear: Modes are not parts, nor pieces of the whole. They each comprise the entire substance in a different simultaneous structure. The same 'stuff', the activity, is STRUCTURED THREE WAYS AT ONCE.

At first, the theory of three simultaneous structurings of a single substance may appear strange. Perhaps an illustration of a different type may make it seem less so. Let us suppose, for example, that a cook bakes two cakes in separate shallow pans. Later, she places them one on top of another, with frosting between, on top of the whole, and around the sides. At this point there is a single two-layered cake, structured in terms of layers no longer visible to the eye but covered with frosting. Now the cake is sliced into ten pieces, but without any of the pieces being removed from the plate. What is the new structuring of the cake? It is structured into ten vertical slices, with no substance left over. Just as obviously, to one who knows cakes and takes out a slice to look at it where it is cut, it is still a two-layered cake, with all the substance in two frosted layers with nothing left over. The cake, then, is simultaneously structured into layers and slices, such that the entire substance of the cake is structured in each way. By special fancy cooking procedures, even more elaborate structurings could be built into the cake — for example, by using different colored doughs. Further structurings can be cut into it, by cutting the cake into concentric rings before cutting it into slices.

It is the thesis of this volume that human behavior must be analyzed as consisting of various simultaneous structurings of its activity, structurings which are here called modes. It contends, furthermore, that an adequate description of such behavior cannot be reached by utilizing a theoretical foundation in which less than three such modes are postulated; and that the penalty for attempting to utilize fewer modes is the distortion or rejection of some data concerning interpenetrating subsystems of this behavior. It claims that no more than three such modes need be used to accommodate the present data.

Wherever there is one such mode there are always two more, simultaneously structuring the same stuff in a different way.

3.6 Bibliographical Comments on Chapter 3

3.61 On Segmenting a Continuum

One of the basic problems which confront us in linguistics in the necessity for a theory and procedure for the analytical breaking up of a physical etic continuum into a sequence of discrete emic units. We began discussion of this problem in relation to chunks, or segments, or waves of activity (§ 3.2). The problem will continue to come into attention throughout the book from a theoretical point of view.

Sapir illustrates the language problem by reference to music: "Even the most resplendent and dynamic symphony is built up of tangibly distinct musical entities or notes which, in the physical world, flow into each other in an indefinite continuum but which, in the world of aesthetic composition and appreciation, are definitely bounded off against one another, so that they may enter into an intricate mathematics of significant relationships" (1933, in his Selected Writings, 8). For illustrations in terms of mathematics, see Joos (1950: 702-04).

The problem covers areas much more general than that of linguistics, for example that of epistemology and the theory of perception. Compare Sinclair: "The real difficulty is... to understand how we come to experience the world as containing particular things" (1951:176-77; and cf. Koffka, 1935). Or note the anthropologist Nadel: "If scientific insight is insight into an order of things, observation must be directed towards breaking up the continuum of data into units — units which can be manipulated and ordered in a fashion more systematic than the ambiguous and fortuitous ordering inherent in naïve observation" (1951:75). Compare also the relationship of an analogical computer (with some characteristics of a continuum) to the digital computer (dealing with discrete elements) in reference to the analysis of a continuous physical variable and of some characteristics of the central nervous system (Gerard, Von Neumann, and others, in Cybernetics, 7th, 1951: 26-37); e.g., "in almost all parts of physics the underlying reality is analogical, that is, the true physical variables are in almost all cases continuous, or equivalent to continuous descriptions. The digital procedure is usually a human artifact for the sake of description" (27, Von Neumann), and "You treat them as if these transition states did not exist" (30, Stroud). Compare statements of Z. Harris (1951:22).

Two types of continua occur in linguistic data. The first is a stream of continuous speech or action. The second type is a continuum of physical characteristics of members of a class of units (such that no 'absolute' physical criterion can determine by a simple measurement which of two units one is observing, since the ranges of their physical variants may overlap under certain contextual influences). Here the units being compared do not occur in the same sequence, adjacent to one another, but occur at separate times and places, and must either be analyzed as the 'same' emically, or 'different' emically. (If, for example, one hears at one moment, in a strange language, one variety of [t] sound, and at another moment another variety of [t], he must determine in some way whether the two sounds are members of the same emic unit, or of different emic units.) The emic analytical process must deal simultaneously with emic units as discrete parts of a system of units, and as discrete parts of sequences of units in sequences of complex events.

The approach here to etic segments as waves of physical activity is a development of my earlier analysis of the sounds of a speech continuum in which I observed the peaks and troughs of stricture, and set them up as centers of segments which had indefinite borders. In succeeding chapters — especially in Chapter 14 — this approach will be helpful as it is extended to the theoretical treatment of problems presented by fusion, where centers of segments are again under attention with borders sometimes left indeterminate in theory as well as in empirical fact. The earlier material came as a result of a struggle to determine the sequence of articulatory happenings in the production of certain complex sounds called 'glottalized stops', 'clicks', etc., and was presented first to a seminar at the Linguistic Institute of the Linguistic Society of America and the University of Michigan, 1940, as part of a dissertation in progress, which appeared later in Pike, 1943a: 107-12 (cf. also 42-55, and diagrams on 90, 92, 94, 96, 98-99; for a different type of segmental diagram, showing both peaks and indeterminate crossing glides, see Pike, 1947c:9-10, 30, 41). Hockett built on this material (1942:5 — text and fn. 4), but with a modification which focused attention on the 'change-point' (5) and segments between any two such points (a view useful for certain purposes, provided one leaves the change-point indeterminate so that a working procedure can in fact identify the *area* of most rapid change without being committed to the impossible task of setting up, in theory or practice, absolute sharp points of change; and provided that the statement of this view does not conceal the fact that the anticipation of the component articulatory movements which produce a sound, or the decay of such components, may spread over several sounds in a sequence — e.g., Carnochan, 1953:94, building on an approach highlighted by Firth — and do not occur exclusively at a change point or even at a change area between segments). Bloch follows Hockett's outlook in this matter (1948:12), but neigher of them seem to me to give adequate safeguards of the kind mentioned here.

For the problem of boundaries in describing discrete units, see also Mathiot (1963b), and Halliday (1961:249). Compare also discussion of units as waves, in §§ 8.42, 12.1, 14.1, and Pike (1959 and 1962b). Note also, below, index references to items in double function, portmanteaus and indeterminacy. For segmenting nonverbal behavior episodes note references to Barker and Wright in § 17.71. For earlier segmentation, note also G. Mead (1938).

3.62 *On Hierarchical Structure*

For epistemological problems related to hierarchical matters see Sinclair in reference to "the focus of our attention, and the wider situation which contains it" (1951:223; also 96, 182-83, 201, 205); or for 'grades of abstraction' note Whitehead (1925:168). For size of unit in a particular setting, in relation to observation, see Lewin (1951:157, 159), Nadel (1951:76), or Linton (1945:158).

For an emphasis on a hierarchy of behavior, note Zipf, "Every act of behavior may be viewed as a complex of ever smaller acts, and as a component in ever larger complexes of action; we might well be in doubt as to the proper size to select as a unit" (1935:12). Linguistic structuring in a hierarchy of some type has been implicit in the work of the immediate and of the remote past. In Bloomfield: "Every utterance is made up wholly of forms" (1926:155); for an attempt to make explicit some of the hierarchical ordering which is implied by Bloomfield's work, see Pike (1943b). Other references to linguistic hierarchy may be seen in Hockett (1947b:284-85), Ege (1949: 21), de Groot (1948:436), Hjelmslev (1953:18, 24). Numerous other items directly or indirectly have reference to hierarchical materials. A number of these will be referred to in Chapters 9-11, and 15; see, for example, Z. Harris (1946).

Carroll points out that the notion of hierarchy of units applied to goal-directed behavior comes from linguistic theory (1953:106-07).

The term 'closure' is taken from Koffka (1927:60; 1935:151); cf. Lewin (1951:159). For closure as not autochthonous but "an abstraction based upon a sampling of various situations in which different expectancies have made different trace systems available for communication with input stimulus information" see Bruner (1951:310). In Chapter 4 we shall deal more extensively with hierarchical matters in reference to focus (§ 3.3), which is related to closure.

Hierarchical levels for phonology will be treated in Chapter 9 (bibliography § 9.7); for grammatical structures see Chapter 11; for interlocking hierarchies and systems, Chapter 15; for semantic hierarchy, Chapter 16; for society as a whole, Chapter 17. For a different variety of three-fold structuring see Trager (1963). I am unable, however, to find any simple way of translating his units and concepts into mine.

3.63 *On Units*

For units as well-defined, in reference to contrast, variation, and distribution in class, sequence, matrix, see Pike (1962a, 1963b). For an insistance on the necessity of retaining units, note Hill (1962); see also Halliday (1961:247). For the thesis "that there are units underlying social structure which are analogous to those which underlie language structure", and an attempt to symbolize these, see Bock (1962); here discussion of social structure includes reference to segmentation, identification, and matrix relations of the units, as well as their contrastive complementary and distributional elements (155, 162; see below, § 17.73, for quotations).

Lamb, for linguistic units, suggests that "one need recognize only three primitive relationships existing among linguistic units: that of a *class* to its *members*... that of a *combination* to its *components*... and that of an *eme* to its *allos*", (1962:4). Chomsky, on the other hand, has replaced attention to units by the development of rules: "A generative grammar is a system of explicit rules" (1961b:220) — rather than a set of inventories (compare 222, n. 10).

See, also, references in §§ 9.71, 11.71-72.

CHAPTER 4

FOCUS ILLUSTRATED

4.1 *A Football Game in Focus*

Some years ago (October 25, 1952) I saw a football game played between the teams of the University of Michigan and the University of Minnesota.

By comparing notes on my own observations, made there, with data from my recordings of a radio broadcast of the same game, and with several newspaper reports of it, it is possible to illustrate and develop further some of the problems of focus introduced in the preceding Chapter.

4.11 *The Length of the Game*

Throughout the broadcast data there are many cultural indications that the game was just sixty minutes long: 8/3/11.7... *and that's the scoring picture from Ann Arbor with the ball game twenty-three minutes old;* then a few minutes later, *and we still have thirty-four minutes of football remaining.* This sixty-minute period is initiated by a signal from one of the officials and then by the first significant player-participant action, the kickoff: 8/2/1.1 *We're just about set to go from Ann Arbor... Minnesota kicks off; kicking off is C —, a low kick, down to the 15, to the 10, to the 5.* The hour ends with a signal gun: 8/6/23.4 *He's over the midfield stripe, to the 40, to the 35, cuts back in, and is dropped out of bounds, on the Minnesota 32-yard line in a — please — that will be it; that's it, that's all there is, there isn't any more; the gun goes off; it's been sixty minutes of Gopher-Wolverine football... the final score at the end...*

The focus is lifted, in the report in the Michigan Daily the next day: ...*The Gophers left the field after 2 hours and 20 minutes of football.* The 60-minute count included only such official times as those for which the broadcaster stated that: 8/3/19.5 *Time is in down on the playing field here.* The longer count included the 15-minute half-time intermission, shorter intermissions following the first and third quarters, numerous time-outs requested by the teams, and other periods of time during which the official clock was not in motion (such as the interval between the time that a forward pass was incomplete and the next play was begun).

The University of Michigan Marching Band represents Eddie Cantor during the Mid-Game Spectacle (Photo by Boyce Photo Co., Ann Arbor, Mich.)

4.12 The Spectacle

After the official game was over people began rapidly leaving the stands. My wife, however, said: *Let's wait, I want to see the whole thing.* This 'whole thing' was on a focal level higher than that of the other two mentioned: It was the game as a *spectacle*, including the activity of the players (both those in the game and those on the sideline), the activity of the officials (who were not carrying the ball but who are very important to the game), the half-time activity of the bands, the activity of the fans, and activities before the game began.

(For this term note the Ann Arbor News for Nov. 6, 1952: *The scramble for teams for the Jan. 1 football bowl spectacles was on today.*)

After the official game, the band lined up in the form of a large M, played, and marched off the field, and out of the stadium. They continued to play until they were so far away from the field that they could hardly be heard. It was not until then that my wife said: *Well, it's beginning to thin out; I guess we can go, almost.* The game as a spectacle was then over, for her, even though at no specific point could one say that it had ended just there, since the gradual thinning of the crowd left a fuzzy slur of group activity following unrelated activities of the individual fans.

The unofficial spectacle had begun early. A half hour before the opening kick-off, ticket keepers were busy at the gates; local and state police were directing the thousands of cars, and using an overhead airplane at strategic points to send squad cars to help take care of potential traffic jams. Venders of hot dogs, banners, toys and Presidential campaign buttons were plying their trade. A few thousand fans were already in the stadium, buying sunshades, enjoying the game atmosphere, and waiting for the scheduled pre-game activities. A blimp advertising beer and an airplane extolling a brand of bread were flying overhead, and the shadow of the blimp occasionally struck the fans and diverted their attention from the events in the stadium.

The spectacle, already under way, soon had a more formal opening. The loud speaker at the stadium announced the first official part of the pre-game program, and the band from Minnesota spelled out 'Hello'. A bit later the Michigan band came on to the field; and with a formal: *Ladies and gentlemen...* the announcer asked the people in the stadium to rise and sing the national anthem. Further band numbers followed, with the crowds standing once more as they sang the Michigan Alma Mater.

After a fifteen-minute pre-game performance the announcer inaugurated the official game (as distinct from the more inclusive spectacle) by saying over the loud speaker: *Good afternoon, and welcome to the...* The larger spectacle continued simultaneously with the official game. Fans yelled or cheered; school cheer leaders led in organized yells more or less closely related to the progress of the game, as when they shouted in unison: 8/2/3.3 *Go, go, go, go, go, go, go,* as the home team penetrated deeper and deeper into its opponent's territory. Some of the action, however, was quite unrelated to the official game: the seating of late comers; a call over the loud speaker for a doctor in an emergency; the police insisting that a drunken man be led from the stands.

The spectacle program took over in full force during the half time, with first one and then the other band marching in patterned lines so as to show, among other things, a Paul Bunyan frying pan, a gun with coeds for bullets, a violin with moving bow (in reference to Jack Benny), a comedian with rolling eyes of giant size (Eddie Cantor), and a top hat (for Ted Lewis).

4.13 *The Season*

The following pre-game statement by the broadcaster shows that he has simultaneously available several levels of focus higher than those I have referred to thus far:
8/1/17.5 *And so the picture from the University of Michigan stadium on homecoming day of this 1952 season is Michigan versus Minnesota with the famed Little Brown Jug going to the winner, and first place in the Big Ten.*

The official game is referred to here in the phrase *Michigan versus Minnesota*, and the next higher layer in the series is indicated by the phrase *of this 1952 season* which includes all of the games to be played by the team of the University of Michigan that year — and the statement reveals that the goal of the season's activity is to win the conference championship (*first place in the Big Ten*). On the other hand, the reference to the *Little Brown Jug* refers to a long period of rivalry between the two universities. The printed 'Official Program' for the game states that a water jug seems to have been forgotten by the Michigan trainer, and was picked up by the Minnesota custodian, in the post-game excitement in 1903. *Later*, it says, *the jug was missed and Mr. Yost wrote to Minnesota authorities asking for its return. The Gopher authorities, in a bantering spirit, suggested that Michigan 'come and get it'.* And now each year the winner of the game takes the trophy until the next season.

These two higher-level goals came in conflict for the focal attention of the fans. The Michigan Daily stated, the next day: *And the Little Brown Jug, nearly forgotten in the scramble for the Conference lead...*

The spectacle, however, fitted into a somewhat different hierarchy which was referred to, in the quote above, by the phrase: *on home-coming day*. The Daily describes it thus: *Pennant-waving alumni, descending on Ann Arbor in nostalgic droves, had their day yesterday, and the public relations couldn't have been any better.*

Temperatures were pleasant, the Wolverines trounced Minnesota 21-0, the Michigan band deserved the usual superlatives, and the many homecoming displays, the later housewarmings and receptions added a sentimental touch to 'dear old Michigan'. Homecoming day was for the alumni to come back home — and come they did, with an old grad band to help play during part of the half-time activities.

Some of the sports writers hinted at a further high focal level in which the winner of the Big Ten Conference season was scheduled to participate, namely, the game between the winner of the Big Ten and the winner of the Pacific Coast championship, at the Rose Bowl in Pasadena, California. Note, for example, the Detroit Times:

Minnesota may request that you omit flowers from their Big Ten football funeral, but the spunky Wolverines of Michigan are not shying away from bouquets, as long as they contain roses.

Yes, there is a fragrance floating in from a place called Pasadena where the Rose Bowl roses bloom. Both Michigan football players and their ardent supporters are starting to think in those terms. (A week later the Michigan Daily states: *A flood of ineptness in the first half yesterday doused Michigan's Rose Bowl hopes and washed the Michigan Wolverines right out of the Big Ten lead.*)

Other teams were simultaneously engaged elsewhere, during the contest in Ann Arbor. Thus the broadcaster: 8/3/10.9 *Illinois playing down at Purdue, the other key game, as far as the Big Ten championship is concerned this year.* Similarly, over the loud speaker during time-outs the announcer occasionally gave last minute scores of games in progress elsewhere. Here the focus was much broader than that of the Big Ten, and included teams from all sections of the country. Announcements of scores frequently got a strong response from some large segment of the 70,000 or more fans present.

4.14 *Miscellaneous Overlapping Hierarchies*

Numerous hints throughout the game gave evidence of other hierarchies of activity which temporarily merged with the spectacle. Thus the stadium announcer: *I want to thank the many scouts* for helping to usher during the game. The activity of the scouts was just one element in a larger series of activities which overlapped on those of the football season, as part of the spectacle. The students, cheering, found their activities here merely a part of the long series of studies and extracurricular events. Likewise the alumni from many different occupations were gathered together as spectacle observers, but each with his own personal hierarchy of activity elsewhere. The vendors, coaches, broadcasters, officials, and others, likewise would find their observing activity here just one small bit in a large hierarchy of their own activities.

In general, no evidence would occur in the public data to lead us to focus on these personal hierarchies. Occasionally, however, reports would do so. The most striking incident of this type was the publication in the Ann Arbor News of the picture of two children recuperating from polio, one of them still with his respirator, who attended the game in wheel chairs, sitting at the 50-yard line in the box of the athletic director, and being wheeled across the turf after the game and the spectacle were over, to be returned to the hospital. In the official program, also, there were numerous references to personal hierarchies of activity of certain individual players, giving their athletic history and a discussion of their injuries — although the concealment of unhealed injuries became a part of the pre-game strategy to prevent the opposition from taking advantage of this knowledge; thus the radio announcer told us: 8/1/23.8 *Both coaches have been very mum about injuries to key men; we'll give them to you fans as* [*soon as*] *we know at kick-off.*

4.15 Abstraction Focus (Hypostasis)

A sharply different kind of focus could also be seen in the material concerning this game. This was the focusing of attention not on the game as such nor on any part of the game as part of that game, but rather a focusing upon an etic *summation* of events not directly related to each other but classified in terms of a prior format and called the 'statistics' of individual or team performance. Thus (The Michigan Daily): *He [K—] completed 11 of 14 tosses from the left halfback position. All told this year K— has hit on 23 out of 40 for 268 yards ...End L— P— enters the game tied with K— for the team scoring lead.* Or note the following tabulation (the Detroit Times):

U-M Statistics

	Mich.	Minn.
First Downs	22	10
Rushing Yardage	264	85
Passing Yardage	118	50
Passes Attempted	20	21
Passes Completed	8	8
Passes Intercepted	2	1
Punts	6	9
Punting Average	37.5	33.4
Fumbles Lost	4	3
Yards Penalized	45	30

Score by Quarters:
Michigan   7 7 0 7 — 21
Minnesota   0 0 0 0 —   0
Touchdowns — Michigan: B — (2), T — Points after touchdown: R — (3).

The most important part of the abstracting of the game concerns the scoring: 8/6/25.3 *As far as the scoring was concerned the first score of the game went to Michigan... The final score came after...* The hypostasis here is a very important one since the emic structure of the game involves the attempt to win it, and winning it necessitates scoring. Hence the particular series of plays which lead to the winning of the game, or to opponent's insufficient scores, constitute the highlights and are included in the 'recap' (recapitulation of the principal features of the game) for the benefit of listeners who turned on the radio late, or in the news columns to give a quick understanding of the way the game worked out. This particular game, as the tabulated statistics show, ended with a score of 21 to 0 in favor of Michigan. The score was attained by three touchdowns, each counting 6 points, plus a special point after each of those. In this particular game each of the touchdowns was made by a Michigan man carrying the ball across the goal line and the follow-up point was made by having the ball kicked over the cross bar between the goal posts.

4.16 *Periods in the Official Game*

The official game consisted of timed activity divided into four quarters of fifteen minutes each: 8/6/26.1 *And the score board showed 7 minutes remaining in the fourth and final quarter of the ball game.* Here the focus was simultaneously on the quarter itself and on the quarter as constituting a part of the game. At other times the quarter is focused on in reference to an intermediate unit, the half: 8/4/13 *The third quarter, the second half, just getting under way from Ann Arbor; a beautiful October afternoon.* The activity of the first two quarters is separated only by a lapse of a couple of minutes, but the activity of the two halves is separated by fifteen minutes of rest time for the players, filled with a program for the fans watching the spectacle.

The periods are marked in special ways. Before the first half begins one of the teams wins the toss of a coin and can choose either to defend a particular goal or to receive or kick the ball: 8/6/25.4 *The Wolverines elected to receive, after Minnesota won the toss and [Minnesota] elected to defend the goals with the wind.* After the first half: 8/4/11.9 *Michigan now has the choice, and they elect to receive.* For the quarters there is no new kick-off but the teams are turned around to play in opposite directions on the field.

4.17 *Plays, Play Sequences, and Closure*

The game is further divided up into a series of attempts by one side or the other to carry, pass, or kick the ball toward the oposite goal line until it can be carried or passed over for a touchdown. Each attempt at advancing the ball is called a play. Frequently attention is focused on these plays as such; for example the broadcaster: 8/4/11.9... *ready to begin the [description of the] second half play by play.* The plays may be focused on one at a time: *Michigan took the opening kick-off*; or in retrospect several may be looked at together as consituting a single sequence: 8/2/1.8 *The injured P — is in there to start this opening sequence of plays. The Wolverines took the opening kick-off and marched 71 yards in 10 plays to score.*

A sequence like this last one may draw to it the arbitrary focus of the observer, so that he views it as a unit, a sustained drive heading toward the goal without the team losing the ball. Officially, however, there is a different grouping which is often focused on as well — namely the fact that one team is given four tries to cover a distance of 10 yards; if it fails to cover this distance in the four attempts allotted to it, then the opposite side gets the ball and tries to carry it in the opposite direction. Each play in such a series of four is called a 'down'. If in four downs or less the required yardage is achieved, then the team begins with 'first down' again, with four more potential attempts for a further ten yards: 8/2/4.4 *It brings up second down and still — oh — probably 10-1/2 to go; he lost a half yard on the play; so on two spinning plays D— B— has failed to pick up any yardage.*

Particular plays, also, may be looked on as units and as such viewed from the point of view of closure. An attempt to pass the ball into the opponent's territory, for example, counts officially as a completed down, that is as a play; but if the pass is not caught by a member of the team throwing it, but rather is dropped, the pass itself is ruled 'incomplete' and does not add yardage to the progress of the team: 8/4/27.2 *He was already looking at where he was going to run instead of grabbing the ball. He had it momentarily and then dropped it. It goes as an incompleted forward pass for Minnesota.* Here then there are simultaneously two layers of closure: For the first — the attempted pass as such — there is an official failure to have closure if the pass is dropped; from the point of view of the play as a play, however, there is closure, and the play is officially ended.

4.18 *Plays in Slots with Choice and Variants*

At the opening of each half the particular play used is determined in advance by the rules of the game. It must be a kick-off with the ball starting from the ground and kicked by one of the players toward his opponents. At other points in the game, however, the particular play can vary. It may be a pass, a run, a kick, etc. Thus, the potential for each play, in a series of four plays constituting the four downs, itself constitutes a 'slot' where a selected play may be used.

The choice of the particular play used is determined by the quarterback: 8/2/2.9 *T— [quarterback] looks over Minnesota's 6-2-2-1 [defensive position] now; and then the 'T' formation; he gives the hand-off this time to H—.* The quarterback's strategy is therefore to choose plays considered by him most likely to succeed at any particular time. In addition to the basic possibilities of running, passing, or kicking there are many varieties of plays within each of these major types. If the player runs with the ball, for example, he may run around either end of the opposing lines or he may attempt to run through the center of the line or between players at either end of the line, etc. Here is the first play of the Michigan-Minnesota game which followed the opening kick-off: 8/2/1.9 *T— [quarterback] looks over Minnesota's 5-3-2-1 defense, then he shifts the Wolverines unbalanced to the right, single wing. K— deep. B— close. B— spins, and he's hit for a two-yard loss. Getting in there very nicely is C— S—, the right guard for Minnesota — submarined those would-be Michigan blockers, and moved in very nicely and dropped Michigan's fullback D— B— for a 2-yard loss.*

Passes, similarly, may occur in numerous varieties. They may be thrown directly ahead of the line or to one side; a short distance or a long distance; or may be thrown laterally to one side to a teammate who then carries it forward. For a sample passing play note the following — the final play of the game: 8/6/23.3 *Minnesota looks over that defense of Michigan; it's a 5-3-2-1*. Then *G— from the tailback goes back, cocks his arm on the Minnesota 29-yard line, throws way down field — and it is intercepted by Michigan's number 19 K—; he's over the midfield stripe, to the 40, to the 35, cuts back in, and is dropped out of bounds on the Minnesota 32-yard line.*

4.19 *Wholes Smaller than Plays*

Often the announcer focuses temporarily on a bit of activity much smaller than one constituting an entire play: The quarterback looking over the field preparatory to calling the play; the shifting of the line; the spinning of a player to reverse direction while carrying the ball; the defensive man's rushing in to the offensive field of play in order to pull down the runner before he can get away; the falling of the offensive runner after he is tackled by his opponent; also the backward movement in preparation for a pass; the lifting or cocking of the arm to pass; the throwing of the ball; the catching of the ball by an opposing player; the progress of his running; the changing of direction by cutting back into an open spot; the fall of the player when he is tackled out of bounds just off the official playing surface.

4.1.10 *Homomorphic Activity and Indeterminacy*

In general the purpose of the plays, or of the activity smaller than that of a play, can be deduced from the place it would normally occur in a sequence of activities in the game. Occasionally, however, two elements occur which are physically alike but which are emically different. The blowing of the whistle by an official, for example, may on the one hand signal the players that the game has begun, or, on the other hand, may signal an interruption of the official timing of the game while a penalty is inflicted on one of the teams.

Some deliberate deception is used: 8/6/8.4 *That was the fullback fake buck lateral, W— handing off to S— he faked a buck through the line and S— went back to pass.* Here one player moves toward the line as if he were going to carry the ball directly forward, and this activity is designed to draw the defensive players to that particular spot where the ball would have gone had be done what it appeared he was going to do. By this maneuver the offensive team hopes to have an opening for their ball carrier or for the person who is to receive a pass. There is a technical parallel between the activity of the faked buck through the line, and a filibuster (cf. § 2.2) or a lie. In each of these activities an alien observer (or even a domestic one) who saw only that small segment of activity would not know whether that part of the play was designed to go ahead as it seemed, or whether it was designed to be a feint, to draw away the opposition. Just as verbal elements which are similar in form but different in meaning are said to be HOMOPHONOUS (§ 2.2; cf. *pair* and *pare*), nonverbal ones may be called HOMOMORPHIC.

4.2 *Height of Focus*

Starting from some arbitrarily chosen but culturally documented level of focus, documented in terms of verbal or nonverbal activity which indicates closure, as in the preceding section or in Chapter 3 exponents may be used to symbolize hierarchical layers culturally or analytically recognized as embracing a larger or smaller sequence of activity than the starting focus level.

4.21 *Predominant Focus*

As a starting point we may try to pick a PREDOMINANT FOCUS UNIT, around which the cultural evidence indicates that other included or simultaneous larger units are oriented. For the data of § 4.1, we chose the official game as the predominant whole. The cultural evidence in support of this choice is the frequent reference to *pre-game activities*, *half-time activities*, and the like, in press and broadcast; the loudspeaker announcement; *Game's over!* personal comments from the fans: *Say, that's pretty good, I got here just in time for the kickoff;* and the nonverbal activity of mass arrival and departure.

4.22 *Exponents in Formulas*

If, then, we start with the official game symbolized as U, the seasonal series of official games might be U^2, the Rose Bowl post-season contest as U^3, and the long series of contests for the Little Brown Jug as U^4. On lower focus levels, the first (or second) half, as a whole, would be U^{-2}; a quarter, U^{-3}; a minimum sequence of downs, U^{-4} (first through fourth; or first until the next first by the same or opposing side if less than four); a single play, U^{-5}; a sub-unit of activity within the play, U^{-6} (cocking arm to pass, passing, running, changing direction of running, blocking a tackler, catching a pass, kicking the ball, dropping the ball, etc.). Below this are further hierarchical layers — U^{-7} and so on — which get below the normal limit of focus (cf. § 3.33) of the fans; these low-level elements would include muscle movements, heart beat (though the trainer might conceivably check this for some injured player), molecular movements, and so on.

If the analyst chooses to start with a different initial point, in reference to the experience of some particular participant, or because no predominant point of focus could be usefully postulated, then the same kind of symbolization would be used with U representing the new starting point. If, for example, he were to start with a fumble made by a player who played in the game for only a few minutes. dropped the ball, was removed from the game by the coach, and could remember little about the game but that horrible experience, then the analyst might for some purposes consider the fumble as U, that play as U^2, the two minutes' game activity of that player as U^3, etc. It is evident that observer status affects the focal hierarchy.

4.23 *Hypostasis Formulas and Types*

The units in the preceding paragraphs have been symbolized as members of an activity sequence in a structural hierarchy, with the units distributed directly into slots (§ 3.4) in larger units of activity. When, however (in order to give it separate analytic attention for etic classification or analysis, or for statistical treatment), any unit of activity is abstracted from the kinds of purposive activity sequence expected by regular participants, this essential distributional characteristic may be temporarily ignored. In such an instance, i.e., in HYPOSTASIS (§ 4.15), the unit in its focal level is symbolized as U^0; *participant focus* (§ 3.32) implies attention within a normal hierarchical purposive context, whereas *classificatory focus* implies hypostatic attention on a unit abstracted away from such contexts.

In addition to the hypostasis of football statistics mentioned in § 4.15, many other types of such abstraction appear in our culture: a quotation, abstracted from a lecture and repeated out of context; or a quotation of one's own speech (for example: *I said 'cat'*); a word used out of its normal distribution (as *if* in *the ifs on this page*); part of a word referred to, as such, in grammatical discussion (for example: *the suffix "s" of boys*); the related usage of lexical elements by nongrammarians [See *Time*, June 21, 1963, p. 10, quoting Martin Luther King, Sr.: "We're through with tokenism and gradualism and see-how-far-you've-comeism. We're through with we've-done-more-for-your-people-than-anyone-elseism."] (for example: *There are lots of isms*); each of the entries ("words") listed in a dictionary; each of the vocal sounds mentioned as such in a general lecture on phonetics; practicing passing, by itself, in preparation for use of that activity in a football game; or the repeated practice of a specific medical operation on a cadaver.

The activity of hypostasis itself — the bringing to attention or the repeating of a unit outside its normal emic context — is in turn part of a structural hierarchy of activity. This activity sequence is an activity of analysis, rather than of participation in the activity being analyzed (see § 4.4). Just as the dissection of a live bug to look at its parts destroys the part as a functioning part of the whole bug — and destroys the bug — so abstraction of parts of behavior leaves the parts in a different distributional matrix from that which they had before analysis.

Occasionally hypostatized elements are formally marked. Hebrew prayers, for example, when quoted for reference rather than being used for prayer are changed so as to prevent sacrilegious implications: in such quotations of a prayer the sound [h] of ordinary speech may be changed to [k]. The most familiar example is a change of *ellohenu* 'our God' to *ellokenu*. (Communication from Prof. Abraham Kaplan, University of Michigan.)

Spelling words aloud is a form of hypostasis — the naming of parts of a formal sequence of letters normally utilized for reading as wholes. Here, too, special forms occur, since the naming or pronunciation of a consonant often carries with it a vowel not part of the sound sequence in the word spelled — as, for example, 'b' pronounced as /bi/ in spelling *boy*; or the vocalic and consonantal change in 'h' pronounced as /eč/ in spelling *hat*.

When the abstraction is part of the normal activity of the participants, as when the participating official signals that there have been four downs (counting their number without reference to the manner in which the particular downs were activity sequences or to the specific context in which they occurred), we will call it FUNCTIONAL HYPOSTASIS. When, however, some nonparticipant is abstracting elements in a manner not observed in participant activity, we shall call it ANALYTICAL HYPOSTASIS. If the analyst or reporter abstracts in the way that the participants do, then it is ANALYTICAL FUNCTIONAL HYPOSTASIS. When the coach after a game discusses with the players the movies taken of the game, his activity is in part of this type.

4.24 *Modal Elements in Focus Formulas*

Before treating participant types further, we will do well to observe that modal elements (§ 3.5) in the units can also receive hierarchical (or focus) symbolization. The potential for a 'first half' of activity as a slot in the pattern of the football game, a slot to be filled by the particular playing of this particular half on this specific occasion, would be UD_s^{-2}, in which U is the official game as a whole, subscript $_s$ refers to the slot-characteristic of the distribution mode (§ 3.51), D symbolizes the distribution mode itself, and the $^{-2}$ exponent indicates a lower focal layer of that mode. UD_s^{-3} might be the quarter slot, UD_s^{-4} a slot for a sequence of downs, UD_s^{-5} the slot for a play to be selected by the quarterback, and UD_s^{-6} a slot for an optional unplanned variant in the execution of one phase of the play (e.g., cutting back to avoid a defense player who had evaded the offensive blockers).

A hierarchy of purpose might start from UF_p, in which the official game is U, with a total set of identifying characteristic features F, and the immediate purposive component of that complex is subscript $_p$ — the attempt to win the official game as a whole. On a higher layer, UF_p^2 might be the attempt to win the championship of the Big Ten. On lower layers UF_p^{-2} might represent the determination to hold an aggressive, chance-taking, opposing team scoreless in the second half while they themselves play cautiously to preserve a lead gained in the first half; UF_p^{-4} might be an attempt through a series of plays to make enough yardage for a first down; UF_p^{-5} an attempt to gain yardage by a pass; UF_p^{-6} the attempt to evade a tackler.

With subscript $_m$ indicating one particular physical variant of form of the manifestation mode (§ 3.52) of the unit, UM_m^{-3} might be physical activity recorded by a camera and tape recorder during one of the quarters; UM_m^{-6} the bodily motion by which a tackler was evaded.

4.25 *Diagram of Changes of Focus Height*

If the layers of hierarchical structure within a unit are plotted on a graph, with the smallest internal unit layer as at the zero point horizontally and vertically, but the more inclusive units occurring on a higher level and extending farther to the right, focus differences can be symbolized by drawing a horizontal line at any level where a unit occurs. In Figure 4.1 the attention may be centered at various levels — the season games, the specific game, the half, the play, or even molecular action.

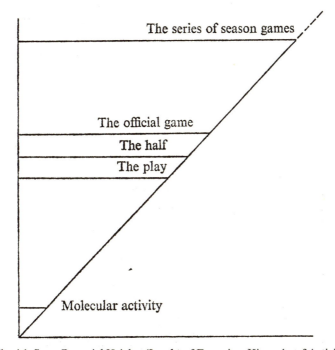

Fig. 4.1 Some Potential Heights (Levels) of Focus in a Hierarchy of Activity,

4.3 *Depth of Focus*

4.31 *Shallow and Deep Focus*

In photography the focus may be shallow, so that — say — only those objects between six feet and seven feet from the lens are in focus while the remainder is blurred,

110   FOCUS ILLUSTRATED

or the depth of focus may be deep so that everything, for example, from eight to one hundred feet away is clear cut in the picture and in focus. Similarly there may be a CULTURAL DEPTH OF FOCUS so that numerous levels of the activity hierarchy are simultaneously in focus. Depth of focus can be seen in some quotations already given: 8/4/13 *The third quarter, the second half, just getting under way* (where focus includes attention on the half as a whole and simultaneous attention to a quarter within it); or: 8/6/26.1 *The fourth and final quarter of the ball game;* and so on.

Depth of focus seems to be increased if the observer has a longer time to study the activity — that is, if he can study a record of it a number of times by seeing movies repeated, or by hearing a musical composition over and over again, or by re-reading a written account. Much more of the intricate detail of activity and the inter-relationships between those details can then be brought under attention without losing the simultaneous focus on, and the enjoyment of, the unit as a whole.

This focus characteristic, like the series of shallow focuses seen in Fig. 4.1, can be shown on a hierarchical diagram. In Figure 4.2 the lower limit of focus likely to be reached by many of the fans is set as point A, a maneuver within a play; top limit is arbitrarily set at B, the end of the post-seasonal Rose Bowl game. The relationship between points C and D represents one possible (culturally identified) focal depth likely to be used by some fans at some period of the game, a depth embracing a series of four downs in which each of the separate plays within the series is 'simultaneously' in focus.

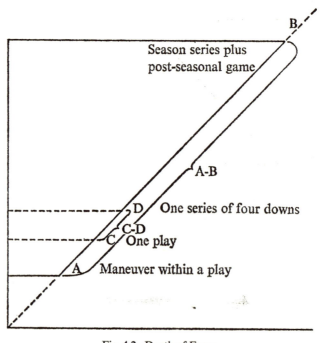

Fig. 4.2. Depth of Focus

A-B represents a large depth of focus, with brief activities simultaneously in focus with the season-plus-post-season activity. C-D represents a much smaller depth of focus (but one larger than D as a single top focus by itself).

4.32 *Thresholds, With Lower and Upper Limits to Height of Focus*

Limits to the lowest level of focus are set by the purpose of the participant or observer, but with a large margin of indeterminacy. When the controlling purpose of the churchgoer was worship (§ 3.2), the lower limit of focus did not tend to go below 'paragraph' size (whereas critical attention to the speaker's pronunciation would move focus lower, to single sounds). In conversation of a nontechnical type, where the purpose is communication, focus probably stays on or above the sentence level. Again, however, there is considerable indeterminacy. In a room full of many people talking all at once, for example, the listener may be forced to ask for and to focus on the repetition of a single word — or syllable — in order to understand it. This instance, however, is probably best treated as a kind of hypostasis in which the hearer becomes analyst for a moment — and then, with relief, may repeat the whole sentence including the analyzed word, as he 'shifts gears' back into normal communication status. Similarly, in the heat of the game, the attention of the fans is perhaps seldom directed to a focus lower than that of a maneuver within a play, except under hypostasis — as when a time out is called after an injury or for other reasons: 8/5/23.8 *B— is winded and so Michigan calls time out.*

Whenever a certain change in focus is necessarily accompanied by a sharp change in observer attitude or participant type, we may say that a THRESHOLD must be crossed to pass from one to the other. Such a threshold is crossed when one passes from a participant kind of observation to an analytical kind of observation of the same events. When the focus is lowered to units (say, muscular or molecular activity) so small as to be outside of the range of observation by the football fans, another threshold has been crossed.

Scientists in a SYSTEMIC hypostasis (i.e., in the abstraction of one or more systems), may arbitrarily set upper and lower limits to their field of inquiry so as to be able to concentrate on a smaller body of data. This fact, in part, is what constitutes differences between disciplines. And this point of view, in turn, can be used to define one of the purposes of this book, that is, an attempt to demonstrate that for best results linguists must at times raise their focus to include nonverbal behavior as part of their data, and anthropologists must sometimes, and in some senses, treat language data within a single hierarchical structure along with nonverbal activity.

The upper limit to focus fluctuates greatly in accordance with permanent or temporary purpose and interest. It seems to be much less rigid culturally — i.e., the thresholds are often less sharp — than the lower limit. The cultural evidence collected concerning this football game sets the highest focus at least as far back as the start of the rivalry between the football teams of the two schools in competition for the Little Brown Jug. In that connection the Official Program says: *Next year will be the fiftieth anniversary of the rivalry that began just 49 years ago.* (A higher focus is elsewhere in view in the Program, but probably should be treated as part of the spectacle hierarchy, rather than of the official game: *The prologue to the Stadium Story... had its beginning in 1865 when cricket was all the student rage and the wickets were set up on State Street to block traffic and frighten horses until the complaints of Ann Arbor residents resulted in an appropriation of $50 by the Board of Regents for a playing field.*)

A high-level focus, however, often constitutes a hypostasis (viewed without reference to the slot which it fills in the larger sequence of activity of which it was — or is normally — a part). Such a unit in hypostasis (U^o), however, may be large (like the series of games for The Little Brown Jug) or small (as in considering 'the sound [t]').

The lower limit of total focal depth, likewise, is sometimes a large unit when, in hypostasis, past games are being discussed. In such instances the entire set of details of the specific activity sequence may be ignored or forgotten, and only the total outcome be focused on in retrospect. Thus, in the Official Program: *The game was one of the most important ones of its time, for 'the championship of the West' and it ended in a 6-6 deadlock.* At the opposite extreme a game and all its official activity and score may be temporarily out of focus in retrospect, and only the resultant state of one of the players may be in view: 8/2/1.3 *The injured P— is in there to start...*

4.4 *Breadth of Focus*

4.41 *Focusing Processes*

The activity of bringing an item into focus is itself a unit of activity, but when the process of focusing includes the use of memory, it is not directly observable by us. For this reason we used indirect means (the objective study of concrete verbal utterances of the participants and of observers, as well as the observation of nonverbal behavior) to deduce the presence of, and the beginning and ending points of, the crucial units of focusing behavior in the experience of the participants.

In some situations, however, focusing as a physical act can in part be directly observed. A player may turn his head, or eyes, or both, so as to look at a teammate when we call to him. In such an instance, part of the physical activity of focusing is OVERT, rather than covert only. To a slight extent, the change of lens adjustment in the eye can be detected even without special equipment, as when a person is first observed to be staring into space or 'looking through' a person and then has his attention attracted to something else.

Each overt or covert type of physical movement must ultimately enter into the analysis of activity into waves or segments of movement (§ 3.23). The focus of attention in vision need not necessarily be identical with the physical focus of the eye, however, since one may outwardly center the eye on one object, but concentrate inwardly rather on observing something quite different 'out of the corner' of the eye.

In spatial focus, as in a time sequence, the larger whole and the parts may be kept in some kind of simultaneous awareness. The areas in focus may not have a sharp boundary, but rather become blurred in progressive degrees, in a kind of indeterminacy of segmented borders. In the transition stage from one visual focus to another there may be fuzziness also, as when something 'catches one's attention' and leads to a shift of focus — as when a tackler comes toward a runner.

Possibly a visual hypostasis can be postulated as parallel to the types already discussed. If, while running, a player looks at one opponent with such concentration that he fails to observe through the corners of his eyes another opponent coming toward him, he is in danger of drifting into the path of the second, and of being tackled. In this case the hypostasis consists in focusing on a bit of the spatial (instead of temporal) field to the exclusion of its place in the larger field.

Physical focus by ear is covert, and hence not directly observable by us, except in the grossest component in which one can see the head rotated in an effort to locate the source of a sound. By ear, however, there can be selectivity of attention which can be deduced by an objective study of the verbal utterances (naïve or sophisticated) of the participants in an event, or by tests to determine the accuracy of their powers of discriminating components of sound. All of us experience the effort needed to pick out one voice from a roomful of speaking people. As it is for vision, so in hearing, the covert concentration focus can differ from the overt physical one — a person can be taking part in one conversation while really trying to listen more intently to another.

There can be hypostasis in hearing, analogous to that in vision, when a person concentrates on one component of sound so strongly that he is unaware of any of the other simultaneous sounds around him. Negatively one can train oneself to ignore an alarm clock; positively one can train oneself to focus quickly and consciously on the ringing of an alarm clock, a baby's cry, the snapping of a twig, an instrument playing a wrong note in a band. Whereas the average person can be taught to listen for a particular musical instrument in an orchestra, the conductor of the orchestra would seem to have a wide focus, since he responds to the playing of the composition as a whole, but is simultaneously keenly aware of the product of the activity of each member of the orchestra. Similarly, the football player may ignore the shouts of a crowd, while listening for the voice of a teammate; the fan in the stands may be unable to 'see' the play of more than one or two men at a time on the field (and often enjoys the game best if he by turns concentrates on the activity of a linesman, or a back, etc., for some time), whereas the trained observer seems to be able to 'see' much more of the play at once — to follow a developing pattern of activity in which the whole makes sense.

Focus activity in tasting, touching, and smelling parallels the focus elements already mentioned for seeing and hearing, and each act of focusing, of whatever type, constitutes a unit of behavior. Each type may take noticeable conscious effort — as when one is attempting to locate a particular person in a crowd, or to see an airplane heard distantly somewhere in the sky, or to find a four-leaf clover in the grass, or to detect a misprint in reading a printed page, or to decide what the characteristic flavor is in the soup.

Here, as elsewhere, there may be homomorphic activities. The person looking at a page in order to proofread it may at first *appear* to be carrying on the same activity as a person studying the content of that same page. Yet everyone who has himself read proof extensively knows that a focus adjusted for misprints may at times completely fail to follow the contents — i.e., may fail to widen focus so as to include purposive elements. It is difficult to enjoy an article and to proofread it at the same time. The experience of typing seems to be similar. For example, I once had some work done by a typist who was an almost perfect 'machine'; in some 250 pages there occurred only two stenographic copying errors — yet she also accurately copied a number of 'obvious' mistakes in the manuscript which I had submitted to her.

4.42 *Wide versus Narrow Focus*

The incident comprised of the singing of the national anthem at the beginning of the football spectacle was a single unit, a sub-unit within the whole scene. Yet this incident itself was extremely complex in that many hierarchies combined to form a composite of hierarchies. In fact there were many sub-groupings of hierarchies which constituted sub-composites of the entire event. One component was composed of the hierarchy of vocal movements for the singing; another of the movements of the musicians during their playing; others: the arm movements of the conductor, the standing up of the fans, the taking off of hats, the saluting by the few military, the activity of the person who slowly raised the flag during the singing.

BREADTH of focus, or wide focus, is a term used here to suggest attention simultaneously directed to a number of different kinds of component hierarchies included in the unit under attention, such as those just mentioned.

Focus on speech can be narrowed to include only the sounds, words, and phrases, or may be widened to include the hierarchy of the pitch sequences of the voice, or may be widened further yet to include general voice quality as well.

4.43 *Relevance in Reference to Composites*

It should be easy to see that if all components of the spectacle were to be treated on a par, that the data would be unmanageable, and a description hopelessly unwieldy and unintelligible. If an indiscriminate mixture were made, let us say, of the solemn voice quality of the announcer, with the movement of the little finger of the clarinetist, with the eye movements of a fan who is watching one of the ushers, no emic structural form would emerge from the description.

In order to avoid this chaotic result we must assume that there are SUB-ASSEMBLIES of component hierarchies, which bring together in analytical focus via sub-units of hierarchical activity those items which are structurally closely related. One such sub-assembly (or sub-composite) would be the total verbal activity of the announcer; another might be the total activity of fans singing, standing, and taking off their hats; another, the movements of the person raising the flag; and so on.

RANDOM movement would not be structureless, but would be movement relevant only to a hierarchical composite much larger than the official game as such — a part of personal activity — which does not forward the purposes of that activity which is in focus. For example one player, after dropping a pass, made a gesture of disgust with both hands toward the ground. This activity did not forward the ball, nor had it any connection with the official game; it was random and irrelevant in reference to the play. At the same time, nevertheless, that gesture was highly relevant in reference to the overlapping simultaneous hierarchy of that player's total personal or social participation in the game.

Part of the strategy of the game seems occasionally to involve an element homomorphic with random movement — the attempt at deceptively leading the opponents into the casual assumption that a small segment of activity of one of the players is random, irrelevant, or accidental, when actually it is craftily designed to provide a quick surprising advantage. This strategy is based on the fact that activity will appear 'random' to the opponents if it seems to be an irrelevant manifested variant of a unit which includes a very wide range of variants — e.g., the variety of specific steps a player may use in taking up his position. Inasmuch as such variants are non-emic, they appear 'aimless', since aim or purpose is tied to emic structure. Yet a structurally relevant activity is here disguised as a nonrelevant variant of a different emic unit.

Occasionally elements may appear to be so widely removed from the point of analytical interest as to be irrelevant, whereas later study may indicate that the ignored residue is relevant at an unexpected point in the analysis. It is the argument of this volume, we repeat in this connection, that nonverbal behavior as a whole is highly relevant to a theory of the structure of verbal behavior, and vice versa.

In general, relevance may be objectively studied if one assumes that a hierarchy is relevant to a second (often larger) hierarchy in which occurs a set of units with which the first is in some way regularly co-terminous or co-extensive, or with which it is either regularly, or predictably, or exclusively associated. The football player's motion of disgust is not predictably or exclusively associated with the dropping of a pass, but usually occurs, if at all, associated with some situation in which the person assumes that he or someone else should have acted in a more pleasing way. The fan's looking here and there is regularly associated with his activities during various parts of the spectacle, and is relevant to the hierarchy of the spectacle as such, as well as to the hierarchy of the fan's own personal activities and history. Voice quality (harsh, happy, sad, solemn), on the other hand, is not relevant on a syllable level, since it tends to change or be co-extensive with much larger linguistic segments such as phrases, or even a sequence of a number of sentences (a 'paragraph', let us say). When a set of elements as one component of a behavior sequence occurs only when a second set of elements occurs — and especially if the two elements always begin at the same time and end at the same time — they are both relevant to the same larger system. This we observed in the relation of Junior church to Senior church.

Finally, two items which are regularly associated together in fulfilling a purpose — in reaching a particular goal set forth in advance — are both considered relevant to the purposive unit which includes this goal; regular association of units in activity which advances a person toward the fulfillment of his goal is evidence for the mutual relevance of those units.

4.44 *Segmental Borders of Composites*

We have previously seen (§ 3.2) that behavior consists of waves of activity, in which each change of movement direction, or of speed, or of acting body part, or of actor, or of activity type introduces a separate small etic segment of activity, as when one's hand is waved back and forth (or the tongue goes up and down for [a-i-a-i-a]). This point of view can now be made more explicit for composites as wholes: A new etic segment is encountered every time a composite of regularly associated moving body parts, or of associated actors, is replaced by another composite, or is changed in direction, or type, or speed. For example, when a person stops talking and begins to run, a segmental change occurs since the composite of vocal-apparatus movements has been replaced by a composite of nonvocal movements (even though, as for the segment sequences discussed earlier, the exact border is often indeterminate). An etic segmental change occurs, according to the same criterion, when one person stops talking (i.e., one composite ends) and a second person begins (even though, if the second person interrupts the first, overlap may bring indeterminacy of borders).

In the spectacle there were a large number of segmental breaks between composites, at various hierarchical levels: e.g., when the Minnesota band left the field and the Michigan band came on; when extra members of the Michigan squad left the field, with only eleven of its men remaining there; each time a defensive platoon of players replaced an offensive one; when a running player cut back in a different direction; when a player held out his arms to be ready to receive a pass; when an official took the ball from one of the players; when the fans left the stands; and so on, down to such small composites as the saying of *Oh!* by a particular fan.

4.45 *Segments as Simultaneously Members of Separate Intersecting Hierarchies*

There was a vast interlacing network of activities represented in the actions of the official game, the spectacle, and the personal hierarchies of players, fans, officials, and other persons. The spectacle, for example, was witnessed by thousands of people, yet for each of them the witnessing of the spectacle was just one event in a whole series of events in their lives. If the analyst were to trace the hierarchical progression of the activities of the lives of ten of these people, each hierarchy would be different, but overlapping in at least this one point — their over-all attendance at the spectacle — but not in the minutiae of some of their facial expressions, for example, or most of their verbal utterances (though, in cheering, students shout in unison), restless activity, and so on.

In general, then, we can summarize the principal elements of focus analysis by suggesting that the study of the *breadth* of focus indicates the composite range of diverse component hierarchies included in attention at any one time; *depth* of focus covers the degree of simultaneous attention on both the high and low hierarchical units of one or more hierarchies; *height* of focus indicates the hierarchical element cut out for attention from a particular sequence, or the particular place of such a unit in a hierarchy.

4.46 *Composites in a Setting*

The behavioral setting within which any one activity hierarchy (or unit thereof) occurs is a complex of such hierarchical composites of activity. The behavioral spectacle of the football game is composed of a NETWORK OF INTERWOVEN HIERARCHIES of activity. The activity of one fan or one player provides one component of the larger activity of a more inclusive hierarchy, — that is, part of the setting within which it occurs, in reference to which it is viewed or focused upon, and along with which it is simultaneously hierarchically structured.

In diagramming a kinship system the chart of the systems may at first appear slightly different, if one begins by focusing attention on, say, a female child as 'ego', from what it would appear if her father were set up as being 'ego'. The two charts, to be sure, would be very closely correlated. If, now, the individual genealogies of two hundred randomly selected individuals from a small community were separately plotted and then superimposed one on another, the composite chart would symbolize an intricate network of partially overlapping relationships in which a newcomer to the community would not be as closely related to the older members as they are to each other. Similarly, the hierarchies of *activity* of persons at the spectacle form a network. Persons who are of a similar participant type (say, all the fans seated in Row 70 of Section 41) may engage in activities (e.g., looking in such and such a direction during a touchdown) which would overlap heavily. A charting of the activity hierarchies of an adequate number of persons of different participant types (fans, officials, coaches, quarterbacks), then, would lead toward an understanding of the pattern of the enormously complex network of activity which comprises the behavioral component of the spectacle as a whole.

The total field within which any one composite occurs, however, includes not only (1) this larger network of simultaneous hierarchically-structured human activity, but also (2) the products or the behavior of products of previous human behavior which are structured relevant to the official game (e.g., the stadium, playing field, goal posts, whistle, horn, or 'products' composed of the achievement of points, touchdowns, past victories — or of status such as winner of the toss of the coin), or not so structured (e.g., coats, hats, cigarettes, blimp, coffee urn), and (3) the presence or behavior of nonhuman elements which are not products of human behavior (e.g., that of stray dogs, the shining sun, drifting clouds, blowing wind, or of molecules, and so on).

Many of the elements in the setting of human behavior, like that behavior itself, are also trimodally structured. The demonstration of this part of the theory, however, will not be attempted until § 17.5. We proceed rather to discuss in detail the structured units of human behavior itself.

4.5 *Bibliographical Comments on Chapter 4*

The whole problem of focus as treated here, and the ability of a person to select for attention one complex of elements of activity out of a total setting, with variants in the time span, breadth of composites viewed, and clarity of details within a large pattern, could be profitably studied in comparison with the figure-ground situations analyzed by the gestalt psychologists. Since this chapter was written, for example, I have read Koffka (1935) and find in his treatments of simple spatial figures, and other matters, a number of illuminating parallels.

For focus as applied to relevant semantic components of situations, see R. Allen (1962).

The term hypostasis is taken from Bloomfield (1933a:148), where he refers to it as "the mention of a phonetically normal speech-form". Our approach, however, refers the hypostasis to its function as an abstraction from a much larger systemic structure, rather than to repetition or mention as such.

The theory of games, as developed by mathematicians, has as its goal something quite different from that of the discussion of this football game. "The chief problem of the theory of games is thus the problem of distinguishing good strategies [i.e., for winning, etc.] from bad" (McKinsey, 1952:98), whereas the chief purpose of our approach is to study the structuring of the patterns of behavior which go into the playing of the game. Yet the two approaches are not mutually exclusive, since the theory of games must study something of their structure in order to find optimal strategies, while our structural approach must include among its components the intention of players to choose a strategy which will be aimed at winning. The mathematical theory of games, seen from our point of view, comprises a significant attempt at an etic classification of some game strategies and structures.

CHAPTER 5

THE BEHAVIOREME (INCLUDING THE SENTENCE)

In Chapter 1 we argued that a theory of the structure of behavior was needed which would allow the treatment of verbal and nonverbal behavior within a single framework.

Chapter 2 indicated that such a theory would need to treat of behavioral structure in reference to the difference between a physical or cross-cultural etic approach, and a functional mono-cultural emic approach, with emic units composed of points in a structural system to be discovered by the analyst in one culture at a time.

In Chapter 3, and again in Chapter 4, one large behavioral emic unit was studied. Both the church service and the football spectacle contained a large enough variety of materials, verbal and nonverbal, to test the possibility of crossing over the linguistic-nonlinguistic border without serious jar, while treating these elements as structurally integrated parts of a single unit rather than as a mere aggregation of components of essentially distinct, non-interlocking types. Both of these units, furthermore, were sufficiently formal and repeatable to allow us to find a relatively rigid structural framework within which their variants could without too great difficulty be seen to operate.

The theory indicates that for adequate description and understanding one must start with some knowledge — even if crude or incomplete — of large units of behavior before studying smaller units within them. Chapters 3 and 4 helped us here, also, by allowing us to apply this general principle to the presentation of material in this volume: In each of these chapters, one concrete illustration of a large behavior unit served as a context within which details of the theory could begin to emerge without forcing the reader to memorize long lists of definitions of terms, dependent one upon another in the structural hierarchy of the system in which the first term of the series is not adequately understandable until the last is known. Now, however, we are ready to describe in more technical terms the kind of emic unit represented by the church service and the football spectacle. Chapters 6 through 11 will describe certain sub-units wihin the large ones. In order, however, to test the approach on material which appears to be less rigidly structured than the church service and football game, we will use for further illustrative material excerpts from recordings of a series of family breakfast scenes.

5.1 The Behavioreme Defined or Described[1]

A unit of behavior such as the church service or the football game we shall call a BEHAVIOREME. At the end of this name is the suffix *-eme*, which is generalized from the ending of the well-established linguistic term *phoneme* (just as the term *emic*, used in Chapter 2, was abstracted by us from the term *phonemic*). This suffix has received wide usage, especially since Bloomfield (1933a), and it is almost certain to become one of the productive suffixes of our general English vocabulary, in linguistic circles at least. It is also convenient in some contexts to use EME as a noun, meaning an emic unit. The nonlinguistic reader should note, then, that it is worth considerable effort to understand the way this useful suffix is entering the literature. To be sure, its use is sometimes too frequent, or applied when other terms are available, or used awkwardly, but such infelicities should not lead us to refuse to use the term at all, since a judicious application of it may allow us very economically to signal to the reader when we have moved from nonstructural grounds to a consideration of similar elements within the framework of an entire emic system.

As a first approximation of the meaning of the term behavioreme, we suggest that it be used to label an emic unit of top-focus behavior which is related to its cultural setting in such a way that cultural documentation may be found for its beginning, ending, and purposive elements.

We need a more rigid description of the behavioreme, however, which makes more explicit some of the characteristics of its internal structuring in relation to the emic system of which it is a part. The following will give us a closer approximation to such a description:

A BEHAVIOREME is an emic segment or component of purposive human activity, hierarchically and trimodally structured, having closure signalled by overt objective cultural clues within the verbal or nonverbal behavior of the domestic participants or domestic observers, and occurring thorugh its free or conditioned, simple or complex variants within a behavioral system (or composite of systems) and a physical setting which are also emically, hierarchically and trimodally structured. A verbal behavioreme is an UTTEREME (§ 5.5).

The various components of this definition have all been discussed, tentatively, and illustrated in earlier chapters. References to the pertinent sections are these: emic characteristics, § 2; segmentation, §§ 3.2, 3.42, 3.61; purpose, §§ 3.53, § 2.2, § 4.1.10;

---

[1] Some readers would feel more comfortable if here we were to talk in terms of *well-described units*, rather than *well-defined units*. The description desired here is one which will allow an outsider to utilize the unit — to act — as would a native member of the culture. We are not interested in definition solely to differentiate or to catalog units, or to provide expanded paraphrases. (We wish the description to be useful for productive — generative — purposes in the community setting, not merely to serve classificatory aims.) A unit is well-described if and only if its contrastive components (and identification resulting from these components), range of variability (free or conditioned, simple or complex) and distribution (as member of a class, as member of a hierarchical sequence, and as filling a slot in a dimensional matrix) are specified (1962a: 241-42; 1963b:fn. 6). Note also the implication in reference to units as in some sense particle, wave, and field (1959, and §§ 12.1, 14.1-4).

hierarchical structuring, §§ 3.31, 3.62, 4.14, 4.45; trimodal structuring, § 3.5; closure and objective cultural clues, §§ 3.35, 2.73 (and see also focus, § 4); domestic participants, §§ 2.11, 3.32; 4.23; variants, §§ 2.3, 3.52; emic system, §§ 2.5, 2.6, 2.74; composite, § 4.4; setting, § 4.46. Additional discussion of many of these points in later chapters will gradually sharpen up our understanding of them, but in the meantime the illustrations help us to get a preview of many of the important parts of the theory as a whole.

5.2 *The Behavioreme Illustrated by a Breakfast Unit*

As a further illustration of a behavioreme I have chosen mechanical recordings of 'family breakfast' scenes. For the first recordings of these breakfasts the microphones were hidden, and the children of the family being studied did not know that recordings were being taken. Later, the microphones were in sight (where higher fidelity recordings could be secured), and caused some comment — but after eight weeks of work the novelty had worn off, the equipment rarely caused comment, and as nearly as I could tell did not often interfere with completely normal expression — from laughter to tears. Similarly, there was little interference caused by the notations which I was making simultaneously concerning nonverbal activity. In referring to these recordings, below, the letter 'B' indicates the breakfast materials, the first number signifies the arbitrary file marker of the incident — a different breakfast occasion, for example — and the remainder identifies the place on the record where it is heard; M — represents Mother; F—, Father; J—, a girl of twelve years of age; B—, a girl of seven; S—, a boy who turned four during the period of recordings.

The following verbal elements are typical of those comments which contribute cultural evidence for the total breakfast unit as one with closure. First we give samples, from a single record, signalling that breakfast is about to begin that day: B84/1.2 M—: *B—, would you please bring in the little white pitcher?* B84/3.6 M—: *Children!* [i.e. *Come*, with calling intonation]. B84/4.8 M—: *B—, it's late!* [*so hurry*]. B84/4.9 B—: *We're having dry cereal?* B84/5.4 M—: *All right...* [we're ready now, let's begin]. B84/5.5 F—: *Sit down, B—*. B84/5.6 F—: *Father, we thank Thee for Thy blessings.* B84/6 M—: *There's your cereal B—*. B84/6.7 M—: *Pour Cheerios into your* [*bowl, and start eating*].

Nonverbal elements that signalled the beginning that same morning included setting the table in preparation for breakfast, ringing the breakfast bell (B84/1), opening a box of dry cereal, sitting down at the table, toasting bread while at the table, and so on.

Various bits of evidence signalled the end; for example: B84/2/5.1 S—: *I'm done, I beat you! ... I beat Daddy!* B84/2/6.2 S—: *Could I be excused? Can I Mother?* M—: *No, not now, we're just about ready for worship.* B84/2/6.7 B—: *We have just a few minutes, ... we got to get to school!*

Nonverbal evidence signalling the end includes the fact that persons leave the table, the washing of the dishes, etc.

One of the most interesting evidences of closure of sub-units included in the breakfast materials is the way in which S—, on an occasion when he is being fed by F—, will refuse to take a bite in the middle of an utterance (or even, at times, a series of utterances on some topic) but will dodge to avoid a proffered spoonful until he has spoken fully, then will accept food easily. That is to say, he resists interruption. Cultural evidence for such resistance, or cultural evidence for hesitation or the unfinished nature of a unit, constitutes evidence that some behavioremic pattern is under way but is uncompleted. Note, for example, the following (B69/21):

S—: *Daddy, I want the floor!* [Shouting, in the midst of an uproar over the description of a fight at a hockey game; the children had been taught to take turns when too many wanted to talk at once]

F—: *OKay, S—, you've got the floor.*

S—: [Starts shouting a tale, too loudly to be heard clearly]

M—: *All right, now, we'll listen. Speak softly.*

S—: [Quietly] *Once upon a time...* [starts a story about a boy hunting tigers]

B—: *Sugar please J—.*

S—: [Shouts] *Stop interrupting me!*

M—: *Just a minute, no she can get the sugar, that's all right, she isn't really interrupting, continue.*

S—: *Oh.* [Quietly] *And know what?* [Story goes on].

Similarly, the numerous calls by S— in B37 (*Daddy, go on with the story*) are evidence that the story was an included unfinished behavioreme in process of development. In this particular instance, furthermore, the story was not finished on that day, but on several succeeding days a continuation of the jet-plane story was called for (B40/10.1, B49/5.7), so that here the included story-telling behavioreme was partially included in each of several breakfasts.

Through the characteristics of its feature mode, breakfast is identified as breakfast, or contrasted with dinner and supper, by features of the matrix[2] in which it occurs (especially by the time of day), by the menu (fruit juices, and usually by cooked cereal — although dry cereal might occasionally be found at breakfast or at a light evening supper, say on Sunday night), and so on. Purpose, present in every behavioreme as one of its identificational-contrastive features, is detected, also, in the cultural evidence: 43/1.1 J—: *Excuse me, I'm thirsty* [Begins to drink her milk, before the official opening, on a dinner record]. At times, however, the purpose is not to satisfy immediate hunger, but to care for one's future needs even if one does not feel hungry at the moment. In these materials the purpose is sometimes provided by proxy, from F— or M—, and received through (partial) obedience, on the part of the children:

---

[2] Contrast (see § 5.1, fn.) would now be treated as in reference to vectors in various dimensions of the embedding matrix (compare 1962a). For two uses of the term matrix see also second fn. to § 11.225.

B73/4.8 M—: *...It's very good; B— you're just going to have to learn to eat more.*
B—: *I'd rather drink vitamins instead of having to drink oranges.*

The manifestation mode of the breakfast eme is seen through its particular physical variants — i.e., in the differences and likenesses between breakfast on various days. The variants may be free, with differences not caused by the particular environment. Breakfast conversation, for example, may range over various topics without reference to the immediate environment. On one particular day (B18), pre-breakfast verbal elements included S— discussing a neighbor boy; B— and S— singing to themselves and discussing a bassoon with F—; and M— signalling *There now [we are ready]*. Breakfast verbal elements included grace said by M—; discussion of clothes by M—, J—, and B—; problem of getting slippers back on S— discussed by S—, M—, and B—; interjected elements regarding toast, etc., by various persons; discussion of the making of napkin rings, by J— and M—; of report cards, by J— and M—; of eating needs of S—, by F—; of water boiling in altitudes, by J—, F—, M—; taking of written notes by F—. Pre-breakfast nonverbal activity had included B— ringing a bell to call the other children to the table; S— gesturing to the neighbor's house; M— putting away the ironing board; B— putting on a dress; S— moving his chair, and playing with plate and spoon; M— opening refrigerator and pouring milk, then mixing and serving the cereal and scraping out the cereal bowl, and putting the toaster on the table. Breakfast proper included physical nonverbal items in which M— worked the toaster, ate grapefruit; J— looked for slippers for S—, B— daydreamed (with chin cupped in hands, elbows on the table); F— gave cod-liver oil to S— in drops; J— got socks for S—; B— ran to J— to whisper in her ear behind cupped hands, then got Kleenex from kitchen; M— finished fruit and put it to one side, then buttered toast, and passed it; etc.

On some days the activity may be different, but freely variant. On other days, however, variants may be conditioned. On Saturday morning, for example, breakfast may start a bit later, and does not end with a slur into school-going activities. Complex variants also occur, in which one of the slots normally filled by a single segment is filled by a sequence of segments — e.g., when in B84/11.8 J— arrives late, says grace silently, and then has her breakfast activity merge with that of the rest of the family behavioreme.

The distribution mode of this emic unit contains a number of slots filled by relevant classes of items. The pre-breakfast preparations, in this data, often include the playing of Tschaikovsky's Fifth Symphony on the phonograph to wake the children up to get dressed for breakfast, the calling of the children to come, the sitting down to the table. Then the official breakfast opens with a slot for the saying of grace. This slot may be filled in two major ways, one of which is the offering of prayer by the active family head (the father, or in his absence, the mother), while the other contains two subslots which are filled respectively by the active head's request, directed to another member of the family, to say grace, and the saying of grace by that member. In general, there is next a slot for eating fruit or drinking fruit juice, although S— may be required to delay his until his cereal is eaten, as an inducement to hasten the latter (e.g., B40/6.6). Toast eating fills part of a larger composite slot which also embraces a slot for cereal eating. The two sub-slots for toast and main course (usually cereal-eating) are not fixed in a definite time sequence, but mutually interrupt each other. Simultaneous with the fruit-eating and main-course-slots — but specifically excluded from the slot constituting the official opening of the breakfast, already referred to — is a large slot for general conversation. Occasionally this verbal activity is closely integrated with the nonverbal activity; e.g., B84/6.2 M—: *May I have the bananas please? ... Thank you.* Or J—: *Don't blow bubbles here at the table, B—!* Or B84/11 M—: *Where's your napkin, sister? Go get something and wipe that up.*

More often, the conversation was unrelated to the eating — so much so that except for occasional quiet asides or interjected bits one would scarcely know from the conversation that a meal was in progress. This conversation is itself trimodally structured, but without rigid, repeatable organization of its major features from day to day. The most prominent slots are those for give and take, i.e., utterance and response, between two speakers. A larger grouping is characterized by a series of such exchanges between two or more speakers on a single topic, or on merging topics (where one topic changes to another through association with some minor point in the first).

A series of this type may be broken — i.e., desire for a new slot may be signalled — by an interruption from a third person so as to change the topic and the immediate speech participants. Similar change of conversation unit can be signalled, without change of actors, by special vocal cues, of which one of the most frequent is change of voice quality: B84/2/12.9 B—: [With change from normal tone to low, shocked, husky warning] *Hey S—, take that [Ping-pong ball] out of your mouth!* B84/7 [After a pause] B—: *My gourd is getting bigger!* [With excited happy voice quality, changed from a rather apathetic refusal of bananas on cereal: *Not right now*] Or B84/9.4 M—: *Well what kind of a day do you think it's going to be outside?* [With cheery brightness of voice].

During the main part of the meal, before the official major closing slot, conversation types — or parts of conversations — occur which on occasion it is convenient to label etically as (a) merging (where two conversations become one, as one pair of speakers stops its discussion and joins the other), (b) diverging (where two people break off from a conversation involving more people, and carry on a simultaneous but different discussion), (c) simultaneous (two conversations at the same time), (d) overlapping (simultaneous at the end of the one discussion and the beginning of the other), (e) interrupted and unresumed, (f) resumed (whether from a preceding day, or from a moment earlier, to constitute the last part of a discontinuous type), (g) discontinuous (with attention focused on two or more noncontiguous parts) (h) inserted, and so on.

In order to indicate the way in which a single breakfast table conversation can illustrate the complex interweaving of a number of these characteristics, we give here excerpts from B37, beginning right after the official opening of the meal (B37/5.8):

... [B— talking about a book. S— calls for attention, overlapping on B—, who continues talking for a while]

S—: *Daddy, Daddy, Daddy, Daddy, tell a story about a jet airplane and about a cowboy in that story, will you please?* [With the topic stimulated by a picture of a zooming jet airplane on the cover of a book beside his plate]

... [B— still persists; S— calls again and gets the attention of F—] ...

F—: *Well, if you eat your cereal well, maybe I'll tell you a story.* [Note indication of purpose of this sub-unit, from parents' point of view]

... [A bit of discussion, before commencement]

F—: *Well, I tell you, there's the book so you can see a picture of what it looks like...* [Further bit of laughter and settling down] *Once upon a time, Mother, there was a cowboy.*

[Note high-level lexical formula to indicate beginning of the story sub-unit]

M—: Oh!...

M—: *Come on, J—.* [Note inserted conversation unit, as J— comes to the table]

J—: *I'm coming.*

M—: [to J—] *Don't you think it would be nice to wear something else today?...*
[Discussion of dresses, and related matters].

J—: *May I have, ah,—*

M—: *—the sugar?* [With utterance begun by one speaker completed by the other]

... [Continued discussion, overlapping again in the last several utterances with S—]

S—: *Daddy, go on and tell the story!*

F—: *Ohhh kay...*

F—: *So,—*

S—: *Go on!*

B—: *Go on!* [Gruffly]

M—: *Please Daddy!* [To B—, hinting, to soften voice quality]

F—: *So, this cowboy S—, he went out and he got himself into a — jet — airplane, where—*

... [Further discussion of same topic]

F—: *So he got in the jet airplane, pulled the lever* [Sound imitating a motor], *out came the jet* [plane noise] *off it went!*

S—: *And it made some fire.*

...

S—: *And it went so fast it came bumpin' an' crackin' and crackin', make — ah — that it bust to pieces.*

... [Further discussion of jet]

S—: *I saw a jet flying over my head when it was dark.*

J—: *Did you?*

S—: *Mhm. With a flashlight.*

B—: *You don't need a flashlight to see those junks.*

M—: *What did we look for with a flashlight over in Australia?* [Conversation diverging, switched on term *flashlight*]
S—: *Ah, mm. Possums.*
M—: *Possums, wasn't it.*
B—: *Not pirates!* [laughing]
M—: *No, possums...*
S—: *And it made some noise like this, pxxx!*
... [Further discussion of possums]
M—: *Who brought us some baby possums to see?*
S—: *A—.*
M—: *A— did, yes sir, A— then brought us some lovely baby possums to see.*
B—: *Mommie, what was that boy's name that S— was playing with* [*in Australia*]? [Conversation shifts again, to new sub-unit, switching on the term *name* in reference to *Australia*]
M—: *What was tha— Who was that boy that let you ride his tricycle every now and then?*
S—: *John!* [With vowel of *John* pronounced fairly well back in the mouth]
M—: *Yes, John, he is a lovely boy, isn't he?*
S—: *He's living over there.* [In reference, now, to a house across the street]
M—: *That's another John, isn't it?*
S—: *Uh huh, there's two Johns, isn't there?* [With vowel of *John* much farther front]
M—: *Yes.*
M—: *Who was the one that you played with over in Australia?*
S—: *John.* [With front vowel]
...
M—: [to F—, a moment later, with change from participant focus in discussion with S—, to analytical focus in a separate analytical etic discussion with F—] *You know when he first referred to J— D—, his vowel in 'John' was much farther back than it was when he referred to the one across the street.*
F—: *Oh.* [apathetic voice quality]
M—: *At first, then after he'd said the one across the street then his — when I asked him again about the one in Australia, he —* [F— overlaps last word, cutting it off]
F—: *This morning, you mean just now?* [Voice quality change shows interest picking up]
M—: *Just now!*
S—: *Daddy, tell the story, I don't know this story.*
... [Story discussion continues, with all members of the family participating; S— makes noises to simulate the plane, which brings on a discussion of noise making]
S—: *Daddy, will you take* [*for*] *me two* [*spoonfuls*]? *I* [*w*]*ant two, Mom. I* [*w*]*ant two. Mommie I want two. Daddy I — Daddy, Daddy, when you weren't here I took two, two.* [On last word, F— begins, but stops as his first sound overlaps on S—, then begins

again. Further discussion of the vitamin topic follows, ending with various play noises of B—, then —]

S—: *Daddy, know how — kitties — drink their milk?*
F—: *How do they drink their milk?*
S—: *Like this* — [demonstration]

... [Discussion of kitty topic; toast request; further play noises by B—, e.g., voiced velar implosives in sequence; S— again asks for story; B— asks for it in Spanish; the story begins; J— gets 'motherly', asking B— if she should take away her milk and drink it; a considerable pause, then S— changes the topic]

S—: *Daddy, there's really snow on the ground, see? Daddy want to come and see?* ...
F—: *Back in your seat son.* [After they had arisen to go to the window] ...
S—: *B— know what Daddy's going to do for us?* [F— simultaneous with end — *Pass the sugar please*] ... *He's going to make us a big snowman. OH BOY* [Ends with a long high squeal]

[... A whirl of rapidly changing topics and rapidly changing speakers, as various items become simultaneous and cannot be separated in the record. Then —]

M—: *Well shall we clear the table?*

The total breakfast, as part of its distribution mode, has a slot-filling function in the total activities of the day. It follows getting out of bed, precedes going to school, and so on.

The physical setting in which the breakfast scenes were embedded, on the other hand, includes the house with the dining room, table, chairs, toaster, cups, bowls, window shades; the kitchen with stove, sink, pots and pans, drawer for spoons, etc. In terms of our perception of them, we note that these physical items have a distribution mode via the wider setting in which they occur, with a physical hierarchy in the size of environment focused on (from cup, to room, to house, to community, etc.); a feature mode in reference to the contrastive differences (culturally formulated) between bowl and plate, or dining room and kitchen; a manifestation mode in reference to the precise way in which the table setting differs from day to day, or variants in the heat of the stove, the cloudiness of the sky (partially correlated with amount of artificial light or time of year), and so on.

5.3 *Included Behavioremes, Minimum Behavioremes, and Thresholds*

The breakfast scene constitutes a variant of a single behavioreme. It contains within it all the elements to identify it as such and to contrast it with other units of the same general class such as dinner or supper. Yet, as we saw illustrated in the quotations from Record B37, there are elements which are smaller than the breakfast as a whole, but which are included within the breakfast scene and which themselves also contain evidence of closure, purpose, and structuring which identify them as behavioremes. This forces us to conclude that within a large behavioreme there may be INCLUDED

BEHAVIOREMES which are smaller than the behavioreme containing them, but which are analyzed as behavioremes on the basis of the same kinds of criteria. Thus, the various conversational units referred to in our discussion of Record B37 are probably best treated as varieties of verbal behavioremes included within the breakfast eme; a single complete utterance such as *yes* is a small included behavioreme. Similarly, one may argue that the receiving and eating of a piece of toast is a nonverbal behavioreme.[3] It would be a verbal-nonverbal-composite behavioreme if one handles the verbal request (that the toast be passed) within the pattern.

If behavioremes may be included within behavioremes, the question then arises: Are there lower limits to the size of behavioremes? Upon the answer to it hangs the possibility of knowing when one's analysis is complete. If one cannot determine the lower limit to behavioremic segmentation, then one can only end with an arbitrary consideration of some of the intermediate units within the hierarchy of behavioremes included the one within the other.

The elements of an answer to this question have already been given, in other terms, in §§ 3.32-35, 4.23, 4.32: First, MINIMUM BEHAVIOREMES must be located relative to the kind of participant action being studied. Minimum behavioremes in the action of an analyst, or in the activity of a critic, may be considerably smaller than the minimum behavioremes in the action of normal participants. If one fails to treat separately such activities, one must inevitably end in confusion, since two homomorphic activities (§ 4.1.10), alike in physical set-up but differing in purpose, may have different minimum closure elements. Secondly, this attention to participant type in reference to analytical attention implies that units obtained by observing hypostasis (§§ 4.15, and 4.23) must not be treated in the same hierarchical set as units not obtained in such a manner. Third, the THRESHOLD for minimum behavioremes (§§ 4.32, 3.33) must not be allowed to go lower, for any one hierarchical set, than can be culturally, objectively documented as having closure and as being purposive. In spite of the fact that we have earlier shown that there is an area of indeterminacy in the matters of participant type (§§ 3.34, 4.1.10, 2.2), and so on, the insistence on such a threshold, indeterminate as it may be, is essential to a useful, practical handling of the theory; we assume that the indeterminacy in the theory is reflecting some of the ambiguity which exists, in fact, in the activity of the community itself, and that a concealing of this ambiguity in order to get 'clear cut' theory at this point would not contribute to fidelity of description but to concealment of the facts of behavioral structure.

Nevertheless, within this range of uncertainty of analysis of behavior the determination of a threshold of minimum behavioremes is important. It is this threshold

---

[3] A problem remains here. Dwight Bolinger has suggested to me the posibilities (1) that a behavioreme should be socially recognized as a unit; (2) that separate act tokens should be recognized by native actors as summing up or as manifesting such a unit; and (3) that we do not have a behavioreme unless we have occasion to refer to it as a unit. The absent-minded plucking of a blade of grass — or the routine eating of toast — might not qualify. (Compare, also, our discussion in § 6.43.)

which allows us, in the present volume, to stop short of the *reductio ad absurdum* of treating the movement of some particular molecule in some particular nerve fibre in some particular muscle of some part of the vocal organs during the production of some particular sound as constituting a behavioreme on a theoretical par with the football game. Without a threshold *somewhere* in the theory — even though it be a vague one which shifts with participant type — there would be no such stopping place.

It is the setting up of such a threshold, also, that serves as the practical base for the establishing, in the next three chapters, of minimum units of the three modes of a behavioreme. Without a minumum threshold for the size of behaviuoremes, there could be no 'minimum' units within them. Since our minimum for a behavioreme is tied, in this theory, to the presence of purpose, and of closure reflecting that purpose, the minimum unit of the feature mode of the behavioreme can be set at a threshold level which is also tied to purpose or meaning in some way, and yet constitute part of an integrated theory in which the small modal units of a behavioreme are defined in reference to and dependent upon their function relative to the larger unit. Once this is done, the minimum unit of the manifestation mode of the behavioreme can in turn be set as in direct relation to and dependence upon the minimum unit of the feature mode of the behavioreme, so that the threshold of units of the physical hierarchy are not allowed to descend to the level of molecular action, but are also held to a manageable size, for behavioral purposes. There will still arise problems and room for disagreement as to the exact place the threshold should be set, and as to the way in which subthreshold units should be handled, as we shall see in Chapter 8, but at least this approach gives us a method of getting at the problem.

So far, I have been able to find no evidence leading to criteria for setting up theoretical limits for a *maximum* behavioreme. We have already seen, in Chapter 4, that the maximum can surely be large, varying from a football game to a series fifty years long. Provided that the analyst can find cultural evidence for showing purpose and closure in normal participant action, the theory allows for behavioremic size without any top limit.

It frequently proves convenient, however to contrast minimum behavioremes within some hierarchical set with larger types within that same set, without stating what the top limit is. In conversational material, for example, the minimum behavioreme is either a short statement or question, and so on, or a brief reply to such a statement or question. The utterance plus its reply may constitute a higher layered behavioreme in the same hierarchy, and the entire conversation containing that exchange may be another. (When we wish to refer in general terms to any behavioreme larger than a minimum one, we may call it a HYPERBEHAVIOREME. Thus the utterance-reply sequence, and the total conversation, are both hyperbehavioremes as against the minimum behavioremes composed of the utterance itself, or the reply. We shall have occasion in later chapters to utilize the prefix HYPER- in similar ways in contrasting minimum units of the modes of a behavioreme with hyper-units of those same modes.)

A terminological problem arises at this point since certain emic units which we wish to call minimum emes may at one time have variants which are shorter than at another time. For both the minimum behavioreme and the hyperbehavioreme an analysis must distinguish between those variants which contain only OBLIGATORY elements essential to the shortest variant of the type, and those variants which are EXPANDED by containing one or more nonobligatory portions as well. Thus an imperative sentence type with a simple variant such as *Come!* may have an expanded variant such as *Come here!* Each of these variants of the imperative sentence type would be manifestations of that minimum type as a whole, contrasted with a nonminimum verbal behavioreme such as a form of verse which must contain several elements within it. 'Minimum', in the sense used here, refers to the presence of a single set of obligatory parts in the emic structure, and not to the particular length of its variants.

In a different set of contexts, the term minimum may be used to refer to *variants* of units rather than to the unit types themselves. A minimum variant is a non-expanded variant, containing only its obligatory elements. Units, may have variants which are expanded or non-expanded; a minimum structural eme, then, may have nonminimum variants of that eme, and a nonminimum emic unit — a hyper-unit — may have minimum variants or nonminimum variants. The phrase *Come here!* is a nonminimum variant of a minimum eme, i.e., an expanded variant of the imperative utterance type in English. A nonminimum emic unit such as the singing of the hymn discussed in Chapter 3 might have just one of its stanzas sung during a service in which time was at a premium, and in that instance the singing of the single stanza would constitute a minimum variant of that nonminimum eme.

5.4 *Systems of Behavioremes*

A behavioreme is a manifested part of an emic system of behavioremes. If this were not true, there would be chaos in our description more severe than would result from the lack of a threshold of minimum behavioremes; purposive movements of the lips and feet, or manipulation of footballs, baby buggies, and cabbage seeds would form an unorganized aggregate of activities, or might be arbitrarily classified without reference to their function in life as we live it.

Any emic system of emic units is characterized by the fact that emic units occur in distribution classes (§ 3.4) of units. A distribution class, in turn, is determined in relation to the occurrence of contrastive emic units within the same emic slot (§ 3.4) of a behavioreme. When various emic classes of units are included within the variant manifestations of a single behavioreme — in different slots within that behavioreme — or in a class of behavioremes, this group of classes constitutes an emic system of classes by virtue of this distribution. Thus the family-breakfast behavioreme is included within the group of family activities, and is part of the system of those activities. Similarly, the individual's participation in that family breakfast is part of the system of his personal activities.

Within a behavioreme with focus as broad (§ 4.4) as the family breakfast there occur so many kinds of activities that there is confusion unless they can be treated in terms of a set of composite hierarchies, as some kind of component sub-assemblies (§ 4.43) within the larger whole. The classes of units of one such INCLUDED HIERARCHY constitute a SIMULTANEOUS COMPONENTIAL SYSTEM of that hyperbehavioreme or of a system of hyperbehavioremes. Two of the most important and obvious simultaneous componential systems within the breakfast unit are composed of the verbal hierarchy and of the nonverbal one, respectively.

The question must be raised, here, as to whether the setting up of componential systems of this type has not defeated our attempt for the volume as a whole to show that behavior cannot be treated in water-tight compartments. The answer to this query is that it does not, precisely because we indicated that the component hierarchies are only relatively or partially independent, not completely so. At certain points in the argument it is highly important to indicate places where there is not rigid separation of the hierarchies, but interpenetration between them (as in the instance where two activity types are closely integrated in a sub-unit which involves the phrase *Pass the toast*). In addition, in this matter there is a marginal area of activity where indeterminacy of componential systems occurs, just as there is an indeterminate area at the borders of many other units postulated by the theory. Both of these facts will be treated in more detail, later. Interpenetration of systems will be treated especially in Chapter 15. Indeterminacy of other types will be mentioned as the various emic units come before us.

NONSIMULTANEOUS CONGRUENT SYSTEMS, or STYLES, will be treated in more detail in § 16, and are composed of two (or more) systems of units so related that, in general, they share most of their units, though often with slightly different physical manifestations of these units. Two styles of speaking constitute two such systems. Two or more congruent systems make up a single HYPERCONGRUENT one. Hypostasis, to which we have already been forced to refer on a number of occasions (§§ 2.1, 4.15, 4.23), is caused by the displacement of a unit from one such system (one where the participant is playing the game which is under attention) to another (one in which the participant is analyzing or discussing the game). One of the most fascinating situations in which two componential systems overlap is in the situation of "April Fool". On April first, the trickster tries to achieve a result by statements designed normally to get that result — say, to get a person (who is operating in one system) to look out the window to see an elephant. When (as intended) the 'lie' is detected by the deceived person, the normal penalties for a detected falsehood are avoided by the speaker and turned into a joke by saying *April Fool*, which apprises the listener of the fact that the speaker was operating in the special system permissible only on that one day of the year. Note the cultural reaction to this system when misplaced: B 84/2/1.2 F—: *J—, is that an elephant out there?* J— looks, and replies something noncommittal

(*Why should I know?*). F—: *April Fool.* J—: *To-day isn't April Fool...* M—: *Daddy's just at the wrong end of the month isn't he? This is the last of April, and not the first.*

5.5 *The Uttereme (The Sentence Syntagmeme) and The Etics of Utterances*

Since the balance of the volume will deal much more with verbal behavior than with nonverbal behavior it proves useful to have a set of terms which may be applied exclusively to verbal elements without reference to their nonverbal or composite verbal-nonverbal counterparts. We have illustrated at some length in this chapter verbal behavioremes included within composite verbal-nonverbal ones; these verbal behavioremes we shall call UTTERANCE-EMES or, with the term abbreviated for convenience, UTTEREMES;[4] utteremes constitute a subdivision of behavioremes, such that every uttereme is a behavioreme but not all behavioremes are utteremes. When we wish to distinguish, as for minimum behavioremes versus hyperbehavioremes, between small and large verbal types we will speak of MINIMUM UTTEREMES and HYPER-UTTEREMES: one of the large conversation units (say the story mentioned above, § 5.2) would be a variant of a hyper-uttereme; a single sentence would be a variant of a minimum uttereme. From an etic point of view, similarly, we may speak of etic utterances or etic hyper-utterances, without committing ourselves in advance to a particular emic analysis of these utterances for any particular language.

In discussing the etics of utterances, we need to note especially: (1) the problem of segmenting utterances from a continuum, (2) the kinds of criteria which serve to identify or to differentiate utterance types, (3) the types of utterances or hyper-utterances which are the end product of classification by such an etic scheme, and (4) the kinds of distribution classes of utterances and hyper-utterances which are determined by their function in particular languages.

For discussion of the internal structure of sentences, see also §§ 7, 11.

5.51 *Segmentation of a Continuum into Utterances and Hyper-Utterances*

In the analysis of a language, one needs to make an etic segmentation of the data. The large hyper-utterances need to be cut tentatively and perhaps inaccurately (i.e., nonstructurally) into smaller hyper-utterances or minimum utterances included within the larger hyper-utterances. A number of clues for a procedure and criteria for doing this have already been given. Others are available. The following list is not intended to be exhaustive, since a separate detailed treatment is needed of these matters, but may be suggestive: (a) Each change of speaker within a hyper-utterance

---

[4] In recent publications on tagmemics, the term *syntagmeme* is extensively used for a construction of tagmemes at any level of the hierarchy. An uttereme would then be a *sentence syntagmeme* — a syntagmeme on the sentence level. See also §§ 11.22, 11.44 (especially Table 3).

implies the beginning of an included utterance or hyper-utterance. (b) Each change of topic also implies the beginning of an included utterance or hyper-utterance. Other clues include (c) a lull, or long pause in the conversation, or (d) a sharp change of voice quality, (e) a quick audible catching of breath by the speaker, (f) a 'running down' intonation pattern, (g) other vocal signs which are not words (e.g., a slow indrawn air stream to the mouth, through partially closed lips, or the clearing of the throat, or a cough), (h) special wording indicating a new subdivision in the topic (e.g., *Now another thing*...), and so on. Other verbal signs may signal endings (*Thanks for your attention;* etc.), or continuance rather than an ending (e.g., a quick speed-up to prevent interruption, or an increase of loudness to shout down someone trying to interrupt, or a pause put after the first word of a succeeding grammatical unit instead of between two such units, also to prevent interruption; or special words or word groups such as *yes... yes... yes* to signal continuance of listening rather than of talking; and so on).

Many nonvocal elements help the listener to segment out the relevant changes of hyper-utterance types. An accompanying change of stance, or of facial gesture, or a raising of the hand to stop someone from speaking may contribute in this way. Whenever this is the case, we note once more that verbal and nonverbal activity cannot profitably be completely separated in analysis. (Yet the analysis of words or sentences outside of normal behavioral contexts may itself constitute an activity, and the analysis of that analytical activity in structural terms is also part of the total analytical necessity facing the student of human behavior. This is a study of the activity of analytical hypostasis — and a very profitable one provided its results and procedures are not allowed to vitiate the results of an analysis of normal participant activity. For the general theoretical problem, see §§ 2.1, 4.23, 7.321.)

In the analysis of utterances in this way one is not discussing the meanings of words or sentences in themselves, apart from verbal and nonverbal context, but is rather attempting to analyze verbal behavior as a subsystem of total human behavior and as embedded within. From this fact that we deduce the theoretical validity of the use of FRAMES, which prove so useful in practical working with behavior units. A frame is merely the identified context which surrounds an identified, filled slot, such that a series of items may be observed in a single slot, one after another in a repeated context, without the functional relation being changed between the context and the (changing) item within the (unchanging) slot. Thus, for example, the words *big, tall, ugly* constitute a substitution list, or distribution class, which may fill the slot in an utterance frame *The... house fell down.*

We shall have occasion to refer to this kind of situation in many different places in the subsequent discussion. For the moment, however, it is sufficient to indicate that part of the segmentation procedure for isolating utterances is built upon an extension of this principle, in which the frame is exclusively nonverbal but the slot-filling material is verbal. For example, the minimum uttereme may often best be seen as one which comprises the smallest obligatory parts which may fill a slot in such a (nonhypostatic) nonverbal frame — e.g., an exclamation such as *Ouch!* filling a slot after a person hits his finger with a hammer. (Another minimum utterance type may be seen in a different nonverbal frame, as when a person in some physical context gives a verbal minimum order which is carried out by the second person without reply; when the reply is verbal, an utterance-plus-response unit is similarly isolable within the nonverbal context. Note: One person comes up to another in a queue, and says: *A line, is there?* To which the other replies: *Yup.*)

Once a minimum uttereme has been isolated within a nonverbal frame, moreover, this uttereme can then itself serve as part of a frame for identifying other segmental borders. A command, isolated within a nonverbal frame, may serve as part of a frame in which a verbal reply is given, and the distribution class of such replies can be studied as an uttereme class relative to this appropriate context, and dependent upon it, and so on, to higher and higher layers of the hyper-utteremic hierarchy or parts thereof. Inasmuch, however, as this procedural start is keyed into observations made when verbal activity begins within a nonverbal context, and inasmuch as different distribution classes of utteremes occur in different such contexts, it follows that in our next section, discussing the criteria for differentiating utterance types, we must also include some criteria of a nonverbal type. This, in turn, gives further evidence that our outlook set forth in Chapter 1 must be sustained: In some instances, verbal activity cannot be adequately analyzed without reference to the manner in which it is interlocked with nonverbal activity.

5.52 *Etic Classificatory Criteria for Utterance Types*

It is not possible at this point in the discussion to give detailed instructions for identifying utterance types since some of the criteria involve a study of smaller-layered included units which have not yet been presented in relation to this theory. It is desirable, however, that some indication be given here of the kinds of criteria which could go into making up a detailed study of UTTERETICS — i.e., a classification of criteria such that their application would lead to groupings useful for comparison of utterance types around the world, for training of students before they attempt to analyze a particular language. Unfortunately, such a listing is not complete, and since the order in which the criteria are applied affects greatly the kinds and usefulness of resultant groupings, this listing is only a first approximation to that which the field needs.

Following the application of each criterion, a grouping of utterances will result, with one group which does and another which does not contain that feature. As successive criteria are applied, the groups get smaller and smaller, until after the application of the final criterion there should be only a single utterance type in each group, — provided that the list of criteria is complete and adequately arranged in the most useful order (which we have not assumed for this particular tentative listing):

Sample criteria for utterance and hyper-utterance etic types:

(a) Is it essential that the speaker have in advance of delivery the knowledge of the precise wording which he is to use (e.g., in reciting a poem), or is no such knowledge or partial knowledge necessary?

(b) If (a) is essential, is it also essential that the wording have been prepared by the speaker (as in giving a reading of his own words), or may it have been prepared by someone else?

(c) If (a) is essential, is it also essential that the wording be preserved orally only, or may it have been preserved in writing?

(d) Is there an essential relation of the utterance type to its inclusion in a specific kind of larger behavior pattern or to its inclusion in some structural slot of such a pattern (e.g., a sermon in a church service), or is it not dependent upon such specific hierarchical occurrence?

(e) Is there an essential number of speakers (e.g., in a soliloquy, or a quartet)? If so, how many?

(f) Is there an essential type of speaking functionary or functionaries (e.g., judge versus witness), or is there no prescribed difference in function?

(g) Is it essential for an audience to be present (e.g., an audience for a sermon, since a sermon preached without an audience would be a different utterance type, in hypostasis, and a sermon given from a radio studio without a visible audience might give 'mike fright' to the speaker), or not? If so, is there an essential audience type?

(h) Is there an essential time (e.g., Easter Sunday, for an Easter church program), or is it tied to no particular time or occasion?

(i) Is there an essential place (e.g., for a British coronation ceremony), or may it occur in various unspecified places?

(j) Are there essential props, or an essential setting (e.g., the baseball diamond where the umpire says *Strike!*), or may it occur in undefined places?

(k) Are there essential concomitant actions (e.g., in a gesture song), or may the utterance occur with none other than vocal movement?

(l) Is there an essential specific voice quality (e.g., in song)? If so, what is this quality?

(m) Is there an essential (even though only partially definable) purpose or meaning of function of this utterance type (e.g., for amusement, learning, analysis, etc.; or for a question, or command; a rehearsal differs from a regular performance, or hypostatic activity from that of regular participant activity, by this criterion) — and if so, what — or is the utterance an accident physiologically conditioned (e.g., a cough) or not in accordance with the normal intent of the speaker (i.e., interrupted and truncated by another person, or by some other event).

The *topic* of a discussion may for these purposes be treated somewhat like the meaning of a morpheme.

(n) Is this a minimum utterance type (a sentence type), or a nonminimum one (a hyper-utterance)?

(o) If this is a nonminimum type, is there an essential symmetry, or essential size, or essential and optional number or kind of slots and their correlated distribution classes (e.g., number of lines, or size of lines in verse, or rhyming patterns in verse, or the number of acts in a play, or the speeches versus rebuttals in a formal debate, or greeting versus leave-taking elements in a formal conversation), or is there no such formal limit (other, for example, than utterance and reply slots and changes of topic in an informal conversation)? What are these slots and classes?

(p) If this is a minimum type, what are its specific essential internal slots and what are the distribution classes of elements filling these slots? And what are the permitted optional expanding slots and classes filling these slots?

See, also, tagmemic structures of sentence constructions, §§ 7, 11.[5]

As a brief indication of the way in which such a set of criteria could be applied, note the following two illustrations:

The jet plane story (partially quoted in § 5.2) (a) [see sections just above for these divisions] had no wording planned in advance; (d) it was part of one variant of the breakfast hyperbehavioreme, told during the main course, but was not essentially so since it might have been told at bed time or while travelling in the car (though in these instances one might argue that it constitutes a different unit, since its purpose would be different — although we shall for the present attribute this meaningful difference to the functional slot in which the story occurred rather than to the internal structure of the story as such); (e) at least two persons were always involved; (f) usually the respective functions of these two were teller and listener, but occasionally the normal listeners (i.e., S— and usually B— and J—) reversed roles and contributed to building up the plot; (g) an audience of at least one was essential, or the story would not be told; (h) the time was at breakfast, and (i) the place at the breakfast table would be concomitant with the time; (j) the breakfast setting would also provide the essential props; (k) the eating of S— was an essential concomitant set of actions, since the story stopped if they did not continue; (l) voice quality was not uniform throughout; (m) the essential purpose of the story as such was to arouse interest, but combined with this structural slot was to induce S— to eat his cereal happily; (n) the story was definitely a hyper-utterance, composed of many smaller hyper-utterances or minimum utterances; (o) the size was indeterminate — and could have been very shortly completed (though it carried over several days); the formal parts included an official announcement of its beginning drawn from a class of such special elements (*Once upon a time*), with various changes from one included incident to another, and with slots

---

[5] As reports of sentences continue to reach us in the form of matrices with contrastive dimensions, the etics of sentence types should be made more complete, and more parallel to the usefulness of a phonetic chart. Various kinds of dimensional displays of different languages should eventually lead to a display of sentence types — or, on different levels — of clause types, phrase types, etc., comparable to the phonetic chart. Such a chart may be assumed to be the conflated results of all reported sentence systems. For matrix dimensions of constructions, see Pike (1962a, 1963b); for the concept of conflation of matrices — but within the context of the merging of cells of morphemic or submorphemic components — see Pike (1963d), and Pike and Erickson (1964).

for elicited or voluntary contributions from other members of the family.

As a second illustration, we may take one utterance from that recording, the *Yes*, by M— (the utterance which follows the statement of S— *Uh, huh, there's two Johns isn't there?*): Here (a) the wording is not planned in advance; (d) it is part of a larger utterance-response — part of a conversational hyper-utterance, — and occurs, in this function, only as a dependent part of such a hyper-utterance (though it may occur in other slots, as a signal by a listener to a speaker that the speaker should continue, etc.); (e) it implies, in this function, at least two speakers, (f) one of whom (g) is responding to the other; (h) time, (i) place, (j) props· and (l) voice quality are not determined, since the type of conversational hyper-unit containing it may occur in various kinds of contexts; (k) there are no essential concomitant actions; (m) the meaning of the particular element filling the slot is 'affirmation' whereas the total slot function is 'reply' (which might have been negative, instead of positive); (n) it is a minimum utterance type, (p) in this non-expanded form it has only the one internal grammatical, lexical slot, filled by one of a class of items such as a simple *Yes*, or *No*, or a complex *I think so* with its own internal slots (but in an expanded form it might contain two or more major slots in such a reply as *Yes I think so*), plus the slot for the superimposed intonation, which in this particular instance (37/12) falls from high to mid pitch.

5.53 *Etic Utterance Types*

If the preceding etic criteria are applied to a large number of utterances and hyperutterances, various groups will emerge after the application of each criterion in the set. If the order of application of criteria is changed, the resultant groupings will correspondingly differ; hence, for different purposes, the analyst may choose to use a different order of application of these or other diacritica of utterances. A much more extensive investigation needs to be made, and trial of various alternative orders of application of criteria, before we shall know which is the most useful for linguistic purposes.

As an indication of a few of the groupings which might emerge when various criteria are given prominence in the descriptive order of application of some such set of criteria, we give the following miscellaneous examples:

A joke, limerick, parody, pun, or comedy (criterion in prominence early in order of application: humorous purpose).

A song, chorus, vocal solo, cantata, oratorio, aria, chant, choir practice session, opera, lullaby (criterion in prominence: sung voice quality).

A presidential address, welcoming address, after-dinner speech (criteria in prominence: single speaker, special audience, long hyper-utterance).

A sermon, invocation, prayer, litany, recited creed, marriage ceremony (criteria: religious purpose and setting).

A slogan, motto, proverb, epigram (criteria: size, familiarity, aptness, etc.).

Conversation which is formal, informal, over the phone, in a discussion group, in an oral examination, in an interview (criterion: give and take between speakers, etc.).

A judge's giving sentence, a lawyer's argument, the President's annual message to Congress, a sermon, an umpire's decision (criterion: with the person speaking having his individuality subordinated in importance to the role which he is representing in the society at that moment; note that this leads to overlap with some of the other groupings).

Sentences which are narrative (*John ran away*), actor-action (*John ran away*), command (*Come!*), sentence-word type (Italian *canto*, 'I sing'), goal-action (Latin *cantātur* 'it is being sung'), equational (Russian *beātus ille* 'happy (is) he'), instrument-action (Tagalog *ipi 'nu:tul nja aŋ 'gu:luk* 'he cut with the bolo'), sensation (Georgian *'m-e-smi-s* 'me-sound-is' i.e., 'I hear'), impersonal (German *mir ist kalt* 'to-me is cold' i.e., 'I feel cold'), explicit-action (*I did hear him*), emphatic (*RUN home* [*don't walk*]), informal question (*John ran away?*), formal question with inverted order (*Did John run away?*), negative (Menomini *kan upianan* 'not he-comes [negative]' i.e., 'He does not come'), surprise (Menomini *piasah!* 'and so he's coming!'), disappointment (Menomini *piapah!* 'but he was coming!'). Also minor sentence types: interjections (*Please*), completive (*This one*), exclamatory (*John!*), aphoristic (*First come, first served*). (The sentence types in this group were abstracted from Bloomfield [1933a: 171-77], who gave as his first criterion the fact that they occur in "absolute position" [170], and not as part of a larger form. Further subordinate criteria had to do with their use of pitch units [171], full versus minor types [172, 176-77], constituent parts [172], relation of these parts [173], occurrence of special elements in the form [174], order of elements in the form [174], their meanings as determined from their occurrence in the cultural setting [e.g., 176], and so on.) (For favorite and minor sentence types in Chinese, note Chao [1959].)

5.54 *Utterance Distribution Classes*

A listing of sentence types for a single language, English, has been made by Fries (1952), using a different set of criteria, or criteria applied differently: In a first dichotomy, utterances are divided into (1) communicative and (2) noncommunicative types (Fries, 53).

Noncommunicative types of utterances are in general those exclamations "characteristic of situations such as surprise, sudden pain, prolonged pain, disgust, anger, laughter, sorrow".

Communicative utterances are divided into (a) those "regularly eliciting 'oral' responses only" — further subdivided by formal criteria (Fries, 42-47) into greetings, calls, and questions (53); and (b) those "regularly eliciting 'action' responses, sometimes accompanied by one of a limited list of oral responses" — i.e., requests or commands; and (c) those "regularly eliciting conventional signals of attention to continuous discourse (sometimes oral signals, but of a limited list, unpredictable in place, and not interrupting the span of talk or utterance unit)" — i.e., statements (53).

Various utterance types are further subdivided in accordance with the order of occurrence of the distribution classes of words within them (142-72).

A further classification (Fries, 240-55), cutting across some phases of his earlier classification, is one into (a) 'situation' sentences (which may occur at the beginning of a conversation, for example), (b) 'sequence' sentences (in which some word in a sentence ties it to an earlier word in the same conversation unit; e.g., the situation sentence *The quoted price of the books we need is sixty-five dollars* is followed in Fries' materials with the sequence sentence *That amount is just about what we figured*, in which the sequence signal for the second sentence is the word *that*), and (c) 'included' sentences (in which a sentence becomes part of a larger sentence, as *they're all clogged with roots* is included in the sentence *The boys we've had out there couldn't do anything satisfactory with the lines because they're all clogged with roots*).

The reader will note that Fries' classification of utterances is much more easily related to our emic approach than is that of Bloomfield, since the work of Fries utilizes more directly and explicitly the relationship of a sentence classification to the occurrence of these sentences in specific slots in verbal, nonverbal, and composite verbal-nonverbal behavioremes. Without such reference to nonlinguistic items, the helpful classification given by Fries could not even have gotten under way, since by its first dichotomy it had reference to the setting of speech within speech or to its setting within nonverbal bahavior, and in the classification of the communicative utterances there was in turn further essential reliance upon nonverbal criteria in the form of the regular presence of action responses. Here, once more, we see clearly that language study must, in order to be useful or theoretically valid, be treated within its hierarchical framework of nonlinguistic as well as of linguistic behavior.

Distribution classes of utterances, as distinct from groupings determined by criteria other than that of distribution within particular functional slots in a particular language, can in principle be determined for only one language at a time. No general etic classification can provide for the distribution classes of utterances of all languages within a single listing, since languages differ as to the particular functional slots within their hyperbehavioremes, and as to the distribution classes within these slots. If one looks again at the data in the last two paragraphs as taken from Fries, one will notice that it is in fact a grouping of distribution classes, for a single language (English), identified in relation to their occurrence in slots in particular hyperbehavioremes whether verbal, or nonverbal, or composite verbal-nonverbal in nature. It was precisely this fact which makes it appealing to us, in the light of behavioremic hierarchical structure. Nevertheless, this advantage from the hierarchical viewpoint brings with it a limitation of application to a generalized etic approach: To whatever extent these particular kinds of classes are restricted in ocurrence to English, to that extent the English system of classes lacks the generalized character of a purely etic scheme which should simultaneously and with equal facility serve for classifying the utterance types of all languages at once.

If, however, one takes these particular distribution classes of English utterances and treats them as suggestive of the *kinds* of classes which might — or might not — occur in some other language, and if one then adds to this listing as many other kinds of distribution classes as can be found in other languages, then a systematization of the etics of distribution *classes* of utterances can be developed to supplement a systematization of the etics of kinds of individual utterances in which the principal dichotomies in the classification are based on other than distributional criteria. Unfortunately, such an etic classification of kinds of classes of utterances, if it is to be adequately representative of the world picture, must await more studies of other languages.

Classes of hyper-utterances determined by their distribution in typical slots in sample languages need also to be systematized into some etic conceptual scheme. The criteria given in § 5.3 lead to groupings of various kinds, in accordance with the priority given to the order of application of these criteria. Special attention, for the purposes of training students to be prepared for the structural analysis of the hyper-utterances of a particular language, needs to be placed upon a classification in which top priority is given to distributional characteristics. These, to be sure, differ from language to language, as they do for minimum utterance types, but there is probably sufficient similarity in all languages to justify a generalized scheme which could serve as systematized background data to make the student observe more quickly the particular emic distribution classes of hyper-utteremes which he was meeting in a language just then being studied by him. We are not yet ready to present such an etic classification here, however. It would constitute a volume in itself.

5.55 *Emic Procedure in the Analysis of Utterances and Hyper-Utterances*

In order to pass from a prestructural etic description of the utterances and hyper-utterances of a language to a structural, emic description of the utteremes and hyper-utteremes of that language, the analyst must go through various procedures, or operations, to process his etic data. It is evident that this procedure assumes that the linguist has made a preliminary recording and analysis of some small part of his data in terms of some general etic outlook before his emic procedures can be utilized. Yet it also assumes that there may be a wide margin of error in this early etic work. If the student has had little training, the etic error will be greater than if he has been exposed to a wide variety of languages, and if he is a monolingual speaker with no training, his etic outlook will be in fact completely conditioned by the emic structures of his own language as seen, if at all, distorted by traditional presentations in the schools, which in our western culture have for many years used Latin forms as a kind of generalized background for viewing English and other languages. If the student is well trained, certain of these errors will disappear, though distortions may be introduced, say, in the form of an etic scheme heavily weighted in the direction of non-Indo-European languages, as a protest against present distortion in their favor. Even with perfect training and wide experience, however, one must always assume a large margin of emic error in early etic analysis, (1) since etic training and observation includes more elements than can be relevant in any one language — hence there would be over-recording or analysis in the early stages, — and especially (2) since relevance in a particular language is dependent not on the absolute nature of the etic data but upon the relationship of any bit of data to the whole system of the language which contains it — but this relationship cannot be known until the language is first known, so that etic absolutes must be modified in terms of the relativity of the parts of the system to each other (§ 6.7).

For this same reason, it is impossible to give a complete statement of procedure for the emic analysis of utterances until we have covered the general characteristics of a system as a whole, since part of the procedure must draw upon elements of the system which at first sight might not appear to be relevant at all. Just as we have thus far argued that language must be analyzed in relation to the nonverbal setting in which it occurs, so we are now limited by the fact that sentences can not ultimately be analyzed in full until something is known about *smaller* parts of the linguistic system. We shall return to procedural matters, then, after the smaller units of the language system have been discussed (§§ 6.8, 7.7, 8.7, 9.25, 11.5).

Nevertheless, it will probably be helpful to the reader if we indicate, now, the general principles upon which an analysis of utterances or hyper-utterances within such a larger framework can be based.

Every etic utterance may be assumed to comprise: either

    (a) a free variant of an emic utterance

or (b) a conditioned variant of an emic utterance

or (c) part of an etically-complex variant of an emic utterance

or (d) a sequence of manifested variants of two or more emic utterances

or (e) a fused composite variant of two completely simultaneous or partially simultaneous emic utterances

or (f) an error of phonetic recording which would be eliminated upon re-hearing or an error of analysis which would be eliminated upon further study;

and (g) the emic utterances composed of these etic variants are members of emic distribution classes of emic utterances within the larger system of classes of emes which comprise the language.

Thus, for example, the call *Mommie Mommie!* is a free variant of the calling emic utterance which includes among its members, also, *Daddy Daddy!* since the general pattern is unchanged by the choice of the particular member of the distribution class which may fill that slot. For a particularly interesting example from § 5.2 note that when J— says *May I have, ah* —, it constitutes an etic utterance by the criterion of change of speakers, since M— follows that with a second etic utterance, which is — *the sugar?* Nevertheless, it is obvious that there is some kind of unity between the two such that together they form a single entity of some kind. Here we would treat them as separate etic utterances which together constitute an etically-complex variant of the simple question uttereme.

The transfer from the etic treatment of hyper-utterances to the identification of the hyper-utteremes in a language is parallel to that of passing from etic minimum utterances to utteremes. Other than the fact that we are dealing on a higher level of the hierarchy of utterances, no new principles need to concern us here.

After a discussion of some bibliographical matters which are relevant to this chapter, we shall be ready to go on to the discussion of units which are smaller than the vocal or nonvocal behavioremes. The pattern for the next six chapters is as follows: First we discuss, in one chapter each, the minimum units of each of the three modes of the behavioreme, verbal and nonverbal. Then we discuss units within these modes which are intermediate in the hierarchy between the minimum unit of the mode and the total behavioreme in which they occur. Chapter 6 treats the minimum unit of the feature mode; Chapter 7 the minimum unit of the distribution mode; Chapter 8 the same for the manifestation mode. Chapter 9 continues with the manifestation mode, with higher layered units in the hierarchy of that mode; Chapter 10 with the higher-layered units of the feature mode; and Chapter 11 the same for the distribution mode. A small chart may help the reader to see the plan more clearly:

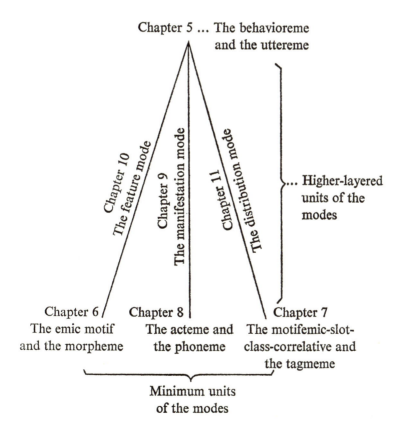

5.6 Bibliographical Comments on Chapter 5

5.61 On Behavioremes

In the anthropological literature, Nadel has a passage that sets up a unit which in some features is close to our behavioreme: "...no legitimate isolate can be discovered more basic than that of a standardized pattern of behaviour rendered unitary and relatively self-contained by its task-like nature and its direction upon a single aim. On this basic level the behavior pattern runs its course in time; it consists of a sequence of part-actions which has a beginning and an end — the assumption of a particular task, its execution, and completion. The essential aspect is biographical, and the unit of action so viewed is best termed a *behaviour cycle*" (1951:75-76). This is followed by a paragraph which implies an optional focus on various levels of a hierarchy of such patterns. Unfortunately, for our purposes, Nadel does not attempt to follow up this initial outlook with an analysis of the internal structuring of the behavior patterns themselves, in reference to a system of such patterns of activity, but rather turns his attention more specifically to an analysis of society and the institutions and groups of persons acting in that society. His term 'behavior cycle', however, should be useful to persons who dislike the term 'behavioreme' — a term which we continue to utilize in this volume since it is more easily related to our entire system of terms and the structural point of view which they represent.

For a similar related concept see now Barker and Wright for "an easily discriminated part of the stream of behavior and situation which we have called a *behavior episode*" (1955:4) such as a child moving a crate across a pit; "The behavior in this and every other episode has three basic attributes: it has *constant direction* [towards a goal], it is within the *normal behavior perspective* [emic], and it has approximately *equal potency* throughout its course [toward goal, uninterrupted, with concentration on it]" (1955: 5). Similarly, behavior episodes are the "smallest units which appear to be of value in ecological studies. They can be considered the particles of ecological research" (1955:7). For episode analysis by contrastive features see also Oliver (1958). Note also Vogt for "long-range cultural phenomena [which] have a beginning, a middle, and an end, and their own natural forms" ... but which "then do not recur" (1960:22). Note Aristotle, who long ago stated "Now a whole is that which has beginning, middle, and end" (*Poetics*, Chapter 7).

Related to our description of the breakfast unit there has now appeared an analysis of eating, given by Halliday (1961:277-79). His analysis however, is largely of the content of the menu, rather than of the eating activity itself. Symbolism with slots and class (note 'E:1 [breakfast]') appeared, as well as a hierarchy from the meal "down to the gastronomic morpheme, the 'mouthful'" (1961:277, 279).

For question frame procedure for analysis of Ladino weddings, leading to symbolized contrastive units, and sub-units, and network of relations, see Metzger and Williams (1963).

For purpose, use, and function in relation to meaning or intent, note § 17.5. For Morris, "signs are identified within goal-seeking behavior" (1946:7; see also 9). For Skinner, on the other hand, purpose is not a property of the behavior itself, but a way of referring to controlling variables (1957:87-90). Note also Carroll for whom "the distinctive feature of each unit, whatever its size, is a specific goal-directed character" (1953:106).

5.62 *An Etic Classification in Anthropology*

For an etic listing of a great many general kinds of behavior units, as well as an etic listing of many elements of the social and physical setting of behavior, one may consult the Outline by Murdock, Ford, and others (1950). This outline is serving as the basic conceptual scheme for an etic collection of cultural matters, with its "ultimate objective ... to organize in readily accessible form the available data on a statistically representative sample of all known cultures ... for the purpose of testing cross-cultural generalizations", etc.; by 1943 the Survey had "filed some 500,000 cards with full or substantial information on nearly 150 cultures" (xii). One of their chief problems of a practical nature was the necessity for using various criteria which were overlapping, and which could not be used with complete rigor there lest the result be "an intolerably cumbersome system of classification" which "would seriously fragment the descriptive materials"; so that their actual work reflects "now one principle of classification, now another, oftentimes two or more in combination" (xx). This difficulty is similar to the one discussed in our materials for the classification of utterances, §§ 5.3 and 5.4. Apparently they also faced the necessity of rejecting an emic classification in favor of an etic one, for their purposes (cf. xvii, and their rejection of a configurational approach adapted to the 'particular content and institutions' of a culture, in favor of "an elaboration of what Wissler called 'the universal culture pattern'"). Although there are provisions in their outline for linguistic materials, the works processed by them do not yet contain enough detail of the necessary kind to provide adequate background excepts for the development of the etic utterance classifications.

Folktales have been analyzed with extremely elaborate etic typology (S. Thompson, 1955-58; Aarne, 1928). For attempt to treat these, however, as emic units within particular tales, note Dundes (1962b, 1963). Much earlier works done on lists of culture traits have served as etic classificatory devices for initial study of cultures; note, for example, Kroeber (1936); see also below, § 6.91.

For etic classification of gesture, note also E. T. Hall (1959).

5.63 *On Linguistic Units Larger than Sentences*

Linguistics in the past three decades made its most striking progress by dealing with units no larger than sentences: with sounds (especially since Sapir, 1925, in his

Selected Writings 33-45), with significant parts of words, i.e., morphemes (especially since Harris, 1942a), and with sentences (e.g., Bloomfield, 1933a, who adopted his sentence definition from Meillet — see Bloomfield 1926:154). Study of the structure of large language units has been left largely to the students of literature (who have worked more with written than with spoken materials) or students of metrics, and with the students of public address (for the structure of speeches of various kinds). See Wellek and Warren for an attempt to give an etic summary of literary types, or genres (1949: 235-47, with bibliography 337-40). See Jakobson and Lotz (1952) for one of the few structural studies (by linguists) of a large language unit; in this study verse patterns are correlated with the structure and sequence of syllables, words, and phrases, and are diagrammatically and formulaically represented. This analysis by Jakobson and Lotz is much closer to the structure of the hyper-utterance, as we see it, than the more widely-known recent attempt of Harris (1952a, 1952b) at 'discourse analysis'. Harris' approach differs radically from ours in starting assumptions, working procedures, and kinds of results obtained; his approach seems to me to be essentially atomistic, with attention directed to (assumed, not procedurally identified) sentences in juxtaposition rather than as integrated in a close knit but larger structure. Fries' attention to sequence signals (1952:240-55) and his insistence, for example, that "the question itself is part of the frame in which the answer as an utterance operates" (165, 169) strikes me as revealing more of the higher-layered structural form. (cf. also Karcevskij, 1937:59). On the other hand, Harris' stimulating handling of a "chain of substitutions" in a particular text may be very useful for "content analysis" (cf. Lasswell, Lerner, and de Sola Pool, 1952) inasmuch as the chain is dependent on correlations (within that particular text) which in turn are in part dependent upon content, even though the content as such is specifically ignored. Bloomfield did not go as far as Jakobson and Lotz, or Fries or Harris, in that he stated that "each sentence is an independent linguistic form, not included by virtue of any grammatical construction in any larger linguistic form" (1933a:170), and did not attempt to see ways in which sentences were tied together in larger structures. It was perhaps this limitation which has prevented, in this country, the development of linguistics so that it would be integrated more closely with studies of literary form. When linguistic study deals with units larger than the sentence, a bridge may be built between linguistics and some kinds of literary study. Similarly, these larger units must furnish the structural approach which can serve as the bridge between the study of linguistic form and of nonverbal behavior patterns.

See, now, various studies by Hill (e.g., 1955), and articles in H. Allen (1958, revised 1964), with some bibliography in Pike and Pike (1960).

Bloomfield states, in a passage highly commending de Saussure, that he "should differ from de Saussure chiefly in basing [his] analysis on the sentence rather than on the word" (1924:319). J. R. Firth, in his analysis of "prosodies", likewise uses an approach which "has the great merit of building on the piece or sentence as the primary datum" (1947), going beyond the word or syllable or individual sound. But it would appear that, as the further step, building on hyper-utterances has some further advantages. Yet even this unit is still not large enough — linguistic analysis must begin with the composite verbal-nonverbal behavioreme.

Numerous recent authors continue to treat the sentence as the basis of linguistic analysis. Note Lees "We take the central problem of linguistic science to be the study of the formal, or syntactic, properties of sentences" (1960a:1). Benveniste states that "Les phrases n'ont ni distribution ni emploi" (in Preprints... 1962:497). W. Haas has the sentence as most inclusive, also (1955).

Compare Chomsky: "From now on, I will consider a *language* to be a set (finite or infinite) of sentences" (1957a:13); and Z. Harris: "no higher-order strings [than sentences] exist (in English)" (1962:49; and cf. 1954b:260); and Postal: "The assignment of sentencehood or grammaticalness can be taken to be the most general feature of the structural description" (1962:2-3).

Our view, on the other hand, continues to be (as in the first edition of this book, 1954) that the sentence is a totally inadequate starting or ending point. Sentences themselves cannot be analyzed without reference to higher-level relationships. A number of writers hold related conclusions. Hjelmslev wishes linguistic theory to prescribe lexical analysis (1953:61). Z. Harris takes the "discourse of one or more persons ... as the fullest environmental unit for distributional investigation" (1954a:158); Gudschinsky followed up Harris' discourse analysis with application to an American Indian language (1959b). Loriot has made studies of intelligibility destroyed when sequence structure beyond sentence length have been distorted in Shipibo (Peru; analysis unpublished; comments based on mimeographed material 1957); for studies concerning paragraph and narrative structure of a related language, see Loos (1963). Various signals which show the relationship of sentences in sequence to English discourse are given by Fries (1952). Yen gives some monologue and paragraph analysis (1960). Jakobson has long been interested in poetic form — insisting (in Sebeok, 1960:350) that poetics may be regarded as an integral part of linguistics. Sebeok, similarly, has discussed the lyric, giving diagrammatic presentation of double structure — of images chosen from human life versus subject matter form non-human nature or objects — linked by conventional devices (in For Roman Jakobson... 1956:438); see also his study of Cheremis charms (1953). With Saporta he has also studied the formal structure of nursery rhymes (in de Sola Pool, 1959). Stennes has discussed "five positions which are filled by clauses [in a discourse]: *Announcement Introduction* BODY *Conclusion Closing*" (1961:9). Longacre has discussed the bearing of context on translation theory (1958b). Law has discussed lengthy introductory greeting forms in Nahuat (1948). Halliday suggests the possibility of the reference of sentence structures to units "above the sentence" for revealing "the range, and cline, of the determination of probabilities by the occurrence of a member of each class" (1961:272, fn. 69). See also Diver (1963:167-68, 172).

I find it of interest to note that a way to tease a child who insists on having a story told him by the unwilling parent, is for the parent to reply with a story which fulfills formal requirements above the sentence, but gives no topic content: *I'll tell you a story about Jack and Madorry, and now my story's begun. I'll tell you another about his brother, and now my story is done.*

The immediate need of analyzing sentences in a larger setting lies in the necessity for separating dependent and independent types in terms of their occurrence in slots in larger structures. Sentences occurring in a slot following a question may differ from those occurring in a slot following a statement. The utterance-response slots and the distributional restrictions which they impose are relevant to the description of the sentence. Waterhouse points out that the independent-dependent relationship occurs on various levels — not only morpheme level, but also for words, clauses and sentences; independent sentences "are defined distributionally as those which can occur as a complete utterance without ambiguity, or which can initiate discourse without necessity for some type of defining context"; dependent sentences are "those which cannot occur as a complete utterance or initiate discourse without some defining context, and which are formally marked for dependence" (1963:46). This grouping crisscrosses with the relation between complete and incomplete. For independent-complete note *Jack threw the ball straight at Susie*; for independent incomplete: *Just got back from Austin yesterday*; for dependent complete: *Consequently there's no water left in the well*, or *He is every inch a man*; dependent incomplete: *But not now,* and *Very nice, really* (1963:46). The article gives an etic listing of dependent and independent types.

Compare Weir, in analysis of the syntax of a solemnant child: "The linguistic material ... could not be presented satisfactorily if it were confined to sentence analysis" (1962:101) since it must account for 'paragraphs' or 'build-up' segments such as *Block — Yellow block — Look at all the yellow block* (82); and *I'm fixing the door — Door's open — I'm locking* (110).

See also § 11.723 for further references.

5.64 *On Meaning in Definitions of Sentence Types*

Among the criteria given in our list in § 5.2, note that item (m) was the presence or absence of an essential (even though only partially definable) purpose or meaning, which seems to differ from Bloomfield. Thus in 1931 he stated that "Needless to say, these meanings [such as 'complete and novel' for favorite sentence form] cannot be defined in terms of our science and cannot enter into our definitions; for every definition of the favorite largest-form types (and of everything else) is to be made in terms of forms, constructions, phonemes, or other linguistically determinable features" (207). How is this to be reconciled with the quote from Bloomfield utilized at the end of § 2.73 that "In language, forms cannot be separated from their meanings" (1943: 102)? The answer seems to me to be that Bloomfield overstated his case in emphasizing two points: (1) that "we must *start* from forms and not from meanings" (1943:103;

italics added; cf. also 1933a:172); and (2) that "to define this (or any other meaning) *exactly*, lies beyond the domain of linguistics" (1933a:172; italics added). The essential nature of the protest against using meaning as a starting point seems overworked when on that basis he excludes meaning from sentence definitions entirely, even though he knew that "In studying a language, we can single out the relevant features of sound only if we know something about the meaning" (1943:102, et al.). In our view, however, we reject *both* the start from meaning *and* the start from pure form, by insisting on treating language as a form-meaning composite, and by insisting on the necessity of working with both of them from the beginning, and of keeping both of them in our definitions. We grant Bloomfield's second protest, that meanings can not be known exactly, but deny his conclusion (that, since meanings cannot be known exactly, they cannot be utilized in definitions of sentence types). Rather we insist that the form-meaning composite must always be treated as such, in any study of nonhypostatic units (but for hypostatic units see § 6.43), and that just as form is always to some extent physiologically and acoustically indeterminate and incompletely known to us (since the ultimate minutiae go beneath nuclear size within the atom, and beyond our powers of direct or indirect observation), so also to some extent meanings and purposes are certain to be ultimately somewhat indeterminate (since the internal neurological events are not subject to our direct observation, and the physical contexts contributing components to meaning are infinite in number within the commuity usage of a form over a period of years). Yet neither of these facts should prevent our utilizing form and meaning as basic, useful hypostatized components in definitions of emic structures. For further discussion of related problems see §§ 6.46, 6.91, and 2.72-73.

Note also Fries' refusal to use meaning as the defining characteristic of structures (1954:60). But for some control of meaning needed during analysis see 1954:74, fn. 6. Chomsky attempts to present a grammar theory which is "completely formal and non-semantic" (1957a:93; cf. also 94, 97, 99-104). He insists that grammatical structure be identified "independently of any semantic consideration", since he affirms that "those who regard semantics as providing the basis, in some sense, for grammar" have implicit to this view the claim that "there are semantic absolutes, identifiable in noises independently of the grammatical structure (in particular, the lexical items) assigned to them" (1961b:232, fn. 25). Note that in this book I affirm the necessity of dealing with form and meaning at the same time, to some degree, and deny the necessity of treating semantic elements as absolutes independent of all lexical and grammatical data. See, also, discussion of transformationalism below, §§ 11.6-7. For Lamb, semantic and phonetic elements are "considered to be outside of the linguistic structure" (1962:15). Note, however, that there are 'sememic' strata in spoken languages (1962:27).

For older convictions about the relations of sentences to ideas expressed by them note Paul (1889:111) and Vendreys (1925:73).

CHAPTER 6

THE MINIMUM UNIT OF THE FEATURE MODE OF THE BEHAVIOREME
(INCLUDING THE MORPHEME)

Thus far we have been talking principally about large units of behavior. Now, in accordance with the outline sketch at the end of § 5.55, we are ready to begin a series of three chapters discussing certain small units within a behavioreme, with one unit as a threshold minimum for each of the three modes. We begin with the minimum unit of the feature mode, since it is from units of this mode that we are operationally first able to establish the threshold which later is the basis for determining a comparable minimum for the units of the other modes (the manifestation mode and the distribution mode).

6.1 *Definition of the Emic Motif*

As a first approximation toward a useful definition of the emic motif we may state:
  Condensed definition: An EMIC MOTIF (or MOTIFEME) is a minimum unit of the feature mode of the behavioreme.

This definition is especially useful in emphasizing the fact that these minimum motif units are not defined by themselves, but can be defined only as relative points in the larger units and systems of which they are a part. Likewise it is useful in emphasizing that ultimately the behavioreme can not be defined without reference to these smaller units which in part comprise the behavioreme, and which are referred to in the definition (§ 5.1) of the behavioreme itself by the phrase 'hierarchically and trimodally structured'. The large units and the small ones, within this theory, are therefore in part mutually defining. Ultimately, neither can be identified nor defined nor described without some degree of explicit or tacit reliance on the other.

Nevertheless, it is important for purposes of detailed study of these units that a more complete description be given which parallels that of the behavioreme (§ 5.1) so that likenesses and differences may the more easily be observed.

  Expanded definition:[1] An EMIC MOTIF (or motifeme) is a minimum, active, trimodally structured, emic segment or component of human activity, within the hierarchy of the feature mode of a minimum or included behavioreme or hyper-behavioreme; it is manifested by free or conditioned, simple or complex, fused or clearly segmented

[1] See fn. for §"5.1.

variants, through the manifested variants of the emic units (or components of the emic units) of the hierarchy of the manifestation mode of a behavioreme; it is co-extensive with and distributed within one or more manifested minimum active slots of the distribution mode of a behavioreme; and it occurs within a trimodally and hierarchically structured system of emic motifs and system of behavioremes, and hence within a structured physical matrix. In any one non-artificial emic system of motifs, all but a relatively small percentage of the motifs must be purposeful or lexically meaningful.

A verbal emic motif is a MORPHEME: a verbal etic motif is a MORPH.

Many of the elements of this definition have been illustrated in earlier sections: the general nature of emic relevance, § 2; problems of segmentation, §§ 3.2, 3.42, 3.61, 5.51; hierarchical structuring, §§ 3.31, 3.62, 4.14, 4.45, 5.3, 5.63; trimodal structuring, §§ 3.5, 5.2; variants, §§ 2.3, 3.52, 5.2, 5.3; emic system, §§ 2.5, 2.6, 2.74, 5.4; setting, § 4.46, 5.2; purpose or meaning, §§ 3.53, 2.2, 4.1.10, 5.52, 5.64; slot, §§ 3.41, 4.18; behavioreme, § 5.

Various other elements in the expanded definition need additional treatment here or in later chapters: the minimum and active characteristics of such a segment; illustrative types of variants of emic motifs; correlation of motif with slots of the distribution mode; and systems of motifs. We will discuss and illustrate most of these elements in connection with the trimodal structuring of morphemes. First, however, we wish to enable the reader to follow the discussion more easily by giving him a few (incomplete) illustrations of emic motifs, both non-verbal and verbal, and by comparing the emic motif with the behavioreme.

6.2 *The Emic Motif Partially Illustrated*

Within the breakfast materials, perhaps 'adults eating a bowl of cereal' is an emic motif,[2] with its feature mode containing a component of purpose-meaning, i.e., in part, 'eating cereal for sustenance.' (Compare B49/13.7 S—: *Daddy, can you help me with my — with this [cereal] so I can be a big man? Will you?*) Movements within this unit — the picking up and filling of the spoon, swallowing the cereal, etc. — are physical components of the feature mode of the cereal-eating motif. Simultaneous composites of such movements constitute physical segments of the manifestation mode of that emic motif; each day the specific sequences of movements in the cereal eating differ etically — the specific way in which the spoon is carried to the mouth, etc. — and constitute etic differences within the manifestation mode of that unit. Variants within the manifestation mode of the cereal-eating eme differ, also, in the extent to which they are discontinuous. On one occasion a toast-eating motif causes the cereal-eating one to be interrupted at numerous points; on another occasion there is

---

[2] See fn. for § 5.3.

less interference. Similarly, it may be relatively little interrupted by conversation, or greatly so, or on brief occasions the records show overlap (speaking with one's mouth full). As for the distribution mode, the cereal-eating motif fills, in most of these records, the slot for the 'main course' at breakfast, and is accordingly usually co-extensive with that slot. Only rarely, in this particular family, is the cereal-eating motif replaced by or followed (or preceded) by a bacon-and-eggs-eating emic motif. The latter, however, occasionally functions as a part of the main course in a heavy breakfast when visitors are present; dry cereal occasionally substitutes for cooked cereal, but two kinds of cereal would not be expected to fill the two parts of the main course for a visitor's breakfast. A further problem remains: the cereal-eating motif is perhaps simultaneously an included behavioreme (§ 5.3); this overlap will be discussed in the next section.

Verbal emic motifs — i.e., morphemes, — like nonverbal ones, occur in the breakfast materials. Note the utterance portion (B36/5.9) M—: ... $^{2\text{-}}$*when we* ^{o2}*fished* $^{2\text{-}}$*in that* ^{o2}*riv*$^{\text{-}1}$*er* | $^{4\text{-}}$*wasn't that* $^{o3\text{-}2}$*fine* |. Here the morphemes include the segmental ones: *when*; *we*; *fish*; *-ed*; *in*; *that*; *river*; *was*; *n't*; *it*; *fine*; and the intonational ones: 2-; ^{o}2; 2-; ^{o}2-1; 4-; ^{o}3-2; the significant breath group type symbolized at its end by the tentative pause mark [|]; and possibly some others of voice quality, rhythm, and so on, which characterize the style of the speaker at that particular moment. (There appear to be four relative, non-absolute but contrasting emic pitch levels in the English intonation system; these we have numbered from high to low, with high pitch as number 1. Where we wish to indicate pitch morphemes we will write the sequence of contrastive pitch levels by superscript numbers preceding the syllable or sequence of syllables over which the pitch contour is spread; the superscript degree sign indicates 'sentence stress', the beginning of a primary contour; hyphens join members of a single total contour; the single vertical bar indicates the pause at the end of a 'poised' or 'tentative' breath group, whereas a double one would have signalled a 'relaxed' or 'final' breath group and pause. For a detailed analysis of the intonation system of English, see Pike, 1945; for a differing analysis, see Trager and Smith, 1951. For the relation of pitch materials to the present theory see § 13.)

Each morpheme is trimodally structured. For example, the morpheme {*not*} (which we enclose in braces — cf. Hockett, 1947b: 278 fn. 11 — and Z. Harris, 1951: 15, fn. 16 to indicate that all variants of this morpheme are being referred to as a group) has a purposive component in its feature mode, meaning 'negation.' The variant *n't* is but one manifested variant of the morpheme, which also includes the variant *not*, with a vowel. These variants are sometimes free and sometimes conditioned; following *was*, in such a colloquial non-emphatic context as that given above (i.e., in *Wasn't that fine*) only *n't* occurs. Under such a context as *He's not...* (following the variant *'s* of {*is*}), only the variant *not*, with a vowel, occurs. As for one sample characteristic of the distribution mode of {*not*}, as a whole, we may see that it is a unique member of a distribution class of morphemes in that it, and it alone, fills the slot after *was* in *Wasn't it?* whereas the morpheme *was* is one member of a distribution class of several morphemes which can come at the beginning of that phrase (e.g., *is*, *has*, *wo-* (*won't*), *would*, and so on).

6.3 *The Emic Motif Contrasted with the Behavioreme*

By comparing the definition of the emic motif (§ 6.1) with that for the behavioreme (§ 5.1) we may note two principal differences: (1) an emic motif is sometimes smaller than a minimum behavioreme — in fact it would usually be so — whereas a behavioreme can never be smaller than an emic motif; and (2) the emic motif as such does not of itself in nonhypostatic contexts carry with it top focus or closure. For example, one expanded minimum (§ 5.3) verbal included behavioremic variant in these materials is (B18/8.5) M—: $^{4\text{-}}Don't\ ^{o3\text{-}}take\ ^{\text{-}2}your\ |\ ^{o3\text{-}}slipp^{\text{-}2}ers\ ^{o1\text{-}2}off\ |$. Within it are the segmental morphemes *Do* (with changed vowel), *n't*, *take*, *your*, *slipper*, *-s*, and *off* plus the simultaneous intonational morphemes 4-, $^{o}3\text{-}2$, $^{o}3\text{-}2$, $^{o}1\text{-}2$, and two breath-group morphemes. No one of these by itself would be likely to constitute a nonhypostatic included behavioreme within the breakfast scene (though as a reply to special situations a combination of *slipper* with an appropirate intonational accompaniment is conceivable, whereas this could never happen with *-s* except in some form of analytical hypostasis).

It is possible, however, for a particular manifested variant of a behavioreme to contain only one emic motif, such that the variant of the behavioreme would begin and end with the beginning and ending of that emic motif. In such an instance the manifested variant of the motif constitutes the manifested variant of the behavioreme. The purposive-meaning components of their respective feature modes is only partially overlapping, however, while the expanded variants of the same emic minimum behavioreme might contain several emic motifs in sequence, and components of their respective distribution modes (including specific and potential function as wholes, and their internal slots) would differ. If, for example, we ignore for a moment the intonational units but look only at the segmental ones, then in the English sentence syntagmeme of 'command', the variant *Come!* is comprised of the single morpheme *come*; yet the same verbal behavioreme could be manifested by different morphemes as in *Run!* or *Jump!*, in which the meaning in the feature mode (i.e., the meaning of 'command') is unchanged, while the morphemes with their meanings are replaced. Other variants of the same emic unit may be of an expanded type, and contain a sequence of several morphemes, as in *Come here!* or *Run fast!* or *Come over here!*

In English we never find a single morpheme as the total manifestation of a total uttereme variant, since in English the latter always contains at least one intonational morpheme simultaneously with the segmental one. In (B18/1) $^{o3\text{-}2}What$, for example, there is the segmental morpheme *what* plus the intonational morpheme which rises from relative pitch level three to relative pitch level two. In Comanche, of Oklahoma, no such obligatory duality of segmental and intonational morphemes seems to occur, since the bulk of the emotional overtones of surprise, fear, disgust, and the like (which in English are often carried by intonational elements) are in Comanche signalled by other means (cf. Smalley, 1953).

In nonverbal behavior I suspect that included behavioremes are much more frequently manifested by single motifs than they would appear to be in English speech even were intonation to be ignored, although not enough work has been done on nonverbal emic motifs for us to be at all certain. Even if the eating of a bowl of cereal is best treated as an emic motif, as we implied above (§ 5.2), it would seem also at times to constitute a manifested variant of the included behavioreme[3] 'eating main course', since there is cultural data indicating that it occasionally comes into focus (e.g., in *What are we going to have to eat?*).

6.4 *The Feature Mode of the Morpheme*

6.41 *Minimum Purposive Units in Reference to Hypostasis in a Componential System*

If, however, we assume that the eating of a bowl of cereal constitutes a minimum purposive unit in the feature mode of the breakfast behavioreme, we must now face a considerable body of evidence which appears to contradict this conclusion and to indicate that there are smaller purposeful elements within such an episode. Cultural evidence demonstrates that attention does sometimes focus on parts of the cereal-eating event in a manner that makes them appear to be purposive. Note such phrases as: *Pick up your spoon*; *Hold it this way*; *Open your mouth*; *Swallow*; *Let go of the spoon* (*held by the teeth*); *Put it down*; *Take another bite*; etc. Why, then, should not these smaller and apparently purposive units be considered the minimum ones, rather than the cereal-eating event as a whole? Why was not the 'threshold' of the minimum unit of the breakfast scene lowered to this point?

The answer seems to be that items such as these occur in special kinds of situations — situations in which the parent is teaching the child or is giving him orders — and this kind of situation and this kind of unit is quite different from the normal (e.g., adult) eating of breakfast which we analyzed. A teaching episode constitutes part of a system which may be included within the larger breakfast eme as a whole. The separate teaching orders constitute hypostatic bits which are not part of a behavioreme of normal breakfast eating. The included teaching or commanding situations are not smaller emic motifs within the normal cereal-eating unit as such, but are rather bits of functional hypostases (§ 4.23) which serve as minimum, emic motifs in a teaching behavioreme included within the eating units, as parts of a simultaneous system in which the teaching units partially overlap in their manifested forms with the larger eating unit.

[3] For portmanteau levels, see §§ 11.222, 11.722.

Similar types of situations where hypostatic elements of the teaching scene are very clearly in evidence are to be observed when one is watching a coach teaching people to swim, or to high jump, or to sing. Specific instructions may temporarily focus attention on details which later must drop below the threshold of participant focus if one is to perform will under competitive situations or in public.

Another type of situation which makes the necessity of such an approach even more clear is the vocal activity in a phonetics class. For the pronunciation of a particular vowel one may hear utterances like *Spread your lips wider*, or *Raise your tongue*, but this very useful attention to details of vocal articulation should not lead the analyst to regard a temporarily purposive and conscious 'raising of the tongue' to be analyzed on a par with verbal items such as *boy*, *cat*, *-ish*, and *-ing*, which — on the basis of nonhypostatic material — are treated as the minimum elements of the feature mode of English verbal emic utterances. It would cause utter confusion, also, to attempt to treat these items of hypostatic behavior on the same level as (that is, in the same system of behavior with) the normal pronunciation of sounds when one is talking rapidly a language which he knows thoroughly. Similarly, it would ultimately prevent a behavioremic analysis if one attempted to equate, on the same threshold level, the items *boy* and *-ish* merely on the basis of their hypostatic use in quotation by a linguist (i.e., in *I said 'boy'*, and *I said '-ish'*).

It is unprofitable to attempt to treat emic motifs of purposive behavior from one system within the framework of the system of another type of behavior even though the two may, as in the breakfast scene, be occurring at the same time, with the same or with different actors (e.g., an adult eating normally while a child is being instructed to eat). We may, indeed, go further and point out that on a larger scale it is ultimately an approach related to this one that allows us to separate French utterances from — say — Chinese utterances, in the speech of a bilingual, or a colloquial from a formal style (see § 16). It is for reasons such as these, also, that words — and even sentences — must not be studied outside of total concrete behavioral contexts under the misapprehension that valid conclusions concerning these isolated, hypostatic data are valid for the description of the units of normal, contextual speech. Normal (i.e., nonhypostatic) and hypostatic verbal systems may be partially congruent without being completely so.

6.42 Sources of Analytical Knowledge of Purposes and Meanings

Purpose and meaning may nevertheless be found, in part, (1) by observing analytical hypostasis within the culture itself — by observing the things that participants say about their purposes and meanings, when trying to give an analysis of them for technical purposes. More important (2) is the observation of what participants imply indirectly or state directly in their conversation at times when they are 'off guard' and are merely acting a normal participant part within which some functional hypostasis

(§ 4.23) does occur. If we were limited to verbal comments by informants, important though these may be, the margin of error would be wider than it actually is, since people sometimes deliberately give false statements about their purposes and meanings, or their observational and analytical ability may be poor, or the range of variation of purpose within a body of participants may be so large as to leave verbal reports confused or conflicting. When a person, for psychological comfort, persuades himself that his purposes are different from those which an objective analysis would indicate are the underlying motives, a further problem arises. Finally, and most important, the analyst (3) may by-pass the use of such materials, by observing regularities of sequence in events, with the assumption that human activity is purposive if it regularly elicits either (a) a positive response activity to the eliciting activity (e.g., shutting the door in response to a request), or (b) a deliberately verbalized or nonverbalized resistance to or rejection of the elicited response (e.g., *I won't*); and from this objective point of view purpose and meaning largely consist of such response elicitations. Note, for example, Fries:

In the study of the language records of a former time we have, because of the nature of the evidence, usually had to try to arrive at the meanings of the language forms by connecting them with recurring elements in the situations in which they were used. In the study of living languages it is often possible to observe directly the responses which particular language forms elicit in a speech community. We assume that if a particular response regularly follows the utterance of a language pattern, then this pattern 'means' this response. Upon such regular recurrences rests the kind of prediction that makes possible the social functioning of languages (1954: 65).

Insofar as the analyst is concerned, in each of these three kinds of data, the objective study of objective responses, whether in the form of verbal activity or of nonverbal activity, is the source of his determination of the presence and nature of meaning and purpose. In utilizing meaning and purpose it is not necessary to have direct access to mental events; the objective data indicated above are sufficient. The detection of this component is possible for the analyst provided that he utilizes all available, observable elements within the cultural data itself, and that he allow for an ample margin of error — especially in situations where lying may be present (§ 6.44).

6.43 *Conceptualized Hypostasis in Participant Awareness of Purpose and Meaning*

One of the observable elements of human behavior, however, and an extremely important one, is precisely the fact that participants in that behavior affirm an awareness or knowledge of meaning or purpose, but without analyzing these meanings or purposes as an awareness of that potential for elicitation of response which we have set forth as the principal component of these meanings. What, then, is the technical analysis of this awareness itself? Or can our theory find room for it, without destroying the objectivity of its approach? Our reply is, first, to accept this fact of affirmed awareness of meanings as an objective observable datum on a par with other observable verbal events; people say things about meanings, and these sayings we collect and study as part of our total corpus of material to be described. Our later step is to treat this awareness in a manner analogous to other situations in which participants in an activity abstract some part of it for observation and discussion outside the immediate context of normal usage — i.e., as some form of hypostasis (cf. § 4.23); this participant awareness of meaning or purpose, and the focusing of attention upon it for discussion or understanding, would be a CONCEPTUALIZED HYPOSTASIS of a potential (i.e., successful or unsuccessful) response elicitation. And it is this characteristic, rather than the more technical matters of response elicitation, which is likely to constitute the predominant usage of the term 'meaning' by the non-analytical participant in speech behavior. The analyst, however, must have a theory which allows the popular hypostatic reaction to meaning to be treated as a specialized instance of a broader technical principal of responses elicited in context, whether that context be an ordinary one or one involving technical or lay personnel performing an analysis. (Cf., for conceptualized hypostasis in regard to slots, § 7.321.)

A similar problem occurs in the analysis of nonverbal materials: Is the analyst to ignore completely the elements which the participants in that activity allege are its purposes? Or is he to take the stated purposes at their face value as being the 'real' purposes of that activity? Our answer is neither of these two. We assume that the basic purpose or meaning of a nonverbal activity, like that of a verbal one, is to be detected by the objective evaluation of objective distributional data of elicited responses as observed by the analyst. Included within the ultimate data to be analyzed, however, are the statements of the participants as they attempt to verbalize their purposes. The units of purpose analyzed in this second type of data may be quite different from those detected in the first data, and the second type constitutes an analysis of the participants' conceptualized hypostatic purposes, whereas the first — the nonverbalized — type of data lead to an analysis of units of behavior of which one component is the nonhypostatic purposive one. For a similar outlook, which seems to me to be arrived at without reference to any over-all theory, note Opler, who says: "Moreover, I continue to believe that a culture is what the investigation of its carriers by the anthropologist proves it to be and not what informants think it is or ought to be. The amount of rationalization, idealism, self-righteousness, and hope evidenced by carriers of a culture is quite properly a part of the culture or at least a [conceptualized hypostatic] commentary on the culture, but it is not a definition of the [nonhypostatic] culture" (1948:116); cf. also Greenberg (1948:143).

At this point we return once more to the difference between a behavioreme and an emic motif: A verbal behavioreme to be analyzed as such must at some point in the data be found as a kind of unit which receives participant focus in nonhypostatic situations. A meaning for a particular variant of an uttereme (but not, sometimes, for the abstracted pattern as a whole) may often easily be found. Since, however, the particular verbal emic motif — the particular morpheme — may be below the threshold of focus of non-analytical members of a culture, they will be unable to report, on questioning, any meaning for some of the morphemes, even though the analyst can satisfy himself by objective study that such items are meaningful and can describe the nature of that meaning. Thus, for example, an English-speaking child may be able to give some reasonably good reply to a question such as *What does 'house' mean?* but be unable to reply adequately to the query *What does '-ly' in 'beautifully' mean?* Adults in a literate society are made aware of many of these items through dictionaries, which in essence are hypostatic listings, but in a pre-literate society the linguist frequently — usually, it seems to me — finds that an adult has little or no understanding of the meanings of his morphemes below the threshold size of included utteremes (cf. 'words', § 11). Some well-planned experiments on such matters might prove very interesting, and are needed for theoretical purposes. (See, now, experiments such as that by Berko [1958, in Saporta, 1961].) For correlation of intention with meaning, see Osgood (1963:741).

6.44 *Indeterminacy and Margin of Error in Analyzing Purpose and Meaning*

In spite of the problems which are involved, it is absolutely essential, if one is to study behavior *as it actually functions*, that one assume that the analyst can detect the presence and to some degree the nature of meaning and purpose. It should be strongly emphasized, however, that this by no means implies that we assume that the analyst is able to detect meaning and purpose without error — rather it is assumed that he does so crudely, with a margin of indeterminacy and of error. Nevertheless his possible degree of accuracy is sufficiently high to enable him to utilize this feature of the morpheme and of the uttereme to help identify these units, provided that from the earliest stages of his analysis he always accompanies the study of this purposive-meaning component of the emic units with a study of the formal components of their physical activity, and attempts the analysis neither of form nor of meaning by itself without reference to the other (cf. §§ 6.46, 5.64, 6.91).

Error in analysis differs from indeterminacy in analysis. Errors in analysis can in principle, at least, be corrected by the analyst or his successors by utilizing more adequate data or more adequate procedures. Indeterminacy, on the other hand, is of a type which in the nature of the case can never be resolved regardless of the amount of data collected; in fact, certain types of indeterminacy increase as one attempts to resolve them the more vigorously. An error, for example, might be quite simple: The analyst may have thought that an informant pointed at a person's eye when he spoke a word, when in fact the informant was pointing at the eyebrow. Or the foreign analyst might assume that for English he had all the usages of the word *table* and define it in reference to four-legged pieces of furniture, before coming across the same term applied to three-legged pieces of furniture.

Indeterminacy of meaning is much more subtle: Is the element *port* the same, in the items *port of entry, to reach port, portal, porthole, portmanteau, portcullis, porter, portentious, Portland, Portugese, portrait, portly?* The data may be such that there are partial phonetic and partial semantic resemblances between certain of these items, but the decision at some point must be arbitrary as to assignment of some of the most perplexing of these items. A theory of the structure of behavior must leave room for variants in both form and meaning, but whithout being able to provide any absolute measure of just how much alike or just how different either form or meaning of the form-meaning composite may be before one can no longer equate two items. In our present theory we state that the indeterminacy lies in the data, within the structure, and that any arbitrary attempt to force a decision one way or another in certain instances does violence to the structure rather than clarifying it.

If, in the face of this problem, we attempt to 'leave it up to the informant' or to ask the informant whether two such items are 'same' or 'different' (§ 2.73), a practical decision may thus be reached for better or for worse, but the technical situation may have deteriorated and become increasingly indeterminate, insofar as the very questioning may itself have *changed* the structure which we were investigating. This follows from materials which we have already indicated; namely, that the meaning of an item is determined by the contexts in which it has been used (§ 2.5). The use of this item *port* in a context composed of the linguist speaking to the informant is part of the total data which now constitutes the background circumstances within which the informant has heard the items used and which determine the meaning for him. The linguist, therefore, has by his process of investigation changed the very data he is investigating: An informant is to this extent 'dissected' — i.e., 'spoiled' as a so-called 'naïve' (i.e., normal) native speaker — and can never again be reconstituted exactly as he was before. Conclusions arrived at by such techniques (which sometimegreatly speed up the analytical process), therefore, must be checked against fresh data unbiased by such questioning. In practice, structural conclusions for which informants are used are often checked against a body of textual material into which this bias could not have entered — say by using recorded conversational material of other speakers.

This problem becomes especially acute, however, if one wishes to investigate the awareness of purpose and meaning rather than these elements without reference to the awareness threshold. It is evident that if an informant has been exposed to a direct question such as *Do you think of 'port' in 'porthole' as the same as 'port' in 'to arrive in port?'* his awareness of such a possibility will then be present whether it was before or not — and in delicate instances the informant finds it impossible to recall how he reacted to such matters before he was questioned. For such reasons, linguists find it necessary to exercise caution in utilizing themselves as their own informants since their analytical procedure can so easily modify the system they are studying, without their being conscious of the fact that a shift in the data is going on at the very time they are working. If two morphs — e.g., two of the above instances of *port* — share the same formal elements of sound or of nonverbal activity, it is still possible for them to be emically distinct, in spite of their likeness in form; such a verbal pair constitutes a set of homonyms; a nonverbal pair is a set of homomorphic motifs. Intentional acts, for example, constitute different emic motifs from unintentional acts homomorphic with them: the obviously deliberate spilling of milk on the table at breakfast differs from the nondeliberate spilling of milk and elicits a different parental reaction. The intentional grounding of a forward pass in football differs from the mere failure to pass it accurately (§ 4.1.10). As we have already indicated (§ 2.2) a culture may have specific procedures, in courts of law, to determine intention and purpose in retrospect in order that the culture may know what are the next acts appropriate for that culture; even the culture itself provides for indeterminacy at such points in that there are courts for appeal against the decision of lower courts. An analysis of the culture therefore must not distort the structural picture by concealing the fact that it is the culture itself which allows for such indeterminacy. In the instances in which it is possible to differentiate emically between homonyms or homomorphic units, however, the fact that they are different must be determined (1) by the difference of distribution of the two units within larger units, (2) by their structural function within the total system, and (3) by differences of purpose or meaning which are sufficiently sharp to warrant their being handled as emically separate. Here the word 'sufficiently' leaves an ultimate area of indeterminacy.

It is clear, furthermore, that the meaning of a morpheme can be so greatly weakened in certain contexts that the respective variants of the morpheme in these contexts have little meaning in common (compare the use of *terrible* in the phrases *terribly good*, *terribly bad*, *terribly funny*, and *a terrible sight*). The amount by which any two members of a morpheme can differ in meaning and yet remain variants of that morpheme is dependent upon the total system to which it belongs.

6.45 *Morphemes Without Lexical Meaning*

For the moment, we shall use the term 'lexical meaning' or 'dictionary meaning' without attempting a detailed technical discussion of it (but see §§ 10 and 16). For our present purpose it is sufficient to state (a) that this is the kind of meaning which is analytically assigned to the units of the feature mode of a verbal behavioreme whenever such meanings are found at all, (b) that it is sometimes above the awareness threshold of the untrained native speaker, in conceptualized hypostasis of the potential response elicitations (§ 6.43), and (c) that it specifically excludes certain types of meanings derived from the manifestation and distribution modes of the behavioreme — meaning types which have not yet been discussed (§§ 7.321 and Chapter 16). The lexical meaning of *boy*, for example, is roughly 'male child'; of *-ish*, 'having the traits of'.

Where no lexically-meaningful component can be detected for a morpheme it may be called an EMPTY one. Such empty morphemes can be carefully identified only as a residue following the analysis or partial analysis of elements which are meaningful. Some of the reasons underlying the necessity for this procedural delay are probably (1) the fact that the large majority of those sequences of sounds which early in the analysis appear to be meaningless will later prove to be (a) lexically meaningful, with the meaning at first obscure but later identified, or (b) mistakenly segmented into a tentative morpheme, so that it is later shown to belong to a part of a large sequence of sounds as part of a larger morpheme manifested by that longer sequence (or mistakenly segmented in such a way that it comprises parts of two morphemes, etc.) or (c) proves to be not a live morph, but a dead one, and hence part of an etically complex morpheme (see § 6.54 and § 6.1, definition), and (2) that a system of utteremes is functionally a communicative (as well as an esthetically expressive) device on a level of conceptual awareness — but that that function could not be served by a language with too large a proportion of lexically-meaningless elements as members of its feature mode which must carry the major portion of the conceptual burden. If, however, this reasoning proves to be inadequate, and not replaceable by a more fruitful argument, then we would change our justification to a purely empirical one — that few such elements are in fact found.

Empty morphemes are sufficiently infrequent in English to make it difficult to find examples which are not open to challenge. Perhaps the element *does*, in the sentence *Does he go to the school here?* is adequate (cf. Fries, "this *does* has no lexical meaning whatever" 1952:149). If so, then the reader should be prepared to find this type discussed again, when their grammatical function is under consideration (§ 7.324). Occasionally one (or more) sounds occurs between two apparent morphemes, without being clearly assignable to the one or to the other, yet with no clear meaning of its own. It might prove more useful to analyze such an element as one morph of a morphetically-complex morpheme whose other morph is one of the adjacent ones. Compare *meritorious* where the *merit* and *-ous* are separated by *-ori-*; in this instance my preference would be to treat *-ori-* as not an active element, since it is not found with a wide variety of stems and suffixes, but to treat it as an etic part of the total etically-complex variant *-orious*.

Certain English exclamatory elements in which the meaning is largely obtained by the intonation superimposed upon them might be illustrative of another kind of empty or partially empty morpheme. I am uneasy about such an analysis, however, since an item like *mhm*, which seems at first to be almost an empty morph, cannot be quite handled in this way. The rising intonation which accompanies it, and which together with it means 'yes', does not by itself mean 'yes' — so part of this lexical meaning seems to come from the segmental unit itself. Furthermore, it seems to be in some quasi-contrast with the segmental part of such an item as *mʔm*, with morpheme-medial closure of the vocal cords, since this morpheme plus its accompanying intonation means 'no' even though that intonation on other items does not necessarily imply negation.

A further kind of empty morpheme would be an ARTIFICIAL one. These are delibe-

162   THE MINIMUM UNIT OF THE FEATURE MODE OF THE BEHAVIOREME

rately created by some individuals. Note, for example, the following, from W. Kelly (1952:19):

> *With his filibeg fair filligreed*
> *With finest filiform,*
> *He fleetly footed froo and fro*
> *The figwort in the storm.*
> *A flaught of borealis and a*
> *Firkin fine of fat*
> *Was fimbricated on the fringe*
> *Of Frelinghuysen's hat.*

Quite different from these are the empty morphemes which occur in structurally active classes, and hence are structurally active themselves even while lexically nonproductive. These are found as elements of frequently repeated stereotyped phrases or 'formulas'. Consider, for example, *rack* in the phrase *rack and ruin*; or *shrift* in *to make short shrift of*; or *wax* in *wax and wane*. In terms of nonverbal behavior similar problems arise. Thus the activity of sewing buttons on the sleeve of a man's coat is a process with little current purpose outside of its 'formula' value as it fits into the pattern of making a coat in a fashion acceptable to society.

6.46 Contrastive-Identificational and Meaningful-Formal Characteristics of a Morpheme

The sum of the physical components of the feature mode of any morpheme will be seen to cover the same data as the sum of the components of all the variants (§ 6.5) of the manifestation mode of that morpheme. The structuring of the data, however, is quite different in the two modes. In the analysis of the manifestation mode of a morpheme into variants, we will find (§ 6.5) that the basic product is a number of NON-SIMULTANEOUS SEGMENTS of activity, no two of which occur at the same moment and place in any one behavior event. In the analysis of the feature mode of a morpheme, however, a basic product is a number of SIMULTANEOUS COMPONENTS which cut 'horizontally' through time, instead of 'vertically', so that several of them may be occurring at a single moment of time in one of the variants of that morpheme.

For any one particular culture, these components may often be divided into distinct sets in accordance with their membership in certain simultaneous componential systems — especially, for verbal motifs, with pitch as a component versus articulatory components. Such an outlook, on a higher level of focus, underlies the analysis of a complex behavioreme into verbal versus nonverbal elements or systems.

Although we have discussed the formal characteristics of the morpheme here as if they were separable from the meaning characteristics, which we discussed in §§ 6.41-45, a correction must now be made: *Neither the formal component nor the meaning component of a morpheme must be treated as a nonhypostatic eme*[4] *in its own right*, even though both are given a hypostatic unity in the activity of the analyst (cf. conceptualized hypostasis in §§ 6.43, 7.321). Rather a lexically-meaningful morpheme constitutes a FORM-MEANING COMPOSITE (but for lexically-meaningless morphemes see § 6.45) in which both analytically-observed components are so fused in actual activity that neither may be abstracted as a unit for normal participants acting in a nonhypostatic manner. This point of view has been relevant to our discussion on two previous occasions (§§ 2.2, 5.64), and is certain to recur again (e.g., § 6.91).

Similarly, every eme is simultaneously *identificational* as well as *contrastive*. That is to say, that once a morpheme is discovered, by observing its contrastive relationships to other morphemes in a system of morphemes (§§ 6.7, 16), that morpheme can then be identified in other circumstances where some of the contrastive morphemes do not occur. Here, again, a composite label is necessary to represent this point of view: a morpheme is an CONTRASTIVE-IDENTIFICATIONAL COMPOSITE of features. Only in analytical conceptualized hypostasis (§§ 6.43, 7.321, can we view these elements as separate; they are not assumed, in this theory, to constitute separate emes in their own right in nonhypostatic behavior.

6.5 *The Manifestation Mode of the Morpheme*

The basic elements of the manifestation mode are the separate repetitions, or different occurrences, of that same morpheme. The sum of the occurrences of a morpheme makes up the total manifestation mode of that morpheme.

6.51 *Identical Manifestations*

In referring to the SAME VARIANT OF A MORPHEME, we shall mean, except when it is stated specifically otherwise, that two or more instances or occurrences of that morpheme (a) have the same verbal emic units of sound — the same phonemes — manifesting them, and (b) have meanings so similar that the analyst at that moment does

---

[4] Our recent studies in the permutation and conflation of matrices of morphological formatives (1963e) bring the term 'category' into the theory as a formal component of a vector of an emic matrix. Within such a matrix the category either comprises an emic semantic unit, or an emic component of the matrix itself as an emic form-meaning composite. This could later force an amplification of the theory. A simple morpheme with a one-to-one correspondence of form and meaning would represent a simple instance of a vector-patterned formative in a matrix. When vector formative is not consistent specific treatment is necessary. Recent generative approaches will perhaps raise a quite different set of questions concerning the treatment of conventional morphemes, as it has done for phonemics (see § 8.815). Note Householder: "Taxonomic morphemes are of little value for generative grammar" (in Saporta, 1961:20; compare Voegelins' hunch in 1963:29). For further discussion of lack of correspondence — while insisting on a form-meaning relationship of a nondirect kind — see also F. Palmer (in Preprints... 1962).

not detect differences between them. If, however, the analyst notices that two same variants of a morpheme nevertheless differ slightly phonetically, in that the phonemes in the two instances are the same but the manifesting variants of the phonemes have differed slightly but nonphonemically, he may choose to refer to these instances as different PHONETIC VARIETIES OF THE SAME PHONEMIC VARIANT OF THAT MORPHEME. Such phonetic varieties of a phonemic manifestation of a morpheme occur at every repetition of a morpheme, inasmuch as no two physiological movements can be exactly duplicated (§ 2.3; for phonetic variation, see also § 8.44).

Repeated utterances of *cat*, therefore, or the word *cat* in the two utterances *I saw the cat*, and *My cat is here*, would be the 'same' variant of the morpheme *cat* in so far as its emic sounds were concerned, even though some slight physical variation in those sounds is certain to occur in the various repetitions. On the other hand, *am* does not have the same variants in the two utterances *I am going* and *I'm going*, since the loss of the vowel in the second utterance is the loss of an emic unit of sound.

6.52 *Free Variants of a Morpheme*

Phonemically-different morpheme variants each of which (1) has the same effect on the hearer, (2) with no predictability of occurrence (a) in reference to the local linguistic environment or (b) in reference to the social environment or to the general style are COMPLETELY FREE. In my dialect the different pronunciations of the noun *address*, with stress on first and on second syllable, respectively, seem to illustrate such completely-free variation. On the nonverbal level, there are completely-free variants within the breakfast scene, as for example the precise manner in which one alternates bites of toast with spoonfuls of cereal. Every completely-free variant of a morpheme is LOCALLY free. The particular environment of the morphemes in sequence with it neither causes the selection of nor prevents the presence of the particular variant under attention.

Whenever an emic unit is manifested by two different variants, it is sometimes convenient to speak of each variant as a ALLO-UNIT, or allo-eme. Variants of a morpheme, therefore, would constitute allomorphic variants of a morpheme, or ALLOMORPHS.

6.53 *Locally-Conditioned Variants of a Morpheme*

On the other hand, a morpheme may be manifested by LOCALLY-CONDITIONED variants, in which the selection of variant is determined by the surroundings within which the manifested unit is occurring. Within the present theory, this conditioning can perhaps be most easily described by stating that the manifested form of the morpheme can be modified under the impact of its occurrence in or adjacent to any of the three kinds of units of the respective modes of the uttereme: It may be conditioned by occurring adjacent to a minimum unit of the manifestation mode of the uttereme (which would be an emic unit of sound, a phoneme), or to the minimum unit of the feature mode of the uttereme (i.e., another morpheme), or within — i.e., manifesting — a slot-class correlative of the distribution mode of the uttereme (i.e., a tagmeme).

Note that these enter a matrix of types of variants:

Conditioned Variants of Morphemes

	Phonological Variants	Semantic Variants
(A) Locally Conditioned		
(1) by adjacent morpheme	-s ~ -en	*drive a car/horse*
(2) by adjacent phoneme	-s ~ -es	*flip flap*
(3) by manifested tagmeme	I ~ me	*terribly beautiful*
(B) Systemically Conditioned	*can't*	*queer bird*

An illustration of a morpheme modified by its phonological environment is the 'plural' morpheme in English. Following the words *cat, bat, cup,* etc., it has the variant *-s*, without the vibration of the vocal chords. A different variant (*-es*) of the same morpheme follows the words *house, mouse, juice,* and other words which end in a sibilant sound; it is this minimum unit of sound which determines the selection of the *-es* variant of the plural morpheme, just as it is the particular type of articulation at the end of *cat*, and *cup*, which determines the occurrence of the *-s* variant after those words. The evidence leading to this kind of conclusion is the large number of examples following these patterns. In general, it may be said that this kind of conditioning is REGULAR and produces PHONOLOGICAL VARIANTS OF MORPHEMES, PHONEMICALLY CONDITIONED.

Local conditioning by adjacent morphemes may be illustrated by another manifested variant of the same plural morpheme, the *-en* plural on *oxen*. Here the occurrence of that particular variant of the plural morpheme is limited to a position immediately following the particular morpheme *ox*; the occurrence of *-en* is conditioned by the occurrence of *ox*. In general, this kind of conditioning is IRREGULAR, and produces PHONOLOGICAL VARIANTS OF A MORPHEME MORPHEMICALLY CONDITIONED.

The variant *me* occurs in certain slots in the distribution hierarchy of the behavioreme where *I* does not occur, and vice versa — e.g., in the instances *I came home; He met me*. It may be assumed that the two variants of {I} are PHONOLOGICAL VARIANTS OF A MORPHEME, TAGMEMICALLY CONDITIONED.

Is there any essential degree of similarity in sound to which two variants of a morpheme must conform, if they are to be considered variants of that morpheme? We have implied, so far in this discussion, that there is no such restriction, since we have treated *-en* and *-s* both as variants of {-s plural} and *I* and *me* as variants of {I}. We wish, now, however, to add a general empirical type of restriction similar to that given for the presence of meaningless emic motifs in a system (§ 6.1.). In any one system, there can be only a relatively SMALL NUMBER OF MORPHEMES WITH PHONOLOGICALLY-UNRELATED VARIANTS. If any system were at some time to contain a great number of phonologically-unrelated members of units, it would presumably disintegrate as a system, or else undergo a reorganization of its parts; communication depends upon the ability of the users of a system to recognize its signals upon the repetition or reoccurrence of those signals, so that the mass of them must have manifested variants which are phonologically alike to a recognizable degree. From an operational point of view, therefore, any phonologically-nonsimilar variants should be accepted as members of a single morpheme only as a residue of elements after the bulk of the language has been analyzed without reference to such units.

Morphemic variants, however, are not limited to changes in their phonological content. Their semantic characteristics, also, may be modified (as we implied in § 6.44), and give SEMANTIC VARIANTS OF MORPHEMES. This modification may be caused by their juxtaposition to a morpheme or morpheme sequence, as *drive* in *to drive a car* means something slightly different — i.e., is a different semantic variant — from what it does in *to drive drive a horse*. An allomorph is a SEMANTIC VARIANT OF A MORPHEME, MORPHEMICALLY (or LEXICALLY) CONDITIONED when the neighboring morpheme is the conditioning element. The degree of semantic variation which can occur in any of these conditioned changes of meaning is indeterminate (§ 6.44). (Changes in the meaning of morphemes which are forced on them by their occurrence in certain tagmemic slots — i.e., SEMANTIC VARIANTS OF MORPHEMES, TAGMEMICALLY CONDITIONED — will be discussed in § 7.323.) If phonemes of neighboring morphemes affect the meaning of a morpheme, a SEMANTIC VARIANT OF THAT MORPHEME, PHONEMICALLY CONDITIONED is produced. This may occur in verse, if the semantic impact of a particular morpheme is heightened by its relation to other morpheme which rhyme or are in alliteration with it. Note, for example, the effect of the use of [f] in the verse by W. Kelly, § 6.45. Here, also, we could include 'symbolic' elements such as *flip flap*; size change from small to large is suggested by the vowels. (See also § 16.83.)

6.54 *Morphetically-Complex Variants of a Morpheme*

A variant or member of a morpheme is etically SIMPLE when no smaller meaningful morphs can be observed within it. It is this type of morpheme which we have discussed thus far. Occasionally, however, it is useful to postulate single morphemes which have etically COMPLEX variants. Within them two (or more) meaningful units can be detected, but in a sequence which as a whole must be analyzed as a single minimum active variant of that morpheme. (Much of the relevant discussion pertaining to these complex items will be delayed until § 6.61, but an illustration or two may be helpful at this point.)

A morpheme may be morphetically simple in those instances in which a single morph such as *boy* constitutes the only variant of the morpheme. In a word like *hamlet*, in which the morph *ham-* occurs with the same active morph *-let* as occurs with *brook* in *brooklet*, we conclude that the *ham-* is not active (since it does not seem to occur with other suffixes, nor by itself, nor have any present functional relation to a word like *home*); we then further conclude that the total word *hamlet* is a single active but morphetically-complex variant of a morpheme composed of the two morphs *ham-* and *-let*. (The word *oxen*, however, would be a sequence of two morphemes, since the *-en*, though not occurring with other morphemes, is nevertheless analyzed — see § 6.53 — as a variant of an active morpheme.) The word *breakfast* would here be analyzed as a single active morpheme. If, however, *break-* and *-fast* were to be treated as separate morphs (on the alleged ground that the present native reaction to the parts of the word would allow for the analysis of a present structural connection with the full words *break* and *fast*, or because of the clustering of consonants in the middle of it), then *breakfast* would be treated as morphetically complex, but a single morpheme. Similarly, if one concludes (because of parallels with *conceive*, *deceive*, *convict*, *depict*, etc.) that *receive* contains two morphs *re-* and *-ceive*, then in our treatment we would further state that the two morphs are members of a single morphetically-complex morpheme. My personal preference (for semantic and distributional reasons) is to treat *receive* as a single morph, and not to divide it etically. The theory here allows for both starting points, but each arrives at the same essential conclusion for the word as a whole — that it is but one morpheme. Some of the linguists who treat words like *conceive* as containing two morphemes (Bloomfield, 1933a:209, 240-46, 366; Nida, 1949:59) likewise treat words like *hammer* or *spider* as containing two (Bloomfield, 1933a; Nida in 1946, but not in 1949:60). Here, likewise, we would treat the words as single morphs rather than sequences of morphs. The net result would be somewhat the same in our theory for both approaches, since were we to treat them as composed of two morphs in sequence, we would then further analyze them as comprising a morphetically-complex variant of a single morpheme. Similarly, were we to follow Bloomfield (1933a:245) in setting up the 'symbolic' element *-ash* of *bash*, *clash*, *crash*, *dash*, *flash*, *gash* as a 'root-forming' morpheme meaning 'violent movement', we would then indicate further that the entire word *flash* is a single morpheme which would turn out to be morphetically complex.[5]

It would seem, moreover, that a word like *truth* could be treated easily in this way as containing two clear morphs — *true* and *-th* — but only one active, morphetically-complex morpheme. The approach allows us to postulate a substructuring of morphs without destroying its functional analysis as a single unit.

A special instance of an etically-complex morpheme is one in which the member is DISCONTINUOUS; the total variant is interrupted by a second morpheme, so that the 'first' morpheme occurs split into two or more noncontiguous parts. For a nonverbal

---

[5] For possible treatment of these elements as a variety of formative in a matrix, compare footnote to § 6.46, and Pike 1963d.

illustration of a discontinuous emic motif, note that the cereal-eating motif may be interrupted by a bite of toast, and then continued.

Within this theory, however, there is a restriction as to the application of this principle of discontinuous morphs of a morphetically-complex morpheme: Two noncontiguous members of a single morphetically-complex morpheme cannot be members respectively of two distinct words. A single morpheme whether morphetically simple or morphetically complex can be simultaneously a member of two hypermorphemes only at a point of fusion between them. Words would be instances of such hypermorphemes if they were composed of a stem, let us say, plus an affix, so that this principle rules out the approach of Z. Harris who sets up, as single morphemes, combined discontinuous elements in concord (1945a; 1951:166, 182, 205, 210) such that within *filius bonus* the ... *us* ... *us* "together constitute one broken morpheme, meaning male" (1951:166; and see, for a discussion of the theoretical implications of this problem, Bazell, 1953:6-7, 9-10). See also §§ 7.322, 7.56.

6.55 Fused versus Clearly-Segmented Variants of Morphemes

The etically-simple morphemes so far discussed have been relatively simple to segment one from the other. (It has been easy to see where one morpheme stopped and the other began, provided that we assume, as we have done, that we know what the emic units of sound are and do not become concerned with drawing any line between the physical manifestations of these sounds in sequence — a problem which will concern us in § 8.4.) In *cats* there are clearly the two units, *cat* and *s*. The determining of this fact, were English language strange to us, will be discussed in § 6.81; here we wish only to mention the results of such analysis and its simplicity. The problem becomes more difficult, however, when we try to find *will* in *won't*, since the change of vowel leaves us at first uneasy, because of the changed physical form of the variants; nevertheless, the *will* is clearly not phonemically reflected in the *n't*, so we would divide the two morphemes as *wo- -n't*. The problem becomes acute, however, when a single sound joins two morphemes in sequence and cannot be assigned to either of them. In a rapid pronunciation of *as you* (*like*), the *as* and *you* sometimes have such a sound, [ž], between them. Even more difficult is a situation in which two words are completely coalesced into a single emic unit of sound; compare, for example, the slow pronunciation of *Did you enjoy it?* with a very rapid, slurred /jɪnǰoi ɪt/, in which the first syllable (pronounced the same as *gin* in *ginger*) contains such a fusion. Our definition, in § 6.1, made provision for such elements, and hence needs to be illustrated here; our analysis of these items and of zero variants, however, will be given in Chapter 14.

6.56 Locally-Free but Systemically-Conditioned Variants of Morphemes

A morphemic variant is SYSTEMICALLY CONDITIONED when it is determined by — and in turn helps to signal the presence of — the particular nonsimultaneous componential system (§§ 5.4, 16) or style within which the morpheme is being produced, but is not determined by the morphemes, as such, which are adjacent to it. If a particular analyst is ignoring the social connotations derived from such systems or styles, these variants are likely to appear in his analysis as completely free variation, inasmuch as no local factors are determining their occurrence.

In the nonverbal materials such systemically (stylistically) conditioned variants of emic motifs occur in the breakfast scene: There may be more formality, for example, when visitors are present. Specifically, the family might be more careful to all begin their cereal-eating together, after waiting for each person to finish his fruit juice.

Of the verbal motif variants, note those morpheme abbreviations which are used in good colloquial speech but which would be avoided by some speakers in formal contexts. There appear to be some speakers, for example, who instead of saying *can't*, try always to say *cannot* in public address, but who would use the abbreviated form in conversation. Here the variants *n't* and *not* constitute locally-unconditioned but SYSTEMICALLY-CONDITIONED PHONOLOGICAL VARIANTS OF A MORPHEME, inasmuch as the neighboring morphemes are not responsible for this difference; they are stylistically conditioned in that the general formality system determines for that particular actor the variant of *not* which he will use.

Similar systemically-conditioned but locally-unconditioned elements will meet us in various places in the analysis (see, for example, § 8. 441). This implies that the system of morphemes must be determined separately for each system or style, and that then we may find that two or more systems have many (or most) of their morphemes in common, even though the variants manifesting some of them differ.

Occasionally a hypercongruent system (§ 5.4) will contain two variants of a morpheme, distributed in such a way that only one of the variants occurs in one style, but that either of the variants may optionally occur in the other. Here it is the option which is conditioned by the style, not a single variant form as such. This would be the situation for a person who uses both *can't* and *cannot* in non-emphatic public address, but who uses only *can't* in non-emphatic conversation.

We also find SYSTEMICALLY-CONDITIONED SEMANTIC VARIANTS OF MORPHEMES (cf. § 6.53) which are in part conditioned by the style or congruent system (§§ 5.4, 7.313(4)) or by the lexical context (§ 7.313(4)) or setting (§§ 4.46, 7.313(4)) in which they happen to be occurring at the time. Note, for example, the semantic variant of *bird* in *He is a queer bird* as over against a different linguistic (and, presumable, physical) setting in *That is a queer bird*.

6.6 The Distribution Mode of the Morpheme

6.61 Activeness of Morphemes

In § 6.1 we indicated that morphemes were ACTIVE (or live, productive); see also § 7.51.

This chracteristic is important but its delineation meets with serious practical difficulties, since structural indeterminacy leads not merely to a static blurring of borders but to a dynamic readiness to change.

As a first test for activeness, we suggest that when a slot in a pattern can have any one of a large number of purposive or meaningful elements occurring there, each of these elements is active. Thus in the sentences *I saw John*; *I saw Bill*; *I saw Jim*; *I saw Tom*; the items *Tom, Bill, Jim* are seen to be active.

(Similarly in the utterances *I saw the great big boy*; *I saw all the men*; *I saw ten sheep*; the items *the great big boy, all the men*, and *ten sheep* are active. These latter, however, are not minimum elements and hence not single morphemes even though they are active ones. That they are not minimum can be demonstrated by further active substitutions, thus: *the great big man, the great big sheep, the great big house*, etc.).

A second test for activeness is that the item joins in a larger unit where elements are so substituted, even though it cannot itself be replaced by substitutions of this type. In *cats, houses, dogs, pigs, tables, chairs* the plural element is active because of the active materials preceding it, even though no other morphemes can substitute for the plural one.

A third test for activeness is seen when a particular purposive unit can occur in a wide variety of different kinds of functional slots. Note, for example, the morpheme *big* in the utterances *I saw the big boy*; *He is too big*; *He is not big enough*; *Bigness is not of itself desirable*.

A fourth test is that new combinations previously unknown to the language can be demonstrated to have occurred within recent times. Thus *-burger* in *cheeseburger* seems now to be active, in parallel with its usage in *hamburger*.

This, however, poses a problem of indeterminacy: Is one such new usage sufficient to indicate that an item is active? Does that one particular element have to have widespread usage throughout the community, or only in the speech of a few of its individuals? At some point it would appear certain that elements such as *-burger* become active and productive; at other times it would seem certain that an item has no such productive activeness; in between there is a fuzzy border line.

A former active morpheme may become so joined to a neighboring morpheme that it loses its productivity, and constitute with its neighbor a single etically-complex active form. I would suggest, for example, that both *brook* and *-let* are still active in *brooklet*, but that *hamlet* constitutes a single etically-complex morpheme in which the first part is now certainly not active (cf. § 6.54).

This raises a further question as to whether, when an inactive element is coalesced to an active one, the active element still retains its active character in the new combination. Our solution is to suggest that some etic morphs (like *cran-*, and like *ham-* of *hamlet*) are inactive, while others, like *-let* and *berry* may constitute fully active morphemes in some environments, but in other environments constitute SEMI-ACTIVE members of etically-complex morphemes.

The question may be raised as to whether a single morpheme may comprise two etic morphs both of which may be semi-active. Possibly a word like *greenhouse* (which is not green, but a place where green plants are grown) would fit such a category. If so, then compounds which are not regularly formed (and especially those which have a specialized meaning) might be handled in some such way. If we were to treat *greenhouse* as a single etically-complex morpheme, then *Jack-in-the-pulpit* would likewise be a single etically-complex morpheme, but one in which there were four semi-active morphs. If this does not prove useful, however, then in the present theory they would be treated on a higher level of the hierarchy of the feature mode of the behavioreme, as a special unit in such a higher layer (Chapter 10).

This leads to a fifth criterion of activeness, namely, the presence of a meaning (a) which is relatively easy to determine and (b) which is seen to contribute in a regular fashion to the total meaning of the morph sequence of which it is a part. The *green-* of *greenhouse* meets condition (a), but fails to meet condition (b), which is rather met in the phrase *a green house*. Completely-inactive items such as the *cran-* of *cranberry* fill neither of these conditions.

As a sixth criterion, related to the fifth, we are likely to consider active any morph which the native speaker, upon questioning, can describe, or discuss easily, or define; e.g., one occasionally hears a linguist say to an informant: *Does X mean anything?* If the answer is *No*, or a shrug, the test does not prove activeness — nor does it prove passiveness. This test, however, may increase the indeterminacy of the ultimate analysis and the errors within it, by modifying the linguistic structuring of the informant, as we indicated in § 6.44.

As a seventh criterion, we recognize as fully active any morph at the time it is constituting the only segmental morph manifesting an uttereme, as *boy* in the exclamation *Boy!*[6]

As an eighth criterion, we note that there are oftentimes intonational or pausal options on or at the borders of active morphs which are normally (i.e., apart from hesitation, hypostasis, etc.) absent from an inactive morph. A glide and stress may optionally occur on the active *re-* of *re-cover* (meaning 'to cover again') which would not appear under the same conditions on the first syllable of *recover* ('to gain back').

As a ninth criterion, one may note that the investigator is more likely to consider a morph active if it is easily segmented out of a continuum, so that its borders are clear, than he is if the morph is fused (§§ 6.55, 6.66, 7.45, 14) to another morph or morphs.

Inactive etic morphs are passive (or nonproductive, "dead"). These (1) may constitute morphs which previously were active but now have lost their productivity (cf. *break* in *breakfast*; *-th* in *truth*) or (2) they may appear as the end product of borrowing from a second language certain elements which there patterned actively, but which the borrowing language does not treat as such (as *re-* and *-ceive* in *receive*; but cf. § 6.54); or (3) they may constitute inactive elements coupled to elsewhere active ones

---

[6] Bolinger suggests to me that a further type of bondage should be recognized — one in which items like *Ouch!* are limited to a particular type of utterance, such as exclamation. Otherwise *ouch* would be analyzed as fully free.

(*cran-* in *cranberry*; *-eteria* in such a neologism as *wash-eteria* modeled after *cafeteria*). At the border line there is considerable indeterminacy, since, for example, an item like *-eteria* may at some uncertain point become active if it is used freely and naturally by enough people in a variety of combinations; here the passive element itself becomes active, while the semi-active element to which it is attached becomes fully active by becoming part of a productive class of items occurring in that position. Even a passive morph, however, may often have a somewhat explicit, or else a vague contribution to the total semantic meaning of the element of which it is a part. Note, for example, the semantic function of passive morphs[7] in many neologisms, as for the *utter-* in *uttereme* (as an abbreviation of *utterance-eme*, § 5.1).

6.62 Parasitic (Latent) Morphs, and Differences in Participants

Certain other kinds of elements become partially active in quite a different way, as PARASITIC morphs which are the result of a kind of folk etymology, which finds within a word of one overall meaning an included sequence of sounds which is homophonous, or partially homophonous, with some other word historically unrelated to the host word. Thus some persons react in their avoidance or usage of words as if they observed *fake* in *fakir*, *bust* in *robust*, *sex* in *sextet*, *nigger* in *niggardly*, *noise* in *noisome*, *religious* in *sacrilegious*, *pun* in *pundit*, etc. (A. Read, 1949:306-12, whence the terms 'parasitic' and 'host' also are borrowed). I was mentioning this linguistic characteristic to one adult, for example, and illustrating it with the word *fakir*; this person replied: *I thought 'fakir' was where we got the word 'fake'!* Such reactions can be observed in young children, as well as in ordinary conversation or in puns of adults; note these I have observed: S—: *Daddy, are those your alligator shoes?* F—: *Yes.* S—: *What do you alligate 'em with?*; or F—: *...without alloy!* S—: *Daddy, What's "loy"?*; or B69/10.1 B—: *... terramycin [medicine].* S—: *[No!] It's mine!*; or F—: [teaching the name of Webster Lake, Mass.] *... Chargoggagoggmanchaugagoggchaubunagungamogg.* S—: *Ladies chaugagogg*; or S—: *In the middle of 'leggings' they start with 'guns', don't they?* (in which *leggings* contained a mid central vowel in the second syllable). Or note the following incident: 72/13 F—: *His little toe's awfully big, isn't it?* S—: *His little toe, is off?* F—: *Is big!*

Any meaningless sounds not included in such a parasitic part of the host word would constitute a passive morph; the part under attention would therefore be parasitically semi-active. In *pundit*, when viewed in this way, the *-dit* would be passive, the *pun-* parasitically semi-active, and the whole would constitute a single morpheme which temporarily or optionally (or dialectally) is etically complex with an included parasitic element.

Occasionally the nonparasitic part would also become fully active, or be equated to

---

[7] Compare the intricate crisscrossing of submorphemic formatives (Pike and Erickson, 1964) in a morphological matrix.

an active element; note that the *-r* in *fakir* becomes equated with the *-er* in *farmer*, once the first part is equated to *fake*. Note also, in written humor, the near-activeness of *-minton*, with near-emptiness of meaning (§ 6.45), in the following conversation: Elephant: ...*join in a game of badminton*; Donkey: *I'm playing a game of good-minton* (W. Kelly, 1952:185); also, same author, *ignoromnibus* (20), *rebellicosely* (22), *stuck on a technicalorie* (28), in which the analysis involves further partial identifications of forms. Recently a colleague called to my attention that his daughter said *I don't want to go to your ami, but to mother's ami* (she had been told that they were going to *Miami* — and since they had been visiting her mother's uncle she wanted to insist on the particular relationship).

I recall the incident when I first heard someone read in a Church of England service the phrase *manifold blessings*, with the pronunciation *many-fold*; for the first time it occurred to me that this *mani-* was the 'same' as *many*. My reaction to that word *manifold*, regardless of pronunciation, has never been the same since. It seems to me, on the basis of such experiences as this, that the actual morphemic system of some individuals must be considered to be different from that of others, as mine differed before and after this incident. Specifically, for example, a Latin scholar, who is very intent at understanding the etymological sources of his English words, reacts differently from the man-in-the-street. This becomes objectively visible — not a mere subjective judgment — when the Latin scholar becomes annoyed if the man-in-the-street uses certain affixes in ways which are not etymologically consistent, whereas the man-in-the-street may himself be unmoved by this problem. It appears to me that the strong emotional reaction of some of these scholars may not be due exclusively to the fact that they are aware of etymological inconsistencies, but may be based upon a far deeper situation — namely, the fact of a different morphemic system which they have as over against that of the man-in-the-street, but largely congruent with his.

Just as we had differences of observers and of observer types in the church service, and in the football game (§§ 3.1, 4.23), so there are differences of speakers in reference to their morphemic systems within the community. Even though the actual manifestation (pronunciation or use) of the systems may be almost identical, language systems of such individuals are in fact not quite the same.

6.63 *Morphemic-Class Membership and Potential-Distribution as Components of the Distribution Mode of a Morpheme*

Another characteristic of the distribution mode of the morpheme intimately related to its activeness is the fact that the morpheme is an ALTERNATIVE FOR THE MANIFESTATION OF AN EMIC SLOT, a possibility of selection, one of the range of options (cf. § 7.311) which the actor may exercise in his living. Thus the morphemes *boy, dog, horse* are among the alternatives for selection for occurrence in the slot after *My* in the phrase *My dog came home*. By virtue of the fact that for any one particular emic slot a number of morphemes constitute the available options at that slot, this list of morphemes constitutes a DISTRIBUTION CLASS OF MORPHEMES. One of the principal components of the distribution mode of a morpheme is its MEMBERSHIP in such a class, and in a system of such classes, and, in connection with its membership in such classes, its POTENTIAL and observed distribution in various kinds of slots in various utteremes.

It is worth noting, further, that TIME, as embedded in the distribution mode, has been implied in the previous paragraph, but that time does not need treatment as a separable component of the mode. Class membership can only be determined in reference to events which are past (verbal utterances which are past, when the emic motifs under attention are verbal ones); and only by a comparison of the structure and meaning of two or more utterances which have occurred in the immediate past, or in the somewhat more remote past, can the analyst begin to tell that two items should be classified distributionally together. No one utterance by itself, in an unknown language, gives the analyst a clue as to where the borders of morphemes occur within it, nor the classes into which they fall. An element of time past is therefore implicit in the assumption of the presence of distribution classes.

Similarly, future time is embedded in the theory at this point as a function of the potential for occurrence of a member of a distribution class (cf. Bazell, 1953:12, "The distribution of a unit is the totality of its possible relations"). Once the membership of a class is known, and the slot-distribution of that class is known, one can PREDICT the possibility of occurrences of certain morpheme sequences,[8] before they have occurred; one may also predict even more specifically the native reaction to a certain utterance (with a moderate degree of indeterminacy via negation or misunderstanding, cf. § 6.44) which the analyst may use in speaking to an informant, in testing that utterance. These elements of essential predictability carry with them a certain amount of the 'future' into the formulation of the distribution mode of the morpheme (and cf. § 7.52 for potential as a component of the tagmeme).

From the point of view of the analyst-observer, the 'near-past' and 'near-future' seem in these particular instances to be essentially undifferentiated. Both are simultaneously represented within the components of the distribution mode of his emic units at each level of the theory, with an area of indeterminacy for 'error' or 'invention' of native speakers who may on rare occasions depart from the norms of the community. Both, furthermore, involve predictions as to data which the observer may, within this margin of error, expect to find on a previously recorded tape, or in future utterances of informants.

Similarly, the 'present' enters into the linguistic formulations as a flexible element which is neither an extensionless razor edge between the past and the future, nor a

---

[8] Some current linguistic discussion often refers to the generative nature of a system where I have used predictability or (§ 6.61) activeness or productivity (and see Wonderly, 1951-52:2-3). Note here, however, a more insistent joining of a corpus of past productiveness with the intuition of future possibility of generativeness. For our earlier discussion of bibliographical references on productiveness, see § 7.84.

fixed span of hours or seconds, but rather a flexible span of attention. The terms 'focus' (§ 3.3) and 'height of focus' (§ 4.2) cover this element of time, provided that the focus so considered is that of active participants in an event in progress, which in turn involves some part of the event completed and some part of it always uncompleted.

Once an event is finished, and is looked on as finished, the detachment with which it is viewed in retrospect is a kind of functional hypostasis (if a non-analytical member of the culture is doing the viewing — § 4.23) or of analytical or analytical-functional hypostasis (if an outsider or analyst is considering the completed event — § 4.23). It would seem to follow that a morpheme never constitutes a 'present' in this sense, unless it happens to be manifesting a complete uttereme under conscious attention (as in *Boy!*) or is under the immediate scrutiny of the analyst; ordinarily a morpheme (except in a hypostatic dictionary listing) is below the threshold of participant awareness and shorter than a unit of 'present' focus of utteremic size and character. Time, to the behavioremic analyst, appears only as a kind of useful participant or analytical conceptualized hypostasis (cf. §§ 6.43, 4.23) of a sequence component of events.

6.64 *The Internal Structure of a Morpheme*

In § 6.61 we discussed the possibility of elements being active, as one component of the distribution mode of morphemes — a component which involved their occurrence in larger situations, that is in slots within utteremes. We now add the further statement concerning the distribution mode (already implied within the course of our discussion, § 3.51) that the internal structure of the morpheme has one of a number of kinds of sequences of actions which occur within that particular componential system of morphemes.

In morphemes these actions result in some typical sequences of sounds. In English, for example, we have many morphemes manifested by three emic units of sound in the sequence consonant-vowel-consonant, as in *cat*, *run*, *sit*, *tip*. In addition to this CVC pattern (in which C represents an emic unit of consonant sound — not consonant letter — and V represents vowel), there are patterns of CCVC (*trip*), of CCCVC (*strip*) of CCCVVC (*stripe*, i.e. [straip]), VC (*is*), VVC (*ice*), VCC (*ant*), C *-s* in *cats*), CVCVC (*ticket*), VCVCVCC (*elephant*), and many others. Yet these patterns do not all have the same functional burden, inasmuch as morphemes with a distributional component of the internal pattern C, for example, may serve as suffixes (e.g., the plural variant *-s*), or as abbreviated variants of longer forms, in rapid speech, as [-v] in *I've gone*, but do not constitute morphemes in the same class with *cat, dog, tree, elephant, automobile*. Similarly, the form VC is frequent in words like *of, in, at*, but relatively less frequent in the class containing *dog, automobile*. Such patterns, especially the frequent ones, in any language, may be called SHAPE TYPES (after S. Martin, 1952:16; cf. canonical forms, Hockett, 1947a:333; or prosodies, Firth, 1949:141).

Each language must be analyzed one at a time, in determining its own shape types and the functional part each plays. Nevertheless, there is sufficient uniformity throughout the world so that the analyst in the early stages may utilize his knowledge of this fact to make early guesses concerning the probable functioning type of morphemes as they emerge in his analysis. On the one hand, morphemes of the form V, or C, or VC, or CV, are likely to be suspected as constituting prefixes, suffixes, or grammatical markers of some kind. On the other hand, apparent morphemes composed of several syllables are likely to be immediately suspect, in that they may prove to have been incompletely analyzed, and to be composed of two or more morphemes in sequence.

Not only do these shape types have a bearing on the functional load of a form and the identification or signalling of its class membership, but they may also have some effect upon the occurrence of parasitic morphs (§ 6.62). Other things being equal, a sequence of sounds which is homophonous with a morpheme of a frequent shape type, but which is included within a larger sequence of sound, is more likely to be treated by some speaker as a parasitic morph than is a sequence which does not comprise such a pattern. Thus it was much more probable that S— would abstract *man* from the sequence ...*oggmanchauga*... (§ 6.62) than that he would have abstracted the sequence *an* which is simpler but manifesting a less frequent shape type.

A further characteristic of a morpheme is its relationship to a class of morphemes of which it is a member and, through its class membership, its relationship to a system of morphemes. Earlier in this section we attributed to the distribution mode of a morpheme its distribution (or relationship to) sequences of morphemes; so, now, we attribute to the distribution mode of a morpheme its occurrence within and relationship to a class (or classes) of morphemes and a system (or systems) of morphemes. The classes and systems in which morphemes occur will be treated, however, in §§ 6.7, 7.31.

6.65 *An Occurring Allomorph Viewed as Constituting an Occurring Morpheme*

Here also I adopt a further convention which I feel strongly is necessary and legitimate, but for which the theoretical justification is only partially worked out: WHENEVER A VARIANT OF A MORPHEME HAS OCCURRED THE MORPHEME ITSELF HAS OCCURRED. If one has just heard a variant of a morpheme (say, the variant [-z] of the English plural) he has heard that morpheme (i.e., he has heard the English plural morpheme). Cf. also Lounsbury, "A morpheme may be said to OCCUR when one of its phonemic forms occurs" (1953:6). This does *not* say, however, that hearing a variant of a morpheme is hearing all the variants of that morpheme at once. It does *not* say that when hearing a variant of the morpheme the listener 'thought he heard' an ideal of some type. It states, rather, that insofar as human reaction to human behavior is concerned, a variant *is* the unit, at that time and place, in its normal distribution. Cf. also Hockett, for whom grammatical and phonological elements occur — but for whom morphophonemes occur "purely as symbols" (1961a:50).

An analogy from far afield may be useful to help the reader understand this point of view for morphemes (but for a contrasting attitude towards morphemic classes, see § 7.313(4)). Let us think, for the moment, of the person John Doe as if he were a 'morpheme': To-day he is one 'allomorph'; yesterday he was a different 'allomorph' (of himself as an emic unit); after eating a T-bone steak he will be a still different 'allomorph'; each 'occurrence' of John Doe on these different days, with different physiological variants (or even different clothing variants), we will pretend is a separate 'allomorph' of that individual. For purposes of stydying the behavior of John Doe and his colleagues, it is more convenient to say that when we meet John Doe in the variant of a 'post-T-bone-steak-satiation-allomorph' we have 'actually met' John Doe, than to say that human behavior is analyzable only under the assumption that a person never meets John Doe himself, but only an 'allomorph' of him. To be sure, some kinds of philosophical discussion of John Doe can be made — perhaps must be made — without this assumption, but they seem to constitute a kind of etic analysis of his structure. Any analysis of John Doe AS THE CULTURE REACTS TO HIM, i.e., any emic analysis, must assume that anyone who has just met Allo-John-Doe has in fact just met John Doe.

Cf. Quine for the "summation of person stages" (1953:72; see also 65-70 for discussion of river stages, and further discussion of the identity of the individual). (See fn. to § 17.4.)

6.66 *Border Limits of Morphemes in Reference to Tagmemes*

In § 6.1 we implied that a morpheme was co-extensive with and distributed within a tagmeme. This would seem to imply that there are limits to a morpheme. How rigid are these limits, how sharp cut are the borders between them, and is there an element of indeterminacy such as has been met at other points in the theory?

In general, the answer is probably clear. Usually one morpheme can be separated from another, and we can see where one begins and ends without too much difficulty. The rule-of-thumb procedure for identifying these borders and units will be given in § 6.81. Similarly, we can state that wherever a morpheme ends, a tagmeme ends wherever a morpheme begins, a tagmeme begins.

A number of special difficulties arise when one attempts to apply these principles, however. Some of them may be listed here, though the treatment of them will be left to later sections (especially Chapter 14) where the problems can be dealt with against a background of more elements of the theory as a whole. (1) Two morphemes may partially fuse together so that no clear border can be discovered between them; the border comes within a phoneme (cf. §§ 6.55, 14.12). This situation, like the next one, carries with it the blurring of the boundaries of the tagmemes which they are manifesting and within which they are distributed. (2) Two morphemes may in some particular manifestation be completely fused, so that no border at all can be found between them in that instance (§§ 6.55, 14.12). (3) A single morpheme may in certain instances manifest two fused tagmemes (§§ 7.45, 14). (4) A morpheme sequence can manifest a minimum (expanded) tagmeme (§ 7.44). (5) Morpheme boundaries which may appear to be sharp cut in a phonemic transcription of those sequences may be seen to be blurred if one looks at them etically, in reference to the slurring of the borders of the emic units of sound (Chapter 8); phonemically the border may be clear when phonetically it is blurred. (6) A morpheme may have discontinuous parts (§ 6.54), so that the segment between the borders beginning and ending the morpheme is interrupted, raising the problem of two internal borders which are either clear or fused also.

6.7 *Systems of Morphemes as Composed of Emic Classes of Morphemes*

The detailed study of the nature of classes of morphemes can best be postponed until Chapter 7, and the next few chapters. Enough of that material needs to be briefly foreshadowed here, however, to give an initial broader perspective concerning the kind of setting within which a morpheme occurs.

Whereas a morpheme is a member of a distribution class of morphemes (§ 6.63), a distribution class of such morphemes is in turn a member of an emic class of emic distribution classes of morphemes, which we shall call an emic SYSTEM of morphemes and/or of their classes. Within any one large system there may be included various simultaneous smaller componential systems of morphemes — e.g., one for segmental morphemes and one for intonational morphemes. Likewise, when different styles involve some differences in the number of morphemes, the congruent systems of morphemes will not have quite the same inventory — e.g., *thee*, *thou*, and *-est* (as in *knowest*) are special members of one such congruent system of morphemes used in some verse or in prayer (§ 7.313(3-4)). A set of all systems of morphemes which are congruent and/or simultaneous, together with all other verbal units congruent with them (including those to be discussed in Chapters 7 through 13), constitute a single, larger, emic system of verbal behavior as a whole (§ 5.4), a LANGUAGE; the nonverbal units of behavior constitute other high-layered emic systems.

Just as a morpheme may have its different manifested variants, so two morph classes, each largely alike but partially different, may constitute variants of a single emic class of morphemes. These characteristics of morpheme classes will be discussed in § 7.313(3); for the moment it will be sufficient to indicate that since morph classes are composed of variants of those morphemes, the morph classes vary with the morphs contained in them, so that the manifestations of a morpheme class may be locally conditioned (§§ 6.53, 7.313(3)) (1) by its phonemic surroundings, (2) by its morphemic surroundings, and (3) by its tagmemic slot occurrence; and may also be conditioned (4) by its occurrence in a componential or congruent system (§§ 6.56, 7.313(3-4)). The illustrations given for morpheme variants apply here if the class containing the morphs is considered instead of the individual morphs themselves.

An additional problem needs to be mentioned. From one point of view a unit is a composite of CONTRASTIVE RELATIONSHIPS within a system. One of the most difficult of the theoretical problems which must be faced by such a theory as this one is the balance to be struck between giving priority to the relationships[9] themselves on the one hand or to be given to the items which are at the poles of the relationships, on the other (e.g., cf. discussion in Bazell, 1953:110; Z. Harris, 1951:370-71). In this theory, we have ended by putting emphasis on unity rather than on diversity; we have set up emic units for our basic attention.

6.8 Morphetics

Just as a special linguistic term is provided for a verbal behavioreme (i.e., the uttereme), so a linguistic term was provided in § 6.1 for a verbal motif. Every etic verbal motif is a MORPH, and every emic verbal motif is a MORPHEME; thus *boy*, *-ish*, and the plural {-s} are morphemes; the English plural variants *-s*, *-es*, *-en* of *cats*, *houses*, and of *oxen*, etc., are each morphs which constitute members of the morpheme {-s}.

6.81 *Segmentation of a Continuum into Morphs*

Just as it was necessary to suggest (§ 5.51) means by which etic utterances could be identified within a larger continuum of speech, so it is necessary to discover the morph units within utterances.

The procedure for identifying morphs is (1) to obtain two utterances which are partly alike in form and meaning, and whose general meaning is known by gesture, translation, or paraphrase, and (a) to find the least common denominator of form and meaning by which the two are alike (as *the boy* in *the boy came home* and *the boy ran away*), or (b) to find an identifiable element by which the two differ in form and meaning (e.g., *yesterday* in *the boy came home* and *the boy came home yesterday*). Then (2) the same kind of comparisons are made on a large body of data, including the material already obtained as a result of the first step, and the smallest meaningful forms in the resulting elements are morphs (e.g., *the boy*, obtained earlier, would be broken down into morphs *the* and *boy* after one also obtained — in addition to *the boy came home* — phrases such as *the man came home* and *a boy came home*). In one respect this may be considered a frame technique (§ 5.51) applied to morphs.

Early errors in drawing morph boundaries have to be corrected by later comparison with other occurrences of these tentative morphs in various environments to check to see that neither too much nor too little phonetic material has been attributed to any

---

[9] Attention in these chapters, therefore, has been on (segmental) *units* as well-described by contrast, variation and distribution rather than on relationships (see §§ 7.85-86). In our more recent materials (1962a, 1963b, 1963d) we have developed matrices as units of field. In the matrix, vectors lead to field relationships. Then a matrix itself may be seen as a different type of well-described emic unit (1963d).

one morph (e.g., a stranger, upon hearing only *long*, without a [g] pronounced, and *longer*, with [g] pronounced, might for some time include the [g] as part of the morph *-er*). In addition, morpheme boundaries may be fused (§ 6.55, and Chapter 14), causing further difficult problems or indeterminacy in boundary identification.[10]

6.82 *Etic Classificatory Criteria for Morph Types*

Various criteria of an etic nature may be used to describe morphs in a manner comparable to that used for an etic utterance in § 5.52.

A first set of criteria may allow the analyst to make initial observations according to some characteristic of the manifestation mode (§ 6.5) of the morph:

(a) Is the sound pattern (§ 6.64) of the morph composed exclusively of segmental sounds? or of one component (or more) of a sound? or of a pitch unit or sequence? or of stress? or of length? or of some combination of these? or of a process of change from one sound (or sounds) to another?

(b) How many units of sound are in this pattern?

(c) What are the types of sounds (or sound components) in this sequence, and how are they arranged (e.g., as stopped consonant plus vowel plus consonant, etc.)?

A second set of criteria may allow a rough, highly tentative, semantic classification of a morph. (In current linguistic practice such a grouping is seldom handled formally, and is not used after the early stages of analysis, although probably all workers get quick clues from such meanings, leading to profitable hypotheses of distribution-class membership and grammatical function — hypotheses rigorously tested, discarded, or revised by later emic procedures):

(d) Is the meaning concrete, or objective, or such that experience would suggest that the morph is likely to be found serving as a stem or as a principal word? Or would experience suggest that because of its meaning (and possibly its size) it is more likely to be found here as a affix, or functioning as an small grammatical particle?

(e) If it seems to fall within the first of these two groups, does it signify an object? or an action? or process? or a state? or a quality? or other comparable element? What specific range of meaning, within one of these groups, does it have?

(f) If it appears to be of the second kind, is its meaning somewhat like that of a conjunction? article? personal pronoun? relative pronoun? preposition? or other similar item? or does it indicate gender of item mentioned (size shape, sex)? or of speaker (men vs. women or children)? animate or inanimate? number (singular, dual, triple, plural)? case? possession? alienable or inalienable? time (past, present, future, near, remote)? aspect (complete, incomplete, continuous, repeated, begun)? visibility or invisibility? transitive or intransitive? subject or object (direct or indirect)? active or passive? direction of action (from, to)? cause? certainty? source of knowledge (first

[10] Morphemes when fused may be viewed as waves rather than as particles. Compare §§ 14.12, 14.2, 14.52, 12.1 (and fn.).

hand, hearsay)? or other factor (see listing and illustration in Nida, 1949:149, 168-69, 181-86, from which the last part of this paragraph in part draws).

We shall proceed now to a further kind of criterion — the occurrence of the morphs of a particular language within distribution classes in that language. For structural purposes, morph groupings should be arrived at in relation to morph distribution classes. By implication this rejects as structurally invalid any grouping arrived at on purely semantic grounds, and also rejects as incomplete or as inaccurate any definition such as that 'a noun is the name of person place or thing', since (a) distributional criteria are, in fact, utilized in identifying the group of items labelled 'noun', and (b) the grouping retains some items such as *seizure* which the semantic criterion, by itself, would have eliminated.

6.83 *Etic Classificatory Criteria for Morphs in Relation to their Distribution Classes*

An etic distribution class of morphs is a group of individual morphs which occur in a particular structural slot in some specific utterance or utterance type, or is a group of morphs each of which can occur in a number of such slots, manifesting the same morph class (§ 6.7). The characteristics of a morpheme class — their specific relationships to the distribution mode of the uttereme, their relationships to one another in an utterance, etc. — will be treated later (cf. §§ 7.31, 7.32, 11). Here we wish to list a few criteria which have more specific reference to the membership of a morph in a class than to the analysis of the class constituted of such morphs:

(a) Is the morph in a class which is relatively large (say with 200 or more morphs), or is it in a class which is small (say with half a dozen)? (For discussion of this point, see § 7.313(1).)

(b) Is it in a class which constitutes a subclass of a large morph class which appears in another slot or slots?

(c) If it is in a subclass of a larger class, is the subclass determined by the fact that it correlates in some way with one or more specific members of another class (say with *he*, or *she*, or *it*, or *they*, etc.)? (§ 7.313(2).)

(d) Is the morph in a class whose membership is determined by its occurrence in one slot, only, or in various slots? (§§ 7.313(2-3), 7.321.)

(e) Does this morph occur in a class in which many of the morphs in the class contain a meaning-component in common (such as 'object', or 'action', or 'tense')? If so, what is that meaning? (§ 7.313(1).) Does this particular morph share that class meaning?

6.84 *Summary of the Relation of Morphs to Morphemes*

In order to pass from a prestructural, etic description of the minimum units of the feature mode of utterances to an emic description of these minimum units a set of emic procedures is necessary, as it is for the emic analysis of the utterances themselves (§ 5.5). In both procedures, advanced etic training affords a means of faster handling of the data of an unfamiliar language, but carries with it an inevitable degree of etic distortion of the local pattern, but a distortion which the emic procedures are designed to eliminate more or less successfully.

Alternatives underlying the equating of any specific morph with some morpheme or part thereof during the analysis can be summarized in a manner used for utterances (§ 5.5). Once a morph is identified in accordance with the criteria mentioned in § 6.82, it may be assumed that it is one of the following:

either (a) a free variant of a morpheme (§ 6.52)
    or (b) a conditioned variant of a morpheme (§ 6.53)
    or (c) part of an etically-complex variant of a morpheme (§ 6.54)
    or (d) a sequence of manifested variants of two or more morphemes, such that it needs to be segmented further into (morphs and) morphemes (cf. § 6.81)
    or (e) a fused composite variant of two partially-simultaneous[11] or completely-simultaneous morphemes (§§ 6.81, 14)
    or (f) an error of morphetic analysis, or of recording the sounds, which would be eliminated upon further study;
    and (g) the morphemes composed of these morphs are members of emic distribution classes of morphemes within the larger system of emic classes within the language as a whole; in this respect the morphs must be analyzed as morphemes only in reference to a system of contrastive relativity for all of the morphemes, the classes of morphemes, and the language system within which they occur and which they in part constitute (§§ 6.7, 16).

6.9 Bibliographical Comments on Chapter 6

There has been a great deal of work on morphemics in this country and elsewhere, especially since the important article by Harris (1942a) which went beyond Bloomfield (1926, 1933a) by attempting to make articulate certain of the distributional parallels in the methodology of phonemic and morphemic analysis. Some other publications dealing directly or indirectly with morphemics include Trager (1944), R. A. Hall (1945), Z. Harris (1945a, 1946, 1951), Hockett (1947a), Bloch (1947b), Voegelin (1947), Nida (1948b, 1949, 1951), Bazell (1948a, 1948b, 1949, 1952, 1953), Pike (1948, 1953a), Bolinger (1948, 1950), Wells (1949), Hoenigswald (1950), Trager and Smith (1951), Wonderly (1952a), Lounsbury (1953), Pickett (1953), Hjelmslev (1953), Pittman

---

[11] Since this section first appeared (1954), we have developed much more elaborate techniques for handling simultaneity of morphemes, through postulating formatives at the intersection of categories in a matrix (1963d). Note further description in § 14.12 fn., and see § 15.33 for system).

(1954b), and various studies of the morphemics of individual languages in connection with a more comprehensive study of their grammars.

For more recent studies see now S. Martin for morphophonemics of Japanese (1952), Pickett for diagram of verb sequence limitations (1955), Shell for tagmemic analysis of transitive and intransitive verb patterns (1957), Mayers (1957), Law (1962), Hill (1958), Robins for extensive charting of derivation types (1959a:346-65), Pike for compound affixes (1961c).

Cox (1957) illustrates the value of utilizing separate morpheme-order charts for each verb type; this is a major contribution of tagmemic theory, without using tagmemic terminology. Otherwise, one frequently finds verb composite charts with transtive, intransitive, subordinate, and independent elements all put into a single ordering. The difficulty with these approaches is that they do not allow productive (generative) usage of the formulas without many errors. In practical field work it has proved necessary to insist on the separate tagmemic charting of verbs according to the constructions in which they occur, and the co-occurrence restrictions within them, if the productive power of the formulas is not to be lost. For comment on the development of this article note Pike (1957a).

6.91 On Morpheme Definition

The first use of the term 'morpheme' is attributed tentatively by Jespersen (1937:105-06) to Noreen. The term morph seems to have been introduced by Hockett (1947a:322), supplementing the term 'alternate' or 'alternant' as used by Z. Harris (1942a) and Bloomfield (1933a:209).

I have not found in anthropological literature a term which parallels precisely the use here of emic motif. The phrase 'culture element' or 'culture trait' seems to refer to such 'minimal definable elements of culture' as were compiled in 1928 by Kroeber (cf. Kroeber, 1936), but includes not only action elements of varying size, but also many objects or beliefs which are the products of culture or used by the culture. Gifford and Kroeber (1937), for example, include among such culture traits the following: a sea-otter fur blanket, a beard, dogflesh not eaten, person in moon, fear of twins, eagle dance, and swimming breast stroke. Similarly, the various terms in Opler (1948) do not correspond with the unit of behavior discussed in this chapter.

See, now, Dundes, using etic and emic units in analysis of folklore motif (1962b, 1963); structural analysis allows more useful typological statements; and "If a folklorist aligns all the tales with the same structure reported in a given culture, that is, aligns them motifeme by motifeme, he may then easily note whether or not a specific motifeme is manifested by a particular motif" (1963:126) as the interdiction-violation motif sequence allows one to see striking structural differences between European and American folktales where the difference "concerns the number of motifemes intervening between a pair of related motifemes" (1963:127). In reference to the study of folktales, Dundes states that "It seems safe to say that the emic unit of the motifeme (Propp's function) marks a tremendous theoretical advance over the etic unit of the motif" (1962b:103). Compare, also, studies on units of cognitive systems (Frake, 1961, 1962; Conklin, 1955, and in Householder and Saporta, 1962, with "cultural categorization of reality" in the "folk taxonomy"; Mathiot, 1962, 1963a).

The terms 'kinemorph' and 'kinemorpheme' of Birdwhistell (1952:15-16, and addendum revising 22) seem to be applied to certain nonverbal motifs, in an attempt to parallel the terms morph and morpheme which are applied to verbal motifs.

For a discussion of some earlier uses of the term morpheme, and problems in connection with them, see Jespersen (1937:106-08); compare Skalička (1936, on sèmes), Bloomfield (1926:155), Projet (TCLP IV, 1931:321). Even recent use in this country is not completely uniform — as when Z. Harris speaks of "morphemes of order" (1952a:18; and cf. 1951:186 fn. 63, 184-85, 190 fn. 70, 211 fn. 28, 213 fn. 31); an opposite extreme, in limitation of the term, is the use of the Danish linguist Hjelmslev such that "the term *morphemes* is restricted to use in the sense of inflexional elements, considered as elements of the content" (1953:15 fn.)

One of the difficulties in handling morphemics in terms of a form-meaning correlation is the lack of a permanent unchanging core of meaning (cf. Bazell, 1948a:2-5, in contrast to Bloomfield's opposite working assumption, 1933a:162). This problem has led to the attempt to reach an essentially "negative formulation" such that the meaning of morphemes "sets them apart" from other forms; this avoids the necessity for assuming that the forms have an identical meaning, though it still allows for "some semantic feature in common which remains constant in all their meanings" (an older formulation of Nida's, 1948b:421 fn. 15, building on Bloomfield, 1933a:161; and cf. S. Martin, 1952:11), or it allows a formulation in which the meaning of the morpheme is "the total of the semes" in the various contexts in which the morpheme occurs (a revised formulation of Nida's), since in some instances "There is practically no common denominator [of meaning] left" in a series of uses of a morpheme (Nida, 1951:9). Compare Bazell, who also attempts a negative formulation since he feels that the extremes of meaning of a morpheme do not always have a common core (1948a:2-4; and see his negative description as a "systematic irrelevance of any distinctions of meaning" in 1949:4-5; cf. Hjelmslev, 1936:50). Any definition involving meaning of any kind is further complicated by the presence of meaningless "empty words" (a phrase early attributed to the Chinese scholars — Müller, 1876:77-78; for modern treatment of the problem, see Bazell, 1948b:286; 1949:11; Hockett, 1947a:331-33; Nida, 1948b:416-17; Wonderly, 1951-1952:155). We attempt to meet the problem, in the present volume, by leaving room for variants of meaning but more especially by defining the morpheme only in relation to a larger structure of which it is a part, the behavioreme, and to the feature mode of that larger unit (§ 6.1; cf. also § 6.45); by doing so we hope to avoid the extreme of treating "morphological systems" "in essence" as "systems of meanings" (de Groot, 1948:440), as well as the extreme of "the fundamental purely formal definition" in which "a morpheme is an arrangement of phonemes" distributed within morphemes and utterances, etc., but in which one can only "use meanings as hints" to help find morphemes, without the meaning as part of the basic definitions themselves (Hockett, 1949a:40; cf. Z. Harris, 1951:8 fn. 7, 173, 189, 365 fn. 6; and the reply to Harris in Fowler, 1952:506-08; compare Trager and Smith, 1951:68, 54, 81). In such a formalistic approach, the analyst affirms that he separates homophonous morphemes not on the basis of meaning but on the basis of distributional criteria. These criteria include, among other items, the fact that "It is therefore convenient to let the various morphemes of the language have identical distributions" in order to get a "compact description" (Z. Harris, 1951:199-200) — but this goal could not be obtained if *too* and *two* were treated as manifestations of a single morpheme, instead of two morphemes which were respectively members of different classes.

Before this item of Harris' appeared, Nida had rejected such a solution on the ground that it would necessitate "repetitions of forms in listing" (1949:57, fn. 52). He also rejected the solution that would make *man, horse, fish* as basically nouns (with verbs to be derived from them by zero) and *swim, jump, run* as verbs (with nouns to be derived from them by zero), on the ground that "it is impossible to arrive at any valid basis for determining the basic class memberships of homophonous forms" (1949:57 fn. 52). Instead, he concluded that he should assign "*fish*, meaning an object, and *fish*, meaning a process, to the same morpheme" on the ground that "these differences in meaning are paralleled by distributional differences" (1949:57; cf. Principle 5:55-56). Others of his principles are also of interest here: His criterion that nonhomophonous items might be "treated as submorphemic if the difference in meaning of the allomorphs reflects the distribution of these forms" was a principle which was set up to apply to instances where there was "Contrast in identical environments" — i.e., in instances such as *shown* versus *showed*, in matters of style (1949:42 item 4, illustrated on 43, item H — and very useful in that connection, as we shall see presently); the instance of *fish* versus *fish* is not illustrative of this principle, since the different meanings of these two homophones do not so contrast, and are not matters of style. We suggest that *fish* and *fish* might possibly have been subsumed under the principle that "Occurrence in the same structural series has precedence over occurrence in different structural series in the determination of morphemic status" (1949:42 item 1), and that this consideration would lead to treating *fish* and *fish* as two separate morphemes, members of two sharply different classes or series of morphemes, with widely different tagmemic distributions. Here, however, as elsewhere in the present theory, we may expect some indeterminacy, and instances in which any forcing of a decision one way or another would be arbitrary and not justified by the data; in such instances the indeterminacy would be either as to class membership (or memberships) of a specific morpheme (or morphemes), or as to the presence or absence of emic contrast between the classes of morphemes.

For a very different treatment suggested for the handling of semantic variation in the morpheme, note Bolinger, who says that "We need to trace associations rather than identities" (1950:118), and "In an ideally constituted lexicon, the elements of the word would relate it to more inclusive genera precisely and scientifical[l]y (connotation), and the word itself would refer to a species [of semantic component], or to a less inclusive genus [of semantic component], something at a higher level of specificity (denotation)" etc. (1950:124). Note that this implies a generalized etics of meaning (cf. §§ 6.82, 6.94).

Failure to see that meanings can vary non-emically within a morpheme has led to some conclusions different from those reached here. Note Bloch: "According to our assumptions, if a verb that belongs to a given conjugation differs in meaning or connotation, however slightly, from a verb with a phonemically identical base that belongs to another type, the verbs are different morphemes: the *shine* whose preterit is *shined* is a different verb from the *shine* whose preterit is *shone*; and by the same argument the *show* whose participle is *shown* is a different verb from the *show* whose participle is *showed*" (1947b:406-07); also: "The form *n't* is best regarded as a separate morpheme, not as an alternant of the full form *not*. The two forms contrast, at least stylistically and in their connotations, in such phrases as *I cannot go* : *I can't go*" (1947b:406 fn. 14). It is to Nida that we are indebted for the first major suggestion towards the solution of this problem in terms of submorphemic variation in reference to the sociolinguistic environment (1948b:432); he uses the same approach to avoid Bloch's conclusions that /hæv, hev, ev, v/ (i.e., variants of *have*) are distinct morphemes (Nida, 1948b:432-33; and 1949:42 item 4, and 43 item H).

Problems of meaning affect the morpheme definition in several other ways. The presence of lexically-meaningless morphemes (§ 6.45) forces us to utilize a definition in which the morpheme is identified in relation to its position in the total structure in a behavioremic hierarchy, rather than to adopt a definition in which the morpheme is assumed to be a 'minimal meaningful unit' per se. Two solutions have been suggested to meet this problem, both of which attempt to eliminate some lexically-meaningless morphs from morphemic status. The first is by Hockett, who proposes that we recognize "EMPTY MORPHS, which have no meaning and belong to no morpheme" (1947a:333). Cf., also, discussion by Lounsbury (1953:12-13).

The second attempt to avoid this difficulty is one made by Pittman, and focuses especially upon morphs which have grammatical significance but not a strong or easily-seen lexical meaning. Thus he says that "Certain phonological sequences, however, which have usually been described as morphemes, might perhaps be more neatly described as 'overt valences'" which "may appear to be very similar to morphemes, or, indeed, they may be 'carried' by specific morphemes. Possible examples of this might be the unit *to* in English infinitive expressions and the suffix *-r* in Spanish infinitives. The English auxiliary 'do' in expressions such as *I do not know* is another likely example" (1954a:7). Perhaps the chief difficulty in the way of following Pittman's suggestion is that he gives neither theory nor methodology which would let one see what a morpheme is, or how it is to be defined, or related to his total theory of linguistics; as a consequence, it is impossible to determine which specific phoneme sequences in the language would constitute (a) morphemes but not valences, (b) valences but not morphemes, (c) valence-carrying morphemes (e.g., he gives no reason for treating conjunctions differently from *to* and *do* other than his saying that "conjunctions, although identifiable as real, contrastive morphemes, may be said to 'carry' valences" (1954a: 7-8).

Our insistence that lexically-meaningful morphemes constitute form-meaning composites (§ 6.46, and cf. §§ 2.2, 5.64) serves as a convenient point at which to contrast this part of the theory with comparable sections of certain other approaches. Whereas on the one hand this theory forces us to reject de Groot's point of view that morphological systems are "systems of meanings" (since our theory insists on the essential physical manifestation of a morpheme), on the other hand it leads us to reject what I take to be Bazell's point of view, when he states that "it would be preferable not to introduce semantics on the morphemic level as a positive factor" (1953:59), and that "the sememe like the morpheme is a distributional unit, and the reason for purging the one level [presumably morphemes] of positive semantic criteria of differentiation..." (59), and "The linguist who has got it into his head that a morpheme is a meaningful unit, cannot possibly be supposed to understand semantic change" (105). Cf. also Trager and Smith who seem to treat morphemes as "formal units" without essential semantic relationship (1951:68, where the term "formal units" includes intonational affixes, and 55, where segmental morphemes are defined exclusively in reference to their phonemic and formal structure).

At the same time, the present theory forces the rejection of any theory which sets up emes of meaning — i.e., sememes (Bloomfield, 1933a:162; Nida, 1951; Bazell, 1953:81; compare Goodenough 'significata or sememes' 1956:198) — which are other than units of functional or analytical conceptualized hypostatis (§ 6.43) and are on an entirely different plane of behavior from that of a nonhypostatized morpheme. This, in turn, carries with it a rejection of the dualism of Hjelmslev, which starts with a basic assumption of a functional dichotomy of expression and content (1953:30, 36-37) which, if pursued in emic terms, would presumably lead to emes of meaning which have no constantly-present physical manifestation but which are merely abstracted relationships.

The elimination of this dualism from a basic theory of nonhypostatic language is necessary, further, if one is to arrive at a unified theory of verbal and nonverbal behavior which includes items for which such a conceptually-hypostatized dichotomy could not easily be postulated. The retention of the dualism as a basic postulate would prevent the analysis, in a framework which could accommodate linguistic analysis, of any kind of human behavior in which such a dichotomy could not be seen; it would lead to a theory in which 'signs', 'symbols', and 'semiotics', in general, were of a structural type too widely divorced from other types of human behavior to be easily included in a single structural approach with them.

Similarly, this theory rejects the approach of Hjelmslev to whatever extent he sets up any emic unit without permanent reference to the substance manifesting it, whether that unit be a distributional one, or one of content or of expression (cf. Hjelmslev 1953:68, "Substance is thus not a necessary presupposition for linguistic form"). The present theory would indicate that it is invalid to utilize 'substance' or physical manifestation of units in order to arrive at those units but then to discard reference to such physical components as being irrelevant to the structure, as if they were a mere scaffolding for the erection of a theory, with the scaffolding to be discarded once the theory is attained. Our theory insists, rather, upon a return to the implications of Bloomfield's assertion (which he, himself, departed from in setting up sememes) that the fundamental assumption of linguistics is that "In certain communities (speech-communities) some speech-utterances are alike as to form and meaning" (1933a:144; and cf. above, § 5.64 and § 2.73); cf., also, Bloomfield: "In language, forms cannot be separated from their meanings" (1943:102).

Just as the utilization of an outlook in terms of form-meaning composites avoids some problems in theory, so the utilization of reference to identificational-contrastive composite components (§ 6.46) also allows us to by-pass a difficult theoretical problem. If we were to assume that the meanings of morphemes were only contrastive, then they would have that meaning only when the items with which they were assumed to be in contrast could be found also in the same environment in different utterances; if, however, the meaning is also an identificational feature, then the meaning once identified in one environment may be recognized and treated as the same meaning in a different environment even if no set of contrastive morphemes is permitted there. Note the argument of Bazell, who seems to take a different view: "since meaning presupposes a choice, every syntactic limitation implies zero-meaning. In those positions in which a past but not a present morpheme is possible, the morpheme is voided of whatever semantic role it may have in other positions, if the opposition is binary" (1953:11); and in *many feet*, vs. *many hands* "the plural morpheme is necessarily voided of meaning" [i.e., because one cannot say *many foot*, etc.] (1953: 11). If one insists that components of the morpheme are simultaneously identificational and contrastive, this problem does not arise; *cat* means *cat* in both of the first two instances, and in the latter two instances the plurals both mean plural. (Bazell's point of view represents, I think, one variety of analysis in terms of 'neutralization of oppositions' which is more often encountered in reference to phonological questions; in both instances the identificational nature of emic units should be taken into account.)

Since our first edition (1954) numerous discussions of the relation of morphemic analysis to semantic components have appeared. For continuing definition in semantic terms, note Hockett: "*Morphemes are the smallest individually meaningful elements in the utterances of a language*", (1958:123); "to get to the grammatical stratum" certain information which "is always at bottom semantic, no matter how disguised" must be "added to phonological information" (1961a:46). Note W. Haas who protests against delay in use of meaning (1960:254-59); Pulgram has a protest against "the stultifying exclusion of linguistic meaning" (1961:324). Gleason has the morpheme "as the smallest unit which is grammatically pertinent" (1961:52) or "the smallest element in the expression which has a direct relationship with any point in the content system" (1961:79). F. R. Palmer emphasizes that some of our criteria "may be semantic" in our analytical procedures — and that these must not be dismissed as mere "heuristic guides" (in Preprints..., 1962:324); but for Palmer the relationship of phonetic elements to categorical meaning need not be one-to-one — he requires only that all its categories have phonetic exponents (in Preprints..., 1962:233). Here, as in our matrix-formative material (1963d; Pike and Erickson, 1964) the form-meaning composite necessity is retained, but a biuniqueness — one to one — relationship requirement of form to meaning is relaxed. For a general discussion of the relation of meaning to morphemics note Strang (in Preprints..., 1962:250). Bazell rejects the notion of a morpheme as a meaningful unit (1962:132). Z. Harris has proposed a procedure that "yields the morphemes of a language without any reference to meaning or informant response" (1954a:155); here Harris studies successor counts and predecessor counts of phoneme sequences, arriving at tentative segmentation of morphs or morphemes.

For Hockett a "morpheme is not composed of phonemes, but a morph is" (1961a:31); Lamb treats a morpheme or its allomorphs as "represented by" phonological elements (1962:9).

Considerable discussion has arisen under the need to relate morphemes to some hierarchical structure. For Hockett, the phoneme in the phonological hierarchy is analogous to the word in the lexical-grammatical hierarchy, and the phonemic component is analogous to the morpheme; he feels that this view destroys "the last vestiges of the long-standing parallel between the terms 'morpheme' and 'phoneme'" (1961a: 45, 48); similarly, by his approach, the lexical hierarchy merges into the grammatical one, rather than being in contrast with it. Halliday has three hierarchies, and treats the morpheme as "the minimal element of grammatical structure" (1961:286 fn. 95); the lexical items may be of various types and lengths, and hence "may not be coextensive with any grammatical unit at all" (273). The morpheme "has no structure" (Halliday, 1961:256 fn. 37).

For relations of morphology to syntax, note Pittman, for whom there is an "inescapable interdependence" in the language studied (1954b:239); he proposes the use of the term 'word root' as defined as any "sequence of phonemes of a given language which belongs to a class of unlimited membership, and which is not analyzable into a combination containing a shorter sequence belonging to a class of unlimited membership" — versus restricted classes of marginal morphemes — so that morphology can then be defined as the "set of structural signals which relates its word roots (and/or their expansions) to one another in substitutions" and syntax as "the set of structural signals which relates its word roots... to one another in sequences" (1959:200).

For problems in morphology-syntax division due to fusion, note Pike (1959) and H. Hart (1957:162). Compare also Sivertson (1960:763). Theoretical problems arise due to the fact that phonological variants of allomorphs are not sporadic, but occur in patterned groups. For insistence that allomorphs cannot be listed indiscriminately, if one wishes to see the system, and for necessity of setting up allomorph classes comprising basic forms of morphemes, see Pike (1953a); this proves necessary both for a process statement and for description via item and arrangement. For the problem seen through transform grammar, note Chomsky, in connection with the word *telegraph* (1962, § 2.1). For moneme as a term used to represent minimum meaningful units which can be lexical with experiential reference (e.g., *yesterday*), or lexical with functional reference (e.g., *in*), or nonlexical function (e.g., subject function in a clause), see Martinet (1960a:4-7); note, there also, problems of lack of one-to-one correlation of form and meaning. For formal statement of morpheme treatment by mathematical symbols, see Hockett (1952b). For summary and bibliography of Soviet and East European work on morphemics see van Schooneveld (in Sebeok, 1963b:22-34).

In reference to a trimodal approach to morpheme definition, I am not acquainted with any attempt to describe the data in this fashion. In reference to sociological matters, however, Parsons in reference to "interactional orientation" does suggest an analysis of social action by means of three modes: "the cathectic, the cognitive, and the evaluative" (1951:12, and 7-14), but I find nothing in common between his approach and that developed here.

6.92 On Active Elements

Active elements enter into regular analogies. Hence another (cf. § 6.61) criterion for activeness is that "The speaker can use a form in a regular function even when he has never heard the resultant form" (Bloomfield, 1933a:274-75; cf. Z. Harris, 1951:255). This is in turn related to "the statistically determinable readiness with which an element enters into new combinations" (Bolinger, 1948:18; even with "the appearance of only one in a lifetime", 21; but cf. Bazell, 1949a:8-9; and cf. new problems raised in Bolinger, 1950:135, where new forms are created by phonetic analogies to which one would hesitate to assign morphemic status). For a large collection of new formations, see Mencken (1945, I, e.g., 350-72, 362, 399, 401, 406). For an earlier discussion of the problem see Jespersen who protests against treating the *pre-* of *preparation* as parallel to that of *pre-suppose* since only the latter kind "deserve a place in English grammars: the other words belong to the dictionary"; whereas fixed phrases are "formulas" (1924:43, 32). Similarly, Fries treats the ending of *truth* as "not now a live or productive pattern and has only historical significance" (1945:18 fn.; cf. Sapir, 1916, in his Selected Writings, 441), though he recognizes indeterminacy, since for some it is "difficult to draw a line" (1940:36). Problems in determining such elements are frequent: e.g., discussion in de Groot (1948:463, regarding Latin), Bloomfield (1933a: 275, for *duchess*), S. Martin (1952:103, for Japanese, and *tycoon/typhoon* for English), Nida (1948b:425, 429, 431, general problems, and 1949:60-61), etc. Related problems in the treatment of items like *was* or *is* are found in Hockett (1947a:343); Bloch (1947b:416-17); Nida (1948b:429); Z. Harris (1951:201 fn. 9). Note also Harris.:

"...the {wh-} 'interrogation' morpheme" [i.e., as in the first part of *when*] (1951:210 fn. 23, 192-93). The fullest treatment which I have seen of the logical but unacceptable results of utilizing a theory of morpheme definition which implies the use of form-meaning correlations for morpheme identification without reference to active and passive structure occurs in Bolinger (1950), where a large number of passive items with semantic effect are discussed (see list, for example, 119-20). For numerous examples of stems changing form, as learned roots are borrowed, note Bloomfield (1933b:19-20 — such that we might now have difficulty in determining morphemic status of these elements).

The uncertainty concerning compounds (§ 6.61) may imply that more than three degrees of activeness (active, passive, semi-active) are in force. There may, in fact, be a progressive gradation from highly active to completely inactive, with a number of stages in between. It would be necessary to qualify such a point of view with the restriction that at certain points in this graded series there seem to be sharper jumps than at others. For discussion of problems of this type, continuing up to the phrase level, and with several such jumps or types indicated, see Bolinger (1948).

For a considerable period of time I have felt an objection to Bloomfield's treatment of primary derivatives, primary affixes, and root-forming morphemes in words such as *receive*, *hammer*, and *crash* (1933a:208, 240-46). I first reached a solution to the problem in terms of morphetically-complex morphemes, however, in a paper entitled "Complex Morphemes" presented to the Linguistic Group of the University of Michigan, Apr. 11, 1949 (unpublished). This approach was developed as a result of combining an interest in 'native reaction' (for which *slush* and *receive* appeared in some undefined way to be units) with a testing for parallels between phonetically-complex phonemes and morphological data. Cf. also below, § 7.87. For a different approach to this problem, with *receive* analyzed as two morphemes in sequence plus a verbal 'long component', see Z. Harris, 1951:301-302, 161.

For psycholinguistic tests to indicate that certain forms are members of a productive class, by tests with children at the language-learning stage, note Berko (1958, in Saporta, 1961:371-75); the children were asked, for example, to fill in words which required them to create plural forms of nonsense words.

6.93 *On Indeterminacy in Morphemic Analysis*

Zipf pointed out for nonverbal behavior "the problem of establishing criteria of comparison to determine how similar two acts of behavior must be before they can be considered the same" and at the same time implied that too rigorous a direct attempt to observe a person might indeed change his reactions, "making self-conscious the person whose behavior was under consideration" (1935:12). Both of these elements have already entered into our discussion (§§ 6.43, 6.44, 6.5). Bloomfield met the problem, in reference to semantic elements, by assuming for linguistic purposes that "each sememe [meaning of a morpheme] is a constant and definite unit of meaning" (1933a:162), with "*some speech-utterances... alike as to form and meaning*" (144), but granted that this "basic assumption" was "true only within limits" (145) since the "linguist cannot define meanings" (145) and this ultimately implies that for certain specific problems (e.g., root-forming morphemes such as the *-ash* of *crash*) the analysis "is bound to be uncertain and incomplete" (246), or indeterminate (cf. *sloth*, 145). Compare Nida, who states that for certain situations "The decision rests with the native speaker of the language" and that "This subjectivism in the analysis of a language is completely legitimate, since it reflects the actual usage of the language by the native speaker and reveals the live associations ..." (1949:57). More specific discussion of indeterminacy as such has recently appeared in Bazell (1952:34-36: 1953:111, where he states that "Indeterminacy is the price paid for discreteness"; and see also 1951:116); de Groot has for some time been impressed with the frequent necessity to allow for borderline cases of all kinds (1948, e.g., 480-81). For a discussion as to the limits (largely paradigmatic, or for inflectional morphemes) of 'suppletion' — i.e., the situations in which two morphs of a morpheme may have nothing phonemically in common, see especially S. Martin (1952:102); for earlier reference to suppletion, see Bloomfield (1926:161); cf. discussion of criterion of phonetic similarity in Hockett, 1952a:92-93; and for other dilemmas, 1950a:83.

Problems of segmentation have led to uncertainty in many areas. Z. Harris has emphasized the need to start the segmenting process "independent of any particular distributional criterion" (1954a:158). This segmentation by phonological sequence has been carried further and more formally by Hiż (1957).

General discussion of segmentation is found in Greenberg (1957) — considered by Chomsky (1959c:214) to be the best segmentation treatment.

Numerous specific problems arise in segmentation. Hockett treats the absence of stress on *-man* "as a separate morpheme" (1958:180). Yngve indicates that discontinuous constituents are difficult, or not found "in mathematical notation" (1960:448-49, 462). A fusion of two morphemes leads to many problems; for implications in morphology-syntax division note Pike (1949). For fused morphemes in blends note Hockett, with "*shell* a 'blend' of *shout* and *yell*" (1961a:52). For portmanteau — simultaneous — morphs note bibliography in § 14.52, with further bibliography on the problem of arbitrary cuts in segmentation. For fusions leadings to zero, see § 14.53.

For problems in folklore segmentation note Dundes (1962b:35).

For fusion seen through formatives of a matrix see Pike (1963d) and Pike and Erickson (1964).

For further bibliography on segmentation note also § 3.61.

6.94 *On Etic Classifications*

Some brief etic summaries of phones, or morphs, or other etic elements, have appeared for various areas. Note, for example, Capell, for Oceania (1933), and for New Guinea (1940). For a more general listing see Nida (1949): semantic etics of inflectional morphs (166-69); semantic types of non-inflectional morphs (178-83); for small morph classes of various kinds (1949:107-48); groupings by structural shapes (62-77); and for larger morph classes (149, and Fries, 1952); cf. also Kantor (1936:198-341), and Hoijer (in Symposium, 1954: 9-10). Attempts at a semantic etics go back much farther, especially to Wilkins with subdivided criteria for the etics of meaning, and a symbolism for such (1668), who (so David Abercrombie informs me) was in turn indebted to Dalgarno (repr., 1834, of items 1661, 1680). Note, also, Roget's Thesaurus (1933, revised) and Sweet's discussion of an earlier edition (1875-76, in Collected Papers 1913:15-16, where a sample objection is that "theft" comes under "transfer of property"). Recent attempts at some phase of the etics of meaning occur in Sapir (1944, in his Selected Writings 122-49; and 1930), Sapir and Swadesh (1932), and Bull and Forley (1949); the latter feel that "the study of verbs and many phenomena associated with them should begin with an analysis of reality and the patterns and limitations which it dictates to man" (65; but for a different point of view, cf. Hjelmslev, 1953:49). Note also the implication of the need for a hierarchically-structured etics of meaning, but with no attempt to develop such materials, in Bolinger (1950:124). Reifler discusses the general problem (1953:371-72), and indicates that the need for such classifications was suggested earlier by Vendryes; on the other hand, he illustrates the manner in which it may be difficult to decide whether two items should or should not be considered similar or "compatible" in meaning (1953:379); Paul, however, had long before insisted that "There is no such thing as a perfect concord between the logical [etic] and the grammatical [emic] categories" (1889:300), as a caution concerning attempts to utilize etic classifications as a basis for analyzing a language.

For an attempted etics of word types according to frequency, archaic versus non-archaic usage, and words needed for grammatical or social purposes, note Bull (1949:474). For category contrasts note Sapir and Swadesh (1946). For gesture, see E. T. Hall (1959), Birdwhistell (1952, 1959), Hayes (1957); for folktale note Propp (1958).

CHAPTER 7

THE MINIMUM UNIT OF THE DISTRIBUTION MODE OF THE
BEHAVIOREME (INCLUDING THE TAGMEME)

In Chapter 5 we discussed the behavioreme, and its simultaneous structuring into three modes. In Chapter 6 we studied the minimum unit of the feature mode — and observed (§§ 6.63, 6.7) that it had, among other characteristics, certain distributional relationships to classes occurring within functional slots. In Chapter 7 we shall discuss this characteristic in reference to the unitized structure of the distributional mode of the behavioreme.

7.1 Definition of Motifemic-Slot-Class-Correlative

Just as for the emic motif it proved convenient to have a simple definition followed by one which included explicitly some of the items implicit in the shorter definition, so it is useful here:

Condensed Definition:[1] A MOTIFEMIC-SLOT-CLASS-CORRELATIVE is the minimum unit of the distribution mode of the behavioreme.

This definition emphasizes the fact that such a unit cannot be defined as something discoverable or describable in and of itself, but that it occurs only as a part of — and mutually definable with — a larger unit of behavior. The definition is useful, however, only when it is convertible into a series of operations which allows the analyst to discover these units. The expanded definition contains nothing which is not present by implication in the shorter one, but lends itself more readily to being used as a basis for building a methodology of analysis and description of these units:

Expanded Definition: A MOTIFEMIC-SLOT-CLASS-CORRELATIVE (or ROLE-EME) is a minimum, active, trimodally-structured emic segment or component of human activity within the pyramided hierarchy of the distribution mode of a minimum or included behavioreme or hyperbehavioreme; it is characterized by an emic slot correlated with a morpheme class (or with a composite class of morphemes plus morpheme sequences); it is manifested by free or conditioned, motifemically-simple or motifemically-complex, fused or clearly-segmented variants through the mani-

---

[1] See fn. to § 5.1.

fested variants of its manifesting emic motifs or classes of emic motifs, and it occurs within a trimodally- and hierarchically-structured system of motifemic-slot-class-correlatives and within a system of behavioremes, and hence within a structured physical setting. Some motifemic-slot-class-correlatives have a recognizable structural meaning or structural purpose as one of their characteristics.

A verbal motifemic-slot-class-correlative is a TAGMEME; a verbal etic motif-slot-class-correlative is a TAGMA.

Many of the elements in this expanded definition have been treated in earlier chapters. See, for example, the references following the definition in § 6.1. Add to that list the following: emic motif, § 6; motifemic class §§ 6.63, 6.7, 6.83; motifemic variants, § 6.5, 6.84. Before discussing the further elements entering into this expanded definition we shall illustrate its general application to the breakfast materials.

7.2 The Motifemic-Slot-Class-Correlative Partially Illustrated within the Breakfast Unit

For a family-breakfast behavioreme we have already illustrated, in the discussion of its distribution mode (§ 5.2), the occurrence of slots within the structure of the pre-breakfast preparations. These slots include places for the official opening, for the various courses, and for the official closing. The kind of activity which fills these slots was also discussed.

Within this breakfast behavioreme, a motifemic-slot-class-correlative would constitute the unit 'breakfast-main-course'. Its slot-filling relation to the breakfast behavioreme which contains it indicates that the main course is a component of the internal structuring of the distribution mode of that behavioreme. This slot-filling characteristic, furthermore, is one of the principal elements which simultaneously characterize, on a lower level of the hierarchy, the distribution mode of that motifemic-slot-class-correlative itself. Another of its distributional characteristics is its potential for occurring in other meals — say a party breakfast — as well.

The manifestation mode of this motifemic-slot-class-correlative would be seen in its variants — namely, either a cereal-eating motif filling that slot, or a bacon-and-eggs-eating motif filling the same slot. Thus the manifestation of the 'breakfast-main-course' is by a class of emic motifs or, more specifically, by some one member of that class at any one time. The specific emic motif manifesting the motifemic-slot-class-correlative at one particular breakfast scene, furthermore, would in turn be manifested not by all the variants of that emic motif simultaneously, but by one specific variant of that one specific motifemic member of that motifemic class — that is, by the particular eating of a particular kind of cereal in that particular fashion on some one particular day at the family breakfast.

The feature mode of this motifemic-slot-class-correlative of 'breakfast-main-course' would in turn be characterized by all the elements identifying it and contrasting it with other units — especially (a) by the class membership actualizing it, and (b) by the added functional 'meaning' component of 'slot for eating main course for sustenance.'

7.3 *The Feature Mode of the Tagmeme*

The feature mode of certain of the units in the breakfast scene has just been illustrated briefly, but we now wish to treat that mode in more detail in reference to certain technical problems which arise during its analysis.

A series of verbal motifemic-slot-class-correlatives — i.e., tagmemes — may be seen in the included uttereme B18/9.1; B —: *I don't care but you ran off with mine*. Here the word *I* is manifesting a tagmeme whose distribution mode includes (1) its occurrence as both (a) constituting and (b) filling the first slot in that manifested uttereme, (2) its potential for occurrence in other utteremes where it comes in a different physical place in the uttereme (as *I* manifests the same tagmeme, filling the 'same' (i.e., emic) slot, with the 'same' manifesting emic class in a 'different' uttereme, in *Why should I care?*), and (3) the fact that its variants are 'tied to' (i.e., correlated in distribution and form with) the manifested variants of emic classes manifesting certain other tagmemes in the same uttereme (as *I* is 'tied to' *do* in *I don't care*, but *He* is tied to *does* in *He doesn't care*).

This tagmeme is manifested by a member of the class which includes morphemically-simple members such as *we, he, you, John, Bill, Jim*, and morphemically-complex ones such as *the dog, ten boys, all the men*, etc. These items constitute part of the total manifestations of the manifestation mode of that tagmeme.

The feature mode of this same tagmeme — the first in *I don't care* — includes the structural meaning of 'actor-as-subject'. (This is not the same tagmeme as occurs at the beginning of *I was hit by the ball*, as we shall see later; i.e., not all 'subjects' are members of the same tagmeme, though all such types do constitute a class of various different subject tagmemes, cf. §§ 7.321, 7.43.) The feature mode would also include among its components all the potential internal markers of the class which can identify this tagmeme or contrast it with others. Thus the fact that *big John* can be an extended member of the manifesting class of that tagmeme is also one of the characteristics of its feature mode.

7.31 *Distribution Classes of Morphemes as Tagmemic Components*

One of the characteristic components of the feature mode of a tagmeme (a verbal motifemic-slot-class-correlative) is the particular distribution class which manifests it. These classes, by their presence, contribute to the tagmeme a number of important elements which need separate discussion.

7.311 *Choice in Relation to Classes of Morphemes*

The tagmeme, through the membership of its manifesting class, is very important to human behavior since, among other reasons, it is here that deliberate, conscious CHOICE (cf. § 6.63; see also Index, under Choice and under Meaning and Choice, Native Reaction) is frequently exercised as to alternative purposes or goals to be pursued or meanings to be suggested to others, although at other times the factor of choice does not reach the threshold of awareness. When an author is 'hunting for the right word' the process of choice or selection becomes highly conscious; it can be made conscious, even if it was not so before, when a teacher asks *Why did you use that word?* Whenever alternative morphemes are being discussed culturally it is evidence that one is looking at a slot where a tagmeme is involved, while the particular alternatives which may be chosen are themselves the members of a DISTRIBUTION CLASS OF MORPHEMES (§ 6.63) which manifest — and hence in part constitute — that tagmeme.

Every morphemic alternative implies the presence of a tagmeme on some level of analysis, just as the exercise of these choices implies the utilization of some morpheme or hypermorpheme (Chapter 10) which manifests the tagmeme at that particular time and place. This should not be interpreted to mean, however, that such alternatives are always highly conscious since, on the contrary, when one speaks rapidly the attention is likely to be focused only on the higher layers of choices and purposes (e.g., in behavioremes, Chapters 4 and 5) with the internal elements representing a highly intricate unconscious slection of alternatives within the larger patterns. Selection of items within the smaller layers is likely to become conscious when one's activities are disapproved by other persons in the culture, or when disputes arise, or when motives are challenged, or under new situations. When a new situation forces on one of the participants an unprecedented conscious choice, this very fact makes the total event into a different kind of behavioreme, however, from that involved when the participant is just following a routine which has been established by others (cf., on participant differences, §§ 3.32, 3.34, 4.1.10, 4.22).

(Before leaving this topic one word of caution may be given: In discussing choice, we are not attempting to argue the metaphysical problem as to whether, on the one hand, a person has freedom of the will to choose to act in certain ways or whether, on the other hand, biological and cultural determinism rule out such choice other than as a name for a resultant of physiological and cultural forces. Rather in this theory we are discussing human behavior AS PEOPLE REACT TO IT, i.e., in reference to its emic structuring. In order to reach this goal, choice and purpose must be included in the theory, whether one is a mechanist or whether one believes — as I do — in some degree of free will, since many of our daily activities are structured relative to the working assumption that we do so have it; people in certain circumstances seem to talk, and to act nonverbally, *as if* they thought they had free will, purpose, and choice, and as if they thought other people had these characteristics, and this fact is an important part of the data which must somewhere be accommodated in any *emic*

198   THE MINIMUM UNIT OF THE DISTRIBUTION MODE OF THE BEHAVIOREME

description of their behavior. In this theory, it is handled within the tagmeme [or in the hypertagmeme], or within its nonverbal counterpart, the nonverbal motifemic-slot-class-correlative.)

7.312 *A Class of Morphemes as a Tagmemic Clue*

Since a distribution class of morphemes is a component of the feature mode of the tagmeme, it is therefore one of the identifying-contrastive features of that tagmeme: once the tagmeme has been determined by various procedural steps, and once the class can be identified in terms of its internal characteristics, then in any specific utterance the naïve or analytical listener who hears and unconsciously or consciously identifies the presence of some member of that morphemic class, by the help of one or more characteristics of such a class, has a clue as to the presence of some one of the tagmemes which may be manifested by members of that class. Once a listener is aware of the fact that English has an 'actor-as-subject' tagmeme, and that it is manifested by members of a class including *Bill*, and *Jim*, then when he hears the form ...*Bill*... he is alerted to the possibility that an actor-as-subject tagmeme may be present. Since, however, the morpheme may happen to be manifesting one of the other gramemes (say, 'object-of-an-action') which also are manifested by members of that same morphemic class, other identifying-contrastive features of the tagmeme must then be used to determine which of the tagmemes is, in fact, being manifested at that moment by the morpheme *Bill*.

7.313 *Etic Classes of Morphemes versus Emic Trimodally-Structured Classes of Morphemes*

The emic classes of morphemes are trimodally structured, as are the morphemes themselves, and this structuring affects the analysis of the variants of the tagmemes which they manifest (§ 7.4).

7.313(1) *The Feature Mode of an Emic Class of Morphemes*

Sometimes the feature mode of a class of morphemes includes, as one of its components, the class meaning of its membership. Many classes of morphemes, however, lack such a detectable meaning. The CLASS MEANING is in part observable in terms of the statistical probability that any one member of the class will have a certain kind of lexical meaning, or some specific semantic component. That is, if the bulk of the words of a class have some kind of semantic component in common, this component may constitute the meaning for the class as a whole, in spite of the fact that there may be a number of members of that class which do not of themselves include that particular semantic component. The class meaning is determined in reference to the generalized semantic nature of the bulk of the elements comprising the class, and not in reference to a hundred percent of the members of that class. Thus the morpheme class containing items like *house, dog, cat, stone* has as a class meaning 'an object' in spite of the fact that other items in the same distribution class do not have the meaning of 'object' but signal some kind of process, as in the words *a fire, a loss,* or *a thought*.

This class meaning, furthermore, is not determined exclusively in reference to an a priori etic classification of its semantic components, but is in part determined in reference to the function which the class fills within tagmemic slots of the language and of the nonlinguistic culture and the structural meanings of those slots (§§ 7.321, 7.324). Thus 'an object' is not defined solely in reference to an etic scheme of physics (which might point out that a table, for example, is a composite of processes or motions of molecules, atoms, electrons, and so on, or that in terms of a period of time the table as a whole is subject to decay and hence constitutes a process), but also has reference to the function of a word like *table*, as the people of that culture react to it. In this instance, a table would be treated by members of the culture as an object in the sense that the word *table* can fill tagmeme slots as 'actor' or as 'recipient' of an action (e.g., in *the table fell on my toe and hurt me*), and this fact contributes to the class meaning of that class of morphemes of which *table* is a member.

Some emic classes of morphemes have no apparent class meaning; semantically, these classes are 'empty' in a manner somewhat analogous to the way in which single morphemes can be empty of meaning (§ 6.45). Classes which are semantically empty are likely to be small and to be restricted to occurrence in one or a few tagmemic slots which are lacking in any obvious structural meaning (§ 7.321); the membership of an empty class is also likely to be composed of morphemes with semantic components which are very diverse, so that it is difficult to find a semantic component which serves as the 'least common denominator' of the class. A class of suffixes which occurs in only one tagmemic slot, which contains only a half dozen morphemes, and whose morpheme meanings are very diverse, would constitute such a class type.

Where a morpheme class has a strong class meaning, it may sometimes be detected — or tested — in ways beyond those implied thus far. If, for example, a word is borrowed from another language, and if the native speaker who first borrows that word knows immediately what morpheme class to place it in, and what tagmemic slots to use it with, without help of clues other than the semantic ones in the word being borrowed, the probability is that the class to which he assigns it has a strong class meaning. On the other hand, if native speakers react with considerable surprise when it is pointed out to them that a word has a particular etic semantic character (as *fire* represents a process), the probability is that his surprise is caused by the clash of a class meaning with an etic component of a lexical meaning which it is modifying. The feature mode of a morpheme class may (or may not) contain any such strong class meaning as one component; other feature-mode components help to differentiate it from other classes.

In a composite morphemic distribution class which includes some morpheme sequences, as distinct from a distribution class composed of single morphemes, there can be some markers of the class which are composed of one or more special morphemes of such sequences — and this fact constitutes another component of the feature mode of such a class. A case suffix may identify a noun, for example, as distinct from a verb; or items such as *the* or *a* may identify a noun phrase as distinct from a verb phrase. In a composite class composed of some single morphemes plus some morpheme sequences, the sequence members of the class could likewise be identified by some one morpheme of the sequence. Thus the occurrence of *the* in *the boy* serves to identify it as a noun phrase, as a morphemically-complex member of a class which also includes single-morpheme items such as *Bill*; similarly *-ize* in *verbalize* helps to identify that word as part of a morphemic class which also contains the word *run*.

When a member of an emic morpheme class is composed of a sequence of two morphemes, it is a MORPHEMICALLY-COMPLEX member of that class. *John* and *Bill* are morphemically-simple members of a class which contains the morphemically-complex members *the boy*, *a man*, and *Johnny*, each of which is composed of two morphemes. Morphemically-complex members must be distinguished, however, from MORPHETICALLY-COMPLEX (BUT MORPHEMICALLY-SIMPLE) members of a morpheme class. If, for example, one concludes that *hamlet* is a single morphetically-complex morpheme (cf. § 6.54) with one passive and one semi-active morph, it is a morphemically-simple member of the class which contains *town;* a subclass which is composed exclusively of morphetically-complex but single morphemes would in turn constitute a morphemically-simple but morphetically-complex class. A morphemic subclass which is entirely composed of morphemically-complex members, however, would itself constitute a morphemically-complex class. Likewise, one may find a PASSIVE MORPH CLASS which is composed exclusively of passive morphs (§ 6.61) in a certain tagmatic slot within a subclass of morphetically-complex morphemes. Classes of morphs are active or passive in a reciprocal relationship with the activeness or passiveness of their membership; a decision as to the activeness of a class of morphs automatically forces the same decision concerning its membership, and vice versa.

The principal component of the feature mode of an emic class of morphemes, however, is probably best considered to be composed of its TOTAL MEMBERSHIP rather than the morphetic or morphemic characteristics of its individual members. One class may be composed of members such as *boy, twig, scissors,* and another of items such as *brown, tall, ugly*. The membership of a class is an identifying-contrastive characteristic of that class. It is important to notice that the knowledge of the total membership of a class is one fact which enables the analyst to recognize the presence of a morphemic class through any one specific morphemic manifestation of that class, once the membership of class has been determined by prior study. Such membership, however, cannot constitute a clue for the analyst in his search for the classes in the first place; the class and some or all of its membership must first be discovered with the aid of clues which come from the distribution mode, as we shall see presently (§ 7.313(2)). Membership in a class of morphemes serves most usefully as a differential clue to the identification of the particular class being manifested at a particular moment, when the two classes under attention are MUTUALLY EXCLUSIVE IN MEMBERSHIP so that no morpheme is a member of both of those emic classes. Two classes of morphemes are composed of mutually-exclusive memberships if the members of these classes are in turn mutually exclusive as to the tagmemic slots which they occupy (§ 7.313(2)).

Class membership of a morphemic class may be limited, or CLOSED, such that no new members are known to have been added in recent times, and such that the analyst observes that a native speaker in borrowing words from another language adds them to other classes, but not to a closed one. As an instance of a closed class, note one of the groups of 'function words' in Fries, 1952, e.g., Group G, composed exclusively of *do, does, did,* as in the sentence *Do the boys correct their work promptly?*

An OPEN class is one to which new items are known to have been added in recent times, and one to which the linguist may by chance observe a native speaker add new words by borrowing or by direct invention — e.g., the linguist may be able to watch a scientist at work developing the terminology in some field, or may be able to observe a native speaker of a primitive technology borrow into open classes words for new gadgets which the linguist brings to the area. As an instance of an open class, note that class to which the following words have been added: *radio, television, meson*.

Closely related to the closed and open membership of a class may be its size. A class is SMALL which has only a few members — say three to thirty; but a class is LARGE which has many — say two hundred or more. Small classes are likely to be closed in membership; open classes are likely to be large ones. Small classes often comprise special grammatical elements, such as case, or tense, or connectives (cf. § 6.82(f)). Occasionally a morphemic class is found which contains only one member, but which must nevertheless be treated as a bona fide total morphemic class since it is the only morpheme occurring in a particular gramemic slot, and as constituting one part of a slot-class-correlative. Such a morpheme may be called a UNIQUE member of a morphemic class. Note Group H, composed of the one morpheme *there*, in Fries (1952:97).

7.313(2) The Distribution Mode of an Emic Morpheme Class

The principal differential element of two morphemic classes consists of differences in their respective distribution modes. This characteristic is more important than the phonemic shape (§ 7.313(1)) of its member morphemes, or its class meaning (§ 7.313(1)).

An attempt to make class meaning a basic starting criterion for determining the classes is fatal to any structural analysis.

The distribution mode of a morphemic class includes its occurrence or potential for occurrence in one or more emic slots. Two etic classes which are mutually exclusive as to the emic slots in which they occur thereby constitute two different emic classes. By this provision the classes containing respectively *Bill* and *sing* are considered to be emically different. Etic classes with different distributions in their respective emic slots are themselves emically different, and this distributional difference is the crucial element in the distribution mode of such simple morphemic classes. (In § 7.313(1) it was the total mutually-exclusive membership of a class that was treated as part of the feature mode of that class (§ 7.313(1)), whereas here it is the mutually-exclusive distribution of that total membership which is analyzed as a component of the distribution mode of the class.)

In § 6.64 we indicated that the PHONEMIC SHAPE TYPE of a morpheme constituted one component of the distribution mode of that morpheme in reference to its internal structure. Similarly, in terms of a distribution class of morphemes, any characteristic shape type which is present for each morpheme of that class is in turn a component of the distribution mode of that class.[2] If, for example, all stems of a certain language are of the phonemic shape CVC or larger, whereas some (but not all) affixes are of phonemic shape V, or of shape C, then the shape-type CVC (or larger) is one component of the distribution mode of each morphemic class of stems, and the option of having shape-type V or C is a characteristic shared by some manifesting members of each morphemic class of affixes. In Tzeltal (a Mayan language of Mexico), for example, all noun stems and all verb stems begin with CV, and some of them end with one, or two, or three consonants; numerous affixes, however, are composed of VC, or even simply of C (Slocum, 1948:77-86).

Another component of the distribution mode of some classes of morphemes or of subclasses of morphemes — in fact a component which is frequently the element which separates a class into two or more subclasses — is the POTENTIAL FOR CORRELATION OF A MEMBER OF ONE CLASS OR SUBCLASS WITH A MEMBER OF ANOTHER CLASS OR SUBCLASS, such that both have the same referent, either within the same utterance or within different utterances of an including hyperutterance. Thus *John, Bill, the man*, etc., may optionally be included in the following sentence, substituting for *Bill* in correlation with *who* and *he: Yesterday I saw Bill, who had come from the grocer's, just as he was crossing the street*. Or the following: Query: *Did you see John yesterday?* Reply: *Yes, I saw him crossing the street*. Note also *John, the man, him*, and *secretary, in John is the man I mean; they made him secretary*.

A somewhat different distributional component of the distribution mode of a morpheme class is its OCCURRENCE IN A SYSTEM OF MORPHEME CLASSES and, in this connection, in a HIERARCHY OF CLASSES or of subclasses within classes. Characteristics of these systems will be treated briefly in §§ 7.313(4), 16.15.

In § 6.65 we argued that it was useful, and emically valid, to assume that when a

[2] But see fn. to § 3.5(3), which would suggest that the analysis of shape-type sequence might better be treated as a component of feature mode.

listener was hearing an allomorph, that he was hearing the morpheme — that when an allomorph occurred, the morpheme could be viewed as occurring. It does not seem to me similarly valid and useful, however, to apply the same conclusions to a multiple-member class of morphemes and its variants. The difference lies in the fact that in between the manifesting morpheme and a total morphemic multiple-member class is an etic multiple-member variant of that class, an alloclass (§ 7.313(3)). (A single-member 'class' § 7.313(1) is not under consideration here; such a class would present a border-line case in this instance even as it leads to indeterminacies in other directions — § 7.324.)

For this reason, a person who has just heard a morpheme spoken has *not* heard a total alloclass; it is necessary for him to have heard at least two morphemes in that same tagmemic slot before he can react to the multiple-member nature of such a class. Even if he hears a particular sentence repeated a number of times, but with one word deleted at a certain point each time, with a different member of the same morpheme class replacing it, he has never heard the morpheme class uttered all at one time — but only members of the class at different intervals. If he tries to hear a morphemic alloclass as such, by having a list of items repeated in isolation one after another, this too fails to meet emic conditions, since this abstracting of the class is a kind of hypostasis which leads to a morphemic class quite different from the one he was trying to hear (inasmuch as one of the components of the class he wanted to hear is its distribution in nonhypostatic circumstances, whereas his hearing it in isolation is a hypostasis which destroys those conditions). A morpheme, from this point of view, seems to be an 'event', whereas a class of morphemes is not an event. Any one total variant of a morpheme may occur at one time in such an event; but the total variant of a multiple-member class of morphemes cannot all occur at one time as an event. A class unit is in this respect a step further removed from behavior as such than is the morpheme unit.

A class of morphemes, then, cannot be said to 'occur' in the same sense that a morpheme does. In order to indicate this difference in our discussion, we will say that a morpheme both occurs and is manifested when an allomorph of it occurs, but will speak of an emic class of morphemes as being manifested by the occurrence of one of its morphemes, without saying that the class itself has occurred.

This problem is the source of one of the reasons why a tagmeme seems, at first glance, so much less concrete than a morpheme. Since an emic class of morphemes is one of the components of the feature mode of a tagmeme, the tagmeme carries with it some of the difference between a manifested morpheme and a manifested class which is manifested by that morpheme. Nevertheless, the tagmeme is treated as an objective emic unit occurring within normal participant behavior — not a mere conceptual construct of the linguist (but cf. tagmemic slot, § 7.321) — because of its function and structural relation to the uttereme; it is assumed always to have a physical basis in terms of some of its manifested variants, and no tagmeme is postulated as being present in an utterance unless such a manifestation may be present.

We shall return to this problem again in § 7.55, insofar as it concerns tagmemes as wholes, rather than their manifesting classes of morphemes (and cf. §§ 7.313(4), 16). Meanwhile, the discussion has proceeded far enough to allow us to indicate that it is this difference between a morpheme and an emic class of morphemes — and between comparable elements in the structure of phonemes and tagmemes — which has led us to treat morphemes, tagmemes, and phonemes as more elemental within the theory of the structure of behavior than are the emic classes of morphemes, the classes of tagmemes or the classes of phonemes.

(It should also be pointed out here that on the basis of this decision as to the nature of the structure of human behavior it is by no means helpful to define a morpheme as 'a class of allomorphs' or to define a phoneme as 'a class of allophones'. The two uses of the word 'class' reflect groupings which are structurally so different that such a terminology is confusing. This difficulty is increased when we find it necessary for descriptive purposes to identify and name certain classes of allomorphs in which each allomorph in the class comes from a different morpheme (§ 7.313(3)). Hence we avoid the use of the term 'class' as applied to a group of sub-emic allo-units of a single morpheme or phoneme. To ignore the distinction — although, of course, it could be handled by a very different terminological device — is to ignore an important structural threshold within the emic activity of man.)

7.313(3) *The Manifestation Mode of an Emic Class of Morphemes*

The manifestation mode of a morpheme class is composed of the sum of the nonsimultaneous variants of that class. These variants may be optional ones, or conditioned by the immediate environment whether (a) phonemic or (b) morphemic, or may be conditioned (c) by the particular tagmemic slot and (d) by the congruent system in which they are occurring (§§ 6.5, 6.7).

For a chart showing intersection of these kinds of conditions note § 6.53; see also § 7.43 for chart showing conditioned variant types of the tagmeme as a whole.

Two morphemic classes may be etically different classes but emically the same class, for example, if they occur in different tagmemic slots (§ 7.321) but contain the same morphemes as members. It is convenient, however, to call two such etic classes the SAME VARIANT OF A MORPHEMIC CLASS, or 'two instances of the same etic class of morphemes', just as repetitions of a morpheme are the 'same variant' (§ 6.51) of that morpheme if the emic sounds are the same at each repetition.

A morpheme class has FREELY-VARIANT MANIFESTATIONS of that class whenever, in the same tagmemic slot, one member of the class is substituted for (cf. § 7.321) or replaced by another morpheme which is a member of that class. The replacement of *John* by *Bill* in *John came* and *Bill came* is an instance of this freely variant manifestation of a class of morphemes.

Three types of LOCALLY-CONDITIONED VARIANTS (CONDITIONED ALLOCLASSES) OF EMIC CLASSES OF MORPHEMES may be distinguished, in accordance with the kind of modification which is produced in the class by the environment: (1) In the first of these, the membership is reduced or increased so that the number of morphemes in the class is changed. (2) In the second, the phonemic content of the manifesting morphemes is affected. (3) In the third, the meaning of one or more of the manifesting morphemes is modified. The conditioning elements may be phonemic, or morphemic, or tagmemic, or systemic.

The first kind of locally-conditioned etic variant of a class of morphemes occurs whenever two etic classes of morphemes, which are members of the same emic class of morphemes, differ as to the presence or absence of one or more morphemes, provided that this difference is caused by its position in relation to a contiguous or noncontiguous emic class or subclass of morphemes in the same uttereme. In English such an instance may be seen in the composite morpheme-hypermorpheme class which includes the members *John, the boy*, and *the boys* in the tagmemic slot after *I saw* in the sentences *I saw John, I saw the boy*, and *I saw the boys*. Of these three sample members, however, only *John* and *the boy* can manifest that class in the tagmemic slot before *is* in *John is here;* and of these three only *the boys* can manifest that class in the same tagmemic slot in the utterance *The boys are here*. The partial lists of members of the larger total composite morpheme-hypermorpheme class which may occur in these respective limiting tagmemic slots constitute etic subclasses of morphemes or hypermorphemes, and these subclasses in turn constitute TAGMEMI-CALLY-CONDITIONED LEXICAL VARIANTS OF THAT COMPOSITE EMIC CLASS OF MORPHEMES AND HYPERMORPHEMES. Just as *will* in the form *wo-* conditions *not* to *n't* in *won't*, and vice versa, on a submorphemic plane, so the etic singular subclass of the emic class which contains *John, the boy*, and *the boys* reciprocally conditions the occurrence of the singular subclass of the emic class which contains both *is* and *are*. The conditioning factor, here, is the manifesting morpheme (i.e., *is*) of the subclass (i.e., singular) of the emic morpheme-hypermorpheme class (including *live, lives, come, comes*, etc.) which may occur within the emic slot following it.

Note, also, the conditioning of occurrence of members of a subclass by tagmemic arrangements of correlated forms such as *John* and *him* in *John came home yesterday and I saw him there* (cf. § 7.313(2)).

When the conditioning factor affecting the membership of the etic variant of an emic class of morphemes consists of a neighboring morpheme or morphemes, a MORPHEMICALLY-CONDITIONED (OR LEXICALLY-CONDITIONED) LEXICAL VARIANT OF AN EMIC CLASS OF MORPHEMES is obtained. In the tagmatic slot filled by *work* in the phrase *to make quick work of*, the manifesting etic class of that tagma potentially includes items such as *time*, but does not include *shrift*. In the phrase *to make short work of* the word *work* is a member of the same emic class as seen manifested by *work* in the preceding sentence, but the etic class is different, since it may now include *shrift* as one of its members, since one hears the phrase *to make short shrift of*.

In certain types of verse, a PHONEMICALLY-CONDITIONED LEXICAL VARIANT OF AN

EMIC CLASS OF MORPHEMES is seen, in that at certain points in a stanza the only appropriate (cf. §§ 3.42, 1.3) words which may fill a certain tagmatic slot will be items which rime. This riming limitation constitutes a phonological subclass of the larger class of items which might otherwise fill that slot.

The conditioned variation of morpheme classes thus far illustrated has involved the presence or absence of complete morphemes. In the next type, however, it involves submorphemic phonological variants of morphemes and hence of their manifesting classes. These kinds of variants have already been discussed from the point of view of morphemes (§ 6.53). A further word about them is needed here to show their relation to etic distribution classes of morphemes (and cf. § 6.7). When a type of conditioning of morphemes is phonologically regular (§ 6.53) and widespread so that it affects the phonemic content of a number of morphemes of a particular emic class of morphemes, it produces in the emic morpheme class a locally-conditioned etic variant which may be called a PHONEMICALLY-CONDITIONED PHONOLOGICAL VARIANT OF THAT EMIC CLASS OF MORPHEMES. Such a class variant is an ALLOMORPH CLASS which might be composed, for example, of the variants of the members of a class of morphemes in which each variant has been modified by the palatalization of its final consonant under the influence of a following morpheme which begins with a palatal sound.

When, however, the change of phonemic content of the variants of one or more morphemes of a morpheme class cannot be traced to the regular phonological influence of an adjacent morpheme or morphemes, but the change is irregular and phonologically unpredictable, the locally-conditioned allomorph class in such a situation constitutes a MORPHEMICALLY-CONDITIONED PHONOLOGICAL VARIANT OF THAT EMIC CLASS OF MORPHEMES. The *wo-* (of *won't*), and the *sha-* of *shan't* thus constitute some of the members of an allomorph class of that morpheme class which contains *shall*, *will*, *can*, etc.; and this morphemically-conditioned class variant comprises that group of morpheme variants arbitrarily modified and abbreviated in phonemic content under the influence of the morpheme *not* which follows them in a context such as *I can't go today*.

Similarly, there may occur a TAGMEMICALLY-CONDITIONED PHONOLOGICAL VARIANT OF THE MORPHEME CLASS which it manifests. This type would constitute an etic class variant which contained among its manifesting members some allomorphs which were phonologically conditioned by their occurrence in a particular tagmemic slot. Thus *he* and *him* would belong respectively to different tagmemically-conditioned allomorph classes (cf. § 6.53) of the same morpheme class.

The third type of locally-conditioned variant of an emic morpheme class is one in which the local environment affects (a) the meaning of some of the morphemes manifested within it, or (b) the meaning of the class as a whole. When it is the tagmemic slot in which the morpheme class is occurring that affects the meaning of the morpheme or of the morpheme class, a TAGMEMICALLY-CONDITIONED SEMANTIC VARIANT OF THAT EMIC CLASS OF MORPHEMES is produced. The effect of the meaning of a tagmemic slot upon the meaning of individual morphemes will be discussed in § 7.323 (i.e., *terribly* in *terribly pretty;* and cf. § 6.53); the effect upon the analysis of the meaning of a morpheme class will be treated in § 7.324. A MORPHEMICALLY-CONDITIONED (or LEXICALLY-CONDITIONED) SEMANTIC VARIANT OF AN EMIC MORPHEME CLASS would be an etic class of morphemes which had one or more of its members modified in meaning because of its occurrence in the same context with another morpheme or class of morphemes (cf. *drive* in *drive a horse*, versus in *drive a car*, § 6.53; in that section it was the individual morpheme which was under attention whereas here it is the class of morphemes which contains *drive*, etc., which is under attention). A PHONEMICALLY-CONDITIONED SEMANTIC VARIANT OF AN EMIC CLASS OF MORPHEMES, paralleling morphemically- and tagmemically-conditioned types, occurs when the phonemes of neighboring morphemes force a submorphemic but semantic change in the morpheme or morpheme class under attention. The heightened semantic impact of some words in verse is presumably to be handled as a modification of their less colorful meanings, as a conditioned result of the patterned phonemic content of some part of that verse (cf. the verse quoted in § 6.45).

An ETICALLY-COMPLEX VARIANT OF AN EMIC MORPHEME CLASS (analogous to a morpheme containing two morphs in sequence, § 6.54) occurs as a hypermorphemic subclass within a composite morphemic-hypermorphemic class, manifesting that larger class under certain conditions. In a distribution class which contains, among other items, *John, Bill, the boy*, and *a dog*, the items *the boy* and *a dog* are members of such a morphemically-complex subclass within the larger composite class. In certain tagmatic slots the occurrence of this morphemically-complex subclass is freely variant with the morphemically-simple subclass, since either of them may be found in such sentences as *John came home* and *the boy came home*. Under other circumstances — in different tagmatic slots — the occurrence of the morphemically-complex subclass may be conditioned. In the tagmatic slot filled by *boys* in *Boys like to run fast*, for example, only a morphemically-complex subclass occurs, conditioned by that tagmatic slot in its relation to the plural form of the morpheme *like* which is manifesting the next tagmatic slot; in the tagmatic slot filled by *John* in *John likes to run fast*, however, that subclass does not occur, whereas the simple subclass which includes *John* does occur, and the morphemically-complex subclass containing *that boy* may also occur, since these two latter subclasses are in free variation with each other in their occurrence in this tagmatic slot.

FUSED VARIANTS OF EMIC CLASSES OF MORPHEMES also occur, but discussion of them will be postponed until Chapter 14 (and cf. § 6.55).

There may occur SYSTEMICALLY-CONDITIONED BUT LOCALLY-FREE (cf. § 6.56) VARIANTS of an emic class, analogous to the three types of locally-conditioned variants of emic classes already discussed.

A SYSTEMICALLY-CONDITIONED (BUT LOCALLY-FREE) PHONOLOGICAL VARIANT OF AN EMIC CLASS OF MORPHEMES would constitute a distribution class of allomorphs which includes one or more allomorphs whose phonological character is modified because of the style which the speaker is using (§ 6.56, where *not* occurs in certain formal styles at points where *n't* would be inappropriate).

Also, a SYSTEMICALLY-CONDITIONED (BUT LOCALLY-FREE) SEMANTIC VARIANT OF AN EMIC CLASS OF MORPHEMES would constitute any allomorph class among whose allomorphs are some which have semantic variation conditioned by the style in which they are occurring (cf. § 6.56, with the illustration *He is a queer bird*; cf. also § 7.313(4)).

A SYSTEMICALLY-CONDITIONED LEXICAL VARIANT OF AN EMIC CLASS OF MORPHEMES is seen when certain morphemes of a class occur during the utilization of one congruent system (or style) of a language, but are omitted during the utilization of a different congruent system. To the class containing *you*, *he*, *we*, etc., in ordinary speech is frequently added *Thou*, for example, in the congruent system of prayer (§ 6.7). In the same congruent system, *-est* (verbal suffix, second person singular) is added to the class containing *-s* (verbal suffix, third person singular). An emic class of morphemes which is composed of the combination of two classes of morphemes from two (or more) respective congruent systems constitutes a HYPERCONGRUENT CLASS OF MORPHEMES: within such a hypercongruent emic class of morphemes, an etic subclass which is limited in part to one of the congruent systems is a conditioned variant of that hypercongruent class. Similarly, formal versus informal congruent systems of speech may contain different variants of a particular morphemic class. In English, for example, many polysyllabic nouns would certainly enter a variant of composite morphemic-hypermorphemic noun class which is used in very formal style, which would not be likely to constitute part of an etic variant of the same emic class which occurs in informal speech. That is, the use of too many 'big words' in informal speech would appear inappropriate — and inappropriateness is evidence of the use of items outside their accepted class (§ 3.42) or system.

7.313(4) *Lexical Sets and Systems of Morpheme Classes*

It is likely, furthermore, that a congruent system (§§ 6.7, 6.56, 5.4) which contains a special etic subclass of one morphemic type will contain several such subclasses for other morpheme classes. In such an instance, the sum of the morphemes and morpheme sequences in the subclasses of all the variant morphemic classes for that particular STYLE-CONGRUENT SYSTEM constitute a SYSTEMICALLY-CONDITIONED LEXICAL SET (i.e., CLASS OF COMPATIBLE CLASSES) OF MORPHEMES. It is appropriate to that particular style to use any member of the lexical set in any relevant emic slot in that congruent system: formal-style verbs may be used in formal-style slots where verbs occur, while formal-style nouns may occur in their permitted slots, and so on, so that a text constitutes a uniform document insofar as permitted lexical-style types are concerned. When, however, a particular morpheme or morpheme sequence is a member of two such lexical sets, it may occur in speech in both styles.

Occasionally words are excluded from certain contexts, not because a style-congruent system rules them out, but because a CONGRUENT SYSTEM makes them inappropriate. These are the situations in which it does not "make sense" to put certain morphemes together, even though the grammatical conditions and style do not prevent their juxtaposition or use in the same context in that manner: these are SEMANTICALLY-CONDITIONED LEXICAL SETS. The fact that it 'makes sense' in a fairy tale to say that *The fox ate up the moon*, but that it would not be appropriate in normal contexts, is due to such context conditioning.

In a number of instances (§§ 7.313(2), 7.313(3), 6.83(c)) we have had occasion to refer to subclasses within larger classes. This implies the presence of a HIERARCHICALLY-STRUCTURED SYSTEM OF CLASSES within any one single congruent system of the language under attention.

A system of morphemic classes is not an event. It is rather a class of classes, and its variants are therefore classes. Just as the classes are one step removed from events (cf. § 7.313(2)), so a system of two or more emic classes is one step further removed from such events. A system of classes of morphemes is not itself an event, and hence it is not convenient to state that it 'occurs' when an utterance occurs; rather the system of classes of morphemes, like its classes, in this theory is said to be manifested in utterances but not to occur in them.

Since in one of its aspects a language may be viewed, however incompletely, as in part a system of classes of morphemes (§ 6.7), it is highly instructive to keep in mind an abbreviated and over-simplified schematic set of etic possibilities or 'models' of the manner in which different systems may contribute to the structure of different kinds of languages.

In Schematic Class-Type A we will assume that the language contains only one emic distribution class of morphemes. All elements other than those signalled by the individual lexical items must be signalled by the emic slots in which they occur (§ 7.32); subordination, modification, 'an action' versus 'to act', etc., must all be signalled exclusively by the relative physical order of the elements. Every morpheme must be able to occur in every slot that any other morpheme may occur. If one tries to build a language artificially to meet these requirements, one starts satisfactorily, but cannot continue very far, since there are not enough kinds of signals available to handle the many kinds of relationships which develop in any culture. Nevertheless, the exercise is very useful, in showing basic language characteristics. Note, for example, the following sentences from an artificial 'language'. In them there is just one emic distribution class of morphemes composed of *los*, which means 'having some reference to one or more characteristics of smoke', *mif* 'having some reference to one or more characteristics of a ball', and *kap* 'having some reference to one or more characteristics of an eye or eyes'. The specific differences in the meaning of these items, such as 'it is smoke', 'smoking condition', 'smoke as a subject of discussion', 'smoke-like activity (of the eyes)', 'smoke-like character (of the eyes)', constitute tagmemically-conditioned semantic variants (§§ 7.323, 6.53, 7.313(3)) of the morpheme *los*, etc. The different functions of these items are characteristics of the tagmemic slots in which they occur (§§ 3.4, 3.51, but especially 7.321 below; for symbolization of the tagmemic structure of this problem, see § 7.74). (The data for illustrating Class-Types A, A', B, B', and C were prepared to these specifications by Evelyn G. Pike).

SCHEMATIC CLASS-TYPE A (Artificial Language Material with Only One Emic Distribution Class of Morphemes):

1. *los*   'It is smoke'
2. *mif*   'It is a ball'
3. *kap*   'They are eyes'
4. *losmif*   'The ball is smoking'
5. *miflos*   'The smoke is rolling'
6. *mifmif*   'The ball is rolling'
7. *mifmiflos*   'The smoke is rolling in round puffs'
8. *mifmifkap*   'He is rolling his eyes around' or 'The eyes are rolling around'
9. *losmifkap*   'His eyes roam darkly'
10. *mifkaplos*   'The smoke is trying to escape' or 'The smoke looks around'
11. *kapmifmif*   'I can see the ball rolling' or 'The rolling ball is visible'
12. *mifkapkap*   'He is looking around' or 'The eyes are looking around'
13. *losloskap*   'His eyes are smoldering menacingly'

Also, with no translation provided:
14. *kapmiflos*   ...
15. *kapkapkap*   ...

For building Schematic Class-Type B we will assume that the language — a different language from that illustrated by Schematic Class-Type A — contains two or more emic distribution classes of morphemes. These classes are mutually exclusive as to the tagmemic slots which they may fill; any tagmemic slot which may be filled by a member of one of the classes cannot be filled by any member of any other of the classes; but any tagmemic slot which may be filled by one member of a class can be filled by any other member of that same class, in principle, though there may be gaps in observation such that some apparently 'possible' sentences do not happen to occur in the recorded data. Each class contains a number of morphemes with easily detected, fairly objective meanings, even though a few of the meanings may be much less so than others. In this language, the tagmemic slot and its physical order (relative to other emic slots with their functions, *not* relative absolutely to the beginning of the sentence) continue to be an important signal beyond that of the lexical item itself but, in addition, the class as such is also a signal, since once the linguist has finished his slot-class analysis of the language, the recognition of a particular morpheme as belonging to a particular class signals the fact that the tagmemic slot which it is filling must be one of a limited number of tagmemic slots which may be filled by such a morpheme. This added provision makes for much greater flexibility for Type B than for Type A; a much more extensive artificial language can be built to this model than to Type A. Note the following brief sample: one emic distribution class of morphemes in this artificial 'language' is composed of *som* 'boy', *fik* 'donkey', *mul* 'cow'; the other emic distribution class of morphemes is composed of *lok* 'having reference to noise', and *mis* 'having reference to stopping', with semantic change from 'speak' to 'mooed' and to 'bray' constituting a morphemically-conditioned semantic variant of the morpheme *lok* (§§ 6.53, 7.313(3)), the semantic change from 'mooed', etc., to 'did this loudly' constitutes a tagmemically-conditioned semantic variant of the same morpheme (§§ 7.323, 6.53, 7.313(3)), etc. The different functions of these items are characteristics of the tagmemic slots in which they occur (§§ 3.4, 3.51, but especially 7.321 below; for a tagmemic analysis of this data, see § 7.74). Note that the place of a tagmemic slot is not to be counted mechanically, say from left to right, but in reference to its total function in which a morpheme sequence can serve as a morphemically-complex member of a class of items which fills a higher-layered slot. Thus in *sommislok* 'The boy spoke haltingly', below, note that *mis* is not in the same tagmemic slot in which it occurs in the sentence *sommis* 'The boy stopped', but rather joins with *lok* to make a hypermorphemic sequence *mislok* which fills the same slot as occupied by *mis*, alone, in *sommis* (cf. morphemically-complex sub-members of a distribution class of morphemes, § 7.313(3), and of a tagmeme manifestation, § 7.44).

SCHEMATIC CLASS-TYPE B (Artificial Language Material with Two or More Major Emic Distribution Classes of Morphemes):

1. *somlok*   'The boy spoke'
2. *sommis*   'The boy stopped'
3. *fiklok*   'The donkey brayed'
4. *mulmis*   'The cow stopped'
5. *sommislok*   'The boy spoke haltingly'
6. *fikmismis*   'The donkey kept balking'
7. *mulloklok*   'The cow mooed loudly'
8. *fiklokmis*   'You could hear the donkey stop'

Also, with no translation provided:

9. *somloklok* ...
10. *mulmislok* ...

For the next generalized situation, Schematic Type A', we add to the single major large distribution class of morphemes of Type A a small number of morphemes which constitute one or more distribution classes which are very small (some of which may contain only one morpheme per class); which occur in relatively few emic slots; which signal grammatical relationship or hypertagmemic function of a morpheme sequence more than they do a particular lexical meaning, so that the lexical meaning may be difficult to find, or impossible to separate in part or in whole from the tagmemic meaning (cf. §§ 7.324, 6.45). In the following brief sample, the reader is to assume that *kol* and *pav* constitute two members of a major emic distribution class of morphemes which is very large, but which is illustrated here by only these members; on the other hand, he is to assume that *em* and *sa* are the only members of their minor class. We do not supply the meanings of the morphemes, here, but they may be deduced (1) from the general meaning of the utterances in which the morphemes occur, in contrast to the general meaning of utterances in which they do not occur, etc., and (2) from the observed structural relationships of the morphemes in sequence, once the general meaning has been vaguely understood; tagmemically-conditioned semantic variants of these morphemes occur, as they did in the two earlier artificial languages used for illustration; the meanings of the morphemes *sa* and *em* are less 'concrete' than for *kol* and *pav*, and cannot be easily equated with the English translations implied in the translations of the sentences as wholes. The general meaning of the utterances as wholes, referred to in item (1), must either be obtained from some kind of crude translation by a bilingual, or must be deduced by the linguist as he observes the physical and cultural situation within which the utterances are made and the gestures or activities which accompany them; that is to say, that the analysis of the individual morpheme must begin with some kind of vague understanding of the total verbal-non-verbal pattern in which it occurs; morphemic analysis begins with a crude etic appraisal of the behavioremic situation.

SCHEMATIC CLASS TYPE A' (Artificial Language Material with One Major Emic Distribution Class of Morphemes and One or More Minor Classes):

1. *emkol* — 'They are learning'
2. *sakol* — 'It's a school'
3. *empav* — 'They are playing'
4. *sapav* — 'They are players'
5. *sapavkol* — 'The players are well trained' or 'They are well-trained players'
6. *sapavpav* — 'The players are playful'
7. *sakolpav* — 'The school is playful' or 'It's a play school'
8. *emkolpav* — 'They are learning in a playful way'
9. *emkolkol* — 'They are learning in a skillful way'
10. *empavsakol* or *sakolempav* — 'The scholars are playing'
11. *empavkolsakol* or *sakolempavkol* — 'The school plays skillfully'

Also, with no translation provided:

12. *sakolempav* — ...
13. *sapavemkol* — ...

This type of class situation, Schematic Type A', is patterned to reflect *some* of the characteristic phenomena seen in many of the languages of China. The reader should note, however, that such a type makes no pretense at 'classifying' a language as consisting of these characteristics only; every language is sufficiently complex so that at some point it is likely to have elements which are similar to each of the types we are using here to illustrate general principles. The proportionate amount by which languages differ in such respects, however, gives to them a pattern of their own which may impress a person from a different language area as being strange.

Such characteristics of a language do not necessarily have this effect upon the observer early in his study of that language. It is quite possible that an analyst in the early days of his study might be convinced that the data he was meeting were of a somewhat 'conventional' type (i.e., of a more Indo-European pattern). Then, however, a few residues might begin to trouble him — a number of morphemes which do not fit his preconceived ideas as to how a language should operate. It is sometimes such a crucial residue, rather than a large initial mass of data, which forces him to consider casting his entire description in a different format. For purposes of illustration, however, we find it necessary to condense, into a small space, material which in an actual situation might be much more diffuse. The procedures implied here, and illustrated more at length in § 7.74, are designed to be applicable to actual situations, not just to artificial ones.

Just as Schematic Class-Type A could be made much more productive by an addition, in Type A', of one or more minor emic classes of morphemes, so also Schematic Class-Type B may be made much more flexible if it is modified into Schematic Class-Type B' with one or more added minor emic distribution classes of morphemes to supplement its major classes. In the following artificial sample, one major class is composed of *mana, fukos, kiti,* and *sat*. A second major class is composed of *tesu, soki, kuni* and *samo*. One minor class is composed of *kil;* a second is composed of *top*.

SCHEMATIC CLASS-TYPE B' (Artificial Language Material with Two or More Major Emic Distribution Classes of Morphemes and One or More Minor Classes):

1. *manatesu*   'The lady makes dresses (or clothes)'
2. *fukostesu*   'A friend makes dresses'
3. *kititesu*   'The man makes clothes'
4. *sattesukil*   'Does the clown make dresses?'
5. *kititesutop*   'The man does not make dresses'
6. *sattesutop*   'The clown does not make dresses'
7. *manatesufukos*   'The lady makes dresses for a friend'
8. *manatesukitikil*   'Does the lady make suits for the man?'
9. *manatesukititop*   'The lady does not make suits for the man'
10. *kitisokimana*   'The man sells groceries to the lady'

11. *fukoskunisat*   'A friend keeps accounts for the clown'
12. *kitisamotop*   'The man is not singing a song'
13. *satsoki*   'The clown sells groceries'
14. *kitisamotopkil*   'The man is not singing a song, is he?'

Also, without translation provided:

15. *fukossamokititopkil* ...
16. *manasokitopkil* ...

Sometimes a language which contains phenomena associated with Schematic Type B may have within its major classes a number of subclasses of those major classes which operate grammatically in ways analogous to the minor classes for Type B'. Such a type might be labelled Schematic Class-Type B″. The difference between Schematic Class-Type B' and Schematic Class-Type B″ is that the minor classes of the latter are composed of emic subdivisions of the larger classes, instead of being completely independent of the membership of the larger classes. The Mixtec language of Mexico has as one of its most characteristic sets of features a group of classes which are similar to those mentioned for both Types B' and B″; for a list of some members of a subclass which manifests a Mixtec directional-locational tagmeme, see § 7.323.

In our next type, Schematic Class-Type C, we wish to illustrate the manner in which a language may have several major emic classes of morphemes, and several minor emic classes of morphemes, but so arranged into a hierarchy of classes that one major class (let us say Class I) may occur with one or more minor classes (say Classes 1a, 1b, 1c) in an intimate association with them such that a member of Class I plus a member of Class 1a (or of I plus a sequence of 1a, 1b, and/or 1c, etc.) enters into a class of close-knit hypermorphemes which as a whole is itself one of several major mutually-exclusive hypermorpheme classes. A further close-knit higher-layered class might be composed of members which have as one of their morphemes a member of Major Class II, and as another morpheme in sequence with it, a member of Minor Classes 2a, 2b, and 2c. (No member of Class 1a, 1b, or 1c occurs in association with Class II as comprising a hypermorpheme; and no member of Classes 2a, 2b, 2c occurs with a member of Class I as comprising a hypermorpheme.) Such hypermorpheme classes, we may call respectively Class I' and Class II'.

These emic distribution classes, like all other emic distribution classes of morphemes or of hypermorphemes are determined in reference to the tagmemic slot or slots which they fill. In the following artificial language material, emic classes of morphemes and hypermorphemes are therefore to be determined in this way; since, however, we shall not be discussing tagmemic slots in detail until later in § 7.32 and § 11, and hypermorphemes, as such, until § 10, some of the reasons for our analysis will not appear until those sections are reached. (Similarly, phonological considerations are relevant to the ultimate treatment of such morpheme sequences, and these phonemic and hyperphonemic items will not be treated in detail until Chapters 8 and 9. Nevertheless, we are anticipating here some of the conclusions concerning morphemic classes which in fact cannot be completely justified within behavioremic theory unless *some* data — the precise amount, whether much or little, we do not specify — are gathered from these various modes of the uttereme, as well as from the nonverbal behavioremic setting within which the distribution of the uttereme may aid in determining cultural relevance and function — i.e., meaning or purpose of some kind, as well as the slot-filling function of the utterances within a larger nonverbal-verbal context.)

It is very useful for the advanced linguistic student[3] to take a number of hours to attempt to analyze these data *before* seeing a solution or partial solution of them. Within this material are many kinds of interlacing problems which, stated in words, may not appear very surprising to him but which, when 'worked through', make concrete a number of the principles of linguistic structure which otherwise may remain unassimilated, and which cannot be appreciated in the same way if the solution is read before the data are viewed with care. For this reason, and because of the interlocking of morpheme classes with tagmemic slots, we shall give the data here, but delay the listing of the members of the morpheme or morpheme-hypermorpheme classes until § 7.74. At that time, also, we shall give some tagmemic and syntagmemic formulas for the same materials. The student will find the effort more profitable, in some ways, if he attempts to analyze, first, the data for 'Stage A' from these several (morphemic, tagmemic, utteremic, phonemic) points of view and only then proceeds to inspect the data of 'Stage B' from these same points of view, in order to correct or amplify his conclusions based upon the first stage. Next he proceeds to 'Stage C', etc.

The reason for such a MULTIPLE STAGE PROBLEM is that it allows for an extremely important element: It makes it possible to view all the data from many viewpoints so that he can treat the problem as a whole; he 'dives in' to the structure as a whole, vaguely, crudely, inaccurately, but nevertheless with the advantage that he can begin to see each componential system or mode of the language in reference to other systems or modes. In addition, it makes possible in a practical, working situation that which behavioremic theory asserts in principle — that various parts of the language, such as morphemic class structure and tagmemic structure, hypermorphemic structure and hyperphonemic structure, in some instances constitute reciprocal components in their respective definitions. Such a multiple-stage and multiple-level approach reflects, furthermore, something of the actual working procedure of every practicing descriptive linguist — even of those who most vigorously attempt to eliminate such matters from their theoretical statements and from their written final presentation of

---

[3] The beginning student is likely to find this problem too complex for solving readily. For his purposes, a more gradual approach is needed, and one which introduces him to problems in an order quite different from that adopted in this theoretical treatment. A detailed step-by-step procedure was begun in 1950 and announced (1954) for this volume. The methodological task, however, has been taken over in some of its introductory phases by Elson and Pickett (1962), and for more advanced stages by Longacre (1964a).

data. (For documentation of this fact, see Pike 1952a:115-19, e.g., in reference to Trager and Smith, 1951:54, 81, 68.)

If the student is not acquainted with methods of phonemic analysis at the time he starts the analysis of this material, he may ignore the phonological theoretical problems (which are not treated until §§ 8 and 9); otherwise he may utilize current phonemic techniques (e.g., Pike, 1947c). (The low dot [.] represents syllable division. The line slanting to the right [\] represents the end of an abdominal pulse, a stress group. The single vertical bar [|] represents the end of a tentative-ending breath group; the double vertical bar [||] represents a final-ending breath group. The raised dot [·] indicates the lengthening of the sound immediately preceding it.)

SCHEMATIC CLASS-TYPE C (Artificial Language Material with Two or More Major Emic Distribution Classes of Morphemes Linked in Close-Knit Hypermorphemes with One or More Minor Emic Classes of Morphemes, respectively; and with the Hypermorphemes Thus Formed Constituting Further Major Emic Distribution Classes of Hypermorphemes, or Entering Composite Morpheme-Hypermorpheme Classes):

Phonetic Data Stage A:

1. *to.'mik.sa*\|| 'The food is good'
2. *to.'mi.ku*\|| 'The food is hot'
3. *ti.'pa.ku*\|| 'The fire is hot'
4. *ti.'pa.suf.ku*\|| 'The fires are hot'
5. *ti.'pam.to.mim*\|| 'The food on the fire is cooking'
6. *ti.'pam.to.mis*\|| 'The food on the fire is done'
7. *sti.'fo.\mit.·i.pa*\|| 'The man is stirring the fire'
8. *sti.'su.\mit.|·i.pa.suf*\|| 'The man will stir the fires'
9. *sti.'ka.\mi.'tuf.sto.mi*\|| 'The old men stirred the food'

Phonetic Data Stage B:

10. *tu.'pa.pi.\mit.'mi.tuf.m*\|| 'The man sees the children'
11. *ksa.'tu.pa.pi.\mit*\|| 'The man sees well'
12. *lil.'ksa*\|| 'Life is good'
13. *ksa.'ta.ta.\mi.tuf.m*\|| 'The children ate well'
14. *tu.'pa.ka.\mit.'ka.puf*\|| 'The man saw the berries'
15. *lil.m.|·it*\|| 'The man is living'
16. *lil.m.|·it.m*\|| 'The child grows'
17. *lil.m.|·its*\|| 'The old man is living'
18. *lil.'smits*\|| 'The old man is dead'

Phonetic Data Stage C:

19. *tat.'su.\mi.tuf*\|| 'The men will eat'
20. *ta.tak.sa.mi.tuf.m.ku.to.mi*   'The good children ate the hot food'

21. tu.pa.ka.mit.ksa.ka.puf 'The man saw the good berries'
22. ka.ˈpuf.ksa\‖ 'The berries are good'
23. lil.m.ˈka.puf.m\‖ 'The growing berries are ripening'
24. lil.m.ˈka.pufs\‖ 'The growing berries are ripe'
25. lil.ˈska.pufs\‖ 'The berries on the dead vine are ripe'
26. tu.ˈpa.su.\ksa.'mi.tuf.ti.pa.suf\‖ 'The good men will see the fires'
27. tu.ˈpa.ka.\mit.'ksa.to.mi.suf\‖ 'The man saw the good meal'
28. tat.ˈpi.\mits\‖ 'The old man is eating'
29. tat.ˈsu.\mit.m.'kap\‖ 'The child will eat the berry'

Phonetic Data Stage D:
fon.m.ˈskim.\‖ tu.ˈpa.ka.\mit.ˈsmit.m.\‖ ta.ˈta.\mit.m.ˈka.puf.nos\‖ tu.ˈpa.tu.pa.ka.\mit.\‖ ta.ˈta.\mit.m.ˈka.puf.\‖ mit.m.\| fon.ˈsmits.\‖ ka.ˈpuf.ksa.nos.\| fon.ˈ-smits.\‖ ka.ˈpuf.ksa.\| fon.ˈsmit.m.\‖ mits.\| tu.ˈpa.pi.\sil.ˈska.puf.nos.\| fon.ˈsmit.-m.\‖ tu.ˈpa.pi.\ski.ˈsuf.ka.puf.\| fon.ˈsmits.\‖ ka.ˈpuf.ksa.\| fon.ˈsmits.\‖ tat.ˈsu.-\ski.'suf.ka.puf.\| fon.ˈsmit.m.\‖ tat.ˈ·a.ta.\mi.ˈtuf.ksa.ka.puf.\‖ lil.ˈksa.\| fon.ˈ-smi.tuf.\‖ fon.ˈs:kim.\‖ "I'm telling you a story. An old man saw a child. Was the boy eating berries? He looked again. Yes, the boy was eating berries. 'Hello, fellow', said the old man. 'Are the berries good?' asked the old man. 'The berries are good', replied the boy. 'Old man, can you see the berries?' asked the boy. 'I can see the berries and they are good', replied the old man. 'Let's eat berries, then', said the boy. They ate and ate the good berries. 'Life is good', they said. I'm finished telling my story."

Although we shall not be discussing in detail the problem of 'words', or of 'morphology' versus 'syntax', until Chapter 11, the preceding problem is built to lead to certain units which would clearly be recognized as 'words', and to illustrate a language type in which a morphology-syntax division is structurally basic. The terms 'stems', 'affixes', and 'words' are much more useful in discussing Class-Type C than they are in discussing a language which utilizes morpheme distribution classes which are more like Class-Type A or B.

If Class-Type C is augmented with further minor classes which are like the minor classes of Class-Types A' and B', rather than like those of Class-Type C which are so closely knit to major classes in further classes of hypermorphemes, it becomes Class-Type C'. Such a type may serve to initiate the student into some of the theoretical problems which are met in — say — Turkish, or Aztec, or Latin (though certain other problems, e.g., those of tagmemic fusion, need a supplementary model for Latin or Spanish; fusion problems will be discussed in Chapter 14).

7.32 Tagmemic Slot, Proportion, and Structural Meaning as Tagmemic Components

A morphemic distribution class is determined by its occurrence in one or more tagmemic slots (§§ 3.41, 6.63), and it is the structural, reciprocal correlation of a class of morphemes with a tagmemic slot which constitutes the tagmeme — a verbal motifemic-slot-class-correlative. Therefore just as the contrastive-identifying criteria of morpheme classes constitute one set of contrastive-identifying criteria for tagmemes, so the contrastive-identifying criteria of the tagmemic slot also constitute another major set of contrastive-identifying criteria for tagmemes.

7.321 *Tagmatic versus Tagmemic Slots*

With this in mind, it is now necessary to make a distinction between a tagmatic slot and a tagmemic one — which we have not done on occasions earlier, when emic slot was mentioned (e.g., § 6.63).

A TAGMATIC SLOT has at least three important elements to identify it, or to contrast it with other slots, in addition to those resulting from the class filling it. First, a tagmatic slot has a single, rigid physical ORDER or physical POSITION in reference to the place it occurs in some one variant of an uttereme. Thus, to be in the 'same' tagmatic slot, in two utterances, a word must precede or follow the same morphemic classes in the same tagmatic slots in those two utterances: *John* and *Bill* are in the same tagmatic slot, for example, in the utterances *John, they say, came home yesterday*, and *Bill, they say, came home yesterday*, but the tagmatic slots would differ slightly or considerably from them in the utterances *They say that John came home yesterday*, and *My big John came home yesterday*, and *Did John come home yesterday?*

Second, a tagmatic slot is such that there is a constant relationship between the function of any one of the morphemes optionally filling it and the morphemes filling other tagmatic slots in the same uttereme; there is therefore a constant functional PROPORTION which can be seen between any set of morphemes filling two tagmatic slots of an uttereme. For example, the relationship of *John* to *ran* is the same as that of *Bill* to *ran* in the sentences *John ran home*, and *Bill ran home*. Set up in the form of a proportion, this would read:

John : *ran home* :: *Bill* : *ran home*.

In these utterances, *Bill* and *John* are HOMOLOGOUS; and *John* is here a HOMOLOGUE of *Bill*, while *Bill* is a homologue of *John*. Two morphemes which are proportionate in filling the same tagmatic (or tagmemic) slot, then, are homologous; homologous items fill a comparable place in the next layer of the hierarchy of which they are a part.

It needs emphasis at this point that we have not stated here that any one 'meaning' — or *any* meaning — has been carefully and minutely identified in order to discover that proportionate relationship. Rather we have indicated that, whatever the meaning is, or whether or not there is any detectable meaning, the relationships are parallel between the utterances, and between the elements substituting one for another within the tagmatic slot. It is not necessary that one be able to define more accurately than this the function of elements in order to be able to identify slot-class relationships, and to identify membership in the same tagma constituted of that slot-class correlation.

Third, however, we note that in spite of the necessity for this last word of caution, we can state that often there is a discoverable — though perhaps vague — function, or STRUCTURAL MEANING which is one of the identifying-contrastive characteristics of such a tagmatic slot as manifested by its morphemic class. For example, the function or structural meaning of the slot-class unit manifested by *John* in *John ran home* may be labelled 'actor-as-subject'. On the other hand, it may not be profitable to try to describe a specific structural meaning, for the morphetic-slot-class-unit (the tagma) manifested by *to* in the utterances *He wanted to sing* and *He wanted to write*, etc.; in accordance with the second (i.e., proportion) characteristic of a tagmatic slot all that is necessary to enable one to identify the presence of that tagma is to separate it from others which do not enter the same proportion.

Nevertheless, once a structural meaning has been clearly found for any one tagma, it must be assumed to be a different tagma from a slot-class-correlative which has a distinctly different structural meaning. Once the structural meaning of a tagma has been discovered, it is as legitimate a criterion of the identity of that tagma as any of its other criteria; two tagmas can be differentiated by any one of their respective characteristics — whether of meaning, or of order, or of proportion, or of class membership, etc. It is in part by this provision, for example, that we indicate that in English there must be more than one subject tagma: the tagma manifested by *John* in *John ran home* means 'actor-as-subject-of-the-sentence' but the tagma manifested by *John* in *John was hit in the eye* is a different tagma with a different structural meaning such as 'recipient-of-action-as-subject-of-the-sentence'.

A TAGMEMIC SLOT is composed of one or more tagmatic slots joined into a single tagmatic functional unit. Tagmemic slots, from this point of view, are variants of tagmemic slots. (A slightly different point of view, not under consideration here, is that involved when the analyst is first attempting to analyze a language. At such a stage, a tagmatic slot may in some instances be merely a tentatively-regarded tagmemic slot. The two views do not conflict, and often merge into one.) Variants of tagmemes including their variant slots, would normally be scheduled for treatment in § 7.4; it is convenient, however, to transpose a bit of that material to this section in order to clarify the relation of the tagmatic slots to their corresponding tagmemic ones. Several types of such relationships may be listed:

(1) A sequence of two tagmatic slots in two respective utterances may be assumed to constitute the same sequence of tagmemic slots if their function, proportion, structural meaning, and physical order are the same in reference to each other in the two utterances, even if some material in the second utterance interrupts the two slots under attention in the first utterance. Thus, in *John ran home* the relationship between the slots filled by *John* and *ran* is unaffected by the intervening *they say* in the utterance *John, they say, ran home;* hence the tagmatic slot filled by *John* in the first utterance

and the tagmatic slot filled by *John* in the second utterance are assumed to be variants of the same tagmemic slot.

(2) The physical order of a tagmatic slot (in reference to other tagmatic slots in that utterance) may differ from that of a functionally similar tagmatic slot in a second utterance and yet be a variant of the same tagmemic slot. Thus the tagmatic slot filled by *away* in *John ran away* is the same tagmemic slot but a different tagmatic slot from that one filled by *away* in *Away ran John*, but the style difference carried by this tagmatic variation must be accounted for in a manner analogous to that for other kinds of locally-free but stylistically-conditioned variants (§§ 6.56, 7.313(3)).

(3) Two tagmatic slots may be assumed to constitute the same tagmemic slot if they differ only in the functional relation between these slots and, respectively, the neighboring slots in the utterances in which they occur, provided that this functional difference seems to be noncontrastive in the language, and is rather conditioned by the particular lexical elements filling these slots. Thus, for example, the relation of *fire* to *burns* in *Fire burns* is a bit different from the relation of *man* to *sings* in *Man sings* (since *fire* cannot voluntarily perform its action, etc.), but this difference is not emic; the tagmemic slot filled by *fire* is the same[4] tagmemic slot as is filled by *man;* the language treats *fire* "as if" it were an actor, precisely by constituting it a member of the same morphemic class as *man*, filling the same tagmemic, and manifesting the same slot tagmeme in the same uttereme.

There may, however, be some permanent indeterminacy or early but temporary procedural error in deciding just how similar two tagmatic meanings must be before one may assume that they may or may not constitute variant meanings of the same tagmeme; this, however, is no different in principle from the indeterminacy in deciding whether a certain pair of homophonous morphs, different somewhat in meaning, are members of the same morpheme (§§ 6.43, 6.44; and cf. § 7.43).

(4) Tagmatic slots from two different utteremes may constitute a single tagmemic slot if the functions (or structural meanings) and classes filling them are the same. Thus, for example, the tagmatic slot filled by *John* in *John is here* is the same tagmemic slot but a different tagmatic slot from that filled by *John* in *Is John here?*

Before ending this discussion of tagmemic slots it is necessary to draw attention to one erroneous conclusion which a reader might easily be led to deduce from our terminology, but which must be rejected within the framework of the total theory. If the analyst assumes that a tagmemic slot is to be considered an emic unit of behavior on a par with the behavioreme, uttereme, morpheme, tagmeme, phoneme, he will encounter crippling difficulties; although a number of tagmemic-slot characteristics such as we have discussed in this section can be shown to be in line with the conclusion that a tagmemic slot is itself an emic unit, there is one element that rules it out. This latter characteristic is the fact that the tagmemic slot *as such* has no physical manifestation within non hypostatic behavior. But since *every* emic unit within this

---

[4] Judgment concerning any one particular illustration such as this may need revision in the light of the contribution of transformationalists. See fn. to § 7.322.

theory does have its manifestation mode, a tagmemic slot cannot be considered one of them; that is to say, a tagmemic slot is not an eme.

The question is likely to be raised at this point as to why the 'filling' of a slot does not constitute a 'manifestation' of that slot, and so fulfill the requirements of a manifestation mode for the slot. The answer is in two parts: First, the reason for discussing slots as slots is specifically to study their distributional relations *as if* there were no filling in them; to drop this approach would necessitate the reworking of the presentation of the nature of tagmemes, without the advantage of being able to discuss the situations, considered abstractly, within which tagmemes have their manifesting classes occurring; it can be done, and would not injure the basic trimodal emic theory we have been setting forth, but it would make it more difficult to talk about, since more things would have to be said 'at the same time' without being able to break up components for separate contemplation. Secondly, if we grant for the sake of argument that the filling of a slot is a manifestation of that slot, and hence that a slot is an eme without the restriction mentioned above, then our resultant eme turns out to be a slot-plus-filling correlative. But since the filling is a morphemic class, we have ended up with a slot-class correlative; and the morphemic-class-tagmemic-slot-correlative is already accounted for in our theory: it is, specifically, the tagmeme. Furthermore, once we see that the result would in fact be the reestablishment of the tagmeme under a different label, we can then point out that there is considerable advantage in retaining our present approach: In practical matters, we gain by being able to discuss slots apart from their filling; in theoretical matters, we gain by having our term — tagmeme — represent by definition the entire slot-class correlative, with the filling constituting one component and the slot another component, rather than having the term focused on just one of these components. It allows us to retain the point of view, also, enunciated in § 3.56, that the distribution mode [of a unit] is *not* a system of empty slots within empty slots, but a system of filled slots, in which the substance filling the slot — the particular item at the time, and the class of potential items so occurring — is part of the distribution mode.

Two questions concerning this problem still remain: Why, one might first ask, do we use the term 'emic' for a slot, if the slot is not a nonhypostatic eme? The answer is that it proves convenient to have a term to refer to a characteristic of or component of an eme without committing ourselves as to whether this particular component is or is not an eme itself. An 'emic unit' is an eme; an emic characteristic or component may in some instances constitute an eme, and in other instances may not constitute a nonhypostatic eme.

The second question follows: What kind of unit, then, is an emic slot, within this theory, if it is not an eme? The answer to this query is that it is either an analytical abstraction made by the linguist, or — in an instance where non-analytical participants in an activity discuss slots where activity may or does occur (§ 3.41, the omitted choir number) — an analytical abstraction made by the participants. In both instances, the result would be a CONCEPTUALIZED HYPOSTASIS (§§ 6.43, 16.7) of a component of an eme; but this hypostasis is neither a functional hypostasis nor an analytical functional hypostasis of an eme in the sense described in § 4.23, since it is not the hypostasis of a unit which is a part of, and an *activity* normal or essential to, the behavioreme in which the slot normally occurs. In this sense, 'slot', as a unit is analyzed as a creation of the analyst, in a manner which we have rejected for emes of non-analytical behavior (cf. §§ 2.1, 2.72) but which we accept as valid for conceptualized hypostasis and which we have accepted for the etic systematizations of the analyst (§ 2.1). It is, however, a *conceptualized* functional hypostasis when normal participants focus on slot characteristics minus the particular activity which might fill such a slot (cf., again, § 3.41 — the omitted choir number noted by the participants), and it is a *conceptualized analytical* functional hypostasis when the nonparticipating analyst studies such a slot from the point of view of the normal participants in its containing activity.

Both of these conceptualized types differ from the nonconceptualized types of hypostasis of § 4.23 in that the only physical activity which manifests this analytical activity is constituted of the verbal utterances of the analyst himself (especially the verbalization of the names, such as 'slot', which he uses to label these abstractions), and of his neural activity as he ponders the problem (cf. § 16.7). The analytical activity of abstracting for discussion a 'slot' without its filling is itself an activity emic to the analyst. If one chooses to eliminate from one's data all analytical activity, whether performed by a professional or by normal participants in an activity, such problems may be in part by-passed. If this is done, however, the resultant theory cannot be a complete theory of the structure of human behavior since any such theory must include the theorizing of the theorist himself, as we have indicated in § 2.1. Yet a confusion of analytical and non-analytical types of activity paralyzes effective analysis; they must be treated separately within the theory without a distortion of that theory.

7.322 Recognition of Proportion

In the preceding section we indicated that one of the elements essential to a tagmeme was the homologous nature of its various manifesting morphemes. The question which we raise here is the means by which the linguist can recognize such homologousness when he sees it, i.e., how he can tell that

John : came :: Bill : came.

Our conclusion is that there are some tests which lead one to an assurance that his first guesses are right, or that they are wrong and must be corrected, but that there is no technique which can by-pass the necessity for the initial crude etic guess nor which can lower to zero the margin of error of that initial guess.

If, for example, the analyst for some reason suspects that two sentences have homologous parts, he may use an 'expansion' approach to test that guess: Two sentences which can be similarly expanded by the addition of extra words in the same places in those sentences can usually be assumed to have the same tagmemes and to have corresponding morphemes or words proportionately placed in these tagmemes, whereas two sentences which cannot be so expanded have to be assumed to contain different tagmemes in whole or in part, or to be in some way different as regards the arrangement of their tagmemes. Thus, the utterance *Come John!* can be expanded to read *Come here quickly John!* whereas the utterance *No John!* cannot be expanded to read *No here quickly John!* and make sense; the two utterances do not have homologous parts; *come* and *no* are not homologues of each other in these instances. On the other hand, *Come John!* and *Run John!* can both be expanded by the addition of *quickly* before *John;* they have homologous parts.

A second test for homologousness, one which is not conclusive but which helps to support the first, is the fact that if two morphemes are homologous in one tagmemic slot and if each of these morphemes occurs in numerous other tagmatic slots, there is a strong probability that the two morphemes will be homologous in at least some of these other slots as well.[5]

Thus, if the analyst is uncertain as to whether two morphemes are homologous in a slot under attention, but if he is certain that they are not homologous in other slots, then he should hesitate to consider them homologous in the first slot. This is another way of viewing the fact that morphemes occur grouped into emic classes, and once a member of a class is identified in a particular tagmemic slot, there is some probability that other members of that same class, occurring in the same sequence of morphemes, will be homologous with it. There is some caution needed in this test, however, since there sometimes occur homophonous but contrasting manifestations of tagmeme sequences — i.e., structurally ambiguous sentences do occur — which are not distinguished by this second test, although they would be so distinguished by the first test (compare *John paid for a bench in the park*, with *John paid for a bench which was in the park*, and *John paid for a bench yesterday when he was in the park*).

Further techniques of tagmemic identification are implicit in the balance of this chapter, but none of these later additions eliminates the necessity for a man to make at least *some* of the first crude etic guesses as to proportion when he is analyzing a language for which no interpreter is available. If the analyst has bilingual informants sufficiently sophisticated, he may try to pass on to them the onus of such an analytical leap, by asking them to tell him whether items such as *John came* and *Bill came* are the same or different. This is by no means a simple question to ask of a native

---

[5] Note that transformational tests underlie our early methodology here. In general, homologous items transform alike. Current availability of transformation theory allows us now to make much more explicit the nature of the tests than was possible a decade ago when this was written for our first edition — and to locate with more assurance smaller emic subclasses of nouns, verbs, or other classes.

speaker, however (cf. discussion in §§ 2.73-74), since in this instance sameness or differentness has to be interpreted not on the level of morphemes (in which these two sentences are different) but on the level of tagmemes (in which the two sentences are the same).

Even if the analyst succeeds in destroying the naïveté of his informant (§ 2.73) so that the informant learns to react on the tagmemic level at the appropriate time, the essential question still remains: How does the quasi-analyst — i.e., the informant who has now in part become an analyst — recognize that two items are homologous? And how is this knowledge related to an initial guess of the nonnative analyst, when both native and nonnative may be only partly right?

If one tries to escape this difficulty by stating that the analyst utilizes structural and/or lexical meaning to recognize proportion — which he certainly does, for this early guess — the question then becomes: And how does he recognize this structural meaning — is it not by proportion? And how does one separate that structural meaning in his *first steps* from lexical meaning — does not tagmemic proportion enter?

If the analyst tries to escape these difficulties by affirming (without demonstrating) that he uses neither lexical meaning nor structural meaning nor intuitive recognition of proportion nor any combination of these, but that he uses only 'distribution', he has once again changed the focus of attention for the question, but has neither answered it nor by-passed its implications. How does he recognize that things are in sequence — that one comes after the other? And how does he recognize that two sequences are comparable, or the same, or different, so that he can compare distributions? Or how does he recognize slots in a sequence without labelling the slot as such (since that would lead back immediately to the difficulty of recognizing proportion) so that 'distribution' is not treated as a crude occurrence of one morpheme next to another, but of morphemes in *relevant* sequence? And how does he recognize the fact that two items are the two items which he thinks they are, or that one is a recurrence of the other, if no such identification insight occurs prior to the study of the distribution of the items identified crudely or tentatively by that insight?

I am not competent to handle the philosophical and psychological problems involved in the analysis of the initial insight of the analyst, whether that insight has reference to the recognition of proportion (or of structural meaning) or the recognition of the first items of lexical meaning (or of purpose). Our linguistic theory and the procedures based upon it, however, must take as a basic working assumption the fact that proportion and lexical meaning are part of the data, as well as the fact that the linguist can identify, crudely, etically, with a wide margin of error, something of these characteristics in the data *before* he applies his rigorous emic procedures to this material to arrive at a structural refinement of that material. We have chosen — perhaps unwisely — to call these essential activities of the analyst INTUITIVE STEPS[6]

---

[6] Our emphasis on the need for intuition in some steps of discovery procedure is retained from our 1954 edition. Now, however, we would point out two factors: The continuing insistence that an

(or ANALYTICAL LEAPS). By them the analyst sets up his ETIC HYPOTHESES for testing, and in relation to them any emic analysis of human behavior must ultimately be in part initiated.

An intuitive step is implicit or explicit in the application of every major part of the theory. One will occur, for example, at the introduction of the phoneme where the analyst assumes the presence of speech segments and his ability to recognize — crudely and etically only — some of them. Another occurs at the introduction of each hyper-unit.

It is at this point, then, that I refer again (cf. § 1.2 end) to a monolingual approach to the analysis of a language — the analysis of a language approach through gesture, without an intermediary interpreter — emphasizing that it constitutes my basic method of testing whether those points which must be bridged by intuitive steps are fatal to the theory by being procedurally unworkable; or whether on the contrary it can be demonstrated, objectively and repeatedly, by independent observers, that those steps can in fact be taken within the limits of time and equipment available to the practicing linguist, and with a degree of accuracy sufficient to allow success. In reference to the two instances mentioned here (proportion and lexical meaning) in which such intuitive initial steps are essential to the theory, there is no doubt whatever — these steps can be taken: on the one hand, people have for years been learning the meaning of words by gesture, where an interpreter is not available, and my test of the monolingual demonstration of this procedure is merely putting the process under conditions for more rapid testing and better control. On the other hand, in the same manner, persons have been learning and responding to the analogies or proportions or patterns of language from their childhood — and, once more, a laboratory monolingual test of this ability (seen, for example, in our Record 53) merely shows that under controlled conditions one can indeed recognize linguistic proportion between similar items rapidly enough and with a sufficient degree of accuracy to be useful. Therefore there is no procedural reason for eliminating such

---

intuitive component in analysis enters at every point in field procedure where tagmemic theory brings in a new emic term at every emic level of each emic hierarchy.

More recent studies by the transformationalists have emphasized that there is no *mechanical* discovery procedure possible. This is another side of the same coin. We have insisted for a decade that intuitive components must enter. It is the necessity for these intuitive components in analysis which makes a mechanical discovery procedure impossible. We would equally strongly insist, however, that the impossibility of a *mechanical* discovery procedure (and see fn. to § 7.87) does not eliminate the possibility of procedures which allow us to discover things. The gratuitous adding, by implication, of the word 'mechanical' before the phrase 'discovery procedure' we vigorously reject. Rather, we have discovery procedures which are of the guess-and-check type (Longacre, 1964a, or Pike, 1960c). Once a system is arrived at by such procedures, with intuitive components, then description (as over against discovery) can choose to present only part of the data (the formal part) and leave out the semantic component. I have chosen, on the other hand, to retain semantic components in presentation for a simple reason: I wish to be able to know, after I have presented a linguistic structure, *what* it means — not merely that it is well-formed — since language is a communicative system. (For continuing indeterminacies in tagmemic analysis — as in any analysis — see also § 7.71.)

recognizability from the basic theory itself even though the philosophical statement of these matters may be far from adequate.

It is also important to see that within this theory a morphemically-complex item cannot be considered as homologous with a morphemically-simple item, unless the morphemically-complex item occurs within the boundaries of a single expanded tagmeme; it may not occur partly in one (nonfused) hypertagmeme, and partly in another (nonfused) hypertagmeme. This follows from the phrase in the definition of § 7.1 which reads: "...within the pyramided hierarchy of the distribution mode of a minimum or included behavioreme or hyperbehavioreme." The phrase 'pyramided hierarchy' implies that a tagmeme, except at a point of fusion of two tagmemes, cannot be divided in such a way that half the manifested form of a morphemically-complex variant of one tagmeme and half the manifested form of a morphemically-complex second tagmeme, constitute a coherent higher-layered unit, since, rather, in this theory the higher-layered unit beyond a tagmeme would be constituted of a hypertagmeme, and a hypertagmeme is composed of the manifested forms of two (or more) tagmemes — not parts of two manifested tagmemes. Similarly, we would not, within this theory, group into a relevant high-layered unit half the manifested form of a hypertagmeme with the manifested form of part or all of a simple or morphemically-complex variant of a tagmeme. (See, now, Halliday: "Only whole units can enter into higher units"; 1961:251.)

Specifically, this would mean, for example, that we would not grant that *John...s* is homologous with *you* in *John sings* and *You sing;* although *John...s* occurs when *you* does not occur, and vice versa, we would not state that one substitutes for the other, since the tagmemic-slot occurrence, and hypertagmemic analysis of the totals, is not the same. (This point of view is related to that within which we stated that Latin *...us ...us* of *filius bonus* could not in this theory be considered a pair of discontinuous morphs of a single morphetically-complex morpheme, but had to be considered a noncontiguous sequence of morphemes; cf. § 6.54.) We would state, rather, that *John* substitutes for *you*, and that *sings* substitutes for *sing*.[7]

7.323 *Tagmemic Meaning in Relation to Morphemic Meaning*

Occasionally the tagmemic (i.e., structural) meaning may be strong enough to modify, or even eliminate or reverse the meaning which the manifesting morpheme would have in other tagmemes. If we say that something is *terribly* good or *terribly* bad or *terribly* pretty the meaning 'degree of' seems to be implied by the tagmeme rather than by the morphemes, since almost any morpheme (or hypermorpheme) in the same slot will have much of its ordinary meaning lost whereas the meaning of the tagmeme will continue. Compare, for example, *awfully good, awfully bad;* or *fright-*

But for a quite different approach through sentence generation by rules, see now Chomsky, 1957a.

fully good, frightfully bad, frightfully ugly, frightfully beautiful. In some languages this is even more striking. In the Mixtec language of Mexico, for example, there are the nouns *čìi* 'stomach', *žatà* 'back', *ʔinì* 'innards, heart', *ʔici* 'road', *nuù* 'face'. All of these are used as ordinary subjects and objects of verbs with the meanings given. When, however, they are manifesting a special 'directional-locational' tagmeme, the normal lexical meaning is partially superseded by the meaning of the tagmeme so that translation of these items is changed: 'stomach' becomes 'under', 'back' becomes 'back of', 'innards' becomes 'inside of', 'road' becomes 'direction toward' or 'to, toward', so that prepositions might then be used in translating them into English. Note, for example, *hikán-de kee-dé nuù náà-de* 'He asks [eggs] from his mother', in which 'from' is the word 'face' in the special directional-locational position. For other Mixtec illustrations note the following: *ni hakù ʔuʔù-de* 'He laughed bitterly' in which the *ʔuʔù* is a verb meaning 'to hurt' but manifesting here a tagmeme which has as its function the modification of the preceding verb; hence the morpheme 'to hurt' has its meaning modified by an accretion of the tagmemic meaning until it must be translated as 'bitterly' (i.e., 'hurtingly').

7.324 Tagmemic Meaning in Relation to Morphemic-Distribution-Class Meaning

When a tagmeme is manifested by a class of morphemes which occur only in this tagmeme and not elsewhere, then it is impossible to separate the structural meaning of the tagmeme from the meaning of that distribution class as a whole. We have already indicated (§§ 7.313, 6.83(e)) that a distribution class of morphs or morphemes may, as a whole, have a kind of meaning in which a large number of the members of that class — but by no means all the members of that class — have some meaning component in common. Since, however, this morphemic-class meaning is in part a product of its distribution in one or more tagmemic slots, and since tagmemic meaning is likewise a product of distribution of elements in a set of functional environments, these meanings coalesce if the distribution class occurs only in the one tagmeme and does not occur in other tagmemic slots in such a way that the total class-meaning component could have been differentiated from any one tagmemic meaning. For example, the morphemic class composed of *and, or, not, nor, but, rather than* is such that "All the words of this group stand only between words of the same part-of-speech or subgroups" ... and "are signals of 'leveling', of connecting two units with the 'same' structural function" (Fries 1952:94-95); hence the semantic component of 'connection' or 'leveling' which is part of the class function is simultaneously part of the tagmemic function as well.

The indeterminacy becomes even more striking, however, when the morphemic class manifesting the tagmeme is not only limited in occurrence to that one tagmeme, but when that class is itself composed of only one member. In the prior situation there could be some lexical semantic differentiation among the words of the class by observing the contrast of one of them with another in the same tagmemic slot —

since any semantic difference between them while within that slot could not be attributed to the slot, but could only be attributed to the morphemes (i.e., the semantic difference between *and* and *or* is lexical, not tagmemic). In this new situation, however, no lexical contrasts can occur within the single manifested morpheme of the tagmeme and so there is no way of determining which part of the semantic com- already been set forth incidental to the discussion of the feature mode of the tagmeme.

The contrastive-identificational characteristics of the feature mode of the tagmeme meme which may also be said to carry the implication of 'plural modification'. It is not possible, therefore, to state what percentage of the plural meaning is carried by the tagmeme, and what percentage is carried by this one morpheme which alone can manifest it — nor is it necessary to do so since the analysis may be left indeterminate, with the statement that this is the way in which the structure itself is built, and that the analysis is designed to reflect that structure. For purposes of reference, however, the semantic label may be applied indiscriminately to either or both — one may refer either to the 'plural morpheme -*s*' or to the 'plural tagmeme manifested by the plural class which contains a single member, the plural morpheme -*s*.'

7.4 *The Manifestation Mode of the Tagmeme*

Turning from the feature mode of the tagmeme to the manifestation mode of the tagmeme, we find that much of the data relevant to the manifestation mode has already been set forth incidental to the discussion of the feature mode of the tagmeme. The contrastive-identificational characteristics of the feature mode of the tagmeme constitute its simultaneous components (e.g., the morphemic class which manifests it, the tagmemic slot which this class fills, the structural meaning — if any — pertaining to it, and so on). Each of the contrastive-identifying features of a tagmeme may vary freely, or under the impact of a particular environment, and each such variation of a contrastive feature, or simultaneous variation of several contrastive features of a tagmeme, produces a separate nonsimultaneous variant of that tagmeme, i.e., an ALLOTAGMA. We may mention briefly certain of these types, and refer to the sections in which the varying components were earlier treated; they are mentioned again here in order to help the reader see the variation as it affects the total tagmemic variant rather than just the abstracted class component of the tagmeme.

7.41 *Identical Manifestations of a Tagmeme*

Just as a morpheme which is repeated after a few minutes' interval is considered the same variant of that morpheme, provided that no emic units of sound are lost, or added, or replaced, and in spite of differences of surroundings in various utterances

(§ 6.51), so two instances of a particular tagmeme may be considered the SAME VARIANT (the same allotagma) of that tagmeme if all of the emic contrastive features are the same in the two instances. If, for example, we at one period of time hear the utterances *John came home, Bill, came home, Joe came home,* and at another period of time we again hear *John came home, Bill came home, Joe came home,* the allotagma manifested by *John, Bill,* and *Joe* is the same in each instance. Similarly, this same allotagma is seen in a different context in the manifesting phrases *Did John come home? Did Bill come home? Did Joe come home?* In each of these instances, the manifesting class was the same morphemically (§ 7.313(3)); in each the structural tagmemic meaning ('actor as subject' § 7.321) was the same; and in each the functional tagmemic slot (§ 7.321) carrying that meaning was the same.

7.42 *Free Variants of a Tagmeme*

There occurs a FREELY-VARIANT MORPHEMIC MANIFESTATION OF A TAGMEME when one member of its manifesting class is freely substituted for another member of that class (§ 7.313(3)). HOMOLOGOUS members of two utterances (§ 7.32) are freely variant morphemic manifestations of a tagmeme; cf. *John* and *Bill* in *John came home* versus *Bill came home.*

On the other hand, FREELY-VARIANT MORPHETIC MANIFESTATIONS OF A TAGMEME occur when two instances of an utterance contain two respective members of a morpheme which are in free variation with each other (§ 6.52), as in *I am going* versus *I'm going.*

Likewise, FREE TAGMATIC-SLOT-VARIANTS (or POSITIONAL VARIANTS) OF A TAGMEME would vary their physical order of occurrence without any change in their linguistic signal, or meaning, or style; compare, in § 7.32, *John ran away,* with *John, they say, ran away.*

7.43 *Locally-Conditioned Manifested Variants of a Tagmeme*

Conditioned variation of a component of a tagmeme results in the conditioned variation of the tagmeme itself. If an emic class of morphemes (§ 7.313) has two conditioned etic variants which are phonologically different, and each of which, in different environments, may manifest a particular tagmeme, the occurrence of each of these alloclasses leads directly to the occurrence of a LOCALLY-CONDITIONED PHONOLOGICAL VARIANT OF A TAGMEME manifested by these respective alloclasses. This local conditioning may be of several types, in accordance with the respective types of conditioned alloclasses (§ 7.313(3)).

Note, again, that the types of local conditioning can be shown as the intersection of conditioning types: phonological, lexical, tagmemic, and (§ 7.46) systemic; and the elements affected can be the lexical class, the phonological shape of the manifested members of the class, and the shade of meaning of the class or of the members of the class. Note accompanying chart:

		Conditioned Component		
		Lexical	Phonological	Semantic
Conditioning	Lexical			
Environment	Phonological			
	Tagmemic			
	Systemic			

The tagmeme has (1) a morphemically-conditioned phonological variant when one or more members of the morphemic class manifesting the allotagma is submorphemically but phonologically modified in an irregular manner due to the influence of a specific neighboring morpheme or morphemes (§§ 6.53; e.g., as *will* is modified to *wo-* in *won't*). A tagmeme has (2) a phonologically-conditioned phonological variant when the morphemes of the class or subclass manifesting the allotagma are submorphemically but phonologically conditioned in a regular manner (§ 6.53, say by a regular process of palatalization). There occurs, also, (3) a tagmemically-conditioned phonological variant of an allotagma when one or more of the members of the morphemic class manifesting the allotagma is submorphemically but phonologically modified in an irregular manner, due to the influence of a neighboring tagmeme or tagmemes; if we assume that in §§ 6.53, 7.313(3) we were correct in concluding that *I* and *me*, *he* and *him*, and also *she* and *her* are respectively members of single morphemes, with locally-conditioned phonological variants determined by their occurrence *within* particular tagmemes in utterances such as *She came home* and *The people met her*, we would assume furthermore that the same phonological variants are conditioned by *neighboring* tagmemes in such instances as those which Jespersen calls 'relative attraction' in utterances like *I have come to be known as her whom your uncle trusted* (1949, § 7.226, where *her* is used rather than *she* under the influence of the manifested tagmeme following it). For a different type of example in which it may perhaps be helpful to assume that a morpheme receives a phonological variant under the impact of a neighboring manifested tagmeme, note *wiv-* in *wives;* here, and possibly also in the earlier illustration, it is indeterminate as to whether the conditioning element is the single morpheme 'plural', or the tagmeme uniquely manifested by that one morpheme.

The membership of the class of morphemes manifesting the tagmeme may be controlled locally, leading to a LOCALLY-CONDITIONED LEXICAL (or MORPHEMIC) VARIANT OF A TAGMEME. The conditioning element (§ 7.313(3)) may be (1) morphemic (such that certain morphemes are limited to sequences in which certain other specific morphemes occur — as in *to make short shrift of*), or (2) phonemic (such that only certain words, of a particular phonological structure, may be used in certain places where they must rhyme with other words, etc.), or (3) tagmemic (such that there is concord — plural noun occurring with plural verb, etc.).

When, however, the tagmemic component which is affected is a semantic one, then there occurs a LOCALLY-CONDITIONED SEMANTIC VARIANT OF A TAGMEME. The semantic component which is affected may be one of the individual semantic components of the individual morphemes comprising the class of morphemes manifesting the tagmeme, and in this situation one may see semantic components of the morphemes affected (1) by local morphemic conditions (§§ 6.53, 7.313(3), e.g., in *to drive a horse* versus *to drive a car*), (2) by local tagmemic conditions (§§ 6.44, 7.323, 7.313(3), e.g., in *terribly pretty*), or (3) by local phonemic conditions (§§ 6.53, 7.313(3), e.g., in rhyme or alliteration).

On the other hand, the vague, general meaning of the manifesting class of morphemes may contribute to the meaning of the total tagmeme (§§ 7.312, 7.313(1)), and in this way be considered to affect that structural meaning indirectly. In instances where only one tagmeme is ever manifested by a particular class of morphemes there may be indeterminacy between the class meaning and the structural meaning of the tagmeme (§ 7.324).

In addition, the semantic conditioning may be local but the semantic component directly affected may be structural meaning of the tagmeme itself, rather than the meaning of the class of morphemes (or its members) which manifests the tagmeme. Thus, for example, the meaning 'actor-as-subject' in the first tagmeme in *Fire burns* is slightly different from the meaning 'actor-as-subject' in *Man sings*, since the relationship of the subject to the remainder of the sentence is slightly different in each instance (§ 7.321).

Just as, however, differences of meaning which are sufficiently great may force the analyst to treat as different a pair of homophonous morphemes, so it is necessary to treat as separate tagmemes any two tagmas which are sufficiently different in meaning (§ 7.321), even if they are manifested by the very same morphemes; such tagmemic manifestations are homophonous[8] but not homologous (cf. § 7.321, where *John* is seen to manifest two separate tagmas — which may now be said to constitute separate tagmemes as well — in the utterances *John ran home* and *John was hit in the eye*). For an illustration of longer phrases which are homophonous but not homologous — and which therefore, by this theory, are seen to contain the same morphemes but different tagmemes — note Fries (1952:223): "these *Spanish students* (those who are studying the language, Spanish, *or* students from Spain", "a *deaf* and *dumb teacher* (one who teaches those who are deaf and dumb *or* one who is himself deaf and dumb)"; the expanded environments which indicate that the relationships of the parts of the sentences are not the same for the alternate interpretations are there

---

[8] Note (unchanged from our 1954 edition) that I have long been interested in ambiguous utterances; but that here ambiguous utterances are treated as homophonous sentences (or phrases) via homophonous manifesting morphemes of contrasting tagmeme sequences. Tagmemic theory shares with more recent transformationalist studies (Chomsky, 1957a:86-87) the concern with phrases undifferentiated by a mere sequence of morphemes or of morpheme classes. In our most recent tagmemic studies, we are dealing with tagmemes in relation to grammatical roles as well as to situational roles; see fn. to § 7.6).

supplied by Fries, as indicated. The degree of difference of meaning necessary to be sure that such homophonous items are or are not homologous (i.e., are or are not freely variant manifestations of the same tagmeme) is indeterminate, as the degree of difference necessary to separate homophonous morphemes is indeterminate (§§ 7.321, 6.43, 6.44); a number of doubtful instances might be included among those modifiers for which Fries states: "I have not been able to find formal features that differentiate the more precise meanings included here" (1952:224 fn. 15).

Turning now to the membership of a class of morphemes manifesting a tagmeme, we see that conditioned changes in the membership (§ 7.313(3)) of an emic class within any one emic slot lead to conditioned changes in the etic variants of the tagmeme which it manifests, i.e. to LOCALLY-CONDITIONED MORPHEMIC (or LEXICAL) VARIANTS OF A TAGMEME. These variants (1) are morphemically (or lexically) conditioned when the class membership which may manifest the tagmeme is limited because of the specific morphemic or lexical items in its immediate surroundings (§ 7.313(3), e.g., the etic class containing *shrift* in *to make short shrift of* versus the etic class in *to make quick ... of*). The variants (2) are phonemically conditioned when the class membership which may manifest the tagmeme is limited because of the necessary phonological shape of the lexical item required to fill the slot (§ 7.313(3), e.g., in those instances in verse where a particular grammatical slot must be filled by words of a specific rhyming character). The variants (3) are tagmemically conditioned when the class membership which may manifest the tagmeme is limited because of the subclass of morphemes manifesting a different tagmeme in some other part of the uttereme or hyperuttereme (§ 7.313(3); e.g., in concord or agreement of various types, as plural subject with plural predicate; or § 7.313(2), in the correlation of a member of one class manifesting a tagmeme with a member of a different class manifesting a second tagmeme, as *he* correlates with *man* — in the same or different utteremes of a hyperuttereme — or as *Bill* correlates with *secretary* in *They made Bill secretary*).

7.44 *Morphemically-Complex Manifested Variants of a Tagmeme*

In reference to the membership of the classes of units manifesting tagmemes, it is not only the changes in the individual morphemes of the manifesting subclasses which must be discussed, but the morphemically-simple versus morphemically-complex membership of these manifesting classes. The problem assumes considerable importance, since the threshold between tagmemes and hypertagmemes must be determined relative to considerations of this membership.[9] We have already

---

[9] The reader needs to be aware of an important change in the use of terms which has entered tagmemic discussion at this point. Shell's morphological study (1957) was written from this viewpoint — with a tagmeme requiring at least a filler manifestation of length no more than one morpheme long, and a hypertagmeme with at least two obligatory parts manifesting it. Longacre felt that this dis-

faced a similar problem in noting the difference between a behavioreme and hyperbehavioreme; between minimum and nonminimum (expanded) manifested variants of a behavioreme; between a minimum behavioreme and a minimum manifested variant of a behavioreme; and between top focus and included behavioremes (§ 5.3).

The crucial difference between a tagmeme and a hypertagmeme is that a tagmeme is sometimes manifested by a single morpheme, whereas a hypertagmeme is never manifested by a single morpheme; some tagmemes may on some occasions be manifested by a sequence of two or more morphemes, whereas a hypertagmeme is manifested exclusively by sequences of two or more morphemes or by a simultaneous composite or fusion of two or more morphemes; the manifestation of a tagmeme is optionally morphemically complex (but with the essential reservation that some of its manifestations are morphemically simple), whereas every manifestation of a hypertagmeme is essentially morphemically complex; except that here, as at many other points in behavior, there may be discovered an area of indeterminacy.

The difference in the permitted manifestation of tagmemes versus hypertagmemes can also be stated in reference to the classes whose membership comprises the manifestation of the tagmemes and hypertagmemes. Thus (see § 7.313(1)) the emic class manifesting a tagmeme must either be morphemically simple, or it must contain a morphemically-simple subclass as part of the total class which is a morpheme-hypermorpheme composite class (e.g., *John, Bill, the boy, Johnny, the big boy*, as members of a class which may manifest the last tagmeme in the sentence *I just saw John*).

Similarly, data in § 7.313(1) can be utilized to indicate that a manifested variant of a tagmeme can be morphetically complex but morphemically simple, since a single-morpheme manifestation is morphemically simple whether the morpheme itself be morphetically simple or morphetically complex. If, for example, the word *hamlet* is analyzed as composed of two morphs but one morpheme (§§ 6.54, 7.313(1)), then the tagmemic slot next after *the* in the sentence *The hamlet is over there* is the one filled by *hamlet;* this tagmemic slot would be tagmatically complex but tagmemically simple, filled by a morphetically-complex but morphemically-simple member of an emic class.

On the other hand an actor-as-subject plus action expression such as *John saw Bill* in the sentence *John saw Bill but I saw George* would constitute the manifestation of a hypertagmeme, not of a tagmeme, since at least two morphemes are essential to the emic slot filled by *John saw Bill* if the structural relationship of that expression to the rest of the sentence is not to be changed.

Within the discussion of the morphemically-complex manifested variants of a

---

allowed the analogy of a phonological hierarchy in which syllable need not be longer than one phoneme, etc. Hence he treated tagmemes as occurring at various levels of the grammatical hierarchy. This view is now widely adopted, but not integrated into the early chapters here. For extensive discussion of its theoretical implications, see below, §§ 11.1-4, and fn. to § 10.1; for pedagogy see Longacre (1964a).

tagmeme it is useful to introduce a further subdivision: an ESSENTIALLY-COMPLEX VARIANT OF A TAGMEME is one in which both members of the complex (or substitutes for them) must occur if either of them occurs. Thus *the boy* is an essentially-complex variant of a tagmeme in *The boy came home*, since, if *the* occurs, *boy* (or a substitute) must also occur; if *boy* occurs, then *the* (or a substitute) must occur; yet the emic slot at that point is tagmemic rather than hypertagmemic since *John* could substitute for the sequence *the boy*. An OPTIONALLY-COMPLEX (or EXPANDED) VARIANT OF A TAGMEME, however, is one in which one morpheme (or a substitute for it) of the two-morpheme sequence is essential but the other is optional. Thus *My John* in *My John came home* is an optionally-complex manifestation of the actor-as-subject tagmeme, and an expanded variety of the simple manifested variant *John* in *John came home*. The MINIMUM VARIANT OF A TAGMEME would be a single morpheme such as *John* (but the minimum variant of a hypertagmeme would be a two-morpheme sequence).

It should be further pointed out that the reason why a morpheme sequence such as *my John* must be treated as manifesting the same tagmeme as *John* does, in the sentences *My John came home* and *John came home*, is that the emic proportion is unchanged by this relation; i.e.,

John : *came home* :: *My John* : *came home*

insofar as the basic structural relationships of the emic slots in that sentence are concerned (cf. § 7.321). *John* and *My John* are here homologous.

A complication arises at this point in the discussion: By earlier implication of the theory (§§ 6.1, 6.66), a morpheme occurs only as it is manifesting a tagmeme; every occurring morpheme manifests a tagmeme; the beginning of every occurring morpheme coincides with the beginning of a tagmeme and the ending of every occurring morpheme coincides with the end of a tagmeme; within the theory, every morpheme is co-terminous with a tagmeme. How, then, is it possible for a single tagmeme to be manifested either by an optionally-complex variant or by an essentially-complex variant if such a variant contains two morphemes each of which is co-terminous with a tagmeme?

The answer implied by this theory is that there may be an INCLUDED TAGMEME within the manifestation of another tagmeme, when an emically-minimum tagmeme happens to be manifested by an essentially-complex or by an optionally-complex variant. When the tagmeme manifested by *John* in *John came home* is expanded to *my John*, the tagmeme 'actor-as-subject' continues with the same structural meaning and function as before, but with an expanded manifested variant. Within that manifested variant of the tagmeme, however, on an inner layer of structure, two included tagmemes are now to be seen, one of which is manifested by *John* in *my John* and the other of which is manifested by *my*, and both of which manifest minimum tagmemes included within an expanded variant of the minimum tagmeme 'actor-as-subject'. A different set of included minimum tagmemes within the same tagmeme 'actor-as-subject' (but with that tagmeme and its manifesting class occurring with etic semantic variants, cf. §§ 7.321, 7.313(1), 7.313(3)) can be seen in the essentially-complex variant *to sing* in the utterance *To sing takes effort* (contrast *Work takes effort*).

7.45 *Fused versus Clearly-Segmented Variants of Tagmemes*

Since morphemes are distributed within tagmemes (§§ 6.1, 6.66), and a tagmeme begins or ends wherever a morpheme begins or ends, and since, furthermore, there are various kinds of fusion between morphemes (§§ 6.55, 6.66), it follows that there are tagmemic fusions; there will be as many types of such tagmemic fusion, also, as there are of morphemic fusion. The morphemic types are listed in § 6.66; the gramemic fusions will be discussed in § 14; some of the problems of discovering tagmemic borders will be discussed in that section, and in §§ 7.56, 11.

7.46 *Systemically-Conditioned Variants of Tagmemes*

In § 7.43 we indicated the manner in which the locally-conditioned variants of emic classes (§ 7.313(3)) resulted in locally-conditioned manifestations of the tagmeme. We now turn to the manner in which a systemically-conditioned but locally-free class of morphemes can also affect the manifestation of the tagmeme, so as to produce a LOCALLY-FREE BUT SYSTEMICALLY-CONDITIONED MANIFESTED LEXICAL (or MORPHEMIC) VARIANT OF A TAGMEME. This conditioning of tagmemes may be of two types, in accordance with the kind of systems (§ 7.313(4)) which affect the tagmemes. A tagmeme has (1) a style-conditioned lexical manifested variant when the matrix system affecting the tagmeme is a congruent linguistic style (e.g., when the content of the lexical set of classes is conditioned by the style which includes *thee* and *thou*, or an extra-large number of polysyllabic words). It may have (2) a matrix-conditioned lexical manifested variant when the matrix system affecting the tagmeme is that of the general cultural and physical setting (e.g., when it 'makes sense' to say that *the fox ate up the moon* in a fairy tale but not in serious discourse). The occurrence of lexical items, or the COMPATIBILITY of particular sets of classes of lexical items in particular lexical, cultural, or physical contexts, is the element affected by these two types.

Similarly, a tagmeme has a LOCALLY-FREE BUT SYSTEMICALLY-CONDITIONED MANIFESTED PHONOLOGICAL VARIANT when the style or matrix system affects the phonemic content of some member of the morphemic class manifesting that tagmeme (see § 7.313(3), for choice of *not* versus *n't*). Likewise, a LOCALLY-FREE BUT SYSTEMICALLY-CONDITIONED MANIFESTED SEMANTIC VARIANT OF A TAGMEME is seen when the semantic content of some member of the morphemic class manifesting the tagmeme is affected by the style tagmeme in which an utterance is given (§ 7.313(3), *He is a queer bird* versus *That is a queer bird*).

When a style allows or causes a change in the etic slot occurrence of a tagmeme, this results in a SYSTEMICALLY-CONDITIONED SLOT (or POSITIONAL) VARIANT OF A TAGMEME (as in *Away ran John* versus *John ran away* or *Away John ran*, § 7.321). This in turn may result in a SYSTEMICALLY-CONDITIONED STRUCTURAL-SEMANTIC-VARIANT OF A TAGMEME (in that, conditioned by the tagmatic slot change in the style, the grameme manifested by *away* has livelier story-telling connotations when it is placed early than when it is placed late in the sentence).

7.5 *The Distribution Mode of the Tagmeme*

Just as we found many parallels between the characteristics of the manifestation mode of a tagmeme and the manifestation mode of the morpheme, since the morphemes were the elements which manifested the tagmeme, and since any variation in the morphemes was therefore reflected in the variant manifestations of the tagmeme, so also we find many parallels between the characteristics of the distribution mode of the tagmeme and the distribution mode of the morpheme.

Through its external distribution a tagmeme integrates with the rest of the system of grammar. The tagmeme, like units of any system, must have some mechanism by which it can be integrated with the balance of the system. In tagmemic theory units are described as having a distribution in a slot of a larger system; this leads to its hierarchical and functional integration with the system.

7.51 *Activeness of Tagmemes*

Within the definition of the tagmeme (§ 7.1), for example, there is provision for the fact that it is ACTIVE (or live, productive), just as this provision was in the definition of the morpheme (§ 6.1) and in its analysis (§ 6.61). The relationship is much closer than that of mere parallelism, however; the activeness is in part reciprocal, because of the relation of the morpheme to the tagmeme or, more specifically, because of the fact that the borders of the two in part coincide (§§ 7.45, 6.66). This fact is the result, furthermore, of the relationship of the morpheme to the uttereme: the morpheme occurs only as an integral part of the manifestation of an uttereme,[10] and its relationship to such an uttereme is its distribution within the minimum units of the distribution mode of the uttereme, namely within the tagmemes of that uttereme.

Since a morpheme's boundaries are determined in reference to its activeness, we may then conclude that the criteria for an active morpheme may be used as criteria for the activeness of a tagmeme as well, although there must be a rephrasing of the criteria from the tagmemic point of view. Note, then, the criteria essentially repeated, but modified in statement, from § 6.61:

[10] Or, of course, of some lower-level syntagmeme included within the sentence syntagmeme.

(1) A tagma is active (and hence constitutes a tagmeme or a variant of a tagmeme) if its feature mode has as one of its characteristics an emic class of morphemes (or an emic composite class of morphemes and hypermorphemes) which is relatively large (e.g., the tagmeme manifested by *John* in *I saw John, I saw Bill, I saw the boy*, etc.).

(2) A tagma is active if it is the second part of a two-tagmeme hypertagmeme in which the first tagmeme meets the conditions of the first criterion just given (e.g., the tagmeme manifested by {-s} in *cats, houses*).

(3) A tagma is active if the emic class of morphemes constituting one of the contrastive features of its feature mode is also a contrastive feature of various other tagmemes (e.g., the tagmeme manifested by *big* in *I saw the big boy;* compare *He is too big; big enough, bigness*).

(4) A tagma usually may be considered to be active if the emic class of morphemes constituting one of the contrastive features of its feature mode has had its membership increased within recent times (e.g., the tagmeme manifested by *radio* in *The radio works well*). There is indeterminacy, however, as to how many such additions there must have been, and how widespread their usage must be, before this conclusion is certain.

There is a further element of indeterminacy which can be very difficult to handle when a particular morph appears to be semi-active (§ 6.61) in a morphetically-complex morpheme. Here the difficulty lies in deciding whether the tagma under consideration is being manifested by just one morph of a two-morph sequence, or whether it is being manifested by the total sequenc. For example, are we to assume that the semi-active morph *berry* in the sentence *That is a cranberry* is manifesting the same tagma as is being manifested by *berry* in *That is a big berry*? Or is *berry* in the first of those two sentences manifesting the same tagma as is *berry* in *That is a blueberry*? Or, on the contrary, are *cranberry* and *blueberry*, as wholes, manifesting the active tagma manifested by *berry* in *That is a berry*? Note that the sentence *That is a green blueberry* would seem to force us to treat *green* as in the same tagma with *big;* hence *cranberry*, as a whole, in *That is a cranberry* manifests the same tagma as *berry* in *That is a berry*. We conclude, then, that a sequence of two passive morphs, or of a passive and a semi-active one, must be assumed to fill only a single active tagmemic slot; an indeterminacy as to the active or semi-active status of a morph will therefore be reflected in the analysis of the sequences containing them.

Wherever a single but morphetically-complex morpheme occurs, there one also finds a sequence of two PASSIVE (or dead, nonproductive) tagmas or of a passive and a SEMI-ACTIVE tagma; such a sequence constitutes a tagmatically-complex but single tagmeme (cf. § 7.44). Tagmas may be PARASITICALLY semi-active or parasitically passive when they occur as the result of the occurrence of parasitic morphs (§ 6.62).

(5) A tagma is usually active if it has a structural meaning clearly identifiable by the linguist (e.g., the actor meaning carried by the actor-as-subject tagmeme in *John ran home*), although not all active tagmas have such a meaning (§ 7.321).

(6) Any tagma for which relatively-unsophisticated native speakers are able to describe a structural meaning, upon questioning, is very likely to be active; but, as it did for the activeness of morphs, such a test leads to a different kind of indeterminacy, by changing the structuring of the informant and rendering any further tests less reliable at any point where such a test assumes that the speaker is still linguistically naïve.

(7) A tagma is active if it is the only segmental tagma in an uttereme (e.g., the tagma manifested by *boy* in the exclamation *Boy!*).

(8) A border between two active tagmas may be assumed to occur at any point where pauses or intonational breaks frequently occur in nonhypostatic or nonhesitation situations (e.g., after *John* in *John so they say has come home*, but not after *cran* in *cranberry;* and not in the middle of a morph); but there is some indeterminacy in such matters, in that in very 'careful' speech, or to get intelligibility after a misunderstanding, pauses may be introduced where no tagmemic border occurs; such social situations must be added to the other excluded types (hypostasis and hesitation) before this supporting criterion may usefully be used. In addition, an occasional individual may have a style differing from that of the average person in the community precisely by the fact that his style is marked by pauses coming frequently where they would not be expected in the speech of his colleagues. One public speaker whom I heard recently, for example, used the following utterances among many which were so marked: *That is used in/Brazil but not the very same language*. Also: *It is altogether possible that within/the sound of my voice...*

7.52 *The Tagmemic-Class Membership and the Potential Occurrence of a Tagmeme as a Component of Its Distribution Mode*

Just as the distribution mode of a morpheme contains among its components the actual occurrence of that morpheme at some one point of time in a particular utterance, and its potential for occurring in various other places in utterances (§ 6.63), so a tagmeme has like components. Not only does the actor-as-subject tagmeme occur as manifested by *John* in *John came home*, but this same actor-as-subject tagmeme may also occur, manifesting part of a different uttereme, in *Did John come home?* The total actual and potential occurrence of a tagmeme in various utteremes or hyper-utteremes is part of its distribution mode.

The occurrence of a tagmeme as a member of a class of tagmemes is likewise a component of a distribution mode of a tagmeme — a component correlated with its potential distribution, since two tagmemes which have certain distributional potentials in common (e.g., the tagmeme 'actor-as-subject' and the tagmeme 'recipient-of-action-as-subject') are members of the same emic distribution class of tagmemes, as we shall see in § 7.6.

Problems as to time in relation to the potential distribution of the tagmeme are analogous to those discussed for the morpheme and the predictability of its past or future occurrence (§ 6.63). Here, as there, we are interested in "distribution" not only as an element in the recorded history of the behavior of a people, but are also interested in the distribution of this behavior in the potential future. Potential for occurrence in predictable structural positions must be a legitimate functional part of behavior, *from the point of view of the manner in which people react to it* and act within group-behavior patterns; otherwise, language and nonverbal behavior could not constitute components of culture on which people could rely for building useful activity. In tagmemics, a STATIC analysis would be one which refused to grant the relevance of potentials of various kinds and their legitimate place in a description of a language. We must reject such a purely static analysis of behavior materials at whatever point it is found, if this static analysis purports to be an emic analysis; an etic analysis may in some instances be a static view, and highly useful (§ 2), however, provided it is not allowed to dissuade one from accepting the underlying postulates necessary elsewhere for working emically. One such postulate, which must be included *somewhere* in any theory which attempts to analyze behavior in reference to the manner in which participants in that behavior react to it, is the descriptive validity of the use of the composite of characteristics of predictability and potentials which occur in a culture. Such a view is an emic one and leads to a DYNAMIC approach to the analysis of tagmemics. This view is related, furthermore, to the conviction that the emic analyst of any part of human behavior must be prepared to utilize all kinds of objective, observable behavior which are relevant to that particular part of behavior which he has selected for study, as we indicated in §§ 2.73-74, 2.5-6. One who holds a dynamic view of behavior, then, must reject any analysis of language which attempts to define behavior exclusively in terms of the past, or in terms of a very small sampling of fixed examples without reference to the productive potentials[11] or productive analogies of the speakers of that language. See § 7.84.

7.53 *Potential for the Correlation of the Manifestations of One Tagmeme with the Manifestations of Another Tagmeme*

One of the characteristics of a tagmeme which may conveniently be considered as a component of its distribution mode is the fact that there is frequently some kind of relationship between the specific manifested form of one tagmeme and the specific manifested form of another tagmeme in the same uttereme or hyper-uttereme. Three kinds of such correlation may be mentioned here:

(1) There is a SUBSTITUTION CORRELATION when the manifesting class which constitutes a component of the feature mode of a tagmeme is subdivided into groups of morphemes (or morphemes and hypermorphemes) by their correlations with a small

---

[11] See fnn. to §§ 6.63, 3.51.

number of special morphemes such as *he, she,* or *who, which,* etc. (cf. § 7.313(2)). Cf. *There is a boy who is a friend of mine,* versus *There is a dog which is friendly with me.*

(2) There is REFERENT CORRELATION when members of the same major class of morphemes — not members of a major class and of a minor class, as in the preceding type — are essential to the respective manifestations of two tagmemes of an uttereme or hyper-uttereme, provided that it is also required by this structural correlation that the two be in some way identifiable by objective cultural tests as referring to the same person, or object, etc. (cf. § 7.313(2)). Cf. *John is president.*

(3) There is AGREEMENT CORRELATION (or a TIE, or CONCORD) when the occurrence of the manifested form of one tagmeme forces within another tagmeme of the same uttereme or hyper-uttereme a manifestation — usually morphemically-complex — which indicates its correlation with the first tagmeme in number, case, gender, or the like. Cf. Spanish *la casa blanca* 'the white house', with the article, the noun, and the adjective containing a feminine ending. The reader should note, however, that if each of the two elements so correlated is morphemically-complex at every occurrence — i.e., if each is composed of a stem plus an affix which is in agreement with an affix attached to the stem of the second element — the essentially-complex nature of the two would remove these complexes from tagmemic consideration and lead to their consideration within the discussion of the internal construction of the respective hypertagmemes involved.

(4) There is SYSTEM CORRELATION when the manifested forms of the tagmemes of one system or subsystem of tagmemes partially limit the occurrence of the manifested forms of an interlocking but different system or subsystem of tagmemes. Thus a system of tagmemes manifested by segmental morphemes may interlock with and partially limit the occurrence of the forms of a tagmemic system which is manifested by intonational morphemes. For the latter kind of system, see §§ 13,3, 13.5 and Pike, 1963c; for a discussion of interlocking of systems, see § 15.2.

7.54 *The Internal Structure of the Tagmeme*

We have previously indicated (§§ 3.5, 6.64) that components of the distribution mode of an eme include not only its actual distribution within a sequence under attention, and its potential distribution in other sequences, but also the internal distribution of its parts.[12] For the tagmeme, as for other emes, this fact is relevant. For reference to its distribution in larger units, for example, see §§ 7.52, 7.6, 11.

A morphemically-simple manifestation of a tagmeme has only one morpheme within it, so that no problem of morpheme-sequence constructions is relevant in tagmemic manifestations such as *John* in *John is coming.* When, however, the

---

[12] But see fn. to § 3.5(3).

tagmeme has an expanded manifested variant composed of a morpheme sequence, the internal structuring includes the relationship between the morphemes of such a sequence or — more specifically insofar as this theory is concerned — between the sequence of included tagmemes (§ 7.44) within the syntagmeme including them.

The structuring of the manifestations of a tagmeme in terms of morpheme-sequence types is limited to the particular tagmemic variants which are optionally complex or essentially complex. See § 7.44 for initial illustration of these items (*My John* versus *John* in *My John came;* and *To sing takes effort* versus *Work takes effort*). For a more inclusive etic listing of such tagmemic types, see also § 11.52.

The phonological structuring of the manifestations of a tagmeme will be composed of the shape types of its manifesting morphemes (§ 6.64).

7.55 *An Occurring Tagmemic Manifestation Viewed as an Occurring Tagmeme*

In § 6.65 we argued that it was useful and emically valid to assume that when an allomorph occurred the morpheme could be viewed as occurring; in § 7.313(2), on the other hand, we stated that the conclusion must be quite different for an alloclass of an emic class of morphemes: A person who heard a morpheme manifesting that alloclass should not be considered as hearing the alloclass itself. In turning now to the tagmeme, it is not at first apparent which viewpoint will prove most useful and valid, inasmuch as the tagmeme is manifested by a morpheme (and hence might seem to 'occur') but this morpheme is a member of an emic class of morphemes (§ 7.31) which constitutes one component of the feature mode of the tagmeme (and hence might seem not to 'occur').

Our decision is to treat an occurrence of a manifestation of a tagmeme as an occurrence of that tagmeme. This is useful, since it allows us, for example, to say that 'the tagmeme actor-as-subject in the sentence *John came home* is *John*' or, more simply, that 'the subject of the sentence is *John*'; but this usage would be partially invalid if we could not assume that an occurring manifestation of a tagmeme can rightly be viewed as the occurrence of that tagmeme. Furthermore, it allows us to count the number of tagmemes in a specific sentence, which we could not do if tagmemes could not be said to occur in a specific sentence. Ultimately, on higher levels of the hierarchy, we must be able to speak in this manner, or we will be forced to state that no sentence type ever occurs, but that manifestations of sentence types do occur. This, too, seems less useful than the implication growing from our decision, which allows us to speak of the sentence types (utteremes) occurring in a particular paragraph, for example. On grounds of general theory, it makes our theory more consistent and symmetrical to treat *every* unit of a behavioreme as occurring when it is manifested, rather than treating a morpheme as occurring when manifested, but the tagmeme and phoneme and some other units as not so occurring. Similarly, we shall generalize and treat all emic classes as not occurring, but as being manifested only, so that here too the treatment of emic classes of morphemes is parallel with that given to other emic classes of behavior. (For further support to our decision in terms of an analogy with reference to native reaction to persons, see § 6.65.)

7.56 Border Limits of Tagmemes in Reference to Morphemes and Hypermorphemes

The relationship between the identification of tagmeme boundaries and morpheme boundaries is partially but not completely reciprocal.

All of the problems met in the identification of single-morpheme boundaries are immediately relevant to the identification of tagmeme boundaries, in view of the fact that wherever a morpheme begins a tagmeme begins, wherever a morpheme ends a tagmeme ends, and wherever there is morpheme fusion there is fusion of the manifestations of two or more tagmemes. Thus the kinds of problems mentioned in § 6.66 may be re-phrased here: (1) The manifested elements of two tagmemes may fuse in part, so that no clear border may be discovered between the tagmemes; this occurs when the border between the two manifested tagmemes occurs within a single phoneme (cf. §§ 6.55, 14; e.g., when the morphemes *as* and *you* manifesting their respective tagmemes have the border fused to /ž/ in a rapid pronunciation). (2) The manifestations of two tagmemes may be completely fused, so that no border can be found between them, and the same phonemic sequence simultaneously manifests both (cf. §§ 6.55, 14; e.g., when the morphemes *did* and *you* manifesting their respective tagmemes are fused to /ǰ/ in a rapid pronunciation of *Did you enjoy it?* as /ǰɪnǰoi ɪt/). (3) Tagmemic manifestations which appear sharp cut at their borders when seen in phonemic transcription may nevertheless be phonetically blurred if one looks at the subphonemic characteristics of their sound-producing movements (§ 3.25; e.g., the etic border between [a] and [i] is slurred and indeterminate in a pronunciation of the sequence [ai] without intervening glottal stop); phonemically the border may be clear when phonetically it is blurred. (4) A tagmeme may be tagmatically-complex, with two tagmatic slots making up the total, single tagmatically-complex tagmemic slot; this situation results whenever the manifesting morpheme occurs in two etic parts, and in such an instance no tagmemic border occurs at the internal tagmatic border, as no morphemic border occurs at the morphetic border between the two morphs (cf. §§ 6.54, 6.61, 6.62, 7.313(3); a tagmatic but not a tagmemic border occurs between *ham-* and *-let* in *hamlet*).

These various items will not be discussed further here, but will be treated in a special section (§ 14), along with certain other related problems. Another item should be mentioned, however, which is relevant to the finding of tagmeme boundaries: (5) A tagmemic manifestation of an optionally-complex or essentially-complex type contains within it a sequence of included tagmemes (§ 7.44; e.g., the included tagmemes manifested by *big* and by *John* in the including tagmeme manifested by *big John* in the sentence *Big John came home*). In such an instance, the problem of tagmemic segmentation is not reciprocal with that of morphemic segmentation, since a tagmeme manifestation including within it two included tagmemes has within it a morpheme boundary which is not as such relevant to either of the boundaries of the including tagmeme itself. The boundaries of the manifested variants of the included tagmemes, however, are reciprocal with that of the morphemes manifesting them, as indicated in the preceding paragraph. (The nonreciprocal nature of some of the boundaries of morphemes with the boundaries of including tagmemes will concern us again in § 15.13, where it is seen to carry very considerable theoretical importance).

In addition, (6), this theory leads to the postulation of some situations in which fused tagmemes are manifested by single morphemes which are not fusions of two morphemes. Note that the *-o* of Spanish *ablo* 'I speak' is treated as a single nonfused morpheme (with various semantic components) which is manifesting two tagmemes fused in this instance within a single morpheme; but in other instances these two tagmemes are manifested, nonfused, by a sequence of two or more morphemes, as by *-a-* and *-mos* in *ablamos* 'we speak'. (This problem will be treated further in § 14.1; and now cf. Pike 1963d; and Pike and Erickson 1964.)

A problem in determining the borders of included tagmemes is involved, (7), when the analyst tries to determine whether an addition to a two-tagmeme sequence is an expansion of one member of that sequence, or is an expansion of the sequence as a whole; a decision in this matter will affect one's analysis of the borders of the included tagmemes. Thus, *the* and *boy* manifest included tagmemes in the including tagmeme which is manifested by the sequence *the boy* in the sentence *The boy came home;* but in *The big boy came home* does *big* expand the included tagmeme manifested by *boy* or does it expand the essentially-complex manifestation of the actor-as-subject tagmeme manifested by the morpheme sequence *the boy*? The ultimate implications of a decision on such a simple matter are far reaching, and to some extent involve the analysis of the IMMEDIATE CONSTITUENTS of an utterance — the morphemes or hypermorphemes which comprise manifestations of the most basic and highest-layered tagmemic or hypertagmemic units of an utterance or part of an utterance. A decision on these matters can be rephrased as constituting a decision as to which simple morphemes are homologous with which potential morpheme sequences, or which morpheme sequences are homologous with other potential morpheme sequences. This, in turn, involves a first etic guess based on apparent membership in morpheme-hypermorpheme classes, on apparent tagmatic position, on apparent tagmatic function or structural meaning, and on the formal and semantic unity of the manifesting hypermorpheme. The emic refinement of such initial hypotheses must be handled by any procedures available for checking homologousness (see § 7.322 or hypermorphemic unity § 10) and is subject to the errors and indeterminacy of such procedures and such recognition of proportion. In this particular instance, we conclude on the basis of such tests that in *the big boy came home* the phrase *big boy* is homologous with *boy* and constitutes an expansion of one of the included tagmemes within the essentially-complex manifestation of the actor-as-subject tagmeme which in turn might have been manifested by the single morpheme *John*.

The alternative analysis, which would make the optionally-occurring morpheme *big* an expansion of *the boy*, at first seems attractive (since it leaves as the innermost layer of the phrase *the big boy* the two essentially-occurring morphemes *the* and *boy*) but may carry with it an implied analysis of certain expansions which is in contradiction to the structural relationships (structural meanings) etically observable in the cultural situations, i.e., in the larger behavioremic setting. If, for example, *big* is optional to the sentence *John saw Bill* as in *John saw Big Bill*, it would be structurally unprofitable to state that *big* modified the entire obligatory sequence *John saw Bill*, since (a) on a level of structural meaning 'bigness' is not a quality of the action *John saw Bill* but of *Bill;* and (b) on a level of formal emic classes *Big Bill* appears to be homologous with and an expansion of *Bill*. In some such instances, there is certain to be indeterminacy, but (c) in general we suggest the principle that one should try to analyze such items so as to avoid adding further high-level tagmemes to a phrase (as there would have appeared an additional one if *big* were analyzed as modifying *John saw Bill*). We should treat options, other things being equal, as included tagmemes which are expansions of tagmemes already there (as *big* expands *Bill*, rather than modifying *John saw Bill*).

It is also useful to emphasize (8) that it is not necessary to postulate an additional including tagmeme every time a tagmeme is expanded, and it is not necessary in every instance to insist on attributing a hierarchical order to every such multiple expansion of a tagmeme. That is to say, that since *Big Bill* is analyzed as a morphemically-complex manifestation of the tagmeme which may also be manifested just by *Bill*, there is no necessity for setting up a new tagmeme to accommodate the phrase *Big Bill;* the one tagmeme can be treated as being manifested in the one instance by the single morpheme *Bill*, and in the other by the morpheme sequence *Big Bill*. Similarly, by this provision, it is not necessary to force a decision as to whether, on the one hand, *little* in *my little boy who knew John* is related to (modifies) *boy*, and *who knew John* is related to (modifies) *little boy*, or whether on the other hand, *who knew John* modifies *boy*, and *little* modifies *boy who knew John*, etc. Here a SERIAL EXPANSION[13] is indicated, in which various items may expand a tagmeme, with the included tagmemes of various kinds relating to the original item which manifested the non-expanded form of the tagmeme without a determinate hierarchy of this expansion. In such a situation, that is to say, 'immediate constitutents' are not to be considered as always binary, but may sometimes operate in a serial or nonhierarchical fashion within the larger including tagmeme. Nevertheless, there must be allowance for some hierarchical subgroupings of constituents within such a series (as when *very* is immediately related to *big* whereas *very big* is related to *boy* in the sentence *That very big boy knows John*). In all such matters, however, there continues

---

[13] See, now, the discussion of string constituents by Longacre (1960). See also § 11.23(6).

the necessity for initial etic hypotheses of homologousness, with the necessity for formal emic checking, modification, or rejection of these hypotheses in reference to other data in the language and in the nonverbal features of the verbal-nonverbal composite behavioremes containing the utterance under consideration.

Although in the preceding instance we pointed out a situation in which hierarchical order is not necessarily present internal to certain low-layered serial situations in expanded tagmemes, we must also point out an instance in which analysis, according to this theory, must include careful attention to hierarchical matters, and must refrain from setting up units which lead to hierarchical clash. This negative principle (9) can be stated tentatively as follows: A morphemically-complex item cannot be considered as homologous with a morphemically-simple item, unless the morphemically-complex item occurs within the boundaries of a single expanded tagmeme; it may not occur partly in one (nonfused) hypertagmeme, and partly in another (nonfused) hypertagmeme. In the terms of our definition of the tagmeme in § 7.1, and expressed positively, this implies that a tagmeme is distributed within the PYRAMIDED HIERARCHY of the distribution mode of a behavioreme or hyperbehavioreme. For example, if one grants that *sings* is a unit in *John sings*, or if one grants that *John* is by itself manifesting an actor-as-subject tagmeme, then it would be invalid to treat as a hypermorpheme unit the noncontiguous morpheme sequence *John ...s*. If one attempted to argue that *John...s* is substitutable for and homologous with *you* in *You sing*, and hence a unit, the theory here would lead to deny that statement and to reply that *John*, on the contrary, is homologous with *you*, and *sing* with *sings*, and that the agreement correlation of *John* with *sings*, and of *you* with *sing*, is to be treated, as indicated in §§ 7.313(2), 7.313(3), 7.43, as representing the potential for such correlation within the distribution modes of their respective emic classes and tagmemes; the observed resultant forms (of *sing* versus *sings*, etc.) are the tagmemically-conditioned lexical variants of the manifested respective tagmemes. (For a comparable problem in respect to morphemes, where the view was rejected that *...us ...us* of Latin *filius bonus* constitutes a single morphetically-complex morpheme, see §§ 6.54, 7.322). All such considerations affect the points in a sequence of morphemes where the theory allows one to conclude that tagmemic borders occur.

7.6 *Systems of Tagmemes as Composed of Emic Classes of Tagmemes*

In § 5.4 we indicated that behavioremes were members of systems of behavioremes some of which might on occasion be manifested simultaneously in a composite hierarchy; other systems of behavioremes (especially styles) were nonsimultaneous, but congruent, so that units of one were related to units of another and the systems formed a hypercongruent system of behavioremes. In § 6.7, morphemes were shown to enter comparable simultaneous componential systems, or nonsimultaneous congruent systems. In § 7.313(4), a similar approach led to viewing certain emic classes of morphemes — not the individual morphemes themselves — as members of systems which were either style congruent, or matrix congruent. Finally, in § 7.52 the present section was anticipated in part, when it was indicated that tagmemes occurred as members of distribution classes of tagmemes. Now we wish to discuss in more detail the nature of distribution classes of tagmemes and the manner in which they may constitute members of systems of tagmemes.

A DISTRIBUTION CLASS OF TAGMEMES is constituted (1) of a number of tagmemes which have in common the potential for occurring in an anlogous included slot in an uttereme, but which differ both in the formal structure of their manifesting classes and in the structural function or structural meaning of those tagmemes; or a distribution class of tagmemes is composed (2) of two or more tagmemes which have in common a constellation of one or more distributional components such as physical order in a number of utteremes in which they occur plus agreement or concord of the manifesting subclasses of these tagmemes with the manifesting subclasses of neighboring tagmemes in these utteremes.

Many of the items in English which are ordinarily called 'subjects' of statements would seem to constitute an etic distribution class of tagmemes of the second type. Note the following sentences: *John runs home. John has been hit in the eye. John was given the map. John was given to the city for a manager. John is the teacher. John is tired.* At least some of these sentences must be considered as beginning with separate tagmemes because of the sharp differences in their structural meaning[14] and proportion (§ 7.321; e.g., actor-as-subject, versus recipient-of-action as subject), and in their potential expansion (§ 7.43; e.g., *To John was given the map* but not *To John ran away*). Nevertheless, there is some kind of distributional unity among them, in that each precedes the predicate in these utterances and each is manifested by a singular etic subclass (§ 7.313(3)) of its total emic class which is in agreement correlation (§ 7.53) with a reciprocally-conditioned subclass of the class of morphemes which manifests the tagmeme following the subject (i.e., singular predicate follows singular subject). The morphemes *John*, *Bill*, and *George* have lexical meanings which are different, but these morphemes are members of a single emic distribution

---

[14] Some of our recent material has made striking advances at this point. We are now (see Pike, 1964d) trying to follow the flow of dramatis personae, and of other situational roles of the real world (action, time, location, etc.) through a discourse. This allows us to describe one kind of lexical chain structure in the discourse (quite different from that of Z. Harris, 1942a). It leads also to an analysis of further tagmemic types, of contrastive structural meaning. More importantly, it allows us to see the relationships between situation invariants and grammatical change — or between grammatical invariants and situational change. Thus, in change from active to passive expressions the *presence* of a (grammatical) subject *position* is invariant (tied in position and number concord to the predicate), but the dramatis personae shift — the 'logical subject' of the active becomes agent in the passive clause whereas the 'subject' slot is filled with 'logical object'. From the viewpoint of the tale as a whole, however, the dramatis personae remain invariant, with the grammatical shift. Not only can an actor shift from subject slot of an active clause to agent slot in a passive clause, but a name such as *John* can be replaced by *he*, *the boy*, or *the one who got hurt*, etc.

The PLOT is the 'meaning' component of the form-meaning composite which is the tale and the tale itself become a linguistic unit above the sentence level (cf. §§ 5.53, 5.63, 11.723).

class of morphemes; likewise, the distinct tagmemes which are manifested by *John* in the above sentences have tagmemic meanings which are different, but the tagmemes are members of a single emic distribution class of tagmemes.

Two or more etic distribution classes of tagmas may combine into a single emic distribution class of tagmemes. If, for example, one concludes that the tagmas manifested by *John* in the preceding sentences are a single distribution class of tagmas, but are the same tagmemes which are manifested respectively by *John* in the questions: *Did John run home? Has John been hit in the eye? Was John given the map?* etc., then this etic distribution class of tagmas from the statements would combine with the corresponding etic distribution classes of tagmas from the questions to form larger emic distribution classes of tagmemes.

A second distribution class of tagmemes in English is composed of a group of tagmemes which may occur as 'modifiers'; the data quoted here concerning formal arrangements, statements concerning structural meanings, and sample phrases, are largely taken from Fries (1952:202-27); the difference in my interpretation of his data lies in the fact that I am suggesting that several different tagmemes, in a distribution class of tagmemes, are involved in that which he calls 'The modification structure with Class 1 word as head' such that the structure 'signals a variety of meanings' or even a 'great diversity of meanings' (217). He seeks, 'as far as possible, to connect each [structural] meaning with the distinctive formal features which operate to distinguish it'; at the points where he succeeds, we suggest that, within our theory, separate tagmemes are in general identifiable — that as, elsewhere, a combination of phonemic form and lexical meaning help to identify or contrast morphemes, so here a combination of form and structural meaning help to identify or contrast tagmemes. Fries names as 'Class 1' a group of items which we could assume constitute an emic distribution class of morphemes and hypermorphemes, including items such as *hat, cushion, clerks, failures, companions, committee, streets, worker, performance, Spanish* [*people*], *criminal* [i.e., *one who has committed crimes*]. His 'Class 3' is an emic distribution class including items such as *pure, open, unsightly, crooked, continuous, rapid, flat, perfect* [as in *perfect stranger*], *hard* [as in *a hard student*], *criminal* [as in *a criminal lawyer who handles cases of crime*], *Spanish* [as in *a Spanish student who is studying the language*]. By referring to these emic classes of morphemes and hypermorphemes as descriptive components of tagmemes, two or more separate tagmemes can then be identified within a single distribution class of 'modification' tagmemes:

(1) A tagmeme characterized and manifested by Class 3, with a significant contrastive tagmemic meaning of 'character of' or 'quality', and distributed in an emic slot preceding a tagmeme to which it is related as a head in a higher-layered hypertagmeme. (This following tagmeme is in turn characterized and manifested by Class 1 and has the meaning of 'substance'.) Note, for example, the tagmeme manifested by *pure* in *the pure water*, or by *open* in *the open book*.

(2) A tagmeme characterized and manifested by Class 1, with a significant, contrastive, tagmemic meaning of considerable variation, but in part summarizable

under the label 'identification', and distributed within a hypertagmeme such that it precedes a head tagmeme which is characterized and manifested by Class 1, and which has a vague and non-uniform tagmemic meaning of 'material' or 'item'. Note, for example, *budget* in *the budget committee*, or *bath* in *his bath robe*, or *milk* in *the milk delivery*, or *birthday* in *a birthday remembrance*.

Several problems arise in connection with the further analysis of these two tagmemes, however. When a word in Class 3 is homophonous with and related in meaning to a word in Class 1, for example, ambiguous phrases can result (Fries, 223). Nevertheless, two such structurally-ambiguous phrases would be tagmemically different, within this theory: the phrase *a criminal lawyer* (i.e., *who handles cases of crime*) is homophonous with, but not composed of the same tagmemes as, the phrase *a criminal lawyer* (i.e., *who has committed crimes*) cf. also § 7.43.)

Another problem lies in the fact that, as an emic unit, a tagmeme may have some sub-emic variants (§ 7.4), which may in part be reflections of sub-emic variants of emic classes of morphemes and hypermorphemes (§ 7.313(3)). The variation may occur either in the form, or in the structural meaning, or in both of these components. It is clear in Fries' material that there are other 'modification' tagmas, similar to these either in form or in meaning, which I have not mentioned. Are they to be interpreted as the same or as different tagmemes? In some instances I am not at all certain; a further study might lead to reasonable certainty on some of these, and to a realization of permanent indeterminacy for others.

It would seem probable that in situations where Class 1 words modify certain other Class 1 words and the structural meanings are "somewhat diverse", but Fries has "not been able to find formal features that differentiate the more precise meanings included" in that group of phrases (224 fn. 13), that the variation in the structural meanings is lexically conditioned (note locally-conditioned semantic variants of tagmemes, under the influence of neighboring morphemes, in §§ 7.43, 7.321). That is, the difference in the modification relationship of *truck* to *driver* and of *milk* to *delivery* and of *rug* to *sale* would seem to be conditioned by the particular lexical items involved, in the phrases *a truck driver*, *the milk delivery*, and *a rug sale*.

It seems possible, however, that separate tagmemes should be postulated for the tagmas manifested by *purified* and *purifying* in the phrases *the purified water* and *the purifying water* since there are "formal characteristics within the 'modification' structure" which "provide significant contrasts to distinguish certain of the meanings that attach to the 'modifier' relation" (219). The formal indication in the word *purified* is the presence of one of the members of 'Class 2-d' — i.e., a word from 'Class 2' such as *remember, want, see, purchase*, plus "the *-ed* form (the so-called past participle)" (220). The formal indication in the word *purifying* is the presence of a word of the same group (Class 2) plus the *-ing* form. The semantic component of the tagma manifested by *purified* is "indication that the following modified item is the undergoer"; the semantic component of the tagma manifested by *purifying* is "indication that the following modified item is the performer". This composite form-meaning difference would seem to indicate that the two tagmas are separate tagmemes.

It is possible, however, that in this instance someone would choose to argue that the manifesting classes are the same, in that they are merely subclasses of the larger emic class labelled Class 2, and that therefore the semantic difference is no more than a subtagmemic variation conditioned by this subclass occurrence. Now we should recall that in the instance of morphs which differed both by form and by meaning, or which differed by meaning alone, we assumed that they constituted different morphemes if their meanings were sufficiently different; the use of the word 'sufficiently' however, left an area of indeterminacy (§ 6.44). Likewise, we indicated the same problem for tagmas in § 7.321. Here, it appears to me that the difference of meaning is sufficiently great, coupled with the formal difference, to justify analyzing them as separate tagmemes within a single distribution class of tagmemes.

In some instances, the Class 1 word being modified is derived from a Class 2 word, as *student* from *study*, *denial* from *deny*. When such a word is modified by a Class 3 word which has a contrasting form with a Class 4 word (as *continuous* contrasts with *continuously*, *rapid* with *rapidly*), "the meaning in the modification is not that of 'quality of substance' but rather 'manner of action'" (222), as in *a continuous worker* (*who works continuously*) or *a flat denial* (where a person *denies flatly*). In this data, it seems to me that no new tagmemes are involved, but that the meaning of 'quality of action' instead of 'quality of substance' is conditioned by the lexical subclass of the following Class 1 manifestations, rather than being a component of a contrasting tagmeme.

If, however, the various modifiers are in fact composed of a distribution class of tagmemes, is there any justification left for the vague title given to them as a group? Possibly so, though such a grouping might need structural refinement, or some subdivision. Note, for example, that morphemes also come in distribution classes, and that such a class may sometimes have — but does not necessarily have — a detectable class meaning (§ 7.313(1)). The meaning of an emic class of morphemes, furthermore, may be vague, or inconsistent, but in the latter event it continues to function as one of the components of response-behavior elicited within the culture, even though it 'logically' is inconsistent, or is applied to some of the morpheme-class members with which it is in obvious lexically-semantic clash. It should not surprise us unduly, therefore, once we have established the presence of a distribution class of tagmemes, to find that this total set of tagmemes, as a whole, has a very high-layered and vague but none-the-less effective impact on the activity of a culture. In Fries' terms, we might say that such a component is no more than 'connection' of a type which is in structural contrast with other connective patterns; i.e., "'Modification' is a structure of connection, but it is a connection of a particular kind" (207). Or a phrase which he uses in describing the meaning of 'direct object' might be suitably rephrased to serve as a model for describing the meaning of some 'modifiers': "The meaning of 'undergoes the action' in this kind of object includes *everything that is linguistically grasped in the pattern of 'undergoer'*. From a practical point of view there may be no actual 'receiving' or 'undergoing' of any action" (184; note that Fries seems to handle the kinds of inconsistencies which we mentioned, above, in the phrase "From a practical point of view...").

If, now, we ask where the impact of such a semantic component of a distribution class of tagmemes can be seen in our English-speaking culture, I suspect that the best answer is this: It can be seen precisely in the fact that in the history of the development of the study of English grammar, many persons have reacted to some kind of unity in the undifferentiated or partially differentiated tagmemic members of that class, and this reaction took the form of developing the label 'modifier'. More direct evidence from non-analytical or non-hypostatic data is more difficult to find, but might be found by procedure similar to those which would indicate that native speakers of English react to words such as (*the*) *fire* as if it were an object instead of a process, as indicated by the fact that they may show surprise when it is pointed out to them that some of these words represent processes rather than objects.

Without attempting to discuss in detail the nature of the evidence, we might suggest a third possible emic distribution class of tagmemes and hypertagmemes in English, in addition to the one composed of 'subjects' and the one composed of some 'modifiers'. This third tagmemic-hypertagmemic class would be composed of 'predicates'. It is precisely the fact that predicates are not uniformly composed of a single tagmeme which forced Fries, I think, to utilize three separate "minimum free utterance test frames that formed the basis" of his examination of English structure (75, 80-82). 'Frame A' was illustrated by the sentence *The concert was good* (*always*); 'Frame B' by the sentence *The clerk remembered the tax* (*suddenly*); 'Frame C' by *The team went there*. The various items which here enter his 'Class 2' form 'subgroupings of these words' of that class. The structural evidence for separate predicate tagmemes or hypertagmemes is in part composed of the distinctions between these subgroups of morpheme-hypermorpheme classes which manifest the tagmemes under discussion. The evidence for uniting these tagmemes into a single larger distribution class of tagmemes or hypertagmemes is in part the kind of data which led Fries to group together these manifesting subclasses of words into his Class 2, which contains not only *is*, *was*, *are*, *seem*, *become*, but also *remembered*, *saw*, *signed*, and likewise *went*, *came*, *ran*, *started*, *talked*.

If one finds it useful to analyze subjects, modifiers, and predicates as composing distribution classes of tagmemes, it would seem likely that further distribution classes of tagmemes would also appear in a more extended study of such matters. The sum of all such emic distribution classes of tagmemes of a language, within a single componential system of behavioremes, would constitute a COMPONENTIAL SYSTEM OF CLASSES OF TAGMEMES. Two such componential systems from two congruent styles would constitute a single hypercongruent class of tagmemes or of tagmeme classes. The distribution classes of tagmemes within a formal style, for example, would be congruent with — and in many respects identical with — or supplemental to the distribution classes of tagmemes in a less formal style; for some sample etic differences in the physical position of etic slots, or the membership of morpheme distribution classes, note *Away ran John* (§§ 7.321, 7.46), *-est* of *knowest* (§§ 6.7, 7.46).

In general, two componential systems of distribution classes of motifemic-slot-class correlatives are distinct the one from the other, even though simultaneously manifested in a behavioreme. Thus, separate motifemic-slot-class correlatives of verbal and nonverbal types may be simultaneously present in the church service (§ 3), the football game (§ 4), or the breakfast scene (§ 5). Nevertheless, there is some indeterminacy between them, and some overlapping, in that some one motifemic-slot-class correlative may be manifested optionally by morphemes or by nonverbal motifs, or by a composite of verbal-nonverbal motifs. It was precisely at this point that we began the volume in Chapter 1. In that chapter, the gesture song as a game was specifically built upon the possibility of substituting, for party purposes, nonverbal for verbal units in the artificial motifemic-slot-class situations (§ 1.1). A bit later in that same chapter (§ 1.3) a non-artificial situation entailed the possibility of substituting a shake of the head for the verbal *no*, a nod for *yes*, etc., and illustrated again the fact that there are emic distribution classes of behavior units which are of a composite verbal and nonverbal type; here, also, there is interpenetration or overlapping or indeterminacy between the verbal and nonverbal systems of emic slot-class correlatives.

7.7 *Tagmatics*

A verbal etic motif-slot-class-correlative is a tagma (7.1), with numerous characteristics which allow for its identification or for its contrast with another tagma. In this section we wish to bring together a listing of a number of these characteristics, many of which have already been discussed and illustrated, and to give a brief indication of the way in which tagmas may be discovered and analyzed tagmemically.

7.71 *Segmentation of a Continuum into Tagmas*

In §§ 5.51 and 6.81 we discussed briefly the manner in which a continuum of speech could be segmented into utterances and morphs. A similar problem must be met in the segmentation of a continuum into a sequence of manifested tagmas. Since, however, the borders of morphs coincide with the borders of tagmas (§§ 6.66, 7.56), except that an expanded tagma may contain several included morphs (§§ 7.44, 7.54), the problems of tagma segmentation are in part reciprocal with morph segmentation: every morph boundary will simultaneously be a boundary of a tagma of some type, whether included within another tagma, or not so included.

In addition, however, for tagma segmentation it is necessary to make initial judgments as to substitutability, since borders of segments are here relative to borders of substituted items. Two homologous items are members of the same tagma and are substitutable (§ 7.321). Judgments must therefore be made as to whether two items are or are not homologous, with tests of expandability, etc., for checking on the accuracy of these initial judgments (§ 7.322).

A further problem of tagma segmentation arises that is of a type which does not affect morphetics or morphemics as severely: a minimum tagma must have among its manifestations at least some which are composed of single morphs,[15] but others of its manifestations may be composed of morph sequences for which each included morph simultaneously manifests an included tagma (cf. §§ 5.3, 7.44). The fact that a tagma, the minimum etic unit of the distribution mode of an utterance type, can have nonminimum variants, increases the analytical difficulty; homologousness must be judged for a pair of morph sequences, or for a morph sequence and a morph, in terms of the function of such items relative to the remainder of the utterance in which it occurs. Thus one must judge not only whether one morph substitutes for another in a sequence — which is relatively simple — but whether a morph sequence substitutes for a single morph, which is sometimes a judgment very difficult to make and to test.

The initial margin of error in such tagmatic segmentation may be larger than in morphetic analysis. Here, as there, the theory does not lead to error-proof initial procedures, but rather provides for an initial start in tagmatics which is a first approximation, and for further procedures which lead to a tagmemic analysis which eliminates many of these errors, while leaving a margin of indeterminacy.[16]

7.72 Etic Classificatory Criteria for Tagma Types[17]

In §§ 5.52 and 6.64 we listed some criteria for classifying etically various kinds of utterances and morphs. Similarly, we can summarize here a number of the kinds of tagmatic criteria which have appeared directly or by implication in earlier pages of this volume, or which are of comparable types.

First we list criteria which permit the analyst to classify tagmas in accordance with class characteristics of their manifestation mode:

(a) Is the class which manifests the tagma composed of single morphs only? or of morph sequences? of single morphemes only? or of morphemes and hypermorphemes as well? (§ 7.44)

(b) Is this manifesting class composed of segmental morphs? or of morphs mani-

---

[15] But see, now, fn. for § 7.44.
[16] See also fn. to § 7.322.
[17] With tagmemic analysis under way in a substantial number of languages, it is hoped that within a few years this classification can be amplified until it will be useful in grammatical work as a phonetic alphabet is in phonological study. The types of tagmas suggested need to have an 'alphabet' of symbols for them. When these can be agreed upon, then formulas will be read with an ease analogous to that of phonetic script. See, also, Longacre (1964a).

fested by pitch, stress and length only? or by a phonological process of some kind? or by some combination of these? (§§ 6.64, 7.74)

(c) Are some or all of the members of this class phonologically modified under certain phonemic, morphemic, tagmemic, or systemic conditions? or lexically modified under some such conditions, so that the class membership varies under these conditions? or in tagmatic concord? or semantically conditioned? (§§ 7.43, 7.45, 7.46, 7.53). Must the manifesting member of this class have the same referent as the manifesting member of a class manifesting another tagma in the same utterance? or does it correlate in some other way? (§ 7.53)

(d) Is the manifesting class relatively large? small? (§§ 6.83, 7.313(1))

(e) Is the class limited to occurrence in this tagma? if not, where else does it occur? or is it a subclass of a larger class? (§§ 6.83, 7.313(2-3), 7.313(4), 7.74)

(f) Is there a class meaning detectable within many members of the class? and is it separable from the structural meaning of the tagmatic slot in which it occurs? (§§ 7.313(1), 7.324). Is the class meaning, if any, that of action? object? quality? quantity? substance? state? process? person? tense? aspect? gender? number? case? connection? manner? degree? identification? negation? exclamation? imitation? relationship? (cf. § 6.82(e-f))

(g) Are the members of the manifesting class active? passive? semi-active? (§§ 6.61, 6.62, 6.92, 7.51)

Secondly, we list criteria which have relevance to tagmatic slots as a component of the tagma:

(h) In what physical order does the tagma come in reference to other tagmas? Is this order fixed, or is it freely variable with other orders? (§§ 7.321, 7.42)

(i) Is this tagmatic slot manifested only by minimum variants or by minimum and by expanded ones? (§§ 7.44, 7.54)

(j) Is this tagmatic slot obligatory to the higher-layered tagmatic or hypertagmatic unit in which it is occurring? or optional? (§§ 7.44, 7.54, 11)

(k) In relation to the tagma or hypertagma with which it is most closely associated structurally is it subordinate (marginal, satellitic, affixal)? head (nuclear, central, stem)? coordinate?

(l) Is the tagmatic slot an active one? passive? semi-active? (§§ 7.51, 6.61, 6.62, 6.92, 7.56, 6.66)

(m) Can it constitute the only tagma in an utterance? (cf. § 6.3)

(n) Is it related in occurrence to the occurrence of pause, intonation, or other phonological events? (cf. §§ 7.746, 15)

(o) Is there a tagmatic structural meaning detectable within some or all of the manifestations of the tagma? and is this meaning separable from the meaning of the class manifesting it? or from the morpheme(s) which in turn constitute the manifestation of the class? (§§ 7.321-324). Is this meaning — if any — that of performer of an action as constituting the subject of an utterance? recipient as subject? identified item as subject? other relation as subject? goal of an action as object of an utterance?

indirect object? agent? object complement? identified item as a predicate nominative? or as in apposition with some other item? transitive action? intransitive action? a relating action, or state, or affirmation? or impersonal action? a direct or indirect question indicator? quotation types? formality or informality indicator? quality? quantity? substance? connection? exclamation? specified position, time, degree or other relation? or gender, number, person, tense, aspect, case, direction, instrument, emphasis, formality, mood, emotional flavor, command, negation, etc.? (cf. §§ 5.53, 6.82(e-f), 7.321, 7.6, 11).

7.73 Etic Classificatory Criteria for Tagmas in Reference to Their Distribution Classes

We have seen that tagmemes may occur in distribution classes (§§ 7.6, 7.52), and we now list a few of the criteria for distribution classes of tagmas as we previously did for distribution classes of utterances (§ 5.54) and for distribution classes of morphs (§ 6.83):

(a) Do the tagmas in this distribution class of tagmas all occur within a single style or system? (§§ 5.4, 6.7, 7.313(4), 7.46, 7.6)

(b) Is the class of tagmas composed of several tagmas? or of only two or three? or is it a unique member of the class? (§ 7.6)

(c) Do these tagmas have the same manifesting morphemic or morphemic-hypermorphemic class (i.e., are they homophonous)? or are they manifested by different morphemic classes? (§ 7.742-746)

(d) Do the tagmas in such a class have similar rules of agreement concord — if any — with other tagmas in the same utterance? (§ 7.53)

(e) Do the tagmas of this distribution class of tagmas occur in only one sentence type (one uttereme) or in several? (§ 7.6)

(f) Do the tagmas of this class occur in the same utteremes, or do some of them occur in certain utteremes which do not permit one or more of the others? (§§ 7.52, 7.6)

(g) Is there a distribution-class structural meaning — even though vague — which may be detected in a number of the occurrences of the members of this class? If so, what is it? subject? object? modifier? action? relator? or other? (§ 7.6)

7.74 Utteremic-Tagmemic Formulas Following Tagmatic Analysis

7.741 Summary of the Relation of Tagmas to Tagmemes

In order to pass from a prestructural, etic description of the minimum units of the distribution mode of utterances to an emic description of these minimum units, an

THE MINIMUM UNIT OF THE DISTRIBUTION MODE OF THE BEHAVIOREME   255

emic procedure is necessary, and etic training is highly desirable, as it is for utteretics (§ 5.55) and for morphetics (§ 6.84). The same general kinds of principles are applicable here, as there.

Every tagma may be assumed to comprise: either
- (a) a free variant of a tagmeme (§ 7.42)
- or (b) a conditioned variant of a tagmeme (§§ 7.43, 7.46)
- or (c) part of a tagmatically-complex variant of a tagmeme or of one of its manifested forms (§ 7.44)
- or (d) a sequence of two or more manifested variants of tagmemes, so that the tentative tagma needs further segmentation (§ 7.71)
- or (e) a fused composite variant of two or more partially simultaneous or completely simultaneous tagmemes (§ 7.45)
- or (f) an error of tagmatic analysis which would be eliminated after further study;
- and (g) the tagmemes composed of these tagmas are members of emic distribution classes of tagmemes (§ 7.6) within the larger system of the language as a whole, which in part they reciprocally constitute.

Once the tagmas have been studied and reinterpreted tagmemically in these respects by the appropriate techniques, the utteremes of a language can then be described in tagmemic terms. In order to give an abbreviated view of the manner in which such a description can be presented, we return to the artificial language materials which were used in § 7.313(4). The total analysis of these artificial languages cannot be given here,[18] however, since the mechanism for describing hypermorphemes, hypertagmemes, phonemes, hyperphonemes and the interpenetration of modal units, awaits further theoretical development in Chapters 9-11, 15. Nevertheless, some additional characteristics of these 'languagettes' can now be profitably discussed.

7.742 *Utteremic-Tagmemic Formulas for Languagette A*

If the reader will refer back to the artificial data illustrating Schematic Class-Type A in § 7.313(4), he may note that there are various alternate utteremic analyses which may be given of this data. In order to determine which is preferable, more data, and longer contexts, would be necessary.

---

[18] Since these artificial exercises appeared in the 1954 volume, numerous partial tagmemic analyses of natural languages have been made and published. They should be given more serious attention than these earlier hypothetical problems. These, however, illustrate some components of early tagmemic theory where they can be seen more readily than in longer studies. The later view (1960) of § 11.41 would alter in some degree the suggested solutions of this chapter, by having constructions which contain two obligatory tagmemes find their description in a slightly different place in the grammar — but the relevance of obligatory items continues to be very strong, and cannot be eliminated under any theory. Similarly, the analysis of a subject with and without an optional modifier is revised in § 11.222.

For our purposes we present first the tentative solution suggested by means of the following utteremic-tagmemic formulas:

Languagette A:
Uttereme I ('affirmation concerning an item'):
Minimum, obligatory form:

$$+ S(ubject)^{W(ord)}$$

Potential maximum expanded form:

$$+ (\pm[\pm M^W + A^W] + S^W)$$

Utteremes: In this formula the only uttereme present is seen first in minimum and then in expanded form.

Tagmemes: Only one tagmeme, symbolized as S^W, is obligatory to this uttereme. It is composed (1) of a tagmemic slot (a) which has the structural meaning of 'item concerning which an affirmation is made', (b) occurring in Uttereme I in physical sequence after an action tagmeme, if any such is present in the manifested uttereme; the tagmeme is also composed (2) of the manifesting class ^{W} which fills the tagmemic slot just mentioned. As an illustration of this minimum manifestation of the uttereme, note the utterance *los* 'It is smoke'.

In the expanded manifestations of Uttereme I, two further included tagmemes may occur. One of these, A^W, is manifested by and in part composed of the same word class ^{W} — but with the morphemic meaning of members of the class modified (conditioned) by the meaning of the tagmemic slot in which they are occurring (see § 7.313(4)). The tagmemic slot which constitutes its other component has the structural meaning of 'activity going on' and in physical sequence precedes the tagmeme S^W in that uttereme. Note *losmif* 'The ball is smoking'. This included tagmeme A^W, furthermore, may be optionally expanded by the included tagmeme M^W which (1) is manifested by the morphemic class ^{W}, with its membership semantically conditioned by the tagmemic slot it is filling, and (2) has a tagmemic slot with structural meaning of 'modification of activity' and a sequential order preceding the activity tagmeme. Note *losmifkap* 'His eyes roam darkly'.

The brackets in the expanded utteremic formula enclose the tagmeme A^W expanded by the optional addition of the included tagmeme M^W.

Morphemic classes: The one emic morpheme class in Languagette A is composed of the items *los*, *mif*, and *kap* (cf. § 7.313(4); this emic class is in turn composed of several etic classes of the same membership, but with their lexical meanings affected by the tagmemic meaning. The symbol used here to label the emic class is ^{W}. An alternate symbol type — more useful under some circumstances — is the symbolization of the entire class by placing one of their members in pointed brackets, thus: ⟨*los*⟩; the same tagmemic formula would then read: $S^{<los>}$. (The pointed brackets follow Pittman, 1954a; the formula is to be interpreted to read 'the class of which *los* is a member'; if two emic classes contain some of the same members, the choice of the illustrative morpheme should be such as to lessen the possible ambiguity.) The definition of this emic class includes not only its membership and etic semantic variants but its distribution in the tagmemes S^W, M^W, and A^W of Uttereme I.

Each of the specific utterances of two or more morphemes constitutes a separate hypermorpheme; e.g., *losmif* 'The ball is smoking', and *miflos* 'The smoke is rolling' constitute two hypermorphemes manifesting the same uttereme. Each specific sequence of two morphemes manifesting the included but expanded tagmeme $[\pm M^W + A^W]$ constitutes a member of a class of such included hypermorphemes; e.g., *losmif* is an included hypermorpheme in the utteremic manifestation *losmifkap* 'His eyes roam darkly'.

The preceding analysis of Languagette A was based on the assumption that $\pm A^W + S^W$ is here an expansion of $+ S^W$. This assumption could only be substantiated or refuted by observing such items in larger contexts, to see if in a slot in hyper-utteremes these two utterances were homologous (sustaining the analysis above) or not homologous (refuting the analysis above). If the items proved to be *not* homologous, the analysis of Languagette A would then have to be reworked into two utteremes, as follows:

Languagette A, alternative analysis:
Uttereme I ('identification of an item'):

$$\text{Minimum and Maximum: } + S^W$$

Uttereme II ('activity affirmed concerning an item'):

$$\text{Minimum: } + A^W + S^W$$
$$\text{Maximum: } + (\pm M^W + A^W) + S^W$$

In this analysis, Languagette A, though having the same number of tagmemes as in the preceding analysis, has an extra uttereme, so that tagmemic definition must be reworked to mention the distribution of tagmeme S^W in each of these utteremes. Only one emic class of morphemes appears in the solution, as before, and it is related in distribution to the same tagmemes. The hypermorphemes remain unaffected. On the other hand, Uttereme II now is in part composed of a hypertagmeme, $(+ A^W + S^W)$, because, in this alternate analysis, two obligatory tagmemes are involved.[19]

The possibility of this kind of an alternate analysis emphasizes once again the necessity for *working with units larger than the sentence*, and for checking homologousness within the structure of such hyper-utterances; no mere distributional study of morphemes as such is adequate without ultimate reference to such larger structures. In Languagette C, such data is provided as part of the problem.

[19] See fn. to § 7.741.

7.743 *Utteremic-Tagmemic Formulas for Languagette B*

For the languagette illustrating Schematic Class-Type B, see data and discussion of its class types in § 7.313(4); utteremic-tagmemic formulas for it might be as follows:

Languagette B:
 Uttereme I ('affirmation of the activity of an item'):

$$\text{Minimum, obligatory form: } +S^N + A^V$$
$$\text{Maximum: } + S^N + (\pm M^V + A^V)$$

In general, the description of this languagette can be handled in a way comparable to that for Languagette A. Note, however, that here ^{N} and ^{V} symbolize two emically-distinct classes (with membership listed in § 7.313(4)), which may be conveniently labelled as 'noun' and 'verb'.

Three tagmemes are present — S^N, A^V, and the included tagmeme M^V; A^V has an expansion to $(\pm M^V + A^V)$.

Note, as illustrating the minimum variant of this uttereme, the utterance *somlok* 'The boy spoke'. For an expanded variant, note *sommislok* 'The boy spoke haltingly'.

7.744 *Utteremic-Tagmemic Formulas for Languagette A'*

For the languagette illustrating Schematic Class-Type A', see data in § 7.313(4), p. 112b-113a and note the following formulas (other analyses are possible):

Languagette A':
 Uttereme I ('affirmation of state or action'):

$$\text{Minimum: } + StI^P + St^W$$
$$\text{Maximum: } + StI^P + (+ St^W \pm M^W)$$

Uttereme II ('affirmation of the activity of an item'):

$$\text{Minimum: } + P^{(+ AI^{em} + A^W)} + S^{(+ StI^{sa} + St^W)}$$
$$\text{Maximum: } + P^{(+ AI^{em} + [+ A^W + M^W])} + S^{(+ StI^{sa} + [+ St^W + M^W])}$$

For the analysis implied[20] by these formulas we have assumed that Utteremes I

---

[20] The data are too simple to allow a conclusive answer which parallels natural language adequately. In this analysis the assumption is that the two particles *em-* and *sa-* both fill the same emic slot in Uttereme Type I and carry the same tagmemic function there — but manifest contrastive tagmemes and functions in Uttereme Type II.

 If, on the contrary, one were to guess that elaboration of the data to approximate more closely a

THE MINIMUM UNIT OF THE DISTRIBUTION MODE OF THE BEHAVIOREME   259

and II are not homologous in large hyper-utteremes: we assume they would come in some different slots or in different uttereme sequences in such larger structures.

A number of elements in these formulas need to be explained, since they have not been described in the discussion of the preceding languagettes. In the minimum formula for Uttereme I, for example, StI means 'state indicator', with ^{P} meaning emic 'particle class' composed of *em* and *sa;* St is 'slot for functional state (as a thing or as an abstracted activity)', and ^{W} is the 'full word' emic class which may fill that slot. For an example of this uttereme, manifested, note *emkol* 'A state of learning is present' or 'They are learning'.

In Uttereme II, the 'action indicator' tagmeme AI^{em} differs from the 'generalized state indicator' tagmeme StI^P of Uttereme I in that the only member of the particle class which can fill that slot is *em;* ^{em} therefore is a subclass of ^{P}; and AI is an 'activity indicator' tagmemic slot. Similarly, the grameme StI^{sa} is composed of the tagmemic slot 'specific-state indicator' plus the manifesting class ^{sa} which is a different subclass of ^{P} from that represented by the subclass ^{em}.

In addition, $P^{(+ AI^{em} + A^W)}$ is a construction with a meaning of 'performance', and is manifested by the two obligatory tagmeme AI^{em} and A^W; similarly, $S^{(+ StI^{sa} + StW)}$ is a construction meaning 'subject of performance', manifested by the two tagmemes StI^{sa} and St^W.

The arrows pointing to the "+" symbol before each of the constructions, with the slant line cutting the line connecting the arrows, here symbolizes the fact that there is free variation in the physical order in which these two constructions may occur relative to one another.

As an example of Uttereme II, manifested, note *empavsakol* 'an item or state in which scholarly activity occurs is serving as the subject of an activity in which the state is one of playfulness', or 'The scholars are playing'.

7.745 Utteremic-Tagmemic Formulas for Languagette B'

For the languagette illustrating Schematic Class-Type B', see data in § 7.313(4), and note the following formulas:

---

natural language would force *em-* and *sa-* into demonstrably different slots and relations in discourse structure, then an alternate analysis might be required. Specifically, one uttereme (syntagmeme) would be a Stative in which *sa-* but not *em-* appears; a second uttereme would be one in which *em-*, but not *sa-* appears, with a meaning of affirmed action. There would remain the uncertainty as to whether the utterances containing both *em-* and *sa-* would best be treated as expansions of the second uttereme type, or as comprising a third type in themselves.

It should be pointed out, furthermore, that one cannot guarantee uniformity of judgment in such matters in natural language; non-uniqueness of solutions will remain here, as elsewhere, as long as observer intuitive components must enter analytical procedure (see §§ 11.75, 7.322); the best which can be expected are alternative, simple, mechanically-convertible solutions.

Languagette B':
Uttereme I ('affirmation of the activity of an actor'):

$$\text{Minimum: } + S^N + A^V$$
$$\text{Maximum: } + S^N + (+ A^V \pm G^N)$$

Uttereme II ('negation of an affirmation of the activity of an actor'):

$$\text{Minimum and Maximum: } + \text{Aff}^{U\text{-}I} + \text{Neg}^{top}$$

Uttereme III ('query as to the presence of the activity of an actor'):

$$\text{Minimum: } + \text{Aff}^{U\text{-}I} + Q^{kil}$$
$$\text{Maximum: } +(+ \text{Aff}^{U\text{-}I} \pm \text{Neg}^{top}) + Q^{kil}$$

In these formulas, tagmemic items different from the kind illustrated in the discussion of Languagettes A, B, and A' include the 'negative' and 'question' tagmemes Neg^{top} and Q^{kil} (each manifested by a morpheme class composed of a single morpheme each) and the 'goal' tagmeme G^N. Note, for example, the minimum Uttereme I illustrated by *manatesu* 'Lady clothes-makes', i.e., 'The lady makes clothes'; compare *manatesufukos* 'The lady makes dresses for a friend', in which the included tagmeme G^N occurs.

For Uttereme II the symbol U-I indicates 'any manifested form of Uttereme I', and Aff implies an affirmative utterance slot.

Uttereme III is similar to Uttereme II in that Uttereme I is included within it: *manatesukitikil* 'Does the lady make suits for the man?'

Three utteremes are postulated for Languagette B', under the assumption that the three would not be quite homologous in the slots in a large hyper-uttereme; note that the negative type, in this data, seems only to precede a query of some kind. If, however, a larger body of material were to show that all of these sentences could in fact come as manifesting each of the major slots in a conversation, then the solution would require a single uttereme, instead of three, as follows:

Languagette B', Alternate Analysis:
Uttereme I ('query or negation or affirmation of the activity of an actor'):

$$\text{Minimum: } + S^N + A^V$$
$$\text{Maximum: } + (+ S^N + [+ A^V \pm G^N]) \pm \text{Neg}^{top} \pm Q^{kil}$$

In both Languagette A and in Languagette B' there appeared the need of hyper-utteremic data. Some of this has been supplied for Languagette C.

7.746 Utteremic-Tagmemic Formulas for Languagette C

We turn now to a partial analysis[21] of the data of Languagette C which were presented as an illustration of Schematic Class-Type C, § 7.313(4).

We are pretending that the data of Stages A-C were gathered by a linguist asking in one language for the general translation equivalent in Languagette C, by using some such query as 'How do you say...'. A linguist of more extensive training than the one we are assuming here might have started differently, merely by recording utterances which he overheard in the course of a day's activities — but this would have necessitated, in order to get a sufficiently large number of forms partly alike and partly different, a much larger body of material than it would have been feasible to publish for this illustration, and much more experience before attempting the task with any hope of efficient, rapid work being done. Stage D represents a story which the native speaker is assumed to have told to the linguist.

We shall not present here the full analysis of each stage of these data, because of limitations of space, nor shall we indicate all of the phonetic-phonemic or morphetic-morphemic elements which are relevant to their analysis, since our purpose here is rather to set forth the tagmemic elements entering into utteremic formulas. A few comments, however, will be made concerning some of the problems which arise in a stage-by-stage analysis of a language.

In Stage A, for example, most of the phonetic data seem quite simple, with phones [p, t, k; m; f, s; i, u, o, a]. The hyperphonetic segments include open and closed syllables of patterns CV, CCV, and CVC; abdominal pulses (stress groups) have stress on the second syllable of the group; breath groups are composed of one or two stress groups. The only complication which is likely to bother the beginning student is the long [t·] interrupted by syllable division, in [sti. ˈfo.mit. · i.pa↘‖], Utterance No. 7.

The morphetics of Stage A is much more difficult. Students in the class room frequently try to segment Utterance No. 1 into *to* 'food', *sa* 'good', *mik* 'is' — an analysis biased by the here-irrelevant syllable division, by the accidental fact that *ku* 'hot' has a morphetic shape-type CV which, they seem to feel, 'ought' to be reflected in the word for 'good' which contains at least the sounds [sa]. A further morphetic start by them often treats the *m* of *tipam* (Utterance No. 5) as a 'locative', meaning 'on', because of the translation 'on the fire', but with the *m* of *tomim* from that same utterance as constituting a morph meaning 'is in process'. The analysis of some of the morphs of Utterances 7-9 is likely to be quite uncertain at this stage.

The utteremic and tagmemic guesses[22] at Stage A are sharply in need of revision at

---

[21] This description (of 1954) is now incomplete — see fn. to § 7.741 — but still highly useful pedagogically. It needs more attention to emic levels (see §§ 11.22, 11.4, 11.72) following Longacre, and illustrated extensively by Pickett (1960). In addition, it needs supplementation by matrix techniques (e.g., Pike, 1962a, 1963b).

[22] See, now, extensive discussion of guess-and-check procedures in Longacre (1964a).

later stages, if the morphetic guesses are those just indicated, since the analysis of the one affects the other.

During the analysis of Stage B, the student, while revising his phonetic analysis, adds the phone [l], and may reach the phonemic conclusion — if he has not done so earlier — that a phonetically-long consonant is phonemically a sequence of two like consonant phonemes. This conclusion either aids and supports the morphetic analysis of *tipa* in No. 7, and of *mit* in Nos. 15-17, or the morphetic identification of the latter helps the student to arrive at the phonemic hypothesis to be checked distributionally.

In Stage B, also, he may need to have it called to his attention that the descriptive statement of the structure of stress groups can be retained as in Stage A (with every stress group stressed on the second emic syllable), only if the syllabic [m] of Nos. 15-17 is treated as an etic syllable which with the etic syllable preceding it constitutes a single etically-complex emic syllable.

Morphetically, in Stage B, there is likely to come the most important insight needed for the appreciation of the morpheme structure of this languagette. By observing *ksa* in No. 11, part of the erroneous analysis of *sa* of No. 1 may be corrected; if in Stage B the student arrives at the conclusions suggested in the last paragraph concerning the syllable, then the way is open for him to see that in No. 1 the morph *tomi* is 'food' — and to eliminate any 'copula' from his utteremic pattern, since no morphetic material remains there to manifest such a morpheme. Further, the repeated occurrences of *mit* in Nos. 10-18 force the student to try to identify that morph in relation to the various translation meanings of 'man', 'old man' (where no specific morph of shape-type CV or larger, for 'old', can be found), 'dead' (where a similar problem arises), 'living', and even for 'children'. For this reason he reconsiders the meanings of *m* and *s*, and may hypothesize that the two *m* morphs of No. 5 were in fact occurrences of the same morpheme.

Provided that he reaches this conclusion in Stage B, the entire utteremic-tagmemic structure earlier postulated by him will now undergo complete revision. Whereas he may in Stage A have treated *tipa* in Nos. 5-6 as a 'verb', homophonous with *tipa* as a noun in No. 3, he may now begin to see that in this languagette there occur affirmation sentence types without 'verbs', as well as one in which verbs do occur. The preparation of formulas of these utteremic types should lead to a major break through in understanding the structure of the language.

In Stage C, hypotheses set up in Stage B can be checked on new data, and gaps in the pattern filled in. Items 20-21 lack some phonological data, but since no evidence has appeared to show contradiction to the tentatively-suggested breath-group structure, it is assumed that these two would follow that pattern. Here, too, it can be seen that there is some correlation between the grammatical structure and the ending of a stress group within a breath group.

Stage D, by adding narrative material, allows some new kinds of data. A 'tentative' breath group contrasts with the 'final' type seen in earlier stages. New sentence types appear in the more complex situation, and the narrative, as a whole, itself shows a hyper-utteremic structuring.

We are now ready to suggest certain formulas which will show some characteristics of an utteremic-tagmemic analysis of this material, but with a minimum of reference to the phonological data.

Languagette C (data in § 7.313(4)):
Uttereme I ('affirmation of quality'):
$$\text{Minimum: } + \text{Item}^{\text{Noun}} + \text{Quality}^{\text{Adjective}}\backslash\|$$
$$\text{Maximum: } + \text{Item}^{\text{Noun}(+ \text{ Item}^{\text{noun}} \pm \text{ pl. } \{^{suf.}\})} + \text{Qual.}^{\text{Adj.}}\backslash\|$$
(See Utterances 1-4, 22; and text of Stage D.)

Uttereme II ('affirmation of state'):
$$\text{Minimum: } + \text{State}^{\text{Noun}_2(+ \text{ Item }^{\text{noun}} + \text{ asp. }^{\text{asp.}})} + \text{Item}^{\text{noun}}\backslash\|$$
$$\text{Maximum: } + \text{State}^{\text{Noun}_2(+ \text{ Item}^{\text{noun}} + \text{ asp.}^{\text{asp.}})}$$
$$+ \text{Item}^{\text{Noun}(+ \text{ Item}^{\text{noun}} \pm \text{ pl. } \{^{suf.}\} \pm \text{ asp. }^{\text{asp.}})}\backslash\|$$
(See Utterances 15, 5, 16-18, 23-25; and text of Stage D.)

Uttereme III ('affirmation of action'):
Assumed Minimum:
$$+ \text{Action}^{\text{Verb}(+ \text{ Action}^{\text{verb}} + \text{ tense}^{\text{teo.}})} + \text{Actor}^{\text{noun}}\backslash\|$$
Assumed Maximum:
$$+ (\pm \text{ Qual.}^{\text{Adj.}} + \text{Action}^{\text{Verb}} \pm \text{ Action}^{\text{verb-r.}} + \text{Action}^{\text{verb}} + \text{ten.}^{\text{ten.}}])\backslash +$$
$$(\pm \text{ Qual.}^{\text{Adj.}} + \text{Actor}^{\text{Noun}}[+ \text{ Actor}^{\text{noun}} \pm \text{ pl. } \{^{suf.}\} \pm \text{ asp.}^{\text{asp.}}]) \pm$$
$$(\pm \text{ Qual.}^{\text{Adj.}} + \text{Goal}^{\text{Noun}}[+ \text{ Goal}^{\text{noun}} \pm \text{ pl. } \{^{suf.}\} \pm \text{ asp.}^{\text{asp.}}])\backslash\|$$
(See Utterances 7-11, 13-14, 19-21, 26-29, and text of Stage D).

Uttereme IV ('query of affirmation of quality or of action'):
$$\text{Minimum-Maximum: } + \text{Aff.}^{\text{U-I/U-III}} + \text{Ques.}^{nos}\backslash\|$$
(See text of Stage D, for samples).

Uttereme V ('quoted affirmation or query'):
$$\text{Minimum-Maximum: } + \text{Aff.}^{\text{U-I/U-III/U-IV}}\backslash| + \text{Quote}^{\text{U-II}}\backslash\|$$
(See text of Stage D, for samples).

Uttereme VI ('calling affirmation or query'):
Minimum-Maximum:
$$+ \text{Call}^{\text{Noun}_2(+ \text{ Item}^{\text{noun}} + \text{ asp.}^{\text{asp.}})}\backslash| + \text{Aff.}^{\text{U-II/U-IV (and others)}}\backslash\|$$
(See text of Stage D, for samples.)

Hyper-Uttereme I ('a story-telling episode'):
$$+ \text{Intro.}^{\text{U-II}} + \text{Narr.}^{\text{U-III}}$$
$$+ \text{Sequence}^{\text{U-I/U-II/U-III/U-IV/U-V/U-VI}} + \ldots + \text{Concl.}^{\text{U-II}}\backslash\|$$

(Note: The analysis here is to a considerable extent an etic guess, and incomplete; more complete stories in the same emic pattern are needed if one wishes to explore the limits of substitution in such a pattern.)

From these utteremic formulas we now abstract certain tagmemic data:
List of unincluded tagmemes and of included tagmemes:

Item^{noun}; (in which the 'noun' spelled with lowercase 'n' implies the single-morpheme stem); occurs obligatorily in U-I, in U-II (as a tagmeme by itself, and as included in the 'state' construction, and in included occurrences of these utteremes. The expanded form is symbolized as Item^{Noun} since in the formulas this symbol represents any manifestation of the tagmeme, whether expanded or unexpanded;

plural$\{suf\}$; occurs, optionally, only as included in an expanded form of Item^{Noun}, Actor^{Noun}, or of Goal^{Noun};

aspect$^{asp.}$; occurs, optionally, as an expansion included within Item^{Noun}, Actor^{Noun}, or Goal^{Noun}; or obligatorily as a tagmeme included with the construction State-Noun$_2$;

Actor^{noun}; occurs, obligatorily, unexpanded, or occurs expanded (symbolized as Actor^{Noun}) by plural$\{suf\}$ or aspect$^{asp.}$, in unincluded and included U-III;

Goal^{noun}; occurs optionally, unexpanded, or expanded (as Goal^{Noun}) by plural$\{suf\}$ or aspect$^{asp.}$, in unincluded and included U-III;

Quality^{Adjective}; occurs obligatorily in U-I, but optionally as an expansion of the construction Action^{Verb} or of the tagmemes Actor^{Noun} and Goal^{Noun} of unincluded and included U-III;

Action^{verb}; occurs obligatorily in the construction Action^{Verb}; or occurs also in that construction as a reduplicating optional expansion tagmeme Action^{verb-r}, in unincluded and included U-III;

tense^{tense}; occurs obligatorily in the construction Action^{Verb}, in unincluded or included U-III;

Question^{nos}; occurs obligatorily in unincluded and included U-IV.

A few constructions may also be listed (their component included tagmemes have already been recorded above):

State$^{Noun}_2$ (in which the subscript 2 indicates that this noun structure is different from that recorded as Noun without a subscript numeral; it contains exclusively but obligatorily the included tagmemes Item^{noun} and aspect$^{asp.}$); occurs obligatorily in unincluded and included U-II;

Action^{Verb}; (composed obligatorily of close-knit Action^{verb} and tense^{tense} tagmemes; may be optionally expanded by close-knit Action^{verb-r} or by loose-knit Qual.$^{Adj.}$); occurs obligatorily in unincluded and included U-III;

Affirmation$^{U-I/U-II/U-III/U-IV}$; any of the utteremes may serve as the manifestation of this construction when included in an affirmation slot in U-IV, U-V, or U-VI;

Quote^{U-II}; the uttereme U-II may fill a quotation-indicator slot, and with it constitute a hypertagmeme, in U-V;

Call^{Noun2}; this 'call' construction is manifested by Noun$_2$, as was the 'state' construction; it occurs in U-VI;

Intro.$^{U-II}$; this 'introduction' construction is manifested by Uttereme II, and occurs in the opening slot of Hyper-Uttereme I.

Concl.$^{U-II}$; a 'concluding' construction, manifested by U-II, and occurring as the termination of Hyper-Uttereme I.

Morphemic classes were also symbolized in the utteremic formulas, and may now be listed separately, with a note as to their tagmemic and hypertagmemic occurrences:

noun stem: *tomi* 'food', *tipa* 'fire', *mit* 'human being', *lil* 'life', *kap* 'berry', *fon* 'utterance', *ski* 'I', *sil* 'you'; manifests the following tagmemes: Item^{noun}, Actor^{noun}, Goal^{noun};

plural suffix: *suf* ~ *uf* 'plural' (with allomorphs occurring after vowels and consonants respectively); manifests the tagmeme plural$\{^{suf}\}$, only, in the expanded tagmemes Item^{Noun}, Actor^{Noun}, Goal^{Noun};

aspect suffixes: *m* 'continuative', *s* 'completive'; manifests the tagmeme aspect$^{asp.}$, only, in the expanded tagmemes Actor^{Noun}, Goal^{Noun} (and possibly — though not occurring in the data, and hence not listed in U-I — in Item^{Noun});

verb stem: *sti* 'stir', *tupa* 'see', *tat* 'eat'; manifests the tagmemes Action^{verb}, and Action^{verb-r}, in the construction Action^{Verb};

tense suffixes: *fo* ∞ *pi* 'present' (with occurrence of the allomorphs morphemically conditioned), *su* 'future', *ka* ~ *a* 'past' (with allomorphs occurring after vowels and consonants respectively); manifests the tagmeme tense^{tense}, only, in the construction Action^{Verb};

Adjective: *ksa* 'good', *ku* 'hot'; manifests the tagmeme Qual.$^{Adj.}$, only, in U-I, and in the phrasally-expanded constructions Action^{Verb} and Goal^{Noun};

Interrogative: *nos* 'query'; manifests the tagmeme Ques.^{nos}, only, in unincluded or included U-IV.

Certain of the symbols in the utteremic formulas represented classes of hypermorphemes:

Noun$_2$: a class of hypermorphemes composed of noun stem plus aspectual suffix;

Verb: a class of hypermorphemes composed of a verb stem, or sequence of two identical verb stems, plus a tense suffix;

U-I, U-II, U-III, U-IV: classes of utterances which, when used as manifestations of slots included in larger utteremes, serve as large hypermorphemes.

One composite class of morphemes and hypermorphemes was also symbolized:

Noun: composed of noun stem, or of noun stem plus one or two optional suffixes.

It is convenient, in this languagette, to give the label of 'words' to members of the following classes: Adjective, Interrogative, Noun, Noun$_2$, and Verb. (Note that these words are not internally interrupted by a pause, nor by the border of an abdominal pulse, nor by other 'words'. Noun occurs as manifesting numerous tagmemes, and hence in numerous positions in the phrase; the tagmeme manifested by Adjective occurs in various utteremes and in various expanded constructions.)

7.75 *Languagettes for Student Analysis*

The student who has worked through the formulas given in the preceding section might like to have available a number of further languagettes, for his own analysis. (These languagettes were prepared by Evelyn G. Pike.)

THE MINIMUM UNIT OF THE DISTRIBUTION MODE OF THE BEHAVIOREME

Languagette 1

1. molikilosipami — 'The dog bit the cat'
2. takumulusumoli — 'The cat scratched the boy'
3. katolusisotaku — 'The boy struck the horse'
4. pamitiposikato — 'The horse kicked the dog'
5. pamitipositukukato — 'The vicious horse kicked the dog'
6. molikilomipami — 'The dog is going to bite the cat'
7. katolusimotaku — 'The boy is about to strike the horse'

Languagette 2

1. at — 'They are playing'
2. no — 'They are running'
3. si — 'They are sleeping'
4. atat — 'The playing is good' or 'They are playing happily'
5. atno — 'The playing is fast' or 'They are playing fast'
6. noat — 'The running is good' or 'They are running well'
7. nosi — 'The running is slow'
8. sino — 'They are going to sleep quickly'
9. noatat — 'Running happily makes a good game' or 'They are running well for fun'
10. noatatno — 'Running well leads to a fast game'
11. nonono — 'Fast running makes a race' or 'It's a fast race'
12. atatatat — 'Playing well gives a happy game' or 'The happy game is being played well'
13. atatatsi — 'Playing well gives a slow game'
14. atatatno — 'Playing well gives a fast game'
15. nonosi — 'Running fast makes for sleepiness'

Also, with no translation provided:

16. atatsi — ...
17. noatnono — ...

Translate:

18. ... — 'The running is fast'
19. ... — 'The game is going fast'

Languagette 3

1. losisanfelopinmotu — 'The man saw the flower in the garden'
2. losifelopinmotu — 'The man looked in the garden'
3. losifelomotu — 'The man saw the ball'

4.	losipinmotu	'The man saw the garden'
5.	losimotu	'The man saw it'
6.	litomotu	'The teacher saw it'
7.	litolakimotu	'The pretty teacher saw it'
8.	litolakipinlaki	'The pretty teacher made the pretty garden'
9.	nasulaki	'The children made it pretty'
10.	nasulakilaki	'The good looking children made it attractive'
11.	sanlakitokanlositon	'The pretty flower is in front of the man'
12.	santokanton	'The flower is in front'
13.	litofelokol	'The teacher showed it inside' or 'The teacher showed the ball'
14.	litofelopinkol	'The teacher showed it inside the garden'
15.	nasutokanlakimotu	'The children saw the pretty face'
16.	felofelopinton	'The ball is in the garden'
17.	losilakifelolakifelopinmotu	'The handsome man saw the pretty ball inside the garden'
18.	nasustankonolo	'The children ate the cake'
19.	nasustankokani	'The children made the cake well' or 'The children did well at making the cake'
20.	losipinlakikani	'The man did well at making a pretty garden'
21.	litokanisanlakitokannasukani	'The good teacher did well at making a pretty flower before the children'
22.	sankanipinlaki	'The good flower made the garden attractive'
23.	litofelotokannasukol	'The teacher showed the ball to the children'
24.	litolosikaniton	'The teacher is a good man'

Languagette 4

STAGE A:

1.	kinazviŋazzunvi	'Will the man shoot the lion?'
2.	viŋazkinazzamatvi	'Will the lion spring at the man?'
3.	ŋitkakinazzuŋku	'The man prepares to shoot'
4.	ŋitkaviŋazpumazamatku	'The hungry lion prepares to spring'
5.	pumakapatka	'It hungrily turns'
6.	zivzamatka	'It quickly springs'

STAGE B:

7.	pitkaviŋazkinas	'The lion sees the man'
8.	zunvikinazzivviŋas	'The fast man will shoot the lion'
9.	zuŋkuviŋazmuka	'Does the shot kill the lion?'
10.	mukvikinazpumaviŋazzif	'The hungry man will kill the fast lion'

STAGE C:

11. kinazzuŋkupitka   'Does the man see the shot?'
12. mukvizamatkuvinas   'The spring will kill the lion'
13. kinazmukuzivpitvi   'Will the man see the fast killing?

Languagette 5

STAGE A:

1. kimatapkansutso
2. tapkansutsokima
3. sutsokimatapkan
4. kimasutsotapkan
5. tapkaŋkimasutso
6. sutsotapkaŋkima

'You are speaking to him'
(Utterances 1-6 are alternate utterances with the same meaning).

7. sutsotapkantapma   'You are speaking to me'
8. sutsosutkantapma   'You are listening to me'
9. sutsosutkaŋkima   'You are listening to him'
10. kimsosutkantapma   'He is listening to me'
11. kimsosutkansutma   'He is listening to you'
12. kimsokimkantapma   'He is working for me'
13. kimsokimkansutma   'He is working for you'
14. sutsokimkantapma   'You are working for me'

STAGE B:

15. sutsokuptapkantapma   'Are *you* speaking to me?'
16. sutsotapkaŋkuptapma   '*Are* you *speaking* to me?'
17. kupsutsotapkantapma   'Are you speaking to me?'
18. kimsotapikimkan
19. kimkaŋkimsotapi

'He who is talkative is working'

20. tunaskaŋkimsotapi   'He who is talkative is studying'
21. tunaskantapso   'I am studying'
22. tapkaŋkimsotunaši
23. kimsotunašitapkan

'He who is learned is speaking'

STAGE C:

24. kimsotapkantunaši
25. tapkantunašikimso

'He is speaking learnedly'

26. kimsotunaši   'He is learned'
27. tapkansuti   'The speech is audible'
28. kimsotapkansuti   'He is speaking audibly'

29. tapso — 'There is a speaker'
30. tapkan — 'There is speech'
31. suti — 'There is audibility'
32. sutso — 'There is one who listens'
33. sutkan — 'There is listening'
34. kimso — 'There is a worker'

STAGE D:

35. tapsotunaskantapi ⎤
36. tunaskantapitapso ⎦ 'I am studying aloud'

37. kimtapso ⎤
38. tapkimso ⎦ 'There is a speaker and a worker'

39. kimtapsosutkan ⎤
40. tapkimsosutkan ⎬ 'He and I are listening'
41. sutkaŋkimtapso ⎦

42. sutsotapkimkan ⎤
43. sutsokimtapkan ⎦ 'You are talking and working'

44. kimsotapkansutunaši ⎤
45. kimsotapkantunasuti ⎦ 'He is speaking audibly and learnedly'

46. kimtapmakimsotunašisutkan ⎤
47. sutkantapkimakimsotunaši ⎦ 'The learned one is listening to him and me'

48. kimtapkantunaskimikimsokimi ⎤
49. kimsokimitapkimkaŋkimtunaši ⎦ 'He, an industrious person, is working and speaking learnedly and industriously'

STAGE E: The following utterances are recorded without translation:

50. kimtapi ...
51. suttapkan ...
52. tunastapso ...

STAGE F:

53. tapkan‖ 54. tunaskanotoki‖ 55. sutsotunaskaŋkup| tapkantapso‖ 56. tapsotunastunaskan| kimsotapkan‖ 57. sutsotunaskankupma| tapsotapkan‖ 58. tapsotunaskan| tapkan| kimsotapkan‖ 59. kupsosutkanfopisutma| tapsotapkan‖ 60. tapkaŋkimatunaši| kimsotapkan‖ 61. sutsotunaskanotokikup| tapkan| tapkantapso‖ 62. notoki| kimsotapkan‖ 63. sutsotunaskanfopikup| tapkantapso‖ 64. fopi| kimsotapkantapma‖ 65. tapsosutkanfopisutmakup| tapkantapso‖ 66. sutsosutkantapma| kimsotapkan‖ 67. fopso‖ 68. taptapsosutkaŋkima‖ 69. tapkansuti‖ 70. tapkan‖ 'Here's a story. Once there was a student. "Are you studying", I asked. "I am studying very hard", he answered. "What are you studying", I asked. He said that he was studying a speech. I asked who would listen to him. "It is for the students",

he said. "Did you study the speech yesterday?" I asked. He said, "Yes". I asked if he would study the next day. He said to me that he would. "May I listen to you", I asked. "You may hear it", he replied. The day arrived. We all listened to him. It was an acceptable speech. That's the story.'

7.8 Bibliographical Comments on Chapter 7

It will be evident to the reader acquainted with the linguistic literature that this chapter is a crucial one to the theory in that it proposes a third linguistic unit — the tagmeme — to join the phoneme and the morpheme, which are two small units that serve in some fashion as a starting point for some of the work of current linguistics (e.g., Bazell, 1953:5-6).

The outlook of this chapter, by setting up the tagmeme, takes issue with Z. Harris's conviction that

The linguistic structure of an utterance is presumed to be fully stated by a list of the morphemes which constitute it, and by their order. The difference between two utterances is expressed by the difference in morphemic constituency between them (1948: 87);
Past this point [i.e., the formal basis of getting phonemes and morphemes, etc.], however, there is often no agreement, even though it might seem that agreement would be almost automatic, since all that has to be done is to state the distribution of the elements which have been obtained (Harris, 1944a; 198; and cf. Lounsbury, 1953: 11).

We would say, rather, that the distribution of morphemes must be handled in reference to tagmemic units, which must also be obtained.

For a mathematical argument that many definitions which have been condemned as circular are in fact scientifically valid, as a variety of 'recursive definitions' from which "the definienda are not always eliminable", or "where [it] seems inevitable to define some term A with the help of B and B with the help of A", see Bar-Hillel (1953b). In our view, the descriptions of uttereme, morpheme, tagmeme, etc., make up a set of such simultaneously recursive definitions, and hence constitute a system.

In the nonverbal sphere the empirical usefulness of some kind of motifemic-slot-class correlative may perhaps be more easily seen than it is in linguistic analysis. The reason for this difference lies in the greater difficulty in locating a minimum motifemic unit in the analysis of nonlinguistic events than in verbal ones. It is relatively simple, by utilizing the communicative function of speech, to arrive at morphemes as minimum lexical units, with some residue; it is much more difficult to determine when one has a minimum nonlinguistic but purposive unit. This difficulty is in part due, according to this theory, to the fact that different participant types of activity or participant focus analysis of some units are clearly homomorphic but broken into subunits of different sizes and thresholds in accordance with their actor's participant type (§§ 3.32, 4.15, 4.1.10, 4.23, 4.32, 6.44, 6.62). By utilizing a theory which builds on a slot-class correlative as a basic occurring unit, however,[23] the analyst can start his analysis in the middle of the hierarchy, without waiting to find maximum and/or minimum units. This makes a slot-class starting point much more useful, for behavior as a whole, than is one which by implication insists on identifying a threshold that defines some kind of minimum before analysis can go further.

This does not mean, however, that the nonlinguistic analyst is not to be interested in the possibility of thresholds and minimum units of various types, but that he can get started and can delay a decision concerning them until after he has collected and partially analyzed a considerable body of material which may help him understand something of participant types or systems of activity which may cause such thresholds to differ within events which appear to be homomorphic.

For relation of tagmemes to constructions, and for relation of tagmemics to transform grammar, see § 11.6 with bibliographical comments throughout § 11.7. For tagmemics in phonology, see § 12.5, and § 8.66.

Since our first edition (1954) the idea of unit itself has come under subtle attack. From the direction of glossematics, Uldall states that to "the scientific view the world does not consist of things, or even of 'matter', but only of functions between things, the things themselves being regarded merely as points in which the functions meet" (1957:8). He still leaves some room for units defined as terminals (47) but in general disposes of "the Aristotelian bath-water" (9, fn. 1) of a thing existing with properties, performing activities (8). Lees specifically rejects "certain fictitious 'units of grammatical form', called 'gramemes', [tagmemes] along with a host of other fanciful '-emes'" (1960b:211). Some of Chomsky's statements imply that the nodes in the tree diagrams of a phrase structure grammar are pure symbols — neither names nor units: "we no longer have any reason to consider the symbols '*NP*', '*Sentence*', '*VP*', etc., that appear in these rules to be names of certain classes, sequences, or sequences of classes, etc., of concrete elements. They are simply elements in a system of representation which has been constructed so as to enable us to characterize effectively the set of English sentences in a linguistically meaningful way" (Third Texas Conference 1962:129).

Tagmemics takes a sharply different view and sees a variety of structural units: classes (noun, verb), constructions (noun phrase), tagmemes (subject, predicate), and so on. These may be labelled by names or by sheer numerals, arbitrarily chosen afresh without reference to any system of units. Any strictly formal use of numerals, without reference to class, construction, or tagmeme, however, would lead to a description which — if extended to a total language — would be extraordinarily opaque. This opaqueness, I believe, would not be due merely to the clumsiness of the representational symbols, but to the fact that we perceive a structure as made of units, and that the interrelated units are part of the system. Longacre, from the

---

[23] Note that this same possibility, carried over into linguistic analysis, helps to justify Longacre's contribution referred to in the fn. to § 7.44.

tagmemic viewpoint, argues that "The speaker acts as if he were using units which start and stop" (1964a:14); and cf. his 1963:475 fn. 6 in relation to native reaction of speakers.

Other authors, from differing theoretical backgrounds, have also come to the defense of the basic need of units in the study of a language structure. Jakobson implies units in taxonomy, as underlying a system, when he says that "It took time to realize that a description of systems without their taxonomy, as well as a taxonomy without description of single systems, is a flat contradiction of terms: both imply each other" (in *Proceedings of the Eighth...* 1958:18). Both a tagmemic theory and a transformation theory of grammar — in my view — need an explicit statement of units on which their processes operate. Note, for example, Stockwell: "we must assume a variety of 'elements' or 'formatives' on which the rules operate to generate sentences" (1960a:546); these elements in the tagmemic view are not "fictitious" but are part of the structure of the language being described. Note also Halliday "A structure is always a structure *of a given unit*" (1961:255); also Bach: "Without the possibility to specify a level of shiftable units intermediate between the 'word' and the sentence, the formulation of transformational rules which include permutations would be enormously complicated" (1962:264). Hill, reacting to the threat to their exclusion from current descriptions, has written an article to defend the need for moveable units in our grammars: "The first implication is that any utterance is separable into discrete units, since only chunks and pieces can be arranged and manipulated" (1962:345). Lamb, in retaining units, says that "one need recognize only three primitive relationships existing" among them: "that of a *class* to its *members*... of a *combination* to its *components*... and that of an *eme* to its *allos*" (1962:4).

For further discussion of unit, see § 11.765.

7.81 *On Classes of Morphemes*

The discussion of classes of 'words' as such (rather than of morphemes, or of morpheme-hypermorpheme composites) and of 'parts of speech' will be reserved for Chapter 11. A number of references to classes are useful here, however, even though they overlap on that discussion.

Thus, for example, according to our theory Fries was reacting to the emic — as distinct from an etic — view of morpheme or morpheme-hypermorpheme classes when he made the following statement:

A part of speech in English, like the strike in baseball, is a functioning pattern. It cannot be defined by means of a simple statement. There is no single characteristic that all the examples of one part of speech must have in the utterances of English. All the instances of one part of speech are the 'same' only in the sense that in the structural patterns of English each has the same functional significance (1952: 73).

Note also his important statement about lexical sets:

As we record more specifically the details of the experience of language learning, we realize increasingly that we 'learn' not only the shape of a lexical item and the recurrent stimulus-response features that correlate with it, but also the sets of other lexical items with which it usually occurs (Fries, 1954: 66, fn. 32).

Certain etic variants of classes, in which the membership is lexically conditioned (§§ 7.43, 7.46), were treated by Fries in reference to "lexical compatibility" (1952: 223-24), and lexical set (1954:66); cf. also Harris ("culturally determined limitations", 1951:253-54, and 1946:163-64), and Wonderly (1951-52:3).

For discussion of the meaning of a class, note Sweet who says that

I may remark at once that the real difficulty of determining the meaning of the parts of speech lies in the fact, which logicians and grammarians obstinately ignore, that they often have no meaning at all. Indeed the whole of language is an incessant struggle and compromise between meaning and pure form, through all the stages of vagueness, ambiguity, and utter meaninglessness (1913:16),

so that the "definition of a part of speech must be a purely formal one" (18). Contrast Bloomfield:

The functional meanings in which the forms of a form-class appear constitute the class-meaning (1926: 159; cf. also 1933a:266-68, 166, 202-05, 247-51).

For a recent use of semantic labels for classes, see Pittman (1954a:10). For vague meanings of classes of classes, see Z. Harris (1951:252, fn. 21).

For a theoretical rejection of class meanings, but with a simultaneous practical retention of class meanings under a different label, note Voegelin:

One after another, the meaning content of an older generation's use of a category is abandoned, leaving nothing but distribution, that is, position in an utterance or part of an utterance, as a word or phrase. Thus, from the older use of verb (V) as an action word and noun (N) as a thing word, and so on, modern analysts of natural languages use V and N and other parts of speech in a strictly formal sense, divorced from meaning (1952:222);

but, later,

the overriding meaning of the paradigm is *possessor relation to N*. ... To obtain an overriding meaning in this sense implies that a given language will show at least two sets of forms with parallel or analogous specific meanings, but with contrastive or overriding meaning (232).

On the other hand, Voegelin has been responsible for stimulating one of the most useful approaches to the labelling of morpheme classes, through a numbering technique. Any morpheme labelled with a 'decade' number (i.e., 21-29, or 31-39, or 41-49, etc.) is a member of that class. For an illustration, note Wonderly (1951-52), and Garvin (1948, 1951).

For instances in which class meaning, lexical meaning, and structural meaning are indeterminate or problematical, in 'function words', cf. Fries (1952:106). Whereas for Fries the function words seem to constitute one part of a basic dichotomy of his theoretical approach, in our theory they are less prominent, and rather form a marginal group of lexical items[24] in which tagmemic meaning, morphemic meaning, and morphemic-class meaning become fused or indeterminate (§§ 6.45, 7.323-24). Compare, also, references to Pittman in § 6.9, and compare Sweet:

It need hardly be said that there is no absolute line of demarcation between the two [grammar and dictionary]; thus the prepositions and many of the particles belong both to the grammar and the dictionary (1900b: 74).

Extensive discussion of morpheme classes occurs in Harris (1951:243-324). Cf. also Bazell (1953:69-80); Fries (1952:110-41).

For recent discussion of classes note Quine, with classes as constructions rather than discoveries (1953:125). For affix classes charted separately according to variant word structures, note Cox (1957), with differences in result according to whether one charts from the end or beginning of the word structure. Substitution techniques via "diagnostic environments" are treated by Lees as "simply a misleading way to present a proposed grammatical analysis — more accurately, a proposed morpheme-order analysis" (1960b:209). Nida has begun to give "increased recognition [to]... the significance of classes as determined by the function of the words rather than classes determined on the basis of form" (1960:220); this emphasizes external distribution as over against internal structure. Halliday, similarly, says that "*classes* are derived 'from above' (or 'downwards') and not 'from below' (or 'upwards')" (1961:261), and classes "are set up with reference to the *form* of the unit next above" (261); he also quotes Robins as giving preference to syntactic function as over against morphological paradigms when there is a conflict of classification (262).

For Martinet, substitution is choice (in Preprints... 1962:504). For Brown, the meanings of word classes are probabilistic (in Saporta, 1961:508); "nouns *tend to have* a different semantic from verbs, and that the native speaker detects this tendency while he is in the process of learning the language" (504). Chomsky suspects that continued refinement of "the category hierarchy" may converge "with what has been called logical grammar" as grammatical rules "become more detailed" (1961b:237, fn. 32, see also 235, fn. 29) leading to elements which we can — given the grammar — "recognize as a semantic feature of some sort"; note also doubt about the "natural bond between grammar and 'logical grammar'" (1962:524 § 2.3). Halliday seems to imply that there will be a cline — continuum — (1961:249) in the "delicacy" of membership of classes (258).

For disjunctive classes, with included division subclasses, see H. Hart (1957:121-52).

---

[24] For limited classes — even a class of one member — treated as a special instance of a matrix, see now Pike 1964c.

For a class of classes, or hierarchy of classes, note Hjelmslev (1953:18), and Jakobson (in *Proceedings of the Eighth...*, 1958:19). For subclasses of noun and verb, note Lees (1960a:22, 23); see also F. R. Palmer (1958); and see below, § 11.43. For an emic subclass as part of a larger class — and criteria thereof — note H. Hart (1957: 147-50). For 'shifter' classes which are "distinguished from all other constituents of the linguistic class solely by their compulsory reference to the given message" — for example *I* — note Jakobson (1957b:2, with term taken from Jespersen). For criteria of word classes, note also Uhlenbeck (1953); compare various markers of classes in Gleason (1961:255 — *a piece of iron* versus *a piece of an iron*); Hill, with form classes marked by derivational morphemes (1958:166-72). Representational formulas of the variants of a class are found in Lamb (1962:9); a cover symbol is followed by vertical double bars which are in turn followed by alternate environments and the variants represented on the next lower stratum. Problems in the categorization of Vietnamese word classes are discussed in Honey (1956).

For a contrasting view of the relation of slot to class, note Lees: "No matter how class-membership is designated, whether honestly by listing or subscripting, or whether by the misleading technique known as substitution in frames..." (1963:551).

For monologue practice, by solemnant child, of substitution in slot, however, see Weir (1962); compare Braine: "the child learns, one at a time, that each of a small number of words belongs in a particular position [e.g., first or second of two] in an utterance" (1963:13); "pivot words" are those for which the position is already learned; all other words group indiscriminately with them in "the X-class".

7.82 *On Slot or Position*

Bloomfield early suggested that 'Each of the order units in a construction is a *position*' (1926:158). The conception of a sentence as containing places for substitutable items had, nevertheless, been a part of practical grammatical apparatus before that (e.g., Sheffield, 1912:107).

For positions as diagnostic, see Bloomfield (1926:158-59), Pike (1943b:81), Z. Harris (1946:165), Fries (1952:75-86). For position as having a strong priority over morphemes in analysis, see Z. Harris:

We may therefore speak of interenvironment relations, or of occupyings of positions, as being our fundamental elements (1951:371, and cf. 1946:171, 181),

although this point of view of Harris' is not integrated with his more frequent attention to morphemes and morpheme classes (e.g., "The method described in this paper will require no elements other than morphemes and sequences of morphemes, and no operation other than substitution repeated time and again" 1946:161; and cf. quotations in § 7.8, above).

J. R. Firth would refer to "place and order" in a way similar to our handling of the term etic slot (1957a:5); for him, however, etic slot would be "successivity of bits and pieces in a unidirectional time sequence" (1957a:5). Cf. Palmer, with "order (grammatical)" as emic slot and "sequence (exponential)" as specific etic data (in Preprints, 1962:235); see also Sprigg (1954:138-39); Halliday (1961:255 and 251, fn. 24). For handling of formulas in a manner related to that of tagmemics, note the use of letter symbols for tagmeme and tagmemic slot, with numerals for the classes, in such a statement as "1 (at X)", in Halliday (1961:264); concord is shown by subscripts or decimals: "2.1 (at Ya)"; versus "2.2 (at Yb)" (264).

Note, for position in discourse, Stennes: *Announcement Introduction Body Conclusion Closing* (1961:9). Note Waterhouse, for extensive discussion of independent versus dependent sentence types and their relation to position in discourse (1963).

For slot in reference to word-class definition see § 7.81. For external distribution in definition of emic class note Longacre (1964a, Chapter 3). For slots relevant to folktale structure and its units note Dundes — with topic versus comment in proverbs (1962a:37) and various other motifemic slots (1962b, 1963).

My insistence on the relevance of external distribution (their occurrence in higher-level slots) in description of tagmemes (or constructions or other units) provides, in tagmemic theory, a place where context restrictions enter — versus Lees who, in rejecting tagmemics, claims that "context restrictions" are "never in fact utilized by structural linguists whose conception of grammatical structure is equivalent to a theory of labeled bracketing" (1963:551).

Householder seems to have external distribution of units as primary: "the primes themselves have no other properties than those of making up higher units" (in Saporta, 1961:24); but a tagmeme is not a prime, but "is a shorthand statement of two rules" — one regarding parts of the construction, and the other concerning replacement of its parts (25); yet a tagmemic relation or rule between primes may be "just as primitive and important as the units themselves".

7.83 *On Proportion, Positional Meaning, and Substitutability*

Bloomfield stated that "The meaning of a position is a *functional meaning*" (1926:159), and that it

would be more concrete, but perhaps less useful, if we said: the meaning common to all forms that can fill a given position, when they are in that position, is a functional meaning (1926: 159).

Since that time, the prevailing climate of opinion has led workers to try to eliminate such reference to meaning from their structural definitions, while on occasion granting the presence of such meanings. Note, for example, the following quotations from Fries:

The grammar of a language consists of the devices that signal structural meanings (1952:56),

nevertheless,

For a grammar that will give an understanding of the working of a language we must turn aside from all definitions that strive to state the identifying characteristics of grammatical structures in terms of meaning content. Structures do signal meanings, it is true; and these meanings must be described. The meanings, however, cannot serve successfully to identify and distinguish the structures (1952:203).

As far as analytical procedures are concerned, however,

Meaning of some kind and of some degree always and inevitably constitutes part of the framework in which we operate (Fries, 1954:61),

and

The use of the technique of substitution in investigation always demands control of certain features of 'meaning'. The investigator must, in some way, either through an informant or by using his own knowledge, control enough of a particular kind of meaning to determine whether the frame is the 'same' or 'different' after any substitution is made (1952:74-75, fn. 6),

but

Of course, the object of our search here is not the meaning but the strictly formal features which make a difference in the 'meaning' (1952:75, fn. 6).

furthermore,

it is necessary to insist that such terms as 'subject', 'indirect object', 'direct object' have no relation to the actual facts of a situation in the real world. As grammatical terms they are simply names for particular formal structures within an utterance (1952:175).

Although Z. Harris finds it necessary to add to his scheme a "position-morpheme" (1951:211, fn. 38; cf. also 185-86, 357 and 195) presumably because it adds, for example, "the 'object' meaning to *you* in *I saw you*", he fails to integrate this addition into a coherent theory with the main stream of his thought (which "will require no elements other than morphemes and sequences of morphemes" 1946:161, from which morpheme types he normally omits morphemes of order, without comment). Even in reference to meaningful or structural positions, however, he elsewhere states that

It may be necessary to point out that this positional analysis is strictly formal, as compared with form-and-meaning analysis like the one in Otto Jespersen's analytic syntax (1946:177, fn. 26).

At this point, Z. Harris seems on occasion to share with Fries the recognition of structural, positional meaning, and the desire to eliminate this factor from his structural definitions. Trager and Smith go even further, in that they wish to see such structural meaning eliminated not only from the resultant definitions but from the procedures of analysis as well:

The procedures for syntactic analysis do not differ essentially from those already used. With the phonology completely established, and the morphological analysis completed, the syntax of a language like English can be constructed objectively, without the intervention of translation meaning or any resort to metalinguistic phenomena (1951:68).

The reader will recall that we have earlier insisted that, in our view, neither an approach through meaning alone, nor one through form alone, is valid, but that in every step in linguistic analysis we must retain a form-meaning composite as essential to analysis and definition (§§ 5.64, 2.73).

Here, likewise, we reject with Fries and Harris an analysis by meaning *alone*, and reject with Fries an analytical procedure which purports to be handled by form alone; but I find it valid to include structural meaning within the various components which enter into a definition of a tagmeme, if for that particular tagmeme a structural meaning is clearly identifiable (but for Fries' discussion of some of these problems, see 1952:203, 188-89, 175-76, 178, 191, 201, 204-06, 217, 219, 224).

One of the chief reasons for insisting on the validity of and necessity for the use of meaning along with form, to identify and control *proportion* (§ 7.321) in substitution, is illustrated in a problem met by Z. Harris when he ignored this component:

Since our procedure now permits us to make any substitutions of any sequences, it may become too general to produce useful results. For example, we might take the utterance *I know John was in* and substitute *certainly* for *know John*, obtaining *I certainly was in* (1946: 166);

know John is not proportionate to *certainly* in that utterance. Harris, in that paragraph, states that this substitution conceals several important facts of sentence structure, distribution and concord. He affirms that "such substitutions as *certainly* for *know John* can be precluded by analyzing the utterance into immediate constituents", but that such a technique does not serve him there since "the analysis into immediate constituents is not used here and we must state other methods of excluding such substitutions as *certainly* for *know John*" (1946:166, fn. 9); no such methods are provided in that article, however, and the problem does not seem to be raised in the same way in 1951 (compare, however, the discussion of related but different problems on 249-51, 257, 259-60, 296-97, 311, 311 fn. 21, 350-51, 365 fn. 6). For a quasi-mathematical attempt to discuss such a problem, see Bar-Hillel (1953a:48).

For an extensive critique of Harris' substitution methods, see Fowler:

But the methodical use of frames requires a kind of control not possible at the beginning of an analysis in which distribution or arrangement is the only relevant relation| (1952:508),

and

But (as, again, it can hardly be too often repeated) no substitution classes are yet in existence the choice of another frame (no matter whether one or all of the constituent elements be changed) is necessarily therefore either random (and not a method at all) or determined by a criterion other than 'distribution or arrangement' (508), and

It is this prime criterion — the additional element of function or of meaning — which Harris would put aside in favor of 'distributional investigations'. Until it is brought back and placed in first position, the job simply cannot be done (509).

To Wells we are indebted for the term 'expansion' (1947a:81, 83). We use it, however, within a framework of control which embraces both form and meaning (or proportion) from the early etic beginning of an analysis, rather than trying 'in our exposition to leave the factor of meaning out until much later (Part III)" (Wells, 1947a:85 — a goal he fails to attain, cf. 81, 85, 92).

For the term 'substitution' used for open classes, vs. 'commutation' for closed ones, see reference to Firth in Carnochan (1953:79 fn. 5).

For some descriptions of tagmemic meanings, within a different theoretical framework, note Jespersen, e.g., 1949:

The tertiary serves to qualify not the real content signified by the verb, but the stylistic choice of the following word, which is then strongly stressed, as in '*she fairly screamed*', or as in '*I absolutely blushed*' (84).

On language as choice see now R. Brown (1957a:171) and Longacre (1964a:14).

Since the publications of Fries which were referred to earlier in the section, he has stated that "*the language itself is not the meanings. A language is a code of signals*" (1962:99); he continues to deal with "*grammatical meanings*" which "are definite and sharp, essential features of every utterance" (1962:70). Chomsky, however, has attempted to set forth a grammatical theory which is "completely formal and non-semantic" (1957a:93-94, 99-100, 103-04); as such he implies a rejection of the idea of Fries' structural meaning; later Chomsky states that "it seems evident that perception of grammatical relations in a sentence does not depend on a prior and independent identification of semantic properties, and that the study of grammatical structure seems to be, in fact, quite independent of meaning" (1961b:232). His emphasis seems to be to reject "semantic absolutes, identifiable in noises independently of the grammatical structure" (1961b:232, fn. 25). (Note that my emphasis does not at all set up semantics independently of the grammar, but emphasizes a form-meaning composite, to avoid a trap of totally independent meaning, or a trap of totally independent form.) Compare Chao's reference to subject and predicate as having "grammatical meanings" which "should better be described as topic and comment rather than actor and action" since the action can be "outwards from the subject", or "inwards to the subject", or "not related to it except by way of general comment" (1959:1). Compare, similarly, Hockett (1958:205; see also 194, 197, 201).

Longacre suggests that a "background of meaning would seem to be essential to the analysis" but "that meaning nowhere come[s] into the foreground" (1964b:23); yet names of units are useful since "it is difficult to compare things that do not bear names" (14).

As far as I am concerned, the linguist's task is not done when he knows — or shows — *that* we are saying something (in 'well-formed' sentences) but only after he knows — and shows — approximately *what* we are saying. Thus our grammatical formulas must have reference to grammatical meaning if we wish to generate sentences which are meaningful and usable by the speaker. If we generate the meaning of sentences, none of which we can use, or join into larger relevant and structured sequences (see § 5.63), why bother?

7.84 *On Potential and Prediction*

In §§ 2.6 and 2.74 we discussed some of the possibilities of predicting behavior in reference to clashing emic systems. Within the tagmeme, the productive 'potential' for substitution leads to the 'prediction' of sequences which may occur. For a discussion of such productive potential see Wonderly (1951-52: 2-3; compare Fries, 1952:65). For potential as prediction, see Hockett (1948a:269-70); but for his adverse reaction to potential in another connection, note 1949a:47-48, and reply by Pike (1952a:109-11).

Note also Z. Harris:

Therefore any differences in substitution potential which can be recognized from the structure of an utterance are relevant even to that utterance alone [i.e., by itself] (and are certainly relevant to the whole language) (1951: 273 fn. 27);

and, in reference to the ability to "predict utterances", see 365 — though predictions of difficulty in learning a second language are "outside the techniques and scope of descriptive linguistics" (21).

For an earlier reference, note Bloomfield: The totality of utterances that can be made in a speech-community is the *language* of that speech-community. We are obliged to predict; hence the words 'can be made'.

Where good informants are available, or for the investigator's own language, the prediction is easy; elsewhere it constitutes the greatest difficulty of descriptive linguistics (1926:155).

In reference to nonverbal behavior, note Sapir:

It is easy for an Australian native, for instance, to say by what kinship term he calls so and so or whether or not he may undertake such and such relations with a gvien individual. It is exceedingly difficult for him to give a general rule of which these specific examples of behavior are but illustrations, though all the while he acts as though the rule were perfectly well known to him. ... It is, rather, a very delicately nuanced feeling of subtle relations, both experienced and possible' (1927, in his Selected Writings: 548).

For an extensive discussion, favoring the use of the term 'choice' in nonlinguistic situations, see Nadel (1951:68-72). Compare Kluckhohn (1949:31, 43, 67-68, 260), and Twaddell,

we notice in our own language the meanings, the acts of choice

and

Language is one of the points of intersection in that network of habit and choice which is the pattern of human beings (1949:6, 4).

But for this term sharply rejected (and, in 1933, replaced by the word "selection"), as reflecting "the primeval drug of animism", see Bloomfield (1930b:554). Contrast the activity of the parrot who, according to Hoijer,

learns single and unrelated (to him) morpheme utterances. The trick learned by the primate, like the utterances of the parrot, is not seen as a frame in which substitutions are possible but only as an act complete in itself and discrete from all others (in Kroeber, 1953: 555).

For reference to selection potential as basic to communication theory, note Shannon:

The significant aspect is that the actual message is one *selected from a set* of possible messages. The system must be designed to operate for each possible selection, not just the one which will actually be chosen since this is unknown at the time of design (in Shannon and Weaver, 1949: 3).

Attention to the generative power of a grammar has come to the fore in the past few years; note Chomsky (1957a:13). Halliday claims, however, that "any theory-based grammar, transformational or not, can be stated in generative terms" (1961:241, fn. 2). Compare Longacre's demonstration of the generative power of tagmemics (1964a:Introduction). It has been only slowly recognized that the terms prediction, potential, and productiveness are closely related to the term "generative power". Thus Wonderly's claim "We need, therefore, to balance our formulas representing the productive potential of the Zoque language as a functioning, productive system..." and "the productive potential is relevant to any study of the language" (1951-52:2-3) sounds strangely up-to-date, if one makes the appropriate transformation from the term productiveness to generativeness. (See also, above, our fn. for § 6.63.) Then, as now, any incomplete formula would lead to incomplete or erroneous results, under any system. There remains, under all theories, the problem of the relationship between production by the speaker and recognition by the hearer; note differences between reading versus spelling discussed in Fries (1962:170-71). See, also, Chomsky's claim that "attempts to construct a model for the speaker or hearer are quite premature at this point" and that it is a "mistaken view that a generative grammar in itself provides or is related in some obvious way to a model for the speaker" (1961a:14, fn. 17); yet I find myself unable to match this disclaimer against the current work of some transformationalists (especially when they are using contrastive transformational studies as a basis for the preparation of pedagogical textbooks for teaching people to speak the language). See also § 7.52.

7.85 *On Morphemic Slot-Class Correlatives versus Constructions or Relationships*

We have already discussed (§ 6.7), to some extent, the advantages of giving priority in the theory to physically-manifested units, rather than to abstracted relationships as such. This view must not be distorted, however, to make it appear to imply that such units exist *apart from* their occurrence in any relationship; rather the units are treated as occurring only as points in a system[25] of relationships (§ 6.7), with unity and relationship both relevant, but with attention focused on the first. Thus the present theory is *neither* that of relationships apart from substance *nor* of substance apart from relationships, but a theory in which the 'relationships' into which units enter are interpreted as conceptualized hypostatic constructs viewed by the analyst as components of those units. Thus the view here is neither the one accepted nor the one rejected by Hjelmslev:

The recognition of this fact, that a totality does not consist of things but of relationships, and that not substance but only its internal and external relationships have scientific existence, is not, of course, new in science, but may be new in linguistic science. The postulation of objects as something different from the terms of relationships is a superfluous axiom and consequently a metaphysical hypothesis from which linguistic science will have to be freed (1953: 14);

and

Linguistics ... must establish the science of the expression without having recourse to phonetic or phenomenological premisses (50);

and

'substance' cannot in itself be a definiens of language (66; cf. 61, 68, 81).

In the tagmeme we have insisted that the filling of the slot (i.e., the manifestation mode of the tagmeme; cf. §§ 3.56, 7.4) is relevant to its nature, and that the relational functions of the emic slot (§ 7.321(2-4)) are also relevant.

We also insist that focus of analytical attention in theory and practice must be placed on units as total elements — though with a relevant placement in a hierarchy of larger forms — and not on bipartite 'constructions' as the principal elements. WE REJECT A VIEW IN WHICH THE MOST BASIC RELATIONSHIP IS, PRIMARILY, BETWEEN UNITS OF EQUAL RANK, OR OF THE SAME 'LEVEL', AS TERMS OF A RELATION IN A BINARY CONSTRUCTION; and we PROPOSE A VIEW IN WHICH THE MOST BASIC RELATIONSHIP IS BETWEEN A UNIT AND ITS SLOT-OCCURRENCE. This view has lead to the treating of the tagmeme, with its slot-class correlation, as more basic than that of 'immediate constituents' as such. The underlying reason for this decision we argued in 1944, under the phrase "Positions: as theoretically primary, establishing form classes and parts

---

[25] For focus of attention on a system of relationships as itself an emic unit, see our more recent matrix papers (e.g., 1962a, 1963b, 1963d; Pike and Erickson, 1964).

of speech" (1944:114; compare a re-working of this point of view, above, in relation to tagmemes, §§ 7.31, 7.321), and affecting lexical meanings (1944:114, 124-25, 129-32, 134-36; compare above, §§ 7.323-24). The crucial part of the argument as regards unit vs. construction, however, is contained in an extensive footnote:

In a large phrase, each of the immediate constituents, i.e., each member of the relationship, has a unit function with in that relationship, whether the member is simple or complex. For example *Tom* and *Big Tom* both function as subject in *Tom likes apples* and *Big Tom likes apples*. Now since *Big Tom* likewise has members of an internal relationship — *big* in modifying position and *Tom* in modified position — it is evident that a relationship as a whole can function as a unit in one position of a larger relationship as in *Big Tom likes apples*;

and

one may deduce that the basic characteristic of a large complicated relationship is not its internal structure as such, but rather its total function as a unit in relation to the physical and linguistic environment in which it is uttered.

The note then continues to discuss the labelling problems of hierarchical structures, in which

the labelling of a top layer and function in terms of a lower layer and function steals the source material for labelling, in due course, [from] the lower layer,

so that the analyst may then be tempted to affirm

that only relationships exist since everything would seem to have been described about the simple forms [the ultimate constituents] already (127-28 fn. 7).

Six years after the publication of this note I was startled to find that much earlier Bloomfield had met one phase of this problem:

E. A. Esper calls my attention to an error in my English wording of Meillet's definition, LANGUAGE 2.158: 'A maximum construction in any utterance is a *sentence*'. For 'construction' one must, of course, read 'form', since otherwise, the definition, if it meant anything at all, would exclude largest-forms that happened to contain only a single morpheme; e.g. *Come! Ouch! Yes.* (1931:209 fn. 6);

yet in 1933 Bloomfield had not assimilated this lesson, and was still setting up multi-partite constructions as basically distinct from simpler items:

The grammatical forms of a language can be grouped into three great classes: (1) When a form is spoken alone (that is, not as a constituent of a larger form), it appears in some *sentence-type* ... (2) Whenever two (or, rarely, more) forms are spoken together, as constituents of a complex form, the grammatical features by which they are combined, make up a *construction* (1933a:169).

In 1952 Pittman gave a paper, at the August meeting of the Linguistic Society of America, entitled "The Priority of Valence over Phonological Attachment and

Relative Order in Descriptive Statements". Developing this point of view in his grammar of Nahuatl, he argues that

'It is possible to conceive of the relation between two immediate constituents as a sort of link, or bond, between the constituents. ... called a 'syntagmatic relation' by Hjelmslev ... a sort of 'bond' or 'valence' connecting the terminals' (1954a:5-6).

Here Pittman attempts to make such an abstracted 'valence' his principal theoretical construct. (For an early use of this term, see de Groot, who attributes it to Reichling (de Groot, 1948:437, 439, 441, 443-44; there it is used in reference to "suitableness for combinations with certain other words in a certain way").

It seems improbable that Pittman's abstracted covert valences — i.e., abstracted relationships — could attain nonhypostatic emic status within our theory since they lack, in such a treatment, a manifestation mode (cf. § 7.321, for our treatment of abstracted tagmemic slots as denied emic status, other than as a conceptualized hypostasis).

Compare, in this connection, a statement of Bloomfield's which implies that relationship is part of an emic unit, not a nonhypostatic emic unit to be abstracted in itself:

To earlier students, language appeared to have a third aspect, intermediate between form and meaning; this aspect was usually called *function*. Thus, a word like *apple* not only meant a certain kind of fruit, but also functioned as a noun, serving as the subject of verbs, as the object of prepositions and transitive verbs, and so on. Careful study, however, showed that features like these are a part of the form; they are the formal features which come into being when two or more forms are combined in a larger form. ... In sum, the function of a speech form consists merely of formal features which appear when it serves as part of a more inclusive form (1943:103).

Pittman's overt valences we have already discussed in § 6.91, in reference to Fries' "function words" or, in this theory, to morphemes which have empty meaning (§ 6.45) or meaning indeterminate with tagmemic meaning (§§ 7.323-24). The kind of data leading to such a problem of function words or of overt valences has been neatly stated by Bloomfield, for Tagalog:

Some of the particles seem, however, to stand in none of these relations [attribution, predication, serialness], but rather to express these relations themselves. Thus the particle t *and* in the preceding example is expressive of the serial relation. So further: malakì ŋ baháy *large house*; the particle ŋ expresses the attributive relation (1917:146);

and some of the same relationships may be expressed by word order without the particle — but in this instance the word order differs from that which occurs when the particle is present.

There continues to be discussion of the relation of units to constructions — or of terms to their relationships. This issue goes far deeper than linguistics alone. Note Lévi-Strauss: "L'erreur de la sociologie traditionelle, comme de la linguistique traditionelle, est d'avoir considéré les termes, et non les relations entre les termes" (1945:48). Copi quotes Wittgenstein approvingly concerning the suggestion "that the relation between *a* and *b* should not be represented by placing a term between their names, but rather by a *relationship* of their names '*a*' and '*b*' (in Henle, 1958:113); I interpret this to mean that rather than setting up the relationship as a separate, independent element, the construction *ab* includes the terms in relationship; this is similar to our treatment of tagmemes — as including relational components — comprising a construction rather than the abstraction of the relationship as an emic unit in itself. W. Haas states that "To select an element by commutation is to state a syntagmatic relationship of it to the *whole remainder* of the sign" (1959:3); Halliday includes as "fundamental categories" of the theory of grammar "'unit', 'structure', 'class', and 'system'," — elements which are "mutually defining" (1961:247-48), "but all structures presuppose classes and all classes presuppose structures" (261). Longacre handles as primitives of linguistic structure both the syntagmeme (construction) and tagmeme (element of a construction) (1964a). For further discussion of item-in-slot versus construction, note also § 11.711. For both slot and construction in folktales, see Dundes (1963:123).

Note, from a different viewpoint, Garner's assumption that *"The search for structure is inherent in behavior"* (1962:339) but "behavior is primarily relational" (341).

7.86 *On the Etics of Relationships*

The most consistent and rigorous attempt to provide a theory behind the etics of grammatical relationships is that of Hjelmslev (1953). This, to me, seems to have been potentially his greatest contribution — the building of a general, logical 'grid' of relations, of a quasi-mathematical type, through which languages can be etically seen and etically compared. Such an etic classification, however, should not be confused with the kind of operational prescriptions which must constitute part of any generalized emic approach to a particular language. Note, also, H. J. Uldall (1949), with some symbolism for such relations. Much work has also been done by Bazell, in attempting to classify the etics of relationships (1953:13-39, and references to numerous other articles in the 1949 and 1950 volumes of the Linguistic Bibliography published by the International Committee of Linguists). For a bibliography on glossematics, see Spang-Hanssen (in Trends, 1961:163-64).

Problems concerning the relation of logical function to actual grammatical distribution have been under attention for many years. Note, for example, Paul (1889: 311-38), with a heading "The divergence of psychological and grammatical distribution", and with a formulaic representation of certain of these elements. Contrast Sheffield: "It is easier, however, to 'muckrake' the parts of speech than to replace them with word-categories valid for every language" (1912:90) — where logical etics and descriptive emics are confused. For an argument that the environment in which man finds himself imposes its (etic) pattern on man's language (especially as regards nouns and verbs), note Bull (1949:474-75); it fails, however, to account for languages in which the noun-verb dichotomy is not basic to word classes (e.g., cf. the quote from Bloomfield, regarding Tagalog, in § 7.85).

Perhaps the best known discussion of language types, including a discussion of relational elements, is that of Sapir (1921:59-156, with summarizing chart on 150-51). Here, too, is the best discussion of the difficulties inherent in such a task (e.g., 129-33).

Various studies are giving us partial lists of emic slots of various kinds. Note Bendor-Samuel (1961); Stennes, with slots in discourse (1961:9-13); Guthrie (1961).

7.87 On the Initial Development of Tagmemic Theory

In a paper, "Syntax of the Mixteco Noun", presented in 1941 to the Mexican Society of Anthropology (published by title only, in the Revista Mexicana de Estudios Antropologicos Volume V, nos. 2-3, 1941), I first analyzed the manner in which a subclass of Mixtec nouns was changed in meaning in certain syntactic positions (cf. above, § 7.323, and 1944:131-32). It was this bit of descriptive work which laid the groundwork and provided the stimulus for the later development of that part of the present tagmemic theory which has reference to the interrelations of lexical meaning, class meaning, and tagmemic meaning.

Meanwhile I was attempting to apply to Mixtec the taxeme-tagmeme outlook of Bloomfield's *Language* (1933a). In trying to do so, three difficulties which are now relevant to tagmemic analysis became clear: (1) structural layerings needed explicit formulation, in a hierarchical structuring not developed by Bloomfield; (2) the study of immediate constituents needed explicit criteria for its application; and (3) taxeme and tagmeme had overlapping definitions.

To meet the first of these difficulties and to make layered structure explicit, I proposed an analysis in a kind of 'pyramided' structure, with a chart to show the layerings (1943a:70, a procedure which in some form or other has now been frequently used in the discussion of immediate constituents — e.g., Nida, 1949:87; Fries, 1952:266). For the second, I proposed a list of criteria for immediate constituents (1943b:74-81). This list proved incomplete, and not sufficient for a full procedure. Since that time, additional criteria have been suggested by other writers — especially by Wells (1947a) and Pittman (1948b), but further criteria and theory were needed.

In order to try to solve some of these problems, William Wonderly and I attempted in the summer of 1948 to devise a set of formulas which would lead, without reference to meaning, to the immediate constituents of any utterance. After trying many formulas such as "If ab and abc but not ac occur, c is subordinate to ab", etc., we repeatedly ran into situations which made the conclusions untenable in the light of grammatical junctures which were obvious from other criteria. In the meantime, however, we noticed that we could with a fair degree of ease and agreement recognize the consistent proportion of one item to its environment and of a substituted item to that same environment — and that this recognition occurred long before we could be reasonably sure of the immediate constituents of that utterance. Therefore, in the present theory, I have given the recognition of proportion in substitution an important place in tagmemic treatment (§§ 7.321-22), and have eliminated from the theory any attempt to determine immediate constituents without reference to structural meaning or proportion.[26]

For the third of the difficulties in Bloomfield's analysis — the confusion in the relation of taxeme and tagmeme — a discussion of their overlapping analyses in Bloomfield's work was given, with an attempt to revise the usage of the terms so as to eliminate such overlap (Pike, 1943b:65-74). In the next few years the basic criticisms raised at that time continued to appear valid, but the revised solution did not prove particularly useful: it seemed that some basic difficulty must still remain with the fundamentals of the approach. The taxemes of selection, order, modulation, and phonetic modification did not seem to be parallel or analogous one to another; the postulation of a new over-all tagmeme for every expansion of a basic construction became highly unwieldy; and several components of the tagmeme which we can now distinguish clearly — though with some residual indeterminacy — were not differentiated by the terms of the definition of the Bloomfieldian tagmeme, so that morphemic class, class meaning, tagmemic slot, structural meaning, correlation of various types, intonational versus segmental tagmemes, productive versus nonproductive morphs, etc., were not consistently handled. In the present theory, therefore, the attempt to salvage the Bloomfieldian tagmeme has been abandoned, and morphemic-class theory, the theory of hierarchical structuring of the various modes of utteremes, and the theory of componential but interpenetrating systems, etc., take over miscellaneous areas covered in part by the older term.

Our particular approach to the tagmeme, however, began in 1948. In the spring of that year, I asked myself: "If the discovery of the phoneme was long delayed, and came after investigators began to see that the naïve reaction of native speakers was quite different from what phonetic theory would have predicted (e.g., see Sapir, 1933, in his Selected Writings, 47-58), is it possible that some currently unknown unit of grammar, equally important and equally clearly implied by naïve native reaction to grammar, is waiting to be discovered by someone who would search for such ignored clues?" I set myself to this search, without much success, for a year: I looked for clues in both meaning and form, with no useful result.

Then I decided to try to duplicate for grammar the technique Sapir had utilized in demonstrating the necessity for a structural approach to phonology. As he had built, in 1925, two artificial systems of sounds which had the same list of phones, within entirely different phonemic structures, so I would try to build various artificial languagettes with some constant list of starting elements but with different gram-

[26] Note that this also implied abandonment of an algorithm for analysis. See § 7.322.

matical structures. This approach proved more fruitful: a list of morphs provided the constant for the various languages; and differences in morphophonemics, morphemic order, bound versus free classes, word class groupings, agreement, structural meanings, sentence patterns, and so on, provided the variables.

Early in 1949 I was trying out a number of these characteristics with constructions as theoretically basic, and met again the problems inherent in such a starting point (§ 7.85). Turning once more to the treatment of structural, positional unity as having priority over construction, and labelling the structural position plus its manifesting class as a 'grameme' (now called tagmeme).[27] I tried to list its defining characteristics. A comparison with the phoneme and morpheme led to the conclusion that all three could be given comparable definitions, with an over-all term for any structural unit of language behavior.

Two important adjustments in definition had to be made, however, before this approach was possible. The first was the addition, to each definition, of the distribution of such a unit in a larger structure as a component in the definition of the included unit. This caused no problem for phoneme, morpheme or tagmeme, since the tagmeme, for example, could be defined as included in, or distributed within, the sentence. But what was the largest linguistic act to be distributed within? Here we were inevitably committed to the relevance of culture, or nonverbal behavior, as a distributional setting for large linguistic units. It was only a matter of time, therefore, until the total theory, in order to survive at all, had to embrace nonverbal as well as verbal human behavior.

The second necessity was the probing for possible — but not essential — parallels, in all unit types. Since all must have distributional components, and all must have identificational-contrastive features (with their 'identificational' aspects indicating that two units might be the 'same', and their 'contrastive' aspects indicating that they might be 'different'), so all might prove to have variants, free or conditioned, simple or complex. It was at this point that our initial search for an incentive toward or confirmation of analytical theory in naïve native reaction to linguistic structure received its first strong integration with our newer structural definitions: if phonemes might be manifested by two phones in sequence, in a phonetically-complex variant of a phoneme, would analogy suggest the possibility of morphetically-complex morphemes, in which the two morphs were not productive or active in that combination? The answer was definitely 'Yes'. If, with Bloomfield (1933a:209, 240-42), *receive* was treated as two units, here the two could be combined into a single morphetically-complex morpheme, for which the activeness was restricted to an etically-complex unit which as a whole manifests a tagmeme. In this way, not only would the possible structural parallels of phonemics, morphemics and tagmemics be realized, but — more important — we would have found a theoretical framework (cf. §§ 6.54, 6.61-62,

[27] In the 1954 volume I called the new concept a grameme. The term met with objection, and was replaced with Bloomfield's term, but not Bloomfield's concept. For discussion of the relationship, see § 11.74.

6.92, 7.44) within which would be accommodated our long-standing native aversion to the treatment of *receive* as a sequence of two morphemes. The new approach was embracing a large variety of phenomena in a coherent theory, and at the same time 'making sense' of many structural phenomena to which speakers had been intuitively reacting. The new theory, then, was leading to an emic analysis — the analysis of human behavior in reference to the manner in which participants react to their own behavior and respond to the behavior of their colleagues.

7.88 *On Tagmemic Method*

The beginner will find a useful introduction to some early tagmeme concepts in Elson and Pickett (1962). More extensive methodology in terms of an etic-emic approach to tagma and tagmeme in the analysis of a construction is developed in Longacre (1964a). Special problems are treated in descriptive statements of various languages (see, bibliography in Pike, 1965b).

The necessity for intuitive components in the action of the analyst rules out an analytical algorithm for procedure (see fn. to § 7.322). The demand for the study of observables allows us to find system in the speech of someone outside ourselves. Prevention of a solipisistic attitude toward analysis or methodology (in which only the study of one's own speech can have validity) is by-passed here by belief in the possibility of empathy with other persons (note the term 'human' in the title of the volume), an intuition made possible or elicited by the study of *observable* behavior of these other people (of our own or of another language).

For further bibliographical discussion of the relevance of psycholinguistic factors, see § 8.815.

For further discussion of tagmemes in relation to constructions, see Chapter 11.

CHAPTER 8

THE MINIMUM UNIT OF THE MANIFESTATION MODE OF THE BEHAVIOREME (INCLUDING THE PHONEME)

In Chapter 5 we set forth in a technical fashion our largest units of human behavior, the behavioreme and hyperbehavioreme, which we had illustrated in a less technical fashion in Chapters 3 and 4. In Chapters 6 and 7 respectively we dealt with the minimum units within the feature mode and the distribution mode of the behavioreme. Now we turn to its manifestation mode to look at those structural units of movement which constitute the manifested elements of all the modes. It is these units of physical motion which underlie all the physically manifested units of purpose and meaning, or of distribution and structural function, which we have already discussed. These units of motion, nevertheless, are not the same structures as those discussed in Chapters 5-7, even though they ultimately include the same substance; they are separately structured, with different criteria and often but not always with different borders. In this chapter we will deal with the minimum active units of the manifestation mode of the behavioreme, following which, in Chapter 9, we shall treat the larger units of the same mode of the behavioreme.

8.1 *Definition of the Acteme*

Condensed definition:[1] An ACTEME is the minimum unit of the manifestation mode of the behavioreme.

This brief definition, like the condensed definitions of §§ 6.1 and 7.1, points to the fact that no minimum unit of nonverbal or of verbal behavior can be described or defined adequately in and of itself, but can be defined and delineated only in reference to its relationship to a hierarchy of larger units of which it is a part. In addition, it implies that units of one such mode cannot be defined exclusively in reference to other like minimum units of that same mode of a behavioreme or behavioremes, but that the units of one mode must somehow be identified in relation to and in contrast with other modes of that same behavioreme or set of behavioremes. The large units, the minimum units, the various modes of such units, and the systems of such units, together constitute a single set of units which are in part mutually defining, and as such constitute a larger system of behavior.

[1] See fn. to § 5.1.

THE MINIMUM UNIT OF THE MANIFESTATION MODE OF THE BEHAVIOREME

The discussion of many of the details of this interpenetration of elements of units will be delayed until Chapter 15, when the problem of such interpenetrating systems will be specifically treated. Some of these details, however, must be mentioned here as we analyze the acteme.

Expanded definition: An ACTEME is a minimum, active, trimodally-structured emic segment or component of human activity, within the pyramided hierarchy of the manifestation mode of a minimum or included behavioreme or hyperbehavioreme; it is characterized by identificational-contrastive components constituted of physical activity; it is manifested by free or conditioned, simple or complex, fused or clearly-segmented variants; it is distributed not only within the larger units of the manifestation mode of the behavioreme, but is simultaneously distributed within minimum or large units of the feature mode of the behavioreme (and hence indirectly within units of the distribution mode of the behavioreme); and it occurs within a trimodally- and hierarchically-structured system of actemes and system of behavioremes, and hence within a structured physical setting.

A verbal acteme is a PHONEME.

A nonverbal acteme is a KINEME.

All of the terms in this expanded definition have been discussed at least tentatively in earlier chapters (see §§ 6.1 and 7.1 for references), although some of these elements will receive more extensive treatment here and in later chapters.

8.2 *The Acteme Partially Illustrated within the Breakfast Unit*

Within a single breakfast scene there occur a great many verbal actemes and nonverbal actemes.

8.21 *Nonverbal Actemes (Kinemes) Illustrated*

The presence of nonverbal actemes in a breakfast scene, for example, can be seen in the buttering of a piece of toast, which itself is an emic motif (§ 6.2). The grasping of the knife is the first acteme (kineme) in a sequence of actemes which makes up the manifestation mode of that emic motif. Other nonverbal actemes in the sequence include the following: arranging the knife for cutting the toast in half, the cutting motion, releasing the knife, passing the toast to some other person, or putting it on a serving dish.

Each acteme in this sequence is trimodally structured. Each contains features which allow the analyst to identify it, and which contrast it with other emic units within the same system of emic units and in analytical reference to the same set of purposes, type of participant, and hierarchical thresholds.

The grasping of the knife at the beginning of the emic motif is contrasted, as part of its feature mode, with a distinct acteme which is composed of pushing the knife to a neighbor who is expected to do the buttering. It is probably convenient to consider such an initial grasping as but one variant of an acteme which includes, as part of its manifestation mode, many variants conditioned by the nature of the object to be grasped: a glass has to be picked up by finger movements quite different from those used in grasping a knife, and a pitcher must be handled differently from both. Free variants, also, occur within the limits imposed by the objects themselves: a cup may be grasped around its bowl, without the fingers holding it by the handle, or the cup may be picked up by the handle, with further variants as to the manner in which the handle is held. Style variants also occur, as when a glass, in the family circle, might occasionally be grasped so that the palm of the hand is above the top of the glass, whereas the more usual, and more formal, variant would dictate that the palm of the hand should be at the side of the glass. If the type of participant is changed, further variants would occur: a young child may be urged to hold a glass in two hands, and may delay some years before grasping knife or fork or spoon in the manner used by the adults. As for the distribution mode of this acteme, grasping actions are likely to come at the beginning of a number of the eating or drinking motifs of a meal, and in the middle of discontinuous eating motifs, when eating is resumed, etc.

None of these grasping and arranging actemes is the result of a single movement of a single muscle, but is a highly complex coordinated movement of many muscles, with one or more moving parts of the body — e.g., one or more fingers, wrist, etc. — moving either simultaneously or in some kind of complex unit sequence. When two such motions occur simultaneously (as two fingers moving together), they constitute simultaneous components of one variant of the acteme. When they move in sequence, they constitute two or more segments of an etically-complex variant of the acteme, if the sequence can be shown to constitute a single contrastive event from the point of view of the behavior pattern and purpose threshold then under attention. Such a unitary characteristic can be deduced for a movement sequence (1) when no smaller part of the sequence can be shown to be contrastive within the same sub-system of behavior and within comparable participant circumstances, or (2) when the total sequence can be shown to constitute a unit member of a slot-class of elements which are mutually substitutable for each other under special circumstances which we shall discuss more in detail in reference to phonemes (§§ 8.445, 8.53, 8.66). For utilization of the first provision, it is essential that participant type be comparable, lest, as we showed in § 6.41, teaching situations completely upset all thresholds of attention, and hence all analysis of the borders of emic motifs, of behavioremes, and — now — of actemes.

A teaching hypostasis, such as is indicated by the verbal materials in *Pick up your spoon; Hold it this way;* etc., can break up that which in one sub-system is a unit sequence, so that in the hypostatic situation it constitutes several units. Similarly, microscopic and physiological analysis might lead to the detection of an enormous number of movements — even down to submolecular size — but from the point of view of an analyst who is trying to analyze behavior AS THE ACTORS THEMSELVES

THE MINIMUM UNIT OF THE MANIFESTATION MODE OF THE BEHAVIOREME   293

REACT TO IT, such elements appear noncontrastive as such, or grouped into sequences of motions which are reacted to as if they were units of themselves.

In this connection it is interesting to note that many movement complexes which in normal, nonhypostatic situations are not of themselves emic motifs, but merely one acteme of a series of actemes which make up the manifestation mode of the emic motif, are under teaching hypostasis simultaneously emic motifs and actemes; an acteme of picking up a knife, in nonhypostatic behavior, is part of the larger emic motif of buttering the toast, whereas under direct tuition from the parents it may become the subject of direct focus, and hence an emic motif in its own right. It is the change of purpose, and change of focus, incidental to the change of type of participant, which lowers the purpose threshold and gives to the smaller unit a motifemic status.

If, however, for one reason or another we are temporarily unable to determine a lower limit of purpose or a theoretically-sound motifemic threshold within the particular system of actions which we are investigating, we must then start at some arbitrary but convenient point in the hierarchy of those actions, using this point as an arbitrary threshold, and work both above and below that threshold within the hierarchy. As we indicated in the introduction to § 7.8, one can usefully begin his analysis in this way, even before resolving threshold problems such as those discussed in reference to the behavioreme in § 5.3.

8.22 *Verbal Actemes (Phonemes) Illustrated*

As an illustration of a verbal acteme, we take the English sound /l/ from the record B19/8.2 M—: *Ah — Don't take your slippers off.* (The slant lines indicate phonemic writing, but square brackets phonetic writing, after Trager and Bloch (1941:229). When I refer to a symbol as an orthographic element, I place it in double quotes, thus: "m".)

The feature mode of this acteme includes numerous components such as a tongue motion (or tongue position attained by prior motions) which brings the tip of the tongue into contact with the upper gum, while the sides of the tongue are lowered so that air can pass over them, a position of the soft palate such that it touches the back wall of the pharynx so air cannot pass out the nose, a vibration of the vocal cords for voicing, and a movement of the abdominal muscles to squeeze the lungs and force air out through the mouth.

The manifestation mode of this verbal acteme /l/ includes a number of variants. Within the sentence B18/7.9 M—: *Well I'll say that doesn't look bad at all does it?* the sides of the tongue for the [l] sound in *I'll* and *all* are much lower than for the [l] — the same verbal acteme — in *slippers*, giving to the lower variety a more 'hollow' acoustic effect than for the higher variety; the lowered position of the sides of the tongue occur at the ends of syllables and words, whereas the raised position is encountered at the beginning. A prolonged variety of [l] in a thoughtful, deliberate style, implying resignation, occurs, also, in the word *well* in B18/8.1 M—; *Well you can wear* [...] *that way if you want to*. A sharply different variety occurs when there is a sharp change of topic and M— uses a 'light' or cheery tone with the implication *Let's start off a happy day*. An additional variety of [l] occurs in *well*, again, in the phrase B18/7.5 M—: *Well, sir, Mommie's dressed S— in his new jeans*, and is pronounced without the vibration of the vocal cords, but with the latter half of the word unvoiced, breathy, and prolonged.

The distribution mode of the verbal acteme /l/ includes its actual and potential occurrence at the beginning and end of English syllables; in clusters of consonants, e.g., after /p, k/ as in *Play, clay;* in stress groups; in morphemes; and in grammatical units.

8.3 *The Feature Mode of the Phoneme*

8.31 *Simultaneous, Sequential, and Contrastive-Identificational Features*

In the previous section (§ 8.22) we used physical components of the phoneme /l/ to illustrate the feature mode of one characteristic phoneme. We now wish to state that these physical components are, within any one phonetically-simple variant of the phoneme, simultaneous components, and are contrastive-identificational.

At the nucleus (§§ 3.21, 8.42) of the segment [l], the tongue tip is at closure, while the sides of the tongue are lowered, and the vocal cords are vibrating because of the air simultaneously thrust out from the lungs by the action of the abdominal muscles. These simultaneous movements, or relevant positions resulting from prior movements, are SIMULTANEOUS COMPONENTS of the feature mode of the phoneme /l/. (Cf. § 6.46 for simultaneous components of morphemes.)

When a phoneme is phonetically complex (§ 8.445, and cf., for morphemes and tagmemes, §§ 6.54 and 7.44), with two segments in sequence constituting a single manifested variant of that phoneme, certain of the physical components of the phoneme are SEQUENTIAL rather than simultanous only; even here, however, each of the segments in sequence has, in turn, its simultaneous components. For example, Spanish "ch" in *chamaco* 'boy', represents the single phoneme /č/, which is composed of the two segments [t] and [š] in sequence, with each of the segments composed of several simultaneous physical components. In the sense in which we shall often use the terms, the total of the simultaneous components of a phonetically-complex phoneme include all its sequential components as well.

The simultaneous components of a phoneme differentiate it from every other phoneme in that same system of phonemes. Thus, the movement or position of the tongue tip for the English phoneme /l/ contrast it with the English phoneme /s/, in which the tongue movement allows the air to escape over the tongue tip; the movement of the sides of the tongue contrasts /l/ with /t/, in which air cannot escape over the sides of the tongue; the position or movement of the soft palate contrasts /l/ with /n/, in which air is allowed to escape through the nose; the vibration of the vocal cords for /l/ (ignoring, for the moment, that special variant cited in § 8.22 during which the vocal cords were not vibrating and for which the voiced-voiceless contrast is not relevant) contrasts it with /s/ and /t/, in which there is no such vibration; and the abdominal movement which forces air from the lungs out through the mouth contrasts it with such an exclamatory sound as may be found written as "tsk", in which the click sound is caused by a column of air drawn into the mouth by the backward and downward moving tongue.

Ultimately, every phoneme of a system is contrasted with every other phoneme of that system by its contrastive features, the simultaneous and sequential components of its variants. The simultaneous features of a phoneme, then, whether the phoneme is of a single-segment type or of a multiple-segment type, are CONTRASTIVE FEATURES of that phoneme, in that they differentiate it from other phonemes of that system, and a physical component of a phoneme may be considered structurally relevant to that phoneme, or to that system of phonemes when, and only when, it can be shown to thus contrast with its absence in another phoneme (as vocal cord vibration in some variants of /z/ but not in /s/) or to contrast with another physical component in another phoneme (as labial closure in /p/ but lingual closure in /t/).

Phonemes, from this point of view, are sounds with contrastive features, such that the sounds are in contrast within the phonological system of which they are a part, and — within the hierarchical structure of the behavioreme — constitute sequential contrastive components of the formal contrastive features of morphemes (cf. the articulatory components mentioned in § 6.46). In order to be contrastive, such sounds must not only enter such a hierarchy, but at some point in the system must be partially independent of one another (i.e., be not completely conditioned in their physical character and their occurrence or distribution), though partial conditioning of physical character and some limitation as to distribution is normal.

In general, it is most easy to see such nonconditioned independence when two phonemes constitute the only differentiating elements between two words or phrases, which then constitute a 'minimal pair' of words differing phonologically only by those respective phonemes. Thus, *seal* and *zeal* differ by /s/ and /z/ only, and demonstrate most effectively the contrast between those two phonemes. Although such minimal pairs are a great help in analysis, the theory presented here does not require that they be present for every pair of sounds in a language: in order to prove that two sounds are separate phonemes it is sufficient to demonstrate that they occur in environments where the difference between the sounds can be shown to be contrastive and nonconditioned. (For specific detailed procedures for determining these facts, one may consult the chapter on Contrast in Analogous Environments, in Pike, 1947c: 73-77. It is not relevant to our immediate purpose to discuss them here.)

An important theoretical question must now be raised: If a contrastive feature is relevant because it contrasts with a second feature at one point, can the first feature be considered relevant at a second point in the system, if, at that second point, that second feature does not occur (since the first member, but not the second member of the reciprocally contrastive pair, is the only one permitted at that second point)? Or does a phoneme, which gets its contrastive relevance by virtue of an unconditioned contrast with a second phoneme at one point in the system, lose its contrastive relevance — and hence its phonemic identity — when, at some other point in the system, this sound occurs but its contrastive counterpart does not? The answer given by the theory of this volume is that a sound which is once seen to have the status of a phoneme at one place in the system is assumed to retain its phonemic status in other places in that same system, even when in those places the contrastive counterpart does not occur, provided that the phoneme can be clearly identified by the same contrastive features it had elsewhere, and provided that these two phonemes always have the same approximate phonetic characteristics at every point in the system where they do occur in contrast. (These provisions are to allow for special treatment when the physical character of either of the sounds changes in special conditioning environments. See § 8.34 for sound types intermediate between two contrastive phonemes, and §§ 8.33, 8.441 for problems when in a special environment a sweeping change can affect the physical characteristics of a whole series of phonemes.) Since, for example, /s/ and /z/ are seen to be contrastive phonemes in the English morphemes *seal* and *zeal*, we assume, within this theory, that in *zebra* the first sound is the phoneme /z/ (though there is no morpheme *sebra*) and that in *stick* the first sound is an occurrence of the phoneme /s/ (though there is no consonant cluster /zt-/ at the beginning of English words); similarly, the voicing of /z/ is relevant in *zebra*, and the lack of voicing in *stick*.

The reason that this conclusion is reached in the present theory is the fact that each component of the feature mode is considered to be an IDENTIFICATIONAL FEATURE, as well as a contrastive one; there are no contrastive features separate from identificational ones, nor identificational features separate from contrastive ones, but only the composite CONTRASTIVE-IDENTIFICATIONAL FEATURES of the feature mode of any emic unit. (This we have already indicated in connection with other units, §§ 6.46, 6.91, 7.87, 3.53, 5.2, 7.2.) The tongue-tip contact for /l/, the lowered tongue sides, the vocal cord vibration, the closed nasal passage, and the egressive air stream all help to identify the unit /l/ as that unit, as well as to separate it from /t/, /s/, /n/, etc.

These features serve not only to identify different occurrences of the same emic unit in different morphemes such as *all, tall, call, skill, little, slip*, but also serve the extremely important function of allowing the identification of repetitions of the same phoneme in different repetitions of the same morpheme. Without some such possibility of identification of repeated occurrences of a specific phoneme or morpheme, linguistic analysis could not be established on an emic basis. (Cf., for some problems of sameness and repetition, the discussion in §§ 2.14, 2.73, 2.74, 3.61, 6.44, 7.321, 7.41, 7.87.)

8.32 *Units versus Relationships or Poles of Contrast*

The element of our theory just treated, which emphasizes the joint role of identification and contrast, leads to another important and related element of the theory. Since phonemes are composed of bundles of contrastive features, and since contrast implies an opposition between two elements, it is attractive to conclude that a phoneme has no unity other than as an intersection of a network[2] of contrasts — but our basic theory rather indicates that such a point of view would be incomplete, in that it would fail to give adequate weight to the identificational characteristic of components of the feature mode of a unit. Once such components are viewed as identificational, as they are in the theory set forth in this volume, the identificational characteristic must be considered as leading to the identification of a unit, and not *merely* as adding one more fiber at a point of intersection of various contrasts. The identificational view leads to the establishing of units which may be identified as units (phonemes, morphemes, tagmemes, etc.), and which have theoretical validity and great theoretical importance; the identificational view leads to the theoretical priority, if any priority must be assigned, to such units rather than giving priority to the 'relationship' between such units or to poles of oppositions or contrasts between these units.

Such a conclusion is based on the conviction that satisfactory analysis of human behavior must lead to the description of units which are emic ones and that leads to the discovery of units which in some way reflect the structure of human behavior AS PEOPLE REACT TO THAT BEHAVIOR (as we have indicated in earlier chapters, §§ 6.65, 7.311, 2.74, 3.35, 5.1, 6.42, 6.43, 6.93, 7.322).

Another advantage derived from the treatment of components of the feature mode as identificational as well as contrastive is that it makes it a bit simpler, it appears to me, to speak of the identification of a phoneme when it contrasts with its absence, than it does to treat such a phoneme as merely one pole of a relationship for which the other pole is zero. Once 'absence' of a contrast is treated as the pole of a relationship between two contrasting elements of which one never occurs, it is a delicate theoretical matter to keep from multiplying zero constructs out of all proportion to their possible validity in reference to analyzing behavior as people react to that behavior as composed of concrete units of behavior (and, for another reason, cf. § 8.84). If an element can be treated as identificational, the lack of contrast at some

---

[2] Note carefully here the phrase *other than*. We have been developing matrix theory to supplement study of elements (for example constructions) as unit particles by their treatment in reference to their occurrence as points in a field (or matrix, network; see Pike 1962a, 1963b, 1963d and Pike and Erickson, 1964). There must be complementarity of analysis, and presentation, not mutual exclusion (see §§ 12.1, 14.2, 14.4, and Pike, 1959). Without its particles, a field disappears — no units would be in its cells to comprise its manifesting phenomena. Without field, emic particles do not occur — since the contrastive categories (necessary for differentiation and recognition of the units) derive from the vectors of the field.

In a moment (§ 8.33) the field point of view will come temporarily into focus.

point may perhaps be more easily handled. (We will not discuss problems of 'zero' further here, however, since we are reserving them in general for § 14.53.)

8.33 *Relativity of Features and Phonetic Overlap*

The identificational characteristic of components of the feature mode must not be given more weight than it warrants, however. Specifically, the analyst must not conclude that because such components are identificational they cannot be contrastive; the contrastive nature of the components must simultaneously be kept in view.

It is because of the contrastive nature of the components of the feature mode of a phoneme that variants can occur in the manifestation of that phoneme without destroying its communicative value. These variants are to be treated in §§ 8.42, 8.44, but it is desirable to mention here that no such variants could occur if the contrastive features of the phoneme were physically unchanging absolutes. The possibility of such identificational utility of a varying signal is founded on the fact that variation which does not cancel the contrast of a physical component of one phoneme with that of the other phonemes in the system does not of itself destroy the identificational value of that physical component.

A phoneme, made up of such fluctuating components, must not be considered as an unchanging physical absolute, but as a unit which occurs only as a 'point' RELATIVE to a system[3] of points in a phonemic system, which in turn is identifiable only as part of and RELATIVE TO ITS PLACE IN THE MUCH LARGER BEHAVIOREMIC SYSTEM which it in part comprises; the total abstraction of a 'phonemic level of analysis' away from its behavioremic and objective context does not constitute, within this theory, a possible emic analysis — though a description of this type can be achieved by relying tacitly on behavioremic material, through unstated assumptions.

From one point of view, relative units may be pictured, in an analogy, as 'centers of force' kept apart from other centers of force by their mutually repelling nature. The center of force itself, plus its outgoing 'lines of force' is the phoneme; the keeping apart of two particular centers of force is an 'opposition' or a 'contrast' so that each of the two centers contrasts with the other.

From an *emic* point of view the phoneme, not the abstracted poles of the contrast, must be considered a unit, just as in an *emic* study of human behavior a stone, being thrown by a man, would have to be considered a unit even though for certain other purposes it is hoped that the stone as such can ultimately be ignored, and that the moving of the stone can be considered merely as a moving change in the density of the field of forces. (Cf. Einstein and Infeld, 1938:258).

[3] See fn. to § 8.32. Now attention goes beyond a matrix of phonology to which phonemes are related, to a matrix of matrices — the phonological matrix as one cell in the larger including behavioremic matrix of human activity as a whole. (The total language matrix, intermediate between these two in the matrix hierarchy, is not under attention here).

Within the 'center of force' in the phoneme there may be a number of contrastive features which work together to keep this phoneme apart from others within the system. Within any one contrasting situation, any one or more of these features may vary to or toward zero, without loss of phonemic identity and phonemic contrast of that phoneme provided (a) enough of the remaining features are retained to assure the retention of the contrast between this and other phonemes, or (b) the varying feature does not quite reach zero effectiveness, but continues to signal the contrast.

The physical character of a phoneme may change but leave the contrasts unaffected if the total environment has so changed — through the change of a congruent or componential system (§§ 5.4, 6.41, 6.56, 7.46) — that the change in the contrastive feature of the one phoneme does not destroy the contrast of that phoneme with the second phoneme, in that the second has been affected in an analogous fashion by the total environmental change (so that the relative contrast is left undisturbed in spite of the absolute changes; if one speaks in a loud voice, then repeats the same material in a soft voice, then in a high-pitched harsh voice, the phoneme /l/ in each instance continues to be separated from /t, o, n, s/, etc., since they likewise are affected in a comparable way).

If the immediate, local phonological environment — rather than the general system — is changed in such a way that another contrasting phoneme of the system is changed in an analogous fashion when it likewise comes in that same local phonological environment, the phonemes retain their differentiation relative to each other; before phrase-final /l/, for example, both /i/ and /u/ may be slightly longer than they would be before /t/ (cf. *feel, fool, beat, boot*). Two or more etic sounds that have RELATIVELY THE SAME PLACE IN A CONGRUENT SYSTEM OR SUBSYSTEM are the same phoneme.

A contrastive feature is not a constant. Nevertheless, there seems to be a RANGE of variation beyond which a phoneme such as /l/, /t/, /s/, /o/, etc., does not go. (At the moment we are not discussing phonemes of tone or stress.) Within a particular local phonological environment this range must be small enough that a contrast is retained between that phoneme and other phonemes with that narrow environment and within that particular congruent system in which they are occurring (i.e., such that there is no 'intersection' of phonemes, in which the identical physical entity within the identical physical environment is at one time attributed to one phoneme as a variant of that phoneme and at another time to another phoneme as a variant of that second phoneme; in this theory we grant no homophonous phonemes within identical environments).

On the other hand, there is nothing within the theory to prevent certain variants of two phonemes from being homophonous within certain restricted but distinct environments (i.e., it allows 'overlapping' of phonemic variants): for example, there might occur phonemes A and B in which phoneme A had the variant [i] (a high, front, unrounded vocoid) after /t/, and phoneme B had the variant [ɨ] (a high, central, unrounded vocoid) after the same phoneme /t/, but in which phoneme A had the variant [ɨ] after the phoneme /k/, whereas phoneme B had the variant [ɨ] (high, back, unrounded vocoid) after /k/. In this instance (reported orally, by Sapir, in 1937 for Southern Paiute) we assume that the two occurrences of [ɨ] are perceptually homophonous (though instrumental studies would presumably show them to be slightly different because of the on-glide from a different consonantal position). Nevertheless, in spite of this phonetic overlap, the high central vocoid after /t/ is analyzed as a member of phoneme A, but after /k/ as a member of phoneme B. Here the range of variation in phoneme A has overlapped the range of variation of the phoneme B, except that the overlapping variants never occur in the same local environment, and hence is not rejected as intersection. Stated in other terms, the contrastive features of phonemes A and B were not absolutes, but CONTRASTIVE TO ONE ANOTHER RELATIVE TO THEIR PLACE IN A SUBSYSTEM of sounds. The variants of phoneme A were both assigned to phoneme A in the analysis because they occupied the same relative place in their respective subsystems (i.e., the contrastive set of sounds after /t/ and /k/ respectively) as both being in contrast to phoneme B. It is in an instance such as this that one sees most clearly that identificational features serve as such only in a framework within which the identificational features may be characterized in a way which is relative and contrastive, rather than absolute. (See diagram in § 8.34.)

8.34 *Fused Ranges of Features with Intermediate Phonetic Manifestations*

Occasionally the total contrastive nature of a phoneme, which gives contrasts in numerous directions, separating it from all other phonemes in the system, is weakened in one particular direction in one particular kind of local environment so that in that environment the phoneme is no longer differentiated from a certain other phoneme of the system as it is in one or more other environments. In such an instance the second phoneme is reciprocally weakened in its contrast in reference to the first phoneme. The result in such a special environment is the occurrence of a sound intermediate in phonetic type, perceptually 'half way' in character between the two phonemes which elsewhere are poles of a contrast. In my phonetics classes, for example, I have had speakers of American English who use a sound before /r/ in *for* or *four* which is somewhat like the /o/ of *coat* (as they pronounce the word) and somewhat like the /ɔ/ of their *caught*, but which is perceptually so close to a sound intermediate between the two that neither I nor the speakers themselves after phonetic training could decide whether it phonetically was more like their /o/ or like their /ɔ/; before such an /r/ no contrast occurred between the two phonemes. To what phoneme, if any, did the intermediate sound belong?

Within this theory, a sound intermediate between the norms of two phonemes, and within the same componential and congruent system as those norms but differing only in the local environment, is treated neither as a member of the one phoneme nor as a member of the other, nor as a third phoneme in the system of phonemes, but as an ambiguous phonological unit composed of the fused ranges of the two; such a unit we term an ARCHIPHONEME (a term long known to the field but used here in a much more restricted sense, cf. § 8.85). It is convenient to indicate the phonetic nature of such an item by a diagram, as follows, indicating the manner in which two phonemes may contrast in one environment or many environments but have fused non-contrastive ranges in another:

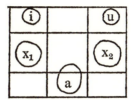

Contrastive Ranges of Phonetic Norms of Phonemes in Environment A; Circles indicate limits of fluctuation in that congruent system.

Fused and Limited Range of Medium-High Vowel Phonemes in Environment B of the same language and the same congruent system; x_1 and x_2 indicate the two archiphonemes.

When we compare this conclusion with those of § 8.33, we note that the postulation of archiphonemes is quite different from that of overlap, since in overlap the manifestation of two phonemes becomes homophonous or nearly so, but this overlap involves two manifestations of each of two phonemes in each of two local environments (or in each of two congruent systems), such that one of the manifestations of the one phoneme is perceptually homophonous with one of the manifestations of the other phoneme (whereas our archiphoneme is not homophonous with any phone or either phoneme in the same congruent system). Compare the following crude diagram of phonetic overlap with the diagram at the end of the preceding paragraph:

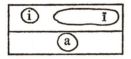 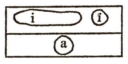

Phonetic Range of the Phonemes /i/ and /ī/ after /t/ in Southern Paiute

Phonetic Range of the Same Phonemes after /k/

Similarly, the archiphoneme, as used here, is not the same as intersection which is not accepted in this theory as a legitimate interpretation of phonemic data, since in intersection a single sound in a particular phonological environment is attributed now to one phoneme and now to another, even though it be in each instance perceptually identical with one of the phonemes of the elsewhere-contrastive pair but not with the other. (Our archiphoneme is not homophonous with either pole of the contrast, but is left as a fusion of ranges rather than being arbitrarily assigned now to one range and at other times to another; the fusion of phonemic contrastive ranges which results in the archiphoneme at a particular point in the distributional system is also very different from the fusion of two phonemes in sequence, which we shall mention in § 8.446.)

8.35 *The Possibility of Contrastive-Identificational Features of Phonemes as Emes*

Should the contrastive-identificational features of phonemes be considered emes in their own right, i.e., as "featuremes"? (And, if so, is it not inconsistent to treat phonemes as minimum units of the manifestation hierarchy, instead of treating featuremes in this way?) The question is by no means an easy one, since there is evidence both positive and negative.

Our first answer would have to be a positive one: There is some evidence to indicate that these features could be treated as emes. Specifically, (1) it can be argued that it is the contrastive-identificational feature, not the phoneme as a whole, which actually signals semantic differences in word pairs such as *seal* versus *zeal*, *sip* versus *zip*, since the phonological difference between the words is the difference in the contrastive feature which /z/ has as over against those of /s/ whereas /z/ and /s/ contain other contrastive features in common which are not replaced in the pairs of words (i.e., both /z/ and /s/ are fricative and continuant). Then, (2) the differential feature can be seen to be trimodally structured relative to a system of such features and to the particular congruent system and subsystem in which it is occurring; the manifestation mode of this feature has variants which in *zeal* is seen as voiced (or at least as ending in voicing), whereas in *his* or *buds* pronounced in context or in isolation without exaggerated 'clearness', the feature is often seen in a variant which is unvoiced but weak, or voiced at the beginning but unvoiced at the end. The distribution mode of this feature includes its potential for occurrence on some consonants, and on all vowels in speech aloud; on consonant clusters within a single syllable it may occur in sequence with itself at the end of the syllable (e.g., in *hand*), or in sequence preceding a voiceless consonant or consonants (in *hence* [hents]), or following a voiceless consonant at the beginning of a syllable (e.g., *plow*). As for the feature mode of this feature of a phoneme or phonemes, one could argue that voicing is one component, but that it is not always present, and that weak articulation is another simultaneous component of this feature, which is present except in a congruent system of a special type which, in isolating words, exaggerates the voicing component to make the word intelligible against a noisy background, etc. With care, the trimodal structuring of such featuremes could be demonstrated. The status of the feature emic unit could be further argued, (3), on the basis of the fact that all emes are in some sense componential. Even the abstraction of verbal emes from large behavioremes shows that componental elements may be emic units. In addition, the treatment of tones in tone languages as phonemes is evidence that componential features of phonological segments are legitimately treated as emes themselves, inasmuch as such tones have been treated as phonemes by practically all workers for years; tones, it can be claimed, are on the same level in this respect, as are other significant features of the phonological system. Finally, (4), such features can be shown to be substitutable one for the other much as can phonemes (see *keel, feel, seal, zeal, kneel, deal*).

Our second answer, however, is a negative one: For a number of reasons, it is desirable to avoid analyzing the contrastive-identificational features as emic units, as emes, even though they are obviously emic features, i.e., contributing contrastively to emic units. (Often in the early stages of analysis, or occasionally in later stages, it is convenient to say that a phonetic characteristic — say aspiration — is 'emic' or 'phonemic', indicating that the feature is relevant to the system of emes, but without implying by that terminology that the feature is itself an eme, and before one knows whether a two-segment sequence composed of a stop plus an aspirated release is a sequence of two phonemes or is a single etically-complex phoneme in contrast with single-segment non-aspirated stops.) (1) It is very convenient, for example, to treat as emes only those items which can be considered as chunks, or segments, of activity substitutable in active slots; the term 'emic segment' has thus entered into our definitions of the behavioreme (§ 5.1), the morpheme (§ 6.1), the tagmeme (§ 7.1), and the phoneme (§ 8.1). In this respect the contrastive-identificational feature, since it is so obviously componential and simultaneous rather than a chunk of activity, is not easily handled as an emic unit. The objection is not fatal to the possibilities of treating features as emes, however, since we have already indicated that in some respects such features can indeed give the appearance of substitution, and since those elements which we do accept as emes can be considered as total chunks of activity cut out of a sequence of activity only when we have first abstracted from the total behavioreme the componential system and sequences of that system of which the chunks are a part. A phoneme, that is to say, is also not a complete chunk of a behavioreme in which both verbal and nonverbal activity are going on simultaneously, but can be treated as a chunk or segment only when the verbal sequence has first been abstracted. Perhaps some kind of sequence abstraction of features could be imagined of which the features would then be chunks; I do not at present think so, however. There is, nevertheless, at least one instance in which we do so abstract a sequence of componential sound or a sound characteristic away from the remainder of the verbal sound, and treat it as a series of phonemes. Intonation or tone is treated as a sequence of phonemes suprasegmental to the segmental chunks themselves. It is precisely this difference, however, which raises serious problems in respect to tonal analysis. In Chapter 13 we shall attempt to show how this does not destroy the theory.

The next objection (2) to treating features of phonemes as emes is that the consequences of doing so lead to a difficulty insoluble by linguistic means and presumable ultimately by science as it is now constituted: If the arguments for eliminating the phoneme as the minimum emic unit of the manifestation mode of utteremes is valid, and the contrastive-identificational feature is a smaller emic unit, then there is an infinite regress, such that the feature, in turn, cannot possibly be the legitimate minimum, since the features of these features, and then the features of the features of these features, etc., would be relevant and smaller emic units. Specifically, behind such a feature as voicing are the many muscle movements involved, in numerous variant combinations; behind each muscle group is the movement of each muscle and its parts, etc. As we have already indicated (§ 5.3), however, such regress[4] leading to sub-atomic structure is scarcely a fruitful field for the anthropologist who is interested in the purposeful reactions of members of a culture to other members of that culture, and in the structuring of such reactions; even the study of the movement of muscles, rather than of the parts of the body moved by such muscles, is probably lower than he can in general profitably go, and more complex than his techniques of observation can handle.

Yet is there, we now ask, structural justification for setting up a threshold such that phonemes are emic units, within the behavioremic hierarchy, but such that contrastive-identificational features of phonemes are below that threshold and are not emes? I believe so. The emic threshold is intimately and structurally related to our starting point in Chapters 3, 4, and 5. In the definition of the behavioreme (§ 5.1), purpose, culturally documented, is one of the elements essential to the emic analysis of human behavior. It is only in reference to a hierarchy of units in which purpose (or meaning) enters, that such a threshold can be established. The alternative to including meaning or purpose in such behavioremic definition is to abandon the most useful structural threshold between the reciting of a poem and the minutiae of atomic structure.

In § 5.3 we discussed briefly the manner in which the minimum units of the behavioreme were related to a threshold tied to purpose or meaning in some way. We can now be more specific: The lexically-meaningful morphemes of verbal behavioremes, by their meaningful character, first set the threshold for the minimum units of the feature mode of utteremes, and then indirectly set the minimum of the manifestation mode of the uttereme. It would appear that the units of the phonological hierarchy which are the *largest* which can conveniently serve to define by their sequences the formal character of the morphemes of languages of the world should be considered the *minimum* units of the manifestation mode of utteremes in general. Syllables are too large to easily constitute the defining phonological sequences within morphemes, since often they comprise more than one morpheme. In addition, morpheme boundaries are often not correlated with syllable boundaries, with the result that morpheme boundaries often come in the middle of syllables and syllable boundaries often come in the middle of morphemes. This lack of coincidence of boundaries makes it difficult, in many languages, to use the syllable as a grammatically-convenient phonological

---

[4] As an analog to our insistence here, note the growing conviction among physicists: "we believe that nature as a whole has a structure of inexhaustible depth... [with units] disclosed one after another by deeper studies" (Sakata, 1961).

minimum. On the other hand, contrastive-identificational features of phonemes are smaller than necessary for defining the large bulk of morpheme occurrences. Phonemes, however, meet both of these objections, since — unlike the syllable — they are small enough to provide a phoneme boundary at most morpheme boundaries and — unlike the contrastive feature — are as large a phonological unit as can be used if all but a few of the morpheme boundaries are to coincide with a phonological boundary. Hence phonemes are convenient threshold units.

The phoneme is a convenient minimum, furthermore, since this characterization of morphemes is largely accomplished by a transcription of a series of single phonemes linearly, rather than by bundles of simultaneous units, such as would have to be postulated if the features were here treated as emes. Since the uttereme is a sequence of activity in time — not a spacial portrayal like a picture — the most convenient unitary division, if obtainable, would seem be one in which a sequence of basic threshold units is a sequence of single chunk-like units.

Exceptions to this situation do occur, however, as when a phonological feature of voicing might be interpreted as the morphemic element in the verb *believe* as against the noun *belief*, or in *bathe* versus *bath*. Cf. Bloch, who suggests that here "the quality of voice (at least when accompanied by the quality of constriction)" be considered "as defining a separate phoneme /V/" (1950: 93 fn. 16). In other languages occasionally a phonological feature has definite and active morpheme status, as in Comanche *Puʼkuʔokʷekʷaiʔu* 'she went to render it' versus *PuʼkuʔokʷEkʷaiʔuʔ* 'she rendered it and went on' where the unvoicing is analyzed by Canonge (1957) as a morpheme. Nevertheless, we are convinced that it is preferable to set the emic threshold between phonemes and phonemic features, in spite of the possible morphemic status of some features, rather than to accept the consequences of considering the features as emes. One can, moreover, in some of the instances of the kind just cited, adopt a description of the data which bypasses the apparent exceptions of morpheme borders within a single phoneme, by treating the change as a replacement of one phoneme such as /v/ by another such as /f/ rather than as the loss or addition of the one feature such as voicing. We would not rely on this as eliminating the difficulty, however, but would prefer rather to grant that the threshold, though essential, and though tied to the morphemic structure of the uttereme, is not in all details clear cut, but in some of them is fuzzy or perhaps indeterminate, as are many other classificatory boundaries within the theory.

A further hierarchical fact is also in support of treating the phoneme, rather than the feature, as the minimum eme. This is the fact that an entire uttereme might be composed of a single morpheme (cf. § 6.3) which in turn is a single syllable, which in turn is a single phoneme. Since, however, a phoneme is separated simultaneously from various other phonemes in the system, no phoneme could have just one contrastive feature; and since no uttereme can be less than a single segment — hence not less than a single phoneme — it could therefore not be composed of a single contrastive-identificational phonological feature. It leads to a more consistent hierarchical structure, therefore, to assume that the phoneme is the threshold minimum for other verbal emic units, as it must in fact be the minimum for a total utteremic manifestation. (See § 9.5 for a further threshold.) I suspect that evidence of another kind might also be obtainable, either to support this conclusion or to force us to lower the emic threshold to include emic features as emes. This would be evidence from experimental phonemics, in which some kind of observable native reactions were elicited under controlled conditions by careful experimental techniques, so that one could determine whether or not the phoneme does have a sharply greater response value as a unit than do the features themselves. At the moment, however, we base our judgment in terms of the relation of the phoneme to the other units of the other modes of the utteremic hierarchy. In addition, we should emphasize the fact that the affirmation of the emic nature of phonemic units does *not* deny the structural value of, nor the trimodal structuring of, the features — any more than does the affirmation of the structural relevance of molecules deny the structural relevance of atoms on a lower hierarchical level.

8.4 *The Manifestation Mode of the Phoneme*

Within this theory there are no emic units without a physical manifestation, as we have indicated earlier (§§ 3.52, 3.56, 6.91), and for all such linguistic units their manifestation occurs through phonemes, sequences of phonemes, features of phonemes and hyperphonemes. In discussing the phonemes themselves, however, we affirm that they too have their manifestation mode, their essential, structurally-relevant physical components.

8.41 *Movement as Basic to Phonemic Manifestation*

The phoneme, in this theory, is viewed primarily as an emic unit of behavior — not as primarily a unit of acoustics. The essential physical substance of the manifestation mode of such a unit of behavior, therefore, is the physiological MOVEMENT of the body parts involved in the production of the phoneme, or the position resulting from such movements. The affirmation of the relevance of such movement does not, however, deny the relevance of other components; on the contrary, the distributional component is also relevant, and will be treated when the distribution mode of the phoneme is discussed. Nor does the affirmation of the relevance of movement in the phoneme imply that such movements are absolutes, or constants. Rather the movements as simultaneous components of the entire manifested physical character of the phoneme are relative to other identificational-contrastive features of the phoneme in any one congruent or componential system, and to the units of other congruent and componential systems, as we have already indicated in the treatment of the feature mode of the phoneme (§§ 8.31, 8.33). The phoneme, therefore, is *not* 'a movement' as such, but a unit of the manifestation mode of the uttereme, established relative to other such units and to the entire system of units of various types, and composed, insofar as its own manifestation mode is concerned, of a physical component which may fluctuate.

The treatment of movement as basic to the phoneme is an important point in reference to the theory as a whole. It is this starting point which allows us to unite football games and phonemes in a single theory, since movement is one common denominator of them both (just as both of them also attain emic status, eventually, only in relation to a cultural unit in which purpose and closure can be documented).

If instead of treating movement as basic we had analyzed the phoneme as an acoustic phenomenon — as a sound wave — the correlation with football games would have been much more difficult. What, for example, would have been the equivalent, in the football game, of the acoustic phenomena? Presumably it would have been the visual phenomena, the light waves reflected from the players as they moved about the field. Such light waves, to be sure, are essential to the game, since the players cannot intercept a pass, for example, without following the play visually. Nevertheless, it seems much more difficult at present, at least, to construct a theory of the structure of behavior if we build it upon those wave phenomena which connect participants in the behavior, or participants with results of behavior, than if we build it such that our basic starting point is the sequence of waves of movement of the participants. It is interesting, also, to note in this connection that Cooper, Delattre, Liberman, Borst, and Gerstman have begun to feel that "the relation between perception and articulation may be simpler than the relation between perception and the acoustic stimulus" (1952: 605).

8.42 *Waves of Activity in Phonemic Manifestation*

Although we have not founded the theory of phonemic manifestation upon sound waves, nor of the passing of a football upon light waves, we have nevertheless used a different kind of wave as constituting the essence of the etic characteristics behind all emic units as they are seen in sequence in context. These waves which we do accept as basic to the structure of behavior units are the WAVES OF MOTION, waves of activity, discussed in §§ 3.21-25, 3.61. Several phases of the problem illustrated there warrant further mention here, as being especially relevant to an understanding of phonemic structure, but need no further extensive discussion:

(1) A phonemic sequence is often a continuum of constant physical movement and of sound with no physical breaks between the movements or sounds (§§ 3.2, 3.61). Note, for example, the following sequence which is composed of a voiced continuum: *a boy I knew*. There is no factual justification for the belief of Ross (Professor of Linguistics, University of Birmingham) in the existence of "minute periods

of silence between the speech-sounds of continuous speech" (1944: 103), although the fact of his reaction to speech as if it were so composed is a very neat psycholinguistic datum supporting the validity of the treatment of speech sounds as emically discrete 'particles'. (2) The emic problem in such an instance is to determine what chunks of the continuum constitute emic segments (§ 3.61), as emically discrete but etically slurred parts of the total system. (3) The etic units of such a sequence are the waves of motion, separated by a change of motion, even though the point of change is slurred and often indeterminate (§§ 3.22, 3.25), as when the tongue change from [a] to [i] in [ai] is smoothly accomplished so that the border can be located at no precise point, even though on occasion a general area of change can be roughly determined (§ 3.61). (4) The nucleus of such an etic wave can be composed either of the moment during which an articulating movement is reaching its greatest degree of closure, or when it is reaching its greatest degree of opening (§ 3.21); thus in [aiai], the first [i] symbolizes the nucleus of a segment, as the tongue reaches the point higher in the mouth than it is immediately before or after it; likewise, the second [a] symbolizes the nucleus of an etic segment, where the tongue reaches a point lower than the positions of the tongue immediately before or after it. In addition, nuclei are found before and after a change of speed of movement of an articulator, such that the articulator moves rapidly, slows down but continues movement in the same direction or in the same manner, and then speeds up; a humming of notes up the scale, with a momentary slightly slower movement as each half-tone is passed, produces a series of such nuclei (cf. 'time bulge', Pike, 1943a: 111-13). (5) As the articulator approaches the point at which the nucleus occurs, an 'on-glide' is produced; as it leaves the nucleus, an 'off-glide' occurs. Such approaches and releases, as well as the nuclei themselves, may constitute part of the physical elements which comprise contrastive-identificational features of the phoneme in one or more of the congruent systems in which it occurs. For the nasal consonants, for example, the moments of approach to oral closure, or release from such closure, are perhaps more useful in detecting the point of closure than the moment of closure is in itself; nasals dictated in isolation, with no on-glides or off-glides, are extremely difficult to tell apart, whereas this separation is relatively simple if a vowel precedes or follows so that transition glides do occur. (6) If two movements approach their highest degrees of closure at the same time, and leave that position at the same time, the simultaneous movements produce only one etic segment; if the movements are simultaneous, but in opposite directions, a single etic segment is heard also (cf. Pike, 1943a:111, 114); in [am], for example, only one segment is heard after the [a], though two changes occur — one, the closing of the lips, and the other, the opening of the nasal passage. (7) The smaller waves of movement may form 'ripples' on larger waves of movement; the phones may form ripples of movement (§ 3.23) on the syllabic movement, for example. (8) Two etic segments may be combined in one phonetically-complex phonemic segment (§ 3.61), as when [ph] constitutes in English the phoneme /p/ in *pie*. (9) From one point of view, the basic problem of the emic analysis of all human behavior is the task of deriving discrete emic units from an etic continuum of waves of movement (§ 3.61); it is the problem of the simultaneous handling of 'particles' of activity as 'waves' of activity (cf. §§ 12.1, 14.2, 14.4).

Diagrams may help to illustrate some of the principles given above.

First, we show a simple wave of movement in which a single articulator is in action — the tongue moving up and down:

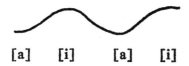

Next we indicate the same movement, but with the diagram transformed so that all nuclei, whether peaks or troughs of movement, are shown as peaks of the wavy line:

With two or more articulators involved, and with both peaks and troughs shown as the top of a wave, the next diagram shows schematically the manner in which nuclei of segments can succeed one another even though the DECAY of a movement affects several following segments, and the ANTICIPATION of a movement affects several preceding segments:

Much more complicated diagrams can be drawn to indicate possible permutations of such elements, and to illustrate specific sequences. (See Pike 1947c: 10, 29, 30, 38, 40, 41, for numerous illustrations.)

8.43 *Participant Type in Relation to Phonemic Movement*

By rejecting sound waves as our starting point, and by accepting activity of an individual as basic to our analysis, we have tacitly rejected the sound wave as the locus of the phoneme. Instead, the LOCUS of the phoneme, in this theory, is the individual actor and his actions. This conclusion, however, leads to a further problem: Is it the speaker, or the hearer, who is relevant? or is it both? or do they have separate emic analysis due them? Thus far, we have focused almost exclusively on the speaker, but it is clear that language cannot function with speakers alone. Yet how can a listener 'hear' a phoneme, if part of the nature of that phoneme is in the movements of the speaker?

There are several possible ways out of this difficulty. The first is to assume that the listener also reacts to the physiological movements of the phoneme, as productive movements, by a kind of empathy in which the sounds caused by the speaker's movements elicit some kind of neurological correlate in the brain of the hearer, and that this neurological activity is a subphonemic variant of the more overt physical activity of the speaker, but similar to the activity of that speaker as he thinks of what he is saying — or as either of them may on another occasion talk silently to himself.

A second possible analysis is sharply different. In order to sense the weight of it — since it is quite opposed to our ordinary thinking — we first return to the football pass. Here it is clear that the emic activity composed of passing the ball is utterly distinct from the emic activity which includes the visual movements by which one observes from the stands the passing of that ball, and completely distinct from the activity of catching that pass on the field. The initiating activity, the receptive activity, and the activity of analysis or observation of the interconnecting medium are distinct; the type of participant — the actor status — dictates a differential emic unit as the product of the analysis of each of the three elements (cf. §§ 2.2, 2.4, 3.32, 4.23). This would seem to imply, by analogy, that the emic units of speaking (with their manifesting physiological movements composed of articulations) and the emic units of listening (with their manifesting movements composed of the movements of the ear drum, of components of the inner ear, and of chemical or electrical movements in the nerves and brain) are emically distinct. The relationship between the units of the spoken system and the units of the listening system would then have to be treated as relations between closely correlated systems.

We reject the analogy of pass throwing and reception in relation to speaking and listening, and do not accept, therefore, this second analysis. In speech, the sequence of (spoken or heard) phonemes preceding and following /m/ in the phrase *John saw him yesterday* is the same for both the speaker and the hearer; the spoken and heard sequences of phonemes are either the same, or the same with some distortion due to interfering noise, etc. The equivalence[5] of the spoken and heard phoneme sequence leads to the treatment of them as being sequences in two respective systems which are congruent one with another, and which have the same phonemes. Just as a phoneme may have one voice quality, from one set of physiological movements in speech aloud, but another voice quality from another set of physiological movements in song, and yet comprise two variants of the same phoneme in the respective congruent systems (§ 5.4), so here we may assume that the same phoneme may have

---

[5] But see now speculation by Osgood that the phoneme but not the syllable is relevant to hearing, and that the syllable but not the phoneme is relevant to speaking (1963: 742). I find his hunch is unconvincing, since the scheme proposed appears too simple to account for the kind of empirical data I have had to analyze — or for poetics, where an ignoring of the syllable would leave hearer reaction unexplained.

articulatory plus neurological movements in the congruent system of speech aloud, but auricular plus neurological movements in the congruent system constituted of speech being heard.

The phonemes in a thought sequence, similarly, would be equated with the phonemes of the same sequence spoken aloud or heard, but with variants conditioned by their occurrence in the congruent system of thought for which the manifesting physical elements are neither articulatory (in the sense we have thus far used the term, though there may be some degree of suppressed articulatory movements), nor auricular, but are neurological. This activity in the brain would be assumed to constitute the manifestation mode of those particular variants of the phonemes of a thought sequence, even though this activity is not accessible to observation in phonemic detail (but only through gross patterns of electrical activity at various parts of the brain), and in spite of the fact that the person thinking may have no proprioceptive sense of the details of that neural activity.

8.44 *Variants of Phonemes*

In the preceding section, and in other places throughout earlier chapters, we have had occasion to refer to variants of phonemes in order to illustrate some characteristic of behavioremic systems. Here we bring together a number of these items in a more systematic form.

8.441 *Systemically-Conditioned but Topologically-Same Variants of the Phoneme*

We have just finished discussing in § 8.43, for example, differences which may be found in the manifested form of phonemes if they occur in spoken speech, heard speech, or thought speech. In each of these instances, the difference in the variant of — say — the phoneme /t/ is due to its occurrence in one or another of these congruent systems (§ 5.4), rather than being due to any characteristic of the phonemes immediately surrounding it. Similarly, phonemes in speech aloud differ from the variants of the same phonemes in whisper, or in song, or in shouting, or in a high-pitched tone of voice, or in harsh speaking, and the like; in such instances, as for spoken speech versus heard speech, the differences are the result of the occurrence of the phonemes in differing congruent systems. All such instances of conditioning by occurrence in a particular congruent system, or style, may be labelled as LOCALLY-FREE BUT SYSTEMICALLY-CONDITIONED VARIANTS OF A PHONEME.

Inasmuch as one systemically-conditioned variant of a phoneme is equatable with another systemically-conditioned variant of that same phoneme in a different congruent system by its relation to all the other similarly-distorted variants of the other phonemes in that system, we see once more the necessity for understanding that a phoneme is not a physical absolute, but a unit identifiable in relation to its relative, comparable place in a congruent system (§ 8.33) of phonemes. Two such systemically-conditioned variants are physiologically different but TOPOLOGICALLY THE SAME, in that the two total patterns are identifiable point-by-point, with certain point-characteristics relatively unchanged, but with distortion in respect to the absolute relations one to another. TOPOLOGICALLY-SAME SOUNDS ARE MEMBERS OF THE SAME PHONEME IN SPITE OF ETIC DISTORTION.

8.442 *Phonemically- and Hyperphonemically-Conditioned Variants of the Phoneme*

The distortion of an entire group of phonemes, by its occurrence in a special congruent system such as in song, is not the only circumstance in which a group of phonemes as a related whole can have the phonetic character of each of its members affected uniformly (so that the variant of the first phoneme in the first congruent system is modified in the second congruent system in a manner analogous to the way in which the second phoneme of the group is likewise modified in that same congruent system).

Local circumstances can likewise cause distortions in an entire subgroup of the phonemes of a language. All vowels of a language, for example, may have more open tongue positions in closed syllables than they do in open syllables, such that the tongue is not quite so high in the mouth before a syllable-closing consonant as it is for the same vowel phoneme when no such consonant follows it in the syllable. Such variants, caused by the neighboring sounds of the immediate local environment are LOCALLY-CONDITIONED VARIANTS OF THE PHONEME, and because of their like place in a comparable series of variants of a group of phonemes, they are TOPOLOGICALLY THE SAME, with their identification made relative to the subsystem of sounds which such a group constitutes. (In such an instance, the phonetic character of the phoneme variant is relevant to its identification, but this character may have a range of variation which is sufficiently large to allow some phonetic overlap with the variant of another phoneme of that subgroup within a different conditioning place in the permitted distribution of these sounds; for an illustration, see § 8.33.)

Another view of locally-conditioned variants of phonemes is the one seen when one considers the manner in which the articulation of one phoneme slurs into the articulation of the next (cf. § 2.3). Since, as we have indicated (§ 8.42), the sound-producing movements are not separated one from another, but slur into each other with indeterminate borders, every phoneme has a different variant for every sound it precedes, for every sound which it follows, and for every combination of every preceding-following sequence of sounds, and for some modifications induced by sounds at a greater distance whose influence does not decay even within the immediately succeeding sound. The phoneme /b/, for instance, differs slightly before /o/ (note lips already pursed for the vowel) from what it does before /i/ (note the high tongue position for the vowel formed while the /b/ is being pronounced). Such variants are PHONEMICALLY-CONDITIONED VARIANTS OF PHONEMES.

A second kind of locally-conditioned variation is one in which the phonemes are seen to be HYPERPHONEMICALLY-CONDITIONED, in that the local conditions causing the change are not the relation of the phoneme to other neighboring phonemes, but the relation of the phoneme to its place in a larger unit of the phonological hierarchy — to its place in the HYPERPHONEME (§ 9.1). One such hyperphoneme which frequently affects the manifested form of phonemes occurring within it is the stress group (or the abdomineme, as we shall call it in § 9.3). Sounds occurring at the peak of the stress group — in the stressed syllable — are likely to have variants which are longer than elsewhere, stronger, or more tense in articulation. Sounds occurring at the borders of stress groups are also likely to have variants differing from those occurring at the peak of the stress group or elsewhere in the stress group than at the peak or at its borders. Phoneme variants at the end of such a stress group may be especially long, or weak, or unvoiced, or unaspirated, or changed in other ways; in one language the variants in such a position may be affected quite differently from what they are in another language, so that in the one language the variants of stop phonemes in this position may be aspirated, whereas in another language the variants of stops in this position may be unaspirated. Similarly, at the beginning of stress groups special variants may occur, but these variants are not uniform from language to language, but must be identified for one language at a time. Other hyperphonemic units, such as the syllable and breath group, may have further effects upon the phoneme, when it occurs at their peaks, or borders, or between their peaks and borders. When a number of phonemes are affected in a comparable manner at some point in a hyperphoneme, their respective variants in these situations are topologically the same as their variants in other conditioned situations.

It is oftentimes a great convenience, when discussing the members (allophones) of a phoneme, to have available certain terms which distinguish between that variant which occurs most frequently, with its phonetic nature least affected by its environment, and that variant or group of variants which occurs less frequently, with greater demonstrable effect upon them from their environment. The more frequent, less affected member, may be called the NORM; the less frequent, but more affected members, may be called SUBMEMBERS of that phoneme. If in a certain language no such clear distinction exists among the members of one of its phonemes, then these terms would not come into service, unless by analogy with other instances in which a norm is easily found and conveniently used; there an arbitrary labelling might sometimes conveniently be given.

8.443 *The Possibility of Grammatically-Conditioned Variants of the Phoneme*

Before the recent development of etic theory concerning phonological units larger than the phoneme (especially under the influence of Stetson, 1951), and the current development of techniques to observe borders between these etic units in mechanical recordings of connected text (by Voegelin and others at the University of Indiana;

cf. Voegelin, 1953, 1954; N. Hickerson, 1954:298-99, Yegerlehner, 1954:283), it appeared to me impossible to reach a phonemic analysis which was on the one hand internally consistent and which, on the other hand, did no violence to the kinds of data derived from observed cultural reaction (§§ 2.73-74), without postulating subphonemic variants conditioned by position in the word, or in other grammatical units of the hierarchy. Now, however, a large part of the data handled as grammatical conditioning can be handled as conditioning by hyperphonemes (syllables, stress groups, breath groups), as indicated in the previous section, within the emic theory of the structure of these higher units to be developed in the next chapter. To a considerable degree, therefore, we shall lighten our reliance in phonemic description on such word-conditioning, or the like (for my earlier emphasis see Pike, 1947c:87b, 89a, 161, and 1948:162).

Nevertheless, lest we be too hasty in this matter, inasmuch as a few residues may prove still to be best described as the result of grammatical conditioning,[6] once the bulk of the conditioning has been handled phonologically, we shall indicate here the place in the theory into which such subphonemic grammatical conditioning will fall, for that part of it which proves ultimately to be sustained.

Nonsystematic residues within a system, as unassimilated INTRUSIVE variants from another dialect or from another language, might be described as MORPHEMICALLY-CONDITIONED variants of phonemes. Such a description might be useful to handle MISPLACED ALLOPHONES of which I have heard Professor Kurath, dialect geographer at the University of Michigan, speak often; it might also be a way to handle some of the phonetic problems of scattered, nonsystematic, unassimilated loans of 'coexistent systems' (Fries and Pike, 1949).

Similarly, though word-conditioning can be expected to be largely replaced by stress-group conditioning (i.e., by abdominemic conditioning), it is possible that some word conditioning — i.e., HYPERMORPHEMIC CONDITIONING — of phoneme variants may occur as a special residue. If, for example, consonants such as [r], [l], [v], [y] are unvoiced at the end of words with or without suffixes, but not internal to the word even at the end of a suffix, and if such a word constitutes a single stress group, the unvoiced variants could be described as abdominemically conditioned; thus far, the

---

[6] This section of the 1955 volume was written too early to reflect the more radical views suggested by some of the (Chomsky) transformationalists. They would start presentation (it is not analysis which they have in view) from grammatical symbols, generating, by rule, sentences in phonetic form. The grammatical rules, under this approach, are prerequisite to phonological representation. The Trager model of phoneme-to-syntax has by them been turned upside down (as Longacre has pointed out, 1964a; see below, § 9.71). Hence the appearance of grammatical considerations in a phonological discussion (see Chomsky, Halle and Lukoff, 1956, and Chomsky, 1957a:57) seems less surprising than it once did. Our view, however requires both a phonological hierarchy and a grammatical one, interacting (see Chapter 15) in both analysis and presentation. Some fifteen years ago the academic climate made it important that certain grammatical requisites enter phonemic analysis (1947a, 1952a); now I would add that, similarly, certain phonological requisites must enter grammatical analysis. See bibliographical discussion in § 8.87.

suggested data seems to parallel that of Cakchiquel of Guatemala. Enclitics, however, may be added to these words. Here our data for Cakchiquel is incomplete; if the unvoicing continues to disappear before the enclitic, and if the enclitics themselves constitute separate abdominemes, no change in the description of the unvoicing is necessary; if, however, the enclitics become part of the stress group, with no secondary stress characteristics, etc., but if the unvoicing continues preceding them, there might here be an instance in which conditioning by the word unit would still be the best available description.

A further possibility which, the theory indicates, should now be investigated, is that of TAGMEMICALLY-CONDITIONED variants of phonemes, in which the relationship of two variants of a phoneme could not be satisfactorily described by their relation to larger phonological units, but might be better described by their relation to tagmemic situations of some kind, such as the relation of stem to affix. If, for example, stem vowels were found to be lengthened, but affixal vowels were not, and no difference in stress or other such hyperphonemic characteristic marked the two positions, there might be some value in analyzing these variants as tagmemically conditioned.

Likewise, it would be well to study further the possibility of UTTEREMICALLY-CONDITIONED variants, in which a grammatical sentence is in contexts unmarked by hyperphonemic border characteristics, but nevertheless is paralleled at its borders by sub-phonemic variants which would then be considered as utteremically conditioned.

It should be noted, however, that even such a partial abandonment of reliance on grammatically-conditioned phonemic variants in description is in part programatic — not a present achievement in fact — so long as linguists are forced, as they have often been, to postulate phonological junctures at points where they have not heard them, in order to justify a description of phonemic variants in phonological terms rather than as grammatically conditioned. Such a device has been used, for example, when (a) in certain grammatical situations segmental changes have been observed, (b) these have been attributed to a 'juncture' or even defined as the manifested total form of that juncture, and (c) the juncture symbolized by space or other device at such points, but (d) also written at other points in the system, grammatically parallel to these, but with no segmental changes involved — i.e., where the juncture was then written grammatically, with no phonological evidence (see, for example, quotations from Bloch, Trager, Welmers, Harris, and Lukoff, in Pike 1947a:160-62). In such instances, in the future, a linguist must either (a) identify the hyperphonemic characteristic present in the phonetic data, or (b) set up the slight differences as phonemic rather than as subphonemic, abandoning the psycholinguistic evidence and theory which would have led to the treatment of them as phonemic, or (c) conclude that, after all, subphonemic variants can indeed be grammatically conditioned. (For an unsuccessful attempt to follow the first of these alternatives, see Trager, 1948, as discussed in Pike 1952a:108). In addition, such grammatically-defined distributions of sounds served for a long time as clues for places to look for abdominemic borders

— until phonetic teaching techniques developed far enough to make the requisite ear training part of the regular procedure in a phonetics class.

For the theoretical basis of this practical work see Pike (1962b); for analysis see bibliography in §§ 9.63, 9.74.

Note, also, the continuing necessity for describing one component of the distribution mode of the phoneme in grammatical terms (§§ 8.52, 8.1), with its possible theoretical reflection on this subphonemic problem such that *at times* the conditioning environments may prove to be 'combined grammatical-phonological border points' (Pike, 1947c:161n), etc.

8.444 *Free (Nonconditioned) Variants of the Phoneme*

In § 2.3 we indicated that it was impossible to repeat any movement exactly; delicate measuring instruments are certain to detect some variation in such an attempt. The numerous differences of uncontrollable variation of articulatory movement (or of the resultant sound) in the repeated production of a phoneme — differences unconditioned by any style, or surrounding sounds, or grammatical or hyperphonemic environment — constitute a SCATTER of FREE VARIANTS OF THAT PHONEME.

When such variants are so minute as to be undetectable by auditory means, they may be called, for linguistic purposes, the SAME VARIANT, or the SAME ALLOPHONE of that phoneme (Pike, 1952b:623); for purposes of instrumental analysis, however, it may be necessary to treat a series of such subperceptual free variants as different subliminal allophones.

A phoneme may also have free variants, unconditioned by any environmental factor, which are above the perceptual threshold. Sometimes such fluctuation may be quite large — as when in Zapotec, of Mexico, a voiced [z] may fluctuate freely with a lenis [s] in the same phoneme with it, but contrast phonemically with a fortis [s] sound (Leal, 1950:133 fn. 11; Pickett, 1951:60 fn. 3). Variants of this type are also called FREE and UNCONDITIONED, but are less likely to be called the 'same' allophone; even if the fluctuation is over an infinite range, it is often convenient to label the poles of the fluctuation as separate allophones, and to symbolize them in a phonetic transcription, but to cover the intermediate varieties with a general descriptive statement with none or only a few of the intermediate stages symbolized in the phonetic transcription of the data.

A variation which is systemically conditioned (§ 8.445) will appear to the investigator as a free variant, if he fails to note the specific style which the speaker is using at the moment of change. Thus, for example, the systemically-conditioned aspirated variety of American /t/ in the middle of a word like *matter* may seem to be a free variant of the normal flapped variety — since it is not locally conditioned — if the analyst fails to note that the aspirated variety is used under circumstances where the speaker is struggling to be heard above noise, or to make the pronunciation 'clear' to a foreigner, or that it occurs in 'careful' public address, or in other special circumstance.

8.445 *Phonetically-Complex Variants of the Phoneme*

When the manifested form of a phoneme is composed of a single phonetic wave of activity (§ 8.42), it may be called phonetically simple; thus [f], [m], and [s] are phonetically simple. When, however, a manifested form of a phoneme is composed of two or more phonetic waves (i.e., phonetic segments) in sequence, the form is PHONETICALLY COMPLEX; English /p/ in *repay* has such a phonetically-complex variant, composed of the segment [p] and the segment [h] in the etic sequence [ph]; the same phoneme /p/ has a phonetically-simple variant in the word *happy*, where the transition to the final vowel occurs without the segment of aspiration. As this pair of illustrations shows, a phoneme may contain both phonetically-simple and phonetically-complex members among its allophones.

The interpretation[7] of an etic sequence of two phonetic segments as the manifestation of a single phonemic segment is dependent upon its occupying a single place in the system of phonemes (§ 8.6) and a unitary (i.e., active) slot in the internal structure of an emic class of emic syllables (i.e., in a CVC pattern, §§ 8.53, 9.244); in this respect its function must be comparable to single-segment phonemes (Pike, 1947c:128-38).

8.446 *Fused versus Clearly-Segmented Variants of the Phoneme*

We earlier indicated (§ 8.34) that the contrastive ranges of two phonemes can be used in special environments in such a way that an archiphoneme is produced intermediate in phonetic character between the norms of two phonemes, within a general congruent system in which the norms also occur. We now turn to situations in which two phonemes in sequence may fuse into a single phonetic segment which may be called a PORTMANTEAU PHONE. In rapid 'uncareful' speech, for example, an English vowel with a following /n/ may occasionally fuse to a single-segment portmanteau nasalized vowel, with loss of a nasal segment; in such an instance it may be necessary to interpret the nasalized vowel phone as a single etic segment that simultaneously constitutes a vowel phoneme and a following consonant phoneme, as in [ˈwa̧ičəgo] for *Whyn't you go?*, i.e., *Why don't you go?* (Pike, 1949).

The fact that every two contiguous sounds within a rapid sequence of sound reciprocally affect one another (§ 8.442) is related to the same portmanteau phenomenon — in fact, their slurred sequence could be considered as a partial portmanteau, with the two-segment character of the sequence preserved. Thus, a diagram may indicate the stages of fusion:

---

[7] Once again the reader should be warned that in discussing analysis we have specifically insisted on the necessity of intuitive, nonmechanical steps in the procedure. See § 7.322 and second fn.

It is inconceivable that we should permanently repudiate any attempt to systematize and to understand to whatever degree is possible this heuristic and its relation to the possibility of knowledge. No virtue resides in encouraging starvation in the presence of — only — sandwiches. See also, end of § 8.52.

318   THE MINIMUM UNIT OF THE MANIFESTATION MODE OF THE BEHAVIOREME

In Stage A, a pause occurs between the sounds, sufficient to prevent any conditioning of one by the other. In Stage B, the sounds occur in normal sequence within a hyperphoneme, and the first decays after the second begins, while the first begins before the second is finished. In Stage C, the peaks of the waves are still not simultaneous but

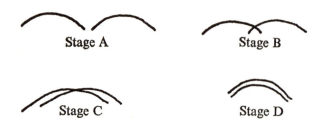

the anticipation and decay stages of second and first overlap much more. In Stage D, the phonemes are sequentially completely fused, within a single portmanteau phone.

The interpretation of a single phone as a fused sequence of two phonemes is dependent upon its functioning in a hyperphonemic pattern as a sequence of two phonemes, or its complementary or fluctuating occurrence with the phonetic-phonemic sequence it represents (§ 8.445, and Pike, 1947c:138-40).

For further discussion of fused emic units, see Chapter 14.

8.5. *The Distribution Mode of the Phoneme*

Like all other emes, the phoneme has a distribution mode within its trimodal structure:

8.51 *Actual and Potential Distribution of the Phoneme in Hyperphonemes*

Every phoneme occurs within a syllable — a small hyperphoneme — or at the joint borders of two hyperphonemes in sequence in a still larger hyperphoneme; the general pattern of phonemic distribution within these hyperphonemes limits the distributional occurrence of the single phoneme. Hence one component of the distribution mode of the individual phoneme is its POTENTIAL FOR OCCURRENCE (a) within certain slots in one or more emic classes of emic syllables or larger hyperphonemes, and (b) in certain sequences of phonemes within contiguous structural slots of these hyperphonemes. Thus, for example, English vowels may fill the slot for the peak of the syllable; most English consonants (with /ŋ/ an exception) may fill the pre-peak slot in a syllable which has only one pre-peak consonant; /s/, and only /s/, may fill the consonant slot at the beginning of a three-consonant pre-peak sequence in the syllable; etc.

Instead of speaking of the potential for occurrence, one might start from a slightly different point of view and speak either of all reported occurrences, or speak of

THE MINIMUM UNIT OF THE MANIFESTATION MODE OF THE BEHAVIOREME 319

limitations upon occurrence. Our choice is to focus attention upon the DYNAMIC phases of language structure and its positive, productive potential, rather than on static phases, when the alternatives are otherwise equally possible. In this connection, it can be seen that phonemic manifestations treated as waves of motion (§ 8.42), rather than as static mouth 'positions', represent a further choice of dynamic outlook rather than a static one.

One of the advantages of this point of view is that we can now use it to show how the two dynamic elements of potential distribution in hyperphonemes, and phonemic manifestations as waves of activity, combine to allow us to describe fruitfully a further characteristic of the distribution mode of phonemes at the boundaries of hyperphonemes which are included in higher-layered hyperphonemes. Let us label the different parts of a sequence of two syllables, successively, as the rising phase (which also is the starting phase), peak phase, falling phase, trough phase (which is also the indeterminate border phase), rising phase, peak phase, and falling phase (which is also the end phase) respectively. Similarly, several phonemes in sequence may in these terms have successive rising, peak, falling, trough, rising, peak, and falling phases, etc. These may be illustrated in diagrams A and B below:

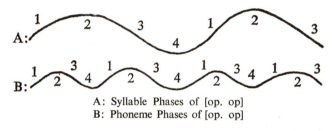

A: Syllable Phases of [op. op]
B: Phoneme Phases of [op. op]

1: rising; 2: peak; 3: falling; 4: trough

Note that the trough phase between the second and third phonemes corresponds with the timing of the trough phase between the syllables.

Let us suppose, further, that the sequence of phonemes in B is composed of /o/ followed by /p/ followed by /o/ followed by /p/ (using a sequence studied intensively by Stetson, 1928, with second edition, 1951). What would be the distribution of these phonemes in reference to the phases of the syllable sequence A? A static description might mention the fact that one possibility, the most frequent, is [o.pop] (in which the low dot indicates the trough between the syllables), that a less frequent arrangement is [op.op], and that a third arrangement would be [opop] (with no labial release and no perceptual syllabic border between the components of the ambisyllabic consonant; for further discussion of this type, see § 9.236). A dynamic description, however, is more flexible; it could describe these relationships and, in addition, could much more easily describe the manner in which one of these types (the [op.op]) passed by infinite degrees into the others, by stating that the phoneme /p/ occurred at different points in the transition from the first to the second syllable, changing from its occurrence at the falling phase of the first syllable, in a slow congruent system, to the rising phase of the second, in a rapid congruent system.

In the following diagram note that when the syllables of [op. op] are at their trough phase the second phoneme reaches its peak phase:

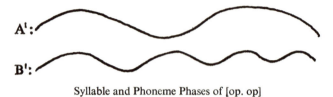

Syllable and Phoneme Phases of [op. op]

From this it follows that it is not always convenient to state that phonemes are distributed within syllables, directly, since at times it may be necessary to move to a higher-layered unit — say the abdomineme — to find one in which the borders of the higher-layered unit will coincide with some phoneme border. Similarly, if a phoneme peak occurs at the trough phase of a sequence of two abdominemes, it may become necessary to describe its distribution relative to the larger, breath-group unit. A dynamic approach to the problem in terms of simultaneous or overlapping waves of activity provides a convenient way of discussing these matters.

A similar approach will prove helpful when we discuss fusion at more length in Chapter 14, and interpenetrating levels and systems in Chapter 15. Note, also, that this is related to the technique we have already used, in § 8.446, to show the relation between the slurring of contiguous phonemes, and the complete fusion of such phonemes — which can now be stated as different degrees of overlapping of various phases of these respective phonemes.

8.52 *Actual and Potential Distribution of the Phoneme in Grammatical Units and in the Behavioreme*

In a fast congruent system which contains some elements like [o. pop] which in a slow congruent system of the same language revert to [op. o p], there are likely also to occur some sequences like [o. pop] which do not change to [op. op] in the slower system. Since the two kinds of sequences are in the fast system homophonous, there is nothing in the phonetics which serves as a basis for predicting which of the sequences will and which will not so differ in the slow style. If, however, the lexical characteristics of the elements of the fast form are known, i.e., if the morphemes are identified, one can know which of the fast forms will be heard in the respective slow-form syllable types, if one has prior knowledge of the phonemic distribution in morphemes in that slower congruent system. It seems evident, then, that for the understanding of the phonological relations between phonemes and their hyperphonemic matrices in the language as a whole, the hyperphonemic distribution alone is not sufficient; for this purpose one needs to know the potential lexical distribution as well, and the correlation of distribution between related congruent systems. In the fast and slow systems of the schematic type just indicated, for example, the distributional potential for consonant phonemes would differ: in the fast system it would include, in the center of a stress group, only syllable-initial position; in the slow system it would include also syllable-final position in the center of a stress group. Thus the distributional mode of a consonant phoneme would differ in the two systems, and this difference would be distributionally controlled through the MORPHEMIC structure of the language (cf. shape types, § 6.64), not through the hyperphonemic structure alone. For specific instances, compare English *a name* with *an aim*.

The permitted sequences of phonemes are also restricted by the grammatical arrangement. In § 7.313(2), for example, we indicated that in Tzeltal it was not the individual morpheme which controlled the limitations within which the phonemic shape type of morphemes could vary, but the more general relation of stem (which could have only shape type CV or larger) versus affix (which might have shape type VC or even C); this control was by TAGMEMIC DISTRIBUTION CLASS — not by individual morpheme, nor tagmeme, nor uttereme (nor by phonological unit, inasmuch as the syllable break often interrupts the CVC pattern of a morpheme, syllabifying the second C with a following vowel-initial morpheme).

Elsewhere, restrictions on the potential for the occurrence of a particular phoneme may be imposed by its position in a unit conveniently called a WORD; syllables at the end of words frequently have different permitted structure than those at the beginning of words. Note, for example, that in Tamil the three lateral phonemes "do not occur after word juncture" — i.e., at the beginning of syllables which are at the beginning of words — but do occur at the beginning of syllables elsewhere (Fowler, 1954:364); in Zoque, "Syllables beginning in CCC or CCCC occur only in word initial position" (Wonderly, 1951-52:116). Since restrictions of a word-conditioned type may be imposed when the word is not coterminous with any hyperphonemic unit, such restrictions are lexical or grammatical, not hyperphonemic.

One further component of the distributional mode of a phoneme is easily overlooked: It occurs within a particular LANGUAGE, and within particular UTTEREMES of that language, and within the BEHAVIOREMES of a particular culture or individual which contain the utteremes of that language. These are behavioremic prerequisites[8] to the identification of or analysis of any phoneme. Together with the fact that the distributional components of the phoneme include reference to smaller grammatical elements, this forces us to define the phoneme not as an entity by itself, but exclusively in reference to the behavioreme and system of behavioremes of which it is a part: the definition of a phoneme as the minimum unit of the distribution mode of the uttereme (cf. § 8.1), and the expanded definition which must include reference to more details of this relationship (cf. § 8.1 for the expanded definition of the acteme, of which the

---

[8] See, also, fn. to § 8.443.

phoneme is a verbal type), are merely defining sentences which are constructed to insist upon and in part delineate these relationships. Since, furthermore, the morpheme — and every other emic unit of a language — must similarly be related to the behavioreme, and with a manifested component composed to some degree of phonemes, the grammatical units are identifiable and analyzable only in relation to the phoneme; hence phoneme, morpheme, tagmeme, uttereme, hyperphoneme, etc., all are parts of a complex set of interrelated elements which enter into each other's definitions in a simultaneously recursive form (cf. quotation from Bar-Hillel, § 7.8) as part of a coherent system.

8.53 *The Internal Structure of the Phoneme and Its Active Membership in a Class of Phonemes*

The distribution mode of the morpheme (§ 6.64) and the tagmeme (§ 7.54) contained a component consisting of a sequence of their manifesting phonemes (except for the few morphemes containing only one phoneme). With the phoneme, however, no such sequence internally of smaller emic units occurs; a phoneme, this latter statement implies, is composed exclusively of one phoneme, and not of a composite of two phonemes in sequence. The internal structuring of the phoneme is largely that of the simultaneous components which constitute its contrastive-identificational features. There is, however, the small residue of sequential features, as indicated in § 8.31, composed of the etic segments of multisegment phonemes, such as the [t] and [š] of Spanish /č/, or the [p] and [h] of English *pie*. On a subphonemic level, these segments constitute a sequential part of the distributional mode[9] of that phonetically-complex phoneme.

The fact that a phonetic sequence may under certain circumstances be interpreted as a single phoneme is intimately linked to another characteristic of the distribution mode of the phoneme: each phoneme is distributed contrastively within, and is a member of (or, in rare instances, constitutes) an emic CLASS of phonemes (§ 8.6) whose membership is ACTIVE by virtue of the fact that it occurs within an active slot in a class of hyperphonemes (§§ 8.445, 9.243-44). A two-segment (or on rare occasions a three-segment) sequence of phones which as a whole fills a single active hyperphonemic slot is a single emic unit, a single phoneme; in this distributional respect, furthermore, such a phoneme would parallel other phonemes, of a single-segment type, which also fill that active hyperphonemic slot. Such a slot might be composed, for instance, of the C position in a CVC syllable pattern. The separate phones which comprise a two-segment phonetic manifestation of a single phoneme would be passive, since neither of them completely fills such an active lot. It is this theoretical consideration which justifies and is the source of the empirical

---

[9] But see fn. to § 3.5(3).

"interpretation procedures" of Pike, 1947c:60-61, 131-40. Further discussion of these slots will be delayed until the next chapter, which deals with hyperphonemic units.

8.54 *An Occurring Allophone Viewed as Constituting an Occurring Phoneme*

In § 6.65 we argued that "whenever a variant of a morpheme has occurred the morpheme itself has occurred". Our basic point of view was that the analysis of behavior — morphemic behavior — AS THE PERSONS IN THAT CULTURE REACT TO THAT BEHAVIOR, demands that a morpheme should be repeatable, and that variants of that morpheme should be identifiable as the same morpheme in spite of its variants, just as John Doe is treated as if he were the same person today as he was yesterday and as if John Doe can in fact be seen (rather than an 'Allo-Doe' being the only visible entity). The same kind of argument had to be repeated for the tagmeme (§ 7.55).

Similar considerations lead us to the conviction that an occurring allophone should be viewed, in an emic analysis (not necessarily in a philosophical discussion of the nature of reality) as an occurring phoneme. But compare Twaddell: "What occurs is not a phoneme, for the phoneme is defined as the term of a recurrent differential relation" since "What occurs is a phonetic fraction or a differential articulatory complex correlated to a micro-phoneme", (1935:49); compare also Carnochan: "as units they [the vowels] are not pronounceable" (1950:1041). An argument similar to mine occurs in Bolinger (1954:10).

8.6 *Systems of Phonemes*

We turn now from the discussion of separate phonemes to a brief mention of some of the characteristics of the phonemic systems of which the phonemes are members.

8.61 *Congruent Systems of Phonemes in a Hypercongruent System*

Within any one voice quality — harsh, singing, pouting, happy, baby talk by adults, etc. — the phonemes constitute a system. Similarly, within any one speed — fast, slow — the phonemes likewise constitute a system. Two such systems in the same language are CONGRUENT (§ 5.4), in that all or most of the phonemes of the one system are topologically related (§ 8.441) to the phonemes of the other system. In addition, we indicated in § 8.441 that two topologically-related phonemes of two congruent systems are in this theory considered to constitute the same phoneme of the total language system, i.e., of the HYPERCONGRUENT SYSTEM (§ 5.4), but systemically conditioned as to their physical manifestations. For example, F— thought he heard B— say: *What is that you ride in Mexico?*, and so F— answered: *A horse*, to which B— replied: *I said WRITE [rait·h]!*. On another occasion, M— said: *I didn't get that shirt ironed very well, did I?*; to which F— answered, with a facetious glottalization of the final stop: *Nope* [*nopʔ*]*!;* on which S— commented: *Daddy said* [*nopʔ*] — *you slipped your mouth*, indicating that in this instance the distorted phoneme signalled a specialized pronunciation which was picked up as such. S— himself often uses special stop allophones for vocal play; for example, I have noted glottalized stops in his speech on the end of *gallop*, and *elephant*.

The congruent systems of phonemes in a hypercongruent system are NOT EQUALLY DISTINGUISHABLE, as the first of the illustrations in the set just given indicate — and as anyone experiences, who shouts to be heard in a subway, or who must learn to enunciate clearly, and to adopt a syllable and abdomineme pattern which leaves all vowels with a certain amount of emphasis but with none of them shouted.

Occasionally there are more phonemes in one congruent system than another — in which case it is sometimes convenient to call the systems only partially congruent — when the phonemes of the one system are not all in a one-to-one topological relation with phonemes of the other system. Thus in 'careful speech' there may be OVER-DIFFERENTIATED PHONEMES, i.e., a pair of phonetically-similar phonemes which between them divide the functional load of the single phonetically-related phoneme of the normal congruent system. For example, in some dialects of Mexico a bilabial voiced stop and a bilabial voiced fricative are members of a single phoneme, conditioned or in free variation in the normal system; but in schoolroom discussions, or the like, /b/ and /v/ may be contrastively treated, as a reflection of the spelling system (Pike, 1947c:142; contrast this situation with the one in which UNDERDIFFERENTIATED archiphonemes occur, with a single phonetically-ambiguous phone filling the contrastive range of two phonemes within a limited subsystem of a particular congruent system, § 8.34).

The overdifferentiated phonemes just mentioned occur in morphemes of the major morpheme classes of the language. Occasionally, either in the normal congruent system, or limited to a special congruent system, EXTRASYSTEMATIC PHONEMES occur as part of the manifestation of special morphemes. Such phonemes may contain kinds of articulatory movements which are not part of any phoneme of any morpheme of the major morpheme classes of the normal congruent system. One such sound is the click of commiseration in English, that includes a movement of the tongue as it pulls air into the mouth (the sound often written *tsk*); compare, also, the mention of misplaced allophones, in § 8.443.

Listeners must also be prepared to interpret topologically any DISTORTED PHONEMES[10] in which the distortion is not deliberate, hence not part of a congruent system, but

---

[10] We are currently working on matrix theory (see § 15.336 and fnn. to §§ 11.225, 11.6, 14.12, 14.3, and to title of chapter 17). It appears to us that it should illuminate some of the problems of phonemic distortion and many of the difficulties encountered in trying to find acoustic constants (note for example, problems reported in G. Miller and Nicely, 1955; Hoffman, 1958; Liberman, Delattre and Cooper, 1958; Mol and Uhlenbeck, 1959; Lisker, Cooper, Liberman, 1962; Cooper, Liberman, Lisker, Gaitenby, 1962).

See, also, the use of matrix in phonetic ranking, fn. to § 8.623.

produced by the communication medium — as in a radio broadcast — or by some temporary impediment in the person's speech. On the breakfast recordings, for example, distortions occur when someone is talking while food is still in the mouth. Stuttering may bring in further temporary distortions. Liquor may produce other distortions in speech or articulation. In Puebla, Mexico, a young fellow told me, for example, that one evening some police officers who accosted him insisted that he whistle, to give a quick proof of his sobriety.

8.62 *Trimodally-Structured Classes of Phonemes*

Phonemes are structurally grouped into etic and emic classes (1) in accordance with their distribution in slots and sequences within hyperphonemes and grammatical units and (2) in accordance with their contrastive relations and phonetic ranking.

Described in reference to the trimodal structuring of the phoneme classes, these same relevant components of the classes appear: An emic class of phonemes has, as components of its feature mode, its membership, and the fact that it contrasts with other classes, and that each member of the class is in contrast with every other member of that class. Another frequent component of the feature mode of an emic class of phonemes is a set of articulatory subgroups comprising the class, in a hierarchically-ordered RANK of phonetic relations. As a component of its manifestation mode, the emic class of phonemes may have one or more etic classes as variants. As a component of its distribution mode, an emic class of phonemes has the potential to be distributed within one or more active slots of one or more emic classes of hyperphonemic units, and within one or more active slots of the shape types of one or more grammatical units.

A more extended description is now given:

8.621 *The Distribution Mode of an Emic Class of Phonemes*

An ETIC DISTRIBUTION CLASS OF PHONEMES comprises the group of phonemes which occupy any one active (§§ 8.445, 8.53) slot in the phonemic shape type (cf. § 6.64) of a hyperphoneme, of a morpheme or of a hypermorpheme, of a tagmeme or hypertagmeme, of an uttereme or hyper-uttereme. A syllable type such as CVC, for example, is manifested by the respective manifestations of three etic distribution classes of phonemes, in sequence. Similarly, for the morpheme shape type CVC there are also three etic distribution classes, respectively manifested in the sequence, some of which may and some of which may not be homophonous with the distribution classes determined by the shape type of the syllable, previously mentioned.

One of the tasks of an emic analysis of etic distribution classes of phonemes is to determine which of the etic classes are emically the same, and which are emically different. An EMIC DISTRIBUTION CLASS OF PHONEMES is composed of one or more etic distribution classes of phonemes united into an emic unit by their comparable function in phonological and grammatical units, or by the phonetic similarity of the etic groups and their complementary distribution within their respective slots. Samples of etic and of emic classes of phonemes, and an indication of the kinds of conditioning which affect the distribution of their variants, will be given in the next section. First, however, a few more general characteristics need mentioning.

The distribution mode of a phoneme class includes a POTENTIAL FOR CORRELATION of one manifested member of that class with a manifested member of a particular subgroup of another emic class with which it occurs in sequence: A voiced phoneme of one class for example, may be so correlated with another emic class which is to follow it that only a voiced member of that next class may fill the next active slot in the sequence (cf. singular and plural correlations of morpheme classes as they manifest tagmemes, § 7.313(2); cf., also, these restrictions in relation to phonemically-conditioned membership variants of phoneme classes, in § 8.622).

A further component of the distribution mode of an emic class of phonemes may be its membership, as a subgroup, in successively larger emic classes of phonemes, in a HIERARCHY OF CLASSES OF PHONEMES. A group of liquids and semivowels, (/r, l, y, w/) for example, might by themselves in one slot constitute an emic class of phonemes, but in a different active slot they might be part of a much larger emic hyperclass, one which contained all voiced consonants, as contrasted with the emic hyperclass of vowels.

In addition, there may occur SETS OF CLASSES OF PHONEMES such that, in any one congruent system of phonemes, certain sets occur and constitute the entire possible number of phonemes occurring in that congruent system, but in a different congruent system of the same language, the set of classes might be slightly different in membership, conditioned by that system. If, for example, in a congruent system of 'careful speech' an overdifferentiated pair of phonemes (§ 8.61) occurs, this pair will enter one or more classes of phonemes, and modify the containing sets accordingly (cf. also § 7.313(4), for comparable problems in morphemics, and § 7.6, for tagmemics).

Just as our usage of 'class' in reference to morphemes occurring in tagmemic slots made it inconvenient to speak of a morpheme as a 'class of allomorphs' (§ 7.313(2)), so here we use the term 'class' in reference to a group of phonemes substitutable in a slot in a phonological or grammatical sequence, and avoid using it, insofar as is possible, in reference to the group of allophones which makes up a phoneme.

8.622 The Manifestation Mode of An Emic Class of Phonemes

Two etic classes of phonemes, determined by the fact that they occupy different slots in the sequences of a language, are the SAME VARIANT of an emic class if the membership is identical, i.e., if they contain the same phonemes: an utterance-initial etic class of phonemes and an utterance-final etic class, for example, would constitute the same variant of an emic class if they contained the same phonemes (cf. §§ 6.51, 7.313(3)).

The emic class has FREELY-VARIANT MANIFESTATIONS whenever one phoneme or another is momentarily the member which occurs, representing the class as a whole, in a particular slot; thus /p/ and /m/ are freely-variant manifestations of a class which comes syllable initially in *pail* and *mail* (and cf. § 7.313(3)).

LOCALLY-CONDITIONED VARIANTS OF A CLASS OF PHONEMES may be composed of changes in membership, or of changes in the subphonemic articulatory character of the members as a group. The changes may in turn be caused by the manifested membership of another class of phonemes in sequence with it, or by the particular slot it fills in the shape type of the morpheme, word, hypermorpheme, tagmeme, hypertagmeme, uttereme, or hyper-uttereme (cf. the kinds of variants indicated for morpheme classes, in § 7.313(3), which are partly like these and partly different).

Thus a PHONEMICALLY-CONDITIONED MEMBERSHIP VARIANT OF A CLASS OF PHONEMES occurs when the etic subclass of the larger emic class is limited to one phonetic type of member before a manifesting member of similar phonetic type in a class following it in the sequence of phonemes under attention: i.e., for example, there may be a limitation to phoneme sequences such that only voiced members of the first class may precede, in a certain language, a voiced member of a following class, and vice versa, in accordance with the potential for correlation of manifested members of classes as mentioned in § 8.621. (Compare the morphemically-conditioned lexical variants of an emic class of morphemes, discussed in § 7.313(3)). A HYPERPHONEME-SLOT-CONDITIONED MEMBERSHIP VARIANT OF A CLASS OF PHONEMES, on the other hand, would occur when a restricted subclass of the whole class is limited in distribution to a particular place in the syllable, or stress group, or breath group; for example, if all consonants may occur in a breath-group-initial slot, and all but /h/ may occur in a breath-group-final slot, the etic class of phonemes which occurs in breath-group-final position (and is composed of all the consonants but /h/) would be a hyperphoneme-slot-conditioned membership variant of the full class.

Similarly, GRAMMATICAL-SLOT-CONDITIONED VARIANTS OF AN EMIC CLASS OF PHONEMES occur when the restricted classes, as subclasses of a larger class of phonemes, are limited in distribution to special places in the morpheme, the word, other hypermorphemes, or utteremes or hyper-utteremes, tagmemes or hypertagmemes. Occasionally, furthermore, the conditions may be combined in such a way that the restricting position is definable only as a composite limitation produced by a particular grammatical slot within a particular hyperphonemic one, or vice versa, in a GRAMMATICAL-SLOT-HYPERPHONEMIC-SLOT-CONDITIONED VARIANT OF THE PHONEME CLASS. Every such etic class is an ALLOCLASS of the emic class.

Whenever all the members of a class of phonemes are affected by a succeeding phoneme in such a way that each of the phonemes in the class has a subphonemic variant conditioned by that following phoneme, the phoneme class as a whole is represented in that position by a PHONEMICALLY-CONDITIONED ALLOPHONIC VARIANT (or ALLOPHONE CLASS) of that emic class of phonemes. If, for example, an emic class of phonemes contains a single group of stops, and the phonemic membership of the class is always the same in every slot, such that there is only the one 'same membership variant' of that class at every occurrence, and if that group of phonemes is voiceless in initial phrase positions but voiced between vowels, then two allophone classes (the voiceless one and the voiced one) make up the emic class. (Here, again, is a reason for avoiding the term 'class of allophones' as applied to a single phoneme; cf. §§ 8.621, 7.313(2), 7.313(3).)

If within an emic class of phonemes some of the members are phonetically-complex (§ 8.445), these members constitute a PHONETICALLY-COMPLEX SUBCLASS OF THAT PHONEME CLASS. If, furthermore, in some positions all members of the emic class were phonetically complex, and in other slots all the members were phonetically simple, the two-segment members would constitute a phonetically-complex allophone class. Similarly, if in a particular slot all the members of a class are fused to the following phonemes, a FUSED VARIANT OF THE EMIC CLASS would be present.

In addition to the locally-conditioned etic variants of an emic class of phonemes, such a class may have a SYSTEMICALLY-CONDITIONED ALLOPHONIC VARIANT in which the style affects the entire class phonologically — e.g., as in song. A SYSTEMICALLY-CONDITIONED MEMBERSHIP VARIANT OF AN EMIC CLASS OF PHONEMES would be one in which the system, or style, led to extra phonemes in a class through overdifferentiation of that class (§ 8.61), or to fewer members in the class through underdifferentiation. When, however, the new system includes phonemes of a special type which are not members of any of the previous emic classes in the normal congruent system, and occur in different slots, the added emic classes — composed of one or more members, as for example in the interjections of emphatic style — enter the system of classes of phonemes, and produce a variant of the phonemic system as a whole, a SYSTEMICALLY-CONDITIONED ALLOSYSTEM OF CLASSES OF PHONEMES. An allosystem of classes of phonemes is a variant of the total system of phonemes within the phonological-grammatical structure of the hypercongruent system which constitutes the language.

8.623 *The Feature Mode of an Emic Class of Phonemes*

There is often a very close relation between an etic or an emic distribution class of phonemes and certain articulatory features of the members of those classes. One would be startled to find, for example, the sounds /o, m, l, p, t, s, x/ constituting one major emic class of phonemes of a language, and /i, n, r, k, f/ constituting another major emic class of phonemes in the same language. On the other hand, one would not be surprised, at all, to find in one major emic class /p, t, k, b, d, g/, in another /f, s, x/, and in another /a, i, o, u/. The PHONETIC SIMILARITY of the members of a class or of the members of a subclass within a larger class (as /p, t, k/ are similar in type of articulation and constitute a phonetic subclass different phonetically from the /b, d, g/ of the class suggested above) is definable as a relevant CONTRASTIVE-IDENTIFICATIONAL FEATURE OF THE FEATURE MODE OF A CLASS, composed of a CONTRASTIVE-IDENTIFICATIONAL FEATURE COMMON TO THE MEMBERS OF A CLASS OR TO THE MEMBERS OF

A SUBCLASS OF THAT EMIC CLASS. (Such a feature or group of features is not composed of a phonetic absolute, however, but is determined relative to the congruent system of sounds in which it occurs, and to the slots within the sequences of phonemes in which it occurs, as it is for the phonemes when they are treated as separate units, for which see § 8.33.)

Traditionally, such articulatory classes are presented as a generalized phonetic scheme in the form of a phonetic chart in which sounds made at the same point of articulation are placed in columns, and sounds with the same set of contrastive features, otherwise, are placed in rows, with rows close together in the chart if they have features in common, thus:

```
p  t    k ʔ
   c č
b  d    g

m  n    n

f  s    x h

   i  u
     a
```

More recently, a theory of RANK OF ARTICULATION (or RANK OF STRICTURE), of phones has been elaborated by Eunice V. Pike which modifies the presentation somewhat, but which allows the groupings to be charted much more rigorously. We give in slightly abbreviated form her seven criteria of rank (1954:26-29); the first two concern the ranking of articulations *within* a phone (and were based on Pike, 1943a), whereas the next five make the specific contribution referred to here, in the ranking of phones in respect to *one another*: (1) An articulation in the oral cavity ranks higher than a stricture in the nasal cavity, which in turn outranks one in the pharyngeal cavity. (2) Within a cavity, a stricture causing complete closure outranks one causing localized friction, which in turn outranks one causing little or no friction in that same cavity. (3) When the highest ranking articulation of one phone has higher rank than the highest ranking articulation of the second phone, the first phone as a whole outranks the second: e.g., /p/ outranks /f/, /n/ outranks /s/, /a/ outranks /ʔ/. (4) When two phones have the same highest-ranking articulation, but different nonhighest ones, the rank is determined on the basis of the next-highest articulation of each, or an additional articulation of one of them, in accordance with the above criteria: e.g., /b/ outranks /p/, /p/ outranks /m/. (5) Of two oral strictures of the same degree of closure, the one farthest front has the higher rank, so that /f/ outranks /s/, /t/ outranks /k/, /i/ outranks /ɨ/. (6) In a phonetically-complex phoneme, the articulations of the phones of which the phoneme is composed are treated in rank as if the strictures were simultaneous in time; this criterion must be used, then, in combination with Numbers 1-4: e.g., /č/ outranks /t/, /sʷ/ outranks /s/, /ⁿd/ outranks /d/, /ʔb/ outranks /b/, /kˣ/

outranks /k/. (7) A phoneme of high pitch outranks one of low pitch. (8) And, we add on the suggestion of May Morrison, an initiator (Pike, 1943a:87-88, 129-30) acts as a further stricture, with oral initiator outranking a pharyngeal one, and a pharyngeal initiator outranking a pulmonic one, so that a click /t$^<$/ would outrank a glottalized /tʔ/, and /tʔ/ would outrank ordinary /t/.

The same criteria, when applied to a group of sounds as a whole, allow its relative SERIES RANK (or CLASS RANK) to be established. Thus /f, s, x/ as a group outranks the group composed of /a, i, u/. The same criteria allow the relative ranking of groups composed of sounds at one point of articulation, such that the group /b, p, m/ outranks the group /d, t, n/. A group of stops, by these criteria, would also outrank a group of labials, since, for example, /k/ outranks /m/; but the group of labials /p, m, f/ outranks /f, s, x/ since both /p/ and /m/ outrank each of the fricatives.

A partial ranked generalized phonetic chart[11] gives a bit clearer picture of a few of the changes in charting which such a theory would bring in (and the dotted line indicates the change which would occur in the chart if [h] were treated as a glottal spirant instead of a vocoid; for the chart of Mazatec phonemes, see E. V. Pike, 1954:30):

```
       <---------   Degree of Fronting   <---------
  ^              c  [ts]
  |           b  d          g
  |           p  t          k
  |           m  n          ŋ
  |           v  z          g
  |           f  s          x
                  ü     u
                  i     ï
                     a
                     h....
                         .
                         . ʔ
  ^                      .
  |                     ..>
```

(Degree of Closure — vertical axis label)

By glancing at the chart, a phonetician will readily see that it comes close enough to traditional charts of phonetic sounds to indicate that reaction to characteristics of ranking may have been an important but not necessarily conscious source of them. Close inspection of this and similar charts, however, shows a number of striking

---

[11] I would now call this chart a two-dimensional matrix. The field structure of the matrix is ordered (1) according to a ranking of nearness (by adjacency of matrix cells) (a) of individual units and (b) of classes of units, and (2) according to a ranking of greater to lesser degree of closure (by upper left to lower right diagonal). See also fn. to § 8.61. It is from the matrix (field) characteristics that a phonetic chart derives its validity or value.

differences. Chief among these is the manner in which both /h/ and /ʔ/ (glottal stop) rank below all the consonants and below all the (nonnasalized) vowels, rather than having /ʔ/ grouped with the stops, and /h/ with the fricatives. As E. V. Pike then states, "this low ranking of /h/ and /ʔ/ may be the reason that, as a pair of consonants, they so frequently pattern [in distribution in hyperphonemes, etc.] differently from other consonants, and at times are so closely allied to the structure of the vocalic nucleus" (30). Nor is the /h, ʔ/ group the only one which, as a phonetic class, is frequently found to have a function in a distributional fashion: voiceless stops, voiced stops, nasals, voiceless fricatives, vowels, consonants, and other such large or small phonetic groups are frequently found together as members of distributional classes or subclasses. The attempt to describe phonemic distribution without reference to the phonetic character of the groupings — i.e., in direct disregard of the manifestation mode and feature mode of the phoneme classes — is an attempt to operate without reference to a prominent part of the RELEVANT LINGUISTIC STRUCTURE of the language — one which has historical implications (41).

8.63 *An English Illustration of Emic Classes of Phonemes*

In order for the reader to see the effect of the emic analysis of phoneme classes on a scale larger than was convenient to illustrate in the preceding paragraphs, we give here a tentative structural restatement of the material in Bloomfield's Language (1933a:131-34). We are attempting neither to justify nor to disagree with his analysis of the individual phonemes, although a different analysis at any one point would affect the rest of the description here, but to regroup his data into emic classes, with their phonetic features, their variants, and some of their distributional characteristics stated.

Six emic classes of consonant phonemes may be deduced from Bloomfield's 1933a materials. Our emic classes differ sharply in kind and in membership from the groups which he presents, however, since his goal was to "show that no two of them play exactly the same part" (130) in distribution — negatively or positively — and by this technique "to define every non-syllabic phoneme in our language" (134), whereas our goal here is to show the positive slot groupings in structural, emic classes. The detailed data on vowel groups are not given by him in 1933, and the nuclei in such syllables as *beat, bait, boat, bout, bite, boot,* and the phonetic sequence between the initial and final consonants in *beauty,* are classified by him in the vocalic section of the phonemic system, so that none of their consonantal on-glides or off-glides occur within the materials analyzed. I utilize his orthography:

Emic Phoneme Class 1:

Membership: The phonemes (in order of rank) /ǰ, č; b, d, g; p, t, k; m, n, ŋ; v, ð, z, ž; f, θ, s, š; l, r; w, j; h/.

Phonetic Type or Rank: Contoids and nonsyllabic vocoids
(a vocoid is any sound in which the air escapes out of the mouth, over the center of the tongue, without pronounced or localized friction in the mouth; contoids are nonvocoids. Sample vocoids: [i], [o], [a], [r] (nonflapped), [w], [h]).

Distribution (only insofar as we are discussing it here):
In the first and last consonant slot in CVC syllable structure at the beginning and ending of words or stress groups (V represents any occurring vowel or any nuclear combination of vocoid followed by [j] or [w] — called "compound phonemes" by Bloomfield — or the sequence [juw] which Bloomfield treats as compound); also in the slot filled by C in a CV structure; in the main-final slot sometimes followed by a post-final slot in reference to a sequence VCCC-C which appears to reflect word structure (stem final, plus inflectional element, but not specifically so labelled by Bloomfield in 1933); in pre-final slot, and second pre-final slot, in the same structure. Two of these structures may be usefully shown by using S for syllable matrix, W for word matrix, hyphen for separating stem and inflectional element, V for syllable nucleus, number 1 for the first emic class of phonemes and number 2 for the class occurring in post-final position: S1V1, and WV111-2.

Membership Variants (Alloclasses):

1^a: Composed of /ǰ, č; b, d, g; p, t, k; m, n, –; v, ð, z, –; f, θ, s, š; l, r; w, j; h/ (in which the hyphens are used to indicate those items of the emic class which are omitted from this etic class of phonemes); distributed in WS1V1 in the first slot, WS1^{a}V1, with hyperphonemic-hypermorphemic-slot conditioning of the membership of the class; lacks /ŋ/ and /ž/ (Bloomfield's Group 1); i.e., we find /hæŋ/ (*hang*) but not /ŋæh/, nor words beginning with /ž/.

1^b: Composed of /ǰ, č; b, d, g; p, t, k; m, n, ŋ; v, ð, z, ž; f, θ, s, š; l, r; –, –; –/; distributed in main-final slot as WSV1^b, with hyperphonemic-hypermorphemic-slot conditioning; lacks nonsyllabic nonretroflexed vocoids, i.e., /w, j; h/.

1^{b1}: /ǰ, –; b, –, g; –, –, –; m, n, ŋ; v, ð, z, ž; –, –, –, –; l, r; –, –; –/; a subvariety of the hyperphonemic-hypermorphemic-slot conditioned alloclass 1^b, further conditioned by the following phoneme /d/ which is in post-final position manifesting Class 2 of the phoneme groups, i.e., in the formula WV1^{b1}-2$^{/d/}$; lacks voiceless contoids, /d/, and nonsyllabic nonretroflexed vocoids; seen in *grabbed*, etc. Note the phonetic-feature correlation, of the phonemically-conditioned membership distributions, which permits only voiced contoid or /r/ with voiced contoid here, and the restriction which prevents doublets such as /d/ plus /d/. Note, also, that /d/ in diagonals within the formula refers to a phoneme, but the "b" in 1^{b2} is a numbering device only — not the phoneme /b/.

1^{b2}: /–, č; –, –, –; p, –, k; –, –, –; –, –, –, –; f, θ, s, š; –, –; –, –; –/; a subvariety of the hyperphonemic-hypermorphemic-slot conditioned alloclass, further conditioned by the following phoneme /t/ which is in postfinal position; in formula WV1^{b2}-2$^{/t/}$; lacks voiced contoids and vocoids, /t/, and voiceless vocoid; e.g., *helped*, etc.

1^{b3}: /–, –; b, d, g; –, –, –; m, n, ŋ; v, ð, –, –; –, –, –, –; l, r; –, –; –/; a similar kind of conditioning, with formula WV1^{b3}-2$^{/z/}$; lacks voiceless contoids, sibilants, assibilants, and nonsyllabic nonretroflexed vocoids; e.g., *grabs*, etc.

1^{b4}: /–, –; –, –, –; p, t, k; –, –, –; –, –, –, –; f, θ, –, –; –, –; –/; a further subvariety of 1^{b}, similarly conditioned by the specific manifesting member of the following class, in formula WV1^{b4}-2$^{/s/}$; lacks sibilant or assibilant, voiced contoids, and nonsyllabic vocoids; e.g., *helps*, etc.

1^{c}: /j, č; b, d, –; p, t, k; m, n, –; v, –, z, –; f, θ, s, š; l, –; –, –; –/; distributed in mainfinal slot after a pre-final filled slot, i.e., with conditioning by a hyperphonemic-hypermorphemic shape-type arragement with formula WV11^{c}; lacks /g, ŋ, ð ž/ and nonsyllabic vocoids; contains many sub-alloclasses of this alloclass, conditioned by the specific phonemes manifesting the adjacent classes:

1^{c1}: /j, č; b, d, –; p, t, k; m, n, –; v, –, –, –; f, θ, s, š; –, –; –, –; –/; distributed, as the result of hypermorphemic-slot conditioning, in main final after a pre-final, with conditioning, further, by the preceding phonemes /l, ř/ which occur in pre-final position manifesting Class 1, in formula SV1$^{/l,\ r/}$1^{c1}; lacks voiced velar stop and nasal, nonlabial voiced fricatives, as well as liquids, and nonsyllabic vocoids; *bulge, filch, bulb, held, help, belt, milk, elm, kiln, delve, pelf, wealth, else, Welsh, barge, march, barb, hard, harp, heart, hark, arm, barn, carve, scarf, hearth, farce, harsh.*

1^{c2}: /j, č; –, d, –; –, t, –; –, –, –; –, –, z, –; –, –, s, –; –, –; –, –; –/; distributed in the same hypermorphemic slot as 1^{c1}, with a different phonemic conditioning of its membership by the preceding phoneme /n/ which is in the pre-final slot, in formula WV1$^{/n/}$1^{c2}; contains only voiced and voiceless alveolar affricates, stops, and sibilants; *range, pinch, sand, ant, bronze, month, once.*

1^{c3}: /–, –; –, –, –; p, t, k; –, –, –; –, –, –, –; –, –, –, –; –, –; –, –; –/; in formula WV1$^{/s/}$1^{c3}; contains voiceless stops only; *wasp, test, ask*; homophonous with Class 4.

1^{c4}: /–, –; –, –, –; p, –, –; –, –, –; –, –, –, –; f, –, –, –; –, –; –, –; –/; in WV1$^{/m/}$1^{c4}; contains only voiceless labial stop and fricative; *camp, nymph* (and we omit Bloomfield's *dreamt*, as seeming to be structurally divergent from the balance of his material, since it includes a main final out of place in his classification).

1^{c5}: /–, –; –, –, –; –, t, –; –, –, –; –, –, –, –; –, –, s, –; –, –; –, –; –/; in WV1$^{/p,\ k/}$1^{c5}; contains only alveolar voiceless stop and sibilant; *crypt, lapse, act, tax.*

334   THE MINIMUM UNIT OF THE MANIFESTATION MODE OF THE BEHAVIOREME

1^{c6}: /–, –; –, –, –; –, t, –; –, –, –; –, –, –, –, –; –, –, –, –; –, –; –, –; –/; in $WV1^{/t/}1^{c6}$; contains only alveolar voiceless stop; *lift*.

1^{c7}: /–, –; –, –, –; –, –, k; –, –, –; –, –, –, –; –, θ, –, –; –, –; –, –; –/; in $WV1^{/ŋ/}1^{c7}$; contains only velar voiceless stop and interdental voiceless fricative; *link, length*.

1^{c8}: /–, –; –, –, –; –, –, –; m, –, –; –, –, –, –; –, –, –, –; –, –; –, –; –/; in $WV1^{/ð, z/}1^{c8}$; contains only /m/; *rhythm, chasm*.

1^{c9}: /–, –; –, –, –; –, –, –; –, –, –; –, –, z, –; –, θ, –, –; –, –; –, –; –/; in $WV1^{/d/}1^{c9}$; contains only /z/ and /θ/; *adze, width*.

1^{c10}: /–, –; –, –, –; –, –, –; –, –, –; –, –, –, –; –, θ, s, –; –, –; –, –; –/; in $WV1^{/t/}1^{c10}$; contains only tongue-tip voiceless fricatives; *eighth, Ritz*.

1^d: /–, –; –, d, –; p, t, k; m, n, ŋ; –, ð, z, –; f, –, s, –; l, r; –, –; –/; (we have added to Bloomfield's list Number 23 the phonemes /θ, ž/ as not occurring among his illustrated pre-finals); distributed in pre-final slot in formula $WV1^d1$; lacks affricates, nonretroflexed nonsyllabic vocoids, bilabial voiced stop and fricative, alveopalatal sibilants, and /g, θ/. The sub-alloclasses of this alloclass are largely nonsystematic in reference to their articulatory or ranking groups, though all but one of them includes the liquids /l, r/. In order to save space, and since the same phonemes are involved as in 1^c (but in different groupings), we will list only the positive members of the sub-alloclasses, and the environmental formulas (i.e., without indicating the missing members by the use of hyphens):

1^{d1}: /d; t; n, ŋ; l, r; in $WV1^{d1}1^{/θ/}$; *width, eighth, month, length, wealth, hearth*.

1^{d2}: /d; n/; in $WV1^{d2}1^{/z/}$; *adze, bronze*.

1^{d3}: /p, t, k; n; l, r/; $WV1^{d3}1^{/s/}$; *lapse, Ritz, tax, once, else, farce*.

1^{d4}: /p, k; (m), n; f, s; l, r/; in $WV1^{d4}1^{/t/}$; *crypt, act, (dreamt), ant, lift, test, belt, heart*.

1^{d5}: /m; s; l, r/; in $WV1^{d5}1^{/p/}$; *camp, wasp, help, harp*.

1^{d6}: /m; l, r/; in $WV1^{d6}1^{/f/}$; *nymph, pelf, scarf*.

1^{d7}: /n; l, r/; in $WV1^{d7}1^{/ǰ, č, d/}$; *range, pinch, sand, barge, march, hard, bulge, filch, held*.

1^{d8}: /ŋ; s; l, r/; in $WV1^{d8}1^{/k/}$; *link, ask, milk, hark*.

1^{d9}: /ð, z; l, r/; in $WV1^{d9}1^{/m/}$; *rhythm, chasm, elm, arm*.

1^{d10}: /l, r/; in $WV1^{d10}1^{/b, n, v, š/}$; *bulb, kiln, delve, Welsh, barb, barn, carve, harsh*.

1^e: /–, –; –, –, –; –, –, k; m, –, ŋ; –, –, –, –; –, –, –, –; –, –; –, –; –/; distributed in the second pre-final slot of W, as $WV1^e1^{f}1^g$; contains only non-alveolar nasals, and velar voiceless stop.

1^{e1}: /k/; in $WV^{e1}1^{/s/}1^{/t/}$; here the phonemic conditioning which provides the limitation to the membership of 1^{e1} is not just the following /s/ in the pre-final slot, but the following /s/ *plus* the main-final /t/; *text*.

1^{e2}: /m/; in $WV1^{e2}1^{/p/}1^{/t, s/}$; where the limits of distribution are again laid down by the joint conditioning of the pre-final and main-final slots; *tempt, glimpse*.

1^{e3}: /ŋ/; in WV1^{e3}1$^{/k/}$1$^{/s/}$; *minx*.

1^{e4}: /r/; in WV1^{e4}1$^{/t/}$1$^{/s/}$ and WV1^{e4}1$^{/m/}$1$^{/\theta/}$; *warmth, quartz*.

1^{f}: /−, −; −, −, −; p, t, k; m, −, −; −, −, −, −; −, −, s, −; −, −; −/; distributed in the pre-final slot following a second pre-final and preceding a main final; contains only the voiceless stops, and /m, s/.

1^{f1}: /p/; in WV1$^{/m/}$1^{f1}1$^{/t, s/}$; *tempt, glimpse*.

1^{f2}: /k/; in WV1$^{/ŋ/}$1^{f2}1$^{/s/}$; *minx*.

1^{f3}: /m/; in WV1$^{/r/}$1^{f3}1$^{/\theta/}$; *warmth*.

1^{f4}: /s/; in WV1$^{/k/}$1^{f4}1$^{/t/}$; *text*.

1^{g}: /−, −; −, −, −; −, t, −; −, −, −; −, −, −, −; −, −θ, s, −; −, −; −, −; −/; distributed in main-final slot after two pre-finals; contains tongue-tip voiceless stops and fricatives.

1^{g1}: /t/; in WV1$^{/k/}$1$^{/s/}$1^{g1} and WV1$^{/m/}$1$^{/p/}$1^{g1}; *text, tempt*.

1^{g2}: /θ/; in WV1$^{/r/}$1$^{/m/}$1^{g2}; *warmth*.

1^{g3}: /s/; in WV1$^{/m/}$1$^{/p/}$1^{g3} and WV1$^{/ŋ/}$1$^{/k/}$1$^{g3/}$ and WV1$^{/r/}$1$^{/t/}$1^{g3}; *glimpse, minx, quartz*.

1^{h}: /−, −; −, −, −; p, t, k; m, n, −; −, −, −, −; f, −, −, −; l, −; w, −; −/; distributed in the second slot of a two-consonant pre-syllabic cluster which begins with the phoneme /s/, in the hyperphonemic pattern S/s/1^{h}v; conditioned, therefore, jointly by hyperphonemic slot and by phonemic environment (since /s/ elsewhere constitutes an emic class with a unique member, numbered Class 3, we may re-formularize this item as S31^{h}V, and restate the conditioning as caused jointly by the hyperphonemic slot and by the phonemic class, which in turn leaves it indeterminate as to whether the individual phoneme is the conditioning element, or the class composed of that phoneme — but similar indeterminacies are inherent in any situation involving emic classes of unique membership, as we indicated in § 7.324); contains voiceless stops and labial fricative, the nasals, the lateral, and the labial vocoid; *spin, stay, sky, small, snail, sphere, slew, swim*.

Emic Phoneme Class 2:

Membership: /d, t; z, s/.

Phonetic Type or Rank: Voiced and voiceless alveolar stops and sibilants.

Distribution: Occurs as the post-final consonant in the structures WV1-2, WV11-2, and WV111-2, in which the inflectional elements constituting the morphemes manifested by this phoneme class constitute, in addition, the manifested forms of a class of tagmemes (§ 7.6) which occur in the same relative slot — a suffixal slot — in numerous hypermorphemic structures (i.e., in morphemically-complex words).

Membership Variants (Alloclasses):

2^a: /d, –; –, –/; occurs after, and conditioned in membership by, the class 1^{b1} (for which see above) in WV1^{b1}-2^a (or other formulas with added pre-final, or pre-final plus second pre-final), i.e., after a slightly restricted list of voiced contoids and /r/; e.g., *grabbed*, etc.

2^b: /–, t; –, –/; occurs after, and conditioned by, the members of phoneme class 1^{b2} in WV1^{b2}-2^b etc.; e.g., *helped*, *glimpsed*, etc.

2^c: /–, –; z, –/; in WV1^{b3}-2^c, etc.; e.g., *grabs*, etc.

2^d: /–, –; –, s/; in WV1^{b4}-2^d, etc., e.g., *helps*, etc.

Emic Phoneme Class 3:

Membership: /s/.

Phonetic Type or Rank: Voiceless alveolar sibilant.

Distribution: Occurs, as we indicated at the end of the discussion of Class 1, in the hyperphonemic structure S3$1^h$V. In addition, it occurs in the hyperphonemic structure S345V as the first of a sequence of three pre-syllabic consonants. (Note that just as an emic class of morphemes may occur in one of several tagmemic slots §§ 7.742-46, 7.313(2)), so a class of phonemes may occur in several hyperphonemic or hypermorphemic slots.) Limitations as to the membership of Class 5 after Class 3 plus Class 4 give some specific distributional restrictions of the groupings in which Class 3 occurs, as follows: S3$4^{/p/}5^{/l/}$V, S34$5^{/r/}$V, and S3$4^{/k/}5^{/w/}$V, yielding the forms *split, spray, stray, scratch, squall*, in addition to *spin, stay, sky, small, snail, sphere, slew, shrink, swim*, from S3$1^h$V, illustrated above with 1^h.

Membership Variants: None.

Emic Phoneme Class 4:

Membership: /p, t, k/.

Phonetic Type or Rank: Voiceless stops.

Distribution: We turn now to the second class of the sequences of classes in the structure S345V, and note that the second position in that sequence defines the distributional characteristics of Class 4, which, within the data of Bloomfield's with which we are concerned, occurs only here as a separate class (but the same phonemes constitute part of the larger Class 1, also, in the hierarchy of such classes, and the emic subclass is homophonous with the etic class 1^{c3}).

THE MINIMUM UNIT OF THE MANIFESTATION MODE OF THE BEHAVIOREME   337

Membership Variants (Alloclasses):

4ª: /p, t, k/ — the complete membership — occurs in S34ª5/r/V, i.e., between /s/ and /r/ in an initial cluster of three consonants; *spray, stray, scratch.*

4ᵇ: /p, –, –/; in S34ᵇ5/l/V; *split.*

4ᶜ: /–, –, k/; in S34ᶜ5/w/V; *squall.*

Emic Phoneme Class 5:

Membership: /l, r; w/. (Probably most analysts would add /j/ to this list; Bloomfield does not do so since he treats /juw/ as a compound phoneme in his list *beauty, gules, pew, cue, muse, new, view, few, spew, skew*):

Phonetic Type or Rank: Liquids, and labial vocoid.

Distribution: Occurs as the third of a three-consonant sequence in the hyperphonemic structure S345V, and as the second of two consonants in the structure S65V.

Membership Variants:

5ª: /l, r; w/; S6/g, k/5ªV; contains the full class membership; after the velars of Class 6; *glue, clay, gray, crow, Gwynne, quick.*

5ᵇ: /l, r; –/; in S6/b, p, f/5ᵇV; contains the liquids; conditioned by the labials of Class 6; *blue, play, flew, bray, pray, fray.*

5ᶜ: /l, –; w/; in S6/s/5ᶜV; *slew, swim.*

5ᵈ: /l, –; –/; in S34/p/5ᵈV; *split.*

5ᵉ: /–, r; w/; in S6/d, t, θ /5ᵉV; contains the nontongue-tip consonants of 5; conditioned by the nonsibilant tongue-tip contoids of 6; *dray, dwell, tray, twin, three, thwart.*

5ᶠ: /– r; –/; in S345ᶠV, conditioned by the slot in the three-consonant sequence of the hyperphonemic pattern, *spray, stray, scratch*; and in S6/š/5ᶠ, *shrink.*

5ᵍ: /–, –; w/; in S34/k/5ᵍV, *squall*; and in S6/h/5ᵍ, *when* [hwen].

Emic Phoneme Class 6:

Membership: /b, d, g; p, t, k; f, θ, s, š; h/.

Phonetic Type or Rank: voiced and voiceless stops, voiceless fricatives, and voiceless nonsyllabic vocoid.

Distribution: Occurs as the first of a two-consonant sequence in the structure S65V.
Membership Variants:

6ª: /b, d, g; p, t, k; f, θ, –, š; –/; in S6ª5/r/V; *bray, dray, gray, pray, tray, crow, fray three, shrink*.

6ᵇ: /b, –, g; p. –, k; f, –, s, –; –/; in S6ᵇ5/l/V; lacks the flat tongue-tip contoids, and /š, h/; *blue, glue, play, clay, flew, slew*.

6ᶜ: /–, d, g; –, t, k; –, θ, s, –; h/; in S6ᶜ5/w/V; lacks the labials, and š (which for many speakers also has something of a labial character); conditioned by the labial of Class 5 following it; *dwell, Gwynne, twin, quick, thwart, swim, when*.

Further Emic Phoneme Classes in English:

The list of emic classes of phonemes in a language is by no means infinite; once the conditioned classes are treated as submembers of the total class, the apparent inexhaustible number is greatly reduced, even as the fifty four groups above have been analyzed as constituting just six emic classes.

Bloomfield in his 1933 treatment hints at further groupings, and conditioning restrictions, but these still leave a relatively small number of classes. Thus the syllabic elements of the syllable nucleus are themselves in part complex — composed of sequences of elements — and in part simple, and in part are vocoids and in part syllabic contoids, and have distributional restrictions in reference to hyperphonemic and hypermorphemic slots. These various kinds of nuclei have additional restrictions and subgroupings in reference to subgroupings of consonants which can precede and follow them. Some of the distributional sequence types (both grammatical and phonological) not discussed in 1933a are treated in his work of 1935. (I presume further such details occur in his work on the structure of learned words (1933b), which I have not seen.)

8.64 *A Hierarchy of English Classes of Phonemes*

In the previous section we on occasion indicated that a small emic class of phonemes was distributed, within the system of phonemes, in a larger class of phonemes, in a hierarchy of such phonemes. It is useful to refer to some of these data in a further paragraph here.

The groups of phonemes distributionally united into classes usually have one or more contrastive-identificational features of these phonemes in common. The smaller the group of phonemes in a class, the more features they may each contain in common, such that each is separated by only one such feature: thus Class 4, of /p, t, k/, have in common the characteristics of nonsyllabic and contoidal nature, occlusion of the air stream, oral articulation, and voicelessness, but are separated from each other by the specific point of articulation in the mouth. This class is included in Class 6, however, which also includes the phonemes /b, d, g, f, θ, s, š, h/; in the larger class, voiced sounds are included, as well as one vocoid (/h/), and oral fricatives, so that the members have fewer elements in common. Class 1, at the top of the consonantal hierarchy, includes all of these, as well as the affricates, nasals, voiced fricatives, liquids, and voiced nonsyllabic vocoids.

Occasionally, furthermore, on the lower levels of the hierarchy, there may occur classes which include among their membership consonants which by CLASS CLEAVAGE belong to more than one other low-level class. Thus, for example, Class 2 contains /d, t, z, s/, of which /t/ occurs in the small Class 4; the /s/ elsewhere constitutes the entire membership of Class 3, and also enters Class 6; the /d/ and /t/ and /s/ enter Class 6; whereas /z/ occurs additionally, within the materials analyzed here, only in Class 1.

8.65 *Phonemically-Complex Members of an Emic Class of Phonemes*

The phonemes enter hierarchies of more than one kind, however. Not only do they enter hierarchies of more inclusive groupings whithin the system, but they also enter hierarchies in more and more inclusive structural units in sequences. It is precisely this characteristic which gives rise to and is implied by the mutually-restrictive membership of alloclasses in sequence — the correlation restrictions mentioned in §§ 8.621, 8.63. Even more inclusive are the unitary patterns implied, by this argument, when one studies the mutual restrictions between consonantal occurrences and vocalic occurrences in a structure such as CCVC — restrictions hinted at, but not illustrated, toward the end of § 8.63. The fact (illustrated in § 8.63) that the consonants in a structure such as CCCV may have different potential sequential relations and occurrences than in the structure VCCC is a further reason why we must conclude that phoneme sequences have some kind of unitary structure, in an expanding hierarchy of sequential units, and that different sequences in different slots may have a different unitary and hierarchial structure.

As we have morphemically-simple, morphemically-complex, and morphemically-simple-plus-morphemically-complex classes of morphemes (§§ 7.313(1), 7.313(3), 7.44), so we can have phoneme classes whose membership is not only in part composed of single phonemes (as illustrated in § 8.63), but which is also composed (or even exclusively composed) of two or more phonemes in sequence, as PHONEMICALLY-COMPLEX MEMBERS OF A PHONEME CLASS. It is at this point that we begin to justify the treatment of a CONSONANT CLUSTER as a unit of some kind — it is a phonemically-complex unitary member of a certain class of phonemes occurring in some slot in some larger structure of hyperphonemic, morphemic, hypermorphemic, tagmemic, hypertagmemic, utteremic, or hyperutteremic type. Similarly, it is this approach which in part justifies our speaking of the NUCLEUS OF A SYLLABLE (whether it is composed of one or more phonemes, or of vowels only, or of vowel plus consonant) as we have done tentatively already (§ 8.63) in reference to the syllable nucleus in *bite*, and shall do more so later (§§ 9.223, 9.243, 9.73). Since, however, these phonemically-complex classes of elements can only be determined in reference to their distribution or function in larger units, the further justification for treating clusters and nuclei as units[12] of some kind must wait until the discussion of the PHONEMIC SHAPE TYPES of these units in later chapters (but see § 6.64, for morphemic shape types, and § 7.313(2), for shape types of morpheme classes as components of the feature mode of tagmemes).

8.66 *Emic Slot-Class Units in Phonology*

Since we have been dealing with classes of phonemes, and with slots within which these classes are distributed, and since the classes in part define the slots and the slots in part define the classes, we next inquire: Should we postulate an emic unit composed of a correlation between an emic phonological or grammatical shape-type slot and an emic phonological class, as we did earlier between a tagmemic slot and a morphemic class (i.e., the tagmeme, Chapter 7)?

Our answer is in the affirmative: A structural correlation between an emic class of phonemes and an emic slot in the shape type of some phonological or grammatical unit must itself constitute a kind of emic unit. The "C" (or the "V") in the CVC formula of an emic syllable type, or in the formula of a morpheme shape type, etc., is the symbolization of a PHONEMIC SLOT-CLASS CORRELATIVE.[13] It differs from the tagmeme, which is a morphemic slot-class correlative, (1) in that its manifesting elements are members of classes of phonemes, instead of classes of morphemes, and (2) in that it is not a minimum unit of any mode of the uttereme, but is a unit in the phonological hierarchical system of the manifestation mode of the uttereme, whereas the tagmeme must be set up as the minimum unit of the distribution mode of the uttereme, for reasons discussed in Chapter 7. It is this latter reason which made it highly desirable to coin a short name for the tagmeme, paralleling the other minimal terms — morpheme and phoneme — but which makes it much less necessary to do so for the phonemic slot-class correlative. The structural place of the tagmeme in the entire system makes reference to it very frequent, furthermore, and a short term desirable — more so than the disadvantage of an extra term in our linguistic vocabulary — whereas the need for a short term is not so pressing for the phonological unit, and hence we have not felt the necessity of multiplying coined terms further at this part of the system.

Further discussion of the specific function of such a phonemic slot-class correlative in hyperphonemes will be delayed until §§ 9.243-45.

---

[12] See, now, Crawford's analysis of phonological strings and phonological tagmemes (1963), and implications for our model discussed in §12.5.

[13] Crawford (1963) has gone farther than this, treating the phonemic-slot-class correlative as a phonotagmeme on a par with our grammatical one. See below, § 12.5.

8.67 *Order or Relationship as a Conceptualized Hypostasis*

Before reaching those sections, it may be wise to make specific rejection of one point of view which the reader might feel is implied by the acceptance of the slot-class correlation as leading to an emic unit. Is the order, itself, in which two or more phonemes occur to be considered an emic unit of nonhypostatic behavior? Our answer is negative. Just as we previously rejected the tagmemic slot as an emic unit of nonhypostatic behavior, treating it rather as the conceptualized hypostasis of the analyst (§ 7.321), so here we reject both the phonemic slot and the abstracted ORDER of phonemes as emic units of nonhypostatized behavior, and treat them as emic units of conceptualized hypostasis in the behavior of the analyst. Since the arguments to reach this conclusion are approximately the same as for the handling of the tagmemic slot, it is not necessary to repeat them here.

Even when it is convenient to call order phonemic, where one has contrastive arrangements such as in *act* /ækt/, *tack* /tæk/, and *cat* /kæt/, the order does not constitute an eme of nonhypostatic behavior. Rather one notes that, as we suggested in § 7.321, an emic unit is always an eme, whereas an emic characteristic may in some instances constitute an eme in its own right, and in other instances may be only the contrastive-identificational feature of an eme, or of some mode of an eme. This same point of view was given also in relation to phonetic contrastive-identificational features of phonemes, in § 8.35.

Similarly, we reject RELATIONSHIP (or OPPOSITION) between phonemes, or between phoneme classes, or between phonemes within phoneme classes, as constituting an emic unit of nonhypostatic behavior. We accept it, however, as an emic unit of conceptualized hypostasis in the behavior of the analyst. This again leads us to treat physical activity as essential to all of our emic units (with neural and verbal activity as the manifestation of emic units of conceptualized hypostasis). For the earlier discussion of this problem, as regards relationships between morphemes, see § 6.7; in reference to tagmemes versus constructions, see § 7.85; cf. also § 8.84.

8.7 *Phonetics*

In Chapters 6 and 7 we listed numerous characteristics of etic units discussed in those chapters, after having given a more specific discussion of the structural, emic matters. It is useful to do the same here, but more briefly.

8.71 *Segmentation of a Continuum into Phones*

In determining the number of phones within a particular continuum, the analyst attempts to observe the number of articulatory movements or changes of articulatory movement within that continuum, in accordance with the theory discussed in §§ 8.41-

42 (and Pike, 1943a:107-16). Each time an articulatory change occurs, the analyst assumes that a different phone has begun, often with the border indeterminate. These changes he may sometimes observe directly, as when sounds are involved in which lip movements are relevant; or he may deduce them, if invisible, by determining the kind of movements which he would have had to have made to produce such a sound; or he may utilize X-ray machines or the like to take still or moving pictures of such movements. On the field the last device is seldom possible, however.

8.72 *Etic Classificatory Criteria for Phone Types*

In order to give an etic classification and etic description of a phone once it is segmented from a continuum, a number of criteria are available. Since I have written at length concerning these characteristics elsewhere, I shall only allude to them briefly here.

(a) Is an air stream involved in the production of the sound, or is some non-airstream mechanism used? (Pike, 1943a:85-106, 154) Since air streams are present during the production of almost every sound with which we as linguists are concerned, we shall assume below that the phone is one of these types.

(b) How and where is the air stream initiated? by lung pressure? by pharyngeal movement? by tongue movement? by other movement? (Pike, 1943a:87-103, 129, 154)

(c) Is the direction of movement such as to move the air stream inward? outward? (Pike, 1943a:87-103)

(d) Is there a closure (or closures) which prevents the air stream from escaping by one vocal cavity while permitting it to escape by another? If so, which? oral? nasal? (Pike, 1943a:129-30, 136, 154)

(e) What is the degree of interruption of the air stream? complete? partial? with strong localized friction? with little or no localized friction (i.e., cavity friction)? (Pike, 1943a:137-48)

(f) How many strictures (points of contact or near contact) are there in the articulatory production, and where are they? at lips? teeth? tongue tip? tongue blade? tongue mid or back? tongue root? velum? uvula? velic? faucal pillars? pharyngeal wall? epiglottis? vocal cords? arytenoid cartilages? esophagus? (Pike, 1943a:122-24, 154)

(g) What is the rank of each stricture? primary? subprimary? secondary? tertiary? adjunct? acme? (§ 8.623, and Pike, 1943a:130-36).

(h) What is the degree of stricture at each of these points of articulation, in addition to that indicated in (e)? in degree of closure? in time? in extension of point of contact, lengthwise or sidewise? in height of opening between the articulator and the top of the passageway? (Pike, 1943a:137-48)

(i) What is the type of articulation? flapped? trilled or vibratory? normal? spasmodic? (Pike, 1943a:124-29, 154)

(j) What is the relative strength of articulation or of the resulting sound? strong? weak? (Pike, 1943a:128-29)

(k) What is the shape of the articulator? flat? grooved? rounded? convex? retracted? expanded? protruded? with central air escape? with lateral air escape? with central or lateral adjunct contact? (Pike, 1943a:121-22, 136-37)

(l) What is its segment type? a crest of movement? a trough? a crossing glide with simultaneous crest and trough? a bulge of stricture, or a time bulge? (§ 8.42; Pike, 1943a:107-16)

(m) What is its placement in relation to the syllable in which it is contained? nuclear? vocalic? syllabic? nonsyllabic? consonantal? marginal? presyllabic? postsyllabic? at an indeterminate syllable juncture? (§§ 8.51, 9.221-25; Pike, 1943a:116-20, 145)

(n) What is its placement in relation to the stress group? in a stressed syllable? in an unstressed syllable? (§ 8.51; Pike, 1943a:119)

(o) What is its placement in relation to the breath group, or other phonological unit? (§§ 8.51, 9.232, 9.32)

(p) What is its placement in relation to various grammatical units? the morph or morpheme? higher-layered grammatical units? (§ 8.52)

8.73 *Etic Criteria for Phones in Relation to their Distribution Classes*

(a) Do the phones in this distribution class occur in only one congruent system? or more than one? whisper? song? formal? informal? rapid? slow? other? (§ 8.61)

(b) Is the class large relative to other distribution classes in the language? small? with only one member? (§ 8.63)

(c) Is it a subclasss of a larger class? If so, is the subclass membership determined by correlation with the membership of other classes? or by specific hyperphonetic slot occurrence? or grammatical occurrence? (§§ 8.621-22, 8.63-64)

(d) Does the class occur in more than one hyperphonetic or grammatical slot? If so, which? (§§ 8.621, 8.51-52, 8.63)

(e) Is there a phonetic characteristic common to all members of the class? or more than one such characteristic? if so, what is this characteristic or group of characteristics? or characteristic common to phonetic subgroups of the class? (§§ 8.623, 8.3)

(f) What is the relative rank of such a group of sounds, in accordance with its phonetic characteristics? Is it in a hierarchy of rank, or does it cut across the characteristics of various other groups? (§§ 8.623, 8.63 Class 2)

(g) Are there phonetically-complex members of the class? (§ 8.65)

8.74 *Summary of the Relation of Phones to Phonemes*

In order to pass from a pre-structural, etic description of the minimum units of the manifestation mode of the uttereme to an emic description of these minimum units, an emic procedure is necessary, and etic training highly desirable, as it is for utteretics (§ 5.55), for morphetics (§ 6.84), and for tagmatics (§7.74).

Basic to such a procedure is the understanding of the relationship of phones to phonemes.

Every phone may be assumed to comprise either
- (a) a free variant of a phoneme (§ 8.444; Pike, 1947c:122-27)
- or (b) a conditioned variant of a phoneme (§ 8.441-443; Pike, 1947c:84-104)
- or (c) part of a phonetically-complex variant of a phoneme or one of its manifested forms (§ 8.445: Pike, 1947c:131-37)
- or (d) a sequence of two or more manifested variants of phonemes, so that the tentative phone needs further segmentation (§ 8.71; Pike, 1947c:67, 117b-120)
- or (e) a fused composite variant of two or more partially or completely simultaneous phonemes (§ 8.446; Pike, 1947c:138-40)
- or (f) an error of phonetic recording which would be eliminated by more accurate rechecking;
- and (g) the phonemes composed of these phones are members of emic distribution classes of phonemes (§§ 8.62-65) within the larger system of the language as a whole (§ 8.61), which in part they reciprocally constitute.

8.8 *Bibliographical Comments on Chapter 8*

The term *acteme* is taken from Zipf (1935:301-02); *kineme* from Birdwhistell (1952); *phoneme* from current usage, which begins with Baudouin de Courtenay and his pupil Kruszewski (1779 and 1881, reference in Firth, 1934).

8.81 *The History of Phonemics and of Articulatory Phonetics*

8.811 *On Early Phonemics*

For the term phoneme, Bloomfield also mentions (1932:228-29), its early use by de Saussure "in much the present value" in his Mémoire (1878), and "explicit formulations" in Baudouin de Courtenay, *Versuch einer Theorie der phonetischen Alternationen* (1895), 9; Sweet, *The Practical Study of Languages* (1899), 18; Boas, *BAE Bulletin 40*, Vol. 1 (1911), 16; [Daniel Jones] *Principles of the International Phonetic Association* (1912); de Saussure, *Cours de linguistique générale*² (1922), 55; 63 (first edition, 1915, from much older lecture notes); Sapir, *Language* (1921), 18, 47, 57, and in *Language* 1.37 (1925); though "not all these authors use the term *phoneme*, and the term phoneme has been used also in other senses". Daniel Jones learned about phonemics from Ščerba (pupil of Baudouin de Courtenay) and first mentions it in a lecture in 1917, printed in the Transactions for 1917-20 (private communication). For the relation of scholars of the Prague school to Baudouin de Courtenay and to Ščerba, see Trubetzkoy (1949:xxvii). Note, also, the reference to "distinctive sounds" by Sweet (1900b). Phonemic principles were used very early, to some extent, in all alphabetical writing; thus Haugen (1950a) points to the use of minimal pairs for contrasting phonemes, used in the middle of the twelfth century by an unknown author. For further reference to early phoneme materials, see Arend (1934), Hjelmslev (1947: 72n), Pedersen (1928).

For the early history of phonemics, from a British point of view, see D. Jones (1957); for recent British material, see summary and bibliography in O'Connor (1957); for history of the phonetic alphabet, see Albright (1958).

8.812 *On Phonemics in the United States*

In this country, however, phonemics has had a development to a considerable extent independent of these European elements, and still reflects in its interests the differences which are rooted in its origin. Although Bloomfield early spoke of "distinctive" features and sounds (1917:9, 134), presumably under the influence of Sweet of England (Jakobson, private communication, who says that Bloomfield mentioned this fact to him, in reference to Sweet 1900b), the character of American phonemics seems to be due more especially to the influence of Sapir. Sapir's outlook, in turn, grew from his observations of the reactions of persons to the SYSTEM of their CULTURE as a whole (note quotation above, § 2.1), and to their systems of sounds, more specifically, as he watched American Indians try to write their own languages (1921:58; and see further references above, § 2.74). It was on the basis of such experiences that he elaborated the material on the contrasting relationships of systems of phonemes (1925, in his Selected Writings: 33-45) which set the tone for the kind of interest in a system of *units* that has been evident here — and which is quite in contrast to the interest in a system of *oppositions*, which engrossed much of the attention of European phonemicists soon after that, and which began without their knowledge of the work of Sapir (for example, it was some months after the presentation by Jakobson and others, of the phonemic propositions at the First International Congress of Linguistics in 1928, that Sapir's work was called to his attention — private communication from Jakobson — and a year before references to Sapir's materials are found in the writings of members of the Prague School, as in Mathesius, 1929:67, and Trubetzkoy, 1929:66n). For a detailed listing and brief characterization of the many items on phonemics which appeared during the next decade and more, see Fischer-Jørgensen (1941).

The early work on Sapir, showing how two different systems could be created from a single set of phonetic elements (1925 in his Selected Writings), the careful discussions of Bloomfield (1933a), and the methodological work of Swadesh showing how phonemic principles were to be applied and how interpretation of long consonants grew out of such principles (1934, 1935a, 1937a) largely comprise the basis upon which my own understanding of phonemics grew.

A careful review of the various early attempts to define the phoneme is given by Twaddell (1935), along with a critique of then-current phonemic theory, in reference to the theoretical difficulty of equating phonemic variants. To the questions which he raised, various persons attempted answers — e.g., Vachek (1936), Andrade (1936, with reply by Twaddell, 1936a), Swadesh (1935b, with reply by Twaddell, 1936b). For summary of early phonemics see also Chao (1934:363-67).

Work by Trager and Bloch on English vowels (1941; cf. also Bloch and Trager, 1942) set the pattern for much American work for the next decade; both of these authors had written earlier papers — Bloch (1935) differing radically and Trager (1935) differing mildly from the 1942 positions — Bloch followed up the problems of analysis by discussing phonemic overlapping (1941), while Trager engaged in special studies such as that of allophones of the English /t/ (1942). The early six-vowel system for over-all pattern suggested by Trager and Bloch was later replaced with a nine-vowel system by Trager and Smith (1951); here the technology — but not the explicit theory — involves the start on a lexical-phonological basis by choice of sets of dialectal variants found in certain lexemes. From this tacit assumption of lexemic-phonemic identity there was developed an explicit system of over-all pattern of nine vocoid types as points of reference for all English dialects. Reviews of this crucial part of American linguistic development are found in Sledd (1955), and — adversely — in O'Connor (1951). Note also Haugen, for whom the Trager-Smith material should be regarded "as a useful phonetic alphabet" (1960:62-63) in reference to its attempts to treat various dialects.

For more recent developments in the United States, including the rejection of conventional phonemics by Chomsky, note references in §§ 8.814, 8.815, 8.84, 8.87. Note also historical statement of linguistic development by R. Hall (1951, 1952) and by Lane (1945, 1946). For some discussion of phonological universals, see Saporta (in Greenberg, 1963:48-57) and Ferguson (in Greenberg, 1963:42-47).

8.813 *On Articulatory and Acoustic Phonetics*

The study of the articulatory production of sounds has a much longer history than the study of phonemics, even though in the former — phonetics — a large amount of phonemic data was implicit. Not only have there been competent phoneticians in England for three hundred and fifty years (e.g., J. Hart, 1569; note many others mentioned in J. R. Firth, 1947, and in Abercrombie, 1949) and on the continent (e.g., Montanus, 1635), but also there were phonetic elements in the grammars of ancient Greece and Rome (cf. Sturtevant, 1940) and several hundred years B.C. in India (see documentation in W. S. Allen, 1953a). In the present generation a great deal of further work has been done (bibliography in Pike, 1943a). It has been only two decades, however, since the appearance of the first attempt to give a systematic exposition of articulatory phonetics without a tacit reliance on unanalyzed phonemic matters (Pike, 1943a). Since then, the primary attention in respect to phonetics in this country has shifted to interest in acoustic analysis of sounds, under the impact of the invention of the sound spectograph (e.g., R. Potter, Kopp, and Green, 1947; Joos, 1948; Jakobson, Fant, and Halle, 1952). Within the theory of this volume, however, it is evident that the study of physical articulations continues to hold a highly important place, since study of waves of movement constitutes a point of contact with behavior in general, more readily than can the study of waves of sound.

The attempt to put the study of articulatory phonetics on a sound experimental basis goes back to 1874, to a committee appointed by the Société Linguistique de Paris, with Hovet, Morey, and Rosapelly; Abbé Rousselot in 1885 began to work with them, and is considered the founder of experimental phonetics, followed later in the USA by Sheldon, Grandgent, Weeks, Josselyn, Scripture, and others (data from Phonetics, 1927; cf. also Stetson, 1951, 10a).

The need for continued, careful study of articulatory phonetics as a basis for linguistic description is emphasized by Ladefoged who deplores the fact that "...most of the auditory-articulatory descriptions of American linguists are simply personal impressionistic remarks" (1960a:390). For a summary of recent British work note O'Connor (1957). For a summary and bibliography of palatography see Moses (1962). Summary and new articles on work in phonetics are found also in Kaiser (1957). Extensive discussion of physiological phonetics occurs in Husson (1959), including reference to physiological studies much more extensive than are reflected in earlier treatments of tongue movements. The introduction of electromyographic techniques and of high-speed ex-rays bring to articulatory studies new tools and contributions. Note the extensive studies of syllable production by investigation of electrical discharge of the muscles, and of other techniques for the study of syllables (Broadbent and Ladefoged, 1959, 1960; Ladefoged [with Draper and Whitteridge], 1958). (Note fuller bibliographic discussion of the syllable in §§ 9.72-73, and fnn. to §§ 9.221, 9.222, 9.225, 9.232, 9.311, 9.312.) Techniques have also been developed for studying vocal cord vibration by shining a light through the neck; a photo electric cell records changes in the light which gets through the opening and closing vocal cords (Fant and Sonesson, 1963).

Typologies of the phonetic characteristics of phonemic systems have continued to occur; note Hockett (1955), Wolff (1959), and Voegelin and Yegerlehner (1956). Need for a universal etics — "a universal phonetic theory" — is found in Chomsky (1962, §§ 4.2, 4.3 — pp. 531, 537, 554).

Acoustic study of phonetics has had a tremendous development since the invention of the sound spectrograph. Note Joos' basic summary of the technique (1948); and Pulgram (1959). For bibliographical listings note Fant (in Proceedings of the Eighth..., 1958) and summary in Fischer-Jørgenson (in Proceedings of the Eighth..., 1958).

Of immediate relevance to our theoretical discussion is Jakobson's attempt to set up a universal phonetic etics in terms of a dozen or so distinctive features (polar oppositions, in which a feature is a relationship between a contrastive pair, not one term of the opposition). Some confusion arises in their materials since in some instances it is the binary oppositions, as wholes, which are treated (and counted) as the distinctive features: "The inherent distinctive features which we detect in the languages of the world... amount to twelve binary oppositions", Jakobson, Fant and Halle, (1952:40; repeated in Jakobson and Halle, 1956:28-29). "The choice [sic] between the two opposites may be termed *distinctive feature*" (1952:3); in "the strictly relational terms of distinctive features" the "invariant is the opposition" (5). Elsewhere, however, these authors treat the poles or terms of the opposition as if they were features, since the poles are given names ("vocalic vs. non-vocalic") and a particular phoneme can possess or contain a "bundle of distinctive features" which are invariant properties (cf. 1956:13) and, for example, sounds with a single periodic source are "phonemes possessing the vocalic feature" [not the two poles of the opposition] (1952:18) with the components extractable (1956:33). (And see discussion of binarism below, in § 8.84). For criticism of the "distinctive function of distinctive features" which "may be taken over by the (normally) redundant features" such that "the spurious elegance surely backfires", see Bar-Hillel (1957:327). For discussion of redundancy, and native awareness of it, see Garner (1962:282).

There has been a great deal of difficulty in finding a one-to-one (bi-unique) correlation between acoustic properties, distinctive features, and articulatory features. Ferguson, in discussing Halle's work, considers that one of "the most encouraging developments in Halle's treatment is the tacit abandonment of the assumption that there is an acoustical property, no matter how complex, corresponding to each distinctive feature" (1962:297); for some components there is a "multiplicity of cues", (298). Similarly, Trim states that we may say, in general, "that no single phonetic cue is indispensable to the identification of a phonological unit" and that they may be found "in any number of acoustic dimensions over an indefinite stretch of the utterance" (1962:776); Fant tells us that "Alternative solutions or formulations of the acoustic counterpart of a feature or even alternative choices of features are possible so that the system chosen by the structural linguist may not be the same as that adopted by the engineer or phonetician" (1960:213). Specifically, there is a strong developing conviction that there is a more immediate correlation between perceptual units and articulatory units than between perceptual and acoustic ones (see references in §§ 8.41, 8.815).

Voegelin's claim also needs to be given close attention — that, although the distinctive feature scheme comprises the best componential typology available, it is "still a typology whose prerequisite, as for all typologies, is a prior structural statement — here, in terms of unit phonemes" (1959:14).

For the assigning of zero to a cell of a distinctive feature matrix in order to avoid redundancy in specification of the same features once sounds have been assigned to a particular place in the tree underlying the matrix see Halle (1959a:34-36, 40, 46) but an alternative choice for the first binary branchings lead to different placement of the zeros.

For a feature as "best regarded as a proportion between two phonemes" see Haugen (1962:654).

Acoustic material is continually appearing in the journals, and in laboratory reports — for example in those of the Speech Transmission Laboratory, Royal Institute of Technology, Stockholm. Note also various authors in Proceedings of the Fourth International Congress of Phonetic Sciences.

For reference to the general phonetics of units larger than the phoneme note Chapter 9.

Problems of segmentation have given much difficulty. For bibliography of problems in acoustic segmentation and commutation, note Lisker, Cooper and Liberman (1962:89, fn. 14). For one attempt at speech synthesis from stored segments note Sivertsen and Peterson (1960). The assumption of Peterson, Wang and Sivertsen that intelligibility "is carried by the more sustained or target positions" is rejected by Liberman, Ingemann, and others (1959:1493). Conventional phonemics continues to have difficulty in segmenting materials; note Hockett, in discussing alternatives of segmenting English vowel nuclei (1955:160), and discussion of English affricates, some of which he refuses to segment (161).

8.814 *On the Validity of the Phonemic Principle*

The validity of phonemic theory has been called in question. W. S. Allen's objection is based on the assumption that some features "are relevant to the development of the language" (1951b:133), and that ordinary phonemic descriptions do not necessarily include these features: "and 'Grimm's Law' became a law only when Verner recognized the phonological incomparability of pre-tonic and post-tonic *-t-, etc." (131). "In short", he continues, "it does not seem to be the best structuralism to set up categories [presumably phonemes] which break down in diachronic and comparative study: the only existing phonemic theory which comes near to meeting the comparativist's requirements is that proposed by Freeman Twaddell, which has little but the name in common with other theories" (131). Also, "The trouble is that the letters of a phonemic or near-phonemic transcription are exclusively concerned with those particular features which happen at the time to be significant from the narrow viewpoint of word-differentiation; they tell us nothing of the more stable processes of which the articulatory spectrum is composed, and little of the features whereby the continuum of utterance is maintained" (135-36); for more recent statements by Allen, see 1953b:84-85; 1954:556 fnn. 2, 4; and cf. 1953a:8, 65). In reply, the theory presented in this volume would maintain (1) that the study of language as a functioning system of human behavior is not a narrow viewpoint, but far more basic to the study of man than is the hypostasis of the changes which have occurred through time; (2) that it is more easy to have hindsight as to which features *have been* relevant in any one particular language at any one particular time than it is foresight as to which *will certainly be* relevant in any one direction (since the same phonological conditions do not always produce the same results — else no uniform dialect could ever develop divergent dialects); (3) that the phonemicist may describe all the phonetic components which he can identify — and hence have them available for comparativist purposes — even though treating in a special way those features contrastively relevant in communication; and (4) that the components of a continuum which so frequently are relevant to change of phonemes are handled, in this theory, within the contrastive-identificational components of higher-layered structural units such as the emic syllable and emic stress groups and breath groups (Chapter 9), so that a structural, emic approach need not be abandoned in order to make room for them — on the contrary, the structural approach becomes even more relevant.

Specifically in this latter connection, for example, many of the phonological characteristics subsumed under the label of 'prosodies' by Hjelmslev (1936), H. J. Uldall (1936), Firth (1949, 1951a, 1952), and others, find their place in a coherent emic theory within higher-layered units of the phonological hierarchy and the interpenetration of the phonological with the grammatical hierarchies. In the following quotations, note the extent to which 'prosodies' subsume certain phonological contrastive features of hyperphonemes and hypermorphemes: Firth stated that "For the purpose of distinguishing prosodic systems from phonematic systems, words will be my principal isolates" and in his "new order of abstraction" "we may abstract those features which mark word or syllable initials and word or syllable finals or word junctions from the word, piece, or sentence, and regard them syntagmatically as prosodies, distinct from the phonematic constituents which are referred to as units of the consonant and vowel systems" (1949:128, 129). Robins, who bases his theoretical outlook on Firth's prosodies, states that "members of the London group of linguists have been developing techniques of phonological analysis not based on purely 'phonemic' principles, and to some extent rejecting certain of the tacit assumptions of strictly 'phonemic' analysis" (1953a:138). Sharp attempts a "tonal analysis of the disyllabic noun" of Chaga "without recourse to tonemic analysis as a prerequisite" since he finds it "more appropriate to think in terms of prosodic patterns that are features of the word as a whole" (1954:169). For further references to members of the London group as regards handling phonological contrastive features of hypermorphemes as prosodies, see § 10.51; and for hyperphonemic characteristics as prosodies, § 9.73; see also §§ 11.711, 13.82, 14.5.

For our integration of the various hierarchies — phonemic, morphemic, tagmemic — and our attempted solution of some of the problems with which they have been struggling, see chapter 15.

Extensive discussions of prosodic techniques by those closely associated with this approach are now available. Notice especially Robins (1957b), and Bursill-Hall (1960 and 1961). Note also bibliography in Firth (1958), and in Pike and Pike (1960).

The prosodic approach of Firth has some relationship to the componential analysis of Jakobson (1939 and 1949b). For the prosodic approach applied to American Indian languages, see Wallis (1956) and Bendor-Samuel (1960).

A quite different rejection of former phonemic analysis has been made by Chomsky, who insists that the recognition of contrasts between phonemes has no necessary reference to semantics — the pair test is not a meaning test (see 1955, and 1957a:99, where he affirms that randomly presented sequences of elements, consistently identified by the native hearer as different, are in contrast). (But for failure by Saporta and Contreras to follow their own criteria from alleged pair tests, see Garcia 1963: 261-62).

Chomsky goes further in rejecting post-Bloomfieldian phonemics, saying that "the level of taxonomic phonemics [conventional phonemics] is not incorporable into a descriptively adequate grammar" (1962: § 4.5, p. 553; and see 1963:309), on the grounds that assumptions of linearity, invariance, biuniqueness, and local determinacy are implied in post-Bloomfieldian phonemics, and in each instance are inadequate or inaccurate. He retains, however, what he calls "systematic phonemics" — but this "would now generally be called 'morphophonemics'" (1962, § 4.2, p. 532). He feels that no phonemic level is needed beyond the morphophonemic one since there is visible to him "no other significant level of representation". He uses the term "systematic" in this connection since it is related to the system of syntax out of which the phonological rules grow as a lower level of rules. Halle joins Chomsky in rejecting the phoneme since "a phonemic transcription is redundant and should be eliminated as a separate level in the scientific description of a language" (1960:145). For our discussion of the psycholinguistic problems involved, see § 8.815.

For mathematical treatment of phonemic theory see Peterson and Harary (in Structure of Language..., 1961); for phoneme distribution in a general calculus see Harary and Paper (1957). Šaumjan attempts to build a theory of two-level abstractions — the "observation level" and "the level of [theoretical] constructs" (1962:758).

For overall pattern see §§ 15.2 and 15.33; for juncture phonemes see § 9.74.

Householder feels that "In phonological grammar the two chief nuisances are biuniqueness and 'once a phoneme, always a phoneme'" (in Saporta, 1961:19).

For summary and bibliography of Soviet and East European work on phonology, see various authors in Sebeok (1963b).

8.815 *On Psycholinguistics*

One of the most interesting developments in phonemics is a renewed interest — but under a different label, that of PSYCHOLINGUISTICS — in the phoneme as it elicits responses from its hearers, or, more specifically, "with the way in which the speaker of a language encodes his behavior into linguistic responses, depending on the structure of his language, and, as a hearer, decodes linguistically coded messages into further behavior" (Carroll, 1953:111, with earlier use of the term psycholinguistics in Pronko in 1946, referred to by Carroll: 75); and that "there are publically observable indices of subjective events" (Carroll: 72) which must not be "taken at face value" but are nevertheless valuable, in studying language behavior. Such a point of view is congenial to the theory of this volume; for some time I have insisted on the fact that *"explicit observable reactions"* of speakers to linguistic material are part of the data which must be analyzed as essential to the founding of an adequate phonemic theory and procedure (Pike, 1947c:64b, 160bn; Fries and Pike, 1949). I have been using the phrase "experimental phonemics" to describe situations in which such reactions are elicited under experimental situations (note the references to Marckwardt, above, § 2.74, and related discussion in §§ 2.73, 3.35, 6.44, 7.311, 7.87; Gimson, 1945-49; Cooper, Delattre, Liberman, Borst and Gerstman, 1952; cf. also last paragraph of § 8.35).

Now, "in an atmosphere of frank experimentalism", a number of workers have collaborated on an extensive programmatic statement which should lead to valuable data which may help test such assumptions as that "The *phoneme* is probably the one unit which can be demonstrated to exist both linguistically and psychologically" (Sal Saporta, in Osgood, Sebeok, and others, 1954:62; but cf. references in §§ 9.72, 9.76). This emphasis, however, is utterly different from the point of view — rejected by all scholars in this country, so far as I know — that one must consider "phonemes as 'Ideas' in something like the Platonic sense" (Brøndal, 1936:45), or that "the abstract sound of my vowel *u* must be considered as always existing, whether there is any concrete manifestation of it or not" (D. Jones, 1939:3). It continues to be my conviction (cf. §§ 2.73-74, and Pike, 1947c:64b, 160b) that *all* linguistics which deals with language as a functioning part of human activity — i.e., as an emic structure — must have its underlying premises founded solidly on the linguist's observations of the reaction of native speakers to the utterances of each other, to their attempts to learn a language foreign to them, or to write their own language, etc. Within this theory it is considered to be an illusion, therefore, if one thinks he has sought for any *emic* units of language without some response criteria — in this language or in those whose studies gave rise to his experience — having affected implicitly or explicitly his starting assumptions and his selection of data (say a corpus of one language, not a corpus composed of a miscellaneous undifferentiated or unidentified mass of utterances from thirty distinct languages).

More recently still, Chomsky has insisted that "we are trying... to find a basis for intuitive [grammatical] judgments" and that "data of this sort is available to the native speaker" and it "is pointless to refuse to make use of such data in evaluating the success of a particular attempt to formulate the rules of some grammar" (1961b:225); for him "descriptive adequacy" includes such psychological reality (1962, § 4.5, p. 548); in fact "data of this sort [introspective judgments in reference to grammaticalness, for example] are simply what constitute the subject matter for linguistic theory" and we "neglect such data at the cost of destroying the subject" (1962, § 3, p. 526).

In view of such strong statements in reference to grammatical intuition, it seems to me that Chomsky is, on the other hand, insensitive to available intuitive or psycholinguistic support for the conventional phoneme level which he rejects; his model does not call for it, and in his reading of Sapir (see Chomsky, 1962, § 4.2, p. 532), he senses support for the psychological relevance of morphophonemic units but not the equally-available support for the relevance of conventional phonemes.

Note the handling, by Sapir, of reaction to the allophones of the vowel *a* of *bad* and *bat* as a single unit, in spite of difference of length conditioned by the voiced and voiceless consonants (1925, in his Selected Writings: 37); and of "a single objective phoneme" which at times manifests ("is a pool of cases of") a "'true *s*' and 'pseudo *s*'" — i.e., of /s/ directly related to its source in morphophonemic *s* (a "true element of the phonetic pattern") and of instances of /s/ where it is derived from a morphophonemic alternation with /z/ (with this latter *s* as "a secondary [morphophonemically alternating] form of another such element", the /z/).

More recent material giving evidence for native reaction both to a phonemic and to a morphophonemic level are found in Gudschinsky (1958b:343-45); for best results in literacy, sounds need to be written phonemically inside of words, but morphophonemically at word borders (344). Note also Hockett (1955:45; 1958: 441-42); Hoijer (1958).

For experimental evidence that there may be sharp differences of discrimination when phoneme differences are involved, but when the acoustic data itself would not lead one to expect such differences, note Liberman, Harris, Hoffman and Griffith where the "perceived shifts from one phoneme to another were rather abrupt" (1957:367); similarly, Liberman, Harris, Kinney, Lane (1961:387); likewise Liberman, Cooper, Harris and MacNeilage, but with the perception of stop distinctions as "nearly categorical [that is, very sharp]" but with "a perception of the synthetic vowels" as "continuous" (1962:5) such that "although the stop consonants lie in an acoustic continuum, the perception is essentially discontinuous" and "at the phoneme boundaries, the incoming sounds are heard categorically — that is, in absolute terms" (1962:3). See also Liberman, Delattre, Cooper (1958:153).

The assumption is that the peaks of consonant recognition are the results of learning, and — furthermore — that "what has been learned is a connection between speech sounds and their appropriate articulations" (Liberman, Cooper, etc., 1962:4), since the discontinuities occur precisely where articulations are discontinuous. That is to say that phonemes are more closely related to articulatory dimensions, and not "so simply along the psycho-acoustic dimensions, ...thereby forcing the perception to reveal an affiliation with articulation rather than with sound" (Lisker, Cooper, Liberman, 1962:97-98) since a small articulatory change from front to back with velar stops gives a larger acoustic discontinuity. (Note also, for bibliography on discrimination of morpheme boundaries, 101, fn. 29.) For further discussion of the same problem note Liberman, Harris, Eimas, Lisker, Bastian (1961:177), with further emphasis on the connection between "speech sounds with their appropriate articulations"; also Fry, Abramson, Eimas, Liberman (1962:171). Note, however, that Liberman, Cooper, Harris and MacNeilage go further and suggest that perhaps the relation is not between articulation as such and perception "but rather in the motor commands that actuate the articulators" (1962:7-8). Jakobson and Halle, however, have felt that the "surmise of a closer relationship between perception and articulation than between perception and its immediate stimulus" was "theoretically unlikely" and without "corroboration in experience" (1956:34).

For production through articulation by way of rules, see Liberman and others (1959:1493, — "with the rules in terms of subphonemic dimensions". See also Halle, for generative rules for the "dual processes of production and perception" (1962c: 433). For objection to the Spanish generative rules of Saporta and Contreras (the rules do not generate the sequences in loan words) see García (1963:261). For relativity of perception of sounds to various elements of the environment such as "the normal resting level" so that "the acoustic structure of a sentence alters the perception of succeeding vowel sounds", note Broadbent and Ladefoged (1960:390, 384). See also Trim (1962).

Note the relationship of these problems to the problem of phonetic similarity (§ 8.83), and of phonetic substance (§ 8.82).

For bibliography on psycholinguistics, note Zwirner (1962); for some recent articles reviewed, see Ervin (1962); for an extensive collection of reprinted articles on speech perception, meaning, language learning, and bilingualism, see Saporta (1961). See also, above, §§ 2.73, 2.74, on extralinguistic data and systemic clash. Note also intuition in tagmemic analysis, §§ 7.322, 7.84. Note also Longacre's insistence that we "can observe behavior; we can only affirm intuition" (1964a:13), and hence the continued need for study of observable native reaction not merely the non-observable intuitions of native speakers as they report them to us. See above, § 7.88, for discussion of observation and intuition in reference to tagmemes. For sound symbolism, see § 16.83.

For some discussion of psycholinguistic universals, see Osgood (in Greenberg, 1963:236-54).

Pimsleur, Mace, and Keislar discuss from a psychological point of view the addition of cues other than acoustic ones for hearing (1961:26); that is, the speaker reacts to meaning in context.

8.82 *On Substance*

In § 6.91 (and cf. § 2.13) we indicated that this theory rejects any morphemic approach to whatever extent it sets up an emic unit without reference to the substance manifesting it. In § 7.85 the implications of the point of view were developed for the tagmeme. The same contrasting views are present in phonemic discussion. Note, in our theory, how phonetic data ('substance') is treated as relevant to the nature and function of classes of phonemes (§ 8.62), and to the phoneme as a wave of activity (§§ 8.41-42).

For writings which emphasize the theoretical importance of the phonetic data (or the 'substance') to linguistic theory, note Sweet, "the main axiom of living philology is that all study of language must be based on phonetics... It is equally necessary in the theoretical and in the practical study of language" (1900b:4); Paget (1936:36); Zipf (1935:60); Stetson (1937); Trager, who grants that "the acoustic and articulatory phonetician... will be legitimately included in the fellowship of linguists, as practicioners of prelinguistics, in so far as they orient their observations to data sought for as the basis of microlinguistic analysis" (1949:3); Meader and Muyskens (1950:29-30); Bazell (1951:34, 38); Eunice Pike, who states that "phonetic ranking of sounds is structurally relevant" (1954:41); Jakobson and Halle (1956:16-17).

For the opposite point of view, note Bloomfield, who feels that such things as phonetics "do not form part of linguistic theory" (1924:318), and "Tables [of sounds charted phonetically] like these... are irrelevant to the structure" (1933a:130-31; cf. also 128); de Saussure, with linguistic elements "indépendamment des lettres [sounds] qui le composent" (3rd ed., 1931:57; and 43, where the material making up chess pieces is irrelevant); Hjelmslev, "No extra-lingual criteria can be relevant, i.e. neither physical nor physiological nor psychological criteria" (1936:49), and "there is no necessary connection between sounds and language" (1936:51); "language is a form and outside that form, with function to it, is present a non-linguistic stuff, the so-called substance" (1953:49), "Substance is thus not a necessary presupposition for linguistic form, but linguistic form is a necessary presupposition for substance" (1953:68; cf. also 50, 66, 71, and 1947:73), and "In this respect, then, there is no difference between, *e.g.*, chess and pure algebra on the one hand and, *e.g.*, a language on the other" (1953:71); Joos (1950:704); Martinet (1949a:37); and cf. Z. Harris, commenting on Trubetzkoy, "... the types and degrees of phonetic contrast... have nothing to do with the classification of phonemes" and "the selection of phonetic criteria vitiates the structural value of his phonemic patterns" (1941:348), since "only distributional contrasts are relevant, while phonetic contrasts are irrelevant" (347).

8.83 *On Phonetic Similarity*

This problem is closely related to another, as to whether or not it is essential that members (variants) of phonemes be phonetically similar. Z. Harris argues that phonetic similarity is not essential (1951:367 fn. 9). R. Hall feels, however, that "We should be suspicious of any phonemic identification established on the grounds of distribution alone" (1950a:478). Trager uses phonetic similarity in his definition of the phoneme (1942:145; cf. Trager and Smith, 1951:19); note also Bloch in his postulates (1948:28, 30), and more recently (1950:89); cf. Bazell (1951:34, 38); cf. also Twaddell (1953:418); cf. W. S. Allen (1953b:81). For an objection to the criterion see Jakobson (1949b:212), who would replace it with one concerning phonetic oppositions, and the exchange of views between Twaddell (1936b:54, 56-57, 59) and Swadesh (1935b:250). Cf. Welmers (1947:99-100), Carnochan (1953:80), and Hjelmslev (1953:39-41). For problems of psychological similarity, see Osgood, Sebeok, and others, (1954:78, 80-82).

Bloomfield claims that "Such a thing as a 'small difference of sound' does not exist in a language" (1926, in 1949:197). This point of view, in conjunction with his statement quoted in the last section to the effect that phonetics is not structurally relevant leads me to assume that he would conclude that the phonetic similarity or dissimilarity of any two phonemes is irrelevant to the system, or that the phonetic gap between any pair of phonemes is likewise irrelevant in comparison with the phonetic gap between any other pair of phonemes in that language. Such a view we have implicitly rejected in § 8.623.

If we were to adopt as an assumption that which to me seems to be Bloomfield's position, it would then appear that the linguistically-trained informant should never be in doubt as to which of two phonemes a particular phone is actualizing (cf. R. Hall, 1950b:36, "clearly noticeable to every native speaker"). The empirical facts seem to me to contradict this conclusion, and lead to the rejection of such an assumption (cf. our treatment of archiphonemes in § 8.34). We leave room for indeterminacy as to the degree of phonetic similarity present in reference to a particular pair of phones or phonemes. The uncertainty is at times permanent, due to an indeterminacy inherent in the data, and at times is temporary, due to the lack of etic training or emic training on the part of the investigator. A summary of experience which serves as a somewhat useful rule-of-thumb for the beginner who wishes to know whether or not two phones are to be considered phonetically similar for phonemic purposes may be found in Pike (1947c:70; for techniques to discover when this starting point is inadequate, note 1947c:94a, 119a).

For phonetic similarity of the allophones of a phoneme in reference to phonetic features "recurring in recognizable and relatively constant shape in successive utterances" such that "The phonemes of a language are not sounds, but merely features of sound" note Bloomfield (1933a:79-80). For a phonetic constant denied, note Twaddell, who states that "it is a fact that acoustic analysis reveals nothing which all these [t]s have and which no [p] or [d] ever has" (1936a:294, and 1935, versus Andrade, 1936:4); cf. also Cooper, Delattre, Liberman, Borst, and Gerstman (1952:605).

For the possibility of phonetic similarity between two phonemes which under certain conditions approaches perceptual identity or near-identity (§ 8.33) see Bloch (1941). Compare the exchange between Swadesh (1935b:246) and Twaddell (1936b: 53-54, 59); in the latter, note especially the phrase, attributed to correspondence from Swadesh, a "like place in a comparable series"; cf. Martinet (1948:43-44). (For laboratory conditions in which sequence or pattern relations override objective acoustic similarity, such that the same acoustic cue (an artificial 'stop' or burst of noise) may at times be interpreted before [i] and [u] as a kind of [p], but before [u] as a kind of [k], see Liberman, Delattre, and Cooper, 1952:501, 504, 506-14.) We conclude that English [h] and [ŋ] are not members of a single phoneme, in spite of complementary distribution in reference to syllable-initial and syllable-final position, since (1) they are phonetically quite dissimilar (though both are similar to the extent that they are nonsyllabic), and (2) they are not members of a "comparable series" (in that [h] is in the phonetic series with [f] and [s] whereas [ŋ] is in the phonetic series with [m] and [n], and the [m] contrasts with [f] while the [n] contrasts with [s], etc.); see also Pike 1952b:623, and Hjelmslev, 1953:40). Note that here, however, the concept of 'series' is itself based on an assumption of a degree of relevant phonetic likeness — of relevant common phonetic components of a matrix — and of proportional relations among those components (such that [m] is to [f] as [n] is to [s], etc.). In addition, the concept of series is in many specific instances probably in part based on a tacit reliance on the emic structure of emic classes of phonemes (see §§ 8.62-63) and on contrasts between these classes. At present, however, we have neither the theory nor methodology to specify just how far such considerations should be relied on in any particular instance, nor do we have theory to determine whether this uncertainty is permanent or temporary.

To whatever extent one rejects a criterion of phonetic similarity as being relevant to phonemic analysis, he must heighten his reliance upon the relativity of contrasts in relation to a total system of sounds (cf. § 8.33). In our view, the phonetic characteristics of phonemes and the relative characteristics of phonemes must be kept in balance without a denial or neglect of the one or the other. If one rejects the phonetic component of phonemes to the extent of claiming that "that which is relevant in phonemics is only the contrast between one group of sounds and another" one is likely to conclude that "Phonemes are points in a network of contrasts" (Z. Harris, 1941:346) — a point of view which we consider to be true, insofar as it goes, but not complete, since in our opinion it does not do justice to the trimodal structure of a phoneme (cf. Vachek, criticing "purely relational units" as having "nothing to relate", 1936:38). In our view, neither the relevance of and the relativity of the contrasts as such, nor the relevance of and the phonetic character of the poles of the contrasts should be denied.

For discussion of a phoneme center in a range of allophones, through synthetic vowel recognition, note Wiik (1962). Peterson discusses perceptually equivalent vowels in terms of the requirement that absolute values of formant frequencies lie within certain limits (1961:27; bibliography included). Phonetic similarity in reference to limitations on historical change is discussed by Austin (1957). Problems in specifying sameness and differences are discussed by Chomsky (1961b:227-28); and see above §§ 2.73, 2.74, 8.814, 8.815.

8.84 On Feature versus Opposition, and Identification versus Contrast

Is a phonemic feature of a phoneme composed of an opposition between two poles of a contrast, or is it rather composed of one of the poles themselves? Phonemic theory will look very different in accordance with the decision which one makes at this point, or still different if one does not commit himself in some way in the face of this issue; the consequences are far reaching. Much of the different flavor in the writing of persons who were members of or have been strongly influenced by the Prague school is due to an inclination to favor the first alternative (with emphasis on oppositions, as such, as the focus of attention), as over against some American work (with attention focused on the terms or poles of the oppositions). (Interestingly enough, though comparable problems are equally important in grammatical matters, there has been much less difference of approach here, since many American writers have followed a view which places priority on dichotomous constructions, for example, rather than on unity. It is by adopting the emphasis upon unity, however, while retaining in the theory a place for constructions, that the theoretical advance in this volume has been possible. Note the discussion in §§ 7.85, 6.7, 8.32, 8.67). Lévi-Strauss, for example, says of Trubetzkoy that "elle refuse de traiter les *termes* comme des entites indépendants, prenant au contraire comme base de son analyse les *relations* entre les termes" (1945:35). Jakobson states for Serbocroatian that "The whole pattern is based on eight dichotomous properties; among them six *inherent* (or *qualitative*) features concerning the axis of simultaneity only (vocality, nasality, saturation, gravity, continuousness, and voicing)" (1949b:208); note that the properties are not the poles but the oppositions themselves. (See also discussion and quotations in § 8.813 above.) Contrast this with Bloomfield, who implicitly refers to the poles of contrast when he says that "These distinctive features occur in lumps or bundles, each one [i.e., each bundle] of which we call a phoneme" (1933a:79).

On the other hand, the poles of contrast and the contrasts of poles cannot ultimately be separated, as Hjelmslev indicates by saying that "There will always be solidarity between a function and (the class of) its functives: a function [an opposition] is inconceivable without its terminals [the poles of the opposition], and the terminals are only end points for the function and are thus inconceivable without it" (1953:30). It is not surprising, therefore, that there is a struggle to keep the two in balance, and that consistency in balance should be difficult to maintain, if one puts emphasis either on the opposition or on the poles of an opposition.

To me it appears that only an emphasis on the opposition as such rather than on the poles of the opposition could have led Jakobson and Lotz to affirm that "Our basic assumption is that every language operates with a strictly limited number of underlying ultimate distinctions which form a set of binary oppositions" (1949:151). Yet this leads to difficulties. In some instances, one pole of an opposition is treated as the *absence* of a phonetic characteristic, even though elsewhere, in order to maintain the dichotomous principle, this feature defined as an essential absence is treated as essentially *present* in a complex whose very essence is a combination of absence and presence, thus: "We mark by a plus sign only the presence of the feature in question; the absence (as its opposite) is indicated by a minus sign only there, where no plus sign occurs at all. A complex combining both opposite terms is represented by the ± sign" (Jakobson, 1949b:208-09); cf. above, § 8.32.

If in such a situation one grants, however, the structural validity of phonetic data, as such, in reference to its place in a system which in turn has its points defined relative to all the points of that system and relative to the environments of the points of that system at any one time, then contrast, relativity, and phonetic relevance can all be preserved without an insistence on binary oppositions to the exclusion of ternary oppositions or of a ternary series such as [f, s, x]. Similarly, for a number of units we have argued in previous sections that emic elements are simultaneously identificational as well as contrastive, and that to ignore either of these two phases of the characteristics of an emic unit is to invite difficulties elsewhere (cf. §§ 6.46, 6.91, 8.31, as well as §§ 3.53, 5.2, 7.2, 7.87).

For further approaches to related problems, note the Projet (1931), Twaddell (1935), Jakobson (1939), Sebeok (1953:381n), Jakobson, Fant and Halle (1952), Martinet (1952), Garvin (1947), Cherry, Halle, and Jakobson (1953).

The possibility of treating contrastive features as trimodally structured has been mentioned in § 8.35; for indications of the manner in which variants of the manifestation mode of such a unit would be treated, note Jakobson (1949:208, 211), and Jakobson, Fant, and Halle (1952:6-7).

Jakobson insists that "*Per definitionem* every distinctive opposition is binary" — and that language patterning in a binary fashion is not due to the "hypnotic influence of machines" but that it is the "most advantageous way of coding... any verbal behavior" (1962:454-55). See also §§ 8.813, 11.712; and Halle (in Studies Presented to J. Whatmough, 1957). Horalek gives a criticism of binarism (in Preprints..., 1962: 46-47); yet Jakobson and Halle have committed themselves to the belief that the "binary opposition is a child's first logical opposition" (1956:47), claiming for the approach not only linguistic analytical convenience but deeper psycholinguistic reality. For objection to binary insistence, note Bazell (1953:4-5, 108) and Andreyev (1962:191)

8.85 On Neutralization, Overlap, Archiphoneme, Intersection, and Related Matters

For discussion of the 'neutralization' of a contrast at one or more points in a system, see Projet (1931), Trubetzkoy (1935, and 1949 [1939]:246-61), Martinet (1936, 1949b:4-5), Jakobson (1949b:211), Jakobson and Lotz (1949:152), Z. Harris (1941: 349; 1942b:316; 1945:239), Trnka (1939:29), Hockett (1950b:55), Pike (1947c:233, 241, 243). Oswald (1943:25), D. Jones (1950:92, 94, 97, 98, 100), H. J. Uldall (1936:54, 56-57), Bloch (1941), Bloch and Trager (1942:44), Wells (1947b:256n), Welmers (1946:16), Rowe (1950:140), Sapir (1933, in his Selected Writings: 47), Swadesh (1935b:246-48), Twaddell (1935:31, 55; 1936b), Halpern (1946:26), Hoijer (1945:17), Berger, (1949). See also above, § 8.31.

For more recent discussion of neutralization see also W. Haas (1958:136-47, 146-50),

Bazell (in *For Roman Jakobson*, 1956), Gregg (1957:83), Gleason (1961:294-95); Jakobson — for whom the "embarrassing problem" of the neutralised phoneme "disappears on the level of distinctive features" (1962:449).

For "some phonological feature" which can be "significant in some positions but not in others" see Robert Hall (1960:197); and compare our use of the term "overdifferentiation" (Pike, 1947c:142).

8.86 *On Emic Classes of Phonemes*

If one treats an emic class of phonemes as a subsystem of phonemes, one finds interesting points of contact in the work of certain scholars in London for whom the term "commutation" is restricted in application to alternation of terms within "closed and exhaustive systems" whereas "substitution" labels an open system or one seen in "the early procedure in research" (references to Firth, in Robins, 1953a:140 fn. 3, and in Carnochan 1953:79 fn. 5; cf. also 'alternances' — lists of items in contrast in phonemic contexts in various parts of the syllable — in Firth and Rogers, 1937). There is a major difference, however, in that in a language for which "In the stem a five term vowel system operates" but "In the ending a three term system operates" such that the "similarity of sound" in certain of the vowels of the two systems "is not sufficient reason for considering these sounds to be necessarily forms of the same phonological unit" (Carnochan, 1953:80). Although we would grant that the "function of the terms in the stem is different from the function of the terms in the ending" in such a situation, we would want to be able to identify — in some situations at least — items from different emic classes of phonemes or from variants of these classes when they are phonetically similar. Otherwise, we would have to reject, for example, the phonemic identity of the various occurrences of the /t/ phoneme in the English classes following, listed by number from § 8.63: 1, 1^a, 1^b, 1^{b4}, 1^c, 1^{c1}, 1^{c2}, 1^{c3}, 1^{c5}, 1^{c6}, 1^d, 1^{d1}, 1^{d3}, 1^g, 1^{g1}, 1^h, 2, 4, 6, 6^a, 6^c. This, in turn, would force us to employ distinct letter symbols (which could not be called phonemic symbols) for each occurrence of the [t] phone in a different phonological, grammatical, or phonological-grammatical environment somewhat after the manner of Carnochan (who, however, applies this only to a small fraction of the areas which it would affect if the principle were carried out to the bitter end of its far-reaching implications). On the other hand, our symbolization of emic classes and of variants of these classes is clearly related to Mitchell's symbolization of certain — not all — "prosodies" (1953, e.g., p. 384).

A point of contact with American work is the relation between emic classes of phonemes and charts of syllable structure. For the latter, note Whorf (1950[1940]:12), Z. Harris (1951:73-74, 153).

See also the work of the Danish scholars Fischer-Jørgensen (1952, on "phoneme categories") and Hjelmslev (1953:18, 22, on "paradigms").

Note also Scott (1956:556) — and compare his prosodic treatment of phonematic units in a system in a structure; cf. §§ 8.815, 9.73. Note also the term "virtual cluster" to represent one "whose emergence would not change the patterns exhibited by the actually occurring clusters", in H. Vogt (1954:31).

For phoneme classes following up the suggestions of the tagmemic approach, with etic and emic classes of vowels and consonants, note Faust and E. G. Pike (in Serie Linguistica Especial 1959:28-39); and Clark, with illustration of alloclasses (1959); see also phoneme classes in Crawford (1963), and various articles in *Studies in Ecuadorian...* (1962) and *Studies in Peruvian...* (1963).

8.87 *On the Relation of Grammar to Phonemic Analysis*

For the view that grammatical considerations should not enter into phonemic analysis, note, Wells (1947b:259), Trager and Smith (1951:53-54, 68, 81). Compare Welmers, for whom it seems legitimate to obtain "a shove along the road of phonemic analysis by our knowledge of morphology" though "the final test of our phonemic analysis must be that of phonetic justifiability" (1947:100). Welmers (100) feels also that "our choice of one out of several possible phonemic analyses may be determined by the morphology" — a view shared by Hockett (1950a:69). Bloch feels that "Morphological and syntactic criteria must not be used to influence the basic analysis leading to the discovery of distinctive qualities and their distribution; but they are often helpful in deciding how to group these qualities, one they have been discovered, into combinations defining phonemes" (1950:92-93n.), although "no phonemic description is valid if it fails to account, explicitly or implicitly, for any of the qualities of a dialect, or if these qualities are not the sole basis on which it is built" (92). Earlier, Trager had argued that "*Contrasts with* means that meanings may be distinguished" and that we "find, for each given situation, which sound-types are distinctive (serve to identify different speech elements — that is, differentiate meanings)" (1942:145), and Bloch and Trager said that "Some considerations of meaning must enter, it is true, even into phonemics... we need to ask only whether two utterance fractions are the same in meaning or different" (1942:53). More recently, Bloch has attempted to set up postulates which, in theory at least, would allow one to avoid this reliance (1948); serious difficulties arose with this attempt, and the crucial postulates were reworked (1953). It seems to me, however, that they still do not reach his goal, since, for example, English /n/ and /ŋ/ are in obvious contrast in /sən/ versus /səŋ/, but they would apparently show up as noncontrastive by his revised postulates (inasmuch as a 'general' statement of the utterance-initial distribution of /n/ can easily be distinguished from the 'joint' distribution of the two in utterance-final position — a condition which, he seems to imply, would prevent their being considered contrastive; i.e., any pair of "allophones P and Q in overlapping or incorporating distribution, such that the communis of their ranges cannot be distinguished from either propria by any general definition", "are *in contrast* with each other" but pairs "to which the provisions of this postulate do not apply are *noncontrastive* with each other", Bloch, 1953:60-61, — but since the utterance-initial distribution of /n/ is part of its propria and can thus easily be stated in general phonological terms, and the utterance-final distribution of both is part of their communis, the two sounds of English would be considered noncontrastive by his assumptions). For discussion of a related problem concerning Bloch's newer assumption, in reference to a non-English language, see Smalley, 1955. For references to brief mention by Lotz and Fischer-Jørgensen of some related problems, see Bloch (1953:59); for the discussion of the free-variation problem of Bloch, see Pike (1952a:112-115). For references to further problems of the relation of phonemics to grammatical analysis, with points at which the two have been combined in the literature, with the theoretical implications of this overlap, see Pike (1947a, 1952a). See also Voegelin, who has a discussion "of the Pike heresy — introducing morphological considerations in phonemic analysis" (1949:78a), supporting the use of grammar in techniques for searching for phonemes (84a), but rejecting it in presentation (83-85). For an opposite view, note Bazell (1951:34; but see 1953:46), Uhlenbeck (1950:254-55), Bar-Hillel (1953b:161; 1954a:234). See also Jakobson (1949a) and Z. Harris (1951:344).

Since the first edition of this chapter appeared (1955), views concerning the relation of grammar to phonology have undergone much debate.

Persons adopting Firth's prosodic approach (see above, §§ 8.814, 9.73) continue to insist on the possibility of dealing with phonetic material whenever they choose, directly in reference to the word or some other unit rather than strictly in terms of phonology; see, for example, Sprigg in reference to tones (1955:134).

Joos, however, continued to object to mixing levels of phonology and grammar: "the ghost of the slain dragon continued to plague the community of linguists under such names as 'grammatical prerequisites to phonemic analysis' and has not been completely exorcized to this day" (1957:96). That same year Chomsky was insisting that "considerations on all higher levels, including morphology, phrase structure, and transformations, are relevant to the selection of a phonemic analysis" (1957a:60n). See also Chomsky, Halle and Lukoff, of analysis of English stress in reference to grammatical placement (1956). Chomsky's interest in grammatical prediction of stress morphophonemics continues, and affects his setting up of linguistic theory itself (1962, § 2.1, pp. 516-17).

For Chomsky, "what the phonetician hears as stress level is determined in part not by the acoustic event but by an ideal stress pattern that is assigned to the utterance by the rules of a generative grammar" so that "the phonetician may be 'hearing' something that is not present in the sound wave in full detail" (1961b:227 fn. 17).

Chomsky sets up "ordered rules constituting the phonological component" of the grammar which "cannot be undertaken in isolation from the study of syntactic processes", and vice versa (1962, § 4.4, p. 547).

Compare, however, Hockett's "continuing conviction with Smith and Trager" that "the phonological system of a language can be discovered and described without any criterial use of grammatical facts " (1961a:49); but note Hockett's use of grammar heuristically in phonology (1955:16).

For generative treatments of phonology note Saporta and Contreras (1962), and Halle (1962a). For "positions in which morphological and syntactical structures have phonetic effects" see Chomsky and Miller (in Luce and others, 1963:308).

Ferguson (1962:285-86), however, points out the anomaly of Halle's insistence on a transformational grammatical analysis prior to the derivation of phonetic elements out of this analysis, when Halle himself wrote a full book on the phonology of a language — presumably from a transformational point of view — without a full transformation statement of the grammar preceding it. (Similarly, Ferguson points out that while Halle rejects discovery procedures, he nevertheless gives useful instructions of a heuristic type on branching diagrams.)

For my view that some grammatical data are needed for adequate phonological analysis and presentation, and some phonological data for adequate grammatical analysis and presentation, see fn. to § 8.443.

For a complex instance of morphophonemic changes used to identify portmanteau fusions of /y/ with other sounds, see Powlison (1962). For discussion of an attempt to describe a language without postulating vowel phonemes, but at the price of morphological elements entering the phonological description, see Pittman's review (1963) of Kuipers.

CHAPTER 9

HIGHER-LAYERED UNITS OF THE MANIFESTATION MODE OF THE UTTEREME (INCLUDING THE SYLLABLE, STRESS GROUP AND JUNCTURE)

In accordance with the plan indicated in § 5.55, we now wish to discuss the general character of some of the units which are intermediate in size between the behavioreme itself and the minimum units of the respective modes of the behavioreme. In this chapter we shall discuss the intermediate units of the manifestation mode of the behavioreme, in Chapter 10 the intermediate units of the feature mode, and in Chapter 11 the intermediate units of the distribution mode. We shall restrict our discussion, however, to verbal behavioremes — i.e., to utteremes — in order to conserve space and in order to develop the implications of the theory within an area where considerable attention has been directed to characteristics of such intermediate units.

9.1 *Hyperphonemes*

We shall label as a HYPER-ACTEME any unit, larger than an acteme, which is a member of the hierarchy of the manifestation mode of a behavioreme or hyperbehavioreme. Similarly, the term HYPERPHONEME will be applied to any phonological unit which is larger or higher ranking than a phoneme and which is a member of the hierarchy of the manifestation mode of an uttereme or hyper-uttereme. (For the special meaning given to the term 'larger' in this context, see § 9.5.) There is no set number of kinds of such intermediate hyperactemes or hyperphonemes required by the theory. Usually, however, it will be found structurally necessary to deal with hyperphonemes composed of emic syllables (but see § 9.76), emic stress groups, emic breath groups, emic rhetorical periods, and larger units or possibly units intermediate in size between those mentioned.

Each hyperphoneme, like every other emic segment (cf. §§ 5.1, 6.1, 7.1), is an active, trimodally structured emic segment of human activity; it contains physical features identifying it relative to and in contrast with other emic units on its own and/or on other levels of the phonological hierarchy; it is manifested by free or conditioned, simple or complex, fused or clearly segmented non minimum phonological variants; it is distributed within the still larger units of the manifestation mode of utteremes or hyper-utteremes, and whithin a system of hyperphonemes of its own level and of higher levels of the manifestation hierachy, as well as within a structured grammatical and physical setting.

Since no terms are used in this definition which have not been used in earlier chapters, further discussion of them is not necessary at this point. Note, however, that the crucial difference between the description of the hyperphoneme and the phoneme is the occurrence here of the term 'nonminimum' as against the term 'minimum' used in describing the phoneme in § 8.1.

9.2 *The Emic Syllable*

9.21 *Definition of the Emic Syllable*

The EMIC SYLLABLE (or SYLLABEME) is a hyperphoneme, containing all of the characteristics of hyperphonemes which were mentioned in § 9.1, and is further characterized by the fact that most of the manifested members of the system of emic syllables of which it is a part are coterminous with a physical chest pulse, or composed of an etic complex of a strong and a weak etic chest pulse, or composed of part of an etic chest pulse in which each part comprising an emic syllable is identified as such in reference to the stress pattern or potential, the pitch pattern or potential, the quantitative pattern or potential, and the phonemic shape type of the hyperphonemic, morphemic, or hypermorphemic sequences in which it occurs and which it in part comprises.

The chest pulse will be discussed in § 9.221, etically-complex syllables in § 9.235, stress, pitch, and quantitative potential in § 9.225, system and emic classes of emic syllables in §§ 9.244-45.

9.22 *The Feature Mode of the Emic Syllable*

9.221 *The Chest Pulse*

In all except a few emic syllables (cf. §§ 9.225 and 9.235-36), the feature which differentiates it from other syllables in the sequence of syllables, and from units higher or lower in the hierarchy of the manifestation mode of the uttereme (i.e., from phonemes as such, or from stress groups as such) is the presence of one CHEST PULSE,[1] or SYLLABLE

---

[1] Since this chapter was first published (1955) Ladefoged and his associates have published extensively on the physiology of the syllable. Ladefoged concludes that "there is insufficient basis for a chest pulse theory of the syllable" (1962:91). Elsewhere, however, he calls on some kind of subglottal organization of sounds: "Two points are immediately obvious: firstly there is a general increase in the amount of muscular activity as the utterance proceeds; and secondly the *muscular*

PULSE. "Basically", according to Stetson, from whom we take the initial *etic* material on the syllable, "the syllable is a puff of air forced upward through the vocal canal by a compression stroke of the intercostal muscles" (1951:200a), "the muscles between the ribs which produce the syllable pulses" (196a). The contractions of these muscles "produce a separate pulse of pressure for each syllable; the pressure falls between the syllable pulses" (3b), except for instances where "a sudden rise in intensity marks the entrance of the new pulse" (172a). It is the sequence of syllable pulses which we assume causes the sequence of etic syllables.

Stetson assumes that every syllable pulse is in part characterized by a "ballistic movement" (1951:4b, 8a, 29a, 194a), i.e., a rapid "movement started by the momentary impulse of the driving muscle group" such that the rib cage moved in this way is then "carried by the momentum" with no further force acting on it (194a). Every syllable must, he believes, have one such movement, but none must have two — not even if the syllable is a long one, since "the one thing essential to a long continuous syllable is simply that no second ballistic movement occur" (171b). (This point of view we accept for etic purposes, but not for emic ones, as we shall see in § 9.235.)

Whereas the ballistic movement of the rib cage constitutes the feature which separates syllable from phoneme or from stress group, the second feature of the syllable which we mention is an optional one, and brings in a contrast between two types of syllables. This feature is the optional prolongation of a syllable, after its ballistic beginning, by the action of further muscular movements, in a slower, 'controlled' form (Stetson, 1951:8a, 9, 28a). This mechanism allows the production of 'long' vowels in contrast to short, rapid ones in syllables which otherwise contain the same phonemes.[2]

---

activity occurs mainly *in bursts* which immediately precede each syllable" (Ladefoged and others, 1958:5-6, italics added). In addition, Ladefoged and Broadbent find it necessary to deal with "units which are somewhat larger than the duration of a single speech sound" (1960:169); and, as for stress, Draper, Ladefoged, and Whitteridge find "a consistant pulsing action of the muscle before stresses in the sentence" (1960, Fig. 6). It would seem to me that Ladefoged has no intention of returning to a theory which makes sequences of consonant-vowel totally random in theory; the distributional expectancies seem to require some physiological control (see below, § 9.76). In this sense the chest pulse theory seems to me to need revision rather than rejection.

Ladefoged finds that the intercostal muscles produce bursts of activity in the middle range of the breathgroup. Muscles must *hold back* the pressure when the lungs are very full (almost a reverse-action to result in pulse production) whereas extra muscles must be called into play when the pressure is low at the end of the breath group: "a long conversational utterance after a deep inspiration is therefore: first decreasing activity of the external intercostals; then increasing activity of the internal intercostals; and finally increasing activity of the accessory respiratory muscles, probably beginning with the external obliques, and then bringing in rectus abdominis, and then, right at the end, latissimus dorsi" (Ladefoged and others, 1958:13); further description of the mechanism designed "to maintain a constant mean background pressure in the lungs" during this process is seen in Ladefoged (1962a: 76); see also Draper, Ladefoged, and Whitteridge (1960:17).

For reasons underlying Ladefoged's rejection of the chest pulse which can in part be solved by an etic-emic treatment see fn. to §§ 9.225.

[2] Compare Ladefoged: "the internal intercostals can contract in a variety of ways. They can regulate not only the degree of stress, but also the manner of onset of stress. Possibly their activity

A further contrast may develop if the syllable begins — instead of ending — with a controlled movement before the ballistic pulse occurs. Stetson suggests this type, beginning with a fricative (1951:8a).

Although for the purposes of this discussion I have adopted Stetson's assumption that a ballistic pulse occurs on every (etic) syllable, I do not do so without reserve. This hesitation can be expressed in the form of three questions, which I am not competent to answer:

(1) If a syllable can begin with a controlled movement, as he admits (1951:8a), and can end with a controlled movement (same reference), why should it be impossible to pass from a beginning controlled movement to a continued controlled movement without the intermediate ballistic pulse?

(2) Why should it be assumed that it is impossible to move the muscles of the abdomen in a surge to drive out air without a simultaneous pulse of the muscles between the ribs? Surely we have the kinesthetic feeling that these abdominal muscles may work to drive out air during one variety of breathing, without[3] intercostal pulses — and if that feeling proves to be physiologically justified, why should it be impossible to utilize the same mechanism in speech, to make a rapid abdominal pulse on — say — a CV sequence which we hear perceptually as a syllable, but which does not contain a synchronized chest pulse?

(3) Is it not possible to make a series of weakly articulated CVCVCV sequences with breath pressure gradually changed during the process of exhaling, but with the pressure change caused by a single strong, easily-felt movement of the abdominal muscles? This might account for the fact that in American English there occur occasional very rapid 'slurred precontours' in which articulation seems lax, syllables in the sequence do not have a 'separate' effect, but rather produce a smooth, gliding, integrated whole. This contrast of slurred (or glissando) to nonslurred syllable sequences is significant to speech, and must be accounted for somewhere in a complete descrip-

---

can also be correlated with vowel length and many other prosodies of the syllable and the breath group. However, speculation on the subject is somewhat pointless, since objective evidence can be recorded by any team of physiologists and phoneticians who care to insert an electrode into the relevant muscle" (Ladefoged and others, 1958:14).

I feel that we *must* assume a physiological basis for long vowels and for other perceived contrasts in syllable types. If speculation encourages instrumental phoneticians to provide tests of old guesses, or gives us new guesses or solutions, the speculations will have profited us all. In the meantime, practical phonetics operates via imitation-label techniques (Pike, 1943a:16-24).

[3] Some of Ladefoged's data seem to me to supply substantial evidence, now, of some of this kind of action — and to comprise a crucial part of the data by which he challenges the chest-pulse hypothesis. Only if an etic-emic approach can account for these pulseless syllables, without losing the relevance of chest pulses elsewhere, can chest-pulse theory survive. We attempted to meet this problem on the basis of a small amount of earlier data from Stetson, which he himself did not handle adequately — see reference to *a-la* in (3) below. It is by no means certain, therefore, that Ladefoged's data add further theoretical difficulty at this particular point, even though he further documents the problem. It is by no means necessary for *every* syllable to have a pulse in order for the chest pulse to be relevant to the system; see § 9.225 for emic reorganization of such etic data, and footnote there, commenting on Ladefoged.

tion of English; note our description and illustrations in 1945 (67-68, 135, 136, 140, 142, 147) and in 1947c (52b); certain of these illustrations are included on the phonograph records accompanying the intonation volume. (If, however, these slurred types must be treated in a fashion other than that of syllable contrasts, note our alternate suggestion below, § 9.76; for a further possible instance in which syllable differentiation might be possible without a chest pulse, note Stetson, who suggests that "In very rare cases, it may be that the chest movement is a continuous, slow, 'controlled' movement of expiration, and that the syllable is due to the ballistic stroke of the consonant... it is possible that '*a-la*' may be so uttered. There is no experimental evidence for such a correlation" 1951 [1928]:58.)

As an instance in which the chest pulse by itself, without articulatory changes, is seen to be contrastive, in that it affects the presence of syllables, note the syllabic consonants in Stetsons' illustrations *Lil' 'll lie low* and *Runnin' n' neighin'* (1951:101, 186, 119, 187). Compare the many 'syllables' which can be heard in whistling rapidly a sequence of syllables on a single pitch; and cf. Stetson (1951:36b).

For instances in which syllables with the ballistic syllable pulse are followed by a controlled movement in contrast to syllables in which the ballistic movement is not so followed, one may utilize word pairs from any language in which there is a contrast between long and short vowels within single emic syllables. Note, for example, German *Beet* [be:t] 'flower-bed' and *Bett* [bet] 'bed' (Bloomfield, 1933a:107).

In English the controlled versus the ballistic types seem also relevant, but in a more complex set of interrelationships with hyperphonemes than can be handled by a simple long-short dichotomy:

(1) The first English problem for which this approach is useful is in the handling of certain differences between the final syllables of *insult* versus (rapidly pronounced) *tinsel*, or of the final syllables of some pronunciations of *refugee* versus *effigy*, or of *separate* /'sɛpəret/ (verb) versus *separate* /'sɛpərɪt/ (adjective), or of the second syllables of *mailman* pronounced as /'melmæn/ versus /'melmən/; cf. also *access* versus *axis*. The word-final syllable of the first member of each of these pairs has frequently been treated as carrying 'secondary stress' whereas the second has been considered as being 'unstressed'; see, for example Kenyon and Knott (1944:266, 357, 384), D. Jones (1940:229-232), Trager and Bloch (1941:227-29, with the labels "medial stress" and "weak stress"), Trager and Smith (1951:36-37, with the labels "tertiary" and "weak" stress). In earlier work, I had tried to treat the "somewhat prominent" final syllable of *separate* (verb) as probably due to "its vocalic quality", and that of *refugee* as "probably due to the fact that the relationship of a semantically full suffix like *-ee* to a full free underlying word like *refuge* is grammatically quite different" from the relationship of the parts of *effigy* (1945:78-79, 188n. 118, 83-84); in addition, these syllables do "not readily serve as the beginning of primary contours" (though they more readily carry glides at the end of contours than do the final syllables of *separate* [adjective] and *effigy*); hence I there called them 'unstressed' in spite of their prominence. (Note, however, that we are not dealing here with the first syllables of words like *hesita-*

tion, educability, which then — as now — we treated in a different way.)

A third possibility, a "more attractive" one than either their treatment as phonemically stressed or unstressed has recently been proposed by Twaddell, and we adopt this scheme tentatively, i.e., until further experimental evidence be available, since it seems to by-pass the more serious deficiencies of the other two approaches. This solution starts by granting a contrast between the final syllables of words like *separate* (verb) and *separate* (adjective) which is more than vocalic; instead of attributing this added difference to contrastive stress arrangements, however, it attributes it to contrastive syllable types — the verb *separate* ends in "a controlled movement" and the adjective *separate* ends in a "free ballistic movement" (Twaddell, 1953:444); no reference to vowel quality or to grammatical constituents is necessary to grant a contrastive difference at this stage, since potentially one might find minimal contrastive pairs in which vocalic and grammatical constituents were identical (compare *refugee* with *chicadee* or *filigree*). If we indicate the controlled movement by a til [~] (to prevent confusion with the current use of the ordinary length sign [·]) after the vowel or segment during which the movement is controlled, we can rewrite some of these words as follows: /ˈsɛpəre~t/ versus /ˈsɛpərɪt/, *insult* /ˈɪnsə~lt/ versus *tinsel* /ˈtɪnsl̩/ (or even /ˈtɪnsəl/).

(2) A second problem in English which might be illuminated by such an approach is the sharply different strength which is contrastive upon syllables which are emphatically stressed but are otherwise phonologically identical. Note the following (taken from Pike, 1945:86): *What is it?* meaning "Quick, let me know what you want", or "What you are looking at" and pronounced as /hwət ǁɪz ɪt/ with especially short vowel on *is*, in contrast with *What* ǁ*is it?* meaning "What could that particular thing possibly consist of?" and pronounced as /hwət ǁɪ~z ɪt/ or /hwət ǁɪ~zɪ~t/ with elongated /ɪ/. Such a contrast is especially important as indicating that the [~] item is not part of a stress series as such, since it is independently variable, with either degree of length occurring on an emphatically stressed syllable (but not with the same frequency of occurrence — a fact which is here not relevant to the argument).

(3) Possibly this approach would contribute to a solution of problems raised by an "early drop or rise of pitch" in certain intonation contours; note, for example, the symbol [~] added to one of the items given in Pike (1945:74-75, 86):

I ǁ*am tired* versus *I* ǁ*a~m tired.*
3- º2- -4 /   3- º2-4- -4 /

(4) It might also contribute to an understanding of the contrasts between long and short level contours preceding a second contour beginning on the same pitch. Here again, for details, see Pike (1945:61-65, 71) where "Long level contours occurring on single open syllables produce long vowels: on syllables closed with voiced [or sometimes voiceless] consonants, the length is to a considerable extent spread over

these consonants", etc., but "Level contours may be either long or short." Contrast, for example,

>   a big black bu˜g   with   a   bi˜g bla˜ck bu˜g
>   3- º2   º2   º2-4 /   3- º2-2   º2-2   º2-4 /

(in each of which there occur three syllables with heavy stress of perceptually-same intensity).

(5) As for instances in which the controlled movement precedes the ballistic movement, these also may be available in English examples. Note, for example, the elongated initial consonants in the following exclamations: *Gr˜eat Ceasar's ghost!*, *Get s˜et now!*. (For discussion and further examples see Pike, 1945:97-98.)

Not all length can be attributed to this chest-pulse mechanism, however. Some lengths are sustained for too long a time for that. Compare, for instance, extreme elongation of the vowel in *It's a lo::::ng long way home*, where the abdominal mechanism must be chiefly relevant. At present, it is not at all clear where one mechanism leaves off and the other begins, or just how they function together. Specifically, for instance, it is not easy to be certain that the mechanism which separates *some pre˜tty shady work* ('genuinely pretty') from *some prett˜y shady work* (i.e., "quite underhanded", Pike, 1945:97-98) is the chest pulse, or that the same mechanism operates in *Don't˜d˜o it!*

9.222 *Releasing and Arresting Margins of the Syllable*

In addition to the difference between controlled and ballistic movements of the syllable, there are other differences important to the initiation of syllables:

Syllables beginning with vowels are "released by the chest"; i.e., "the rapid rise of pressure of the syllable is generated by the intercostal muscles of the chest" (Stetson, 1951:7b). On the other hand, syllables "like '*pay, day, die*', are released by a consonant... The intercostals act as before, but the consonant constriction occurs at the same time, so that the air pressure develops behind the consonant closure" and "the 'release' is always due to the combined action of intercostals and articulation" (Stetson, 1951:7b).[4] The chest-released type of syllable may be symbolized, after Stetson, as

---

[4] Ladefoged rejects Stetson's assumption that external intercostals check the open syllables and states that these "bursts occur irrespective of whether the word ends in a consonant closure or not" (Ladefoged and others, 1958:10), and "in the majority of conversational utterances which we have recorded there is no action at all of the external intercostals" (1958:10-12). Draper, Ladefoged and Whitterage point out that in "speech such as loud talking or shouting, the checking action of the external intercostals occurs for short periods only after a very deep inspiration". The internal intercostals come into action before the volume of air in the lungs has decreased; but quiet speech "involves more prolonged use of the external intercostals" (1959:24-25). Note chart which illustrates the muscles involved at the beginning of the utterance, as distinct from those involved at the middle or at the end (24). Their insistence here is that there is an important relation "between the respiratory muscles and the relaxation pressure" (26).

OVO; the consonant-released type, as CVO. Compare the initial syllables of *able* and *table* for illustrations of this contrast.

A modification of the consonant-released type is found when a consonant cluster occurs at the beginning of a syllable, such that the chest pulse builds up during the articulation of the entire sequence of consonants (Stetson, 1951:83-88). Such syllable beginnings can occur in syllables like *play*, and *try*, or even in a rapid pronunciation of *sty* (but for instances in which the [s] constitutes here a second pulse, see §§ 9.225, 9.235).

The syllable pulse can be stopped — "arrested" in Stetson's terms, "braked" in Twaddell's — in a variety of ways comparable to those in which it can be begun. On the one hand, syllables of the type OVO have the "pulse arrested by the intercostal muscles which take up the momentum of the pulse" as in the word *I* or *oh* (Stetson, 1951:7b). On the other hand, "the 'arrest' may be due to the action of the articulation alone" which "blocks the air flow and raises the pressure in the trachea and so takes up the momentum of the pulse" (7b). These are the 'closed' syllables, of the type OVC, such as are seen in the words *ape*, *ire*, and so on. Here, too, a cluster of two consonants may act together, arresting the chest pulse instead of releasing it (and here, also, there are instances in which the release of the first or second consonant may constitute the nucleus of an additional etic syllable which is not an emic one); see §§ 9.225, 9.235; examples may be constituted of words such as *ask*, *sink*, *apt*.

The combinations of these chest-released or arrested and consonant-released or arrested beginnings and endings allow for four contrastive possibilities: OVO, OVC, CVO, CVC (Stetson, 1951:2a, 200a), and in each of the two latter types "the delimiting consonants are integral parts of this chest-pulse movement" (Stetson, 1951:27b). (For a further type with indeterminate border see § 9.236.) For illustrations in which the type of syllable beginning or ending is contrastive in sequence, note Stetson: OVO.CVO, OVC.CVO, *I do*, *I'd do*; OVC.OVC, OVC.CVC, *I'm Ike*, *I'm Mike*; CVC.OVC, CVC.CVC, *whole ode*, *whole load*; OVO.CVO, OVC.CVO, *I lie*, *I'll lie*; OVC.CVC, OVC.OVC, *unknown*, *unown*; CVC.OVO, CVC.CVC, *this eye*, *this sigh*; CVC.OVC, CVC.CVC, *top egg*, *top peg* (1951:175-76); and note OVC.CVC *a name*, *an aim*; CVC.CCVO, CVCC.CVO *more stew*, *Morse too* (the latter from Bloch, reference unidentified). In all these illustrations, we use the lowered dot to indicate that syllable division occurs between two phonemes. (For types like *Topic* versus *top pick*, however, see § 9.236.) It is convenient to call consonants or consonant sequences which release or arrest the syllable pulse the MARGINS of the syllable.

9.223 *The Syllabic and the Syllable Nucleus*

We assume here that the SYLLABIC part of an etic syllable, in contrast to its margin, is that part of the syllable during which the chest pulse is emitted. Stetson does not favor the term syllabic, but refers rather to "the *vowel shaping* movements of the vocal canal" (1951:200a; also see 2b, "vocal-canal shape through which the pulse is emitted"; 37a, 91). He specifically defines the vowel, furthermore, in reference to this canal-shaping *function*: "The characterized syllable factor which emits the syllable pulse, usually with tone from the glottis, is counted the vowel" (1951:200-01; also, 27b, 91b), and "the pulse must occur if there is to be a vowel" (2b). This leads him to an internal inconsistency, however, when those particular sounds which he wishes elsewhere to call consonants are here functioning as the nucleus of the syllable: "On occasion the vocal canal may be shaped by a continuant consonant; a fricative which makes emission possible, like 'sh....' or '*pst*', may act as a vowel" (though there is no theoretical apparatus which allows for items to "act like vowels" but not "constitute" vowels in his materials), and "any continuant may be given the [vowel or syllabic] function" (91b, 34a; cf. also 42a). The presence of these syllabic consonants as shaping the vocal canal is not allowed for in his basic thesis that "The functional difference of vowel and consonant as constituents of the syllable, as characterized factors of the syllable, is an essential phase of the motor theory of phonetics" (9).

In the present theory we attempt to utilize Stetson's concept of the point of emission of the syllable pulse while avoiding the inconsistency in reference to vowels or syllabic consonants. We do so by several related devices: (1) We label the point of emission of the etic syllable pulse as the SYLLABIC, or syllabic sound, without reference to its specific articulatory phonetic character. (2) We utilize a second term, NUCLEUS OF THE SYLLABLE, to refer to the core of an emic — rather than an etic — syllable. This core includes the syllabic part of that emic syllable, if any, but may also include some elements structurally correlated in distributional function with the syllabic rather than with the margin; such nonsyllabic nuclear components may, for example, include a glottal stop, or nonsyllabic vocoids, or voiced sonants such as [l] and [n]. In an emic syllable which is not composed of an etic syllable (see § 9.225), the nucleus contains no syllabic, though it may contain a vowel. (3) The term 'vowel' is utilized in reference to emic sounds and their distributional function, whereas the term 'vocoid' is used when referring to the phonetic character of certain sounds (those in which air enters or leaves the mouth over the center of the tongue without friction in the mouth) without reference to their emic or distributional function (see Pike, 1943a; 1947c:13bn). This terminological provision allows us, when it proves advantageous in a particular language, to refer to vocoids which are nonsyllabic and consonantal, or to vocoids which are vocalic, syllabic, and nuclear, or to vocoids which are vocalic, nonsyllabic, but part of a nuclear vocalic VV sequence. It also allows us to refer to consonants (or to nonvocoids) as syllabic, when they are the canal-shaping part of the syllable, without getting into contradiction as to vowel-consonant definitions. (For further discussion of the content of nuclei of emic syllables, see § 9.243.)

For illustrations in which the placement of the syllabic peak or peaks in an utterance is contrastive, note *stirring* ['stɹɪŋ] in contrast to *string* [strɪŋ] and *erring* ['ɹɪŋ] in contrast to *ring* [rɪŋ] (from Bloomfield, 1933a:122).

As an illustration of a syllable in which the syllabic is only part of the syllable nucleus, note English *style* /stˌaiˌl/ (with the nucleus enclosed in half-brackets, as in

Pike, 1947c:148-49a; an alternate phonemic analysis would represent the syllable as /st˻ay˼l/, in which the nonsyllabic phoneme in the nucleus is treated as a consonant). For instances in which the nucleus is composed of vowel plus glottal stop, see Aschmann (1946:41-42); for a more complex situation, with nuclei of types ˻V˼, ˻VV˼, ˻VʔV˼, ˻VʔV˼, ˻VVʔ˼, and ˻VʔVʔ˼, see Pickett (1951:61), Leal (1950:134), Longacre, (1952:75-76; 1955:189-94), Robbins (1961). Note, furthermore, that the kinds of contrasts between controlled and ballistic chest pulses discussed in § 9.221, are often largely contained within the syllable nucleus.

9.224 The Phonemic Content of Emic Syllables

Two etic syllables which contain different phonemes are assumed to constitute different emic syllables. One of the contrastive-identificational features of an emic syllable is its phonemic content. (Or at least part of each of the same phoneme the latter reservation allows a slight variation in content, in that under certain circumstances an etically-ambisyllabic phoneme might be treated as belonging to two emic syllables. See fused variants of syllables in § 9.236.)

9.225 The Emic Syllable as a Potential Carrier of a Unit of Pitch, Stress, Length, or Morphemic Shape Type

Whereas the discussion of the characteristics of etic syllables, up to this point, has been heavily indebted to the instrumental studies of Stetson, we now turn more to the possibility of and the relation between etic and emic syllables, the validity of which Stetson was not ready to concede. In these matters, therefore, we must rely more on the implications of the theory itself and on descriptions and foreshadowings of this point of view in our earlier publications, or in the publications of others, until further instrumental and structural studies are available.

In many languages, if one holds rigorously to an analysis of emic syllables such that one maintains with Stetson that every functional syllable must have one but only one chest pulse of the kinds which Stetson has described, one arrives at a language description which is in strong clash with other evidence which points to the nature or grouping of the structural units as the native speakers react to those units while they speak the language, discuss its structure, write it, or learn a language foreign to them. As they speak about the language, they may discuss the number of syllables in an utterance, for example, and two speakers of that language are likely to agree quite closely as to the number of and identification of the syllables in any one utterance of that language. Yet when speakers of two different languages listen to the same utterance from one of those languages, they may disagree strongly as to the number of syllables in one or more words of that utterance. I have heard Spanish speakers insist that they heard two syllables in the English word *cow* (Pike, 1947c:65a), Japanese speakers that they heard two, three, or four syllables in *skates* (and Y. R. Chao tells me that Chinese speakers hear three in this word); Bloch states that "In the English word *asks*, pronounced with a long vowel and distinctly released consonants, a Japanese will hear five syllables" (1950:92 fn. 14).

Since we are convinced that reactions of this and of related types are, at some level of linguistic or nonlinguistic structure, emically determined, we further have concluded (1947c:65, 144-48, 246a) that in a particular language the etic syllables may be structurally realigned into emic syllables which are only partially co-terminous with the etic syllables of that language.

Specifically, for example, we would object to treating the English word *at* as composed of two emic syllables, even in those pronunciations of it within which Stetson's techniques would indicate that there is one chest pulse in which the vowel constitutes the syllabic and a second pulse in which the aspirated release of the consonant constitutes a second, silent, syllabic. Similarly, we would object to treating as composed of two emic syllables the word *ski*, in spite of the fact that by Stetson's techniques there would appear in some pronunciations of the word one chest pulse for the /s/ and another for /ki/. For over two decades evidence of this kind has appeared in his publications. For references to his 1928 edition of Motor Phonetics, see Pike (1947c: 65bn). For more recent data, note his 1951 edition, with reference to "an unvoiced preceding syllable and a bi-syllabic form" in groups such as *sf* (84b); an illustration of this in his Fig. 72, syllable number 8, p. 85; further illustration and comment in Fig. 75, p. 86b, and Fig. 76, p. 87. Note, furthermore, that "The motor phonetic tracing Chest Pulse for the syllables parallels the acoustic intensity line" (179b) so that "This marks the identity of the syllable as it appears in the acoustic patterns and as it appears in the motor phonetic tracings" (179b); then compare the amplitude of the intensity for the syllabic nasal and the syllabic lateral on 187, 186, and note that they are less distinct from their surrounding sounds in intensity than are the amplitudes of the intensity lines for the adventitious syllables composed of the aspirated releases of the final /p/ of *pap* on 183, of final /t/ of *Lafayette* on 185, and of the first *at* on 184. I can not conceive of any native speaker of English seriously arguing that we should treat *at* and the like as composed of two syllables, however, and even Stetson himself completely ignores his own data concerning such adventitious or silent syllables when later in his work he discusses rhythmic groupings of words (e.g., 106-23) — a happy oversight which prevented his approach from collapsing.

In the light of such problems, we must either reject the entire syllable-pulse concept or allow for an overriding emic reorganization of etic syllables by other factors. If we adopt the first expedient, and reject the chest pulse as a pertinent physiological base for etic syllables, it leaves us, I think, with no adequate substitute at a crucial point in our theory, where a physical base must be provided as part of the manifestation mode for every emic unit. We have, then, chosen the second alternative, seeking for those factors which would allow for such emic reorganization of the data.[5] Fortunately, it seems that these can be found, and that they do not come into conflict

---

[5] Precisely here is where Ladefoged and his associates fall short of adequate reworking of phonemic theory on the basis of their new data. Ladefoged continues to assume that for a chest-pulse theory

with the demands of other parts of the theory. For our approach to these criteria, and for some of our illustrations, we draw on Pike, 1947c (60b, 246a, 144-49).

One of the most important factors in the emic reorganization of the etic syllables in some languages is that of timing. A part of an etic syllable may constitute a separate emic syllable if it fills a patterned place comparable to that of other emic syllables which are coterminous with etic syllables, and two etic syllables in sequence may constitute a single emic syllable if together they fill a patterned place comparable to that of other emic syllables which are coterminous with etic syllables. In patterned English verse, for example, the syllables *at* and *ski*, even though each may constitute two etic syllables, fill the same function in metrical feet as *to*, or *he* which constitute single etic syllables. On the other hand, Japanese seems to constitute our best illustration of a language in which many single etic syllables must be analyzed as constituting sequences of two emic syllables because of the timing-reorganization of the etic syllables. Thus, Bloch tells us that

The number of syllables in a phrase is therefore not found by counting peaks of sonority or chest pulses, but only by counting the temporally equal fractions contained in it, or by comparing its duration with that of another phrase in which the number of such fractions is known. In short, the Japanese syllable is a unit of duration. Such a unit is often called a mora; but the term 'syllable' is better established in descriptions of Japanese (1950: 92 fn. 14).

---

of the syllable to be useful there must be physiological evidence to support the presence of the pulse on every unit which one wishes to call an [emic] syllable. Since he does not find this, he rejects the syllable-pulse concept. For evidence of this note his objection that "Provisional results do not support his [Stetson's] contention that there is nearly always a peak of sub-glottal pressure corresponding to each syllable" (1960b:175); and "Stetson's main conclusions were: (1) *Every* syllable is accompanied by a 'ballistic chest pulse' produced by the action of the internal intercostal muscles" (1962:73; italics Ladefoged's).

It is Ladefoged's emphasis on "*every*" that leads him to difficulty: he finds that "words such as *pity* and *around*" are sometimes pronounced such that "a single increase in tension spans a group of articulations including two vowels separated by a consonant closure", "and sometimes there are two separate bursts of activity in what is normally regarded as a single syllable (e.g., in *sport*, *stay*, and other words beginning with a fricative followed by a plosive)" and since there is therefore "no simple correlation between intercostal activity and syllables" (1962:78-79) he rejects the chest-pulse theory. Note, again, that "Very often there is not even a correlation between the number of bursts of muscular activity and the number of segments perceived as syllables in an utterance" (Ladefoged and others, 1958:6). It is most unfortunate that Ladefoged did not notice that the same kinds of problems had already been discovered by Stetson. Note the quotation in the preceding paragraph of the text (retained from our 1955 edition) concerning words like *ski*, *pap*, including "an unvoiced preceding syllable" for the voiceless syllable of *pap*; references were also available in Pike, 1947c (65, fn. 4); elements as complex variants of a single emic syllable in § 9.235, below. Similarly, Stetson had instances of one etic syllable containing two emic syllables — one physiological syllable containing two perceived syllables — in his items like *Lill' 'll lie low*, quoted above in § 9.221 (from Stetson, 1951:101, 186, 119, 187). We reassert our earlier claims, therefore (1) that we need a physiological basis for syllable, welcoming the greater accuracy of the newer materials available; (2) that we must expect that no physiological material will ever, no matter how refined, give us the complete correlation of phonetic elements with perceived syllables; and (3) that we must also deal with situations in which a single etic syllable may be perceived by foreigners as a single syllable but by native speakers as two or more syllables. A rigid etic view must give way to a theory which allows for emic use of etic material in some such fashion as we have proposed here. See, also, fn. to § 9.221.

The kinds of adjustments which his data indicate that one would have to make in order to move from Japanese etic syllables to emic syllables (which in this instance seem to be equivalent to functional moras) include the following: Each vowel of a vowel sequence, regardless of the number of chest pulses in the sequence, would constitute the nucleus of a syllable; in [aoi] 'blue', for example, there are three such moras or emic syllables. A long nasal consonant following the syllabic of an etic syllable leads to a separate emic syllable; in [kŏm·bān·] 'tonight' there would be four emic syllables. Similarly, a long voiceless consonant may constitute an emic syllable; in [s·teru] 'throws away' there are three emic syllables; in [ip·pai] 'full' there are four. A voiceless vowel, like a voiced one, constitutes the nucleus of an emic syllable; note the first (voiceless) vowel in [sʊsumu] 'advances'. A long vowel constitutes a single syllabic of a single chest pulse but two nuclei of two respective emic syllables; in [šo·sa] 'major' there are three emic syllables. (Cf. Bloch, 1950:91-92). In each instance, it is fractions which "are heard as having the same time value" which constitute the emic syllables.

A second factor in the emic reorganization of etic syllables in some languages is that of permitted placement of contrastive tone. Mixtec gives one of the most striking instances in which such emic reorganization must be postulated, though the criterion of permitted tone placement is paralleled by the timing factor, and by that of units of morpheme structure. In a word like [katā] 'to sing, is going to sing' there are two emic syllables, each of which is composed of an etic syllable, a unit of timing, a unit of morpheme structure, and — the item under attention here — a unit of tone placement; in [kátā] 'is singing', the level tone of the preceding form is replaced by a high tone on that syllable. Completely parallel to these two forms in tonal structure, however, is the pair of words [kā·] 'to climb, is going to climb', and [ká⸱] 'is climbing', in which the first part of a long tone is replaced by a high tone, producing a phonetic glide from high to mid tone. Phonetically-long, non-rearticulated vowels, it is known from other evidence such as contrastive words like [kāī] 'to eat' and [kàí] 'to bend' (and, for other evidence, see Pike, 1948:79n), constitute sequences of two vowel phonemes, and those long vowels as in [kā·] /kāā/ 'to climb' clearly seem to constitute a single etic syllable. Because of their one-to-one correlation with phonemic tones, however, and their correlation with units of timing and morpheme structure, every vowel phoneme is best considered the nucleus of an emic syllable. In [kā·], therefore, only one etic syllable is found, but two emic syllables.

Further complications occur, moreover, since in Mixtec the initial /ⁿd/ begins with a nasal segment which appears to constitute by itself a chest pulse in such a word as /ⁿdátá/ 'to split'. Here, however, no contrastive tones appear on the nasal segment, but its pitch is conditioned by the environment in which it occurs, and the nasal part of the /ⁿd/ phoneme is not to be considered an emic syllable even though it may constitute an etic one. Note, then, that in Mixtec one etic syllable may comprise two emic syllables (i.e., /kā-/ and /-ā/ in [kā·]); one emic syllable may comprise two etic syllables (i.e., /ⁿdā-/ in /ⁿdākōtō/ 'to look up'); two etic syllables may comprise two emic syllables in which the boundary between the etic syllables coincides with the boundary between the emic syllables (i.e., as in /kātā/); or, instead of being coterminous, two etic syllables may comprise two emic syllables, but with the boundary between the two emic syllables being different from the boundary between the two etic syllables (as in [ⁿdā·]/ⁿdāā/ in which the first etic syllable ends with the nasal, but the first emic syllable ends with the first vowel).

As a third factor in the emic reorganization of etic syllables we may mention the distribution of an etic syllable type or types in some part of the stress groups of a language, especially as the carrier of the stress itself, i.e., as the nucleus of an abdominal pulse. Perhaps one of the reasons that the etic chest pulse composed of the /s/ in English *stay* is not an emic syllable is that such items by themselves do not serve as the peak of a stress group in non-interjectional forms (ignoring, that is to say, items such as *pst!*).

A fourth factor in the emic reorganization of etic syllables is probably composed of the relation of etic and emic syllable types to the dominant phonemic shape types of the morphemes, or words, or morpheme classes of a language (§§ 6.64, 7.313(2), 8.52). In Mixtec, for example, the fact that isolated morphemes each contain at least two vowel phonemes, but no more than two vowel phonemes (Pike, 1944:122; 1947a, 167-69; 1947c:147a; 1948:79) leads to the implication that it is the morpheme, through its shape type, which here controls the vocalic sequences. Since, furthermore, the control works through a prescription of a permitted minimum and maximum number of vowel phonemes, it seems that the vowel count is equivalent to mora count, and in turn this is equivalent to the number of postulated emic syllables in that language. We conclude, then, that it is certainly valuable to take into account the predominant shape types of morphemes or classes of morphemes when trying to determine the relation between the etic and the emic syllables of a language, and that this methodological advantage probably reflects some theoretical correlation, as well, in at least some languages. If this proves to be the case, it would be one more instance of an interpenetration of phonological and grammatical layerings (cf. §§ 8.443, 8.52, 15).

The particular manner in which these various criteria overlap and affect one another is not yet known, nor the priority which one may have over another. Until these problems can be solved there are likely to be considerable differences in the manner in which different investigators handle any particular set of syllable data in any particular language.

9.23 *The Manifestation Mode of the Emic Syllable*

Just as we treated nonsimultaneous variants of the manifestation mode of the morpheme (§ 6.5), of the tagmeme (§ 7.4), and of the phoneme (§ 8.44), so we have nonsimultaneous components — i.e., variants — of the emic syllable. The kinds of situations which led to variants within the phoneme lead also to variants within the emic syllable.

9.231 *Systemically-Conditioned but Topologically-Same Variants of the Emic Syllable*

Within a sentence uttered in a song, or in a shout, in a whisper, or in a harsh voice, any one syllable spoken in the one style will differ from the comparable syllable in the same sentence spoken in a different style. These differences are assumed to be caused by the congruent system — the style — as a whole, and hence are not assumed to constitute distinct emic syllables. Rather etic syllables of this kind are considered to be LOCALLY-FREE BUT SYSTEMICALLY-CONDITIONED PHONETIC VARIANTS OF AN EMIC SYLLABLE; they are considered to be topologically the same.

9.232 *Phonemically- and Hyperphonemically-Conditioned Variants of the Emic Syllable*

Any one syllable may be heavily affected by its position in a larger hyperphoneme. Specifically, an emic syllable which is relatively unstressed at the margins of an abdominal pulse may occur in a heavily-stressed variety at the peak of that abdominal pulse; the stressed and unstressed etic syllables may constitute variants of a single emic syllable.[6] This same distributional difference may also cause a difference in the length or intensity of the syllable nucleus: for example, at the unstressed position in the abdominal pulse the syllable might be of a ballistic type only, whereas at the peak of the abdominal pulse a controlled variant of the same emic syllable might occur.

Similar differences may affect the length or intensity of margins — especially the arresting margin — of an emic syllable. Occurrence at the borders of a breath group might have further comparable etic effects upon an emic syllable. In addition, distribution in the larger hyperphonemes may affect the voicing of the manifesting phonemes of an emic syllable — e.g., at the final margin of a breath group the final phoneme of an emic syllable might be unvoiced although the other variants of that phoneme were voiced. (See § 8.442 for a discussion of this same conditioning relationship, but with the phoneme as the starting point.) Similarly, the discussion of the effect of one phoneme upon another phoneme in sequence with it may be rephrased to focus the attention upon the change insofar as it affects the syllables: i.e., one syllable may affect another subphonemically, in that one syllable may affect an adjacent phoneme of an adjacent syllable.

---

[6] Probably the work of Crawford (1963) will force this judgment to be reversed. If the stress is treated like other phonemes, then as /pa/ differs from /ba/ so /pá/ differs from /pa/. The implications for our theory here are not yet clarified. It seems, however, to leave all variation in syllables to occur below the phoneme threshold.

9.233 *The Possibility of Grammatically-Conditioned Variants of the Emic Syllable*

If one concludes that it is empirically and theoretically valid to describe some subphonemic variants as grammatically conditioned (see § 8.443 for a discussion of this possibility), he should also conclude that etic differences within the variants of emic syllables could likewise be caused by their distributional relation to certain grammatical units.

9.234 *Free (Unconditioned) Variants of the Emic Syllable*

In the discussion of the phoneme we indicated (§ 8.444) that in the attempted repetition of any phoneme there would be a scatter of free variants of that phoneme, since no physiological movement can be actually repeated. A similar consideration applies to repetitions of emic syllables, and leads to free variants of them. When these variants are below the perceptual threshold of a particular observer at a particular time, such variants are labelled as the SAME VARIANT of that emic syllable. When, on the contrary, the variants are unconditioned by the environment, but are above the perceptual threshold of the observer, and noticed by him, these may be labelled as FREE UNCONDITIONED PHONETIC VARIANTS of that emic syllable. (Syllable variants which are locally free, but which are caused by the particular congruent system in which they are occurring, are not treated as totally free variants, but as systemically conditioned; see § 9.231.)

9.235 *Etically-Complex Variants of the Emic Syllable*

In an earlier section (§ 9.225) we cited some of the evidence from Stetson showing that the English word *at* frequently appears as composed of two etic syllables, but indicated that we would wish to treat it as a single emic syllable for English. Without repeating the evidence and references given there, we wish here to add a descriptive label to emic syllables of this type — a label which will allow the reader to see them in relation to other problems of linguistics which we have treated in earlier chapters (§§ 5.55c, 6.54, 7.44, 8.445): An emic syllable composed of a sequence of two or more etic syllables constitutes a single ETICALLY-COMPLEX EMIC SYLLABLE. The little puff of breath which in some pronunciations of *at* follows the release of the /t/ is registered on Stetson's instruments as an etic syllable, and is treated in this theory, for English, as an etic syllable which is the second part of an etically-complex emic syllable whose first etic component has the vowel /æ/ as its nucleus. Similarly, for such a word as English *ski* we assume only one emic syllable, whether it be composed of one etic syllable — with a rapid initial consonant cluster which registers on Stetson's instruments as a single releasing consonant complex — or whether it be composed of a sequence of two etic syllables — with the phoneme /s/ registering on Stetson's instruments as a separate etic syllable. (The principal kinds of criteria used in reaching such a conclusion for a particular language have been given in § 9.225.)

380 HIGHER-LAYERED UNITS OF THE MANIFESTATION MODE OF THE UTTEREME

Inasmuch as Stetson's data indicate that not all pronunciations of a word like *ski* are composed of two etic syllables, furthermore, we must conclude — in an instance where the same word varies from a one-etic-syllable pronunciation to a two-etic-syllable pronunciation — that there is free variation between an etically-simple variant of such an emic syllable, and an etically-complex variant of that syllable. (Compare the conditioned variation between the etically-simple [p] in *happy* with the etically-complex variant [pʰ] in *pie*.)

9.236 *Fused versus Clearly-Segmented Variants of Emic Syllables*

In the previous section we listed variants of a syllable which were etically complex. Here we wish to mention, in reference to variants, the reverse situation — one in which a variant of an emic syllable is composed of only part of a single etic syllable. Illustrative data from Japanese and Mixtec, and the criteria for analyzing this data, have been given in § 9.225: In each of these languages certain phonetically-long single etic syllables were analyzed as sequences of emic syllables because of the two units of duration in the one etic syllable (Japanese and Mixtec), or because of the two units of tone placement on the single etic syllable (Mixtec), or because of the morphemic structural shape-type parallels which lend support to the assumption of a bi-emic-syllable interpretation of some of the etically-single but phonetically-long syllables (Mixtec).

The reason for mentioning these data again is to call attention to the fact that, from the point of view of phonetic segmentation, the bi-emic syllables within the single etic syllables may be considered as a case of segmental FUSION OF SYLLABLES parallel to the fusion of phonemes discussed in § 8.446. A syllable such as Mixtec [kā·] 'to climb' may be considered a PORTMANTEAU ETIC SYLLABLE inasmuch as its emic analysis breaks it into the emic syllable /kā/ plus the emic syllable /ā/.

Whenever the etic segmentation of the emic syllables is etically clear, however, a perceptual break between etic syllables is coincident with the border between two emic syllables and is simultaneously coincident with the border between two phonemes.

Occasionally, however, a kind of partial fusion of two English syllables occurs in which, at the border, the arrest of a stressed syllable and the release of a following unstressed syllable are both handled by the chest musculature, but with a consonant — coincident with the intersyllabic border — pronounced so rapidly and/or lightly articulated that it neither plays a noticeable part in the arrest of the first syllable, nor in the release of the second, nor in a combination arrest-release of the two. In such circumstances it is neither profitable to assign such a consonant to the first syllable in the analysis, nor to the second, nor to treat it as functioning ambisyllabically as both arresting and releasing, since it is neither comparable to the /g/ in a deliberate pronunciation of *big apple*, nor in *by gone*, nor to the two /g/ phonemes in *big goat*. What, then, should be done with such a /g/ as occurs in a rapid pronunciation of *rigor*? Our solution is to grant that in such instances there is an indeterminacy within the data — that one must not try to insist that there be a clear-cut boundary between every two syllables, when the data do not warrant it, any more than we try to do so for boundaries between the phonemes /a/ and /i/ in an /ai/ glide (§ 8.42). In addition, we set up a further formula to indicate that the indeterminate syllable division of *rigor* or *topic* comes somewhere within the consonant, but is not produced by that consonant in an arresting or releasing or arresting-releasing function: ꞌVOÇOV (or simply ꞌVÇV) differs from ꞌVC.CV, ꞌVO.CV, ꞌVC.OV (for a different symbolism for this type of contrast, see also Twaddell, 1953:441).

A set of schematic diagrams to show this relationship has already been presented, in a connection with phonemic distribution in hyperphonemes, in § 8.51. In one pair of diagrams the border between [p] and [o] coincides with the border between two syllables; in another diagram pair the sound [p] straddles the point of division between the two syllables. In the latter, the point of syllable division is indeterminate with respect to phoneme borders.

Yet even this bit of indeterminacy is still too definite to show the whole picture — it implies that the sound [p], if it does not come wholly in one syllable or the other (or if there are not two contiguous [p] segments, one in each syllable), comes right at the mid point between the two. It would appear, on the contrary, that the sound [p] in the second syllable following the stressed one might not necessarily come exactly at the point of greatest syllable trough — i.e., insofar as the chest pulse is concerned — but might come a bit to one side or the other, with perceptually more or less the same indeterminate function, by infinite stages. If we call such a changing relationship of the consonant to the intersyllabic border a PHASE DRIFT between the phonemic wave of movement and the syllable wave of movement, we may have a convenient way to label such data. Then we can state, for example, that the phase drift may change with rate of utterance — that a postsyllabic consonant of slow speech may by a gradual phase drift, with gradual increase of speed, move to intersyllabic position. Thus a very slow morpheme-by-morpheme pronunciation of the word *biting* (e.g., as used by a person explaining to another the place where the word should be broken for orthographic purposes at the end of a line) may have the /t/ as a clear arresting consonant of the first syllable, but faster pronunciations may gradually move that consonant to an intersyllabic position.

A somewhat different result occurs when a postsyllabic consonant has a phase change which brings it by gradual increase of speed to a presyllabic position in a following syllable, but with an intermediate stage during which the consonant becomes 'double' such that it is arresting for the first syllable, releasing for the second, with a perceptual syllabic border in the middle of the sound — which now becomes two phonetic segments, [p] plus [p]. (For discussion of the change of a consonant from one syllable to another, with change of speed, and for the change from a single to a double consonant, one may consult many samples from Stetson, e.g., 1951:34, 41, 73-75, 98-99.)

In situations of these kinds, the problem of syllable identity is a serious one. In *biting*, for example, is the *-ting* of a rapid pronunciation, in which the /t/ is of the indeterminate intersyllabic type mentioned above, to be considered the same emic syllable as the *ting-* of *tingle*? Or is the *bit-* of a rapid pronunciation of *biting* to be considered the same emic syllable as the *bit-* in the slow, morpheme-by-morpheme pronunciation of the same word? At what stage in a phase drift does a phoneme pass from one emic syllable to another? And when is it theoretically as well as practically indeterminate? Much more work is needed before such questions can be answered.

We hazard a few general principles, however, which need testing: When it is decided that the data are indeterminate, with a non-arresting, nonreleasing, intersyllabic consonant (such that the [t] of *biting* is demonstrated instrumentally to have its phoneme peak during the center of the syllable trough), we assume that the PHONEME IS IN DOUBLE SYLLABLE-FUNCTION, as a simultaneous member of both syllables. In *biting*, the first syllable would be *bit-* and the second would be *-ting*; the /t/ in each instance would be the same — there would not be postulated a two-phoneme sequence /t-t/, but only one phoneme, which is simultaneously a member of both emic syllables.

This then raises the problem of the relationship, for example, between the syllables of *bedding* /ˈbɛdɪŋ/ and of *'bad dog* /ˈbæ˜d.dɔ˜g/ (with the symbol /˜/ as indicating controlled syllable type; see § 9.221). Since, by the above principle, the first word has two syllables (ending and beginning in the sound /d/ respectively), and the phrase *bad dog* likewise has two syllables (ending and beginning respectively in /d/), is it not implied that the syllable /ˈbɛd/ and the syllable /ˈbæ˷d/, the syllable /dɪŋ/ and the syllable /dɔ˜g/, are comparable, when in fact they clearly differ? The necessary reply, if the present analysis proves useful, would be to grant to some degree the implied parallelism of the syllables as isolated bits, but to deny the implication that the sequences containing them must therefore likewise be parallel; rather the theory would insist that the two sequences differ in that in the first sequence there is a fusion of two emic syllables such that at their borders there is a single phoneme in double function,[7] whereas in the second illustration there is no such fusion, the syllable border is clear cut, two consonant phonemes occur, and the two sequences contrast.

A slightly different diagram of the two sequences may perhaps make the analysis even more clear:

---

[7] We may be here dealing with another instance of etic versus emic analyses. Etically, I have handled the syllable boundary in *bedding* as indeterminate, with the consonant in double function between the two syllables. Sarah Gudschinsky suggests (private communication) that emically this might be treated as analyzable into a syllable ending in a consonant, preceding a syllable beginning with a vowel, when in a two-syllable stress group the first syllable is stressed — i.e., CVC.VC. This would fill out the pattern of CV.CV, CVC.CV, CV.V.

/ˈbɛ|d|ˈŋ/   versus   /ˈbæ~d|.|dɔ~g/

This diagram is designed to emphasize the fact that only one phoneme /d/ is involved in the first instance, with two of them in the second, and that an additional difference lies in the placement of the syllable border. (A further use of the concept of partial fusion of hyperphonemes, with a lower-layered unit serving in double function at the border of the two, will be utilized again later, in reference to abdominal pulses, in § 9.24; see also § 14.)

9.237 *Abbreviated Forms in Reference to Variants, Complexes, and Fusion*

There remain a number of kinds of abbreviated utterances in rapid English speech where the phonetic and pattern data need reporting in much more intricate detail, or in which the theoretical outlook needs further modification or operational development, before emic syllable analysis can be anything but uncertain. The reason for this difficulty is that a particular abbreviated form (1) may have lost one or more syllables as over against the slower, longer form, (2) may constitute a systemically-conditioned phonemic-content variant of the emic form (§ 9.231), (3) may have lost one emic syllable, with the remnants of one former emic syllable now constituting an etic part of an etically-complex single emic syllable (cf. § 9.235), or (4) may have fused borders between two syllables in the fast form which have no fused borders in the slow form (cf. § 9.236). Until there is available in any particular instance a considerable amount of phonetic data in reference to chest-pulse types and borders, and abdominal-pulse types and borders, and data in reference to the patterned forms of very fast speech of that language instead of the traditional presentations in terms of slow or moderately-fast speech, without serious study of the extra-fast types in which the most serious modifications take place, it may be difficult or impossible to tell which of the above numbered possibilities — or others — have been actualized. Even when these data are later available, there will presumably be some continuing examples of indeterminacy within the structure, rather than the current uncertainty due to the incompleteness of the report of the structure.

I would assume that a form such as *It's* (as an abbreviation of *It is*) would illustrate the first type suggested above — the loss of a syllable via the loss of the nucleus of that syllable. Twaddell's phrase *It's cool today* abbreviated to *'s cool today* (1953:424, 446, 447, 450) is much more difficult. If, as he suggests, the two are not homophonous, but contrast, I would infer that the *'s* constitutes a separate emic syllable from the following *cool*. (Compare, also, my handling of /ş/ as a syllable in [*It*]*'s the truth*, 1945:98, although the selection is less useful than Twaddell's, since it does not lend itself to the same type of contrast).

Yet is *'s* a separate emic syllable from *it's*, or is it a sub-emic variant of that syllable? If the *'s* occurs exclusively as a result of the abbreviation of *it's*, the most convenient analysis is to treat it as a speed-conditioned variant of the unstressed form of the emic syllable *it's*, but if an *s* which is syllabic results also from the abbreviation of other syllables than *it's*, one could not emically identify *s* both with *it's* and with another such syllable without falling into a kind of analysis which leads to intersection of emic entities (§ 8.33(6)).

Several other items in the current literature could likewise be profitably re-studied with such possibilities in mind. Note *Ed had ''edited it* [ɛdɛ''dɛdɛdɛdɪt] (or [ɛdɛd''-ɛdɛdɛdɪt] or [ɛdɛ''d̩ɛd̩ɛd̩ɪt] with the low dot for syllable border) in Pike (1945:98), which must be treated at least in part as having numerous partial fusions between syllables, with the /d/ phonemes serving repeatedly in double function within the syllable sequence (§ 9.236). Another problem phrase is seen in Twaddell (1953:424, 446, 449, 450): *If it's squarely in front* as ʼf+ʼts+squarely ʼn+front#. Quite different is the problem raised by D. Jones' analysis of short British *Thank you* as [k̩kyu] (which I presume contrasts with *cue* [kʰyu]?), in 1940 (227). Many more problems would also arise if one followed a suggestion of Eugene A. Nida's (in conversation) that one should analyze the speech of tobacco auctioneers. See also the abbreviations discussed in Pike (1949).

9.24 *The Distribution Mode of the Emic Syllable*

The characteristics of the distribution mode of the emic syllable within abdominemes (i.e., emic stress groups) or within sequences of abdominemes is analogous, on a higher hierarchical layer, to the distribution of the phoneme within syllables or sequences of syllables. By reference to the latter (§ 8.5), therefore, we can shorten considerably the present section.

9.241 *Distribution of the Emic Syllable in Larger Hyperphonemes*

Just as the phoneme has as a component of its distribution mode a potential for occurrence within certain slots in one or more emic classes of syllables, and within certain sequences of phonemes within contiguous structural slots in hyperphonemes (§ 8.51), so an emic syllable has as a component of its distribution mode the potential for occurrence within certain slots in one or more emic classes of abdominemes or in even larger hyperphonemes, and the potential for occurrence contiguous to certain other emic syllables in such hyperphonemes. Thus the syllables *con-* and *pre-* are distributed in the syllable slot preceding the peak (the stressed syllable) of the abdomineme in *conserve* and *preserve*, whereas *-serve* and *-tain* are distributed within the peak slot of the abdomineme in *reserve* and *retain*; and syllables ending in voiced consonants might in some language have the potential for occurring, in an abdomineme, before syllables beginning with voiced consonants but not before syllables beginning with voiceless ones, etc.

Just as a single phoneme could be distributed not only within one of the phases of a single syllable, but may also serve in double function at the border of two contiguous syllables within an abdomineme (§ 9.236), so a single syllable may occur not only at the pre-peak or post-peak phase of an abdomineme, but may also serve in double function by occupying the trough between two abdominemes in a breath group, as a member of both. Compare, for example, the utterance

a ˈbook of ˈstories with a ˈbook of stories.
3- º2-3 3- º2-4   3- º2-   -3- º2-4

In the first utterance, *a book* constitutes one abdomineme, and *of stories* a second (with a down glide on *book* symbolized by the numbers 2-3, and with clear segmentation between the two stress groups symbolized by the lack of hyphens between the º2-3 and 3-). In the second utterance, the syllable *of* serves in double function, completing the first stress group, ˈ*book of*, and beginning the second, *of* ˈ*stories* (symbolized by the hyphens on both sides of the -3- between the two primary contours whose beginning points are symbolized by the degree sign). For discussion of this material, and further illustrations, see Pike, 1945 (esp. 37, 67, 160-61).

This change of the phase relationship between the occurrence of the syllable and the occurrence of the trough between abdominemes can be diagrammed, furthermore, in a manner analogous to that used for syllable-phoneme relations in § 8.51:

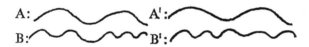

A, A¹: Stress Group Phases   B, B¹: Syllable Phases

9.242 *Distribution of the Emic Syllable in Grammatical Units*

Sometimes the restrictions upon the occurrence of a particular emic syllable are composed, not of their relation to their including stress group, but of their relation to the grammatical units within which they wholly or partly occur. Thus we had occasion to mention, when discussing the distribution of phonemes, that in Zoque no phoneme occurs in a cluster of three or four consonants except at the beginning of a word (§ 8.52). Restated here in reference to syllable occurrence, this datum implies that a particular syllable containing three or four presyllabic consonants in Zoque can be found only at the beginning of words; this is a morphemic or hypermorphemic restriction. Similarly, in Tzeltal (§§ 7.313(2), 8.52) certain tagmemic shape-type distributional restrictions specify that every stem must contain at least a syllable nucleus plus one presyllabic consonant.

It is important to state, however, that there is no theoretical necessity for syllable boundaries to coincide with word boundaries in every instance, nor with morpheme boundaries. Frequently a syllable boundary comes in the middle of a morpheme, and a morpheme boundary in the middle of a syllable — as in Tzeltal (cf. Slocum, 1948:

77-86), where a stem of pattern CVC may combine with an affix of pattern V, producing a hypermorpheme pattern of CV.C-V (in which the dot indicates syllable division, and the hyphen morpheme division). Similarly, in English, *an aim* in slow speech follows the pattern VC. VC, but in fast speech it may follow the pattern V.C VC (with space indicating word division).

9.243 *Immediate Constituents of the Emic Syllable*

As for the morpheme (§ 6.64), the tagmeme (§ 7.54), and the phoneme (§ 8.53), the internal structuring of the emic syllable is a component of its distribution mode.[8] As it did for the morpheme, so for the emic syllable the sequence of consonants and vowels within it constitute its generalized SHAPE TYPE. This shape type for the emic syllable is the abstracted pattern of an emic class of syllables (§ 9.3), or of a subclass of an emic class of syllables of which it is a member, and has by anticipation been utilized repeatedly in preceding sections in the guise of formulas such as CVC or VC (e.g., §§ 8.621, 8.63), where 'C' and 'V' refer to emic classes of phonemes (§§ 8.62-66) filling slots of the slot-classes within an emic class of syllables (§ 8.66). The relationship etically between a presyllabic, a postsyllabic, and a syllabic sound within the syllable has been indicated in §§ 9.221-23; the relationship between the emic interpretation of the syllable and its etic pitch or length has been discused in § 9.225; its interpretational and distributional relations to stress groups have been discussed in §§ 9.225, 9.232, 9.236-37, 9.241. Some characteristics of nucleus and margin of the emic syllable have been anticipated in §§ 9.222-23.

It proves highly convenient, in handling the preceding elements, to assume that just as an uttereme may have a hierarchical structuring in terms of the immediate constituents (§ 7.56) of that uttereme or of the tagmemes and morphemes making up the internal structuring of that uttereme, so, likewise, a syllable may have a hierarchical structuring. Thus in a syllable of pattern CV or CCV or CCVV, the first layering is represented by a dichotomous break between prenuclear margin and the nucleus; these fill the two main high-layered slots in the structure of the syllables. Where a language contains syllables with the patterns CVC, CVVCC, CCVCC, etc., there may be postulated a dichotomous break between the nucleus on the one hand and the two margins on the other (if the nucleus somehow is independent of the two margins), or a dichotomous break between the prenuclear margin versus the nucleus and postnuclear margin (in a language in which the domain of significant pitch extends over the postnuclear margin as well as over the nucleus), etc. These analyses are justified by the distributional relations between the various specific emic syllables manifesting the emic classes of syllables represented by these syllable-type formulas. The possibility of substitution of one phoneme for another in a particular slot in the margin, for example, is likely to be more dependent upon the particular phonemes manifesting

[8] But see, now, fn. to §§ 3.5(3), 7.313(2).

other slots in that margin than it is by the particular phonemes manifesting the nucleus of such syllables. I.e., if a formula CCV is manifested by the phoneme /s/ in the first consonant slot, and the nuclear slot is filled by the phoneme /a/, the list of phonemes which may fill the second consonant slot are more likely to be controlled by the presence of the /s/ than they are by the presence of the /a/ — e.g., they may be limited to voiceless consonants after the voiceless /s/, etc. Such considerations indicate that a closer relationship exists between the two consonants than exists between either consonant and the vowel.

Similarly, in Totonaco a postvocalic glottal stop is treated as part of the nucleus, rather than as a postnuclear consonant or part of a postnuclear consonant cluster, in CVʔ and CVʔC pattern, since (1) the postnuclear distribution of the consonants /p, t, q, y, w, m, n/ can be stated simply if /Vʔ/ is treated as a nucleus (any of these consonants follow any nucleus, whether composed of /V/, or /V·/, or /Vʔ/), but the statement is more intricate if /ʔ/ is treated as part of a postnuclear cluster of consonants (since the final consonants much then be treated as occurring singly following a nucleus, and in clusters of which the first member must be /ʔ/); (2) the postvocalic glottal stop as a nuclear element would have a frequency not out of balance with nuclear components, but treated as a postnuclear consonant it would be strongly skewed from the distribution of other consonants in postnuclear position, in that it would occur with much greater frequency; (3) Spanish loans entering the Totonaco system frequently have glottal stop as a postvocalic accretion, which can be treated as a nuclear change if the glottal stop is considered a nuclear component, and in this characteristic it would parallel many other loans which have nuclear accretions composed of vocalic lengthening — but if the glottal stop is treated as postnuclear, then it is the only consonant which is added to Spanish words when they are borrowed; (4) there is often phonetic fusion between the postvocalic glottal stop and the vowel preceding it, leading to a portmanteau sound which phonetically is composed of a single-segment laryngealized vocoid — a kind of fusion which seldom unites the nuclear glottal stop with a succeeding postnuclear consonant; (5) in certain grammatical situations the initial consonant of the second morpheme of a two-morpheme sequence is lost, following a morpheme ending in a vowel nucleus or in a vowel plus glottal stop nucleus, but is not lost after a morpheme ending in a consonant other than glottal stop — and further similar grammatical situations indicate that vowel-plus-glottal-stop acts as a unit, comparable to a nucleus composed of single vowel (Aschmann, 1946:41-42; for further references, see end of § 9.223).

If, now, we wish to extend the hierarchical analysis to further internal layerings, the argument becomes much more difficult and more tenuous, though useful. Within a phonemically-complex syllable margin, we suggest, there are sometimes further hierarchically-ordered arrangements: In a sequence of two consonants the first may function quite differently from the second in that it may in some sense be considered subordinate to the second, or on the other hand the second may be subordinate to the first; in a sequence of three consonants, two of the three may be linked in a structural block within which the two are structurally more closely bound to each other than either is to the third; and the two may or may not be subordinatie to the third; similar subordinations and groupings may occur in groups of two or three vowels, or of two or three tones. Criteria for determining such groupings and subordinations are found in Pike and Pike (1947), and in E. V. Pike (1954:34-37): (1) A distribution class of phonemes containing members of lower phonetic rank (with criteria for rank listed in § 8.623) is frequently, but not always, subordinate to a distribution class of phonemes containing members of higher phonetic rank (Mazatec /h/ is subordinate to /k/ in /kha/); any member of the class partakes of the subordinate or nonsubordinate nature of the class as a whole. (2) When, of two distribution classes, one has a smaller membership than the other, the one with smaller membership (the 'lack of diversity') is likely to be subordinate to the other (Mazatec V_1 is subordinate to V_2 and V_3 in CVVV, since only /e/ and /a/ occur in the first vocalic slot, but more vowels occur in the other slots). (3) If members of one distribution class are perceptually less prominent than members of another class, due to shorter length, or greater distance from the peak of the syllable, or other reason, such less prominent members are likely to constitute a subordinate distribution class (in Mazatec CV_1V_2, V_1 is very rapid, weak, and hence subordinate). (4) In a sequence of three consonantal distribution classes which may occur together as the prenuclear margin of an emic syllable class at the beginning of an utterance, two of the three classes are likely to be more closely joined to each other structurally than they are to the third if, in the middle of an utterance following a vowel, part of the prenuclear margin of the second syllable shifts phase so that the new syllable boundary comes after the two consonantal slot-classes and before the third, etc. (in Mazatec CCCV, the first consonant "occasionally syllabifies partially with the preceding syllable in the middle of utterances"). (5) In a sequence of three marginal phonemes or of three nuclear phonemes, the immediate-constituent border is likely to occur between the first and second (or second and third) if a morpheme boundary occurs at that point in the sequence (in Mazatec CVVV, a morpheme break always occurs before the third vowel). (6) In a sequence of three phonemes, the criteria utilized for sequences of two phonemes may be successively applied (if the immediate constituent analysis cannot be arrived at otherwise), such that, for example, the three are graded in series according to rank of articulation of their respective memberships. The Mazatec syllable ntiai$^{4\text{-}2\text{-}4}$ in khoa^{1}ntiai$^{4\text{-}2\text{-}4}$ 'we (exclusive) will travel' (with *ntia*$^{4\text{-}2}$ constituting the morpheme 'road'), for example, by these criteria has the following constituents: ([n/t]) ([{i/a}] [{$^{4/2}$} {^{4}}]).

E. V. Pike (1954) has shown that such analyses have much more than exclusively descriptive interest: She demonstrates that the subordinate status of consonants in clusters has a considerable effect on the most efficient way of introducing consonantal combinations in a sequence of lessons for teaching people to read. They allow for generalizations as to the particular consonants of a consonant cluster which are more likely to be utilized or omitted by very young children as they begin to talk. They also lend themselves to supplementary summarizing statements of certain kinds of consonantal and vocalic losses which lead to cluster reductions in some instances of dialectal change over a period of time in different geographical areas.

9.244 *Emic Classes of Emic Syllables*

It follows, on the basis of the discussion in the last section, that the analysis of the immediate constituents of a single emic syllable by itself cannot be made: An immediate-constituent analysis of an emic syllable is possible only in relation to the respective emic classes of phonemes (§§ 8.62-66) of which each phoneme of such a syllable is a member, and in relation to the particular emic class of syllables of which the emic syllable itself is a member. Identification of emic classes of phonemes is likewise in turn possible only in relation to their occurrence within slots of the shape type of the emic syllables which they in part constitute. Here, as many times before in the theory, we find that two kinds of analysis must proceed together, since their components are reciprocally relevant to each other.

The feature mode of an EMIC CLASS OF EMIC SYLLABLES is composed of the components which identify that class and which distinguish it from other classes. One such important component is the specific set of emic classes of phonemes which make up any one emic class of emic syllables. Some of these classes were illustrated, for English, in § 8.63, where Emic Phoneme Class 4, composed of /p, t, k/, composed the filler for the second slot in emic syllable patterns beginning with three consonants (as in *split*).

We shall not attempt to justify here the treating of a syllable type like CV as distinct from one like CCV, beyond referring to the demonstrated usefulnes of the concept as it has already appeared in earlier sections — e.g., the last — and as we shall have occasion to refer to these units again. Every reference to 'syllable type' or 'syllable pattern' or *generalized* phoneme sequence in syllables has tacit reliance on some theory related to this one, even though such a theory may not have been made explicit. The phrase 'syllable pattern' may be restated, in our terms, to read: "abstracted pattern of the emic slot-class sequences within an emic class of emic syllables", and the emic classes of phonemes entering the slots in emic syllables are one component of the feature[9] mode of such an emic class of emic syllables.

The manifestation mode of an emic class of emic syllables includes, as components, all of the nonsimultaneous variants of such an emic class. Identical variants of a manifested member of the class would be composed of repetitions of that particular emic syllable. Free variants of an emic class of emic syllables would consist of the occurrence of different specific emic syllables of the same general pattern, manifesting the same class, as /pa/ and /ta/ might both manifest a class CV. Locally-conditioned variants of an emic class of syllables might find their controlling conditions linked to the place of occurrence of the manifesting syllables in reference to the stress group or

---

[9] Note that here we were close to the analysis recommended by Crawford. See fn. to § 3.5(3) for the kind of reworking of other sections which would make them more consistent with this one.

breath group; for example, with the nucleus of each of the manifesting emic syllable of the class being subphonemically lengthened when they are stressed. Systemically-conditioned variants might be composed of syllables of the class pronounced in a staccato style, or a decrescendo manner, when occurring within a congruent system of 'syllable timing' (Pike, 1945:34-35, 109-10). Fused manifested variants of emic classes of emic syllables may occur when specific members of emic classes in sequence are fused (§ 9.236).

The distribution mode of an emic class of emic syllables includes its internal structuring[10] into emic slot-classes of phonemes (§ 8.66). In a CVC pattern — i.e., in a CVC emic class of emic syllables — the C slot and the consonant class of phonemes occurring in that slot make up part of the internal distributional relations of that syllable pattern, inasmuch as that particular consonant class precedes rather than following the nucleus, etc. Each such slot must be active, in order to be relevant to the internal distributional structure of the emic syllable. A passive slot may be filled by one segment of a phonetically-complex single phoneme (§ 8.445) without constituting a structural slot which needs symbolization in the CVC formula. Although a number of rules-of-thumb can be set up to decide in many instances whether or not a particular two-segment sequence of phones constitutes a single phoneme or a sequence of phonemes (Pike, 1947c:131-40), and whether the slots in which they occur are correspondingly active or passive, further work needs to be done before some of the theoretical reasons underlying such useful judgments are clearly understood. Presumably, however, such reasons, once clearly known, will in part be analogous to those adduced for the activeness of morphemes and tagmemes in § 6.61, 7.51.

9.245 *Emic Hyperclasses of Emic Syllables*

A further component of the distribution mode of an emic class of emic syllables is its membership in an EMIC HYPERCLASS OF EMIC CLASSES OF EMIC SYLLABLES — i.e., within a hierarchy of classes of syllables. Thus in some languages, for certain purposes, it is convenient to point out that an emic class CV, an emic class CCV, and an emic class CCCV, comprise together a larger composite class whose smaller member classes have certain distributional features[11] in common, as over against, say, various classes of emic syllables ending in a consonant.

Such emic hyperclasses of emic classes of emic syllables sometimes play a prominent role in artifically-patterned hyper-utteremes — e.g., in certain types of patterned verse, say of Latin. A particular poem format, for example, may constitute a special subsystem of the language, containing certain functional contrasts (not merely physical

---

[10] Here we fall back into the less-desirable view — of the internal shape as distribution mode. The external distribution should have been highlighted instead, for coherence with the theory. See, again, Crawford (1963).
[11] External distribution is again, fortunately, in focus.

differences) between such emic hyperclasses of emic syllables — hyperclass contrasts which do not occur in ordinary speech within the same language, even though the specific individual syllables and morphemes are the same in its verse as those which occur in its prose. A verse pattern, for example, may at certain slots in its included abdominemes require the presence of a manifested member of a 'heavy' emic hyperclass of syllables, composed of CVC or CV· sequences, etc., whereas at other slots in the verse the pattern may require the occurrence of a manifested member of a 'light' emic hyperclass of syllables, composed of a CV type only. In such a situation, the manifested CVC and CV· sequences would be variants of one emic hyperclass of emic syllables, and the manifested CV sequences would constitute variants of a distinct, contrastive, emic hyperclass of emic syllables.

Since, however, the verse pattern here introduces a specific hyperclass overdifferentiated (§ 8.61) dichotomy which does not occur in non-controlled speech, the verse hyper-uttereme pattern may be assumed to represent a different PARTIALLY-CONGRUENT SYSTEM OF EMIC HYPERCLASSES OF EMIC SYLLABLES. The emic hyperclasses of emic syllables of the verse and of speech would be topologically related in many details, but not identical at this particular point where the hyperclass is overdifferentiated in the verse system.

A further value obtained from the postulation of emic hyperclasses of emic syllables is that it lays part of the foundation for the theoretical justification for treating a syllable nucleus as a unit, even though some nuclei may contain only one phoneme and other nuclei may contain two or more phonemes (whether two vowels, or vowel plus consonant, or vowel plus glottal stop plus vowel, § 9.223). Such nuclei would have in common the fact that they fill a single active slot in a hyperclass of syllables; single phonemes in the nuclear slot might be homologous with phoneme sequences, for example, from the point of view of their relations to the distributional potential of consonants in the margins before and after them.

The sum of the emic hyperclasses of emic syllables in all the congruent systems of a language would make up the total syllabic pattern or syllable system of that language.

9.25 *The Etics of Syllable Structure*

Paralleling the treatment of the etics of the morpheme, tagmeme, and phoneme in §§ 6.8, 7.7, 8.7, it is possible to summarize here certain characteristics of syllable structure:

Segmentation of etic syllables is determined in reference to articulatory waves of motion constituted of chest pulses (§ 9.221), with borders delimited clearly or in fused fashion according to the arresting and releasing phonemes of the etic syllables, or chest relase and arrest of such syllables (§§ 9.222, 9.236, 9.237, 9.241).

Etic classificatory criteria for types of etic syllables include at least the folowing, which are given in the form of questions: (a) Does the etic syllable pulse begin with a ballistic stroke? end with one? Does it begin with a controlled movement? end with one? (§ 9.221). (b) Does it begin with a contoid? vocoid? consonant? vowel? groups of two or more of these? end with such elements? (§ 9.222). (c) Is the border clear? fused? (§§ 9.223, 9.236-37). (d) Is the nucleus composed of a vocoid? contoid? vowel? consonant? vowel sequence? one or two vowels plus glottal stop or other consonant? (§§ 9.223, 9.243, 9.245). (e) What is its phonemic content? (§ 9.224). (f) What is its relation to pitch? to length of sounds? to the peak of abdominemes? or to the unstressed part of abdominemes? to breath groups? (§ 9.241). (g) Is there evidence for hierarchical structuring within the syllable? (§ 9.243). (h) What is its relation to a class of syllables, as regards congruent system, size, subclasses, distribution, shape type, and rank of included phonemes? (§§ 8.623, 9.244-45).

Basic to the operations which allow one to pass from a crude etic analysis to an emic one is the assumption, furthermore, that every etic syllable is either (a) a free variant of an emic syllable (§ 9.234), (b) a conditioned variant of an emic syllable (§§ 9.231-33), (c) part of an etically-complex emic syllable (§ 9.235), (d) a sequence of two or more manifested variants of emic syllables, so that the tentative etic syllable needs further etic segmentation (cf. § 9.221), (e) a fused composite variant of two or more partially or completely simultaneous — portmanteau — emic syllables (cf. § 9.236), or (f) an error of etic recording which would be eliminated by more accurate rechecking; and (g) the emic syllables composed of these etic syllables are members of emic distribution classes of emic syllables within the larger system of the language as a whole (§§ 9.244-45).

9.3 *The Emic Stress Group*

The EMIC STRESS GROUP (or ABDOMINEME) is a hyperphoneme, containing all the characteristics of hyperphonemes which were specified in § 9.1, and is further characterized by the fact that most of the manifested members of the emic-stress-group system of which it is a part are coterminous with a physical abdominal pulse (but for two-pulse emic stress groups see §§ 9.312, 9.32).

9.31 *The Feature Mode of the Emic Stress Group*

9.311 *The Abdominal Pulse*

The physiological feature which most certainly differentiates an emic stress group from emic units of lower levels of the phonological hierarchy (i.e., contrasts it with syllables and phonemes) and from higher levels (i.e., contrasts it with breath groups, etc.) is a wave of movement which may be called an ABDOMINAL PULSE. For the initial physiological description of and emphasis upon the etic abdominal pulse we are indebted to Stetson: "The [rectus and parietal] muscles of the abdomen compress the viscera and force up the diaphragm, thus reducing the volume of the chest. The movement of the abdominal muscles[12] makes the stress, grouping the feet, and breath groups" (1951:193a, 31b); such movements "group the syllables" (57b) "about a single stressed syllable" (3b). (Further quotations from Stetson may be seen in Twaddell, 1953:427-29; a diagram of the musculature involved may be seen in Stetson, 1951:16a, with action-potential recordings of its operation on 12-13.)

One may sense kinesthetically the surges of the abdominal musculature by pronouncing a sentence with highly exaggerated stresses. This necessitates especially-strong muscular movements, and frequently will bring them above the threshold of attention, as tension in the abdomen parallels the recurrence of stresses.

Before one has learned to notice these movements in exaggerated or in normal speech, however, the abdominal pulse is often most easily noticed as "a single rush of syllables" with a single stressed syllable making up a "simple rhythm unit" (Pike, 1945:34), or a "foot" (Stetson, 1951:3b).

Our empirical data, however, suggest that we most assume contrastive differences in abdominal pulses of types not postulated by Stetson. For the syllable, he noted contrasts between ballistic movements and those with controlled movement, even though he did not develop these differences in as much detail as we needed for the theory above (§ 9.221). For abdominal pulses he provides much less: that is, the

---

[12] Ladefoged rejects the assumption that abdominal muscles are the *normal* producing source for stress groups: "Our observations are that in normal conversational English the abdominal muscles are in action only at the end of a very long utterance. In most utterances the air pressure is regulated solely by the intercostals" (1962:81; also 1958:13). But for the intercostal muscles, "Close examination of the records shows that in each utterance there is consistent pulsing action of the muscle before stresses in the sentence" (Draper, Ladefoged, Whitteridge, 1960:14, Fig. 6).

Thus it seems clear that *some* kind of pulsing activity must be maintained as a physiological component of our theory. Whether or not this must ultimately be stated in terms of some kind of hierarchy of movement types, or wave characteristics, of the one or the other set of muscles, or whether it involves various sets of muscles, it does not change the fact that we must leave room in our phonetic and phonemic theory for both the syllabic and rhythm-unit levels of pronunciation. In addition, there must be some room for the rhythm units specifically involving abdominal pulses, as Ladefoged admits: "Of course on the prade ground or in other ceremonial languages (Pike, 1957c), the abdominal muscles may play a more important part" (1962:81; Ladefoged and others, 1958:13).

I personally like to treat the physical organization of syllables into rhythm units as some type of hierarchical organization of waves, since it allows more ready adaptation to my approach via particle, wave, and field. Note, also, that it seems to be possible to obtain support for this view in the physiology claims of Lashley: "I believe that there exist in the nervous organization, elaborate systems of interrelated neurons capable of imposing certain types of integration upon a large number of widely spaced effector elements; in the one case transmitting temporally spaced waves of facilitative excitation to all effector elements" so that "They contribute to every perception and to every integrated movement" (in Saporta, 1961:192); they result in "a series of hierarchies of organization" which make a "syntax of movement" (187). For our purposes here the precise physiology of the techniques is less important than the fact that *some* physical phenomena underlie the etics of syllable and of rhythm unit. While these are being further investigated by the instrumentalists — and until they investigate special parade-ground effects and the perceptually-contrastive types of unit reported here — I leave the early tentative statement as before.

occasional use of the term "pulse" in the phrase "abdominal pulse" may imply a ballistic stroke, but his descriptions uniformly imply exclusively a controlled movement, as when he says that "In reality, the primary stress is the climax of the single slow movement which underlies and constitutes the unity of the foot, and of the breath group" (1951:97b, and cf. 106b). I am convinced, on kinesthetic evidence, that we must for the abdominal pulse, as for the syllable pulse, postulate types which are (a) ballistic, (b) controlled, (c) beginning ballistic and ending controlled, (d) beginning controlled and ending ballistic.

The abdominal-pulse type which is ballistic, with neither ending nor beginning constituted of a controlled movement, seems to be illustrated by the 'barking' of military[13] count such as *hup! two! three! four!* in which each syllable constitutes a ballistic abdominal pulse. I also have a suspicion that a mild variety of ballistic-type abdominal pulse is characteristic of the normal speech of certain speakers of American English (e.g., some persons in northwest Arkansas), producing in almost every sentence a sequence of stressed syllables some of which are likely to end in a sharp, rapid decrescendo which fades into a weak articulation, or are followed quickly by syllables with such decrescendo.

The abdominal-pulse type which is completely controlled, with neither ballistic beginning nor ending, is, perhaps, the mechanism behind that variety of SYLLABLE TIMING (Pike, 1945:35) during which each syllable is sharp cut, of approximately equal duration, and during which no one syllable is suddenly given a stress sharply distinct from its neighboring stresses even though the peak of the abdominal pulse does involve a stressed syllable. Syllable timing may occur, in English, as an identificational-contrastive feature characteristic of a particular style (i.e., of a congruent system) such as chanting, or in a mild form it may be a characteristic of the normal congruent system of a language other than English, such as Spanish.

An abdominal-pulse type which begins with a ballistic stroke, ends with a controlled movement, but with the total length of the pulse determined approximately by the pulse movement rather than by the number of syllables within it, would presumably represent the type occurring in such an utterance as *telephone* or *telephone number* in the majority of English dialects. This would include stress groups which begin with a stressed syllable and end with one or more unstressed syllables — and includes, also, stress groups composed of one syllable only — provided that the decay of intensity is relatively slow, of approximately the same duration in each instance, where one or several post-stress syllables are present.

An abdominal-pulse type which begins with a controlled movement but ends with a ballistic movement would be illustrated by those stress groups which begin with several

---

[13] Our military illustration is now supplemented by contrastive types in natural languages. Aguaruna has a special very sharp decrescendo type for rapid phrases (continuing for a couple of hours) in greeting ceremonies; no electrode studies have been made to check on the assumed musculature, however. Similarly, Culina has very sharp decrescendo types used for emphasis in story telling (Pike, 1957c). For English, see discussion, below, of *Well!*

not-too-fast syllables before the stressed syllable, and end with a stressed syllable with rapid decrescendo. Such a pattern in English would be rare, since the beginning would be appropriate to an unhurried, deliberate style, and the ending to a rapid or emphatic style; only special effects, or surprise, etc., would bring the two together. One such special effect I think I have heard in the syllable *Well!*, as a kind of hearty response; it began with the voice weak, built up to a rapid, strong crescendo, with quick breathy release on the final consonant.

An unhurried, controlled beginning, with an unhurried, controlled ending after the central ballistic pulse, however, seems to occur frequently in American English of non-special style (i.e., in normal style, other than chanting, etc.). It would be illustrated by such an utterance as *What's his telephone number* if stress occurs on *telephone* but does not occur on *What's* or *his*. A ballistic beginning of the stressed syllable, with a controlled post-stress end of the stress group and an optional controlled pre-stressed beginning, appear to comprise some of the crucial features of the basic pattern of somewhat-even timing of recurrent stress groups which makes up the characteristic STRESS TIMING of English (Pike, 1945:36, 41).

9.312 *Nucleus and Margins of the Stress Group*

Just as the syllable has nucleus and margins, so does the stress group.[14]

The nucleus would be composed of the stressed syllable, in a simple stress group of pattern sSs (for which the upper-case S symbolizes the stressed syllable, and the lower-case s symbolizes one or more unstressed syllables).

As on occasion (§ 9.223) we have postulated syllables with phonemically-complex nuclei, patterned as CVVC, so here it may be convenient to postulate an occasional single emic stress group which contains a complex nucleus composed of two adjacent stressed syllables which together stretch over the time during which a single abdominal pulse is reaching its peak of movement. Such an emic unit may be symbolized as

---

[14] I have now attempted a systematic treatment of the practical phonetics of rhythm units (1962b). In it I set up an etics of the rhythm unit, cutting the wave — the contour — into premargin, preslope, nucleus, postslope, and postmargin.

Nuclei may be marked by loudness, high pitch, or length, or by a special segment sequence, or by some combination of these characteristics. The nucleus may be determinate — marked by these characteristics — even when the boundaries are left indeterminate. Premargin and slope may be marked by crescendo, by rising pitch, or by extra-rapid pitch, or by special segments. Postslope and postmargin may be marked by decrescendo, by extra length, by falling pitch, by special segments, or by some combination of these.

Borders between rhythm units are sometimes — not always — clearly marked by some one or more devices; in such an instance, the nucleus need not be marked — it may be indeterminate — while the rhythm unit as a whole is determinate.

A frequent pattern for American-English contours is rapid premargin (and preslope), with crescendo and rising pitch; followed by a nucleus which is loud, high, long; followed by postslope which with decrescendo, falling in pitch, and a bit slower than the premargin but faster than the nucleus; with the end of the postmargin falling off heavily in loudness and pitch, while being drawled.

sSSs, and be illustrated by the phrase *a ⎜big ⎜boy* (in which the word *big* is pro-
$$3\text{-}\ ^02\text{-}\ \text{-}^02\text{-}4$$
nounced rapidly, but stressed) as over against the two-group sequence of *a ⎜big ⎜boy*
$$3\text{-}\ ^02\text{-}2\ ^02\text{-}4$$
(in which the word *big* requires more time for utterance, with an intonation break before the final word of the phrase; cf. Pike, 1954:39; cf. also, in relation to syllable types, § 9.221(4), above). For the symbolism involved, see § 6.62. In an item such as *Tom!*, the nucleus is composed of the first part of the only syllable in the stress group, and may be symbolized as S.

The margins of a stress group may be composed of the last part of a stressed syllable, as in the previous example, or of one or more syllables following and/or preceding the stressed syllable, as in *of the ⎜telephones*.

Constrastive nuclear types include differences as to the intensity-decay characteristics of the nucleus (a normal stressed syllable, versus one with rapid decrescendo — cf. § 9.311), as to the controlled versus noncontrolled character of the syllable at the nucleus (§ 9.221(3)), and — as in English — the specific intonational pitch phonemes on that nucleus. Contrastive marginal types may differ by the number of syllables, or by the presence versus absence of any syllables, by the staccato versus glissando character of these syllables, or as to their ballistic versus controlled types, and may differ in accordance with the pitch phonemes which occur on their manifesting syllables, etc.

A system with two or more contrastive degrees of intensity on nuclei of abdominal pulses would correspondingly have two or more sets of emic stress groups, differing respectively by the occurrence of one or other of these degrees of stress. In English, however, one should note that if one treats the last syllable of the verb *separate* /⎜sɛpəreˇt/ as a controlled-syllable-pulse type — as we do above, § 9.221, following Twaddell's suggestion — rather than as carrying 'secondary stress' then one finds in ordinary spoken English no emic stress group in the verb *separate* other than the same emic stress group seen in the adjective *separate* [⎜sɛpərɪt]; the prominence of the last syllable of the verb is attributed to the character of its contrastive syllable type, and the rhythmic difference of the verb is analyzed as a conditioned variant of the rhythmic pattern caused by its included emic syllables.

Metric verse, however, may constitute one or more hyper-utteremic patterns in which certain overdifferentiated hyperclasses of emic stress groups are in turn composed of member groups which occur relative to one another at certain points in the hyper-utteremic pattern — i.e., they are selected and so placed as to RHYME. In such an instance, the vocalic and consonantal content of certain syllables at certain places in the emic stress groups are relevant identificational-contrastive components of those classes or hyperclasses of emic stress groups which may be emically overdifferentiated in English verse (cf. also §§ 9.245, 8.61, for a similar problem as regards syllable weight and overdifferentiated classes; cf. also § 10.4, for this phenomenon in reference to hypermorphemes).

The number of syllables in an emic stress group and their placement relative to the peak of the group also becomes relevant in much English verse, leading to further overdifferentiated hyperclasses of emic stress groups such as iambic or trochaic feet, etc. The control of tone rhymes in some Chinese verse (see Pike, 1948:34-35fnn. 42-43, for references) likewise leads to further relevant classes of syllables and/or of emic stress groups. In English, furthermore, in such overdifferentiated situations, emic stress groups which contain no unstressed controlled-chest-pulse syllables are members of different hyperclasses of emic stress groups from those to which emic stress groups belong which do contain controlled-chest-pulse syllables (since the controlled-pulse syllables may function, in the metric verse, as if they are stressed; cf. Twaddell, 1953:444). Some writers of verse, however, studiously avoid the setting up of those special hyperclasses of emic stress groups which depend upon number of syllables, by utilizing the normal system (rather than the overdifferentiated one), and exploiting the patterns of recurrent timing of stresses much as they occur in regular speech (note references for Old English in Pike, 1945:180; for modern English, see discussion of the 'sprung rhythm' of Hopkins, in Weyand 1949:93-174, and W. H. Gardner, 1949:98-178).

9.32 *The Manifestation Mode of the Emic Stress Group*

An emic stress group may have locally-free but systemically-conditioned variants if a particular style affects any of the characteristics of its nucleus or margins: A rapid style might lead to more ballistic and less controlled characteristics; an emphatic style in one language might occasionally do the same — but is more likely to achieve emphasis, on the contrary, by 'drawling out' the stress groups with excessively controlled movements. The singing of a stress group would make further changes.

An emic stress group may be modified sharply by its relation to larger hyperphonemes. At the end of a breath group, for example, certain characteristics may be manifested within the particular stress group at that point, even though we attribute these characteristics emically to the larger unit (see § 9.4).

Free variation within the emic syllables or phonemes which are contained within an emic stress group imply concomitant free variation within the containing stress group.

In English, a variation in the number of syllables in a precontour is best considered as free variation in the emic stress group: the phrases *the ˈhouse* and *to the ˈhouse* manifest the same emic stress group; so also do ˈ*telephone* and ˈ*telephone number* or ˈ*telephone the man*. Similarly, the particular syllable-content of a stress contour, in English, is perhaps also best considered as free variation of that contour, so that the phrases *the ˈboy, the ˈman,* and *a ˈhouse* all manifest the same emic stress group.

On the other hand, I consider that in English two stress contours are emically different if the emic pitch on the stress syllable or after the stressed syllable are different: the stress group º2-4 is emically distinct from the stress group º2-3 or º2-4-3, etc.

The reader should note carefully that this approach now provides the theoretical basis for that which in 1945 I postulated on empirical grounds. At that time I found it essential to treat a simple rhythm unit, a stress group, and an intonation contour as in some way the same, with the relevant intonation sequences identified in reference to the beginning point of their primary contours, and this primary contour identified in reference to the placement of stress. It is now seen that the theoretical reason for the necessity of this joint treatment is that the *rhythm unit* is an emic stress group which contains, in addition to its abdominal-pulse peak (the stress) certain pitch phonemes as relevant contrastive-identificational features.

Contrastive pitch on the pre-stress syllables (the PRECONTOUR) as well as a contrastive pitch sequence on the stressed syllable-plus-post-stress syllables (the PRIMARY CONTOUR) leads to a contrastive emic stress group, a STRESS-PITCH CONTOUR (or TOTAL CONTOUR, Pike, 1945:27-30). This implies that the emic stress group is different for |*permit* (with º2-4) and *per*|*mit* (with 3-º2-4), though the primary contours are the same in pitch. The phrases *a* |*permit* (assuming the pitch sequence 3-º2-4) and *per*|*mit it* (with the same pitch sequence), however, constitute manifestations of but one emic stress group. In any particular sequence our approach demands the indication, therefore, of the particular syllable upon which the peak of the abdomineme is to fall — a placement which is in part determined by the lexical structure of the phrase (§ 9.32) and in part is variable as a function of the semantic emphasis carried by the placing of the peak of stress in such sentences as *He must* |*do it* versus *He* |*must do it*. Just as /k/ can occur early in the word *cat*, or late in *tack*, and be a relevant component of each, so the º2-4 primary contour may occur early in |*permit* or later in *per*|*mit*, and constitutes a relevant component of each of the total contours, with its placement in this particular instance determined by the lexical structure.

A special problem arises when a longer sequence contains only one heavy stress — and hence is constituted of a single stress-pitch contour — but contains a number of words of which the lexical stresses are not quite completely suppressed. The resulting slight alternation of one or more partially-suppressed stresses with completely unstressed syllables has in the past required treatment as sequences of SUBSIDIARY contours within the primary contour (Pike, 1945:73, with illustrations and discussion). It now seems much simpler, and in line with the theory, to treat such a composite of a main stress group plus one or more included partially-suppressed subsidiary stress groups as an etically-complex but emically-simple stress group; i.e., a single emic stress-pitch contour. Similarly, our data in 1945 included a number of rhythm units which seemed to require treatment as single contour entities, even though they were interrupted by pause. Such items, with a single relevant major stress, can now be treated as etically-complex single emic stress groups in which the margins may be pausally separated. Interruption of the unstressed precontour or of the unstressed ending of the primary contour, in a hesitation or quoting form, for example, would result in an

etically-complex stress group, in that one of the etic pulses of a two-pulse stress group would contain a stress, and the other would be unstressed (with the unstressed part called a "weak rhythm unit" in Pike, 1945:39-40 — or in certain instances a "postcontour" syllable, 74), as in *This is the one, the teacher said*. A slightly more
$$°2- \quad -4-/ \quad -4//$$
complicated etically-complex contour would be seen when the ending of the contour is repeated (without pause) in unstressed form (Pike, 1945; note "resumed contours", 72-73, and "deferred contours", 73): e.g., *The class studies in the house (but ...)*.
$$3- \quad °2 \quad -4-3 \quad 4- \quad -4-3/$$
Just as two syllables can partially fuse, with a phoneme in double syllable function at the border between them (§ 9.236), so two emic stress groups can partially fuse, with a syllable in double function constituting the end border of the first and the beginning border of the second stress group. Thus there occurs a contrast, in English, between the sequence sSs/sSs (in which the low diagonal slant line indicates the clearcut border between the two stress groups (i.e., an "intonation break", in terms of Pike, 1945:37), and the sequence sSsSs (in which there is no clear intonation break, since the syllable occurs on the border). (For an illustration, see the phrase *a book of stories* in § 9.241, or in Pike, 1945:37, 67, 160-61); for diagrammatic analysis of the articulatory-wave relationships, see § 9.241.)

9.33 *The Distribution Mode of the Emic Stress Group*

An emic stress group is distributed within a sequence of emic stress groups which make up the next higher layer in the phonological hierarchy of the language under attention. In many instances, perhaps in most of them, this would be within the pause group. Certain stress-group types might be restricted to particular parts of the pause group, or might come at any point in the pause group..

The distributional relationship of emic stress groups to the morphemic or hypermorphemic, tagmemic or hypertagmemic structure of a language is in some instances very important to the total structure of the language, and differs considerably from language to language. In some languages, the emic stress group is coterminous with certain hypermorpheme classes which are called 'words' (and in part constitute the definition of the word in such an instance), in that every word is composed of a single emic stress group. In such an instance, the distribution of emic stress groups within hypermorphemes larger than individual words will in some sense parallel the distribution of the words within these larger hypermorphemes. In other languages, however, the boundaries of emic stress groups within the phrase are frequently not identical with the boundaries of hypermorphemes within the same segment of speech. In such instances, the stress groups, like syllables (§ 9.242), may have their boundaries within hypermorphemic or hypertagmemic units rather than co-incidental with them. In English, for example, the pronunciation of ׀*I*׀*m 'going* (with two stresses), brings the intonation break between '*m* and ⎮*going*, whereas the grammatical structure has its most crucial internal border between ⎮*I* and '*m* ⎮*going*.

In addition, in English, the lexical and grammatical structure constitutes the setting for the *placement* of the stress-pitch contours (cf. § 9.32) which constitute the emic stress groups. Each polysyllabic morpheme or hypermorpheme in English contains a syllable which is highly likely to be the one at which the peak of the emic stress group will occur, if a peak of the stress group occurs anywhere within the word at all; the first syllable of *telephone* is likely to be the stressed one, if any syllable is stressed (though the whole word may be unstressed, if it comprises a precontour of a larger stress group, etc., and the last syllable may be specially stressed if there is need for emphatic contrast with *telegraph* in a particular context — say after a misunderstanding). Note, however, that this actual or potential control is considered a lexical characteristic of the controlling words, not a part of the emic contour itself as such. Similarly, the placement of the peak of the emic stress group is variable, for purposes of emphasis and so on, in reference to monosyllables as well as polysyllables, but this, too, may be more limited by some particular morphemes than by others (cf. Pike, 1945:82-84, 118).

Lexical control over stress placement may, in addition, specify *two* potential places of stress on a single word, one or both of which may be actualized in some one particular pronunciation: a word like *fifteen* in some dialects is pronounced as ⎮*fif*⎮*teen* in isolation, ⎮*fifteen* in a sequence ⎮*fourteen*, ⎮*fifteen* ⎮*sixteen*, and as *fif*⎮*teen* in other contexts (cf. D. Jones, 1940:232-33). For certain words of three or more syllables the stress on one syllable gets priority over a stress on another syllable, in that the one will occur if any stress occurs on the word, but the other is optional — sometimes being present in addition to the first, sometimes absent, and sometimes present but not as strong as the other (cf. words like (⎮)*inton*⎮*ation* for which the stress in parenthesis is the optional one, and see discussion in Pike, 1945:84).

Lexical control over abdominemic placement in English affects the placement of the endings and beginnings of such emic stress groups, as well as their peaks: "Primary contours and rhythm units may end coincidentally with the end of any word... Every word end is potentially the end of a primary contour or rhythm unit, and appears as such, at any time, at the semantic option of the speaker" (Pike, 1945:79-82, 29, 35-36) and "The beginning of any simple or complex rhythm unit... almost always coincides with the beginning of a word" (36), though various factors may cause this potential to be ignored or overridden.

The emic stress group, as part of its distributional mode, has an internal structuring into immediate constituents. Certain of these constituents have already been mentioned and symbolized, i.e., the nucleus and the margins (§ 9.312). In most of its characteristics, the approach to the analysis of these constituents is presumably analogous to that for the immediate constituents of emic syllables (§ 9.243).

There is one element in the analysis of English, however, which it is well to emphasize, since for me it has been especially surprising and helpful: During my first attempt at identifying the immediate constituents of emic stress groups in English, it seemed likely that the included syllables, as such, would be the most useful point of reference (paralleling the phonemic content of syllables, in the syllable analysis). This approach met with the difficulty, however, that the number of syllables seemed irrelevant to the timing-function of the English emic stress group, and hence did not serve as a fruitful structural basis for differentiating adequately their structural parts. It then occurred to me that the constants which I had previously postulated for certain contours had been identified and described in terms of stresses and pitch phonemes at key contour points — contour points which occurred at certain syllables where the pitch movement changed direction from rise to fall, or fall to rise, or where the stress changed from crescendo to decrescendo (i.e., at the stressed syllable), or from decrescendo to crescendo (i.e., at the border between two partially-fused stress groups), or where a stress group began or ended (cf. Pike, 1945:26-29; notice especially that "one does not classify the pitch of every syllable or part of a syllable, but only those points in the contour crucial to the establishment of its characteristic rises and falls"). The analysis of the intonation contours (which are now seen to be emic stress groups), furthermore, had there been accomplished in terms of a primary contour which contained a beginning point which was stressed and crucially pitched, an ending point with a crucially-pitched unstressed syllable, and sometimes an additional medial crucially-pitched change point; it optionally contained a 'precontour' — i.e., one or more syllables before the stress, with one crucial pitch or with a slurred pitch sequence (1945:29-30, 65-68). The sequence of the precontour with the primary contour then was considered to constitute a "total contour" (30). If, now, we assume that a total contour of English is the same as an emic stress group (as in § 9.32, above), then the parts of the total contour as earlier identified are now seen to constitute the elements of the product of an analysis of an emic stress group into its immediate constituents: The beginning point of a primary contour would constitute the nucleus of an emic stress group (with the "early fall in pitch" as part of an emically-complex nucleus, § 9.312, and 1945:74-75); the ending point of the total intonation contour would constitute the postnuclear margin in the immediate constituents of the emic stress group; and the precontour of the total intonation contour would constitute the prenuclear margin of the immediate constituents of the emic stress group.

Further implications follow from the immediate-constituent analysis of the stress-pitch contours of the emic stress groups of English. Just as the emic-class analysis of phonemes was a product of the occurrence of the phonemes within slots of the immediate-constituents of the emic syllable (cf. § 9.244, and §§ 8.62-66, 8.53, 8.62-66), so emic classes of components of the emic stress group are found by noting the occurrence of elements at the various points in its shape-type structure. Specifically, the precontours constitute one optional class of such items; the primary contours constitute a larger, obligatory class of those stress-pitch sequences, one of which manifests the nucleus and postnucleus of each English emic stress group; a class of single-pitch and pitch-sequence components also are found in the nucleus of the emic stress groups.

The emic stress groups, moreover, may be assumed to enter a hierarchy of classes within classes of rhythmic groups in English. The precise character of this structuring, however, needs further study, in relation to the potential and actual distribution of each specific emic stress group within the various slots in breath groups or even larger phonological units.

In rare instances it may be possible to find languages in which the syllable has no structural relevance. For describing such instances, the term syllable may be eliminated from the preceding discussion. See §§ 9.76, 9.221 for this possibility.

9.4 *The Emic Pause Group*

Various hyperphonemes which are larger than the emic syllable or emic stress group may occur in a language. One such unit which is relevant to English is the EMIC PAUSE GROUP. The general mechanism for the production of the pause group would appear to be composed of muscular movements similar to those which produce the stress group (§ 9.311), but may contain one, two, or several stress groups within it.

The feature mode of an emic pause group is marked by its producing movement and by a pause following it. In addition, it may contain one of several contrastive kinds of endings. In English, two contrastive emic pause groups are differentiated by the fact that one of them ends in a POISED or FIXATED manner (like the stance of a swimmer who has been told to 'take his mark' and 'get set'), and the other in a RELAXED musculature. The poised type is diaphragm-arrested (cf. Stetson, 1951:54b) and implies a TENTATIVE meaning, or uncertainty, or incompleteness. The relaxed type often may allow the muscular movements to 'coast' to an 'unbraked' stop (cf. reference to 'sigh' or 'groan' of unbraked syllables, in Stetson, 34a) and implies FINALITY of some type or to some degree. The poised type, furthermore, is characterized by the somewhat sustained or 'level' intonational pitch which is found on the latter part of the pause-group contour, whereas the relaxed type ends with a 'fade' of pitch and stress (i.e., in pause groups with a simultaneous falling intonational-pitch phoneme sequence) or with a 'lower than normal' final pitch (on the last syllable of a pause group which contains a falling-rising intonational-pitch sequence). A detailed discussion of this contrast, with illustrations, may be found in Pike, 1945 (vii, 31-33, 135-50, 154), and the accompanying phonograph records; in that discussion, however, the various identifying characteristics were abstracted and treated as contrastive 'phonemes of pause' (and written with single diagonal [/] and double diagonal [//] respectively (or verticaly, as [|] and [||] in Pike, 1947c:45, 50b-52), whereas there the characteristics are assumed to constitute contrastive-identificational features of the pause-group contour as a whole (for further discussion of the relation of the two approaches, see § 9.6). Further contrastive features of emic pause groups can develop by overdifferentiation in verse — e.g., alliteration, or the 'drawling' of the last syllable in the reading of a line (see references in Pike, 1945:11, 180).

If an EMPHATIC STRESS in a particular utterance is more intense than other stresses of other emic stress groups in sequence with that emphatic stress group in the same emic pause group, then the pause group has one major peak, rather than several equal peaks for each of its respective included stress groups. A non-emphatic SENTENCE STRESS might function in a similar way, with the connotation of attention given to the most important element of the sentence but without the emotional overtones which we often associate with the label of emphatic stress. In English, however, it appears to me that sentence stress is best analyzed as a special placement of the regular stress contour rather than as an emic stress contour of a special type (1945:84, 27-28). Similarly, for English 'contrastive stress', appears to be rather a special placement of stress than an additional emic degree of stress (Pike, 1945:45).

The manifestation mode of an emic pause group would include manifested variants composed of the particular emic syllables or emic stress groups included within it, and differing in accordance with the style in which the including passage is uttered, and the immediate context within the passage. Occasionally, moreover, it is necessary to differentiate between etically-simple and etically-complex variants of an emic pause group. Certain etic pause groups which contain no perceptually-stressed syllable are best treated as parts of an etically-complex emic pause group which includes an adjacent etic pause group which does contain a stress (illustrations, and references, are seen in § 9.32, where various types of such stressless pause groups are seen as weak rhythm units, postcontours, resumed contours, deferred contours, — and as the second part of etically-complex emic stress groups which, we now note, partially overlap with an emic pause group in that such an etically-complex emic stress group may constitute the sole or final emic stress group in an emic breath group).

The distribution mode of the emic pause group includes its actual or potential occurrence in larger units of the phonological hierarchy, as well as its distribution within units of the grammatical hierarchy (e.g., pauses frequently occur at the borders of utteremes, etc.). The various emic pause groups would constitute one or more emic classes of emic pause groups, in accordance with the distribution of these groups in certain slots in larger hyperphonemes or grammatical units. The internal structuring of the emic pause group, on the other hand, includes its component parts viewed as manifesting a hierarchy of immediate constituents within the slots of the abstracted shape type of an emic class of emic pause groups.

9.5 Further Hyperphonemes

The top of the phonological hierarchy has been by no means reached when one has dealt with the emic pause group. Still larger hyperphonemes occur.

An EMIC BREATH GROUP, for example, may be larger than an emic pause group, in that several of the latter may be contained in one of the former, though some breath groups may be composed of a single pause group. An emic breath group has, in addition to the characteristics of a pause group, an intake of air which marks its initial boundary.

Perhaps the term EMIC RHETORICAL PERIOD would be useful to label the kind of unity which is detectable in the 'emic phonological paragraphing' of some kinds of public address. Possibly the term EMIC PHONOLOGICAL SECTION might be used to represent even larger physiologically-identifiable phonological parts of an address — as when a 'change of pace' is deliberately accomplished by changing the speed of utterance, quality of voice, intensity, pitch, or gestural stance, in order to indicate a change of topic, a break in the outline of the address, or to elicit a relaxed attention from the audience before working up to the next climax in a series of climaxes in the address.

A total address, likewise, is often marked phonologically, so that a person identifies the approaching end of the address by phonological clues — e.g., a 'let down' or over all decrescendo of intensity contours, general intensity contour for the address as a whole, or a decrescendo of the general pitch level or speed — or, with some speakers, an emic structure whose ending is signalled (and known to their regular listeners) by the opposite — a crescendo of general levels of pitch, intensity, speed, which these speakers are known to use only at the final moments of the address.

Within a conversation, we frequently find it useful to focus on the total material stated, for example, by the second speaker after the first speaker stops and before a third begins (or before the first speaker begins again). Etically, such a chunk of speech, whether composed of a single word or of a long disquisition, may be called an UTTERANCE. From this point of view, a long public address is also a single utterance. When a series of exchanges in conversation can be so analyzed that each chunk of speech between change of speakers can be shown to be structurally relevant — or relevant within a range of etic deviations from the norm of a pattern — then each such emic chunk may be called an EMIC CONVERSATIONAL UTTERANCE-CHUNK. If, furthermore, two such chunks by the speakers in sequence can be shown to constitute a single higher-layered emic unit, these may be called an EMIC CONVERSATIONAL EXCHANGE (or an EMIC UTTERANCE-RESPONSE EXCHANGE).

Even larger emic phonological hierarchical units may, perhaps, be adduced, yet we for the moment shall stop here, as we approach a certain kind of structural threshold: Thus far, with the exception of utterance-response exchange, every kind of emic class of hyperphoneme which we have mentioned (i.e., emic syllable, emic stress group, emic pause group, etc.) has, potentially at least, one or more members which are *no larger than a single phoneme* — and which, in fact, may all be simultaneously manifested by (or at the time of) the manifestation of a single phoneme. (Hence the term 'larger' applied to hyperphoneme versus phoneme in earlier sections must be interpreted to mean "higher in the hierarchical scale and a member of a class of units *some* of which are larger than the longest units in the next lower kind of unit in the hierarchy".)

If, for example, we assume (as some analysts do not) that the English vocoid glide on /bot/ 'boat' constitutes a single phoneme /o/, then the exclamation *Oh!* begins and ends with a phoneme /o/, begins and ends with a syllable whose margins are bounded by that same phoneme, begins and ends with an emic stress group whose margins are bounded by that same phoneme (provided that the ending is interpreted as contrastive for the stress group, but not a separate 'juncture' phoneme — see § 9.63), begins and ends with an emic pause group, and an emic breath group, and begins and ends with an emic utterance chunk of some type. When, however, two persons are involved, and a response as well as an initial utterance are both essential components of the emic unit, such a single phoneme can no longer carry within its borders the manifested margins of the larger emic utterance-response chunk involved. Here, then, is the kind of high-level THRESHOLD at which we for the moment rest, and refrain from pursuing further the possibility of even higher-ranking units of the phonological hierarchy. This threshold, however, is different from the low-level one from which we took our departure as the minimum unit of the same hierarchy, though a co-terminal factor constituted one of the reasons which led to establishment of that threshold at the opposite end of the hierarchy (§ 8.35).

9.6 *The Possibility of Contrastive-Identificational Features of Hyperphonemes as Themselves Emes*

We now turn to an important problem for which, so far as I can see, the theory thus far gives only a partial solution, though later some aspect of the theory may force a decision. The question is: Does each contrastive-idenficational feature of a hyperphoneme constitute an eme?

Emic features are not always emes themselves (see first footnote in § 8.35); specifically, we avoided the treatment of simultaneous components of phonemes as themselves emes (§ 8.35). This, however, does not solve our question as posed for hyperphonemic features.

We shall give our tentative answer to this question by discussing three alternatives, the first of which we reject, and the third of which has some theoretical advantages over the second. Nevertheless the second at present has some important advantages, and may ultimately prove more fruitful than the third.

9.61 *Juncture and Peak Emes: Solution A*

The first attempted solution to the problem assumes (1) that every peak of a hyperphoneme is an eme, and (2) that every 'joint' *between* two hyperphonemes in sequence and/or every *transition* between a hyperphoneme and silence is an eme.

For a sequence of emic syllables, this implies that there are as many occurrences of emes of syllabicity as there are occurrences of emic syllables — one for each nucleus of a syllable. It also implies that there are as many kinds of syllable-juncture emes as there are kinds of contrastive transitions between syllables, and between syllables and silence. For emic stress groups, it implies one or more emes of stress, and as many juncture emes as there are transition types between the stress groups, and between stress groups and silence. For emic pause groups, or emic breath groups, it implies at least one eme of sentence stress, with as many further kinds of juncture emes as there are transition types between pause groups or breath groups, or transitions between these groups and silence.

The advantages of this approach include the following: (a) It treats these emic features as emes, simplifying statements concerning the relation of emic contrasts to emic units. (b) It seems to simplify the consideration of the phonological hierarchy, by treating all phonological emic units as simple *linear* sequences of emes. (c) It leads, therefore, to a simple linear orthography. (d) By so doing it gives the appearance of neat compartmentalization of linguistic data in a linear 'single-level' sequence of phonological forms in contrast to or parallel with another 'level' of grammatical forms. (e) It preserves the treatment of stresses as phonemes, in the traditional way, in such a linear sequence.

The disadvantages are that its apparent gains are to a large extent illusory. (a) The treatment of such emic features as emes merely leads to an infinite regress, since these new emes in turn have contrastive features, which likewise must then be considered emes, so that the problem of a threshold is acute once more. (b) The simplicity gained by treating the phonology as a simple linear sequence of segmental and suprasegmental and junctural phonemes is purchased at too great a price — the price of concealing the hierarchical structuring of the data, and the implicit rejection of hyperphonemes as relevant to the system of language. No apparent gain is worth such distortion of the structure. Such linearity must be abandoned in the face of the empirical evidence of the presence of a relevant phonological hierarchy; and the hierarchical structuring of the immediate constituents of the grammar so necessitates the admission of hierarchical structuring at one point in the system of language that there is nothing in ultimate simplicity of assumptions to be gained by omitting it from the assumptions concerning the phonological part of the language system. (c) A linear orthography is indeed a gain for practical alphabets, but we consider such an element as irrelevant to our discussion of the structure as it functions in speech, and to our description of that structure. (d) Rigid compartmentalization — especially that which consists of orthographic levels rather than of functioning levels within the data — represents a bias in favor of fragmentation which I do not accept as being as elegant or as rigorous in scientific description as a theory which builds upon the empirically demonstrable integration of functioning levels.

Three further disadvantages: (e) If the contrastive features of the hyperphonemes are treated as juncture phonemes, then the empirical data would seem to imply that at times certain of the allojunctures are phonologically zero (cf. Moulton, following Bloch, in 1947:220, and Wells, 1947a:108, with discussion by Pike, 1947a:170-72), and other allojunctures "have nothing in common" phonetically (Hockett, 1949a: 38-39, with discussion by Pike, 1952a:107). This lack of a common characteristic, and the presence of zeros in the phonological material (which above all other material in the language system is assumed to be essentially concrete) is awkward (especially so if one rejects grammatical considerations in phonemic analysis but attempts to discover a phonological zero by grammatical clues inconsistent with that starting rejection).

(f) If the concept of juncture is explicitly stated as the joint between two units of the same hierarchical level, or of two diverse levels, or as a 'disjuncture' between two such units, it is awkward to treat this kind of juncture as the same as that between a phonological unit and pause. Similarly, (g) if one starts operationally with the transition to pause as the source of the juncture-eme concept (cf. Trager and Bloch, 1941: 225), it strikes me as highly inelegant to treat joints between phonological units in the same terms — a treatment which Stetson refers to as "the inconsistency of an 'external open juncture' which does not join anything" (1951:170a).

9.62 *Terminal and Peak Emes: Solution B*

Solution B attempts to retain some of the advantages of Solution A while avoiding several of its more serious disadvantages. It attempts to treat certain contrastive-identificational features of hyperphonemes as emes, but does so *in relation to the hyperphonemes which it also retains as emes*. Thus, emes of stress of some kind may be assumed to occur as the manifesting peaks of the various hyperphonemes (with syllabic stress, stress of the emic stress group, and sentence stress of the pause group or breath group as all possible emes in some particular language), and one or more kinds of contrastive TERMINAL EMES may occur at the end of the respective hyperphonemes (contrastive syllable ends, contrastive stress-group ends, contrastive pause-group ends, etc.).

This approach has several advantages: (a) It treats these emic elements as emes. (b) It retains the traditional treatment of stress as an eme, or of pauses as emes (Pike, 1945:31-33), as well as necessitating less radical reworking of 'juncture' analysis than is demanded by Solution C. (c) It avoids an over-compartmentalization approach which would implicitly reject the structural relevance of hyperphonemes. (d) It allows variants of a peak or terminal eme to be related to the core of the total hyperphoneme of which it is a part. (e) It avoids Objection (f) cited under Solution A, since the 'external open juncture' eme is now seen at every occurrence as manifesting the end of a particular kind of hyperphoneme whether that hyperphoneme occurs before silence or occurs before another hyperphoneme.

On the other hand, Solution B has the disadvantage that it fails to provide a way to avoid the most serious phases of the problem of infinite regress of contrastive emes. Not only is this problem acute in reference to the possibility of treating the contrastive movements leading to voicing or other *simultaneous* components as emes (cf. § 8.35), but also it is relevant to *sequential* contrastive components (cf. § 8.31) as well: If contrastive peaks and contrastive ends of hyperphonemes are to be considered emes, why should not contrastive peaks and contrastive ends of phonemes be also considered emes? If the off-glide of the /m/ in *man* is sometimes a more useful contrastive-identificational auditory clue to the difference between *man* and *Nan* than is the period of bilabial closure, and if the on-glides are similarly more efficient differential clues to the nasals in *ran, rang* than are the moments of lingual closure, why should not each of these off-glides and each of these on-glides be themselves treated as emes within phonemes, if contrastive phonological terminal emes are once admitted to the theory in relation to the hyperphonemes? And, when this is done, would not the peaks of closure for the three nasals similarly constitute three emes distinct from and in addition to the six gliding pre- and post-terminal emes? And would not the same considerations apply to every other phoneme, with its endings and peak? More difficult yet, would not the comparable situation force one to go another step in regress, and treat each off-glide, etc., as in turn involving muscular movements which would have to be analyzed as a sequence of emes, etc.? At *some* point in the regress one must either stop arbitrarily, with no structural reason for doing so, or one must find a structural threshold which gives him structural reasons for a change in the technique of viewing his data from that point onward.

9.63 *Contrastive-Identificational Features of Hyperphonemes: Solution C*

Solution C, which we propose with some misgivings,[15] is designed to avoid all of the disadvantages of the preceding two solutions, but introduces additional ones of its own, which may prove fatal to it in the long run. Specifically, it postulates emic phonemes, emic syllables, emic stress groups, emic pause groups, emic breath groups, etc., but specifically excludes contrastive-identificational features of these emes as emes themselves. It rejects emes of syllabicity, of stress, of pause, and of juncture, but treats the peaks of phonemes and hyperphonemes and the terminal characteristics of phonemes and hyperphonemes as contrastive-identificational features of these including emes.

The advantages of Solution C include the following: (a) It operates with a threshold, discussed in § 8.35, to avoid the necessity of infinite regress of emes *from the point of*

---

[15] There is something elegant about this solution which leaves me wistful, but I cannot make it work. Hence it appears that some variety of Solution B must be utilized for the moment.

view of behavior as people react to that behavior (but makes no claims about the structural regress from the point of view of the physiologist, or biophysicist, or philosopher). (b) It operates within an avowed hierarchical and modal theory of which the phonemes, the emic syllable, the emic stress group, the emic pause group, etc., are the basic isolates of the hierarchy of one mode. This approach, in turn, allows for a statement of the integration of the phonological components of the uttereme with the lexical and tagmemic components at various interpenetration points in their respective hierarchies, without doing violence to the theory. (c) It avoids a monolevel linearity assumption. (d) It retains the advantage of permitting minimum manifestations of an emic syllable, an emic stress group, an emic pause group, etc., to be coterminous with a single phoneme. (e) In English, it helps to explain the linkage of stress and intonation within single stress-pitch contours composed of emic stress groups, i.e., abdominemes.

As disadvantages, however, Solution C carries with it the following: (a) Traditional treatment of stress as a phoneme is rejected, which forces elaborate reworking of one's approach at various places in a descriptive statement — a task we have not yet completed (e.g., instead of stating that the word *per|mit* is stressed on the second syllable if stressed at all, one would say that *per|mit* sometimes constitutes the entire manifestation of an emic stress group, and in such a situation the peak of the emic stress group falls on the second syllable of the word — with the potential placement of the peak under lexical control (§ 9.33)). (b) Rejection of juncture phenomena as phonemes requires similar reworking of statements which have listed junctures along with segmental phonemes in a phoneme inventory. (c) It forces a reworking of the traditional statement of prosodic phonemes as composed of stress, pitch, and length — a task we shall touch on in § 13. (d) It implies that each separate abdomineme must have a separate symbol, as each phoneme does; but such an orthography would be unwieldy.

9.7 Bibliographical Comments on Chapter 9

9.71 On Pyramiding from Phoneme to Syllable versus to Morpheme

Traditionally, linguists have often assumed that phonemes combine to make morphemes, morphemes to make words, words to make sentences, etc. (see, for example, Baudouin de Courtenay, quoted by Jakobson, 1949b:205). Note that this point of view is rejected here, in favor of three hierarchies with partial overlap — the phonological (of phoneme, to syllable, to stress group, etc.), the lexical (of morpheme, to morpheme cluster, etc.), and the grammatical (from tagmeme to hypertagmeme). It is presumably the former approach which has made it difficult or impossible for many linguists to integrate the syllable into their structural theories.

For Trager, the essential progression of levels of structure has been from phonetics (outside linguistics proper), to phonemics, morphemics, syntax, and metalinguistics (outside linguistics proper) (1949), in "ascending levels of complexity of organization" (Trager and Smith, 1951:81; see also 8 and 54). The view is continued by Hill (1962:131). For further comment on the "sin" of mixing levels of analysis note Martin (1956:705). This view I have rejected, as being far too simple. It does not allow for the hierarchical organization of the phonology itself — with phonemes, syllables, rhythm units and so on; it is a linear projection of hierarchical data (and see § 15.31). Recently (1961:212) Trager has attempted a reworking of his older view. The phoneme-through-morpheme pyramiding is also rejected by W. Haas (1960:264).

Longacre has suggested (1964a:7) that "Generative grammar has turned this model upside down", and therefore "has not challenged the model in any essential way". Ultimately, however, generative grammar starting from syntax may be able to handle some of these problems through a "transformational cycle of the phonological component" cutting down from syntax to morphemes, to phonetics, and then back through stress shifts or other phonological material necessary (see Chomsky, 1962, § 2.1, p. 517; and § 4.2, p. 533).

For scholars who have adopted a hierarchical point of view in phonology, note Hockett (1955:2), emphasizing the immediate constituents of the syllable (building on Pike and Pike, 1947), with the "phonological structure of an utterance" showing "a *hierarchic* organization" (43). He deals largely — but not exclusively — with the syllable. Haugen carries the view further (1956a). Sebeok, following a tradition of formal analysis, points out that "Cheremis meter has the following relevant constituents: syllable, word, member, line, line-pair, song. These form a hierarchy, such that every constituent contains some whole number of every preceding one" (in *For Roman Jakobson*, 1956:436). For a different approach to phonological hierarchy, growing out of the theories of Firth, note Halliday (1961).

9.72 *On the Nature of the Syllable*

For treatment of the syllable as a unit with a peak of sonority, see Sweet (1906:65-66), L. R. Palmer (1936:35), Kantner and West (1933:62), Noel-Armfield (1919:39), Kenyon (1943:68-69), Bloomfield (1933a:126); as a "minimum phonemic unit of utterance", R. Hall (1946:77); as "a sequence of sounds containing one peak of prominence", D. Jones (1940:54-55); as "that recurrent sequence of sounds, in terms of which the phenomena of linguistic timing can be described", Haugen (1949a:281, and cf. Brøndal, quoted by Eliason, 1942:146); as a weakening and then a strengthening of pressure, Ripman (1899:127-28, and cf. Sommerfelt, 1931:156-60); as "the maximal unit in which there are no oppositions of order", Bazell (1949b:86n.); as "a chain of expression including one and only one accent" which may be manifested by different degrees of stress or pitch, or by different movements of stress or pitch, or by diacritic signs or graphic devices, etc., Hjelmslev (1939b:267); as a unit composed of a "cadre phonématique" and a "contenu phonématique", Jakobson (in Trubetzkoy, 1949:374); as "a device of convenience for giving the distribution of consonant allophones", Voegelin (1949:79-80n.); as a minimal encoding unit or skill unit, Osgood, and others (1954:57-59, and 41); as a "minimal acoustic unit", Cooper, Delattre, Liberman, Borst, and Gerstman (1952:598); as a physiological unit, Stetson (1951, plus the first edition of 1928 and various other publications of which the material is largely included in the latest work), Pike (1943a:116-20 — including syllables by pulses made by the tongue or pharynx acting as the initiator of the air stream, 118-19), Twaddell (1953), and many other references to the older literature in Stetson; with discussion of CV model versus the "autocorrelation function", Carroll (1953:86; with a statement as to the manner in which a structural view is here more fruitful than statistics).

For a quite different attempt at a suggestion as to a possible physiological analysis of speech sequences larger than the phone see also Muyskens (1925) who tries to establish a unit, called the "hypha", which seems to stretch from the peak of one consonantal constriction to the peak of another after an intervening vowel (i.e., constriction followed by dilation). It suffers from a linguistic point of view, I feel, by assuming that the on-glide to a consonant constitutes part of a preceding hypha, and that the off-glide is part of a following one, so that there is no possibility of treating the phonological hierarchy as composed of syllables which are in general composed of phoneme sequences, since the phoneme — or sound — as a unit disappears from view in this approach; in addition, there are operationally-unfeasible subjective elements, since "There is always attention of the listener to aid in determining the boundaries [of the hypha]" (50) — whereas it seems to me impossible that syllable division could possibly be expected to cut up a sequence in any such fashion as the hypha demands.

More traditionally-identified syllables, however, have a "reality [which] to the native speaker is pragmatically undeniable, at least in the languages with which I am familiar" (Haugen, 1949a:280-81), and which may lead to a "syllabary, [which, in Japanese], must reflect the speakers' naive structural analysis of their language", Bloch (1950:92n); so that "The three psychological units which emerge from a native speaker's analysis, then, are the *syllable*, the *word*, and the *sentence*", (Osgood and others, 1954:60 — but cf. quote in § 8.815 regarding the phoneme, and reference in § 9.76).

For the syllable seen in whistling, note Stetson (1951:36b). For reference to it as "the smallest rhythmical unit of speech", see Vereecken (1939, credited there to de Groot).

Our approach utilizes both a phonetic syllable and a phonemic one (Pike, 1947c: 60b, 65b, 90, 141a, 144-47, 181a); Fischer-Jørgensen likewise utilizes both phonetic and phonemic syllables (1952:15-19). Hoenigswald, however, suggests a view which is quite different from this one: he postulates no need for operating with phonetic syllables, but suggests the presence of phonemic syllables which would serve as the distributional matrices for phonemes of segmental, accentual, and junctural types (1944:155). For an early reference which foreshadows certain aspects of the etic-emic contrast in syllable analysis, see Hjelmslev (1939b).

Granted that the syllable is extremely important to speech, there is a limit, however, beyond which we must not attribute function to it. Stetson seems to attribute to the syllable certain "invariant" functions which to me seemed to be reserved to the morpheme or hypermorpheme. Thus he alleges that "the identity of the series of symbols is maintained though the signals of the series undergo mechanical change. The identity of the symbol is verified by the reversion of the signal to the slow, careful form when the original rate and stress are restored" (1951:9b; cf. also 1945). To me, however, it seems preferable to state that, when a sequence like op. op has changed to o.pop in fast speech, the syllables op and op have been replaced by o and pop; similarly, in *I am* versus *I'm* it seems unfruitful to try to maintain that the syllables are the same. The invariant factor here, in our theory, is the presence of a sequence of identifiable morphemes, with morpheme variants manifested by differing emic syllables. The recognition of the morphemic invariants, in turn, demands a semantic factor — precisely because the phonemic and syllabic content of the morpheme may vary — and this again emphasizes the necessity of treating the morpheme as a form-meaning composite, lest neither variant morphs nor variant etic syllables be recognizable as recurrences of some emic unit. Stetson's *op*, from this point of view, is merely an artificial morpheme in an artificial language system. Nonsense syllables utilized for testing purposes achieve similar morphemic status in such a system, whenever recognition of them is achieved in spite of phonological changes.

For the need of "units that are more than one phoneme in length" into which phonemes are combined or encoded, note Liberman, Ingemann, and others (1959: 1491, 1499). Jakobson and Halle say that "the elementary phonemic frame, the syllable, is established" by the "polarity between the minimum and the maximum of energy" or stop versus open vowel which sets up contrast between these two successive units (1956:37). F. Robbins (1961, and in *A William Cameron Townsend...*, 1961) has syllables of much more complicated structure, containing various types of internal groupings. I would interpret his data as having microsyllables and macrosyllables, such that the domain of fusion of [m] to [i] into a syllabic nasal defines the domain of the macrosyllable (intermediate in the hierarchy between microsyllable and stress group), even across glottal stops and in sequences including various kinds of pulses; for example (in *A William Cameron Townsend...*, 1961:654) M·Ɂ²⁴² 'our (inclusive) sandal', M·²⁴MɁM²⁴ 'our (exclusive) sandal', M·³¹MɁ²⁴ 'your (plural) sandal', with raised dot for length, tones numbered from high to low.

Arnold believes that "the syllable is best considered as a structural unit in terms of which vowel and consonant combinability within a given language can be most economically stated" (1956:253). Note our insistence in § 9.76 that randomness of sound distribution does not occur, and that this requires some syllable concept in the theory — but that the universality of such restrictions requires a physiological base, not a mere distributional construct. The opposite point of view is found in W. S. Allen who has affirmed that for some purposes particular combinations of consonant and vowel elements were given so that "the concept of 'syllable' was not introduced, simply because it was not found necessary" (1956:170); compare also O'Connor and Trim (1953). See also Householder for English phoneme distribution according to rule, without the syllable (1962c:187).

Haugen has believed that "Without the syllable, the factors of timing are meaningless. Its reality to the native speaker is pragmatically undeniable" (1949a:280-81). (This view is called in question by S. Martin, 1956:701; for quotation and discussion, see § 9.76, below.) Note, also, native reaction to support syllable elements through syllable division in teaching people to read (Gudschinsky, 1959d), and spectrographic evidence in which the release of a syllable "often appears as a spike" and so "is visibly marking the syllable boundary" (Lehiste, 1962:178-80, 187; and 1960a:66-71). Lehiste attributes the syllable-marking data to "subglottal activity"; but acoustic cues for syllable types differ between languages; in English, versus Estonian, "Syllable peaks are phonetically present" but "No clear-cut syllable boundaries could be identified" (1962:187).

For references to recent physiological material obtained by Ladefoged and others through electrodes inserted into the muscles, note fnn. above to §§ 9.221, 9.311. For the syllable as "the minimal [phonological] construction which has independence", see Smalley (1961:xvii) with the ratio of internal (greater) to external (lesser) limitations of distribution.

9.73 *On the Structure of the Syllable*

For discussion of various phases of the internal structure of the syllable see Malone (1936), Hjelmslev (1939b), J. R. Firth and Rogers (1935-37), Pike and Pike (1947; with attempt to analyze the syllable into immediate constituents), Scott (1947; with "systemic transcription" having reference to structural groupings, which may be larger than single phonemes, within the syllable), Henderson (1948, with diagrams of distributional types within the syllable, and with reference to a "structural dividing line" which differentiates implied immediate constituents from phonemic content as such), Togeby (1951), Fischer-Jørgensen (1952:35-39), Hockett (1953), McKaughan (1954; with relationships between shorter and longer consonantal sequences within the syllable), E. V. Pike (1954), Sharp (1954).

For Hockett, syllables contain "onset, peak, and coda" (1955:52 — with further discussion of syllable, 51-61). For further discussion of immediate constituents of syllables, see, now, extensive discussion in Hockett (1955:150-62); and Smalley (1961). Note also, for discussion of nuclear matters, Bloomfield (1933a "compound phonemes": 90-91, 124); H. Vogt (1942 with a "syllabic centre" composed of vowel plus consonant); Aschmann (1946); Pike (1947b, with close-knit syllable nuclei:158); Twaddell (1953:431); Longacre (1952, 1955); Hamp (1954); Faust and Pike (in Serie... 1959:28, 40-48, 52), with close-knit nuclei in Cocama), Minor (1956, with up to seven contiguous vowels in a string, syllabically grouped, in Witoto); Clark (1959, with phoneme classes in Popoluca).

For various aspects of the problem of the analysis of English syllable nuclei, see S. Newman (1946) and Swadesh (1947), with nuclei treated as two vowels; Bloomfield (1927); H. J. Uldall (1939); Hockett (1953:169b); Kenyon (1943) and Pike (1947b), with some vowel-phoneme sequences and some single-phoneme vocoid glides; Trnka (1935:11, 14) and D. Jones (1950:70-74, 76-77, 167), with the vocoid glides treated as single phonemes, but written with sequences of two vowel letters; a similar point of view seems to appear in Bloomfield, 1935, (97-98, 100), where he uses the terms "compound symbols" and "digraphs" instead of the term "compound phonemes" which he used in 1933; cf. also Bloch (1935); but contrast Trager (1935), Trager and Bloch (1941), Bloch and Trager (1942), Whorf (1943), and Trager and Smith (1951), with some of the syllabics treated as sequences of vowel phoneme plus phonemes /j/ or /w/ or /h/. Compare Swadesh (1935a), with vocoid glides treated as single phonemes and written by single symbols; see Haugen and Twaddell (1942) for a critical review of some of the problems of the vowel plus glide-consonant approach of Trager and Bloch. See also McDavid (1952), Thomas (1947), Chao (1934), Sweet (1900a, 1906), A. Ellis (1869-1889).

Lehiste and Peterson have now pointed out that $[a^v]$ $[a^I]$ $[ɔ^I]$ have extra duration; and "Criteria are suggested by which the formant movements due to transitions may be distinguished from movements that have linguistic signalling value within the syllable nucleus" (1960:27, 50; 68, 72); and a diphthong "is a vocalic syllable nucleus containing two target positions" (1961a:277); this would seem to imply that the two target items contain a sequence of two vowel phonemes in English, versus those two vowels such as in the words for *bait* and *mate* which contain only one position and only one vowel phoneme (compare Pike, 1947b).

Nuclei composed of syllabic consonants, analyzed in different ways, also are discussed: e.g., in Sweet (1900a:229); Bloomfield (1933a:121-23); Swadesh (1934), Bloch and Trager (1942:50), Malone (1942). In some materials, this leads to the suggestion of the possibility of a "syllabic stress" (Bloomfield, 1933a:122, 130, 136), or of a "phoneme of syllabicity" (cf. possibility mentioned in Pike, 1947c:141an; rejected for German in Moulton, 1947:218).

There has been considerable question as to whether or not the syllable is structurally composed entirely of a sequence of phonemes. Certain phonetic segments which by some scholars would be considered phonemes within the syllable are by others considered "prosodies"; thus Hjelmslev finds certain "prephonemes which by a further phonematic analysis turn out to be not phonemes, but *prosodies*. I understand by a prosody an element not constituting the series, but consolidating the series" (1936:51, for glottal stop in Danish; cf. also H. J. Uldall, 1936). This approach is related to the discussion of prosodies by Firth, who states that "we may abstract those features which mark word or syllable initials and word or syllable finals or word junctions from the word, piece, or sentence, and regard them syntagmatically as prosodies, distinct from the phonematic constituents which are referred to as units of the consonant and vowel systems" (1949:129; cf. also 1951a:84). Earlier, Firth and Rogers maintain that in Hunanese certain phonetic components (which might traditionally be written phonetically as [y] and [w] "may be regarded as syllabic diacritica and not as being 'placed'" (1937:1060, 1059). This carries over to small phonetic segments the kind of argument which we advanced for peak and border of emic syllables in § 9.63, in which we treat the peaks as emically-contrastive features of syllables rather than as themselves emes. (But it is clear that these authors did not consistently apply the approach to all phonemes within the syllables, since if they had done so, they could then have had no 'vowels' or 'consonants' in their descriptions, but merely features of syllables — an extreme to which they do not carry their point of view). A few more references may help clarify this view: Certain "diacritica of the monosyllable are not considered as successive fractions or segments in any linear sense" (Firth, 1949:136); "The syllable is a whole, not merely a number of pieces added to one another. If Roman letters are used to represent it, it must not be taken that their space-order corresponds point for point with an order in the syllable" (Scott, 1947:199); "...significant aspiration and nasalization, for these characteristics may not only be features of the whole syllable of the verb stem, but also features of certain derived forms in their entirety" (Carnochan, 1948:424).

These writers do not seem to see that such a view, pressed to its logical conclusion, would completely prevent the treatment of a sequence formula such as CVC as relevant (formula types which they use extensively), since it would destroy the validity of the 'placement' of C in such a formula. (Henderson, however, has pointed out a partial limitation, by refusing to treat for Lushai the "*Yotization* and *Labio-velarization* as unplaced syllabic features" because of the contrastive placement of the palatal segments in pre- and post-nuclear positions in words such as *hmiay*; 1948:713.) Rather Firth and Rogers set up "alternances" — a list of items in contrast with each other in local phonological contexts composed of the parts of the syllable (1937). Their view has been developed further, by the use of the term "substitution" for reference to an open alternance system, but "commutation" for reference to a closed system, with no structural congruence possible of phonemes in one commutational slot in a syllable to phonemes of similar phonetic character to a different commutational system in a different slot in the syllable or elsewhere (for references, note § 8.86). Yet none of these matters are structurally relevant if sounds are not 'placed' in the syllable structure.

For further prosodic treatment of syllables note Sprigg (1955:141); with tonal system in Burmese stated for the word rather than the syllable 134-35); Shorto (1960:544, with "syllable classes" as "principal constituents of word structure").

For bibliography on prosody note J. R. Firth (1957), Robins (1957b:12), Bursill-Hall (1961). See also §§ 10.51, 8.814.

For our discussion of emic classes of phonemes see §§ 8.53, 8.61-66, 8.86 and for the discussion of the shape types of emic syllables see §§ 9.243-45.

For a phonotagmemic approach to syllables as having positional alloclasses of phonemes comprising internal structural components, and for external distribution in terms of higher-level slots, see Crawford (1963). A somewhat different approach to hierarchical matters involving the syllable, in Estonian, involves the embedding of syllables in word structure which determines "contrasts between phonemic syllables", (see Lehiste, 1960a:63).

For rejection of a linearity assumption, note Stetson, who says that "Speech can be indicated by a native by a row of signs in a line; but the signs give no hint of the pattern and connections of the articulatory movements" (1951:1a); and — now — Chomsky (1962, § 4.3, pp. 538-43). For specific reliance on a linearity assumption, note Hockett, for whom it has become part of his operational framework: "A juncture PHONEME is then a grouping of such phenomena which makes for unambiguous and simple linear transcription" (1949a:38; but see 1947c:258, where Hockett for componential analysis attempts to eliminate this assumption).

For discussion of the borders of syllables, note Stetson (1951, with juncture phonemes rejected, 169b-170, 4b, 173-74), Twaddell (1953, with the possibility of juncture phonemes of syllables mentioned, but with the final structural solution of these pertinent phenomena left in abeyance until further data are available, 426, 418, 423), Haugen (1949a, with "juncture as a morphologically determined displacement of syllable timing", 280), Moulton (1947:217), Eliason (1942, with indication that in certain instances "there is no evident point where one syllable ends and the next begins", 145-46), D. Jones (1940, with "valley of prominence", 56-57), Sweet (1906, in which it is pointed out that syllable boundaries are not always clear, 160). For significant syllable division see also Sommerfelt (1936:33), Hockett (1947a:324, commenting on the phonemicity of syllable division in the work of Newman on Yokuts). Stetson feels that "no one has assumed that two syllables could in any sense overlap or coincide" (1951:27); contrast, however, our portmanteau analysis in § 9.236.

The most extensive study of acoustic evidences of syllable juncture occurs in Lehiste (1960a:60, 63; 1962); see also Lehiste and Peterson, 1959b; see also, above, § 9.72. For a phoneme in double function within the syllable, called an "interlude" which is "coda-like and onset-like at the same time, and structurally it belongs *both* to the syllable which contains the preceding peak *and* to that which contains the following peak" note Hockett (1955:52). For extensive bibliography on juncture note Lehiste (1960b:49-54). Lehiste also shows through acoustic evidence, juncture contrasts in "such words as *solely* and *coolly*" in which "an actual boundary between a final-like and an initial-like allophone of /i/ could be observed" (1962:186); morpheme freedom seems to be involved in some of these pronunciations.

9.74 On the Nature of the Stress Group and Juncture

For the stress group as an organized movement, see Stetson (1951, e.g., 3b, 19b, 28a, 106b, and further page references in the text of this chapter), Twaddell (1953:427-29, 434); as a correlation of timing with concentration of energy, Haugen (1949a:279). For stress as subjective prominence, note D. Jones (1950:59-60), Kenyon (1943:76).

For physiology of stress movements, studied through electrodes inserted into the muscles, note various studies of Ladefoged and others; and see above, footnote to § 9.311.

For the probability "that the perceived loudness of words which are within the normal speech range is largely dependent on the physiological effort required to produce them" see Ladefoged (1962:89; also Ladefoged and others, 1958:9). Note also Fonagy (in *Preprints...*, 1962:27). For a relation of loudness to pressure "required below the vocal cords" note also Draper, Ladefoged, and Whitteridge (1959: 20-21). There continues to be much difficulty in determining physical and acoustic characteristics underlying perceived stress. For the "conclusion that stress is actually physiological", with parameters of "speech power, fundamental voice frequency, phonetic quality, and duration" see Lehiste and Peterson (1959a:429); compare Ladefoged, for intensity correlated with pressure differences (1962:84). For perceived stress affected by vowel quality in reference to vowel power, note Lehiste and Peterson (1959b:59). Note also articulatory force as relevant, in Arnold (1956: 440-41).

For Bolinger "pitch is our main cue to stress" (1958:111), via "pitch PROMINENCE", as a wide departure from a smooth contour (112, 149); and the differentiation of stresses "often calls for a repertorial cue... knowledge of the morphs" (149, 130-33). For Bolinger, duration also is important (138); and see Fry (1955:765). I feel, however, that Bolinger has not adequately included in his treatment sentence pairs which retain the same perceived stresses but contrast by pitch — e.g., *He's going.* (with fall) versus *He's going?* (with rise). Compare, nevertheless, the instrumental material for "stressed syllables" in Fore of New Guinea, with pitch as more prominent than intensity in the physical records (Pike and Scott, 1963). The pitch accent in Fore applies to the phrase as a whole; unaccented syllables rise on a gentle slope (rather than being sharply stepped up as they often are in a tonal situation) and variability occurs in pitch on the non-accented syllable. More recently, Eunice Pike finds in a similar neighboring language structure (Chuave of New Guinea) that the pitch in angry discourse may be spoken in a high angry monotone, wiping out pitch differences; here the intensity contrasts come out more clearly (1964). For discussion of pitch and stress problems in Slovene, note Lehiste (1961:60-65). For accent as predominantly pitch see also Rigault (1962:735).

Chomsky, Halle and Lukoff conclude that stress is such that "it seems pointless to regard suprasegmentals as separate elements at all"; rather, accent should be "a distinctive feature similar to such distinctive features as voicing, nasality..." so that

"All suprasegmentals would then appear as features of phonemes, or as utterance-long or phrase-long components"; then "one can considerably simplify linguistic theory by restricting it to the consideration of linear systems" (1956:79).

For junctures as boundary signals, see Trubetzkoy (in *Proceedings of the Second...*, 1936); as phonemes, Trager and Bloch (1941:225-26), Bloch and Trager (1942:47), Trager and Smith (1951:44-52), as "fictions created ad hoc to account for the difference between certain sets of phonetically different segments", Bloch (1948:41); as phases of movements, Stetson (1951:4b, 154b, 169b, 173b); recorded from tapes, N. Hickerson (1954:298-99). Compare the term "suture" in such contexts as "la suture des morphèmes diffère souvent de l'intérieur d'un morphème par ses propriétés phonologiques" (Principes, 1931:325); also Trnka (1935:12-13, where the term is attributed to Trubetzkoy). Note also "prosodies" in reference to "word junctions", in Firth (1949:129).

For a large variety of specific measured acoustic signals at perceptual junctures, varying widely according to the particular item chosen, note Lehiste (1959), with initial [n] being approximately but unexpectedly twice as long as final [n]; also some formant differences, aspiration, etc.

Lehiste has open juncture as "a point in time, not a phoneme in its own right" leading to hierarchies of such bounded sequences (1960b:48-49); contrast the more frequent attitude of juncture as a phoneme (Reyburn 1954:210; Joos, 1957:216).

Note Lehiste's extensive bibliography on juncture (1959:106-13; 1960b:49-54); and bibliography in Rischel (in *Preprints...*, 1962:155). These acoustic studies give major support to and amplification of the early perceptual work done by D. Jones (1931); and see his more recent discussion (1957:99) of Sweet's earlier treatment of such matters.

For the relation of juncture to grammar such that "junctures should appear only at morpheme boundaries", and "should correspond, by and large, to different morphological and syntactical processes", see Chomsky, Halle, Lukoff (1956:67); note, more recently, Chomsky (1962; § 4.5, p. 553) with "no known method for assigning junctures in terms of phonetic evidence alone". For objection to Chomsky's work on stress, note Second Texas Conference (1962). For a discussion of British versus American views of stress and juncture, note Sharp (1961). For morphemic status of stress, see Hill (1958:102-05).

For the phonological or phonetic word, or phonemic phrase: Sweet (1913:4, where phonetic word is synonymous with the stress group, but, he says, "I would abolish the ordinary word-division altogether", 12-14), D. Jones (1931, with lists of modifications at word boundaries), Brøndal (1936:43, where the term 'phonetic word' is attributed to Vendryes, and sharply rejected), Hockett (1949a:36, where phonological word represents "any stretch of phonemes which occurs as a whole utterance, and which cannot be broken into two or more stretches which also so occur, quite regardless of pause"), Togeby (1949:103, where the phonetic word comprises all the part of the speech chain which is spoken with a single breath), Trager and Bloch (1941:226, with "phonemic phrase" labelling an utterance with one loud stress).

For practical etics of rhythm units, with possible variables, note Pike (1962b); for illustrations of different contour shapes of abdominal pulses note Pike (1957c). For analysis of stress groups in a phonological hierarchy of a particular language structure, note E. V. Pike and Scott (1962); Kensinger (in *Studies in Peruvian...*, 1963:214-15); Rich (in *Studies in Peruvian...*, 1963:201-06); Lindskoog and Brend (in *Studies in Ecuadorian...*, 1962:39-44); Borman (in *Studies in Ecudorian...*, 1962:57-59). For double stresses note Lutstorf (1960:32-37) as well as Pike and Scott (1963) and Pike and Kindberg (1956). For Hill's claim that verse has only two levels of stress, versus speech with four see 1955 (in H. Allen, 1958:20). For a discussion of the history of the bringing in of syllable-timing into meter, and its current clash with stress-group timing, note Allison (1962:62-71).

For loss of intelligibility when English is spoken on the Gold Coast without English stress and rhythm, note Strevens (1954:83).

9.75 *On Breath Groups and Pauses*

For the physiological basis of a breath group, see Stetson (1937; 1948; 1951:3b-4, 54, 106b), Twaddell (1953:427-28, 434, 438-39). For mention in a practical phonetics handbook, see Noel-Armfield (1919:43-44). For problems in the phonemic interpretation of pause, see references to juncture, in § 9.74. See also J. M. Cowan and Bloch (1948:99); S. Martin (1952:16); Hockett's macrosegments (1955:44); see also fn. to § 9.311.

For specific language data on phonological units above the level of the stress group see now Lindskoog and Brend (in *Studies in Ecudorian...*, 1962:39-44), Kensinger (in *Studies in Peruvian...*, 1963:214-15), Rich (in *Studies in Peruvian...*, 1963:201-06), Eunice Pike and Scott (1962), and Eunice Pike (1964).

9.76 *On the Possibility of Languages without Syllables or Stress Groups — or Vowels*

Is it possible for a language to contain no etic syllables? no emic syllables? no etic abdominal pulses? no emic abdominal pulses?

Hjelmslev has argued that "A language without accents will be a language without syllables. French is an example of such a language" (1939b:270). Later in the article he grants the presence in French of "pseudo-syllables" (270), which would presumably be interpreted as etic syllables within our theory. Yet we would insist on the structural relevance, the emic nature, of these etic syllables if they constitute the distributional setting which controls the occurrence of patterns of phoneme distribution, such that one never gets in French a word like /aouiooiueoiaoau/, nor one like /tspffsxtpsk/. Even if one assumes that there is only one pattern of the syllable, nevertheless contrast would be observed between its function as a distributional matrix and the function of the single phoneme — and such a contrast between levels gains for the syllable a place in the total contrastive system of the emic units of the language. For an argument that in French "la syllable est un réalité phonématique" see Frei (1950:167). (See also our discussion of etic versus emic syllables in footnote to § 9.225.)

A similar line of reasoning might affect our decision as to whether a language had an emic stress group. If some unit larger than the etic syllable serves as a relevant matrix for distribution of sounds, then it must be considered as emically structured in some way. It does not seem necessary to assume, however, that in every language a stress group has its peak occurring at a particular slot; rather we may conclude that a stress group is an emic structural unit, in spite of fluctuation in the placement of the peak of stress, if it is sufficiently delimited (a) by being physically an abdominal pulse and (b) by detectable borders of this pulse so that the etic abdominal pulse may serve as a distributional matrix of syllables in spite of the peak fluctuation. On the other hand, we might encounter a language with abdominal pulses which were emic, and had peaks of stress, but in which the placement of the peak is determined not by lexical considerations but by matters of emphasis, attention, and the like. (Such a language could be assumed to have stress groups somewhat like the groups which contain sentence stress in English, but would lack the counterparts of those English stress groups which are in part lexically determined.)

It seems possible, furthermore, to imagine a language in which there are emic abdominal pulses serving as rhythmic units of timing and as matrices of phoneme or syllable distribution, but in which the abdominal surges contain no detectable peak — but in which the syllables occur as a smooth 'patter' within the rhythmic units, with no one syllable outstanding in loudness, length, or prominence. Here the borders of the abdominemes would be relevant, but a peak component would not occur. We have hinted above at a somewhat comparable problem in relation to slurred, glided syllables, in which one might search instrumentally for possible syllables without sharp physiological peaks (§ 9.221). Compare the problem of the "trill or run", in Stetson (1951:67b-68a). We seem to be able artificially to produce rhythm units which are bounded off by beginnings and ending of abdominal movement but within which each syllable is given force so even that we have difficulty in detecting perceptually any difference between them (e.g., in a sequence [pa.pa.pa pa.pa.pa pa.pa.pa] versus [pa.ˈpa.pa pa.ˈpa.pa]). See Culina in Pike 1957c.

In Bella Coola we may see a number of these problems highlighted (with quotations and data taken from S. Newman, 1947):

When two or more syllabics occur in a word or sentence, one can clearly hear different degrees of articulatory force. But these relative stresses in a sequence of acoustic syllables do not remain constant in repetitions of the utterance (132b).

So we begin the problem with this language without lexical stresses, and there are

no distinctive suprasegmental phonemes involving stress or pitch (132a).

The "acoustic syllables" just mentioned, however, are "phonetic syllables" which are in part a conditioned result of the phonemes themselves: glottalized consonants are stronger than others, vowels and certain continuants "stand out acoustically" above other phonemes so that

There are no syllables in Bella Coola

(132a); — a viewpoint based, furthermore, on the fact that there are

no characteristics of phoneme grouping that require or that can be stated in terms of a structurally significant unit such as the syllable (133a).

For example:

Bella Coola words made up entirely of consonants are frequent, as łmk'młp *jack-pine tree*, sk'lxlxc *I'm getting cold*, ti łq'ʷlxc'ntx *that which is fading out*. And words containing only non-syllabic consonants are not rare, as k'xłc *I looked*, łk'ʷtxʷ *make it big!* łxʷtłc *I went through an opening* (132a; his use of the term 'syllabic', etically, is not too clear here).

On the other hand, long groupings of vowels do not occur, and in some consonant groups there are conditioned voiced or voiceless vocoidal releases, treated as non-phonemic, which might conceivably affect any discussion of etic syllables. The distribution of such aspirated and unaspirated allophones is too complicated to be repeated here, and in some phonological contexts is subject to much free variation (which I assume is a major reason why the voiced releases are treated as nonphonemic rather than as occurrences of a phoneme /ə/). In the following illustrations (in which my symbolization is modified slightly from Newman's) [ʰ] is used for aspiration, and [$^I,^U$], etc. for unvoiced vocoids of specified but apparently noncontrastive timbre: /płt/ [pʰłʰtʰ] *thick*, /qnqnklxitxʷ/ [qənqənkəlxitʰxᵁ] *lower it!* /k'nc/ or [k'ᴵntsʰ], or [k'intsʰ], or [k'yəntsʰ] *whale*, /nmnmk'/ [nəmnəmk'ᴵ] *animal*, /ti kʷtmmcctx/ [ti kᵁtəmtsʰtsʰtʰxᴵ] *my husband*, /kʷllx/ [kwəl·xᴵ] *it's getting hot*, /smt/ [səmtʰ] *mountain*, /qaxqx-i/ [qaxqʰx-i] *rabbit* (diminutive form). In this language, then, it appears to Newman that no emic syllable should be postulated, nor any abdomineme with peak of stress. Newman's distributional matrix of "the word as a structural unit which has phonological as well as morphological characteristics" (132a), however might quite possibly prove to be an abdominemic unit without stress peaks, were it to be restudied with this question in mind.

Just as Newman gives illustrations of words with long consonant clusters, so Minor presents from the Witoto language of Peru long sequences of vowels. Note the following: /eíode/ *he grew old*, /makáoiakade/ *he wants to walk much*, /uíia/ *many parrots*, /húiauaí/ *many barbasco roots*, /ráuaioiakade/ *he always wants to hunt far off*, /haĩaide/ *hard*, /náĩio/ *night*. Here the included [i] and [u] segments cannot be interpreted as /y/ and /w/ because of contrast with stressed /í/ and /ú/ in comparable situations. (Compare, also, the vowel clusters illustrated by Shell, from Cashibo: /ʔeei̯/ *to swallow*; /kʷai̯o̭o̭s̭i̭/ *(he) played yesterday*; /či̭o̭i̭o̭/ *group of cicadas*; /paíɔia/ *it is hurting*, 1950: 202). Minor reports that the sequences of vowels do not all have the same timing.

From this he argues that syllabic groupings *do* occur among these vowel sequences. Two or three rapid vowels in a single emic syllable nucleus, therefore, are joined by a ligature; vowel sequences not joined by a ligature constitute sequences of nuclei of two or more emic syllables.

A different kind of data (from that of Newman) has been used to support a rejection of the necessity of the syllable as a universally-necessary contruct. S. Martin (1956: 701), on the basis of recordings by Peterson "of a patient paralyzed from below the throat so that her breathing was completely at the mercy of a machine" but "the patient's speech sounded normal... we were hearing the full range of stress, juncture, and syllable phenomena", rejects "any significant role in speech articulation" to sublaryngeal mechanisms (whether of syllable or of abdominal pulse, etc.). I do not know how this data can be most easily handled. I suspect that we bring to it a perceptual bias from normal speech — that we respond *as if* the tired-sounding patient *could* use sublaryngeal mechanisms for contrastive styles if she chose to do so. If it could be demonstrated that we do not project a potential commutation of syllabic and abdomenic contrasts into this data, then I would suspect that we are responding to subtle timing cues which once were redundant (conditioned by the physiological pulse) but which are now retained by the patient, and made relevant in the absence of the physiological pulse itself.

A third objection to the syllable comes from generative phonology in which "it does seem to simplify the description to introduce intermediate units between word and phoneme, units like the *syllable* and its constituents, the *onset, nucleus*, and *coda*" (Saporta and Contreras, 1962:4). Garcia, however, inquires whether there is any gain in simplicity if three transformations are required by them to avoid syllable boundary (1963:260).

See also Kuipers (1960) for an analysis in which the vowel does not enter.

Osgood would now feel that the syllable (but not the phoneme) is psychologically relevant for encoding a message, while the phoneme (but not the syllable) is relevant for decoding it (1963:742).

Since the first edition (1955) I have become increasingly convinced that syllables must be postulated to provide some nonmystical control on phoneme sequences. Haugen has seen that "the structural principles of distribution" are best brought out "if one adopts the syllable as one's descriptive unit" ... "if a syllable means anything at all, it is a unit of limited and therefore recurrent phoneme sequences" (1956b:196); but to me it seems necessary to have a physiological basis behind that which in fact leads to some universal control on phoneme sequences. Thus Jakobson emphasizes that "There are languages lacking syllables with initial vowels" but "there are no languages devoid of syllables with initial consonants" (in *Proceedings of the Eighth...*, 1958:21); and Smalley states that "When we reach the construction which has internal limitations greater than its external ones... we call it 'syllable' or 'word'" (1961:xvii). Greenberg has suggested that "frictionless continuents may function as vowels" (1962:79).

Note what happens if we take a Swadesh-type analysis of English diphthongs (1947:145) along with a Jakobson, Fant, Halle interpretation of presyllabic w and y vocalic (1952:20) but ignoring stress (with related stress-group juncture) and syllabic peak (with related syllable juncture). We would come out with /ouuiiouiuuaiouəoil/ for *Oh we owe you Iowa oil*; compare also the sequence /veiaioiaaeuhenio/ in Spanish *veía y oía a Eugenio* 'he came and heard Eugene'. Some organizing principle must underlie the groupings of such sequences; intonation groupings, abdominal-pulse groupings, morpheme groupings, and the like are not sufficient to take care of the syllable groupings. Their universal presence requires a universal physiological mechanism determining their existence, even although the underlying etic stratum can be emically reworked and occasionally in part overridden.

Kuipers has now raised a related problem — can a language exist which has no vowel phonemes: "The evidence does not go beyond proving that a 'vowelless' language, as envisaged by van Ginneken, can and indeed does, exist" (1960:106); "The most striking characteristic of the Kabardian phonemic system is the absence of an opposition consonant-vowel" (104). He arrives at this conclusion by treating long central low vowels phonemically as /ha-/ or /-ah/ (33); and a short central low vowel [a] as part of the preceding consonant — analogous, say, to the aspiration of a consonantal series — (51); by treating higher central vowel [ə] as sometimes part of preceding consonants and in part as representing juncture distinction (49, 65). A careful review is given by Pittman (1963).

From the viewpoint of tagmemic theory Kuipers fails to sense the full significance of this juncture material. He must use *either* emic vocalic segment (i.e., vowel phonemes) *or* emic syllabicity as seen in his emic junctures (which are also related to grammatical matters, 63). If he rejects vowel, he must bring in emic hierarchy of syllable — and also of stress group (see 64). Compare problems in English *button* where alternate analyses may treat [n̩] as /n/ plus a phoneme of syllabicity, as /ə/ plus /n/ plus syllable status (see Pike, 1947c:141 n., and discussion of syllable variants and portmanteau syllables above in §§ 9.231, 9.236; cf. also Bloomfield, 1933a:92). That is, first of all, *phonological hierarchy must be preserved* here as relevant to Kuiper's data on Kabardian. Secondly, the possibility of notational elimination of the letter 'a' (which, inconsistently, he does not do) would have to be tested against psycholinguistic considerations (above, § 8.815) to which he gives no discussion or theoretical place. If he follows current interest in utilizing grammatical data for determining his analysis, he might well be expected to bring to bear — because of grammatical components of intuition in the same climate — the intuitive 'particle' rightness of the segmented vowel /a/ reflected in his final orthography.

CHAPTER 10

HIGHER-LAYERED UNITS OF THE FEATURE MODE
OF THE UTTEREME

We turn to a more restricted analysis of units of the feature-mode hierarchy[1] of the uttereme which are larger than the single morpheme.

10.1 *Hypermorpheme Definition and Types*

The morpheme fills a tagmemic slot, manifesting a tagmeme, but is not itself that tagmeme which it manifests (cf. §§ 6.1, 6.6, 7.1, 7.4). A HYPERMORPHEME is a multimorphemic[2] manifestation of an expanded tagmeme, or of a hypertagmeme (cf. § 7.44); i.e., it is any morphemically-complex manifested variant of a tagmeme or hypertagmeme, or of an uttereme or hyper-uttereme; it is emically — trimodally — structured.

Samples of hypermorphemes would include morpheme groups at various levels of the feature-mode hierarchy of the uttereme. When, for example, a SUFFIX CLUSTER

---

[1] This chapter covers only a small part of the formal and semantic problems of the lexical hierarchy, and is probably the weakest in the book; the reader should note revision of the multimorphemic viewpoint of the hypermorpheme in §§ 11.52, 11.41. If the phonological hierarchy needs to be treated as some kind of a dual hierarchy of phonemic string and phonotagmemic slot-plus-class, furthermore (see § 12.5 concerning Crawford), then the implications for the lexical hierarchy need study. Special discussion of interlocking between hierarchies is given in Chapter 15 — but there the full implications of the contributions of Crawford and Longacre are not yet clear. Problems of meaning, in general, are very relevant to this Chapter — as evidenced by the importance to it of idioms and compounding; these special semantic problems are treated in Chapter 16.

One possible reworking of the lexical hierarchy would include reference to dramatis personae and situational roles (1964d) and their flow through the grammatical roles of a discourse. Items like *he* refer in cross reference to long items such as *the boy I used to know*, without going up the specific hierarchy of structure from word to phrase to clause, etc. To Postal, however, such specification of situational role would appear as an "unhappy path" (1964: 88 fn. 64).

[2] A crucial revision in §11.222 (and cf. fn. to § 7.44) withdraws the multimorphemic requirement for hypertagmemes, under the impact of Longacre's work. This in turn forces its withdrawal from the definition of hypermorpheme.

The effect on this chapter: (1) It leaves multimorphemic hypermorphemes as representing *special instances* of hypermorpheme types rather than as comprising the *entire* class; (2) it leaves room for single-morpheme hypermorphemes. The latter cannot be presented adequately however, until we have discussed the problems related to the concepts (a) of emic level, and (b) of simple versus complex manifestations of a tagmeme or hypertagmeme, which we do not develop until §§ 11.13, 11.22, 11.41, 11.52, 11.53. (3) It eliminates some inconsistencies (cf. our next fn. to § this same section).

composed of two suffixal morphemes fills a single expanded tagmemic slot in a chain of suffixes, this bimorphemic cluster constitutes a hypermorpheme. Likewise, if two morphemes together fill the tagmemic slot for a noun stem, these constitute a bimorphemic hypermorpheme; *starlet* would be one such type (occurring in the same slot before plural *-s* as is filled by the morpheme *star* in *stars*), whereas *bluebird* might be another type (but for the possibility of an analysis of some such COMPOUNDS which treats them as composed of a sequence of morphs but not of morphemes, see §§ 6.54, 6.61, 6.92; under the latter analysis, the items would be morphetically complex but single morphemes rather than hypermorphemes).

The particular structurally-relevant types of hypermorphemes which may be expected to occur in a particular language cannot be predicted in advance. The theory requires that there be successively-larger groupings of morphemes, but it specifically does *not* indicate just what these grouping types must be. In a language which has some of the characteristics of Schematic Class-Type C (§§ 7.313(4), 7.746), certain of the close-knit units may conveniently be called WORDS, with combinations of words called PHRASES, which are higher-layered hypermorphemes. In a language with characteristics more like that of Schematic Class-Type A' (§§ 7.313(4), 7.744), the term 'word' is more likely to be used for application to single morphemes than to be applied to hypermorphemes alone; the hypermorphemes of such a language may nevertheless be labelled phrases, whether or not the 'words' are monomorphemic[3] or multimorphemic. Hypermorphemes which are higher-layered than the short phrase, furthermore, may make advantageous the use of further labels — such as CLAUSE (a term especially useful for application to a hypermorpheme which has as immediate constituents a subject and a predicate); SENTENCE (a term useful for application to a specific occurrence or manifestation of an uttereme); RESPONSE (applicable to a manifestation of an uttereme which is not a conversation initiator, but the reply to a comment by another speaker); UTTERANCE-RESPONSE (applicable to the combination of manifested initial uttereme plus manifested reply uttereme, etc.); TOPIC-DISCUSSION (applicable to that part of a particular conversation which revolves around a single topic); CONVERSATION (with a higher-layered sequence of numerous utterance-response units within one or more topic-discussion units); LEAD SENTENCE (initiating the topic-discussion unit of a particular conversation); GREETING-FORMULA (stereotyped non-topic initiation of a particular conversation); CONVERSATION SERIES (a sequence of conversations revolving around some unifying purpose or situation); LECTURE, READ VERSE, and other MANIFESTED UTTEREMES OR HYPER-UTTEREMES, etc. (cf. uttereme and hyper-uttereme types referred to in §§ 5.53-54).

Since some of the same terms (such as conversation, lecture, etc.) may be employed

---

[3] Note the inconsistency built into our first edition here: Some words which act like phrases in the higher-layered slots of the syntax are treated as hypermorphemes even though they are (counter to our older definition) monomorphemic. Our revision allows for this — for both multimorphemic and monomorphemic phrases as hypermorphemes — at the price of making the higher layers of structure into emic points of reference.

here as were used in listing etic utterance types in §§ 5.53-54, however, it is important that the reader notice the crucial difference between the two usages. In Chapter 5 we were discussing the *type*. Here, we are discussing any one specific member which manifests the type; that is, *John came home* and *Bill came home* are manifestations of the same uttereme, but are distinct hypermorphemes. Each sequence of two or more morphemes is a separate hypermorpheme even though they may be members of the same hypermorphemic class and manifest the same uttereme. Each morphemically-distinct manifestation of an uttereme, or hyper-uttereme, or expanded tagmeme, or hypertagmeme, constitutes a separate hypermorpheme.

10.2 *The Feature Mode of the Hypermorpheme*

A hypermorpheme has, as components of its feature mode, the formal and semantic characteristics which make it contrast with other hypermorphemes or with morphemes, phonemes, utteremes, etc., and which permit its recognition or identification.

As to its formal characteristics, the feature mode of a hypermorpheme is in part composed of a specific sequence of two[4] or more specific morphemes, and of the specific phoneme sequences making up these included morphemes (or of the fused composite phonological content of the manifested forms of these two morphemes).

This characteristic would be expected, on the basis of material already discussed for the morpheme. Less easy to realize, however, is the possibility that some *subphonemic* phonological characteristics may be relevant as contrastive features of hypermorphemes — e.g., of certain words — in that they may mark or signal the boundaries of such units. When the word and the stress group coincide, and when phonemes have variants conditioned by placement in the stress group (§ 8.442), then a variant of the phoneme, occurring on a word-initial stressed syllable, may constitute an important signal of the beginning of the lexical[5] unit. Likewise, if it proves advisable in some instances to consider that lexical units have, in the absence of coterminal borders jointly with a hyperphoneme, the ability to cause conditioned variants of phonemes (cf. §§ 8.443, 9.233), then the subphonemic variants of the phonemes when they occur at such boundaries would constitute phonological contrastive features of the units without themselves constituting phonemes. None of these types are quite like the instances in which a specific phonetic segment such as glottal stop is clearly not a variant of any consonant phoneme of the regular consonantal system, but nevertheless

---

[4] See fnn. to § 10.1.
[5] The earlier edition read "grammatical unit". By changing to "lexical unit" we make clearer in this context that the single hypermorpheme, like the single morpheme, is part of the lexical hierarchy — as we have elsewhere treated it, e.g., in § 10.52.

A problem remains, however, as to the precise status of a *class* of morphemes or of hypermorphemes. A lexical class plus a tagmemic slot makes up a tagmeme unit of the grammatical hierarchy, but the class itself is assumed to be relevant to the lexical hierarchy directly. See also fn. to § 12.5.

constitutes a specific signal that a particular kind of morphemic or hypermorphemic boundary is present. See § 10.51.

Certain additional special phonological characteristics may occur, however, such as alliteration, in which one or more of the included morphemes or hypermorphemes or words within the larger hypermorpheme begin with the same sound. In a poem considered as a single hypermorpheme, furthermore, the rhyming sounds may also be viewed as a phonological characteristic of that total unit (and see § 9.312 for the same elements as components of hyperphonemes, or of the patterns of hyper-utteremes — which in turn, manifested, lead to single high-layered hypermorphemes).

The semantic component of a hypermorpheme may include the (predictable) sum of the meanings of its comprising morphemes and manifested morpheme classes and tagmemes (plus, in a larger hypermorpheme, the meaning of its manifested included utteremes and hyper-utteremes), but it may sometimes also contain an additional or overriding HYPERMORPHEMIC MEANING (or IDIOMATIC MEANING) which is not predictable from its included parts. Thus the hypermorpheme *John is a big boy* has a meaning composed of its manifested morphemes, tagmemes, and uttereme, but to *step on the gas* has an added hypermorphemic meaning beyond the sum of the meanings of its included parts. (For further discussion of idiomatic and metaphorical uses of morphemes and hypermorphemes, see § 16.13.)

10.3 *The Manifestation Mode of the Hypermorpheme*

A particular hypermorpheme may have variants of types analogous to those of a single morpheme (§ 6.5). Variants can be regular or irregular, phonological or semantic in character, locally conditioned — by phonemic, morphemic, or tagmemic context — or systemically conditioned. Thus *won't* is an irregular phonological variant of that hypermorpheme which contains as a second variant the form *will not*, and is in part systemically conditioned inasmuch as it is more likely to occur in informal style than in formal style. Further variants of other hypermorphemes, at various levels of the hierarchy, can be classified by analogy with allomorphic variant types, and need not be illustrated in detail here. (But for fused types, and morphophonemic change at morpheme boundaries in hypermorphemes, see § 14.)

The additional element added to the discussion at this point is the treatment, by the same kind of operations and criteria which have been used for single morphemes, of a short or long morpheme sequence *as a whole*. The recital of a particular poem, with errors, would constitute a variant of that hypermorpheme, for example. Similarly, a child, in learning to speak, may learn an entire phrase or sentence as a unit — as a hypermorpheme. If this particular hypermorpheme is sufficiently distinct from other hypermorphemes in the child's speech to be contrastive with it, and is sufficiently unique to be easily identified, then from one point of view it is irrelevant whether the variant used by the child is phonologically identical with the variant used by the adult

— the child's variant is systemically conditioned, with partial topological correspondence (cf. §§ 8.441-42) with the comparable unit of the adult.

Distortion can be utilized by adults, furthermore, for specific effects, with parasitic (§ 6.62) elements deliberately introduced as partial replacements of the phonetically-related normal morphemes of the sequence: *He said I didn't have no sign of kodiak trouble around the heart or no coroner's trombone disease where the blood gets shut off in the artillery... I think they call it the I Oughta* (purported quotation from Heavyweight Champion Rocky Marciano, *Time*, Jan. 25, 1954:82).

Possibly, also, certain pattern errors can be analyzed as leading to variants of hypermorphemes.

Note the following which I overheard: *Mother, Where do kitties find mouse-es* [maᵘzɛz]*?* (as a variant of *mice*); *Mother letted us* (*go*) (as a variant of *let*); *Daddy, can I take your comb in case somebody mess ups my hair?* (variant of *messes up*); *This is a good way to get spankened, isn't it?*; *I don't want no toast* (perhaps to be treated as a variant of *I don't want any toast?*); *Daddy, I have that kind of feelness* (variant of *I feel that way too?*); *I can color nicelier than anybody in this room*; *It stucks* (finger in the handle of a scissor); *He was the goodest one, he fighted outside*; *I liketed it*; (*The tin cup stuck on my mouth and chin*) *because I blewed up* (i.e., *sucked*); *I wish I can!* (variant of *could?*); *Here is the picture we promiseted to send you.*

10.4 *The Distribution Mode of the Hypermorpheme*

The distribution mode of any one particular hypermorpheme may have several components. Among them are the following: (a) The inclusion of the hypermorpheme within a higher-layered hypermorpheme, as *Big John* is included in *Big John came home*. (b) Its membership in a hypermorpheme class, or in a morpheme-hypermorpheme class, as *Big John* is a hypermorpheme which is a member of the class containing *Little Joe*, or the single morphemes *John* and *Joe*. (c) Its further membership, as a member of a class, in a still larger class, a HYPERCLASS OF HYPERMORPHEME CLASSES or a hyperclass of morpheme-hypermorpheme classes. In some languages, for example, one may find several classes of hypermorphemes, each of which is a subclass of a hyperclass NOUN. (d) Its distribution, actual and potential, as a whole, in one or more tagmemic or hypertagmemic slots, as *Big John* may manifest the subject-as-actor tagmeme, or the object tagmeme, etc. (e) Internally, a further distributional component may be one or more elements of a relevant phonological shape type, as, for example, the sequence of its phonemes or types of phonemes may affect its potential occurrence in slots where the rhyming of metric qualities is important to its inclusion in a higher-layered hyper-uttereme.

10.5 Bibliographical Comments on Chapter 10

10.51 On Phonological Characteristics of Hypermorphemes

From our point of view scholars such as Firth and his colleagues appear to have had as one of their goals the attempt to describe directly the phonological characteristics of the hypermorpheme without doing it in relation to prior or concomitant analysis of phonemic units of the phonological hierarchy. On occasion they wish, that is to say, to describe the phonological characteristics of specific words, sentences, 'pieces', or 'stretches' of speech, or of abstracted classes or systems of such utterance pieces, without necessary reference to phonemes as such. The hypermorpheme becomes for them a threshold emic unit such that the postulation of included phonemic units is assumed to obscure the picture rather than illuminate it — though the phonological contrastive features may be treated as being present in the form of 'prosodies' of hyperphonemes or hypermorphemes or classes of these units.

See, for example, the quotations from Firth in § 8.814 (where phonological contrastive features of hyperphonemes are also in view); also, Firth: "I have suggested the use of the terms *prosody* and *prosodies* to refer to structural features of words, pieces and sentences as wholes or to features marking beginnings, endings and junctions" (Firth, 1951a:84; continuing his view in the earlier quotation that such components are "distinct from the phonematic constituents"); Sharp: "A polysystemic approach to linguistic analysis... assumes *inter alia* that such grammatically recurrent elements as the morpheme or word may just as profitably be subjected to systemic analysis as such phonologically recurrent elements as the syllable", and "We have been able to classify our material without recourse to tonemic analysis as a prerequisite: we have worked directly on our phonic material and made a separate analysis at a different level of abstraction", so that it is frequently "more appropriate to think in terms of prosodic patterns that are features of the word as a whole" (1954:168-69); Carnochan: "These features [i.e., phonetic criteria differentiating grammatical categories] are abstracted from the sentence as a whole" (1953:79; see also 1950:1040-41); Mitchell: "Given the complexity of the linguistic text and that phonology is 'phonetics become grammar', it is not surprising that phonological features have significance at other levels and supply in Berber criteria for the two sub-categories of pre-nominal P" (1953:378). In addition, Mitchell has provided us with an elaborate attempt to treat as prosodies the shape types of grammatical constituents in relation to their phonemic content, CVC patterning, and subgroupings of permitted consonants and vowels (1953; compare Sprigg, 1955:134-43, 149-53, 320-22, 340-48). For glottal stop as word marker, note Robins, who refers to zero "realized as ʔ initially at word boundaries" (1953a:141, 143), and note that "The term 'prosodic feature' is used here and in the next paragraph to designate phonetic features occurring at specific places (initial, medial or final) in syllable or word structures, and so acting as markers of such places" (1953b:137n);

for clause, in Sundanese, "established and delimited solely by reference to features of intonation and the associated features of pause", see 1953b:120.

For earlier important attempts to treat phonological components as contrastive features of grammatical units, in somewhat different ways, note Bloomfield (1930a, 1935), D. Jones (1931), Trubetzkoy (1936 in *Proceedings of the Second...*, 1949 [1939]:292-96, 307-14).

10.52 *On Hypermorphemic Meanings*

For a discussion of meanings of hypermorphemes beyond their predictable meanings, see especially the article by Nida, who distinguishes between the endocentric macroseme of *applesauce*, as food, and the exocentric macroseme of *applesauce* as an exclamation (1951:11-13). See also the problem of hypermorph meanings discussed by Bazell (1953:84, and 1949a:2).

Bolinger (1948:22) has one of the most interesting discussions of problems of hypermorphemic unity — though not, however, under that label.

Bloomfield indicates that "In every language, moreover, many complex forms [i.e., hypermorphemes] carry specialized meanings which cannot figure in a purely linguistic description but are practically of great importance. The linguist... cannot evaluate these meanings although in practical life they are fully as useful as any sememe" (1933a: 276). Nevertheless, he also stated that "It is a very common mistake to try to use this difference [specialization of meaning] as a criterion [for compounds]. We cannot gauge meanings accurately enough; moreover, many a phrase is as specialized in meaning as any compound..." as *a queer bird* and *meat and drink* are "fully as specialized as they are in the compounds *jailbird* and *sweetmeats*" (1933a:227-28). Compare, however, from his basic postulates: "E.g., *the book*, or *The man beat the dog*; but not, e.g. *book on* (as in *Lay the book on the table*), for this is meaningless" (1926:156); here he did use meaning, but used it to identify the *borders* of a hypermorpheme, or the presence of a hypermorpheme, rather than to differentiate between *kinds* of hypermorphemes. If meaning must enter operationally into the identification of a hypermorpheme in the one instance, and if a hypermorphemic meaning is admittedly as useful to native speakers as morphemic meanings, and if the definition of morphemes in general can include the presence of meaning (as, for Bloomfield, it does on 264, where the "Smallest meaningful unit of linguistic signalling" on a lexical plane is the morpheme, etc.), it is difficult to see why the meaning of a hypermorpheme should not be utilized in linguistic description and definition provided (a) that we do not assume that these meanings are *exactly* and precisely describable and (b) that we treat it as only one contrastive component of the entire complex of contrastive-identificational components of the hypermorpheme, and provided (c) that we leave an area of indeterminacy in the differentiation of some semantically-related hypermorphemes as we must between certain morphemes.

This implies, furthermore, that hypermorphemes must be listed in our dictionaries, when their specialized meanings are nonpredictable from their included morphemes. This, however, should not surprise us since in practice dictionary makers have long been doing this very thing. Long ago Sweet said that "grammar deals with the general facts of language, lexicology with the special facts" (1913 [1875–76]:31). Specialized hypermorphemes are therefore treated as lexical items, as units. For problems in dictionary making, see Sebeok (1962b); and Householder and Saporta (1962:279-82).

Psycholinguistic techniques may some day demonstrate in other ways that hypermorphemes are units. Note implications of Osgood, Sebeok and their collaborators (1954:17-59, 118). Carroll suggests that activity of reciting a poem "would appear to involve a different set of encoding or response selection units from the set involved in the original creation of the poem" (1953:91).

Numerous instances in which clusters of words are beginning to emerge as single semantic units are appearing in the literature. The term lexeme is useful for this. Note, for example, Hockett (1958:174; with reference to Swadesh 1947a); note also semantic units sometimes manifested by single word and sometimes by word sequence in the taxonomic hierarchy of Conklin (in Householder and Saporta, 1962:121-24).

For lexical items in reference to the relation of cells to a matrix or to a paradigm, note also Lounsbury (1956:162), Goodenough (1956:209), Pike and Erickson (1964, with formatives covering one or more cells of a matrix), and Mathiot (1963b:2 fn 7, with "Pike's concepts of 'slot' and 'filler'" determining the "cognitive content of linguistic 'slots'" for "the units of the lexicon that enter into them").

For more extensive discussion of problems of meaning note Chapter 16.

CHAPTER 11

HIGHER-LAYERED UNITS OF THE DISTRIBUTION MODE
OF THE SYNTAGMEME

In Chapter 9 it seemed possible to find criteria by which syllables, rhythm groups, pause groups, and so on, could be treated as units higher than the phoneme in the phonological hierarchy. Essential threshold criteria were chosen which differentiated each kind of higher-level unit from lower ones. The chest pulse, for example, differentiated the syllable from the phoneme, or from a sequence of sounds which was less than a syllable; an abdominal pulse differentiated a rhythm unit from a syllable or from a sequence of syllables less than a rhythm unit.

Once such units were determined, each of them or classes of them could then be further differentiated and described in terms of the trimodal approach.

In Chapter 10, a similar attempt was made to treat morpheme sequences in terms of hierarchically-ordered units, each of which is trimodally structured. The attempt proved fruitful, but the threshold criteria for determination of the level involved seemed to need further amplification before the results were comparably as satisfactory as those for the phonology.

Now, for Chapter 11, we pose the question: Granted that we have a grammatical hierarchy, and that the tagmemes may be set up as the minimum units of that hierarchy, what components of the data could best be treated as units of higher grammatical layers? And what criteria can be used to determine that we have passed over a threshold from a lower grammatical layer to a higher type?

11.1 *The Term OC-Hypertagmeme Tentatively Applied to Obligatorily-Complex Units*

Various kinds of structures may be treated as high-level, non-minimum members of the grammatical hierarchy — i.e., as HYPERTAGMEMES.[1]

Some of these structures can more easily be treated as analogous to high-level phonological units than can others — i.e., are more fully integrated with the total model. There are differences, also, in the degree of difficulty in finding criteria which allow us to identify or differentiate such units.

---

[1] In many recent publications on tagmemics, the term hypertagmeme has been dropped (under Longacre's influence) and authors are referring to "tagmemes on various levels". This seems to leave no deep-seated confusion.

11.11 *Definition of Tentative Obligatorily-Complex Hypertagmeme*

In this section we tentatively choose for diagnostic purposes a criterion which proved fruitful in the earlier stages of the development of the model and in the analysis of research materials. A bit later we will show how problems emerged in the process of integrating this criterion with the model as a whole, and implications of steps taken to revise the manner in which it is used.

A unit of grammar will be considered an OC-HYPERTAGMEME, for the purpose of this section,[2] if and only if all the manifestations of it are obligatorily complex (i.e., necessarily composed of two or more morphemes or morpheme sequences).

As a unit of grammar, furthermore, each unit is required to be emically relevant, and is describable in reference to contrastive-identificational components of the feature mode, as well as in reference to free or conditioned, simple or complex variants of the manifestation mode, and in reference to its occurrence in sequences, classes, and systems as part of the distribution mode.

This kind of unit would include the structures illustrated, for example, by *the boy, a man, the man*; or by *John came, Bill sang, John sang*; or by *beside him, past me, beside me*, and so on. In each of these there is a mutual dependence of occurrence which characterizes the structure. (One does not say, for example, *The came*, nor *He sat me*.) In these structures the words *boy* and *beside* — or substitutes for them — do not occur without their concomitants *the*, *him*, or the like.

Concerning the feature mode, we must look (a) for manifesting class and (b) emic meaningful slot, if we wish to parallel for hypertagmeme the treatment of tagmeme (§§ 7.31-32). The manifesting class of such a proposed hypertagmeme is easy to find. It would be precisely the list of hypermorphemes fulfilling the requirements of the structures already referred to. That is, *the boy, a man, the man, the big man*, would be members of such a class. This appears to be satisfactory, since for tagmeme, also, the class of morphemes and morpheme sequences manifesting the internal structure of a tagmeme were seen to make up one of these two crucial contrastive-identificational features of the tagmeme (§ 7.31).

When, however, we try to find the emic slot which would make up the second crucial component of its feature mode, a difficulty sets in. Instead of the one emic slot which is associated with a single tagmeme, and which by its function in the system brings the structural meaning to that tagmeme, we find that our postulated obligatorily-complex hypertagmeme occurs in a variety of structurally-meaningful slots. The sequence *the boy* occurs not only in subject slot, but also in object slot, and so on; no one functional slot or meaning is associated with it. It appears impossible to reconcile this fact with our desire to parallel the tagmeme of Chapter 7 with the hyper-

---

[2] The term SC-Hypertagmeme, defined and adopted for all other remaining sections of the book, is introduced in § 11.4. The reader who wishes to move more directly to that solution, however, should not fail to read the discussion of levels of structure in the various subsections of § 11.22. For earlier comment on multimorphemic tagmemes and hypermorphemes, see fnn. to §§ 7.44, 10.1.

tagmeme, in basic structural characteristics. At this point, then, a consistent development of the tagmeme model requires a rejection of the criterion of obligatory complexity as crucial to the tagmeme-hypertagmeme threshold.

11.12 *Disadvantages and Advantages of the Definition of OC-Hypertagmeme as Obligatorily Complex*

Once difficulty has been encountered with the usage of the term hypertagmeme as restricted to obligatorily-complex types of units, various problems can be seen which it raises. One has just been discussed — that no emic slot and its functional meaning is directly applicable to such a unit.

A second problem was pointed out to me by Longacre on analogical grounds some time before this first one had given us difficulty. He noted that in the phonological hierarchy the theory did not require that every syllable be longer than one phoneme, nor every rhythm unit longer than one syllable, and so on. Why, then, should one require — if the analogy were by chance to hold across the two hierarchies — that higher units in the grammatical hierarchy must be obligatorily complex? There seemed to be no way within our earlier model to counter this objection.

A third disadvantage, of a theoretical type, also developed: In principle, the model emphasized unit as primary as over against construction or relationship (see §§ 6.7, 7.85); and unity was determined by over-all function in a higher-level slot. Yet the setting up of obligatory complexity as the principle diagnostic criterion of hypertagmemes would seem to have overridden this view.

A fourth difficulty was that the approach led to a larger number of types of levels than could be easily paralleled with a phoneme, syllable, rhythm-group progression. A single word might have several such layers in it, for example. Thus in a Cashibo word it appears (Shell, 1957) that such complex items sometimes occur inside the core of a word, inside the base, inside the margin, and inside the word as a whole, in a variety of forms. Further layers within layers occur pyramided in the sentence. Yet within this plethora of levels there was no simple way to abstract out, as a special set of levels, the particular ones which (like word, phrase, and clause) intuitively seemed most important. An obscure complex buried in a series of suffixes has the same theoretical status as a clause type.

It was further disturbing when in field studies it became obvious that a crucial diagnostic test of a clause type occasionally turned out to be an optional tagmeme rather than obligatory one. Compare, for example, the transitive and intrasitive clauses in Shell's sixth formula (1957:203) where she has an optional object which, combined with a special class of verbs, differentiates it from the the intransitive clause which never has such an object. This brought into question the implied assumption that the diacritica of a grammatical structure must be its minimum, obligatory tagmemes.

A further theoretical problem arises related to the first one mentioned: If we look for an OC-hypertagmemic slot, or even a group of slots, to which *the boy* can be assigned as filler, we find subject and object slots already assigned to simple tagmemes since single morphemes like *John* fill the slots (§§ 7.313[1], 7.44). This, in turn, is awkward when we compare it with the phonological hierarchy, since no phoneme is there included within the manifestation of a phoneme, but here a determiner tagmeme (manifested by *the*) would be included within the subject tagmeme (manifested by *the boy* as a whole).

The collapse of the obligatorily-complex definition of the hypertagmeme leaves us, however, with an interesting question: What was it that made the definition useful in the first place? Fruitful it was, indeed. It opened the way for Shell (1957), for example, to structure her Cashibo data in an elegant, concise fashion which left the data in a form which is easily transferable to pedagogical treatment for language learning. Other studies by Mayers (1957), and H. Hart (1957) also profited by the approach.

The obligatorily-complex solution had several advantages without which it could not have made this contribution. It is important to review them, to see of they can be salvaged: (1) The solution was simple. The definition was sharp cut, easy to state, easy to understand, and relatively simple to apply. This of itself was of enormous advantage in the processing of data. (2) It appeared to lead to a relatively-simple discovery procedure: If the two included tagmemes of a construction did not always appear in the construction, it was excluded as a hypertagmeme. (3) It led to hierarchical results. If one constituent of a hypertagmeme were itself obligatorily complex, and so on, this showed up in formulas as successive layers of double-plus structure: $+(+[+...+...]+...)+....$ (4) It led to crucial, quick recognition of many important minimum (versus expanded) formulas, without which analytical and pedagogical procedures are difficult to make operable. (5) It led to a quick rule-of-thumb separation of exocentric from endocentric constructions. (6) It allowed the analyst to work immediately with substitution frames and matrices without determining or hypothesizing in advance the point of word boundaries.

Especially by those persons who have struggled with the analysis of unwritten languages it will be recognized that this is no mean list of advantages. How — if at all — can they be preserved? Some of the advantages of the obligatorily-complex criterion can undoubtedly be retained by a new approach to delimiting a hypertagmemic set of units.

11.13 *An Obligatorily-Complex Structure Re-Analyzed as a Special Kind of Emic Class of Hypermorphemes*

Another possibility, however, lies in checking to see if the obligatorily-complex unit treated under the term OC-hypertagmeme can in fact be re-introduced elsewhere in the over-all system. With this in mind, if we re-examine the expected characteristics of the unit as described in § 11.12, we note that only one gap appeared: For trimodal description as a hypertagmeme it lacked only the characteristic of having one particular, structurally-meaningful emic slot. Otherwise, trimodal features can be found for it.

Does this tell us anything? The answer is definitely yes. The characteristics of membership, variants, internal and external distribution are similar to those noted for an emic class of morphemes described earlier (§ 7.313). The principal difference is the very point in question — namely, that the members of this class are obligatorily complex. Each specific member of the class is a hypermorpheme — i.e., a morpheme sequence — but differs from those optionally-complex hypermorphemes which only one of the morphemes is necessarily present. That is to say, that we now have an OBLIGATORILY-COMPLEX CLASS OF HYPERMORPHEMES — rather than a hypertagmeme — with members defined and described by the very criteria earlier postulated for the hypertagmeme.

The obligatorily-complex units postulated earlier as OC-hypertagmemes are thus retained, but renamed. The classes of these units fit a gap left in an earlier stage in the development of the theory, which would sooner or later have given trouble in any case. Chapter 10 (Pike, 1955) did not show sensitivity to this impending clash.

In addition, the classes of optionally- and obligatorily-complex hypermorphemes are made available as contrastive-identificational features of any newly-to-be-defined hypertagmeme, just as classes of morphemes have served in describing tagmemes.

Various difficulties remain. For example, at this stage in the discussion it must be noted that in the tagmemes of Chapter 7 some of the classes of forms filling a simple tagmemic slot were composites of classes of single morphemes, of optionally-complex hypermorphemes, of obligatorily-complex hypermorphemes, and of the latter expanded, optionally, still further. Any use of a hypermorpheme class in hypertagmeme definition must either be able to account for this state of affairs, or lead in turn to a modification of distribution-class treatment on the simple-tagmeme level.

11.2 *The Terms RL-Hypertagmeme and RL-Tagmeme Tentatively Applied Relativistically to Levels of Focus*

A sharply different use of the term hypertagmeme has been set forth by Longacre (1958a, 1964a). It, too, has been very fruitful in actual use in field situations (e.g., Elliott, 1960) and has lent itself to detailed pedagogical development and presentation.

11.21 *Definition of Relativistic RL-Tagmeme and RL-Hypertagmeme*

The starting point of this approach is quite different from that of our Chapter 7. Instead of treating the tagmeme as a minimum unit of the grammatical hierarchy as a whole, it treats the tagmeme as a constituent unit of a larger unit on some one level of the hierarchy which happens to be under analytical scrutiny at the time. An RL-HYPERTAGMEME (i.e., a relative-level hypertagmeme) would be some one unit type of a general class of types at that particular level; if one is focusing on the clause level, then the equational-clause type and a transitive-clause type would both be RL-hypertagmemes, whereas the subjects would be tagmemes.

That is to say, if 'X' represents a particular type of structure at a particular focus, then 'X^{-1}' is a tagmeme. If one focuses on a particular phrase, that phrase type is considered to be an RL-hypertagmeme (as a setting for the distribution of included words); but that phrase will itself be considered a tagmeme type when the clause is in view as an RL-hypertagmeme with the phrase included within it. A unit which is seen as an RL-hypertagmeme on one level is viewed as a tagmeme as part of a higher level.

By this view, both tagmeme and RL-hypertagmeme are relativistically defined. And choice of a particular level as a starting point for description is arbitrary. One may start with a higher level, or a lower one, focus on it — as an RL-hypertagmemic level — and study the contrasting *total* units at that level, or the included ones which are its constituents.

11.22 *Levels of Structure*

The 'levels', on the other hand, are quasi-absolutes. They have an absolute character in that, etically, there are criteria which, in general, differentiate clause level from phrase level, phrase from word level, word from morpheme level, and so on. They are still somewhat relative in that the specific details of the available criteria, and the specific numbers of levels which are structurally relevant to any one language are emically determined.

One language may contain more structurally-relevant levels than another, and the levels may have somewhat — but not completely — distinct diagnostic characteristics.

Crucial to the setting up of one level as over against another, however, is the analytical requirement that unit types on one level must in some sense (1) control the occurrence and relative (fixed or free) order of included constituents, and (2) be structurally organized in a manner which in some sense is sharply in contrast with the layer next higher or lower in the hierarchy.

Some of the levels which are most likely to be treated in such an approach are word, phrase, clause, sentence. Others might be stem, utterance, conversation.

11.221 *Word Level*

In setting up the word level as over against a lower or higher one, various general (etic) criteria are available. Not all of these criteria are applicable in any one instance;

nor do they always lead to the same results. Border-line instances occur between word and bound forms, and between word and phrase. That is, these are generalized etic criteria which may be used to provide initial starting evidences for discovery of units at various relevant levels, but the preliminary results must be emically reworked before presentation of the system and — even then — there may be indeterminacy between the levels just as we have found indeterminacy of borders between units in sequence.

Etic criteria for possible use in the tentative separation of units on a WORD level from subword units or sequences of subword units include the following (we draw especially on Bloomfield, 1933a:178-83, and Nida, 1949:102-06): (1) isolatability, as the standard criterion (a word like *boys* may conceivably be used as a call — *Boys!* or as a total sentence constituting a response form, whereas *-s* would normally be bound rather than free in this fashion; note here that, in reference to isolatability, word is analogous to syllable, and morpheme to phoneme); (2) versatility of occurrence (*boys* may be subject, object, etc., whereas *-s* 'plural' occurs only as a suffix); (3) rigidity of order (subword units are likely to be rigidly fixed as to the places they occur in a sequence of morphemes, whereas a word may be more loose in reference to the place it comes in a sequence of words — cf. the parts of *un-gentle-man-li-ness* versus *away* in *Away he ran*, *He ran away*, *Away ran he*); (4) interruptibility (a word is not easily interrupted by a parenthetical expression as a sequence of words may be — cf. *black — that is bluish-black — birds* where *bluish-black* may not be inserted in the middle of the compound *blackbird*, and compare the expansion potential of *green house* in *greener house* versus *greenhouse*); (5) special relationship (nonsyntactic patterns between morphemes may occur within words which are not found in phrases, cf. *the outcast* vs. *to cast out*); (6) potential phonological markers: (a) it is often possible to pause at the end of any word, but seldom after a nonfinal morpheme within a word; (b) in various languages words may constitute a rhythm or pause group, but affixes seldom do (compare the possibility of pause in the phrase *a black bird* with no such normal possibility in the word *blackbird*); (c) special junctures or (d) phoneme sequences or (e) allophonic occurrences or (f) morphophonemic rules may also help mark word borders; (7) analogy of doubtful items with items more certain (e.g., *the* as more or less non-isolatable, analogous to isolatable *this*, or *-m* in *I'm here* analogous to *am*).

Various word types continue to raise problems of determining word boundaries: non-isolatable words or variants of words (cf. *a*, or *-m* in *I'm*), rigidly-ordered words (*to* in *to go*), words joined into compound single words (*bluebird*), cited parts of words (*isms*), words with affix bound to a phrase (*the King of England's*), and so on. It is precisely these problems which were tentatively by-passed by using earlier tagmemic techniques, but which arise again when one attempts to set up basic levels of structural type.

11.222 Phrase Level and Portmanteau Levels

Having discussed criteria to differentiate word units from subword units, we now turn to those criteria which help differentiate PHRASE level from word. As a first criterion, we use the diagnostic that a unitary sequence wholly made up of two or more words is on a level higher than that of the word — it is a phrase, clause, or sentence, etc. (*The boy* may by this criterion be a phrase, but not a word.)

Negatively, however, we do not use here the requirement that *every* phrase *must* be made up of two or more words. This criterion, as the principle component of the classical definition (cf. Bloomfield, 1933a:178), was useful to us so long as we were treating a hypertagmeme as a sequence of two or more obligatory tagmemes. If, however, we wish to apply that term rather to levels somewhat analogous to the syllable and rhythm group, the obligatorily-complex criterion for phrase prevents the parallelism whereby a single vowel phoneme may, under proper conditions, simultaneously constitute a syllable and rhythm unit. Here, then, we allow a single morpheme, under certain conditions, to be treated simultaneously as a word and as a phrase. Readers of Parts I-II, (1945-55), should note: *The requirement that a hypermorpheme must contain two (or more) morphemes (§ 10.1) is accordingly withdrawn.*

This requires, then, a further diagnostic criterion to apply in such instances: A phrase is a unit, other than a clause or sentence, (a) which fills an emic slot in a clause or sentence structure and (b) which is either composed of a sequence of two or more words or is one word which is optionally expandable in that same slot into a sequence of two or more words.

The boy would illustrate a multi-word obligatorily-complex phrase; *John* and *big John* would illustrate respectively a single-word phrase and its multi-word optionally-complex counterpart. A particular emic phrase *type* would then be made of the sum of all the variant manifestations of it. Both *John* and *big John* would be phrases manifesting the same emic personal-noun-phrase type. Both *John* and *big John* may fill the slot 'actor-as-subject' in the clause *John came home*, for example, and it is the boundaries of this emic slot (and others) which give the unitary character to *big John* as a whole. In terms of formula, a phrase is $+(+ \text{ word} + \text{ word})$ or is $+(+ \text{ word} \pm \text{ word})$ but is not $+(+ \text{ word})$.

(It is worth mentioning that the treatment of a single word as a phrase, when expandable, is in principle similar to the mathematical treatment of parallel lines as a special instance of an angle. By the latter convention a single generalization is made to cover both types of data. So, here, the convention allows us for certain purposes to cover an expandable filler of a slot by the same statement with the expanded filler. The convention runs counter to 'common sense' but is extremely useful. For its application to phrase, see Pickett, 1960. Compare, for earlier material related to this view, Wells, for whom "every expression is a sequence of one or more morphemes", 1947a:82.)

As we earlier had portmanteau phones (§ 8.446) and syllables (§ 9.236), so here we must now postulate PORTMANTEAU LEVELS — two or more levels simultaneously manifested by a single morpheme or morpheme sequence. The necessity for postulating portmanteau levels first was brought to mind by problems raised by Ilah Fleming. She pointed out (private communication) that in Chapter 7 (1954) there was an inconsistency implied when an item such as *John* (as subject) symbolized by +(S) was treated as the same unit as *John* in *big John* symbolized as ±(*big*) +(*John*) — i.e., ±(modifier) +(S) of the sentence *Big John came*. Inasmuch as I had implied that *big John* as a whole was subject, it was inconsistent now to treat *John* in the phrase *big John* as subject. It was this consideration which forced me to start dealing with simultaneous levels in the structure. Thus *John* in *Big John came* is now treated as head of a noun phrase within a phrase-level structure, and so as representing a word-level structure. *John* in *John came*, however, is treated as simultaneously (1) a word-level structure, i.e., head of the noun phrase, and (2) as a total phrase-level structure, within the clause. In the sentence *John came* the word-level and phrase-level structures share the same manifesting unit, which thus serves in double function between levels.

Turning now to the first numbered component above — the slot-filling requirement — we see that the utilization of phrase or sentence-level slots as relevant to the definition of phrase requires definition of these higher structures before the phrase can be more than tentatively identified. To this extent the definition is relative to the system as a whole (or is in part 'circular', or mutually defining, as are all the terms of any system, in our view). We need, then, to check the criteria for differentiating clause from phrase.

First, however, it is useful to mention a few other relationships between units at word and phrase levels: Like the word, the phrase is isolatable, is often versatile as to the number of kinds of slots in which it is found, and occasionally has phonological markers. The phrase is more likely to be interruptible by parenthetical forms or by phonological junctures than is the word. Often the order of words within a phrase is as rigid as the order of affixes within a word, but occasionally word order within a phrase varies freely more than does affix order within a word. From language to language there is considerable overlap between the class meanings of tagmeme types within words and within phrases. Either may contain tagmemes of aspect, time, number, person, emphasis, possession, definiteness, location, size, cause, shape, gender, animateness, movement, agreement, and so on. The difference here is in the level of structure within which the particular language handles the data, rather than in the kinds of data treated; a sharp division in allocation of these elements between two levels of a particular language, however, constitutes a supporting criterion for those levels once they are postulated for such a language. Similarly, a sharp discontinuity in any other of the mentioned characteristics — e.g., distributional versatility of parts, phonological markers, interruptibility, rigidity of order of parts, expansion possibilities, etc. — may for a particular language be diagnostic. In English, for example, within the word there is shown — amongst other items — time (*walks*, *walked*), process (*walking*), possession (*John's*), nominalization (*truth*), size (*brooklet*), sex (*tigress*), and so on. In the phrase may be seen time and process (*was walking*, *a finished product*), possession (*his book*), size (*a big brook*), sex (*a female tiger*), and so on. Yet in the phrase a vastly greater set of meanings can be carried by free forms than can the few carried by affixes (cf. *a good man*, *a likely story*, etc.). Similarly, the English phrase has a much greater expansion potential than the word (e.g., *my very great big and tall John* versus *Johnny's*).

11.223 *Clause Level*

We turn now to the clause level to seek diagnostic criteria to separate it from the phrase level.

Longacre (1958a, 1964a) — who almost alone of current structuralists has faced this problem — suggests that the CLAUSE level though definable separately for each language nevertheless typically (1) has a place in the grammatical hierarchy between phrase and sentence (as the syllable is between phoneme and rhythm group). (2) It is (a) noncoordinate (excluding phrases like *John and Bill* and sentences like *John came and Bill stayed*), and (b) may have various structural patterns such as 'non-centered, centered, or relator-axis'. (3) It typically has an over-all structural meaning of predication, or equation, or query, or command, or related type (e.g., *John came*, *John is president*, *Is he there*). (4) In addition, for a particular language, the internal organization of clause units may differ sharply from that of phrase-level units in terms of number and type of constituent tagmemes making up a particular clause type versus a particular phrase type.

We note, also, (5) that, when transforms change one clause structure into another clause structure, the structure of included expanded phrases may sometimes be unchanged (cf. *My great big John saw Bill* and *Bill was seen by my great big John*). This makes the treatment of phrase structures essential to efficient description of such situations, where during the transform a phrase such as *my great big John* constitutes a constant, an unchanging block of words within the clauses.

Portmanteau levels involving clauses also occur. A single word may on occasion constitute an entire clause. For many languages, a pronominal subject is indicated in the verb, and clause types may have single-word manifestations. Compare Spanish *Voy* 'I am going' with *Voy yo* of the same meaning, but with added independent pronominal subject. In such instances, the total range of possible expansions differs greatly as to the kinds and arrangements of affixal tagmemes within the included obligatory words, and the kinds and arrangements of optional tagmemes which may expand the clause as a whole.

11.224 *Sentence Level*

For criteria separating levels above the clause, Pickett's work (1960) provides the first extensive treatment, although this is in its beginning stages. (1) The SENTENCE level may be portmanteau with that of clause: *John came home* is simultaneously clause and sentence. (2) The potential expansion types, however, are different, and force treatment of the two as separate distributional matrices. Whereas the clause expands in terms of satellite tagmemes of time, manner, location, etc., the sentence expands by the addition of further clauses in coordinate, subordinate, or paratactic relation to each other. Furthermore, (3) a sentence is by definition isolatable in its own right — isolatability is a specific characteristic of the sentence itself (Bloomfield, 1933a:170). Hence, when isolatability is used as a criterion for word or phrase or clause as over against a part of a word, we are saying that word — or phrase or clause — may occur as constituting a portmanteau manifestation of a sentence.

In turn, however, (4) isolatability must be defined structurally. Here we treat it as the potential of an item for constituting an entire utterance. A sentence, in this view, would be a minimum utterance. Some, but not all, sentences are clauses; some sentences are made up of two or more clauses, whereas other sentences — especially those filling an utterance-response slot — may be made up of nonclause phrases or words. (Thus *tomorrow* is a nonclause sentence in the query-response unit *When are you coming? Tomorrow.*)

11.225 *Monologue, Utterance-Response, Conversation, and Intra-Word Levels*

The sentence level must be differentiated from monologue level: (1) A sentence is a minimum monologue; that is, a sentence may be simultaneously manifesting the monologue level, in portmanteau relation with it. (2) The monologue, however, may be composed of two — or many — sentences in sequence. (3) The monologue constitutes the connected discourse of a single speaker — whereas a sentence may be one of several sentences in a single monologue. An extended monologue would be made up of a lecture, soliloquy, or the like.

An UTTERANCE-RESPONSE level may be set up as higher than the monologue. (1) As its crucial component it would contain an exchange between two speakers. (A minimum example: *Going? No.*) (2) In turn, it would be a minimum conversation, in portmanteau relation with it.

CONVERSATION, with its minimum just defined as an utterance-response unit, would be expandable into a sequence of such interlocking units in a variety of forms.

In between the utterance-response unit and extended conversation, however, we leave room for an intermediate unit — a TOPIC unit, with conversation centered about some area of discussion.[3]

---

[3] Some studies in preparation are seeking to establish a formal unit which may be called a PARAGRAPH, identified by sentence-sequence restrictions — or other markers — and by some kind of topic or focussed attention as its semantic components. See Pike, 1964d.

Returning, now, to small units, it must be noticed that within the word there is a possibility of various included distributional matrices.[4] A STEM may contrast with an affixal part of the word, for example. Criteria for stem versus word include (1) the fact that the stem may be followed by non-isolatable morphemes — i.e., affixes, as -*s* in *boys*. (2) Yet the same stems may be simultaneously words, in a portmanteau level, as *boy* is both word and stem. (3) The stem matrix may exclude some of the affixal tagmemes of the word matrix as a whole (cf. *blackbirds*, where -*s* is part of the word but not of the stem). (4) Where the stem is not a word it is restricted to distribution in a word, whereas the word may directly enter into phrasal slots.

Within the stem, furthermore, there is the possibility of additional levels as matrices of distribution. When in a particular language such as Cashibo (Shell, 1957) these are set up, they are used to provide a framework for contrastive expansion of included sequences of tagmemes.

The levels, even when analyzed as contrastively distinct by criteria mentioned here, are nevertheless not kept completely separate. Occasionally one finds a unit of a higher level included within a lower one. It is this situation which in part leads to some of the problems of boundary discussion referred to, for words, above. Thus a phrase fed back into a word-structure before a word-final suffix leads to phrase-word types such as *the king of England's* (*hat*). Similarly a clause may serve as subject, as in *I want to go is always his cry*.

11.23 *Advantages and Disadvantages of a Relativistic RL-Hypertagmeme*

A number of advantages come to us by adopting an RL-hypertagmeme and an RL-tagmeme. (1) When level of structure is under focus, rather than obligatory complexity, the way is open for a unit to simultaneously represent a low level and a higher one — for a word to simultaneously represent the word level and the clause level, for example. This opens the door to see a parallel between the phonological hierarchy and the grammatical hierarchy. As a single phoneme may in some instances constitute an entire syllable or an entire stress group, so a single morpheme may constitute an entire word, a phrase (defined as one or more words expandable into a sequence of two or more words), or a clause, and so on, in portmanteau level with them, as we discussed in § 11.222.

In addition (2) this allows us to put attention upon unity as such, rather than attention upon a construction with two parts, as a primitive starting point. This, too, is

---

[4] Note that the term matrix in the phrase 'distributional matrix' refers to the structured setting within which a unit occurs. Elsewhere in this revised edition the term has been utilized more frequently for dimensional matrices, as displays of the intersecting contrastive vectors of a system. See, for example, § 15.336, and fnn. to §§ 5.2, 5.52, 6.46, 7.6, 8.33, 8.61, 8.623, 11.6, 12.1, 14.12, 15, 15.13, 16.3, 16.5, 17.

in better accord with the theory as a whole (see §§ 7.85, 6.7, 8.32). Thus the second and third disadvantages of the obligatorily-complex OC-hypertagmeme pointed out in § 11.12 are avoided by the relativistic one.

In addition, the relativistic-level approach avoids two more difficulties of an obligatorily-complex requirement. (3) The presence of an optional tagmeme as diagnostic to a particular clause type fits into the relativistic RL-hypertagmeme without jar, whereas it was highly awkward to the obligatorily-complex approach within which an optional diagnostic criterion was an embarrassment.

A further advantage (4) is seen in that some of the end results of the RL-hypertagmemic model approximates our traditional feeling as to relevance of certain components of language structure: Phrase, clause, sentence, and word receive a much more overt recognition than they do in the other approach — even though levels of structure may have earlier been brought implicitly into the description where they were not very prominent.

(5) In sentences it is also easier by this approach through levels to abbreviate complex formulas into simple high-level formulas in a less arbitrary fashion than under the other system. Here, once the analyst decides that phrase level and clause level, for example, are relevant, abbreviation can be made specifically in terms of some symbol indicating these levels as a whole, or their immediate tagmeme constituents, without feeling on the one hand the pressure to include symbolized detail due to the minute included components on these levels, or, on the other hand, without arbitrary crisscrossing of inclusion or exclusion of certain kinds of information. Consistency of abbreviation is accordingly easier to maintain by this approach.

(6) This relativistic approach in the grammar also has the advantage that it is much closer to the kind of advantage which we suggested for tagmemics in general when applied to the nonverbal anthropological materials. Thus, in § 7.8, we pointed out that "By utilizing a theory which builds on a slot-class correlative of a basic occurring unit, however, the analyst can start his analysis in the middle of the hierarchy, without waiting to find maximum and/or minimum units. This makes a slot-class starting point much more useful, for behavior as a whole, than is one which insists upon identifying a threshold to find some kind of minimum before analysis can go further." This possibility of a relativistic start is exploited in detail by Longacre and Pickett on the grammatical level.

In addition, we have emphasized on several occasions that a 'serial expansion' is more useful in some instances than one which requires division into binary immediate constituents, in that our tagmemic approach insists that groupings be made in reference to substitution in slots in the structure — and that any binary structure which is present in the analysis be treated only as the end product of the analysis, rather than as the requirement of an initial decision for binary division at the beginning of the analysis itself. (See § 7.56, and see Pike, 1958a:278.) Here is a further advantage (7) to the RL-hypertagmeme, in that it builds directly into the procedure of analysis and presentation of results this kind of view. That is to say, that Longacre with string constituents (a term which we adopt to replace our term 'serial expansion') makes this fact of structure more obvious to the beginner, by tying the nature of tagmeme into the idea of a string of constituents on a particular RL-hypertagmemic level.

These advantages, however, are purchased at an expensive price. Numerous disadvantages are the result: (1) The solution is no longer that of a simply-defined absolute, which the obligatorily-complex criterion brought in from the bottom to the top of a hierarchy. (2) The analytical methodology cannot be made as nearly mechanical, since relativistic levels are involved. (3) Although minimum and expanded formulas are involved in the ultimate symbolization, the minimum as such is not as directly seen as in the other approach. (4) Similarly, the relation between exocentric and endocentric constructions is not so immediate or direct. (5) By the relativistic approach, one has to hypothecate, early in his work, units on the various levels — he must, for example, assume certain word boundaries. This leads to some of the difficulties which were avoided by the earlier approach in which delayed word-boundary definition was postponed to a later stage of the procedure. The difficulty is by no means fatal, however, since a temporary 'as if' choice of units as matrices for studying distribution allows one to reach tentative conclusions which may be modified in the light of fuller knowledge, so that in the long run this difficulty can be met. (6) By setting up levels as primitive terms, the relativistic approach requires threshold criteria for determining when one has passed from one level to another. This is a very serious requirement and by no means easy to meet — though our attempt to do so has in part been seen in the preceding section.

(7) Another serious difficulty is that if one adopts the RL-hypertagmeme, the tagmeme follows as relativistic also. When the tagmeme is defined as X^{-1}, as a constituent one level lower than the temporary focus of attention, then the tagmeme as the minimum of a hierarchy is lost. This is serious for the total coherence of the theory as it has been developed thus far. In our earlier chapters we used as a primitive notion a minimum phoneme in a phonological hierarchy, a minimum morpheme in a lexical hierarchy, and a minimum tagmeme in a grammatical hierarchy. If, now, tagmeme is tied rather to floating levels of attention, then a tagmeme as a minimum analogous to phoneme and morpheme is lost. The adoption of this point of view, then, would require changes in the earlier development of the foundations of this theory which would be far-reaching.

(8) In connection with this it should be noted that the crucial difficulty that we mentioned for the obligatorily-complex OC-hypertagmeme has not been avoided for the relativistic one. This difficulty consisted in the fact that no single emic slot with its particular specific slot-meaning was discovered for the OC-hypertagmeme. Here, also, no single emic slot is found in which the RL-hypertagmeme must be distributed, nor is there any one meaning found in all the emic slots in which these RL-hypertagmemes may appear. This becomes very clear if one looks at a particular word type

— a noun — and studies the types of slots in which it is found. In fact, it was this very datum in Chapter 7 which was used to separate morpheme class from tagmeme. When we attempt to find a solution for this difficulty such that the RL-hypertagmeme itself can be preserved, rather than being abandoned for the same reason as the OC-hypertagmeme was rejected, we find no specific data which allow us to do so. If, however, we compare this situation with that seen in the phonological hierarchy, we note that the parallelism is closer than it was before. That is to say, that a single phoneme is distributed in slots in various syllable types, and that a particular type of syllable may come in various rhythm-group matrices and the like. Similarly, when a phrase type or a word type comes in particular slots in various clauses, then clause type becomes similar in relationship to its included components as the rhythm-group matrix was to its included syllables, or the syllable was to its included phoneme types.

Two further difficulties remain which presently we should like to try to avoid. In the first of these (9) we note that there is a considerable disadvantage in having a unit called an RL-hypertagmeme only at the particular moment it is under attention. In this approach, a certain unit — let us say a modification-head-noun-phrase — can be called an RL-hypertagmeme when one is looking at its internal components; but when viewed as a constituent entering into the slot of a clause, for example, this noun phrase is no longer an RL-hypertagmeme but an RL-tagmeme. This we find disconcerting in terms of general discussion of the language structure. One could no longer say meaningfully that a language has 'x number of RL-hypertagmemes' because the number would fluctuate in reference to the particular area under attention at the moment. In *some* sense, these terms need to be made absolutistic.

In addition, (10) there is the problem that arises when one tries to determine the limits to the number of levels which can be postulated either in the general theoretical framework or for one language at a time. There seems to be no easy 'stopping place' as to the number of levels that can be set up. When one finds phrases within phrases (compare *very big* in *very big boy*), or when one studies the possibility of proliferation of levels within word stem (compare Shell, 1957; Wise, 1963), it seems difficult to state that any limited number of levels is in theory available. At some point this becomes embarrassing. If some way could be found to limit this number, in principle it would make the RL-hypertagmeme more palatable.

We turn now to consideration of ways of meeting these last two difficulties.

11.3 *The Terms AL-Hypertagmeme and AL-Tagmeme Tentatively Applied in Reference to Levels as Absolute*

The first attempt to avoid some of the difficulties in the use of a relativistic type of RL-hypertagmeme involves a slight redefinition of terms. If we define the AL-HYPER-TAGMEME (i.e., an absolute-level hypertagmeme) as a matrix of distribution of slot-class correlatives, we give it an absolute status. In this instance a particular phrase type would be referred to as an AL-hypertagmeme throughout the entire discussion of the language — whether it were viewed as the top distribution matrix under discussion, or viewed as an AL-hypertagmeme within a higher-levelled AL-hypertagmeme. Thus a complex word type would be an AL-hypertagmeme, and within a phrase it would be an AL-hypertagmeme within an AL-hypertagmeme, and the phrase within a clause would be a word AL-hypertagmeme within a phrase AL-hypertagmeme within a clause AL-hypertagmeme, and so on. Provided the levels were labelled, reference would be clear.

11.31 *Advantages of the AL-Hypertagmeme*

This has the advantage that one could then list the kinds of AL-hypertagmemes found in any one language, and discuss their contrastive features in that language, without having them disappear with change of focus. The AL-hypertagmeme utilized in this way would retain the advantages discussed for the RL-hypertagmeme in the preceeding section, insofar as these advantages are due to the avoidance of the obligatorily-complex definition earlier attempted and insofar as they leave the way open for the treatment of high-level distribution matrices as units of particular structural levels — levels which are emically relevant.

11.32 *Disadvantages of the AL-Hypertagmeme*

A few difficulties would be raised by this change, however. The first: What would then be the AL-tagmeme?

Perhaps this difficulty could be met in a manner which we shall suggest in the next section. It is scarcely relevant to do so here, however, since a more serious difficulty is present.

Neither the RL-hypertagmeme nor the AL-hypertagmeme meets our basic desire: Neither of them provides a hypertagmeme which itself has a single emic slot, possibly with a specific functional meaning, as an identificational-contrastive characteristic. On the contrary, both of these types of units refer to types of structures at specific levels, and may occur in various slots in distribution. A noun phrase, for example, continues to occur in subject slot, in object slot, and in others. The adoption of either of these views, then, would at this point lead to a discontinuity with the basic thrust of the theory as developed in Chapter 7. Unless we are willing to abandon the point of view developed there, we must decide that neither of these units proposed can usefully be termed hypertagmeme.

We return, then, to an expansion of the conclusion reached in § 11.13: The structural units described on these levels, whether optionally or obligatorily complex (with or without portmanteau units involved) fit more neatly into the requirements of a hypermorpheme class than of a slot-class correlative. Each emic phrase type, each emic word type, each emic sentence type, and the like, would better be treated as an emic class of hypermorphemes rather than as hypertagmemes.

Where, then, can we turn — if anywhere — to find something which might nevertheless fit the requirements to set up a hypertagmemic unit? A solution to this problem requires a reconsideration of some of our basic material. To this we now turn.

11.4 *The Term Hypertagmeme (or SC-Hypertagmeme) Applied to Slot-Plus-Class Correlative on Nonminimum Levels of Structure*

The goal we have set ourselves in this section, therefore, is to try to find a unit which will meet the requirements (a) of having a single slot relevant to it, and (b) of having a manifesting class of items which may occur not only in this particular slot but also in various others.

11.41 *Implications of Reworking the Hypertagmeme into a Slot-Plus-Class Correlative in Reference to Levels*

That is to say, we are looking for slots into which a particular phrase type fits, or a variety of slots into which a particular phrase type fits, such that each of these slots plus its total list of fillers might be termed an SC-HYPERTAGMEME — or simply a hypertagmeme. Similarly, we look for a slot or series of slots into which a clause type fits, for example, such that the filler type might be a class of hypermorphemes.

This inevitably forces us — once the question is raised — to note that a noun phrase, for example, comes in a subject slot and object (or other) slots. Similarly, a transitive clause of an independent type comes in an independent slot or a coordinate slot in a sentence. Must subject slot-plus-filler, and independent sentence slot-plus-filler be, therefore, treated as hypertagmemes? The implication is strongly affirmative.

This, however, raises serious questions. Chief among them is the fact that a subject-as-actor with its emic slot and its emic class of fillers has already been treated as a tagmeme — not a hypertagmeme — in Chapter 7. If this is now treated as a hypertagmeme, how would the previous analysis be affected? Would a further unit which is a tagmeme be found which would differ from hypertagmemes such as subject-as-actor?

At this point a suggestion from Wise became important. She strongly objected to the fact that a tagmeme could be included within a tagmeme in the treatment of Chapter 7 (as *the boy* had two included tagmemes in the manifestation of the subject tagmeme in *the boy came home*). This, she maintained, was non-analogous to the situation with morpheme and phoneme, since no morpheme is included within a morpheme, nor phoneme within a phoneme. Rather, she insisted, we needed a minimum tagmeme which would be comparable to a minimum morpheme; this minimum tagmeme would be included in larger units, but would not itself have tagmemes included within it.

The first implication of handling such a suggestion was not too difficult, in the light of the development of portmanteau levels. Thus we might assume that in a phrase like *my big Johnny* the morpheme *John* was simultaneously a stem in *Johnny*, a word in the phrase *my John*, and a potentially-expandable phrase in *John came home*. Then, just as a morpheme by our newer treatment could be simultaneously a word and a phrase with three simultaneous functions as morpheme, word, and phrase — or even as a response-sentence — so we could leave room for a portmanteau which included the simultaneous manifestation of a tagmeme and of a hypertagmeme. *John* in *John came* would be simultaneously a manifestation of a stem tagmeme and of a subject-as-actor hypertagmeme.

An item such as the *-ny* in *Johnny* or the *-ish* in *biggish*, would then appear to be clearly a minimum. This was esthetically satisfactory in that these minimum chunks of words would now be represented by a special term, whereas the expandable units would be represented by a higher-level term.

The application of this approach was more difficult, however, with such an item as *to*, in the phrase *to sing*. On the one hand, it was clear that the *to* seemed to be manifesting a minimum; it appeared impossible to expand that part of the phrase. On the other hand, this left a serious objection in terms of elegance which Longacre's presentation had bypassed. In the relativistic approach, Longacre's treatment guaranteed that, on any particular level, the immediate string constituents of that level were all treated as somehow on a par. This was obtained by calling every string constituent a tagmeme-on-a-level, relative to that particular level. Thus a phrase was split into two, three, four, or more phrase-level tagmemes, regardless of the internal complexity of those relativistic tagmemes.

If we are to retain this advantage of Longacre's treatment, then *to* — like *John* above — must be treated as simultaneously manifesting two levels. As a minimum, it manifests a tagmeme. As a member of a string of slot-class units within a phrase, it manifests one of the hypertagmemes making up that string. The tagmeme-hypertagmeme relation, then, would be in part relative to levels in the Longacre sense, and in part relative to size.

Part of the difficulty of having tagmemes included in tagmemes, in Chapter 7, was related to the fact that an emic class of fillers of an emic slot was not always uniform in internal structure: *big John, the boy*, and *he* were quite different in spite of being potential subjects-as-actors. In dealing with the fillers occurring in slots, Pickett was disturbed by the implied necessity of treating all the members of a filler class as in some way the same. She frequently found it inadvisable to give a single-unit symbol to represent all the fillers of that class. Often, in fact, it was more convenient to break down the members of the class into subtypes of fillers. She noted that this had in fact been done in Chapter 7 (Pike, 1954), and in some other early tagmemic work where the filler for a subject slot, for example, might be symbolized as a composite of noun, pronoun, noun phrase, clause, etc. But she felt that this breakdown into subclass components was not integrated with the theoretical view; rather it was left as a more-or-less practical handling of materials not coherent with the theory as a whole.

H. Hart (1957:151-61) had earlier pointed out such differences in the internal structure or function of parts of a filler class, and had labeled them as DIVISION SUBCLASSES of the larger class. This treatment was useful, since the filler class was obviously subdivided in structural fashion, and at some point this structural difference had to be dealt with. Pickett, on the other hand, set up a subclass of members of the total filler class (a) if the subgroup was found to occur elsewhere as a unit in another slot. Thus a group of nouns in subject slot might elsewhere serve as a special class of members — a division subclass — of words or phrases in a location slot. Her second criterion (b) was the internal structure of the subclass seen as a sequence of tagmemes. Pickett not only adopted this double classificatory criterion, but insisted that in some manner these subdivisions were fully as crucial to the structure of the language as a whole as was the fact that various subclasses together made up a particular filler class for a particular tagmemic slot.

We note, further, that the presence of included tagmemes in a higher-level tagmeme occurred precisely in relation to the internally-structured subclasses of Hart and Pickett. Tagmemes were said to be included within tagmemes (§ 7.44) only when a filler class contained at least two division subclasses, one simple and one complex.

Now, however, we come to the problem with the aid of conclusions developed earlier in this chapter: The former obligatorily-complex unit — and some optionally-complex ones — instead of being treated as an OC-hypertagmeme is analyzed as an emic class of hypermorphemes (§§ 11.14, 11.32). From this it follows that certain of the division subclasses of a filler class are also internally structured in this way, and must be analyzed as emic classes of hypermorphemes making up part of an emic filler class of units.

We can see, then, that tagmemes (or hypertagmemes) are in every instance distributed not into a higher slot-class correlative, i.e., not into a hypertagmeme, but rather into a hypermorphemic structural type or class. It is this hypermorphemic type which in turn is distributed into a larger slot.

We now come to a stage in the discussion where various of these components are brought together and a major change is required in the theoretical framework. *We must abandon the theoretical requirement that tagmemes are distributed directly into tagmemes of a higher level, and replace it with the following requirement: Tagmemes or hypertagmemes (that is, all slot-plus-class correlatives) are distributed directly into hypermorpheme classes (i.e., into syntagmemes) and these in turn are distributed into higher level slot-plus-class correlatives as the total filler or as a division subclass of that total filler class.*[5]

[5] The diagrammatic problem which this raises for the model is seen in §§ 12.2-3. The implications of this change have not yet been fully worked out.

Tagmemes are distributed into hypertagmemes not directly, therefore, but mediated through hypermorphemic classes. Viewed as a *structure*, a unitary, emic sequence of tagmemes is a SYNTAGMEME. Viewed as manifested by a set of instances, it is an EMIC CLASS OF HYPERMORPHEMES. Viewed as a typical group of such members of an emic class, it is a HYPERMORPHEME CONSTRUCTION, a syntagmeme.

The minimum English tagmeme made up of plural slot plus plural filler may first of all be distributed into (a sequence of tagmemes which makes up) that particular hypermorphemic class in English called 'plural count nouns', e.g., *boys*. This hypermorpheme type in turn comprises a distribution subclass which may fill — among others — the hypertagmemic slot head-of-noun-phrase, as in *the boys*. Thus the tagmeme 'plural', by this view, is distributed into a unit which is a class of hypermorphemes (a word construction, here). Then the word construction is distributed into a hypertagmemic slot in the phrase construction. Similarly, the hypertagmeme (as head) is distributed into this particular hypermorpheme construction which then is distributed into (the sequence of hypertagmemes which make up) that clause construction. This clause construction as a whole then is a division subclass of all the potential fillers of a particular slot (of a particular hypertagmeme) which might be called independent-sentence-slot, or the like.

11.42 *Advantages and Disadvantages of the Hypertagmeme as Slot-Plus-Class Correlative on Higher Levels*

It may be useful to summarize the advantages and disadvantages of this further attempt to define hypertagmeme, in reference to our earlier attempts in previous sections. In general, the SC-hypertagmeme retains the advantages of the RL-hypertagmeme or the AL-hypertagmeme. These can be consulted in § 11.23 and § 11.31. These advantages, however, are transferred from the RL-hypertagmeme as a whole to the hypermorpheme class.

This newer view has as an advantage the positive avoidance of the chief disadvantages of the relativistic or the absolutistic hypertagmemes. Instead of treating a unit abstracted from a slot as a high level of focus separated (i.e., in hypostasis) from the total context, it integrates with the total tagmemic theoretical view in which function in the slot of a higher structure (i.e., external distribution) is always immediately relevant to the nature of a unit. Whenever the relevant specific emic slot under attention has a structural meaning, furthermore, this meaning becomes one of the contrastive features of the SC-hypertagmeme which identify it and separate it from comparable constructions on the same level of structure.

In addition, it avoids some of the difficulties pointed out by Crawford (1963), it seems to me, in that the internal distribution of a unit type is referred specifically to the internal slot-class sequence of a hypermorphemic construction rather than to the hypertagmeme directly. When different phrase types, for example, may fill the same subject slot, the varying types of internal tagmemic construction (in phrases such as *big John* or *the boy*) are now not embarrassing to the theory since they are attributed to the respective division subclasses rather than to the total SC-hypertagmeme as such. After emphasis has been placed upon external distribution as primary, the internal distributional structure can be referred more readily to the division subclasses of the filler of that hypertagmeme slot without leaving the SC-hypertagmeme itself without identifying features.

Furthermore, by refraining from calling *big John* a hypertagmeme (as a phrase type), and *the boy* another hypertagmeme (as a phrase type), we avoid the embarrassment of saying that these two AL-hypertagmemes are somehow the same AL-tagmeme when they are subject. Rather the subject-as-actor would be an SC-hypertagmeme within a clause types, manifested by two or more different internally-structured phrasal subclasses, each of which was composed of a hypermorpheme construction with its own internal SC-tagmemic or SC-hypertagmemic structure.

The advantage of the SC-hypertagmeme approach, in sum, is that the theory as a whole becomes more coherent since in one point of view are included reference to minimum units, to portmanteau levels, to division subclasses, and to hypermorpheme classes.

On the other hand, the disadvantages of this newer treatment are relatively few, and where they occur seem to be clearly related to complexities of the data themselves. For example, this new view treats levels — word, phrase, clause, sentence, discourse, etc. — as relevant, emic, preserving Longacre's basic contribution, though at the price of complexity. It requires a careful distinction between hypertagmeme and hypermorpheme types — but this too simply increases the observed differences between the grammatical and lexical hierarchies. It requires room for simultaneous tagmemes or hypertagmemes on various levels at once. Yet portmanteau elements cannot be avoided elsewhere within our approach, so the complexity here adds no new basic principle.

11.43 *Illustrations of Hypermorpheme Constructions (Syntagmemes) and of Slot-Plus-Class Hypertagmemes*

Since we have discussed various applications of terms, it seems advisable now to have an interlude in which we illustrate the application of the terms as we intend to use them throughout the remaining chapters. For this purpose we choose a small corpus of some twenty English sentences, for which see Table 1, selected to illustrate many of the problems involved.

Although the noun phrases in the subject slots have been chosen for more detailed labelling than the verbs, the same approach is relevant to all parts of the lexico-grammatical structure, including other types of subjects in other clauses.

(For pedagogical purposes, one reduction in complexity of terminology might well

UNITS OF THE DISTRIBUTION MODE OF THE SYNTAGMEME   453

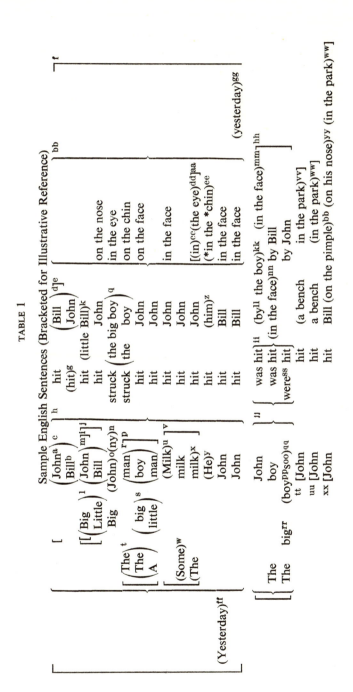

TABLE 1

be used: If for the term tagmeme one utilizes the phrase 'minimum tagmeme', then for hypertagmeme one may utilize the phrase 'tagmeme within a particular higher level structure' such as 'tagmeme within phrase'. For technical reasons we shall not adopt this expedient here in our theoretical treatment, but there seems to be little objection to it on practical grounds. The minimum tagmeme is much less frequently in view in grammatical studies, especially in syntax studies, than are slot-plus-class correlatives on higher levels. Thus in some of these discussions the sheer frequency of repetition of hypertagmeme as against tagmeme may become burdensome and avoided by some such expedient as this. If this change were adopted, our use of the term tagmeme, in pedagogical literature, would be very similar to that of Longacre.)

In the following commentary on Table 1, letter symbols refer to the same symbols in the table:

(a, b as items): *John, Bill* — separate morphemes.

(c, d as class): *John*, etc., members of a personal-noun distribution subclass, manifesting two different hypertagmemes within the clause.

(c as slot): subject-as-actor hypertagmemic slot in a transitive independent clause structure, filled here by the personal-noun division subclass of the total filler class of that slot.

(d as slot): object hypertagmemic slot in transitive independent clause structure, filled here by same division subclass of personal nouns.

(e as item): *John hit Bill*, a particular hypermorpheme; manifesting a particular class — i.e., a construction type — of hypermorpheme; a specific independent transitive clause.

(f as class in hypostasis): *John hit Bill*, etc., members of the class of that independent-transitive-clause type. Since the class is abstracted (i.e., in hypostasis) for citation purposes from various slots (e.g., independent slot in a complex sentence) in various contexts, no f-slot can here be identified in which they might have occurred. (Note: this clause construction is *not* of itself a hypertagmeme, in our revised usage, but a particular hypermorpheme type; in § 11.1-3, however, it was tentatively given a label as an OC-, RL-, or AL-hypertagmeme.)

(g as item in class, in slot): *hit*, single-morpheme member of transitive-verb class; here filling hypertagmemic transitive-predicate slot in independent-transitive-clause construction.

(h as class, in slot, hypertagmeme): a large class, containing various division subclasses — especially of noun types, pronouns, and types of substantive expressions — distinguished either by contrastive distribution elsewhere (as *John* versus *milk*) or by internal structure within the subclass (as *the boy* versus *big John*). The slot in which the class comes here is the subject-as-actor slot in the independent-transitive-clause structure — but the same class occurs in the object slot also. The subject-as-actor slot plus this filler class constitute the total subject-as-actor hypertagmeme (while the meaning of the slot here, as often, provides the name for the total slot-plus-class correlative).

UNITS OF THE DISTRIBUTION MODE OF THE SYNTAGMEME   455

(i as item): *Big John* is a hypermorpheme, of a type composed of adjective as modifier, with personal noun.

(j, k as class): Items of this structure, such as *big John*, make up a hypermorpheme subclass of the total filler class which may be in the subject-as-actor slot, in the object slot, etc.

(c plus j as class): The morpheme class of personal noun (c) together with hypermorpheme class (j) enter a larger class of personal-noun phrases. *John* is treated as a phrase — a single-word phrase — precisely because it is optionally expandable into multiple-word phrases such as *big John*, filling the same slot in clauses.

(l as class, in slot): *big* and *little* are members of a word class of adjectives in a modification slot of the modification-personal-noun phrase construction. Since in this slot the items are expandable to *very big*, etc., the word *big* — like *John* above — is not only a word but is simultaneously to be treated as a one-word phrase.

(m as class, in slot, hypertagmeme): *John* and *Bill* are members of the personal-noun class, as indicated above in (c), but are here manifesting the personal-head hypertagmeme, as they fill the personal-head slot in the modification-personal-noun phrase type.

(n as item, in class, in slot, tagmeme): *-ny* is a morpheme, occurring in the diminutive affixal slot of a variety of the personal-noun word structure. (Other affixal slots sometimes follow it — e.g., the possessive or the plural as in *several Johnnys*, or *Johnny's ball*; but these hypermorpheme types do not come in this same phrase slot in this clause slot; *the* is allowed before the plural word, but not here, whereas *Johnny's* as a subject is expandable to *Johnny's ball*, and hence manifests a different underlying structure.) This morpheme constitutes the entire filler class. The class plus the slot constitute a minimum slot-plus-class correlative. The tagmeme may be labelled as diminutive (with three-way indeterminacy of meaning between morpheme meaning, class meaning, and tagmeme meaning).

(o as item, in slot, tagmeme): *John* here is in another slot — the stem (or head) slot within a personal-noun word structure (whereas in [m] it was in the head slot of the personal-noun phrase structure — i.e., in a higher level construction). The item seems to manifest a minimum slot-plus-class correlative, a personal-word head tagmeme.

(o, i, a as levels): *John* illustrates simultaneous — i.e., portmanteau — function on various levels. In (o) it manifests only the word-head tagmeme. In (i) it continues to be word-head tagmeme (unexpanded) while also manifesting the phrase head, as a simultaneous slot-plus-class correlative on a higher-than-minimum level, a hypertagmeme. In (a) it continues to manifest word-head tagmeme and simultaneously phrase-head hypertagmeme, while in addition simultaneously constituting the entire single-word phrase and manifesting the hypertagmeme subject-as-actor, within the clause. When totally filling a slot of the word level, *John* manifests a tagmeme; when totally filling a slot of the phrase level, a hypertagmeme; when totally filling a slot of the clause level, a hypertagmeme of still higher rank (plus simultaneously filling slots of the lower-ranking hypertagmeme and of the tagmeme).

(p, q as class, in slots): *the man*, etc., are members of a hypermorpheme class, a phrase type different from *big John*, of determiner-determined structure. They constitute an internal-structure subclass of the larger class (h); here occurring in clause slots subject-as-actor, and object. Note that this class differs from (c) plus (j) in optional versus obligatory tagmemes and in the word-class of the phrase head.

(r as class, in slot, hypertagmeme): *man*, etc., a further class of words — count-noun class — filling head slot in count-noun phrase structure, and manifesting the count-noun-phrase-head hypertagmeme (simultaneously filling head slot of word, as a portmanteau level).

(s as class, in slot, tagmeme): *big*, etc., manifests the same class, emic slot, and tagmeme as (l), but occurs in a different hypermorpheme phrase construction.

(t as class, in slot, tagmeme, hypertagmeme): *the*, etc., a class of determiners, in determiner slot, together constituting the determiner tagmeme and hypertagmeme in the determiner-determined hypermorpheme class.

(u, v as class, in slot): *Milk*, a minimum form of a further structural subclass (v) of the subject-as-actor filler class; (u) as a class of mass nouns, (v) as a class of mass-noun phrases.

(w as class, in slot, hypertagmeme): *Some* manifests a further class and hypertagmeme in the expanded mass-noun phrase.

(x as item with overlapping class membership): *the milk* is a member of class (p). Therefore *milk* is a member of both class (u) and class (r).

(y as item, in subclass): *He* is a morpheme, member of pronoun subclass. Treated here as simultaneously morpheme, word (since isolatable), and minimum phrase (since expandable to *he whom I used to know*). The negative expansion potential (one does not hear *big he* as subject) differentiates it from subclass (c) and from the obligatorily-complex (p).

(z as item): *him* is treated in this approach as a phonemic variant (allomorph) of *he*, with its phonemic shape modified due to (conditioned by) its occurrence as manifesting the object tagmeme.

(aa as item): *in the eye* is a specific hypermorpheme, a phrase of the location-determiner-determined type.

(bb as class, in slot, hypertagmeme): The phrase (aa) is a member of hypermorpheme class (bb), in the (bb) locational slot of the clause. (bb) slot plus (bb) class constitute (bb) location-phrase hypertagmeme in the independent transitive clause.

(cc as item, member of class, in slot, tagmeme): The word *in* is a morpheme, member of the location subclass of prepositions (a distribution subclass which in this context excludes *toward*, *from*). In conjunction with the location slot of the location phrase it makes up the location tagmeme. Since it is minimum in length — a single morpheme — the class plus the location slot makes up a location tagmeme, in the phrase level structure.

(dd as item, in class, in slot, hypertagmeme): Item (dd) *the eye* is a hypermorpheme, a phrase of determiner-determined type (p), in hypertagmemic head slot of construction type (aa).

(ee as item): Some specific sequences are unlikely to occur — suggested on Table 1 by asterisks. Some of these etic co-occurrence restrictions — or lack of them — are arbitrary (collocational, idiomatic, or determined by meaning or universe of discourse). Note *in/on the face* but perhaps not *in the chin.

(ff as item, in class, in slot): *Yesterday* is a one-word member of a class of forms which may fill a time slot in the clause (a hypermorphemic member of the class might be, for example, *on that occasion*). There is an etic co-occurrence restriction between the manifested members of this class and the class in predicate slot; the time of each must be compatible; *tomorrow* is incompatible with *hit* outside of science fiction, etc.

(gg as allohypertagma): We assume *yesterday* to be the same word as (ff), in a different etic slot which must nevertheless be analyzed as the same emic slot. The pre- and post-slot etic distributional variants of the emic slot imply the presence of two distributional etic variants of this time hypertagmeme. One variant — one allohypertagma made up of emic class in etic slot — precedes the clause nucleus, whereas the other follows it.

(hh as class in hypostasis): Members of a further clause type — a passive one — are listed in hypostasis (i.e., without immediate reference to any one of the slots from which it might be taken).

(ii as class, hypertagmeme): *was hit*, etc., are members of a class of passive-verb expressions, in passive-predicate slot — a passive-predicate hypertagmeme — in the transitive passive-clause structure.

(jj as class, in slot, hypertagmeme): The emic class manifested by *John*, etc., is the same as (h), (d-k-q), and (dd). Here it is in a different slot (subject-as-goal) and with it constitutes a subject-as-goal hypertagmeme homophonous with (i.e., with same class filler as) subject-as-actor hypertagmeme.

(kk as class, in slot, hypertagmeme): This class (*by the boy*, etc.) is in agent slot, and with it comprises the agent hypertagmeme, in the transitive passive-clause structure. It contrasts with class (mm, aa).

(ll as emic subclass, in slot, hypertagmeme): This class is restricted to items like *by, by means of*. With the agent-indicator slot, in which it occurs, it constitutes the agent-indicator hypertagmeme in the passive clause structure.

(mm, nn, bb as class in etic slots, hypertagmeme): Further distributional etic variants of emic slots (with physical position changed but function structurally unaffected) are seen in that the location hypertagmeme may follow the object hypertagmeme in transitive active clause structure (cf. bb) or the agent in the passive structure (cf. mm). In the passive clause, however, the etic position of the location hypertagmeme is frequently before the agent (cf. nn). Less frequently, and not shown in the table, the location hypertagmeme may precede the object in the active clause, especially if the object is long, as in *He hit in the face the great big bully that was always bother-*

ing the children. (Note the potential ambiguity if the location phrase comes at the end of the clause.)

(oo as class, in slot, tagmeme): *-s* plural, constitutes a morpheme, sole member of a morpheme class in the plural slot, with which it constitutes the plural tagmeme.

(pp as in slot): *boy*, member of single-morpheme word-head tagmeme.

(qq and ss as reciprocally-conditioned co-occurrence subclasses): The plural subclass (qq) of count nouns is, in the head hypertagmeme of the noun phrase in the subject-as-goal passive-clause slot, reciprocally conditioned in occurrence by a plural subclass of the auxiliary class (ss) within the passive-verb phrase. Similar division subclasses determined by co-occurrence restrictions of subject and predicate hypertagmemes occur in transitive and intransitive active clauses, but are not illustrated here. (1) This co-occurrence factor plus (2) similar order and (3) related or same membership of the manifesting classes are the criteria leading us to set up a class of subject hypertagmemes (h) and (jj), and a class of predicate hypertagmemes illustrated by (g) and (ii), cutting across clause types.

(c, m, o-n, r, u, ff, qq grouped into a hyperclass): The term NOUN,[6] as a part of speech, is applied to a nondistribution class called a HYPERCLASS. While it as a whole comes in no one emic slot in these structures, and manifests no one tagmeme or hypertagmeme, its members are grouped for convenience of reference into a hyperclass since (1) they sometimes have accompanying them the same, related, or overlapping tagmemes (or hypertagmemes); cf. modifier hypertagmeme (l) with (m) and (o-n); (s=l) with (r=m); (w) with (u) — compare *some boys*; (r=l=s) with (qq); (c, j, o-n, p, qq each with possible *whom I liked*, and (u) with *which I liked*; plural tagmeme (oo) with (pp=r). (2) They are single words. (3) They have a hyperclass meaning of object, or name of item which — though vague — applies to many members of the hyperclass. (4) In general, they as a whole, or the phrases of which they are head, manifest the same hypertagmemes, such as subject-as-actor, subject-as-goal, object, and location. An English noun class, it must be emphasized, can only be arrived at by such a special grouping of distribution classes; it is not a class determined by uniform external distribution in a specific slot or group of slots in these structures. (5) As for internal composition, presence of plural tagmeme (oo) is the most widely used clue to noun identification. Among problems involved in this inconclusive test, however, note that class (c) and class (u) cannot take plural while retaining the meanings which they have in these slots, but rather only when with a different meaning such as they have as members of class (r) in *the two Johns* or *the two milks* (and there it must be decided whether different morphemes are involved — *John* homophonous with *John* — or whether the same morpheme occurs, with semantic variants which are tagmemically conditioned). In addition, clauses or phrases sometimes occupy subject slot and take the plural, etc.; yet it is awkward to call such items nouns.

---

[6] Note also discussion in § 11.73.

(tt, uu): These sentences are included (adapted from § 7.322, and from Pike, 1943b: 79) in order to illustrate further the fact that items made up of the same morphemes in sequence may nevertheless manifest different tagmemes or hypertagmemes (and require different tagmemic formulas). This has been demonstrated for subject versus object, but needs illustration for other hypertagmeme types in order to show that, in principle, this characteristic may be found at any point in language. In (vv) the phrase *in the park* manifests only one part of the total object hypertagmeme, with the expansion being *a bench which was in the park*; *in the park* here is a hypertagmeme of post-modification of the noun phrase. Yet in sentence (uu), the phrase (ww) *in the park* manifests a different hypertagmeme which here means location-of-action. The expansion of the sentence which tests for this difference (§ 7.322) is *John hit a bench yesterday when he was in the park*. Thus the tagmemic structure of *hit a bench in the park* must be separately symbolized for the two sentences. The sentences are morphemically same but tagmemically different (cf. §§ 7.43, 7.6). Without appropriate expansions or transforms, the sentences are structurally ambiguous (§ 7.322).

(xx): One further sentence is added in order to show that neither of the uses of *in the park* manifests the same hypertagmeme as (bb) in the earlier examples: In (xx), the phrase *on the pimple* manifests the hypertagmeme (bb); *on his nose* manifests the hypertagmeme (yy); and *in the park* manifests the hypertagmeme (ww). If *on the pimple* (bb) were to be omitted, then *on his nose* (yy) would probably be reinterpreted by hearer as (bb); if *on his nose*, rather, were omitted, then *in the park* (ww) would become humorous since contiguity implies that it should be interpreted as the hypertagmeme (vv), whereas the lexical meaning makes this interpretation unlikely.

11.44 *Trimodal Structuring of Hypertagmeme as Slot-Plus-Class Correlative*

In Chapter 11 (versus §§ 1-10) we have adopted a number of changes which must now be reflected in the general trimodal schema of the new hypertagmeme. Many of the details have been treated in earlier sections of the chapter, but a listing of some of them may be useful here: (1) The development of the concept of portmanteau levels, as a solution to the problem raised by Fleming; (2) the introduction of word-phrase-clause-sentence levels, etc., as emic and relevant to tagmemic theory following the work of Longacre (1958a, 1964a); (3) more detailed treatment of division subclasses and sub-assemblies as emphasized by H. Hart (1957), but (4) with further attention to differences between these division subclasses in terms of distributional definition versus internal-structural definition, following Pickett (1960); (5) treatment of word constructions, phrase constructions, clause constructions, etc., as classes of hyper-morphemes (rather than as hypertagmemes, after withdrawal of the obligatorily-complex requirement of my earlier hypertagmeme); (6) rehandling of the definition of minimum, following the suggestion of Wise, in reference to tagmeme versus hypertagmeme.

In addition to these items, we have (7) generalized dependent-independent characteristics of items at all levels of the hierarchy, following Waterhouse (1962). Further (8) we have reassigned internal structure of a hypermorpheme type, in terms of tagmeme sequences, to the feature mode of the construction under the impact of work of Crawford (1963). (This last change is related to the fact that the hypermorpheme type undergoes a change of definition related to that which affected the hypertagmeme. The double-plus requirement for hypermorpheme set down in Chapter 10 is abandoned here, just as it is abandoned for hypertagmeme. See fn. to § 10.1.)

We will assume that from the illustrations of the preceding section the reader now is, in general, familiar with the kinds of units to which we apply our terms. In this section, therefore, we are concerned rather with giving, in outline, a framework to show the organizational interrelation of these terms within trimodal concepts.

We give Table 2 to show the initial broad breakdown of a hypertagmeme into its modal components. This analysis is designed to apply in principle to any hypertagmeme whether highly complex, with intricate internal structure, or simple. It purports to fit any level of structure from the word-head of a phrase (or even smaller in languages where there are complex stems) on up to the hypertagmemic slot-plus-class correlatives which comprise a conversation construction.

We give cross references from the components of Table 2 to some of the illustrations in Table 1. We do this by adding reference numbers to Table 2 and referring back to the reference letters inserted in Table 1. On occasion we add illustrations not provided in Table 1. The commentary for Table 1 may be consulted in order to see the manner in which the letter symbols may be used to refer simultaneously to a class and/or to the tagmeme and/or hypertagmeme which it manifests.

TABLE 2

Trimodal Components of Hypertagmemes[1]

Modes	Components of Modes
Feature Mode	Hypertagmemic Form: Total emic distribution class (i.e., filler class) plus an emic slot. The Class Form: Either an emic class of hypermorphemes[2] — a syntagmeme — with membership open[3] or closed,[4] large[5] or small[6] (symbolizable with a single hypertagmeme-string formula with trimodal characteristics for the class, for which see Table 3), or an emic class of classes[7] of hypermorphemes (requiring two or more hypertagmeme-string formulas for the respective division subclasses[8] involved). The Slot Form: The emic place[9] of the class in an arrangement of hypertagmemes in a higher-level hypermorpheme structure. (For etic variants of emic slots see manifestation mode.)

Modes	Components of Modes

	Hypertagmemic Meaning:
	  The Class Meaning[10]: If the filler class has no structurally-diverse division subclasses, there is often a hypermorphemic class meaning observable; if the filler class has several division subclasses, the composite meaning is likely to be vague or absent.
	  The Slot (Function) Meaning: The meaning of the hypertagmeme as a whole — its functional meaning (especially detected as the meaning of its emic slot).[11]

Manifestation Mode	Variants of Filler Class Viewed as a Whole (leading to allohypertagmas, even when change affects only some members of the whole manifesting class):
	  Simple vs. Complex: A single-[12] vs. a multiple-morpheme member[13] manifesting the hypertagmeme.
	  Free: Any one member of the class[14] manifesting the hypertagmeme in the slot.
	  Conditioned: Any change in the manifesting class is assumed to affect the manifested hypertagmeme, producing an allohypertagma. Therefore, the hypertagmeme may be viewed, as a whole, as being affected in the same manner and under the same circumstances as are the manifesting class and subclasses. (For detail,[15] see Table 3.) A class may be modified in membership, in the phonemic shape of its members, in the meaning of its members; under conditions defined morphemically, phonemically, tagmemically, or systemically.
	  Fused vs. Clearly Segmented: A partially-fused sequence of two higher-level hypertagmemes occurs when a single lower-level hypertagmeme occurs in double function between them. (For discussion of fusions, see §14.)[16]
	Variants of Slot Occurrence (leading to positionally-different allohypertagmas):
	  Free: Alternate physical positions[17] relative to other hypertagmemes in one or more hypermorpheme structures.
	  Conditioned: Placement of hypertagmeme conditioned by — changed because of — some manifesting subclass of that hypertagmeme or of an accompanying hypertagmeme.[18]

Distribution Mode	Sequence Distribution: Active external distribution obligatory[19] or optional,[20] of the hypertagmeme in one or more higher-level[21] hypermorpheme structures (i.e., in one or more syntagmemes).
	Class Distribution:
	  Membership of the hypertagmeme in a distribution class of hypertagmemes.[22]
	  Membership of the hypertagmeme in a (nondistribution) hyperclass[23] of classes of hypertagmemes.
	  Membership in the total slot-plus-class grammatical structure of a particular style,[24] or of a universe of discourse,[25] or of the language as a whole.

Commentary on Table 2:

(1): (h, jj, bb) as hypertagmemes. Additional illustrations would include introductory or finalizing hypertagmemes in conversation, etc.

(2): (p) as hypermorpheme class.

(3): (p) with open membership.

(4): The head hypertagmeme of (y) is manifested by a class with closed membership; extensions such as *he whom I used to know* leave the hypermorpheme class as a whole with open membership.

(5): (p) with large membership.

(6): (y) with small membership.

(7): (h) as a class of classes of hypermorphemes.

(8): (j), (p), (v), (y), as division subclasses of (h).

(9): (h) as subject-as-actor hypertagmemic slot in the transitive-active-clause hypermorpheme structure.

(10): (u), as 'mass' noun, one of a class of hypermorphemes, partakes of a more specific class meaning than does (h), which is a member of a hyperclass of hypermorphemes which has an over-all but inconsistent meaning of 'an object'.

(11): (h), with meaning of subject-as-actor.

(12): (a) as a single-morpheme member of a class.

(13): (i) as a multiple-morpheme member.

(14): (a) or (b) as free variants of the hypertagmeme (h) and of its manifesting class.

(15): illustrations keyed likewise into Table 3.

(16): illustrations of fusion also given in Chapter 14.

(17): (ff) versus (gg) as alternate positions.

(18): (nn) with statistical preference following predicate before a long agent, but without the same statistical preference following a short agent — note commentary on (mm, nn).

(19): (t) and (r) obligatory in (p); (h), (g), and (d) in (f); (cc) and (dd) in (aa).

(20): (s) optional in (p); (ff) in (f); (bb) in (f).

(21): (h) as hypertagmeme, in (f) as higher-level hypermorpheme structure.

(22): (h) as subject-as-actor hypertagmeme, in a distribution class of subject hypertagmemes including (h) plus (jj) and others.

(23): for example, the list of all hypertagmemes in English.

(24): Table 1 as normal style, matter-of-fact; compare, in lively style, *On the chin he struck the big bully.*

(25): Table 1 as normal universe of discourse, such that *(ee) is unexpected; however, *in the chin* would be normal if the universe of discourse in a fiction story were about an oriental idol with a hollow chin in which were hidden jewels.

We next present Table 3 in which we suggest the generalized trimodal components of any syntagmeme.[7] As for Table 2, so for Table 3 we give numbers in cross reference with the lettered illustrations of Table 1, along with occasional added illustrations to amplify the scope of the application of the tabular material to available data.

---

[7] In these sections the terms syntagmeme, emic class of hypermorphemes, hypermorpheme type, hypermorpheme structure, and construction overlap in reference. The term hypermorpheme class, however, highlights for the data the manifesting individual membership; syntagmeme (or construction) has more specific reference to the included tagmeme sequence; type, as a term, often implies attention to the contrastive relevance of a class of units to a larger including class; structure has a broad implication of organizational unity.

TABLE 3

Trimodal Breakdown of Emic Classes of Syntagmemes[1]

Modes	Components of Modes
Feature Mode	Form: An included string of tagmemes[2] or hypertagmemes,[3] obligatory[4] or optional.[5] (Each of these included hypertagmemes, in turn, has modal components, as in Table 2). Meaning: A class meaning sometimes — not always — observable in the syntagmeme. It is a common denominator of meaning[6] of some or many — not necessarily all — of the most typical or frequently occurring members of the manifesting class. ('typical', left undefined.)
Manifestation Mode	Variants (Allo-Units) in Reference to Manfiesting Class: Simple vs. Complex (Minimum[7] vs. Expanded[8]): A simple variant of a syntagmeme — i.e., of a hypermorphemic structure — occurs when all its obligatory included tagmemes or hypertagmemes, but only these, are manifested. A complex variant occurs when one or more optional tagmemes or hypertagmemes is also manifested. Free: In substitution,[9] when one manifesting member of a class replaces another without stated restriction. Fully Free: Variation may be said to be fully free if no restrictions are known. Locally Free but Externally Conditioned: It is locally free, but not fully free,[10] if nothing in the immediate hypermorpheme class under attention controls its manifestation; but it is externally conditioned if an item in a higher-level hypermorpheme or in the system does restrict its occurrence. Conditioned: Here we present a tentative chart to indicate some types of interplay between kinds of effect and the sources of these modifications. (The list is not exhaustive, and the classification will need revision after further empirical data are available). The variety of such changes is much greater — and with more extensive consequences — than is ordinarily suspected:

	Kinds of Modification (or restriction)	Environmental Sources of Modification of Syntagmemes			
		Lexical (Morphemic)	Phonological (Phonemic)	Grammatical (Tagmemic)	Stylistic (Systemic)
	Lexical: via membership of the alloclass	'semantic' restriction in membership of an alloclass of a construction containing a particular morpheme[11]	rhyming restrictions, etc., on alloclass[13]	subclass of forms restricted by a particular slot[15]	class members which are used only in a particular style[17]
	via meaning of the members of alloclass, i.e., semantic	semantic variant of members of an alloclass due to collocation with specific morphemes of another class[12]	heightening of semantic impact contributed by rhyme, vowel quality etc.[14]	change of lexical meaning due to occurrence in a particular slot[16]	change of lexical meaning due to occurrence in a particular universe of discourse, or style[18]
	Phonological: phonemic shape of the members of the alloclass	morphophonemic changes adjacent to an arbitrary list of morphemes[19]	phonological process, regular morphophonemics (choice of allomorph alloclass adjacent to certain sounds)[20]	phonological changes in morphemes (choice of class of allomorphs) due to occurrence in a certain slot[21]	phonological changes or abbreviations due to a specific style of speech[22]

TABLE 3 (Continued)

Modes	Components of Modes				
	Kinds of Modification (or restriction)	Environmental Sources of Modification of Syntagmemes			
		Lexical (Morphemic)	Phonological (Phonemic)	Grammatical (Tagmemic)	Stylistic (Systemic)
	Grammatical: via alloclasses (viewed as types of concord between allotagmas)	correlation of co-occurrence variants of included allohypertagmas by cross reference to particular lexical types of items[23]	correlation of co-occurrence variants of included allotagmas in phonological alliteration or rhyme[25]	correlation of co-occurrence variants of included allohypertagmas, by markers of grammatical agreement or concord[27]	special style as affecting collocational concord of included tagmemes, or hypertagmemes; or resulting in specially included or excluded tagmemes or hypertagmemes[29]
	via position	positional variant of hypertagmeme affected by specific hypermorpheme[24]	positional variant of hypertagmeme affected by phonological elements[26]	positional variant of hypertagmeme affected by presence of optional hypertagmemes or by optional allohypertagmas[28]	positional variant of hypertagmeme affected by style[30]
	Fused[31] vs. clearly segmented variants: A partially-fused sequence of two hypermorpheme types occurs when they share a hypertagmeme in double function at their joint border.				

Distribution Mode	Sequence Distribution: Occurrence in one or more hypertagmemic slots[32] (external distribution); independent[33] (free) or dependent[34] (bound) in its over-all occurrence.
	Class Distribution:
	    Membership of the hypermorpheme division subclass as part of a larger filler class.[35]
	    Membership of the hypermorpheme class in a (nondistribution) hyperclass of hypermorpheme classes,[36] i.e., the syntagmeme as a member of a nondistributional class of syntagmemes.
	    Membership in the total class of classes of hypermorphemes of a particular style,[37] or of a universe of discourse, or of the language as a whole; and in a dimensional matrix.				

Commentary on Table 3:

(1): As illustrations of syntagmemes (or of emic classes of hypermorphemes) of the type treated in Table 3, note (c-j, o-n, p, v, bb, hh) from Table 1.

(2): For a string of tagmemes included in a hypermorpheme structure, see tagmemes (pp) and (oo) in hypermorpheme type (qq).

(3): Hypertagmeme types (jj, ii, kk, mm) in the hypermorpheme type (hh).

(4): obligatory tagmeme (pp) in hypermorpheme structure (qq); obligatory tagmeme-hypertagmeme (cc) and obligatory hypertagmeme (dd) in (aa); (t) and (r) in (p).

(5): optional tagmeme (n) in hypermorpheme structure (o-n); optional tagmeme-hypertagmeme (l) in hypermorpheme structure (j); optional hypertagmeme (bb) in (f); (s) in (p).

(6): general meaning of 'person' in (c-j plus o-n); 'passive predication' in (hh).
(7): *John*, (a), as minimum of class (c-j plus o-n).
(8): (j, o-n) as expanded manifestations of same class.
(9): (a) as free variant of (c-j plus o-n).
(10): '*m*/*am* — locally-free — abbreviation controlled by style.
(11): **in* with **chin* as local semantic restriction of (ee); *big* and *little* of (s) restricted in reference to *milk* of (u, x).
(12): If one assumes that *hit* and *nose* in *John hit$_1$ Bill on the nose$_1$* are the same morphemes as *John hit$_2$ the point on the nose$_2$* (the latter meaning that *he delineated precisely the crucial component of the problem*) then *hit$_1$* and *hit$_2$*, *nose$_1$* and *nose$_2$* are semantic variants of morphemes conditioned by the morphemic environment. Probably *hit* in *hit oil* (i.e., *found oil*) is best treated as a separate morpheme, however.
(13): in rhyme, selection from classes restricted to members of phonologically-defined subclasses.
(14): Heightened semantic attention or impact under alliteration is hard to prove; but cf. Kelly's jingle in § 6.45. For semantic implication of vowel quality, note *flip flop*, and see §§ 16.83, 13.81.
(15): (v) as here including *milk*, but excluding *boy*.
(16): *terribly*, *awfully*, etc., semantically changed in hypertagmemic slot before *pretty* (or before *ly*) in *awfully pretty* (and see § 7.323).
(17): class (y) with special members *Thee*, *Thou*, in elevated poetry or in prayer.
(18): *Morphology*, in a linguistic universe of discourse, refers to internal structure of words; in anatomical discussion it may refer to the form and structure of plants and animals; *articulation* in linguistics refers to vocal movements or arrangements leading to production of vocal sounds, whereas in anatomy it may refer to joints between bones or cartilages of a skeleton.
(19): plural *-en* after *ox*.
(20): voiced variant of plural, (oo), expected after voiced stops, etc.
(21): *him*, allomorph of morpheme (y), elicited by occurrence in object hypertagmemic slot (z).
(22): cf. (10), '*m*/*am*.
(23): concord of allotagmas: co-occurrence lexical subclasses via cross reference of *he* (y) versus *she* versus *it* to lexical subclasses of (c, o-n, r, u, y, qq, etc.): *John, Johnny, man, he*; versus *Jane, Susie, woman, she*; versus *dog, milk, it*, etc. An allotagma of (h) may be manifested wholly or in part by such a co-occurrence subclass, in cross reference with an allotagma of subject, object, location-head, etc., of an immediately- or remotely-preceding clause.
(24): For positional allotagmas affected by specific adjacent hypermorphemes, see discussion of (mm), § 11.43, with commentary there on *in the face* with reference to long or short agent forms. For a positional allotagma affected by its own manifesting hypermorpheme subclass, rather than by the alloclass of an adjacent

hypertagmeme, not the position of *to him* versus *him* in *I gave the book to him* versus *I gave him the book*; and compare positions of object in *Did you see John? Whom did you see?*

(25): membership of allohypertagmas: class membership chosen both to maintain rhyme or alliteration and to preserve grammatical concord.

(26): positional allohypertagmas conditioned by phonology: as when grammatical order is changed in verse to allow words to fall where they will rhyme.

(27): with predicate (ss): co-occurrence subclasses of plural subjects (h) and (jj) with plural predicates (g) and (ss), i.e., plural concord from subject to predicate allohypertagmas.

(28): positional allohypertagmas conditioned by other hypertagmas: A hypertagmeme may occupy one physical position in the minimum form of the hypermorpheme structure, but a different position when a particular optional hypertagmeme happens also to occur. (In Zapotec [Pickett, 1960], for example, several third person dependent pronouns occur, and one of them must immediately follow the verb in an independent transitive declarative clause. If the [optional] independent subject *precedes* the verb, then any one of the third person dependent pronouns may fill the obligatory slot after the verb. When, however, the optional independent subject comes *after* the verb and the obligatory dependent subject pronoun, only a certain one of the dependent pronouns — the 'third person singular identified' — can be chosen.)

(29): style concord of allohypertagmas: co-occurrence lexical sets of words lead to appropriateness of vocabulary in reference to uniform types — e.g., consistent collocational uses of levels of learned vocabulary — cf. *segmental material* rather than *segmental stuff*. Note, also, the specially included hypertagmeme beginning the clause *Oh that I might!*

(30): positional allohypertagmas conditioned by or permitted within special styles: *Away ran John* for *John ran away*; and syntax distortion within some verse.

(31): See § 14.

(32): Hypermorpheme type (j) occurs in subject slots (h) and (jj), object slot (g), location-phrase slot (dd), etc.

(33): In general, words are independent if they can fill totally either the utterance or the response slot in an utterance-response unit (i.e., must potentially be word-sentence portmanteaus). Clauses, to be independent, must be able to fill the utterance slot of an utterance-response unit. Sentences to be independent are in turn potentially portmanteaus of sentence and total discourse. Hypermorpheme class (hh) is independent.

(34): Both a morpheme class and a hypermorpheme class may be grammatically dependent. Dependent forms may be found on any level of structure. Note the dependent morpheme classes (n) diminutive, and (oo) plural. Some items which are part of a grammatically-independent class occur sometimes or always in phonological variants which are dependent: *'m* of *am*. A dependent sentence or clause may fill a response slot, as part of a higher-level discourse slot.

(35): hypermorpheme class (p) as member of total filler class (h).

(36): distribution class (g) plus distribution class (ii) as members of nondistribution hyperclass 'verb expression'.

(37): appropriate congruent vocabulary of words and expressions in a lexical set (§ 7.313[4]) of a particular style.

11.5 *Etics and Emics of Hypertagmemes and of Hypermorpheme Types*

In Parts I-II, §§ 5.5, 6.8, 7.8, 8.7, we discussed, in reference to the units treated, (1) problems of segmentation. Then we listed briefly (2) etic criteria for the classification of types of units and (3) distribution classes of these units. We next (4) summarized problems which were analogous, for all of the unit types, in passing from etic to emic units. Similar kinds of material are relevant here. There is considerable overlap between the new material and Chapter 7.

11.51 *Segmentation of Hypertagmemes and of Hypermorpheme Structures*

Segmentation of tagmas or hypertagmas is treated in § 7.71. This material must now be supplemented, for relevance of levels, by §§ 11.2-4. Tests for homologousness (§§ 7.71, 7.322) via expandability can in part be restated in terms of transform grammar (see § 11.76).

Borders of hypermorphemes and hypermorpheme types continue to be related to the borders of hypertagmemes (see tagma vs. morph, §§ 7.71, 6.66, 7.56, 7.44, 7.54). As in the earlier materials, internal constituents of hypermorpheme structures are not required to be binary; they may occur in serial expansion (§ 7.56), i.e., as string constituents (§ 11.24). This, too, affects the determination of borders of hypermorphemes included in higher-layer hypermorpheme structures. Defined borders of hypermorpheme types change, also, with the withdrawal of the requirement of two morphemes per hypermorpheme (§§ 11.22; 10.1). For some purposes this leaves us weaker in ability to segment our materials. Hence there is the tentative suggestion, here, of the possibility of using the wave character of a hypermorpheme (§ 11.32) as a possible supplementary criterion:

In attempting to restrict the number of hypertagmemic levels postulated to a useful small number, Pickett 1960:54-62 ran into a particular difficulty: Within a Zapotec clause or a phrase it is often exceedingly useful to group together for reference certain included string constituents which are especially relevant for identifying that hypertagmemic type or for contrasting it with others. In comparing a transitive with an intransitive clause, for example, a subject of some type, a predicate of some type, and an object were much more relevant than constituents given manner, degree, location, time. Not only were the former items diagnostic in separating the types, but they seemed to function as a unit string. This unity was especially evident in that they frequently constituted the minimum form for such a type. A minimum intransitive clause in Zapotec has a dependent subject and an intransitive verb. A minimum transitive clause has a subject, a transitive verb, and an object. It was convenient to refer to such a constituent complex as a CLAUSE NUCLEUS in contrast to the margin or satellite groups of tagmemes.

But a question arose: If the nucleus may function in some way as a unit, was it not, itself, a matrix of tagmeme distribution — a hypermorpheme type — as over against a different included hypermorpheme type made up of the margin? And if this should apply to the clause, would there not also be nuclear hypermorpheme types in phrase, in word stems, and the like? And if it were true in these, would not the number of levels of analysis which were treated as emically relevant become so great that the very concept of level as a useful term would itself disappear? And would not hypermorpheme and hypertagmeme segmentation become highly indeterminate?

Within the considerations so far developed in setting up contrasting levels, there seems to be no way of meeting this objection fully. It seemed wise, therefore, to try to find an overriding criterion which would be necessary to apply before a separate level should be set up as emically in contrast with another level of analysis in the grammatical hierarchy. That is, one needs a criterion in grammar analogous to the physical difference of levels which were used in Chapter 9 to separate syllable from phoneme and from rhythm unit. A syllable was there assumed to have some kind of physical characteristic — a chest pulse — which differentiated it from the phoneme, even when the levels were in portmanteau relationship such that a single phoneme simultaneously constituted a total syllable and a total rhythm unit. If in the phonological sphere a criterion was used to distinguish such levels, what might we find to perform a related task in the grammatical hierarchy?

The suggestion which Pickett and I have been using is that in order to be considered an emic level in the grammatical hierarchy, a level must in some sense be a GRAMMATICAL WAVE. The nucleus would be analyzed as the peak, or center, of that wave. The margins would in some sense be composed of constituents which are at the borders of the grammatical wave. The constituents which serve simultaneously as part of two adjacent hypertagmemes would be a constituent analogous to a syllable in double function between rhythm units which have an indeterminate border.

This criterion is beautifully simple in principle, and elegant in its relating to the general outlook treating the phonological hierarchy. The possibility of having a total theory of language structure which is on the one hand a particle view — dealing with specific units — and on the other hand a wave view — dealing with the manner in which these have their required components and by which they fuse one into another in sequence — is highly attractive. (See Pike, 1959, and chapter 12.)

If this view is adopted, constituent clusters constituting nuclei of hypermorpheme structures would then not necessarily receive the status of emic hypermorpheme structures themselves. They would be analogous to a vowel cluster, in the nucleus of a syllable, which would not itself be a syllable. A marginal cluster of hypertagmemes would be analogous to a consonant cluster in the syllable.

The extent which this approach will help solve the problem of segmentation of hypermorphemes and hypertagmemes is not yet clear. Pickett has used it in setting up Zapotec material (1960:90-91). Until it is tested more widely, however, we cannot be sure whether it will run into indeterminacies in application which will force its heavy modification or even its abandonment. Meanwhile, however, we hold to it tentatively as part of the definition of any syntagmeme which we set up.

In practice, however, we have difficulty in applying the criterion. For example, in a phrase such as *a very big boy whom I used to know*, the nucleus of the phrase would be the obligatory sequence *a boy*. The margins would include, however, not only the post modifier *whom I used to know*, but the included *very big*. Thus neither the marginal string nor the nuclear string is completely continuous. This makes the figure of speech less attractive than it would be otherwise. In addition, there is the problem that it can be argued that *very big* itself has a wave-like form such that *big* would be the nucleus, and *very* the margin. Such situations would frequently arise whenever modifications of modifications occur nested within larger structures. The question: Should *very big* then be considered as a separate hypermorphemic wave within the total phrase *a very big boy*, or should this be treated in some fashion as part of the total phrase type, but an elaboration of it internally? At the moment we lack clear criteria for answering this question.

Perhaps some solution can be found whenever the total phrase can serve as an isolatable entity (as a response utterance) in contrast to the included phrase which would not so serve excepting in reference to the implied fuller phrase.

11.52 *Etics of Hypertagmemes and of Syntagmemes*

The listing of etic criteria for slot-plus-class correlatives in § 7.72 continues to be useful with the following modifications: (1) Criteria for tagmas and hypertagmas may be broken down into (a) those which are relevant to *all* structural levels, and (b) those few which are useful only to one level. Certain of the possible meanings — such as subject-as-actor, in § 7.72(o), for example — may be restricted to a single level. (2) A criterion must be added for minimum tagma and nonminimum hypertagma (§ 11.41). (3) Further structural meanings of hypertagmas must be added to the list in § 7.72(o). Morphological work by Shell (1957), Cox (1957), and Delgaty (in *Mayan Studies* I, 1960) make it evident that this list will have to be expanded — Delgaty shows very great intricacy of detail in such structures — but the list already contains many of the general kinds of things to be expected. Similarly, Pickett shows very intricate detail of slot-plus-class correlation on the phrase level but the general types found are within the framework implied in § 7.72(o). When more tagmemic studies are in print, the whole range of tagmatic types and contrastive criteria around the world will need treatment in a separate monograph; it would be premature to attempt it here.

Similarly, separate monographs are needed to study the etics of the tagmemic structure[8] of word types, of phrase types, of clause types, of sentence types, and of higher-level discourse structures. The suggested criteria in § 7.72(a-g) are still largely relevant. They must be modified somewhat, however, in order to be applied to problems of the re-defined (§§ 11.22, 10.1) hypermorpheme where level becomes relevant to it, and where single words, for example, may be variants of a phrase type.

The lists will need supplementation for further varieties of types, however, as soon as enough empirical studies are available to justify separate treatment. As one sample set of sentence types note Waterhouse (1962, for Oaxacan Chontal, where contrastive internal tagmemic composition and intonation patterns are given for each). There one finds a class of nine sentence types of affirmation: of action, of action toward goal, or toward recipient, of process, of state or quality, of reflexive action, of relation, of identity, of location; a class of three sentence types of negation: nonintensive, intensive, negation of question or of command; two types of interrogation: for information, for corroboration; five types of exclamation or sequence (a miscellany possibly needing further analysis): vocative, imperative, hortatory, response, sequence. Pickett (1960: 76:84), also giving tagmemic breakdown, lists 21 sentence types — the number, however, may vary considerably in accordance with one's judgment as to grouping allo-types into single units.

For application of the lists in §§ 5.52-53 to hypermorphemic types on levels below the sentence — and for better fit on higher levels as well — the following modifications are needed: (1) Criteria must be added to determine the level of structure — e.g., clause, phrase, word (cf. § 11.22, for suggestions). (2) The criterion of independence versus dependence must be extended to all levels of structure (cf. § 11.44, commentary on items 33 and 34 of Table 3). (3) More extensive treatment is needed, on all levels, of included tagmeme or hypertagmeme sequences, pointing up the suggestions of § 5.52(o-p). (4) Etic listing of clause types, phrase types, etc., must be expanded (since only sentence types, and higher levels, are included in § 5.53).

---

[8] Tagmemics continues to look forward to a universal etics of grammatical types, growing out of our first volume (1954, §§ 6.82-84, 7.72-73), and analogous to the etics of phonological types. With the number of articles now appearing on clause and phrase types, some such general etics of these constructions should be much farther along soon. Compare Chomsky's desire for a "general semantic theory of some sort, independent of any particular language" (1962:§2.3, p. 525), and his desire for language universals (1961a:5; 1961b:219; 1962:§4.2, p. 531). Although he has noted in the latter reference that a phonetic matrix helps provide components of a universal phonetic theory needed for phonological study, he has not yet seen the need for comparable grammatical matrices like ours (Pike, 1962a, or 1964d, for tagmemes).

We are reaching toward an 'alphabet' of tagmeme types. As soon as we can get somewhat uniform agreement as to the particular symbols that may be used for comparable tagmemes throughout the world (a goal which may take as long or longer than the present degree of agreement on a phonetic alphabet) tagmemic description, and description of construction types, should be as easy to read a our phonetic materials today. In addition, it should allow for easy comparability from language so language.

An intricate example of phrase types is seen in Pickett (1960:36-54) who gives nine major and fifty-three minor phrase types, each with formula showing contrastive tagmemic components. Phrases are first grouped according to the specific clause slots, phrase slots, and sentence slots which they fill. Within independent object and subject slots, for example, a different list of phrase types is found from that occurring in dependent subject slot; or in location, or time, or manner, or purpose slot; or in the various predicate slots. The range of their meanings (sometimes identical with the meaning of the slot in which they occur) includes possession, modification, apposition, nominalization, addition, compounding, personal, demonstrative, quantity, location, time, manner, purpose, augmentation, negation, query, aspect, speed, intransitive, transitive, imperative, equational, exclamatory, vocative, and so on.

11.53 *Summary of Relation of Hypertagmas to Hypertagmemes and of Etic to Emic Classes of Hypermorphemes*

The relations between the hypertagma (an etically viewed slot-plus-class correlative) and hypertagmeme are those stated in § 7.741: A hypertagma may be (a) free or (b) a conditioned variant of a hypertagmeme; or (c) part of an etically-complex hypertagmeme; or (d) a sequence of hypertagmemes nonfused or (e) fused; or (f) erroneously set up as a hypertagma in the initial stages of the analysis.

Similar relations exist between a particular sentence and the sentence type — i.e., the emic hypermorpheme type — as indicated in § 5.55. Likewise, phrases and emic phrase types, clauses and emic clause types, must be similarly viewed.

For the development of the procedural application of these principles, analogous to those used by us for the phoneme (Pike 1947c), see Longacre (1964a).

Perhaps the single most important procedural addition to the etic criteria in §§ 5.52, 7.72, and to the principles involved in passing here from etic to emic units, is a suggestion of Longacre's (1958a, 1964a) about contrastive types. He points out a danger that — unless there are adequate safeguards — a single structure such as $(+A \pm B)$ might be restated, by a simple juggling of symbols, as the two structures $(+A)$ versus $(+A+B)$. In this latter instance the optional minimum would be treated as one total unit, and the optional expansion defined as a distinct unit with two obligatory parts. This difficulty had, in fact, plagued us in classroom usage of the practice problems in §§ 7.313(4), 7.74, 7.75. Up to this point our only solution had been, on occasion, to grant alternate answers as theoretically correct even when one of the two was empirically undesirable. Longacre overcame much of this difficulty by insisting that a *single* contrastive difference in a pair of phrase (or clause, or sentence) formulas is insufficient to show that they are emically distinct structures; always there must be at least two correlated formal differences. The differences may be of various types — based on order of included tagmemes, included manifesting classes, nature of included tagmemes, potential transformations, of which the following formulas may suggest samples: (1) $(+A+B)$ versus $(+A+C+D)$; (2) $(+A+B)$ versus $(\pm D \pm E+A)$; (3) $(+A+B_1[=+a+b+c])$ versus $(\pm A+B_2[=+c\pm d])$; (4) $(+B_1[=+a+b]+A$ [with A in cross reference with a]) versus $(+B_2[=+b\pm c]+A$ [with A in cross reference to b]); etc.

In my own view, we must retain the provision (see § 7.745) that a structural contrast can meet the requirement of a double difference if one of the two major differences consists in a sharply different external distribution — often carrying with it a different structural meaning — of the item as a whole in a higher-layered hypertagmemic slot. Compare, for example, $(+A+B)$ occurring only in one type (or slot) of utterance-response sequence, versus $(+A+B+C)$ occurring in a different type (or slot) of utterance-response sequence. (For Pickett's use of this criterion to separate a dependent from an independent time clause, note 1960:69).

Problems remain — as when we wish to treat a double difference in class membership (e.g., singular to singular and plural to plural internal relations) as representing co-occurrent hypertagmatic restrictions (§ 11.44, Table 3, manifestation mode, conditioned variants of grammatical form) rather than separate clause types. It is here that our last suggestion, about external distribution, aids us by implying that if external function and expansions or transforms — are *not* different, and if the manifesting classes are overlapping or members of larger distribution classes, the units may sometimes be treated as etic variants of one another in spite of the double difference. Contrastiveness of types must not be determined, in my view, by formal considerations alone, but by the relationships of the data to a total form-meaning composite, whether in morphemics (§§ 6.46, 6.91) or tagmemics. See, now, Pike (1962a: 236-38).

11.6 *Tagmemic System in Reference to Kernel Matrix and Transforms*

In previous sections we have utilized the concept of wave with nucleus and margin to help express in analogical form a number of relationships within our data. In § 8.42 we refer to waves of motion in reference to the articulatory motions which lead to segmentation of a continuum of speech into phonemes or phones. Higher-level waves were referred to in reference to syllables in §§ 8.51, 9.223, 9.241. Earlier in the present chapter (§ 11.51) we utilized the concept to help in understanding the relationship of the nucleus of a clause to its margin. We now ask the question whether or not the same concept might help us in treating a further problem:

Z. Harris discusses "elementary sentences" which "will be called sentences of the kernel of the grammar" (1957:334). The grammar as a whole consists of a kernel made up of a "set of elementary sentences and combiners, such that all the sentences of the language are obtained from one or more kernel sentences (with combiners) by means of one or more transformations" — and these kernel constructions seem to be very few (for English he lists seven principal sentence constructions, all of which are active ones, plus a few minor ones, 335). In addition, there are other sentence types arrived at by transformations of the underlying sentence structures. Thus a passive may be derived from an active, and question types may be derived from the simple transitive statements. Earlier treatments of kernel and transform sentences are found in Z. Harris (1952a:4; 1954b:260) in which it is suggested that kernel sentences of the language might be the best starting point to get at machine translation from one language to another.

In tagmemic terms it might be possible to treat as the 'kernel' of the grammar those structures which make up the nucleus of the grammar system as a whole. Items which could be derived from these would then be treated as marginal sentence types.

Such an approach would ease one problem which has faced people writing monographs on tagmemics: H. Hart, for example, after setting up sentence types of affirmation of activity, of description of item, and of identification of an item, then treated emphatic and query types as separate sentence types on a par with the first three. To do this, however, the full structures of the first three types had to appear in the emphatic and query formulas with additional descriptions which were in fact made in transform terms. For example, in a commentary of the emphatic utterance type she states that the symbolized but included affirmation sentence has one or two of its included tagmemes (there labelled grammemes) "selected for special attention and moved to the emphasis slot" (1957:143). Since, in fact, for these marginal sentence types a transform rule was included as a commentary to the added sentence type, it would seem more elegant if these two kinds of sentence types — nuclear and marginal, basic and derived — could be given systematic status as nuclear and marginal respectively. The precise effect of this suggestion must await further[9] study, but it seems a promising lead at least.

11.7 *Bibliographical Comments on Chapter 11*

Much of the bibliographical material relevant to Chapter 7 is also relevant to Chapter 11. The reader should consult § 7.8, therefore, as well as the comments here.

---

[9] Since the first edition of this chapter was published (1960), our techniques for handling derivation from kernel (nuclear) matrices have been developed. Categories comprise the rows and columns (with, for example, independent versus dependent on one dimension, and transitive, intransitive, equational on another) of the particular level of the construction under attention. Construction types (syntagmemes) of that level come in the cells. Derivation is achieved by multiplication of the matrix by a constant — that is, modification of each of the cells of the matrix by an interrogative component, or an imperative one, or both, etc. (Pike 1962a:226-29). The determination of conditioned variants of the constructions (so that no alloconstructions enter the emic cells) is also discussed (236-39). Different kinds of matrices provide a display of tagmeme sequences which demonstrate contrasts between the constructions (232-35), or for illustrating these contrasts in the form of citations in a syntax paradigm (1963b). The approach works also on the morphological level (1963d). Note also second fn. of § 11.225 for list of other fnn. commenting on matrices.

11.71 On Hierarchical versus Combinatorial Grammar

Types of grammatical presentation may be compared with one another as to the proportion of emphasis they give to 'vertical' relations — relations of an item to higher-levelled structures — on the one hand, or, on the other hand, the emphasis which they give to 'lateral' relations — relationship of one item to another in sequence with it. Where emphasis is heavily vertical, with emphasis upon inter-level relations, the grammar may be called HIERARCHICAL. Where emphasis is upon sequential or combinatorial relations a grammar may be called COMBINATORIAL (or CONSTITUENT). No one approach can be exclusively dedicated to either of these matters; over-all approach is a matter of emphasis.

For discussion of a monohierarchical view of the Trager type, note § 9.71 (and Longacre's comment that generative grammar has turned this model "upside down", leaving the model essentially unchanged, 1964a:7). A bi-hierarchical view, with phonology as over against the grammatical-lexical elements of language, see Hockett (1961a). The tagmemic approach considers three hierarchies — lexical, phonological and grammatical — as the minimum which can handle the complexity of language; rather than dropping to fewer hierarchies, tagmemics may eventually move to splitting each of the three into component hierarchies (see § 12.5, in reference to the Crawford contribution).

Chomsky protests that certain taxonomic theories are "highly simple" — too simple to reflect the process of the learning capacity of a child (1962: § 5, pp. 555-56). To this tagmemics heartily assents — but insists that the addition of transforms as a process or the inverted Trager model is still far too simple to handle our data; at least three simultaneous hierarchies must be observed in the phrase structure. Without such an approach, one is unable to find — in my view — an adequate source of the reaction of human beings to pattern. Longacre has pointed out, following Walter, that patterning is essential to human behavior — that "man abhors chaos" (1964a:13); the tagmemic view asserts that a very long list of rules, which are supposedly 'ordered', in fact appear to the intuition of some of us as being disordered in that they lack pattern. Pattern must be found in the intricate interplay of the three hierarchies and in the intersection of categories or vectors of a matrix of a field structure. In addition, from the tagmemic view, it is highly inelegant — and far from simple — to have a set of ordered rules so arranged that the change of one minor rule in the middle, at some level, will drastically affect many of the rules at other levels. To those interested in tagmemics, a far greater measure of stability of the system, of simplicity of pattern, and of ordering of data, is seen in the handling of emic levels such that an 'exception' or minor deviation of regularity is less able to change the looks of the broad outline.

Other approaches to hierarchy are found in Halliday (1961, see comments below, in § 11.77), in Bendor-Samuel (1961), in Bloch (1946b), and scattered throughout tagmemic literature (see § 11.77 for bibliography). A substantially different approach, in terms of stratificational hierarchy, shows — from top to bottom — semantic, sememic, semimorphemic, morphemic, morphophonemic, phonemic and phonetic levels — with the first and last "outside of the linguistic structure and in the 'real world'" (Lamb, 1962:15-16; compare Haas, 1955:82, for levels of semantic value in the hierarchy; and note also hierarchies of semantic taxonomies in the work of Conklin, 1955; in Householder and Saporta, 1962, Frake, 1961, and Nida, 1961, in A William Cameron Townsend). For Householder, phonology and morpho-syntactic structure "are not successive 'levels', but parallel systems (each with its own levels)" (1959, in Saporta, 1961:22). For Garvin, "An integrative sequence of units on the next lower level of integration constitutes a unit on the next higher level" (in Tax, 1952:220).

Chomsky considers "the idea that each level is literally constructed out of lower level elements" to be a "rather dubious" position, with "its origin in the attempt to develop a discovery procedure for grammars" — a goal which he renounces (1957a: 59). Chomsky rejects Yngve's production ("from top down") since he "selects grammatical constructions before he selects the words they will use" (1961a:11; see also Miller and Chomsky in Luce and others, 1963:475). I do not see how Chomsky avoids the same objection. (See comment by Longacre, above.)

Lees misinterprets the three hierarchies of tagmemics, assuming that they are "independent from one another, but interwoven in the sentence" (1960b:211) and feels that "this theory of separate grammatical, morphological, and phonological hierarchies is, I regret, a backward step for him to take"; he fails to have realized that we would insist upon the interlocking of the hierarchies, with "certain points or regions at which some of the units of the hierarchy *are* coterminous, or co-nuclear, in order for the units of the various hierarchies to be relevant to one another" (§ 15.1), and that we therefore deny any totally-separate view of three hierarchies. We leave them only sufficiently independent to have identities of their own within the interlocking total fusing system.

Tagmemic views would insist that *all three* hierarchies be relevant not only in the analysis of any structure — including any sentence — but in the evaluation of any grammar; phonological considerations help determine certain boundaries; semantic considerations help determine grammatical functions, and certain elements of lexical function; grammatical construction types enter as well, of course. For problems in which one must be ready to "edit the corpus of utterances judged grammatical by an informant so as to include metaphors, mentioned words, foreign words " — with criteria which are semantic, since the use of *if* in *How many ifs do you see on this page* since this is not a "grammatical intuition" see Lackowski (1963:213); and therefore when we "ask an informant for judgments of grammaticality we implicitly require an interpretation" (213); compare, above, our discussion of problems in using informant reaction for 'same' or 'different', § 2.73. Note, further, that Lackowski excludes from the grammar proper specific morphemes or words; rather the grammar separates types (215)... generates types such as indefinite article, plus temporal, plus post temporal (214-15). Note that this use comes closer to tagmemics than does transformation theory, in that it leaves lexicon outside of the grammar (see our lexical hierarchy) but leaves structural class — and perhaps tagmemes — in the grammar.

The Lackowski material points to the need, therefore, of a much more radical reworking of the Trager model than that of a reverse-type Trager hierarchy; nothing less complex than a trihierarchical approach is complicated enough. Tagmemic theory has thus far not attempted to give priority to any one of the three hierarchies. If, however, it were forced to make a decision in this direction, it would give the nod to the lexical hierarchy, as over against the phonological and grammatical ones, in that it is here that we determine, perhaps, something of 'what we want to say' — and therefore is the closest to our fundamental assumption that language is designed for communication and for understanding between peoples.

For further discussion of hierarchies in reference to simplicity, note §§ 15.31, 15.32.

11.711 *On Item-in-Slot versus Construction*

In § 7.85 of Part I we emphasized the fact that, in our view, the relationship of an item to a slot which it fills in a higher-layered structure needed to be given priority in theory and analysis over the relationship between one item and another on the same level, or in the same structure with it. (Our earliest presentation of this view is in 1944: 114, 127fn. 7.) Priority, however, does not mean exclusive domain — both characteristics of language remain important to any grammatical approach. (Bloomfield, for example, though emphasizing constructions and the order of arrangement of items in them (e.g., 1933a:168-69), includes statements such as "The regular analogies of a language are habits of substitution" (276); this sentence can be reinterpreted as implying the necessity of an item-in-slot view.) It was our crucial assumption of item-in-slot theoretical priority, however, which seemed to be the point at which, above all, the approach to hierarchical grammar differed from the approach to combinatorial (or constituent) grammar.

Perhaps the difference can be pointed up by contrasting a summary statement by Z. Harris with one of ours: "Each element is defined by the *relations among elements* at the next lower level" (Harris, 1951:369, italics ours). We would say, rather, that each unit is classified primarily by its occurrence — its external distribution — in one or more slots of one or more higher-layered structures, and secondarily by its internal organization; both criteria are crucial, but in any clash of analysis the first gets priority.

Firth (1957:17, and 5) treats both of these components of analysis but seems to assign priority to them in a reverse order: "The first principle of phonological and grammatical analysis is to distinguish between *structure* and *system*. We have already mentioned the interior phonological relations connected with the text itself: firstly the syntagmatic relations between elements of structure prosodic and phonematic, secondly the paradigmatic relations of the terms or units which commute within systems set up to give values to the elements of structure." For colligation as the "syntactic juxtaposition of two or more categories", note Simon (1953:327).

For substitutability as a fundamental concept, with some historical discussion going back to Dionysium Thrax, note Quirk (1958:37), with expansion and abbreviation of a segment in a frame, explored in the 17th century. For tactical pattern via construction, positions, markers, and morpheme sets, note Hockett (1954a:215). For Pittman's insistence on markers in relation to constructions note discussion in § 7.85; compare also McKaughan (1962:51, for particle marking sentence relationships).

Longacre, though dealing with tagmemic theory and practice, pays much less attention to external distribution in construction definition than I do. He does not wish to treat external distribution as a countable contrastive feature, since he feels that it obscures structural distinctions proper to contrastive levels (1964a). I continue to feel that emphasis upon external distribution of a unit is necessary to assure the retention of hierarchical structuring such that units of one level are thoroughly integrated into the system through their occurrence in slots in higher levels. This insistence on the occurrence of a construction in a slot in a larger construction has as a consequence the insistence that one must somehow start analysis and description in reference to a *total* system — not in reference to any part of a system, nor in references to abstracted sentences or constructions. By dealing with external distribution as an essential relevant component of a unit one implies that one must start with total system, since all items are linked *by this means* into larger systeme of which they are a part. (I would now — 1964 — find less objection, however, to a view which gives *equal* priority to tagmemic class-in-slot and to construction — as a neither-the-hen-nor-the-egg-first view.) For external distribution relevant to commands, see Brend (1964:45).

For an attempt to find grammatical universals in a perspective of word order, see Greenberg (1963:58-90).

11.712 *On Immediate Constituents as End Products of Analysis Rather than as Starting Points*

"Immediate constituents of constructions appear within our theory, but in a sharply different role from that of current linguistics or of Bloomfield. Instead of being the point of initial attack on grammatical analysis, they appear as an end product of analysis" (Pike, 1958a:277). The question arises as to why it is that there seems intuitively to be such great validity to immediate constituent analysis, whereas it has proved so extremely difficult to handle empirically. Our judgment is that binary immediate constituents are a special instance of the end product of a much more inclusive analytical principle. The analytical principle necessary is to treat items in slots in a higher level. When, as a matter of fact, it turns out that all items in a particular sequence can be conveniently treated as occurring in two successive slots of a higher-level structure, then the end product of this decision is a pair of binary immediate constituents. When the end product of this item-in-slot analysis leaves us with more than two, the end product is a series of serial (§ 7.56) or string constituents (Longacre, 1960).

The source of the difficulty is in part an underlying assumption in the traditional approach that items go together to make up constructions, and that this combinatorial start is the essence of grammar. This starting assumption forces one to begin analysis by looking for 'cuts' in the string of materials. If, on the other hand, one starts with unity as a basic assumption (Pike, 1944:114, 127), and units are in turn assumed to occur in higher-level slots and to be analytically identifiable in reference to the slots which they completely fill as units, then the approach is to first look for unitized items or groups of items in reference to such high-level slots. (See §§ 7.85, 11.711.)

For earlier treatment of immediate constituents in these chapters, note §§ 7.56, 7.83, 7.85, 7.87. Although immediate constituents have been implied for centuries in grammatical analysis, the starting point for attention to this view in American linguistics is generally Bloomfield (1933a:161). The first attempts to deal with the problem on a theoretical front is Pike (1943b). Note there an early attempt to show hierarchical structuring in grammar; note especially the chart on 70, followed (with modifications) by numerous recent writers such as Nida (1949:87) and Hockett (1958:152). Wells made a major advance in interpreting immediate constituents in reference to expansions and substitutions (1947a). Though Pike had suggested the use of frames for class analysis and the study of immediate constituents (1943b:81), and Z. Harris (1946) had contributed extensively to the study of progressively-inclusive constructions, it was Wells who brought forcibly to attention the immediate-constituent implications of expansions. Pittman, in turn, made a further advance, in pointing out criteria for nuclear versus satellitic relations (1948b). Protest has occasionally been made against treating immediate constituents as binary (Bazell, 1953:5). In spite of attempt to set up rules for determining immediate-constituent breaks (Pike, 1943b:74-81; Nida, 1949:91-99), wide divergence continues to occur in applying the principle to — let us say — English (Sledd, 1957:270, in reference to work of Roberts, Whitehall, and Lloyd-Warfel). Hockett has recently improved charting of immediate-constituent relations (1958:188-89). For more recent immediate-constituent charting of English construction types, see Nida (1960 [1943]). Compare, also, Gleason (1961:121-48).

Smith argues that "the binary principle must be followed throughout in syntactic analysis" (1962, in Third Texas Conference:113); Yngve also "would expect that binary rules would predominate... even to the almost complete exclusion of ternary or other larger rules" (1960:454). Note Longacre's string-constituent analysis, in which a binary assumption must be eliminated from the working norms of the analyst (1960:65-70). Longacre has given the most vigorous attack on the binary assumption of immediate constituents — insisting, rather, that strings of constituents are often preferable, leaving binary elements as a special case rather than vice versa (1960). For further objection to binarism, note also Worth (in *Preprints* ... 1962). (And cf. serial expansion, § 7.56). (In defence of binary analysis in reference to phonology, see Halle in *Studies Presented to...*, 1957; and see also, §§ 8.813 and 8.84.)

Yngve has a recent attempt to defend an immediate-constituent framework, assuming that it "can be used as the basis for a model of sentence production and that any shortcomings can be overcome" (1960:445). He does this with a left-to-right convention, assuming that the model "should share with the human speaker of the language" relation to proper time sequence (445; see also 452, 465). With this in mind, Yngve attempts to show that the degrees to which modifiers of various kinds can be elaborated to the left of the construction are substantially different from the much less restricted development to the right, so that "depth considerations are among the most important factors in the grammar of any language" (1960:452; with techniques for calculating depth, 451). He assumes, further, that "the set of constituent-structured rules is unordered" with "no grammatical significance... attached to the order in which the rules are listed in the memory" (445); and the "rules for parentheses, instead of being stated in terms of resolution of ambiguity, are stated in terms of the kinds of nodes in the tree that are being expanded" (448, 461). Some of his output strings include not only words in sequence, but structural symbols interwoven with them (447).

For mathematical treatment of several grammar types related to analysis, note Bar-Hillel, Gaifman, and Shamir (1960).

11.72 *On Emic Levels of Grammatical Structure*

It may be a bit difficult for the reader to appreciate the sense in which the treatment of levels in this chapter differs from that which I have in earlier chapters. The difference seems to be that in previous instances I had dealt with levels on an etic basis; here I am treating them emically.

In 1943b I pointed out that Bloomfield's work needed to be revised in order to bring to the fore of our thinking pyramiding structures in terms of layers, or levels (70). At that time it seemed quite clear to me that a hierarchical approach was certainly necessary, and that this would affect grammar. In Part I layerings of structure are involved in many of the formulas: Whenever parentheses occur within parentheses, and further parentheses within these former, layering is implied. I indicated that on occasion morphological layering must be treated as differing from syntactic layering, and so on. On the other hand, I had equally strongly insisted that there were times when the setting up of layer distinctions — such as between morphology and syntax — could be highly misleading. In fact, tagmemics in part developed as a specific attempt to be able to analyze grammar for languages such as Mixtec where the boundary between word and phrase is not necessarily a sharp one.

In this current chapter, however, levels are re-established, under the influence of Longacre (1958a, 1964a), as primary working tools. The difference, however, is considerable. For the first time, so far as I know, it has been suggested to us that levels themselves may be set up by contrastive techniques — techniques similar to those which we have already used for differentiating morphemes or phonemes. To be sure, this emic view has been foreshadowed in many earlier publications — as one can see once one looks for it — but this, also, is to be expected. When phonemes were first treated explicitly, there seemed to be little difference between a phonemic description and the older treatments of the phonetic description of a language and its orthographical representation. The difference between phonemic statements and the older orthographical works lay in the precision of the techniques and in the clarity of the conceptual framework — and here the same is true for treatment of emic levels of grammatical structure.

Starting from Longacre's contribution, it seems possible to treat a level not only as contrastive, but as trimodally structured — with its identificational-contrastive features, its variants and manifestations, and its distributional relations to other levels, This allows the integration of the emic character of a level with other emic units of the tagmemic approach.

The term "level", however, is being used in an entirely different manner by Chomsky: "A linguistic level is a method of representing utterances" (1957a:109, also 59), rather than — as for us — an attempt to represent some phase of structuring assumed to be in the material examined. Phonemic, morphemic and phrase-structure levels are referred to by Chomsky (86-87, 109), with a still 'higher' level of transformational analysis added (87). Lees considers that one of the two most far-reaching results "of Chomsky's study is then his discovery of a new level of linguistic structure" — the transformations (Lees, 1957:387), with a basic idea "obviously derived from those manipulations characteristic of Harris' discourse analysis".

Occasionally, however, one senses some feeling that the hierarchical structure is from the "lowest level" of "morphophonemic and phonemic rules", to the "'intermediate' transformation level", to "a 'highest' level, the level of phrase-structure" (Lees, 1957:388-89, and see Chomsky, 1957a:46, but contrast 59, where he denies that higher levels are constructed out of lower ones).

Chomsky specifically objects to the model which treats phonology as a level separate from grammar, especially if used to imply that in language learning — especially for the child — phonological learning precedes syntactic learning (1962, § 4.5, p. 552).

For levels as rules, see Bach (1964:57-59). Smalley feels that we pass from a threshold to another when we reach "the construction which has internal limitations greater than its external ones" (1961:xvii). Lamb has "levels of analysis and description" which are mainly "different types of analytical activity which linguists perform on different sections of a grammatical description" — such as "Phonemics, Phonotactics, Morphophonemics, Morphemics... Sememics" and so on; whereas representational levels and tactic levels "belong to the language" (1962:29); an Xemic stratum may have representation on a lower stratum in terms of alloXs (1962:6, 30).

Halliday insists that "a unit can include... a unit of rank higher than or equal to itself, but not a unit of rank more than one degree lower than itself; and not, in any case, a part of any unit" (1961:251; see above, § 7.32 for our related view). Compare, however, Rosbottom, with tense markers on a derivational level (within the verb stem) as inflectional suffix, versus as phrasal enclitic, for habitual, past, and future, respectively in Guaraní (1961:345). For a language with six contrastive levels of structure within the stem, symbolized and identifed by successive degrees of closure, note Wise (1963); levels of verb structure are chartered also by Chafe (1961). For compounding of suffix clusters, note Pike (1961c). For evidence that independent versus dependent types of constructions occur on all grammatical levels, see Waterhouse (1963). For nucleus and margin note Pickett (1960:91, with construction as a wave) and Longacre (1964a, with nucleus of construction as relevant to its contrastive features); see also Pittman (1948b, for criteria of nucleus versus satellite).

For transformationalist implied rejection of portmanteau levels, see § 11.722, in reference to Postal. For transformationalist neglect (or repudiation) of an emic clause level see § 11.724, reference to Bach.

11.721 *On Words and Morphology versus Syntax*

Must a morphology-syntax border be treated as basic for every language, and as an initial start of analytical attack? We previously answered in the negative. We did this on the basis of the fact that in some languages such as Mixtec it was difficult to find a sharp morphology-syntax boundary (1944:113-14, 126, 128; 1949), which appeared to be structurally relevant to the language, since (1) in general theory, a prime component of word definition was isolatability, yet (2) in this particular language many items which grammatically functioned as words were phonologically dependent, and (3) higher layerings in increasingly inclusive units seemed to have equal priority as over against a single dichotomy between an arbitrarily-imposed morphology-syntax boundary. Note a similar discussion in H. Hart (1957:142, 161-64).

Firth, recently, suggests also that the distinction between morphology and syntax is perhaps no longer useful in descriptive linguistics (1958:14). See also, Z. Harris (1951:262), W. S. Allen (1951b:126), Hjelmslev (1953:16). Compare Hockett: "This does not mean that every morpheme should be taken to be a word in its own right; the real implication is that THERE ARE NO WORDS IN CHINESE. The whole tradition of 'words' as worked out with western languages is useless in Chinese' (1944: 255).

If, now, we bring a word level back into the structural purview, how is this to be related to our previous statements? The answer is in some respects now quite clear: (1) The word level is only *one* level which may be set up in reference to several other levels which can be equally relevant, such as phrase, clause, utterance-response, conversation, etc. Hence, no single dichotomy of morphology-syntax necessarily makes sense. (2) The setting up of any level must now be an *emic* matter, not an ad hoc or etic one. Thus, we can now state that a word level should be postulated for any language whenever it can be demonstrated that it is structurally relevant and useful to do so — that is on emic criteria. This parallels our treatment of phonemics, in that we set up a phonemic system for one language at a time. We now set up word level for a single language at a time, provided that that particular language requires it. Longacre has recently been consulting with some students of languages of the Mayan family, where word level was not useful, but in which a single over-all level called word-phrase was more relevant and easier to handle — (Elliott in *Mayan Studies*, I, 1960); Delgaty has recently adopted this point of view for his treatment of a related language, Tsotsil (in *Mayan Studies*, I, 1960). (3) Some of the problems which led to indeterminacy of the morphology-syntax levels included the feedback of higher-level structures within lower-level structures. This continues to cause difficulty, but will be treated in Chapter 15 as important to the theory. At this point it is only relevant to state that just as there are indeterminacies at the junction of morphemes or of phonemes, so items with this kind of feedback of higher into lower structures may lead to an indeterminacy as regards levels. Just as, however, we did not completely abandon the relevance of phonemic segmentation just because of built-in indeterminacies in the system, so here we would now indicate that there are times when a word level is emically relevant even though there may be indeterminacies in the application of the emic criteria in some particular instances in analyzing such a language.

Other views of the word: The sentence is "the unit of language, not the word", Sweet (1900b:98); and Cassirer, after Humbolt (1953:303-04); but for Whitney "the whole structure of our science rests upon the study of individual words " (1867:238). The word is "an ultimate, or indecomposible sentence", for Sweet (1913:5). It is not, however, a phonetic unit (1900b:98), and the sentence-test does not work well on words like *the* (1913:6). Various problems in word delineation are discussed in Vendryes (1925:89), Projet (1931:321), Bloomfield (1933a:178-82), Pike (1945:79-82), Hockett (1947b:275-80; 1948b:2, 6-7; 1958:167, 178), Guthrie (1948), Bazell (1948b: 284-85; 1949b:86), Nida (1949:102-06), Z. Harris (1951:327-28), Milewski (1951:249-50, 252), Pittman (1954b:239), Osgood, Sebeok and others (1954:66), F. R. Palmer (1956:574-75), and others.

For a summary of recent discussion in morphology-syntax division, note Nosek (1961). For problems in word definition, see Hiorth (1958), Togeby (1949) and Sivertsen (1960:763). For word as universal, note Hymes (1956:286). For an initial attempt to show some universals in reference to word order see Greenberg (1963:33-34). For the word as the "highest among the linguistic units compulsorily coded" note Jakobson and Halle (1956:71). Compare Gudschinsky for focus shifting from words to morphemes to allologs and to phonemes — with word sometimes but not always basic for encoding tone (1958b:342, 344); compare also Sprigg for tones in relation to words (1955:134). Robins treats the word as "a unique entity in grammar" and "not just a stage in the progression 'from morpheme to utterance'" (1960:137). Pittman builds heavily on word roots, rather than on full words, leading to morphology as paradigmatic and syntax as syntagmatic (1959:199).

For items with *'s* as part of the word, so that the whole unit is brought out from permanent memory and so that "depth is reduced to five" note Yngve (1960:463).

For description of morphology and syntax combined in a single tagmemic treatment, note Clark (1962). For a morphological paradigm analogous to a syntax paradigm, note Pike and Erickson (1964). For an extensive discussion of the tagmemics of a verb structure note especially Shell (1957); see also various morphological sequence charts in other theoretical frameworks (for example, Olmstead, 1961: 107-111). See also Delgaty (in *Mayan Languages*, I, 1960, with complicated etic groupings of pronouns, but awkward description); Derbyshire (1961a); Waterhouse (1962:72, 87-88, for noun and verb structures). For summary and bibliography on Soviet and East European work in syntax, see various authors in Sebeok (1963b).

11.722 *On Portmanteau Levels*

In § 11.22 we pointed out that levels may be simultaneous — i.e., portmanteau. Some illustrations are given in § 11.43(o-i-a). The integration of portmanteau levels into the theory had to wait for the treatment of levels as themselves emically contrastive. This allowed the criterion of obligatory complexity to be withdrawn for hypertagmemes, and this in turn allowed for a simple unit to simultaneously manifest two levels of units.

Here, also, details as such are not new; it is the emic treatment within a hieararchical framework which represents the advance. Note, for example, that single words as constituting entire sentences have long been under attention (Sapir, 1921:118), Bloomfield (1933a:172), Nida (1949:103). Compare also Z. Harris (1946:165-66, sequences as single).

Recent psychological studies have been treating the same problem from a different point of view. Note, especially, Carroll's discussion, and comments on Skinner (1959a:42): "Skinner takes pains to insist that a mand is not the same as a tact, even when it is of the same phonetic shape. *Water!* learned as a mand, he thinks, does not automatically transfer to *water* learned as a tact", and "Specific morphemes or morpheme-groups such as *water* and the *ball* are then merely 'subroutines' called by these constructions, and no longer have the behavioral status of mands or tacts — they are simply general-purpose responses which may be fitted in to either type of response pattern". Various instances of units in double function are found in Pickett (1960). See also Brend (1964:59, 65-66, 71).

Compare, also, fusions resulting in double function (see Index); note, for example, *sheep* in § 14.12. Simultaneity may sometimes be best treated as involving overlap of neighboring forms. Compare morpheme alternants in Spanish, with resultant problems as seen in Saporta (in Kahane and Pietrangeli 1959:31). Compare, also, Halliday, for whom "a given formal item can be at one and the same time, and in the same sense, an exponent of a unit, a structure, an element of structure, a class, and a term in a system" (1961:265).

Postal fails to sense that tagmemes can be simultaneous, and therefore treats the presence of two as the presence of but one with deletion of the other (1964:42); similarly, he has no place for simultaneous levels of emic structure (1964:13).

11.723 *On Sentences in Relation to Higher-Level Units*

For bibliography on sentences and units higher than sentences, note also §§ 5.63-64.

Bloomfield set the pace for American linguistics when he said that "When a linguistic form occurs as part of a larger form, it is said to be in *included position*; otherwise it is said to be in *absolute position* and to constitute a *sentence*" (1933a:170). Hockett follows up this view by saying that "A *sentence* is a grammatical form which is not in construction with any other grammatical form; a constitute which is not a constituent" (1958:199). By insisting that units have first relevance in reference to occurrence in a higher-layered slot, we reject this definition of sentence. It is precisely for this reason, furthermore, that we are forced to insist that linguistic analysis must take as part of its essential domain the treatment of units larger than the sentence. Without these higher-level units there are not available adequate distributional matrices for determining sentences themselves. A sentence is first of all a unit which occurs in a slot in a higher-level structure — as part of a monologue, or as a total utterance, or as response in an utterance-response structure, etc.

Hierarchical structure does not stop with the sentence, nor begin with it. Rather it must begin with the total language event in a total cultural setting — which, in turn, is in a total physical setting. It is precisely this interlocking on higher and higher levels of integration that forces us to treat language as merely one phase of human behavior, and structurally integrated with it.

On the other hand, since one cannot in fact describe the entire universe in a single sentence, nor analyse it in a short article, it is essential that we slice out from all phenomena available to us some section to treat. For such purposes, the abstracting out of sentences for study is a legitimate and useful procedure. It should be pointed out, however, that this is treating sentences in hypostasis. It is a deliberate distortion introduced in order to handle the data. The distortion is not to be regretted, provided it is recognized and allowances are made for its ultimate effect upon the description. An 'as if' procedure is a useful one, provided one does not forget that it is an abstraction which one is dealing with.

J. R. Firth has repeatedly emphasized the abstract nature of isolates in analysis (see 1958:7-8, 23). In addition, he has emphasized treatment of the abstraction in terms of levels. The "basic assumption of the theory of analysis by levels is that any text can be regarded as a constituent of a *context of situation*" (1958:7) and congruent levels of various grammatical and phonological types (cf. 22, 27, and 1951b:126-28). He suggests a brief listing of (etic) characteristics of linguistic units higher than a sentence (1958:9-10 — which adds some items beyond the list which we gave in

§§ 5.52-53). For special emphasis on sentence types, with their differential characteristics, and for contrastive formulas, note Waterhouse (1962:16).

Note that we reject the assumption of Lees who takes "the central problem of linguistic science to be the study of the formal, or syntactic, properties of sentences" (1960a:1). So, for Chomsky, a grammar is a "device of some sort for producing the sentences of the language under analysis" (1957a:11); a language is considered *"a set... of sentences"* (in Luce and others, 1963:283). For Katz and Fodor grammars "seek to describe the structure of a sentence IN ISOLATION FROM ITS POSSIBLE SETTINGS IN LINGUISTIC DISCOURSE (WRITTEN OR VERBAL) OR IN NONLINGUISTIC CONTEXTS (SOCIAL OR PHYSICAL)" (1963:173). This, too, we reject. For us, the sentence is merely *one* level in a hierarchy which includes *larger* and *smaller* elements. I similarly object to Benveniste's handling of the sentence as the top (in *Preprints...*, 1962:498). We would be closer to Hoenigswald who claims that "Discourses are the true minimal free forms" (1959:410 fn. 5; cf. Leopold where, for the child "syntax comes before morphology" (in Saporta 1961:356). For material larger than sentences note discourse analysis of Z. Harris (1952a, 1952b); with application to an Indian language by Gudschinsky (1959b). For monologue and paragraph structure in a descriptive statement, see Yen (1960); Stennes (1961:9, with function words and stereotyped utterances signalling "the change from one division of the discourse to another"); Loos has narrative sentences comprising elements of narrative paragraphs, in contrast to conversational sentence types of discourse (1963:701-08); paragraphs have markers; change of subject or of tense from sentence to sentence may be marked. Brend shows that requirement of certain elements in independent sentences may — as dependent-derived ones — be met by the occurrence of these elements in remoter verbal context (or even in the nonverbal physical context) (1964:13, 119). Sarles suggests methods for utilizing question-response frames (1963). For "three basic types of sequences" — *"build-ups, break-downs,* and *completions"* in verbal play of a solemnant child see Weir (1962:81-84); for necessity of analysis of discourse beyond the sentence see (101).

For relation of plot (as the meaning of a story analogous to the meaning of a morpheme) to a story, involving relations of tagmemes to nonverbal context, and for flow of situational roles of the plot through grammatical roles of a text, see Pike (1964d). For chains of lexical items in discourse, see Z. Harris (1952a). For folktales with stereotyped structural slots and their fillers — amenable to tagmemic analysis — note Dundes (1962b, 1963); reflecting earlier work of Propp (1958 [1928]). Riddles are treated by Georges and Dundes (1962). Note myths treated as sequences of successive segments but with the sequence type repeated in variant fashion (yielding a display like a sequence of musical cords) in Lévi-Strauss (1955). Note that I would deal with such forms as representing construction types with some tagmemic slots and fillers specified by the system. This implies agreement with Jakobson who states that poetics may be regarded as an integral part of linguistics (1960:350). See above, § 5.63. For a collection of essays on the theme, see Poetics (1961).

It is only in reference to discourse structure, furthermore, that many important characteristics of sentence structure can be adequately handled. Note, especially, the treatment of independent and dependent structures which can be either complete or incomplete (Waterhouse, 1963:46). The crisscrossing of these categories involves discourse relationship, such as occurrence in a unit — as we would propose it — of utterance-plus-response types. Certain omissions are permitted only within special discourse slots; or in relation to the total situation of language in nonverbal context. Note, in this connection, the discussion of Vigotsky (1961 [1928] in Saporta, 1961); he gives extensive discussion of the manner in which understanding between people depends upon the situation — thus, as people see a bus coming for which they have been waiting for a long time, they will say *It is coming*, not *The bus for which we are waiting to go here and there is coming*. The relation of discourse to the external situation, therefore, must be treated in a larger theory in which some unit of situation-speech is involved which is larger than speech itself. (Compare our initial approach to the whole theoretical problem of language and behavior as set forth in Chapter 1); see also, above, reference to Firth and context of situation.

11.724 *On Clause versus Phrase*

Once one has decided to treat the phrase level as an emically-distinct level from that of clause, and then begins to search the literature to see what earlier treatments or anticipations of this approach are present, he may be astonished at the lack of relevant data in places where he would expect it. In American studies this is undoubtedly due to the great influence of Bloomfield, and his treatment (1933a). For him, the word 'clause' remains undefined. In searching his volume I find only scattered usages of the term in reference to particular illustrations, and never as an integral part of his description of units or structure, as such (1933a:192, 197, 204, 251, 263, 273, 407, 437). The clause crept into his description without treatment. It seems to me that this points up as clearly as anything could do the fact that clause was utilized merely as a traditional etic category, rather than a structural emic level.

The phrase, in Bloomfield, is utterly different in treatment from that which we have here, and likewise has affected the American scene heavily. He defines it as a "free form which consists entirely of two or more lesser free forms, as, for instance, *poor John* or *John ran away*, or *yes, sir*" (1933a:178). Note two major differences between his usage and ours: (1) He utilizes the criterion of multiple words, rather than allowing for a phrase consisting of a single word. (It was precisely this starting point which we utilized in §§ 1-10 for hypermorpheme, which we withdraw now that emic levels have been postulated.) (2) Although he treats a multi-word sentence as a phrase, and a multi-word clause as a phrase, a single-word sentence or a single-word clause would not, in his view, be a phrase. Here the obligatory-complexity of the phrase definition makes phrase units cut across clause and sentence, but never lets them be in portmanteau function with a single word. For the phrase as multi-morphemic, see also Jesperson: "A *phrase* is a combination of words which together form a sense unit, though they need not always come into juxtaposition" (1936: vol. 2, sec. 1.87).

Even as late as 1964 the transformationalists have repudiated such emic levels. Bach, for example, in a transformationalist text states that a "comparison with the system described in Chapter 3, for instance, will show that there is no fixed set of 'levels' such as word level, clause level, phrase level, sentence level in the systems of PS rules and P markers" (1964:59).

It is to Longacre, therefore, that we owe emphasis upon the clause as a useful starting point in analysis, and as an unavoidable emic level (see his pedagogical treatment of 1964a, with mineographed edition, 1958a). Longacre provides structural criteria for distinguishing various clause types — obligatory or preferred order of elements, different internal tagmas, or number of tagmas, presence or absence of a tagma, difference in manifesting classes of clauses, or a difference in grammatical transforms. For Longacre, obligatory tagmemes are nuclear (though not all nuclear tagmemes are obligatory). Peripheral tagmemes are less likely to be diagnostic of clause types than are nuclear tagmemes, and are less likely to be affected by transformations. Nuclear tagmemes are often marked by special case endings or particles in some languages (Longacre, 1964a, § 1); they may be centered (with bound subject), noncentered (with free subject) or relator-axis, (with a subordinating conjunction or particle or phrase).

For tagmemic treatments of clause in specific languages note H. Hart (1957), Thomas (1958), Elliott (in *Mayan Studies*, I, 1960), C. D. Ellis (1960), Pickett (1960), Derbyshire (1961b), Law (1962), Clark (1962), Hess (1962), Zvelebil (1962) Peeke (in *Studies in Ecuadorian...*, 1962), Waterhouse (1962), Abrahamson (in *Studies in Ecuadorian...*, 1962), Orr (in *Studies in Ecuadorian...*, 1962), Matteson (1963), Huestis (1963), Eastman (in *Studies in Peruvian...*, 1963), Minor and Loos (in *Studies in Peruvian...*, 1963), Brend (1964). For clause in relation to matrix see Pike (1962a), Larson (in *Studies in Peruvian...*, 1963), Snell and Wise (in *Studies in Peruvian...*, 1963), Engel and Longacre (1963). For a somewhat different treatment of clauses note Stennes (1961); with verbal nucleus, or equational with optional verbal, or clauses with no verbal. For tagmemics and transforms in Old French, see Belasco (1961). Hockett (1958:194-95, 203-07) surveys different clause types for English, giving the observation that a clause is "usually, though not always, a composite form built by a predicative construction". Potter has both subject and predicate in clause definition, and lack of predication in a phrase word-group (1957:105).

It is the setting up of phrase and clause and sentence as emic levels which allows us in appropriate contexts to treat a single word as simultaneously a phrase, clause, and sentence.

Andreyev points out that A. A. Xolodivič breaks phrases into nucleus and environment, with environment as deficient (zero), optimal, or superfluous (1962:190). Compare Pickett (1960:91, with construction as wave, with nucleus and satellite tagmemes), Z. Harris (1962, with structural strings).

Longacre treats phrase as being single-centered (*the great black, shambling, bear*), double-centered (*John and Mary*) or relator-axis (*to the store*); the head element of the phrase may be related to other elements by modification, by overt linkage, or by overt relator; criteria are given for isolating phrase units from the corpus (1964a; § 2).

Numerous treatments of English verb phrase continue to appear. Among them are Hill (1958:191-229), Lambek (1959), Twaddell (1960), Joos (1961; with some tagmemic reference: 38-41), Pittman (1963).

For further analysis of English syntax, note Trager and Smith (1951), Fries (1952), Roberts (1956, 1962, 1964), Francis (1958), Sledd (1959), Chomsky (1957a), Lees (1960a, 1960b), Hill (1958), Hockett (1958), Stockwell (1960b), Nida (1960 [1943]), R. L. Allen (1962, verb phrase), Pittman (1962), Joos (1963, verb), Diver (1963, verb tense), Fillmore (1963, a summary in transformational terms), etc.

For diagramming concord and some other relations between sentence slots of fifteenth-century English, see Reszkiewicz (1962).

For a mathematical approach to phrase structure note Bar-Hillel, Perles and Shamir (1960). Compare, for a calculus of syntactic types, Lambek (1959).

For early chart of phrase structure of Mixtec verbal elements, note Pike (1944). For some tagmemic analyses of phrases see Thomas (1958), Pickett (1960), C. D. Ellis (1960), Guthrie (1961), Derbyshire (1961b), Bendor-Samuel (1961), Hess (1962), Abrahamson (in *Studies in Ecuadorian...*, 1962), Eastman and Eastman (in *Studies in Peruvian...*, 1963), Clark (1962).

11.73 *On Parts of Speech*

The history of the study of parts of speech is a long one. Aristotle talks about the problem in Chapter 20 of his Poetics. Robins has an extensive discussion of the history of the problem (1951:17, 20, 40, 72, 79; see also 1952:291-95). For the semantic view that a "Noun is the name of a person, place, or thing" see Barrett (1860:87). Compare, more recently, House and Harmon (1950:20), or Blake (1931:53), and de Groot (1948:479-80). For a philosopher's view, note Urban (1939:85-6, 150-58), and Sinclair (1951:121, 129-30), both of whom attempted to retain some contact with modern linguistics. For the possibility of classes being set up with a calculus of probablility in which each item is "an instance to some degree or other of a class" with probability rankings in membership, note Kaplan and Schott (1951:168); see also Brown, in Bruner, and others, 1956:266-67). For formal class definition note Bloomfield (1933a:264-72), Harris (1951:243-61; 1952b:212), Nida (1949:107-10), Hockett (1939:235-48; 1958:215-17, 221, 227, 264). Difficulties in determining membership in parts of speech have long been known: Paul (1889:403, 406-07), Jesperson (1940-1949:2). The problem of the universality of parts of speech has come in for considerable discussion: Sapir (1921:126), Whitfield, quoting Magnusson (1955:245), Meredith (1956:11-12), Bull (1949), Sheffield (1912:90).

Fries attempted to avoid the problems raised both by functional definition (1952:

204-05) and by meaning definition. He did this by avoiding traditional labels and using definition of new terms (numbers) by their occurrence in frames. Note that near the end of § 11.43 we treat this difficulty in definition as being due to the fact that the noun — if it be set up at all as a part of speech — is a nondistribution class (a hyperclass of an elaborate type, requiring criteria similar in complexity to the kind which Fries called on to delimit a strike in baseball, 1952:60-61).

The need for setting up hyperclasses occurs in other areas also if we wish to preserve some of the groupings of traditional grammar. One of these, especially, is the PARADIGM, in which nouns of different cases do not occur in the same functional slot; the pulling together of these nondistribution classes of nouns into comparable paradigms is not by distribution of the total word, but rather by a complex of criteria including identity of stem across the paradigm, comparability of kinds of relations between stem and affix, mutual exclusiveness of the stem in this hyperclass with stems in a verb hyperclass, etc. For a different attack on the problem of retaining paradigms, note Voegelin (1959:23, in which a paradigm is a group of items which makes an isosemantic set). For a view otherwise, in which a paradigm of this nondistributional type seems to be disparaged, since "These inter-relations are not between words as such nor are they properly stated by interrelating the exponents", Firth (1957:20).

For matrix treatment of morphological paradigm, emphasizing submorphemic components and patterns, see Pike (1963d), Pike and Erickson (1964), and Pike and Becker (1964).

For a type of syntactic paradigm (growing out of tagmeme theory) in which the listing of forms includes just one member from each kind of construction (rather than an exhaustive listing of all members of one type of construction class), see Pike (1963b, 1963d). A transformation paradigm based on clause roots is seen in Thomas (1964).

In reference to co-occurrence classes of government, concord, agreement, or other tie, much work has been done. Note Bloomfield (1933a:165, 190-94), and Fries (1952:144-48, 176, 214). Hockett attempts to treat the relevance of such co-occurrence classes as due to "deep-level relationships", in contrast with "surface grammar" which deals with obvious class relations (1958:250-51). For co-occurrence in reference to transformation, see Z. Harris (1957). For singular versus plural concord sequences treated as leading to alloconstructions, see Pike (1962a).

General discussion of word classes may be found in Honey (1956, for Vietnamese); F. K. Chao (in *Preprints...*, 1962:15, for classical Chinese); H. Hart (1957, for emic subclasses); Chomsky (1961b:239 fn. 36, impossible to define word classes by inflection); Sledd (1955, in H. B. Allen, 1958:89, with protest at Fries' system where "*Wednesday* is in Class 1 in *The abstract came Wednesday*, but *Thursday* is Class 4 in *The service is Thursday*"); Lees (1960a:22-23, with subclasses of noun and verb); F. R. Palmer (1958); Robins (1952, in reference to universal grammar); Waterhouse (1962:87-88, with noun structure table); Norman (1958). See also above, §§ 7.81, 11.43; Pittman (1959:200, with word roots rather than words as starting points for describing syntax); Quine (1960:113-14, for pronouns being supplanted only by definite singular terms — rather than standing for the grammatical antecedents which may be indefinite singular); Gleason (1961:202, with a mixture of class notation and tagmemic notation in items such as adjective-subject-verb as in *Good boys behave*); Lamb (1962:4, with "only three primitive relationships" relevant to linguistic units, one of which is that of a class to its members); and (1962:9, 12, with basic representational rule such as $X || env_1/Y$, meaning that X in a stated environment " is represented (on the next lower stratum) by Y", as an allo of class manifestation by the subrule indicated); C. Smith (1961, with construction rules for generating adjectives, or complex modifiers by transforms); Jesperson (1933:308-13, for problems in traditional definitions of word classes). Note also Kulagina, summarized by Andreyev (1962: 186-87, with a set-theoretic scheme in which the construction is the "family" of the word form, and the paradigm is its "neighborhood" — and families group into types "somewhat similar to the parts of speech").

11.74 *On Tagmemes née Gramemes*

In our earlier material we utilized the term grameme — or grammeme (1954, 1955, and others). The term grew up as a neologism intended to imply 'unit of grammar.' The term was abandoned and replaced by Bloomfield's term 'tagmeme' because of objections raised, on etymological grounds, by other linguists. The theory as such is unaffected by the change. The principle difficulty is the danger of confusion with Bloomfield's use of the term tagmeme which we borrow. For discussion of the difference see Pike (1958a); note also discussion in § 7.87.

Bloomfield lacked a clear concept of a slot-plus-class correlation as an essential characteristic of tagmemic form. Rather, for him, the tagmeme was a label applied to *any grammatical characteristic* provided it were meaningful. For him the tagmeme was a *component* of grammar rather than the kind of segmental unit which we set forth here. Thus the term *duchess!* for Bloomfield contained the three tagmemes (as well as taxemes) of selection, order or arrangement, and exclamatory final pitch (for summary and page references, see Pike, 1943b:68-69). For us, however, the 'selection' of a form would be rephrased as the manifestation of a tagmeme by an emic class of forms which in turn is manifested by one particular manifesting morpheme or morpheme sequence; order would be found as a distributional characteristic of one or more tagmemes (or hypertagmemes) within the slots of a hypermorpheme structure; exclamatory final pitch might be a contrastive feature of a hypermorpheme class or of some tagmeme associated with it. No one of these grammatical components by itself would be a tagmeme in our usage.

Another source of confusion in reading tagmemic material of our type must be watched carefully. For us, a detailed tagmemic formula usually symbolizes and always implies *both* the emic slot and the emic class at each point in the structure.

Occasionally, however, a person may utilize the meaning of a slot as the source of an abbreviated symbol for the tagmeme as a whole; or one may use the symbol of the manifesting class as the symbol for the tagmeme as a whole. When either of these choices is made, a tagmemic formula may look more like a traditional formula than the analysis itself warrants.

Thus in schematic form an extremely simple tagmemic formula might be $S^N\ P^V\ O^N$ which is to be read as: a structure containing three tagmemes of which the first and third contain Nouns as a manifesting class, with the second manifested by the Verb class, while the functional tagmemic slots are respectively Subject, Predicate, and Object.

Occasionally, for simplicity's sake, the fillers may be lowered to the line following a colon, as S:N P:V O:N (following Waterhouse, 1962 [1958], based on a suggestion by Paper). Or the formula may even be abbreviated to SPO. In the latter instance however, if it is intended as a tagmemic formula the fillers are always indirectly implied. Longacre is encouraging this type of symbolization in his formulas for ready perception of the total structure. Yet this abbreviated symbolization should not be confused with an essentially-semantic analysis, without formal content, which could be shown also as subject, predicate, object, but in which the rigid formal requirements of the manifesting classes in an emic structure are not in view.

A tagmemic formula continues to imply classes, inter-relationships, and total formal system, even though semantic labels may be used for convenience. It should be seen that the first slot-plus-class formula above could be replaced by a formula such as $I^A\ II^B\ III^A$, and the second by I II III. The semantic nature of the labels is a mnemonic device, not essential in any respect to the *presentation* of the system as a formal structure.

The semantic labels are, however, of high value when one is presenting the system as a part of a pedagogical device to teach people to speak the language. Just as a lexicon must be provided the learner in order that he may have the meanings of the words which he wishes to use, if he is to use them at all, so the meanings of the tagmemes must be presented to the learner if he wishes to use them for communication. This pedagogical or communication requirement, however, does not as such affect the presentation of the materials as a quasimathematical structure when one so desires.

Yet the tagmemic formula with slot-plus-class requirement must be kept distinct from a structural formula of the type used by Z. Harris (see, for example, 1946:180) where the basic structural content is principally that of classes in sequence — symbolized as N V N, for example. Similarly, the advance in Fries' grammar in English was built by exploiting the view that "*An English sentence then is not a group of words as words but rather a structure made up of form-classes of parts of speech. ... Our description ... will ... be in terms of the selection of these large form classes or parts of speech and the formal arrangements in which they occur*" (1952:64).

It is here, also, that there is one of the crucial differences between the hierarchical grammar of a tagmemic type and the grammar proposed by way of the transforms of

Harris or Chomsky. The tagmemic approach insists on grammatical structures as made up of *formal segmental units* which are other than and beyond mere classes of words or sequences of classes. Tagmemics insists upon a formal segmental unit which is a grammatical one, a unit of which the manifesting class is just one component whereas function is another.

11.75 *On Discovery versus Presentation*

Much of the linguistic literature of the past has concentrated on discovery procedures, or has treated linguistic theory as if techniques for discovery of units within a language were somehow immediately relevant to the techniques for presenting this data in a systematic fashion — or else the difference between discovery and presentation has not been kept in focus. It has only been on rare occasions that this approach has been seen to cause difficulty. (See, for example, my suggestion 1952a:118, that some of the differences in approach between Bloch and me were due to lack of sharp delineation here.)

Chomsky and Lees have forced into sharper focus the necessity of keeping the two apart in our thinking. Chomsky, for example, has "disclaimed any intention of finding a practical discovery procedure for grammars" (1957a:56, and 59 where "we renounce this goal") and would treat earlier methodology as the much more trivial matter of providing "a manual of suggestive and helpful procedures" or of arriving "at a grammar by intuition, guess-work, all sorts of practical methodological hints, reliance on past experience, etc." (1957a:56). The emphasis on rejection here is specifically rejection of the possibility of *mechanical* ways to arrive at units (57). Lees strongly emphasizes this view (1957:378-79). And, Lees points out, Chomsky is seeking rather for an evaluation procedure, "a mechanical way to evaluate two proposed grammars on the basis of explicit criteria of excellence and reject one as inferior to the other" (380), so that "It would then no longer be the responsibility of the grammarian to state rigorously HOW he managed to find the particular grammar proposed. Any manipulatory or heuristic principles or devices which he may have found useful or stimulating play no role within the theory itself, once it is constructed" (380). Lees points out a number of ways in which this view affects previous work in linguistics — affecting the concept of grammatical levels, for example, (381).

It should be noted that this view differs from the underlying approach of Bloomfield stated explicitly for historical matters and implied for his descriptive approach: "The following assumptions and definitions for historical linguistics are added for the sake of completeness. Insofar as they are correctly formulated, they will merely restate the working method of the great majority of linguists" (1926:162). That is, basic postulates are closely correlated with working procedures. I assimilated as part of my own working assumptions Bloomfield's view.

I feel that theory of language structure should not lose sight of the fact, furthermore, that we are interested in language as communication — not as design, only. Our presentation formulas, therefore, should be considered elegant not solely when they meet the test of efficient description of design, but also when they best lead to a structural presentation efficient for learning to speak. I shall attempt, however, to keep investigation and analysis, versus presentation, labelled as such throughout the succeeding chapters.

I continue to retain strong interest in the methodology of grammatical analysis. The tagmemic approach, growing out of the desire to develop analytical techniques, has indeed proved fruitful in this regard. It is now easier to see, however, why certain of the characteristics of tagmemics were presented as they were in 1954. The recognition of proportion, reference to structural meaning, and recognition of lexical meaning or purpose, were all referred to in § 7.322 as "activities of the analyst" which were "INTUITIVE STEPS (or ANALYTICAL LEAPS)" such that by them "the analyst sets up his ETIC HYPOTHESES for testing, and in relation to them any emic analysis of human behavior must ultimately be in part initiated." It turns out that there is no clash here with Lees and Chomsky. They deny the possibility of a mechanical discovery procedure. I affirm the necessity of certain intuitive components in an analytical procedure. I now merely add that it is the necessity of these — or other — intuitive components which make a mechanical discovery procedure impossible.

I indicated in § 11.74 that in *presentation* of a grammatical structure, tagmemes do not have to be represented by semantic symbols. Numbers, letters, or algebraic formulas can replace every contrastive feature of a tagmeme, such as emic slot and emic filler class, or may symbolize directly the tagmeme as whole. Once this is done, it is then clear that in the presentation of the system as a whole no semantic component need obtrude itself. The tagmemic grammar would then be available for evaluation in terms of its formal characteristics, alongside of any other type of grammar description available. Tagmemic analytical methodology requires reference to meaning, and requires certain intuitive judgments and hypotheses. Tagmemic presentation, on the other hand, requires none of this.

This is not to say, however, that we ourselves prefer a tagmemic symbolism which is devoid of all reference to structural meaning or the like. The burden on the memory imposed by a symbolism which has no reference to tagmemic function such as subject, object, head of a construction, modifier, or time relation, etc., is exceedingly great. Any one who has read morphologies prepared with a morphological index of the Voegelin type, labelled by numbers (see Wonderly, 1951-52, Cox, 1957) knows quite well that from the mechanical numbering he gets the big advantage of succinctness of reference, but a very heavy memory burden indeed. (Even the author himself of one such monograph told me that after a couple of years he could not recall his own symbol references, but had to check them.) How much greater would be this difficulty if extended to the entire grammar. Thus it seems unlikely that for pedagogical grammars, or for grammars designed to be read by other linguists, we can afford to dispense with semantic labels in favor of purely algebraic symbols. For machine translation, or the like, on the other hand, formal symbolization of tagmemic units would seem to be called for.

Nor is it clear to me that the goal of a *mechanical evaluation* procedure (see quote above, from Lees, 1957:380) has ultimately any greater hope of success than does the dream of a mechanical discovery procedure. Are we to assume that all matters of esthetics can be eliminated from evalutation? Are we to assume that no elements of simplicity, or of value, or of purpose are unrelated to intuition of form, or of purpose, value, usefulness, beauty, and elegance? A non-unique mechanical evaluation procedure would be possible only if there were prior agreement on nonmechanical esthetic matters. On would have to decide which criteria would enter into the value judgments underlying the particular procedure — criteria which are far from being mechanically evaluatable — elegance of description, beauty of presentation, perspecuity of format, priority of competing but conflicting patterns (should priority be given to simplicity of inventory or simplicity of rule, to simplicity on high grammar levels or on low grammar levels, etc.). A counting of symbols, for example, cannot automatically determine evaluation. One would first have to use nonmechanical devices to determine what symbols were worth counting, the circumstances under which symbol complexes could be replaced by unitary symbols, and so on. Evaluation itself must first be evaluated in reference to some purpose of usefulness, insight, or beauty.

Already, however, it is clear that transformational grammars are non-unique; Schachter, for example, poses numerous alternative approaches to English transformations (in *Preprints...*, 1962).

For evidence of the mechanical hope lying behind the evaluation procedure, however, note Halle: "The theory of generative grammar postulates, moreover, a *mechanical* [italics mine] procedure by means of which preferred descriptions are chosen from among several alternatives", and "The basis of this choice ... is termed *simplicity*" (1962a:55). Contrast Andreyev who insists that we "cannot put the links between words, notions, and reality-objects into a machine"; thus "quasi formal" versus "really formal" approaches (with and without a man involved) both "have their advantages and consequently, their legitimate rights to existence" (1962:196-97). Note also Garvin who insists that "a purely distributional analysis will not account for all intuitively observable syntactic relations" but "will have to be coupled with the use of a form-meaning technique" (1962a:120). A related hope of a mechanical procedure underlies the transformationalist recognition procedures — one which "AUTOMATICALLY assigns to each sentence a correct structural description" (Postal, 1964:3, 15).

Eventually, also, it seems intuitively clear to me that the dream of mechanical *generation* of all and only the well-formed linguistic units is hopeless — if one believes as I do that elements beyond the sentence (epics, sonnets) also have claim to the status of being linguistic units. Not only are poems intricate beyond our dreams, in structural interrelations, but in addition they deliberately exploit departures from (otherwise) well-formedness. Mechanical generation and recognition of *beautiful* departure from the rules seems to require a nonmechanical element.

As for discovery of the relation of speech to speaker, Chomsky claims that generative grammars "take a completely neutral point of view" and only erroneously have attributed to them the assumption that "sentence-generating grammars consider language from the point of view of the speaker rather than the hearer" (1959b:137-38 fn. 1). Assuming for the moment that I accept his judgment of what generative grammar has been doing yet it seems to me that there is no possible mechanical way by which an evaluation procedure can determine that a presentation *ought* to be neutral as to speaker or hearer. Nor do I find transformationalists consistent in this claim. Lees, for example, states for transformationalists: "Our belief that speakers, both in producing and in understanding sentences, make use of the 'generation' of sentences by the grammar of their language" (1959:1). (Compare Hockett, speaking not as transformationalist, for whom grammatical description "is an operational parallel to part of the speaker's internal apparatus" 1954a:218.) More recently, Chomsky has specified that a "generative grammar" is "a partial theory of what the mature speaker of the language knows", not at all "a description of his actual performance" (in Luce and others, 1963:326); his competence (328); compare Bach (1964:64). In the same volume, however, Miller and Chomsky attempt a few speculations concerning "models for the *user*" — i.e., "talker and listener" (in Luce and others, 1963:422, 465-67).

11.76 *On Transform Grammar and Tagmemics*

Recent developments of transform grammar by Z. Harris (1952a, 1954b, 1957, 1959) and Chomsky (1957a, 1961b, 1962) and others, lead to many fruitful points of contact with the tagmemic approach. For annotated bibliography of transformation materials see Boyd and King (1963). For discussion of the differences between the Harris approach with transformational analysis as decompositional, versus the Chomsky approach with transform grammar as generative, note discussion by Fries (1962:88-90). For Chomsky's discussion of his relation to Harris, see Chomsky (in Third Texas Conference; 1962:124-29); for Harris' comment on Chomsky's contribution, note Z. Harris (1957:283, fn. 1). For Harris' early statement that "A grammar may be viewed as a set of instructions which generates the sentences of a language" see 1954b:260.

On generativeness (mathematical) versus productivity (actual possibilities with finite memory) note Yngve (1960:450); a well behaved grammar should generate only sentences which can actually be produced. Compare Lamb on recognition or decoding grammar versus generative grammar (1962:28), and Gleason (1961:204).

Numerous references have already been given above to transform grammar. Note, amongst others, references concerning the nature of facts of language, § 2.73; nonsemantic pair test, § 2.73; linguistic universals, § 2.74; rules versus unit, § 3.63; sentence as basic, § 5.63; nonsemantic grammar, § 5.64; segmentation problems, § 6.93; nodes versus names, § 7.8; intuition, § 7.88; rejection of conventional phonemics, § 8.814; descriptive adequacy in relation to psychological reality, § 8.815; stress and grammar, § 8.87; hierarchy, § 9.71, 11.71; kernel of a grammatical system, § 11.6. See also below for early sources of transformation, § 11.761; intuition, § 11.763; process, § 11.764; derivational history, § 11.765; levels, § 11.71, 11.72; discovery procedure, § 11.75.

For transformationalist rejection of a tagmemic approach, see discussion by Postal (1964:33-51), based, however, on only a few of the tagmemic concepts in the introductory text of Elson and Pickett (so, similarly, Bach, 1964:41-44). Postal feels that the tagmemic approach lacks precision (a telling point in view of the very great contribution of transformational grammar — perhaps its greatest contribution — to precision of statement and hence testability of statement; see, however, fn. to § 12.1) and that the relation of slot to class merely leads to redundancy of nodes in an implicit tree diagram (and compare Chomsky, in Luce and others, 1963:329). Postal and Bach imply that a rewrite of a tagmeme slot and class symbol such as X:a as X → a preserves the material of X in a; this is false from the tagmemic viewpoint, since the function of a tagmeme is implicit in the symbol X but not in the symbol a (since Subject: *John* written as Subject → *John* loses the symbolization of subject function of *John* which elsewhere could be object, and so on; their formalism misinterprets us here). Postal feels that tagmemics is but one variety of phrase structure grammar, each of which — in his view — assigns wrong analyses to coordinate constructions, fails to handle deletions, does not meet requirements of simplicity, does not account adequately for the speaker's understanding of grammatical relations or of relations between sentences, does not adequately handle sentence types, or provide simplest correct analyses of sentences, nor handle elegantly various overlapping selectional or concord restrictions (72-74); compare Lees' list (1963:551:52). Many of these problems are discussed explicitly by Longacre from the tagmemic viewpoint (1964a), others have received brief mention within the analyses of specific data in articles not examined by Postal (e.g., for concord, or for relations between sentences, see Pike, 1962a).

On the other hand, a tagmemic view would feel that a rigid transformationalist approach does not give adequate theoretical attention to the nature of units in general (contrast, variation, distribution); to emic levels such as clause; to patterning by way of field theory (vectors of a matrix — experience of pattern is not *merely* perception of a rule); the necessity for more persistent attention to the correlation of form with meaning in a unit of grammar (a tagmeme); to etic versus emic elements of units or levels; to the structure of units beyond the sentence; to partially-independent but partially-overlapping hierarchies of lexicon, of phonology, and of grammar, in reference to particle, wave, and field; to the relation of verbal to nonverbal structure. For a different defense of phrase structure, through a critique of Chomsky's defined restrictions imposed upon such a structure, see Harman (1963); note that (as in tagmemics) lexical rules "are not considered part of the syntactical rules" (610) — but tagmemics at the moment leaves an indeterminate boundary between grammatical versus lexical co-occurrence.

My feeling that tagmemics and transformationalism should ultimately merge in the main stream of linguistics is denied by Postal (1964:51) on theoretical grounds.

11.761 *On Sources of Transformational Grammar*

Transform grammar grows out of earlier approaches to language and logic. Note, for example, Morris: "Logical syntax deliberately neglects what has here been called the semantical and pragmatical dimensions of semiosis to concentrate upon the logico-grammatical structure of language, i.e., upon the syntactical dimensions of semiosis. In this type of consideration a 'language' (i.e., L_{syn}) becomes any set of things related in accordance with two classes of rules: *formation rules*, which determine permissible independent combinations of members of the set (such combinations being called sentences), and *transformation rules*, which determine the sentences which can be obtained from other sentences" (1938:14).

Z. Harris developed the use of transforms in an attempt to analyze language units longer than the sentence (1952a). By transforming certain kinds of sentences into simpler types, he was able to see more clearly certain characteristics of the structure of a text. Harris' treatment of transforms in reference to co-occurrence of members of word classes or of other elements is found later (1957). For an application of Harris' transforms to a total grammar structure, see Gudschinsky (1959a) and for the application to discourse analysis for the same language note Gudschinsky (1959b).

Chomsky, working with Harris' materials in the early stages of their development (see Harris, 1957:283n.) seems to have added to the approach a basic emphasis upon evaluation procedures and generativeness as over against investigation procedure (1957:51, 54-57, and see above, § 11.75). The term generative is attributed by Chomsky (1957a:7 fn. 3) to Post (1944). Misra feels that Panini, some twenty-five hundred years ago, utilized generative rules (in *Preprints...*, 1962). Some students find the easiest introduction to generative transformations through Gleason (1961).

Chomsky, in dealing with formal presentation of transformations or in dealing with evaluation of grammar, concludes "that grammar is autonomous and independent of meaning" (1957a:17); he considers his approach to be "completely formal and non-semantic" (93). In contrast with this, Harris, who had been especially interested in investigation procedures, had felt that "The consideration of meaning mentioned above is relevant because some major element of meaning seems to be held constant under transformation... But aside from such differences, transforms seem to hold invariant what might be interpreted as the information content" (1957:290) — though this semantic relation is not "merely because the same morphemes are involved" inasmuch as *The man bit the dog* and *The dog bit the man* contain the same morphemes but describe "quite a different situation". (Note my comment on this semantic characteristic as constituting a crucial difference between his former work on word classes and his current work with transforms, Pike, 1959.) More recently, however, Harris seems to put less stress upon the meaning involved (1959:28).

11.762 *On Some Problems in Description*

In transform grammar one sometimes has successively inclusive class symbols (carried over from Harris, 1946). Both tagmemic grammar and transform grammar insist however that an attempt to describe grammatical structure in terms of morpheme classes alone — even successively inclusive classes of classes — is insufficient. Tagmemics, however, does it by insisting on the necessity of both emic slot and emic class as being relevant to grammatical structure (Pike, 1945, §§ 7.1, 7.31, 7.32; 1958a:276). In this latter we state that an analysis of sentence structures solely in terms of sequences of word classes such as N V N is rejected, and one such as $S^N P^V O^N$ — with both slot and filler explicit or implicit, see § 11.74 — is essential.

Chomsky, on his part, gives very strong evidence that a phrase structure description couched in terms of linear sequences of word classes cannot conveniently handle some problems of grammatical design — e.g., sentences made up of two sentences plus conjunction, certain discontinuous contructions, certain components of verbal phrases (items like *have...en*), and certain restrictions of subject in relation to object in sentences like *John admires sincerity* but not *sincerity admires John* (1957a:36-44). (From Lees we seem to get the caution that it might be ultimately possible to handle some of these problems in a phrase structure grammar, though the price of doing so might be much greater complexity: "There is as yet, however, no rigorous proof that a phrase-structure grammar of a natural language is inherently impossible", 1957:402.)

Note also Chomsky's important insistence on the necessity of language as being able to handle embedding or nesting of structures (1957a:21-22, 1962; § 2.2, 520). For tagmemic handling of these matters, note Longacre, who points out specific formula types through which tagmemics handles "infinite branching, infinite nesting and coordinate constructions, admitting formation of an infinite series" (1964a, fn. 20). One — but not all — of the theorems of Bar-Hillel and Shamir to show that "English is not adequately representable" by a finite state grammar depends on the acceptance, as an English sentence, of utterances such as "*If it rains then it pours then if it rains then it pours*"; but, they add, "Most linguists as well as most ordinary speakers of English — in contradistinction to most logicians" would not regard such a string as an English sentence (1960:162-63).

Problems of concord or government or agreement of referent have also been difficult or awkward whether handled by rewrite rule at various depths (note, for example, Chomsky, 1957a:29 fn. 3; Postal, 1964:46); or by superscript or subscript (Bach,

1962:264-65; Fries, 1952:189); see tagmemic treatment in terms of conditioned alloconstructions (Pike, 1962a:237).

Andreyev lists "initial data" which are "necessary for the operation of Chomsky's transformational model", including words classified grammatically, selection of kernel sentences, lists of elementary transformations, and latitude of applicability of each transformation (1962:190).

Tagmemic grammar and transform grammar also agree that the treatment of ambiguity in recent approaches to grammatical study is inadequate. Both tagmemic and transform grammar require that English be analyzed in reference to a much finer grid than is possible with a few parts of speech, if ambiguities are to be taken care of.

Transform grammar separates ambiguous sentences "by providing two or more different automatic derivations for them"; "Thus, *He bought stock for me* can be understood in one of two ways: either it means *He bought stock; the stock was for me*, or it means *He bought stock; he did it for me*", and the two have different transforms (Lees, 1957:383). See also Chomsky (1957a:86-90); 1962: § 2.2, 520, § 4.1, 530. Tagmemics has analyzed such ambiguous sentences as different sequences of tagmemes (Pike, 1954, § 7.6[2], § 7.43). Tagmemics utilizes various types of expansions and of transforms — though not under the latter label — to test for such differences (§§ 7.322, 7.6[2], 7.321). Transform grammar, however, should enable us to make some of these tests more rigorous. Bar-Hillel and Shamir point out that "Chomsky... does not seem to have been aware" of the ability of a finite state grammar "to discriminate homonymities by constructional methods" (1960:161). For ambiguity in Tagalog transforms, note Schachter (1961b). One difference of usage should be noted here, however. Whereas Chomsky treats the sentence as that which is written with a "fixed phonetic alphabet" (1961a:7), I would refer to the ambiguous element as an utterance, representing two distinct but ambiguous sentences. From this point of view Chomsky is interested in generating utterances, whereas I am interested in generating structured sentences. Just as I would not treat two homophonous words in a pun as being the same word, so I would not treat two homophonous utterances as being the same sentences. For types of ambiguity, see Weismann (in Flew, 1953 [1951]).

11.763 *On Intuition and Meaning*

In §§ 7.322, 11.75, 8.815 we indicated that tagmemics utilizes intuitive reaction to structure as data to be exploited by a practical analytical methodology. Transform grammar expresses this somewhat differently: "It is undeniable that 'intuition about linguistic form' is very useful to the investigator of linguistic form (i.e., grammar). It is also quite clear that the major goal of grammatical theory is to replace this obscure reliance on intuition by some rigorous and objective approach" (Chomsky, 1957a:94, see also 84). Lees goes even further: "It is precisely this Sprachgefühl, this intuitive notion about linguistic structure, which, together with the sentences of a language, forms the empirical basis of grammatical analysis; and it is precisely the purpose of linguistic science to render explicit and rigorous whatever is vague about these intuitive feelings" (1957:399n.). Compare also Lees, for whom the empirical data include "various kinds of judgment they [the native speakers] can make and feelings they may have about linguistic data" (in reference to judgments of rhyme, grammatically-permitted sentences, etc.), as over against the intuition of the linguist qua scientist about the data (1957:376, and 392-93).

See, now, Chomsky's more sweeping statement that "data of this sort [i.e., of introspective judgments as to a difference between sentence types] are simply what constitute the subject matter for linguistic theory" and "We neglect such data at the cost of destroying the subject'" (1962, § 3, 526). For implication concerning phonemics, see § 8.815. See also, Chomsky with the "major goal of grammatical theory is to replace this obscure reliance on intuition by some rigorous and objective approach" (1957a:94; and see idem in Luce and others, 1963:329, with intuition as knowledge; cf. also 293). Compare Miller and Chomsky on the "psychological reality of transformational grammars" (in Luce and others, 1963:482-83); Postal feels that deleted elements are nevertheless "ACTUALLY PRESENT" (1964:73); but Uhlenbeck is inclined "to doubt its psycho-linguistic validity" (1963:10).

Chomsky assumes his theory to be "completely formal and non-semantic" (1957a: 93, 99, 94, 100, 103, 107), "with the study of grammatical structure ... quite independent of meaning" (1961b:232). Perhaps this belief — a hyperbole in my opinion — is due to an assumption that people who do utilize meaning operate on the assumption that meaning can be handled without reference to grammar: "It seems evident that perception of grammatical relations in a sentence does not depend on a prior and independent identification of semantic properties, and that the study of grammatical structure seems to be, in fact, quite independent of meaning" (Chomsky, 1961b:232), and "a reasonable perceptual model would have the property that grammatical structure is identified independently of any semantic consideration" and the alternative claim "must be that there are semantic absolutes, identifiable in noises independently of the grammatical structure (in particular, the lexical items) assigned to them" (Chomsky, 1961b:232, fn. 25). It is this last belief of Chomsky's about the supposed alternative that I reject. Compare Uhlenbeck, who affirms that "every single sentence ... has to be interpreted by the hearer with the help of extra-linguistic data" (1963:11-12, 17); and that failure to sense this will lead transformational grammar to "hundreds of rules" for "pseudo-restrictions" and hence the approach will "turn out to have been a blind alley" (18).

In tagmemics, on the contrary, we insist that neither the grammar *nor* the meaning can be identified independently of the other; and that neither exists independently of the other. Rather, in tagmemic terms, the empirical basis of grammatical analysis is a *composite* of structured meaning and structured form.

(See §§ 6.46, 2.2, 5.64, 6.91, 7.83, 9.72). Our insistence on a form-meaning composite is best paralleled, insofar as transform analysis is concerned, by the work of Worth.

He states that "Two phrases which are transforms of each other are correlated in meaning as well as in form" (1958:258). And "One cannot of course have recourse to meaning alone, but a sharp difference in meaning may well be the clue to an equally sharp, if not equally obvious, difference in form" (259n.). In addition, "Perhaps the major flaw in the traditional approach, however, has lain in the fact that it has divorced meaning from form, and in so doing has departed from the realm of the demonstrable fact to enter that of the unprovable assertion." So that in this study "all the class labels and semantic interpretations ... are firmly grounded in demonstrable formal features" (287) and a "distinctive feature of transform potential" "is inherent in the sub-type and is as much a formal characteristic thereof as, say, the fact of belonging to a particular set of correlated morphemes is characteristic of membership in a certain word class" (289).

Tagmemics is set up as part of a theory of the structure of behavior, not merely as a formal algebraic system. For this reason also — in addition to our attention to analytical methodology and to the nature of the form-meaning composite — it refers to meaning more extensively than does transform grammar. Chomsky observes that when he some day extends his studies to cover such matters, then, too, semantic considerations will enter. Note, for example, his reference to a "metatheory that deals with grammar and semantics and their points of connection" and that "To understand a sentence we must know much more than the analysis of the sentence on each linguistic level" but "We must also know the reference and meaning of the morphemes and words of which it is composed; naturally, grammar cannot be expected to be of much help here" (1957a:102 and 103-04).

In the tagmemic approach we would point out that, to Chomsky's acknowledged use of the meanings of morphemes and of words to understand a sentence, we must also add the meanings of the tagmemes. We consider it inadequate to assume that intuition of linguistic form divorced from a larger theory of semantics is a sufficient explanation of tagmemic meaning.

Note that Lackowski says that "if we attempt to formulate our observations in strictly grammatical terms there is no possibility of success, for the tools used by the grammarian are hopelessly inadequate to do the job of answering these questions" — questions concerning metaphor, mentioned words, and foreign words (1963:215, 213); statistical statements must be included to help handle these same problems (215), or as the mention of the word *if*, or citations from a foreign language.

For important handling of recurrent elements in transformation, in terms of a "battery" of related sentences, note Hiż (in *Structure of Language...*, 1961), and Thomas (1964).

11.764 *On Transformation as Process*

One other difference, of a major type, may be indicated between tagmemics and transform grammar. It can be seen best by way of an analogy with problems earlier treated in linguistic theory. With Sapir, and others, morphological analysis was treated frequently in terms of items and processes — in terms of base forms which were modified by some process of affixation, phonological change, or the like. Especially with the work of Harris, the approach through item and process was largely replaced for a decade by attention to items and their arrangements (see, especially, Harris' introduction of this view in 1944a:204, in which "we no longer talk about process and change or the priority of the base"). Thus treatment of the distribution of allomorphs without reference to basic forms became popular. Transform grammar is essentially a view of grammar in reference to item and process. Thus a kernel grammar is treated as a set of basic forms which are modified by certain rules to lead to derivative types of constructions. For further suggestions that a transformation "is a statement of the structural relation of a pair of constructions which treats that relation as though it were a process", see Gleason (1961:172, 215); similarly, Lamb (1962:19). Compare Bach, for whom process statements are "usually implicit transformations" (1964: 104).

Tagmemics, on the other hand, developed as an item-and-arrangement type of approach. Tagmemes were postulated as being segmental units of grammar. The distribution of the units in reference to each other and to the larger including structures made up an item-and-arrangement grammar. (But my morphological work consistently retained process statements whenever they appeared to be useful; note, especially, perturbation types of tone rules, in Pike, 1948.)

In order to show process relations between statement types, our newer tagmemic materials are choosing to set up basic matrices first (showing constructions as intersects between various categorical components). Once basic matrix types have been set up, transformations are first shown directly from matrix to matrix, as multiplication of matrices (Pike, 1962a:226-29). Tagmeme formulas are then provided in detail — or by rule, or by summarizing symbols (Pike, 1964c:90) — for the constructions implied by the cells of the derived matrices. From these formulas, in conjunction with a phonological description and a dictionary, generation (Longacre, 1964a) of specific sentences can be achieved. Perhaps some points of contact with our transformations across matrices would be found in the work of Lekomcev, reported by Andreyev, "with three additional kinds of transformations" which are "transplantation from one paradigmatic class to another, transference from one syntagmatic scheme to another, and the cycle of expanding an element into a string of elements" (1962:191).

Any grammar can in principle be stated *either* in terms of item and process or in terms of item and arrangement. (For further discussion of these two approaches, and references to some of the earlier literature, note § 14.51.)

Any item-process approach inherits both the strengths and weaknesses of that approach. As one strength it may gain in compactness in handling some data. As a weakness it may be accused of pseudo-historical statements (§ 11.765). For process as "this pitfall of reification", see Voegelin and Voegelin (1963:18; they prefer "typology" as "approaching the ultimate subtlety — the nature of language", 19).

11.765 *On Derivational History and Tagmeme Units*
Chomsky implies that the history of a derivation must be known before the transform can be treated or the structure identified (that is, "we must know not only the actual form of S_1 and S_2 but also their constituent structure — we must know not only the final shape of these sentences, but also their 'history of derivation'" 1957a:37; cf. 40, also 92; so also Lees, 1957:392).

Statements of this type easily become related to implications of behavior — that the speaker or hearer 'first' acts thusly and 'then' modifies that behavior to produce the observed result. Such implications seem to be the source of Carroll's uneasiness: "There is also no behavioral reason why a child, for example, could not learn an interrogative structure before he learns a declarative structure; therefore, one would be surprised to confirm Lees' expectation that the order in which a child learns constructions corresponds to the logical taxis of transformations" (1959a:43). Similarly, although Carroll assumes that transform grammar "seems to imply that in the composition of any utterance, the basic building blocks are the kernel sentences and that the speaker seeks out appropriate kernel sentences and combines and 'transforms' them to suit the total linguistic and socio-psychological situation", Carroll feels that "before the speaker chooses any kernel sentence, he is more likely to 'choose' whether he is going to respond with a *generic mand* or a *generic tact*" (e.g., a command statement versus a declarative statement, 1959a:42-43). Lees feels (1959) that he has answered this objection, but I do not find his reply convincing.

Note, more recently, Chomsky's tie of transform grammar to language learning with these concepts as "the set of tools used by the learner in constructing an internal representation of his language (i.e., a generative grammar) on the basis of presented linguistic data" (1962: § 2.2, 518).

Not only is Carroll's comment well taken about the learner, but a further structural difficulty emerges. If a transformation rule is to be applied to a sentence which itself is the result of a generative process, the results should turn out to be a structure comprising the initial tree plus a transformation. But this leads to difficulties — since a *direct* analysis of tagmemic function can be made of elements in the transformed string. It is by no means necessary to go through the transformation in order to find, for example, that there is some structure in *John and Bill went home*, or in *John was seen by Bill*. Nor must one go through derivation and transformation in order to analyze something of the structure of *Did John and Bill go home?* If it is possible to move directly into the analysis of the question construction with its tagmemic components, why should one accept the implication that the *only* structure in the query is an underlying structure plus transformation? A tagmemic view of these problems would insist that there is a tagmemic structure present both in a basic sentence, and also in a derived sentence. Even when transform relations can be shown between two sentences, one has not eliminated the possibility for setting up the internal structures of the two. If one attempts to avoid these difficulties by setting up derived trees (derived P-markers) as defining structure-after-transformation (compare Chomsky, 1961a:19-23), and if units are granted as present in the primitive strings, then a dilemma lies before us: either the derived tree is distinct in type from the primitive tree (since the former but not the latter has a constituent structure with tagmemic units in it), or the structure of the derived tree is directly accessible to tagmemic analysis (since it contains a tagmeme sequence like that contained in the primitive string). (If *no* units are allowed to enter a system, an approach runs into skepticism. If units are in fact brought into the system, but are not given theoretical status in the system, they may then be treated merely as irrelevant names or labels.)

The transformationalists have begun to sense some of these problems, and to search for solutions within their frame of reference. Note that the term 'derivational history' is given less prominence; the term 'phrase marker' for 'a labelled tree' has taken its place (Chomsky, 1961a:8); this takes the pseudo-historical label from the data, but — in my opinion — not from the generative process itself.

Note, for example, Lees: "In particular, transformations will have to be so formulated that the transform is provided with a constituent structure which is capable of entering another following transformation as argument, since some sentences will be generated by the use of more than one transformation" and "Some other way, then, will have to be found to specify the grammatical status of the transform elements" (1957:400). Also (400), "For the second or question transformation [*Bill was hit by John* (question) → *Was Bill hit by John?*] to apply properly, we must be able to recognize automatically that *Bill* is a subject noun-phrase (NP) of the intermediate sentence" — but noun-phrase as subject *is* a tagmeme with manifesting class plus slot.

Note also Lees, with "nor shall we offer any solutions to the still unsolved problems involved in providing the transforms with reasonable sources for the new generated constituent analysis" (1960a:30). (For an extensive review of Lees, with many problems of detail, see Householder, 1962b; e.g., difficulties in ordering of transformations, 330-31.)

Chomsky, more recently still, has now admitted in a discussion session that "the result of the transformation must itself have constituent structure, because the next transformation must apply only to something with constituent structure" but that "the structure is not given by the phrase-structure rules ... the question is difficult" — and "all the answers I have seen so far are ad hoc" so that "at this point there is some important insight that is still lacking" (in *Third Texas Conference*, 1962:158).

Compare, also, Chomsky (in Luce and others 1963:300-03). Bach considers that optional transformational rules should apply to something other than terminal strings — to something more like our emic classes (in *Preprints*..., 1962:317; i.e., to strings with "detailed subcategories" and "only indirectly between particular sentences"). Compare also Stockwell: "we must assume a variety of 'elements' or 'formatives' on which the rules operate to generate sentences" (1960a:546); or Worth (in *Preprints...*, 1962); — or Hill, who feels it to be "quite obvious that the formulae for 'deriving' a passive sentence from an active one could not be stated as a manipulation unless the active sentence contained isolable items capable of being manipulated" (1962:345). Note, further, that Bach insists on "a level of shiftable units intermediate between the 'word' and the sentence" (1962:264). This would rule out Chomsky's implication that intermediate units are not essentially relevant to the theory of grammar other than as a help to apply the rules: "instead of a rule of procedure for constructing an inventory of elements, we have no longer any reason to consider the symbols '*NP*', '*Sentence*', '*VP*', etc., that appear in these rules to be names of certain classes, sequences, or sequences of classes, etc., of concrete elements. They are simply elements in a system of representation which has been constructed so as to enable us to characterize effectively the set of English sentences in a linguistically meaningful way" (in *Third Texas Conference*, 1962:129). If, furthermore, units intermediate in the tree are denied structural status other than that of representation of the tree itself, then the whole thrust of the distinction "between kernel and non-kernel sentences may end up as a 'trivial' one" (Schachter, in *Preprints...*, 1962:323). And "the symbols and structures that are manipulated may bear no very direct relation to any of its concrete subparts" (Chomsky, 1962: § 1, 511).

At some point, it would seem, transform grammar needs a further unit to be identified and transformed. It is our belief that the tagmeme, or something very much like it in structure, is needed for this purpose in transform grammar. A statement in terms of item and process needs an adequate statement of the item units before the processes can be most effectively implied.

It may very well be that segmentation and classification has on occasion been overemphasized — but that does not make them unnecessary. Recurrent use of terms like noun phrase, or subject, reflect the need, I believe, of units of some such type in a total grammatical description — units which are primitives in a tagmemic theory. Longacre states, however, that even where terms like 'verb phrase' are used in transform grammars, they would not usefully serve as units in a tagmemic sense, since they cover material much too broad to be useful (including all sorts of complements and objects as well as modifiers of time, place, and manner, 1964a).

Tagmemics rejects the implication that grammar is *merely* "a system of explicit rules" alone (cf. Chomsky, 1961b:220); a grammar must include units (particles), rules (related to the dynamism of a wave view), and a matrix system (field). The conviction that a minimal pair is "not an elementary notion" (Chomsky, 1962: § 4.3, 541), that the commutation test is of "marginal interest", (541) and that the principle of complementary distribution is "devoid of any theoretical significance" (547) is therefore the end product of an attempt to handle a grammar of rules without explicitly identified units — units which must be justified in reference to contrast (and identification), variation (free or complementary), and distribution (ultimately into discourse beyond the sentence, and into field system). See also Diver's insistence on units

(1963:181); or, for units beyond the sentence, Armstrong (in de Sola Pool, 1959:157-59, 164-65).

Lees, however, would reject the "recognition of certain fictitious 'units of grammatical form', called 'gramemes' [tagmemes], along with a host of other fanciful '-emes'" (1960b:211). Chomsky mentions units (1959a:33) and "discrete atoms" (in Luce and others, 1963:274) but does not integrate them into a theory of units in a way satisfactory to a tagmemic view — since he claims that "by a grammar we mean a set of rules" without adequate reference to units on which they operate (284). For further discussion of unit see § 7.8. For relation of rule to context, according to Chomsky, note that "it is the *rules* that are sensitive to or free of their context, not the elements in the terminal string" (in Luce and others, 1963:294, 360, 366-409).

11.77 *On Halliday's Prosodic Approach to Grammar*

We have earlier discussed at some length bibliography on matters of Firth's prosodies (§§ 8.814, 9.73, 10.51). Apart from the insistence that phonological matters could be described directly in reference to word as a base, there was little relation between the prosodic approach and the kinds of interest which have directed the development of tagmemic grammar. Since our first volumes (1954, 1955), however, Halliday has gone beyond the earlier views of Firth to develop a more extensive theory of grammar. Many of his points of view can be correlated with components of tagmemic theory. For the remainder of this section, page references will refer specifically to Halliday (1961) unless otherwise indicated. (For presentation of a development of this view, see Dixon, 1963.)

Halliday's fundamental categories include "unit", "structure", "class", and "system" (247). His attention to items relates to the crucial effort of tagmemic theory to make *well-defined* items. Halliday, on the other hand, provides no theoretical specifications for units in a generalized sense (comparable to tagmemic contrast, variation, and distribution; 251-255). Translate his "unit" (252) by "syntagmemic level".

Comparable to tagmemic slot, one may find in Halliday (following Firth) the term "place": "A structure is thus an arrangement of elements ordered in 'places'" (255). Etic slot — as distinct from emic slot — has its analogy in the "successivity of bits and pieces in a unidirectional time sequence" (251 fn. 24); "the more abstract dimension of order" (251) overlaps with the kinds of problems which we would treat in terms of emic slot. To our distribution class, compare: "The class is that grouping of members of a given unit which is defined by operation in the structure of the unit next above" (260) — that is, it comes in a slot of a construction. Such a distributional class may allow differing internal structures (compare, in tagmemics, distribution subclasses) since a "class is *not* a grouping of members of a given unit *which are alike in their own structure*" (261).

For our construction read "structure": "the structure is the highest abstraction of patterns of syntagmatic relations" (254). As I have tagmeme distributing into construction, and construction distributing into tagmeme in an upward zigzag (§ 12.3), Halliday has structures alternating with classes (266 fn. 58).

Halliday utilizes units such as subject, predicate, complement, adjunct, head, qualifier (257) which overlap with our tagmemes. Formulas for slot and class in tagmeme find their closest equivalent in Halliday when he uses an Arabic numeral for the filler and a capital letter for emic slot. Compare his "1 (at X)" or his "2.1 (at Ya)" with a reversal or order in tagmemic formula of X:1 (or X^1); and Y:2.1 (or Y^1) (264, especially fn. 54).

There are also many relationships as to hierarchy, although the terminological differences are substantial. Thus sentence, clause, phrase, word, morpheme are related by rank in Halliday's terms, (252, fn. 28) but as levels of a hierarchy in tagmemic discussion. Tagmemics deals with three hierarchies — lexical, phonological and grammatical. Halliday also deals with three, calling them lexis, phonology, and grammar, but labels them as "levels". (Halliday also uses the term level for a different relationship in which "the primary levels are 'form', 'substance', and 'context'," 243.)

Both the tagmemic view and Halliday's treatment protest against a mono-hierarchical view (tagmemic terminology) or a mono-level view (Halliday, 269); each insists that the lexical, phonological, and grammatical hierarchies should be kept distinct: "The separation of levels [hierarchies] has been taken as a starting-point" (Halliday, 268).

Halliday objects to conflating the hierarchies as leading to "confusion of level with rank" (281) (that is, he objects — as tagmemics does, see §§ 9.71, 11.71 — to building a single hierarchy from phoneme to morpheme to word to sentence, etc. (see 281 under the label "confusion of level with rank").

There are some important differences between us however. Halliday treats the morpheme as "a grammatical unit" (256 fn. 37; also 286 fn. 95) whereas I would treat it as lexical. (But Longacre is developing a tagmemic model with morpheme as in the grammatical hierarchy and lexeme as in the lexical hierarchy.) Halliday, however, rejects lexicon as having hierarchy (276) and hence does not leave room for the extensive development of lexical theory, in an analog to phonology or grammar, which tagmemics expects.

As for phonological hierarchy, Halliday follows Firth in dealing with phonematic units which are phone components limited to specific contrastive sets of substitutable items in particular slots in a structure, rather than setting up phonemes which can be equated in different slots; so that the various t occurrences of English do not comprise "'the phoneme /t/'" since "no such entity will be postulated" (284 fn. 91). On the other hand, Halliday makes explicit the necessity of phonological distinctions: "*All* formal distinctions presuppose *some* distinction in substance" (282) even though the proper handling of this dependence on that phonological material is often indirect through a hierarchy of forms or procedures.

In the grammatical hierarchy, the status given to class and to slot in Halliday's approach (as in the formulas we mentioned) leave room for partial translation in terms of tagmemics, even though Halliday does not set up such a grammatical unit directly.

As for interlocking between hierarchies, Halliday insists that "A meaningful account of how grammar and phonology are related in English must be based on a prior separate statement of the two" (269). Similarly, when grammar and lexicon "have been described separately, the next stage is to relate them" — a statement which applies "equally" to phonology and lexicon (274 fn. 72, and 275). Yet "the units may not be coextensive" (283) even though the phonology is a necessary underlying substance to grammatical units (281); phonological and grammatical categories on the clause boundaries, for example, should not be sought in a one-to-one relation (285).

Halliday's treatment of system emphasizes that various of the terms are "mutually defining" "since no one category is defined until all the others are, in the totality of the theory" (248). Those who have used the tagmemic approach would find further correlations with the approach in this book in which the total theory is treated as a unit.

As for particle, wave, and field, Halliday's interest in items overlaps with tagmemic attention to particles. His interest in long components of higher units, and in the prodosic approach of Firth, overlaps with tagmemic interest in high-level phonology — in the phonetics of rhythm waves and the like. His suggestion that "The formal meaning of an item is its operation in the network of formal relations" (245) suggests that his approach would not prove hostile to matrix theory, even though he does not currently move in that direction.

Like tagmemic theory, Halliday protests that language is not just a code (280). Rather, language is patterned activity (250) — which leads to a view similar to that of tagmemics in which language is treated as a type of social behavior. In fact, his illustrations of a nonverbal type show the possibility of close correlation: Halliday (278-79) gives an analysis of a menu — the components of types of meals during a day's activity, with a "mouthful" as the "gastronomic morpheme" whereas tagmemics has dealt with the structure of a particular meal and the activity of that meal (§ 5.2).

The tagmemic implication that units ultimately derive from native reaction is perhaps at long remove related to Halliday's insistence on behavioral context as relevant. Of more direct relevance, however, is the relationship between the tagmemic treatment of etics and Halliday's treatment of "delicacy" (258, 260, 268, 272). Since "The limit of delicacy is set by the means at one's disposal" (272) rather than by internal structuring of the system, one treats delicacy as an etic — alien — component rather than an internal one. Halliday's use of "cline" has reference to "a continuum carrying potentially infinite gradation" (249). Such a cline may lead to indeterminacy of the number of units or of the number of levels of a hierarchy. Apparently, however, Halliday would not refer to a hierarchy if the elements in it are discrete (cf. 249); here, possibly, is the closest approach to the tagmemic search for emic levels of a hierarchy which can be contrastively determined; that is, tagmemics treats emic levels of the grammatical hierarchy as not a cline. (But see his "unit", 252.)

Halliday does not deal with etic versus emic relationship between the levels of a hierarchy. But for him "delicacy is a cline" (287 fn. 98), when dealing with classes as a result of finer and finer analysis. Tagmemics, however, holds out the hope of finding emic classes versus etic classes. Emic subclasses would be determined by structural criteria rather than by an arbitrary arresting of the analytical process.

In terms of desired elegance of results, Halliday, to me, seems to put emphasis on the desire "to provide a framework of logically interrelated categories (so that it can be evaluated as a theory, and compared with other theories) from which can be derived methods of description... which show us something of how language works" (291-92). He wishes to have the "scheme of interrelated categories" set up in such a way as "to account for the data" and a way to "relate the categories to the data and to each other" (243). His theory leaves room for method to be derived from it; description is "a body of method derived from theory and *not* a set of procedures" (249). Halliday sets up theory from which method is to be derived — but refuses to equate theory with procedure. Tagmemics preserves a little closer relation between the theory and procedure in that it feels that fruitful theory must to some extent be limited by analytical techniques for processing or evaluating data. Tagmemics has oscillation between theory and method rather than a one-way priority.

Halliday finds little direct need occurring for adding simplicity as "a separate criterion" since it turns out "to be a property of a maximally grammatical description" (246, fn. 15) and hence is often an unnecessary addition to theory (but see 249, where occasionally it is used to decide between "fewer systems with more terms and more systems with fewer terms"). Halliday makes no use of generatability as distinguishing a theory since "any theory-based grammar, transformational or not, can be stated in generative terms" (241, fn. 2), and a grammar is "a set of properties of what the linguist accounts for grammatically" or "that part of a language which is accounted for by grammatical description" (246 fn. 17). Presumably generative rules, therefore, would be used by Halliday or by tagmemics when they are useful for descriptive or explicative purposes, but would not be given theoretical status to the exclusion of other devices which would aid our *understanding*.

CHAPTER 12

TRIMODAL RESTRICTIONS ON SETTING UP EMIC UNITS

We have now treated the basic kinds of elements of sample behavioremes, including their total structure, minimum units of their three modes, and the hierarchies within each of these modes. Numerous severe problems remain as to the precise relationships between the modes (especially as affected by special kinds of componential systems), by fusion of units, and by interpenetration or interdependence between the modal hierarchies.

Before discussing these difficulties, however, we would do well to face a danger which could easily grow out of the use of behavioremic theory. This is the danger that persons might find alleged emic units everywhere in such miscellaneous and uncontrolled profusion that the approach would collapse into an arbitrary multiplication of units which are not in fact relevant to the internal structure of the cultures studied.

What analytical controls can be applied which would exclude the postulation of unnecessary trimodal units? We suggest several which are by no means final, and which we ourselves may not yet be able to apply in every instance. In fact § 13.6 shows some relaxation of the controls for one particular purpose.

There remains, in view of the difficulties, the possibility that the basic trimodal model may need modification while the general 'tagmemic' approach is maintained. See § 12.5.

12.1 *Restrictions Imposed by the Trimodal View of Language as Particle, Wave, and Field*

In setting up further emic units within the trimodal model it is helpful to keep in mind that certain general characteristics of the modes seem to be so frequently present that it is unwise to assume too quickly that one has found additional emic units unless they too are structured modally in some such way.

The first set of characteristics to be summarized in this manner indicates how behavioremic modes reflect the basic principles of phonemic theory of the last decades. The feature mode seems to be the one which especially covers elements of CONTRAST and IDENTIFICATION. The manifestation mode includes elements which characteristically show nonsimultaneous variants in COMPLEMENTATION or FREE VARIATION. The distribution mode is the one which most specifically has reference to various aspects of SYSTEMIC DISTRIBUTION and CLASS MEMBERSHIP. In dealing with emic units, their internal modal structuring may in general be expected to follow this pattern.

The second set of characteristics of the modes, to be summarized here, shows a quite different set of relations between them. A system of units which is seen principally through the identificational-contrastive units, or feature mode, of that system may appear as STATIC (seen typically in face diagrams of the phonetics of a system). When, however, the system is seen through the units of its manifestation mode and the physical basis of units as they flow into one another in a sequence of fusing, changing segments, the units of the system appear as DYNAMIC (seen, for example, in segmentation diagrams of the phonetics of a sequence of sounds in an utterance). When the same system is viewed by way of its distribution mode and the manner in which the units of that mode operate within the matrix of larger units and in relation to the hierarchical structure of the sequences and classes of the system as a whole, the system appears as FUNCTIONAL (for example, with phonemes functioning as components of syllable types).

A third set of characteristics of the modes of emic units further specifies characteristics of emic units. The units of the feature mode, more than those of the other modes, are analytically seen as DISCRETE PARTICLES or SEGMENTS of activity. That is, they can be symbolized by discrete signs without violence to their most prominent characteristics. The units of the manifestation mode, on the contrary, have as an essential prominent component the factor of movement as a physiological basis — movements which slur into one another without necessarily discrete border points. Thus, even though the included emic units of the manifestation mode may be symbolized by discrete signs, nevertheless an approach which focuses on their essential physiological components leads to a view of units of the manifestation mode as CONTINUOUS WAVES of behavior within the system. The units of the distribution mode, if viewed in an analogous manner, force one to place attention upon the contexts in which they occur, on the classes and systems of which they are a part, and without which neither unit nor context nor system exist. In this view, the units of the distribution mode are functioning manifestations of concentrations within, or parts of the TOTAL FIELD[1] of the relevant behavior under study.

---

[1] Since first publication of this chapter (1960) our researches in matrix (see 1962a, 1963b, 1963d, Pike and Erickson, 1964) have greatly strengthed our conviction that the analogy of particle, wave, and field will be a fruitful one. The principle of complementarity of viewpoints which one must adopt to perceive a unit adequately forces us to view elements in three separate ways, through three separate technologies and theoretical concept sets. Units must be viewed as particle (with their elements of contrast, variation, and distribution in class, sequence and matrix); this allows for perception of segmentation, for classification, and for taxonomic structures. The same units must be viewed as waves; this allows for fusion, sequential hierarchies, and process statements of various types — including transformations. Finally, the unit sets must be viewed as items in a field — as cells in matrices

Whenever any emic unit is proposed, it is well to attempt to study the internal modal units or components which such a new unit would imply. One asks: Are the internal components of the feature mode of this proposed unit contrastive-identificational? or static? or discrete? Are the internal components of the manifestation mode composed of variants complementarily distributed or freely variant? or dynamically changing and wave-like in their physiological basis? Are the internal components of the distribution mode of the proposed unit clearly related to contextual or class-membership problems? or do they enter into, become related to, and in some way form part of the total field of the units which are embedded in them?

Similarly, as one views the proposed unit in reference to its relation to larger units, one may ask: Does the proposed unit form part of a modal structure of a higher-layered unit? If so, of which mode of that unit are they included parts? If it appears to be part of the feature-mode hierarchy of the larger unit, does the included unit serve as an contrastive-identificational component of the including unit? If the included unit appears to be part of the manifestation-mode hierarchy of the including

---

with dimensions of various kinds; this allows pattern and system an explicit place in overall theory. Whereas these volumes (1954, 1955, 1960) gave special attention to the development of particle — with the tagmeme as a grammatical particle — and lesser attention to wave functions (through fusion in sequence) our publications since then have given more attention to system pattern, to theory of field, through matrix studies; numerous articles applying these concepts in the field are already revealing pattern which has previously been obscure. For list of other sections where matrix references are given, see second fn. to § 11.225.

Compare Andreyev who states — in reference to various mathematical linguistic models — that no model can be of a completely unilateral kind (1962:190). Our model of particles cannot work without some reference to waves and field; nor the model of waves without reference to particle and field; nor that of field without reference to particle and wave.

For structure as a network of relations see Z. Harris (1954a:149).

Goodman discusses the attempt to provide a "beginning of theory of nonlinear order", a "calculus of order" of square-cell arrays, with reference to notions of besideness' manor (in reference to minimum path between cells), betwixt, nextness, barony (in relation to beside), and so on, in matrices (1951:273, 266-76); once such an approach can be applied with precision, then we should have available a rigorous approach to *ordered arrays* of matrices such as ours, and field theory, comparable to the useful precision of *ordered rules* provided by Chomsky and others. Order — in intuition and in data is *not of one type only*. For mechanical equating of phonological tree (or rules of distinctive feature priorities) with an associated phonological matrix, see Halle (1959a:34-36); note, further, that his non-unique assignment of distinctive feature (alternate analyses) is reflected in alternate placement of zeros in cells of competing matrices.

For rearrangement of matrices as a device for studying the chronology of archeological artefacts, see Tugby (1958, with further bibliography). After our matrix articles referred to here were in press, we found a similar permutation technique developed independently, used for finding significant patterns in displays of data concerning underdeveloped economies (Leontief, 1963). For attempt at a matrix of time concepts in English verb phrases, see Diver (1963).

Dixon (1963:13) has an approximation of our model of particle, wave, and field when he deals with "isolates" (cf. our particles, but "with one part of the continuum emphasized and brought into the most immediate consideration"), "hillocks" (cf. our waves), and "field containing a number of hillocks" (cf. our sequential matrix). Note also some similarities of Lévi-Straus on myth, with timelessness of elements in application, historical sequence, and structural dimensions (1955:52), to our treatment of some poetic form as particle (cf. time standing still), wave (smear into physical time) and field (intersection of universes of discourse) (Pike, 1964f, 1965).

unit, does it contribute variants, dynamic characteristics, and physical wave-like properties to the including unit? If the included unit appears to be part of the distribution mode of the larger unit, does it somehow form part of the matrix, or functional context, or field within which included units of the feature mode and manifestation mode of the larger unit are distributed? If a significant number of the answers to these questions and to those of the preceding paragraph are 'yes', the proposed emic unit is likely to be on a solid footing. If the answers are 'no', one should procede with care — the proposed unit may turn out later to be some kind of arbitrarily abstracted etic element rather than an emic structural one.

In sum, language under this model is viewed as particle, wave, and field (Pike, 1959). Each of the three views of language contributes an insight into its structure. The particle view leads one to study carefully the psycholinguistic data which support segmentation of sequences into chunks of behavior, and the identification of variants as members of units. The wave view accounts better for the physical data of continuous articulatory movements or sound waves. The field view leaves room for a theory of classes and systems of phonemes, morphemes, and tagmemes. Sequence of units is easiest treated under a particle view; smearing of unit borders under a wave view; structure of system, or of universe of discourse, under a field view. (See also §§ 14.11, 14.3.)

12.2 *The Restriction Imposed by the Retention of Simultaneous Modes*

The second safeguard to help one test the validity of setting up a particular emic unit is related to the one just discussed. By it one checks to see whether its basic structural components can be studied as additive 'parts' of the unit or whether on the contrary they must be treated as simultaneous modes of that unit.

Behavioremic theory is slow to accept as an emic unit any unit which is basically made up of 'parts' which are 'added' into a whole. It looks, rather, for units which have simultaneous structures each of which covers the entire substance of the unit (cf. § 3.56).

The following models of an emic unit must therefore be rejected since they imply a mere sum of units in a larger one.[2] A whole which is cut into separate parts:

---

[2] A construction is more than the sum of parts in that it may have a total meaning — a semantic contrastive feature — and a function as a unit in external distribution. Under a transformationalist approach the unity might be expressed as a relation to a tree — primitive or derived.

A further model must also be rejected, not because it implies parts but, on the contrary, because it implies that the modes are merely aspects of a unit, or points of view in looking at a unit, such that a unit could be seen in these aspects without there being present any simultaneous but structurally-distinct modes. The following diagram is designed to suggest that one can approach data from different points of view, even when there are no natural structural divisions residing in the behavioral data:

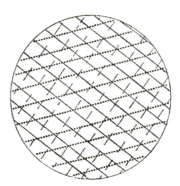

A more useful model is suggested by a diagram in which a long solid line represents a high-layered emic unit as such, while three triangles descending from it represent the included hierarchical structuring of the three simultaneous modes. Each mode has its own included structures, with parts which sometimes do and sometimes do not end at the same places as do the units of the other modes:

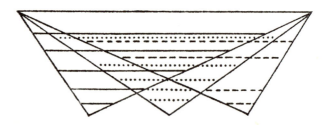

A sentence type — a sentence syntagmeme — might be viewed from this standpoint somewhat as follows — with variations required for particular languages. (For a related diagram see § 5.55; for further modification, see § 12.3 and § 12.5.) The feature mode has units written in roman type, the manifestation mode in italic, the distribution mode in small caps. There is no attempt to symbolize in this particular

SENTENCE TYPE—SENTENCE SYNTAGMEME

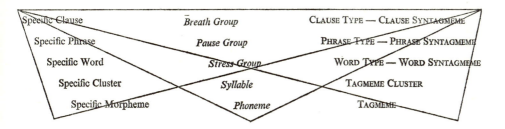

By this set of restrictions a great many three-part groups of data would be eliminated from emic status. An action divided arbitrarily into past, present, and future, for example, would not be considered trimodally structured, in spite of its three 'parts', since these parts would be additive, not simultaneous. Nor are the introduction, body, and end of an action three simultaneous modal structures. Similarly, the mere fact that an action may be seen in various aspects (e.g., economic, political, and religious) does not in itself justify the treatment of that action as trimodally structured. The structural, emic character of each of these aspects would have to be specifically and separately validated if they were to be retained as relevant to behavioremic description.

12.3 'Spectrum' Restrictions on Emic Progression

In seeking further necessary restrictions to prevent the analyst from allowing the emic approach to lead to difficulty by way of unwarranted emic units, one attractive 'blind alley' should perhaps be specifically marked: It is simple and elegant, but not fruitful, to assume that every emic unit is composed of three modes, that each mode is itself an emic unit, and that each of these modes is composed of three modes which in turn constitute emic units which in turn are composed of three modes and in turn constitute three emic units, etc., etc. That is, we reject the conclusion that U, F, M, and D are each units such that $U = F, M, D$ (read: unit comprises feature, manifestation, and distribution modes); $F = F', M', D'$; $F' = F'', M'', D''$; $M = F', M', D'$; $M' = F'', M'', D''$; etc.

I have explored this possibility, but have been unable to come out with anything which can be aligned with the empirical data. Although it may appear at first to be indistinguishable from the kind of EMIC PROGRESSION which we have been using in previous chapters, there is one crucial difference. This blind alley would set up the entire mode of an emic unit as an emic unit in itself. Our working theory, on the contrary, does not set up the total mode of a unit as itself an emic unit but rather selects from the mode various of its components and treats each of them as emic units.

Thus the emic progression is not from units, to modes, to units, to modes; but passes from units, through modes, to component units, and through their modes to further component units of those included modes. That is, $U = F, M, D$; $F = F_a, F_b, F_c, F \ldots n$; $F_a = F', M', D'$; $F' = F_a'', F_b'', F_c'', F'' \ldots n$; $F_a'' = F''', M''', D'''$; etc., in which $_a, _b, _c$ are components of a mode. It is not yet completely clear why this difference has proved crucial.

A mode is a SPECTRUM of components. (For the spectrum used as an analogy in a different manner, in semantics, see Firth, 1951b:132.) The total mode with all its components is like 'white light'. The individual components are like 'colored lights' in which each color has its own specific frequency of vibration. A specific wave length cannot be assigned to white light, but can be assigned only to some specific fragment of the total spectrum. An analysis of white light as a whole can not be made in such a way that it is alleged to constitute a single unitary wave length. By this analogy, then, we suggest that any particular mode of a particular emic unit may be analogous to 'white light' which is a composite of a number of units, and the units would be analogous to the separate frequencies which go in to make up that total composite 'whiteness'.

A second caution concerning emic progression states that it must not be allowed to imply a continuing infinite regress or progress of emic units of any one comparable type. On the contrary, we have indicated at numerous places that there are places where the type of activity changes radically. Some of these have to do with the functioning of communication. Other thresholds differ in accordance with whether one is analyzing the activity of speaker or listener (cf. §§ 2.4, 4.32, 5.3, 6.41), and so forth. Still other thresholds have to do with observable overt activity versus unobservable and covert activity.

The spectrum analogy again is useful in getting a crude understanding of this phase of our point of view. There are many types of activity which are relevant to behavior but which are not observable by the analyst by direct means. Some of these are the smaller units of activity such as the activity of small muscles, or molecules, or subatomic structures. We might compare these small activities to the ultra-violet part of the spectrum. On the other hand, a generations-long event would be invisible to any one person, hence it is INFRA-OBSERVABLE, below the VISIBLE SPECTRUM. The dividing lines would constitute some kind of threshold of activity.

A 'short-wave' event of human activity must be seen through a microscope. A 'long-wave' event, to be seen, must be recorded intermittently with elapsed-time photography over a period of centuries and projected rapidly.

A third caution concerning emic progression has been implied earlier in the insistence that form-meaning composite units must be retained (§§ 2.73, 5.64, 6.46, 6.91, 7.83). If a component of meaning is abstracted as part of the characteristic spectrum of a mode, this component is not itself considered to be in the line of emic progression unless some physical component is preserved which can constitute its manifestation mode. In conceptualized hypostasis of meaning (cf. §§ 6.43, 6.91, 7.85) the neural activity can serve in this way. See also § 16.6.

A fourth restriction on emic progression reflects the problem discussed in § 11.41, where it was indicated that tagmemes (or hypertagmemes) were not distributed directly into higher-level tagmemes, but into syntagmemes, and the syntagmemes then are distributed into hypertagmemes as their total or partial filler classes. Distribution procedes from tagmeme to syntagmeme to tagmeme, not from tagmeme to tagmeme directly. (This restriction is vaguely similar to that shown earlier in this section whereby units were broken down into a spectrum of trimodally-structured emic components of modes rather than into units composed of emic modes directly.)

If the sentence-type diagram of § 12.2 is revised with this provision in mind the right-hand triangle showing the distribution progression would need to be modified, as follows (with arrows showing the direction of distribution of units):

↗ Behavioremes
Conversation-Length Hypertagmemes
   (i.e., slot-plus-class correlatives)
      ↘
      ↗ Conversation Syntagmemes
Monologue-Length Hypertagmemes
      ↘
      ↗ Monologue Syntagmemes
Utterance-Response-Length Hypertagmemes
      ↘
      ↗ Utterance-Response Syntagmemes
Sentence-Length Hypertagmemes
      ↖
      ↘ Sentence Syntagmeme
      ↗
Clause-Length Hypertagmemes
      ↖
      ↘ Clause Syntagmemes
      ↗
Phrase-Length Hypertagmemes
      ↖
      ↘ Phrase Syntagmemes
      ↗
Word-Length Hypertagmemes
   (i.e., slot-plus-class correlatives)
      ↖ Word Syntagmemes
      ↗ (i.e., word-construction types)
Morpheme-Length Tagmemes
   (minimum slot-plus-class correlatives)

12.4 Restrictions in Solving for Modal Components

Much of the discussion of this chapter has assumed that the investigation of a structure is fairly well along, and is being tested in retrospect for over-all coherence and basic internal relations, or at least that a particular unit has been proposed and is being tested. Occasionally the problem is quite different — How can these principles be rephrased to serve as 'sign posts' pointing in the direction of structures to be discovered?

If the investigator suspects that he has in view a unit of the manifestation mode of some unit 'X', for example, how can he set out to try to find — if they in fact occur — the corresponding distribution-mode units and feature-mode units, or even 'X' itself?

To whatever minor extent we can succeed, we wish to lay the groundwork for using the present achievements as an *exploratory* tool for further work.

Assuming M and F, while wishing to solve for D, D must (1) in some way make up the setting for M and F, and (2) must enter into and comprise some kind of temporal sequence. (3) Units of D must always be present when M and F are present, so D should be discoverable in sequences of M or F. (4) D must have no other physical content than that which is seen, in some way, manifested through the variants of M and the units of F, so the investigator looks for a further structuring of the same substance, rather than seeking new substances. (5) He seeks some functional regroupings of units of M and/or F as a unitizing of the setting as such. (6) If item (5) is successfully completed, then 'distribution' will in this sense be unitized through units of D and will not have to be handled solely as an abstracted relational component of the system. (7) These D units should also themselves be tri-modally structured in emic progression with included F', M', D' (except that at minimum threshold points the internal structuring may be obscure), so that the investigator — once he has them before him in hypothesis — looks for their variants and contrastive features. The expectation of emic progression, however, implies (8) that distribution units will comprise a hierarchy which is different from the hierarchy of the units of the manifestation mode.

In solving for M, the investigator can begin (1) by assuming that whenever he observes a form of purposeful activity, it is always, in some way or in some place, a variant of an emic unit (or part of a unit or sequence of units) on some level of the hierarchy of some componential system of behavior. Observation that behavior is 'random' often implies, from this point of view, that the data under discussion are as yet emically unanalyzed, or — frequently — that the units which they are manifesting have a much greater range of variation in their manifestation than some other units which are more narrowly and rigidly fixed in their variant forms. An emic unit of 'exploratory behavior', for example, may vary more widely than the stroke forms used in serving a tennis ball. After selecting some movement of physical activity as a starting point of investigation, he seeks (2) for related events or activities which have the same function and which might prove to be variants of the same emic unit (its included M' characteristics of that unit). (3) He studies such items to see if they are complementarily distributed — or freely variant — in sequences of particular events, and studies the distribution of the unit as a whole (its external D characteristics). He checks to see (4) if they are manifesting units of a sequence of events which are clearly meaningful or purposive. (5) He seeks for the internal identifying or contrastive features of the unit (its included F') (6) He checks to find its relation to a larger manifestation hierarchy, and (7) to note its relation to the entire componential system of which it is a part. (8) M must occur wholly in D. (9) It must be made up wholly of F. He looks to see if the units are (10) 'concrete' or tangible, (11) 'chunk-like' — easily segmented, (12) basically physical and (13) with physical wave-like motion as basic to them.

In solving for F, the investigator may begin with a wave or sequence of waves of motion which at first appear random. He seeks (1) to locate contexts in which the presence, absence, or change of this event appears to elicit contrastive responses. He attempts to determine (2) the significance — meaning or purpose — of the eliciting event (as part of the F' of this F), (3) its physical cues (a further component of F' of F), (4) the range of variation in that physical event (its M), and (5) the appropriateness of its occurrence in certain larger contexts (part of its D) as well as (6) its internal functional slots and their fillers (also part of its D). He looks to see (7) if F is one simultaneous component of M, and (8) is identificational and (9) contrastive. (10) The form of F must be made up of M. (11) It must occur wholly in D. Of F, M, and D, the M is the most tangible, D is the most elusive, and F the most immediately significant or purposeful.

One of the most successful applications of this approach occurred when it appeared wise to try to solve some of the problems concerning the overlapping membership of morpheme classes by looking at classes as special kinds of emic units. The results have already been used in Chapter 7 as a basic part of behavioremic theory. This one achievement, alone, has more than justified the energy spent in developing the point of view, since it has brought into coherent, organized relationship many facts about classes — with their variants, functions and contrastive-identificational features — which before this were isolated, ignored, buried in footnotes, or treated in an off hand manner as 'semantic restrictions', and so on.

The data proved to be sufficiently important, in fact, that they were moved from a scheduled place in a later chapter on classes and systems to an introductory place in the chapter treating tagmemes for which the emic class analysis had become crucial.

The reader is referred to that treatment, §§ 7.31, 7.4, 7.52-55, for illustration of results of the extension of the trimodal approach to new areas where the analysis seems to me to be solidly entrenched.

A further illustration is developed in Chapter 13, however, which is much less certain. It is presented in the hope that the reader will see how the approach leads to an observation of new relationships in old trouble spots of theory. It stimulates the creation of new hypotheses which, even though needing testing and later modification, nevertheless point to new areas where behavioral structures can be observed.

12.5 *Modifications Imposed by a Model which Includes Phonotagmemes*

Crawford (1963 [1959]) notes that in the phonological area the phonemes, as parts of classes, occur in structural slots in syllables. Hence a phonemic slot-plus-class correlative can be posited for phonology.

So far, there is no difference from the point of view developed here — since in § 8.66 we also noted this fact. Crawford, however, goes farther. He sets up the phonemic slot-plus-class correlative — which he calls a PHONOTAGMEME — as on a par with the grammatical tagmeme. This leads to substantially different results from ours, since we had treated the morpheme, phoneme, and tagmeme as comparably minimum members of their respective hierarchies, with phonemic slot-plus-class correlatives not playing a prominent role in the theory.

It is not yet clear just how far-reaching the changes might be which will develop from this Crawford suggestion. At least two major possibilities must be considered:

(1) On the one hand, the setting up of the phonotagmeme as on a level comparable to the tagmeme may force changes in the theory of hierarchies. If phonemes in classes enter phonotagmemic structures just as morphemes in class enter [grammatico-]tagmemic structures, then our trimodal model would be replaced by a doubly bifurcated one: A phonological pair of hierarchies would be balanced by a lexico-grammatical pair. In the latter pair, the grammatical hierarchy would be composed (1a) of [grammatico-]tagmemic slot-plus-class structures of successively including levels. The lexical hierarchy (1b) would be composed in some way of the specific lexical units of larger and larger size (specific morphemes, phrases, clauses, etc.) which fill the slots in the [grammatico-]tagmemic hierarchy. The phonological pair of hierarchies, on the other hand, would be made up (2a) of a phonotagmemic hierarchy of successively higher-level slot-plus-class structures, and (2b) a hierarchy of 'phonemic units' of successively higher levels (i.e., specific phonemes, syllables, stress groups, etc.) which fill the slots of the phonotagmemes. Within this doubly-bifurcated model, however, Crawford retains trimodal structuring of individual units such as phonemes and morphemes.

(2) On the other hand, it is possible that the phonotagmeme may be ultimately accepted as on a par with the tagmeme, and a phonological hierarchy accepted as parallel to the grammatical one, while retaining a third — the lexical — hierarchy. This, however, could only be done under two conditions: (a) A lexico-tagmeme would need to be set up which differed in some crucial way — as yet not delineated — from our grammatico-tagmeme. In addition, (b), the fillers of the two tagmeme types would have to be different. Perhaps the syntagmeme types charted in § 12.3 would comprise the fillers for the grammatico-tagmeme — and even relieve us of

some of the hierarchical problems of present tagmemic treatment raised in that section. The specific morphemes and morpheme sequences would then in turn comprise the fillers of the lexico-tagmemic units. Unfortunately, we do not yet visualize the characteristics required for postulating a lexico-tagmeme.[3] If, however, the lexico-tagmeme can later be usefully set up, it may help solve problems of metaphor, idiom, and universe of discourse — or other matters — discussed in Chapter 16. (And see § 15.13 for supporting reasons for separation of grammatical and lexical hierarchies.)

---

[3] Considerable work is now going on attempting to study the structure of the lexical hierarchy in reference to these problems. Several hypotheses are being tested, but are not ready for publication. See also fnn. to § 10.

CHAPTER 13

MODE-LIKE EMIC UNITS AND SYSTEMS

This chapter shows what happened when some of the exploratory devices of Chapter 12 were applied to a particularly mystifying problem.

13.1 *Background of the Suprasegmental Problem*

In 1949, a year after I had completed Tone Languages, I was intrigued by the possibility that the frame techniques which I had developed for purposes of tonal analysis could be generalized for all kinds of phonemes — that, if we set up the tone procedures in such a way that they could be used for all sounds, only one basic set of procedures would be needed. Furthermore, the technique of determining the structure of tone systems could become a model for determining all linguistic units, a model which might result in greater simplicity and elegance as all phonemes melted into a single large class, theoretically homogeneous in type.

This viewpoint was supported by the growing conviction that "Quality, like pitch, is ultimately relative rather than absolute" (Pike, 1947c:66). Vowels and consonants were seen in the same way (Pike, 1952b). If that were so, then tone techniques were theoretically pertinent to their analysis, since the tone methodology was particularly well adapted to handle units which differed not by absolute quality but only by degree — by degree which is relative to and contrastive within particular contexts or frames.

If such a point of view could be sustained, it would wipe out the contrast between segmental and suprasegmental phonemes and erase one longstanding problem. Instead of trying to keep the two apart, and finding criteria for doing so, we would fit all phonemes into a single kind of system.

In addition, characteristics of tone phonemes would serve as a superb proving ground for phonemic theory, since a tone phoneme would be one of the simplest of all phonemes — with a single pure, abstract characteristic relatively determined. Tests applied to it for establishing theoretical principles would be carried on in an almost 'sterile' context — i.e., not accompanied by disturbing factors of complicated timbre.

Gradually, however, three difficulties come more and more into prominence:

The first is the simple fact that a tone phoneme is not a total chunk of the phonetic sequence. 'Vertical cuts' in a sound continuum might easily result in /s/, /t/, /k/, or frequently might give /o/, /a/, but would never give /'/. Here the two did not act alike.

If, however, the chunk characteristic of a phoneme were abandoned, a second difficulty arose: If a phonetic component such as tone could constitute a phoneme, the consistent application of this principle led to setting up *all* contrastive components such as voicing, labialization, sibilantization, etc., as phonemes, or even as suprasegmental phonemes. (For "secondary" phonetic features such as labialization thus treated as suprasegmental, see Trager, 1941:135.)

To me such a conclusion appeared as awkward, though not necessarily impossible. Behavioremic theory profited from wave-like chunks as units (§ 8.42). Native speakers, furthermore, seemed to react to tone phonemes in a manner sufficiently distinct from their reaction to voicing or labialization that it appeared to me highly probable that they were reacting to some structural difference more deeply rooted than that between two components which differed only in degree. I did not believe that the English speaker, for example, reacted to the second syllable of *per'mit* as containing, on a structural par, the phonemes (among others) of stress, voicelessness (or fortisness), bilabiality, occlusion, retroflexion, etc.

An alternate solution ran into a third difficulty: If one began with the requirement that a phoneme constitute a segment of a continuum, then tone as a phoneme would disappear. Instead, one would obtain single phonemes which were made up, for example, of a vowel plus a tone. Then /á/ would be a single phoneme in contrast to /à/ (rather than /a/ plus /'/, versus /a/ plus /`/ respectively). This of itself is not impossible, though awkward because of multiplying greatly the number of phonemes in any one system.

A much more serious problem arises, however, when one attempts to carry over the same principle to English pitch contrasts. In the sentence *If he could, I'd like to have him do it*, let us suppose a ⁰2-4-3 pitch sequence — a very probably one in such a sentence — on the word *could* (cf. § 6.2 fn. for symbolism). In this instance a consistent application of the same principle would force us to set up three vowel phonemes (/²ʊ/, /⁴ʊ/, /³ʊ/), each with its contrastive pitch component. In spite of the fact this kind of solution has been seriously proposed by highly competent linguists (in public address — I fail to find the material published) it impresses me as quite impossible to accept as basic to a behavioremic analysis which attempts to arrive at emic units reflecting the way in which native participants react to their behavior. I feel strongly — without benefit of the kind of psycholinguistic experimental data which would be helpful — that native speakers of English do not react to three vowel segments in *could*, even while they do react contrastively (with corresponding meaning changes) to replacements of any of the three pitches of the accompanying intonation sequence indicated. Similarly, Mazatec has on occasion two or three lexical tones spread over a single vowel segment, or one lexical tone spread over two or three vowel segments (Pike and Pike, 1947). No simple chunk cuts can be used universally without violence to tone or intonation system.

In the face of these problems, early in 1952 I surrendered to the pressure to treat tone phonemes as different in some crucial but mysterious way from segmental phonemes, abandoning the attempt to treat them all as alike in a structural framework in which a simple tone served as a model for them all.

13.2 *Segmental Phonemes as Analogous to the Manifestation Mode*

What, however, were we now to do? It occurred to me that the approach to many problems through trimodal structuring had brought unexpected help. Could it possibly help here? I decided to try it and see.

Let us suppose, I said to myself, that in some way tone phonemes and segmental phonemes were different from each other in some modal fashion — what would this imply? It would suggest that there are MODE-LIKE EMIC UNITS, so that some of them would be classifiable and describable in a way reminiscent of the feature mode of an emic unit, others as having some resemblance to the manifestation mode of emic units, and still others as having some vague relationship to the characteristics of the distribution mode of emic units.

If this were the case here, would it be the tone phonemes or the segmental ones which more closely paralleled the characteristics of the manifestation mode of units? The answer seemed certain: The SEGMENTAL phonemes such as /s, t, o, m/ were the more concrete, more readily observable, more chunk-like, more easily seen as physical waves. This concreteness made the segmental phonemes, as wholes, the obvious starting point as analogous to the manifestation mode of units.

13.3 *Suprasegmental Phonemes as Analogous to the Feature Mode*

Where, then, would the SUPRASEGMENTAL phonemes of tone, stress, length, and intonation fit? They cannot be observed directly, without prior or simultaneous reference to the segments. In this sense, the suprasegmental phonemes are almost intangible simultaneous components of the segmental phonemes.

Segmental phonemes, also, do not exist except as combinations of intensity, duration, and vibrational frequency. These physical characteristics are in this respect simultaneous components of the segments, and make one segment differ from another. The phonemes of tone, intonation, stress, and length, however, are *organized* in some fashion different from or beyond the mere frequency, intensity, and duration which make up those ordinary segments which have no accompanying suprasegmental phonemes. The suprasegmental phonemes are vaguely analogous to the feature mode of emic units — they carry a 'flavor' of 'feature-like' quality — because of their componential nature. (And their difference in organization will appear in analytical perspective a bit later, § 13.5.)

13.4 *Subsegmental Phonemes (Voice Quality) As Analogous to the Distribution Mode*

The question now arose: Is there, by chance, some set of units which looks, analogously, as if it were mode-like in a distributional sense? A list of requirements (similar to the ones now presented in § 12.4) were drawn up to the ones now presented in § 12.4) were drawn up to serve as a guide as to the kind of unit to look for, and as a test of success in the event such units seemed to be found.

Soon an answer presented itself which seemed at first to meet all the requirements. The syllable constituted the sequential matrix of distribution for segmental phonemes and their variants, and for many pitch phonemes. It entered structured sequences made up of syllables; it was always present when segments were present (except for a rare possible situation in which the abdominal pulse but not the syllable would be relevant — § 9.76). The syllables themselves could be analyzed in an F-M-D manner (§§ 9.22-24). And there was hierarchy involved, in that syllables were distributed in stress groups, pause groups, and breath groups. This analysis looked very attractive indeed.

Presently, however, a flaw in the analysis began to appear: The segments seemed to be part of the same hierarchy to which the syllables belonged. This was disturbing, since the phonological hierarchy had already treated the syllable as a higher layer in the manifestation mode of the sentence. How then, could it serve double duty as also something quite different — as a special distribution unit of mode-like type? This objection obtained even greater force when it appeared that the grammatical hierarchy of the tagmeme must be kept separate in the theory from the lexical hierarchy of the morpheme. If the present data were to be somehow analogous to these, the syllable would not serve as the sought-for matrix unit.

I returned to the search, therefore, to find a phonological unit with matrix characteristics in a hierarchy different from that of the phoneme-syllable-stress group. Presently one appeared. It was VOICE QUALITY.

Every sentence, syllable, and segment occurred in some over-all timbre or vocal organic set which colored it. These qualities changed from time to time with borders frequently the same as those of major units of stress or pause groups, but conflicting with them often enough to give a crucial indication that the quality units were in sequences whose hierarchy was not the same as that of the regular phonological hierarchy previously treated. In my collected materials qualities of voice would occasionally change sharply in the middle of these other units — a fact which had been very disconcerting when in earlier analysis I had at first attempted to treat quality chunks of speech as on some level in the same hierarchy with stress but on a higher layer of that hierarchy.

Some of these settings last only a short time. Thus a sentence may contain a parenthetic utterance which carries its own particular qualitative elements with it. A sharp break in quality may occur within a sentence within a fraction of a second.

Now an exciting implication was forced into attention: Inasmuch as certain of these qualities seemed to be consistently used in the recorded breakfast materials, at certain kinds of points in the conversation or with certain kinds of effects on the hearers, we concluded not only that they were part of the signalling apparatus of speech but also that this signalling apparatus must be considered a basic integrated part of the total of the language and form-meaning modal and hierarchial structure. Voice quality was not just a vague kind of unstructured 'expression' outside the total organization of the culture, nor a mere quasi-irrelevant appendage or isolated compartment of behavior. Voice quality would have to seen as an interwoven part of the intricate total speech network.

The voice quality components could be viewed as SUBSEGMENTAL, modally paralleling the segmental and suprasegmental phoneme types already treated, much as the distribution mode of a unit parallels it manifestation and feature modes.

The thought of quality phonemes as such, however, was not new to me. I had been working with phonetic quality (Pike, 1945:101-02) and phonemic voice quality for some time. It was rather the modal tie-in to the total speech system, as distinct from a mere collection of peripheral phonemes, which was the immediately added factor in my thinking. I had earlier reached the conclusion that quality was phonemic, and had begun collection of materials for analyzing these qualities. In January of 1952 I started writing an article, entitled "Phonemic and Morphemic Voice Quality", exploring "the possibility of finding voice quality contrastive, and used to signal contrastive meanings." From one sample address, I began by noting six contrasting quality types: (1) light, smiling, and reassuring (*God is faithful in promising — yes*), (2) husky, indicating importance, (3) hollow, awesome (*God is love*), (4) shouting, emphatic (*The trumpet shall sound*), (5) chanting (*And so much the more*), (6) dulcet, prayerful (*God — give me a word*), (7) normal (*Second Corinthians, Chapter 15*).

Yet this analysis was not satisfactory — and the article was left unfinished — for several reasons. The first was that *many* such qualities seemed to be involved. Those noted in this attempt were far too few to cover the others which continued to show up in the recorded breakfast, football, and church materials — whining (by the children), amused tolerance (by the parents) unctuousness (as the children try to elicit favors), whispered, devotional, and angry qualities, and so on. Note a few samples:

From Record 37:
Relaxed: *Testing, one, two, three, four.*
Reassuring: *Oh, I think Daddy will be here in a minute.*
Breathy, with surprised protest: *Sweetheart, look at the color of your socks!*
Sad: *That needle can just hurt my S- a great deal.*
Whine: *I want to sew!*
Tender, breathy on last word: *He brought these possums in a box.*
Petulant: *Daddy tell the story; I don't know this story.*

A second difficulty was that several of these qualities could be combined. What was to be the phonemic analysis of a quality which had several such components? Was it a single new composite unit? or was it a simultaneous bundle of several phonemes? If so, were there limits to the combinations?

It later appeared that the answer to these difficulties could not be a simple accretion of more and more phonemic quality types. Rather the various combinations would have to be studied to find any internal structural ordering in them — and possibly even a hierarchical and criss-crossing layering of small quality units distributed in larger ones.

The size of this newer research task — analysis of the recorded materials — was such that it had to be delayed, rather than being prepared for inclusion here as originally planned.

(More recently, other scholars have worked on quality types. Since, however, our purpose here is to indicate how the trimodal model stimulated our thinking in the development of the theory, reference to later studies will be delayed until § 13.81.)

13.5 *Componential Systems of Mode-Like Emic Units*

The conclusion that voice quality was phonemic, and subsegmental, brought in its wake a number of insistent questions: What specific phonemes and types of phonemes of voice quality would be found in particular language — say English? How would these be related to a phonetic conceptual scheme paralleling that for segments? What permitted sequences of these would be found? Would they in turn be hierarchically ordered into larger and larger units? Would characteristics of trimodal structuring apply to each, then? And why should it be that there should occur phonemes of the various mode-like types?

The answer to this last question seemed now available: The mode-like types were not arbitrarily and miscellaneously arranged. Rather there were emic classes of phonemes, just as there were emic classes of morphemes. Evidently sets of these classes comprised simultaneous COMPONENTIAL SYSTEMS MODALLY ARRANGED. Phonological units were structurally arranged not only in sequence groupings, not only in hierarchically-arranged larger and larger types, and in emic classes of phonemes distributed in syllables and stress groups, but also they were arranged in basic systems in a trimodal fashion so that segmental, suprasegmental, and subsegmental types could all comprise simultaneous but distinct structural arrangements of a single sequence of events.

The discussion in the previous section has indicated that voice-quality units would be part of a subsegmental componential system of phonology. It suggested that these would be hierarchically arranged — though the details are as yet unknown to us. Voice-quality phonemes presumably comprise or are parts of voice-quality morphemes and tagmemes in hierarchical structures.

It became evident that intonation studies, in the light of this theory, also needed further development along hierarchical lines. Intonation structure in English should not be viewed as a sequence of intonation phonemes unrelated to higher-layered intonation units. Rather the phonemes of intonation should be seen as combining into larger and larger units. These units must be studied modally also, to see to what extent — or whether — there are simultaneous but distinct phoneme versus morpheme hierarchies of intonation. Terms such as "precontour", "complex rhythm unit", and so on (cf. Pike, 1945, and cf. §§ 6.2-3, 9.22, 9.241, 9.31-33, 9.6) need reassessment in an intonational morpheme hierarchy as units analogous to the prefixes, stems, words, phrases, sentences, of lexical elements. At the same time, their relationship to componential systems in general (§§ 6.41, 6.46, 10.51) and to stress groups (§§ 9.31-33, 9.6) need clarification if a total structural picture is to be obtained. This empirical study, also, is too large to attempt for inclusion in the present volume.

The stress problem itself became acute when the hierarchical articulatory approach was applied to it. If one adopts the view that the stressed syllable is a contrastive component of an emic abdominal pulse but not itself a separate emic unit (a possibility suggested in § 9.63), stress phonemes as such would not occur. The traditional approach to suprasegmental phonemes would thereby be affected, with stress removed from the normal trio of stress, pitch, length. It was partly hesitation at this point which led to some reserve in suggesting Solution C′ of § 9.63, and made it wise to leave room for the possible — I would now say probable — eventual adoption of 'Solution B' (§ 9.62) which would preserve stress phonemes as such. Even so, however, the modal and hierarchical status of stress as it would present itself under 'B' is still obscure.

Length problems also arise. It is clear that length may be both lexically phonemic and also contrastive in various nonlexical manners (see §§ 9.221, 9.225, 9.236). Was it possible, we asked ourselves, that a hierarchical structuring of length types could be found? How would rate of utterance, lexical length, and exclamatory length be related to this structuring if it occurs? Would such an approach shed any light on the problem as to whether, in a particular language, contrastive lexical length should be treated as a separate abstracted phoneme of length rather than as a repetition of the short vowel phoneme, and rather than as an additional but long vowel phoneme?

All of these components — phoneme segments, voice quality, pitch, stress, length — were evidently involved in any speech situation, and needed to be recorded for study. Supplementing the materials of 1945, I decided to test for some of these contrastively, by having texts recorded by different speakers, and transcribed.

The data repeated here are taken from an illustrated paper, unpublished, given at the Michigan Academy of Arts and Sciences, Section on Linguistics and Literary Criticism, Detroit, 1953.

Note Reading Type A. Here a poem by Emily Dickenson is read by a graduate student. The general voice quality — and total effect — is very prosaic. It could have been used to read a news report on lack of progress in a congressional filibuster. No special pitch intervals or height occurred. Phones were conversational types.

Rhythm was controlled by the physical phrasing. and so appeared as rather mechanical, with short and rather evenly-spaced stress groups.

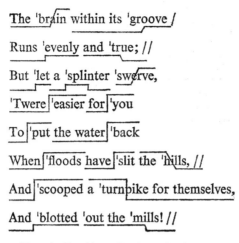

Type A: Read by a Graduate Student

The normal voice quality and pitch height are not given special symbols here — though symbols were available (cf. Pike 1945:101-03, for specific detail). Note, however, that a pitch line hugs the top of the letters for high, may pass considerably above them for extra high, and immediately or further below for mid and low respectively. A break in the line, furthermore, indicates the end of a stress group. Stress is indicated by a vertical stroke, and vowel or consonant length by a raised dot — as after *you*. The single diagonal bar indicates 'tentative' pause, with sustained pitch; the double bar indicates a 'final' pause, with pitch dropping more than the emic levels themselves require.

Type B is very different in voice quality. The whole reading is very soft, low, quiet, with narrow pitch spread. The dynamics of the whole is a sustained even loudness, with very little change of intensity for stress, and very little change of speed. Rhythm groups are frequently identified as much by their borders as by their peaks: ends of the rhythm units are frequently lengthened either by consonant, vowel, or both. A gradual decline in general height of pitch occurs in the latter part, and is only inadequately suggested by the dropping of the 'high' line six to mid pitch in seven, to low in eight. Otherwise, an extraordinary degree of sustained pitch is held throughout, on individual words and phrases. No final fade is recorded for the last word. The only pause in the entire poem comes after the second line. The softening of all phonetic elements of contrast gives a 'pensive' mood to the whole, as if the reader were *pondering* meanings — not trying to point them out to others.

This reading is by James Squires, who is himself a poet. When I showed him this graphic analysis of his recording he commented that the purpose for utilizing this general style was an attempt to subdue the dangerously heavy tendency toward doggerel through a line with characteristic stresses, since the phonological structure

> The 'brain within its 'groove
>
> Runs 'evenly and true; /
>
> But│'let a│'splinter·'swerve;
>
> 'Twere│'easier for 'you·
>
> To 'put· the 'water· 'back·
>
> When 'floods· have 'slit the 'hills
>
> And 'scooped a 'turnpike for them'selves,
>
> And 'blotted 'out· the 'mills!/

Type B: Read by a Poet

tended to obscure the meaning by calling attention to the sound; but that in a different kind of a passage — say some types of prose — his reading might rather have been designed to try to enhance the rhythmic characteristics rather than subdue them.

The contrast between Types B and C could scarcely be greater. In Type C, many phonetic techniques are used to achieve deliberate, dramatic effects, and to force the reader to focus on various aspects of the poem. The pitch range is very large. Pitch falls from extra high to low on the word *groove*. Pitch direction changes in the middle of syllables — as in *groove* and *swerve*. Stress changes are abrupt, intense, and varied — indicated by single versus double vertical stroke. Very great changes of speed show an intensity of implication. Note (f) as showing very fast tempo building up on line four, and (s) slowing down to a very deliberate pace in line six — repeated in lines seven and eight. Rhythm groups are set off by a combination of techniques: Length on *brain* gives a feeling of 'poise' for 'leaping' to the fast precontour *within the* plus

> The│'brain within its│''groove° /
>
> Runs° /│''evenly and│'true; //
>
> 'But^h /│'let a│''splinter 'swerve,^h ←/
>
> ⁽ᶠ⁾'Twere 'easier for you →
>
> To put the│'water back
>
> When⁽ˢ⁾│'floods have│'slit│the│'hills, /
>
> And│''scooped a 'turnpike⁽ᶠ⁾ for them'selves,
>
> And⁽ˢ⁾│''blotted 'out· the 'mills! //

Type C: Read by Literary Critic

the very sharply focused, extra-stressed, pitch-contrasted *groove*; this last word, in addition, is set off at the end by a release of the consonant *v* to a slight voiced vocoid [ə], and pause. Line two utilizes a very similar technique, with *runs* 'poised' by vocoid release plus pause, followed by the extra-stressed, pitch-contrasted *evenly*.

After a relaxed 'final' pause at the end of line two, line three begins in a similar way — though with voiceless vocoid [h] replacing the voiced one of line two. Line three ends, however, very differently. It has audible indrawn breath (see arrow) as preparation for the very fast beginning of line four, without the slow-down of lines one, two, and three.

The last line shows a sharp pitch transition from high falling to low falling, signalling change of mood from excitement at watching the awesome nature scene to one of quiet contemplation of the permanent effects on man's works.

The reader in this instance was Austin Warren, a literary critic who considers Emily Dickenson our greatest American poet and who has made commercial recordings of some of her materials. Professor Warren commented, after he had recorded the material, that he liked a poem in which every word is important — and we have seen that by his rhythmic groupings, extra stresses, high pitches, and rate changes he was able to emphasize many individual words such as *groove, evenly, splinter, scooped, blotted out*.

It should now be evident that the author of the poem exploited, directly, only the segmental system of the various componential systems available. The readers, however, were able to utilize effectively the suprasegmental and subsegmental systems of pitch and voice quality or dynamics.

The written form gives much less opportunity for the composer of the poem or other literary work to communicate to the reader the moods or emotive qualities to which he was reacting as he thought through the poem. In the process of 'thinking through' any such literary production the author would be unconsciously 'hearing' the words with *some* pitch and quality scheme. Yet only part of this which he 'hears' and 'feels' can get into ordinary print. Whatever part of his mood were in fact contained in such unwritten elements would be lost to the reader.

Should one not — we now inquire — consider what would happen if the poet were able to control consciously and write down for us alliterative intonation? or voice qualities contrasting with words proper so as to give special irony? or pitch patterns introduced for delicate surprise at points where the reader would not be expected to produce them for himself? We have already seen humorous selections marked delightfully (by Stark, in Pike, 1947c: 50-52). (I have also attempted to compose a poem or two where special pitch patterns gave part of the essential meaning — but my general artistic ability is too low to be effective.)

Thus far, poets are exploiting only part of available linguistic resources. If literary students could be training to read material marked for intonation — let alone other components — poets might have an interesting time exploiting new art forms for them. By way of encouragement to anyone who wishes to try, I might add that in phonetics classes I have used (for practising the reading of intonation) some poems of Frost marked for pitch as read by the author. To may astonishment I have found a number of the linguistic students suddenly excited by poetry who had never been interested before. The *visual* pitch allowed them to perceive and enjoy thoroughly what they had never been able to grasp in print — nor from phonograph records directly!

13.6 *Larger But Incomplete Modal Analogies*

At this point in the investigation the segmental, suprasegmental, and subsegmental approach made a further contribution. It served as a rather remote analogy to hint at some of the structural relationships between verbal and nonverbal behavior. In the breakfast scene, for example, the ordinary physical activities of eating, of sitting at the table, and so on, would constitute a hierarchy of activity of a type which would be considered partially analogous to the general segmental componential system of the total breakfast behavior, whereas the conversation superimposed upon that physical activity but not directly correlated with it would be a kind of adventitious addition making up a separate hierarchy with a separate set of elements of a 'suprasegmental' type.

The analogy is incomplete, however, in that the criteria set up in Chapter 12, by which one solves for F when one has M, are not met in this instance. One cannot state, for example, that all the eating activity of the breakfast scene is wholly included, even though restructured, in the verbal activity. Nevertheless, the partial success at describing the verbal-nonverbal relationship by this model is, to me, of interest in itself in addition to the fact that it has proved stimulating at other points.

One of these was the search it initiated for a subsegmental system analogous to the verbal and nonverbal components, utilizing the suggestions of Chapter 12 as to solving for D. We were now ready to ask: What would be the subsegmental characteristics of a trimodal structure in which conversation and nonverbal behavior were respectively suprasegmental and segmental? We must seek, again, for an element in which both these activities are combined — units of activity which are larger than either of these two by themselves, within which both of these are simultaneously distributed, which do not add elements which are not visible as parts of the manifestation mode of these other elements, but which nevertheless are distinct from them in the sense that they constitute further higher layers of organization.

It would not do to suggest that a merely larger set of behavior patterns would serve this function, since a larger set of elements of the same general type would merely be higher layers of the same componential systems. It must, rather, be in some respects different in kind.

Our suggestion: That EPISTEMOLOGICAL ATTITUDES or ACTIVELY-HELD BELIEF SYSTEMS (and the active moral character of a person) provide this integrating organization. All conversational activity, as well as all nonverbal activity, is contained within the general FRAMEWORK OF REFERENCE of activity which can be viewed in some such way.

Without a belief system (conscious or unconscious, vague, or organized concerning the nature of the world around him and concerning his own person) the individual could not act purposively.

Character and actively-held belief systems do not exist in a vaccuum, apart from activity. Character and belief systems are built during such activity. Nevertheless, though character may be built — for better or for worse — during a basketball game, the structure of that manifesting basketball game is not itself the structure of the character or belief system of the player.

If one wishes to discover the nature of a particular adult's epistemological attitudes, or belief systems, or character, one can do so only by examining his overt behavior. It is this overt behavior which manifests or constitutes the manifestation of these underlying attitudes, and without this manifestation — both verbal and nonverbal — they could not be discovered by the analyst.

We now return to linguistics, and a second contribution stimulated by the view that speech is suprasegmental to nonverbal behavior. We begin with a puzzling bit of data: At a luncheon one day my neighbor was in the midst of a reply to a question of mine when suddenly he quietly spoke the words *No thank you*, and continued the explanation in normal voice. What was the relation of this phrase to the conversation? None, except as an interruption. The interjected phrase was an 'aside' to a waiter who was holding a serving tray toward him.

The verbal insert was not organized in relation to the hierarchy of the conversation. Within what hierarchy then did it take place, and what hierarchy did it in part constitute? It would seem that this utterance was part of the luncheon *as such*, rather than of the conversation conducted at the luncheon. Yet in relation to the luncheon activity it was suprasegmental. Here, then, were two simultaneous suprasegmental relationships. One of these — seen in *No thank you* — was more closely related to the manifestation mode of the luncheon episode and its basic segmental character. The other — the conversation in general — was more detached from that segmental structuring. Evidently, then, we are in this instance meeting an INNER SUPRASEGMENTAL hierarchical relationship and an OUTER one. Confusion of description would result if this layering were ignored, and all verbal utterance treated as a single linear hierarchy.

13.7 *Overlapping Hierarchies of Mode-Like Emic Units*

The conclusion that behavior as a whole could have simultaneously an 'inner' and an 'outer' suprasegmental verbal system, with the inner one more closely related than the outer one to the segmental nonverbal system, was paralleled and reinforced by a similar query regarding language itself. Was it not possible that a language might have two or even three simultaneous structurings of pitch in different hierarchical relationships? And would this lead to the solution of the very difficult question as to the relationship between lexically-contrastive tones, phrasally-contrastive intonations, and socially-contrastive height of voice? To me the answer is 'yes'.

Phrasal intonation would be analyzed as, in general, an outer suprasegmental layering of speech. Lexical tone would be an inner suprasegmental layer, closely related to the 'segmental' hierarchial system of sounds and words. General height of voice, however, would perhaps be treated as subsegmental, analogous to or part of the system of voice quality.

In Mazahua (Eunice Pike, 1951), for example, there are two heights of lexical pitch which occur contrastively on nonfinal syllables of words, as in items such as *záphə* 'gun', *zàphə* 'lake'. Other contrastive pitches and pitch sequences are of a phrasal, intonation type, and occur on word-final or on phrase-final syllables, with a different number of contrastive heights — three of them. The lexical type contribute as parts of segmental morphemic structure. The intonation type themselves wholly constitute morphemes, as parts of the intonational componential hierarchy; compare *thúsʔə^1* 'a cigar, you say?,' with *thúsʔə^2* 'and a cigar?,' *thúsʔə^3* 'a cigar?' (In these illustrations of Mazahua the acute and grave accents indicate high and low lexical pitch respectively, whereas the numerals indicate intonation levels, with 1 high, 3 low). Note also the glides on *rà-šə̂rə$^{2\cdot 1}$* 'tomorrow?!' and *ʔyahkə$^{2\cdot 3}$* 'Hey, you give it to me!'

Eunice Pike suggests that the two kinds of units should not be combined into a single system of pitch even although an occasional allophone of a tone and of an intonation phoneme may be homophonous. Her reason: "To us, however, it seems that the tonemic material and the intonemic material constitute two separate systems. The presence of these two systems is indicated by their different distribution, by their different types of allotones, and by the different grammatical-semantic characteristics of the morphemes into which they enter, or which they constitute. We do not wish to combine into a single phoneme allophones — even homophonous ones — taken from two different systems." The modal analogies developed here support this view, and indicate that intonational pitch may constitute a componential system different from that to which the units of lexical pitch belong (1951:39n).

Once we had granted the usefulness of the modal analogy for pitch relationships, the question arose as to whether the same approach would be useful for length and stress. It became evident that a comparable situation existed, even though less-extensively developed systems, with fewer included units, might be involved (cf. § 9.221).

For length: Lexically-contrastive length would parallel lexical tone as an 'inner' suprasegmental layer closely related to the sound and word segmental hierarchies. Phrasally-contrastive or expressive length would parallel phrasal intonations, as an 'outer' suprasegmental layer. General rate of speech — fast and slow — would parallel voice quality, as subsegmental.

For stress (cf. § 9.3): Expressive, phrasal stress would similarly appear as an 'outer' layer of the suprasegmental hierarchies. Lexical stress would seem closely related to the segmental systems of sounds and words. General loudness would, in turn, parallel subsegmental voice quality.

Finally, as we look back at all three — pitch, length, stress — we see that the three types in turn have their mode-like relationships as to classes of units. The *lexical* pitches, stresses, and lengths, though all suprasegmental from one hierarchical viewpoint, are all — when viewed 'close-up' (i.e., with attention addressed to their own modal structure) — somewhat segmental in type. The *phrasal* intonation, expressive length, and expressive stress are all suprasegmental, in general, but seem heightened in this quality (i.e., suprasegmental to the suprasegmental system) when compared with the lexical units. The socially-relevant height of voice, the rate, and the general loudness are also all in one sense suprasegmental, but when viewed in this 'close-up' of the suprasegmental components as a system are in another sense subsegmental to that suprasegmental system.

Could this vague relationship in turn be further generalized and clarified, without bringing in concepts other than those seen to be necessary for describing the characteristics of sounds, words, and sentences already studied? It soon appeared probable. As emic progression (§ 12.3) shows units trimodally structured, with the modes containing a spectrum of units each of which may be trimodally structured, and as classes of morphemes are trimodally structured (§§ 7.313, 12.3), so also systems as a whole may be trimodally structured. The total language system may be structured into suprasegmental, segmental and subsegmental systems. It is the internal modal structuring of these larger mode-like systems which, in an internal layering of emic progression, gives rise to the various kinds of suprasegmental relationships which led to some of the puzzles looked at in this chapter. Many of the details, however, remain obscure. Other problems are undoubtedly left untreated — and some may prove to have been distorted — but the general significance of the approach seems to be sufficiently clear to make it evident that suprasegmental units must be studied hierarchically and multi-systemically.

13.8 *Bibliographical Comments on Chapter 13*

Some differences of opinion remain as to whether suprasegmental phonemes should be part of our conceptual framework. Hamp argues that certain stylistic elements "are entities in some other system that runs alongside the linguistic and impinges on it in a peculiarly intimate way" (1957a:141). Chomsky, Halle, and Lukoff, however, question the whole possibility of even stresses as being suprasegmental. They state that "the distribution of stresses is accounted for automatically in terms of the hierarchy of junctures with no intervening 'morphological' level. In such a case, it seems pointless to regard suprasegmentals as separate levels at all", but rather they "can consider accent to be a distinctive feature similar to such distinctive features as voicing" and so they would "have accented and unaccented vowels"; suprasegmentals "would then appear as features of phonemes, or as utterance-long or phrase-long components"; if they can extend this "to other languages, one can considerably simplify linguistic theory by restricting it to the consideration of linear systems" (1956:79); they hope to show later "that a similar treatment of pitch is possible and advantageous" (fn. 14). Note that this view would be counter to our thrust which affirms that intonation systems must be handled with their full gamut of phonemes, morphemes, and tagmemes.[1]

13.81 *On Voice Quality, La Langue and La Parole*

As more and more materials in speech begin to appear structured, the view that 'language' as a structure differs from 'speech' as activity is threatened. In behavioremics, furthermore, the structural units always retain substance as relevant to their manifestation mode (§§ 6.91, 7.85, 8.82). Under the impact of these two factors, we abandon the distinction between *la langue* and *la parole* proposed by de Saussure (1931 [1915]).

Voice quality would, then, in my view be considered linguistically relevant whether, on the one hand, unitized (i.e., 'discretely coded') in contrastive phonemes or in componential systems such as whisper versus song, or whether, on the other hand, it is socially significant but gradient (i.e., 'continuously coded' by degree) as may be rates of speed, degree of voice loudness, or general height of voice. (Though Professor Martin Joos suggested to me some years ago that even the general height of voice may prove to be discretely split into four 'kinds' of pitch levels, which I would call — from low to high — relaxed, normal, intense, excited). Even qualitative characteristics which are considered 'unlearned' may often be modified under social pressures, and so move into the linguistic orbit as signals of social conformity and of social level. Even sneezes, laughter, coughing, and nervous affects on the voice differ sharply according to one's social environment. And the fact that actors — or nonprofessional mimics — can imitate many characteristics of voice quality normally associated with particular individuals shows that these characteristics, also, are cues to the listener which allow him to learn much about the speaker's personality — which may be relatively constant for him, but fixed by his attitudes and habits rather than by physiological necessity. Even those over which the speaker has little control — resulting, for example, from cleft palate — carry a message differentiating one individual from another.

For a different point of view see Togeby (1951:264), and Sebeok, Walker, Greenberg (in Osgood, Sebeok, and others, 1954: 76; from this volume, however, I take the phrases "discretely coded" and "continuously coded" — 85). Compare Hjelmslev (1953:74). Hamp (1957a) in discussing Grimes' treatment of Huichol, feels that the vocal qualifiers may not even be properly labelled by the language name 'Huichol', "since the latter is a linguistic term" and it is "highly unlikely that the other system is

---

[1] See, now, Pike, 1963c, for intonation as a concomitant system with its own grammatical, lexical, and phonological units.

coextensive with linguistic Huichol" (141); rather the qualifier system "runs alongside the linguistic [system] and impinges on it in a peculiarly intimate way".

For physiological conditioning of voice quality, see also Meader and Muyskens, 1950:226). For early attempts at listing discrete voice qualities note, among others, Rush (1867). Some bibliography is given in Pike (1945:5, 12-13, 181-84).

For discussion of gradient problems in quality, see Pike (1945:99).

For an attempt to lay an articulatory groundwork for the phonetics of voice quality, and transcriptional symbols, see Pike (1945:99-104). A relatively high tongue position in the mouth leads to a 'thin' or 'childish' quality. The tongue low in the mouth produces a more 'hollow' or 'sepulchral' sound. With the tongue back, a more 'choked' or 'muffled' variety is likely to be heard. Other effects come from fronting, lip rounding, throat tension, etc.

For voice quality as signalling personality characteristics, see Sapir (1927, in his Selected Writings: 535-36, 540-41, with such phenomena occurring in a "bewildering range" as yet unclassified or named, and yet perhaps "in some way a symbolic index of the total personality"), Newman and Mather (1938, with listing of qualitative and dynamic factors found in patients with classical depressions, gloom, or manic syndromes, etc.), Stevens (1951:1068, 1070, with the possibility of judging one's occupation from voice-quality cues), Kennedy (1953:369, with masculine tone varieties).

For voice quality as part of vowel signals, see Firth (1936:534, tone with breathy vowels), Henderson (1952:151, sepulchral voice).

For recent attempts at listing phonemic "voice qualifiers", see H. L. Smith (1952: 61-63; with overloudness, oversoftness, rasp or stricture, raspIessness or openness, drawling, whining, singing, chuckling, ingressions, and whispering). Stockwell, Bowen, and Silva-Fuenzalida have shown some quality types for Spanish (1956:661-65). McQuown shows sample transcriptions and comments from quality analysis (1957b:82-84). Pittenger and Smith show the implications of vowel quality for psychiatry (1957:72-74), with differentiation of quality phenomena into vocal qualifiers, vocal differentiators, vocal identifiers, and vocal quality and voice set. (These divisions of H. L. Smith are mentioned, but not illustrated, in his review of Jassem (1955:153.) Trager has a similar, but more elaborate, analysis of vocal types (1958): voice set (prelinguistic, including data from background of physiology and physical peculiarities — sex, age, mood, location, etc.); voice qualities (pitch range and control, resonance and rhythm control, tempo, articulation control, etc.), vocalizations — of three types (a) vocal characterizers (laughing, crying, whispering, whining), (b) vocal qualifiers (intensity, pitch height, extent — i.e., drawl or clipping), (c) vocal segregates (*uh-huh*, *sh*).

For voice quality ('vocalizations') as not part of a sentence note Joos (1957:418); similarly Hill (1955, in H. B. Allen 1958:21, as "not parts of larger metalinguistic structures"). Various experiments on voice quality are found in the work of Ochiai and Fukumura (1957). For an attempt to observe and report on many kinds of voice quality phenomena from recordings, note Pittenger, Hockett and Danehy (1960).

For classification of laryngeal components in phonation (normal glottal, ligamental, arytenoidal, ventricular and voiceless, whisper, voice, creak, stop) see Catford (in D. Jones, 1964).

In reference to the possibility of a subsegmental hierarchy suggested in § 13.4, we suggest that voice set might be a high-level unit in a hierarchy whose low-level units would be more localized quality changes affected by specific oral adjustments (Pike, 1945:101). Intermediate between them would be the long units of song, whisper, etc. General rate of speed and local length phenomena might be part of a second such hierarchy. Dynamic factors of stress-group type, with dynamic contour affected by early or late, sharp or gradual crescendo and decrescendo, etc. (Pike, 1957c), might be high-level components of a third hierarchical set with special controlled or ballistic syllable types (§ 9.221) intermediate in range, and single phoneme dynamics at the bottom of the hierarchy.

13.82 *On Suprasegmental Phonemes*

There have been numerous attempts to define suprasegmental phonemes (see collection of definitions in Wells, 1945:28-29). These approaches do not all lead to the same units, however. For Hockett, "Those [features] which clearly extend over a series of several segmental groupings are SUPRASEGMENTAL" (1942:8), so that, for example, voicelessness and "absence of nasality" are both suprasegmental over the last two phonemes of *crypt*. Compare Harris on long components (1944b:191-96; 1951:125-36). Trager included among the suprasegmental components various secondary phonetic characteristics such as labialization (1941:135); cf. Harris, with height of tongue as suprasegmental (1944a:206). In 1947c (65b, 63a) I attempted to define the suprasegmental phonemes as those units that "affect sounds quantitatively but not qualitatively", limiting the list to length, stress, pitch, and possibly glottal stop (147-48a). For glottalization, see also in this connection Harris (1944a:205), where glottalization (but not glottal stop) is suprasegmental because it is "addable to and removable from glottalized continuants" and "a glottalized continuant configurates as one consonant"), and Haugen (1949a:281), where, in Danish, glottal stop is a prosodeme because of "the effect of timing"). Haugen, moreover, wishes to say that "all phonemes are successive" (even if stress could not then be called phonemic) and that "any significant sound feature whose overlap of other features is temporally correlated to syllabic contour should be called a prosodeme" (1949a:282). For other views of prosody, quite different from that of Haugen, see H. J. Uldall (1936:54-55, in which prosodies are defined as "consolidating one syllable" and in Danish include h, not-h, glottal stop, not glottal stop, and others), Hjelmslev (1936:53, in which consonants must be capable of occurring both final and initial, but prosodies in one or the other position only), Firth and others (references and discussion in §§ 8.814, 9.73, 10.51). For suprasegmental elements as behaving like a separate system, see

Wells (1945:28-29). In sum, definitions have been attempted in reference to larger structures (e.g., syllables in reference to segmental spread), in reference to componential analysis, in reference to phonemic analysis, articulatory production, or acoustic form, and in reference to system formation.

Some authors, instead of trying to work their way through these knotty problems, build the foundations of their system without including them (Jakobson, Fant, Halle, 1952:15). Others have assumed that the problem may be structurally irrelevant, and that the traditional analysis of tone phonemes versus voice phonemes "has no doubt been largely determined by our traditional orthography" (Greenberg, in Osgood, Sebeok, and others, 1954:12). McDavid, in reviewing Jones, says that "Not only is this multiplication of technical terms [toneme, stroneme, chroneme] esthetically disturbing; it suggests a hierarchical difference that does not necessarily exist" (1952:381). Hockett, in objecting to the title of my Tone Languages, protests that "Such terms may form no part of an objective linguistic taxonomy" and "the expression 'tone languages' ... may be no more meaningful than, say, 'velar spirant languages'" (1949a:30).

For references to stress, see §§ 9.74-76.

For length, note § 9.22. Note also H. Vogt, on Norwegian (1942:9), where CV·C is contrasted with CVC·, *vi·s* 'wise' versus *vis·* 'certain', and "the distinction must be of a prosodic nature, because phoneme sequences as a whole and not single phonemes are opposed". See also Haugen, where a sound which "extends beyond the boundary of a syllable" "is uniformly interpreted as a new phoneme" (1949a:280). On vowel length in Estonian, see Ariste (1939:277, 279, with three phonemic lengths plus two or more others). For a more recent study of Estonian, based on spectrographic analysis and juncture theory, see Lehiste (1960a). Note also, for Hausa, Carnochan (1950).

13.83 *On Intonation*

A long-standing misconception concerning intonation is rejected by most scholars today, namely that "the tones expressive of sorrow, lamentation, mirth, joy, hatred, anger, love, pity etc. are the same in all nations" (Sheridan, 1798:170). Note, for example, Sapir's rejection of this view (1927, in his Selected Writings:538). In Comanche, no contrastive intonations have been found (Smalley, 1953:297; cf. discussion above, in § 6.41); rather "Greater emotional intensity is sometimes conveyed, not by intonational changes, but by segmental changes", for example in |išapĬ '(You) liar!' versus |isapĬ 'a liar' (Canonge, private communication). Note also contrastive intonation exclusively on a few exclamatory particles, in Oto (Pike, 1945:21). Experimental evidence that intonation patterns are learned is found in Evelyn Pike (1949).

For intonation as a distinct system from tone, in a language containing both, see

Pike (1948:16-17, 36, 85-86), Hockett, on Mandarin (1950a:65), Eunice Pike, on Mazahua (1951), Haugen and Joos, on Norwegian, (1952). Cf. also Von Laziczius (1936:58-59) with reference to "emphatica" which are expressive as against lexical phonemes which are representational, and Bazell, for whom intonation is not in the "central structure of a language" (1953).

See also Siertsema (1963, with terraced tone optionally treated as in part intonational).

The best illustration of the opposite point of view — that lexical and phrasal pitch should be analyzed as a single linear set of pitch phonemes — is seen in Bloch, with four resultant Japanese pitch phonemes (1950, versus 1946, in which the accented syllable of a word and all but the first of a series of syllables immediately preceding it in a word had high pitch, 98 fn. 4).

The presence of four discrete *contrastive* pitch levels in English was first pointed out by Pike (1942:32-34). Extensive analysis was made of meaningful sequences of these pitches, in the same volume (48-86), along with drills for foreign student practice, as well as discussion of problems of quantity and a listing of voice qualities (91-95). The pedagogical material utilizing the contrastive pitches was incorporated in Fries and staff (1943, and subsequent editions). The theoretical material was then expanded and published separately (Pike, first printing 1945; the date of this publication is frequently misquoted, with a 1946 date — that of the second printing — utilized, as by Wells 1947b; most recently Trager [in D. Jones, 1964:267, 270], uses the second-printing date — 1946 — while attributing an earlier date — 1945 — to Wells and adds incorrectly that "the basic analysis of English pitch [was] made by Wells and extensively applied [sic] by K. L. Pike" — in spite of Pike's prior publication several years earlier, in 1942, and the extensive and widely-known use of Pike's work by Fries and staff in 1943).

For other approaches to pitch phonemes in English, see Wells (1945, with reference to pitch morphemes), Trager and Smith (1951, with reference to junctures and terminals). Bolinger rejects the view of four contrastive steps, by showing intermediate pitches (1947, 1951) — but fails to operate within the restriction set by Pike (1945:26) that only the crucial contour points must be treated in this contrastive way. The domain of intonation phonemes, that is, is not the individual vowel but a place in the emic stress group.

Discrete steps of intonation are also rejected by Togeby (1951:38), and by Weinreich (1953a:277). Possibly some of the difficulty here (apart, that is, from failure to deal with contour points) is their failure to seek the contrasts only in frames with general height of pitch controlled. The contrasts occur within any particular general height or style of voice, with some particular spread of intervals. Thus, for example, all the contrastive contours may occur in falsetto; falsetto cannot, therefore, be considered as a special fifth pitch level which breaks the system of four contrastive levels (our reply to Bolinger's attack in his review of 1947:71).

For bibliography on English intonation, see Pike (1945). See, also, references in preceding paragraph. For more recent treatments (but without the structural views needed for behavioremic synthesis) see Jassem (1952), Hockett (1958:33-61), and Bolinger (1947, 1951, 1955b, 1958). For a structural analysis of Spanish intonation, see A. Anthony (1948) and Stockwell, Bowen, and Silva-Fuenzalida (1956). For structure in the intonation of an American Indian language, see Larsen and E. V. Pike (1949).

See, also, Fries (in D. Jones, 1964:242-54, who shows that out of 2561 yes-or-no questions, about sixty percent — counter to continuous assertions to the contrary — had falling intonation).

For work on British English note also Kingdon (1948, 1958), Sharp (1958), J. D. O'Connor and Arnold (1961); Lees (1960c), Schubiger (in D. Jones, 1964:255-65), and E. Uldall (in D. Jones, 1964:271-79). Descriptions of intonation of other languages continue to appear: for Spanish, Wallis (1951); for Swedish, Hadding-Koch (1961); for Cocama (Tupi Guaraní), Faust and E. G. Pike (in *Série Linguistica...*, 1959:26); for Russian, Buning and Van Schooneveld (1960); for Czech, Daneš 1957).

Numerous discussions of general problems of intonation are also appearing: Hockett (1955:46, 223); Sledd (1959:20-34; 1955, in H. B. Allen, 1958:86) "as essential to the definitions of subject and object"; James (1956-57); Koekkoek (1956-57); Lehiste and Peterson (1961b:425); Chomsky (in Third Texas Conference, 1962:122), as "one of the tremendous gaps in the kind of grammar that I have been working on, is its failure to make any kinds of predictions about intonation" — though he doubts the advisability of trying to support a phrase-structure grammar "by giving phonologically-based rules for determining phrase cuts"; see also 19. For an attempt at intonation in transforms, however, note Stockwell (1960b). For intonation universals, see Bolinger (1961); as peripheral, Daneš (1960:54); for the "attitude of listeners to a variety of intonation patterns" experimentally looked at through Osgood's semantic differential, E. Uldall (1960:223); experiments in which the subject attempts to match intonation — which "points up the fallacy of considering the physical pitch to be an adequate representation of the perceived (psychophysically determined) pitch" (J. M. Cowan, 1962:569-70); psychological context of intonation, Vigotsky (in Saporta, 1961:527); tone and intonation overlapping, Grimes (1959); in relation to poetic language, and in relation to music, Žinkin (1962:167, 169); in relation to religious chantings, Weinreich (in *For Roman Jakobson*, 1956:639-40); in relation to sing-song style — stereotyped — as well as chanting, recitative of drama or song, and lexical tone Chao (in *For Roman...*, 1956).

13.84 *On Tone*

For bibliography on tone languages, see Pike (1948). For first treatment of frame techniques in the analysis of tone, stress, and length, see Pike (1938; developed in detail, 1948). For first use of term 'toneme' (pointed out to me by Daniel Jones) see Armstrong and Tin (1925:20).

For minimal pairs with four tone levels, in Chatino, see McKaughan (1954:27; *kItá* 'you wait', kItā 'he waits', *kita* 'cigarette', kItà 'flour' — with [I] representing voiceless vowel, and ['] high tone, [-] mid tone, [(unmarked)] lower tone, [`] lowest tone). For pitch contrasts as differences in timing of the tonal curve, in Scandinavian languages, see Haugen (1949a:279-80). For five tone levels in Trique of Mexico, see Longacre (1952); in Tahua Yao of China, see Chang (1953:375), in Ticuna of Peru, see Anderson and Anderson (in *Série Linguistica*, 1959). For special problems in analysis: tone variants, D. Jones (1944); toneless syllables in Mandarin, Hockett (1949b:211); upper tones with voiceless initial, lower tones with voiced initial, in Kennedy (1953:368); incomplete symmetry, and length pseudo-contrasts in Zapotec, Eunice Pike (1948); pitch pseudo-contrasts in Campa, Pike and Kindberg (1956); pitch analysis of words without reference to tone phonemes, in Chaga, Sharp (1954: 167-68; and cf. above § 8.814); for models of tone systems, Pike (1952b); for historical origin of tone in Swedish, Oftedal (1952); also Jakobson (1931); on African languages, Welmers (1949, 1950a, 1950b, 1952). For intonation in relation to tone, see §§ 13.5; 13.83.

New approaches to problems of tone continue to appear: W. S. Allen suggests that for ancient India, "some of the tonal terminology is really based on gestural movements, which are of course in turn related to the kinaesthetic and acoustic phenomena" (1953a:91). The whole problem of trying to find a neutral point to which tones may appear to be relative may have reference to "the physical ordering of stimuli, and at the middle of a series of responses there is a neutral point" — as in problems of relative weights, and adaptation level for various elements (compare Broadbent and Ladefoged, 1960:384-87). Schachter, for Twi, finds some instances in which change of tone rather than level of tone is relevant (1961a:238); compare the "terrace-system type" reported variously by Welmers (1959), Meeusen (1952), Siertsema (1963:61). Welmers emphasizes the non-uniqueness of tone problems (1959). Kikuyu morphophonemics, with tone reversal for negative, is seen in Harries (1952:143). Rowlands has tone elision in Yoruba (1954:376-77). Various other articles on tone languages can be found by perusing various issues of *African Abstracts*, in the linguistic studies section (for example, 1963, vol. 14). An excellent — one of the few — historical reconstructions of tone, in the proto-Mixtec group, is seen in Longacre (1957:93-112). Psycholinguistics of tone is noticed when, in teaching people to read, the prior humming or whistling of tone apart from segmental context "made faster progress in tone readings", Gudschinsky (1959d:451). For phonetic similarity in tone, note Schachter (1961a); tone handled in relation to word, Sprigg (1955:134); allotones, in Seminole, determined by word position, vowel length, emphasis, neighboring tones, and stress, in West (1962:83-85); tone as an important syntactic signal, but with low lexical load and no morphemic minimal pairs, in Huave, Pike and Warkentin (1961); tones contrastive on a domain of several microsyllables, pronounced with closed lips on a nasal, with only glottal stop interruption, in Chinantec, Robbins (1961 and in A William Cameron..., 1961); tone with variants involving breathy voice quality, Burton-Page (1955:113); nucleus and contour in Norwegian tone, Haugen (1963:160-61); tone problems in dialect geography in Scandanavia, Jensen (1961); also E. V. Pike, with allomorphs of different dialects of Mazatec (1956); a description of several different types of tonal and accentual systems within twenty-five related languages of the Central Highlands of New Guinea, E. V. Pike (1964); continuing appearance of instrumental studies of tone, as in Chinese, for example Shen, Chao, and Peterson (1961).

As for the relative nature of tone, note the following incident told me by E. V. Pike: In the Mazatec village of Huautla, Mexico, four children were playing a game similar to 'Old Maid', in which the object was to call for cards held by their companions. Occasionally when they called for a card, they would mention only the name of the object itself. Among the objects named on the cards, however, was a pair ni^3nta^3 'bone' and ni^4nta^4 'fox' (with tone 4 lower than tone 3). When they called for one of these words by name alone — without using the word in a sentence — sometimes confusion would result. Occasionally they would prefer to ask 'Did you want fox or bone': ni^3nta^3 a^3xo^4 ni^4nta^4. Their reply would be either $ni^3nta^{3-4}ri^3$ 'I said bone, man!' or else $ni^4nta^4ri^3$ 'I said fox, man!'

For singing in a tone language, see § 13.85.

13.85 *On Communication with Abstracted Components*

In Arica, communication by drums may follow the linguistic pitch; for a few references see Pike (1948:36). For similar treatment of drum communication in Bora, Peru, see Thiessen (to appear).

Conversation by whistling, in Mazatec, Mexico, with apparently unrestricted topics, is described by G. Cowan (1948); this also follows the abstracted linguistic pitch.

In a more recent article G. Cowan (1952) describes briefly a different system of communication by whistling — in Tepehua, a language of Mexico — which so far as is known is nontonal, in which the *contrasting consonants and vowels* are whistled. A difference between 'stops' and 'fricatives' is in the whistle talk carried by lip movements. Consonants are palatalized in the whistle. Both consonants and vowels are somewhat labialized, but varying degrees of rounding or spreading retain the contrasts of speech. One is not nasal, but has a front and raised tongue position. Distant whistling is achieved by a doubled finger in the mouth, which fogs the contrasts and reduces the number of possible messages. A bilingual informant illustrating the data, by whistled replies in Spanish, made the same kinds of adjustments for the Spanish sounds. For whistled Spanish. in the Canary Islands, see Classe (1957).

A 'hum talk' on the other hand, is known through an abstracted intonation of Yiddsch, utilized for conversation during parts of certain religious occasions where regular conversation is taboo (private communication from Prof. Abraham Kaplan, who tells me that he himself participates in such conversations, and that a sample conversation — quite legitimate, except that the novelist carries it to excess — occurs in The Passover Guest, by S. J. Rabinowitz [Sholom Aleichem]).

For a discussion of western music stimulated by speech intonations, see R. A. Hall (1953). For references to Chinese, African, and American Indian music based on linguistic pitch see Pike (1948:34); see also A. M. Jones (1958:11-12).

For an extensive bibliography on drum talk and whistling speech, see Stern (1957: 503-06), with some reference to Burma; note also Busnel, Moles, Vallancien (in *Proceedings of the Fourth...*, 1962). In reverse, there is an extensive literature on the whispering of tone languages; for one instance only, note J. D. Miller (1961:15). See also references in Pike (1948:34, fn. 40). A quite different — but partially related — instance occurs in the English spoken by natives of the Gold Coast languages: stress and rhythm of normal English are omitted, leading to serious loss "in terms of intelligibility" since the "habit is to stress all syllables approximately equally", eliminating possibility of sentence stress; similarly, the contrastive intonation tunes of English are lacking — in spite of the fact that these Gold Coast languages are tonal — and therefore one misses "a great deal of the information about the attitude of the speaker toward his subject and his audience", Strevens (1954:83-84).

For the problem of creating song tunes in a tone language note some summary in Pike (1948:34); for discussion of hymn creation under such circumstances, note M. Cowan and Davis (1955); and see special issue of the journal *Practical Anthropology* (Nov.-Dec., 1962). For ability to think even when there are incapacities for speech, with the suggestion that the difference is due to the "physiologic and psychologic structures" of the different performances, note Goldstein (1948:146-47). Further reference to song and tone languages may be found in Wangler (1958) and Bright (1957:28) — with lack of correspondence in the two systems.

CHAPTER 14

FUSED UNITS

In the last chapter we showed how the modal outlook led to a general view of the relationship between suprasegmental, segmental, and subsegmental systems of sound. In this chapter we again use the modal outlook to help us understand the changes which occur when segments come together in sequences. (For earlier mention of these problems, see §§ 6.55, 6.66, 7.56, 8.42, 8.442, 8.446, 9.225, 9.236-37, 9.241, 9.32, 9.61, 9.74.)

14.1 *The Item-and-Arrangement (Particle) and Item-and-Process (Wave) Views of Sequence*

Specifically, we wish to know whether a modal view of the phenomena occurring at the borders of segments in sequence can help us attain an over-all scheme which will apply to a wide range of segment types. Fusion, change, or interference between segments must ultimately be studied in a wide variety of sequence types or JUNCTIONS, if we are to arrive at a framework which will be useful for further inquiry.

We are using 'junction' to refer to a sequence of two abutting segments of any kind. (The term 'juncture' is more generally used to refer to the 'joint' which is 'between' two units, and is usually restricted to postulated phonological units at these joints. Cf. §§ 9.61, 9.74.)

14.11 *The Modal Analogy*

The reader will recall that in § 12.1 we indicated that the characteristics of feature mode and manifestation mode led by crude analogy to static versus dynamic versus functional views of data, or to views of particle versus wave versus field. Here we apply the static (i.e., particle) and dynamic (i.e., wave) analogies to two approaches which have been called respectively 'item-and-arrangement' and 'item-and-process.' (For the field view, see § 14.3.)

Under the STATIC view a sequence of units is treated as a sequence of discrete segments — of PARTICLES or ITEMS. Each unit segment in the sequence is assumed to have, in principle, a specific beginning and ending. Each junction is analyzable, in principle, into two concrete, non-overlapping units. Thus the junction *cats* is analyzed into *cat* and *-s;* /æžu/ *as you* is analyzed into /æ-/ *as* and /-žu/ *you* (or into /æž-/ and /-u/; or into /æz/ and /-ʸu/ in which the raised /-ʸ/ implies an abstracted palatal component).

The strength of this static view lies in the fact (1) that it allows units to be treated as discrete, thus paralleling the basic outlook of emic units as distinct, contrastive components of speech. Also (2), it holds out promise (which in my view cannot be fulfilled) of allowing linguistics to be treated simply and exclusively as composed of two kinds of theoretical constructs — phoneme and morpheme units on the one hand, and distribution on the other — hence suggesting a linguistic theory of considerable simplicity.

Basic techniques to implement this static view would require (1) theory and methods for determining the point at which a junction is to be cut into two — a technique for resolving the junction into two discrete sets of components. They would also require (2) theory and methods for determining the allo-units of a unit, and their distribution, i.e., variants which differ according to the particular junction in which they occur. One must, that is to say, be able to segment /æžu/ in *some* way in principle and practice. It would seem to me that these practices should ideally be consistent, reflect a coherent view of language, and should not in principle permit numerous conflicting alternate analyses. This, for me, would be part of a definition of ideal — unattainable — methodological rigor.

Under the DYNAMIC view, on the other hand, a sequence of units may be treated as a series of WAVES flowing into one another, fusing at their boundaries, with the ending point of the one unit and the beginning of the next frequently indeterminate. While on the one hand an emic unity is postulated for each member of the junction, such that each unit is contrastive and emically distinct from the other unit, nevertheless the manifestation mode of each unit is seen as wave-like, with merging borders. The 'center' or wave peak of a unit may be detected — or, at a minimum, the fact of the presence of the unit may somehow be attested — while the borders of the unit may be indeterminate. Thus the sequence /æžu/ *as you* may have morphemic wave peaks of *as* and *you* at /æ-/ and /-u/ while the borders of both are indeterminate within the phoneme /-ž-/. The junctions composed of *cuts* and *buds* may have peaks somewhere within *cut*, *bud*, and within /-s/, or /-z/, but the borders may be conveniently treated as indeterminate for either junction if (for reasons unspecified here) one wishes to treat the voicelessness of the /-s/ plural allomorph as part of the *cat* morph, or the voicing of the /-z/ plural allomorph as part of the *bud* morph.

The strength of this dynamic view lies in the fact (1) that it allows the indeterminacy-in-fact of segment borders to be treated as indeterminacy-in-theory as well. A cut does not have to be made at any particular spot in the sequence and a phoneme shared by two morphemes does not have to be arbitrarily assigned to one or the other.

Further (2), it allows the wave-like character seen clearest in phonological movement to be generalized to other linguistic levels, so that the wave character of phonology becomes an integral part of a total theory. (3) A large series of events in a particular language can be easily summarized by a simple, elegant statement of changes — e.g.: "any stop will be lost when it would otherwise occur before a second stop across a morpheme boundary within a word". Such a statement eliminates the necessity of making separate statements for the action of each stop or for the distribution of each allomorph. (4) A theory of linguistics emerges, with this as one component, which has a few simple theoretical constructs applying to the whole system of human behavior — constructs which can deal with modal and hierarchical ordering of that behavior as well as with its simple segmentation. (5) The entrance, into the theory, of merging units meets one basic philosophical requirement for any theory which is to portray adequately the universe as a system in which units can in fact interact with one another. This approach contrasts with a purported universe of discrete units which can only, in principle, react at a distance.

Basic techniques to implement this dynmaic view would require (1) theory and methods for determining the degree of fusion of the units in a junction. They also require (2) theory and methods for describing the type or process of fusion within the junction. (3) Theory and methods must be available for handling the implication that every fusion should ultimately be treated in reference to a higher layer of structure in some hierarchy, whether phonological, lexical, or grammatical. (4) Theory and methods are required for determining the actual or reconstructed allomorphic bases from which the fusing process is assumed to start — since statements of fusion, change, and process all imply some real or assumed point of departure. One must, that is to say, be able to determine that /æžu/ is the end product of a fusion between /æz/ and /yu/, and to note that the fusion is partial, with the border phonemes coalescing phonetically into one mutually-shared phoneme which is different from either of the reconstructed phonemes at the border point.

The analyst is tempted to inquire: Which of these two views — item-and-arrangement or item-and-process — is correct? and to try to force the issue one way or the other. The modal approach implies that this question is itself in error, since the question implies that one or the other is wrong. The modal approach utilizes both. Each view shows one phase of language structure. Each must be included in any comprehensive view of language or behavior. Yet neither is complete in itself. Each will by itself lead to distortion (see § 14.2). The two together are still incomplete, needing a field view — § 14.3 — to round out the modal approach and to correct some of the distortion introduced by the other approaches.

In spite of the necessity for the two, they cannot be fused into a single, undifferentiated median approach. Like the modal structures discussed in earlier chapters, these approaches must be treated separately, weighted for the distortion involved in abstracting either of them from the total system, and recombined into a higher synthesis of understanding.

14.12 *Summary of Some Fusion Types*

Before making more explicit the specific distortions involved in the application of the two views, it is useful to list briefly a few of the kinds of fusion which we must meet — and most of which have been mentioned in earlier chapters. This listing begins to show that problems of fusion run throughout all kinds of sequences, all kinds of hierarchies, all kinds of units, and to show that a few principles may be applied to the etic classification of all of them.

For convenience in discussion, the degree of fusion between the segments in a junction may be arbitrarily subdivided (a) into those where there is no audible effect, (b) those with PARTIAL fusion, and (c) those with COMPLETE fusion.

First we note fusions within the phonological hierarchy: Across a pause, even in the middle of a sentence, phonemes often have no effect on one another above the perceptual threshold. Across a stress-group boundary or a syllable boundary there may be some modification of one sound by another. Within a syllable, adjacent phonemes often affect one another much more appreciably. These latter changes may be considered as partial fusions, and include subphonemic labialization, voicing, nasalization, and so on.

Often — especially in a junction of consonant and a vowel — the partial fusion of phonemes is BI-DIRECTIONAL, with the first sound in the junction partly anticipating the articulatory formation of the second, and the second containing the delayed decay of the articulatory formation of the first. At times — especially in a junction of two vowels — the articulation of the one may slur or glide smoothly into the next. (Cf. §§ 8.42, 8.442.) Complete fusion of two phonemes in a junction, however, would result in a single shaved, PORTMANTEAU[1] phone (§ 8.446), as in Record 72/13.7, S —: [aį hat] *I'm hot* where /i/ and /m/ fuse to a nasalized vocoid.

Syllables in sequence may be partially fused through the effect of partial fusions of the included phonemes at their borders. A complete etic fusion of two emic syl-

---

[1] Our recent studies are developing further ways of handling simultaneity. By setting up a matrix with intersecting dimensions of contrasting categories, formatives fill the cells at the intersection of the categories. Whenever a single formative fills a cell, it by definition simultaneously manifests categories from the two or more intersecting dimensions comprising a portmanteau formative. Formatives in such circumstances can form elaborate patterns not easily analyzable in terms of conventional morphemics. A conventional morpheme — a simple morpheme — would be a vector formative in a matrix, with the same formative in every cell of one and only one row (or in every cell of one and only one column). If a row is partitioned by two formatives which occur exclusively in this row, then two allomorphs represent one morpheme, which is a vector formative — which may then be represented by a single morphophonemic symbol for the entire row (or column). In more complicated instances, a formative may occur in various rows while also occurring in various columns. Here ambiguity of the semantic component of the formative occurs. The ambiguity must be cut by the superimposition of different matrices from different parts of the word or utterance.

Analysis of formative patterns is best achieved by permutation of rows and columns so that formatives — wherever possible — form blocks of like units; superimposition — conflation — of matrices then cuts ambiguity. For the theory and illustration of such matters see Pike (1963d), and Pike and Erickson (1964).

lables results in one etic portmanteau syllable of the two emic ones (for an example see §§ 9.236, 9.225; and cf. 9.237 for abbreviations or other types). In addition, at the border point in a syllable sequence a single phoneme in double function (§ 9.236) may simultaneously end the one syllable and begin the next. Two stress groups, similarly, may have their phonemes modified by one another, and may have a mutual border syllable shared in double function (§§ 9.241, 9.32).

Within junctions of the lexical hierarchy there occur the subphonemic phonological changes already referred to in the preceding paragraphs (and see § 6.66[5]). If one looks at the morpheme junctions after they are written phonemically, however, there may appear to be either clear segmentation — with no fusion in evidence — (as in *rain* versus *raining*) or the borders may be blurred by some type of fusion (§ 6.55). As with phonology, so here with morphemes, the fusion modification may be partial as in the voicelessness versus voicing of the plural morpheme of *cut-s* versus *bud-s*). It may be complete, with a resulting morphemic portmanteau (as in French /o/, *à le*, Bloomfield, 1933a:179). Some partial portmanteaus may overlap all the phonemic material of one morpheme with part of the phonemic material of another, or others (cf. /jɪnjoi ɪt/ *Did you enjoy it?*).

The fusion may be UNI-DIRECTIONAL, either anticipatory and affecting the first morpheme (as *in-* in *improbable* versus *incapable*) or with decaying influence, affecting the second (as in *cat-s* or *bud-s*). The fusion or modification may be bi-directional, affecting both morphemes (as *will* and *not* in *won't*). The fusion also may at times be considered as producing a phoneme in double function (as /ž/ would then simultaneously be a member of *as* and *you* in /æžu/).

In addition to these morphemic junction types, which parallel phonological ones, others can be added: Fused forms can at times be clearly segmented even when one morpheme is included within another (as in Zoque /y/ 'his' plus /pata/ 'mat' /pyata/ 'his mat'; Wonderly, 1951-52:117). At other times the analysis of an apparent inclusion is much more difficult, since the segments thus abstracted are not themselves regularly found occurring elsewhere (as /... æ .../ and /r ... n/ in *ran;* cf. also *sold, feet*).

Further complications are made up of irregular forms where the particular morphemes in the junction (rather than the specific phonemes or classes of phonemes manifesting the morphemes) lead to an irregular change (cf. *-en* plural after *ox*). Other irregularities may be due to the tagmemic function of one member of the junction (*him*, in object slot) or to particular morphemes manifesting particular tagmemes after certain particular morphemes (*be*, after *I*, in *am*). Occasionally an irregularity occurs in one of the morphemes of the junction such that the modification of the first morpheme signals to the bearer the interpretation of an otherwise ambiguous second morpheme (the stems *dij-* and *dig-* of *decir* 'to say' in Spanish help signal the preterit *dijo* 'He said' and present *digo* 'He says' in which *-o* is otherwise ambiguously 'I' or 'he').[2]

---

[2] See, now, treatment of *dijo* as a high-level particle, in Pike (1963d:15, 19).

There may appear to be excessive phonemic material in a particular junction (e.g., the -r- in *children*), or apparent complete lack of phonemic material for one morpheme (as in the plural *sheep*, where no phonetic data are present beyond that in the singular *sheep*). Occasionally the lack of a phoneme or phonemes may itself signal the presence of a second morpheme (as when a minus feature signals masculine, in French: *plat* [pla] 'flat' versus *platte* [plat], Bloomfield, 1933a:217).

Tagmeme borders may be blurred subphonemically insofar as the phonemes manifesting them slur together (§ 7.56[3]). They may be blurred also when the morphemes of a junction are partially or completely fused (§ 7.56[1-2]).

The most interesting tagmeme fusion, however, occurs when a single morpheme simultaneously fills two tagmemic slots (§ 7.56[6]), in a tagmemic portmanteau. There is a crucial difference between the morphemic portmanteau and the tagmemic one: In the tagmemic portmanteau only one morpheme is assumed to be present, whereas in the morphemic portmanteau two morphemes are present in a phonologically-fused form. In the tagmemic portmanteau, however, two semantic components or complexes of components may be expected in the manifesting morpheme. In Spanish *ablo* 'I talk', for example, the *-o* carries mood and tense, as well as person and number, but is here treated as a single morpheme (but for treatment as two morphemes, one of which is zero, see § 14.53). In *ablamos* 'we speak', however, mood and tense are covered in *-a-*, with person and number in *mos*. It is the presence of such two-morpheme sequences, plus the paralleling semantic components in *-o*, plus the fact that synchronic data do not supply formal evidence for splitting *-o* into two or more morphemes, that lead us to treat this instance as tagmemic fusion rather than as a morphemic portmanteau (and cf. §§ 7.56[6], 14.53).

Fusions (or modifications) of morphemes within junctions from the various hierarchies may be optional (as for *I'm* versus permitted *I am*) or obligatory (as /kəp-s/ *cups* but not /kəp-z/). Some fusions vary in this respect: *not* is optionally fused in *He doesn't* (or *does not*) *want to go;* but it is obligatorily so, in my normal style, in *Doesn't he want to go?*

(For some special purposes, a morpheme variant which is part of a regular process occurring between morphemes may be called a DYNAMIC VARIANT, a predictable one. On the other hand, an irregular variant which is restricted exclusively to a particular hypermorpheme — as the *-en* of *oxen* is restricted to the hypermorpheme *oxen* — may be called a STATIC VARIANT. Note, however, that *all* variants can be treated from static, dynamic, and field points of view.)

14.2 Distortion Introduced by Arbitrary Cuts and by Reconstructed Bases

Both the item-and-arrangement and the item-and-process approach to allomorphic description, however, lead to serious problems. Whether the one or the other — or both — are used, at some point distortion occurs.

With the static item-and-arrangement approach, the chief difficulty seems to be the fact that it requires a sharp-cut segmentation even when this cannot be achieved without arbitrariness, as we indicated in § 14.1. In order, for example, to abstract segmented allomorphs of *as* and *you* from /æžu/ a cut unwarranted by the data must be made either before the consonant, after the consonant, or between components of the consonant — or one may present to the reader alternate cuts, with pros and cons for each, but with each of them a distortion of the fused borders of the morphemes.

The reader should note carefully, however, that we do not say that this item-and-arrangement approach must not be used. On the contrary, it is very effective whenever one needs to list morphs or morphemes separately, as in a dictionary. In doing so, however, one should acknowledge the distortion, noting that a more complete view must keep in mind static, dynamic, and field approaches as each makes its own essential contribution to a total view. Each simultaneously provides a necessary corrective to the respective distortions of the others.

A second kind of distortion introduced by a static, segmenting approach is seen in an analysis of Spanish *dijo* 'He said', referred to in the preceding section. If the cut is made between the stem *dij-* and the pronominal element *-o*, one might be expected to assume that the *-o* gives the total cue to the reader that the third person is subject. Yet *-o* by itself may be elsewhere the manifestation of the morpheme 'I', as in *digo* 'I say', a different form of the same verb. Actually, part of the hearer's cue to the morphemic (and hence semantic) interpretation of *-o* comes from the stem allomorphs *dij-* and *dig-*. A cut which implies, then, that *-o* is the total manifestation of the form-meaning composite translated by 'I' or 'he' is a distortion. (An attempt to treat the *-j-* and *-g-* as part of the pronoun would lead to even more difficult problems in such forms as *dice* 'He says'. See Pike, 1963d:15, 19.)

One further problem may be mentioned which is not a distortion, in the sense of the latter two problems, but that leads to complications so great that, if no solution is proposed, it destroys the simplicity and usefulness of some descriptions based upon it. When a whole series of regular changes of a single related type occur, such as can be simply summarized in a process statement (as for example, the loss of the first consonant in a cluster, as mentioned earlier), a crude static approach may be forced to list laboriously every stem, with each of its allomorphs, just as if no regularity could be observed. This is especially costly in situations involving tone perturbation where, for example, every stem which has low final tone in its basic allomorphic form (to use process terminology) is replaced by an allomorph with final high tone.

The solution to this problem (Pike, 1953a) is now simple, preserving the usefulness of the item-and-arrangement approach. It consists of setting up CLASSES OF ALLOMORPHS on a phonological, grammatical, or — if necessary in particular instances — arbitrary basis, such that the distribution of an entire group of regular allomorphs can be handled in a single statement. This achieves the same effect as does starting from a basic form in an item-and-process approach, while avoiding calling the members of any particular class 'basic'. In consonant cluster reduction, for example, one may refer to an allomorph class composed of stem allomorphs without final consonant, and a related allomorph class composed of stem allomorphs with final consonant; one may say that any member of the first class may occur before morphemes beginning with a consonant, but any member of the second class before morphemes beginning with a vowel. This descriptive technique allows an item-and-arrangement approach to be used in complicated tone situations where otherwise only an item-and-process solution has so far been feasible.

With the item-and-process approach, on the other hand, the chief distortion seems to occur when it leads to statements which imply that a particular form 'A' and a form 'B' 'first' come together in sequence and 'then' are modified — although in fact the two unmodified forms may never have occurred in sequence in the observed data. The unmodified sequence is a hypothetical construct, a theoretical starting point for description of the observed facts. The basic forms postulated by this approach, then, are frequently present in the description but absent from these particular sequences in the data — though in general, but not always, a form set up as basic to a modified sequence will be found unmodified in some other sequence in the language. If, for example, the form /əz/ as in *houses* is chosen to be considered the basic form of the English plural morpheme, then *cat* plus /-əz/ (which never occurs after *cat*) is 'changed' to *cat* plus /-s/ (in which the term 'changed to' is a descriptive 'as if' expression, not a statement of observed change going on). This pseudo-history, the positing of hypothetical starting points, in the major price one must pay for the very great advantage of the simplicity of some item-and-process statements.

A further distortion within an item-and-process statement may creep into it from a partial combination with the item-and-arrangement approach, if during the process approach there is an attempt at segmentation of the parts. With /æžu/ the process statement need not attempt such segmentation — it can leave the borders fused, and segmentation indeterminate, with /ž/ shared by both morphemes. With a form such as Spanish *dijo* 'He said', however, the analyst is more likely to wish to combine an item-and-arrangement approach with the process approach by calling *dij*- the stem and *-o* the suffix. The moment this is done, however, the segmentation leads to the problem pointed out above in the item-and-arrangement approach. A pure process approach refuses to specify a border between stem and suffix — but this in turn leads to serious practical problems of description which, so far as I know, have not been solved or even carefully explored. It is often still convenient to use an item-and-arrangement approach, specifying stem and affixal allomorphs, in spite of the distortion brought in thereby.

Illustrations for item-and-arrangement and for item-and-process distortion have been drawn here from morpheme sequences since it is for these sequences that the two approaches, as such, have been developed. Inasmuch as our handling of the problem is designed to cover a much larger area, however, a few illustrations from phonology may be added to suggest that the basic issue is not one limited to morphemes, but is crucial to all units of behavior.

An item-and-arrangement approach describes sequences of phonemes as if they were composed of allophones each of which has a sharp border. The concept of 'slur' does not enter this approach. Each allophone is treated as a distinct subphonemic entity, which occurs next to other such entities like beads on a string. This is an obvious distortion of the data, since in a continuum of sounds there is frequently no specific point where one sound ends and the next begins. The cuts between phonemes are arbitrary, as were the morphemic cuts, since characteristics introduced by anticipation and slow decay of phonemic components lead to overlap, and are therefore not completely segmentable.

On the other hand, an item-and-process type of approach to phonemic description elegantly handles slurs and indeterminate borders. It may lead to a different distortion, however, since it in effect sets up basic phonetic forms of phonemes — often called 'norms' — which are treated as convenient theoretical starting points for the description of the observed slurs and observed conditioned variants. These norms, however, are at times arbitrarily chosen, or may even appear to imply some kind of irrelevant normative judgment. As for morphemes, so for phonemes, a sweeping, simple generalization can often be made by a process statement when regular changes affect a class of phonemes. A statement that in a particular language all stops are nonphonemically unvoiced in utterance-final position would be an example. The comparable statement by a rigid item-and-arrangement approach would be strikingly unwieldy, unless here, as for morphemes, allophone classes are set up which are distributionally analogous to classes of allophonic norms.

A phonological problem parallel to the one in which two morphemes share one phoneme (as /ž/ in the morpheme sequence /æžu/ *as you*, is simultaneously part of two morphemes, in a process view) would be seen when the phoneme /t/ is simultaneously part of two syllables in a rapid pronunciation of English *biting* (see § 9.236).

The basic assumption of clear-cut segmentation in an item-and-arrangement approach and of identifiable peaks in the process approach both lead to the most serious dead end, however, in a phonological or morphemic portmanteau, i.e., in a 'sequence' of simultaneous phonemes or simultaneous morphemes. In such an instance neither internal borders nor internal distinct peaks can be found in a junction. (See § 14.12). The treatment of one etic segment as two emic ones, of one etic wave as two emic waves, is a serious distortion of the data which theory in some manner should account for.

14.3 *The Hyper-Unit (Field) View of Sequence*

It is here that the third approach — a field view — serves us well. By it an entire junction, a 'sequence' of two units, is treated as a single hyperunit with no essential requirement of internal specific segmentation or specific peak identification. For this field view it is sufficient to know *that* a junction of two units is present, and to know their semantic function, formal function, and structural interrelations in higher-level structures, without the requirement of being able to separate the components of their respective manifestation modes. Thus a phonetic quadruple portmanteau such as [ǫ̃] (occurring in my record 84/9 S: [ai ǫ̃ ˈwą̃nə] *I don't want to* [*see*]) has one wave peak for both the morpheme *do* and the morpheme *not*, as well as — presumably — for the phoneme /o/ and the phoneme /n/. Both the morpheme junction and the phoneme junction fuse to a single phonetic segment.

In this instance the nasalization is clearly related to the /n/. In some instances, however, the fusion is so irregular that no certain phonetic identification can be made. In *my*, for example, if one concludes that there is a junction of *I* and posessive -*s* (Hockett, 1947a:343) the phonetic character of -*s* is completely lacking. Here the field approach can be used — if the investigator on other evidence is convinced that *my* represents two morphemes — to treat *my* as a morphemically-nonsegmentable hypermorphemic unit. (For a third approach, with the base *mVy*, see Trager and Smith, 1951:62.)

The strength of this field approach is (a) that it gives theoretical support to the formal treatment, as wholes, of complex but unanalyzable units; (b) that it helps to explain the fact that some high-level units (such as *dijo*) are semantically relevant as wholes; (c) that it gives theoretical support to the fact that in practical language learning it is often simpler, faster, more efficient to memorize a few 'exceptions' than it is to learn complex analytical descriptions created ad hoc to treat single examples whose 'segmented' description reflects little or nothing of recurrent pattern in the language; (d) that it points up the fact that eventually every instance of fusion must be described in reference to a larger unit of structure; (e) that it lays the groundwork for understanding the development and use of phrasal idioms, of compounds, or of any high-layered units which show unpredictable unitary semantic or formal characteristics; (f) that it relates junction theory to the theory of learning, since often complex expressions are learned as wholes before the child learner can manipulate the substitutable items which alone can show that the child is reacting to a pattern of units in sequence (and adults never completely leave such principles or early reactions).

It is instructive here to compare the experience of the papyrologist who is attempting to read and transcribe a text written in an obscure handwriting. Professor Herbert Youtie of Michigan tells me that "you read the words and letters after you recognize them", in some sense. That is to say, that in practical operational procedure it is impossible to decipher letter by letter a cursively-written manuscript. The reader must first try to grasp the meaning of a whole document, and of the sentences in that document, before he is able to understand some of the more obscure words or recognize some of the letters within it. Once he has gained this initial over-all understanding, however, he is then able to turn to the specific obscure letters and words and see that 'of course' those were the particular letters and words which were 'there all the time', but which could not be 'seen' until this larger understanding was obtained.

Basic techniques to implement this field view would require[3] (1) theory and methods for determining that a junction — a structural complex — exists even though it is not segmentable; (2) theory and methods for handling the resultant mixture, in a descriptive statement, of some low-layer segments — with some complex unsegmentable hyper-units or junctions — without losing the elegance gained by keeping a description restricted to compartmentalized descriptions of one layer at a time; (3) theory and methods for handling the inventory of such diverse units — as when, in a lexicon, single-morpheme listings need to be supplemented with morpheme sequences which have special meanings not predictable from the included parts; (4) theory and methods for discovering and describing the extent to which fusions are created not only between comparable segments of a single subsystem in the language, but between disparate units of disparate systems; (5) theory and methods to explore the implication that ultimately language must not be viewed as a series of unit segments in a sequence, but rather as one total, continuous field, with various overlapping waves of 'concentrations of energy' of various types (which can in part be factored out 'as if' they were segments, but which never can actually be pulled out of the mass as a list of 'things' which are added in rows with 'gaps' between the units and layers or systems of units).

14.4 *Distortion Introduced by Incomplete Segmentation*

Should we by chance try to adopt the field approach completely, rejecting the approaches of static segmentation and dynamic wave units, we soon find, however, that — if we are consistent — we can no longer find in our data anything which resembles language. Without unit substitution at structurally-relevant places, there is no language pattern and no communication. Unit substitution in pattern slots implies *some* kind of segmentation — whether with clear-cut borders or with indeterminate ones. A field view as part of a larger approach may simplify the study of elements like *ate, sold, ran, won't, went, am, feet,* or *sheep* (*plural*), or idioms such as *to step on the gas,* but by itself it cannot serve as the single foundation stone on which to erect a satisfactory linguistic theory. It must be accompanied by both the item-and-arrangement and item-and-process views. The three complement one another and in part serve as a corrective to their respective distortions. No one of the three can dispense with either of the others.

This conclusion is in line with the entire thrust of behavioremic theory. It emphasizes that systems are composed of mutually-related parts, units, and subsystems which are mutually defining. Neither unit types, nor systems, nor layers of structure can — in the behavioremic view — be discovered or adequately described without

---

[3] Recent papers on matrix have begun to meet many of these requirements. References to these articles can be found by checking sections referred to in the second fn. to § 11.225.

some large or small degree of reliance upon units, systems, and layers of structure which are diverse from those momentarily under most direct attention.

We are ready now to devote a chapter to pointing up some characteristics of this integration. First, however, we will refer to samples of the large body of literature relevant to the topics we have just been discussing.

14.5 *Bibliographical Comments on Chapter 14*

Much of the bibliographical data relevant to this chapter has been mentioned in other connections. For general materials on phonemics, including phonemic variants, see §§ 8.4, 8.8; for the syllable, §§ 9.22-23. Phonemic changes at morpheme boundaries are in general handled under the term morphophonemics — which see in references given in the first paragraph of § 6.9. For some continental views of morphophonemic data, one must watch for the term 'implication' (H. J. Uldall, 1936, and Hjelmslev, 1936; compare also mention of neutralization, intersection, and archiphoneme — § 8.85). For morphophonemic data treated from the viewpoint of prosodies, see Robins (1953a:143). For the approach of the Prague school, see Projet (1931:321-22; with references to work of earlier scholars). For particle, wave, and field, note § 12.1. For transformation, note § 11.76.

14.51 *On Item-and-Arrangement versus Item-and-Process*

The earliest specific discussion which I have noted of the differences between item-and-arrangement and item-and-process descriptions occurs in Harris (1944a:203-05). In this article he seemed to imply that, in general, modern linguistics should preferably not imply "primacy of the base" or a "motion analogy" of process, but deal with distributions. Soon after the appearance of this article, the general trend of American linguistics for the next decade was to use item-and-arrangement statements — with process statements carrying low prestige. Nida, for example, changed largely from process to item-and-arrangement (allomorphic-item-in-distribution) statement between the 1946 and 1949 editions of his *Morphology*. The change was incomplete, since some terms such as "replacive" or "minus feature" remained essentially process in type. Harris, himself, continued to make occasional reference to alternate descriptions by process (1951:373, 367 fn. 9).

Tone studies proved resistent to this trend (Pike, 1948, Mak, 1953), since the available allomorphic techniques were so awkward as to be hopelessly impractical in a situation where complicated tone changes occurred. It was not until the concept of allomorph classes was developed (Pike, 1953a) that an item approach to these tone systems was feasible.

In the meantime, problems inherent in the item-and-arrangement approach, and the continuing advantages inherent in the process approach, forced various scholars to attempt to reconcile the two. While this chapter was in early draft, for example, Hockett published a study urging that neither item-and-arrangement nor process approaches should be rejected (1954a), but that the process approach should be formalized. In the same issue of that journal Harris reassessed the two views, finding the "combinatorial or item style" "more parsimonious and representative for much of linguistic data" but granting that for "certain situations, especially in compact morphophonemics" the "process style ... is useful" (1954a:149). See above, § 11.76.

It is a curious fact that in this respect linguistics during the previous decade was moving counter to the general stream of the philosophy of science. Note, for example, the philosopher Sinclair: "It seems probable that we in our culture are now moving into a stage of our intellectual development in which we are going to think more and more in terms of process and less and less in terms of things" (1951:80), and "Physicists no longer think of atoms and the like as things, ... but in another way which can be described in terms of 'process' while a parallel change can be found in biology and psychology and a wide range of other subjects" (cf. also Whitehead, 1952 [1925]: 74, "The reality is the process", and, 71, "concrete fact is process"). Possibly the best explanation for the recent linguistic unpopularity of process statements is seen in Haugen and Twaddell, in reference to process terms in connection with treatments of phonetics: "historical terms — 'phonetic result', 'raised' etc. — seem out of place in a descriptive statement" (1942:233-34). Compare also the segmentation statement about "the usual notions" regarding the nature of words, referred to by Greenberg, that "every phoneme should belong to only one word" (in Osgood, Sebeok, and others, 1954:66); our view of phonemes or syllables in double function eliminates this requirement and opens up an avenue to process statements. (Compare the discussion of possible description in terms of shared phonemes in Nida, 1949:77, and Lounsbury, 1953:12.)

For a recent attack on the "antiquated and improper process-metaphor", assigning the "phonic data ... to prosodic categories", see W. S. Allen (1954:556). See also Sharp (1954), who rejects a process approach to tone studies. He uses no reference to shifted tones or perturbations of tones or basic tones, preferring to analyze the pitch structure of words without their being written phonemically. He seems to be unaware that desired invariant formulas, in the American approach, are found in rigid morphophonemic symbolization — e.g., Swadesh (1934) and Hockett (1948b) which attain Sharp's goal of invariants without ignoring crucial phonemic contrastive data; see, also, Lounsbury (1953:11-15).

I have not seen in any treatment by way of the item-and-arrangement approach any simple, adequate handling of a morpheme which (seen through the process approach) is itself composed of a process. 'Minus Feature' as a label for a kind of morpheme (e.g., Bloomfield, 1933a:217, and Nida, 1949:75) is essentially a process term. For unvoicing (a process) suggested as a morpheme in English, see Harris (1951:209, with noun *house* composed of verb *to house* plus unvoicing). Note, also, zero treated *not* as "a 'segment' supplied" but as "an *operation* performed on overt forms", W. Haas (1957:42).

Since the above paragraphs were written the turn of the wheel is nearly complete. Approach through particles by way of item-and-arrangement is heavily out of favor with many recent writers, and approach through process — under the guise of rules — is in many places now popular. The linguist is said to have "traditionally and naively" understood "analysis" to mean "'dissection into simple additive segments', and by 'criteria' he usually means 'recipes for segmentation'." But "taking such unsophisticated conceptions as these to be the basis of scientific methodology is tantamount to viewing physiology as a branch of surgery", Lees (1960a:xxv).

Gleason would propose a distinction between an "adjustment model" which involves — in our terms — processes, but processes which are automatic and not carrying semantic relevance to the fusion, and the "process model" proper in which the process is itself a "basic unit in the grammar", meaningful "grammatically or semantically" (1961:215-16). It seems to me difficult to separate the two in such instances as Chomsky's extensive — and useful — discussion of the variants of *telegraph* which are "obviously not capricious" (1962, § 2.1, p. 516).

It seems to me unfortunate that there should be a battle to try to force the issue to either process or to particle — especially since we must leave room as well for pattern and system through a field approach.

14.52 *On Arbitrary Cuts and Hyper-Units*

The problem of making some cuts in an item-and-arrangement approach has been succinctly stated by Lounsbury: "The locations of the cuts are not always uniquely determined" and they are made "to some extent arbitrarily" (1953:12). The advantage of the approach is that "it deals with the segmentation of actual utterances rather than with constructs" (1953:15) [e.g., a reconstructed form] as "a fictitious agglutinating analog" (1953:13) once removed from reality but "the resulting very discrete localizations of meaning associated with some of the procedures under the method of morpheme alternants [i.e., variants of items] are, or may be, highly unrealistic" (1953:15).

For numerous alternate suggestions for cuts, see Harris (1951, Chapter 12), Nida (1949:77). Bloch has effectively shown us the arbitrary end result of insistance on cuts in some especially difficult cases. Of these perhaps the most instructive is his exploring of the price to be paid for segmenting *am* and *are* in English: "Any solution of the problem is inescapably ad hoc; we propose to regard the alternants of the base here as /æ/ and /ah/ in complementary distribution, and to posit a suffix morpheme with two alternants /m/ and /r/, the choice between them being regulated by the shape of the base alternant: /m/ after /æ/, /r/ after /ah/" (1947b:408). Under such circumstances it becomes relevant, also, to note Bloomfield's practical protest against analytical segmentation of some irregular forms: "The partial resemblances between forms which we describe in morphology are often so whimsically irregular that a rigorous statement has practical disadvantages. It may take more discourse to describe a few eccentric forms than it would merely to cite them" (1945:8); and similarly Bloch, 1947b:418 fn. 26, rejects the analysis of English atonic verbs from use in pedogogical materials). In connection with such matters, Bolinger urges that "the statement of a law shall be more economical than the mere enumeration of the phenomena for which it is supposed to account" (1948:136).

For problems in analysis — problems for which I think the 'field' concept is needed — see Harris analyzing English *was*. He says that the phoneme /w/ is there "in one morpheme with the *-t* 'past' [such as in *missed*], with the /əz/ and /ər/ of *was* and *were* allomorphs of be" (1951:209 fn. 9). Later in the same volume he gives an alternate analysis of *was*, by saying that "if we analyze *was* as {*be*} + {*-ed*}, but have no basis for placing the boundary, we do not place it arbitrarily, but recognize no phonemic correlation for the alternants of {*be*} and {*-ed*} in each other's environment, but only for the sequence of them together, which is /wəz/" (1951:372). For references to *my* as *I* plus *possessive*, see § 14.3. For the problem of Spanish words such as *digo*, see Nida (1949:130-38 and Pike, 1963d, 15, 19; compare, also, Lounsbury (1953:17n).

For portmanteau morphs, see Bloomfield (1933a:179); Hockett (1947a:333; 1954a:216), Nida (1948b:417-18), Wonderly (1952a:367), Aschmann and Wonderly (1952), Pittman (1954a:21). For portmanteau under the European term *cumul*, see Bazell (1953:9; and compare 1948a:20-21; 1952:36, where *duke* in *duchess* is "determinate on the part of content, but indeterminate on the side of expression"). For the possibility of portmanteau on a word level, see Trager (1951:129), Trager and Smith (1951:59, 72). For *had* as *have* before *-d* see Harris (1951:213), and for *wh-* as a morpheme in *when* (1951:210 fn. 23, 192-93). For the problem of *went* see Bloch (1947b:410), versus Bloomfield (1926:161); see also S. Martin (1952:102). For allologs see Trager and Smith (1951:59, 72). For detailed instances of irregularity where morphemic segmentation gives extensive difficulty, see, concerning Mazatec, Pike (1948:126, 147-57), and for an instance in Otomí verb morphology see Wallis (1956). See also Kennedy (1953:370), and Wells (1949).

For the possibility that hyper-units of various kinds are learned or utilized as units, rather than as sequences of smaller segments, compare Osgood, Sebeok, and others, where "probably individual words and trite phrases" "are encoded as units and run themselves once initiated" (1954:57). In the same volume, Jenkins indicates that some mechanical movement sequences "are actual integrations", in typing, and "not merely a rapid sequencing of discrete responses" (in Osgood, Sebeok, and others, 1954:25). For further discussion of portmanteau elements, note avoidance of the concept in W. Haas (1957:53); but approval in Lounsbury (1956:161).

Residual problems in segmentation continue to receive attention. For the question of the one-phoneme or two-phoneme analysis of [č] see Hockett (1955:161-62); for indeterminacy of phonemic analysis in temporal or spacial or social transition from one structure to another, note Moulton (1960:182). To the degree that attempts at segmentation are based upon the assumption of phonemes in a linear sequence, Chomsky insists that simultaneity of phonemes violates this condition — as for a vowel plus nasal (1962: § 4.3, p. 540); similarly, the linearity would for him appear grossly exaggerated if the phonemic contrast is carried by the conditioned variation of a preceding phone (541).

Segmentation techniques for lexical items have been carried further by Greenberg in terms of square arrays to show certain types of analogies — one of the most formal attempts available (1957). Problems in tone fusion are seen especially in Longacre (1959); tonal-mechanical processes occur frequently elsewhere, as in Rowlands (1954:383), Cole-Beuchat (1959), Bascom (1959). Tonal fusions, plus segmental fusions, encountered by Longacre in Trique led him to set up macromorphemes, with "each morpheme of the set [as] an alternate of the macromorpheme" (1959:9); compare the morpheme overlap within an ambimorphemic boundary, of Garvin (1957:14-15); Longacre also uses the term "morpheme cluster" from Garvin, and compares it to Martin's use of "morpheme association" for such instances. Compare the handling of affix compounding in Ocaina, in Pike (1961c). A further problem is found in "a tantalizing similarity of certain recurrent partials having less than morphemic status", as in Chatino, in Pride (1961:5); compare the formatives in Fore, in Pike (1963d). Other problems of extensive fusion, or indeterminacy, or overlap can be seen in a conventional description for Oneida, by Lounsbury (1953); for transformational treatment in a related language, Mohawk, note Postal (1962).

For skewing in closeness of relation of morphemic form and morphemic meaning, note F. R. Palmer (in *Preprints...*, 1962:236-37), where phonetic exponents (manifestations) are necessary for each grammatical category, but without needing to be in one-to-one relationship with them. Compare our elaborate development of the similar view by way of formatives (Pike, 1963d:17; Pike and Erickson, 1964). For treatment similar to our matrix view, note Uhlenbeck, where "the Javanese productive verbal categories [are] controlled by 13 oppositions" (in *For Roman Jakobson*, 1956:573, 569) and categorial values were deeply obscured for earlier investigations; note also that the "traditional description of Albanian cases may thus be presented as a matrix of four dimensions: case, number, definity, and gender", in Newmark (1962:315).

For the principle that the highest degree of morphemic irregularity leads to simplest formative relations in a matrix, see Pike (1963d:17-18); note also (19-20) that fusions differ at low speed versus high speed — so that some high-level particles are stable under low-speed conditions, whereas others break up into separate particles.

Special problems of segmentation which involve zero will be treated in the next section.

14.53 *On Zero*

The use of zero in linguistic analysis has had a long history. Bloomfield attributes its development to early Hindu Scholars (1933a:209), stating that it "is necessary for Sanscrit" and "probably economical for English" (1926:160); see also W. S. Allen (1953a:12). Jakobson attributes its emphasis to Bally (in *Mélanges ... Bally*, 1939), following the principle of de Saussure that oppositions may be units opposed to nothing, hence zero is a sign (1931:124). Zero has also been used by many other scholars as an accepted analytical tool, e.g., Project (1931:314); Chao (1934:377, for zero allophone of a phoneme); Harris (1951:213, 256, 334, 356 fn.13).

Zero allomorphs are perhaps the most frequent zeros postulated. Nida recommends the use of zero allomorphs but hesitates about the use of morphemes which are totally zero (1949:46 and fn. 44). Olmsted tries to salvage morpheme zeros from excessive — and fatal — overuse, by restricting zeros to one zero allomorph per morpheme and one zero morpheme per class (1951:163-66). Jakobson and Lotz utilize a "zero-phoneme" for French, although they state that it occasionally has vocalic or aspiration variants (1949:155). Zero allophones are postulated by Moulton (1947:220). Bloomfield claims that distinctions in one or more parts of a paradigm imply homonymy in the remaining forms (1933a:224); rejected by Bazell (1948a:17).

There have been protests against some phases of the use of zeros. Kurath in reviewing Bloch and Trager's Outline says, "In other words, if two forms behave alike syntactically we must act as if they behaved alike morphologically as well, whether they do so or not. A treacherous device indeed!" (1945:210). Voegelin suggests that symmetrical considerations must not be considered adequate justification for zero units, lest, for example, we postulate a "zero nose" in a man (1952, in Tax, 1952:224). Pike (1947a:171-72) criticizes Moulton's zero allophones in German, on the grounds that the variant overt forms are not specified, and might make the analysis contradictory. Compare Hockett, who says that "we cannot assign phonemic status to something when it is not present, and therefore 'potential pause' cannot be phonemic" (1949a:48).

Nida has objected (1948b:427) to assigning semantic-morphemic function exclusively to a covert (zero) allomorph when an overt difference is present (e.g., in *song*, treated by Bloch — 1947b:407 — as a morpheme alternate plus zero, with the zero signalling the nominalization). Nida's solution includes three morphemes in such a word as *feet*; one as the stem, one as the replacive *-ee-*, and one as the zero allomorph of the plural morpheme (1949:54). Lounsbury discussed various alternative possibilities with and without zero (1953:12-13) in an attempt to find solutions which give a more "realistic localization of meaning" since both meanings (of the morphemes of a fused sequence) are associated with the part which is not zero, and "a zero morph cannot otherwise be perceived than through the occurrence of the morph which implicates it".

Pickett gives one of the most instructive specific instances of problems arising when trying to apply rules for allomorphic zero (1953). She suggested that theory be modified from Nida's view so that "If two related forms contain an overt difference and a structural zero difference as the only significant features for establishing a minimal unit for phonetic-semantic distinctiveness, the semantic value should be assigned to the overt difference, not to the zero, unless that overt difference can be established as sub-morphemic on the basis of complementation in cases where no zero is involved" (296).

Extensive discussion of the concept of zero is in W. Haas (1957). He insists that one must not use contrast of the presence of zero with the absence of zero — in a false "*distinction of indiscernibles*" — but that zero must contrast with overt forms "in some of its environments" (36, 41). Further, as 'order' has form consisting only of syntagmatic relations, so 'zero' has form consisting only of paradigmatic relations (42-43). A zero allophone — but not a zero allomorph — "seems to be a contradiction in terms" (47).

For zero in reference to bimorphic members of a class (compare our use of fused tagmemes, § 14.12), see Haas (1957:52-53). See also Frei (1950:171, in reference to cumul types). Frei also has extensive treatment of other problems of zero. For him, "Le nombre des phonèmes zéros successifs est théoriquement illimité" (171).

From the viewpoint of behavioremic theory it would seem that problems involving zero arise when one tries to arrive at a linear sequence of morphemes without adequate reference to hierarchical structure and tagmemic function. The use of zero is one result of an item-and-arrangement approach when that approach is not combined with the hierarchical elements involved in an item-and-field approach. If one is rigorously describing language as exclusively made up of a combination of observable sequences of morphemes and phonemes, only, there is no room for linguistic elements which simultaneously have the characteristics of (1) containing two morphemes but (2) being empirically nonsegmentable. The use of zero in such instances provides a pseudo-segment which allows to function an approach which must, in principle, have every sentence segmentable down to the morpheme level.

A hierarchical item-and-field view, thus, may need to modify Bloomfield's Assumptions 5-8, which seem to imply that every utterance is a small submultiple of phonemes (1926), by leaving room in the segmentation for a few unsegmentable phonological units known to comprise simultaneous (portmanteau) phonemes, or morphemically-unsegmentable units known to comprise simultaneous morpheme composites. It must also leave room for one morpheme to comprise the simultaneous manifestation of two tagmemes.

When, however, one is using an item-and-arrangement approach, the use of zero continues to appear necessary, as part of the distortion price paid for the temporary advantages of that approach. Even so, however, one should try to use caution, as recommended by Nida (1949:46), Olmstead (1951), and W. Haas (1957), so as to avoid an excessive multiplication of numerous zeros in a single system. Otherwise, one arrives at many morphemes which — because they are zero — are all homophonous. But since the reason for setting up zeros in the first place was in part the desire to avoid having in the analytical system units whose structure is morphemically-different but homophonous, the unrestrained use of zeros is self-defeating.

For a study which works out in detail the contrast between analysis with multiple zeros versus analysis with none see Aschmann and Wonderly on Totonac (1952). Certain grammatical categories are treated there "as implicit in stems and affixes rather than as zero morphemes" (130). For a list of Totonac implicit morphemes, see 145; for contrast with Olmsted's and Nida's views, 143. For a sample of the alternate result (rejected by Aschmann and Wonderly) containing six postulated morphemes of zero out of eight morphemes in sequence, we quote from 144:

The Totonac verb pucay *he looks for him* consists overtly of the stem -puca- and the suffix -y, and is now structured as V^{a1} + 71. Implicit in this V^{a1} stem are third person singular identified subject and third person singular object; implicit in suffix 71 is present tense. In Aschmann's earlier analysis he treated certain of these categories as zero morphemes; we now find that if this were done consistently in line with the above paragraph, what we now treat as simply a bimorphemic sequence V^{a1} + 71 would then become a sequence of eight morphemes, six of which are zeros: V^{a1} (lexical meaning only) + 0 (3rd pers. subj.) + 0 (sing. subj.) + 0 (identified subj.) + 0 (3rd pers. obj.) + 0 (sing. obj.) + 0 (present) + 71 (ord. action).

The net result of their preferred (nonzero) approach, according to the authors, gives a simpler morphemics and tactics but somewhat more complex semantics — since all stems and some affixes "are made to be associated with one or more basic meanings, and our structural statement must cover the circumstances under which these additional meanings are present or absent" (145).

An item-and-field approach to these data would presumably leave some of these items as single morphemes, without zero, but would find in them the simultaneous manifestation of several tagmemes. It is possible that such a further step would for certain temporary purposes retain the advantage of using an analysis without zero while finding structural contrast between some of the meanings at another — the tagmemic — part of the system. For other purposes an item-and-arrangement approach might continue to find zeros of some value here. Static, dynamic, and functional contributions can be made by the approaches through item-and-arrangement, item-and-process, and item-and-field respectively.

Note also Saporta, for Spanish: a morpheme may not have zero as its only member, nor a portmanteau as its only member, nor a single member made up of portmanteau and zero (1959:614-15); but in *ám-a* the suffix is one morph, one morpheme, with two semantic components — tense and third person singular; his charts showing the lining up of the separate segmental components of the verb imply, in our terms, some tagmemic fusion.

For zero allotagmas, where we set up an unfilled slot (rather than a morpheme of third person which is itself zero as a morpheme), note Pike (1962a:237); and cf. (1963b:222, 226). Compare also Hill (1962:347); Longacre (1964a:104-06); see above, § 14.12 for *sheep*, and compare Hill (1958:139). Heller (1964) seems to want to set up an allotagmatic zero whenever *any* optional tagmeme is not manifested; this would imply scores of zeros, demanding pseudo maximum forms of all constructions (compare similar implications in morpheme sequence in Frei, 1950).

Further references to zero are found in Stockwell (1959:256-57), quoting W. Haas favorably; Pulgram (1961:305, for zero allophone of /ə/ in French); Hoeningswald (1959:409, especially useful for discussion of change).

CHAPTER 15

INTERLOCKING HIERARCHIES AND SYSTEMS

In this chapter we first wish to take up the particular problem as to the manner in which hierarchies interlock with one another. Then some similar relationships will be discussed concerning systems.

The attempt to show this interlocking is important, since it would appear that tagmemic theory as a coherent approach must eventually stand or fall by crucial demonstrations in this area. If it falls, pieces of the theory (such as attention to slot and class relationships as constituting tagmemes), may be salvaged, but the trimodal hierarchical system as presented here must then be sharply modified. If it is to stand, crucial evidence must be presented indicating above all that the lexical hierarchy is different from the grammatical hierarchy as such. The most crucial evidence is summarized in § 15.13, but we delay that evidence until the background setting for it can be presented.

In Chapter 14, we were largely interested in LATERAL INTERLOCKING of units within any one layer of any one hierarchy. In that chapter two units of a comparable layer and of the same hierarchy fused to a greater or lesser degree at their borders.

Lateral fusion or interlocking can also be demonstrated, however, between units of distinct hierarchies.

At various points, especially in Chapters 9, 10, and 11, we have shown that there can be VERTICAL INTERLOCKING, in which low-layered units of a hierarchy are included within higher-layered units of the same hierarchy: Phonemes may be included in syllables and stress groups, as morphemes may be included in hypermorphemes of various kinds, and tagmemes within syntagmemes. Across hierarchical boundaries, however, vertical interlocking can occur such that low-level units of one hierarchy are specifically relevant to high-layered units of another hierarchy. Progressive inclusion of smaller units within larger units, as well as fusion of units at their borders, are all relevant to the total hierarchical system of language.[1]

---

[1] Units of the various hierarchies, we would now suggest, may interlock as intersects in matrices. As categories of various dimensions — or various matrices — meet, the intersection defines the type of interlocking.

15.1 *Interlocking Between Hierarchies*

Interlocking between hierarchies may relate two or three of the hierarchies as a whole, but when it does so the actual linking must take place between one particular unit or layer of one of the hierarchies and one particular layer or unit of one of the other hierarchies. Multiple linking at the borders and/or nuclei of units of the hierarchies makes up the interlocking of the hierarchical system as a whole.

Language constitutes a system but no language system can occur unless some kind of interlocking also occurs. Lower-layered units within one modal hierarchy must somehow be fused into or integrated with larger units of activity on a higher level of that hierarchy, or else there is no structure joining these units.

Structure, in this sense, is in part a function of the interlocking and interpenetration of levels or layers of a hierarchy. The various hierarchies of such a system, furthermore, must also be relevant to and interlocking with one another or else no structural organization of them occurs. On the one hand there must be certain points or regions at which some of the units of the hierarchy *are* co-terminous or co-nuclear, in order for the units of the various hierarchies to be relevant one to another. On the other hand there must be certain points in the system at which some of the units on various levels of the hierarchies of the modes are *not* co-terminous or co-nuclear. If all units of all hierarchies were always co-terminous and co-nuclear then there would be no trimodal structuring at all, but merely a single structure which could be looked at from three different points of view.

The linking of one unit type or another leads not only to co-terminous and co-nuclear relations, but also to fusion, to double function, and to indeterminacies of various kinds. These fusions and indeterminacies are not to be considered as disastrous to the presenting of a system — nor to be considered as undesirable or as the result of an incomplete analysis. On the contrary, at times they are seen to be essential features of the system itself. It is these which allow for that type of integration which itself is essential to a system.

In addition, it is at these points that change can occur within a system. Without such possibilities of fusions and indeterminacies between units of a system many of the kinds of changes which are empirically observed could not occur. A dynamic system finds change possible at these points of interlocking between units and hierarchies.

A description of the empirical data, if it is to include reference to the dynamics of a system, must allow for such indeterminacies, such linkages, and such fuzzy borders between hierarchies and systems. It is only a static, arbitrary segmentation and arbitrary compartmentalization of systems or units which can in presentation eliminate these empirical data.

We now summarize a few of the ways in which the various hierarchies interlock.

15.11 *Interlocking between the Lexical and Phonological Hierarchies*

Units of the lexical hierarchy and units of the phonological hierarchy often have borders in common. The common borders reinforce each other and make much more easy the segmentation of units in a lexical sequence or of the units in a phonological sequence. This reinforcement however, does not take place uniformly on every layer of the one hierarchy in reference to every layer of the other hierarchy. For each particular language the particular co-terminous relations of the various borders must be specified on the basis of empirical evidence.

Apart from instances where fusion of certain types occurs (§§ 14.12, 14.3) morphemes are likely to begin and end with a phoneme. It is precisely this characteristic of the interlocking of the lexical and phonological hierarchies which made it convenient in § 8.35 to treat the phoneme as occurring just above a threshold of the phonological hierarchy. By starting the phonological hierarchy with the phoneme (rather than treating the componential features as the minimum unit of that hierarchy) one is able to segment a sentence into morphemes at whose boundaries there is usually a phoneme boundary as well.

The beginning analyst is likely to have the false assumption that every word in the lexical hierarchy should simultaneously constitute a unit of the phonological hierarchy — say a stress group. Word segmentation may be neatest and simplest when each word does begin and end with a stress group beginning and ending, but this would be only one special instance of the interlocking of the lexical and phonological hierarchies by border reinforcement of their units.

In another type of language many words may not end with a stress — a stress group may contain several lexical words. Yet the lexical word unit may nevertheless exercise a control over the ending of stress groups of the phonological hierarchy, such that if a stress-group ending is to occur at all, it is highly likely to occur at the end of a lexical word, and such that the end of any lexical word may optionally be reinforced by the ending of a stress group. Here the lexical unit controls, to a considerable extent, the options as to the potential placing of endings of stress groups. English has many characteristics of this type — such that discovery of options in a sequence where stress groups may end is one of the best criteria for determining word boundaries (Pike, 1945:79-82). (Note that there is no normal option to stress the word *ticket* on the second syllable. On the other hand the phrase *Lick it!* may be made into two stress groups with the second one heavily stressed under special circumstances).

Optional lexical placement of phonological borders is by no means restricted to one level of the phonological hierarchy. It affects placement of syllable boundaries even as it does the placement of stress group boundaries. Syllable-boundary placement may change noticeably with change of speed. For example, such items as *a name* versus *an aim* may be quite distinct at slow speed, whereas in rapid speech they may become homophonous. It is important to note, however, that when a rapidly-pronounced sentence is then repeated slowly by the informant, that the syllable divisions 'revert' to their earlier places. The control of the places to which the syllable boundaries revert is based upon the lexical structure and not upon the phonological structure (versus Stetson, 1945:46-47; 1951:74, who implies that control of reversion is in the syllable structure itself; see our comment on this view, in § 9.72; and cf. § 8.52).

Special pronunciations under special circumstances may lead to further changes and may either obscure the syncronization of boundaries between syllables and lexical units, or may sharpen this co-terminous relation. When people speak slowly over a difficult telephone connection these boundaries may frequently be pronounced in such a manner as to reinforce one another, whereas in quick, quiet, secret communication the boundaries may be slurred and the co-terminous relations lost.

In some languages such as those of southeast Asia the syllable of the phonological hierarchy is likely to be co-terminous with a morpheme of the lexical hierarchy. Any one morpheme is likely to begin a syllable and to end with that same syllable. In English, morphemes are likely to end at the end point of a syllable, and to begin at the beginning of a syllable, but many morpheme ends occur in the middle of syllables (as in *boys* where two morphemes make up the one syllable).

In some instances, however, even in English the syllable segmentation clashes with (rather than reinforces) lexical segmentation. Note, for example, that pronunciation of *at all* in which the syllable break comes after the first vowel, while the *t* syllabifies with *all*.

Similarly, on higher levels of the hierarchy, phonological pause groups often — but not always — end at the point where sentence units of the lexical hierarchy end. Here again the lexical units exercise some control over the places where the optional endings of pause groups may occur. Pause groups may also at times embrace units larger than the sentence. Pause-group borders may be made to crisscross with sentence borders, however, so that at the sentence border no pause occurs whereas immediately after the second sentence begins the pause does occur. This is the device by which people talk so that others 'cannot get a word in edgewise'. Note: *That is what she used to say. But ← now she doesn't say it any more* (with no pause at the period-plus-ligature; but with pause and sharply indrawn breath after *But*).

In some languages, furthermore, rhythm groups from the phonological hierarchy at times ignore the lexical word units, such that within the phrase the word units are not marked phonologically.

One should notice, however, that the units of the phonological hierarchy may often have quite different simultaneous analyses at some one point. In the phrase *as you like* (see §§ 6.55, 14.11, 14.12, 14.2) the phoneme /ž/ is in double function as member of the two morphemes *as* and *you*, and of the syllables. In a rapid pronunciation of *a book of stories* (see §§ 9.241, Pike, 1945:37), on the other hand the syllable *of* is in double function between the stress groups, with indeterminate phonological border between the first and second stress groups; nevertheless the lexical and grammatical break between the phrases *a book* and *of stories* is not indeterminate, but clearly segmentable.

It is not only the borders of units of the lexical and phonological hierarchies, however, which may reinforce one another. On occasion the nuclei must be given special attention as they also have particular synchronous interrelations. In the illustration just given, for example, the nuclei of the two stress groups *a book* and *of stories* coincide with and reinforce the nuclei of the lexical phrases so that the head words *book* and *stories* both receive stress. Similarly, it frequently happens that a word composed of two or more morphemes has one — the stem — which is nuclear to the other and is reinforced by being simultaneously the nucleus of a stress group.

There are also interrelations between these hierarchies in reference to distribution. Units of the lexical hierarchy and units of the phonological hierarchy exercise some mutual control as to the patterns of sequence of small phonological units within them. The phonological hierarchy because of its physiological mechanism exercises some ultimate control upon the possible phonological patterns within lexical structure: For example, it seems to be a physiological component of the syllable — the chest pulse — which in part limits languages as to the number of consonants or vowels which they may have in sequence. In the vast majority of languages no more than four consonants occur in sequence within any one syllable, and seldom do more than four vowels occur in sequence. (Cf. § 9.76).

On the other hand, the lexical units exercise detailed control over the distribution of specific sounds within the limits set up by the phonological mechanism. The limits imposed upon the particular structure of particular syllables, the particular sounds within particular classes of phonemes — the particular detail of structural classes and subclasses of such sounds — is determined by the lexical units. Addition of loan words, for example, may lead to considerable change in the over-all distribution of sounds in a particular language. This is a simple instance in which it is clear that the introduction of new lexical items has modified the phonological patterning.

Occasionally control of internal pattern of a unit may best be considered as a composite of lexicon and of phonology. Perhaps one such situation is illustrated by morphophonemic changes where at morpheme boundaries certain phoneme replacements occur. When these replacements are phonologically arbitrary, it is clearly the lexical item which is the basic control. When the changes are phonologically regular, it may be argued that the control is at heart a phonological one as well.

15.12 *Interlocking between the Phonological and Grammatical Hierarchies*

Since there is some type of tagmemic border whenever there is a lexical border (§§ 6.66, 7.56), interlocking of borders of the units of the lexical hierarchy with those of the phonological hierarchy will always in some manner be interlocked also with some units of the grammatical hierarchy. Thus much of what has been said in the preceding section about the relation of phonological units to single lexical items such as single words or particular morphemes or to specific phrases applies equally well to particular distribution classes of morphemes, to particular kinds of phrases, and the like. In this section, then, we need only to emphasize that certain types of interlocking of phonological and nonphonological hierarchies are particularly under the control of tagmemic situations representing a grammatical pattern as such, rather than under the control of some more arbitrary manifesting member of such a pattern. (Cf. § 8.52).

In the preceding section, for example, we indicated that there is a possibility in English that a stress group or pause group may optionally end at the end of any one word. In this section, however, it is important to notice that it is more probable that a pause group or stress group will end at the border of a prepositional phrase — say — than in the middle of one. For many speakers, a pause seldom is noted in the midst of a phrase such as *in the house,* or in the middle of a verbal phrase such as *will come,* or after the subject of a clause such as *He knew the man.* I have recorded data on only one American speaker who frequently ends a breath group in the middle of such phrases. The indrawn breath at an unexpected place in the sentence gives his speaking style a specific individuality. Note: ... *that you write into — the magazine;* ... *who have — solid character; because of his — ability* (where the dash represents breath intake).

Just as one feels that it is esthetically satisfying to find that a lexical word unit is paralleled by a phonological unit — say by the stress group — so it is esthetically satisfying to find a language structure in which a particular grammatical sequence must be paralleled by a particular kind of phonological structuring. When the grammatical hierarchy and the phonological hierarchy coincide in this way it seems to give a neatness of structure which is easy to recognize because there is a reinforcement of the borders of the one kind of unit by borders of the other kind of unit. In such instances the phonological characteristics are diacritica of the grammatical units. In some Mandarin sentence types, for example, one expects a pause between subject and predicate (Chao, 1948:34-5).

Because of this general expectation of grammatical unity and phonological unity to be somewhat parallel, a sequence of words which is grammatically ambiguous in that it potentially can be manifesting either of two sentence patterns will likely be interpreted as representing the grammatical pattern which has internal units most closely paralleled by the accompanying high-level phonological units. That is to say, that the high-level phonological breaks may lead to a perceptual forcing of breaks in the lexical and grammatical structure. Note, for example, the effect of an included pause on interpretation of the triple pun in the next sentence: /ðə sənz rez mit/ *the sons — raise meat* and *the sun's rays — meet.* For further instances where the intonation affects structural interpretation of the segmental materials see Fries (1952:221, 225, 227, 249, 216, 163-64, 157, 254-65), Schubiger (1935:13-23), Trager and Smith (1951:50-52).

One should not, however, assume that the grammatical and phonological hierarchies *must* coincide. Although they often do coincide, and the frequency of such coinciding may be very high at crucial high-level grammatical junctures, they by no means always reinforce one another this way. We have already given illustrations of exceptions both in terms of individual style, cited in this section, and in the style of "not allowing one to get a word in edgewise", but a great many exceptions occur in ordinary speech which go unnoticed unless they happen to lead to misunderstanding. It is a serious methodological and theoretical error to deal only with the frequent form and ignore the many options and exceptions. Failure to observe such deviations — whether for emphasis or for special style or otherwise — allow one to get a false security in his feeling that phonology and grammar are parallel. This in turn makes it difficult for the analyst to realize the extent to which the lexical, phonological, and grammatical hierarchies must be treated as relatively independent. Instances where the phonological and grammatical hierarchies reinforce one another must be treated as special cases of reinforcing border points rather than as illustrating a theoretical norm.

In practical field work analysts have often worked with 'cleaned-up text' — either with text dictated sentence by sentence so that each one is a phonological unit, or with sentences repeated separately by the informant after having been given in consecutive text. Methodologically this is helpful, since (like the isolation of words by an informant) it helps to find psycholinguistically-relevant grammatical (or lexical) units. For theory, however, this may prove fatal. One may, by limiting himself to such artificially-selected data, build a theory of language structure which will not apply to language as it is in fact spoken. Practically, it would fail (a) to account for the lack of phonological juncture between certain units which by the demand of simplicity and coherence must be treated as sentences, and (b) to account for the presence of phonological junctures where they seem not to 'belong'. Theoretically, such an omission of data could lead to an unwarranted rejection of distinct hierarchies of units, inasmuch as the data on which the theory is built have in fact been selected so as to bias the judgment by eliminating empirical areas where multiple hierarchies must be postulated.

Note a few samples, from our recordings, of data in which unit borders of high-level phonology and high-level grammar do not coincide:

B37/6.5 *I always enjoyed-oh-changing ... to wear the — wear the — thing of the day before...* [Note pauses, shown by dashes within the verb phrase and within the noun phrase]. B37/8.3 *... that's the reason you've — had more trouble* [pause within verb phrase]. B37/8.5 *May I have — the sugar please* [pause between verb and object]. 8/1/1.6 *... when — L B got the gun* [pause between conjunction and balance of its clause]. 8/1/4.3 *... more drama ← more strange twists, and more action than anything ← dreamed up for the silver screen//* [← breath group ending with in-drawn breath, between noun *anything* and its post modifier]. 8/2/3.8 *B ... picks up nothing ← as*

T — the right tackle moves in there ← and drops B in his tracks. ͡In fact — he lost a yard on the play [The intonation links *In fact* with the following sentence, but pause with elongated final *t* of *fact* occurs after that second sentence begins.] 8/2/4.9 *L P caught a beautiful pass, right on his — knees* [pause between possessive and head of phrase]. 8/2/5.2 *First and ten for Michigan on the Minnesota 17 yard line ͡Listen to the crowd.* [Ligature indicates that there is no juncture between the two sentences]. 8/2/5.2 *... allowing ... to skirt—the left end* [pause between verb and object] 8/2/5.6 *The battle ˏ is Bitter ˏ and the action ˏ is sweet ˏ Here comes Michigan ˏ out of the huddle now* [juncture between sentences slight, like that between the other phrases, without pause; fortis *B*]. 8/2/6.1 *Those big white jersey boys from — gopher town* [pause within prepositional phrase].

The seriousness of an over-emphasis upon coincidental high-level phonological and grammatical border points becomes acute when one meets a language in which a very high degree of non-conformity at such borders is common. It was this very point of grammatical-phonological non-conformity which started me on the quest for a new grammatical theory. The extraordinary degree to which rhythmic groupings failed to coincide with grammatical groupings in Mixtec forced me to describe Mixtec grammar (Pike, 1944, 1949) without postulating a sharp morphology-syntax boundary. The following sentence will give one example of this kind of criss-cross: *te-nìkaʔàn tuku-i* 'And the youngster spoke again'. Here the first stress group is composed of the word *te-* 'and' as well as of *nì-* and *kaʔàn* 'complete speak', the first two components of the verbal phrase. The second stress group is composed of the last part of the verbal phrase — *tuku* 'again' — and the subject of the phrase, which is *-i* 'child'. Thus the major phonological break comes in the middle of the close-knit verbal phrase. The major grammatical break follows the particle 'and' which is within a stress group. The second major grammatical break precedes the enclitic 'child' (which is an alternate of a full grammatical form *sùčí*, a free form), and so falls within another stress group.

The crisscrossing of borders between phonological and grammatical hierarchies may be seen on phonological units lower than that of the stress group. It is seen frequently on the syllable level in English. Notice the sentence *I'll go*. Here *I'll* constitutes a single syllable of the phonological hierarchy, crossing over the grammatical immediate constituent break between subject and predicate, but interrupting the verbal phrase. An even more complicated illustration is the one which we used for fusion earlier (§ 6.55) /jɪnǰoi ɪt/ *Did you enjoy it?* Here the first syllable includes the subject *you* with the first word *did* of the verb phrase, and the first syllable of the second word *enjoy* of the verb phrase. Occasionally, for some pronunciations, such abbreviations lead to ambiguities which can be exploited for puns. Note, for example: *Why are a mouse and a pile of hay alike?* Answer: /ðə kǽtl ɪt əm/, with ambiguity between *The cattle eat'em* and *The cat'll eat'em*.

Illustrations such as these help to let us see clearly that grammatical theory must be specifically stated so that (1) phonological and grammatical units are not required to be always coterminous, but that (2) the hierarchies interlock at a sufficient number of points to guarantee that we are dealing with a single larger system rather than with various systems which are structurally unrelated.

Similarly, just as there is some relationship between the nuclei of lexical units and the nuclei of phonological units, so there is sometimes a relation between the nuclei of grammatical patterns and the nuclei of phonological units. Thus when there is a regular occurrence of stress upon the stems of words in general, rather than on the stems of just a few words, this regularity indicates that the relation from nucleus to nucleus is between the nucleus of the phonological unit and the nucleus of the syntagmeme, as well as between the nucleus of the phonological unit and the nucleus of the particular lexical units involved. (Cf. §§ 7.313(2), 8.52).

Nuclear interlocking may also occur on higher levels of the grammatical and phonological hierarchies. For example, a 'sentence stress' may frequently occur upon the nucleus of some grammatical pattern such as a phrase or sentence structure. Most frequently, for example, one would expect a stress to occur on the word *house* within the phrase *within the house*. It is only under exceptional circumstances of special attention that the stress would be likely to shift to the word *in* for that phrase (cf. Pike, 1945:84-5).

We conclude, then, that grammatical patterns in part — but by no means completely — control the placement both of the borders of units of the phonological hierarchy and of the nuclei of these units. The control is sufficient to provide for interlocking of these hierarchies. The lack of control is sufficient to allow for the independent structuring of the two hierarchies.

15.13 *Interlocking between the Lexical and Grammatical Hierarchies*

That the lexical hierarchy and the grammatical hierarchy are closely integrated parts of a single larger system is clearly shown by the fact that borders of their units coincide in many ways and in many places. Most important of these facts is that at every point where is a morpheme boundary there is simultaneously the boundary of some tagmeme (§§ 6.1, 6.66, 7.56). In the phrase *the biggest boys* there are morpheme boundaries as well as tagmeme boundaries before and after *the*, *big*, *-est*, *boy*, *-s*. Where there is complete or partial fusion between the morphemes of the sequence, there is therefore simultaneously some correlated fusion between the manifestations of the tagmemes of that sequence.

If the facts of border relations between units of the lexical hierarchy and units of the grammatical hierarchy were to include only these facts, then the analyst would be forced to conclude that there were not two hierarchies structurally differentiable but that there was only the one hierarchy which could be arbitrarily viewed in two or more aspects. It is crucial to the theory of trimodal structure and of tagmemics, therefore, to see that in some other senses the borders between *some* units of the lexical hierarchy occasionally do *not* coincide with *some* units of the grammatical hierarchy. This can be accomplished if one looks at the hierarchies not merely on the layer in which the single morpheme is relevant, but at layers of these hierarchies where more morphemes are in view.

Here the essential, critical observation is that a morpheme at its beginning may be simultaneously coincidental with the beginning borders of two tagmemes (or tagmeme and hypertagmeme) of different layers, whereas that same morpheme in the same morpheme sequence is at its ending coincidental with the ending of only one of the tagmemes mentioned. In this way there is a definite difference in the border relations of the lexical hierarchy and the tagmemic hierarchy as wholes. In the utterance *the boy ran away*, for example, there is one tagmeme which we may call 'demonstrative' which is manifested by the definite article *the*. There is another tagmeme (or hypertagmeme) 'subject-as-actor' which is manifested by the morpheme sequence *the boy*. The demonstrative tagmeme is an included tagmeme within the actor-as-subject tagmeme. We observe that the initial boundary of the morpheme *the* is coincidental both with the beginning of the tagmeme 'demonstrative' and the tagmeme 'subject-as-actor'. On the other hand, the end border of the morpheme *the* is coincidental only with the 'demonstrative' tagmeme and not with the 'subject-as-actor' tagmeme. If, however, the 'subject-as-actor' tagmeme were manifested by a single morpheme such as *John*, then that single morpheme would begin and end at the beginning and ending of the 'subject-as-actor' tagmeme, and no argument could be based upon it alone to separate the lexical and grammatical hierarchies at this point.

We shall return to further ramifications of this argument in a moment, but first wish to refer to some of the data discussed in Chapter 14, in order to indicate how border relationships between units of the lexical and grammatical hierarchies affect the relationship between the hierarchies themselves:

(a) A particular sequence of morphemes may sometimes be ambiguous in reference to its tagmemic structure. Ambiguous items which have the same morphemes but different tagmemes may be called HOMOMORPHIC. The morphemic content in them is the same, but the fundamental grammatical structure is different. If the grammatical boundaries — the immediate constituent breaks — may occur in two or more places within the morpheme sequence and yet make correct speech, then we may observe that there is a certain control of lexical grouping exerted by grammatical structure. See the phrase: *He paid for a bench in the park* (§ 11.43, commentary on [tt], and Pike, 1943b:79).[2]

(b) A single morpheme may, on the other hand, simultaneously serve as manifesting a part of two overlapping grammatical constructions. This morpheme is in double function between the two tagmemes or tagmeme sequences. See the illustrations from Fries: *They have to have the students pay* (in which the second *have* serves

---

[2] Note that we have long been interested in structural ambiguities. See also §§ 7.43, 7.6(2).

simultaneously in reference to the infinitive relation and in reference to the verb *pay* [1948:4-8]; and *They have had to have the students have the money sent*). Such a morpheme in double tagmemic function is further evidence that there is not a one-to-one correlation between units of the lexical and grammatical hierarchies.

(c) A related phenomenon occurs when a single morpheme fills the slot of two fused tagmemes. This is the circumstance in which a morph with two semantic components is nevertheless analyzed as a single morpheme, but the semantic components in part reflect semantic elements of the two tagmemes fused in that one morpheme. An illustration is the *-o* of *digo*, with components which are both personal and tense or mode, (cf. § 14.12, 14.2).

We turn from the study of border relationships between the units of the lexical and grammatical hierarchies in order to study the relationships between their nuclei.

(a) The nucleus of the grammatical structure and the nucleus of the lexical structure are often the same, especially in an endocentric construction. In *big John*, for example, the word *John* is the nucleus of this specific lexical phrase, and in addition is the nucleus of the personal-noun grammatical construction (the syntagmeme) as such. Similarly, in *boyish*, *boy* is nuclear and *-ish* is marginal. When dealing with the particular instance *boyish*, one is dealing with it as a lexical item, in part. When, however, one generalizes on this term and refers to a class of stems any one of which may be modified by the suffix *-ish*, then a statement of the problem in terms of class and affix becomes a tagmemically-orientated statement, with the nuclei of the lexical and grammatical units reinforcing one another.

(b) In some circumstances the relation between nucleus of grammar and nucleus of lexical items may be skewed. This is especially true in the metalanguage of linguistic discussion. Notice, for example, the phrase *the -s*, (meaning *the suffix -s*). Here the head of the construction is obviously the item *-s*. Yet in lexical terms and in normal speech this is a marginal item which in routine use occurs with a stem. In this special metalanguage use the lexically-marginal item is temporarily treated as grammatically nuclear. Related but quite distinct situations occur in normal language. Compare *Those more-or-less-once-a-month-promised-but-usually-not-that-often-forthcoming letters...*, and *It* [*the paper wad*] *went right over the-boy-that-sat-in-front-of-me's head*.

The lexical hierarchy and the grammatical hierarchy exercise to a considerable extent mutual control over each other's distributional and semantic characteristics: Lexical items can occur only in relevant tagmemic slots, whereas tagmemes (and hypertagmemes) have as one of their crucial characteristics the appropriate class of morphemes (or morpheme sequences) which may manifest them. If units of the lexical hierarchy occur, units of the grammatical hierarchy must occur (§§ 6.1, 6.66, 7.56). Neither can occur without the other. Occurrence of fused varieties of the one implies the occurrence of fused varieties of the other (§ 6.66). A lexical meaning may be modified by a tagmemic meaning (cf. *terribly pretty*, §§ 7.323, 7.43, 11.44, commentary 16 on Table 3). Where a class of morphemes occurs as manifesting only one tagmeme in the language, there is an indeterminacy between the meaning of the morpheme class and the meaning of the tagmeme (§ 7.324). When the class which can manifest only one tagmeme is itself composed of only one morpheme, there is a further indeterminacy between the meaning of the morpheme, the meaning of the class, and the meaning of the tagmeme (§ 7.324). In situations where such limitations occur, the presence of any member of a class which is restricted in distribution to the one tagmeme signals the presence of that tagmeme. Similarly, where there is a morpheme which is the sole member of the class, and the class occurs only as manifesting one tagmeme, the presence of this morpheme signals the presence of the lexical unit, the presence of the lexical class, and the presence of the grammatical unit.

When specific lexical items signal grammatical relations because of their restricted distribution, they may be called FUNCTION WORDS (and cf. § 6.45). It is not yet clear,[3] in tagmemic terms, what else is implied by Fries' category of function words (1952: especially 106). Probably some of the structures in which function words fill the same slot, in Fries' analysis, would have to be separated into distinct syntagmemes within the present treatment. That is, I would expect to find that a sentence type or construction which required a particular function word to signal its crucial relationships would have to be set up as a separate sentence type or — at the least — sub-type. The sentences *Who came?* and *John came* would in syntagmemic terms come out as different structures.

In at least two other ways the interlocking of lexical and grammatical hierarchies appears in the work of Fries. In his formulas for sentence types he finds it necessary in some instances to note whether the subject of the sentence does or does not refer to the same person as does an expression later in the sentence. It is important, for example, in understanding the sentence *My husband is the director* that one recognize that *my husband* and *director* have the same referent. Unless this is indicated in some way in the formula, the structural characteristics are not adequately shown (Fries, 1952:191-92, 268-69).

Secondly, in the sentence formulas of Fries there occasionally occurs a specific listing of a specific lexical item such as *-d* for "past tense". These items become crucial parts of his sentence formulas for certain purposes (Fries, 1952:198-99, 211, 220). It is not yet certain to what extent this kind of symbolism will carry over into syntagmemic formulas. If these particular morphemes are always unique members of a class such that no other morphemes enter the class, then the morpheme formula could be replaced by a class formula which in fact would signal the same morpheme, but in principle would avoid the necessity of listing specific morphemes as such. The morphemes could in that instance be listed in reference to their class function even though the class were uniquely composed of a single morpheme.

Whether or not a similar tagmemic reinterpretation[4] would allow one to bypass

---

[3] See, now, portmanteau tagmemes, lexically signalled (compare double-function tagmemes in Pickett (1960:69-71), and see Pike (1963b:222)).

[4] In one of my most recent papers (1964d) I have attempted to develop the symbolization of situa-

the signalling of identity of lexical referents is much more doubtful. I would expect that further study would show that identity of referents would have to be retained in the grammatical formula, but that these would be handled in terms of alloclasses which were made up of potentially-same referents with some type of allotagmemic tie involved. Shell (1957:204) found it necessary for Cashibo, for example, to symbolize allotagmas in accordance with the fact that a subordinate clause had the same subject (same referent) as the principal clause. This seems to be a parallel situation to that symbolized by Fries for English, though in a sharply different construction.

The interlocking of the various levels forces one to take a much more wholistic approach in which data from various levels and hierarchies may need to be called upon in order to explain the layer under attention. Occasionally high-layer material must be anticipated in the presentation of low-layer data, and when one reaches the description of higher layers, one may find it necessary to go deeply into the details of a lower layer in order to make the empirical situation clear.

One of the clues for tagmemic recognition is not just the presence of lexical classes. but the presence of allomorphs of morphemes which are tagmemically conditioned, Note the analysis of *he* and *him* as one morpheme in § 6.53; the presence of the particular allomorph *him* helps to signal the occurrence of the 'goal' tagmeme in *John saw him*. For certain purposes, therefore, one cannot afford to completely eliminate from consideration on a high grammatical level the details of a low lexical level which normally are subsumed in the presentation of intermediate levels of the hierarchies. This is analogous to the manner in which a particular allophone of a phoneme may help signal the fact that one is at the end of a pause group — though this phonologically-relevant clue would be graphically invisible at the time one is working on the pause layer of the phonological hierarchy, if the data at that point had meanwhile been respelled phonemically.

We turn again, now, to one of the most crucial questions of this chapter, and of the book as a whole: Can we be certain that the lexical hierarchy is structurally different from the grammatical hierarchy? Must we indeed deal with three hierarchies — the lexical, the phonological, and the grammatical — or could we deal with only two, one of which is phonological and the other is a composite of grammar with its manifesting bits? In our view, the data which have been presented thus far indicate that the lexical and grammatical hierarchies must indeed be kept distinct. Since the question is very crucial, however, it may be helpful to the reader to summarize here a number of the most important considerations leading to this conclusion. Most of them have been discussed elsewhere and need only be briefly mentioned here. (But see § 12.5).

(1) Units of the lexical hierarchy can be expressed in terms of phonemes, whereas

---

tional role (which would care for identity of referent) in relation to grammatical role (for example, subject-as-actor versus subject-as-goal). See also fn. to § 7.6.

These relations, however, would be different from concord (for which see Pike, 1962a:236-37).

structures of the grammatical hierarchy can be expressed only in terms of formulas. *The cat fell down*, as a lexical structure, can be crudely expressed in the following phoneme sequence /ðə kæt fɛl dawn/. The grammatical structure which that sentence manifests, however, can only be expressed by formulas which indicate subject-as-actor hypertagmeme followed by a certain kind of predicate hypertagmeme, with internal tagmemic construction further symbolized if desired; the symbols must explicitly or implicitly have reference to manifesting classes, structural meanings, rigid or flexible orders of occurrence, potential expansions, etc.

(2) There is a difference between a particular sentence and the sentence type of which that particular sentence is one illustration or sample or manifesting member. We wish to be able to say that *John came home* is a sentence, that *Bill came home* is a sentence, that *John came home* and *Bill came home* are different sentences, but that *John came home* and *Bill came home* both manifest the same sentence type. We can talk this way without contradiction if we differentiate between units of the lexical hierarchy and units of the grammatical hierarchy, but if we fail to make this distinction between the two hierarchies then such descriptive statements will lead to contradiction at some point. Here 'sameness' is defined in one instance in reference to the lexical hierarchy, and in the other instance in reference to the grammatical hierarchy.

(3) A particular idiomatic phrase may have a lexical unity of a type which is quite different from other lexical units manifesting the same grammatical structure. Thus the idiom *to step on the gas* has a hypermorphemic special meaning which is quite different from the hypermorphemic regular meaning which is part of phrases such as *to step on the worm*. Nevertheless, the tagmemic structure of the two seems to be the same. The lexical hierarchy includes specialized hypermorphemes which are not of themselves specialized tagmemes or syntagmemes.

(4) A particular lexical unit may be the same in two utterances, while the grammatical function is different. *John* is lexically the same in the utterances *John hit Bill* and *Bill hit John*, but the tagmeme manifested by *John* in the two instances is different.

(5) A single member of the lexical hierarchy may simultaneously and unambiguously serve as parts of two grammatical structures in a single sequence. A morpheme may be in double function within a sentence. (See reference to *have* earlier in this section).

(6) A lexical item or sequence of such items may simultaneously and ambiguously serve as a member of two contrastive structural sequences of grammatical units. (Cf. discussion of *paid for a bench in the park*).

(7) A single morpheme may serve to manifest two fused tagmemes in a portmanteau tagmeme, as in the *-o* of *digo* (cf. above).

(8) Given a particular sentence such as *John came home*, the lexical entities may be changed without changing the basic tagmemic entities, if one replaces *John* by *big John*. This leads to an important generalization which in part covers several more specific arguments: Units of the phonological hierarchy expand differently from

units of the lexical hierarchy, and from units of the grammatical hierarchy. Starting with a brief sentence such as *John came home*, every added morpheme expands the basic lexical hierarchy. *Big John came home* is a larger hypermorpheme than *John came home;* the two expressions are not the same hypermorpheme. *Big John came home quickly* is a larger hypermorpheme than *Big John came home*. On the other hand, expansion of one of the tagmemes can be made internally without adding to the basic tagmemic structure as a whole. Thus *John came home* and *Big John came home* each have the same basic subject-as-actor hypertagmeme, in spite of their different internal structure. The phonological hierarchy on the other hand may expand in kind structurally from the phoneme threshold up to the breath group threshold without expanding in length or content. A single phoneme such as /o/ may, that is to say, simultaneously constitute a phoneme, syllable, stress group, pause group, breath group. These three different types of expansion can be diagrammed crudely as follows:

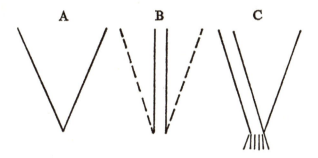

The diagram A represents the lexical hierarchy, which beginning with a single morpheme expands by accretion upwards, such that each added morpheme makes a larger hypermorpheme. Diagram B indicates the phonological hierarchy with the phoneme at the narrowest part of the vertical column at the base of the diagram. Here a single phoneme is present. If that phoneme constitutes a breath group as well, then the breath group of this single-phoneme size is represented on the diagram at the narrow part of the column at the top. If, however, the breath group includes numerous syllables, stress groups, and the like, then there is further climbing of the hierarchical ladder not only by kind of unit, but by size of unit, by accretion, and this is indicated by the dotted lines ascending upward. By the upper part of Diagram C it is intended to suggest that the growth of a syntagmeme may be by several hypertagmemes in a row, just as the growth of a hypermorpheme may be by several morphemes in a row. Yet Diagram C also indicates schematically that one of the hypertagmemes (the one between the parallel lines at the upper left) can be expanded internally by various included tagmemes, as is indicated by the lines at the bottom of the diagram which expand that one hypertagmemic slot.

(9) Since the lexical and grammatical hierarchies expand differently, it means

that at some point in some of their layerings their borders will not be co-terminous. This we indicated, above, by saying that in *Big John came home* the subject-as-actor hypertagmeme begins with the morpheme *big*, but does not end with that morpheme. It is only an included tagmeme which ends with *big*.

(10) The lexical and grammatical hierarchies in some languages expand with a sufficient degree of independence that a high-level unit of either one may occur filling a low-layer slot in the other. A highly-complex lexical unit, such as an intricate verb structure, may fill a low-level tagmemic slot as predicate of a sentence. This causes no surprise. When, however, a complex lexical item of a type which normally fills only slots of a high-level syntagmemic structure is found filling a low-level slot, the result may be unexpected, and cause analytical difficulty if one is using classical procedures. Such a situation occurs in the 'phrase word' *the king of England's hat*. Here the phrase *the king of England* is a high-layered lexical item grammatically structured with a high degree of internal tagmemic complexity. Yet the entire morpheme sequence is put in the slot preceding the possessive -'*s* where normally only a low-layered structure would occur.

It is the criss-crossing[5] of layerings of the two hierarchies which makes this phrase awkward to handle within traditional analyses. If, however, one does not make too rigid, or too early in his theory, a dichotomy between morphology and syntax, but leaves room for independent handling of hierarchical materials in various ways, then this kind of situation is much less difficult to analyze. One describes it as being a high-level structure within a low-level slot; one adds the further note that statistically these are infrequent. Under such an approach a 'phrase-word' is no longer structurally 'queer', inasmuch as it can easily be handled within the structural framework proposed, but is merely statistically infrequent.

15.2 *Interlocking between Systems*

Systems may interact, interlock, and affect one another in various ways. If this were not true, the smaller systems could not be structurally integrated into a single larger language system. In order to be part of a higher-layered system, the included systems must at some point interlock in reference to some of their respective borders and/or some of their respective nuclei.

Perhaps from this point of view we can get further insight into the problem of the relation of the systems of intonation and stress in English. If an abdominal pulse, or rhythm group, or stress group, is part of the phonological hierarchy of the regular segmental system (as is implied in § 9.3), whereas the system of pitches in English constitutes a distinct system or subsystem within the total English structure (as is implied in §§ 13.3, 13.5), how is it possible that stress placement is empirically relevant

---

[5] Now often discussed as nesting, or embedding.

to the structure of intonation groups, or how may it be theoretically valid that an intonation contour should be tied in definition to stress placement such that a primary contour begins with a stress (§ 9.32)? Does this not lead to a 'mixing of levels' of analysis? Does not the stress-pitch interrelation completely invalidate the suggestion that in some sense the pitch system is a separate one in English?

In the light of the present chapter our necessary reply is clear: (1) Unless systems or subsystems at some point interlock through their nuclei or their borders they cannot be parts of an integrated larger system. Language, in order to comprise a system, must have its subsystems integrated in some way. (2) The particular details of this integration must be discovered by empirical research for any particular language, however, even though the fact of such integration can be confidently expected. (3) It is our empirical observation, (Pike, 1945:27-8, 179) that a satisfactory statement of the structure of the English pitch system can only be made in reference to placement of stress. The interlocking of the two systems occurs in such a way that one of the principal structural sequences of pitches in English may be called a primary contour, and this primary contour can only be identified in reference to its initial border, which begins with a stressed syllable.

At this point a unit of the high-level segmental system of the phonology (the stress group) and the pitch sequence units interlock by having nuclei synchronized. Similarly, the end of the primary contour is in general synchronized with the end of a stress group, whereas the beginning of a primary contour frequently comes in the middle of a stress group. The beginning of a stress group, however, is co-terminous with another intonational unit — the precontour — which with the primary contour makes up a total intonation unit which is then co-terminous at its beginning and its ending with the stress group. In the phrase *if I wánt to do it*, there is only one stress group and only one total contour if there is but one stress on the phrase falling on the word *want*. The primary contour begins with that word, and ends with the word *it*. The precontour covers the words *if I*.

Differences in the degree and type of integration of the pitch system with other phonological systems in a language can make a sharp difference in the structural pattern of that language. Where pitch phonemes join with segmental phonemes to make up the basic segmental lexical morphemes of the language, the resultant tone language (like Mandarin, or Mixtec) has a structure completely different from that of English where the pitch phonemes integrate with the segmental phonological units only through the integration of their total systems, which manifest distinct morphemic systems. In English the pitch phonemes constitute contrasting features of pitch morphemes, the pitch morphemes enter into pitch-morpheme sequences such as the total contours, and these into contour sequences. It is this total suprasegmental pitch system with its own pitch phonemes, its pitch morphemes, and its pitch tagmemes, which integrates with the phonemes, morphemes, and tagmemes of the segmental system. (See §§ 13.3, 13.5).

An entirely different type of integration of systems is seen in reference to the subsegmental systems of style or of voice quality (§ 13.4). Each style has its set of phonemes. Yet most of the phonemes of any two sets — such as those of speech aloud and of speech whispered, in English — may be considered the same. The differences between the topologically-same phonemes in the respective systems may be considered as conditioned by the system itself (§ 8.44). The overlapping of phonemes between the systems is such that the phonemes — or most of the phonemes — are structurally the same in a topological sense, even though phonetically different as conditioned by the systems. This topological interrelation constitutes the interlocking bond between the segmental and subsegmental systems.

The morphemes of a language might also simultaneously belong to a number of style systems, and link them together. These styles may lead, however, to systemically-conditioned variants of those morphemes (§ 6.56).

In some instances the difference between the phoneme or morpheme systems of the styles may be greater than that of mere allophonic or allomorphic variants, and may include differences in the membership of their respective phoneme and morpheme classes. In this latter instance one of the styles will have extra phonemes or morphemes that the other does not have (compare the special usages of *thee* and *thou*, § 7.46).

When speakers of a language come from different social strata of a culture, their language subsystems may differ somewhat as styles differ. At most points in the two systems the respective items will be topologically related (§§ 8.44, 8.33[5], 9.231). At a few other points there may be overdifferentiation or extrasystematic features (§ 8.61), or there may be special or extra phonemes, morphemes, or tagmemes in the one or the other subsystem.

Individual dialects may also differ in these ways, as may the dialects of people of different ages. Deliberately-distorted dialects would have to be similarly analyzed; these might include the temporarily-adopted speech of a person who was distorting his usual speech for special effects, as he might by using 'Pig Latin', or mock pronunciations of the dialect of some other person.

Similarly, speakers of a language may have slightly different systems of that language if they come from different geographical areas. Geographical dialects, like the social dialects, may in many characteristics be topologically related while differing structurally in others.

Dialects of one language may also differ over a time span. The structure of earlier dialects may be largely similar to that of later dialects. Their similarity is statable in terms of their topological relations.

It is obvious that systems and subsystems of language change in time. But the mechanism of this change, within the implications of the present theory, requires that some units within the hierarchies of one or more of these systems adjacent in time interlock by continuity of function or by double function within the two systems.

The details of such interlocking, whether it be for social, geographical, or temporal dialects, may be seen, first, in reference to the interlocking of units vertically or laterally within any one hierarchy of any one of these systems. Second, the interlocking is seen between the various units of the hierarchies of lexicon, phonology, and grammar. Third, interlocking occurs between subsystems such as intonational and segmental ones. Fourth, the interlocking comes by way of over-all topological relationships of units from one system to another in all of these layers and hierarchies and systems.

That set of component units of a series of dialects — whether social, geographical or temporal — which are topologically related throughout these dialects may be said comprise the OVER-ALL PATTERN or COMMON CORE of that series of dialects.

There is also interlocking between systems in some instances where it is not useful to assume that there is an over-all pattern since the topologically related bits are so sporadic as not to be systematic. This in turn, implies that the basic lexical, phonological, and grammatical hierarchies of the one system fail to be topologically related to the basic pattern of the lexical, phonological, and grammatical hierarchies of the other systems. Systematic topological relations between units implies topological relation between hierarchies.

There can be language mixture, however, between language systems which are not related topologically to an extensive degree. This occurs when fragments of one language are interspersed non-systematically throughout a second language — especially when bilingual speakers utilize bits from one language while they are speaking another language. There may be FRAGMENTS of one language COEXISTANT within the system of another language. These coexistant injected fragments may be loan words or loan structures of one kind or another.

If the borrowed bits are so modified during the borrowing process, however, that the structural characteristics of their lexical, phonological, and grammatical contents are in pattern indistinguishable from the hierarchical structuring of the language into which they are injected, complete assimilation has taken place. The degree of this assimilation, however, varies from language to language, from speaker to speaker, and from item to item within the speech of any one speaker under any one such situation. There is an indeterminacy as to the point at which a loan word or phrase may be considered as having been completely assimilated. At its first usage by a bilingual the phrase may be especially set off by junctures of some type which serve as the equivilent of 'spoken quotation marks' and which therefore indicate that it has some special status in the language. It may also in the early stages have special phonological characteristics brought in from the lending language. These characteristics may disappear and yet leave special shape types of morphemes which are not present in the native stock. In such instances it is impossible to determine by straight descriptive techniques whether a special shape type is merely a rare form inherited from the native stock due to some unknown historical situation, or whether it is in fact a borrowing.

There is also a further difficult problem raised by such mixture: To what extent does the bilingual act as if he were using a HYPERSYSTEM of language, in which the two languages that he speaks somehow fuse into one larger system? Occasionally when a bilingual is learning to read, the experience which he has had with one of the languages will affect the learning process of the other. Phonemic contrasts in one language which parallel in phonetic content some allophonic occurrences of the other may lead him to react to the allophones of the second language as if they were in fact distinct phonemes, insofar as his demands for their being written separately are concerned.

Speakers who are normally considered to be monolingual, but who nevertheless vary their styles on occasion, must certainly be considered as having a hypersystem (or hypercongruent system, cf. §§ 5.4, 6.7, 7.313[3], 8.61) to the extent that the respective subsystems of the language make up one larger system. The structure of hypersystems of all kinds is obscure and needs further study. Speakers themselves, however, are often quite aware of the complex nature of their system. They may state concerning a loan: 'Oh, that's a word from Spanish', for example. Or they may be unaware of the loan character of the borrowed words. Fully assimilated materials are likely to be unidentified by the monolingual speaker as coming from a foreign source. Psycholinguistic studies are needed at these points before some of the structural problems involved are likely to be clarified.

Just as there is doubt as to how large a unit is conveniently considered as part of the language system or hypersystem, so there is a problem as to how small a part of language is best called a 'system'. Occasionally it is convenient to speak of 'the phonological system' or the 'grammatical system' of a language. Sometimes it is useful to apply the term system to smaller parts of the language structure, such as 'the system of stops'. Linguists differ as to the minimum size unit to which they will apply this term. Occasionally it is applied to very small parts of the language system, such as to the class of vowels which may come in a particular slot in a particular syllable structure, or to a particular lexical class of words. In this latter instance the 'system of phonematic units' which comes in a structure such as $b \ldots t$ would be a different phonematic system from that which occurs at the end of a syllable in a structure such as $b \ldots$.

These problems arise since any list of items is a distribution class of some structural relevance if that set of items occurs within some structural slot in the language. Thus a class of morphemes is relevant if it comes in a subject slot, a class of sentences is relevant if it comes in a certain paragraph slot, and the total utterances of a language make up a language system by virtue of the fact that they come in conversational slots within the matrix of behaviour of a particular society. In this sense distribution class and system tend to merge.

Distribution class (or filler class), from this point of view, is a term applied to a structural set of items seen as a filler of a slot. The same materials seen as some kind of top layer of focus may be viewed as a system. Distribution class and system, then, are to some extent terms of relative focus. Similarly, system, subsystem, and hypersystem are terms of focus. If our top focus is on a particular system, then the included systems within it are subsystems, and within the subsystems may be classes.

When the systems do not come in comparable contexts, then the term hypersystem may be used in this volume for the over-all material under discussion. Thus the two languages of a bilingual are in general sorted out into different language contexts such that the utterances of the one language are in general kept within the matrix of other utterances of that same language. It is for this reason that we speak of the over-all bilingual structure as a hypersystem rather than as a simple system. It is evident, however, that different people will apply the term system to different data according to their area of attention.

If for the moment we speak of classes of words as being a system we can make one further generalization here. When two systems of morphemes — that is two morpheme filler classes — in part overlap, fuse, or interlock, CLASS CLEAVAGE results. Here the tagmemic analyst finds it most fruitful to set up two or more distinct classes of morphemes even though certain of the morphemes are members simultaneously of the two classes (i.e., in double function between the classes). Class cleavage — from this point of view — would be a special instance, on a low focus of attention, of interlocking subsystems.

A further problem confronts us about the relation of the interlocking of systems in general: Can we find any fruitful use of the terms 'border' and 'nucleus' as applied to systems, as we did for reference to the borders and nuclei of specific units of the system as they fuse and interlock in sequence and hierarchy? Does the concept of wave of motion, which helped us to find a way of discussing fusion at the borders of the units themselves, help in reference to description of system interrelationships? Perhaps so. If two or more dialects are looked at as if they were 'waves' of dialect, then transition areas between them would be areas of indeterminacy as to where one dialect begins and ends, just as we had areas of indeterminacy in the phonetic border between two sounds, or in the border area between two fused morphemes. Similar transition areas might be postulated between temporal dialects, if a brief indeterminate transition area of rapid change comes between two temporal dialects which otherwise are relatively more stable.

Social dialects or systems would be interlocking at their nuclei — that is at their crucial topologically-related structures. They would differ at their borders — at their points of over-differentiation and under-differentiation relative to one another (cf. § 8.61). Two different languages would be sharply distinct as to their nuclei, but overlapping at their borders, to the extent that bilinguals utilize loans from the one in speaking the other. (And see Pike on change, 1960a).

(But note that this use of nucleus in reference to common core of two languages is quite different from the use of 'Kernel' applied to a single language. See § 11.6).

15.3 Bibliographical Comments on Chapter 15

15.31 On Simplicity, Elegance, and Levels of Analysis

Elegance and simplicity of statement in linguistic description can be sought in various ways.

In chapter 15 we point out that by using a few simple concepts, such as the presence and partial independence of the lexical, phonological, and grammatical hierarchies with interlocking at various layers of the hierarchies, we are able to discuss problems of very great complexity. The fact that this enormous complexity of interlocking systems, layers, and units of various kinds can be described in reference to a few simple components leads us to consider behavioremic theory elegant and fruitful.

This view is sharply in contrast with one which a few years ago attempted to get simplicity in linguistic description by a rigid separation of levels in "ascending levels of complexity of organization" (Trager and Smith, 1951:81; cf. also 8 and 54). In the latter, the ascending order is assumed to be first phonetics, outside of linguistics proper, then phonemics, next morphemics, followed by syntax, and then — and only then — the structure of meaning or so called 'metalinguistics' — an unfortunate term, since the term 'metalanguage' is best used in the traditional sense to refer to language talking about language; e.g., Haugen (1951:213). For the earlier statement of this rigid sequence see Trager, 1949. See also above § 9.71.

To me, this latter approach to grammatical layerings appears inadequate for several reasons: (1) It does not easily allow room for a structural syllable, nor a structural stress group, nor for a structural treatment of idioms. If the pyramiding is from phoneme to morpheme to word to sentence, the syllable and stress group and idiom do not easily fit. When phonological, lexical, and grammatical hierarchies are treated separately, however, their respective hierarchies all find structural place in the system. (2) It gives priority structurally to the phoneme as over against the morpheme, and leaves no room for the tagmeme as such. In my view the morpheme has equal theoretical primitiveness with the phoneme. In fact, were I forced to give priority to one or the other, I would give it to the morpheme since it is here that the form-meaning composite is most easily seen — and my theoretical view is based upon the fact that language is a communicating system with form-meaning relationships at its heart. (3) The third reason is related to the second — that this pyramiding from phoneme to sentence through morpheme does not give adequate room for meaning as a primitive concept, but leaves it to some kind of a layering beyond that of the sentence, rather than working it into the most primitive terms. (4) It shows a relationship between levels of structure exclusively as that of an including one, such that one layer is included within the next higher layer, and the higher layer is built up of units of the lower layer. In my view the relationships often are quite different: Rather, the three hierarchies pyramid side by side, with constant cross correlation and interlocking at various points; in addition, the units of one hierarchy are undefinable excepting in some kind of reciprocal relationship with units of the others. It is not possible, in my view, to first define phoneme and then to define morpheme in reference to it. Rather phoneme, morpheme, and tagmeme must all be defined in reference to one another at the start of the handling of the system of language as a whole.

The differences between these two approaches to language can in part be expressed in terms of criteria of elegance. In the interlocking hierarchical view which I have proposed here, the key criterion of elegance is INTEGRATION. The data are considered to be elegantly described when, in terms of simple hierarchies, the relationships of their various units are neatly set forth as a pattern of integration of these units. In the second, the criterion of elegance has as its keynote the concept of COMPARTMENTALIZATION. Here elegance is assumed to consist of distinct presentation of one set of data with no reference to data of compartments later to be described in the analysis. (See Trager, 1949; Bloch, 1950:86; Trager and Smith, 1951). Elegance in this instance is a function of separateness of parts of the language one from another in the presentation.

A third criterion of elegance, which leads to an entirely different approach to language analysis, takes ABSTRACTION at various levels of analysis as its focus. Firth and his colleagues have been developing the view that one can move into a language structure at any point and study *all* the components of the language relative to that one point. If, for example, they have arbitrarily or for some reason started to study language at the word level, they would want to study the phonetics of the word directly (without going through phonemics), both in its segmental aspects and in its high-level prosodic characteristics. For numerous references and discussion of this kind of material see mention of prosodies in §§ 5.63, 8.814, 9.73, 9.74, 10.51. Note also, specifically, Robins (1953a:145), "By this treatment, in what formerly appeared as the arbitrary substitution of individual letters, there is revealed a certain correspondence of systemic patterning between the grammatical and phonological levels of analysis, when Nasalization, as a process in the morphology of the language, is applied to the phonological structures comprising Sundanese words and syllables"). See also, for summary of 'prosodic' approach, Robins (1957b). For further discussion of the strength and weakness of these three points of view see Pike (1958b).

Since then, however, definitions of the nature of economy or simplicity have often had other foci: Percival, as "a function of the number of rules required to state the relations between the phonemic and allophonic levels" (1960:386); Halle, as "relative lengths" of two sets of statements, which lead, in turn, to ordering of rules, building on Quine, in terms of simplicity of laws (in *Structure of Language...*, 1961:91, 94); Saporta and Contreras, as simplicity of generation (1962:9); also, "the fewest number of symbol tokens" for a small corpus, but "analysis into constituents" for a larger corpus (13); Halliday, as the description that "makes maximum use of the theory to account for a maximum amount of the data" (1961:249).

I personally prefer to keep in mind efficiency of communication and understanding — and compare Bach, with readableness of rules as one kind of nonsystematic simplicity (1964:50). Thus, Ferguson finds Halle's "system of notation ... so complicated that it defied repeated attempts on the part of the reviewer to master it" (1962:292); and Quine, under certain conditions, gives pragmatic considerations priority so that "Elegance, conceptual economy", is secondary to effective communication (1953:79). Dixon, in a related view, would consider simplicity as "less important" than "adequate description" (1963:67). Contrast Postal's counting of symbols (1964:14) — but for early discussions of advantages and disadvantages of "parsimony of symbols" see Chao, 1934, in Joos, 1957:47) — or Halle's measure by number of distinctive features (in *Structure of Language...*, 1961). For logical considerations in simplicity, see Goodman (1951:59-68, 73-84).

For a desire — not yet reached — "to encode [natural languages as] to eliminate" redundancy, see Miller and Chomsky (in Luce and others, 1963:450) — but where redundancy of multiple hierarchies is involved, I personally do not wish to eliminate it from representation. In my view, a principle of complementarity, in which a description must eventually be repeated from the viewpoints of particle, wave, and field, must be given priority over a single approach which may be simplistic in its outline, and in its non-overlapping phases, but is less able to treat various phases of a system. Compare Andreyev, for whom "no model can be of a completely unilateral kind", neither "set-theoretic, probabilistic, or algorithmic" (1962:190). Lees would feel, however, that the "three such hierarchies" "would seem merely to triple the effects of whatever difficulties may be encountered in attempting to picture grammatical patterns" and prevent a "coherent description" or "single theory" (1960b: 211).

For our more extensive discussion of the literature concerning hierarchical structuring, see §§ 11.71, 9.71; for relation of grammatical to phonological hierarchy, with grammatical prerequisites to phonological analysis and the like, see bibliography in §§ 8.87, 9.242. For psycholinguistic "shifting of focus within interlocking hierarchies of units", note Gudschinsky (1958b:345); and cf. § 8.815. Interlocking of grammar to phonology is illustrated for Gilyak by Jakobson (1957a:261), with "striking differences between intersectional and intrasectional laws of phonemic combinations"; juncture is often involved in such matters: see also Priest, Priest and Grimes (1961:335), with Sirono having "two simultaneous, partially independent, yet interlocking systems of organization" — one via traditional grammar and one by spans with special "morphophonemic boundary points, enclitic markers, and special groupings". For hesitation, with repeats that "typically involve function words and occur antecedent to lexical items" and also show phonological borders, note Maclay and Osgood (1959:39). On the other hand there may be overlapping or nonoverlapping of grammatical units with phonological units, Halliday (1961: 281); and sometimes "the criteria of both [grammatical and phonological] analyses to some extent coincide", W. S. Allen (1956:145).

Further discussion of simplicity as requiring multiple hierarchies is found in § 15.32.

15.32 On Mixing, Skipping, and Mashing Levels and Hierarchies

Growing out of the different results gained when one applies criteria of integration of levels versus compartmentalization of levels, certain negative views develop and may be mentioned briefly.

Trager and Smith, as compartmentalizers, emphasize "the extreme importance of levels in the observation and classification of events in the whole field of human behavior", and emphasize that it "has been and will doubtless continue to be one of the most important criteria for scientific work in the social sciences", so that "failure to separate and classify data properly in this regard has been one of the main weaknesses of much of what has been done not only in linguistics but in all the social sciences to date" (1951:81). Trager asserts that "one cannot mix up several levels of analysis and get anything but a mess" (1950:157). Trager and Smith object to trying to present simultaneously data concerning phonetics, phonemics, morphemics, syntax, and meaning. This, from our viewpoint, is in part an objection to the mixing of discussion of layers or units across the hierarchical boundaries.

It is further made clear by other writers that there is a second (somewhat different, but related) objection — an objection to bringing considerations of a low member of one hierarchy into the treatment of a member of the same hierarchy two or more levels removed from it. It is assumed by these writers that one should procede to treat all the relevant data of the lowest member in reference to the next higher layer, and then the third-higher layer should be treated in reference to the middle layer without returning to the lowest layer. If I understand him, for example, this is the implication of McQuown's reference to skipping levels, or "level hopping" (1957a: 189-92).

As over against these views, however, we have already indicated that W. S. Allen wishes to be able to refer to some phonetic matters in dealing with sound change — rather than dealing with phonemes alone (1951b:135-36; and see above § 8.814). Our view, also, insists that at any point in communication various items from various levels of the hierarchies involved are simultaneously affecting that communication. For any one purpose of abstracting some particular kind of phonemenon, it may be relevant to look at items from various levels of the hierarchy rather than dealing with only the highest level which seems to be relevant and attempting to subsume all other data under that one.

A third kind of objection in dealing with hierarchies is the one which comes out of our integration point of view. I have objected to "attempts to squeeze such data [of high-level phonological units] into one nonhierarchical sequence of chopped-up disparate segmental phonemes and quasi-segmental juncture phonemes" (Pike, 1957b:35). By this I have meant the mashing of a hierarchy, or the treatment of the symbolization of the units of a hierarchy, in such a way as to make it appear that the units of that total hierarchy were all of one kind, collapsed into a linear sequence. In my view it is a distortion of levels to treat phonemes, syllables, stress groups, and pause groups, etc., as if they could be symbolized with a single sequence of unit phonemes. For one type of linearization of pitch materials see S. Martin, "The emphasis (pitch 4), however is considered to occur after the syllable which is accompanied by the pitch phoneme" (1952:18). For a different type of linearization see reference to and discussion of juncture treatments in §§ 9.61, 9.74.

It is necessary now to deal with a possible charge of contradiction within the theory. In the last paragraph we insisted that levels should not be mashed together. Elsewhere we have insisted that under certain circumstances items be treated in reference to several levels and from several hierarchies. How do we reconcile these two points of view, on both of which we have insisted? Part, at least, of the answer is this: That to whatever degree the data warrant, levels be considered distinct. For levels treated as discrete "insofar as possible", see Mitchell (1953:378). (Cf. also Hjelmslev, 1953: 72, who states that the two planes of form and content must also "not be *conformal*"). The phrase *as far as possible* gives us the leeway needed to reconcile the two points of view mentioned above. Two questions remain, however. The first is, does such a restriction necessarily have to be made at all? And if so, how large a variation is hidden in the phrase *as possible?*

I have no theoretical answer as to the precise limits to which treatment of language in distinct levels may be carried. It seems to me that this answer must be an empirical one for particular structures one at a time. On a theoretical level, however, I have already indicated in various parts of § 15.1 that it is essential that there be some interlocking of hierarchies and of levels within hierarchies if language is to be a unified structure. Both the theoretical treatment and the presentation of the empirical data, in my view, should reflect this necessity, even though the details cannot be predicted in advance. (Cf. §§ 11.1-4).

We do suggest an argument by analogy, however, to show why it seems to us that interlocking of systems or layers must always be kept in mind as a distinct possibility whenever one is dealing with a complicated situation. These analogies are not designed to prove the theory, but merely to illustrate the fact that the problem of interlocking units, layers, and systems, is much more widespread than in linguistics alone. In automobile mechanics, the battery can *almost* be described as separate from the car. Yet if the two poles of the battery are not joined through the frame (or through some other device) the battery has no functional validity and no operating power. It interlocks with the rest of the system.

In physiology there is similar interlocking. In the instance of a pregnant woman, for example, the unborn child may be viewed as an "independent" physiological system, with the mother constituting another. Nevertheless, it is evident that they are closely interlocking so that at one and the same time they count as two systems and as a single higher-layered system. They constitute two systems in spite of the fact that it is impossible to say at exactly what molecule the blood stream of the mother stops and that of the child begins.

The independence but interlocking of two levels of analysis can clearly be seen also in house construction. If one has a house of two floors — of two levels — this house clearly cannot be described adequately without keeping the two levels apart. Any mashing of them to treat them as a single floor plan would be disastrous. Nevertheless, if joining the first floor to the second floor there is a stairway which is unenclosed on the bottom floor, and unenclosed on the top floor, it is impossible to tell at this particular part of the structure as to where the first floor leaves off and the second begins. To insist on rigid separation of levels at this point in the structure is to fail to report the empirical data.

An entirely different set of important interlocking elements and systems has been developed under the concept of 'feedback'. An automatic machine or factory of great complexity may have many separate parts which are not completely separate, in that they are under the partial control of signals from each other. The result of activity of one part of the machine affects a second part so that it in turn feeds back information or activity to affect the activity of the first part. Engineers are well aware of these problems so that, for example, as one approaches the ideals of a completely automatic factory the "chief electrical engineer cannot have exclusive control over all matters electrical, nor the mechanical engineer over all matters mechanical" (G. S. Brown and Campbell, 1952:63). In such a situation "Scores of unit processes are interlocked with a meticulous balance of energy distribution" (Ayres, 1952:85), so that "In the present state of the art there is a growing recognition among engineers and scientists that they cannot deal with control systems part by part, but must design each system as a unitary whole" (G.S. Brown and Campbell, 1952:58).

Linguistics, in some senses, is like an automatic factory with various component parts each of which feeds back on the other. The interlocking of these various parts through the feedback system makes it utterly impossible to give a complete, adequate description of any one part without reference to the degree to which it interlocks with and is affected by other parts. Tustin further develops these materials in terms of factory automation by indicating that the "existence of feedback" is in general a question of "interdependence"; in such instances "each is a cause, and each an effect, of the other" so that "we have a closed chain or sequence" which "engineers call a 'closed loop'" (1952:48). Such concepts of interdependence are closely related to our concepts of interdependence of morpheme classes, morpheme boundaries, and tagmemes. Compare also the phrase "syncrhonization circuits" used by the linguist Twaddell (1953:437-38) in reference to levels of the phonological hierarchy.

There is another way in which it seems possible to make an effective case for the fact that a language system cannot be eventually treated as a purely formal system without reference to semantic elements. Goedel's theorem seems to demonstrate that no system which is sufficient for mathematics can be proved consistent by methods expressible within the system itself — or, more specifically, "the consistency of arithmetic cannot be established by any meta-mathematical reasoning which can be represented within the formalism of arithmetic'." (Nagel and Newman, in J. Newman, 1956:1694).

Similarly we must know from sources outside the language itself that "sound systems we attempt to analyze are indeed real language utterances and the utterances of a single language, not those of several languages — a dozen or a hundred" (Fries, 1954:61). These points of view imply that there is an interlocking of levels of form and meaning which cannot be ignored.

Psycholinguistic considerations show still further different types of interlocking of levels. For example, the "behavioral correlates of tightness of unit formation" (which seems to be to some degree a measure of the coherence of the units of a particular hypermorpheme as in *B'lieve-'t-'r-not*) "should be latencies between elements in production and the existence of skill modifications, such as truncation, amalgamation, and anticipatory and perseverative alteration" (Osgood, Sebeok, and others, 1954:59). Further interlocking may be seen in "the conditional dependencies between input and semantic systems" (120); interlocking pause points are much more likely to correspond with decoding units, however, than with encoding units, in which the "unit of decoding" would "have to be given in terms of speech comprehension" (100). Similarly, "points of decision" have reference to various hierarchies, such that under certain circumstances a unit may have been chosen "as a phonological unit (a syllable) or as a morphological unit (a morpheme)" so that "Obviously the two levels need not exclude one another" (62). Finally, "from the speaker's point of view, selection at each hierarchy is a simultaneous function of *all* of the preceding sequence and of regulating inputs from *all* levels of organization" (97). All of these things lead one "to feel overwhelmed with problems of multiple causation affecting the production of utterances" (112) — another way of indicating that the various hierarchies are simultaneously relevant.

More recently, the problem of interlocking levels has been treated from a sharply different viewpoint. Chomsky and his associates feel no hesitancy about presenting grammatical rules before phonological ones; a different hierarchical view of the relation of grammar to phonology underlies their value judgments.

For bibliographical references, and discussion, see §§ 8.87, 9.71, 11.71, 8.814-15.

15.33 *On Systems*

15.331 *On Overall Pattern*

For an attempt to deal with over-all pattern, see Trager and Bloch (1941:243-45), Trager and Smith (1951:9, 22, 27-29). For common core and over-all pattern as technical terms, see Hockett (1955:18-22, and in Lévi-Strauss and others, 1953: 40); over-all pattern as a graphic device, Stankiewicz (1957:53-54); but for rejection of over-all patterning to the degree that asymmetry, involving neutralization, must be involved, see Stankiewicz (1961:129). Further Discussion of over-all pattern: Hill (in First Texas Conference, 1962:133); Twaddell (in Second Texas Conference, 1962:129-42).

15.332 *On Bilingualism*

For bilingual relationships, see, especially, Haugen (1953), for extensive study of Norwegian in America (1950b, 1954, and 1955); and Weinreich (1953a) with extensive discussion of principles of languages in contact (1954, in Saporta, 1961:388-89, with tables of forms of language interference — phonic, grammatical, and lexical, versus structural and non-structural, also 1957). For bibliography note Haugen (in Saporta, 1961), and Weinreich (1958 in *Proceedings of the Eighth...*, 795-97). Note Swadesh (in *Selected writings of E. Sapir*, 1949:65, for psycholinguistic complications of two phonemic systems); Waterhouse (1949, with local vernacular learned only as an adult, for social reasons); Ferguson (1959); Pike (1960a, with structural change demanding units shared by the two systems; Diebold (1961); Leopold (in Saporta, 1961:358, of the German-English bilingual child); symposium in *Anthropological Linguistics*, January, 1962, for relation of multilingualism to socio-cultural organization).

15.333 *On Dialects*

For studies of dialect, note Trubetzkoy (1931); Bloomfield (1933a, Chapter 19 for useful summary of techniques); Kurath, Bloch, Bloch, and Hansen (1939); H. Kurath (1949); Bloch (1950:88, with dialect affecting phonemic description); Trager and Smith (1951, in reference to over-all pattern, and see above, § 15.331); Atwood (1953, for verb forms); Stankiewicz (1957); Doroszewsky (in *Proceedings of the Eighth...*, 1958); H. B. Allen (1958:137-91); McDavid (in Francis, 1958, on American English dialects); Putnam and O'Hern (1955:29, as marking social status); Haugen (1956-57: 18, with diaphone); Cochrane (1959, with diasystem). For structural dialectology, note Weinreich (1954); Stankiewicz (1957); Moulton (1960); Ivić (1962, with bibliography).

For the social significance of subtle pronunciation cues on Martha's Vineyard, see Labov (1963).

For brief selected bibliography on the relation of phonemics to historical and comparative studies, and a selected bibliography on lexicostatistical dating of dialect divergence, note Pike and Pike (1960:34-35).

15.334 *On Coexistent Systems*

For an extensive study of coexistent systems on various linguistic levels, with charts suggesting various interlockings, see Flydal (1952). For an attempt to set up criteria for the presence of coexistent systems or fragments, see Fries and Pike (1949). For objection to such procedures on the grounds that "the phonemic system of a dialect is necessarily single, not multiple", see Bloch (1950:87; see also his bracketed note in *Language* 26.409, 1950). Note, however, that for him certain sounds which we would treat as extra-systematic, such as the alveolar click of commiseration in English, can either be "excluded" as not part of the relevant material, "or else treated as an organically-separate part of the system (though not as part of an independent system coexisting with the main one)" (1950:87n). At this point it seems to me that the argument is no longer a basic question of analysis as to whether all the material is to be treated in a uniform way or not, but becomes a question of determining what one will call system, subsystem, part of system, independent system, fragmentary system, etc. For further argument that loan words should be included with analysis of other material for arriving at phonemic systems, note especially Wonderly (1946), Trager (1948:159), Hockett (1948a:269). For argument in favor of a "substructure" for foreign phonemes, note Lunt (1950:409). Contrast also the treatment of the vowel in *oops* by Trager and Bloch where the vowel "is not really part of our active vocabulary" (1941:230). For "independent grammatical systems", note Harris (1951:346).

For treatment as a pseudo-problem the question whether English is a Germanic or Romance language, and replacement of such a question with treatment of the languages as containing various types of systems which "can be related to those set up for the languages generally called Indo-European", see W. S. Allen (1953b:91).

Many other scattered references to problems of loans occur throughout the literature. For polysystemic analysis of language, see J. R. Firth (1949:151). For prosodic systems, see J. R. Firth (1949:151), Sprigg (1954), W. S. Allen (1954), and §§ 8.814, 9.73, 10.51.

For further discussion of coexistent systems note Faust and E. G. Pike (in *Serie Linguistica...*, 1959:12, with /e/ and /o/ in loans, only, in Cocama); Cazaku (in *Preprints...*, 1962:13); David Blood (1962:113, with differences between older and younger persons, and differences between women and men in phonetics); Haugen (1961:402, with the need for bilinguals to learn to keep items apart); Weinreich (1954, in Saporta, 1961:383, with "two coexistent systems, rather than a merged single system", probably corresponding "more closely to the actual experience of the bilingual", but with linguistic evidence inconclusive).

On overdifferentiated sounds, see Pike (1947c:142); for extra-systematic sounds, idem. (143); Hockett (1948b:2); Larsen and E. V. Pike (1949:275-76). For insistence on retention of underdifferentiated and overdifferentiated sets, allowing asymmetry into a system, note Stankiewicz (1961:129).

For an instance of accentuated asymmetry in a consonantal system, note Franklin and Franklin (1962). It is difficult to reconcile such problems with Halliday's claim (1961:246) that "a system is by definition closed". Our view includes the possibility of indeterminacy built in to the system itself — an indeterminacy which should be reflected in the description of the structure.

For language as having simultaneous systems in the forms of multiple hierarchies, note discussion of hierarchy in §§ 9.71, 11.71, 15.31, 15.32. For informal versus formal difference in Telugu treated as "the coexistence of two distinctive phonemic systems" see Sjoberg (1962:269; with several aspirated stops missing from unassimilated Sanscrit loans in the informal system, 271, 273; with educated men using informal pronunciation to "womenfolk, children, or servants" since the "sanctity" of the formal language may be preserved only as it is "set apart from the secular", 279).

For synchronic treatment of the contrastive structure of indigenous versus loan words in a language, see Bloomfield (1933b) and Mathesius ([1934] reprinted in Vachek, 1964).

15.335 *On Style*

For consonantal change (or addition) to signal special kinds of style, or persons with certain characteristics, note Sapir (1915, in his Selected Writings:180-81, 190-92; 1910, in his Selected Writings:456-67). For style and metacongruence, see Smith (in Report of the Third..., 1952:60). For the structural status of phonemes in different styles, see Grimes (1955, with related phonemes across two styles as distinct; reply by Hamp, 1957a); and S. Martin (1952:13-14, with the related phonemes across two styles as members of the same phonemic unit but with tempo styles as containing tempo phonemes); see also above, § 8.441. For the term "code-switching" which may also be relevant to style congruence, note Jacobson (in Lévi-Strauss and others, 1953:16).

Note also Pittman (1948a, with levels of honorifics); Yngve (1960:465, with style preferences in reference to degrees of depth in constituent layering); Riffaterre (1959, with style in relation to context type); Spencer (1957, with received pronunciation related to social system); Gumpers (in *Preprints...*, 1962:448, with socio-linguistic styles); Joos (1962); Trim (1962:777, with a formal style which has linguistic units in most elaborate form, with "articulatory-acoustic-perceptual differentiations" as constant and maximal, versus "familiar situations where situational information is high and social constraint on behavior low", where the full system is "rarely explicit" and "the sole criterion" is "successful recognition"); Hill (in *First Texas Conference*, 1962:131, with free variation due to style); Voegelin (1953:1, with tape recordings of slower styles for full forms).

For diagrammatic presentation of a double structure in a lyric monologue, note Sebeok (in *For Roman Jakobson*, 1956:437, with a spiral construction of the two sets of images); compare units of plot and structure as emic units, with contrast between units of plot, of form, and of linguistic level in Dundes (1962b:98); for hierarchy of a phonological matrix pattern, in which "every constituent contains some whole number of every preceding one" note Sebeok (in *For Roman Jakobson*, 1956:436, for Cheremis folk songs). Weinreich indicates rhyme resources of Yiddish benefiting from "the fusion history of the language" (1959:425). For a collection of essays on style, note Sebeok (1960). See also extensive collection of essays on poetics, in *Poetics* (1961).

For multiple systems within a uniform style, as an analytical device, note J. R. Firth (1949:151). For coexistent phonemic systems in reference to dialect geography, note Francescato (1959). For style alternation in Russian note Klagstad (in *For Roman Jakobson*, 1956).

For brief bibliography on linguistics in relation to the analysis of literature note Pike and Pike (1960, § 29). For style in Soviet analysis, see Akhmanova and others (1963:101, with poetry, 109-14).

15.336 *On Field and Matrix*

A high-level system of some kind may serve as 'field' for lower units. See the "backward-working adaptations" of agreement of adjective with following noun as indicative of hierarchy, in Osgood, Sebeok and others (1954:60). Compare the implications of recursive "subroutines" in Carroll (1959a:45). Thus a style may be field for a set of allophones of a particular voice quality § 13.4); or for a set of special morphemes (*thee, thou*, §§ 7.313(3)). Field may affect a system more extensively, as in interpreting the meaning of words (§ 6.56), or even affecting rules of ethical requirements of truth values of statements as in 'April Fool' jokes (§ 5.4) or in science fiction. A relevant UNIVERSE OF DISCOURSE, then, in this system is a field concept (§§ 16.12, 16.81) related to system.

Recent attempts specify some characteristics of field: (1) Grammatical matrices include cells at the intersection of categories of dimensions (Pike 1962a) whether of clause, phrase, or of phonological material and so on; (2) A small dimensional display can serve as a nucleus of a subsystem of the language, which can be amplified by 'multiplication' to cover larger areas of the language (Pike, 1962a). (3) When constructions are to be intersects of the dimensions, evidence of their contrastive relevance can be seen in various types of testing frames of a matrix type, in Pike (1963b). (4) On the morphemic or submorphemic level, pattern can be further displayed in terms of matrices, whose permutation allows blocks of formatives to emerge so that they can in turn be studied in reference to semantic relevance (Pike, 1963d; Pike and Erickson, 1964). (5) Description in terms of particle, wave, and field (see above, § 12.1), allows (a) segmented chunks to be analyzed as linguistic sequential emic units, (b) with these units — even when they have smeared, indeterminate boundaries — to be treated as waves, and (c) to be treated alternatively as points in a network of relations in the matrices of a field structure.

Our assumption, furthermore, is that in the brain there must be some type of organization which has a relevant relation to a multiple model of this sort. It reminds us of what Lashley stated several years ago (1951, in Saporta, 1961:194-97) that "the cortex must be regarded as a great network of reverberatory circuits" such that a stimulus "must produce widespread changes in the pattern"; so that she strongly suspects "that many phenomena of generalization, both sensory and conceptual, are products, not of simple switching, but of interaction of complex patterns of organization within such systems" (196); and only methods of analysis of "a composite of many interacting systems" will be able to point "toward understanding of the physiology of the cerebral cortex" (197) — systems which she has "tried to illustrate at a primitive level by rhythm and the space coordinates" (197). As we see it, not only has structural linguistics "suffered from a failure to appreciate the extent and depth of interconnections among various parts of a language system" (Chomsky, 1962, § 1, p. 513), but transformational grammar — which attempts to handle material too exclusively in terms of rule, and not enough in terms of unit and matrix — is also suffering from a thrust toward a monosystemic nonfield view.

CHAPTER 16

MEANING

The special problem to be treated in Chapter 16 is meaning. Here we are concerned not with the general nature of a theory of meaning, but with the manner in which a hierarchical view of language illuminates a few of the specific problems which arise in a more general study of meanings.

In general, however, we shall assume that meaning has reference to COMMUNICATION between individuals. Meaning, in this view, would have reference to the activity of the communicating individuals. Both covert and overt characteristics of the activity both of the speaker and listener would thereupon be relevant.

On the part of the speaker, there may be a covert PURPOSE or INTENTION of eliciting a response, or of having an IMPACT on the hearer, by means of his overt utterance. The speaker may elicit either a positive or a negative response by his utterances. In addition, there may be overtly communicated to the hearer an UNINTENDED impact from the speaker's attitudes, personality characteristics, and other situational information.

The hearer, on his part, may give an overt response either in the form of verbalization or in the form of physical activity. The response which he gives may be either the one elicited and expected by the speaker, or it may be a negation of the material desired by the speaker, or it may be a response to unintended communication. On the other hand, the covert response of the hearer may consist of UNDERSTANDING or of failure to understand.

Thus the intention of the speaker along with the understanding of the hearer, and the eliciting activity of the speaker along with the responding activity of the hearer together make up the behavioral context of communication in a society. The various components of this communicating situation of eliciting activity and responding activity, of intention and of understanding, constitute the social components of language meaning.

16.1 *Meanings of Units of the Lexical Hierarchy*

When meanings are discussed, it is usually meanings of the lexical hierarchy which are the subjects of such discussion. It is here that one gets the meanings of idioms, words, phrases, or novels. But when one attempts to locate or describe the particular meaning of a particular morpheme or morpheme sequence, difficulties arise. The meaning of the morpheme seems to change from context to context. There is uncertainty as to the identification of particular morphemes — whether two morphs are occurrences of the same morpheme or of different morphemes.

16.11 *Semantic Variants of Morphemes*

We have already indicated that conditioned changes of lexical meaning are treated, within our approach, as components of variant morphs within the morpheme units. Allomorphs differing by meaning may have the semantic difference determined by the neighboring morpheme (note *drive* in *drive a car* versus *drive a horse* § 6.53) or the semantic variants may be conditioned by their tagmemic occurrence, as is *frightfully* in the phrase *frightfully beautiful* (§ 7.323, 7.313[4]). Semantic variants may also be conditioned by the universe of discourse within which they occur — by their style or congruent system, or by their physical matrix (§§ 6.56, 7.313[4]). See also Chapter 11, Table 3, Item 18, and § 15.33.

A severe problem remains, however: When two morphs having related meanings (for illustration and definition of related meanings see Nida, 1949:56-57), how are we to determine that the two morphs do not contrast? How can we be certain that the difference in meaning is sufficiently great, on the one hand, to guarantee that the two morphs are distinct morphemes, or is sufficiently small, on the other hand, to indicate that the two morphs are members of a single morpheme? It seems to me that there frequently is indeterminacy in the lexical system at such points (see *port* in § 6.44). In such a pair of morphs as /sil/ *seal* (meaning an animal) and /sil/ *seal* (meaning a *stamp*) the meaning is sharply different and the larger contexts in which the two occur is also very different. Only occasionally would the immediate contexts be the same as in such a sentence as *There is a seal over there*. This sharp difference of meaning and context makes it easy to determine that these are distinct morphemes. With the two morphs *apple* and *apple*, however, where the one refers to a Baldwin apple and the other refers to a McIntosh apple, there may be two sentences which are ambiguous in *The apple is over there*. The properties of *apple* in each instance are quite different. The contexts in which they occur are also different. For example, concerning the one apple one might say *That is an excellent eating apple* whereas the other would not normally be referred to in that context.

It seems clear that the situations for *seal* and for *apple* are different. It is by no means clear, however, that we have a set of operations which will unambiguously decide between the two kinds of relationships. We continue to treat *seal* and *seal* as two morphemes, whereas we continue to treat the two morphs *apple* and *apple* as one morpheme even though the theory and operations for doing so need further development.

Perhaps the answer will lie in the direction of attempting to find a statistically much greater set of common contexts for the two uses of *apple* than is true for the two morphemes *seal* (*All apples are fruit* and *He likes apples* are presumably much more frequent types than *All seals — both animals and stamps — are things*). A second approach would be by way of tests for native reaction. If careful operations could be worked out, there may be useful 'same or different' tests for allomorphic membership in the morpheme (see Nida, 1949:57).

Sometimes, on the other hand, the specific meaning of a single morpheme such as (*to*) *win* may summarize the common subsequent cultural effect of a large variety of specific physical events. The 'winning' in football may be accomplished by a pass over the goal line, by a run over the same, by a ball kicked over the bar between the goal posts, or by other events such as a touch back. The winning may be a composite of these in a total score. A large variety of such physical behavior may have to enter into the components of the physical behavior which goes into winning. Where the identity of their sameness or difference cannot be determined by physical measurement, it can only be identified in reference to resultant cultural activity of the participants, as attested by careful observation. A win implies standing in a league. A win implies going to higher echelons of battle, a win implies receiving a victory cup, and so on. It is these subsequent activities which constitute the culturally-attested sameness of these behavior patterns or results.

16.12 *Central Meanings of the Hierarchy*

When a morpheme has several meanings, one of these may appear to be clearly CENTRAL, or basic, with the others marginal to it or derived from it. The meaning of *nose* in the phrase *the nose of a projectile* seems marginal to the central meaning observed in the phrase *the man's nose*. This difference, furthermore, seems important to language function. The ability of a speaker to start with a small vocabulary and yet discuss a wide variety of topics is directly related to his ability to take words with central meanings and use them in a wide variety of marginal senses. It is part of the symbolic system of language, a crucial part of the productive potential of language. Without this ability to extend the meanings of words to a variety of contexts which are only vaguely related to the first one, language as we know it could not function.

How, then, do we determine the central meaning of a morpheme? There are several essential components to an answer of this question. The first component in the answer is that, other things being equal, the central meaning will be one which was learned early in life. Meanings early learned are likely to have a certain primacy about them which is lacking in later meanings.

A second component in the identification of a central meaning is the fact that it is likely to have reference to a physical situation — a physical situation which is early encountered by the child as he learns the language. The word *nose* is learned in the context of the child's body rather than in the context of projectiles. It is learned in this physical context rather than in the context of *sticking one's nose into somebody's business*. This early, physical context sets up the central meaning of *nose*. A most instructive confirmation of these characteristics is seen in the anecdote referred to by Bloomfield. "If a speaker has heard a form only in some marginal meaning, he will use this form with the same meaning as the central meaning — that is, he will use the form for a meaning in which other speakers use it only under very special conditions — like the city child who concluded that pigs were very properly called *pigs*, on account of their unclean habits" (1933a:431-32). The early learning of the child involved the local physical context of eating (*eating like a pig*) or of dirt (*filthy as a pig*). The later meaning, applied to an animal, was from the child's point of view an extension of the earlier central meaning. Perhaps both of these criteria are instances of a more inclusive one: If two meanings are related, the more central is the one in terms of which the other can be explained (private communication, William Alston).

Another criterion of central meaning may be that, in general, in the community as a whole it may occur with greater frequency than any one of the marginal meanings. This does not apply to special universes of discourse, however, where a marginal meaning may have a special technical sense for that particular discussion, and be used again and again without the central meaning being mentioned at all.

For the adult linguist who cannot recapitulate the child's experience in a strange language, central meaning may sometimes be detected by studying the learning process of children in the culture, or by some kind of psycholinguistic test to get from the people native reactions which are based upon these early experiences. On the other hand, if the linguist — as an adult — learns the language by a monolingual approach (see §§ 1.4, 7.32), he builds up for himself some of the same reaction to central meanings. Since, however, his experiences differ from those of a child in the same culture who is learning monolingually, he can never attain quite the same reaction to the language that native speakers would have.

Similarly, if in the adult experience of native speakers the physical context in which a word is used changes in frequency greatly as over against the contexts in which this word was used when they were children, the central meaning for the adult native speaker may also change. As the speaker grows older, therefore, the central meaning becomes to some extent relative to the universe of discourse in which it is used.

By analogy with this treatment of central and marginal meanings of single words or morphemes, we may suggest that there is a HIERARCHY OF CENTRAL MEANINGS of sequences of words. The central meaning of a phrase, as against the central meaning of a particular word, would first of all be related to the central meaning of its included words. Thus the phrase as a whole, if treated in its central meaning, would have its included words understood in their central meanings. From this it follows that the central meaning of a phrase is the predictable sum of its parts taken in their central meanings. The meaning of idiomatic phrases would not be considered as a central meaning. The phrase *to step on the gas* would not be interpretable in terms of its central meaning, nor predictable in terms of the meanings of its parts. It would not, therefore, have an over-all central meaning, but rather a special one.

Many samples are collected by Mencken: *to spread it on thick, to do the square thing, to face the music, to keep one's shirt on, to shell out, to go the whole hog, to make a stab at, to go haywire, to get the axe, to pass out,* (1945-48:392-94, 594-95). For further full sentences with special meaning one may note proverbs of various types such as *A stitch in time saves nine*, and *Let sleeping dogs lie*.

Greeting forms such as *How do you do?*, also have a meaning which is quite different from the sum of their parts. Their function, too, differs from the structurally most-closely-related sentences. Thus one says *How do you do?*, but one does not say *How does he do?* — though one might frequently hear *How does he do it?* Similarly, but in a different behavioral framework, a speech such as the Gettysburg address may be repeated by a child as a patriotic memorial in which the communication impact is one of patriotic sentiment rather than of the verbal content of the address.

By and large, words from small distribution classes, such as *if, an, who, the, to*, do not have central meanings which have as their reference physical objects, or physical actions or qualities. The child may be able to use a number of words which have a physical central meaning before he can control any of these terms. It is more difficult, therefore, to state that such words as *and* have a central meaning as distinct from a marginal meaning. Occasionally, however, phrases may occur in which these items are obviously not used with the meanings which — early learned by the child — bring the more concrete terms in relationship with one another. Such a phrase is a marginal one and has a marginal meaning. For an example, note *And how!*

Special meanings relative to the UNIVERSE OF DISCOURSE are seen clearly on April Fools' day when the impact of sentences is not designed to communicate in the ordinary way but to be deceptive. A lie on the other hand is intended to be deceptive within the normal use of discourse by eliciting a response as to the regular meaning of the sentences while actually the normal connection between these sentences and reality is broken.

If a meaning central to a word has reference to a particular universe of discourse, the implication follows that a universe of discourse, as a whole, may also, in some way, be central to the total body of universes of discourse. The possibility of a hierarchy of universes of discourses, with progressive degrees of centrality, is implied by this approach. Such a hierarchy of universes would be part of the field within which metaphorical lexical hierarchies orbit — hierarchies which we shall discuss in the next section.

16.13 *Metaphorical Meanings of the Hierarchy*

The relation between central and marginal meanings does not stop with the word or phrase. It continues up the lexical hierarchy. A verse as a whole may have an over-all meaning which is marginal to its internal contents. An example would be constituted of the counting rhyme *Engine engine number nine, running down Chicago line, please tell me the correct time,* where the meaning or purpose of the rhyme is to determine a person to be selected for a part in a game. One could not predict this from the words *engine, nine,* etc.

In contrast to the central meanings highlighted in the last section, we turn attention now to the special metaphorical meanings which are marginal to the central ones, at all levels of the hierarchy. Some illustrations of special meanings, however, were also given in the preceding section and included the metaphorical meanings of single words such as *nose* in the *nose of a missle,* of idioms as in *to step on the gas,* and of larger units such as *Engine engine number nine.* ...

The regular or central hierarchy is INDEPENDENT in that it can and does occur without the presence in the system of the metaphorical usages. On the other hand, the metaphorical and idiomatic usages are DEPENDENT or DERIVED.[1] These develop as an extension of words used in central meanings, and so are derived rather than primitive. They are dependent, furthermore, since the derived metaphorical use of a word continues to have its strong metaphorical impact only while that same word is also actively in use currently in the system in its non-metaphorical sense. If in the system a metaphorical use of a term develops, and if the earlier central meaning disappears because of cultural change or for other reason, then the former metaphorical meaning automatically becomes the central meaning. A metaphorical meaning requires the presence of a central meaning but not vice versa.

Cultural evidence can also sometimes be found to identify metaphorical use as over against the central use of a term. If one speaker says to another *Why did you call it 'Y' when it really is an 'X'?* while the hearer replies *I called it a 'Y' because it is like 'Y' in that it does thus and so,* the utterance and response constitute cultural evidence that a metaphorical use is involved.

It is useful at this point to introduce a figure of speech to provide an analogy for the distributional change of words and their impact on the hearer when they pass from metaphorical use to central-meaning use. If, let us say, we have a planet with an artificial satellite, then the 'distribution' of the satellite in a wider orbit carries with it more energy than its distribution in a narrower orbit. As the satellite loses energy it spirals down into an inner, closer orbit. Let us now assume that the central meaning of a word has reference to an ORBIT. Words occur in particular distributions which are frequent and close to the physical situation which they name directly. If, however, the same word is used in distributions remote from the original distribution, and especially if they are remote from the physical contexts in which the words were

---

[1] At some future date I hope to exploit the nuclear versus marginal nature of meanings to treat meaning clusters as units like waves. Independent meanings would be nuclear, derived ones marginal.

For the handling of jokes and puns in terms of tagmemic theory — with light pun related to serious poetic metaphor — see now Pike (1964f).

first learned by the child, or within which they have their central meanings, these special distributions carry with them a certain kind of 'communication energy'. These extended symbolic usages, because of their special distributions, have a heavier impact on the listener. Here the outer distributional 'orbit' carries the greater communication energy in the form of hearer impact. If, however, the word is used very frequently in this metaphorical sense, and as such comes in more and more contexts, so that it takes the distributional place of the word which formerly was used for the central meaning relevant to it, the communication energy of this special meaning has been dissipated, and the now 'dead metaphor' carries no more impact than an ordinary word with its ordinary central meaning.

Although in general the metaphorical meaning will be expected to be statistically less frequent for the community as a whole than is the marginal meaning, this percentage of occurrence may be reversed during the time that the metaphorical meaning is spiralling down into the central orbit. As the word in its metaphorical or marginal meaning gradually becomes the only linguistic item easily available to label a particular object or situation, the alternatives to that labelling become less and less frequent, so that in due time the statistical characteristics of distribution are reversed. Metaphorical meaning has then become central meaning.

There seems to be no specific number of distributional orbits or degrees of remoteness from central meaning or degrees of communication energy which words or series of words can carry. It is clear, however, that under some distributions words carry much greater impact than under others. It seems to me that SLANG obtains its power by an extra-special distribution of words in a metaphorical sense. The impact of the slang seems to come in part from its metaphorical use as such, and in part from the fact that in reference to the community as a whole it has a very infrequent distribution (and hence a 'remote' outer orbit). As more and more people use this particular slang, it ceases to be the property of a small group, spreads out more widely in the community, and the distribution therefore has become that of a lower orbit with less communication energy involved. If the slang becomes very frequent indeed for the adult as well as the younger members of the community, it has lost so much of its communication energy that it becomes useless for its original purposes and must be replaced by a new set of slang terms.

On an artistic level the parallel situation seems to involve poetic distributional innovations. A poem may be striking and fresh because of unexpected distributions of words in a symbolic fashion, or in special collocations. If these identical phrases are used a great deal by many authors, however, they become hackneyed, and spiral down to an inner orbit of CLICHÉ which is no longer effective for poetic purposes.

Occasionally a word may have a double function between two orbits simultaneously. Many puns have phoneme sequences which function in two central orbits. Note the three-word pun in *Why was Pharoah's daughter a financier? — Because she drew a little profit* (or *prophet*) *from the rushes on the bank*. In some puns the reader is expected to react simultaneously to the central meaning of the word and to a marginal meaning. Note the word *worst*, in the following sentence I heard recently: *I've always wanted to fly in the worst way — and by the way, the worst way is in a single-engine airplane* [*to fly to South America from the USA*].

16.14 *Collocational Meanings of the Hierarchy*

The frequency of occurrence of items affects meanings in a further way. If a normal sequence of morphemes with central meanings occurs with great frequency, and potential phrases of the same structure but with some different morphemes are relatively infrequent, the high frequency of the particular morpheme sequence may lead to the specialization of this particular sequence. This specialization is made possible, however, by the fact that each morpheme ultimately obtains its meaning only in relation to other morphemes of the total system and other morphemes of the particular sequences within which it occurs. The meanings of the morphemes are affected by these particular sequences (§ 16.11). When a particular morpheme sequence occurs with great frequency, the special characteristics resulting from the particular combination of morphemes is heightened and tends to be fixed. The end product may be a special hypermorpheme which becomes rigid so that it reacts as a total idiomatic unit rather than a regular sequence of substitutable parts. If metaphor is involved in the meanings of one or more of the words of such a phrase, an idiom may be produced which is a special hypermorphemic collocation with fixed symbolic metaphorical meanings. The phrase *to step on the gas*, therefore, obtains its idiomatic value not only from the fact that central meanings are not completely involved, but also because of the frequency of the occurrence of these particular morphemes in sequence. If no metaphorical meanings are involved, the specialized phrases may become trite or clichés and hence to be avoided for effective literary style. Compare such phrases as *abject terror*.

Once a phrase has become thus set, one or more of the morphemes of that phrase may disappear from normal usage elsewhere. When this happens, the specialized hypermorpheme includes rare morphemes within it. Compare *wrack and ruin, might and main, kith and kin, wax and wane*, (and compare their treatment as empty morphemes in § 6.45). These are in turn related to the greeting formulas such as *How do you do?*, and the like, which we discussed in the preceding section.

Many of these phrases such as the *nick of time* allow the hearer, once he has listened to the beginning of the phrase, to predict with considerable probability the ending of that particular phrase. If one has heard *in the nick of* the probability of *time* being the next word is high. The probability, however, is quite different in type from that which has reference to the tagmemic sequence. In the grammatical structure the prediction and expectancy is of a succeeding structural component, without the same degree of prediction as to the particular member which will fill the structural slot involved. In the sentence *I'm going to the store to buy a pound of...*, the blank may be filled by *nails, sugar, salt, glue*, and many other items. The expectancy for some member of the noun class is very great, but the particular noun expected cannot be predicted as well.

On a high level of the lexical hierarchy prediction of completion can be equally strong under special circumstances. If a person begins to quote a well known poem, the hearer, who knows the poem, will expect the ending of the poem to be in the traditional fashion. It is possible, of course, either for the speaker to make a mistake, or for a special effect to introduce a deliberate distortion of the poem. A special kind of impact — a special meaning — will be obtained when these probabilities are overridden. The change puts the misquoted material in an 'outer orbit' with either pleasant or unpleasant effects, and is likely to elicit a comment in reply. (For example I have in my notes: S —: *We use them once in a red moon.* M —: *The expression usually is once in a blue moon*).

16.15 *Class Meanings within the Lexical Hierarchy*

A distributional class of morphemes may as a whole have a class meaning. This class meaning may be vague, and derived from only some of the members of the class. Nevertheless the class meaning may be an effective part of the signalling apparatus of the hierarchy. For discussion of it notice §§ 7.313, 7.324. (For lexical sets of morphemes, showing some congruence between distributional classes or partial distributional classes of morphemes — leading in turn to specific collocations of various kinds, with their respective meanings — see § 7.313[4]).

16.2 *Meanings of the Phonological Hierarchy*

Selection of units of the phonological hierarchy can be used to elicit responses of various types. This is most frequently seen, perhaps, in the use of rhyme or of alliteration in verse.

The choice of particular vowels may call upon a sound symbolism embedded in a particular culture or language such that morphemes containing vowels like [i] can be chosen to reinforce lexical meanings of smallness or sharpness, as the sound of [u] can be used to reinforce the impression of large size, or smoothness, or gliding continuity, or roundness. Patterns of words chosen such that they end with voiceless stops like [p], [t], or [k], may lend a heightened feeling of abruptness or ruggedness.

Certain sequences of phonemes may have a more specific impact, under appropriate circumstances. Thus the sequence *-ush* as in *hush, slush, mush* or the sequence *fl-* as in *flicker, flare, flame*, or the *gl-* in *glare, glimmer, glance, glow* may reinforce the lexical meaning component which is vaguely common to them. The *fl-* in these words, for example, seems to heighten the impact of the component of 'light' in the words referred to. It is not sufficiently uniform in this impact, however, to seem to have effect on words such as *flow, flimsy, flute, fly, flower, float, flat, flag.* Usually the phonological material by itself does not carry this impression. It occurs only as a heightening of a lexical semantic component already present in the morpheme. A possible exception to this generalization, however, occurs when nonsense syllables are put together to carry particular kinds of impacts. For example a vowel sequence such as /ɪ/ /æ/ /a/ as in *flip, flap, flop* may be used in nonsense syllables to carry an impact of progression from a smaller movement to a larger one.

Whenever part of the response is linked directly to the sounds as sounds, rather than to morphemes as morphemes or to words as words, part of the meaning — within this theory — may be attributed to the phonological hierarchy rather than to the lexical one as such. (Cf. § 6.53).

These special items are quite different from the response obtained from one's general phonological pattern as a whole. One also attains an effect from his general over-all style of pronunciation. This style may become indicative of the particular individual and obtain a response from listeners (even when they cannot see the speaker) as 'meaning' that 'such and such a person is speaking'. Similarly, the use of a particular phonological system, from one dialect, in an area where speakers of that dialect are not socially acceptable to the populace, may elicit a strong reaction against the intruder.

On the other hand a person (for example, a politician returning to his home town) may deliberately vary his current sophisticated style in order to conform to the local pronunciation of the group with whom he is speaking at the moment, so as to avoid such unpleasant reactions, or in order to capitalize upon favorable reactions where the local populace is pleased by the phonological adaptation of the speaker in the direction of their own dialect. In this type of a situation, the general phonological style can 'mean' the 'belongingness' to a particular group and as such elicit the significant reactions which are regularly expected between members of such a group. (See also, Labov, 1963). For extensive illustration of the relevance of sound to monologue play of a young child, see Weir (1962:103) — and Jakobson's comment on her data concerning the "predominently metalingual concern of the solemnant child" (19).

16.3 *Meanings of the Grammatical Hierarchy*

Units of the grammatical hierarchy, as over against the particular lexical items filling the slots of the hierarchy, are meaningful. The meanings of the tagmemes, hypertagmemes, and syntagmemes, are functional meanings. The functional meanings of tagmemes of various sorts — such as 'subject-as-actor'[2] — are the meanings of these

---

[2] For grammatical versus situational role, see now fn. to § 7.6, concerning Pike (1964d).

grammatical structures. For illustration and discussion of them note §§ 7.322-24, 7.43, 7.6, 7.83. Meanings of higher structural units are discussed in § 7.74.

For overlap of the lexical meaning of function words with the meaning of a tagmeme see §§ 6.45, 7.324.

16.4 *Meanings of Componential Systems*

Meanings differ considerably as to whether they come from one or another part of the total system. Intonational meanings in English, for example, may have more basic reference to attitudes than to objective reference. Meanings of the segmental morphemes may include reference to attitudes as well, and function in a different way. (For meanings of English intonation contours, see Pike, 1942, 1945).

Alternative systems or styles may signal various types of group solidarity, and include clues from the various hierarchies. (For phonological impact, note § 16.2). The use of particular tagmemic rearrangements and phonological rhyming subclasses may force special attention, as in verse. The utilization of a style in which many loan words from a language of prestige are included — more loan words than the average person commands — signals elegance and social standing in some areas. In reverse, in some radio broadcasts there are 'mock Indian' personalities who speak with English words but whose syntax or choice of words is designed to imply that of the American Indian (whose grammatical structures, in hundreds of languages of North and South America, in fact differ enormously).

Ordinary speech is carried on within a tacit crude agreement as to the semantic value of the hierarchies of speech. This community agreement may be transgressed for purposes of jokes ('April Fool' erroneous statements), or for serious deception (as in lying). On the other hand, people may overtly state that they are changing their system in some way. They may redefine terms for scientific purposes. Or they may change meanings just for play (e.g., *Let's say 'Yes' when we mean 'No'*). That the matrix may be modified by arbitrary fiat, within certain limits, is one of the great points of difference between the speech of man and the calls of birds and animals. In principle, it would seem that extensive, permanent changes of this type could not be made too violently or arbitrarily, however, without disrupting the speech community — since communication would break down faster between those who failed in using the new system than it could build up between those who were learning it. Extensive change of system to system over a period of time, or of meaning to meaning, must therefore be in a wave form rather than in large discrete steps (cf. §§ 12.1, and Pike, 1959:50, 1960a).

16.5 *Meaning of the Total Structure and Semantic Segmentation*

Having treated meaning as if it were fractionated into signals from the units of the various hierarchies, we must now return to the synthesis of these materials. Meaning has its locus not in the individual bits and pieces of the total structure, but within the language structure as a whole functioning within a behavioral matrix as a whole. None of the bits and pieces has meaning of and by itself. Meaning occurs only as a function of a total behavioral event in a total social matrix.[3]

The sharp-cut segmentation of meanings or partial meanings out of this total structure is therefore in principal impossible. There are no sharp boundaries to the meanings of these parts. Meanings fuse and flow into one another on these lower levels — they overlap and occur simultaneously and interpenetrate. The meaning of one unit not only affects the meaning of a neighboring unit in a collocational fashion, but in fact the meaning of one unit in part constitutes and in part is constituted of the meaning of a neighboring unit. The reciprocal action of one meaning on another is such that they cannot be completely disentangled, as collocational studies demonstrate.

How, then, can we ever speak legitimately of the meaning of a particular isolated abstracted item? How can we even have spoken of the meanings of units of the separate hierarchies?

For our answer we turn for an analogy to our segmentation and abstraction of the morphemic shapes out of a continuum. In some instances morpheme boundaries are very clear — especially across pause. In others, there is fusion on a phonetic level but not on a phonemic level when two neighboring phones of two distinct phonemes in sequence slur into one another at their boundaries. In another instance two morphemes fuse in that they have in common a single phoneme, as in the rapid pronunciation of *as you* discussed in § 14.11. In other instances the morphemes may completely coalesce phonemically in a portmanteau morph (§ 14.12). Nevertheless, we isolated out phonemes which slurred together, and morphemes which slurred together, by identifying the peaks of the waves of movement or the peaks of the waves of morphemic identity. In a sequence of several phonemes, each one may affect every one of the others so that in principle no one phoneme can be completely abstracted from the sequence. Nevertheless, the peak of the articulatory wave may be identified, and symbolization be set up to indicate that such phonemes are present in the sequence in such and such an order. Similarly, even though a sharp segmentation of a morpheme sequence may be arbitrary, nevertheless one can usually determine that such and such morphemes are present, and the order in which they occur; and these morphemes can be symbolized in some way within such an order.

Similarly, we now conclude, semantic components cannot be segmented neatly with sharp-cut borders. On the contrary, we must assume that semantic techniques must be prepared to identify the presence of semantic components without identifying the exact boundaries of the semantic components within the collocational stream. Just as we indicated that we have a morphemic field (§ 14.3) which for certain purposes must be treated as a whole, so we have a semantic field in a total communication

---

[3] See, now, wholeness of literary form, treated tagmemically in Pike (1964f, 1965a).

situation in a total social matrix which cannot be completely and neatly segmented or fragmented, but must be treated as a total field with 'concentration of semantic energy' at various points in it.

Technically, therefore, we must leave room for indeterminacy between the boundaries of semantic components. In practice, for certain purposes we will segment between them arbitrarily if necessary, in order to be able to abstract these components from the continuum and present them in list form for classificatory and discussion purposes. For different types of studies, however, we may find it essential to revert to a kind of collocational study in which this segmentation need not be completely sharp or determinate.

An illustration of the manner in which impact must come from a total structure, and not merely from the bits of a structure, is the limerick. The particular structure of the stress groups and their sequence types (i.e., the meter), the number of larger units constituting lines, the morpheme subclasses phonologically defined so that selection from these classes produces rhyme, the particular selection of morphemes and the collocation at a particular phase in the limerick (*there was an old lady from...*), the grammatical structure so arranged that the 'pay off' statement comes in the last line — these and other items all work together to produce the particular impact of the limerick. If one uses a reduction process to analyse such a form into particular words or sentences, the impact as a whole disappears.

In general, one expects the various components of meaning of a large unit to be integrated so that each supports the other. Occasionally this is not true, in the sense that a combination of small components may produce a higher-level component sharply diverse from the components themselves. A double negative, for example, may result in a positive. A conversation which concerns the weather may in fact not be concerned with items about the weather at all, but may rather have as its basic purpose or meaning the putting at ease of people or the getting acquainted with people. Similarly, there may be mixed motives in an event. Internal meanings may contradict one another or may contradict the over-all meaning or purpose of the larger utterance. An address may be given with an overt purpose, but have concealed within it a quite different purpose, and a quite different reaction on the audience from the one which the audience assumes is desired by the speaker: *For Brutus is an honorable man* (Shakespeare, Julius Caesar, Act III, Scene 2).

Where a person gives a discourse or statement whose intention is to confuse the hearer rather than to enlighten him, moreover, it is clear that the over-all meaning and purpose and response elicitation is not the sum of the bits even though these enter into and contribute toward the total effect.

16.6 *Segmental versus Subsegmental Meanings*

The meanings which we have been discussing thus far in the chapter are meanings which were components of structurally-segmented verbal material. For our purpose in this present section it is convenient to call them SEGMENTAL MEANINGS — i.e., meanings which are 'put into words'. Frequently these segmental meanings can be abstracted by the speakers of the language, discussed overtly, and treated on their part with some assurance of accuracy even though the scientists may find a wide area of inaccuracy in their naive treatment. This abstraction of the meanings by the speakers of the language we earlier called — in § 6.43 — conceptualized hypostasis of meanings. As we indicated there, children or adults may consciously inquire *What does 'X' mean?* in an attempt to discover (segmental) meanings which they assume to be present for words which are new to them. Note, for example, R29/ ...S —: *What's a lap?*, and R84/2/2.8 S—: *Daddy, what's 'space patrol' mean?*

We now wish to provide a term for certain other kinds of behavioral situations which we have all experienced and which seem to be related to but different from the ones just mentioned. We sometimes have a 'hunch' or 'feeling' toward a certain conclusion or classification or understanding without seeming to know precisely what this means in a sharply focused way. We go through internal struggle to find a way to label our feeling or understanding, or may even invent a new term to cover the situation. Once such a label has been found and applied to the vague mass of data, covert activity, and prior set of mind (or intention, or purpose, or desire, or crude understanding) the result is explicit. Once it is thus formulated in words the meaning comes under the term 'segmental' given in the preceding paragraph. We call the meaning of the earlier vague state a SUBSEGMENTAL MEANING.

The choice of the term 'subsegmental meaning' is based on an analogy with our use of 'subsegmental phonological features' to label the voice qualities which underlie the segmental phonemes of speech (§ 13.4). It seems to have a vaguely related function in that the voice qualities extending 'under' and 'throughout' speech reflect basic attitudes and intentions of that speech. Similarly the vague subsegmental meanings and dispositions underlying speech and in part prior to the specific mental formulations or overt motor verbalizations of speech provide a covert dispositional background to the segmental meanings and explicit intentions of speech. To some extent therefore they form the background unarticulated field within which articulate meaning takes place.

Perhaps at this point it would be useful to suggest that DENOTATIONAL meanings may prove to be segmental in this sense, whereas CONNOTATIONAL meanings might be in part subsegmental. The denotational meanings, from this point of view, would be more often treated by participants in the culture as 'the' meaning of a word. That is to say, the denotational meanings would be the ones more likely to be given, in their conceptualized hypostasis of meaning, as the 'real' meaning of the word. The connotational meaning of the word would frequently not be defined as part of the meaning by normal participants when they were attempting to give in paraphrase a statement concerning the meaning of the words under attention.

Poets, or literary critics, would in this sense be functioning rather as technicians than as naive participants in the culture, when talking among themselves about the connotative power of words. Similarly, linguists, or dictionary makers, in discussing the connotation of these words would also be acting as specialists who as part of their duties attempt to make segmental — to force into explicit verbalized attention — those meanings which normally are subsegmental. Subsegmental differences would in part differentiate the phrase *to stink* versus *to have an offensive odor*. They would also include the romantic connotations of a phrase such as *the silver moon*. The analyst, however, discovers these meanings by observing the kinds of contexts in which the words occur — as he determines other meanings.

The term subsegmental meaning could also be used to embrace those kinds of meanings which Bloomfield observed in such situations as the child saying *I'm hungry* when as a matter of fact he was trying to avoid going to bed. Bloomfield considered it nevertheless a "remarkable fact" that both mother and child if asked to give the meaning of *I'm hungry* under such circumstances would describe the meaning in terms of hunger rather than of desire to avoid going to bed (1933a:142). Here we would suggest that this situation is an especially-clear illustration of the fact that conceptualized hypostasis by normal participants deals with segmental meanings rather than subsegmental ones — and that the subsegmental meanings may in fact have an extremely important impact on our behavior. Sometimes subsegmental meanings override the segmental meanings just as voice quality as a subsegmental phonological characteristic may on occasion override the impact of the segmental phonemes and of the morphemes which the segmental phonemes symbolize. Great novelists and dramatists are adept "at laying bare the mainsprings of human action" and pointing out some of these subsegmental meanings, purposes, and drives (cf. Kluckhohn, 1949:298).

16.7 *Hypermeanings — Concepts and Ideas*

We turn now to a further problem. Under what label do we subsume the fact that the meaning of a word such as *horse* has something in common with the meaning of a phrase defining it: *a large solid-hoofed, herbivorous mammal* (*Equus caballus*) *domesticated by man.* ... (Webster's Collegiate Dictionary, 1936)? If meanings are to be exclusively handled as components of specific verbal items such as particular words or particular sentences, what are we dealing with when we say that two morphemically-distinct utterances 'mean the same thing'?

We speak of a HYPERMEANING, which is the meaning of two or more utterances or parts of utterances (1) for which there is culturally-attested conceptualized hypostasis of that meaning by native speakers (that is, the meaning has been talked about in some contexts by the participants in that culture), and (2) for which there is evidence that these participants identify the two verbal expressions as having the same meaning. Where the participants claim that two meanings are the same even though the morpheme sequences involved are different, the common identified meaning is a hypermeaning. Since informant reaction is involved in this definition, however, hypermeanings of a particular text may differ for the native naive speaker, native scientist (including native linguist), and native poet.

If two items with the same hypermeaning are both single morphemes (or words), the morphemes (or words) will be SYNONYMS; the meaning of synonyms is a hypermeaning. Where two expressions have the same hypermeaning but the verbalization of at least one of them is extensive so that a phrase or sentence, or more is involved, one of the utterancesis a PARAPHRASE of the other — or 'gives the meaning' of the other.

The native conceptualized hypostasis of a meaning (of morpheme, word, phrase, paragraph, chapter, etc.) or of a hypermeaning (of sets of morphemes, phrases, chapters, etc.) may be given a specialized label such as VERBALIZED CONCEPT or even idea. For identification, meanings and hypermeanings require the test of sameness and difference with informants — or, in vigorous tests of proposed theory, an elaborate distributional substitute for this procedure — such as is used for identification of the sameness or difference of homonyms, or other utterances.

All the problems of a philosophical type which are involved in the recognition of synonymy can carry over to the problem here. As we see it, however, it is ultimately from an etic point of view, alone, that one may claim that there are never any genuine synonyms. Emically, we must reckon with the fact that participants in the culture do claim that — for certain purposes, within certain contexts — some words 'mean the same thing'. Any analysis of behavior designed to study that behavior in reference to the manner in which natives react to that behavior, therefore, must take account of the fact that people identify two paragraphs as talking about the same idea, or that two people may affirm that they are discussing the same concept.

For a few illustrations of implied hypermeanings, note the relationship between *He sent me a wire* and *He sent me a telegram*. Compare also the statement R82/17 J —: *Honestly, it seems too funny to hear [grammar school] kids start calling math arithmetic again ... because in [junior high] school it's always math*. Compare the popular statement *A rose by any other name would smell as sweet* with the statement *Call it what you like just so long as you use the term consistently*. For verbal play in which hypermeanings are retained but pleasure is obtained by changing the formal items carrying these meanings, note R82/13 S —: *Bow-wow ... Mother ... I'm daddy's puppy ... I'm a big doggy — and know what my name is ... when I'm a doggy? Flippo*. (Compare, also, the hypermeanings of the child who says *Let's say 'Yes' when we mean 'No'*).

Within our theory, we treat the overt handling of such cultural sameness and difference as identification or separation of hypermeanings. Within a hypermeaning, however, the linguist — or poet, for that matter — may detect wide etic diversity which may become emic in another universe of discourse. Other etic differences may be conditioned variants — affected by style, particular morpheme collocations, or tructural matters.

Both in scientific discourse and in practical speech there will be indeterminacy at the borders of hypermeanings as there is indeterminacy at the borders of morphemes or phonemes. It may be impossible to state where the hypermeaning revolving around words and phrases discussing *plant* versus *animal* begins and ends, or *liquid* versus *gas*. Here, however, our difficulties are similar, in principle, to the problems of phoneme or morpheme segmentation which we have discussed at length earlier.

Native reaction indicates that hypermeanings are in some sense, for some purposes, in some universe of discourse, discrete one from another. Hypermeanings may be considered as CONCEPTUAL QUANTA. On a technical front, scientific classifications or logical groupings are deliberate placings of variant elements into systematic sets of units with their correlated hypermeanings in order to be able to handle masses of data which would otherwise be unmanageable. In ordinary common sense thinking, similarly, a vast amount of data is made manageable by one's 'mental computers' by having a bewildering variety of data 'indexed' in terms of items filed mentally by means of 'punch cards' in which the actor has been forced by experience or culture to determine the category within which he chooses to view a certain phenomenon. It is only when phenomena have thus been mentally quantized and classified in mental 'storage' that he can call on this experience rapidly for rational manipulation. The process of careful, verbalized thought is dependent upon this prior process of discrete storage of experience.

Hypermeanings, therefore, may lead to STEREOTYPES such as that of the 'typical Frenchman'. Such a stereotype leads the unwary to group together things which lead to stereotyped handling of situations which would better be handled as relevantly distinct. Stereotyped thinking, therefore, may carelessly be considered unwarranted and undesirable. From a linguistic point of view, however, it would appear that some degree of thinking in terms of discrete hypermeanings, each with its range of variations, is an inevitable requirement for useful and rapid reaction to one's environment.

The flexible person, the innovator, or the one sensitive to new experiences, can transcend these culturally or experientially-given straight jackets, see new relationships, and develop new mental categories. Once he has done so, beginning with his subsegmental reaction to new situational features, and working until he has segmental verbalization of them, other people can use his new segmentalized expressions in order to enter into these categories of experience with him.

Education within a culture should ideally include not only the assimilation of the standard hypermeanings available, with practice in reacting to one's environment in terms of the ranges of deviation of these hypermeanings, but should also include training to help a person to transcend these categories where it would prove fruitful. Education, in order to accomplish this, needs to provide the student with a range of etic classifications in various areas of knowledge and to train him in emic analysis of unfamiliar situations. The etic stereotypes give starting components which can be structurally analyzed to find relevant new units and relationships.

Scientific discourse and practical discourse have many hypermeanings in common.

Thus *The sun should be up soon so we can walk without stumbling in the dark* has one or more hypermeanings in common with the scientific description of the earth's rotating relative to the sun and the resultant bombardment of the earth by photons which help a person to get the sensory stimuli needed to keep from stumbling, and so on.

Participants in speech behavior discuss their speech behavior. That is to say, they have a METALANGUAGE by which language can talk about itself. Here it must be seen that a hypermeaning implies the presence of a metalanguage. It implies that language can be used to discuss itself — that speakers of a language (even linguistically-naive speakers) can discuss the meanings of words by functional conceptualized hypostasis of that meaning, and can equate meanings of words, or equate meanings of paragraphs, or of conversations, or of lectures. This characteristic of man makes up one of the most important elements which distinguishes human speech from communication by animal noises. It leaves open the way to the development of science. It opens the door to symbolic representation in poetry. It provides the mechanism for the possibility of metaphor and symbolic development which allows man to go beyond mere verbal responses aroused by physical stimuli and to enter into the discussion of nonphysical problems.

There is a close relation, but one difficult to analyze, between subsegmental meanings and hypermeanings. Let us suppose, for example, that some participant in our culture has never discussed the term 'closure' in technical contexts, nor has ever had the fact of closure in music or art or behavior brought to the level of awareness in his thinking. Suppose, nevertheless, that he begins to get some kind of a vague reaction to closure and is 'trying to put his finger on' something to label the vague reactions he is beginning to sense. At this level in his behavior we would speak of a subsegmental meaning of closure. After he has brought this sharply into focus, however, or after he has met someone who can describe clearly to him the phenomenon that he has been vaguely feeling after, and especially after he has been given the term 'closure' as a label for this kind of event, the meaning of the word closure would have become definitely segmental. It would have become articulated. When, furthermore, he next engages in discussion in which he relates the word closure to such phrases as 'completing a figure' or 'completing a form', the common semantic core of these terms, phrases, and discussions will carry with them a hypermeaning or concept, which he will be discussing overtly in these technical terms. In our approach, the overt discussion of this meaning of his technical concept would be treated as the functional but conceptualized hypostasis of that hypermeaning.

Hypermeanings enter into a HIERARCHY OF MEANINGS such that one meaning is included within another as an illustration of subtype of the more inclusive meaning. Thus *man* and *woman* are both included in *adult person*, *boy* and *girl* are included in *child*, *child* and *adult* are also included in *person* (Nida, 1955). The criterion as to whether or not one hypermeaning is included in another may be obtained from native reaction to this kind of data. Instead of asking an informant whether two items are 'same' or 'different' one asks "Is 'X' a kind of 'Y'?"[4] Presumably the data would include a number of overlapping answers, which would result in crisscrossing hierarchies of meaning, with various kinds of indeterminacies and class cleavage between them.

When dealing with two dialects or two languages a different hypermeaning type comes into play. Thus the translation of English *table* by the Spanish word *mesa* or the German word *tisch* involves a cross-cultural tacit or explicit hypermeaning. Here, however, the hypermeaning which is identified by bilingual participants in these cultures is not the total range of meaning of *table* with the total range of meaning of *mesa* or of *tisch*. Rather the hypermeaning covers in such instances the common core of meaning covered by the various words. This must be evident inasmuch as translations cannot be made by routine substitution of one word for another; in various contexts the translation must be different. That is, hypermeanings have reference to meanings abstracted not from isolated words and phrases, but from words in context.

16.8 *Bibliographical Comments on Chapter 16*

For loss of meaning — semantic satiation — when words are rapidly repeated many times, see Osgood (1963:739), after Lambert and Jakobovitz. For a different type of loss of meaning, see Osgood's sentence "*Light lights lightly light light lights*" (1963:745, with its alternate: "*Pale flames gently illuminate airy lanterns* [in a Japanese garden]").

16.81 *On the Definition or Nature of Meaning*

The problem of defining the nature of meaning is exceedingly complex and has a long history. For a general study of the problem see Ogden and Richards (1952 [1923]), and Urban (1939). Learning theory is also relevant (Carroll, 1953:111).

One of the most influential of the early students of meaning, especially of meaning related to signs and sign situations, was Peirce. For him "the 'meaning' of a concept" included, among other constituents, the "general habits of conduct a belief in the truth of the concept" "would reasonably develop" (1931-35, §§ 6.481 and 6.490). Compare Kluckhohn (1949:146-47) who has language as an "instrument for action". Compare Sinclair, with "language as causative" (1951:120-21, 172, 204; with language causing people to "hold certain attitudes or follow certain ways of selecting and grouping in attention", or "to consider holding" these attitudes). Note, also, Firth with words as both "affecting and effective" so that "They mean what they do" (1937:126, as in the expression *Say when!*).

[4] See, now, work by Frake (1961, 1962), Conklin (1955, and in Householder and Saporta, 1962).

Some of Peirce's chief terms are summarized by Ogden and Richards (1952:279-85); for Peirce, for example, a "type" as distinct from a "token" seems to be a generalized unit or "form" as distinct from an event which is a particular instance or occurrence of that form unit; an "icon" may be some kind of physical graphic symbol of the unit (e.g., a footprint, or an alphabetical letter); a sign itself may be a "sinsign" (a sign event), a "legisign" (a general sign type), a "replica" (a sinsign of a legisign), or a "qualisign" (which seems to be a characteristic of a sign); etc.

The approach by Ogden and Richards themselves, however, postulates a triangular relation between symbol, referent, and thought (or reference); the symbol symbolizes a thought (or reference) correctly or incorrectly, the thought refers to the referent adequately or inadequately, and the symbol truly or falsely stands for an imputed relation between it and the referent (1952:11); similarly, there are five functions of language which include "symbolization of reference", "expression of attitude to listener", "expression of attitude to referent", "promotion of effects intended", and "support of reference" (1952:226-27); for them, any item which is interpreted is a sign (50), whereas a symbol is a kind of sign used for communicating (23).

Morris has attempted to handle the analysis of signs and meanings in a behavioristic context. He avoids the term "meaning" because it usually throws "a handful of putty at the target of sign phenomena" (1946:19). In general, usages can be divided into the "*informative*, the *valuative*, the *incitive* and the *systemic* usage of signs" (1946:95); while "three major factors discriminable in sign-behavior corresponding to the nature of the environment" include "*designative*", "*appraisive*", and "*prescriptive*" components. In reference to a dog acting as he hears a buzzer "the buzzer is the sign; the dog is the interpreter; the disposition to seek food at a certain place, when caused by the buzzer, is the interpretant"; on the other hand, "food in the place sought which permits the completion of the response-sequences to which the dog is disposed is a denotatum and is denoted by the buzzer; the condition of being an edible object (perhaps of a certain sort) in a given place is a significatum of the buzzer and is what the buzzer signifies" (1946:17-18). Rather than token and type, Morris uses the terms "sign-vehicle" and "sign-family" (251, 20) — as he indicates that Carnap uses the terms "sign-event" and "sign-design". A symbol, for Morris, is "a sign which is a substitute in the control of behavior for another sign, signifying" the same material as the sign for which it substitutes (25). Earlier, Morris indicated that the study of signs may have semantical, pragmatic, and syntactic dimensions, when the relations are that of sign to the applicable object, or of sign to interpreter, or of formal relation of signs to one another, respectively (1938:6-7). For Morris, "a language is a set of plurisituational signs with interpersonal significata common to members of an interpreter-family, the signs being producible by members of the interpreter-family and combinable in some ways but not in others to form compound signs" or "*a language is a system of comsign-families*" (1946:36). The "communicative activity" implied in this definition would seem to make it that of a pragmatist, rather than that of a formalist with inclination "to consider any axiomatic system as a language", or that of the empiricist who "is inclined to stress the necessity of the relation of signs to objects" (1938:10).

B. Russell feels that language indicates facts, expresses speaker states, and alters hearer states (1940:256); the "purpose of words, though philosophers seem to forget this simple fact, is to deal with matters other than words" (186). Gardiner considers a meaning as "something mental" (1932:42), with speaking assuming "the form of *an intention to affect the listener*" (74). G. Miller gives four reasons for social communication: "to increase uniformity of information" and "of opinion", "to change status", and "to express emotions" (1951:253). For a summary of various theories of the psychology of language — dualistic, expressionistic, behavioristic, and interbehavioral — note Pronko (1946:215-32).

For intonation as having no encapsulated meaning, note Smith in Lévi-Strauss and others (1953:29). Malinowski objects to the conception of *any* meaning "as *contained* in an utterance" of any type (in Ogden and Richards 1952 [1923]:307).

The basic distinction between an emotive versus a symbolic use of language is considered by Ogden and Richards as one of their basic contributions toward the foundations of a science of symbolism (1952 viii; see also 150-51, 241; for "good" as used in "a purely emotive" manner, see 125). On the other hand, Morris indicates that "no distinction of emotive from referential meaning really issues" from the analysis (1946:71; compare, however, 68-69, 72). For a detailed assertion of the relevance of the difference between descriptive and emotive, however, see Stevenson (1948).

For objection to the notion that "words have meanings just by standing for or indicating something", note Robins (1951:21). For an epistemological argument that knowledge — and, by implication, a specific meaning — is not of a type that is an "entity which can be possessed or shared or conveyed", note Sinclair (1951: 122-23).

In British linguistics, theories of meaning have been heavily influenced by Malinowski's views on "*context of situation*" (in Ogden and Richards, 1952 [1923], reprinted in 1948; and see 1935:73, 214). Firth extends the relevance of contextual relations to include phonetics, grammar, and other functions (1935a:53-54); also Robins (1951:22, 82-83, 91-92, with emphasis upon function).

For insistence that the context of situation is not enough but that one must, to understand meanings, take into account a universe of discourse in which "a mutual acknowledgment, by speaker and hearer creates the context and therefore gives referential content to the word or term in question", note Urban (1939:194-98, 203-04). Compare attention given to the "associative field or the semantic field of an item", in which there are closely organized sectors of vocabulary such as scale of colors, or system of intellectual values, etc., Ullmann (1956:16). For further discussion of fields, note also his summary of early work of Trier (Ullmann, 1957a:295-97); the history of a word can only be fully understood with reference to "what happened to its neighbors in the field".

Lounsbury shows that unitary definition of the meaning of words is impossible without reference to the "semantic field" (or universe of discourse) under attention — as "Our Grandmother the Moon" must be left out of the analysis of the kinship system of Iroquois (1956:193).

For a bibliography of studies on semantic fields and some discussion of the history of this view, note Öhman (1953:125; and Ullmann, 1957b:322-42). Metaphors under this view presuppose an elementary semantic field (Öhman, 1953:129). Sinclair refers to "the whole of the circumstances" and effects (1951:177); J. R. Firth insists on reference to various specific systems (1951a:85). Within these systems, Firth insists that the "modes of meaning may be stated at a series of levels, which taken together form a sort of linguistic spectrum", in which "the meaning of the whole event is dispersed and dealt with by a hierarchy of linguistic techniques descending from social contextualization to phonology" (76).

For evidence from aphasic patients that meaning in part has reference to context learned, such that some patients can formulate a word only when it comes in a series, note Goldstein (1948:6, 64, 211, 258, 268-69).

Bloomfield set the tone of later American linguistics by using the definition of "the *meaning* of a linguistic form as the situation in which the speaker utters it and the response which it calls forth in the hearer" (1933a:139). Emphasis upon response is found in Harris (1951:20), and in Fries (1952:22n., 32-53). For meaning as "the feature common to all the situations in which it is used", see Bloch and Trager (1942:6). For this view rejected, note Kurath (1945:210). For emphasis upon elicitation in language function, note Fries (1954:65n). For a view by an anthropologist, note Nadel (1951:33). For expectations of response, see Parsons (1951:5). For response, see also G. Mead (1934:67-75).

For meanings as the "point-by-point and pattern-by-pattern relations between the language and any of the other cultural systems", note Trager (1949:7). See also Harris (1951:187).

For a completely different approach, note Twaddell, who states that "whatever we notice is a meaning to us" (1949:6), such that "there is an element of choice in language which we call meaning" (4, 6).

For meaning as "privilege of occurring" in contexts, note W. Haas (1955:80); meaning as "operation in the network of formal relations", Halliday (1961:245); semantics as "virtually a branch of logic", R. Martin (1958:vii); see also Greenberg (1957); and Quine (1960). Attempt at summary of kinds of meanings is found in Henle (1958:138, 165, with conceptual content, propositional attitude, emotional tone, purpose, and various other effects, primary and secondary; with the uses of language to express or to evoke conceptual content, belief, attitude, emotion, or fact about the speaker); and with types of meaning, charted with different senses of cognative versus noncognitive (169). For types of dictionary entries, note Sebeok (1962b). For analysis, in terms of rules, of components of dictionaries as seen through a semantic theory, note Katz and Fodor (1963:191, 181-82). Katz and Fodor insist that a semantic theory should contain "theoretical constructs distinct from the markers employed in grammatical description" (210), but should utilize rules to "take account of semantic relations between morphemes and of the interaction between meaning and syntactic structure in determining the correct interpretation for any of the infinitely many sentences which the grammar generates" (183); the theory must also be able to explain that one sentence is a paraphrase of another (182, 175, 195, 205).

For formal definition as a reduction statement — the conditions under which the term can be applied — note Carnap (1939); and cf. problems in the nature of theory, §§ 2.75, 2.72. For formal meaning as referring "to the significant patterns within the raw material" [of language] but contextual meaning as referring "to the patterns observed in the scientific situation" in correlation with form, see Dixon (1963:37).

16.82 *On Meaning in Relation to Structure*

For our repeated emphasis on form-meaning composite, note § 6.46 and Index; similarly, Longacre (1960:88); Garvin (1962a:120); for tagmemic meaning, see above, §§ 7.83, 7.32. For the study of grammatical structure as quite independent of "any semantic consideration", on the contrary, see Chomsky (1961b:232); and his grammar theory as "completely formal and non-semantic" (1957a:93, 94, 99-104). For a protest that some semantic elements are needed for description, however — of proper names, personification, direct quotation, foreign words, and so on — note Lackowski (1963). For recent discussion of the relation of meaning to morphemics, note Strang in *Preprints...*, 1962:250).

For inability of putting into a machine "links between words, notions, and reality-objects" note Andreyev (1962:196); compare, however, certain rules for mechanical output in Katz and Fodor (1963:192) in the form of "projection rules" for "semantically interpretating sentences"; both treatments agree that there is no algorithm for the discovery of semantic components.

16.821 *On Sememes*

The general question as to whether meanings form a structure is discussed by Hjelmslev (1958). Kurath states that "the vocabulary or lexicon of the language does not constitute a linguistic system but refers to the 'practical world' in which the speakers of any given language move and have their being" (1945:207). Chomsky states that "semantic notions are really quite irrelevant to the problem of describing formal structure" (1955:141). Harris has stated that it is impossible "in general to work out a structure of meanings" (1944a:202).

The attempt to set up a minimum structural unit of meaning, the "sememe", was made by Bloomfield (1926:157). He assumed that these could not be analyzed further "by linguistic methods". Although he clearly recognized that for meanings there is no way "of demonstrating their constancy" (1933a:144), nevertheless, in spite of the fact that we know that "the agreement of the community is far from perfect, and that every person uses speech-forms in a unique way" (1933a:75), "we have to take the specific and stable character of language as a presupposition of linguistic study" (144) in order to operate within the fundamental assumption of linguistics that in a speech community "some speech-utterances are alike as to form and meaning". So that the "constant and specific meaning" (145) implied by the fundamental assumption "is true only within limits, even though its general truth is presupposed not only in linguistic study, but by our actual use of language".

An attempt to treat variants of meaning as allosemic within sememes has been presented by Nida (1951). He deals not only with variants, but shows different kinds of relationships of item to context which affect meaning (linguistic versus cultural context, endocentric-predictable-meanings of morpheme sequences, versus exocentric-nonpredictable-meanings of such sequences). Nida indicated that semantic structure was obtained by pattern of substitution without reference to the particular reference involved, and that this reflected the people's world view. In these items the context was not a grammatical one but a semantic one.

Joos, in analysis of the word *code* finds "just one 'sememe' with '14-allosemes'"; the data were approached by putting into piles slips which seemed to form a circle of piles, leading to a semantic structure (1958:64, 61).

Crucial observer viewpoint as relevant to meaning is seen in Haugen, where "An author telling a story from a particular region [in Iceland] would naturally take that region as his point of orientation", so that he would have two semes (cardinal direction versus ultimate orientation for travelling) with complementary distribution between them (1957:457-59); since the two types of meaning could lead to apparent conflict, one must say that meaning may "be defined as the capacity of a symbol... of discriminating between those messages that could be conveyed in a given social situation".

Note also "sememe as a synonym for significatum and alloseme for denotative type" in Goodenough (1956:207). The problem of sememes must also eventually be brought into some kind of relation with the "semantic markers" of Katz and Fodor (1963:185-87); and with categories (note fn. above to § 6.46). Lamb is developing sememes which seem to be related to such categories (1962).

16.822 *On Synonymy*

For many purposes one needs to be able to identify whether two items are the same in meaning or different. Chomsky assumes that this leads to a basic philosophical problem of synonymy, and hence to an almost insoluble difficulty for linguistics, so that "to know difference in meaning is to know synonymy and this is the central term of the theory of meaning. If accepted then, this claim is an open admission that linguistic analysis must be based on precisely the most dubious part of semantic theory" (1955:142). For a logician's discussion of synonymy, see Quine (1953:24-32, 37-38, 48-49, 56-64); and note that for him the phrases *Evening Star* and *Morning Star* "cannot be regarded as having the same meaning" although the two refer to the same object (9).

For problems of synonymy in reference to translation, note Malinowski who argues that in numerous instances translation "cannot, in my opinion, be carried out with any degree of accuracy" (in Ogden and Richards, 1952 [1923]:303; also ix). Contrast the view of Humphrey that "a given thought may be linguistically expressed in different languages" (1951:262). Note also Ogden and Richards who state that it seems "as clear as anything can be in philosophy that the two sentences 'Socrates is wise', 'wisdom is a characteristic of Socrates' assert the same fact ... they have the same meaning, just as two sentences in two different languages can have the same meaning" (1952 [1923]:97n).

Kaplan suggests that the sameness of a concept employed in different contexts of inquiry would be explicated "not by the constancy of a single reference, but by the pattern of its references" so that it is like "the 'same face' in the members of a family" (1946:287). Thus the unity of a linguistic meaning refers not "to the logical sum nor product of these regions [of semantic overlapping], but to the pattern as a whole ... not an entity but a complex of symptoms ..." so that "It is made clear, not by precise definition, but by a specification of the characteristic syndrome" (287). Compare also handling by Kaplan and Schott of characteristic patterns of items for class membership according to a set of profiles of properties of these items (1951:186).

Bolinger indicates that a simple relationship between "identity and opposition" is no longer practical, but rather there must be degrees of likeness and difference (1950:117); if *song* and *sing* represent the same morpheme, why not also *shine* and *sheen* — and if *handle* and *hand*, why not *hear* and *ear* (119)? Similarly, Öhman indicates that words have multiple meanings each of which has a "single unarticulated section of a field" (1953:133 — as in Swedish the words for "playing" blind man's buff versus "playing" chess [*leka* versus *spela*] are different and hence the field is divided differently in English and Swedish). Ogden and Richards, because of such difficulties in similarity identification, define sameness as having "sufficient similarity to allow profitable discussion" (1952 [1923]:91, 133-34).

Žinkin treats sense as "the synonymy or the equation of differently-named things and the distinction between like-named homophonous things" (1962:159). Katz and Fodor find that "the information about synonyms which a dictionary must provide can be given solely in terms of sense-characterizations" with two lexical items "being fully synonymous if and only if... every path of one is a path of the other" in the tree diagram which includes the semantic markers (cf. 1963:184-85).

16.823 On Variants and Universals

The insistence on focusing attention upon variants of meaning (or of items) is one of the characteristics of 'General Semantics'. When variants are numbered, they are sometimes called 'indexes' with references; for example, $house_1$ $house_2$ (W. Johnson, 1946:211-13). The use of dates (213) has a similar function. An extreme attention to such allomeanings (or allo-units) coupled with a denial of the emic unity of such meanings (or units) leads to a distortion of human experience. Note, for example, Korzybski: "Identity appears, then, as a primitive 'over-emotional' generalization of similarity, equality, equivalence, equipollence, and, in no case, does it appear in fact as 'absolute sameness in all respects'. As soon as the structurally *delusional* character of identity is pointed out, it becomes imperative for sanity to eliminate such delusional factors from our languages and s.r. [stimulus reaction]" (1948:400). Also: "The present $\bar{A}$-system is not only based on the complete rejection of the 'is' of identity, but every important term which has been introduced here, as well as the Structural Differential, is aimed at the elimination of these relics of the animal, the primitive man, and the infant in us" (403). It is difficult to conceive of a theoretical effort more directly opposed to ours. For Korzybski, emic units — "allnesses" (404) — are animal relics, and insane. For us they serve at the height of the rational process, though subject to abuse through the formulation of unrealistic stereotypes. Sameness of meaning is emic.

It is not only individual words which have differences of meaning; the entire semantic system is in a fluid state. Without a possibility of change in meanings human communication could not perform its present functions. Note, for example, Urban's claim that in our living "A language is required which is fluid in such a sense that it makes it possible always to be passing from the unknown to the known" (1939:172). This very flexibility is a further differential characteristic between the speech of man and the communication of animals. In the latter, the "non-mobility of signs forever limits communication to the hearer now" (Urban, 1939:229-30). On the other hand, semantic units must be sufficiently "solid" to allow for the communication of common experience, and for the verbal communication to other persons of experience which is otherwise private to an individual. Thus Urban emphasizes that language shall not only be indeterminate in the sense of being essentially changeable, but also must be "completely determinate in its references" within some limits (1939:172). For similar emphasis upon the necessity for language to be stable for communication but mobile for particular needs, note Karcevskij (1929).

There seems to be a further relation between the emic semantic units of speech and that which philosophers have in some other contexts called 'universals'. Some of the kinds of reactions which we have to the necessity of considering the emic structuring of the semantic component of speech — as over against treating everything in etic detail as the general semanticists are prone to do — can be translated into some of the philosophical vocabulary of universals. Note, for example, Urban's claim that "They [the universals] are real at least in the speech community, whatever other reality they may or may not have. They are the *sine qua non* of there being any linguistic meaning and therefore any communication whatever. A word intends an object directly, but it always intends a universal indirectly, and these two intentions can never be separated" (1939:142). Thus one cannot look at a tall man and put the observation into words "without intuiting the seen man as a *man*", and "the individual Nansen is a universal, as a connecting link of his own manifold and varying states, relations, qualities, and activities. We cannot *see* the individual Nansen except through this universal" (142). (Cf. also § 16.86). Nansen is emic — cf. § 17.4.

For an objection to treating universals — or, in our view, emic structural semantic components of words — as real units in themselves, note Aristotle: "nor are the Platonists making the Forms anything other than sensible things" (*Metaphysics*, Book III, Chapter 1, Section 2; compare also Section 1; also Chapters 3, 6, 7).

Morris objects to "looking for meanings as one would look for marbles", rejecting also these "'platonic ideas'" (1938:44; also 1946:19). Ogden and Richards adopt a related view (1952, [1923]:188). Note also rejection by Quine of items such as "'household'" (1953:10). On similar grounds, Brain rejects words as "notional units" (1950:131). Bruner and others suggest that the view that psychological equivalence is determined by similarity of environmental events must be "replaced by the view that psychological equivalence is only limited by and not determined by stimulus similarity" (1956:8). Postman treats stereotypes under the label of "strong monopolistic hypotheses about classes of objects and people" which can be confirmed by small or minimal information (1951:254-55). Humphrey insists, however, that only "by such discernment of similarities can the organism survive; without it organic response must be chaotic in a chaotic-seeming world" and "is, at bottom, the ability to learn from experience" (1951:307). Brazier assumes that the nervous system must have the possibility of choice in "this conflict between the universals" (1950: 43-44).

See also Henle, for conceptualism as the view that "universals exist only as conceived by thinkers" versus the view of the nominalists who hold that "there are no universals at all: there are particular things which do *not* share any common properties" with words which may, however, "refer indifferently to a plurality of particular objects" (1958:27).

Note that our view has treated cross-language universals as comprising specific etic elements (see §§ 2.11, 2.71, 5.52, 5.53, 6.94, 7.72, 8.72, 9.25, 11.52), along with our general — cross-language — conceptual framework. Compare the desire of Chomsky for "a linguistic theory that aims for explanatory adequacy" which must be "independent of any particular language" (1962, § 2.0, p. 515). For some discussion of semantic universals, see both Ullman and Weinreich (in Greenberg, 1963:172-207, 114-71).

Lanz and Stefflre (1964) have shown that measures of "communication accuracy" in reference to "messages that would enable another person to pick out the stimulus it refers to" give useful predictions over a wider range of circumstances than do the criteria of Lenneberg and Broth; the more flexible communication measure allowed for changes introduced by differences in context (e.g., many varieties of blue versus only one blue in the context).

16.824 *On Forms of Perception*

Cassirer assumes that "the concepts of mass and force [are] 'fictions'" since reality is not immediately graspable, but only mediated through such concepts (1953:76); the "fundamental concepts of each science" are "*symbols* created by the intellect itself" (74-75; cf. also 78); so that there is a "copernican revolution" which is "the hypothesis that, instead of human knowledge being shaped to reality, it is our human judgment which determines whatever is to have the character of the reality for us" (6).

Compare, also, Cassirer: "Thus the special symbolic forms are not imitations, but *organs* of reality, since it is solely by their agency that anything real becomes an object for intellectual apprehension, and as such is made visible for us. The question as to what reality is apart from these forms, and what are its independent attributes, becomes irrelevant here" (1946:8) so that "the basic philosophical question is no longer that of their relation to an absolute reality which forms, so to speak, their solid and substantial substratum; the central problem now is that of their mutual limitation and supplementation" (1946:9). Compare also Urban, who says that language "is the mould in which reality as significant is first given" (1939:375).

Experimental evidence that language forms affect our perception is seen in Lenneberg: "Statistically, codable colors [i.e., those for which names can be given rapidly, easily, in short linguistic terms, etc.] are recognized significantly more often than less codable ones, and thus there is good evidence that the particular linguistic fact, codability, affects the cognitive process, recognition" (1953:470). Experimental evidence that language forms affect our perception is seen in Brown and Lenneberg, who indicated that "the codability of a color" "proved to be related" to the subject's ability to "recognize colors" and "accounted for more variance in the recognition task as the task was delayed and complicated to increase the importance of the storage factor" (1954:462). Compare also Doob (1957:98). See, now, also R. Brown (1958:236-37). And see below, § 16.86.

A great deal of discussion concerning the relation of language to thought and perception centered about discussion of the writings of Whorf, who argued that language strongly affects or channels forms of thought prevalent in a culture. See his Selected Writings (1956), especially the article on the relation of language to habitual behavior (134-59). For a detailed discussion of this view, including a historical perspective, note the volumes by Hoijer (1954), and by Lévi-Strauss and others (1953). See, also, analysis in R. Brown (1958:230-37). For a critique objecting to a certain "extreme form" of the Whorf view which may seem "to predict perfect correspondence of cultural and linguistic areas" inasmuch as "the Hopi and the Hopi-

Tewan who share a general puebloan culture ... speak very divergent languages", see Brown (in Bruner and others, 1956:304); furthermore, "most of the conceptual oddities" turned up by Whorf and others "can be found in some group in our complex society" (311-12). Note also that Malinowski rejects the "dangerous" "assumption that language simply mirrors reality" (1935:64-65).

For words as providing "linguistic 'summaries'," note also Nadel (1951:72 and 42). Compare also Kluckhohn (1949:160, 165-66), and Sapir (1924, in his Selected Writings:157, where "the mould of his thought, which is typically a linguistic mould, is apt to be projected into his conception of the world"); (also 1933, in his Selected Writings:10).

For further discussion of the Whorfian view, note Longacre (1956:307), who prefers Urban's high view of language. See also Wells, with language as a "stumbling block" to Whorf (1962:697); with language as a cause of world view, comprising a "red herring" (704); with language as not causing a world view (698, 703). Carroll grants that the "developmental hypothesis of linguistic relativity asserts merely that the process of learning these discriminations requires the speakers... to pay more attention to these aspects of experience" having "certain effects on behavior" (1963: 17). For further study of the relation of language to psychology and perception note R. Brown (1958); G. Miller, with a general limit of seven units which can be readily perceived without reference to higher organization (1956).

16.825 *On Componential and Hierarchical Analysis of Meaning*

A significant recent attempt to treat meaning structurally lies, in my judgment, in work of Lounsbury (1956 and in *Preprints*, 1962), and Goodenough (1956). They each, independently, attempt to illustrate semantic analysis by way of kinship systems. Goodenough attempts to provide analysis to indicate how any speaker of a language "is able to use a given form in new contexts in ways perfectly intelligible to other speakers" (197n). He divides components of meaning into significata, which are prerequisites (and defining characteristics), and into connotata, which are probabilities or possibilities (195). (These characteristics might be rephrased, in tagmemic terms, as obligatory and optional, nuclear and marginal). A person, for example, can be known to be my brother "whether he acts like it or not" (107).

They indicate that the data to be examined must first be selected in reference to a universe of discourse, a "*delimited area*" (Lounsbury, 1956:193), or a "semantic field" (195). Such a field (or semantic system, Goodenough, 1956:107) is then further treated to an abstracting process, so that for one set of dimensions (or poles) the field, or some part of it, may exhaustively be divided into its parts, into a "paradigm of terms" by the one variable (Lounsbury:193). Such classifications (or 'paradigms') may overlap each other. Formulas are provided to show each sub-universe, and for each variable within such a universe.

See, also, § 17.71, below. Some readers find Wallace and Atkins (1960) the most useful introduction to these problems. See also Burling, who feels that we should "stop pursuing the illusory goal of cognitive structures", and rather admit that we are "just fiddling with a set of rules which allow us to use terms the way others do" (1964:27); rejoinder by Hymes, same journal (116-19), with insistence on need for native response to sorting criteria.

Nida discusses the way in which "componential plotting of the semantic field" is related to morphological work, isolating "semantic functional positions rather than occurrence of morphemes" (1958:288). Such a display comes in contact with former attempts to discuss "mutual relations within the chain of speech" and "paradigms of grammar" making up "the system of the language" (Firth, 1956:95, quoting Hjelmslev).

Pike (1963d) and Pike and Erickson (1964) show matrices of pronouns with fused number-person categories; relationship between form and meaning cannot be set up as one category to one form, but must be related in terms of formative blocks in the matrix pattern, for Fore of New Guinea and Potawatomi of USA; the conflation of matrices with different block patterns, or with related block patterns, allows for the total differentiation — disambiguation — of the formal categories. Wells shows, in a related fashion, how two patterns of color names can be conflated to give a composite set of differentiated cells; the "same property" leads to "equivalent predicate" which can be equated with my category (1962:706). E. T. Hall gives a matrix of intersection of various kinds of message systems such that a map of the total culture results (1959:222-23).

For further discussion of lack of one-to-one correlation of form to meaning see Martinet (1960a:7-9), F. R. Palmer (*Preprints*, 1962), Akhmanova (1963, Chapter 1).

For a different approach to semantic components, see Osgood, Suci, and Tannenbaum (1957). Note, also, resumé in Osgood, Sebeok, and others (1954:179, with *gentleness*, for example, scored against the poles *fresh* versus *stale*, *strong* versus *weak*, *hot* versus *cold*). This approach seems an etic one, in reference to gradients of connotation, rather than the emic, structural one of Lounsbury and Goodenough. Weinreich shows some inappropriateness in such scales of semantic differential (1958:360, fn. 16); compare also Carroll (1959b, for review). Compare Hiorth, for measuring degrees of "distance" between meanings, by an interview technique (1959).

A further important semantic development is the treatment of meaning in terms of a hierarchy of successively-inclusive concepts. Note theory and analytical technique in Conklin (in Householder and Saporta, 1962), Frake (1961:121, with hierarchy of skin disease stages and terminal diagnostic categories, 129 with diagnostic questions and answers), Nida (in A William Cameron Townsend, 1961:313). But see Halliday, for whom "in lexis" there is "no hierarchy of units" (1961:276).

These approaches differ from other types of componential analysis: Nida (1952, with components as objects, processes, relationships, and abstracted features; revised list of elements concerning elements, events, and qualities, in *A William Cameron*

Townsend, 1961:322); Harris (1948, on Hebrew); Krupa and Altman (1961:622, with chart of hierarchy of oppositions in semantic analysis of pronouns, in Indonesia); and various others such as McKaughan (1959:101, a Philippine language), and so on.

Ziff (1960) has discussion of many semantic problems — including principles of "composition" (61-66) and "conventionality" (57-58); "regularities" concern him (but not "rules" which "have virtually nothing to do with speaking or understanding a natural language" (34). A detailed analysis of the approach is found in a review by Katz (1962).

Of great importance is the recent attempt of Katz and Fodor to "characterize the form" of a semantic theory of a natural language (1963:170), so that the speaker's ability to interpret sentences is explained (176), by way of "rules which take account of semantic relations between morphemes and of the interaction between meaning and syntactic structure in determining the correct semantic interpretation" (183). They have semantic diagrams in which hierarchy procedes from the word through grammatical markers, to contrastive abstracted semantic markers, to specific distinguishing semantic elements. This gives a formal way of generating certain notions by way of paths through the tree diagram, and shows how — within a sentence — certain kinds of ambiguities can result or be disambiguated. For critique of this work note Osgood who regrets the unresolved ambiguities growing out of the omission from their theory of users' knowledge "about the nature of their world and about the momentary situational, motivational, and linguistic contexts in which particular sentences occur" (1963:738). Compare my attempt to go to linguistic and non-linguistic contexts — e.g., poem or plot — beyond the sentence (Pike, 1964d, 1964f, and references in §§ 5.63, 11.723).

Note Meredith, for a formal theory of semantic matrices whose arrays suggest inferences concerning comprehension (1959:1003, 1021). See also Hiorth, on "conceptual neighbors" in a semantic field (1956:59).

16.83 On Phonological Meaning

For phonological impact as part of the spectrum of meaning, such that "It is part of a Frenchman's meaning to sound like one", note Firth (1951a:83). Compare Harris, with phoneme as meaningful (1951:188n). Cf. Strevens, with Gold Coast pronunciation "identifying members of a community" (1954:84). For Bloch and Trager, however, "A phoneme is meaningless" (1942:53).

Sapir states that "one of the really important functions of language is to be constantly declaring to society the psychological place held by all of its members" (1933, in his Selected Writings:17-28). Thus "'He talks like us' is equivalent to saying 'He is one of us'" (16; compare also 1927, in his Selected Writings:537).

When some characteristics of the language of a speaker are used by the analyst as "a means of gaining information" about the speaker, Morris implies that the point of view is that of "descriptive pragmatics" and may be used in psychoanalysis, in sociology, etc. (cf. 1938:38). For voice quality in reference to psychiatry, see Pittenger and Smith (1957), and McQuown (1957b).

Brown indicates that the psychiatrist studies speech as an expression of characteristics of the patient — rather than as denoting the verbal content (in Bruner and others 1956:296). Here, lying, for example, may characterize one as a liar (295; see also Ogden and Richards, 1952 [1923]:194). Firth indicates that a child's "sense of social and linguistic differences" is quite well developed before the age of six, and has relevance to "snob commodities" (1937:104). Note also that a poem may be written to convey something about the author to the reader rather than to convey the actual data of the poem (Morris, 1946:97).

For documentation concerning the change of dialect "from standard to folk forms according to the audience", note Mencken (1945-48, I:9; II:347). Note also McDavid (1949:74 n 17).

Hill states "that rhyme and alliteration are structures correlated with language structure but not a part of it" (1955:973). An opposite view "that form is a part of meaning, that content expressed in any other way would not be the same content" is expressed by Lynch (1952:104).

In experiments on sound symbolism, S. Newman found, for example, that subjective judgments as to small or large size were consistently made in reference to a symbolic scale which followed t, p, k, or d, b, g, and so on (1933:68). Carroll, however, emphasizes that it "is doubtful, however, whether any general phonetic symbolism exists across various linguistic families" and suggests that the experiments by Sapir and Newman show only "that it exists in an artificial experimental situation" (1953:238). Similarly, on the other hand, others have suggested that sound symbolism is "a myth, or better that it is always a function of particular associations with meaningful words in a given language" (Osgood, Sebeok, and others, 1954:182). On the other hand, Brown, Black and Horowitz feel that there "may be some features of phonetic symbolism which have a universal validity" (1955:388; see also Brown, in Bruner and others 1956:282-84). For a bibliography on phonetic symbolism see Pronko (1946:205-07). Bolinger has tested some impact of sound-symbolism relations experimentally by trying to have observers rate according to preference their various choices of sentences in which some of the words may "echo a number of other forms not very closely related among themselves, and be attracted sufficiently to take on a cast of their meaning" (1950:129).

The Greek dramatists used higher-level phonological units for special symbolic functions, to "express certain specific moods, actions, and reflections" so that "the Ionian phrases, with their initial short syllables, induced a feeling of something softer or more exotic, sentimental and feminine" and "A slightly modified form of a Dorian ... was also used to suggest sensuous beauty or exalted reflection" (W. H. Gardner, 1949:130).

Note also Fonagy, summarizing work of Macdermott, where "dark vowels" refer more frequently "to dark colors, mystic obscurity, or slow and heavy movement, or depicting hatred and struggle", and where /k, t, r/ as against /l, m, n/ "'predominate in those [poems] with aggressive tone" (1961:194-95). Compare the phonaesthemes in such as *snip, snap* in J. R. Firth (1935b) and sound symbolism in similar elements in Bloomfield (1933a:156). Note that, in our view, *flip* versus *flap* and *flop* lead to phonemically-conditioned semantic variants of a morpheme; see § 6.53. See also Bentley and Varon (1933, with some "inherent differences" within the sounds), and R. W. Brown, Leiter, and Heldrum (1957:352, with discussion of the kind of voice Disney might be expected to give to a boulder versus a pebble).

16.84 *On Grammatical Meaning*

See also references in §§ 7.81-83, 11.76.

For grammatical meanings, note Bloomfield (for "constructional meanings", 1926:158; for class meanings, 1933a:146-47, 280; for tagmeme meanings, 1933a:146, 163-68, 190, 202-03, 205, 247, 249, 266-68). For meanings used to name grammatical categories but not to establish them, note Robins (1951:94-95; compare also 1952: 295). For insistence that "the parts of speech ... often have no meaning at all", note Sweet (1875-76, in Collected Papers, 1913). On the other hand, note that Sapir feels that "we can represent a quality or an action to ourselves as a thing" (1921:124), and hence have some kind of feeling for a class meaning. For a similar view of a psychologist note Brown (in Bruner and others, 1956:310 — where "'thingness'" can infect our thought of such things as "'beauty'").

For problems in handling grammatical meaning, note Fries (1952:54-64, 74-75, 201, 203, 206, 217, 223-24; 1954). For tagmemic meanings see also Pike (1943b, 1957a). For discussion of many specific meanings of English grammatical constructions, note Jesperson (1940-49, 1937).

For the fact that meanings are relevant to the study of transformations in English grammar, see Harris (1957:290); Chomsky, otherwise (1957a:96-97); discussion in § 11.763 above. Osgood, however, would assume that "grammatical distinctions are at base semantic in nature" (1963:746).

16.85 *On Meanings of the Lexical Hierarchy*

See references in §§ 6.91, 6.93; 10.52.

The problems discussed in handling lexical meaning are so vast that we can do no more than give a brief sampling. For a convenient summary, note Bloomfield (1933a:139-57, and see index). Note that for Bloomfield "a proper analysis" must be "one which takes account of the meanings" (128). For a list of problems in handling meaning, note the extended discussion in Bolinger (1950; and 1948:18). See also a specific discussion in terms of the technique of differentiating words closely related in meaning, Bull (1950:469). For another problem, note Bloomfield (1933a:145, with the word *charge*). For the reaction that some morpheme differentiations are "essentially terminological and unimportant" (as for "*two, to,* and *too*", which might turn out to be "one morpheme") see the view of Harris (1951:258n).

Harris feels that "In principle, meaning need be involved only to the extent of determining what is repetition" in descriptive (combinatorial) grammatical analysis (1951:7n), while for Fries, one should "Note that lexical meaning does not form part of the apparatus in which to test structural arrangements" (1954:68), although one must be able to "control enough of their meaning to know whether their referents are the 'same' or 'different', what 'substitute group' they belong to, and whether a word of that substitute group is structurally substitutable in the utterance" (1952:196).

Semantic components of morphemes have been broken down in various ways. Note, for example, Osgood, Sebeok and others (1954:179), Wonderly (1952a:366), Lounsbury (1956), and Goodenough (1956). See discussion above, § 16.825. For the rejection of the "least common denominator" approach to meaning, note Nida (1951:9) with the meaning rather the "total of the series" of allosemes than that of a constant component. For a rejection of "words as isolates corresponding to concepts or ideas, often endeavoring to combine a constant core with a field of indeterminacy", note Firth (1952:5). Bazell likewise insists that "Two meanings of a morpheme need have nothing in common providing that they are linked by an indiscrete series of intermediate meanings" (1948b:286). Compare also Ogden and Richards, (1952:128-29; 147).

On the other hand, Bloomfield has referred to the "*distinctive* or *linguistic meaning* (the *semantic* features) which are common to all the situations which call forth the utterance of the linguistic form" (1933a:141). Compare also Nida (1948b:421 n15). For the suggestion that "The remarkable thing about these variant meanings is our assurance and our agreement in viewing one of the meanings as *normal* (or *central*) and the others as *marginal* (*metaphoric* or *transferred*)", see Bloomfield (1933a:149). The "central meaning is favored in the sense that we understand a form (that is, respond to it) in the central meaning unless some feature of the practical situation forces us to look to a transferred meaning" (1933a:149, as with *fox* used in referring to a person; cf. also 402 in reference to slang which dies out if it becomes more frequent than the central meaning). Note, also, reference to *pigs* (431-32, and above, § 16.12). Compare also the treatment of "the 'object language' or the 'primary language'" where "every word 'denotes' or 'means' a sensible object or set of such objects", etc., in Russell (1940:20); this seems to have some reference to our treatment of central meaning in reference to the early physical circumstances in which words are learned. Compare Osgood and Jenkins who indicate that the "strongest and most available decoding habits" for a word such as *ball* will be those "most frequently elicited by the distal cues of the particular objects encountered" (in Osgood, Sebeok, and others, 1954:182).

Another approach to central meaning might be that of identifying the "focus" of uniform naming, in the experiments of Lenneberg and Roberts; certain colors, for example, were named consistently by individuals and consistently from one individual to another, with rapid responses, utilizing short terms; these particular shades of color were treated as the focus of the color concepts (1956:16).

The problem seems to be related, furthermore, to the fact that it may be impossible to invent a language without names[5] since without names there may be an end to the "power of discussing" a question (Russell, 1940:117). Sapir also states that a large stock of basic radical concepts such as objects, actions, and qualities are absolutely essential if language "is to be a satisfactory means of communication" (1921:98).

For meanings as affected by context — for collocational meanings — note Firth (1952:9, and 1951b:123-24, 135). Note also Kaplan, who discusses the way in which a specified meaning grows and changes with context, from a philosophical point of view (1946:287).

For "unusual distribution" as "the cue to metaphor", note Fries (1954:67n). For the pun as "the first step toward the achievement of symbolic metaphor", note J. Brown (1956:18). For metaphor as necessary to reason, note Urban (1939:177-78) For the nonsense which results if one attempts to carry back "the meaning to the primary physical context", however, note Urban (1939:639-40) who quotes an illustration from Anatole France who indicates that the phrase *The Spirit possesses God insofar as it participates in the absolute* would become "The breath is seated by the Shining One in the bushel of the part it takes in what is altogether loosed." See also Count (1958:1072).

Wimsatt, following Stanford, treats metaphor in reference to a synthesis of two concepts, retaining conceptual independence (1954:128). For metaphor, see also Henle (1958, Chapter 7); and Lackowsky (1963:213, as leading to a problem in grammatical analysis). For my relating of pun to metaphor, see (1964f).

For summary of content analysis, concerning intensity, frequency, contingency, and content, tension, valence, note de Sola Pool (in Saporta, 1961:302-05, 315-22); also Saporta and Sebeok (in de Sola Pool, 1959); for bibliography, note de Sola Pool (1959:235-40).

For sentences grouped semantically, by informant judgment in relation to a limited set of partial paraphrases, see Garvin (1962b).

For connotation versus denotation, note Ogden and Richards (1952:188-89). For denotation as an actual referent but connotation as meaning which refers to "other meanings which the form may suggest", note Carroll (1953:95). Osgood has suggested that "connotative meaning" — in reference to the "psychological state of the communicator" may be measured by techniques of "semantic differential". By "a combination of association and scaling procedures" a sample of "potential bi-polar associations to a particular concept is provided for the subject, his task being simply

---

[5] See our insistence on the necessity of conceptual quanta, in § 16.7, and of particles in § 12.1.

to indicate the direction of each association and its intensity on a 7-step scale" (Osgood, in Osgood, Sebeok, and others, 1954:177).

For the pun as giving a kind of "context-linking" within the total context, note also J. Brown (1956:26). For meaning as part of the total hierarchy of structure, note Firth (1951a:76, and 1951b). For meaning in reference to the social-cultural context, note Fries (1954:68, and 1952:294-95, in reference to the difficulties which Rip Van Winkle got into because of changing social meanings). For the "whole context" as giving meaning to a new word, as one first meets it, see Piaget (1955:164). See also W. Haas (1955:80-81, 1957) for meaning of a word as it functions in a total context.

For the "total meaning" of a literary work, note Wellek and Warren (1949:184). For further discussion of total meaning in literature, note Geiger (1953).

For summary and bibliography of Soviet and East European work on semantics see various authors in Sebeok (1963b).

16.86 *On Concept Formation*

Problems of concept formation are related closely to the problem of lexical meaning, since the conceptual categories may be marked out by various characteristics of behavior — by winking, salivating, embracing, and the like but "in all cases" by speech (see Brown, in Bruner and others, 1956:279). These authors consider that the "working definition of a concept is the network of inferences that are or may be set into play by an act of categorization" so that when one calls an item an apple, because he sees an object that is red, shiny, and roundish, one may infer further that it is edible, juicy, will rot if left unrefrigerated, etc. (1956:244). Similarly, Brown assumes that "when someone has learned to understand an utterance his nervous system is partially 'rewired'" so that he "is disposed to behave appropriately with regard to that utterance" (274-75).

From the psychological point of view, "Concepts are responses which tie together, or link, or combine discrete sensory experiences" — concepts that result from collecting data are not the data themselves, they depend on experience, the ties are symbolic, usually in the form of words, and selective factors are at work in the tieing together of these responses (Vinacke, 1951:1-3). So that "A category is, simply, a range of discriminately different events that are treated 'as if' equivalent" (Bruner and others, 1956:231). Cf. also discussion on universals, in § 16.823.

Theories of cognition are summarized by Postman: The Formalists deal with such matters as more-or-less self-sufficient processes, by way of associationism, relating physical stimulus and experience; the Instrumentalists are "interested above all in the relation between cognition and motivated, goal-directed behavior in the role which cognitive processes play in adjustment and survival" (Postman, 1951:242-43), and hence are integrated more with personality dynamics and social processes.

Concept types may be "conjunctive" such that several attribute values must all be present for an object to "be considered as an exemplar of the category" (Bruner and others, 1956:244); a "relational class is one in which the 'rule' of inference requires that values of different attributes bear a specified relation to each other" (244-45); in a "disjunctive concept" the presence of either one of two — or both — attributes must be present for a member of the class to be defined or recognized (245). The latter class type is the more difficult for people to master since it "seems to violate the expectation that to each effect there be but one cause" (245), and "The possibility of using the 'common features' of a collection of positive exemplars is ruled out" and such concepts "have the property, finally, that to locate or learn their defining properties one must begin 'backwards' — by taking as a focus an instance of what the category is *not*" (159). In linguistic terms, a high versus low tone would be relational; a sound identified as being always voiced and continuant would be conjunctional; allophones one of which is sharply different from the other with very little common denominator between them would be essentially disjunctive — compare the *t*'s at the beginning and middle of *tatter* for an approximation of this type in English.

A summary of conceptual types in detail does not leave "much to be gained" even though one may attempt it in some crude way (Sapir, 1921:113 — e.g., basic concrete, derivational, concrete relational, pure relational types).

Vinacke indicates that a person may attain a concept without being aware of its nature, and specifically without verbalizing it (1951:23). Bruner and others insist that the categories are "inventions and not 'discoveries'" (1956:232). Sapir emphasized the relativity of concepts (1924, in his Selected Writings:159).

Development of language in the child, as related to concepts, have been summarized in G. Miller (1951:141-43); "name words appear first, verbs and adjectives later, relational words still later, and pronouns are just beginning to be used by the most advanced children by the end of the second year"; combinations of words do not begin for some time. For bibliography, note Pronko (1946:201-04). The language development of the child is closely related to concept formation: "One might, indeed, go as far as to say that the process of socialization consists of building into the child a system of hypotheses [concepts] which will prepare him to perceive and know his environment in the ways which his culture favors" (Postman, 1951:263).

Concept formation (in which the concept is unknown to begin with and must be learned or developed by the speaker) must be differentiated from concept identification (in which the concept is known to the speaker, but he is trying to identify it by the use of unfamiliar terms such as nonsense syllables) (Brown, in Bruner and others, 1956:298-301); second-language learning is in part related to identification rather than formation (301); concept formation may from some points of view be considered in relation to generalization of stimulus (Vinacke, 1952:151-56), or to generalization of response (see G. Miller, 1951:181-84). Here the response might be affected about sevenfold as to what word one would get according to the context in which it occurred

(G. Miller, 1951:187). Note also D. M. Johnson on cognitive patterns (1955:132-35, 312-17). For related discussions see also Leeper (1951) and Humphrey (1951). For further references, note Carroll (1953:238). Compare also philosophical discussion on universals (see some references in § 16.82).

Abstractions are formed by strengthening "associations between certain invariant aspects of the materials and the particular verbal response that symbolizes this aspect" (G. Miller, 1951:239). Sometimes "nonlinguistic reality" may "serve as a guide to the categorization of speech" just as speech may serve "as a map" of the region of the world mapped (Brown, in Bruner and others, 1956:294). In some respects a concept is a kind of "hypothesis" about the way one should react to one's environment; experimental studies of the development of such concepts have been made with artificial figures (Postman, 1951:267-68); since, after some delay, memory reconstructs figures more in the direction of the conceptual code, it seems that the "process of remembering is often one of active reconstruction, with systems of hypotheses giving direction to this process of reconstruction" (268; the artificial "code" used by Postman was two line figures which could be changed by dropping a piece from the one and adding it to the other).

For testing the learning of a concept, it seems to be essential that a person be able to apply the label for the concept adequately "to new instances" since one must do more than simply learn "to recognize instances encountered" (Bruner and others, 1956:45; Brown, in same, 275, 286).

People "reassure themselves that their categorizations are 'valid'" by the test of the "*ultimate criterion*" [i.e., whether it ultimately works or not in the world] by "*consistency*", by "*consensus*", and by "*effective congruence*" (Bruner and others, 1956:17-21). A "*defining attribute*" is one set up by official sources — such as the law — whereas a "*criterial attribute*" is one by which a person actually operates (Bruner and others, 1956:30, as in a person's feeling of safe driving speed as over against legal driving speed). An attribute is "critical" if it "alters the likelihood of an object being categorized in a certain way", whereas it is "noncritical" if it does not produce such changes (as in the "probability" of an object "being called an apple") (Bruner and others, 1956:31). A further extensive discussion of the strength of such conceptual structures or hypothesis is found in Postman, where hypothesis strength depends on frequency, number of alternatives available, motivational support, frequency of confirmation, amount of stimulus information available, support from the larger cognitive organization, amount of appropriate stimulus information available, and social consensus (1951:252-63).

Availability of concepts seems to be related to codability (Brown and Lenneberg, 1954:456, and Brown, in Bruner and others, 1956:309; and see above, § 16.824). Abbreviation of phrases (as in *TV*) may have reference to frequency of use; concepts such as "damp soft snow" are expressed in long phrases since they "are not only less frequently expressed but less frequently utilized in perception and thought", so that they "are not habitual cognitive modes" and so are "less available to the English speaker" as "manifest in the fact that the concepts are not coded into single words" (Brown, in Bruner and others, 1956:308).

Concepts may be built up which are nonverbal, and may then receive verbalization (see above, § 16.6, see also below, § 16.87). On the other hand, one may first learn a word which is the label for a concept, from someone else, and then learn the attributes of that concept. Thus "If a biology professor in his first lecture uses the word 'coelenterate' he establishes an empty category to be filled in later" (Brown, in Bruner and others, 1956:277-78).

The study of aphasic patients contains a great many items of interest in reference to concept characteristics and loss, and in relation to hierarchical interrelationships within language structure. A massive amount of informtaion is available in Goldstein (1948). Under some types of aphasia the patient may be able to react to a situation as having relevance to a particular *"realm of ideas"* or "sphere" but not be able to pick out from this grouping of words the particular one which is relevant. That is, instead of replying with a term such as *village* he may reply with *house;* instead of *mouse* he may say *cat;* instead of *God* he may say church (226-27). In one instance, however, the patient responded to words in their "totally concrete character" such that he could not mention items such as *dog, cat, mouse*, but could refer to *polar bear, brown bear, lion, tiger,* etc. — animals which he mentioned in the order in which he saw them upon entering the zoo (61-62).

Similarly, a person may be able to report something seen, but not grasp a reported situation (211). Items learned in the concrete situation are not easily extended, for some patients, to situations in a marginal or metaphorical sense. Thus the German word Anhaenger means a pendant hanging on a chain about a girl's neck, or one following a person, or a second car attached to a first street car trailing it, but the patient cited could not understand that once the word was used as follower it could also mean pendant or trailing car (61-63).

In amnesic aphasia the patient may be unable to find names for ordinary objects — or for adjectives and verbs — even though he can repeat words or correctly accept those presented to him orally or written (246).

In visual agnosia, on the other hand, there are "learned motor automatisms" such that a person may be able to count or do multiplication but have no idea what the numbers mean — may not know, for example, "which is the greater, 6 or 8, etc." (133-34). Sometimes 'large' words may be better understood than the 'small' function words, sometimes separate words are better understood than sentences, and sometimes separate sentences are better understood than words, depending upon the particular variety of aphasia present (91). In particular, Goldstein emphasizes that the abstract potential may be seriously affected and this involves (1) loss of "initiative" or "beginning performance on demand", (2) "Shifting voluntarily from one aspect of a situation to another, making a choice", (3) "reacting to two stimuli which do not belong intrinsically together", or "keeping in mind simultaneously various aspects of a situation", (4) "Grasping the essentials of a given whole, breaking up a given whole into parts" voluntarily, and so on, (5) "Abstracting common properties, planning ahead ideationally ... performing symbolically", etc., (6) "detaching the ego from the outer world" (6, 64, 258, 268-69); note also that this has some characteristics of the figure-ground relationship (5).

Miller gives some summary of these matters — as the patient with "receptive aphasia" may confuse "words in the same associative cluster" though he may be "aided by the context"; since a person may "perceive a word correctly when he cannot repeat the individual vowels and consonants that make up the word", and so on. Since other psychological functions may not be effective in the situation, G. Miller concludes that these perceptual processes are "not an indispensible element of the thinking process" (1951:246-47).

Leeper warns against considering, in concept formation, only those having reference to class concepts since the "emphasis on class concepts is consistent with traditional logic, but is inconsistent with our present knowledge that actual deductive thinking usually starts from a premise that states certain cause-and-effect relations on certain sign-significate relations" (1951:754). Deductive and inventive concept formations do not necessarily follow the types implied by formal logic, especially where "the premises are not well established — situations frequently occurring in actual living" (755, 748-54).

Miller calls one an amnesic aphasic when "A group of similar objects cannot be associated in such a way as to form a category" so that "the associative clusters themselves" have been damaged or destroyed and the patient "cannot handle two aspects of a situation simultaneously", etc., since he cannot form abstractions in a normal way (1951:247). For mention of behavioral definition of an abstraction such that one learns to "respond to similarity in a variety of contexts" as applied to learning by monkeys, note G. Miller (1951:169).

The relationship between study of aphasia and language is not yet completely clear for linguistic purposes, though a summary has been attempted by Jacobson (in Jakobson and Halle, 1956:55-82). He calls aphasia a "similarity disorder" when power of combination or of sequence is partly preserved but selective capacity is impaired strongly (70). When the word "is the sole linguistic unity preserved" (74) in atactic aphasia a person can recognize, understand, repeat, and spontaneously produce words like *coffee* or *roadway* but be unable to grasp or discern nonsense syllables which are phonologically comparable to them. When hierarchical levels of language tend to be reduced, the last level to remain is either "a class of significative values, the word", or "a class of distinctive values, the phoneme"; in the latter, phonemes can be identified, distinguished, and reproduced, but words cannot be (75).

Problems of concept formation continue to receive much attention. Note Henle's summary of the problems (1958:27, with platonic realism embracing the "doctrine that there are such abstract entities" as concepts, but in "the logician's sense, a concept is a *property*", a "*universal* and definitely *not* a psychological entity"); compare, in support of the latter, the logician Quine (1953:10). Henle suggests that a "more functional approach" including ability "to discriminate and to classify" is now more likely to be taken "as a cue to the position of concepts" (1958:29-30, with the behavior of grouping, naming, and differential response to stimulus; 27-28, with the problem of the status of mathematical numbers). For Bruner and others, categorizing must be more than learning to recognize instances — one "is also learning a rule that may be applied to new instances" (1956:45). See also Garner (1962:337, for reference to "stimulus equivocation"). For theological overtones of related problems of the nature of truth versus error, dimensions of relevance, dimension of magnification, and problems in ambiguity, note Pike (1961b). For initial bibliography on ethnolonguistics, note Pike and Pike (1960); see also Index below, under Whorf. For theory formation, see §§ 2.72, 2.75.

16.87 *On Subsegmental Meanings and Preverbal Mental Activity*

There is some objection by behaviorists to the treatment of 'Platonic ideas' which in some way are special 'mental entities' in relation to psychical states (note Morris, 1938:44). They wish to have the term replaced by others which "do not stand for isolated existences but for things or properties of things in certain specifiable functional relations to other things or properties" (44-45); nevertheless some kind of mental activity is retained even in behavioristic formulations. Thus Morris prefers a phrase like "disposition to response", rather than "idea", as being "more suitable for scientific advance" (1946:28, 187, 14). For similar views under the label "set", see Woodworth (1938:790-800), Postman (1951:253), D. M. Johnson (1955: 67-79, 83-90, 103-13, 185-86, 311-45, and bibliographical references, 97-101), and Humphrey (1951:105). For "intention", note Osgood and Jenkins (in Osgood and others, 1954:128), Jacobson and Halle (1956:32); for "motivation", Leeper (1951:752-53), and Humphrey (1951:308). For purpose in a behavioral formulation, note Morris (1946:92), see also Brazier (1950:43); for "objective-setting", note Bruner, and others (1956:243); for intent of behavior, Carroll (1953:89, 99) — and further discussion of the problem as to the manner in which "the individual handles information in central mediation processes" (103-04).

Of special relevance to our handling of subsegmental meaning, however, are discussions of the "pre-language stage of thought, which is unarticulated" (Humphrey, 1951:260 after Pick), or those "rapid premonitory perspective views of a scheme of thought not yet articulate ... the feeling of what thoughts are next to arise before they have yet arisen" (Humphrey, 1951:260, after William James); although this may be rejected strongly as not constituting "an 'idea' of what we want to say", so that there is "no more reason why an 'idea' should precede speech behavior than it should precede any kind of behavior" — a view which has been "experimentally disproved" (Humphrey, 1951:259, cf. also 311, where a "hundred years of psychologizing have shown only what statements to avoid", such as the "idea results in action" or "the idea (or image) precedes thought"; cf. also 261n). Vinacke refers to Galton's "antechamber" (1951:24-25). Cf. also Piaget's "ego-centric thought" (1955:63-66). Note, also, Schilder, for whom "every action is based on an anticipatory plan" which is not "in the full light of consciousness" (1950:50-51).

On the other hand, G. Miller specifically sets up subvocal speech where "many reaction tendencies" may "compete and interact" so that at this level "we compare and edit and search for words", and "Several directions of association may run simultaneously" (1951:236). And so we may speculate that "the average talker needs to plan his sentences, on the average, only about five to ten words ahead of his voice" (192, cf. 191). Lounsbury refers to "semantic encoding in a higher mediational system" (in Osgood, Sebeok, and others, 1954:100), while Greenberg, Osgood, and Saporta refer to the "central programming of neural events in the motor cortex" which "is much more rapid than the sequential execution of the movements" (in Osgood, Sebeok and others, 1954:150).

Concepts can be formed and operated upon without awareness of the subjects as to their criteria for these, so that "behavioral attainment" and "verbal attainment" may be different tasks (Bruner and others, 1956:60; cf. G. Miller 1951:238). Malinowski also indicates that words are not in a one-to-one relationship with sociological reality in some instances (1935:65-66; cf. Leeper, 1951:743-55). Long-range strategies for solving a problem may be present, demonstrable experimentally, and yet not constitute a conscious plan (Bruner and others 1956:54-56).

That some kind of thinking can be carried on "without the aid of the sequential habits of normal speech" seems to be demonstrated by the presence of patients with expressive aphasia who can nevertheless think in a manner which is unimpaired — where persons speak and convey their meaning but frequently have difficulty with grammar, often omitting articles, prepositions, and the like (G. Miller, 1951:246; cf. 236, 182); compare also Humphrey (1951:149, 185-216, 262, 264, 310, 315). For subvocal talking to oneself, note Morris (1946:47), Miller (1951:223-24). For a definition of thinking, note Vinacke (1951:2). For a differentiation of the laws of logic from the dynamic laws of thought, note Miller (1951:226); see also Leeper (1951). For further discussion of the relation of language to thought note Adams and Powers (1929:241-47). For an epistemological view in which "it is not possible to divide the sensory and the intellecual into two distinct spheres" such that "the very first perception" of the matter of sensation "contains a reference to the form of space and time" and "the chaos of immediate impressions takes on order and clarity for us only when we 'name' items" and so permeate them "with the function of linguistic thought and expression" in which the world of impressions "acquires a new intellectual articulation", see Cassirer (1953:87, 198; see also references to discussion of world view or Whorf hypothesis in § 16.824).

Bruner discusses "expectancy leading to an alteration in the availability of memory traces" (1951:306); with some bibliography. Schilder — from a Freudian viewpoint — discusses preparatory and transition stages from images to clear conscious thought (in Rapaport, 1951:497-80); compare Kris (in Rapaport, 1951:474-93). Reik (1948: vii) reports Freud as telling him that "When making a decision of minor importance, I have always found it advantageous to consider all the pros and cons. In vital matters, however, such as the choice of a mate or a profession, the decision should come from the unconscious, from somewhere within ourselves. In the important decisions of our personal life, we should be governed, I think, by the deep inner needs of our nature."

Note Bolinger's discussion, based on Jakobson and Goldstein, in which the speaker may be "aware that there is a vehicle for his idea" but be "unable to lay his hands on it" (1961c:113). Much more exciting, because implying "a complex, dynamic process" is the extensive discussion of Vigotsky for whom "units of thought and speech do not coincide" even though they "show unity but not identity"; thought is "there simultaneously, but in speech it has to be developed successively" (1934, in Saporta, 1961:532-33). Compare, also, Lashley, with thought "as a vague feeling of pregnancy, of being about to have an idea" and not identical with words spoken — since "we search a dictionary of synonyms until a word or phrase is found which does seem appropriate" (in Saporta, 1961:184). For a recent discussion of the relation of speech to thought, and some further bibliography, see Verhaar (in *Preprints...*, 1962:377).

16.88 *On Translation*

For extensive discussion of problems of translation, note Nida (1947a); also articles in *The Bible Translator*, organ of the United Bible Societies. For information theory applied to Biblical sources in translation, note Wonderly (1952b). For translation by immediate constituents, note Hockett (1954b). Harris, concerning translation, feels that we "begin by defining differences between languages of the number and content of the grammatical instructions needed to generate the utterances of one language out of the utterances of the other" for certain specialized purposes (1954b: 259); see other articles on translation theory in the same issue of *IJAL*. For artificial pedagogical problems in translation theory, note Pike (1957-58:347). Note also Longacre (1958b, context in translation theory); Brower (1959, with various articles). Compare Householder, who discusses linguistic coding or mapping in reference to "original form ... recoverable" (1962a:183, 185). Lamb suggests that a "recognition grammar for one language and a generative grammar for another provide the basis for a machine translation system" (1962:28). Materials and bibliography in machine translation can be found in the journal of that name; for starting bibliography, see Pike and Pike (1960:36).

For summary of best in Soviet literature on computational linguistics, see Akmanova and others (1963, machine translation, 44-79), with summary of semantic problems and approaches (58-61). A brief speculation on possible tagmemic use in automatic speech recognition is given by O'Malley (in Automatic, 1963:98).

CHAPTER 17

THE CONTEXT OF BEHAVIOR*

Up to this point in our discussion we have been dealing with behavioral events. These events have been both on a large scale — the football game, the church service, the family breakfast, and on a small scale — a football pass, an articulatory movement. Attention in recent chapters has been largely directed to verbal materials. Now we turn from a concentration on verbal behavior with its events and systems to give attention to certain nonverbal materials.

The materials in view in this chapter, however, are not those of behavior as such, but rather the context of behavior as it is affected by behavior. We wish to discuss a society as a structured group of individuals sharing in that behavior. We will discuss the individual as a unit of such behaving groups. We shall turn briefly to the consideration of 'things' and discuss these too from the point of view of their nature as a setting of human behavior and as a product of human behavior. Nor will 'things' be the only kind of item which is considered simultaneously as in part a context of behavior and in part as a product of behavior. Society, and the individual in society, may also be viewed in this double sense. They, too, are part of the setting within which human behavior occurs, and in turn they are in part molded into the structure that they have by the behavior itself.

Specifically, we hope (1) to show that the structure of language shares many kinds of characteristics with the structure of a society (or with the structure of an individual or of a 'thing' in the society). With this we hope (2) to demonstrate that man has certain structural traits which are more pervasive than have previously been suspected, and which therefore tell us something important about man himself. By this technique we would try (3) to build a conceptual framework which will provide a bridge over which, on the one hand, the linguist can travel in order to understand more easily certain problems of the anthropologist or sociologist and, on the other hand, over which the anthropologist may pass in order to understand some problems of the

---

* Our 1960 title to this Chapter, THE MATRIX OF BEHAVIOR has been replaced by the present one, since we now more often use the term matrix to mean an array of intersecting dimensions representing some type of system or subsystem of behavior. Occasionally, however, we still refer to a sequential matrix as the linear setting within which an act is embedded. Order can be linear, or dimensional, or dimensional in linear sequence — or order can be sequence of application of rules. No one kind of order can monopolize presentation of behavior without injury to the multiple dimensionality of observation and other kinds of complementary human experiences. See also fnn. to § 11.225.

linguist. This, we trust, will make it easier for the beginning student (4) to grasp the total field of anthropology as a unit rather than as accidental cluster of sharply distinct, diverse, unrelated disciplines.

Our immediate aim, however, is restricted to the exploring of these analogies in the area of synchronic structural description. We specifically are *not* attempting any testing for analogies (1) in reference to the transmission of culture, nor (2) in reference to change of structure through time or (3) in geographical spread, or (4) in reference to problems of culture contact. Nor (5) are we attempting to discuss postulations concerning cause-and-effect relations between substructures within a culture, or between culture structures and environment.

This is not intended to imply however, that structural components are irrelevant to the transmission and change of a culture whether via its language or its social system. On the contrary, current historical research in language is finding it necessary to restate much of the older historical material precisely because structural — especially phonemic — considerations have been proved to be of great relevance to the kinds of changes[1] which have occurred or may be anticipated. Structural patterns and emic units — not just the sheer physical data — are *part of the cause* and of the end product of change.

We are convinced that analogous structural components are present, and crucial, in change of nonverbal habits and social organization. That is, we believe that to whatever degree cultural studies currently may lack attention to structural, emic contrasts and to structural, emic units, some important insights are yet to be added to the field. Nevertheless, the task we have set ourselves is not to explore the possible implications of structure as such but rather to explore the structural analogies themselves.

In order to facilitate reference to the analogies of society with language, we will from here on in this chapter use S- to mean society, and terms such as S-phoneme, S-morpheme, S-tagmeme, and S-syntagmeme to refer to components of the structure of society which are in some sense analogous to phoneme, morpheme, tagmeme, and syntagmeme of language respectively.

To some anthropologists this approach may seem merely formal, and lacking in insight into the ultimately-important or deeper problems. If so, the same difficulties may be seen in linguistic analysis: Recent study has contributed much to the understanding of the formal structure of systems of phonemes and morphemes but less to the understanding of meaning — the ultimate goal of study of communication. Nevertheless, the growth of formal studies has been very stimulating to understanding the 'mechanics' of language activity, and now — some of us hope — is ready to make substantial contribution to the study of meaning in a manner which previously was

---

[1] I have elsewhere, however, attempted to show the implication of tagmemics for history. Change occurs only over a bridge of shared components. See Pike (1960a, 1961a). Change in a system sometimes involves formative generalization in a vector of a matrix (Pike and Becker, 1964), with oscillation from simple vector-formatives to formatives in a single cell (Pike, 1963d:20, 16-18).

impossible.[2] So, too, a more formal study of some matters in culture may lay the groundwork for later advance in areas which at first seem remote from that of the formal units themselves.

We are well aware, also, of the fact that analogies can be distorted until they misrepresent data and give false leads to the investigator. We are convinced, however, that little creative thought is possible without at some point employing analogies and testing likenesses in areas where they may not have been suspected. In this chapter, therefore, we take the risk of suggesting various analogies in the hope that some of them will prove fruitful in giving direction to our search for unity in the study of the structure of human behavior and of the matrix of that behavior.

17.1 *A Society as a Whole*

We first claim that there is an analogy between a particular society, as a whole, and a language. A particular society, in this view, may be called an S-LANGUAGE.

Comparable characteristics of a language and an S-language include the following:

(1) The structure of each can be detected only by observing individuals in action.

(2) Each language or society is relatively independent of other languages or societies, although there may be fruitful contact between different languages by way of bilinguals, and contact between societies through individuals bi-socially oriented.

(3) Both kinds of structures are relatively stable, outlasting the lives of the individual members of the society or of the speakers of the language.

(4) A language may have dialects distributed in space, or distributed in terms of social levels, or distributed in time, or as differences in style of a particular speaker. Any one style or dialect, furthermore, may be simultaneously structured to contain co-existent systems or fragments of systems of various segmental and suprasegmental types. Similarly, a society may have variation geographically, in spite of over-all unity. There may also be subgroupings (S-social-dialects) according to particular strata in the over-all society. But, in addition, there may be many interlocking groups (S-interlocking-systems) relevant to any one segment of a society at any one time where various individuals are simultaneously members of different groups with different functions.

(5) The structure of a particular society comprises a set of relationships in a network. Individuals having relationships in this network have relevant contacts with other persons not only in a hierarchical ordering of groups within groups, but across such hierarchical lines — the lowest commoner may wave to a passing king. In addition, since a single individual may act in several roles — as father of a son, son of a father, husband of a wife, etc. — the individuals are not members of a single hierarchy but form a network of crisscrossing hierarchies and relationships. In this

---

[2] For current outlook, see § 16.82.

sense a society constitutes a system of individuals within a network — a matrix or field — just as a language has a network of sounds all in contrast directly one with another, of syllables likewise in contrast, of words and sentences in contrast, and so on. As language utterances in sequence form a hierarchy of parts, whereas the language units as an abstract system constitute a network of intersecting hierarchies, so society likewise has the activities of its individuals sequentially but hierarchically structured while the relationships between those individuals themselves are integrated in a total network.

(6) Further parallels between society and language can be seen when we view both within our trimodal conceptual framework. In a society, as in language, we see (a) contrastive-identificational features of units, (b) physically-manifested variants of the units, with problems of their segmentation, and (c) distributional function of the units relative to more inclusive structures and in reference to their internal structuring by way of functional slots and appropriate classes of units filling those slots. We approach this material first in general terms, and then return to it more specifically in terms of hierarchy types and certain units of those types.

(a) The contrastive-identificational mode of a language — or sentence — as a whole involves its meaning, significance, or societal impact. The significance of language is its communicative relevance to a society. Thus the 'meaning' of language might be said to be 'fruitful communication between its members'. Comparably, the significance of society (the S-meaning), might be treated as 'maintaining orderliness of personal interaction'. Whereas the breakdown of language would result in isolation of individuals into communication chaos, breakdown of society would result in the chaos of a struggle in which each was against the other.

Comparable also to language meanings or purposes are perhaps certain related components of a society: self-awareness as a group, essential to its coherence; esprit de corps, contributing to its driving thrust; shared, articulated goals, values, and cognitive orientations giving direction, sustaining motivation, preventing the on-set of disintegrating apathy, and allowing for rational organization; psychological orientation, or ethos, characterizing the outlook of a group or part of a group; rules, customs, rights, and duties of the group or part of the group, outlining some of its expectations or responses. These characteristics, and more, seem to be some of the S-meanings of a society or components of a society.

Analogous to the more tangible contrastive-identificational features of language are the formal features of a society which identify or contrast it with other societies: language, as part of a communications system, essential to maintaining and passing on the crucial S-meanings of the society; habitual shared patterns of behavior, essential for coherence in self-awareness, for maintenance of life, for recruitment and training of members, for regulating emotional situations, for defense against attack by force or fraud from inside or outside the group, and for carrying out tasks set in reference to the shared values and goals — whether the goals be economic, normative, political, or educational. In addition, the specific membership in the society would be a formal contrastive-identificational component of its over-all feature mode, as the membership of a class of morphemes is a contrastive characteristic of that class.

(Similarly, the structural sequence of included obligatory and optional S-tagmemes might be viewed as a characteristic of this mode; cf. § 11.44, Table 3. But see below, Subsection (c), for a slightly different approach).

(b) Within the conceptual framework as we have been developing it here, we have never completely abstracted language or language structure away from the physical setting. We have persistently maintained a manifestation mode as a component of each of our units. This has resulted in retaining the relevance of the physical, phonetic content of sound units or of words as part of their structure. The analogy with the study of society is to retain a physical component in the statement of social structure. That is to say, that the structure of society seen from this point of view would include the grouping of the individuals within the society, rather than be constituted exclusively of a mathematical network of abstracted relationships between its members. As we have dealt with language as a structuring of verbal behavior — as a structuring of the particular verbal events or as the events in a structured pattern — so the structuring of society would in this view involve the grouping of individuals in a structure rather than a pattern of grouping abstracted from their relationships. Our units of society would then always involve a physical component, the individuals organized.

As the manifestation mode of language involves a segmentation of its included units — segmentation which frequently is indeterminate at the borders even though the centers of the units may be clearly identified as being present — so the physical component of social structure would in this view involve the segmentation of a society into groups. The presence of structured groups might be clearly identified, even though their membership at times would be overlapping, or indeterminate at the boundaries, without destroying the possibility of the identification of the presence of the segments by reference to their centers.

The manifestation mode of language emphasizes variants of the occurring instances of its relevant units under different circumstances. Units of society, likewise, have variants in terms of their membership, where the membership varies in time or in terms of the particular situation in which the group is functioning.

(c) As, in language, our conceptual framework involves functional slots with classes of verbal behavior appropriate to those slots in various hierarchical levels and in various systems and subsystems, so the similar concept is crucial to our view of society. The distribution mode of society in reference to its internal structuring would involve the relevant slots or positions in the society which are appropriately filled by individuals or groups of individuals, and which must be manned if the society is to survive. We shall return to this concept in more detail, presently, in reference to role and the S-tagmeme.

The external distribution of society involves the contact of one society with another in larger loose-knit associations (such as the United Nations) or in the network of human society as a global whole. It involves, also, distribution in an identifying geographical area, even though the borders may be indeterminate (or overlap in the case of emigrants retaining nationality abroad). Geographical distribution, in turn, implies not only spacial occurrence as such, but physical restrictions which limit the range of possible behavior patterns concerning travel, building, clothing, food, and the like. Distribution in a time sequence, furthermore, affects available heritage of physical and mental behavior patterns, physical products of prior behavior, both of that society and of others with which it directly or indirectly comes into contact.

(7) One further analogy needs to be explored before we pass on to the study of specific groups within a society. Is there something in society which can be compared to the lexical, phonological, and grammatical hierarchies of language? The answer to this question is by no means clear. Yet the possibility is sufficiently great to warrant study.

As a starting point we note that in every society there seems to be at least a double structuring such that there is the physical grouping of all individuals into kinship elements, on the one hand, and into various kinds of adventitious groups such as football teams on the other. It is possible that this difference — often sharp — shows us where to begin to look for a difference in societal groups which would parallel the difference between phonological versus lexical units in language.

We assume that groups of individuals are comparable to the physical groupings into phonemes, syllables, and stress groups, or the like, if they have identifying criteria (1) which are physical, essential, universal or nearly-universal in all societies, (2) which cut across the entire population of a society, and (3) which have characteristics which make them functioning units in the society (e.g., as an organized warrior class). Within this type of grouping would be included, amongst others, some general kinds of kinship structures.

Age and sex differences can cut across a kinship structure, but would usually be considered as contrastive-identificational components of the kin structures (i.e., as a 'category' rather than an emic unit) — except, for example, where an age group as a whole has certain unifying behavior patterns and cognitive features which weld it into a functioning unit. In this latter instance it might be necessary to treat an age structuring as in some sense S-suprasegmental to a kinship structure, simultaneous with it.

The particular details of groupings can not, of course, be rigidly prescribed for all societies, since that would be attempting to force a generalized etic a priori grouping on to a particular emic situation. As for language, so for society grouping, the general etic categories with which an investigator begins to study a society must be treated as only preliminary starting groupings which must give way to groupings identified by structural criteria for that particular society. In a particular instance, for example, some society-wide groupings such as the strata of a caste system might serve as higher levels in the S-phonological hierarchy.

If the physically-identified but society-wide groups of individuals are considered as vaguely analogous to the phonological units of language, the regroupings of sets of individuals into units for special purposes would be considered analogous to lexical units. This conclusion is based on the fact (1) that the phonological units of language are in this theory assigned to the physical, manifestation mode, (2) whereas in language the lexical meaning is largely found attached to morpheme clusters and (3) meaning of a lexical type is treated by the theory as analogous to purpose in nonverbal behavior. As phonemic units can arbitrarily be joined to form morpheme units such as *cat* and *dog*, so individuals who in their selection cross over kin-group lines may be joined into various units for particular purposes. A high specificity of purpose of such a small group — for example to play football — adds to the strength of this analogy, by paralleling the meanings of many morphemes. The purpose of such a group, when it is specifically goal-oriented, has this lexical-like flavor, as over against the much more diffuse purpose of a kinship group. Just as the analyst may decide that the 'meaning' of a phonemic system is its contributing to group solidarity, so kinship groupings contribute to such solidarity. But this type of meaning is considerably different from that of a specific goal-directed group where the society itself verbalizes the purpose of such a group.

Similarly, (4) the openness of a class of morphemes, such that the number of morphemes can be in principal infinitely expanded, as over against the closed number of phonemes for a language, seems to be reflected in the possibility of developing an unlimited number of specialized groups dedicated to particular purposes in society, as over against the essentially limited number of kinds of kin groups, or functioning age groups, or the like, in that same society.

Groupings of S-morphemes — of small purposeful groups in a society — into larger wholes would constitute the higher layers of the S-lexical hierarchy (i.e., S-words or S-phrases) just as a clan including smaller family units could be a higher unit of the S-phonological hierarchy (i.e., an S-syllable or S-stress group).

We now turn to discuss the presence in society of possible analogies to grammatical units and hierarchies of these units. In language, the minimal unit of the grammatical hierarchy proposed by this theory is the tagmeme.

We may list several of the components or characteristics of this unit which are important to us at the present stage of this general discussion; more detail would be required for elaborate treatment. Each tagmeme has a relevant (emic) slot (or position) in a larger grammatical structure. Thus *John* comes in a subject-as-actor slot in a sentence type of which *John hit Bill* is a particular illustration. Such a slot often has a detectable meaning, for example — in this instance — 'subject-as-actor'. The slot in this particular sentence (chosen from the class of sentences making up that sentence type) is filled by one of the members of a distribution class which in turn is defined and identified (1) by the fact that its members can fill this structural slot in the various manifestations of this sentence type or (2) by the fact that the same members can fill other tagmemic slots in this or other sentence types. Thus *Bill* fills the subject-as-actor slot in the cited sentence, but might be replaced by *Joe, John, the boy*, etc. Similarly, each of these may occur in the object slot, as in *He saw Joe*. This distribution class, the filler of the slot, may also have a meaning — though often vague or inconsistent; in this instance the meaning of the class might be called 'object'. The tagmeme as a whole, then, is in general composed of a significant slot-in-a-structure with an appropriate class of filler.

The S-analogies are perhaps as follows:

An S-tagmemic-slot would be a slot, position, or STATUS (or STATUS-SLOT) in some type of organized group of people. Occasionally members of the society call such an S-slot an 'office' (e.g., the 'office of president') or 'job opening' or even 'position in the company'.

The S-meaning of the S-slot would be composed of the privileges, standing, influence on or power over other people in the society, and expected behavior of the occupant of the status-slot. The S-meaning of the status-slot, in sum, is the ROLE of the occupant, with especial emphasis upon the appropriate behavior in view.

The S-filler of the status-slot is first of all viewed as the immediate occupant, the incumbent of a particular slot in a particular instance of a particular society type, as Mr. John Doe might be president of the federal bank in Jenkins City. In addition, it should be noted that the S-filler is considered to be the total distribution class of members immediately eligible for filling that slot in that society type. Thus, if the organization of certain federal banks is considered to comprise a structural type, then the sum of all the bank presidents of this particular type would constitute the S-distribution-class (or STATUS-CLASS) as an S-filler of that S-slot.

The S-meaning of this total S-distribution-class would then be the abstracted set of personal and professional characteristics of that status-class of federal bank presidents. As it is for language-class meanings, so this general status-class meaning would be inconsistently applicable to some members of the class. It would nevertheless be emically relevant, since members of the community sometimes react to such persons *as if* they had these characteristics. That is, the S-class-meaning is to some degree a stereotype, and functions as such in the community. (The STEREOTYPE meaning would be, thus, a conceptualized hypostasis of the status-class meaning).

The S-tagmeme, as a whole, would include each of these components — it would be a concept combining status-slot, role, status-class, and stereotypic meaning. In addition, however, it suggests that there is a functional unity here which is structurally relevant to the society. (No single, current, common term refers to the S-tagmeme uniformly and unambiguously. The term 'role' is specialized above to refer specifically to the behavior and standing of a person occupying an S-tagmemic-slot. On occasions when no ambiguity is likely to occur, the term might perhaps be conveniently applied to an S-tagmeme as a whole until some other simple but less ambiguous term is found).

The S-tagmeme, like other emic units, may itself be viewed trimodally. In such a view, the status-slot meaning, and filler status-class with its meaning, would be components of the S-tagmeme's feature mode. Its occurrence in larger structures would be characteristic of its distribution mode. The fact that the status-class can be manifested in a particular instance by any one of its members leads to variants of the manifestation mode; in this mode, also, might be found variants in terms of geographical occurrence of a particular type of structure within a particular society, and variants of these kinds.

17.2 *An S-Sentence-Type within Society*

We turn now from the broad generalizations concerning societies and languages as wholes, to a particular group in American society. This particular group is a 'college-football-team'. The structure of the team as a group is now in view, rather than its behavior which we discussed briefly in Chapter 4. The specific structure of a football team is relatively independent of other structures within the society. It would, therefore, imply a fairly high quasi-independent place in this particular part of the society structural hierarchy. Because of its relative independence and internal coherence, we suggest an analogy between a particular 'college-football-team' and a 'sentence-type' (i.e., the football team is an S-syntagmeme).

17.21 *Feature Mode of the Football S-Syntagmeme*

The feature mode of the S-sentence-type 'a particular college football team' includes, among other components, the purpose of "playing the game according to the written rules" (see Official, 1956) and the unwritten customs of sportsmanship. The specifications, by the rules, of number and characteristics of players, kinds of permitted and prohibited activities and goals, and the type and organization of playing field and equipment, allow one to identify this game when one sees it and leads to contrasts between football, baseball, tennis, hockey, or warfare, and so on. A second component purpose is to 'play to obtain the status of winner of the game in hand, and of champion in a league as a whole'. The first is somewhat analogous to 'understanding' in verbal activity, and the second to 'intention', 'elicited response', or 'meaning'. If the second were to override the first, 'cheating' in football would develop in a manner vaguely analogous to verbal 'lying', in that the elicited response — elicited status of winner — is not in fact justified by the actual behavior in reference to principles tacitly or explicitly accepted by the community.

The formal components of the feature mode of the football S-sentence-type include classes of the individual members of the full squad of regular players and substitute players available and eligible to fill any of the slots of the team-on-the-field, and the observable patterned, shared behavior characteristic of these individuals. The full squad may be treated as an S-dictionary for this S-sentence-type. On a program giving the personnel for a game, the members are often listed alphabetically with a key to indicate which are halfbacks, quarterbacks, ends, and so on, as a dictionary labels entries as nouns, adjectives, verbs, and the like. From this point of view, then, the separate players are S-morphemes (or perhaps S-words).

At the top of this S-lexical hierarchy of this S-sentence-type, however, would be the S-sentences themselves. These would be the various actual varieties of the team-on-the-field from moment to moment. At each substitution of a player, a new S-sentence would be formed (as *Bill hit John* is a different sentence from *Joe hit John*). The sum — the class — of these many different S-sentences is one of the components of the feature mode of the team as a whole, i.e., of this S-sentence-type.

In addition, the structural, contrastive sequences of included S-tagmemes (which will be discussed in § 17.23) comprise part of the feature mode of the emic team. The arrangement of frontline slot with its fillers, in relation to the backfield with its fillers, characterizes college football, and contrasts it with unrelated games such as baseball.

17.22 *Manifestation Mode of the Football S-Syntagmeme*

Thus far, however, we have been viewing the *sum* of all substitute groups as *making up* the total team. We now change our vantage point and view any one S-sentence — any particular team-on-field — as somehow representing the team as a whole. If the *team-on-field* scores, the behavioral reaction and status effect is that of the *total team* scoring. The final score and win-status has no essential structural reference as to which team-on-field made this-or-that-part of the score for the total team. All the unplaying-substitutes of the squad win along with the team-on-field which represents them. Disappointment at not getting to play, or at an unfortunate play, is personal rather than team-structural. From the point of view of structural reaction, when a team-on-field makes a play the total emic team — the S-sentence-type — makes the play.

Now since in our theory any one variant of a unit manifests the unit as a whole, these S-sentences are simultaneously components of the manifestation mode of the team unit; there is a strong modal overlap here. Thus a particular team-on-field is a membership variant — a membership allo-unit — of the total emic team unit (i.e., as an S-sentence is an S-allo-sentence-type, an S-allosyntagma).

In between a total team-on-field and the individual-players-on-field are intermediate structural variants. A particular combination of individuals may make up, say the 'first-string-backfield'; another group may be the 'second string'. One of these particular sub-groups, by analogy, may be called an S-phrase; a particular forward line combination would be a different kind of S-phrase.

The variants so far mentioned are made up of substitutions of personnel. Other kinds of variants — a different, crisscrossing kind of S-allo-sentence-type — are constituted of field *arrangements* of personnel, and are conditioned in part by the place of their occurrence in slots in larger structures. For example, the team-on-field when playing defensively (i.e., in the S-response-slot) has various structural options not open to the offensive team which is in the S-utterance-slot). The offensive team-on-field must retain at least seven men in the front line ('the scrimmage line'). The defensive team may have more or fewer there. Thus a four-man front line becomes a part of a team variant of a restricted (partly-conditioned) kind. The defensive team often pulls some of its men to a place considerably back of the line in order to defend against a pass attack. (Such a team variant may be viewed both as an S-allosentence and as an S-allosentence-type, since the particular team-on-field personnel varies in its arrangement at that moment, while this particular arrangement may be preserved through various changes of personnel).

Both the offensive and the defensive team-on-field, however, have certain free structural options as to the precise degree of closeness of the players. The men on the offensive front line may be close together (although no more than the center and one man on either side of him may lock feet), or somewhat far apart (provided that none is more than fifteen yards from the ball, and all are inbounds). Within these limits, free variation in the lateral starting position of men on the offensive front line is permitted. Certain variants are favored — more frequently used than other variants — by certain teams for certain purposes (e.g., a variant in which the two ends are relatively far apart; or a line unbalanced to one side, with four versus two men on one side of the center; and so on). The defensive team has similar variants but without these restrictions: R8/2/1.8: *T — looks over Minnesota's 5-2-3 defense, then he shifts the Wolverine's unbalanced to the right, single wing, K — deep, B — close;* R8/2/2.9: *T — looks over Minnesota's 6-2-2-1;* R8/2/3.8: *Minnesota operating now in the defensive pattern with five men on the line, three line backers,... with two halfbacks,... and the safety man.*

Segmentation problems also enter the area of study of the manifestation mode. And as provision for indeterminacy must be made in segmentation of language units, so it must be here. For example, what is the structural position of eligible substitutes who do not get to play? Since they never become part of an S-sentence — a team-on-field in competition — are they part of the emic team? Or if they are trying out for the squad, but have not yet been accepted or rejected as permanent members of the squad — what then? Or if they are on academic probation and not eligible for official competition? Segmentation in such instances is as arbitrary as it is in linguistics of one tries to draw a line between *as* and *you* (in *as you like*) when they partially fuse in rapid speech. For some purposes (when units as bounded 'particles' are in view), it is essential that the line be drawn, even though this must be done in an arbitrary manner — as when some members of the squad are awarded a 'letter' to wear, as a token of achievement of full team status. For others (when one wishes to study the manner in which units as 'waves' overlap and fuse), no sharp boundary is drawn, but the data are left as indeterminate.

17.23 Distribution Mode of Football S-Syntagmeme

If we treat a particular team as an S-sentence-type, then a pair of such teams in combat with each other may be called an S-utterance-response-unit. At the moment when a team is on the offensive it would be filling the S-utterance-slot; when on the defensive, it would be playing the S-response role.

The single league, say the Big Ten, would constitute a higher layer in the hierarchy — as an S-paragraph, perhaps. If so, the national collegiate league, in turn, would then be an S-conversation.

The distribution mode of the emic team has reference to its occurrence in an S-utterance-response competitive series, and in a league.

Each man on the team has a role to play in reference to the particular slot on the team which he occupies. The person in the offensive-quarterback slot, for example, calls the plays which are to be attempted. The man in the center slot of the front line initiates the play by moving the ball from the ground. The ends of the front line may run down to receive a pass, and so on. These different structural slots are equivalent to the tagmeme slots in a sentence type, and therefore may be called S-tagmeme-slots, or status-slots. The S-morphemes — the individual players — may replace other players in the relevant functional slots on the team.

Sometimes the use of language of those reporting a football game approximates our technical terms. Note, for example, "...and P — and D — O — will alternate at the safety slot" in the defensive field arrangement (Michigan Daily, Saturday, October 25, 1952).

Particular tagmemes may be modally described. The quarterback S-tagmeme has, as part of its feature mode, the responsibility for offensive strategy and the calling of particular plays. The total membership of the quarterback S-tagmeme, including substitutes available on the squad, would be a formal part of that mode. The manifestation mode of the unit would include particular variants represented by the specific individual occupying the slot at a particular time. The distribution mode might include his place among the backs, all of whom by rule are required to be in physical position at least a yard behind the linemen (except that one and only one back is permitted to be immediately behind the center — an option usually exercised, if at all, by the quarterback).

A distinction, however, must be made between S-tagmemes which might be treated as optional, since not required by the rules themselves, and those which are obligatory. The quarter-back S-tagmeme is in this sense optional. Always, however, one is used on offensive. On defense, occasionally one sees a team-on-field with no quarterback present. On defense an optional but expected arrangement would sometimes include a person in safety position, far back on the playing field to defend against a kick or long pass. The player in that slot might well be the quarterback (with this as an added quarterback function in that allodefensive arrangement — i.e., as an alloposition variant of the quarterback S-tagmeme). If the player in safety slot is not the quarterback, the emic arrangement of the defensive team-on-field would involve the reassignment of that etic-safety-slot to a different S-tagmeme.

The position of field captain on the other hand is an obligatory one, required by rule. He, and he alone, is legally permitted to speak for his team in any dealing with officials. He exercises for the team options available to it as to which goal his team elects to defend, calling for time-outs, acceptance or declining of application of penalties which the officials offer to apply to the opposing team, and so on. Any player on the field, however, may be appointed to serve as field captain. This slot is not mutually exclusive with that of quarterback, halfback, end, center, and so on, but can be simultaneously[3] held by a person who is also in one of these other slots. The status of that of captain is superimposed upon one of the individual team functions and has reference to the team as a whole, but is not structurally related to any other one particular playing slot. The field captaincy, therefore, we will tentatively consider an S-suprasegmental-tagmeme.

Sometimes the squad has a small degree of structuring off the field as well as on. Thus for many teams the team captain is automatically the field captain while on the field, but in addition is their squad captain, and speaks for them during the entire season at banquets, and so on. For other teams, the captain may be appointed just for the one game, and function only on the field.

Higher-layered S-tagmemes (S-hypertagmemes) must be postulated to allow for the action of subgroups on the team prescribed by rule and by strategy. The group of linemen manifest one such obligatory unit, with variants as to number, physical positions, and permissible actions differing according to offensive versus defensive function. A group of backs fills another such obligatory S-hypertagmemic-slot, with strategy free variants which differ sharply as to arrangement.

In the larger spectacle of the football game being played, moreover, the player has a participant role in the team. The official has a controlling or judging role. The coach has a teaching and advising role. The onlooking fan has an observer role. The radio announcer describing the game for other listeners has a specific kind of an active observer role in which he is a vicarious observer for others. The spectacle as a whole, therefore, has an S-tagmemic structuring of its participants. This structuring is intricate, with overlapping intricate details which we have only sampled here. We have not mentioned, for example, rules affecting spectator interference with the players (leading to interlocking activity hierarchies of the two groups).

17.3 *An S-Syllable within Society* (*the Family*)

If we adopt the point of view as tentatively suggested in § 17.1 that physical types of

---

[3] For references to simultaneous tagmemes in language, see Pickett (1960:69-79), Pike (1963b:222); and see §§ 14.12, 14.2, 15.13.

grouping cutting across a society may be analogous to the phonological hierarchy of language, and if we take a kinship system as one such S-phonological hierarchy, we must then indicate what would be the analogies to phoneme, syllable, stress group.

The S-syllable analogue might be a family group. Within any one S-syllable the particular individuals in kin roles might be S-phonemes. As different syllables may have similar structure but different specific phonemes, so different families in a society as different S-syllables have different S-phonemes constituting them.

An alternate way of developing the analogy would be to treat a particular kinsman as analogous to phone instead of to phoneme. (See § 17.7, in reference to Lounsbury). Then, in a particular society, the 'father class' rather than the particular father would be analogous to the phoneme. A particular father would be an instance of occurrence of that phoneme. This approach avoids the postulation of a very large number of S-phonemes for any one society, and is therefore closer to results of language analysis.

The feature mode of this family group would contain characteristics identifying the unit and contrasting it with other groups in the society. The particular membership of the family — specific parents and children — would constitute one of these features. The family has a task to perform which is to provide a matrix for harmonious working and growing together in an orderly fashion, just as the syllable provides a physical sequential matrix for communication.

An essential feature of the identification of an S-syllable — comparable to the necessity for a chest pulse in the phonological syllable — would be the presence of a married couple as the minimum but complex S-nucleus of the family. If the nucleus is represented by the married couple, then the children would represent marginal S-consonants. So far so good, but the analogy is then not immediately useful if one returns to the football team where the S-syntagmeme would not then include any S-syllables, since the family unit does not function in the team. The family S-syllables are S-phonological-units for the society as a whole, including the football team indirectly. Once the football team is viewed in its matrix of support, this support comes heavily from the family unit which fosters its members going to school.

When, however, one drops focus to the team alone, the family S-syllable is irrelevant. A different physical structuring of the team membership coexists with the kin relationship and is more immediately relevant. For the team itself, then, an S-phonological analysis would require a hierarchy which by-passes the family. If, however, we had been discussing a society and a game where families, as such, participate, then the S-phonological hierarchy of the society as a whole and the S-phonological hierarchy of the included subgroup of the total S-lexical hierarchy would have been more immediately and mutually relevant on the same levels of their respective hierarchies.

The manifestation mode of the family S-syllable includes its variants. In our family illustration, the addition of children would result in S-allosyllables. Death of one member would also cause variants. If, on the other hand, there were to be remarriage of one of the partners, with additional children by the step mother, say, then half-sibling children would constitute a partial 'portmanteau' overlap of two S-syllables, with an indeterminacy at the boundary.

The distribution mode of the S-syllable would include the function of the particular family as a member of a class of such families (an S-class of S-syllables) in a larger structure. A class of genetically related families functioning as a unit in the society — say a clan — would be analogous, perhaps, to higher-level phonological units. We will suggest, therefore, that a clan may be considered tentatively as a S-stress-group, with a moiety as an S-pause-group.

Internally within the S-syllable is a further distributional structure. In our society the status-position occupied by the father (who in turn is a member of a status-class, one of whose contrastive features is that of adult male), carries with it the S-class-meaning or role of 'breadwinner', 'partial disciplinarian', and so on. The wife and children fill other status-positions. In terms of immediate constituents, the relationship between husband and wife in our society is in some way nuclear as over against a marginal function of the children, as we indicated above.

17.4 *The Individual*

We assume, to begin with, that *the individual is at least as complex in his internal structure as the language is which he speaks* — otherwise, how could he speak a language which is complex? Something within his structure, furthermore, is presumably responsible for the structuring of his language and of his other behavior. It would seem possible, then, that some of the structuring phrases of the individual himself might be analogous to structured components of language. It is this pair of considerations which gives us courage to suggest some of the analogies below. The same observations, however, would suggest that the seeking of these analogous materials in detail would be a very extensive process — a process which we are not prepared for. Our suggestions are merely pointers, therefore, rather than any attempt at analysis comparable to that which we have presented for language structure. As we used the prefix S- for suggested societal analogues of language, so we use the prefix I- as individual, or person analogues.

For the contrastive-identificational features of the individual we look first at elements of I-purpose and I-meaning. Specific characteristics of a goal-directed type, especially when these are in a zone of awareness, would certainly be in this I-feature-mode, analogous to one component of the feature mode of the morpheme. Possibly here, too, would be placed beliefs, values, desires, ideals, standards, and the like. A particular individual has influence on some of his fellows, and in turn is likely to be influenced by others. This component of relative influentialness becomes a part of the feature mode of the individual. Apathy, as over against purpose, could contrast individuals as its presence can fatally differentiate societies, causing their death. Self-awareness itself would presumably be an contrastive-identificational feature of a human individual as over against a tree or a dog. Concepts and ideas, insofar as they can be handled in this conceptual framework, presumably come here also. Emotional states would in general be here — though it is highly possible that the affective characteristics of the individual may be in a different subsystem of the personality, in a further analogy that we shall mention presently.

The presence of components such as value and purpose in the individual is detected in the same way that meaning in language is detected: either by studying distribution of acts by the individual, in which case the presence of meaning and purpose is deduced by the analyst-observer; or by inquiring of the actor directly, or by gathering comments about these matters made by the individual when he is 'off guard'. In each of these instances there are available objective clues for analysis. The analyst may discover the personality structure of the individual as perceived by the individual himself, or the analyst may find something of the personality structure as it is assumed to exist in reference to its relation to the community as a whole or in reference to other objective criteria. Both approaches are relevant to understanding the I-meanings of the individual, as they are to the understanding of language meanings.

The formal features of the individual include reference to his physiology, and any contrastive-identificational components which can be expressed in physical terms. They differentiate man from dogs, trees, and stones, and differentiate one man from another. These characteristics, then, include facial contours, body, sex, age, size, and shape as well as the nature and function of internal organs.

Identity in the form of continuity of personality is an extremely important characteristic of the individual. If continuity were not part of the identificational characteristics of man, a person could not be sent a bill today for something he bought yesterday, as the Greeks seem to have implied. For society to operate, it must assume that John Doe in the morning is the same I-emic individual as John Doe in the afternoon (see § 6.65, and compare § 16.823).

The manifestation mode takes account of the changes within this recognized continuity. John Doe in the morning is an allo-John-Doe; in the afternoon there is a different allo-John-Doe. The allo-units of John Doe do not destroy the identificational-contrastive unity of him as an individual. Changes may come about in his physical nature by age, by environmental impact, and the like.[4] Changes can also affect his cognative, affective, or value components. He learns, he gets angry, and he changes his standards. These changes also lead to allo-John-Does. In an allo-state he may be awake, asleep, alert, tired, careless, and so on.

Just as an informant may have his structure affected by being asked questions (so that the informant is 'spoiled' as an informant, because he is made aware of things to which as a naive informant he would not normally react — see § 6.44), so a person's

---

[4] See Heraclitus, "Into the same river you could not step twice, for other [and still other] waters are flowing" (Fragment 41, p. 94 in Patrick 1889 [1888]) but for unity with — possibly — implied variants, compare: "Into the same river we both step and do not step. We both are and are not" (Fragment 81, p. 104).

cognative and emotional structures are affected when items are forced to a level of awareness. Curiously enough, that which to the linguist is detrimental — since, it changes the structure which he wishes to study, before he can finish that study — is a major tool of a psychoanalyst. By forcing to awareness components of the structure, he succeeds in changing the structure.

In terms of segmentation of the individual, boundaries on the whole are fairly clear. Occasionally, however, segmentation problems arise as when Siamese twins are born. Here there is an indeterminacy of the boundaries of both individuals, inasmuch as there is a partial portmanteau involved where two individuals share a single vital organ or other portion of their bodies.

The internal structuring of the distribution mode of the individual would from a physical point of view leave him a bundle of physiological organs and parts such as nerves, liver, eyes, and feet. From the psychological and social point of view his internal structure has more reference to components of expectancies in reference to his nature as a social actor. He is a bundle of roles, in which the roles on the one hand constitute part of his contrastive-identificational features as an individual, and on the other hand reflect the internal structuring of his social personality. His distribution mode includes components of his status in the kinship network, age groups, sex groups, and other (S-phonological) physical groupings of his society. In addition he has a distributional place within slots of other (S-lexical) groups criss-crossing these, such as religious groupings, groups for playing games, for educational activities, and so on.

It must also be noted that the individual is distributed in a physical matrix, geographically, climatologically, and in reference to the particular kind of physical objects which surround him.

It would appear that the I-meanings of the feature mode, as given above, are highly diverse. Is there some way in which our theory would suggest that this might be accounted for without destroying the modal approach? The answer appears to be in the affirmative. It would be necessary, however, to increase the complexity of the analogies at this point by suggesting (1) that there is an emic progression of structural units within structural units (§ 12.3) within various of these components, and (2) that there are various I-componential systems which are either simultaneous or complementary. The simultaneous systems would in turn have their units modally structured. Diverse items which are assigned, say, to the feature mode as a whole would then be reassigned to the feature mode — or other mode — of various units within components of the respective systems. (Cf. outer units, § 13.6).

This task we have not undertaken seriously. It could probably be undertaken usefully only by someone whose speciality is dealing with the individual. On the other hand, it might be of interest to suggest a few clusterings of elements which might conceivably be treated as components of a subsystem in some such over-all view.

There might, for example, be postulated a subsystem of the personality unit such that its feature mode would include the understanding of what it would be wise to do (i.e., wisdom, reason). This would be analogous to the meaning component of language. The manifestation mode of this subsystem would include the programming of the personality to prepare it for action (i.e., intent, will), in accordance with or counter to wisdom and obligation. Here the analogue would be to the manifestation mode of language in which specific acts and events are in view as physical entities; the will to act would line up the personality ready for such physical action. The distribution mode of this same subsystem on the other hand, would be composed of a conviction as to what one desires or ought to do (i.e., feeling, emotion, desire, or conscience). This would constitute the distributional background within which understanding and the will to action occur. The inclusion of both desire and obligation in the distribution mode, however, hints at a further needed subdivision of subsystems at this point, or may imply that the basic set of analogies itself needs revision. The internal warfare involved in choosing to do what one wants to do versus what one feels one ought to do would suggest that there are clashing subsystems involved. The presence of substructure of this kind in the personality is perhaps supported by instances of double personality in which a person while acting the role of one of his substructures may be unaware of the existence of the other.

If belief systems, standards of morality, and so on, when affecting a person's judgment and actions are not brought to the level of conscious formulation, it might be possible to treat them as I-subsegmental. If, however, these are codified into specific spoken or written laws, it might be necessary to treat them in this case as having been brought up to I-segmental status. (Compare subsegmental and segmental concept formation as treated in §§ 16.6-7, 16.86-87).

17.5 *Things*

We now turn specifically to the discussion of the physical setting of society. All activity of the society occurs within and somehow in reference to a physical setting. People must live and act within a geographical place, in physical dwellings, with physical clothing, and come in contact with these items through their physical bodies.

If this were all that were involved in the physical setting it would not be interesting to add to this chapter. The important point which makes it relevant here is that items as experienced take some of their perceived characteristics from that experience. The individual is unable to experience his background coldly and interpret it completely neutrally. All phenomena, all 'facts', all 'things', somehow reach him only through perceptual and psychological filters which affect his perception of the structuring of and relevance of the physical data he observes. (Cf. §§ 16.823-24, 16.86).

(In my own epistemology I assume that there is some type of ultimate truth, including an ultimate way of looking at the structure of physical reality. This truth, in my view, would be the emic perception experienced by God, who in turn could focus upon the emic perception of individual men as a component of the total reality available to His observation. Since, however, His views on such matters are not available to us, it does not seem to affect our discussion here. This fact, in turn, leaves us always with the empirical possibility of a plurality of equally-true — or equally-false — observations, coming from different standpoints and from different observers).

We seem, then, to be left with some relativity of phenomena — a relativity due to and limited by the fact that the nature of the observer inevitably in part structures his observation of the setting of his behavior, just as it structures significantly and sharply his emic perception of the significance of acts of behavior in his own culture or in that of others. This is merely a way of indicating that *the observer is part of any equation* where perception is involved. The scientist who reads a moving pointer on a dial is in some sense limited by his own internal equipment which determines the nature of his reactions to the perceived reflected light. His perception of the space-time continuum and of his instruments which record data about this setting are in part a product of his own internal structuring. 'Things' and 'man' are not divorced from each other but are involved in a larger complex such that man's own structure is involved directly or indirectly in his perception and discussion of either.

We do, however, make a crude distinction for practical purposes — a distinction which runs into indeterminacies of various kinds — between (1) items of the physical matrix which are not part of the deliberate products of man's behavior (and are affected only in the perceptual sense mentioned) and (2) those which wholly or in part are made by or modified by man's purposive behavior.

Unplanned components of settings include such things as a rainstorm affecting the course of a football game by leading to fumbles of a slippery ball, or of a dog wandering across the field disturbing play. On the other hand they may include a mountain 'just sitting there' but 'waiting to be climbed' and hence the passive setting of planned behavior. These, however, all differ sharply from the football field, in which the planning of the line placement is deliberate, as is the levelling of the ground. This prepared field as a passive setting of the game is in turn different from the football itself which becomes involved in the behavior directly.

We wish to indicate the general direction in which research might conceivably go to try to analyze any one particular physical item through our conceptual framework of feature mode, manifestation mode, and distribution mode. The problem is in part impossible since such a generalized statement requires first that the various types of settings — of which we have hinted at a few — be separated out so that they would not interfere with one another in such a statement. Nevertheless, a few preliminary suggestions can be made.

We begin with a particular football as an item to be analyzed. Here the contrastive-identificational feature which is analogous to meaning and language or purpose in behavior would seem to be USEFULNESS or EXPECTED USE. Note that it is precisely at this point that the observer is brought into the equation in reference to the football. Meaning, purpose, function, and utility seem to be the bridge by which a physical thing or a physical behavior pattern enters into the structuring of society or of the individual and his behavior patterns.

In addition, the observer is brought into the description in that one of the identification features of the football is the individual's specific emic perception of that football. The football in its full utility has its character as an emic component of the emic setting only for those individuals who know enough about football to identify this object as relevant to that game. The football would not 'mean' the same thing to a Hottentot as it would to an American. This, in our view, is one of the contrastive-identificational features of the football itself — that is to say, by 'football itself' we do not mean the concatenation of molecules as a 'thing-in-itself', but an item which has its structure and relevance within the matrix of human perception and behavior. If one attempts to describe the football exclusively as a concatenation of molecules, and all that goes with it for the physicist or chemist, one must note that these concepts in turn are the result of the emic structuring of a person — the scientist — and the proposed units are not immediately perceptible to him. His experiments and his private cultural history structure him so as to use these terms in order to 'understand' the football on a microscopic scale. The observer is not by-passed by going to the microscopic level.

Formal contrastive features would include the length, girth, weight, two-point shape, lacings, seams, bladder and pressure of air in it, and the composition and color of its cover. All are specified by the official rules.

The manifestation mode of the football would include its variations from day to day as it gets more and more worn out. The rules specify maximum and minimum permitted dimensions, i.e., free variants. Conditioned permitted variants are also specified: A white or colored ball may be used for night games, if there is mutual agreement between the teams. A team on the offensive has the option of using a rubber-covered ball instead of the more normal leather one — or both teams may use it by mutual agreement.

Its segmentation from the rest of the physical setting poses no practical problem. The actors know where the football leaves off and the atmosphere begins. On a much more technical level, however, segmentation of the football from the surrounding atmosphere may be very difficult or impossible. There may be an indeterminacy since the gases from the atmosphere penetrate the skin of the football. In addition, the segmentation of the football on the technical ground of perception is also an elaborate procedure. Specifically it involves all the psychological problems of figure against ground — details which we shall not discuss. One may note in passing, however, the perceptual sharpness of break between the edge of the football and the surrounding setting. This sharpness of change is analogous to the perceptual change when one goes from, say, a consonant to a vowel. Movement also is relevant, when one can see the football move against the stadium background — even as a vowel quality may remain constant, as ground, while a tone changes, as figure — or vice versa.

The distribution mode of the football includes internally its inner-bladder structuring in reference to outer cover, with the outer cover having in turn slots for insertion of laces. Replaceable parts in this structure would include the lace itself, and the bladder. In terms of external distribution a football occupies a place in the total matrix of the game. It occurs as part of the total apparatus along with specialized protective clothing, goal posts, and marked field.

The playing field is likewise structured. In the feature mode it contrasts in shape with a baseball diamond, for example, by being rectangular. The purpose of its design reflects the expected activity which is to occur upon it and which likewise differs from that of the baseball game. The field has a continuity of time in spite of replaced goal posts or redrawn marking lines which lead to minute variations in its manifestation mode. Its distribution mode includes its occurrence in the larger area for the total spectacle so that the slot for the playing field is distinct from that where spectators are permitted. The official hundred-yard distance for the play has beyond it certain end zones at either extremity for further limiting the legal area within which the catching of a pass over the end line is effective within the rules. (Other details, of course, are relevant to the game, but are not mentioned here since it is not our purpose to describe the field but merely to suggest the direction in which the analysis would go within this conceptual framework).

The distribution mode of any object, as perceived by man, seems to have — if it is to appear to be structured at all — the requirements that the parts be in some sense 'replaceable'. That is to say, the observer brings to his handling of recognition or understanding of an inanimate structure something conceptually analogous to the slots and the replacing-classes-of-items which occur in language. A particular table, for example, may be observed to be composed of top plus four legs. These four legs are treated perceptually as if in some sense they are replaceable by substitutes if one of them were to be broken, even if in this particular table the top and legs are made from a single piece. (Note that here when we are discussing a table we are talking of a *specific* table, a specific thing, rather than a general concept such as we had in view in § 16.823). Without this perceptual structuring into actual- or potentially-replaceable parts, perceptual structuring does not seem to occur.

Many products of behavior may themselves have behavior. Automatic factories and many kinds of machines have feedback operations which in part control the behavior of the machines. Provided that such a machine is treated as relevant to the persons using it — that is, provided that human observers are brought into the equation — its operation can be analyzed trimodally. Purpose, value, usefulness, quality, and the like, would be treated as components of its feature mode, as attributed to it by the participant observers in the setting of human society within which the machine operates. For this reason, to the stone-age man in New Guinea a mechanical pencil, colored green, with a red eraser and a red-lead point, might not be 'the same object' as to the European. To the European its usefulness and value have to do with writing. To the person who has never known of writing it might appear to be — at a distance — some kind of caterpiller with a stinger to be avoided.

Just as the analyst of language or nonlanguage behavior and the actor of that behavior may have different views of basic purpose, so the builder of the product may see the value or usefulness of that product in slightly different terms from those in which the user sees it — as when gold coins are used for personal decoration. The difference of analytical results which one achieves may in part, therefore, depend upon the kind of observer and the relative values which the analyst has in mind.

Some products of behavior, however, are purposeless and without utility, in the ordinary sense at least. Incidental effects of accidents are of this type. 'Traces' of behavior such as footprints in the sand are also nonpurposive products. Still further products, however, are traces of behavior which are deliberate — as the footprints in the snow if they are designed to form the matrix for a game of tag, or the magnetic recording on a tape as a deliberately preserved 'archeology' of speech, or a picture as a result of painting activity. These distinct kinds of products must be analyzed in different ways. Those products which are the result of purposeful activity have as components of their feature mode their usefulness as seen by the observer. Those which are accidental products have as the comparable component of their feature mode rather the brute cause-and-effect relation as seen by the observer.

If one turns to things perceived by man which are not fashioned or modified by man, nevertheless the modal view of them seems to be obligatory to man's perception, to the extent that he intrudes himself into the observation of the phenomena. In these instances, also, the distribution mode includes — if the item is to be seen as structured — parts which are somehow in principle thought of as replaceable. This is especially true of such things as molecules, where experiment allows one atom or group of atoms to be replaced by another. It seems to be true also, however, of an object such as the moon concerning which the mind divides the surface into mountains, plains, craters, which in fact form a continuum but which the observer perceives 'could have been otherwise'. A crater formed by a meteor might have been placed elsewhere; or the crater rim might later be dispersed by the impact of further meteors, and so on.

During these replacements, or modifications, if the identity of the object is conceived as being constant because of its relationship to man or to some larger item of the setting — as the moon is considered to be constant because of its general over-all relation to the earth — then the modification of the item as a whole would lead to variations in the manifestation mode of that item.

As regards the feature mode of observed phenomena, the observer intrudes into it. Just as in language we have referred to meaning as part of the observer's addition to the language structure, and as in physical behavior we have similarly referred to purpose, and as in reference to items created or modified or appropriated by man we have referred to utility, so in reference to objects such as the moon, or to particular molecules, the observer brings in a related component. In this instance, however, it seems to be the 'perceived or attributed relation between such an object and its environment'. Specifically, just as an utterance is treated as eliciting a response, so in this further area a physical event may be observed as a CAUSE eliciting an 'effect'. Thus we treat cause-and-effect in physical matters as an analog of meaning in verbal behavior. By extension, similarly, the analog of meaning when applied to the particular object entering into such a cause-and-effect relation would be the 'function' or 'relationship' of that object to the order of nature.

A further epistemological note needs to be added here. If the scholar tries to discover and describe structures either of things or of language without reference to the component which man-as-observer brings to these, then similar results occur in both instances: If language is described without reference to man's reaction to it, then language behavior is described as a mathematical system without reference to meaning or purpose. If things and physical phenomena are described without reference to the observer, then they must be described without reference to cause-and-effect. The attempt to eliminate from one's analytical techniques and from one's descriptions all ultimate or explicit reference to intuitive components of man is an attempt to discover and describe structures in the universe without reference to meaning, purpose, utility, function, relationship, or cause-and-effect. Inasmuch as we as observers are ourselves men, we can only partly succeed in such an attempt. At some point hidden assumptions of one or more of these observer-oriented types must creep back into our descriptions, either under their traditional names, or under others, whether at a late stage in the description of results, or in the early overt or covert assumptions and axioms with which the work begins. In our particular approach, we have chosen rather to face this necessity directly and bring overtly into our description these human characteristics. We consider this to be fruitful; and fruitfulness itself — along with elegance and simplicity — is a similar human component brought to the scholar's observation and understanding of the meaningfulness of his own behavior.

We may also suggest that the observer component of meaning, purpose, or usefulness, is part of an outside component which must be utilized to prove the validity or consistency of a presentation of the formal structure of behavior much as Goedel has shown that data from outside the formalism of arithmetic must be used to prove the consistency of arithmetic as a system (see quotation in § 15.32, taken from Nagel and Newman, in J. R. Newman, 1956:1694).

17.6 *The Struggle to Understand*

The struggle to understand is the struggle to sense structure and its criteria. Cultural clues can be found in the language of the participants in behavior or in society which show where they are trying to discover components of structure.

When the child asks *Why?*, he is asking for one essential component of the feature mode of an emic behavior unit. He assumes that there are no units of behavior which lack such a component. If, occasionally, he asks for the purposive component of a product of *accidental* behavior, the question is embarrassing since purpose — as we indicated in § 17.5 — is not then a part of the feature mode of the unit, even though observed cause-and-effect may be. The scholar who does not sense this may be puzzled at the child's insistence. Guthrie, for example, first protests at the "absurdity" of speaking of a goal "as a cause". Rather, goals "do not determine activity; but stimuli may incite activity that is directed toward a goal previously attained by the activity because the stimuli remain associated with the movements that ended in the goal attainment" (in N. Henry, 1942:52). He relates over-emphasis on purpose to a "childish mode of thinking" and the use by children and parents of the question *Why?* Then he states: "I have on occasion found it quite impossible to convince a child who insisted on knowing why I had driven into my garage with a rear door of the car open, that I had no plans for what happened. That an adult should act and that the act have unplanned results were beyond comprehension at the age of five" (52).

Guthrie, it seems to me, failed to sense the fact that the child's understanding of the emic, structural organization life and action *must* include purposive factors. The child must learn the purpose of acts as he must learn the meaning of words.

Thus the question *Why?* or *What for?* in behavior structure or society structure is analogous to the question *What does 'X' mean?* in reference to language.

The question *How?* is a request for information concerning the manifestation mode of a behavior unit. When these details are furnished, the physical activity may be largely portrayed. *Who?* may elicit manifesting physical components of a group unit, or of an S-tagmeme.

If one asks *What then?*, or *Which was first?*, *How are they related?*, or *Who's boss?*, etc., the reply may give information concerning the distribution mode of an activity or of a social group. The physical distribution of behavior may be investigated by asking concerning time (*When?*), or concerning space (*Where?*).

The general nature of a large behavior unit under attention may be explored by such a question as *What's going on?* The matrix of that behavior may be elicited by *What is the set up?*

The class membership of the elements, and the general structural sequence of replaceable parts, may be tested by such a question as *If X had happened then what different things could Y have done?*

Report of an activity — as by a football broadcaster — may cover the same area of components to give understanding to the listening audience. The phrasing, only, differs. Clues occur in such phrases as *in order to ..., by..., after..., so that...,* and so on, or in general descriptive statement.

For further questions utilized by the investigator, or by native actors, to understand taxonomic hierarchies of concepts, note Frake (1961, 1962), and Conklin (1955, and in Householder and Saporta 1962).

17.7 Bibliographical Comments on Chapter 17

For reference to language in contexts larger than that of human society note Sebeok (1962a, with some summary of the literature of animal signals in reference to man's speech). Tikhomirov lists the difference between the speech of man versus animal communication — conditioning in man "does not need to be reinforced every time", "initial generalization may be absent, connections are easily altered", and "reactions may be established to abstract features" so that human speech is "qualitatively different" from animal communication (1959:367). (We have limited our theory to human behavior, so that animal activity comes in only here as it is relevant to humans). For a subsystem of the speech of man in giving commands to animals, note Chandola (1963).

17.71 On the 'Grammar' of Society

E. Thompson has suggested that "society, like language, is something that has a grammar" (1935:512); by this, however, he implies only that there is in society an internal organization below the conscious level; similarly, Freedman and others (1956:12). Sapir insisted that culture, like language, has pattern, but without trying to give analogical detail (and rather indicating that the two types may even be different by suggesting that language is "not significantly at the mercy of intercrossing patterns of a non-linguistic type" [1929, in his Selected Writings:165]); see also 1927 (in his Selected Writings:546) where "All cultural behavior is patterned", though the actor is frequently unaware of the patterning.

An attempt to find a more specific analogy is that of Lounsbury, who analogically relates phones to kinsmen, phone type to kin type, and phoneme to kin class (1956: 191-92). For this analogy he provides both conceptual framework and procedural steps to arrive at the kin analysis. Note that he suggests a parallelism between phoneme and kin class rather than between morpheme and kin class — as we also have suggested that this kin material (according to Lounsbury the "segmentation of a portion of one's social environment" 166) is analogous to the phonological field rather than to the lexical or grammatical one. He utilizes contrastive features, in general chosen from Kroeber, and clusterings of these features to define the kin classes. For example, in Pawnee "the 'father' class, *atías*, can be defined as *males who are uterine kinsmen of Ego's first-ascending-generation agnatic kinsmen*" (174). Related data are found in Lévi-Strauss (1945, emphasizing oppositions between traits, and 1951), and in Greenberg (1948). See also above, § 16.825.

Goodenough, like Lounsbury, has tested for analogues of phonology and kinship structure. He had earlier "found the linguistic criterion of 'complementary distribution' ... exceedingly helpful, though applied to non-linguistic data" (1951:64); some gift types (*niffrag* and *kiis*) were applicable contrastively in similar property-exchange situations, but others were varieties of a unit (of *niffrag*) with responsibilities of food payments differing according to whether the exchange object was a canoe, pig, chicken, house, etc. In kinship analysis, Goodenough's emphasis is upon symbolization of "the particular set of criteria" by which a "judgment is made" as to whether, for example, "A is or is not B's cousin" (1956:195); it is an attempt at applying to "other types of cultural forms" "the methods of componential analysis as they have been developed for analyzing linguistic forms" (195).

See also Hsu (1959, with kin analysis via function, content, and process); A. Healey (1962:26, with basic terms as nucleus of a kin system, but further terms for secondary characterization as peripheral, and a "commentary on the primary classification"); Grimes and Grimes (1962, with diagrams adding a component of distance).

For sources of our statement about double structuring of phoneme versus morpheme analogies in society in § 17.1(7), note Herskovits, with two broad classes of institutions, those that grow out of kinship, and those that result from the free association of individuals (1948:289); Nadel, with charting of a distinction between "recruitment roles" and "achievement roles" 1957:53, and cf. 84, 91); and J. Henry, with "biological involvement" versus "administrative involvements" (1958:829).

Speiser suggests the term "etheme" for "the minimum distinctive political organization in its socio-cultural setting", but does not work out the details of the implication of such an emic term (1953:138-39).

Greenberg (1957) discusses parallelisms between functional approaches in ethnology and linguistics (76-81) suggesting organic, activity, and internal function types. He also shows parallelisms between culture area, diffusion, and linguistic areal classification (66, 73). Other parallelisms, related to change of structure, might also be investigated; compare sounds conditioned in production by their environment, for example, with the "cultural differentiation [which] was produced [in social structure] by process of adaptation under varying technological and environmental conditions" (Sahlins, 1957).

Aberle objects to the use of language analogs for cultural study, especially on the grounds that cultures have a number of role systems, with division of labor and so on, which have not been shown thus far to parallel linguistic systems. This lack is especially acute when one person's idiolect is treated as a small-scale total language. A person's language, he feels, must be sharply differentiated from a society's system of communication since people do not share — but do participate in — the system precisely because of their different roles or positions in the network (in Dole and Carneiro, 1960).

In my view, language-culture analogies or language-society analogies can be profitably maintained, meeting these objections, if on the one hand tagmemes are added to phonemes and morphemes as units in language theory, and if in discussing a language one insists on the relevance of the total lexicon of all speakers of a language as an essential characteristic of that language. By adding the tagmemic concept one is able to provide for analogs to role. By adding reference to multipersonal lexicon, it then becomes fairly evident that no one person in a complex society shares in handling *all* of the vocabulary of that society, but his particular idiolect differs in lexical respects in accordance with his particular position in the society. Thus the communication network contains a total vocabulary even though one idiolect does not. In this respect, language study, as well as culture study, demands a network — field, matrix — concept.

Frake, following Goodenough (1957) "proposes that a description of cultural behavior is attained by a formulation of what one must know in order to respond in a culturally appropriate manner in a given socio-ecological context" (1962:54); rules "by which people decide upon the category membership of objects in their experience", and "for more complex kinds of behavior: killing game, clearing fields", specifically, what one must do in order to live (1962:54-55, 56). Compare Bock (1962:242).

Sahlins suggests that "Polynesian cultural differentiation was produced by process of adaptation under varying technological and environmental conditions" with adaptation taking place in reference to "a variety of ecological niches" where low island atols, with scarce land, required different personnel organization, with changes occurring after various disasters (1957:291, 295-96). Opler emphasizes relation between "dynamic affirmations" — themes — which provide "the link between culture and the assemblage", for example, continuity of the family, or concern for longevity (1959:964).

Barker and Wright have dealt with units which they call "behavior episodes" (1954:4-5, with direction towards a goal, normal behavioral perspective, and approximately equal potency — concentration — through its course); these episodes lead to a segmentation which has points of contact with our behavioral units (see § 5.61); these units are related to a "place thing-time constellation" called "the *non psychological milieu* or *simply the milieu*" (8). French has segments of ceremonial activity, with their occurrence and nonoccurrence, positions occupied, in various ceremony types (1955).

Since our earlier materials appeared, Bock has attempted to apply some tagmemic concepts to the analysis of society. He segments periods of "social time" into "contrasting and complementary units (emic periods)" (1962:162), rejecting the units of Barker and Wright (1955) as entailing "an unwarranted multiplication of units" which employ "a completely arbitrary (etic) criterion to achieve this final segmentation" (165). Bock (166) emphasizes social space — which is not always physical, in contrast to the space of Barker and Wright. It is his thesis that there are units underlying social structure which are "analogous to those which underlie language structure" allowing the contrastive defining and statement of distribution of these units "in their own terms" (155); such that through such units his "hope" is to work out the "'cultural grammar'" and analog of lexicon. Bock develops as his "fundamental entity" a matrix providing slots with roles as the fillers, such that the entity "is the *situation* — an integral unit composed of an emic space/time matrix together with those social roles expected to occur within it" (222); these matrices are emic units with dimensions (169-72). He maintains that social time, areas of social space, and the expected distribution of social roles within the cells of social space/time matrices will "provide the individual with a means of orienting himself toward (and within) his phenomenal world" such as Nation, the Reserve, and Cosmology — or home, high mass, band council meeting, and wake (3); such a dimensional unit is a social space/time matrix (158), comprising a "situation" as a unit, in contrast to the "role" which is also a unit, filling a slot in the matrix (157-58). In social space areas may be nuclear or marginal (192). For the possibility of transformation from a kernel matrix to a derived one by rules, see (225). Distribution involves correlation of cultural forms (emic matrices or roles) (224) — and see below, § 17.73. Bock's matrices (1962) were developed independently from mine (1962a, 1963b, 1963d; Pike and Erickson, 1964); evidently the force of initial tagmemic theory itself pointed in this direction. For a bibliography and discussion of the literature of social time and space see Bock (1962:161-62, 164); for Bock on role structure, note below, § 17.73.

17.72 *On Society Requisites*

We now turn to bibliographical notes which are designed for the linguist, rather than for the sociologist or anthropologist. In general, they are intended to suggest to the linguist some readings in these areas which will be of interest to him if he wishes to see data which will allow him to consider these analogies in more detail.

Among the many books available on social structure which I have found especially helpful are the following: Linton (1936, especially good for early orientation to prepare for society-language analogs with emphasis on the cultural view); Murdock (1949, for worldwide detail); Freedman and others (1956:70-74, with emphasis on the sociological view, and list of kinds of groups). For collections of brief descriptions of cultures and social structures, note Murdock (1934), M. Mead (1937:15-16, with organization around competitive, cooperative and individualistic types of cultures), Service (1958, with economic components under special attention). For theoretical treatments of social structure, note Weber (1947: e.g., 124-32, for orientation to binding rules in 'legitimate order'), Summer (1940 [1906]), Parsons (1951), Merton (1957, [1949]), Herskovits (1948), Radcliffe-Brown (1949), R. Firth (1951), Nadel (1951 and 1957), Parsons and Shils (1951), Levy (1952), Argyle (1957); also, for summary of various aspects of the study of man from the viewpoints of various disciplines, Linton (1945). For various descriptive studies, often with theoretical treatment; see also: Fortes and Evans-Pritchard (1940), Eggan (1950), Lowie (1950), Radcliffe-Brown and Forde (1950, with extensive theoretical treatment), Goodenough (1951), Murdock (1951), Gluckman (1955). For further listing of group types, note Weber (1947:145-46, 151-52, 154-57, 171-73, 250-54, 424-29), Cooley and others (in A. Lee, 1951:70-71).

Prerequisites of a society are summarized most conveniently in Aberle and others (1950). He lists adequate relation to environment, sexual recruitment of members, role differentiation and role assignment (including allocation of scarce values), symbolic learned communication techniques with shared cognitive (meaningful) orientations, shared articulated sets of goals, normative regulation of means, regulation of affective expression, provision for socialization, and effective control of disruptive forms of behavior. Other lists may be found in Linton (1936:91, 98-99, 101-03, 107, 109, 142-52, 157, 233, 271, 422, and 272-74, with universals, specialities, and alternatives), M. Mead (1937:458-59), Malinowski (1945:43, 44-46, 50), Parsons and Shils (1951:190), Levy (1952:ix, 122-34, 149, 157, 166, 168, 173, 182-83, 187, 191, 193, 240, 248, 255, 263, 270, 275; and vii a suggestion toward "a general conceptual scheme" for "comparative analysis of societies" — with a phonetic-like chart 214). Note also Wissler (1935:526), Redfield (in Freedman and others, 1956:2, for folk society), Beardsley (1953:27-28), Summer (1940 [1906]:56, 70), and Honigmann (1954:42-43, for ethos and mores), Parsons and Shils (1951:192, for boundaries), Murdock (1949:3), Wiener (1954:16, in reference to communication theory), Lowie (1950:3, association, versus society, versus community), Parsons (1951:26-36, the language requirement), Nadel (1957:150). For cultural universals found in every society, note Murdock (summary in Linton, 1945:123-42); also Murdock (1949:2-3, the family), Kluckhohn (in Kroeber, 1953), Malinowski (1945:50). See Boulding (1958:69-70) for analogues from economics. For attention to 'institutions' within a social system, note Malinowski (1945:vii-viii, 49-52, 74, with their contrastive features including charter — with reference to personnel, norms, aims, — material apparatus, activities and functions), Nadel (1951:78). See also Sapir (1931, in his Selected Writings:104, 365), Kardiner (in Linton, 1945:107-08), Lowie (1950:3), Parsons (1951:36-58), Radcliffe-Brown (1952:10), Levy (1952:102-03), Leopold von Wiese (in A. Lee, 1951:339), Evans-Pritchard (1954), Freedman and others (1956:189-90).

Characteristics of a society may be "studied from many points of view: demographic, genetic, ecological, symbolic, structural" (Oliver, 1958:802). Oliver gives extensive lists of structural characteristics emphasizing types of emotional interaction of its members (808-09 — affection, avoidance, etc.), transactions (807-08 — symbiosis, altruism, exchange, competition, with further reference to the nature of goods and direction of their circulation, explicitness of the transfer, repayment conditions, and stated or implied purpose), and interactions in reference to duration, sequence, space (802), and in reference to normative, historical, and suppositional kinds (803-04). J. Henry views the personal community rather in reference to the number of persons frequently affecting the individual, the constancy of the relation — the time spent in interaction — and involvement in terms of obligations to heed wishes of others, and the coefficient of reliance of one person on another in support or approval (1958:827).

Emphasis upon purposive activity, with shared goals or aims as relevant or essential to society and/or culture, may be found in Levy (1952:173), Merton (1957, [1949]:

128-29), Park and Burgess in (A. Lee, 1951:17), Nadel (1951:30, 31-33, 76), Malinowski (1945:51), Merton (1957 [1949]:126), Opler (1948:120, with approved 'themes'), Kluckhohn (1949:35-36), Sapir (1927, in his Selected Writings:341).

For the functionalist approach which treats "processes of culture as an explanation of its products" see Malinowski (1945:34, also 26, 75), amplified most clearly by Merton (1957, [1949:51, 61-81, with "manifest" functions as "intended and recognized by participants" but "latent" functions as "neither intended nor recognized"; also 25-26, 50, with emphasis upon "observable objective consequences" versus "*subjective dispositions* [aims, motives, purposes]"). See also Freedman and others (1956:122), Levy (1952:83), Radcliffe-Brown (1952:178-87), Murdock (1949:xii), Linton (1936:404), Murdock (1951:469). As an over-all statement of the relation between the total purpose of language and the total purpose of other behavior patterns in a society, note the usefulness of the statement by J. R. Firth (1951a:82-83) that "normal linguistic behavior as a whole is meaningful effort directed towards the maintenance of appropriate patterns of life".

Lasswell and Kaplan, in discussing political acts, state that conduct "is goal-directed and hence implicates values" (1950:240). Contrast the behavioral psychologist Skinner, who asserts that purpose "is not a property of the behavior itself; it is a way of referring to controlling variables" (1957:87-90); compare Morris, 1946:9, with response to a "stimulus-object as a goal-object". The philosopher Henle employs "the words 'purpose', 'use', 'function', 'point', 'intention' as synonymous, very much as Morris does" (1958:136); compare our handling of the relationships between meaning and language, purpose and behavior, use of thing, fruitfulness of theory, and so on (§ 17.5). W. H. Whyte's irony should move us: "Someday someone is going to create a stir by posing a radical new tool for the study of people. It will be called the face-value technique. It will be based on the premise that people often do what they do for the reasons they think they do" (1956:40).

For the consideration of those end products of activity which are purposeless (and not "functional") even though recurrent (e.g., road accidents), note Nadel (1951:33); for activity without goal, following frustration, note Maier (1949).

For discussion of the difference or relationship between society and culture, note Kluckhohn and Kelly (in Linton, 1945:79), Herskovits (1948:49), Kroeber (1948:268-74), Kluckhohn (1949:24), Radcliffe-Brown (1949:510), R. Firth (1951:483), Nadel (1951:79-80), Parsons (1951:6, 18), Bidney (1953:84-124), Freedman and others (1956:4), Nadel (1957:149).

17.73 *On Role as S-Tagmemic*

There is some confusion in the field in reference to the terms status, position, and role. I interpret this to be due to the fact that on occasion the authors wish to refer to an S-tagmeme of role, and at other times to the components of that S-tagmeme —

i.e., slot, slot-meaning, filler, filler-meaning, total tagmeme, and total tagmeme meaning. Sapir speaks of "a status which that person happens to fill" (1934, in his Selected Writings: 564). Linton refers to "individuals who occupy the statuses and express the rôles in overt behavior" (1936: 253; here status is slot, individual is filler, role is expected behavior). The actor "is performing a rôle" (114); and there is a distinction "between statuses and the people who hold them" "like that between the driver of an automobile and the driver's place in the machine" (113). For a brief reference by Linton to the quarterback in football — which I found only after I had written this chapter — note 114. For Linton, statuses are "polar positions" within social relationships, with the statuses occupied by individuals (256-57); a status "is a position in a particular pattern" (113), although each individual may have "many statuses".

Murdock and others refer to an individual as the "occupant of a status" with status "to connote the position occupied by an individual in any repetitive social relationship", with the role as the behavior or "enactment" of the individual's part in the relationship (Murdock and others, 1950: 77). For Parsons, the fillers are "encumbents as persons" (1951: 400); status "is his place in the relationship system"; role is "what the actor does" in his relations with others; the status-role forms a "higher order unit than the act"; the actor "holds a status or performs a role" (25); while the actor himself "is a composite *bundle* of statuses and roles" as a "social actor" or a "social unit" (26); for further extensive discussion of roles, note vii, 58-88, 399-414.

Radcliffe-Brown refers to the fact that "each person may be said to have a *role*" so that in a "structural system we are concerned with the system of social *positions*, while in an organisation we deal with a system of *roles*"; the "social structure" is referred to "as an arrangement of persons in institutionally controlled or definable relationships, such as the relationship of king and subject, or that of husband and wife" whereas the term organisation is used "as referring to an arrangement of activities" (1952: 11). Levy argues the use of the terms: For him role means "any position differentiated in terms of a given social structure whether the position be institutionalized or not" (1952: 159); by status he means "the sum total of an individual's (or group's) institutionalized positions in a social structure" (160); individuals "occupy" a status (or position), with roles constituting "*aspects of status*" (160); furthermore, "the sum total of an individual's ideal roles may be termed his *ideal social standing*, or alternatively, his status" (160). For Warner, role places "primary emphasis on the person" — how he "stylizes his behavior" — whereas status "emphasizes membership and place in a social universe" (1953: 51), and is a "social position located in a social universe" (49).

Freedman and others have role as "the position which an individual occupies" in a social system (1956: 206-08). Nadel, however, doubts the value of status as positional and role as acting; he tries to fuse the two in a single view of which there are the aspects of the "rule and its application" — of knowledge and performance (1957: 29); presumably he is here feeling toward the S-tagmemic unity of status-role-actor. He is unable, in my judgment, to follow through consistently his treatise of a unitary status and role without reference occasionally to the componential character of the aspects which he has here specifically rejected. Thus, he refers elsewhere in his book to "the flow of the population into given roles" (77, and cf. 69), which is clearly reference to substitute fillers in specific slots. For Nadel's earlier reference to groups in which, for example, "both mother and child have their appointed 'position'," note 1951 (77).

For an economist's view, note Boulding: "Somebody has defined an organization as a set of holes tied together with lines of communication; the hole is the 'job' or the 'role'; and as one person leaves it another must be found to fit it" (1957:6). Or compare *Time* (July 21, 1958): "Into the slot of president ... moved Bob Kintner". See also Parsons (1951:70) concerning the concept of division of labor as developed by Adam Smith.

For contrastive features of roles, note Linton, with statuses ascribed and achieved (1936:115), with status as "simply a collection of rights and duties" (256-57, and 114). For contrastive features of role as a "configuration of prescriptions by which the status is derived", see Goodenough (1951:114). For components of role characteristics in urban communities, note Freedman and others (1956:444, 448-49; for various other contrastive features, 208). Role expectation as a conceptual unit of action may be seen in Parsons and Shils (1951:190); compare Nadel (1951:67-68) and Merton (in A. Lee, 1951, p. 60). For the essential language function, note Parsons (1951:34). For an extensive discussion not only of "obligations, rights and expected performances", but also of features of role differentiation based upon various criteria of age, generation, sex, economic allocation, political allocation, religion, cognition, and in nonhuman environment, and solidarity, see Levy (1952:159, 306-07). For status as having unavoidable "dominance-subordination relationships", see Count (1958:1065).

In any extensive analysis of role, many other features are treated which have analogies with linguistics. Note, for example, in Nadel (1957): distributional characteristics of role — outer distribution with obligations and rights in reference to a wider public, inner distribution with implications to the immediate group (85-88, 92); distribution in a class of people such as the class of 'fathers' and in reference to in-groups and outgroups with focus of various types (89, 92-93); hierarchical characteristics of role in social strata (31-32); free variants in terms of optional activities in role (27, 31-32, 33, 64, 66, 136, 139) versus contrastive features which make a difference to the basic character of the role (32, 43, 65); minimal — contrastive — pairs of roles (67, for example, manager versus worker, elder versus common citizen, priest versus worshipper); a Sapir-like set of two artificial systems of roles, each containing the same common group of elements in different arrangements (67); the taxonomy — etics — of roles generalized, e.g., independent versus dependent (78, 80, 82); simulated role (compare lying in language, 26); recruitment (or membership or kin) type versus achievement type (36, 38, 42, 53, 70, 83-84, 91); active versus passive (56); roles from different points of view — role conception (56-57); number of roles in any one society or subgroup, with one subgroup having "never less than three, never more than five" out of a total of 16-33 female roles in the total society of Nuba (61-62); role from the observer versus participant viewpoints — "structure abstracted" versus "structure envisaged" (140); the role system as a "role map of society in his head" (58); role meaning as reflected in verbal cues (33-34); "purpose and utility" as an essential concept in studying social existance (158); roles "filled discontinuously" — compare discontinuous morphemes (132); originating versus responding actions — compare utterance-response of language (111); the multi-systemic nature of social structure "being always in the plural" — versus Meyer Fortes *"within a single system"* — (155); "social reality" within social structure, as related to short-range constancies (149-50, 145-46); the sum of roles leading to "social being" (65-66).

For status in reference to social strata, note Sumner, where folkways "create status" (1940 [1906]:67); Sapir (1934, in his Selected Writings:567, in reference to etiquette); Linton (1936:110), Weber (1947:424-29, for "control or lack of it" "over goods or services", and in reference to "property holdings", "exploitation of services", and "plurality of class statuses"); Kluckhohn (1949:254, with "division of labor" making "class stratification almost inevitable in a complex society"), Murdock and others (1950:80, with castes lacking mobility but classes having it); Warner (in A. Lee, 1951:245-48, 256, with differentiation of different classes in American society); also Warner (1953, with extensive discussion and with annotated bibliography; chart of levels, 58); Freedman and others (1956:232, with "rank status"; with "class crystallization", 234-35; with "urban stratification", 520-61).

Gross, Mason, and McEachern summarize various views of role (1958:11-20). They also explore position, as location of actor relative to system (48, 51, 62) or multiple systems or roles (55, 323); with role as a "set of expectations" (60, 58, 319), as an evaluative standard; with rights, obligations, actual performance (62, 64). Goffman later discusses extensively the concept of role distance in reference to status, performance, audience, system, self-image, commitment, conflict, obligations, expectations (1961:85-152). Moreno discusses "psychosomatic roles" (1962:116) as self emerges from role clusterings (114-15).

Following up tagmemic theory, Bock has treated roles as emic units within one kind of cultural matrix whose dimensions are space and time, with roles in the cells of the matrix (1962:222, and see above, § 17.71). In a different kind of matrix he places roles on the left, attributes of sex and status at the top, with plus, minus, or zero in the cells (189, and compare 207, 212). His role units have conditioned variants (158, 174) with alloroles depending upon student behavior in the classroom, versus their behavior at study time, complementarily distributed and with the behavior conditioned by the social space or by other roles. He also shows free variants for roles (175, with student role to take notes during class time, but freely alternating to not taking notes); and concord (218, between sex and grade variants of classroom space and role). He discusses the "set of shared expectations, or beliefs", as attributes of the role which influence behavior (183-84, 230-32); note that the expectation revolving around the role we would treat as the analog of the meaning of lexical items. Compare, for value attitudes in reference to women's roles, de Vos and Wagatsuma (1961).

For social role as having dual function as a category "of a kind of person" and as a plan "for structured interaction" — which we would see as analogs of feature mode and distribution mode, note Bock (1962:179); for extensive bibliographical analysis of the literature on role, in reference to his emic analysis of role, see Bock (1962:154-83). See also, for role, Rommetveit (1955); also Park (1936); compare also Oliver on roles and dimensions (1958:802-04). For an attempt "to present a formal analysis of status and role" based on "sets of nominal definitions" see Coult (1964:29).

17.74 *On Personality and the Individual*

For a classification of 'Why' questions of children into types of causal explanation motivation, and justification, see Piaget (1955:175-79). Morris, in reference to signs, refers to "where", "what", "why", and "how" signs (1946:72-73). Burke suggests that for investigation one must look at *"act"*, *"scene"*, *"agent"*, *"agency"*, *"purpose"* (1945:xv).

For use of question types in discovering inclusion hierarchies of semantic concepts, note Frake (1961). Franklin, by following their techniques, shows body parts in a semantic hierarchy (1963).

Note also references in §§ 16.824, 16.825, 16.86, for further relations between language and cultural concepts; for historical relation between vocabulary and cultural material note Longacre and Millon (1961).

If one attempts to look at the literature of psychology, as well as that of personality in reference to culture, one finds it very large, and beyond the scope of this study. The linguist finds useful summaries of the literature on personality, as it applies to cultural problems, in Kardiner (in Linton, 1945:107-22), Kluckhohn and Murray (1948), Bidney (1953:327-44), and Hallowell (1955). For early bibliography see also M. Mead (1937:513-17); for later bibliography see also Honigmann (1954). In them one finds attention to personality structure in reference to culture theory on the one hand, as well as to psychoanalysis, learning theory, and projection techniques such as that of the Rorschach ink-blot test. For the latter, see Klineberg (in Linton, 1945:76). The cultural approach studies many problems — for example the degree to which selfawareness is a cultural or social product (Hallowell, 1955:81). In the psychoanalytic approach Freud has developed the analogy "between the practices of primitive people and neurotic symptoms" (Kardiner, in Linton, 1945:109). In learning-theory technique, one studies the results of drives, cues, responses, and rewards (Dollard, in Linton, 1945:442). Through projection techniques one may discover "emotional combinations which are not identifiable in the psychopathological entities common in our society" (Kardiner, in Linton, 1945:117). Honigmann summarizes "the genetic, descriptive, structural and phylogenetic approaches to the field" (1954:48). For cross-cultural limits to Rorschach testing, note Adcock and Ritchie (1958:886-87).

For super-ego as relating language to total social environment, see R. Hall (1951). Insistence on pattern and brain rhythms as related to personality is seen in Walter (1953:69, 197-232). For semantic differential as a test of multiple personality, note Osgood and Luria (1954, in reference to "Eve White" and "Eve Black" and "Jane").

Insistence on the fact that the individual cannot be treated apart from reference to society is found in Sapir (1932, in his Selected Writings:519; 1934, in his Selected Writings:592), Cantril (1950:81), Rohrer and Sherif (1951:1-2), G. Mead (in A. Lee, 1951:87), Henry (1958:827). The concept of social personality is closely related to this point of view; note Murdock and others (1950:8), Radcliffe-Brown (1952:193-94), and Nadel (1957:65-66). A different view, which emphasizes the independence of culture and the individual in certain limited senses, in that there is "such regularity in the composition of societies of men, that we can drop individual differences out of sight, and can thus generalize on the arts and opinions of whole nations" is found in Tylor (1913: vol. 2, p. 11). More recently, see White (1949:xviii, 78-79, 84, 86, 92, 100); for an opposite psycho-cultural view, note Bidney (1953:47-53, 79-83); note, however, White's rebuttal to Bidney's earlier publishing of this view (1949:108-09). Compare Opler (1948:115-16), and Kluckhohn (1949:23).

For roles as "in themselves, meaningless when abstracted from the social situation" but functioning "in part, to contrast 'kinds of persons'" see Bock (1962:181; and see references to Bock on role in § 17.73, and on society structure in § 17.71).

For an attempted summarizing chart of the components of personality, after Kluckhohn and Mowrer, note Herskovitz (1948:57); cultural, social, biological, and physical-environmental components are each correlated with universal, communal, role, idiosyncratic components. For the individual's "psychological prerequisites for the functioning of a culture", see Spiro (1954:26). It is of interest to compare "the three components of personality structure postulated by dynamic personality theory: id, ego, and superego" with our postulated three structural modes of behavioral units. The individual has "needs (id) [cf. our physical, manifestation mode], values (superego) [cf. our distribution mode, and our discussion of the place of belief systems in this mode in § 13.6], and executive-response processes (ego) [cf. our treatment of meaning, purpose, choice and identificational-contrastive elements as components of the feature mode]" (28). He equates the executive-response processes with the ego-processes of "perception, learning, and cognition" (cf. 27). And in addition to the structural components he gives a fourth psychological prerequisite, the "mechanisms of defense" of the self — the "symbolic techniques of projection, displacement, rationalization, sublimation, and so forth" (28, 26).

For the problem of the point of view of observer of events versus participant, see Levy (1952:101). For "value" as "a relation between subject and an object" see

Radcliffe-Brown (1952:139). For contrasting views of the same data seen by different observers of Pueblo culture, note Honigmann (1954:100-05).

Compare discussion of references on world view, and Whorf, in § 16.824; note also Quine (1953:78-79, with problems in discussing reality, requiring the imposition of a conceptual scheme peculiar to one's own special language — but with meaninglessness in inquiring about the absolute correctness of a conceptual scheme); to change one's views, Quine points out, agreeing with Neurath, is like "a mariner who must rebuild his ship on the open sea" (79). For changing of observer viewpoint such that physical South may be culturally North, since one must "imaginatively place himself in the scene of his narrative", see illustration in Haugen (1957:458). Epistemological relations of language to man and to knowledge are discussed by Mackey (in *Preprints...*, 1962:58); relation of observer to phenomena and physics, in Cherry (in *For Roman Jakobson*, 1956). An earlier field view of personality is suggested by Lewin (1935:106-10, with boundaries of self), with topology as the (then) most promising mathematics for field psychology (106-07, 56, with boundaries to or unity of the self; 43-46). Compare also Thurstone (1947, for a special theorem concerning mind vectors).

For possible personality analogs to our grammatical insistence on use of both internal versus external distribution see Postman (in Rohrer and Sherif, 1951:244), after Krech and Crutchfield, with structural versus functional (or stimulus versus directive) factors, with needs and goals versus capacity to respond.

17.75 *On Things*

The philosophical problem of how we recognize 'things', and of the relation of things to ultimate reality, is very difficult. Extensive discussion of things as a selection and grouping in attention is found in Sinclair (1951: for example 149-50; for the arbitrariness of such groupings as seen in the difference between the perception of adults and children, note 175). The relation "of the word to the thing" as "the key problem about which all culture and all knowledge finally rests" is discussed in Urban (1939:23); our meanings and communication ultimately depend "upon the mutual acknowledgement of values" and "upon the mutual acknowledgement of 'things'" (146). The question of how "one comes to learn to categorize in terms of identity categories is ... little understood", though "a variety of stimuli as *forms of the same thing*" is relevant to all our psychological experience (Bruner and others, 1956:2-4); a simple stimulus-response theory is insufficient to account for the "subtle events that may occur between the input of a physical stimulus and the emission of an observable response" (vii).

Some of these events are, in our terms, an emic reaction; for similar problems in reference to the building of the emic concept "table", note Eddington (1928:ix-xii).

The problem of the relative and the absolute becomes difficult in this respect. Planck feels that "The Theory of Relativity, too, is based on something absolute, namely, the determination of the matrix of the space-time continuum; and it is an especially stimulating undertaking to discover the absolute which alone can make meaningful something given as relative" (1949:46-47).

Kant taught that "a body is extended" and that this proposition "holds *a priori*, and [is] not a judgement of experience"; since "before I proceed to experience I already have in the concept of body all the conditions for my judgement" (1954 [1783]:18). Schilder maintains that one's own body image "is acquired ... and gets its structure by a continued contact with the world" (1950:174), and there "is no primary perception of space" in spite of Kant's "erroneous opinion". "Localization is built up by optic and kinaesthetic impressions" (21). Recent approaches to "maturation of innate behavior-patterns", emphasizing psychoneural activity which includes components both of 'instinctive" and of "learned" acts would probably lead to a synthesis of views of Kant and Schilder (cf. Count, 1958:1051, 1053, 1067, 1069; and Kluckhohn and Murray, 1948:38).

For discussion of relation of figure to ground, note Koffka (1935:177-210).

Morris considers that "A *behavior-family* is any set of response-sequences which are initiated by similar stimulus-objects and which terminate in these objects as similar goal-objects for similar needs" (1946:10). Koffka emphasized the perception of things or objects according to principles of continuity, contiguity, closure, unit formation, simplicity of shape, maximum and minimum properties, regularity or symmetry, attitude of the observer, and so on (1935:153, 302, 332, 437; 164, 482; 167, 151, 449; 125; 107, 171; 109-110; 149); these items are in turn perceived in geographical [etic] space, versus phenomenological [emic] space (69-105).

Hebb, on the other hand, shows how certain of the supposed immediate perceptual organizations are in fact developed, as a square cannot be recognized immediately, but the corners have to be counted, by a person born blind, but who later is made to see after surgery (1949:32). In our terms, certain of the perceptions which Koffka considers to be innate are shown by Hebb to be emic. For the treatment of "things" —especially highly automatic systems — as having "a characteristic pattern of behavior", such that a number of the terms of human behavior (e.g., "rules" and "variation") may be applied to them, note Nagel (1952:44-46), Oliver (1958).

In looking at objects, Lundberg feels that the term "value" should be replaced by "valuating *activities*" (in A. Lee, 1951:400); "we say a thing has value or is a value when people behave toward it so as to retain or increase their possession of it". It is essential to find out values of neighbors, by observing their behavior, if we wish to live satisfactorily in any community. In a factory "engineers are conscious that quality of product is the ultimate objective" (G. Brown and Campbell, 1952:62). Non-physical characteristics — characteristics which are not the result of objective valuation nor utilitarian considerations — affect, for example, the emic reaction to kurdaitcha shoes in Australia, since they are "associated exclusively with evil magic"

(Davidson, 1947:116). Wilf Douglas tells me, however, that in the Western Desert of Australia "footprints in the sand (and in many places where we cannot see them) comprise the daily 'newspaper' of the aborigines, for through them they can check on the movements of everybody in camp".

When the function of a particular object or practice is not manifest, a "latent function" such as maintaining prestige — the wearing of buttons on the sleeve, etc. — may serve to assist "individuals to maintain their security by preserving continuity with the past and by making certain sectors of life familiar and predictable" (Kluckhohn, 1949:27-28).

For construction of reality in the child note various works of Piaget. For concept formation in terms of hierarchical structure and ecological environment, note Frake (1962:58, with a difference between scientific taxonomy of elements versus the ethnographic taxonomy) and Conklin (in Householder and Saporta, 1962); and see above, §§ 16.824, 16.825, 16.86. For discussion of philosophy of an older type which says that "the world consists of substances and their attributes", with its replacement by one "which allows a predicate to connect several subjects and in which the whole notion of subject has nothing like its classical importance" note Henle (1958:12).

Tagmemics in its insistence on well-defined units as having reference to particle, wave, and field, refuses to reject the unit with its substance, but tries to establish it. Yet in doing so — in terms of relations by way of field matrix — it allows for emphasis upon connections between elements which are seen, also, in relation to dynamic, wave processes. This multiple perspective is mediated by language. It seems fitting, therefore, to close this volume by quoting Morris (1946:274) who in turn quotes G. H. Mead as arguing "that the perception of objects as enduring is not possible without language".

REFERENCES

A William Cameron Townsend; *en el vigésimoquinto aniversario del Instituto Lingüístico de Verano*
1961. (México, D. F. Instituto Lingüístico de Verano).

AARNE, ANTTI
1928. *The Types of Folk-Tale, a Classification and a Bibliography*. Translated by Stith Thompson. (Helsinki, Suomalainen Tiedeakaternia, Academia Scientiarum Fennica. [Folklore Fellows Communications], No. 184, [1961]).

ABERCROMBIE, DAVID
1949. "Forgotten Phoneticians", *Transactions of the Philological Society, 1948*, pp. 1-34.

ABERLE, DAVID F.
1959. "The Prophet Dance and Reactions to White Contacts", *Southwestern Journal of Anthropology*, 15.74-83.

ABERLE, DAVID F., and AUSTIN, WILLIAM M.
1951. "A Lexical Approach to the Comparison of Two Mongol Social Systems", *Studies in Linguistics*, 9.79-90.

ABERLE, DAVID; BRONFENBRENNER, URIE; HESS, ECKHARD H.; MILLER, DANIEL R.; SCHNEIDER, DAVID M.; SPUHLER, JAMES N.
1963. "The Incest Taboo and the Mating Patterns of Animals", *American Anthropologist*, 65.253-65.

ABERLE, DAVID; COHEN, A. K.; DAVIS, A. K.; LEVY, M. J.; and SUTTON, F. X.
1950. "The Functional Prerequisites of Society", *Ethics*, 60.100-11.

ADAMS, SIDNEY, and POWERS, FRANCIS F.
1929. "The Psychology of Language", *The Psychological Bulletin*, 26.241-60.

ADCOCK, CYRIL J., and RITCHIE, JAMES E.
1958. "Intercultural Use of Rorschach", *American Anthropologist*, 60.881-92.

AKHMANOVA, O. S.; MEL'CHUCK, I. A.; FRUMKINA, R. M., and PADUCHEVA, E. V.
1963. *Exact Methods in Linguistic Research*. Translated from the Russian by David G. Hays and Dolores V. Mohr. (Berkeley and Los Angeles, University of California Press).

ALBRIGHT, ROBERT WILLIAM
1958. *The International Phonetic Alphabet: Its Backgrounds and Development* (Indiana University Research Center in Anthropology, Folklore, and Linguistics, Publication No. 7).

ALLEN, HAROLD B., Ed.
1958. *Readings in Applied English Linguistics* (New York: Appleton-Century-Crofts, Inc. [Revised and Enlarged 1964]).

ALLEN, ROBERT L.
1962. *The Verb System of Present-Day American English* (The Hague, Mouton and Company, 1966)

ALLEN, W. S.
1951a. "The Indo-European Primary Affix*-b[h]-", *Transactions of the Philological Society 1950*, pp. 1-33.

1951b. "Phonetics and Comparative Linguistics", *Archivum Linguisticum*, 3.126-36.
1953a. *Phonetics in Ancient India* (*London Oriental Series, I.* London, Oxford University Press).
1953b. "Relationship in Comparative Linguistics", *Transactions of the Philological Society*, pp. 52-108.
1954. "Retroflexion in Sanskrit: Prosodic Technique and its Relevance to Comparative Statement," *Bulletin of the School of Oriental and African Studies*, 16.556-65.
1956. "Structure and System in the Abaza Verbal Complex", *Transactions of the Philological Society, 1956*, pp. 127-76.

ALLISON, ALEXANDER WARD.
1962. *Toward an Augustan Poetic* (Lexington, University of Kentucky Press).

ANDERSON, JAMES M.
1961. "The Morphophonemics of Gender in Spanish Nouns", *Lingua*, 10.285-96.

ANDRADE, MANUEL J.
1936. "Some Questions of Fact and Policy Concerning Phonemes", *Language*, 12.1-14.

ANDREYEV, N. D.
1962. "Models as a Tool in the Development of Linguistic Theory", *Word*, 18.186-97.

ANTHONY, ANN.
1948. "A Structural Approach to the Analysis of Spanish Intonation", *Language Learning*, 1.324-31.

ANTHONY, EDWARD M.
1954. "An Exploratory Inquiry into Lexical Clusters", *American Speech*, 29.175-80.

AREND, M. Z.
1934. "Baudouin de Courtenay and the Phoneme Idea", *Le Maître Phonétique*, 3rd series, No. 45, pp. 2-3.

ARGYLE, MICHAEL
1957. *The Scientific Study of Social Behaviour* (London, Methuen and Company, Ltd.).

ARISTE, PAUL
1939. "A Quantitative Language", *Proceedings of the Third International Congress of Phonetic Sciences*, pp. 276-80.

Aristotle, The Basic Works of
1941. McKeon, Richard, Ed. (New York, Random House). Also *Aristotle's Treatise on Rhetoric*, 1833 (Thomas Hobbes) (Second Edition. Oxford, D. A. Talboys).

ARMSTRONG, LILIAS E., and TIN, PE MAUNG
1925. *A Burmese Phonetic Reader* (London, University of London Press, Ltd.).

ARNOLD, GORDON F.
1956. "A Phonological Approach to Vowel, Consonant and Syllable in Modern French", *Lingua*, 5.253-87.
1957. "Stress in English Words", *Lingua*, 6.221-67; 397-441.

ASCHMANN, HERMAN P.
1946. "Totonaco Phonemes", *International Journal of American Linguistics*, 12.34-43.

ASCHMANN, HERMAN P., and WONDERLY, WILLIAM L.
1952. "Affixes and Implicit Categories in Totonac Verb Inflection", *International Journal of American Linguistics*, 18.130-45.

ATWOOD, E. BAGBY
1953. *A Survey of Verb Forms in the Eastern United States* (Ann Arbor, University of Michigan Press).

AUSTERLITZ, ROBERT
1959. "Semantic Components of Pronoun Systems: Gilyak", *Word*, 15.102-09.

AUSTIN, WILLIAM M.
1957. "Criteria for Phonetic Similarity", *Language*, 33.538-44.

Automatic Speech Recognition: An Intensive Course for Engineers and Scientists, Vol. II, Summer 1963 (Ann Arbor, The University of Michigan Engineering Summer Conferences).

REFERENCES

AYRES, EUGENE
1952. "An Automatic Chemical Plant", *Scientific American*, 187.3.82-96.

BACH, EMMON
1962. "The Order of Elements in a Transformational Grammar of German", *Language*, 38.263-69.
1964. *An Introduction to Transformational Grammars* (New York, Holt, Rinehart and Winston).

BAR-HILLEL, YEHOSHUA
1953a. "A Quasi-Arithmetical Notation for Syntactic Description", *Language*, 29.47-58.
1953b. "On Recursive Definitions in Empirical Sciences," *Proceedings of the XIth International Congress of Philosophy*, 5.160-65.
1954. "Logical Syntax and Semantics", *Language*, 30.230-37.
1957. "Three Methodological Remarks on 'Fundamentals of Language' [Jakobson-Halle]", *Word*, 13.323-35.
1959. "Review of R. M. Martin, *Truth and denotation*: A Study in Semantical Theory", *Language*, 35.311-14.

BAR-HILLEL, YEHOSHUA; GAIFMAN, C.; and SHAMIR, E.
1960. "On Categorial and Phrase-Structure Grammars", *The Bulletin of the Research Council of Israel*, 9F.1.1-16.

BAR-HILLEL, Y.; PERLES, M.; and SHAMIR, E.
1960. *On Formal Properties of Simple Phrase Structure Grammars*. (Technical Report No. 4, U.S. Office of Naval Research, Information Systems Branch, Jerusalem, Israel, 8 July, 1960).

BAR-HILLEL, Y. and SHAMIR, E.
1960. "Finite-State Languages: Formal Representations and Adequacy Problems", *The Bulletin of the Research Council of Israel*, 8F.3.155-66.

BARKER, ROGER G., and WRIGHT, HERBERT F.
1955. *Midwest and Its Children: The Psychological Ecology of an American Town* (Evanston: Row, Peterson and Company [Date supplied by publisher]).

BARRETT, SOLOMON, JR.
1860. *The Principles of Grammar: being a compendius Treatise on the languages English, Latin, Greek, German, Spanish and French. Founded on the Immutable Principle of the Relation which One Word Sustains to Another.* Revised edition (Boston, Geo. C. Rand and Avery).

BASCOM, BURT.
1959. "Tonomechanics of Northern Tepehuan", *Phonetica*, 4.71-88.

BAZELL, C. E.
1948a. "On Morpheme and Paradigm", *Edebiyat Fakültesi Ingilizce Şubesi Dergisi*, pp. 1-21.
1948b. "On Some Definitions in Structural Linguistics", *Garp Filolojileri Dergisi* (Istanbul Üniversitesi Edebiyat Fakültesi Yayinlari) pp. 279-87.
1949a. "On the Problem of the Morpheme", *Archivum Linguisticum*, 1.1-15.
1949b. "On The Neutralization of Syntactic Oppositions", *Travaux du Cercle Linguistique de Copenhague*, 5.77-86.
1951. "Glossematic Definitions", Reprint, pp. 107-17.
1952. "Phonemic and Morphemic Analysis", *Word*, 8.33-38.
1953. *Linguistic Form* (Istanbul Üniversitesi, Edebiyat Fakültesi, Yayinlarindan, No. 574. Istanbul, Istanbul Press).
1962. "Meaning and the Morpheme", *Word*, 18.132-42.

BEALS, RALPH L., and HOIJER, HARRY
1953. *An Introduction to Anthropology* (New York, MacMillan and Company).

BEARDSLEY, RICHARD K.
1953. "Hypotheses on Inner Asian Pastoral Nomadism and Its Culture Area", *American Antiquity*, 18.3.II.24-28.

BELASCO, SIMON
1959. "The Psychoacoustic Interpretation of Vowel Color Preferences in French Rime", *Phonetica*, 3.167-82.
1961. "The Role of Transformational Grammar and Tagmemics in the Analysis of an Old French Text", *Lingua*, 10.375-90.

BENDOR-SAMUEL, JOHN T.
1960. "Some Problems of Segmentation in the Phonological Analysis of Tereno", *Word*, 16.348-55.
1961 [1958]. *The Verbal Piece in Jebero. Word, Monograph* No. 4.

BENEDICT, RUTH
1946 [1934]. *Patterns of Culture* (Penguin edition. New York).

BENTLEY, MADISON and VARON, EDITH J.
1933. "An Accessory Study of 'Phonetic Symbolism'", *The American Journal of Psychology*, 45.76-86.

BERGER, MARSHALL D.
1949. "Neutralization in American English Vowels", *Word*, 5.255-57.

BIDNEY, DAVID
1953. *Theoretical Anthropology* (New York: Columbia University Press).

BIRDWHISTELL, RAY L.
1952. *Introduction to Kinesics; an Annotation System for Analysis of Body Motion and Gesture* (Washington, D.C., Foreign Service Institute).
1959. "Review of Francis Hayes, *Gestures*", *Studies in Linguistics*, 14.41.

BLAKE, FRANK R.
1931. "Review of L. Hjelmslev, *Principes de Grammaire Générale*", *Language* 7.49-54.

BLALOCK, H. M., JR.
1960. "Correlational Analysis and Causal Inferences", *American Anthropologist*, 62.624-31.

BLOCH, BERNARD
1935. "Broad Transcription of General American", *Le Maître Phonetique*, Third Series, No. 49, pp. 7-10.
1941. "Phonemic Overlapping", *American Speech*, 16.278-84.
1946a. "Studies in Colloquial Japanese, I: Inflection", *Journal of the American Oriental Society*, 66.97-109.
1946b. "Studies in Colloquial Japanese II: Syntax", *Language*, 22.200-48.
1947a. "Syntactic Formulas for Japanese", *Studies in Linguistics*, 5.1-12.
1947b. "English Verb Inflection", *Language*, 23.399-418.
1948. "A Set of Postulates for Phonemic Analysis", *Language*, 24.3-46.
1950. "Studies in Colloquial Japanese IV: Phonemics", *Language*, 26.86-125.
1953. "Contrast", *Language*, 29.59-62.

BLOCH, BERNARD, and TRAGER, GEORGE L.
1942. *Outline of Linguistic Analysis*. (Baltimore, Special Publications of the Linguistic Society of America, at the Waverly Press, Inc.).

BLOOD, DAVID L.
1962. "A Problem in Cham Sonorants", *Zeitschrift für Phonetik, Sprachwissenschaft und Kommunikationsforschung*, 15.111-14.

BLOOD, DORIS
1962(?). "Women's Speech Characteristics in Cham", *Asian Culture*, 3.3-4.139-43 (reprint, n.d.).

BLOOMFIELD, LEONARD
1917. *Tagalog Texts with Grammatical Analysis. University of Illinois Studies in Language and Literature*, *3*. Nos. 2-4.
1924. "Review of Ferdinand de Saussure, *Cours de Linguistique Générale*", *Modern Language Journal*, 8.317-19.
1926. "A Set of Postulates for the Science of Language", *Language*, 2.153-64; reprinted in *International Journal of American Linguistics*, 15.195-202 (1949).

1927. "American English", *Le Maître Phonétique*, 3rd series, No. 42, pp. 40-42.
1930a. "German ç and x", *Le Maître Phonétique*, 3rd series, No. 29, pp. 27-28.
1930b. "Linguistics as a Science", *Studies in Philology*, 27.553-57.
1931. "Review of John Ries, *Was ist ein Satz?*", *Language*, 7.204-09.
1932. "Review of Edward Hermann, *Lautgesetz und Analogie*", *Language*, 8.220-33.
1933a. *Language*. New York, Henry Holt and Co.
1933b. "The Structure of Learned Words", (in A Commemorative Volume issued by the Institute for Research in English Teaching, Tokyo), pp. 17-23. [Not seen].
1935. "The Stressed Vowels of American English", *Language*, 11.97-116.
1942. *Outline Guide for the Practical Study of Foreign Languages* (Baltimore. Special Publications of the Linguistic Society of America, at the Waverly Press, Inc.).
1943. "Meaning", *Monatshefte für Deutschen Unterricht*, 35.101-06.
1945. "On Describing Inflection", *Monatshefte für Deutschen Unterricht*, 37.4-5.8-13.

BOCK, PHILIP K.
1962. *The Social Structure of a Canadian Indian Reserve*. Harvard University, Ph. D. thesis.

BOLINGER, DWIGHT L.
1946. "Visual Morphemes", *Language*, 22.333-40.
1947. "Comments on Pike's *American English Intonation*", *Studies in Linguistics*, 5.69-78.
1948. "On Defining the Morpheme", *Word*, 4.18-23.
1950. "Rime, Assonance, and Morpheme Analysis", *Word*, 6.117-36.
1951. "Intonation: Levels versus Configurations", *Word*, 7.199-210.
1954. "Identity, Similarity, and Difference", *Litera*, 1.5-16.
1955a. "Intersections of Stress and Intonation", *Word*, 11.195-203.
1955b. "The Melody of Language", *Modern Language Forum*, 50.19-30.
1957. *Interrogative Structures of American English* (Publication of the American Dialect Society, No. 28, University of Alabama Press).
1958. "A Theory of Pitch Accent in English", *Word*, 14.109-49.
1960. "Linguistic Science and Linguistic Engineering", *Word*, 16.374-91.
1961a. "Contrastive Accent and Contrastive Stress", *Language*, 37.83-96.
1961b. "Syntactic Blends and Other Matters", *Language*, 37.366-81.
1961c. "Verbal Evocation", *Lingua*, 10.113-27.
1961d. *Generality, Gradience, and the All-or-None*. ('s-Gravenhage, Mouton and Co.).
1961e. "Review of Kenneth Croft, *A Practice Book on English Stress and Intonation*", *Language Learning*, 11.189-95.

BOLINGER, DWIGHT L., and GERSTMAN, LOUIS J.
1957. "Disjuncture as a Cue to Constructs", *Word*, 13.246-55.

BORGMAN, DONALD M., and CUE, SANDRA L.
1963. "Sentence and Clause Types in Central Waica (Shiriana)", *International Journal of American Linguistics*, 29.222-29.

BOULDING, KENNETH E.
1957. "A Look at the Corporation", *The Lamp* (Standard Oil Co. [of New Jersey], New York), pp. 6-7.
1958. *The Skills of the Economist* (Cleveland, Howard Allen, Inc.).

BOYD, JULIAN C. and KING, HAROLD V.
1962. "Annotated Bibliography of Generative Grammar", *Language Learning*, 12.307-12.

BRAIN, W. RUSSELL
1950. "The Concept of the Schema in Neurology and Psychiatry", *Perspectives in Neuropsychiatry*, Derek Richter, Ed. (London, H. K. Lewis and Co., Ltd., pp. 127-39).

BRAINE, MARTIN D. S.
1963. "The Ontogeny of English Phrase Structure: The First Phase", *Language*, 39.1-13.

BRAITHWAITE, RICHARD B.
1953. *Scientific Explanation: A Study of the Function of Theory, Probability and Law in Science* (Cambridge, Cambridge University Press).

BRAZIER, MARY A. B.
1950. "Neural Nets and the Integration of Behaviour", *Perspectives in Neuropsychiatry*, Derek Richter, Ed. (London, H. K. Lewis and Co., Ltd.), pp. 35-45.

BREND, RUTH M.
1964. *A Tagmemic Analysis of Mexican Spanish Clauses*, University of Michigan, PhD Dissertation.

BRIGHT, WILLIAM
1952. "Linguistic Innovations in Karok", *International Journal of American Linguistics*, 18.53-62.
1957. "Singing in Lushai", *Indian Linguistics*, 17.24-28.

BROADBENT, DONALD E., and LADEFOGED, PETER
1959. "Auditory Perception of Temporal Order", *The Journal of the Acoustical Society of America*, 31.1539.
1960. "Vowel Judgements and Adaptation Level", *Proceedings of the Royal Society*, B, 151, 384-99.

BRØNDAL, V.
1936. "Sound and Phoneme", *Proceedings of the Second International Congress of Phonetic Sciences*, pp. 40-45.

BROWER, REUBEN A., ED.
1959. *On Translation* (Cambridge, Mass., Harvard University Press).

BROWN, GORDON S., and CAMPBELL, DONALD P.
1952. "Control Systems", *Scientific American*, 187.3.57-64.

BROWN, JAMES
1956. "Eight Types of Puns", *Publications of the Modern Language Association of America*, 71.14-26.

BROWN, ROGER W.
1957a. "Review of G. Herdan, *Language as Choice and Chance*", *Language*, 33.170-81.
1957b. "Linguistic Determinism and the Part of Speech", *Journal of Abnormal and Social Psychology*, 55.1-5. (also reprinted in Saporta, 1961).
1958. *Words and Things* (Glencoe, Ill., The Free Press).

BROWN, ROGER W., BLACK, ABRAHAM H., and HOROWITZ, ARNOLD E.
1955. "Phonetic Symbolism in Natural Languages", *Journal of Abnormal and Social Psychology*, 50.388-93.

BROWN, R. W., LEITER, R. A., and HILDUM, D. C.
1957. "Metaphors from Music Criticism", *Journal of Abnormal and Social Psychology*, 54.347-52.

BROWN, R. W., and LENNEBERG, ERIC H.
1954. "A Study in Language and Cognition", *Journal of Abnormal Social Psychology*, 49.454-62.

BRUNER, JEROME S.
1951. "One Kind of Perception: a Reply to Professor Luchins", *Psychological Review*, 58.306-12.

BRUNER, JEROME S., GOODNOW, JACQUELINE J., and AUSTIN, GEORGE A.
1956. *A Study of Thinking* (New York, John Wiley and Company).

BUETTNER-JANUSCH, JOHN
1957. "Boas and Mason: Particularism versus Generalization", *American Anthropologist*, 59.318-24.

BULL, WILLIAM E.
1949. "Natural Frequency and Word Counts", *The Classical Journal*, 44.8.469-84.
1950. "*quedar* and *quedarse*: A Study of Contrastive Ranges", *Language*, 26.467-80.

BULL, WILLIAM E., and FORLEY, RODGER
1949. "An Exploratory Study of the Nature of Actions and the Functions of Verbs in Spanish", *Hispania*, 32.64-73.

BUNING, J. E. JURGENS, and VAN SCHOONEVELD, C. H.
1960. *The Sentence Intonation of Contemporary Standard Russian as a Linguistic Structure* ('s-Gravenhage, Mouton and Company).

BURKE, KENNETH
1945. *A Grammar of Motives* (New York, Prentice-Hall, Inc.).

BURLING, ROBBINS
1964. "Cognition and Componential Analysis: God's Truth or Hocus-Pocus?", *American Anthropologist*, 66.20-28.

BURSILL-HALL, G. L.
1960. "Levels Analysis: J. R. Firth's Theories of Linguistic Analysis, I", *The Journal of the Canadian Linguistic Association*, 6.124-35.
1961. "Levels Analysis: J. R. Firth's Theories of Linguistic Analysis, II", *The Journal of the Canadian Linguistic Association*, 6.164-91.

BURTON-PAGE, J.
1955. "Two Studies in Gurungkura: I. Tone; II. Rhotacization and Retroflexion", *Bulletin of the School of Oriental and African Studies*, 17.111-19.

BUYSSENS, ERIC
1943. *Les Languages et le Discours* (Bruxelles, Office de Publicité).
1961. "Origine de la Linguistique Synchronique de Saussure", *Cahiers Ferdinand de Saussure*, 18.17-33.

CANONGE, ELLIOTT D.
1957. "Voiceless Vowels in Comanche", *International Journal of American Linguistics*, 23.63-67.

CANTINEAU, JEAN
1951(?). "Les Oppositions Signifatives", (reprint from *Cahiers F. de Saussure*), pp. 1-30.

CANTRIL, HADLEY
1950. "Psychology", *Scientific American*, 183.3. 79-84.

CAPELL, ARTHUR
1933. "The Structure of the Oceanic Languages", *Oceania*, 3.418-34.
1940. "Language Study for New Guinea Students", *Oceania*, 11.40-74.
1945. "Methods and Materials for Recording Australian Languages", *Oceania*, 16.144-76.
1962. "Oceanic Linguistics Today", *Current Anthropology*, 3.371-428.

CARNAP, RUDOLF
1939. *Foundations of Logic and Mathematics*, International Encyclopedia of Unified Science, 1.3. (Some quotations are from the combined edition, 1955).

CARNOCHAN, J.
1948. "A Study in the Phonology of an Igbo Speaker", *Bulletin of the School of Oriental and African Studies*, 12.417-26.
1950. "A Study of Quantity in Hausa", *Bulletin of the School of Oriental and African Studies*, 13.1032-44.
1953. "Glottalization in Hausa", *Transactions of the Philological Society, 1952*, pp. 78-109.
1962. "Pitch, Tone and Intonation in Igbo", *Proceedings of the Fourth International Congress of Phonetic Sciences*, 547-54.

CARROLL, JOHN B.
1944. "The Analysis of Verbal Behavior", *Psychological Review*, 51.102-19.
1953. *The Study of Language: A Survey of Linguistics and Related Disciplines in America* (Cambridge, Harvard University Press).
1959a. "An Operational Model for Language Behavior", *Anthropological Linguistics*, 1.1.37-54.
1959b. "Review of Charles E. Osgood, George J. Suci and Percy H. Tannenbaum, *The Measurement of Meaning*", *Language*, 35.58-77.
1963. "Linguistic Relativity, Contrastive Linguistics, and Language Learning", *International Review of Applied Linguistics in Language Teaching*, 1.1-20.

CASSIRER, ERNST
1946. *Language and Myth* (New York, Harper and Brothers).
1953. *The Philosophy of Symbolic Forms, Vol. I: Language* (New Haven, Yale University Press).

CHAFE, WALLACE L.
1961. "Seneca Morphology VII: Irregularities and Variants", *International Journal of American Linguistics*, 27.223-25.

CHANDOLA, ANOOP CHANDRA
1963. "Animal Commands of Garhwali and their Linguistic Implications", *Word*, 19.203-07.

CHANG, KUN
1953. "On the Tone System of the Miao-Yao Languages", *Language*, 29.374-78.

CHAO, YÜEN REN
1934. "The Non-Uniqueness of Phonemic Solutions of Phonetic Systems", Academia Sinica: *Bulletin of the Institute of History and Philology*, 4.363-97. Reprinted in Joos, 1957, pp. 38-54).
1948. *Mandarin Primer* (Cambridge, Harvard University Press).
1959. "How Chinese Logic Operates", *Anthropological Linguistics*, 1.1.1-8.

CHERRY, E. COLIN, HALLE, MORRIS, and JAKOBSON, ROMAN
1953. "Toward the Logical Description of Languages in their Phonemic Aspect", *Language*, 29.34-46.

CHILD, C. M., KOFFKA, KURT, and others
1927. *The Unconscious: a Symposium*, E. S. Dummer, Ed. (New York, Alfred A. Knopf).

CHOMSKY, NOAM
1955. "Semantic Considerations in Grammar", *Report of the Sixth Annual Round Table Meeting on Linguistics and Language Teaching* (Washington, D.C., Georgetown University Press), pp. 141-58.
1957a. *Syntactic Structures* ('s-Gravenhage, Mouton and Company).
1957b. "Review of Charles F. Hockett, *A Manual of Phonology*", *International Journal of American Linguistics*, 23.223-34.
1959a. "Review of B. F. Skinner, *Verbal Behavior*", *Language*, 35.26-58.
1959b. "On Certain Formal Properties of Grammars", *Information and Control*, 2.137-67.
1959c. "Review of J. H. Greenberg, *Essays in Linguistics*", *Word*, 15.202-18.
1961a. "On the Notion 'Rule of Grammar'", *Structure of Language and its Mathematical Aspects*, pp. 6-24.
1961b. "Some Methodological Remarks on Generative Grammar", *Word*, 17.219-39.
1962. "The Logical Basis of Linguistic Theory", *Preprints of the Ninth International Congress of Linguists*, pp. 509-74.
1963. "Formal Properties of Grammars", *Handbook of Mathematical Psychology* (Luce, Bush, Galanter, Eds.), vol. II, 323-418.

CHOMSKY, NOAM, HALLE, MORRIS, and LUKOFF, FRED.
1956. "On Accent and Juncture in English", *For Roman Jakobson*, pp. 65-80.

CLARK, LAWRENCE E.
1959. "Phoneme Classes in Sayula Popoluca", *Studies in Linguistics*, 14.25-33.
1962. "Sayula Popoluca Morpho-Syntax", *International Journal of American Linguistics*, 28.183-98.

CLASSE, ANDRÉ
1957. "The Whistled Language of La Gomera", *Scientific American*, 196.4.111-20.

COCHRANE, G. R.
1959. "The Australian English Vowels as a Diasystem", *Word*, 15.69-88.

COLE, DESMOND T.
1955. *An Introduction to Tswana Grammar* (London, Longmans, Green and Co.).

COLE-BEUCHAT, P.-D.
1959. "Tonomorphology of the Tsonga Noun", *African Studies*, 18.133-45.

COLLINDER, BJÖRN
1962. "Les Origines du Structuralisme", *Acta Societatis Linguisticae Upsaliensis*, 1.1.1-15.

COLLINGE, N. E.
1962. "Phonetic Shifts and Phonemic Asymmetries", *Proceedings of the Fourth International Congress of Phonetic Sciences*, 563-66.

COLLIER, JOHN
1957. "Photography in Anthropology: a Report on Two Experiments", *American Anthropologist*, 59.843-59.

CONKLIN, HAROLD C.
1955. "Hanunoo Color Categories", *Southwestern Journal of Anthropology*, 11.339-44.

COOPER, FRANKLIN S., DELATTRE, PIERRE C., LIBERMAN, ALVIN M., BORST, JOHN M., and GERSTMAN LOUIS J.
1952. "Some Experiments on the Perception of Synthetic Speech Sounds", *The Journal of the Acoustical Society of America*, 24.597-606.

COOPER, FRANKLIN S., LIBERMAN, ALVIN M., HARRIS, KATHERINE S., and GRUBB, PATTI MURRAY
1958. "Some Input-Output Relations Observed in Experiments on the Perception of Speech", *Second International Congress on Cybernetics*, 930-41.

COOPER, FRANKLIN S., LIBERMAN, ALVIN M., LISKER, LEIGH, GAITENBY, JANE H.
1962. "Speech Synthesis by Rules", (paper presented at the Speech Communication Seminar, Speech Transmission Laboratory, Royal Institute of Technology, Stockholm, Sept., 1962 — to appear in proceedings of that seminar).

COPELAND, JOHN W.
1963. "Culture and Man: Leslie A. White's Thesis Re-examined", *Southwestern Journal of Anthropology*, 19.109-20.

COULT, ALLAN D.
1964. "Role Allocation, Position Structuring, and Ambilineal Descent", *American Anthropologist*, 66.29-40.

COUNT, EARL W.
1958. "The Biological Basis of Human Sociality", *American Anthropologist*, 60.1049-85.

COWAN, GEORGE M.
1948. "Mazateco Whistle Speech", *Language*, 24.280-86.
1952. "El Idioma Silbado entre los Mazatecos de Oaxaca y los Tepehuas de Hidalgo, Mexico", *Tlatoañi*, 1.3-4.31-33.
1963. *Some Aspects of the Lexical Structure of a Mazatec Historical Text* (University of North Dakota, M. A. Thesis).

COWAN, J. MILTON
1962. "Graphical Representation of Perceived Pitch in Speech", *Proceedings of the Fourth International Congress of Phonetic Sciences*, 567-70.

COWAN, J. MILTON, and BLOCH, BERNARD
1948. "An Experimental Study of Pause in English Grammar", *American Speech*, 23.89-99.

COWAN, MARION and DAVIS, M.
1955. *Hymn Writing in Aboriginal Languages* (Santa Ana, Summer Institute of Linguistics).

COX, DORIS
1957. "Candoshi Verb Inflection", *International Journal of American Linguistics*, 23.129-40.

CRAWFORD, JOHN
1963. *Totontepec Mixe Phonotagmemics* (Linguistic Series of the Summer Institute of Linguistics of the University of Oklahoma, No. 8).

Cybernetics, Transactions of the Seventh Conference, 1950. 1951. Ed. Heinz Von Forster (New York, Josiah Macy Jr. Foundation).

DALGARNO, GEORGE
1834. [1661, 1680] *The Works of George Dalgarno of Aberdeen*. Reprinted at Edinburgh.

DANEŠ, FRANTIŠEK
1957. "Sentence-Intonation in Present-Day Standard Czech", *Intonace a věta ve spisovné češtině* (Praha, Nakladetelství ČSAV), pp. 1-8.
1960. "Sentence Intonation from a Functional Point of View", *Word*, 16.34-54.

DAVIDSON, D. S.
1947. "Footwear of the Australian Aborigines: Environmental vs. Cultural Determination", *Southwestern Journal of Anthropology*, 3.114-23.

DE GROOT, A. W.
1948. "Structural Linguistics and Word Classes", *Lingua*, 1.427-500.

DELATTRE, PIERRE
1959. "The Physiological Interpretation of Sound Spectrograms", *Publications of the Modern Language Association of America,* 66.864-75.

DERBYSHIRE, DESMOND
1961a. "Hishkaryana (Carib) Syntax Structure I: Word", *International Journal of American Linguistics*, 27.125-42.
1961b. "Hishkaryana (Carib) Syntax Structure: II", *International Journal of American Linguistics*, 27.226-36.

DE SAUSSURE, F.
1931 [1915]. *Cours de Linguistique Générale*, Third edition, (Paris, Payot).
1959. *Course in General Linguistics.* Translated by Wade Baskin. (New York, Philosophical Library).

DE SOLA POOL, ITHIEL, ED.
1959. *Trends in Content Analysis.* (Urbana, University of Illinois Press).
Developing Hymnology in New Churches
1962. *Practical Anthropology*, 9.6 [special issue].

DE VOS, GEORGE, and WAGATSUMA, HIROSHI
1961. "Value Attitudes toward Role Behavior of Women in Two Japanese Villages", *American Anthropologist*, 63.1204-30.

DIEBOLD, A. RICHARD JR.
1961. "Incipient Bilingualism", *Language*, 37.97-112.

DIVER, WILLIAM
1963. "The Chronological System of the English Verb", *Word*, 19.141-81.

DIXON, ROBERT M. W.
1963. *Linguistic Science and Logic.* (The Hague, Mouton and Company).

DOLE, GERTRUDE E. and CARNEIRO, ROBERT L. (Eds.)
1960. *Essays in the Science of Culture in Honor of Leslie A. White* (New York, Crowell).

DOOB, LEONARD W.
1957. "The Effect of Language on Verbal Expression and Recall", *American Anthropologist*, 59.88-100.
1959. "Respiratory Muscles in Speech", *Journal of Speech and Hearing Research*, 2.16-27.

DRAPER, M. H., LADEFOGED, P., and WHITTERIDGE, D.
1960. "Expiratory Pressures and Air Flow During Speech", *British Medical Journal*, Part i, (June 18, 1960), pp. 1837-1843.

DUNDES, ALAN
1962a. "Review of Ithiel de Sola Pool, *Trends in Content Analysis*", *Midwest Folklore*, 12.31-38.
1962b. "From Etic to Emic Units in the Structural Study of Folktales", *Journal of American Folklore*, 75.95-105.
1963. "Structural Typology in North American Folktales", *Southwestern Journal of Anthropology*, 19. 121-30.

EBELING, C. L.
1962. "A Semantic Analysis of the Dutch Tenses", *Lingua*, 11.86-99.

EDDINGTON, ARTHUR S.
1928. *The Nature of the Physical World* (Cambridge, University Press).

EDGERTON, FAYE E.
1963. "The Tagmemic Analysis of Sentence Structure in Western Apache", *Studies in the Athapaskan Languages* (by Harry Hoijer and others). (Berkeley, University of California Press, pp. 102-48.

EGE, NIELS
1949. "Le Signe Linguistique est Arbitraire", *Travaux du Cercle Linguistique de Copenhague*, 5.11-29.

EGGAN, FRED
1950. *Social Organization of the Western Pueblos* (Chicago, The University of Chicago Press).

EISENSTADT, S. N.
1956. *From Generation to Generation* (Glencoe, Ill., The Free Press).

EINSTEIN, ALBERT, and INFELD, LEOPOLD
1938. *The Evolution of Physics: The Growth of Ideas from Early Concepts to Relativity and Quanta* (New York, Simon and Schuster Co.).

ELIASON, NORMAN E.
1942. "On Syllable Division in Phonemics", *Language*, 18.144-47.

ELLIS, ALEXANDER J.
1869–1889. *On Early English Pronunciation, with especial reference to Shakespeare and Chaucer* (London, Trübner & Co.).

ELLIS, C. D.
1960. "Tagmemic Analysis of a Restricted Cree Text", *Journal of the Canadian Linguistic Association*, 6.35-59.

ELSON, BENJAMIN
1958. *Beginning Morphology-Syntax*. (Glendale [now Santa Ana], Calif., Summer Institute of Linguistics).
1960a. "Sierra Populuca Morphology", *International Journal of American Linguistics*, 26.206-23.
1960b. *Gramática del Populuca de la Sierra* (Xalapa, Vera Cruz, México, Universidad Veracruzana).

ELSON, BENJAMIN, and PICKETT, VELMA
1962. *An Introduction to Morphology and Syntax* (Santa Ana, Calif., Summer Institute of Linguistics).

EMENEAU, M. B.
1950. "Language and Non-Linguistic Patterns", *Language*, 26.199-209.

EMMONS, PATRICIA SOMMERLAD
1962. "Junior Linguistics", *Language Learning*, 12.129-32.

ENGEL, RALPH and LONGACRE, ROBERT E.
1963. "Syntactic Matrices in Ostuacan Zoque", *International Journal of American Linguistics*, 29.331-44.

EPSTEIN, EDMUND L. and HAWKES, TERENCE
1959. *Linguistics and English Prosody* (Studies in Linguistics, Occasional Papers, No. 7).

ERVIN, SUSAN
1962. "Articles on Psycholinguistics (Reviews)", *International Journal of American Linguistics*, 28.205-09.

EVANS-PRITCHARD, E. E. et al.
1954. *The Institutions of Primitive Society* (Glencoe, Ill., The Free Press).

FANT, GUNNAR
1960. *Acoustic Theory of Speech Production*. ('s-Gravenhage, Mouton and Co.).

FANT, GUNNAR and SONESSON, B.
1963. "Indirect Studies of Glottal Cycles by Synchronous Inverse Filtering and Photo-Electrical Glottography", *Quarterly Progress and Status Report* (Speech Transmission Laboratory, Division of Telegraphy-Telephony, Royal Institute of Technology, Stockholm, Sweden, Jan. 15, 1963, pp. 1-3).

FAURE, GEORGES
1962. *Recherches sur les Caractères et le Rôle des Eléments Musicaux dans la Pronunciation Anglaise* (Paris, Didier).

FEIGL, HERBERT, and BRODBECK, MAY
1953. *Readings in the Philosophy of Science* (New York, Appleton-Century-Crofts, Inc.).

FEIGL, HERBERT, and SCRIVEN, MICHAEL, Eds.
1956. *The Foundations of Science and the Concepts of Psychology and Psychoanalysis. Minnesota Studies in the Philosophy of Science*, Vol. I (Minneapolis, University of Minnesota Press).

FEIGL, HERBERT, and SELLARS, WILFRED, Eds.
1949. *Readings in Philosophical Analysis* (New York, Appleton-Century-Crofts, Inc.).

FERGUSON, CHARLES A.
1959. "Diglossia", *Word*, 15.325-40.
1962. "Review of Morris Halle, *The Sound Pattern of Russian*", *Language*, 38.284-98.

FILLMORE, CHARLES J.
1962. *Indirect Object Constructions in English and the Ordering of Transformations* (The Ohio State University Research Foundation Report to National Science Foundation, Report No. 1).
1963. "The Position of Embedding Transformations in a Grammar", *Word*, 19.208-31.
First Texas Conference on Problems of Linguistic Analysis in English, April 27-30, 1956
1962. (Austin, Texas, The University of Texas).

FIRTH, J. R.
1934. "The Word Phoneme", *Le Maître Phonétique*, 3rd series, No. 46, pp. 44-46.
1935a. "The Technique of Semantics", *Transactions of the Philological Society, 1935*, pp. 36-72.
1935b. "The Use and Distribution of Certain English Sounds: Phonetics from a Functional Point of View", *English Studies*, 17.12.8-18.
1936. "Alphabets and Phonology in India and Burma", *Bulletin of the School of Oriental and African Studies*, 8.517-46.
1937. *The Tongues of Men* (London: Watts and Co.).
1947. "The English School of Phonetics", *Transactions of the Philological Society, 1946*, pp. 92-132.
1949. "Sounds and Prosodies", *Transactions of the Philological Society, 1948*, pp. 127-52.
1950. "Personality and Language in Society", *The Sociological Review*, 42.37-52.
1951a. "General Linguistics and Descriptive Grammar", *Transactions of the Philological Society, 1951*, pp. 69-87.
1951b. "Modes of Meaning", *Essays and Studies*, pp. 118-49.
1952. Report. *Preliminary Reports of the Seventh Linguistic Congress, London, 1952*, pp. 5-9.
1956. "Structural Linguistics", *Transactions of the Philological Society, 1955*, pp. 83-103.
1957. *Papers in Linguistics* (London, Oxford University Press).
1958. "Applications of General Linguistics", *Transactions of the Philological Society, 1957*, pp. 1-14.

FIRTH, J. R. and ROGERS, B. B.
1937. "The Structure of the Chinese Monosyllable in a Hunanese Dialect (Changsha)", *Bulletin of the School of Oriental and African Studies*, 8.1055-74.

FIRTH, RAYMOND
1951. "Contemporary British Social Anthropology", *American Anthropologist*, 53.474-89.

FISCHER-JØRGENSEN, ELI.
1941. "Phonologie, Bericht über Arbeiten in Germanischer und Romanischer Sprache", *Archiv für Vergleichende Phonetik*, 5.170-200.
1949. "Review of Kenneth L. Pike, *Phonemics*", *Acta Linguistica*, 5.104-09.
1952. "On the Definition of Phoneme Categories on a Distributional Basis", *Acta Linguistica*, 7.8-39.

FLEW, ANTHONY, Ed.
1953 [1951]. *Logic and Language*, Second Series. (Oxford, Basil Blackwell).

FLYDAL, LEIV
1952. "Remarques sur Certain Rapports entre le Style et l'État de Langue", *Norsk Tidsskrift for Sprogvidenskap*, 16.241-58.

FODOR, JERRY A.
1963. "Review of László Antal, *Questions of Meaning*", *Language*, 39.468-73.

FÓNAGY, IVÁN
1961. "Communication in Poetry", *Word*, 17.194-218.
For Roman Jakobson

1956. Compiled by Morris Halle, Horace G. Lunt, Hugh McLean, Cornelius H. Van Schooneveld. (The Hague, Mouton and Company).

FORSTER, JANETTE
1964. "Dual Structure of Dibabawon Verbal Clauses", *Oceanic Linguistics*.

FORTES, MEYER
1949. *Social Structure: Studies Presented to A. R. Radcliffe-Brown* (Oxford: The Clarendon Press).

FORTES, MEYER, and EVANS-PRITCHARD, E. E.
1940. *African Political Systems* (London, Oxford University Press).

FOWLER, MURRAY
1952. "Review of Zellig S. Harris, *Methods in Structural Linguistics*", *Language*, 28.504-09.
1954. "The Segmental Phonemes of Sanskritized Tamil", *Language*, 30.360-67.
1963. "Review of Zellig S. Harris, *String Analysis of Sentence Structure*", *Word*, 19.245-47.

FRAKE, CHARLES O.
1961. "The Diagnosis of Disease among the Subanum of Mindanao", *American Anthropologist*, 63.113-32.
1962. "Cultural Ecology and Ethnography", *American Anthropologist*, 64.53-59.

FRANCIS, W. NELSON
1958. *The Structure of American English* (New York, The Ronald Press, Co.).

FRANCESCATO, GIUSEPPE
1959. "A Case of Coexistence of Phonemic Systems", *Lingua*, 8.78-86.

FRANK, PHILLIP
1957. *Philosophy of Science: The Link Between Science and Philosophy* (Englewood Cliffs, N. J., Prentice-Hall, Inc.).

FRANKLIN, KARL J.
1963. "Kewa Ethnolinguistic Concepts of Body Parts", *Southwestern Journal of Anthropology*, 19.54-63.

FRANKLIN, KARL J. and FRANKLIN, JOICE
1962. "Kewa I: Phonological Asymmetry", *Anthropological Linguistics*, 4.7.29-37.

FREEDMAN, RONALD, HAWLEY, AMOS H., LANDECKER, WARNER S., LENSKI, GERHARD E., and MINER, HORACE M.
1956 [1951]. *Principles of Sociology* (New York, Henry Holt and Co.).

FREELAND, L. S.
1951. *Language of the Sierra Miwok* (*International Journal of American Linguistics*, Memoir No. 6).

FREI, HENRI
1950. "Zéro, Vide et Intermittent", *Zeitschrift für Phonetik*, 4.161-91.

FRENCH, KATHRINE STORY
1955. *Culture Segments and Variation in Contemporary Social Ceremonialism on the Warm Springs Reservation, Oregon, Dissertation Abstracts*, 15.1161-62 [abstract].

FRIES, CHARLES C.
1940. *American English Grammar* (New York, D. Appleton-Century Co.).
1945. *Teaching and Learning English as a Foreign Language* (Ann Arbor, University of Michigan Press).
1948. "As We See It", *Language Learning*, 1.1.12-16.
1952. *The Structure of English: an Introduction to the Construction of English Sentences* (New York, Harcourt, Brace and Co.).
1954. "Meaning and Linguistic Analysis", *Language*, 30.57-68.
1962. *Linguistics and Reading* (New York, Holt, Rinehart and Winston, Inc.).

FRIES, CHARLES C., and PIKE, KENNETH L.
1949. "Coexistent Phonemic Systems", *Language*, 25.29-50.

FRIES, CHARLES C., and staff.
1943. *An Intensive Course in English for Latin-American Students* (Ann Arbor, English Language Institute).

FRY, D. B.
1955. "Duration and Intensity as Physical Correlates of Linguistic Stress", *Journal of the Acoustical Society of America*, 27.765-68.

FRY, D. B., ABRAHAMSON, ARTHUR S., EIMAS, PETER D., and LIBERMAN, ALVIN M.
1962. "The Identification and Discrimination of Synthetic Vowels", *Language and Speech*, 5.171-89.

FU, YI-CHIN
1963. *The Phonemic Structure of English Words* (Taipei, Rainbow-Bridge Book Co.).

GAMMON, E. R.
1963. "On Representing Syntactic Structure", *Language*, 39.369-97.

GARCIA, ERICA C.
1963. "Review of Sol Saporta and Heles Contreras, *A Phonological Grammar of Spanish*", *Word*, 19.258-65.

GARDIN, JEAN-CLAUDE
1958. "Four Codes for the Description of Artifacts; an Essay in Archeological Technique and Theory", *American Anthropologist*, 60.335-57.

GARDING, LARS.
1955. "Relations and Order", *Studia Linguistica*, 9.21-34.

GARDINER, ALAN H.
1932. *The Theory of Speech and Language* (Oxford, The Clarendon Press).

GARDNER, ELIZABETH F.
1950. *The Inflections of Modern Literary Japanese* (*Language Dissertation*, No. 46).

GARDNER, W. H.
1949. *Gerald Manley Hopkins (1884-1889): A Study of Poetic Idiosyncrasy in Relation to Poetic Tradition*, Vol. II (London, Martin Secker and Warburg).

GARNER, WENDELL R.
1962. *Uncertainty and Structure as Psychological Concepts* (New York, John Wiley and Sons, Inc.).

GARVIN, PAUL L.
1947. "Distinctive Features in Zoque Phonemic Acculturation", *Studies in Linguistics*, 5.13-20.
1948, 1951. "Kutenai I-IV", *International Journal of American Linguistics*, 14.37-42, 87-90, 171-87, (1948); 17.84-97 (1951).
1952. "Structure and Variation in Language and Culture", *Indian Tribes of Aboriginal America, Proceedings of the Twenty-Ninth International Congress of Americanists* (Chicago, University of Chicago Press), pp. 216-21.
1954. "Delimitation of Syntactic Units", *Language*, 30.345-48.
1957. "On the Relative Tractability of Morphological Data", *Word*, 13.12-23.
1958. "A Descriptive Technique for the Treatment of Meaning", *Language*, 34.1-32.
1962a. "A Study of Inductive Method in Syntax", *Word*, 18.107-20.
1962b. "Research in Semantic Structure", Reprint of talk presented to the Linguistic Society of America, December, 1962.

GARVIN, PAUL L., and MATHIOT, MADELEINE
1958. "Fused Units in Prosodic Analysis", *Word*, 14.178-86.

GAUTHIER, MICHEL
1956. "Review of Kenneth L. Pike, *Language in Relation to a Unified Theory of the Structure of Human Behavior, Part I*", *Journal de Psychologie Normale et Pathologique*, 53.205-06.

GEIGER, DON.
1953. "New Perspectives in Oral Interpretation", *College English*, 14.281-86.

GEORGES, ROBERT A., and DUNDES, ALAN
1962. "Toward a Structural Definition of the Riddle", *Journal of American Folklore*, 76.111-18.

GIFFORD, E. W. and KROEBER, A. L.
1937. "Culture Element Distributions: IV, Pomo", *University of California Publications in American Archeology and Ethnology*, 37.117-254.

GIMSON, A. C.
1945-49. "Implications of the Phonemic/Chronemic Grouping of English Vowels", *Acta Linguistica*, 5.94-100.

GLEASON, H. A.
1961 [1955]. *An Introduction to Descriptive Linguistics* (New York, Holt, Rinehart and Winston).

GLUCKMAN, MAX
1955. *Custom and Conflict in Africa* (Glencoe, Ill., The Free Press).

GOFFMAN, ERVING
1959. *The Presentation of Self in Everyday Life* (Garden City, N.Y., Doubleday and Co., Inc.).
1961. *Encounters* (Indianapolis, Bobbs-Merrill Co., Inc.).

GOLDSTEIN, KURT
1948. *Language and Language Disturbances* (New York, Grune and Stratton).

GOODELL, R. J.
1964. "An Ethnolinguistic Bibliography with Supporting Material in Linguistics and Anthropology", *Anthropological Linguistics*, 6.2.10-32.

GOODENOUGH, WARD H.
1951. *Property, Kin, and Community on Truk. Yale University Publications in Anthropology*, No. 46 (New Haven, Yale University Press).
1956. "Componential Analysis and the Study of Meaning", *Language*, 32.195-216.
1957. "Cultural Anthropology and Linguistics", *Monograph Series on Language and Linguistics*, No. 9 (Washington, Georgetown University Press), pp. 167-73.

GOODMAN, NELSON
1951. *The Structure of Appearance* (Cambridge, Harvard University Press).
1955. *Fact, Fiction and Forecast* (Cambridge, Harvard University Press).

GREENBERG, JOSEPH H.
1948. "Linguistics and Ethnology", *Southwestern Journal of Anthropology*, 4.140-47.
1957. *Essays in Linguistics* (Chicago, University of Chicago Press).
1962. "Is the Vowel-Consonant Dichotomy Universal?", *Word*, 18.73-81.

GREENBERG, JOSEPH H., (Ed.).
1963. *Universals of Language* (Cambridge, The Massachusetts Institute of Technology Press).

GREGG, R. J.
1957. "Neutralisation and Fusion of Vocalic Phonemes in Canadian English as spoken in the Vancouver Area", *The Journal of the Canadian Linguistic Association*, 3.78-83.

GRIMES, JOSEPH E.
1955. "Style in Huichol Structure", *Language*, 31.31-35.
1959. "Huichol Tone and Intonation", *International Journal of American Linguistics*, 25.221-32.
1960. *Huichol Syntax*. Cornell University Ph. D. Dissertation. [to be published by Mouton and Company, The Hague].

GRIMES, JOSEPH E., and GRIMES, BARBARA F.
1962. "Semantic Distinctions in Huichol (Uto-Aztecan) Kinship", *American Anthropologist*, 64.104-14.

GROSS, NEAL, MASON, WARD S. and MCEACHERN, ALEXANDER W.
1958. *Explorations in Role Analysis: Studies of the School of Superintendency Role* (New York, John Wiley and Sons).

GUDSCHINSKY, SARAH C.
1958a. "Mazatec Dialect History", *Language*, 34.469-81.
1958b. "Native Reactions to Tones and Words in Mazatec", *Word*, 14.338-45.

1959a. "Mazatec Kernal Constructions and Transformations", *International Journal of American Linguistics*, 25.81-89.
1959b. "Discourse Analysis of a Mazatec Text", *Intern. Journ. of Amer. Ling.*, 25.139-46.
1959c. *Proto-Popotecan* (*International Journal of American Linguistics*, Memoir 15).
1959d. "Toneme Representation in Mazatec Orthography", *Word*, 15.446-52.
1960 [1953]. *Handbook of Literacy* (Santa Ana, Calif., Summer Institute of Linguistics).

GUTHRIE, MALCOLM
1948. *Bantu Word Division* (International African Institute, Memorandum 22, London, Oxford University Press).
1961. *Bantu Sentence Structure* (University of London, School of Oriental and African Studies).

HAAS, W.
1955. "On Defining Linguistic Units", *Transactions of the Philological Society, 1954*, pp. 54-84.
1957. "Zero in Linguistic Description", *Studies in Linguistic Analysis*, pp. 33-53.
1958. "The Identification and Description of Phonetic Elements", *Transactions of the Philological Society, 1957*, pp. 118-59.
1959. "Relevance in Phonetic Analysis", *Word*, 15.1-18.
1960. "Review of A. A. Hill, *Introduction to Linguistic Structures*", *Word*, 16.251-76.

HADDING-KOCH, KERSTIN
1961. *Acoustico-Phonetic Studies in the Intonation of Southern Swedish. Travaux de L'Institut de Phonétique de Lund* (Lund, C. W. K. Gleerup).

HADEN, ERNEST F., HAN, MIEKO S., HAN, YURI W.
1962. *A Resonance-Theory for Linguistics* ('s-Gravenhage, Mouton and Co.).

HALL, EDWARD T.
1959. *The Silent Language* (Garden City, N.Y., Doubleday and Co.).
1963. "A System for the Notation of Proxemic Behavior", *American Anthropologist*, 65.1003-1026.

HALL, EDWARD T., and TRAGER, GEORGE L.
1953. *The Analysis of Culture*. Pre-publication edition (Washington, D.C., Foreign Service Institute, Department of State).

HALL, ROBERT A., JR.
1945. "Colloquial French Substantive Inflection", *French Review*, 19.42-51.
1946. "Colloquial French Phonology", *Studies in Linguistics*, 4.70-90.
1950a. "Nasalization in Haitian Creole", *Modern Language Notes*, 65.474-78.
1950b. *Leave your Language Alone!* (Ithaca, N.Y., Linguistica).
1951. "Idiolect and Linguistic Super-Ego", *Studia Linguistica*, 5.21-27.
1952. "Aspect and Tense in Haitian Creole", *Romance Philology*, 5.312-16.
1953. "Elgar and the Intonation of British English", *The Gramophone*, 31.361.6.
1960. "Italian [z] and the Converse of the Archiphoneme", *Lingua* 9.194-97.
1962. "The Determination of Form-Classes in Haitian Creole", *Zeitschrift für Romanische Philologie*, 78.172-77.

HALLE, MORRIS
1959a. *The Sound Pattern of Russian* ('s-Gravenhage, Mouton and Company).
1959b. "Questions of Linguistics", *Nuovo Cimento*, 13.494-517.
1960. "Review of R. I. Avanesov, *Fonetika Sovremennogo Russkogo Literaturnogo Jazyka*", *Word*, 16.140-52.
1962a. "Phonology in Generative Grammar", *Word*, 18.54-72.
1962b. "On the Reality of Generative Grammars", Pre-publication manuscript, mimeographed.
1962c. "Speech Sounds and Sequences", *Proc. of the 4th Intern. Cong. of Phon. Sciences*, 428-34.

HALLIDAY, M. A. K.
1957. "Some Aspects of Systematic Description and Comparison in Grammatical Analysis", *Studies in Linguistic Analysis* (Oxford, Basil Blackwell), pp. 54-67.
1961. "Categories of the Theory of Grammar", *Word*, 17.241-92.

HALLOWELL, A. IRVING
1955. *Culture and Experience* (Philadelphia, University of Pennsylvania Press).

HALPERN, A. M.
1946. "Yuma I: Phonemics", *International Journal of American Linguistics*, 12.25-33.

HAMP, ERIC P.
1954. "Componental Restatement of Syllable Structure in Trique", *International Journal of American Linguistics*, 20.206-09.
1957a. "Stylistically Modified Allophones in Huichol", *Language*, 33.139-42.
1957b. *A Glossary of American Technical Linguistic Usage, 1925-1950* (Utrecht, Spectrum Publishers).
1959. "Graphemics and Paragraphemics", *Studies in Linguistics*, 14.1-5.
1962. "The Interconnection of Sound Production, Perception, and Phonemic Typology", *Proceedings of the Fourth International Congress of Phonetic Sciences*, pp. 639-42.

HARARY, FRANK and PAPER, HERBERT H.
1957. "Toward a General Calculus of Phonemic Distribution", *Language*, 33.143-69.

HARMAN, GILBERT H.
1963. "Generative Grammars without Transformation Rules: a Defense of Phrase Structure", *Language*, 39.597-616.

HARRIES, LYNDON
1952. "Some Tonal Principles of the Kikuyu Language", *Word*, 8.140-44.

HARRINGTON, JOHN PEABODY
1916. *Ethnobotany of the Tewa Indians* (Bureau of American Ethnology, Bulletin No. 55, Washington, D.C.).

HARRIS, MARVIN
1964. *The Nature of Cultural Things* (New York, Random House).

HARRIS, ZELLIG S.
1941. "Review of N. S. Trubetzkoy, *Grundzüge der Phonologie*", *Language*, 17.345-49.
1942a. "Morpheme Alternants in Linguistic Analysis", *Language*, 18.169-80.
1942b. "Phonologies of African Languages: The Phonemes of Moroccan Arabic", *Journal of the American Oriental Society*, 62.309-18.
1944a. "Yokuts Structure and Newman's Grammar", *International Journal of American Linguistics*, 10.196-211.
1944b. "Simultaneous Components in Phonology", *Language*, 20.181-205.
1945a. "Discontinuous Morphemes", *Language*, 21.121-27.
1945b. "Navaho Phonology and Hoijer's Analysis", *International Journal of American Linguistics*, 11.239-46.
1946. "From Morpheme to Utterance", *Language*, 22.161-83.
1947. "Structural Restatements: I and II", *International Journal of American Linguistics*, 13.47-58, 175-86.
1948. "Componential Analysis of a Hebrew Paradigm", *Language*, 24.87-91.
1951. *Methods in Structural Linguistics* (Chicago, University of Chicago Press [1960 impression entitled *Structural Linguistics*]).
1952a. "Discourse Analysis", *Language*, 28.1-30,474-94.
1952b. "Culture and Style in Extended Discourse", *Indian Tribes of Aboriginal America*. Sol Tax, Ed. (Chicago, University of Chicago Press), pp. 210-15.
1954a. "Distributional Structure", *Word*, 10.146-62.
1954b. "Transfer Grammar", *International Journal of American Linguistics*, 20.259-70.
1955. "From Phoneme to Morpheme", *Language*, 31.190-222.
1957. "Co-occurrence and Transformation in Linguistic Structure", *Language*, 33.283-340.
1959. "The Transformational Model of Language Structure", *Anthropological Linguistics*, 1.1.27-29.
1962. *String Analysis of Sentence Structure* (The Hague, Mouton and Company).

HART, HELEN LONG
1957. "Hierarchical Structuring of Amuzgo Grammar", *International Journal of American Linguistics*, 23.141-64.

HART, JOHN (I. H. CHESTER HERALT)
1569. *An Orthographie, Conteyning the Due Order and Reason, Howe to Write or Paint Thimage of Mannes Voice, Most Like to Life or Nature* (London, William Seres).

HART, RAYMOND E.
1963. "Semantic Components of Shape in Amarakaeri Grammar", *Anthropological Linguistics*, 5.9.1-7.

HARWOOD, F. W.
1955. "Axiomatic Syntax: The Construction and Evaluation of a Syntactic Calculus", *Language*, 31.409-13.

HAUGEN, EINAR
1949a. "Phoneme or Prosodeme?", *Language*, 25.278-82.
1949b. "Phonemics: A Technique for Making Alphabets", *American Speech*, 24.54-57.
1950a. *First Grammatical Treatise* (*Language Monograph*, No. 25).
1950b. "The Analysis of Linguistic Borrowing", *Language*, 26.210-31.
1950c. "Problems of Bilingualism", *Lingua*, 2.271-90.
1951. "Directions in Modern Linguistics", *Language*, 27.211-22.
1953. *The Norwegian Language in America* (Philadelphia, University of Pennsylvania Press).
1954. "Bilingualism and Mixed Languages: Problems of Bilingual Description", *Georgetown University Monograph Series on Language and Linguistics*, 7.9-19.
1955. "Problems of Bilingual Description", *General Linguistics*, 1.1-9.
1956a. "The Syllable in Linguistic Description", *For Roman Jakobson*, 213-21.
1956b. "Syllabification in Kutenai", *International Journal of American Linguistics*, 22.196-201.
1956-57. "The Phoneme in Bilingual Description", *Language Learning*, 7.3-4.17-23.
1957. "The Semantics of Icelandic Orientation", *Word*, 13.447-60.
1960. "From Idiolect to Language", *Georgetown University Monograph Series on Language and Linguistics*, 12.57-64.
1962. "On Diagramming Vowel Systems", *Proceedings of the Fourth International Congress of Phonetic Sciences*, pp. 648-54.
1963. "Pitch Accent and Tonemic Juncture in Scandinavian", *Monatshefte*, 55.157-61.

HAUGEN, EINAR, and JOOS, MARTIN
1952. "Tone and Intonation in East Norwegian", *Acta Philologica Scandinavica*, 22.41-64.

HAUGEN, EINAR, and TWADDELL, W. FREEMAN
1942. "Facts and Phonemics", *Language*, 18.228-37.

HAYES, FRANCIS
1957. "Gestures: a Working Bibliography", *Southern Folklore Quarterly*, 21.218-317.

HEALEY, ALAN
1962. "Linguistic Aspects of Telefomin Kinship Terminology", *Anthropological Linguistics*, 4.7.14-28.

HEALEY, PHYLLIS M.
1960. *An Agta Grammar* (Manila, Bureau of Printing).

HEBB, D. O.
1949. *The Organization of Behavior* (New York: T. Wiley and Sons, Inc.).

HELLER, LOUIS G.
1964. "Some Types and Uses of Tagmemic Zero", *Linguistics*, 4.48-55.

HEMPEL, CARL
1952. *Fundamentals of Concept Formation in Empirical Science. International Encyclopedia of Unified Science*, Vol. II, No. 7.

HENDERSON, EUGÉNIE J. A.
1948. "Notes on the Syllable Structure of Lushai", *Bulletin of the School of Oriental and African Studies*, 12.713-25.
1952. "The Main Features of Cambodian Pronunciation", *Bulletin of the School of Oriental and African Studies*, 14.149-74.

HENLE, PAUL, Ed.
1958. *Language, Thought and Culture* (Ann Arbor, University of Michigan Press).

HENRY, JULES
1958. "The Personal Community and its Invariant Properties", *American Anthropologist*, 60.827-31.

HENRY, NELSON, Ed.
1942. *The Psychology of Learning. Forty-first Yearbook of the National Society for the Study of Education* (Chicago, University of Chicago Press).

HERSKOVITS, MELVILLE J.
1948. *Man and His Works* (New York, Alfred A. Knopf).

HESS, HAROLD HARWOOD
1962. *The Syntactic Structure of Mezquital Otomí*. University of Michigan Ph. D. Dissertation.

HICKERSON, HAROLD, TURNER, GLEN D., and HICKERSON, NANCY P.
1952. "Testing Procedures for Estimating Transfer of Information Among Iroquois Dialects and Languages", *International Journal of American Linguistics*, 18.1-8.

HICKERSON, NANCY P.
1954. "Two Versions of a Lokono (Arawak) Tale", *International Journal of American Linguistics*, 20.295-301.

HILL, ARCHIBALD A.
1955. "Analysis of The Windhover, an Experiment in Structural Method", *Publications of the Modern Language Association of America*, 70.968-78.
1958. *Introduction to Linguistic Structures: From Sound to Sentence in English* (New York, Harcourt, Brace and Co., Inc.).
1959. "Review of G. F. Arnold, *Stress in English Words*", *Language*, 35.564-67.
1961. "Suprasegmentals, Prosodies, Prosodemes: Comparison and Discussion", *Language*, 37.457-68.
1962. "A Postulate for Linguistics in the Sixties", *Language*, 38.345-51.

HINCHA, GEORG
1961. "Endocentric vs. Exocentric Constructions", *Lingua*, 10.267-74.

HIORTH, FINNGEIR
1956. "On the Relation between Field Research and Lexicography", *Studia Linguistica*, 10.57-66.
1958. "On Defining 'Word'", *Studia Linguistica*, 12.1-26.
1959. "Distances of Meaning and Semantical Tests", *Synthese*, 11.33-62.

HIŻ, HENRY
1957. "Types and Environments", *Philosophy of Science*, 24.215-20.
1962. "Questions and Answers", *The Journal of Philosophy*, 59.253-65.

HJELMSLEV, LOUIS
1936. "On the Principles of Phonematics", *Proceedings of the Second International Congress of Phonetic Sciences*, pp. 49-54.
1939a. "Note sur les oppositions supprimables", *Travaux du Cercle Linguistique de Prague*, 8.51-57.
1939b. "The Syllable as a Structural Unit", *Proceedings of the Third International Congress of Phonetic Sciences*, pp. 266-72.
1947. "Structural Analysis of Language", *Studia Linguistica*, 1.69-78.
1953. *Prolegomena to a Theory of Language* (Translation, by F. J. Whitfield, of *Omkring Sprogteoriens Grundlæggelse*, 1943) (*Indiana University Publications in Anthropology and Linguistics*, Memoir 7).
1958. "Dans Quelle Mesure les Significations des Mots Peuvent-elles être Considérées comme Formant une Structure?", *Proceedings of the Eighth International Congress of Linguistics*, pp. 636-54.

HOCKETT, CHARLES F.
1939. "Potawatomi Syntax", *Language*, 15.235-48.
1942. "A System of Descriptive Phonology", *Language*, 18.3-21.
1944. "Review of Eugene A. Nida, *Linguistic Interludes*; and *Morphology, The Descriptive Analysis of Words*," *Language*, 20.252-55.

1947a. "Problems of Morphemic Analysis", *Language*, 23.321-43.
1947b. "Review of Eugene A. Nida, *Morphology*", *Language*, 23.273-85.
1947c. "Componential Analysis of Sierra Popoluca", *International Journal of American Linguistics*, 13.258-67.
1948a. "A Note on 'Structure'", *International Journal of American Linguistics*, 14.269-71.
1948b. "Potawatomi I: Phonemics, Morphophonemics, and Morphological Survey", *International Journal of American Linguistics*, 14.1-10.
1948c. "Biophysics, Linguistics, and the Unity of Science", *American Scientist*, 36.558-72.
1949a. "Two Fundamental Problems in Phonemics", *Studies in Linguistics*, 7.29-51.
1949b. "Review of Y. R. Chao, *Mandarin Primer*", *Language*, 25.210-15.
1950a. "Peiping Morphophonemics", *Language*, 26.63-85.
1950b. "Which Approach in Linguistics is 'Scientific'?", *Studies in Linguistics*, 8.53-57.
1952a. "Review of *Travaux du Cercle Linguistique de Copenhague, Vol. V, Recherches Structurales*", *International Journal of American Linguistics*, 18.86-99.
1952b. "A Formal Statement of Morphemic Analysis", *Studies in Linguistics*, 10.27-39.
1953. "Short and Long Syllable Nuclei", *International Journal of American Linguistics*, 19.165-71.
1954a. "Two Models of Grammatical Description", *Word*, 10.210-34.
1954b. "Translation via Immediate Constituents", *International Journal of American Linguistics*, 20.313-15.
1955. *A Manual of Phonology* (*Indiana University Publications in Anthropology and Linguistics*, Memoir 11).
1958. *A Course in Modern Linguistics* (New York, The MacMillan Company).
1959. "On the Format of Phonemic Reports, with Restatement of Ocaina", *International Journal of American Linguistics*, 25.59-62.
1961a. "Linguistic Elements and Their Relations", *Language*, 37.29-53.
1961b. "Review of L. Kaiser, *Manual of Phonetics*", *Language*, 37.266-69.

HOEBEL, E. ADAMSON
1954. *The Law of Primitive Man* (Cambridge, Harvard University Press).

HOENIGSWALD, HENRY M.
1944. "Review of K. L. Pike, *Phonetics*", *Journal of the American Oriental Society*, 64.151-55.
1950. "Morpheme Order Diagrams", *Studies in Linguistics*, 8.79-81.
1952. "The Phonology of Dialect Borrowings", *Studies in Linguistics*, 10.1-5.
1959. "Some Uses of Nothing", *Language*, 35.409-20.
1960. *Language Change and Linguistic Reconstruction* (Chicago, University of Chicago Press).

HOFF, B. J.
1962. "The Nominal Word-Groups in Carib: A Problem of Delimitation of Syntax and Morphology", *Lingua*, 11.157-64.

HOFFMAN, HOWARD S.
1958. "Study of Some Cues in the Perception of the Voiced Stop Consonants", *The Journal of the Acoustical Society of America*, 30.1035-1041.

HOIJER, HARRY
1945. *Navaho Phonology*. *University of New Mexico Publications in Anthropology: I* (Albuquerque, University of New Mexico Press).
1954. *Language in Culture* (*American Anthropologist*, Memoir 79).

HOIJER, HARRY (Ed.).
1958. "Native Reaction as a Criterion in Linguistic Analysis", *Proceedings of the Eighth International Congress of Linguists*, pp. 573-83.

Honey, P. J.
1956. "Word Classes in Vietnamese", *Bulletin of the School of Oriental and African Studies*, 18.534-44.

HONIGMANN, JOHN J.
1954. *Culture and Personality* (New York, Harper and Bros).

HOOLEY, BRUCE A.
1962. "Transformations in Neomelanesian", *Oceania*, 33.116-27.

REFERENCES

HORST, PAUL
1963. *Matrix Algebra for Social Scientists.* (New York, Holt, Rinehart and Winston, Inc.).

HOUSE, FLOYD NELSON
1936. *The Development of Sociology* (New York, McGraw-Hill Book Co., Inc.).

HOUSE, HOMER C., and HARMAN, SUSAN E.
1950. [1931]. *Descriptive English Grammar*, Second Edition (New York: Prentice-Hall).

HOUSEHOLDER, FRED W.
1952. "Review of Z. S. Harris, *Methods in Structural Linguistics*", *International Journal of American Linguistics*, 18.260-68.
1962a. "On the Uniqueness of Semantic Mapping", *Word*, 18.173-85.
1962b. "Review of R. B. Lees, *The Grammar of English Nominalizations*", *Word*, 18.326-53.
1962c. "The Distributional Determination of English Phonemes", *Lingua*, 11.186-91.

HOUSEHOLDER, FRED W., and SAPORTA, SOL, Eds.
1962. *Problems in Lexicography* (Indiana University Research Center in Anthropology, Folklore, and Linguistics, Publication 21).

HSU, FRANCIS L. K.
1959. "Structure, Function, Content and Process", *American Anthropologist*, 61.790-805.

HUESTIS, GEORGE
1963. "Bororo Clause Structure", *International Journal of American Linguistics*, 29.230-38.

HUMPHREY, GEORGE
1951. *Thinking, An Introduction to its Experimental Psychology* (London, Methuen and Co., Ltd.; New York, John Wiley and Sons, Inc.).

HUSSON, RAOUL VON
1959. "Der Gegenwärtige Stand der Physiologischen Phonetik", *Phonetica*, 4.1-32.

HYMES, DELL H.
1955. "Positional Analysis of Categories: a Frame for Reconstruction", *Word*, 11.10-23.
1956. "Review of *Lingua Posnaniensis*, Vols. I-V, 1949-1955", *International Journal of American Linguistics*, 22.281-87.
1962. "The Ethnography of Speaking", *Anthropology and Human Behavior*, Gladwin and Sturtevant, Eds. Washington, D.C.: Anthropological Society of Washington,
1964. *Language in Culture and Society: a Reader in Linguistics and Anthropology* (New York, Harper & Row).

International Bibliography of Social and Cultural Anthropology
1961. J. F. M. Middleton, Ed. (London, University College).

IVIČ, PAVLE
1962. "On the Structure of Dialectal Differentiation", *Word*, 18.33-53.

JAKOBSON, ROMAN
1931. "Die Betonung und ihre Rolle in der Wort und Syntagmaphonologie", *Travaux du Cercle Linguistique de Prague*, 4.164-82.
1939. "Observations sur le Classement Phonologique des Consonnes", *Proceedings of the Third International Congress of Phonetic Sciences*, pp. 34-41.
1949a. "The Phonemic and Grammatical Aspects of Language in their Interrelation", *Proceedings of the Sixth International Congress of Linguists*, pp. 5-18.
1949b. "On the Identification of Phonemic Entities", *Travaux du Cercle Linguistique de Copenhague*, 5.205-13.
1957a. "Notes on Gilyak", *Bulletin of the Institute of History and Philology* (Academica Sinica, Taipai, Taiwan, Vol. 29, pp. 255-81).
1957b. *Shifters, Verbal Categories, and the Russian Verb.* (*Russian Language Project*, Department of Slavic Languages and Literatures, Harvard University).
1960. "Linguistics and Poetics", *Style in Language*, T. E. Sebeok, Ed., pp. 350-77.

1961. "Linguistics and Communication Theory", *Structure of Language and its Mathematical Aspects*, 245-52.
1962. "The Phonemic Concept of Distinctive Features", *Proceedings of the Fourth International Congress of Phonetic Sciences*, 440-54.

JAKOBSON, ROMAN, FANT, C. GUNNAR M., and HALLE, MORRIS
1952. *Preliminaries to Speech Analysis (Technical Report No. 13*. Second Printing with additions and corrections. Acoustics Laboratory, Massachusetts Institute of Technology).

JAKOBSON, ROMAN, and HALLE, MORRIS
1956. *Fundamentals of Language* (The Hague, Mouton and Co.)

JAKOBSON, ROMAN, and LOTZ, J.
1949. "Notes on the French Phonemic Patterns", *Word*, 5.151-58.
1952. "Axioms of a Versification System Exemplified by the Mordvinian Folkson", *Linguistica*, 1.5-13 (Acta Instituti Hungarici Universitatis Holmiensis).

JAKOBSON, ROMAN, and SOMMERFELT, ALF
1962. "On the Role of Word Pitch in Norwegian Verse", *Lingua*, 11.205-16.

JAMES, MAX
1956-57. "A Tentative Study of the Intonation of Japanese", *Language Learning*, 7.3-4.35-49.

JASSEM, WIKTOR
1952. "Intonation of Conversational English (educated southern British)", *Travaux de la Société des Sciences et des Lettres de Wrocław*, Seria A, Nr. 45 (Wrocław, Nakładem Wrocławaskiego Towarzystwa Naukowego).
1959. "The Phonology of Polish Stress", *Word*, 15.252-69.

JENSEN, MARTIN KLOSTER
1958. "Recognition of Word Tones in Whispered Speech", *Word*, 14.187-96.
1961. *Tonemicity* (Bergen-Oslo, Norwegian Universities Press).

JESPERSON, OTTO
1924. *The Philosophy of Grammar* (New York, Henry Holt and Co.).
1928. *A Modern English Grammar: Part I, Sounds and Spellings* (Heidelberg, Carl. Winter's Universitätsbuchhandlung).
1933. *Essentials of English Grammar.* (New York, Holt, Rinehart and Winston).
1936. *A Modern English Grammar.* Part II, Syntax. Vol. I, 4th Edition. (Heidelberg, Carl Winter's Universitätsbuchhandlung).
1937. *Analytic Syntax*, (Copenhagen, Munksgaard).
1940-1949. *A Modern English Grammar on Historical Principles*, Pts. 5-7 (Copenhagen, Ejnar Munksgaard).

JOHNSON, DONALD M.
1955. *The Psychology of Thought and Judgment* (New York, Harper and Bros).

JOHNSON, WENDELL
1946. *People in Quandries* (New York, Harper and Bros).

JONES, A. M.
1958. "African Music in Northern Rhodesia and Some Other Places", *The Occasional Papers of the Rhodes-Livingstone Museum*, No. 4.

JONES, DANIEL.
1925. "The Phonetic Structure of the Sechuana Language", *Transactions of the Philological Society, 1917-1920*, Part I, pp. 99-106.
1931. "The 'Word' as a Phonetic Entity", *Le Maître Phonétique*, 3rd series, No. 36, pp. 60-65.
1939. "Concrete and Abstract Sounds", *Proceedings of the Third International Congress of Phonetic Sciences*, pp. 1-7.
1940. *An Outline of English Phonetics*, Sixth Edition (New York, E. P. Dutton and Co.).
1944. [printed 1948]. "Chronemes and Tonemes", *Acta Linguistica*, 4.1-10.
1950. *The Phoneme: its Nature and Use* (Cambridge, W. Heffer and Sons, Ltd.).

1957. "The History and Meaning of the Term 'Phoneme'", *Le Maître Phonétique*, Supplement (July-December, 1957).
1964. *In Honour of Daniel Jones*. Edited by David Abercrombie, D. B. Fry, P. A. D. MacCarthy, N. C. Scott, and J. L. M. Trim (London, Longmans, Green and Co.).

JOOS, MARTIN
1948. *Acoustic Phonetics* (*Language Monograph* No. 23).
1950. "Description of Language Design", *The Journal of the Acoustical Society of America*, 22.701-08.
(ED.). 1957. *Readings in Linguistics* (Washington, D.C., American Council of Learned Societies).
1958. "Semology: A Linguistic Theory of Meaning", *Studies in Linguistics*, 13.53-70.
1961. "Semology — an Outline with Discussions", Unpublished manuscript, private circulation.
1962. *The Five Clocks* (*Indiana University Research Center in Anthropology, Folklore and Linguistics*, Publication 22).
1963. *The English Verb: Form and Meanings* (Prepublication manuscript, mimeographed).

JORDEN, ELEANOR HARZ
1955. *The Syntax of Modern Colloquial Japanese* (*Language Dissertation* No. 52).

KAHANE, HENRY R., and PIETRANGELI, ANGELINA, Eds.
1959. *Structural Studies on Spanish Themes* (Urbana, University of Illinois Press).

KAISER, L., Ed.
1957. *Manual of Phonetics* (Amsterdam, North-Holland Publishing Co.).

KANT, IMMANUEL
1954 [1783]. *Prolegomena to any Future Metaphysics that will be able to Present itself as a Science*. Translated by Peter G. Lucas (Manchester, University Press. Also, edition of 1902, *Prolegomena*. Edited in English by Paul Carus, Chicago, The Open Court Publishing Co.).

KANTNER, CLAUDE E., and WEST, ROBERT
1933. *Phonetics*. (New York, Harper and Bros).

KANTOR, J. R.
1936. *An Objective Psychology of Grammar*. Indiana University Science Series. [reissued, 1952 by the Princípia Press, Inc., Bloomington, Ind.].

KAPLAN, ABRAHAM
1946. "Definition and Specification of Meaning", *The Journal of Philosophy*, 43.281-88.

KAPLAN, ABRAHAM, and SCHOTT, HERMANN E.
1951. "A Calculus for Empirical Classes", *Methodos*, 3.165-90.

KARCEVSKIJ, SERGE
1929. "Du Dualisme Asymétrique du Signe Linguistique", *Travaux du Cercle Linguistique de Prague*, 1.88-92.
1937. "Phrase et Proposition", *Mélanges de Linguistique et de Philologie Offerts à Jacq. Van Ginneken* ... (Paris), pp. 59-66.

KARLGREN, H.
1962. "Speech Rate and Information Theory", *Proceedings of the Fourth International Congress of Phonetic Sciences*, pp. 671-77.

KATZ, JERROLD J.
1962. "Review of Paul Ziff, *Semantic Analysis*", *Language*, 38.52-69.

KATZ, JERROLD J., and FODOR, JERRY A.
1963. "The Structure of a Semantic Theory", *Language*, 39.170-210.

KELKAR, ASHOK R.
1957. "'Marathi English': A Study in Foreign Accent", *Word*, 13.268-82.

KELLY, GEORGE
1955. *The Psychology of Personal Constructs* (New York, W. W. Norton and Co., Inc. [2 vols.]).

KELLY, WALT.
1952. *I Go Pogo* (New York, Simon and Schuster).

KENNEDY, GEORGE A.
1953. "Two Tone Patterns in Tangsic", *Language*, 29.367-73.

KENYON, JOHN SAMUEL
1943 [1935]. *American Pronunciation*. Ninth Edition. (Ann Arbor, George Wahr).

KENYON, JOHN SAMUEL, and KNOTT, THOMAS ALBERT
1944. *A Pronouncing Dictionary of American English* (Springfield, Mass., G. and C. Merriam Co.).

KEY, HAROLD
1960. "Stem Construction and Affixation of Sierra Nahuat Verbs", *International Journal of American Linguistics*, 26.131-45.

KINGDON, ROGER
1948. "The Teaching of English Intonation, I, II", *English Language Teaching*, 2.85-91, 113-21.
1958. *The Groundwork of English Intonation* (London, Longmans, Green and Company).

KIRK, PAUL L.
1959. " Note on Morphemic Fusion and Empty Morphs", *Studies in Linguistics*, 14.7-9.

KLUCKHOHN, CLYDE
1949. *Mirror for Man*. New York, Toronto, Whittlesey House, McGraw-Hill Book Co., Inc.
1956. "Toward a Comparison of Value-Emphases in Different Cultures", *The State of the Social Sciences*, Leonard D. White, Ed. (Chicago, University of Chicago Press, pp. 116-32).

KLUCKHOHN, CLYDE, and MURRAY, HENRY A., Eds.
1948. *Personality in Nature, Society and Culture* (New York, Alfred A. Knopf).

KOEKKOEK, B. J.
1956-57. "German Pitch Notation", *Language Learning*, 7.1-2.26-32.

KOFFKA, KURT
1927. "On the Structure of the Unconscious", *The Unconscious: a Symposium*, E. S. Dummer, Ed. (New York, Alfred A. Knopf), pp. 43-68.
1935. *Principles of Gestalt Psychology* (New York, Harcourt, Brace, and Co.).

KORZYBSKI, ALFRED
1948 [1933]. *Science and Sanity: an Introduction to Non-Aristotelian Systems and General Semantics*. Third edition. (Lakeville, Conn., The International Non-Aristotelian Library Publishing Co.).

KROEBER, A. L.
1936. "Culture Element Distributions: III, Area and Climax", *University of California Publications in American Archeology and Ethnology*, 37.101-36.
1948 [1923]. *Anthropology* (New York, Harcourt, Brace and Co.).
1953. *Anthropology Today* (Chicago, University of Chicago Press).
1958. "Sign Language Inquiry", *International Journal of American Linguistics*, 24.1-19.

KROEBER, A. L. and KLUCKHOHN, CLYDE
1952. *Culture, a Critical Review of Concepts and Definitions* (Papers of the Peabody Museum of American Archaeology and Ethnology, Harvard University. Vol. 47, No. 1, Cambridge, Mass.).

KRUPA, V., and ALTMANN, G.
1961. "Semantic Analysis of the System of Personal Pronouns in Indonesian Language", *Archiv Orientální*, 29.620-25.

KUIPERS, AERT H.
1960. *Phoneme and Morpheme in Kabardian* ('s-Gravenhage, Mouton and Co.).
1962. "The Circassian Nominal Paradigm: a Contribution to Case Theory", *Lingua*, 11.231-48.

KURATH, GERTRUDE P.
1953. "The Tutelo Harvest Rites: a Musical and Choreographic Analysis", *The Scientific Monthly*, 76.153-62.

KURATH, HANS
1945. "Review of B. Bloch and G. L. Trager, *Outline of Linguistic Analysis*", *American Journal of Philology*, 66.206-10.
1949. *A Word Geography of the Eastern United States* (Ann Arbor, University of Michigan Press).

KURATH, HANS. BLOCH, B., BLOCK, JULIA, and HANSEN, M. L.
1939. *Handbook of the Linguistic Geography of New England* (Providence, Brown University).

KURYLOWICZ, JERZY
1960. *Esquisses Linguistiques* (Wrocław-Kraków, Zakład Narodowy Imienia Ossolińskich Wydawnictwo Polskiej Akademii Nauk).

LABOV, WILLIAM
1963. "The Social Motivation of a Sound Change", *Word*, 19.273-309.

LACKOWSKI, PETER
1963. "Words as Grammatical Primes", *Language*, 39.211-15.

LADEFOGED, PETER
1960a. "The Value of Phonetic Statements", *Language*, 36.387-96.
1960b. "The Regulation of Sub-Glottal Pressure", *Folia Phoniatrica*, 12.169-75.
1962. "Sub-Glottal Activity During Speech", *Proceedings of the Fourth International Congress of Phonetic Sciences*, pp. 73-91.

LADEFOGED, PETER, and BROADBENT, DONALD E.
1960. "Perception of Sequence in Auditory Events", *Quarterly Journal of Experimental Psychology*, 12.162-70.

LADEFOGED, PETER, with the assistance of DRAPER, M. H., and WHITTERIDGE, D.
1958. "Syllables and Stress", *Miscellanea Phonetica*, 3.1-14.

LADO, ROBERT
1957. *Linguistics across Cultures* (Ann Arbor, University of Michigan Press).

LAMB, SYDNEY M.
1962. *Outline of Stratificational Grammar* (Berkeley, University of California Press).

LAMBEK, JOACHIM
1959. "Contributions to a Mathematical Analysis of the English Verb-Phrase", *The Journal of the Canadian Linguistic Association*, 5.83-89.

LANE, GEORGE S.
1945. "The Tocharian Palatalization", *Language*, 21.18-26.
1946. "Review of Stefán Einarsson, *Icelandic Grammar, Texts, Glossary*", *Language*, 22.249-59.

LANZ, DE LEE, and STEFFLRE, VOLNEY
1964. "Language and Cognition Revisited," *Journal of Abnormal and Social Psychology*, 5.472-81.

LARSEN, RAYMOND; and PIKE, EUNICE V.
1949. "Huasteco Intonations and Phonemes", *Language*, 25.268-77.

LASSWELL, HAROLD D., and KAPLAN, ABRAHAM
1950. *Power and Society* (New Haven, Yale University Press).

LASSWELL, HAROLD D., LERNER, D., and DE SOLA POOL, ITHIEL.
1952. *The Comparative Study of Symbols Hoover Institute Studies Series C: Symbols*, No. 1 (Stanford, Stanford University Press).

LAW, HOWARD W.
1948. "Greeting Forms of the Gulf Aztecs", *Southwestern Journal of Anthropology*, 4.43-48.
1962. *Obligatory Constructions of Isthmus Nahuat Grammar*. University of Texas Ph. D. Dissertation.

LEAL, MARY
1950. "Patterns of Tone Substitution in Zapotec Morphology", *International Journal of American Linguistics*, 16.132-36.

LEE, ALFRED McCLUNG, Ed.
1951. *Readings in Sociology* (New York, Barnes and Noble, Inc. [College Outline Series]).

LEE, W. R.
1956. "English Intonation: a New Approach", *Lingua*, 5.345-71.
1960. *An English Intonation Reader* (London, MacMillan and Co., Ltd.).

LEEPER, R.
1951. "Cognitive Processes", *Handbook of Experimental Psychology*, S. S. Stevens, Ed. (New York, Wiley and Sons), pp. 730-57.

LEES, ROBERT B.
1957. "Review of Noam Chomsky, *Syntactic Structures*", *Language*, 33.375-408.
1959. "Automata and the Generation of Sentences", *Anthropological Linguistics*, 1.4.1-4.
1960a. *The Grammar of English Nominalizations* (*Indiana University Research Center in Anthropology, Folklore, and Linguistics*, Publication 12).
1960b. "A Multiply Ambiguous Adjectival Construction in English", *Language*, 36.207-21.
1960c. "Review of Dwight D. Bolinger, *Interrogative Structures of American English*", *Word*, 16.119-30.
1961a. "Grammatical Analysis of the English Comparative Construction", *Word*, 17.171-85.
1961b. "Some Neglected Aspects of Parsing", *Language Learning*, 11.171-81.
1963. "Review of J. Németh, *Turkish Grammar*", *Language*, 39.548-56.

LEES, ROBERT B., and KLIMA, E. S.
1963. "Rules for English Pronominalization", *Language*, 39.17-28.

LEHISTE, ILSE
1959. *An Acoustic-Phonetic Study of Internal Open Juncture* (Report No. 2, Speech Research Laboratory, Ann Arbor, Mich. [see also 1960b]).
1960a. "Segmental and Syllabic Quantity in Estonian", *Uralic and Altaic Studies*, (Bloomington, Indiana University), 1.21-82.
1960b. *An Acoustic-Phonetic Study of Internal Open Juncture* (*Phonetica*, 5, Supplement. [see also 1959]).
1961. "The Phonemes of Slovene", *International Journal of Slavic Linguistics and Poets*, 4.48-66.
1962. "Acoustic Studies of Boundary Signals", *Proceedings of the Fourth International Congress of Phonetic Sciences*, pp. 179-87.

LEHISTE, ILSE, and PETERSON, GORDON E.
1959a. "Vowel Amplitude and Phonemic Stress in American English", *The Journal of the Acoustical Society of America*, 31.428-35.
1959b. *Studies of Syllable Nuclei, Part I* (Report No. 3, Speech Research Laboratory, Ann Arbor, Mich.).
1960. *Studies of Syllable Nuclei, Part II* (Report No. 4, Speech Research Laboratory, Ann Arbor, Mich.).
1961a. "Transitions, Glides, and Diphthongs", *The Journal of the Acoustical Society of America*, 33.268-77.
1961b. "Some Basic Considerations in the Analysis of Intonation", *Journal of the Acoustical Society of America*, 33.419-25.

LENNEBERG, ERIC H.
1953. "Cognition in Ethnolinguistics", *Language*, 29.463-71.
1960. "Language, Evolution and Purposive Behavior", *Culture in History* (New York, Columbia University Press), pp. 869-93.

LENNEBERG, ERIC H., and ROBERTS, JOHN M.
1956. *The Language of Experience: A Study in Methodology* (*International Journal of American Linguistics*, Memoir 13).

LEONTIEF, WASSILY
1963. "The Structure of Development", *Scientific American*, 209.3.148-66 (Sept.).

LEOPOLD, WERNER F.
1952. *Bibliography of Child Language* (Evanston, Ill., Northwestern University Press).

LÉVI-STRAUSS, CLAUDE
1945. "L'analyse Structurale en Linguistique et en Anthropologie", *Word*, 1.33-53.
1951. "Language and the Analysis of Social Laws", *American Anthropologist*, 53.155-63.
1955. "The Structural Study of Myth", *Journal of American Folklore*, 68.428-44.

LÉVI-STRAUSS, CLAUDE, JAKOBSON, ROMAN, VOEGELIN, CARL F., and SEBEOK, THOMAS A.

1953. *Results of the Conference of Anthropologists and Linguists* (*International Journal of American Linguistics*, Memoir 8).

LEVY, MARION J., JR.
1952. *The Structure of Society* (Princeton, N.J., Princeton University Press).

LEWIN, KURT
1935. *A Dynamic Theory of Personality: Selected Papers*. Translated by Donald K. Adams, and Karl E. Lerner (New York, McGraw-Hill Book Co.).
1951. *Field Theory in Social Science: Selected Theoretical Papers* (New York, Harper and Bros).

LIBERMAN, ALVIN M., COOPER, FRANKLIN S., HARRIS, KATHERINE S., and MACNEILAGE, PETER F.
1962. "A Motor Theory of Speech Perception", Paper presented at the Speech Communication Seminar, Speech Transmission Laboratory, Royal Institute of Technology, Stockholm (Sept. 1962); to appear in Proceedings of that seminar.

LIBERMAN, ALVIN M., DELATTRE, PIERRE, and COOPER, FRANKLIN S.
1952. "The Rôle of Selected Stimulus Variables in the Perception of the Unvoiced Stop Consonants", *The American Journal of Psychology*, 65.497-516.
1958. "Some Cues for the Distinction between Voiced and Voiceless Stops in Initial Position", *Language and Speech*, 1.153-67.

LIBERMAN, ALVIN, HARRIS, KATHERINE SAFFORD, EIMAS, PETER, LISKER, LEIGH, and BASTIAN, JARVIS
1961. "An Effect of Learning of Speech Perception: The Discrimination of Durations of Silence with and without Phonemic Significance", *Language and Speech*, 4.175-95.

LIBERMAN, ALVIN M., HARRIS, KATHERINE SAFFORD, HOFFMAN, HOWARD S., and GRIFFITH, BELVER C.
1957. "The Discrimination of Speech Sounds with and across Phoneme Boundaries", *Journal of Experimental Psychology*, 54.358-68.

LIBERMAN, A. M., HARRIS, KATHERINE S., KINNEY, JO ANN, LANE, H.
1961. "The Discrimination of Relative Onset-Time of the Components of Certain Speech and Non-speech Patterns", *Journal of Experimental Psychology*, 61.379-88.

LIBERMAN, A. M., INGEMANN, FRANCES, LISKER, LEIGH, DELATTRE, PIERRE, and COOPER, F. S.
1959. "Minimal Rules for Synthesizing Speech", *The Journal of the Acoustical Society of America*, 31.1490-99.

Linguistic Bibliography for the Years 1939-50 (Utrecht-Brussels, Spectrum [by the International Committee of Linguists]).

LINTON, RALPH
1936. *The Study of Man: An Introduction* (New York, Appleton-Century-Crofts, Inc.).
1945. *The Science of Man in the World Crisis* (New York, Columbia University Press).

LISKER, LEIGH
1957. "Minimal Cues for Separating /w, r, l, y/ in Intervocalic Position", *Word*, 13.256-67.

LISKER, LEIGH, COOPER, FRANKLIN S., and LIBERMAN, ALVIN M.
1962. "The Uses of Experiment in Language Description", *Word*, 18.82-106.

LONGACRE, ROBERT E.
1952. "Five Phonemic Pitch Levels in Trique", *Acta Linguistica*, 7.62-82.
1955. "Rejoinder to Hamp's 'Componential Restatement of Syllable Structure in Trique'", *International Journal of American Linguistics*, 21.189-94.
1956. "Review of W. M. Urban, *Language and Reality*; B. L. Whorf, *Four Articles on Metalinguistics*", *Language*, 32.298-308.
1957. *Proto-Mixtecan* (*Indiana University Research Center in Anthropology, Folklore, and Linguistics*, Publication No. 5).
1958a. *Syntax Procedures*. Mimeographed.
1958b. "Items in Context: Their Bearing on Translation Theory", *Language*, 34.482-91.
1959. "Trique Tone Morphemics", *Anthropological Linguistics*, 1.4.5-42.
1960. "String Constituent Analysis", *Language*, 36.63-88.
1963. "Review of Zellig S. Harris, *String Analysis of Sentence Structure*", *Language*, 39.473-78.
1964a [1958a]. *Grammar Discovery Procedures: A Field Manual* (The Hague, Mouton and Company).
1964b. "Prolegomena to Lexical Structure", *Linguistics*, 5.5-24.

LONGACRE, ROBERT E., and MILLON, RENÉ
1961. "Proto-Mixtecan and Proto-Amuzgo-Mixtecan Vocabularies", *Anthropological Linguistics*, 3.4.1-44.

LOOS, EUGENE A.
1963. *Capanahua Narration Structure. Texas Studies in Literature and Language*, Vol. 4, Supplement, pp. 697-742.

LORIOT, JAMES
1957. *Shipibo Paragraph Structure*. Mimeographed.

LOTZ, JOHN
1949. "The Semantic Analysis of the Nominal Bases in Hungarian", *Travaux du Cercle Linguistique de Copenhague*, 5.185-97.
1962. "Semantic Analysis of Tenses in Hungarian", *Lingua*, 11.256-62.

LOTZ, JOHN, ABRAMSON, ARTHUR S., GERSTMAN, LOUIS J., INGEMANN, FRANCES, and NEMSER, WILLIAM J.
1960. "The Perception of English Stops by Speakers of English, Spanish, Hungarian, and Thai: a Tape-Cutting Experiment", *Language and Speech*, 3.71-7.

LOUNSBURY, FLOYD G.
1953. *Oneida Verb Morphology* (*Yale University Publications in Anthropology*, No. 48, New Haven, Yale University Press).
1956. "A Semantic Analysis of the Pawnee Kinship Usage", *Language*, 32.158-94.

LOWIE, ROBERT H.
1917. "Notes on the Social Organization and Customs of the Mandan, Hidatsa, and Crow Indians", *Anthropological Papers of the American Museum of Natural History*, Vol. 21, Part I, pp. 1-99.
1922a. "The Material Culture of the Crow Indians", *Anthropological Papers of the American Museum of Natural History*, Vol. 21, Part III, pp. 201-70.
1922b. "Crow Indian Art", *Anthropological Papers of the American Museum of Natural History*, Vol. 21, Part IV, pp. 271-322.
1924. "Minor Ceremonies of the Crow Indians", *Anthropological Papers of the American Museum of Natural History*, Vol. 21, Part V, pp. 323-75.
1937. *The History of Ethnological Theory* (New York, Rinehart and Co., Inc.).
1950 [1948]. *Social Organization* (London, Routledge and Kegan Paul, Ltd.; New York, Rinehart and Co.).

LUCE, R. DUNCAN, BUSH, ROBERT B., and GALANTER, EUGENE, Eds.
1963. *Handbook of Mathematical Psychology*, Vol. II, Chapters 9-14 (New York, John Wiley and Sons, Inc.).

LUNT, HORACE G.
1950. "Review of J. M. Kořínek, *Uvod do jazykospytu*", *Language*, 26.408-12.

LUTSTORF, HEINZ THEO
1960. *The Stressing of Compounds in Modern English* (Berne, Buchdruckerei Walter Fischer).

LYNCH, JAMES J.
1952. "The Dilemma of Literature", *College English*, 14.100-05.

McDAVID, RAVEN I.
1949. "Review of H. L. Menken, *The American Language*", *Language*, 25.69-77.
1952. "Review of D. Jones, *The Phoneme*", *Language*, 28.377-86.
1958. "American English Dialects", *The Structure of American English* (by W. Nelson Francis), pp. 480-543.

McINTOSH, ANGUS
1961. "Patterns and Ranges", *Language*, 37.325-37.

McKAUGHAN, HOWARD
1954. "Chatino Formulas and Phonemes", *International Journal of American Linguistics*, 20.23-27.

1958. *The Inflection and Syntax of Maranao Verbs* (Manila, Bureau of Printing).
1959. "Semantic Components of Pronoun Systems: Maranao", *Word*, 15.101-02.
1962. "Overt Relation Markers in Maranao", *Language*, 38.47-51.

McKinsey, J. C. C.
1952. *Introduction to the Theory of Games* (New York, McGraw-Hill Book Co., Inc.).

McQuown, Norman A.
1952. "Review of Z. S. Harris, *Methods in Structural Linguistics*", *Language*, 28.495-504.
1957a. "Review of K. L. Pike, *Language* I and II", *American Anthropologist*, 59.189-92.
1957b. "Linguistic Transcription and Specification of Psychiatric Interview Materials", *Psychiatry*, 20.79-86.

Maclay, Howard and Osgood, Charles E.
1959. "Hesitation Phenomena in Spontaneous English Speech", *Word*, 15.19-44.

Mäder, Hannes
1962. "The Tongues of Tyrants", *Atlas*, 4.92-99 (Translated from Humbolt, no. 9, 1962).

Maher, Robert F.
1960. "Social Structure and Cultural Change in Papua", *American Anthropologist*, 62.593-602.

Maier, Norman R. F.
1949. *Frustration: The Study of Behavior without a Goal* (New York, McGraw Hill Book Co.).

Mak, Cornelia
1953. "A Comparison of Two Mixteco Tonemic Systems", *International Journal of American Linguistics*, 19.85-101.

Malinowski, Bronislaw
1935. *Coral Gardens and their Magic*. Vol. 2: *The Language of Magic and Gardening* (New York, American Book Co.).
1945. *The Dynamics of Culture Change* (New Haven, Yale University Press).
1948. "The Problem of Meaning in Primitive Languages", *Magic, Science and Religion* (Boston, Beacon Press), pp. 228-76. (Reprinted from Supplement I to Ogden and Richards, *The Meaning of Meaning*, pp. 296-336 [1923]).

Malkiel, Yakov
1960. "Paradigmatic Resistance to Sound Change", *Language*, 36.281-346.

Malone, Kemp
1936. "The Phonemic Structure of English Monosyllables", *American Speech*, 11.205-18.
1942. "Syllabic Consonants in English", *Modern Language Quarterly*, 3.5-8.

Marckwardt, Albert H.
1940a. *Scribner Handbook of English* (New York, Charles Scribner's Sons).
1940b. "Folk Speech in Indiana and Adjacent States", *Indiana History Bulletin*, 17.120-40.
1944. "An Experiment in Aural Perception", *The English Journal*, 33.212-14.
1946. "Phonemic Structure and Aural Perception", *American Speech*, 21.106-11.
1961. "The Cultural Preparation of the Teacher of English as a Second Language", *Language Learning*, 11.153-56.

Martin, Richard M.
1958. *Truth and Denotation: a Study in Semantic Theory* (London, Routledge and Kegan Paul, Ltd.).

Martin, Samuel E.
1952. *Morphophonemics of Standard Colloquial Japanese, Language Dissertation*, No. 47.
1956. "Review of Charles F. Hockett, *A Manual of Phonology*", *Language*, 32.675-705.
1957. "Problems of Hierarchy and Indeterminacy in Mandarin Phonology", *Bulletin of the Institute of History and Philology*, Academia Sinica, Vol. 29, pp. 209-29.

Martinet, André
1936. "Neutralisation et Archiphonème", *Travaux du Cercle Linguistique de Prague*, 6.46-57.
1948. "Ou en est la Phonologie?", *Lingua*, 1.34-58.

1949a. "La Double Articulation Linguistique", *Travaux du Cercle Linguistique de Copenhague*, 5.30-37.
1949b. *Phonology as Functional Phonetics* (*Publications of the Philological Society*, London, Oxford University Press).
1952. "Function, Structure, and Sound Change", *Word*, 8.1-32.
1960a. "Elements of a Functional Syntax", *Word*, 16.1-10.
1960b. *Éléments de Linguistique Générale* (Paris, Librairie Armand Colin).

MATHESIUS, V.
1929. "La Structure Phonogique de Lexique de Tchèque Moderne", *Travaux du Cercle Linguistique de Prague*, 1.67-84.

MATHIOT, MADELEINE
1962. "Noun Classes and Folk Taxonomy in Papago", *American Anthropologist*, 64.340-50.
1963a. "A Procedure for Investigating Language and Culture Relations", Paper presented at the 1963 annual meeting of the Southwestern Anthropological Association, Riverside, California, April 11-3, 1963.
1963b. "The Place of the Dictionary in Linguistic Description: Problems and Implications", Prepublication manuscript.

MATTESON, ESTHER
1963. *The Piro (Arawakan) Language*. University of California (Berkeley) Ph. D. Dissertation.

MATTESON, ESTHER, and PIKE, KENNETH L.
1958. "Non-Phonemic Transition Vocoids in Piro (Arawak)," *Miscellanea Phonetica*, 3.22-30.

Mayan Studies I
1960. (Linguistic Series of the Summer Institute of Linguistics of the University of Oklahoma, No. 5).

MAYERS, MARVIN
1957. "Pocomchi Verb Structure", *International Journal of American Linguistics*, 23.165-70.
1958. *Pocomchí Texts* (Linguistic Series of the Summer Institute of Linguistics of the University of Oklahoma, No. 2).
1960. *The Pocomchí: A Sociolinguistic Study* (University of Chicago Ph.D. Dissertation).

MEAD, GEORGE H.
1934. *Mind, Self and Society* (Chicago, The University of Chicago Press).
1938. *The Philosophy of the Act* (Chicago, The University of Chicago Press).

MEAD, MARGARET
1937. *Cooperation and Competition among Primitive Peoples* (New York, McGraw-Hill Book Co., Ltd.)
1952. "The Training of the Cultural Anthropologist", *American Anthropologist*, 54.343-46.
1961. "Review of Russel L. Mixter (Ed.), *Evolution and Christian Thought Today*", *American Anthropologist*, 63.395-96.

MEADER, CLARENCE L., and MUYSKENS, JOHN H.
1950. *Handbook of Biolinguistics*, Vol. I (Toledo, Toledo Speech Clinic).

MEEUSSEN, A. E.
1952. *Esquisse de la Langue Ombo* (*Annales du Musée Royal du Congo Belge*, Vol. 4).
1960. "Tabulation of the Independent Indicative in Algonquian", *Studies in Linguistics*, 15.19-23.

Mélanges de Linguistique et de Philologie Offerts à Jacques Van Ginneken à l'occasion du Soixantième Anniversaire de sa Naissance (Paris, Librairie C. Klincksieck, 1937).

Mélanges de Linguistique Offerts à Charles Bally (Genève, Georg et Cie, S. A., 1939).

MENCKEN, H. L.
1945-48 [1919]. *The American Language: an Inquiry into the Development of English in the United States: Supplement I-II* (New York, Alfred A. Knopf).

MEREDITH, G. PATRICK
1956. "Semantics in Relation to Psychology", *Archivum Linguisticum*, 8.1-12.
1959. "Semantic Matrices", *Proceedings of the International Conference on Scientific Information, Washington, D. C., Nov. 16-21, 1958*, Vol. II (Washington, D.C., National Academy of Sciences; National Research Council, pp. 997-1026).

MERRIFIELD, WILLIAM R.
1959. "The Kiowa Verb Prefix", *International Journal of American Linguistics*, 25.168-76.

MERTON, ROBERT K.
1957 [1949]. *Social Theory and Social Structure* (Revised edition, Glencoe, Ill., The Free Press).

MESSING, GORDON M.
1961. "Review of T. A. Sebeok, *Style in Language*", *Language*, 37.256-66.

METZGER, DUANE, and WILLIAMS, GERALD E.
1963. "A Formal Ethnographic Analysis of Tenejapa Ladino Weddings", *American Anthropologist*, 65.1076-1101.

MEYER-EPPLER, W.
1957. "Realization of Prosodic Features in Whispered Speech", *Journal of the Acoustical Society of America*, 29.104-06.

MILEWSKI, TADEUSZ
1951. "The Conception of the Word in the Languages of North American Natives", *Lingua Posnaniensis*, 3.248-68.

MILLER, GEORGE A.
1951. *Language and Communication* (New York, McGraw-Hill Book Co., Inc.).
1956. "The Magical Number Seven, Plus or Minus Two: Some Limits on our Capacity for Processing Information", *Psychological Review*, 63.81-97.

MILLER, GEORGE A., and NICELY, PATRICIA E.
1955. "An Analysis of Perceptual Confusions among some English Consonants", *Journal of the Acoustical Society of America*, 27.338-52.

MILLER, JOHN D.
1961. "Word Tone Recognition in Vietnamese Whispered Speech", *Word*, 17.11-15.

MINOR, EUGENE E.
1956. "Witoto Vowel Clusters", *International Journal of American Linguistics*, 22.131-37.

MITCHELL, T. F.
1953. "Particle-Noun Complexes in a Berber Dialect (Zuara)", *Bulletin of the School of Oriental and African Studies*, 15.375-90.

MOL, H., and UHLENBECK, E. M.
1957. "The Correlation between Interpretation and Production of Speech Sounds", *Lingua*, 6.333-53.
1959. "Hearing and the Concept of the Phoneme", *Lingua*, 8.161-85.

MONTAGUE, WILLIAM PEPPERELL
1925. *The Ways of Knowing* (London, George Allen and Unwin, Ltd.; New York, The MacMillan Company).

MONTANUS, PETRUS (PIETER BERCH).
1635. *Bericht van een Niewe Konst Ganaemt de Spreeckonst* (Delft, Pietersz Vuaalpot).

MOORE, PAUL
1962. "Observations on the Physiology of Hoarseness", *Proceedings of the Fourth International Congress of Phonetic Sciences*, pp. 92-95.

MORENO, JACOB L.
1962. "Role Theory and the Emergence of the Self", *Group Psychotheraphy*, 15.114-17.

MORRIS, CHARLES W.
1938. *Foundations of the Theory of Signs, International Encyclopedia of Unified Science*, Vol. 1, No. 2.
1946. *Signs, Language and Behavior* (New York, Prentice-Hall, Inc.).

MOSES, ELBERT R., JR.
1962. "Experiments with Tongue-Palate Contacts", *Proceedings of the Fourth International Congress of Phonetic Sciences*, pp. 214-20.

MOULTON, WILLIAM G.
1947. "Juncture in Modern Standard German", *Language*, 23.212-26.

1960. "The Short Vowel Systems of Northern Switzerland: a Study in Structural Dialectology", *Word*, 16.155-82.
1962. "Dialect Geography and the Concept of Phonological Space", *Word*, 18.23-32.

MÜLLER, F. MAX
1876. *Chips from a German Workshop* (*Essays on the Science of Language*, Vol. 4. New York, Scribner, Armstrong, and Co.).

MURDOCK, GEORGE PETER
1934. *Our Primitive Contemporaries* (New York, The MacMillan Co.).
1949. *Social Structure* (New York, The MacMillan Co.).
1951. "British Social Anthropology", *American Anthropologist*, 53.465-73.

MURDOCK, GEORGE PETER, FORD, CLELLAN S., and others
1950 [1945]. *Outline of Cultural Materials*, Third edition (*Behavior Science Outlines*, Vol. I, New Haven, Human Relations Area Files, Inc.).

MUYSKENS, JOHN HENRY
1925. *The Smallest Aggregate of Speech Movement Analyzed and Defined, 'The Hypha'*, being correlated results from kymographic and palatographic records. University of Michigan Ph. D. Dissertation.

NADEL, S. F.
1951. *The Foundations of Social Anthropology* (Glencoe, Ill., The Free Press).
1957. *The Theory of Social Structure* (Glencoe, Ill., The Free Press).

NAGEL, ERNEST
1952. "Automatic Control", *Scientific American*, 187.3.44-47.

NEEDHAM, RODNEY
1958. "A Structural Analysis of Purum Society", *American Anthropologist*, 60.75-101.

NEWMAN, JAMES ROY
1956. *The World of Mathematics*, 4 vols., (New York, Simon Schuster).

NEWMAN, STANLEY S.
1933. "Further Experiments in Phonetic Symbolism", *The American Journal of Psychology*, 45.53-75.
1941. "Behavior Patterns in Linguistic Structure: a Case Study", *Language, Culture and Personality, Essays in Memory of Edward Sapir*. Ed. by L. Speir and others (Menasha, Wisc., Sapir Memorial Publication Fund), pp. 94-106.
1946. "On the Stress System of English", *Word*, 2.171-87.
1947. "Bella Coola I: Phonology", *International Journal of American Linguistics*, 13.129-34.

NEWMAN, STANLEY S. and MATHER, VERA G.
1938. "Analysis of Spoken Language of Patients with Affective Disorders," *American Journal of Psychiatry*, 94.913-42.

NEWMARK, LEONARD
1962. "An Albanian Case System", *Lingua*, 11.313-21.

NIDA, EUGENE A.
1947a. *Bible Translating* (New York, American Bible Society).
1947b. "Field Techniques in Descriptive Linguistics", *Intern. Journ. of Amer. Ling.*, 13.138-46.
1948a. "The Analysis of Grammatical Constituents", *Language*, 24.168-77.
1948b. "The Identification of Morphemes", *Language*, 24.414-41.
1949. *Morphology: the Descriptive Analysis of Words*. Second Edition (Ann Arbor, University of Michigan Press, [First edition, 1946]).
1950. *Learning a Foreign Language*. Second edition. (New York, Committee on Missionary Personnel, National Council of the Churches of Christ in the U.S.A.).
1951. "A System for the Description of Semantic Elements", *Word*, 7.1-14.
1952. "A New Methodology in Biblical Exegesis", *The Bible Translator*, 3.97-111.
1955. "Problems of Semantic Equivalents", Paper Presented to the Linguistic Society of America, July 29, 1955.

1958. "Analysis of Meaning and Dictionary Making", *International Journal of American Linguistics*, 24.279-92.

1960 [1943]. *A Synopsis of English Syntax* (Linguistic Series of the Summer Institute of Linguistics of the University of Oklahoma, No. 4).

NOËL-ARMFIELD, G.
1919 [1915]. *General Phonetics* (Cambridge, W. Heffer and Sons, Ltd.).

NORMAN, ARTHUR M. Z.
1958. "An Outline of the Subclasses of the English Nominal", *American Speech*, 23.83-89.

NOSEK, JIRI
1961. "On the Morphology-Syntax Division", *Acta Universitatis Carolinae — Philologica 1, Prague Studies in English*, 9.69-82.

OATES, LYNETTE
1964. "Distribution of Phonemes and Syllables in Gugu-Yalanji", *Anthropological Linguistics*, 6.1.23-26.

OCHIAI, YOSHIYUKI
1957. "Memoirs on Nasalics", *Memoirs of the Faculty of Engineering, Nagoya University*, 9.147-53.

OCHIAI, YOSHIYUKI, and FUKUMURA, TERUO
1957. "Timbre Study on Nasalics, Part I: Symbolic Description of Timbre Patterns of Generalized Vocalics; Part II: Preliminary Experimental Representation of Timbre-Patterns of Sustained Nasals", *Memoirs of the Faculty of Engineering, Nagoya University*, 9.154-59; 160-73.

O'CONNOR, J. D.
1951. "Review of G. L. Trager, and H. L. Smith, *Outline of English Structure*", *Le Maître Phonétique*, Third series, 96.42-44.
1957. "Recent Work in English Phonetics", *Phonetica*, 1.96-117.

O'CONNOR, J. D., and ARNOLD, G. F.
1961. *Intonation of Colloquial English* (London, Longmans).

O'CONNOR, J. D., and TRIM, J. L. M.
1953. "Vowel, Consonant and Syllable — a Phonological Definition", *Word*, 9.103-22.

O'CONNOR, PATRICIA, and TWADDELL, W. F.
1960. *Intensive Training for an Oral Approach in Language Teaching. The Modern Language Journal* Vol. 44, No. 2, Part II.

Official NCAA Handbook for Coaches and Officials, Containing the Official Football Rules
1956. (New York, The National Collegiate Athletic Bureau).

OFTEDAL, MAGNE
1949. "The Vowel System of a Norwegian Dialect in Wisconsin", *Language*, 25.261-67.
1952. "On the Origin of the Scandinavian Tone Distinction", *Norsk Tidsskrift for Sprogvidenskap*, 16.201-25.

OGDEN, C. K., and RICHARDS, I. A.
1952 [1923]. *The Meaning of Meaning: a Study of the Influence of Language upon Thought and of the Science of Symbolism*, Tenth edition, (New York, Harcourt, Brace and Co., Inc.).

ÖHMAN, SUZANNE
1953. "Theories of the 'Linguistic Field'", *Word*, 9.123-34.

OLIVER, DOUGLAS
1958. "An Ethnographer's Method for Formulating Descriptions of 'Social Structure'", *American Anthropologist*, 60.801-26.

OLMSTEAD, DAVID L.
1950. *Ethnolinguistics So Far* (*Studies in Linguistics, Occasional Papers* No. 2).
1951. "Covert (or Zero) Morphemes and Morphemic Juncture", *International Journal of American Linguistics*, 17.163-66.

1954. "Towards a Cultural Theory of Lexical Innovation: A Research Design", *Georgetown University Monograph Series on Languages and Linguistics*, 7.105-17.
1961. "Atsugewi Morphology I: Verb Inflection", *International Journal of American Linguistics*, 27.91-113.

OPLER, MORRIS EDWARD
1948. "Some Recently Developed Concepts Relating to Culture", *Southwestern Journal of Anthropology*, 4.107-22.
1959. "Component, Assemblage, and Theme in Cultural Integration and Differentiation", *American Anthropologist*, 61.955-64.

ORLANS, HAROLD
1958. "Review of Raymond Firth, *Two Studies of Kinship in London*", *American Anthropologist*, 60.961-62.

OSGOOD, CHARLES E.
1959. "Semantic Space Revisited", *Word*, 15.192-200.
1963. "On Understanding and Creating Sentences", *American Psychologist*, 18.735-51.

OSGOOD, CHARLES E., and LURIA, ZELIA
1954. "A Blind Analysis of a Case of Multiple Personality using the Semantic Differential", *Journal of Abnormal and Social Psychology*, 49.579-91.

OSGOOD, CHARLES E., and SEBEOK, THOMAS A., Eds.
1954. *Psycholinguistics: A Survey of Theory and Research Problems* (Indiana University Publications in Anthropology and Linguistics, Memoir 10).

OSGOOD, CHARLES E., SUCI, GEORGE J., and TANNENBAUM, PERCY H.
1957. *The Measurement of Meaning* (Urbana, University of Illinois Press).

OSWALD, VICTOR A., JR.
1943. "'Voiced T' — A Misnomer", *American Speech*, 18.18-25.

PACE, GEORGE B.
1961. "The Two Domains: Meter and Rhythm", *Publications of the Modern Language Association of America*, 76.413-19.

PAGET, SIR RICHARD
1936. "The Relation of the Deaf Mute Sign Language to the Sign Languages of North America and Queensland, Australia", *Proc. of the 2nd Intern. Congress of Phonetic Sciences*, pp. 28-30.

PALMER, F. R.
1955. "The 'Broken Plurals' of Tigrinya", *Bulletin of the School of Oriental and African Studies*, 17.548-66.
1956. "'Openness' in Tigre: A Problem in Prosodic Statement", *Bulletin of the School of Oriental and African Studies*, 18.561-77.
1958. "The Noun in Bilin", *Bulletin of the School of Oriental and African Studies*, 21.376-91.

PALMER, L. R.
1936. *An Introduction to Modern Linguistics*. (London, MacMillan and Co.).

Papers on Philippine Linguistics,
to appear (*Oceanic Linguistics 1964*).

PARK, ROBERT E.
1936. "Human Ecology", *American Journal of Sociology*, 42.1-15.

PARSONS, TALCOTT
1951. *The Social System* (Glencoe, Ill., The Free Press).

PARSONS, TALCOTT, and SHILS, EDWARD A., Eds.
1951. *Toward a General Theory of Action*. Cambridge: Harvard University Press.

PATRICK, G. T. W.
1889 [1888]. *The Fragments of the Work of Heraclitus of Ephesus on Nature*, translated from the Greek Text of Bywater (Baltimore, N. Murray).

Paul, Hermann
1889. *Principles of the History of Language,* translated from the Second edition by H. A. Strong (New York, MacMillan and Co.).

Pedersen, Holger.
1928. "Review of *Language*, Vol. 1 etc.", *Litteris*, 5.148-59.

Peirce, Charles
1931-1935. *Collected Papers of Charles Peirce.* Edited by Charles Hartshorne and Paul Weiss (Cambridge, Harvard University Press).

Percival, Keith
1960. "A Problem in Competing Phonemic Solutions", *Language*, 36.383-86.

Peterson, Gordon E.
1951. "The Phonetic Value of Vowels", *Language*, 27.541-53.
1961. "Parameters of Vowel Quality", *Journal of Speech and Hearing Research*, 4.1.10-29.

Peterson, Gordon E., and Fillmore, Charles J.
1962. "The Theory of Phonemic Analysis", *Proceedings of the Fourth International Congress of Phonetic Sciences*, pp. 476-89.

Peterson, Gordon E., and Lehiste, Ilse
1960. "Duration of Syllable Nuclei in English", *Journal of the Acoustical Society of America*, 32.693-703.

"Phonetics",
1927, unsigned article, *New International Encyclopedia*, 18.539-42.

Piaget, Jean
1955. *The Language and Thought of the Child.* Translated by Marjorie Gabain (New York, Meridian Books, The Noonday Press).

Pickett, Velma
1951. "Nonphonemic Stress: A Problem in Stress Placement in Isthmus Zapotec", *Word*, 7.60-65.
1953. "Isthmus Zapotec Verb Analysis I", *International Journal of American Linguistics*, 19.292-96.
1955. "Isthmus Zapotec Verb Analysis II", *International Journal of American Linguistics*, 21.217-32.
1956. *An Introduction to the Study of Grammatical Structure* (Glendale [now Santa Ana], Calif., Summer Institute of Linguistics).
1960. *The Grammatical Hierarchy of Isthmus Zapotec* (*Language Dissertation* No. 56).

Pike, Eunice V.
1948. "Problems in Zapotec Tone Analysis", *International Journal of American Linguistics*, 14.161-70.
1951. "Tonemic-Intonemic Correlation in Mazahua (Otomí)", *International Journal of American Linguistics*, 17.37-41.
1954. "Phonetic Rank and Subordination in Consonant Patterning and Historical Change", *Miscellanea Phonetica*, 2.25-41.
1956. "Tonally Differentiated Allomorphs in Soyaltepec Mazatec", *International Journal of American Linguistics*, 22.57-71.
1959. "A Test for Predicting Phonetic Ability", *Language Learning*, 9.1.35-41.
1964. "The Phonology of New Guinea Highlands Languages", *American Anthropologist*, 66.4.II.121-32.

Pike, Eunice V., and Scott, Eugene
1962. "The Phonological Hierarchy of Marinahua", *Phonetica*, 8.1-8.

Pike, Evelyn G.
1949. "Controlled Infant Intonation", *Language Learning*, 2.21-24.

Pike, Kenneth L.
1938. *Phonemic Work Sheet* (Glendale [now Santa Ana], Calif., Summer Institute of Linguistics).
1942. *Pronunciation: An Intensive Course in English for Latin-American Students*, Vol. I (Ann Arbor, English Language Institute. [Intonation materials later incorporated in Pike, 1945; pedagogical materials in Fries, 1943]).

1943a. *Phonetics: A Critical Analysis of Phonetic Theory and a Technic for the Practical Description of Sounds* (*University of Michigan Publications in Language and Literature*, 21).
1943b. "Taxemes and Immediate Constituents", *Language*, 19.65-82.
1944. "Analysis of a Mixteco Text", *International Journal of American Linguistics*, 10.113-38.
1945. *The Intonation of American English* (*University of Michigan Publications in Linguistics*, 1. [See above, 1942]).
1947a. "Grammatical Prerequisites to Phonemic Analysis", *Word*, 3.155-72.
1947b. "On the Phonemic Status of English Diphthongs", *Language*, 23.151-59.
1947c. *Phonemics: A Technique for Reducing Languages to Writing* (*University of Michigan Publications, Linguistics*, 3).
1948. *Tone Languages: A Technique for Determining the Number and Type of Pitch Contrasts in a Language, with Studies in Tonemic Substitution and Fusion.* (*University of Michigan Publications, Linguistics*, 4 [Mimeographed edition; Glendale, Summer Institute of Linguistics, 1943]).
1949. "A Problem in Morphology-Syntax Division", *Acta Linguistica*, 5.125-38.
1952a. "More on Grammatical Prerequisites", *Word*, 8.106-21.
1952b. "Operational Phonemics in Reference to Linguistic Relativity", *Journal of the Acoustic Society of America*, 24.618-25.
1953a. "A Note on Allomorph Classes and Tonal Technique", *International Journal of American Linguistics*, 19.101-05.
1953b. "Intonational Analysis of a Rumanian Sentence", *Cahiers Sextil Puscariu*, 2.59-60. (Reprinted from 1948:16)
Part I, 1954; Part II, 1955; Part III, 1960. *Language in Relation to a Unified Theory of the Structure of Human Behavior*, Preliminary Edition. Glendale [now Santa Ana], Calif., Summer Institute of Linguistics.
1956. "Towards a Theory of the Structure of Human Behavior", *Estudios Antropológicos Publicados en Homenaje al Doctor Manuel Gamio* (México, D. F., pp. 659-71).
1957a. "Grammemic Theory in Reference to Restricted Problems of Morpheme Classes", *International Journal of American Linguistics*, 23.119-28.
1957b. "Grammemic Theory", *General Linguistics*, 2.35-41.
1957c. "Abdominal Pulse Types in Some Peruvian Languages", *Language*, 33.30-35.
1957-1958. "Language and Life", *Bibliotheca Sacra*, 114.141-56; 255-62; 347-62; 115.36-43.
1958a. "On Tagmemes née Grammemes", *International Journal of American Linguistics*, 24.273-78.
1958b. "Interpenetration of Phonology, Morphology, and Syntax", *Proceedings of the Eighth International Congress of Linguists*, pp. 363-74.
1959. "Language as Particle, Wave, and Field", *The Texas Quarterly*, 2.2.37-54.
1960a. "Toward a Theory of Change and Bilingualism", *Studies in Linguistics*, 15.1-7.
1960b. "Nucleation", *The Modern Language Journal*, 44.291-95.
1960c. "Linguistic Research as Pedagogical Support", *National Conference on the Teaching of African Languages and Area Studies* (papers edited by John G. Brodie), March 11 and 12, 1960, Georgetown University, pp. 32-39.
1961a. "Stimulating and Resisting Change", *Practical Anthropology*, 8.267-74.
1961b. "Strange Dimensions of Truth", *Christianity Today*, 5.690-92.
1961c. "Compound Affixes in Ocaina", *Language*, 37.570-81.
1962a. "Dimensions of Grammatical Constructions", *Language*, 38.221-44.
1962b. "Practical Phonetics of Rhythm Waves", *Phonetica*, 8.9-30.
1963a. "Choices in Course Design", *The Teaching of Anthropology* (*American Anthropological Association* Memoir 94), pp. 315-32.
1963b. "A Syntactic Paradigm", *Language*, 39.216-30.
1963c. "The Hierarchical and Social Matrix of Suprasegmentals", *Prac Filologicznych*, 18.95-104.
1963d. "Theoretical Implications of Matrix Permutation in Fore (New Guinea)", *Anthropological Linguistics*, 5.8.1-23.
1964a. "Stress Trains in Auca", *In Honour of Daniel Jones*, pp. 425-31.
1964b. "A Linguistic Contribution to the Teaching of Composition", *College Composition and Communication*, 15.82-88.
1964c. "Name Fusions as High-Level Particles in Matrix Theory", *Linguistics*, 6.83-91.

1964d. (to appear). "Dramatis Personae in Reference to a Tagmeme Matrix", paper presented to the Linguistic Society of America, Seattle, July 27, 1963 (*Oceanic Linguistics*, Supplement).
1964e. "On Systems of Grammatical Structure", *Proceedings of the Ninth International Congress of Linguists* (The Hague, Mouton and Co.), pp. 145-53.
1964f. "Beyond the Sentence", *College Composition and Communication*, 15.129-35.
1964g. (to appear). "On the Grammar of Intonation", *Proceedings of the Fifth International Congress of Phonetic Sciences*.
1965a. "Language — Where Science and Poetry Meet", *College English*, 26.283-92.
1965b. (to appear). "A Guide to Publications Related to Tagmemic Theory", *Current Trends in Linguistics: American Linguistics* (The Hague: Mouton and Co.).

PIKE, KENNETH L., and BECKER, ALTON L.
1964. "Progressive Neutralization in Dimensions of Navajo Stem Matrices", *International Journal of American Linguistics*, 30.144-54.

PIKE, K. L., and ERICKSON, BARBARA
1964. "Conflated Field Structures in Potawatomi and in Arabic", *International Journal of American Linguistics*, 30.201-12.

PIKE, K. L., and KINDBERG, WILLARD
1956. "A Problem in Multiple Stresses", *Word*, 12.415-28.

PIKE, K. L., and PIKE, EUNICE V.
1947. "Immediate Constituents of Mazateco Syllables", *International Journal of American Linguistics*, 13.78-91.
1960. *Live Issues in Descriptive Linguistics*. Second edition (Santa Ana, Calif., Summer Institute of Linguistics).

PIKE, K. L., and SCOTT, GRAHAM
1963. "Pitch Accent and Non-Accented Phrases in Fore (New Guinea)", *Zeitschrift für Phonetik, Sprachwissenschaft und Kommunikationsforschung*, 16.179-89

PIKE, K. L., and WARKENTIN, MILTON
1961. "Huave: a Study in Syntactic Tone with Low Lexical Functional Load", *A William Cameron Townsend*, pp. 627-42.

PIMSLEUR, PAUL, MACE, LARRY, KEISLAR, EVAN
1961. *Preliminary Descrimination Training in the Teaching of French Pronunciation* (Los Angeles, University of California).

PITTENGER, ROBERT E., HOCKETT, CHARLES F., and DANEHY, JOHN J.
1960. *The First Five Minutes* (Ithaca, N.Y., Paul Martineau).

PITTENGER, ROBERT E., and SMITH, HENRY LEE, JR.
1957. "A Basis for Some Contributions of Linguistics to Psychiatry", *Psychiatry*, 20.61-78.

PITTMAN, RICHARD S.
1948a. "Nahuatl Honorifics", *International Journal of American Linguistics*, 14.236-39.
1948b. "Nuclear Structures in Linguistics", *Language*, 24.287-92.
1954a. *A Grammar of Tetelcingo (Morelos) Nahuatl* (*Language Dissertation*, No. 50).
1954b. "Relative Relevance to Total Structure as Criterion for Determining Priority of Statement Sequence in Descriptive Grammar", *International Journal of American Linguistics*, 20.238-40.
1959. "On Defining Morphology and Syntax", *International Journal of American Linguistics*, 25.199-201.
1962. "A Formula for the English Verb Auxiliaries", *Language Learning*, 12.79-80.
1963. "Review of A. H. Kuipers, *Phoneme and Morpheme in Kabardian (Eastern Adyghe)*", *Language*, 39.346-50.

PLANCK, MAX
1949. *Scientific Autobiography and Other Papers*. Translated by Frank Gaynor (New York, Philosophical Library).

Poetics
1961. Edited by D. Davie and others, ('s-Gravenhage, Mouton and Co.).

POLIVANOV, EVGENIJ
1931. "La Perception des Sons d'une Langue Étrangère", *Travaux du Cercle Linguistique de Prague*, 4.79-96.

POSTAL, PAUL M.
1962. *Some Syntactic Rules in Mohawk* (Yale University Ph. D. Dissertation).
1964. *Constituent Structure: a Study of Contemporary Models of Syntactic Description* (*Indiana University Research Center in Anthropology, Folklore and Linguistics*, Publication 30).

POSTMAN, LEO
1951. "Towards a General Theory of Cognition", *Social Psychology at the Crossroads*, J. H. Rohrer and M. Sherif, Eds. (New York, Harper and Bros.), pp. 242-72.

POTTER, RALPH K.; KOPP, GEORGE A.; and GREEN, HARRIET C.
1947. *Visible Speech* (New York, D. Van Nostrand Co.).

POTTER, SIMEON
1957. *Modern Linguistics* (London, Andre Deutsch).
1962. "Syllabic Juncture", *Proceedings of the Fourth International Congress of Phonetic Sciences*, pp. 728-30.

POWLISON, PAUL S.
1962. "Palatalization Portmanteaus in Yagua (Peba-Yaguan)", *Word*, 18.280-99.
Preprints of the Ninth International Congress of Linguists, 1962. Edited by Morris Halle (Cambridge, Mass.).

PRESTON, W. D.; and VOEGELIN, C. F.
1949. "Seneca I", *International Journal of American Linguistics*, 15.23-44.

PRIDE, KITTY
1961. "Numerals in Chatino", *Anthropological Linguistics*, 3.2.1-10b.

PRIEST, PERRY N., PRIEST, ANNE M., and GRIMES, JOSEPH E.
1961. "Simultaneous Orderings in Siriono (Guaraní)", *International Journal of American Linguistics*, 27.335-44.

Principes de Transcription Phonologique, 1931. *Travaux du Cercle Linguistique de Prague*, 4.323-26.
Proceedings of the Eighth International Congress of Linguists. Edited by E. Sivertsen, 1958. (Oslo, Oslo University Press).
Proceedings of the Fourth International Congress of Phonetic Sciences. Edited by A. Sovijärvi and P. Aalto, 1962 (The Hague, Mouton and Co.).
Proceedings of the Second International Congress of Phonetic Sciences, 1936. Edited by D. Jones and D. B. Fry. (Cambridge, Cambridge University Press).
Proceedings of the Third International Congress of Phonetic Sciences, 1939. Edited by E. Blancquaert and W. Pee. (Ghent, Belgium, Laboratory of Phonetics).
"Projet de Terminologie Phonologique Standardisée", 1931, *Travaux du Cercle Linguistique de Prague*, 4.309-23.

PRONKO, N. H.
1946. "Language and Psycholinguistics: A Review", *Psychological Bulletin*, 43.189-239.

PROPP, V.
1958 [1928]. *Morphology of the Folktale*, Edited by Svatava Pirkova-Jakobson; translated by Lawrence Scott (*Indiana University Research Center in Anthropology, Folklore, and Linguistics*, Publication 10).

PROST, GILBERT R.
1962. "Signaling of Transitive and Intransitive in Chacobo (Pano)", *International Journal of American Linguistics*, 28.108-18.

PULGRAM, ERNST
1959. *Introduction to the Spectrography of Speech* ('s-Gravenhage, Mouton and Co.).
1961. "French /ə/: Statics and Dynamics of Linguistic Subcodes", *Lingua*, 10.305-25.

PUTNAM, GEORGE N., and O'HERN, EDNA M.
1955. *The Status Significance of an Isolated Urban Dialect* (*Language Dissertation*, No. 53).

QUILLER-COUCH, SIR ARTHUR
1947 [1920]. *Studies in Literature* (Guild books [published for the British Publishers Guild by the Cambridge University Press]).

QUINE, WILLARD VAN ORMAN
1953. *From a Logical Point of View* (Cambridge, Harvard University Press).
1960. *Word and Object* (Cambridge, The Masachusetts Institute of Technology, New York, John Wiley and Sons, Inc.).

QUIRK, R.
1958. "Substitutions and Syntactical Research", *Archivum Linguisticum*, 10.1.37-42.

RADCLIFFE-BROWN, A. R.
1949. "White's View of a Science of Culture", *American Anthropologist*, 51.503-12.
1952. *Structure and Function in Primitive Society* (Glencoe, Ill., The Free Press).

RADCLIFFE-BROWN, A. R., and FORDE, DARYLL
1950. *African Systems of Kinship and Marriage* (London, Oxford University Press).

RAPAPORT, DAVID, Ed.
1951. *Organization and Pathology of Thought* (New York, Columbia University Press).

READ, ALLAN WALKER
1949. "English Words with Constituent Elements Having Independent Semantic Value", *Philologica: The Malone Anniversary Studies*, Edited by T. A. Kirby and H. B. Woolf (Baltimore, Johns Hopkins Press), pp. 306-12.

READ, K. E.
1959. "Leadership and Consensus in a New Guinea Society", *American Anthropologist*, 61.425-36.

REIFLER, ERWIN
1953. "Linguistic Analysis, Meaning, and Comparative Semantics", *Lingua*, 3.371-90.

REIK, THEODOR
1948. *Listening with the Third Ear* (New York, Farrar, Straus and Co.).

RENSCH, CALVIN ROSS
1963. *Proto-Chinantec Phonology* (University of Pennsylvania M. A. Thesis).

Report of the Third Annual Round Table Meeting on Linguistics and Language Teaching. Edited by S. J. Castiglione (Washington, D.C., Georgetown University Press.).

Report of the Sixth Annual Round Table Meeting on Linguistics and Language Teaching. Edited by Ruth Hirsch Weinstein, 1955 (Washington, D.C., Georgetown University Press).

RESZKIEWICZ, ALFRED
1962. *Main Sentence Elements in The Book of Margery Kempe* (Warsaw, Wydawnictwo Polskiej Akademii Nauk).

REYBURN, WILLIAM D.
1954. "Quechua I: Phonemics", *International Journal of American Linguistics*, 20.210-14.

RIFFATERRE, MICHAEL
1959. "Criteria for Style Analysis", *Word*, 15.154-74.
1960. "Stylistic Context", *Word*, 16.207-18.

RIGAULT, ANDRÉ
1962. "Rôle de la Fréquence, de l'Intensité et de la Durée Vocaliques dans la Perception de l'Accent en Français", *Proceedings of the Fourth International Congress of Phonetic Sciences*, pp. 735-48.

RIPMAN, WALTER
1899. *Elements of Phonetics* (London, J. M. Dent and Sons, Ltd. [Translated and adapted from W. Vietor, *Kleine Phonetik*]).

ROBERTS, PAUL
1956. *Patterns of English* (New York, Harcourt, Brace and World, Inc.).
1962. *English Sentences* (New York, Harcourt, Brace and World, Inc.).
1964. *English Syntax: Alternate Edition* (New York, Harcourt, Brace and World, Inc.).

ROBBINS, FRANK E.
1961. "Quiotepec Chinantec Syllable Patterning", *International Journal of American Linguistics*, 27.237-50.

ROBBINS, WILFRED W., HARRINGTON, JOHN P., FREIRE-MARRECO, BARBARA
1916. *Ethnobotony of the Tewa Indians* (U.S. Bureau of American Ethnology, *Bulletin* 55).

ROBINS, R. H.
1951. *Ancient and Mediaeval Grammatical Theory in Europe; with Particular Reference to Modern Linguistic Doctrine* (London, G. Bell and Sons, Ltd.).
1952. "Noun and Verb in Universal Grammar", *Language*, 28.289-98.
1953a. "The Phonology of the Nasalized Verbal Forms in Sundanese", *Bulletin of the School of Oriental and African Studies*, 15.138-45.
1953b. "Formal Divisions in Sundanese", *Transactions of The Philological Society, 1953*, pp. 109-42.
1957a. "Vowel Nasality in Sudanese; A Phonological and Grammatical Study", *Studies in Linguistic Analysis*. (Oxford, Basil Blackwell), pp. 87-103.
1957b. "Aspects of Prosodic Analysis", *Proceedings of the University of Durham Philosophical Society*, Series B, 1.1.1-12.
1959a. "Nominal and Verbal Derivation in Sundanese", *Lingua*, 8.337-69.
1959b. "Linguistics and Anthropology", *Man*, 283.1-4 (reprint).
1960. "In Defence of WP", *Transactions of the Philological Society 1959*, pp. 116-44.
1961. "John Rupert Firth", *Language*, 37.191-200.

ROGET, PETER MARK
1933 [1911]. *Thesaurus of English Words and Phrases*. Revised. (New York, Grosset and Dunlop).

ROHRER, JOHN H., and SHERIF, MUZAFER, Eds.
1951. *Social Psychology at the Crossroads* (New York, Harper and Bros).

ROMMETVEIT, RAGNAR
1955. *Social Norms and Roles: Exploration in the Psychology of Enduring Social Pressures* (Minneapolis, University of Minnesota Press).

ROMNEY, A. KIMBALL, and EPLING, PHILIP J.
1958. "A Simplified Model of Kariera Kinship", *American Anthropologist*, 60.59-74.

ROSBOTTOM, HARRY
1961. "Different-Level Tense Markers in Guaraní", *International Journal of American Linguistics*, 27.345-52.

ROSS, ALAN S. C.
1944. "The Fundamental Definition of the Theory of Language", *Acta Linguistica*, 4.101-06.

ROWE, JOHN HOWLAND
1950. "Sound Patterns in Three Inca Dialects", *International Journal of American Linguistics*, 16.137-48.

ROWLANDS, E. C.
1954. "Types of Word Junction in Yoruba", *Bulletin of the School of Oriental and African Studies*, 16.376-88.

RUSH, JAMES
1867 [1827]. *The Philosophy of the Human Voice, Embracing its Physiological History, together with a System of Principles by Which Criticism in the Art of Elocution May be Rendered Intelligible* ... Sixth Edition (Philadelphia, The Library Company of Philadelphia).

RUSSELL, BERTRAND
1940. *An Inquiry into Meaning and Truth* (New York, W. W. Norton and Co., Inc.).

SAHLINS, MARSHALL D.
1957. "Differentiation by Adaption in Polynesian Societies", *Journal of the Polynesian Society*, 66.291-300.

SAKATA, SHOICHI
1961. "Toward a New Concept of Elementary Particles", *The Progress of Theoretical Physics, Supplement*, 19.3-9.

SAPIR, EDWARD
1921. *Language: an Introduction to the Study of Speech* (New York, Harcourt, Brace and Co.).
1930. *Totality* (*Language Monograph*, No. 6).
1949. *Selected Writings of Edward Sapir in Language, Culture, and Personality*, Edited by David G. Mandelbaum (Berkeley, University of California Press).

SAPIR, EDWARD, and SWADESH, MORRIS
1932. *The Expression of the Ending-Point Relation in English, French, and German*, Edited by Alice V. Morris (*Language Monograph*, No. 10).
1946. "American Indian Grammatical Categories", *Word*, 2.103-12.

SAPON, STANLEY M.
1953. "A Methodology for the Study of Socio-Economic Differentials in Linguistic Phenomena", *Studies in Linguistics*, 11.57-68.

SAPORTA, SOL
1956. "Morph, Morpheme, Archimorpheme", *Word*, 12.9-14.
1958. "Review of Colin Cherry, *On Human Communication*", *International Journal of American Linguistics*, 24.326-29.
1959. "Spanish Person Markers", *Language*, 35.612-15.
ED. 1961. *Psycholinguistics: A Book of Readings* (New York, Holt, Rinehart and Winston).

SAPORTA, SOL, and CONTRERAS, HELES
1962. *A Phonological Grammar of Spanish* (Seattle, University of Washington Press).

SARLES, HARVEY B.
1963. "The Question-Response System in Language", mimeographed, pre-publication manuscript.

ŠAUMJAN, S. K.
1962. "Two-Level Theory of Phonology", *Proceedings of the Fourth International Congress of Phonetic Sciences*, pp. 757-61.

SAWYER, W. W.
1959 [1955]. *Prelude to Mathematics* (Baltimore: Penguin Books).

SCHACHTER, PAUL
1961a. "Phonetic Similarity in Tonemic Analysis", *Language*, 37.231-38.
1961b. "Structural Ambiguity in Tagalog", *Language Learning*, 11.135-45.

SCHILDER, PAUL
1950. *The Image and Appearance of the Human Body: Studies in the Constructive Energies of the Psyche* (New York, International Universities Press, Inc.).

SCHUBIGER, MARIA
1935. *The Role of Intonation in Spoken English* (Cambridge, W. Heffer and Sons, Ltd.).
1946. "Intonation — Word-Order — Provisional *It*", *English Studies*, 27.129-41.
1949. "The Intonation of Interrogative Sentences", *English Studies*, 30.262-65.
1951. "The Intonation of Interrogative Sentences II", *English Studies*, 32.252-55.

SCOTT, N. C.
1947. "The Monosyllable in Szechuanese", *Bulletin of the School of Oriental and African Studies*, 12.197-213.
1956. "A Phonological Analysis of the Szechuanese Monosyllable", *Bulletin of the School of Oriental and African Studies*, 18.556-60.

SEBEOK, THOMAS A.
1946. *Finnish and Hungarian Case Systems: Their Form and Function* (*Acta Instituti Hungarici Universitatis Holmiensis*, Series B. Linguistica, 3).

1953. "The Structure and Content of Cheremis Charms", Part I, *Anthropos*, 48.371-88.
1959. "Selected Readings in General Phonemics (1925-1959)", *Studies in Linguistics*, 14.43-47.
(ED.) 1960. *Style in Language* (The Technology Press of M.I.T.; and New York, London, John Wiley and Sons, Inc.).
1962a. "Coding in the Evolution of Signalling Behavior", *Behavioral Science*, 7.430-42.
1962b. "Materials for a Typology of Dictionaries", *Lingua*, 11.363-74.
1963a. "Review of M. Lindauer, *Communication among Social Bees*; W. N. Kellogg, *Porpoises and Sonar*; J. C. Lilly, *Man and Dolphin*", *Language*, 39.448-66.
1963b. *Current Trends in Linguistics*, Vol. I: *Soviet and East European Linguistics* (The Hague, Mouton and Co.).
Second Texas Conference on Problems of Linguistic Analysis in English, 1957, 1962. (Austin, University of Texas Press).
Série Linguistica Especial, I.
1959. *Publicações do Museu Nacional* (Rio de Janeiro, Brazil).

SERVICE, ELMAN R.
1958. *A Profile of Primitive Cultures* (New York, Harper and Bros).

SHANNON, CLAUDE E. and MCCARTHY, J., Eds.
1956. *Automata Studies* (Princeton, Princeton University Press).

SHANNON, CLAUDE E., and WEAVER, WARREN
1949. *The Mathematical Theory of Communication* (Urbana, The University of Illinois Press).

SHARP, ALAN E.
1954. "A Tonal Analysis of the Disyllabic Noun in the Machame Dialect of Chaga", *Bulletin of the School of Oriental and African Studies*, 16.157-69.
1958. "Falling-Rising Intonation Patterns in English", *Phonetica*, 2.127-52.
1961. "The Analysis of Stress and Juncture in English", *Transactions of the Philological Society, 1960*, pp. 104-35.

SHEFFIELD, ALFRED DWIGHT
1912. *Grammar and Thinking: a Study of the Working Conceptions in Syntax* (New York, The Knickerbocker Press).

SHELL, OLIVE A.
1950. "Cashibo I: Phonemes", *International Journal of American Linguistics*, 16.198-202.
1957. "Cashibo II: Grammemic Analysis of Transitive and Intransitive Verb Patterns", *International Journal of American Linguistics*, 23.179-218.

SHEN, YAO, CHAO, JESSICA C. Y., and PETERSON, GILES
1961. "Some Spectrographic Light on Mandarin Tone-2 and Tone-3", *Study of Sounds*, 9.265-314.

SHERIDAN, THOMAS
1798. *A Course of Lectures on Elocution: a New Edition* (Providence, Carter and Wilkinson).

SHORTO, H. L.
1960. "Word and Syllable Patterns in Palaung", *Bulletin of the School of Oriental and African Studies*, 23.544-57.

SIERTSEMA, BERTHA
1959. "Problems of Phonemic Interpretation II: Long Vowels in a Tone Language", *Lingua*, 8.42-64.
1963. "Intonation Phenomena in Tone Languages (as compared with those in non-tonal languages)", *Actes du Second Colloque International de Linguistique Négro-Africane* (Dakar, University of Dakar, West-African Languages Survey), pp. 55-65.

SIGURD, BENGT
1955. "Rank Order of Consonants Established by Distributional Criteria", *Studia Linguistica*, 9.8-20.

SIMON, H. F.
1953. "Two Substantival Complexes in Standard Chinese", *Bulletin of the School of Oriental and African Studies*, 15.327-55.

SINCLAIR, ANGUS
1951. *The Conditions of Knowing* (London, Routledge and Kegan Paul, Ltd.).

SIVERTS, HENNING
1956. "Social and Cultural Changes in a Tzeltal (Mayan) Municipio, Chiapas, Mexico", *Proceedings of the Thirty-Second International Congress of Americanists, Copenhagen*, pp. 177-89.

SIVERTSEN, EVA
1960. "Reviews of C. H. Borgstrøm, *Innføring i sprogvidenskap*; H. A. Gleason, *An Introduction to Descriptive Linguistics*; H. A. Gleason, *Workbook in Descriptive Linguistics*; and C. F. Hockett, *A Course in Modern Linguistics*", *Norsk Tidsskrift for Sprogvidenskap*, 19.745-79.
1961. "Segment Inventories for Speech Synthesis", *Language and Speech*, 4.27-90.

SIVERTSEN, EVA, and PETERSON, GORDON E.
1960. *Studies on Speech Synthesis* (*Report No. 5*, Speech Research Laboratory, University of Michigan, Ann Arbor, Mich.).

SJOBERG, ANDRÉE F.
1962. "Coexistent Phonemic Systems in Telugu: a Socio-Cultural Perspective", *Word*, 18.269-79.

SKALIČKA, VLADIMÍR
1936. "La Fonction de l'Ordre des Éléments Linguistiques", *Travaux du Cercle Linguistique de Prague*, 6.129-33.

SKINNER, B. F.
1938. *The Behavior of Organisms* (New York, Appleton-Century Co.).
1953. *Science and Human Behavior* (New York, The MacMillan Co.).
1957. *Verbal Behavior* (New York, Appleton-Century-Crofts, Inc.).

SLEDD, JAMES
1955. "Review of G. L. Trager and H. L. Smith Jr., *An Outline of English Structure*, and C. C. Fries, *The Structure of English*", *Language*, 31.312-45.
1957. "Review of H. Whitehall, *Structural Essentials of English;* D. J. Lloyd and H. R. Warfel, *American English in its Cultural Setting*; and P. Roberts, *Patterns of English*", *Language*, 33.261-71.
1958. "Some Questions of English Phonology", *Language*, 34.252-58.
1959. *A Short Introduction to English Grammar* (Chicago, Scott, Forseman and Co.).

SLOCUM, MARIANA C.
1948. "Tzeltal (Mayan) Noun and Verb Morphology", *International Journal of American Linguistics*, 14.77-86.

SMALLEY, WILLIAM A.
1953. "Phonemic Rhythm in Comanche", *International Journal of American Linguistics*, 19.297-301.
1955. "A Problem in Phoneme Identification without Differential Meaning", *General Linguistics*, 1.62-69.
1961. *Outline of Khmuʔ Structure* (New Haven, American Oriental Society).

SMITH, CARLOTA S.
1961. "A Class of Complex Modifiers in English", *Language*, 37.342-65.

SMITH, HENRY LEE, JR.
1952. "An Outline of Metalinguistic Analysis", *Report of the Third Annual Round Table Meeting on Linguistics and Language Teaching*, pp. 59-66.
1955. "Review of W. Jassem, *Intonation of Conversational English* (*Educated Southern British*)", *Language*, 31.150-53.
1959. "Toward Redefining English Prosody", *Studies in Linguistics*, 14.68-76.

SMITH, WILLIAM B. S.
1950. "Review of R. A. Hall, Jr., *Descriptive Italian Grammar*", *Studies in Linguistics*, 8.5-11.

SOMMERFELT, ALF
1931. "Sur l'Importance Générale de la Syllable", *Travaux du Cercle Linguistique de Prague*, 4.156-60.
1936. "Can Syllable Divisions have Phonological Importance?", *Proceedings of the Second International Congress of Phonetic Sciences*, pp. 30-33.

SPEISER, E. A.
1953. "Cultural Factors in Social Dynamics in the Near East", *Middle East Journal*, 7.133-52.

SPENCER, JOHN
1957. "Received Pronunciation: Some Problems of Interpretation", *Lingua*, 7.7-29.

SPIRO, MELFORD E.
1954. "Human Nature in its Psychological Dimensions", *American Anthropologist*, 56.19-30.

SPRIGG, R. K.
1954. "Verbal Phrases in Lhasa Tibetan", *Bulletin of the School of Oriental and African Studies*, Part I, 16.134-56; Part II, 16.320-50; Part III, 16.566-91.
1955. "The Tonal System of Tibetan (Lhasa Dialect) and the Nominal Phrase", *Bulletin of the School of Oriental and African Studies*, 17.133-53.
1961. "Vowel Harmony in Lhasa Tibetan: Prosodic Analysis Applied to Interrelated Vocalic Features of Successive Syllables", *Bulletin of the School of Oriental and African Studies*, 24.116-38.

STANKIEWICZ, EDWARD
1957. "On Discreteness and Continuity in Structural Dialectology", *Word*, 13.44-59.
1960. "The Consonantal Alternations in the Slavic Declensions", *Word*, 16.183-203.
1961. "Grammatical Neutralization in Slavic Expressive Forms", *Word*, 17.128-45.

STENNES, LESLIE H.
1961. *An Introduction to Fulani Syntax. Hartford Studies in Linguistics*, 2, Hartford, Conn.

STERN, THEODORE
1957. "Drum and Whistle 'Languages': and Analysis of Speech Surrogates", *American Anthropologist*, 59.487-506.

STETSON, R. H.
1937. "The Phoneme and the Grapheme", *Mélanges de Linguistique et de Philologie Offerts à Jacques Van Ginneken*, pp. 353-56.
1945. *Bases of Phonology* (Oberlin, Oberlin College).
1948. "Traits of Articulate Language", *The Quarterly Journal of Speech*, 34.191-93.
1951 [1928]. *Motor Phonetics; a Study of Speech Movements in Action*. Second edition (Amsterdam, North-Holland Publishing Co.).

STETSON, R. H., and HUDGINS, C. V.
1930. "Functions of the Breathing Movements in the Mechanism of Speech", *Archives Néerlandaises de Phonétique Expérimentale*, 5.1-30.

STEVENS, S. S., Ed.
1951. *Handbook of Experimental Psychology* (New York, John Wiley and Sons, Inc.).

STEVENSON, CHARLES L.
1947. "Some Relations between Philosophy and the Study of Language", *Analysis*, 8.1 (reprint).
1948. "Meaning: Descriptive and Emotive", *The Philosophical Review*, 57.127-44.

STIRLING, M. W.
1963. "John Peabody Harrington, 1884-1961 — an Obituary", *American Anthropologist*, 65.370-81.

STOCKWELL, ROBERT P.
1959. "Review of J. R. Firth, Ed., *Studies in Linguistic Analysis*", *International Journal of American Linguistics*, 25.254-59.
1960a. "Review of M. Schubiger, *English Intonation: its Form and Function*", *Language*, 36.544-48.
1960b. "The Place of Intonation in a Generative Grammar of English", *Language*, 36.360-67.

STOCKWELL, ROBERT P., BOWEN, J. DONALD, and SILVA-FUENZALIDA, I.
1956. "Spanish Juncture and Intonation," *Language*, 32.641-65.

STOKOE, WILLIAM C., JR.
1960. *Sign Language Structure: an Outline of the Visual Communication Systems of the American Deaf* (*Studies in Linguistics, Occasional Papers*, No. 8).

STREVENS, PETER
1954. "Spoken English in the Gold Coast", *English Language Teaching*, 8.81-89.
Structure of Language and its Mathematical Aspects

1961. Edited by Roman Jakobson. (*Proceedings of the Twelfth Symposium in Applied Mathematics.* Providence, R. I., American Mathematical Society).
Studies in Ecuadorian Indian Languages: I, 1962 (Linguistic Series of the Summer Institute of Linguistics of the University of Oklahoma, No. 7).
Studies in Peruvian Indian Languages: I, 1963 (Linguistic Series of the Summer Institute of Linguistics of the University of Oklahoma, No. 9).
Studies Presented to Joshua Whatmough, 1957, Edited by E. Pulgram (The Hague, Mouton and Co.).

STURTEVANT, EDGAR
1940. *The Pronunciation of Greek and Latin* (*William Dwight Whitney Linguistic Series.* Philadelphia. Linguistic Society of America).

SUMNER, WILLIAM G.
1940 [1906]. *Folkways: a Study of the Sociological Importance of Usages, Manners, Customs, Mores, and Morals* (Boston, Ginn and Co.).

SWADESH, MORRIS
1934. "The Phonemic Principle", *Language*, 10.117-29.
1935a. "The Vowels of Chicago English", *Language*, 11.148-51.
1935b. "Twaddell on Defining the Phoneme", *Language*, 11.244-50.
1937a. "The Phonemic Interpretation of Long Consonants", *Language*, 13.1-10.
1937b. "A Method for Phonetic Accuracy and Speed", *American Anthropologist*, 39.728-32.
1947. "On the Analysis of English Syllabics", *Language*, 23.137-50.

SWEET, HENRY
1900a. [1892] *A New English Grammar*, Vol. I (Oxford, Clarendon Press).
1900b [1899]. *The Practical Study of Languages*: *a Guide for Teachers and Learners* (New York, Henry Holt and Co.).
1906. *Primer of Phonetics.* Third edition (Oxford: Clarendon Press).
1913. *Collected Papers of Henry Sweet* (Oxford, Clarendon Press. *Words, Logic, and Grammar*, pp. 1-33 [reprinted from *Transactions of the Philological Society, 1875-86*, pp. 470-503]).

SWETS, JOHN A., TANNER, WILSON P., and BIRDSALL, THEODORE G.
1961. "Decision Processes in Perception", *Psychological Review*, 68.301-40.
Symposium on American Indian Linguistics Held at Berkeley, July 7, 1951, 1954 (*University of California Publications in Linguistics*, 10).

TAX, SOL, Ed.
1952. *Indian Tribes of Aboriginal America: Selected Papers of the Twenty-Ninth International Congress of Americanists* (Chicago, University of Chicago Press).

TAX, SOL, EISELEY, LOREN C., ROUSE, IRVING; and VOEGELIN, CARL F., Eds.
1953. *An Appraisal of Anthropology Today* (Chicago, the Univ. of Chicago Press). [Especially "Cultural Anthropology and Linguistics", pp. 225-26]).

THATCHER, JAMES W.; and WANG, WILLIAM S-Y.
1962. *The Measurement of Functional Load* (University of Michigan Communication Sciences Laboratory, Report No. 8).

THIESSEN, WESLEY
"Drum Signalling in Bora", Prepublication manuscript.
Third Texas Conference on Problems of Linguistic Analysis in English, 1958. 1962 (Austin, The University of Texas).

THOMAS, CHARLES KENNETH
1947. *An Introduction to the Phonetics of American English* (New York, The Ronald Press Company).

THOMAS, DAVID
1955. "Three Analyses of the Ilocano Pronoun System", *Word*, 11.204-08.
1958. "Mansaka Sentence and Sub-Sentence Structures", *Philippine Social Sciences and Humanities Review*, 23.339-58.
1964. "Transformational Paradigms from Clause Roots", *Anthropological Linguistics*, 6.1.1-6.

THOMPSON, EDGAR T.
1935. "The Grammar of Society", *Sociology and Social Research*, 19.507-19.

THOMPSON, STITH
1955-58. *Motif-Index of Folk Literature*, Vols. 1-6 (Bloomington, Indiana University Press).

THURSTONE, L. L.
1947. *Multiple-Factor Analysis: a Development and Expansion of the Vectors of Mind* (Chicago, University of Chicago Press).

TIKHOMIROV, O. K.
1959. "Review of B. F. Skinner, *Verbal Behavior*", *Word*, 15.362-67.

TIMASHEFF, NICHOLAS S.
1955. *Sociological Theory: its Nature and Growth* (Garden City, N. Y.: Doubleday and Co., Inc.).

TOGEBY, KNUD
1949. "Qu'est-ce Qu'un Mot?", *Travaux de Cercle Linguistique de Copenhague*, 5.97-111.
1951. "Structure Immanente de la Langue Française", *Travaux du Cercle Linguistique de Copenhague*, 6.

TRAGER, GEORGE L.
1935. "The Transcription of English", *Le Maître Phonetique*, Third Series, No. 49, pp. 10-13.
1941. "The Theory of Accentual Systems", *Language, Culture and Personality, Essays in Memory of Edward Sapir*, ed. by L. Speir and others (Menasha, Wisc., Sapir Memorial Publication Fund), pp. 131-45.
1942. "The Phoneme 'T': a Study in Theory and Method", *American Speech*, 17.144-48.
1944. "The Verb Morphology of Spoken French", *Language*, 20.131-41.
1948. "Taos I: a Language Revisited", *International Journal of American Linguistics*, 14.155-60.
1949. *The Field of Linguistics* (*Studies in Linguistics, Occasional Papers*, No. 1).
1950. "Review of K. L. Pike, *Phonemics*", *Language*, 26.152-58.
1951. "Review of E. A. Nida, *Morphology*, Second Edition", *International Journal of American Linguistics*, 17.126-31.
1952. "Recent Publications", *Studies in Linguistics*, 10.18-26.
1958. "Paralanguage: a First Approximation", *Studies in Linguistics*, 13.1-12.
1959.
1961. "Taos IV: Morphemics, Syntax, Semology in Nouns and in Pronominal Reference", *International Journal of American Linguistics*, 27.211-22.
1963. *Linguistics is Linguistics* (*Studies in Linguistics, Occasional Papers* No. 10).

TRAGER, GEORGE L., and BLOCH, BERNARD
1941. "The Syllabic Phonemes of English", *Language*, 17.223-46.

TRAGER, GEORGE L., and SMITH, HENRY LEE, JR.
1951. *An Outline of English Structure* (*Studies in Linguistics, Occasional Papers*, No. 3).

Trends in European and American Linguistics, 1930-1960, 1961, Edited by Christine Mohrmann, Alf Sommerfelt, and Joshua Whatmough (Utrecht, The Netherlands; and Antwerp, Belgium, Spectrum Publishers).

TRIM, JOHN L. M.
1962. "The Identification of Phonological Units", *Proceedings of the Fourth International Congress of Phonetic Sciences*, pp. 773-78.

TRNKA, B.
1935. *A Phonological Analysis of Present-Day Standard English* (V. Praze, Nákladem Filosofické Fakulty University Karlovy).
1939. "On the Combinatory Variants", *Proceedings of the Third International Congress of Phonetic Sciences*, pp. 23-30.

TRUBETZKOY, N. S.
1929. "Zur Allgemeinen Theorie der Phonologischen Vokalsystem", *Travaux du Cercle Linguistique de Prague*, 1.39-67.
1931. "Phonologie und Sprachgeographie", *Travaux du Cercle Linguistique de Prague*, 4.228-34.
1935. *Anleitung zu phonologischen Beschreibungen* (Brno: Edition du Cercle Linguistique de Prague).

1949. *Principes de Phonologie* (Paris, Librairie C. Klincksieck). Translated by J. Cantineau from *Grundzüge der Phonologie, Travaux du Cercle Linguistique de Prague*, 7, 1939.

TRUBETZKOY, N. S.; JAKOBSON, R.; and KARCEVSKIJ, S.
1938 [1930]. "Propositions", *Actes du Premier Congrès International de Linguistes.*

TUCKER, A. N.
1949. "Sotho-Nguni Orthography and Tone-Marking", *Bulletin of the School of Oriental and African Studies*, 13.200-24.

TUGBY, DONALD J.
1958. "A Typological Analysis of Axes and Choppers from Southeast Australia", *American Antiguity*, 24.24-33.

TUSTIN, ARNOLD
1952. "Feedback", *Scientific American*, 187.3.48-55.

TWADDELL, W. FREEMAN
1935. *On Defining the Phoneme*. (*Language Monograph*, No. 16).
1936a. "Answers to Andrade's Questions", *Language*, 12.294-97.
1936b. "On Various Phonemes", *Language*, 12.53-59.
1946. "Review of R. H. Stetson, *Bases of Phonology*", *International Journal of American Linguistics*, 12.102-08.
1949. "Meanings, Habits and Rules", *Language Learning*, 2.4-11.
1953. "Stetson's Model and the 'Supra-Segmental Phonemes'", *Language*, 29.415-53.
1960. *The English Verb Auxiliaries* (Providence, Brown University Press).

TYLOR, EDWARD B.
1913. *Primitive Culture*, Vols. 1 and 2. (London, John Murray, Albemarle Street).

UHLENBECK, E. M.
1950. "The Structure of the Javanese Morpheme", *Lingua*, 2.239-70.
1953. "The Study of Wordclasses in Javanese", *Lingua*, 3.322-54.
1962. "Limitations of Morphological Processes — Some Preliminary Remarks", *Lingua*, 11.426-32.
1963. "An Appraisal of Transformation Theory", *Lingua*, 12.1-18.

ULDALL, ELIZABETH
1960. "Attitudinal Meanings Conveyed by Intonation Contours", *Languagĕ and Speech*, 3.223-34.

ULDALL, H. J.
1936. "The Phonematics of Danish", *Proceedings of the Second International Congress of Phonetic Sciences*, pp. 54-57.
1939. "On the Structural Interpretation of Diphthongs", *Proceedings of the Third International Congress of Phonetic Sciences*, pp. 272-76.
1949. "On Equivalent Relations", *Travaux du Cercle Linguistique de Copenhague, Recherches Structurales*, 5.71-76.
1957. "Outline of Glossematics. Part I: General Theory", *Travaux du Cercle Linguistique de Copenhague*, 10.1-89.

ULLMANN, STEPHEN
1956. "The Concept of Meaning in Linguistics", *Archivum Linguisticum*, 8.12-20.
1957a. "Historical Semantics and the Structure of the Vocabulary", *Miscelánea Homenaje I a André Martinet* (Canarias, Biblioteca Filológica, Universidad de la Laguna), pp. 289-303.
1957b [1951]. *The Principles of Semantics*. Second Edition. (Glasgow, Jackson, Son and Co.).

URBAN, WILBUR N.
1939 (and second impression 1951). *Language and Reality: the Philosophy of Language and the Principles of Symbolism* (New York, The MacMillan Co.).

VACHEK, J.
1936. "One Aspect of the Phoneme Theory", *Proceedings of the Second International Congress of Phonetic Sciences*, pp. 33-40.

1964. *A Prague School Reader in Linguistics* (Bloomington, Indiana Univ. Press).

VENDRYES, J.
1925. *Language* (London, Kegan Paul, Trench, Trubner and Co. Ltd.).

VEREECKEN, CÉCILE
1939. "Stress-Groups", *Proceedings of the Third International Congress of Phonetic Sciences*, pp. 248-51.

VINACKE, W. EDGAR
1951. "The Investigation of Concept Formation", *Psychological Bulletin*, 48.1-31.
1952. *The Psychology of Thinking* (New York, McGraw-Hill).

VOEGELIN, C. F.
1947. "A Problem in Morpheme Alternants and Their Distribution", *Language*, 23.245-54.
1949. "Review of K. L. Pike, *Phonemics*", *International Journal of American Linguistics*, 15.75-85.
1952. "Linguistically Marked Distinctions in Meaning", *Selected Papers of the Twenty-Ninth Congress of Americanists*, edited by Sol Tax, pp. 222-33.
1953. "From FL (Shawnee) to TL (English), Autobiography of a Woman", *International Journal of American Linguistics*, 19.1-26.
1954. "A Modern Method for Field Work Treatment of Previously Collected Texts", *Journal of American Folklore*, 67.15-20.
1955. "On Developing New Typologies, and Revising Old Ones", *Southwestern Journal of Anthropology*, 11.355-60.
1959. "Model-Directed Structuralization", *Anthropological Linguistics*, 1.1.9-25.
1960. "Anthropological Linguistics: Introduction and Summary", Mimeographed, pre-publication manuscript.
1961. "Review of K. S. Hilton et al., *Vocabulario Tarahumara*; A. McMahan and M. A. de McMahan, *Vocabulario Cora*; V. Pickett et al., *Vocabulario Zapoteco del Istmo*; L. Clark y N. Davis de Clark, *Vocabulario Popoluca de Sayula*", *American Anthropologist*, 63.877-78.

VOEGELIN, C. F., and HARRIS, Z. S.
1952. "Training in Anthropological Linguistics", *American Anthropologist*, 54.322-27.

VOEGELIN, C. F., and VOEGELIN, FLORENCE M.
1957. *Hopi Domains* (*International Journal of American Linguistics*, Memoir 14).
1963. "On the History of Structuralizing in 20th Century America", *Anthropological Linguistics*, 5.1.12-37.

VOEGELIN, C. F., and YEGERLEHNER, JOHN
1956. "The Scope of Whole System ('Distinctive Feature') and Subsystem Typologies", *Word*, 12.444-53.

VOGT, EVON Z.
1960. "On the Concepts of Structure and Process in Cultural Anthropology", *American Anthropologist*, 62.18-33.

VOGT, HANS
1942. "The Structure of the Norwegian Monosyllables", *Norsk Tidsskrift for Sprogvidenskap*, 12.5-29.
1954. "Phoneme Classes and Phoneme Classification", *Word*, 10.28-34.

VON BERTALANFFY, LUDWIG
1955. "General System Theory", *Main Currents in Modern Thought*, 2.75-83.

VON LAZICZIUS, J.
1936. "A New Category in Phonology", *Proceedings of the Second International Congress of Phonetic Sciences*, pp. 57-60.

WALLACE, ANTHONY F. C., and ATKINS, JOHN
1960. "The Meaning of Kinship Terms", *American Anthropologist*, 62.58-80.

WALLIS, ETHEL
1951. "Intonational Stress Patterns of Contemporary Spanish", *Hispania*, 34.143-47.

1956. "Simulfixation in Aspect Markers of Mezquital Otomí", *Language*, 32.453-59.

WALTER, W. GREY
1953. *The Living Brain* (New York, W. W. Norton and Co., Inc.).

WANG, WILLIAM S-Y.
1959. "Transition and Release as Perceptual Cues for Final Plosives", *Journal of Speech and Hearing Research*, 2.66-73.

WANGLER, HANS-HEINRICH
1958. "Singen und Sprechen in Einer Tonsprache (Hausa)", *Zeitschrift für Phonetik und Allgemeine Sprachwissenschaft*, 11.23-34.

WARNER, WILLIAM LLOYD
1953. *American Life: Dream and Reality* (Chicago, The University of Chicago Press).

WATERHOUSE, VIOLA
1949. "Learning a Second Language First", *International Journal of American Linguistics*, 15.106-09.
1962. *The Grammatical Structure of Oaxaca Chontal* (*Indiana University Research Center in Anthropology, Folklore, and Linguistics, Publication* 19).
1963. "Independent and Dependent Sentences", *International Journal of American Linguistics*, 29.45-54.

WEBER, MAX
1947. *The Theory of Social and Economic Organization*, translated by A. M. Henderson and Talcott Parsons (New York, Oxford University Press).

WEINREICH, URIEL
1953a. *Languages in Contact* (New York, Linguistic Circle of New York).
1953b. "Review of J. B. Carroll, *The Study of Language*", *Word*, 9.277-79.
1954. "Is a Structural Dialectology Possible?", *Word*, 10.388-400.
1957. "On the Description of Phonic Interference", *Word*, 13.1-11.
1958. "Travels through Semantic Space", *Word*, 14.346-66.
1959. "On the Cultural History of Yiddish Rime", *Essays on Jewish Life and Thought* (New York, Columbia University Press, pp. 423-42.

WEIR, RUTH HIRSCH
1962. *Language in the Crib* (The Hague, Mouton and Co.).

WELLEK, RENÉ, and WARREN, AUSTIN
1949 [1942]. *Theory of Literature* (New York, Harcourt, Brace and Co.).

WELLS, RULON S.
1945. "The Pitch Phonemes of English", *Language*, 21.27-39.
1947a. "Immediate Constituents", *Language*, 23.81-117.
1947b. "Review of K. L. Pike, *The Intonation of American English*", *Language*, 23.255-73.
1949. "Automatic Alternation", *Language*, 25.99-116.
1954. "Meaning and Use", *Word*, 10.235-50.
1962. "What has Linguistics done for Philosophy?", *The Journal of Philosophy*, 59.23.697-708.

WELMERS, WILLIAM E.
1946. *A Descriptive Grammar of Fanti* (*Language Dissertation*, No. 39).
1947. "Hints from Morphology for Phonemic Analysis", *Studies in Linguistics*, 5.91-100.
1949. "Tonemes and Tone Writing in Maninka", *Studies in Linguistics*, 7.1-17.
1950a. "Notes on Two Languages in the Senufo Group: I. Senadi", *Language*, 26.126-46.
1950b. "Notes on Two Languages in the Senufo Group: II. Sup'ide", *Language*, 26.494-531.
1952. "Notes on the Structure of Bariba", *Language*, 28.82-103.
1959. "Tonemics, Morphotonemics, and Tonal Morphemes", *General Linguistics*, 4.1-9.

WELMERS, WILLIAM E. and HARRIS, ZELLIG S.
1942. "The Phonemes of Fanti", *Journal of the American Oriental Society*, 62.318-33.

WEST, JOHN DAVID
1962. "The Phonology of Mikasuki", *Studies in Linguistics*, 16.77-91.

WEYAND, NORMAN
1949. *Immortal Diamond: Studies in Gerald Manley Hopkins* (New York, Sheed and Ward).
"What is a Long-Eared Animal?", Anonymous, 1952, *The Bible Translator*, 3.143.

WHITE, LESLIE A.
1949. *The Science of Culture* (New York, Farrar, Straus and Co.).
1959. "The Concept of Culture", *American Anthropologist*, 61.227-51.

WHITEHEAD, ALFRED NORTH
1925. *Science and the Modern World* [References in this text are to the Mentor Book Edition, New York, 1952] (New York, The MacMillan Co.)

WHITFIELD, FRANCIS J.
1955. "Review of R. Magnusson, *Studies in the Theory of the Parts of Speech*", *Language*, 31.245-47.

WHITNEY, WILLIAM D.
1867. *Language and the Study of Language* (New York, Charles Scribner and Co.).

WHORF, BENJAMIN LEE
1943. "Phonemic Analysis of the English of Eastern Massachusetts", *Studies in Linguistics*, 2.21-40.
1950. Articles reprinted under the title of *Four Articles on Metalinguistics* (Washington, D.C., Foreign Service Institute, Department of State).
1956. *Language, Thought, and Reality: Selected Writings.* Edited by John B. Carroll (Cambridge, Technology Press of Masachussetts Institute of Technology; New York, John Wiley Sons, Inc.).

WHYTE, LANCELOT LAW
1961. "A Scientific View of the 'Creative Energy' of Man", *Aesthetics Today*. Edited by Morris Philipson (Meridan Books, Cleveland, The World Publishing Co.), pp. 349-74.

WHYTE, WILLIAM H.
1956. *The Organization Man.* (New York, Simon and Schuster).

WIENER, NORBERT
1948. *Cybernetics, or Control and Communication in the Animal and the Machine* (New York, John Wiley and Sons, Inc.).
1954 [1950]. *The Human Use of Human Beings: Cybernetics and Society.* Boston, Houghton Mifflin Co.

WIIK, KALEVI
1962. "Phoneme Boundaries of Finnish Vowels", *Proceedings of the Fourth International Congress of Phonetic Sciences*, pp. 795-99.

WILKINS, JOHN
1668. *An Essay Towards a Real Character and a Philosophical Language* (London, Printed for Sa. Gellibrand, and for John Martin, printer to the Royal Societies).

WILLIAMSON, K.
1959. "The Units of an African Tone Language", *Phonetica*, 3.145-66.

WILSON, JOHN
1956. *Language and the Pursuit of Truth.* (Cambridge, Cambridge University Press).

WIMSATT, WILLIAM KURTZ
1954. *The Verbal Icon: Studies in the Meaning of Poetry* (Lexington, University of Kentucky Press).

WISE, MARY RUTH
1958. "Diverse Points of Articulation of Allophones in Amuesha (Arawak)", *Miscellanea Phonetica*, 3.15-21.
1963. "Six Levels of Structure in Amuesha Verbs", *International Journal of American Linguistics*, 29.132-52.

WISSLER, CLARK
1935. "Material Culture", *Handbook of Social Psychology*, Edited by Carl Murchison. (Worchester, Mass., Clark University Press), pp. 520-64.

WOLFENDEN, ELMER
1961. *A Re-Statement of Tagalog Grammar* (Manila, Summer Institute of Linguistics and the Institute of National Language).

WOLFF, HANS
1959. "Subsystem Typologies and Area Linguistics", *Anthropological Linguistics*, 1.7.1-88.

WONDERLY, WILLIAM L.
1946. "Phonemic Acculturation in Zoque", *International Journal of American Linguistics*, 12.92-95.
1951-52. "Zoque: Phonemics and Morphology", *International Journal of American Linguistics*, 17.1-9, 105-23, 137-62, 235-51; 18.35-48, 189-202.
1952a. "Semantic Components in Kechua Person Morphemes", *Language*, 28.366-76.
1952b. "Information-Correspondence and the Translation of Ephesians into Zoque", *The Bible Translator*, 3.138-42.

WONDERLY, WILLIAM L., GIBSON, LORNA F., and KIRK, PAUL L.
1954. "Number in Kiowa: Nouns, Demonstratives, and Adjectives", *International Journal of American Linguistics*, 20.1-7.

WOODWORTH, ROBERT S.
1938. *Experimental Psychology* (New York, Henry Holt and Co.).

WORTH, DEAN S.
1958. "Transform Analysis of Russian Instrumental Constructions", *Word*, 14.247-90.

WURM, S. A., and LAYCOCK, D. C.
1961. "The Question of Language and Dialect in New Guinea", *Oceania*, 32.128-43.

YEGERLEHNER, JOHN
1954. "The First Five Minutes of Shawnee Laws in Multiple Stage Translation", *International Journal of American Linguistics*, 20.281-94.

YEN, ISABELLA Y.
1960. *A Grammatical Analysis of Syau Jing* (Indiana University Research Center in Anthropology, Folklore, and Linguistics, Publication 16).

YNGVE, VICTOR H.
1960. *A Model and an Hypothesis for Language Structure* (Cambridge, Massachusetts Institute of Technology Research Laboratory of Electronics. Technical Report No. 369).

ZGUSTA, L.
1960. "Review of W. S. Allen, *On the Linguistic Study of Languages*", *Archiv Orientální*, 28.326-27.

ZIFF, PAUL
1960. *Semantic Analysis* (Ithaca, N.Y., Cornell University Press).

ŽINKIN, N. I.
1962. "Four Communicative Systems and Four Languages", *Word*, 18.143-72.

ZIPF, GEORGE KINGSLEY
1935. *The Psycho-Biology of Language: An Introduction to Dynamic Philology* (Boston, Houghton Mifflin Co.).

ZVELEBIL, KAMIL
1962. "How to Handle the Structure of Tamil", *Archiv Orientální*, 30.116-42.

ZWIRNER, EBERHARD
1962. *Deutsches Spracharchiv, 1932–1962* (Munster, Westfalen, Aschendorffsche Buchdruckerei).

INDEX

When an author is mentioned in several consecutive columns, only one inclusive reference is given.

Aarne, 145
Abbreviation, 383-84
Abdomineme and Abdominal Pulse, 385, 392-95; *see also* Stress Group
Abercrombie, 48, 193, 346
Aberle, 666, 669
Abrahamson, 487-88, 691, 704
Abramson, 353
Abstraction, 587, 635; *see also* Hypostasis
Acoustics, 348
——, versus articulation, 353
——, segmentation in, 349
Acteme, 290-93
——, hyper-, 364
——, nonverbal, 291-93
——, verbal as phoneme, 293
Activeness
——, grades of, 190-91
——, of phoneme, 322
——, semi-active, 200
——, of slot in syllable, 390
——, of tagmeme, 236-382
——, tests for, 170
Activity
——, physical, in phoneme, 341
——, preverbal; *see* Subsegmental
——, and role, 671
——, unplanned, 659
Adams, 639
Adaptation, 667
Adcock, 675
Affix, 217
Age, 646
Agreement, 230
Agta, 696
Aguaruna, 394
Akhmanova, 596, 627, 640
Albanian, 560
Albright, 345
Algonquian, 706

Algorithm; *see also* Intuition
——, impossible for analysis, 289
Allen, H., 146, 537, 541, 593
Allen, R., 118, 488
Allen, W., 57, 346, 349, 355, 412, 481, 542, 557, 561, 588-89, 594, 725
Allison, 419
Alloclass, 332-35, 464; *see also* Variant
Alloconstruction, 499
Allolog, 482
Allomorph, 164
——, class of, 206, 551
——, as morpheme occurring, 176
——, relevance in Spanish, 551
——, semantic, 599
——, versus vector formative, 548n
Allophone
——, class of, 328
——, distribution of, 411
Allotagma, 228
——, zero, 563
Alphabet, 345; *see also* Phoneme
——, for tagmeme, 470-71n
Alston, 601
Altmann, 628, 702
Amarakaeri, 696
Ambiguity, 231, 248, 499; *see also* Homophony, Segmentation, arbitrary
——, and expansion test, 459
——, of formative in matrix, 548n, 627
——, and hierarchy intersection, 570
——, homormorphic sequence, 574
——, by matrix conflation, 548n
——, nonverbal, 43-44
——, of segmentation, arbitrary, 550-52
Amuesha, 728
Analysis, 558
——, activity in abstracting slot, 222
——, behavioremic prerequisites, 321
——, as changing structure, 159

── , componential, of meaning, 626-28
── , controls on modes in, 510-21
── , distribution in, 39, 60
── , dynamic, 239
── , of fusion, 547
── , grammar in phonemics, 361-63
── , and intuition, 244-25, 493
── , levels of, 586-88
── , and meaning, 278-79
── , in morphemics, 559
── , native reaction in, 63
── , nonverbal data in, 60
── , phonological and grammatical prerequisites, 314n
── , of sentence, 149
── , static, 239
── , via systems clash, 64-67
── , transformational procedure, 363
Anderson, 542
Andrade, 346, 725
Andreyev, 359, 487, 490, 494, 502, 512n, 588, 620
Animal Communication, 36, 665
Antal, 690
Anthony, 541
Anthropology; *see also* Activity; Behavior; Behavioreme; Society
── , etics in, 145
Apache, 688
Aphasia, 636-37
Appropriateness, of class, 84; *see also* Class
April Fool, 132, 596, 602, 608
Arabic, 695
Arawak, 697
Archeology, and etics, 55
Archiphoneme, 301-02, 359-60
Arend, 345
Argyle, 668
Ariste, 539
Aristotle, 144, 488
── , properties, 55
Armstrong, 55, 506, 542
Arnold, 412, 417, 541, 697, 711
Articulation
── , versus acoustics, 353
── , and perception, 353-54
Aschmann, 373, 387, 414, 559, 563
As If, 59, 63
Atkins, 626, 723
Atsugewi, 712
Attribute, 635
Austin, G., 64, 71, 684
Austin, W., 357, 679
Axiom, in theory, 68-69
Ayres, 591
Aztec, 703

Bach, 272, 480-81, 487, 495-96, 498, 502, 504, 588
Bally, 561
Bantu, 694
Bar-Hillel, 69, 70, 270, 278, 322, 348, 362, 479, 488, 498-99
Barker, 95, 144, 667
Barrett, 488
Bascom, 560
Base, reconstructed, 550-52
Baseball, 52, 54, 272n; *see also* Cricket
Basketball, 29
Bastian, 353, 705
Bazell, 66, 174, 179, 182, 184, 187-90, 192, 270, 274, 285, 355, 359-60, 362, 410, 478, 482, 540, 559, 561, 631
Beardsley, 669
Becker, 489, 712
Behavior; *see also* Native Reaction
── , accidental, 664
── , actual function of, 157-58
── , business letter, 35
── , change as border, 75
── , church service, 73-94
── , conduct, 54
── , context of, 641-78
── , distribution in, 39
── , etic and emic standpoints in, 37-72
── , exploratory, 518
── , family of responses, 677
── , grammar of, 35
── , homomorphic, 43, 160
── , hypostatic, 155; *see also* Hypostasis
── , indeterminate under observation, 159
── , interdisciplinary concepts in, 36
── , non-verbal, 5, 9, 32-33; at breakfast, 122; meaning, 215; need of concepts in, 36; rejected as criteria, 66; structured, 35; units, 96; physical component, 89
── , practice, 54
── , psychological, 32
── , repetition in, 45
── , responses and sentences, 34
── , social, trimodal via Parsons, 190
── , tagmeme in, 501
── , of thing, 661
── , verbal, integrated with nonverbal, 25-36
Behavior Cycle, 144; *see also* Behavioreme
Behavioreme, 120-49; *see also* Sentence
── , breakfast, 122-28
── , chart of modes, 143
── , defined, 121
── , distribution mode of, 194-289
── , episode, 144
── , feature mode of, 150-93
── , included, 128-29

——, maximum, 130
——, minimum, 129-30; manifestation types, 291-363
——, versus motif, 153
——, system of, 131
——, well-described, 121n
Belasco, 487
Belief, 532-33, 658; *see also* Observer; Theory
Bella Coola, 420-21, 710
Bendor-Samuel, 286, 351, 474
Benedict, 53
Bentley, 630
Benveniste, 147, 485
Berber, 429, 709
Berch, 709
Berger, 359
Berko, 158, 191
Bibliography
——, on animal communication, 36
——, on bilingualism, 593
——, on breath group, 419
——, on co-existent systems, 593-95
——, on concept formation, 633-38
——, on context of behavior, 665-78
——, on dialects, 593
——, and ethnolinguistics, 33
——, on etic versus emic, 53-55
——, on focus, 118
——, on fusion, 556-64
——, on gesture, 35
——, on grammatical constructions, 473-509
——, on grammatical meaning, 630
——, on hierarchy, 95
——, on hypermorpheme, 429-31
——, on intonation, 539-41
——, on juncture, 418
——, on meaning, 616-42; lexical 630-33; structural analysis of, 626-28
——, on morpheme, 182-93
——, on over-all pattern, 592
——, on perception, 625-26
——, on personality and individual, 674-76
——, on phonological meaning, 628-30
——, on psycholinguistics: 351-54
——, on role as S-tagmeme, 670-74
——, on segmentation, 94-95
——, on sentence, beyond the, 145-48, 484-85
——, on simplicity, 587-88
——, on society requisites, 668-70
——, on stress group, 417-19
——, on style, 595-96
——, on subsegmental meaning, 638-40
——, on suprasegmental elements, 535-44
——, on syllable, 409-16
——, on synonymy, 621-22
——, on system, 586-97

——, on tagmeme, 270-89
——, on thing, 676-78
——, on tone, 541-43
——, on translation, 640
——, on unit, 96
——, on universals, 623-24
——, on verbal versus nonverbal events, 32-36
——, on voice quality, 536-38
——, on zero, 561-64
Bidney, 670, 674-75
Bilin, 712
Bilingualism, 593
Binary, 244, 348, 359
——, versus serial, 477
Birdsall, 720
Birdwhistell, 34-35, 184, 193, 344
Black, 629, 684
Blake, 488
Bloch, B., 59, 62-63, 66-67, 95, 182, 186, 190, 305, 315, 346, 355-56, 359, 361-62, 368, 371, 373, 376, 407, 411, 414, 418-19, 474, 492, 540, 559, 561, 587, 592, 594, 619, 628, 687, 703, 724
——, on English 'am', 558-59
——, on Japanese syllables, 375
——, without meaning, 60
Bloch, J., 701
Blood, 594
Bloomfield, 54, 62, 67, 96, 118, 139, 146, 149, 167, 183-84, 187, 190-91, 273, 275-76, 280, 283, 286-88, 331-34, 337-38, 344-45, 355-56, 358, 368, 372, 410, 413-14, 423, 430, 439, 442, 476-79, 482-84, 486, 488-90, 492, 549-50, 557, 559, 561-62, 593, 595, 601, 612, 619-20, 630-31
——, and hypostasis, 118
——, and meaning, 63, 188
——, sentence types from, 139
——, tagmeme versus Pike, 490
Boas, 344
Bock, 62n, 96, 667-68, 673-75
——, emics in social structure, 55
——, social role and tagmeme, 35
Bolinger, 129n, 171n, 182, 185-86, 190-91, 193, 323, 417, 430, 540-41, 622, 629-30, 640, 704
Bora, 543, 720
Border; *see also* Closure
——, and closure, 82
——, coterminous, 566
——, hierarchical crisscross, 572
——, indeterminacy of, 77; in rhythm unit, 395n
——, of phonology, 315-16
——, physical versus tagmemic, 220
Borgstrøm, 717
Borman, 419
Bororo, 697
Borst, 307, 352, 356, 411, 687

INDEX 733

Boulding, 699, 672
Bowen, 537, 541, 722
Boyd, 495
Braine, 275-76, 624
Braithwaite, 69, 71
Brazier, 624, 638
Breakfast, 122-28, 154-55, 195
——, acteme in, 291-93
——, actions in, 291-93
——, componential elements in, 532
——, distribution in, 124
——, Halliday on, 144
——, hierarchies of speech in, 571
——, illustrating slot-class, 195
——, motif in, 151-52
——, official slot, 125
——, as slot filler, 128
——, slot-class in, 195-96
——, variant in, 124
Breath Group, 152, 404, 579
——, bibliography on, 419
——, indrawn, 530-31
Brend, 419, 477, 483, 485, 487
Bridgeman, 70
Bright, 544
Broadbent, 347, 354, 366n, 542, 703
Brodbeck, 69
Brøndal, 352, 410, 418
Bronfenbrenner, 679
Broth, 625, 640
Brown, G. S., 591, 677
Brown, J., 632-33
Brown, R., 274, 279, 488, 625-26, 629-30, 633-36
Bruner, 64, 71, 96, 624, 633-35, 638-39, 676
Buettner-Janusch, 57
Bull, 193, 286, 488, 631
Buning, 541
Burgess, 670
Burling, 627
Burmese, 415
Bursill-Hall, 350, 416
Burton-Page, 543
Bush, 706
Busnel, 544

Cakchiquel, 315
Campa, 542
Campbell, 71, 591, 677, 684
Candoshi, 687
Canonge, 539
Canonical Form, 175
Cantril, 675
Capanahua, 706
Capell, 193
Carib, 698
Carnap, 69, 617, 620

Carneiro, 666, 688
Carnochan, 95, 323, 356, 360, 415, 429, 539
Carroll, 33, 96, 145, 351-52, 411, 431, 483, 503, 596, 616, 626-27, 629, 632, 635, 638, 727
Case, 200
Cashibo, 421, 434-35, 443
Cassirer, 482, 625, 639
Category, 163n, 285, 509; *see also* Matrix
——, implicit, 563
——, item-and-field, 562-63
——, in society, 646
——, subcategory; *see* Substitution, correlation
Catford, 538
Cause, 663
Cazaku, 594
Chacobo, 714
Chafe, 481
Chaga, 350, 542, 717
Chandola, 36, 665
Chang, 542
Change
——, as border of segment, 75
——, cultural, 667
——, emic unit causing, 642
——, John Doe, allo of, 656
——, matrix vectors in, 642n
——, by observation, 159
——, during segmentation, 133-34
Chao, J., 543, 717
Chao, Y. R., 56, 62, 67, 71, 139, 279, 346, 373, 414, 489, 541, 561, 570, 588, 698
Character, 533
Chatino, 542, 560, 706, 716
Cheremis, 147, 410, 595, 720
Cherry, 63, 359, 676
Chess, 52
Chest Pulse: 365-69; *see also* Syllable
Child
——, learning, 275
——, solemnant, 148
Chinantec, 543, 714-15
Chinese, 64, 155, 213, 373, 397, 481, 489, 543-544, 685, 720
Choice, 280-81, 624, 640; *see also* Native Reaction
——, as animism, 281
——, of kernel sentence, 503
——, mechanical, 494
——, in morpheme class, 197
——, native reaction to, 197
Chomsky, 53, 71, 97, 147, 149, 190, 192, 231n, 274, 279, 281, 314n, 346-47, 351-53, 357, 362-363, 410, 416-18, 470, 474-75, 480, 485, 488, 492-93, 495-501, 503-06, 512n, 535, 541, 558, 560, 592, 597, 620-21, 624, 630, 704
——, on fact, 57

———, pair test, 64
———, rejecting phonemics, 351
———, semantics in grammar, 149
———, symbol versus unit, 271
Chontal, 470
Chuave, 417
Church Service, 73-94
Clark, 361, 414, 483, 487-88
Clark, L., 722
Class, 457, 543
———, of activity, 31
———, of allomorph, 551
———, of allophones, 204, 327
———, in artificial language, 210-18
———, cleavage, 585; of phonemes, 339
———, compatible sets of, 208
———, disjunctive, 274
———, distribution, of tagmeme, 246
———, emic subclass, with transformation test, 233n
———, not an event, 203
———, hierarchy of, 202, 209
———, hyperclass, 489
———, hypermorpheme, 214, 216, 243, 460
———, major versus minor, 211-14
———, meaning of, 201, 212, 249, 253, 606, 630
———, of morphemes, bibliography on, 272-75; characteristics of, 178; closed, 201; distribution mode of, 201-04; emically conditioned, 205; empty, 199; feature mode of, 198-201; manifestation mode of, 204-08; meaning of, 198; membership as feature, 200; mutually-exclusive, 201; open, 201; small versus large, 201; structure of, 198-216; as tagmeme feature, 198; tagmemically conditioned, 205; unique, 201
———, morphemically-complex members of, 200
———, of morphs, 178; criteria for, 181
———, noun, 458
———, of phonemes, 322; distribution class of, 325-26; emic subdivisions of, 331-38; hierarchy of, 326, 338-39; sets of, 326; variants of, 326-27
———, phonemically-conditioned, 205
———, of phones, criteria for, 343
———, as probability, 488
———, segmental, 83
———, semantic variants of, 206-07
———, sentence types, 140-41
———, shape-type of, 202
———, of tagmeme, 245-50
———, variant of, 461; types of, 204-08
———, of words, 489; meaning of, 273
Clause; *see also* Syntagmeme
———, dimensions of, 9
———, as level, 441
———, nucleus of, 468
———, portmanteau in, 441
———, transform in, 441
———, versus phrase, 486-87
———, wave in, 468
Cliché, 604
Click, 324, 594
Cline, 54, 508-09
Closure, 96; *see also* Juncture
———, Aristotle, 144
———, breakfast, 122-23
———, criteria for, 81-82
———, in game, 103
Cocama, 414, 541, 593-94
Coda, 416
Codability, 635
Code, 63, 508
Coexistent System, 314, 583
Cognition
———, system of, 184
———, world of informants, 35
Cohen, 69, 679
Cole-Beuchat, 560
Colligation, 476
Comanche, 153-54, 305, 539, 684, 721
Communication, 598; *see also* Meaning
Communication Theory, 281
Commutation; *see* Substitution
Compartmentalization, 406, 587, 589; *see also* Levels
———, of meaning, 61
Complementarity, 588; *see also* Particle; Field; Wave
Component, 35, 163, 527-32; *see also* Phoneme; Prosody
———, in breakfast, 532
———, sequential, 294
———, simultaneous, 162, 294, 408
Componential; *see also* Simultaneity; Portmanteau
Compound, 554
Compounding, and morpheme clusters, 560
Computation, 640
Concept, 612-16, 632, 678
———, color, 632
———, formation of, bibliography on, 633-38
———, names, 634
———, need for interdisciplinary, 36
———, nonverbal, 636
———, scientific as invention, 71
———, subsegmental, bibliography on, 638-40
———, types of, 634
———, and word, 626
Concord, 240, 254, 466, 489, 498-99
Congruent; *see* System, congruent; Topological Variant

Conklin, 35, 184, 431, 475, 616n, 627, 664, 678
Connotation, 611, 632
Consciousness; *see* Concept; Subsegmental
Consistency, 635
Consonant
———, cluster, 339
———, long, 370
Construction, 513n; *see also* Syntagmeme
———, bibliography on, 473-509
———, of formal units, 491-92
———, meaning of, 630
———, overlapping, 574-75
———, versus position, 476
———, versus slot-class, 282-84
———, as wave, 9
Content; *see* Form; Form-Meaning Composite
Content Analysis, 146
Context
———, of behavior, 641-78
———, bibliography on, 665-78
———, psychological, 667
———, of situation, 33, 59, 484, 486, 618
Continuum; *see also* Segmentation; Wave
———, segmented, 94, 133-34
Contoid, 332-38
Contour,
———, primary, 398
———, subsidiary, 398
Contrast, 85n, 510; *see also* Contrastive-Indentificational Feature; Feature Mode
———, in analogous environment, 295
———, breakfast, 123
———, between constructions, 471-72
———, and identification, 90
———, relative to subsystem, 300
Contrastive-Identificational Feature, 54n, 90, 162-63, 288; *see also* Feature Mode
———, of class, 328-29
———, of eme, 163, 302-03
———, of hyperphoneme, 405
———, of individual, 655
———, pause in intonation, 402
———, phonological as morpheme, 305
———, simultaneous, 93; versus sequential, 294-96
———, of society, 644
———, of tagmeme, 198, 218, 228
Contreras, 351, 354, 363, 422, 587, 691, 719
Conversation, 125, 404, 425, 442; *see also* Breakfast
Cooley, 668
Cooper, 307, 349, 352-54, 356-57, 411, 705
Copernican System, 70
Copi, 285
Core, common, 583, 585
Correlation, 240; *see also* Agreement; Concord
———, of phonemes, 326

Coult, 674
Count, 632, 672, 677
Cox, 274, 469, 493
———, morpheme-order charts, 183
Cowan, G., 543
Cowan, J. M., 419, 541, 544
Crawford, 85n, 340n, 361, 378n, 389n, 390n, 416, 424n, 451, 460, 520
Creativeness; *see* Potential; Prediction; Productive
Cree, 688
Cricket, 47-49
———, and clashing systems, 64
Croft, 683
Crosscultural, etics, 55
Crow, 706
Crutchfield, 676
Cue, 683
Culina, 394, 420
Culture; *see also* Behavior; Society
———, map of, via verbal, 35
———, and necessary knowledge, 71
Culture Trait, 183, 641
Czech, 541, 687

Dalgarno, 193
Danehy, 537, 715
Daneš, 541
Danish, 415, 538, 725
Davidson, 678
Davis, A. K., 679
Davis, M., 544, 687
Deception, 115, 132
de Courtenay, 344-45, 409
de Groot 96, 184, 187, 190, 192, 284, 411, 488
Delattre, 307, 352-53, 356-57, 411, 687, 705
Delgaty, 469, 482-83
Delicacy, 54, 508
Democracy, 55
Denotation, 611, 632
Dependence, hierarchy of, 148
Derbyshire, 483, 487-88
Derivation, history of, 503-06
de Saussure, 63, 146, 355, 536, 561
Description, 498-99; *see also* Analysis; Procedure
de Sola Pool, 146, 632, 703
Dialect, 361, 582, 593, 596, 607, 629
———, bibliography on, 593
———, social, 585
———, wave, 585
Dibabawon, 691
Dickenson, 528-30
Dictionary, 175
———, and hypostasis, 158
Diderichsen, 63

Diebold, 593
Dimension, 9; *see also* Matrix
——, of sentence, 137
Dinner, 29, 508; *see also* Breakfast
Diphthong, 65, 414, 423
Discourse: 138-39, 485-86; *see also* Sentence, beyond the; Syntagmeme; Uttereme
——, as environment, 147
——, slots in, 147, 276
Discourse Analysis, 146-47; *see also* Plot
Discovery, 38; *see also* Analysis; Nonuniqueness; Procedure and intuition, 224-25n, 493
——, versus presentation, 492-95
Disney, 630
Distinctive Feature, 348, 358; *see also* Contrastive-Identificational Feature
——, binary, 359
Distribution, 85n; *see also* Class; Morpheme; Phoneme; Tagmeme; etc.
——, of behavioreme, 194-289
——, breakfast, 124
——, in business letter, 35
——, class in artificial language, 211-18
——, of class, sequence, and matrix, 85n
——, co-occurrence, 202
——, of emic unit, 39
——, external, 476-77; and context restrictions, 276
——, in hierarchies, interlocking, 568-69
——, of hypertagmeme, 461
——, mode, 85-86; of filled slots, 93; of syntagmeme, 432-509;
——, and voice quality, 525-27
——, in nonverbal context, 35, 39, 59
——, of phoneme, grammatically defined, 315
——, in social structure, 645-46
——, of stress group, 399-402
——, systemic, 511
——, total and external distribution, 477
——, of unit, 35
Diver, 147, 488, 505, 512n
Division Subclass, 450
Dixon, 506, 512n, 588, 620
Dole, 666
Dollard, 674
Doob, 625
Doroszewsky, 593
Double Function, 95, 483
——, of phoneme in morpheme sequence, 568
——, of phoneme in syllable, 382, 384, 416
——, of syllable in stress group, 385
——, of tagmeme, 575
Douglas, 678
Dramatis Personae, 246n; *see also* Plot
Draper, 347, 366n, 370n, 393n, 417, 703

Drums
——, bibliography on, 544
——, and tone, 543
Dundes, 145, 183, 187, 276, 285, 485, 595, 688, 692
Dynamics, 511, 546; *see also* Generativeness
——, and interlocking, 566

Eastman, 487-88
Eating; *see* Breakfast; Dinner
Eddington, 676
Ege, 96
Eggan, 668
Eimas, 353, 692, 705
Einarsson, 703
Einstein, 298
Electromyographic Techniques, 347
Elegance, 587; *see also* Simplicity
Eliason, 410, 416
Elliott, 436, 482, 487
Ellis, A., 414
Ellis, C. D., 487-88
Elson, 9, 298, 496
Eme, 54; *see also* Emic; Morpheme; Phoneme; Syntagmeme; Tagmeme; Unit; etc.
——, contrastive-identificational, 163
——, criteria for, 37-38, 54
——, versus emic unit, 221
——, as grid, 55
——, of level, 480
——, nonminimum, 131
——, phonological, terminal, 407
——, and purpose, 42
——, and social structure, 55
——, of stress, 407
Emeneau, 72
Emic Element; *see also* Eme; Unit
——, and physical description, 39
——, progression, 515-17
——, standpoint, 37-72
——, structure, 55
——, value of approach, 40
Engel, 487
English, 64, 66, 140-41, 153-54, 158, 161, 165, 233, 247, 250, 271-72, 361-62, 367-70, 372, 375-77, 383, 389, 393n, 394-97, 399, 401, 409, 413-14, 419, 423, 441, 478, 488, 498, 523, 540-541, 544, 553, 557, 559, 570, 572, 581, 594, 616, 622, 630, 686-88, 690, 692, 693, 694, 697-702, 703, 704, 706-14, 715, 718-26, 727, 728
——, abbreviation in, 383-84
——, 'am', 558
——, phoneme classes in, 331-38
——, sentences labelled for tagmemic terms, 453
Episode, 667
Epistemology, 51, 57, 532-33, 639, 676; *see also*

Observer
——, analysis of analysis, 58
——, and observer, 658-59
Epling, 715
Erickson, 54n, 63n, 172n, 297n, 431, 483, 489, 511n, 548n, 560, 596, 627, 668, 715
Ervin, 354
Eseley, 720
Esper, 283
Estonian, 413, 539
Ethnolinguistics, 33, 666
Ethnology; *see* Behavior; Society
Etics; *see also* Eme; Emic
——, of anthropology, 145
——, criteria for, 38
——, crosscultural, 37-39
——, not dichotomy with emic, 41
——, external, 38
——, instrumental report in, 46
——, and intuition, 225
——, and perceptual report, 46
——, of relationship, 285-86
——, standpoint for, 37-72
——, of syllable, 391-92
——, system created, 38
——, of tagma types; 252n
——, term, 37
——, threshold report, 46
——, and universals, 624
——, value of approach, 40
——, variant, 44-46
Evaluation, 494
Evans-Pritchard, 668-69, 691
Exercises, in tagmemic analysis, 209-18, 254-69
Expansion, 279
——, serial, 244
Expectation; 673
Expression, *see* Form

Fact, 56, 658
——, versus data, 57
Falsetto, 540
Family
——, as S-syllable, 653-55
Fant, 347-48, 359, 423, 700
Fanti, 724
Faust, 361, 414, 541, 594
Feature; *see also* Component; Contrastive-Identificational Feature
——, componential, 303
——, contrastive, 295-96
——, distinctive, 302
——, identificational, 296
Feature Mode, 85, 89-91; *see also* Contrast
——, of behavioreme, 150-93
——, breakfast identified by, 123
——, and contrast, 90
——, of emic unit, 85
——, of football team, 649
——, and suprasegmental phoneme, 524
——, of tagmeme, 196
Feedback and interlocking levels, 591
Feigl, 69
Ferguson, 346, 348, 363, 588, 593
Field, 297n, 511, 596-97; *see also* Pattern; System
——, April Fool, 596
——, fusion in, 562
——, of grammar, 9
——, item, 562-63
——, playing field structured, 661
——, semantic, 609-10, 618-19, 626-27
——, sequence viewed as, 553-56
Filibuster, 42
Filler Class; *see* Class, distribution; Distribution
Fillmore, 71, 488, 710
Finnish, 724
Firth, J, R., 33, 63, 71, 146, 175, 276, 279, 344, 346, 350, 360, 362, 410, 413, 415-16, 418, 429, 476, 484, 489, 506-08, 537-38, 594, 596, 616, 618-19, 627, 629-33, 670, 685, 718, 722
——, and context of situation, 33
——, ontological status of constructs, 56
——, on prosody, 350
Firth, R., 668, 670, 712
Fischer-Jørgensen, 345, 347, 360, 362, 411, 413
Fleming, 440, 459
Flydal, 593
Focus, 96, 98-119, 175, 584
——, as abstraction, 102
——, of attention, 113
——, bibliography on, 118
——, boundaries of, 80
——, breadth of, 112-14
——, breakfast, 127
——, depth of, 110, 117
——, in football, 98-117
——, height of, 106-09; diagrammed, 109
——, hierarchy, 108
——, indeterminacy of, 80
——, levels of, 78, 80, 106; tagmemic, 436-45
——, limits to, 80
——, and manifestation, 88
——, modal element in, 108
——, and morpheme, 157-58
——, overt, 112-13
——, and participant, 79
——, on play in football, 105
——, and potential, 91
——, predominant, 106
——, and teaching, 155
——, thresholds, 111

——, wide versus narrow, 114
Fodor, 485, 619-22, 628, 701
Folktale, 183
——, etic and emic, 55
Fonagy, 417, 629
Foot; *see* Stress Group
Football, 98-117
——, distribution mode of team, 652-53
——, and focus, 98-117
——, homomorphic activity in, 115
——, meaning of, 660
——, as an object, 660
——, season, 100
——, team as S-sentence, 649-53
Force of field, 298-99
Ford, 145, 707
Forde, 668, 714
Fore, 417, 560, 627, 715
Forley, 193, 684
Form, 604, 606; *see also* Form-Meaning Composite
——, and meaning, 188
Formalism, 184-85
Formative, 163n, 504
——, and meaning, 189
——, shape of blocks of in matrix, 548n
——, symbolic element as, 167n
——, vector, 163n
Form-Meaning Composite, 9, 55, 62-63, 277, 516-17
——, category of matrix, 163n
——, as contrastive-identificational, 188
——, in grammar, 279
——, in morpheme, 163, 187
——, not one-to-one, 63n, 163n
——, in sentence definition, 149
——, of a tale, 246n
——, and transformationalism, 500-01
——, variants in, 159
Fortes, 668, 673
Fowler, 60, 185, 278, 321
Frake, 35, 184, 475, 616n, 627, 664, 667, 674, 678
——, on cognition, 35
Frame, 478; *see also* Substitution
——, in grammar, 250
——, grammatical, 135
——, repudiated by Lees, 275
——, of reference, 532
——, in segmentation, 134
——, for tone, 5, 541-42
France, 632
Francescato, 596
Francis, 488
Frank, 70
Frankl, 58

Franklin, 594, 674
Freedman, 665, 668-73
Freeland, 67
Frei, 420, 562
Freire-Marreco, 55, 715
French, 419-20, 487, 546, 549, 561, 628, 700, 716, 723-24
Freud, 640
Fries, 52-54, 62-65, 68, 139-40, 146-47, 149, 161, 190, 248-50, 272-74, 276-80, 286, 314, 352, 488-89, 491, 499, 540-41, 570, 574-77, 592-93, 619, 630-33
——, classes of words, 247
——, and meaning, 156
——, and responses, 34
——, sentence types, 140
Frumkina, 679
Fry, 353, 417
Fukumura, 537, 708
Function, 511, 575
——, word, 274
Functionalist Approach, 670
Fusion, 192, 318, 545-64
——, bibliography on, 556-64
——, in English, 383-84
——, of morphemes, 168, 177
——, phonetic segment in, 554
——, stages of, 318
——, of syllable, 380-83
——, in system, 566
——, of tagmeme, 178, 562
——, types, summary of, 548-50
——, unidirectional, 549

Gaifman, 479, 681
Gaitenby, 687
Galanter, 704
Galton, 639
Game; *see also* Baseball, Cricket, Football
——, basketball, 533
——, official, 100, 103
——, spectacle, 99-100
Game Theory, 118
García, 351, 354, 422
Gardin, 55
Gardiner, 618
Gardner, W., 629
Garhwali, 686
Garner, 58, 285, 348, 638
Garvin, 273, 359, 475, 494, 560, 620
Geiger, 633
Generative Grammar, 281; *see also* Transformation
——, as machine, 69
——, monistic hierarchy of, 410

Generativeness; *see also* Dynamics; Potential; Prediction; Productive
——, and potential, 86, 281
——, under all theories, 281
Genotype, 55
Georges, 485
Georgian, 139
German, 139, 368, 414, 561, 616, 636, 702, 709
Gerstman, 307, 352, 356, 411, 683, 686, 704
Gestalt, and focus, 118
Gesture, 31-32, 35
——, bibliography on, 35
——, Birdwhistell on, 34
——, in language, 28
——, in monolingual situation, 30
——, segmentation by, 134
——, song with, 25
——, and tone, 542
——, verbal and nonverbal, 25-26
Gibson, 53, 725
Gifford, 183
Gilyak, 588, 699
Gimson, 352
Gleason, 188, 275, 360, 478, 490, 495, 497, 502, 721
Glottal Stop, as syllable nucleus, 387
Gluckman, 668
Goal-Directed Behavior, 145
——, hierarchy of, 96
Goedel, 591, 663
Goffman, 673
Gold Coast, 419, 544, 628
Goldstein, 544, 619, 636, 640
Goodell, 33
Goodenough, 35-36, 64, 187, 431, 621, 626-27, 631, 665-67, 672
——, objective and subjective, 55
——, on theory, 71
Goodman, 69-70, 512n, 588
Goodnow, 64, 71, 684
Grameme, 5, 288; *see also* Tagmeme
Grammar; *see* Morpheme; Structure; Tagmeme, etc.
——, category in, implicit, 563
——, as formal, 279
——, logical, 274
——, as machine, 69
——, meaning of, 630
——, in phonology, 59
——, surface, 489
——, transformational, 495-98; *see also* Transform
——, wave in, 468
Grandgent, 347
Gregg, 360
Greek, 629, 719

Green, 347, 713
Greenberg, 54, 63, 192, 422, 477, 482, 536, 539, 557, 560, 619, 639, 665-66, 686
Greeting, 30, 425
Griffith, 353, 705
Grimes, 536, 541, 588, 595, 666, 716
Gross, 36, 673
Grubb, 687
Guaraní, 481, 541, 718
Gudschinsky, 36, 65, 147, 353, 382n, 413, 482, 485, 497, 542, 588
Gugu-Yalanji, 711
Gumpers, 595
Gurungkura, 685
Guthrie, 286, 482, 488, 664

Haas, 147, 188, 285, 359, 410, 475, 559, 562, 564, 619, 633
Hadding-Koch, 541
Haitian Creole, 693
Hall, E. T., 34-35, 59, 145, 193, 627
——, proxemics, 34
——, verbal versus nonverbal, 35
Hall, R. A., 54, 182, 346, 355-56, 360, 410, 675, 721
Halle, 72, 314n, 347-48, 354-55, 359, 362-63, 412, 417-18, 423, 478, 482, 494, 512n, 535, 539, 587-88, 637, 686, 690, 700
Halliday, 33, 54, 71, 95-96, 144-47, 189, 226, 272, 274, 276, 281, 285, 410, 474, 480, 483, 506-09, 587-88, 594, 619, 627
——, breakfast, 144
——, formula for slot, 276
——, grammatical view, 506-09
Hallowell, 674
Halpern, 359
Hamp, 414, 535-36, 595
Han, 694
Hansen, 703
Hanunoo, 687
Harary, 351
Harmon, 488, 496-97
Harries, 542
Harrington, 55, 718, 722
Harris, M., 34, 54
Harris, Z., 34, 54, 56, 61, 63-64, 67-68, 72, 94, 96, 146-47, 152, 179, 182-85, 189-91, 246n, 270, 273-75, 277-78, 280, 315, 353-55, 357, 359-60, 362, 472-73, 476, 478, 481-83, 485, 487-89, 491-92, 495, 497-98, 502, 512n, 538, 556-59, 561, 619-20, 628, 630-31, 638, 640, 687, 691, 699, 705, 707, 727
——, on broken morphemes, 168
——, description and purpose, 56
——, distribution, 60
——, interrogation morpheme, 191

740 INDEX

——, and structure exists, 56
——, on 'was', 559
Hart, H., 189, 274-75, 435, 450, 459, 473, 481, 487, 489
Hart, J., 346
Haugen, 56-57, 65, 67, 345-46, 349, 410-11, 413-414, 416-17, 422, 538-40, 542-43, 557, 586, 593-594, 621, 676
Hausa, 539, 685, 727
Hawkes, 689
Hawley, 690
Hayes, 35, 193, 682
Healey, 666
Hebb, 677
Heldrum, 630
Heller, 564
Hempel, 69-71
——, real definition, 58
Henderson, 413, 415, 537
Henle, 619, 624, 632, 637, 687
Henry, 666, 669-70, 675
Heraclitus, 656n
Heralt, 696
Herdan, 684
Herskovits, 666, 668, 670, 675
Hess, E., 679
Hess, H., 487-88
Hickerson, 67, 314, 418, 695
Hierarchy, 5, 9, 244-45, 283, 286
——, bibliography on, 96, 588-91
——, Carroll on, 96
——, of dependence, 148
——, and focus, 117
——, fused boundaries between, 571
——, generative as upside down, 474
——, grammatical, bibliography on, 474-75
——, grammar, nucleus in, 575
——, included, 132
——, interlocking, 475, 565-97; lexicon versus grammar, 573-80
——, intersecting at segment, 117
——, and levels, interlocking, 592
——, lexical, 424n, 520-21; meaning in, 598-605; and phonological, 567-73
——, versus linearity, 406
——, of meaning, 603, 615; as basic, 476; central, 601
——, minimum in, 130
——, and mixing levels, 589-91
——, monistic, 409-10
——, network, 117
——, number of 474-75
——, overlapping, 101, 533-35
——, phoneme through morpheme, 409-10
——, phonological, 410, 528; lexical border of,

567; parallel with grammar, 446, 569; thresholds in, 405
——, priority in, 476
——, spectacle in, 100
——, within syllable, 386-88
——, topologically-related, 583
——, wave in, 79; of movement, 393n
Hill, 96, 146, 183, 272, 275, 410, 418-19, 488, 505, 537, 563-64, 592-95, 629, 694
——, separation of levels, 59
Hilton, 722
Hildum, 684
Hindu, 561
Hiorth, 482, 627-28
Hishkaryana, 688
History
——, derivational, 503-06
——, oscillation of matrix type in, 642n
——, and process, 557
——, tagmemics in, 642
Hiż, 192, 501
Hjelmslev, 32, 63, 66, 96, 182, 184, 187-88, 193, 275, 282, 285, 340, 345, 355-58, 360, 411-14, 419, 481, 536, 538, 556, 590, 620, 627, 682
——, on structure, 57
Hockett, 54, 56-57, 59, 61-62, 67, 96, 152, 175-176, 182-85, 188-90, 192, 279-80, 347, 349, 353, 359, 361-63, 407, 410, 413-14, 416, 418-19, 431, 474, 477-78, 481-82, 484, 487-89, 495, 537-42, 554, 557, 559, 561, 592, 594, 640, 686, 707, 715, 721
——, on Chinese words, 481
——, morpheme not analogous to phoneme, 189
——, phoneme, non-phonetic evidence, 66
——, and segments, 95
——, and structure by speakers, 57
——, use of meaning, 61
Hocus-Pocus, 57
Hoenigswald, 182, 411, 485, 564
Hoffman, 353, 703
Hoijer, 10, 193, 353, 359, 625, 681
——, and culture, 34
Homologous, 218, 222-23, 234, 243, 245, 251-52
——, and expansion, 226
——, test for, 222-23
——, transformational test for, 223n
Homomorphic, 160
——, focus, 114
——, sequence, 574
——, unit in football, 105
Homophony, 43, 160; *see also* Ambiguity
——, differentiation of, 160
——, of phoneme variant, 301
——, of tagmas, 220
——, tagmeme variant, 231
——, verb and noun, 185

Honey, 275, 489
Honigmann, 57, 674, 676
Hopi, 625, 726
Hopkins, 397
Hopscotch, 45
Horalek, 359
Horowitz, 629, 684
House, 488
Householder, 35, 72, 184, 276, 351, 413, 431, 475, 640, 616n
———, hocus-pocus, 57
Hovet, 347
Hsu, 666
Huave, 542, 715
Hudgins, 722
Huestis, 487
Huichol, 536-37, 693-95
Humbolt, 482
Humphrey, 622, 624, 635, 638-39
Hunanese, 415
Hungarian, 706
Husson, 347
Hymes, 33, 36, 482, 627
Hyperbehavioreme, 130
Hyperclass, 489
Hypercongruent, 132
Hypermeaning, 612; see also Meaning
———, as conceptual quanta, 614
Hypermorpheme, 205, 211, 214, 424-31, 433, 454; see also Syntagmeme
———, bibliography on, 429-31
———, borders of, 467-68
———, class of, 217, 428, 460
———, close-knit, 216
———, complex class of, 436
———, construction as syntagmeme, 451
———, definition of, 424
———, distribution mode of, 428
———, feature mode of, 426-27
———, idiom, 605
———, manifestation mode of, 427-28
———, meaning of, 427, 430-31
———, phonological character of, 429
———, versus syntagmeme, 462n
———, types of, etics and emics of, 467-71
Hyperphoneme, 364; see also Phoneme; Syllable; Stress Group
———, bibliography on, 409-23
———, contrastive feature of, 408-09
———, defined, 364-65
———, as eme, 408-09
———, feature of as eme, 407-08
Hypertagmeme; see also Tagmeme
———, and absolute level, 446-47
———, definition of, 433, 435
———, etics and emics of, 467-71

———, illustrated, 452-58
———, obligatorily complex, 433-36
———, obligatorily complex as hypermorpheme class, 435-36
———, relativistic, 436-45
———, slot-class level, 448-66
———, table of components of, 460-61
———, as term, 432
Hyperunit, 553-56
Hypha, 411
Hypostasis, 63, 102, 107-08, 132, 292, 454, 484
———, analytical, 108, 187
———, and class, 203
———, conceptualized, 156-58; containing slot, 221-22; of relationship, 341
———, of contrastive-identificational components, 163
———, and dictionary, 158
———, of focus, 112
———, functional, 108, 155, 175
———, in hearing, 113
———, and meaning, 155, 157, 517
———, order, 341
———, and purpose, 154
———, of relationship, 341
———, and segmental meaning, 611
———, and sentence, 484
———, as stereotype, 648
———, systemic, 111
———, and teaching, 154-55, 293
———, term, 118
———, as time, 175
Hypotheses, and analytical leap, 225

I-Unit, 655-58
Iceland, 621
Icelandic, 695, 701
Idea, 605, 612-16, 638, 640; see also Concept; Subsegmental; Translation
———, versus word, 640
Identificational-Contrast; see Contrastive-Identificational Feature
Idiom, 427, 510, 578, 602-03, 605; see also Meaning
Igbo, 685
Ilocano, 720
Immediate Constituent, 5, 243-44, 278, 282-83
———, binary, 477-78
———, as end product, 477-78
———, of intonation, 401
———, and meaning, 286-87
———, phonology, 5, 406
———, pyramid, 286
———, in social group, 655
———, of stress group, 401
———, of syllable, 386-88, 413

——, and taxeme, 286
——, and translation, 640
Inca, 64, 718
Indeterminacy, 95, 159; *see also* Double Function
——, and activeness, 170
——, of class, 84
——, between componential systems, 251
——, versus error, 158
——, of focus, 80
——, in a football, 660
——, homomorphic activity in, 105
——, and legal action, 64
——, in levels of grammar, 482
——, of meaning, 158-59, 614; attributed to class or to tagmeme, 227
——, of modes, 92
——, of morpheme and tagmeme boundaries, 177-78
——, in morphemic analysis, 191-92
——, in morphology-syntax level, 482
——, of noun-verb, 185
——, number of morphs in sequence, 237
——, in phonemic segmentation, 559-60
——, in phonetic similarity, 356
——, in purpose and meaning, 158-59
——, reaction to, 160
——, of segment, 95
——, of segment borders, 77, 192, 546, 558-60; semantic, 609-10
——, and similarity of tagmatic meaning, 220
——, within stress group boundary, 395n
——, in structure, 58
——, of syllable boundary, 381, 382n
——, in system, 566
——, of tagmatic segmentation, 252
——, in tagmeme, 287; analysis of, 244
——, threshold, 111, 129
——, verbal and nonverbal slot-class, 251
Individual; *see also* Society
——, bibliography on, 674-76
——, person, 655-58
——, personality as unit, 657-58
——, and society, 641, 675
Indonesian, 702
Infeld, 689
Informant; *see also* Native Reaction
——, as analyst, 224
——, naïveté destroyed, 224
——, reaction of, 61-62
Ingemann, 349, 412, 705-06
Institution, 669
Integration, 587
Intention, 158, 598, 638; *see also* Meaning; Purpose
Interlocking

——, as intersects in matrix, 565n
——, lateral, 565
——, vertical, 565
Interruption, 125
Intersection, 359-60
Intonation, 134, 153, 161, 369-70, 531, 581; *see also* Stress Group
——, bibliography on, 539-41
——, contour, points of, 401; deferred, 399; total, 401
——, contrastive, 540
——, on Dickenson poems, 529-30
——, distorted in Gold Coast, 544
——, emotive, 618
——, finality in pause group, 402
——, general types, 536
——, hummed abstraction, 543-44
——, and interlocking systems, 581
——, lack of contrast, 539
——, meaning of, 608
——, and meaning, 618
——, morphemes of, 528
——, and music, 544
——, and pause, 402
——, pedagogical, 540
——, phrasal, 534
——, placement of, 400
——, postcontour, 399
——, precontour, 367
——, rhythm unit in, 398
——, slurred, 367-68
——, and tagmeme borders, 238
——, versus tone, 539-40
——, in vowel segmentation, 523
Intuition, 493; *see also* Native Reaction
——, and analytical leap, 224-25
——, empathy, 289
——, and meaning, 499-501
——, and pair test, 64
——, in phonemics, 66
——, presence of vowel, 423
——, psychological correlates, 67
——, reaction, 352
——, and recognition of meaning, 224
——, in recognition of proportion, 224
——, in relation to meaning and purpose, 663
Invariant, situational versus grammatical, 246n
Irony, 42
Iroquois, 619
Item; *see also* Particle
——, and arrangement, 502, 545-52; versus process, bibliography on, 556-57; segmentation in, 551; and zero, 562
——, and field, 563-64; zero in, 562
——, and process, 501-02, 545-52; allomorph class in, 551-52

——, prosodic, as particle, 508
Italian, 139, 718
Ivić, 593

Jakobovitz, 616
Jakobson, 146-47, 274-75, 345, 347-48, 351, 354-56, 358-60, 362, 409, 411-12, 422-23, 482, 539, 542, 588, 561, 607, 637-38, 640, 686, 703, 721
——, distinctive feature, 348
——, on verse, 146
James, 541, 638
Japanese, 64, 67, 183, 190, 373-76, 380, 540
Jassem, 537, 541, 721
Javanese, 560, 722
Jenkins, 559, 631, 638
Jensen, 543
Jesperson, 183-84, 190, 275, 279, 486, 488, 490, 630
John Doe, 323
——, allomorphs of, 177, 656
——, emic, 656
——, in S-slot, 648
Johnson, D. M., 635, 638
Johnson, W., 623
Joke, 603n, 608; *see also* Pun
Jones, A. M., 544
Jones, D., 64, 66, 344-45, 352, 359, 368, 384, 400, 410, 414, 416-18, 430, 542, 706
Joos, 94, 347, 355, 362, 418, 488, 536-37, 540, 595, 621, 696
Josselyn, 347
Junction, 545, 549-50
Juncture, 238, 315, 545; *see also* Closure
——, allos of, 407
——, bibliography on, 417-19
——, as boundary, 418
——, disjuncture, 407
——, as eme, 405-06
——, informant reaction, 67
——, intonation break, 399
——, and mashing levels, 589
——, pause, 407
——, phoneme of, 416
——, versus phoneme, 405
——, phonological interrupting grammar, 571-72
——, rejected, 409
——, in relation to wave, 307-08
——, and segmentation, 134

Kabardian, 423, 701
Kaiser, 347, 698
Kant, 677
Kantner, 410
Kantor, 193

Kaplan, 54-55, 488, 544, 622, 632, 670, 703
Karcevskij, 146, 623, 725
Kardiner, 669, 674
Katz, 485, 619-22, 628
Kechua, 729
Keislar, 354, 712
Kelley, 71
Kellogg, 720
Kelly, W., 162, 166, 173, 465
Kelly, W. H., 670
Kennedy, 537, 542, 559
Kensinger, 419
Kenyon, 368, 410, 414, 417
Kernel; *see also* Nucleus
——, of system, 472-73
Khmu?, 721
Kikuyu, 542, 695
Kin, 117
——, compare phone, 665
Kindberg, 419, 542, 715
Kineme, 291-93
Kinemorpheme, 184
King, 495, 683
Kingdon, 541
Kinney, 353, 705
Kiowa, 709, 725
Kirk, 729
Klagstad, 596
Klima, 704
Klineberg, 674
Kluckhohn, 32-33, 53, 612, 616, 626, 669-70, 673-75, 677-78, 702
Knott, 368, 702
Koekkoek, 541
Koffka, 94, 96, 118, 677, 686
Kopp, 347, 716
Kořínek, 706
Korzybski, 623
Krech, 676
Kris, 640
Kroeber, 32-33, 145, 183, 665, 670, 693
Krupa, 628
Kruszewski, 344
Kuipers, 363, 422-23, 715
Kulagina, 490
Kurath, 314, 561, 593, 619-20
Kutenai, 696
Labov, 593, 607
Lackowski, 475-76, 501, 620, 632
Ladefoged, 347, 354, 365-66n, 367n, 370n, 374n, 393n, 413, 417, 542, 684, 688
Lado, 64
——, and culture, 36
Lamb, 96, 149, 189, 272, 275, 475, 480, 490, 495, 502, 621, 640
——, on primitives, 96-97

——, representation rule, 490
——, semantics, 149
Lambek, 488
Lambert, 616
Landecker, 690
Lane, 346, 353, 705
Language; *see also* Whistling
——, of animals, 36
——, artificial, 211-18, 255-64, 287-88
——, artificial, multiple stage, 215
——, as behavior, 25-36
——, as code, 63; of signals, 279
——, communication basic, 476
——, as communication, 493
——, and endurance of objects, 678
——, meaning as social component of, 598
——, and psychology, 32
——, relation to phonetics, 355
——, as sentences, 147, 485
——, versus speech, 536-38; *see also* de Saussure
——, structure in, 38
——, as system, 178
——, two, in clash, 64-68
Lanz, 624
Larsen, 541
Larson, 487, 594
Lashley, 393n, 596, 640
Lasswell, 54-55, 146, 670
Latin, 139, 141, 173, 190, 226, 245, 723
Law, 147, 183, 487
Leal, 373
Learning, 554, 635
——, difficulty from alien system, 51-53
Lee, 668
Leeper, 637-39
Lees, 147, 274-75, 475, 480, 485, 488-89, 492-94, 496, 499-500, 503-04, 506, 541, 558, 588, 699
——, on speaker, 495
Lehiste, 413-14, 416-17, 539, 541, 713
Leiter, 630, 684
Lekomcev, 502
Length, 528; *see also* Suprasegmental
Lenneberg, 625, 632, 635, 684
Lenski, 691
Leontief, 512n
Leopold, 593
Lerner, 146, 703
Level
——, absolute, 446-47
——, of analysis, 586-88
——, bibliography on, 588-91
——, clause, 441
——, dependent versus independent, 460
——, as an eme, 480-81; of grammar, 479-81
——, of focus, 106

——, of grammar, versus transformationalism, 487
——, in hierarchy, 474-75
——, interlocking, 60, 566, 590
——, mixed, 362, 588-89
——, of monistic hierarchy, 410
——, monologue, 442
——, morphology versus syntax, 482
——, phonotagmeme, 520
——, portmanteau, 442; bibliography on, 483
——, rigid, 59
——, and rules, 480, 592
——, of sentence, 442
——, separation of, 59
——, of slot-class, 448-66
——, of structure, 437-45
——, suprasegmental, 535
——, word as, 437-38
Lévi-Strauss, 33, 59, 284, 358, 485, 512n, 625, 665
Levy, 668-72, 675, 679
Lewin, 96, 676
——, phenotype, 55
Lexeme, 431
Lexical Chain, 246n
Lexical Set, 209; *see also* Meaning; Semantics
Lexicon; *see also* Hypermorpheme; Meaning; Morpheme; Uttereme, feature mode of
——, bibliography, on meaning of, 630-33
——, phonological boundaries in, 567, 569
Lexis, 507
Liberman, 307, 349, 352-57, 411-12, 687, 692
Lie, 115, 132
Lilly, 720
Limerick, 610
Lindauer, 720
Lindskoog, 419
Linearity; *see* Segmentation
Linton, 96, 668-73
Lisker, 349, 353, 687, 705
Literature, 542, 596; *see* Style
Liu Fu, 71
Lloyd-Warfel, 478
Loan Words, 594-95, 608
——, meaning by, 608
Logic, in theory, 68
Logical Grammar, 274
Longacre, 9, 147, 252n, 261n, 271, 276, 279, 281, 285, 314n, 354, 373, 410, 414, 424n, 432n, 434, 436-45, 449, 452, 454, 459, 471, 474, 477-81, 487, 496, 498, 502, 505, 507, 542, 560, 563, 620, 626, 640, 674
——, relativistic hypertagmeme, 436-37
Loos, 147, 485, 487
Loriot, 147
Lotz, 146, 358-59, 362, 700

Loudness, as subsegmental, 534
Lounsbury, 35, 176, 182, 270, 431, 557-61, 619, 626-27, 631, 639, 665
Lowie, 668-69
Luchai, 695
Lukoff, 314n, 315, 362, 417-18, 535, 686
Luncheon, 533
Lundberg, 677
Luria, 675, 712
Lushai, 415
Lutstorf, 419
Lying, 608, 629
Lynch, 629

Macdermott, 629
Mace, 354, 715
Mackey, 676
Maclay, 588
MacNeilage, 353-54, 705
Mäder, 55
Magnusson, 488, 728
Maier, 670
Mak, 556
Malinowski, 33, 68, 618, 622, 626, 639, 669-70
——, and context of situation, 33
——, language as action, 33
Malone, 413-14
Mandarin, 540, 542, 570, 581, 698, 707, 720
Manifestation, 85, 87-89; *see also* Variant
——, of breakfast, 124
——, and focus, 88
——, of football team, 650-51
——, movement basic to, 306-07
——, physical, 187-88
——, waves of motion, 307-09
——, as the whole, 92
Maninka, 727
Maranao, 707
Marckwardt, 36, 64, 66, 352
Margin; *see* Border; Closure
Martin, R., 619, 681
Martin, S., 175, 183-84, 192, 410, 413, 419, 422, 559-60, 590, 595
Martinet, 274, 355-56, 359, 627
——, moneme, 190
Mason, 36, 673, 693
Mather, 537, 710
Mathesius, 345, 595
Mathiot, 95, 184, 431, 692
Matrix, 9, 298n, 324n; *see also* Dimension
——, of behavior, 641n
——, and categories, 560; interlocking, 565n
——, and chronology, 512n
——, conflated, 163n, 548n, 627
——, cultural, 673-74
——, derivation in, 473n

——, distributional, 443
——, and field, 596-97
——, kernel, 472-73
——, multiplication, 596
——, and network, 357
——, nuclear, 473n
——, order in, 512n
——, paradigm, 489
——, and perspective, 511n
——, of phoneme, distorted, 324n
——, phonological, 348, 512n
——, of sentence, 137n
——, simultaneity of vectors manifested, 548n
——, social, 35
——, term, 443n
——, and time, 512n
——, and transformation, 502
——, and tree, 512n
——, as well-described units, 179n
Matteson, 487
Mayan, 482
Mayers, 183, 435
Mazahua, 534, 540, 713
Mazatec, 28, 388, 523, 543, 559, 687, 693-94, 713-15
——, object slot with gesture, 36
——, syllables in, 388
——, tone games in, 543
——, whistle in, 28
McCarthy, 720
McDavid, 414, 539, 593, 629
McEachern, 36, 673, 692
McKaughan, 413, 477, 542, 628
McKinsey, 118
McMahan, 722
McQuown, 60, 589, 629
Meaning, 277, 598-642; *see also* Choice; Purpose; Semantics
——, absent in morpheme, 160-62
——, alloseme, 621
——, in analysis, 149
——, awareness of, 157-58
——, bibliography on, 616-42
——, bisocial equivalent, 60-61
——, of breakfast tagmeme, 196
——, central, 600-02, 631-32
——, central, hierarchy of, 601
——, and choice, 188, 619
——, of class, 249, 252, 606; of morphemes, 198-99
——, collocational, 605-06, 632
——, common denominator, 184
——, compared with use, 659-60, 662
——, componential analysis, bibliography on, 626-28
——, and compounds, 430

——, concept, 621
——, conditioning lexical sets, 209
——, contradictory, 610
——, as contrastive feature of construction, 513n
——, as criterion of tagmas, 219
——, and culture, 619
——, definition of, 616-20
——, derived, 603
——, differential, 61
——, distinctive, 631
——, emes of, 187
——, field of, 618
——, versus form, 62, 188; *see also* Form-Meaning Composite
——, and formative, 560
——, in grammar, 279
——, grammatical, bibliography on, 630; hierarchy of, 607, 615
——, hypermeaning, 612
——, of hypermorpheme, 430-31
——, of hypertagmeme, 461
——, I-Meaning, 656
——, independent, 603
——, indeterminacy in, 42, 158-59
——, intonational system, 608
——, and intuition, 499-501
——, knowledge of, 155-56
——, and larger distribution, 91
——, of lexicon, 598-606; hierarchy of, bibliography on, 630-33
——, in literature, 633
——, locus of, 609
——, marginal, 600
——, metaphorical, 602-05
——, as morph criterion, 180
——, of morpheme, not one-to-one, 189
——, names in, 632
——, negative formulation of morpheme, 184
——, of nonverbal behavior, 215
——, not one-to-one with form, 163n
——, orbits of, 603-04, 606
——, and pair test, 64
——, phonological, bibliography on, 628-30
——, of phonological unit, 606-07
——, positional, 276-79
——, and purpose, 91
——, in relation to proportion, 222-25
——, of role in society, 648
——, segmental versus subsegmental, 610-12
——, segmentation of, 609
——, and sememe, 192, 620-21
——, in sentence definition, 149
——, and slot, 90
——, spectrum of, 619
——, stereotype in, 614
——, and structure, 619-20, 627-28

——, subsegmental, 611-12; bibliography on, 638-40
——, of system, 608
——, of tagmeme, 217-19; versus class, 227
——, tagmemically conditioned, 226-27
——, from total structure, 608-10
——, in transformation, 630
——, variant, 160
——, as wave, 603n
Mechanical, generation, 494
Meeusen, 542
Meillet, 146, 283
Melanesian, 698
Mel'chuck, 679
Mencken, 190, 602, 629, 706
Menomini, 139
Meredith, 488, 628
Merton, 668-70, 672
Metalanguage, 615
Metalinguistics, 586
Metaphor, 602-05, 632
Methods, 10; *see also* Analysis
——, of procedure, 289
Metzger, 144
Mikasuki, 724
Milewski, 482
Miller, G., 363, 475, 495, 500, 588, 618, 626, 634-35, 637, 639
Miller, J. D., 544, 679
Millon, 674, 706
Mimicry, 43
Miner, 691
Minimum
——, behavioreme, 129
——, morpheme, 150-93
——, problems in, 233
——, uttereme, 135
Minor, 414, 421, 487
Minus, 557
Misra, 497
Mitchell, 360, 429, 590
Mixtec, 5, 227, 286, 376-77, 380, 479, 481, 488, 542, 572, 581, 687, 706, 714
——, syllable versus tone, 376
Mixter, 708
Mode; *see also* Contrast; Distribution; Feature; Manifestation; Variant
——, charted, 143
——, component of, 518-19
——, distribution, 86-87
——, indeterminacy of, 92
——, interlocking; *see* Hierarchy, interlocking
——, member of, 85n
——, need of three, 85n
——, restrictions on units of, 510-21
——, simultaneous, 85n, 93, 513-15

——, as spectrum, 516
Modifier, 247-50, 283
Mohawk, 560, 716
Molecules, 32
Moles, 544
Moneme, 190
Monolingual Approach, 30, 34-35
——, and central meaning, 601
——, and distribution, 40
——, and gesture, 61
——, and intuitive steps, 225
——, nonverbal distribution in, 60
Monolog, 442
Montague, 71
Montanus, 346
Moreno, 673
Morey, 347
Morph, 179; *see also* Morpheme
——, criteria for types, 180-81
——, discontinuous, 226
——, etic types of, 192-93
——, inactive, 171
——, latent, 172
——, live versus dead, 161
——, as motif, 151
——, parasitic, 172, 237
——, passive, 171-72
——, portmanteau, 559
——, relation to morpheme, 181-82
——, term, 183
——, types of classes, 181
Morpheme, 179, 184, 189, 454, 507; *see also* Hypermorpheme
——, active, 169-72
——, artificial, 161-62
——, awareness changed, 159
——, bibliography on, 182-93
——, bibliography on classes of, 272-75
——, border of, in tagmeme, 177-78
——, class membership of, 173
——, complex, 191
——, conditioned type of variants, 165
——, contrastive-identificational, 162-63
——, decade numbers in, 273
——, definition, 183
——, discontinuous, 167-68, 226
——, distribution class of, 197
——, distribution mode of, 169-77
——, emic class of, 178, 198-216
——, empty, 160-61, 186
——, etically complex in class, 207
——, etics of, 179-81
——, feature mode of, 154-62
——, as folk-analysis, 67
——, form and meaning in, 163n
——, fused, 168, 177-78, 550

——, as fused tagmeme, 243
——, as fused wave, 180n
——, and hierarchy, 189
——, internal structure of, 175-76
——, of intonation, 153
——, live, 161
——, locally-conditioned, 164-65
——, locally free variants of, 164
——, manifestation mode of, 163-68
——, meaning in, 631; without meaning, 160-62, 186
——, morphetically-complex, 167, 288
——, as motif, 151-52
——, negative definition of, 184
——, neither purely semantic nor formal, 184-85
——, nonsimultaneous segments, 162
——, as phoneme distribution, 331-38
——, phonetic varieties of, 164
——, phonological feature as, 305
——, of pitch, 152
——, positional, 277
——, potential for distribution, 174
——, prediction of occurrence, 175
——, in relation to analysis and semantics, 188
——, in relation to morph, 181-82
——, repeated, 164
——, semantic variant, 599-600
——, shape type of, 175-76
——, simultaneous components of, 162
——, system of classes, 209
——, system of, as class, 177-78
——, systemically-conditioned, 168
——, and tagmeme borders, 242-45
——, tagmemically-conditioned, 165, 212
——, variants of, 163-65
——, verb-noun relation, 185
Morphetics, 179-81
Morphology; *see also* Morpheme
——, versus syntax, 189, 481
Morphophoneme, 353; *see also* Phoneme
Morphophonemics, 557
Morris, 35, 145, 497, 518, 617, 624, 628-29, 638-39, 670, 674, 677-78
——, and sign, 33, 145
——, terms, denotation of, 55
Moses, 347
Motif, 150-53, 183
——, breakfast, 151
——, definition of, 150
——, discontinuous, 292
——, hierarchy of, 293
——, slot-class of, as tagmeme, 195-96
——, slot-class correlative of, 194
——, threshold in, 293
——, variants in, 292
——, verbal, 152

Motion; *see also* Activity, Behavior, Wave, wave of, 76
Moulton, 59, 414, 416, 560-61, 593
Movement as wave, 306-09
Mowrer, 675
Müller, 184
Murdock, 145, 668-71, 673, 675
Murray, 674, 702
Music, 26, 541
——, in gesture song, 26
——, segments of, 94
——, song in tone language, 544
——, and speech intonation, 544
Muyskens, 355, 411, 537, 708
Myth, 485, 512n; *see also* Folklore

Nadel, 55, 63, 68, 96, 619, 626, 666, 668-72, 675
——, behavior cycle, 144
——, units of continuum, 94
Nagel, 69, 591, 663, 677
Nahuatl, 147, 284, 713
Native Reaction, 54, 58, 63, 67, 159, 292-93, 297, 475; *see also* Eme; Etic; Intuition; Perception; Psycholinguistics
——, in anthropology, 63-64
——, awareness of purpose and meaning, 156-58
——, basic to linguistics, 352
——, and central meaning, 600-01
——, changing informant by questioning, 656
——, to choice, 197
——, and complex morphemes, 191
——, and conceptualized hypostasis, 157
——, differential meaning, 61
——, in grouping sentences, 632
——, in hyperphoneme borders, 408-09
——, and immediate constituents, 67
——, and intuition, 64; as linguistic data, 499-501
——, to John Doe, 177
——, and meaning definition, 192
——, to meaning of class of morphemes, 199
——, morphophonemic, 353
——, naïve change, 159
——, nonverbal contrasts, 53
——, observable, 63, 352
——, to occurring phonemes, 323
——, of pair test, 64
——, as phonemic evidence, 65
——, and phonetic principle, 63
——, psycholinguistics, 35-54
——, rejected by glossematics and others, 66
——, and relation, 280
——, same-different, 61
——, and structural meaning, 238
——, and syllables, 67, 413
——, to syllable differences, 375n, 376

——, tone, 523
——, not uniform, 66
Navajo, 694, 712
Negative, 152
Németh, 702
Nemser, 704
Neologism, 172
Neurath, 676
Neutralization, 359-60
——, in meaning, 188
Newman, 414, 416, 420-22, 537, 591, 629, 663
Nicely, 707
Nida, 64, 67, 167, 181-82, 184-87, 190, 193, 274, 286, 384, 430, 475, 478, 482-83, 488, 556-59, 561-63, 599-600, 615, 621, 627, 631, 640, 696, 724
Noel-Armfield, 410, 419
Nominalism, 58
Nonunique, 56
——, arrangement versus process, 547
——, evaluation, 494
——, solutions, in tagmemics, 259n
Nootka, 64
Noreen, 183
Norman, 489
Norwegian, 540, 543, 593, 696, 700, 711, 726
Nosek, 482
Noun, class meaning of, 458
——, definition of, 181
——, as hyperclass, 428, 458
——, Mixtec, 286
Nuba, 673
Nucleus, 487; *see also* Wave
——, of clause, 468
——, of kin system, 666
——, of phonology versus grammar, 573
——, of rhythm unit, 395n
——, S-nucleus, 654
——, of segment, 294
——, of stress group, lacking, 420
——, of syllable, 339, 371-73, 391, 414
——, of system, 472-73
——, of wave, 74-75

Object, 249; *see also* Subject, Thing
——, logical, 246n
Obligatory; *see also* Contrastive-identificational Feature
——, criteria, for utteremes, 136
Observer, 10, 55, 57-58, 675; *see also* Eme; Etic; Native Reaction; Perception; Philosophy of Science
——, as actor, 55
——, alien, 46
——, awareness as datum, 157
——, and epistemology, 58, 658-59

——, and fact, 659
——, infra-observable element, 516
——, intruding into phenomena, 662-63
——, and meaning, 621
——, of native reaction, 352; *see also* Native Reaction
——, and pattern, 57
——, and purpose, 663
——, and universals, 624
——, and usefulness, 663
Ochiai, 537, 560, 712
O'Connor, 345-47, 413, 541
Offglide, 308
Oftedal, 67, 542
Ogden, 616-18, 622, 624, 629, 631
O'Hern, 593, 714
Öhman, 619, 622
Oliver, 55, 144, 669, 674, 677
Olmstead, 71, 483, 561-63
O'Malley, 640
Ombo, 708
Oneida, 560, 704
Operation; *see* Process
Opler, 157, 183, 667, 675
Opposition, 345, 358; *see also* Contrastive-Identificational
Order
——, contrastive, 341
——, nonlinear, 512n
Orlans, 7
Orr, 487
Orthography, 65
Osgood, 158, 310, 354, 356, 411, 422, 431, 482, 541, 559, 588, 592, 616, 627-33, 638-39, 675, 685, 706-07
Oswald, 359
Oto, 539
Otomí: 559, 723
Over-All Pattern, 346
Overdifferentiation, 324, 360
——, of stress group in verse, 396
Overlap, 359-60; *see also* Fusion, Indeterminacy
——, in segmentation, 553

Paducheva, 679
Paget, 355
Pair Test, 351
Paiute, 300
Palmer, 189, 275-76, 410, 482, 489, 627
Pame, 53
Panini, 497
Papago, 706
——, gesture in, 36
Paper, 351, 491, 693
Papyrology, 554
Paradigm, 489; *see also* Matrix

——, syntactic, 489
Paragraph, 147, 442n, 485
Paraphrase, 613
Park, 670, 674
Parsons, 55, 63, 190, 362, 619, 668-72
Participant; *see also* Native Reaction; Observer
——, focus of, 79
——, Particle, 511; *see also* Static
——, as item-and-arrangement, 545-52
——, Part of Speech, 488-90
——, Passive, 453, 473, 505
——, morph class, 200
Pattern, 474; *see also* Field; System
——, of formative blocks, 548n
——, over-all, 583, 592
——, in science, 58
——, of sound, 65
——, system of field, 512n
Paul, 149, 193, 285, 419, 488
Pause, 134, 529-31
——, and grammar, 568
——, group, 402-03, 568; fixated, 402; poised, 402; tentative, 402
——, potential, 561
——, variants of, 403
Pawnee, 663, 706
Pedagogy, 9
——, texts, contrastive, 52, 54
Pedersen, 345
Peeke, 487
Peiping, 71
Peirce, 616-17, 713
Perception; *see also* Eme; Etic; Observer; Perception
——, and articulation, 353-54
——, bibliography on, 625-26
——, on forms of, 625-26
——, of juncture, 418
——, Koffka on, 677
——, in papyrology, 554
——, of phoneme, 353
Percival, 587
Performance, 495; *see also* Activity; Behavior; Eme; Etic; Native
——, Reaction; Phoneme
Periphery; *see* Margin; Nucleus
Perles, 488, 681
Personality, 537
——, bibliography on, 674-76
——, components of, 675
——, identity in, 656
——, multiple, 675
——, social, 675
——, as unit, 657-58
Perspective, 9
Peterson, Giles, 717

Peterson, Gordon, 71, 349, 351, 357, 416-17, 422, 541, 543, 704, 721
——, on paralyzed patients, 422
Phenotype, 55
Philosophy of Science, 68-72; *see also* Native Reaction; Observer
——, and the analyst, 38
——, and creation, 58
——, structure occurring, 38
——, theory in, 68-72
Phone
——, criteria, for distribution class, 343; for types of, 342-43
——, in relation to phoneme, 343-44
Phoneme, 294-363; *see also* Archiphoneme; Hyperphoneme; Phonemics; Phonology; System
——, as acteme, 291, 293
——, bibliography on, 344-63
——, bundle in, 358
——, in class, 322
——, classes of, 325; bibliography on, 360-61
——, and cultural equivalent, 33-34
——, distorted, 324
——, distribution in grammar, 320-21
——, distribution mode of, 318-23, 325-28
——, in double function in syllable, 381-82
——, English classes of, 331-38
——, evidence for structure, 65
——, existence of, 57
——, extrasystematic, 324
——, feature of, not eme, 302-06
——, feature mode of, 294-302, 328-31
——, grammar in, 361-63
——, history of, 344-46
——, in hyperphoneme, 318-20; bibliography on, 409-23
——, indeterminacy of segmentation, 559-60
——, internal structure of, 294-306, 322, 328-31
——, of juncture, 416
——, compare kin, 665
——, levels mixed in, 362
——, locus of, 309
——, manifestation of, 306-17
——, and morpheme segmentation, 567
——, neutralized, 359-60
——, non-phonetic criteria, 66
——, objections to, 351
——, as occurring, 323
——, overdifferentiated, 324, 594
——, overlapping, 299-300, 359-60
——, pair test, 351
——, phonetic rank of, 325
——, pronounceable, 323
——, psychological, 352
——, psychological unit, 353
——, S-phoneme, 654
——, segmental, mode-like, 524
——, shared by morpheme, 546
——, source of concept, 344-45
——, structure of system, 57
——, subsegmental, 525-27
——, suprasegmental, 418, 522-44
——, theory of, 349-51
——, underdifferentiated, 324
——, variants of, 45-46, 311-17; free or contioned, 46
——, as wave, 307-09
——, zero, 561
Phonemics, 54; *see also* Phonology
——, clash in, 64
——, comparable theories, 356
——, experimental, 352
——, generative rules in, 354
Phonetics, 341-44; *see also* Phone, Voice Quality
——, articulatory, 346-47
——, rank in, 329-35, 388
——, relevant to structure, 331; to linguistics, 355
——, similarity in, 355-57
Phonology; *see also* Phoneme; Phonemics
——, versus grammar, 569-73
——, and lexical hierarchy, 568
——, in lexicon, 569
——, meaning of, 606-07
——, style, 607
——, as wave, 9
Phonotagmeme, 520
Phrase, 425, 456; *see also* Syntagmeme
——, versus clause, 486-87
——, as level, 439-41
——, marker, 503-06
——, obligatorily complex, 439
——, structure, 498
——, types of, 470-71
Physical Component, 187; *see also* Phoneme, manifestation of
Piaget, 633, 639, 674, 678
Pick, 355, 638, 688
Pickett, 9, 182-83, 261n, 316, 373, 439, 442, 444, 450, 459, 466-67, 469-70, 472, 481, 483, 487-488, 496, 561, 653n, 726
Pietrangeli, 701
Pike, Eunice, 5, 329, 331, 355, 388, 413, 417, 419, 523, 534, 540-43, 593-94, 703, 715
——, and intonation system, 534
——, on rank of articulation, 330
Pike, Evelyn, 361, 414, 539, 541, 560, 594
Pike, K. L., 690-92, 698, 707-08, 724-26, 727
Pimsleur, 354
Pitch; *see also* Intonation, Tone

——, as accent, 417
——, morpheme, 152
——, on precontours, 398
Pittenger, 537, 629
Pittman, 182, 189, 273-74, 283-84, 286, 363, 423, 477-78, 481-82, 488-89, 559, 595
——, overt valences, 186
Place, 276, 506; *see also* Distribution; Slot
Planck, 677
Plot, 137, 246n, 595; *see also* Discourse Analysis
Pocomchí, 706
Poetry, 147, 396-97, 427, 431, 485, 494, 529-31, 595-96, 628-29
——, Dickensen, 529-30
——, as hyperphoneme, 427
——, phonological hierarchy in, 410
——, phonological pattern, 390-91
——, and subsegmental meaning, 611-12
——, and time, 512n
——, tone rhymes in, 397
——, topologically related to speech, 390
Polish, 700
Polivanov, 64
Polo, 29
Polynesian, 667
Popoluca, 414
Portmanteau, 95, 154, 481
——, in fusion, 554
——, level, 439-40; bibliography on, 483
——, morph, 559
——, morpheme, 192, 549
——, phones, 317, 548
——, sentence and clause, 442
——, in social structure, 655
——, syllable, 549
——, tagmeme, 455, 550, 576n, 578
——, unit, 513-15
——, vectors intersecting as, 548n
——, zero in, 563
Position
——, as primary, 282-83
Post, 497
Postal, 147, 481, 483, 494, 496, 498, 500, 560, 588
Postman, 624, 633-35, 638, 676
Potential, 280-81; *see also* Generativeness
——, and generativeness, 86n
——, of phoneme occurrence, 318
——, productive, 239
——, in slot-class, 86
Potowatomi, 627
Potter, 347, 487
Powers, 639, 679
Powlison, 363
Prague, 358, 556
Predicate, 250; *see also* Tagmeme

Prediction, 280-81; *see also* Generativeness; Potential; Productive
——, of future utterances, 174
Pride, 560
Priest, 588, 713
Procedure; *see also* Phoneme; Morpheme; Tagmeme; etc.
——, discovery, 224-25n; versus presentation, 492-95
——, evaluation, 492
——, guess-and-check, 225n
——, intuition in, 225n; *see also* Intuition; Native Reaction
——, and meaning, 277
——, mechanical, 225n, 494
——, for morph identification, 179
——, optional starting points in hierarchy, 271
——, in seeking modal components, 518-19
——, tagmemic, 289
Process, 501-02, 511n; *see also* Item
——, bibliography on, 556-58
——, and item, 502
Productive, 190, 280-81, 319; *see also* Generativeness; Potential; Prediction
——, active morphemes, 170
——, and generativeness, 174
——, plural forms by children, 191
Projet, 184, 359, 482, 556, 561
Pronko, 618, 629, 634
Proportion, 219, 243, 278
——, bibliography on, 276-79
——, recognition of, 222-25
——, tagmeme meaning in, 217-18
——, between tagmemic slots, 218
Propp, 184, 193
Prosody, 350, 414, 594; *see also* Componential Analysis; Phoneme
——, abstraction in, 587
——, as feature of word, etc., 429
——, Halliday's view, 506-09
——, and the syllable, 415
——, vowel system in, 360
Proxemics, 34; *see also* Behavior, nonverbal; Gesture
Psychiatry, 537, 629, 657; *see also* Voice Quality
Psycholinguistics, 55, 191; *see also* Native Reaction
——, and hypermorpheme, 431
——, and interlocking levels, 592
——, and phoneme, 351-54
——, of tone, 542
——, and transformationalism, 500
Psychology, 32, 57; *see also* Native Reaction
——, reality of units, 352
——, and voice quality, 537
Pueblo, 676

Pulgram, 188, 347, 564
Pun, 603n-04
Purpose, 42, 153, 598, 664, 670; *see also* Meaning
——, awareness of, 156-57
——, in breakfast, 123
——, in football, 116
——, hierarchy of, 108
——, indeterminacy in, 158-59
——, of individual, 655
——, knowledge of, 155-56
——, and meaning, 91
——, minimum unit of, 154
——, and segmentation, 91
——, in society, 647
——, and unit contrast, 42
Putnam, 593

Quantity; *see* Length
Quechua, 714
Quine, 70, 177, 274, 490, 587-88, 619, 622, 624, 637, 676
——, on realism, 58
Quirk, 477

Rabinowitz, 544
Raceway, 58
Radcliffe-Brown, 56, 68, 668-71, 675-76
Rank
——, of articulation, 329
——, as level, 507
——, of phonemes in class, 331-35
——, in syllable, 388
Ray, 33
Read, 172
Realism, 58
Recursive Definition, 270
Redfield, 669
Redundancy, 348, 588
Reichling, 284
Reifler, 193
Reik, 640
Relationship, 284-85; *see also* Construction; Matrix; Tagmeme
——, etics of, 285-86
——, between units and slots, 282
Relative
——, quality, 522
——, to observer, 659; *see also* Observer
——, tone, 522
Repetition, 45
Response
——, as data, 60
——, to utterance, 442
Reszkiewicz, 488
Reyburn, 418
Rhetorical Period, 404

Rhyme, 206, 230, 428, 595, 603, 610, 629
Rhythm, 397; *see also* Intonation
——, unit, 393, 395n, 398; *see also* Stress Group
Rich, 419
Richards, 616-18, 622, 624, 629, 631, 711
Riffaterre, 63, 595
Rigault, 417
Ripman, 410
Ritchie, 675, 679
Robbins, F., 412, 543
Robbins, W., 55
Roberts, 478, 488, 632, 704
Robins, 33-34, 57, 183, 274, 350, 373, 416, 429, 482, 488-89, 556, 587, 618, 630
Rogers, 413, 415, 690
Rohrer, 675
Role, 137, 666, 675
——, and economics, 672
——, grammatical, 607n
——, as S-tagmeme, 670-74
——, situation, 576-77n
——, in society, 648, 668
——, student, 673
Roleme, 194
Rommetveit, 674
Rorschach, 674-75
Rosapelly, 347
Rosbottom, 480
Ross, 307-08
Rouse, 723
Rousselot, 347
Rowe, 64, 359
Rowlands, 542, 560
Rule, 496-97, 597
——, as categories of culture, 667
——, as levels, 480
——, versus pattern, 474
——, not sufficient, 505
Rush, 537
Russell, 618, 631-32
Russian, 64, 139, 541, 596, 725

S-Unit, 642
Sahlins, 666-67
Sameness, 62, 355-57, 613
——, and general semantics, 623
——, varieties of, 62
Sanskrit, 561
Sapir, 32, 39, 53-54, 64-67, 145, 193, 280, 286-87, 344-45, 353, 359, 483, 488, 502, 537, 539, 595, 626, 628-30, 632, 634, 665, 669-73, 675
——, candle blowing, 44
——, and music, 94
——, sound patterns, 49-50
——, on variation, 44

Saporta, 35, 72, 147, 184, 346, 351-52, 354, 363, 422, 431, 483, 563, 587, 616n, 632, 639, 692, 699
Sarles, 485
Šaumjan, 351
Saxton
——, gesture, 36
Scandinavian, 696, 711
Ščerba, 344-45
Schachter, 494, 499, 505, 542
Schilder, 639, 677
Schneider, 679
Schott, 488, 622, 701
Schubiger, 541, 570, 722
Scott, E., 419, 713
Scott, G., 360, 413, 417, 419, 715
Scripture, 347
Sebeok, 36, 351, 359, 410, 431, 482-83, 536, 559, 592, 595-96, 619, 629, 631-33, 665, 704, 712
Sechuana, 700
Segment; *see also* Segmentation
——, borders of, 76; composite, 116
——, in church service, 74
——, indeterminate, 95
——, of intersecting hierarchies, 117
——, class of, in hymn, 83
——, linear sequence versus hierarchy, 406
——, motif, 150
——, overlapping, 126
——, phonetic rank of, 329-31
——, as wave, 76
Segmentation, 192, 505
——, acoustic, 349
——, and analogy, 560
——, arbitrary, 550-52, 558-60, 566
——, bibliography on, 94
——, distortion in, 555-56
——, in football, 103-04, 660
——, frames in, 134
——, gesture in, 134
——, of individual person, 657
——, of meaning, 609
——, into morphs, 179
——, nonverbal behavior, 95
——, into phones, 341-42
——, and purpose, 91
——, of social structure, 645
——, and stress, 567
——, syllable and lexicon, 568
——, of tagmas, 251-52
——, and zero, 562
Sellars, 690
Semantics, 632; *see also* Meaning
——, and allomorph, 551
——, and definition, 181
——, differential, 632-33, 675
——, general, 623
——, and grammar theory, 500-01
——, lexical set, 209
——, in morpheme analysis, 188
——, neutralization in, 188
——, satiation, 616
——, in transformationalism, 497
——, variant of morphemes, 169
Sememe, 621; *see also* Meaning
——, bibliography on, 620-21
Seminole, 542
Senadi, 727
Seneca, 685
Sentence, 283, 425, 444; *see also* Behavioreme; Syntagmeme; Uttereme
——, beyond the, bibliography on, 145-48, 484-485
——, definition of, 146
——, distributed, 148
——, homophonous, 499
——, in larger unit, bibliography on, 484-86
——, as level, 442
——, meaning in definition, 148-49
——, non-included, 146
——, sequence, 146
——, society analogs, 649-53
——, types of, 139-41; in discourse, 276
Sequence; *see also* Distribution
——, field view of, 553-55
——, and particle, 513
——, and portmanteau fusion, 549
——, static versus dynamic, 545-46
Serbocroatian, 358
Setting; *see also* Matrix
——, of breakfast, 128
Shakespeare, 610
Shamir, 69, 479, 488, 498-99, 681
Shape Type, 175
——, and emic classes of phonemes, 325-28
——, phonemic, 202, 340
——, and syllable, 373-77, 386
Sharp, 350, 413, 418, 429, 541-42, 557
Shawnee, 722, 725
Sheffield, 275, 285, 488
Sheldon, 347
Shell, 183, 421, 434-35, 443, 469, 483, 577
Shen, 543
Sheridan, 539
Sherif, 675
Shifter, 275
Shils, 668-69, 672, 712
Shipibo, 147, 706
Shorto, 415
Siamese Twin, 657
Siertsema, 540, 542
Sign, 33, 63, 145, 285, 617

Signal, 279
Silva-Fuenzalida, 537, 541, 722
Similarity
——, in comparable theories, 356
Simon, 376
Simplicity, 509
——, bibliography on, 587-88
Simultaneity, 10; *see also* Field; Matrix; Portmanteau
——, at breakfast, 125
——, of components, 162, 294, 408
Sinclair, 56, 58, 71, 95, 488, 557, 616, 618-19, 676
——, and things, 94
Siriono, 588, 716
Situational Role, 576-77n, 607n
Sivertsen, 189, 349, 482
Sjoberg, 595
Skalička, 184
Skinner, 145, 483, 670, 686, 724
——, and reinforcement, 33
Slang, 604
Slavic, 722
Sledd, 478, 488-89, 541
Slocum, 385
Slot, 485, 506
——, with appropriate class, 31
——, bibliography on, 275-76
——, as conceptualized hypostasis, 222
——, versus construction, 5
——, not an eme, 220-21
——, functional, 31
——, in game, 104
——, homologous, 218
——, in hypertagmeme, 460
——, meaning of, 227
——, sentence in, 148
——, in social structure, 645
——, and status, 671
——, tagmemic versus tagmatic, 217-27
——, verbal and nonverbal fillers, 30
——, in wholes, 82-83
Slot-Class
——, versus construction, 282-84
——, correlative, 86, 194, 218
——, of phoneme, in syllable, 390
——, phonemic, 340n
Slovene, 417, 704
Smalley, 362, 413, 422, 480, 539
Smith, A., 672
Smith, C., 490
Smith, H. L., 34, 56, 59-60, 62, 67, 152, 182, 185, 187, 216, 277, 346, 355, 361-62, 368, 410, 414, 418, 478, 488, 537, 540, 554, 559, 570, 586-87, 592-93, 595, 598, 618, 629, 711, 715, 724
——, differential meaning, 61
Smith, W., 66

Snell, 487
Society; *see also* Individual
——, captain of team in, 653
——, characteristics of, 669
——, family as S-syllable, 653-55
——, grammar of, bibliography on, 665-68
——, kin and phone, 665
——, morpheme in, 647
——, parallels with language structure, 643-46
——, purpose in, 647
——, requisites for, bibliography on, 668-70
——, as S-language, 643
——, as having S-sentence, 649-53
——, segmentation of groups, 651
——, space in, 667
——, tagmeme in, 648, 667
——, units of, 641-55
——, as a unit, 642
Sociolinguistics; *see* Behavior; Ethnolinguistics; Psycholinguistics; Society
Sommerfelt, 410, 416, 700
Sonesson, 347, 689
Sonnet, 38
Sotho-Nguni, 725
Sound Symbolism, 629-30
Spang-Hanssen, 63, 285
Spanish, 64, 354, 373, 387, 423, 441, 483, 537, 541, 543, 549-50, 552, 559, 563, 568, 575, 616, 701, 719, 722, 726
——, allomorph as relevant, 551
Speaker, 495
——, on generation, 495
Spectacle
——, in football, 99-100, 653
Spectrum and mode, 516
Speech
——, compare animal communication, 665
——, versus hearing, 310
——, versus language, 536-38; *see also* Saussure
Speed, 529-30, 534
——, and boundary, 568
——, and fusion, 560
——, and syllable, 567
——, variant by, 384
Speiser, 666
Spencer, 595
Spiro, 675
Sprigg, 415, 429, 482, 542, 594
Spuhler, 679
Squires, 529
Stanford, 632
Stankiewicz, 592-94
Stark, 531
Static, 319, 511; *see also* Particle
——, sequence, 545-46
Status, 648, 670-71

———, class, 648
Steffire, 624, 703
Stem, 217, 443
———, allomorph class of, 551-52
———, in paradigm, 489
Stennes, 147, 276, 286, 485, 487
Stereotype, 614, 624
———, in society, 648
Stern, 544
Stetson, 347, 355, 366-68, 370-75n, 379, 381, 393, 407, 411-12, 416-17, 419-20, 725
Stevens, 537
Stockwell, 272, 488, 504, 537, 541
Strang, 189, 620
Stratification, 474-75
Stress, 152, 366-68, 370, 529-30; *see also* Stress Group
———, absence of, as morpheme, 192
———, contrastive, 403
———, and controlled vowels, 369
———, distribution of, by lexicon, 400
———, double, 400
———, as eme, 406
———, emphatic, 403
———, lexical, 534
———, as outer, 534
———, as phoneme rejected, 409
———, phrasal, 534
———, pitch as cue, 417
———, secondary, 396
———, and segmentation, 567
———, sentence type, 403
———, timing of, 395, 397
———, and vowel length, 368
Stress Group, 392-401; *see also* Hyperphoneme
———, abdominal pulse in, 392-95
———, absence, 420
———, ballistic, 393
———, bibliography on, 417-19
———, borders of, 401
———, complex, 398
———, controlled type, 395
———, crescendo in, 401
———, distribution mode of, 399-402
———, drawled, 397
———, eme of stress, 407
———, feature mode of, 392-96
———, and grammatical phrase, 570
———, hierarchical, 402
———, immediate constituents of, 401
———, and juncture, 417-19
———, manifestation mode of, 397-99
———, military call, 394
———, nucleus of, 395; contrastive, 395
———, pitch in, 398

———, and syllable, distributed in, 384-85; in double function of, 385; as wave, 385
———, variants of, 397-99
Strevens, 419, 544, 628
String Constituent, 244n
Stroud, 94
Structure, 57, 285, 506; *see also* Construction; Syntagmeme; Tagmeme
———, discovered or created, 55-57
———, levels of, 437-42
———, of morpheme, 175-76
———, nature of, 55-59
———, phonetics as relevant, 331
———, simultaneous, 93
———, of society, bibliography on, 665-68
———, after transformation, 503-04
Sturtevant, 346
Style, 446, 582; *see also* System
———, and allophone, 596
———, bibliography on, 595-96
———, phonological, 607
———, in syllable timing, 394
Subanum, 691
Sub-assemblies, 115
Subject, 8, 277, 279, 435, 454, 462, 574, 577n, 607, 691
———, actor versus goal type: 196
———, as distribution class of tagmeme, 246
———, logical, 246n
Subsegmental, 526, 534
———, meaning, 610-12
Substance, 354-55
Substitution, 251, 275-79, 477; *see also* Frame; Slot
———, correlation in, 239-40
———, in syllable, 415
———, of verbal and nonverbal elements, 30
Suci, 627, 685, 712
Summer Institute of Linguistics, 9
Sumner, 668-69, 673
Sundanese, 430, 715
Sup'ide: 724
Suprasegmental, 522-44
———, bibliography on, 535-44
———, conversation at lunch, 533
———, inner versus outer, 533
———, secondary feature, 523
———, socially relevant, 535
Surrogates for speech, 35; *see also* Drum, Whistle
Sutton, 679
Suture, 418
Swadesh, 54, 64, 193, 345-46, 356, 359, 414, 423, 431, 557, 593, 719
Swedish, 541-42, 622

Sweet, 193, 273-74, 344-45, 355, 410, 414, 416, 418, 431, 482, 630
Syau Jing, 725
Syllable, 538; *see also* Hyperphoneme
——, absence of, 419-22
——, ballistic movement in, 366
——, bibliography on, 409-16
——, boundaries of, 567
——, carrier of prosody, 373
——, characteristics of, 410-16
——, chest pulse, 365-69
——, class of, variant, 389
——, controlled, 367
——, countable, 67
——, definition of, 410-13
——, distribution, 384-89; of phoneme in, 319
——, emic, 365, 406; class of, 389-91; versus etic, 368, 373-74
——, emically reorganized, 375-76
——, feature mode of, 365-73, 391-92
——, fused, 548
——, in hearing, 310
——, hierarchy within, 386
——, hyperclass of, 390-91
——, immediate constituents of, 386-88
——, in Japanese, 67, 375
——, and long vowel, 367n
——, manifestation of, 377-83
——, margin, 370-71
——, in Mazatec, 5
——, in Miztec, 376-77
——, need for physical base, 375n
——, nucleus of, 339, 371-73, 386-87, 414; complex, 373; in English, 372-73; in hyperclass, 391
——, after paralysis, 422
——, pattern of, 389
——, phase drift in, 381
——, phoneme in double function, 381-82
——, and phoneme phases, 320
——, physiological, 366n
——, portmanteau, 549
——, and prosody, 415
——, pseudo, 419
——, pulseless, 367n
——, release types, 371
——, S-syllable, 654
——, silent, 374, 375n
——, single phoneme as, 305
——, slot-class in, 390
——, speed variant of, 383-84
——, in stress group, 385
——, timing in, 375, 394
——, variant of, 378-84; complex, 379; fused, 380-83; phonologically conditioned, 378
Syllabic; *see* Syllable, nucleus of

Synonym, 613, 622
Syntagmeme; *see also* Clause, Hypermorpheme, Phrase, Sentence, Unit, Word
——, within church service, 73-94
——, as class of hypermorphemes, 451
——, conditioned types, table of, 463-64
——, distribution of, 464, 517; in tagmeme, 450
——, distribution mode of, 432-509
——, versus hypermorpheme, 462n
——, illustrated, 452-58
——, S-syntagmeme, 654
——, sentence, model of, 515
——, as sequence of tagmemes, 451
——, tagmeme distributed into, 450-51
——, trimodal nature of, illustrated, 463-64
Syntax, 217
——, versus morphology, 481
System; *see also* Overall Pattern; Style
——, of behavioremes, 131
——, bibliography on, 586-97
——, bilingualism, 593
——, change of, 608
——, clash in, 64-67
——, of classes, 209; not an event, 209
——, coexistent, 314, 583; bibliography on, 593-595
——, componential, 132, 527-32; of tagmeme, 250
——, congruent, 132, 173, 299, 323-24; morphemes in, 178; *see also* Style
——, in creation and discovery, 38
——, of cricket, 51-52
——, and dialect, 361, 582, 593
——, emic, contrastive, 47; discovered versus created, 55-57
——, evidence for phonemic structure, 65
——, hypersystem, 583
——, hypostasis and purpose in, 154
——, indeterminate, 594
——, interlocking, 566, 580-85, 590, 592-95
——, language as, 178
——, learning alien, 51-53
——, linguistic analog for culture, 666; *see also* Society
——, meaning of, componential, 608
——, modes in, 86
——, monistic, 9
——, morphemic, 173; of morpheme classes, 178
——, nonunique, 55-56
——, phonological, Sapir, 49
——, phonology and culture, 345
——, physiological, 590
——, relative, 65
——, of sentence, 137n
——, with simultaneous structures, 93, 132
——, of society, status or role in, 670-73

——, style congruent, 208
——, of tagmeme, 245-50
——, topologically-related, 583
——, universal, etic, 54n
——, variants in, 298; systemically conditioned, 328; in syllable, 378
——, verse and speech topologically related, 391
——, of vowels, 360
——, whole versus parts, 41
Szechuanese, 719

Tagalog, 139, 284, 286, 499, 716, 725
Tagma, 195
——, artificial, solutions to, 255-64
——, criteria for, 252-54
——, parasitic, 237
——, passive versus semi-active, 237
——, in relation to tagmeme, 254-55
——, types, 253-54
Tagmatics, 251-59
Tagmeme; *see also* Ambiguity; Hypertagmeme; Tagma
——, and absolute level, 446-47
——, active, 236-38
——, allotagma, 228
——, ambiguous, 248
——, and analysis, 493
——, in artificial languages, 254-69
——, bibliography on, 270-89
——, bibliography on S-tagmeme, 670-74
——, versus Bloomfield, 490
——, borders of, in reference to morpheme, 242-45
——, borders slurred, 550
——, of breakfast, 195-96
——, chart of variant types, 230
——, as choice, 197
——, class of, 238-39
——, versus class formula, 490
——, componential system of, 250
——, as conditioning change, 463
——, conditioning morphemes, 165
——, conditioning semantics of class, 206
——, contrast between, 471-72
——, contrastive features of, 198
——, contrastive types of subject, 196
——, versus derivational history, 503-06
——, distributed into syntagmeme, 450
——, distribution mode of, 236-44
——, in double function, 575
——, exercise in, 209-18, 254-69
——, feature mode of, 196, 463
——, and Fries' classes, 247-48
——, fused, 178, 243, 550, 562; variant, 235
——, generative approach to system of, 281

——, versus grameme, 5-6, 490
——, history of development, 286-89
——, homologous, 218, 226
——, homophonous variant, 231
——, hypertagmeme table, components of, 460-461
——, included, 234
——, illustrated, 452-58
——, and intonation, 238
——, and intuition, 493
——, in item-and-arrangement, 502
——, level of, 432n; *see also* Hypertagmeme
——, versus lexical hierarchy, 574
——, manifestation mode of, 228-35
——, meaning of, 226-27, 501, 575, 607
——, and morpheme borders, 177-78
——, motifemic-slot-class, 196
——, as occurring, 241
——, as particle, 512n
——, phonological, 340n
——, phonotagmeme, 520
——, physical versus emic border, 220
——, portmanteau, 455, 550, 576n, 578
——, slot, meaning of, 199
——, social role in, 35
——, symbol, 491
——, in syntagmeme, 463
——, systemically conditioned, 235
——, versus transformation, 495-98
——, and transform strings, 503
——, types of, 470
——, variant, complex, 232-34; of breakfast, 196; semantic, 231
——, verbal and nonverbal, 30
——, zero in, 564
——, zig-zag diagram of distribution, 517
Tamil, 321, 729
Tannenbaum, 627, 685, 712
Tanner, 723
Taos, 724
Tax, 561
Taxeme, 5, 286; *see also* Tagmeme
——, types of, 287
Taxonomy; *see also* Analysis; Class; Segment; Segmentation
——, hierarchy of semantics, 475
Teaching Episode, 154; *see also* Hypostasis
Telefomin, 695
Telugu, 595, 721
Tennis, 54
Tepehua, 543
Tewa, 626, 695
Theology, 58
Theory; *see also* Frame of Reference; Intuition; Observer; Structure
——, for communication, 70

——, creation of new hypotheses, 519
——, formation, 68-72
——, Goedel's theorem, 591
——, of human behavior, 32
——, intuition in, 499-501
——, linguists' reaction to, 71-72
——, and methods, 509
——, pragmatic view, 70
——, semantic, 628
——, sociological component of, 70
——, as tool, 70
——, and universals, 71
——, verbal plus nonverbal, 25-26
Thiessen, 543
Thing, 658-63; *see also* Fact
——, baseball diamond, structured, 661
——, bibliography on, 676-78
——, as emic, 676
——, a football as structured, 660-61
——, and observer, 663
——, replaceable parts in, 661
——, use of, 662
Thinking; *see* Concept; Idea; Native Reaction; Observer; Subsegmental; Theory
Thomas, 414, 487-88, 501
Thompson, E., 665
Thompson, S., 145
Thrax, 477
Threshold
——, of awareness, 159, 175
——, of focus, 111
——, indeterminate, 129
——, minimum, 129-30
——, and a non-analytical start, 271
——, of phoneme, 304-06
——, in phonological hierarchy, 405
——, variant, 130
Thurstone, 676
Tibetan, 722
Ticuna, 542
Tigre, 710
Tikhomirov, 665
Time, 512n, 515; *see also* Length; Speed
——, as hypostasis, 175
——, long-wave event, 516
——, matrix with space, 673
——, social, 667-68
——, stress, 395
——, of syllables, 390, 413
Tin, 542, 680
Togeby, 413, 418, 482, 536, 540
Token, 617
Tone, 350, 523, 539; *see also* Intonation; Suprasegmental
——, and arrangement-and-process, 556
——, bibliography on, 541-43

——, and drums, 543
——, fusion in, 560
——, games played by, 543
——, versus intonation, 534, 539-40
——, minimal pairs in, 542
——, problems in, 542
——, reconstruction of, 542
——, rhymes in, 397
——, song in, 544
——, in syllable, 415
——, and whistle, 28, 543
Toneme, 542
Topic, 136, 276, 279, 442
Topological
——, variant of phoneme, 378; of syllable, 378; of system, 583; *see also* System, congruent
Totonac, 387, 563
Trager, 34, 56, 59-62, 67, 96, 152, 182, 185, 187, 216, 277, 314n, 315, 346, 355, 359, 361-62, 368, 407, 410, 414, 418, 474, 476, 488, 523, 537-38, 540, 554, 559, 561, 570, 586-87, 589, 592-94, 619, 628, 682, 694, 702, 711, 721
——, motion and language, 34
——, on phoneticians, 355
——, separate levels, 59-60
Transformation, 487-88
——, battery of, 501
——, and discovery, 492-94
——, as a level, 480
——, from matrix, 502; kernel, 472-73
——, meaning in, 630
——, as process, 501-02
——, as test for homologousness, 223n
Transformationalism, 496
——, characteristics of, 495-96
——, and derivational history, 503-06
——, grammar, in semantics, 149; intonation in, 541
——, as monosystemic, 597
——, semantics in, 497
——, source of, 497-98
Translation, 622
——, bibliography on, 640
Tree, and matrix, 512n
Trier, 618
Trim, 348, 354, 413, 595, 711
Trique, 542, 560, 705
Trnka, 66, 359, 418
Trubetzkoy, 54, 345, 355, 358-59, 411, 418, 430, 593, 695
Truk, 64, 693
Tsonga, 686
Tsotsil, 482
Tswana, 686
Tugby, 512n
Tupi, 541

Turkish, 702
Turner, 67, 697
Tustin, 591
Twaddell, 66-67, 323, 346, 349, 355-56, 359, 371, 381, 383-84, 393, 396-97, 411, 414, 416-17, 419, 488, 557, 591, 593, 696, 711, 723
——, versus introspection, 66-67
——, phoneme exists, 57
——, syllable, controlled, 369
Twi, 542
Tylor, 675
Type, 617
Typology; *see also* Class; Etic; System; Style
——, as etic, 54
——, phonological, 54
Tzeltal, 321, 385, 721

Uhlenbeck, 275, 362, 500, 560, 707
Uldall, E., 541
Uldall, H., 271, 285, 350, 359, 414-15, 538, 556
Ullmann, 618-19
Understanding, 598, 663-64
Unit, 8-9, 96
——, active, 190-91
——, allo-eme, 164
——, in anthropology, 145
——, bearing meaning, 63
——, behavior cycle, 144
——, beyond the sentence, 75; rhetorical period, 404; *see also* Sentence; Uttereme, etc.
——, bibliography on, 96-97, 271-72
——, category of matrix, 163n
——, as center of force, 298
——, of contrastive relations, 179
——, created construct, 57
——, crosscultural, 37
——, discontinuous, 226
——, discovered, 37; *see also* Native Reaction; Psycholinguistics; Structure
——, and distribution, 35
——, emic, as derived from field vector, 297; as part of cause of change, 642; system of, 131
——, episode, 144
——, etic, 37; *see also* Etic
——, expanded, 131
——, feature mode of, 85
——, fused, 545-64
——, of game, 104
——, homomorphic, 105; differentiated, 160
——, hyper, 131; *see also* Hyperphoneme, etc.
——, interlocking, 565-97; in matrix, 565n
——, largest linguistic, 288
——, levels of, 586
——, minimum, 130; of behavioreme, 150; purpose of, 154
——, modes of, 84-91
——, perspective on, 511n
——, phonological section as, 404
——, physical component of, 39, 187
——, and purpose, 42
——, and relationship, 282, 297
——, in relation to slot, 282; *see also* Slot
——, restricted by human organism, 37
——, simultaneous, 513-15; *see also* Portmanteau
——, social, 129n
——, of society, 641-55
——, suprasegmental, 522-44
——, in system, 271
——, thing as, 658-63
——, transformed, 504-05
——, trimodal restrictions on, 510-21
——, variant of, 44-46; *see also* Variant
——, as wave, 95; *see also* Wave
——, well defined, 96
——, whole, as manifested, 92
Universals, 54, 347; *see also* Etics
——, and etics, 54n, 624
——, etics of grammar, 470n
——, group in society, 646
——, of intonation, 541
——, and meaning, 623-24; of John Doe, 624
——, and psycholinguistics, 354
Universe of Discourse, 462, 513, 619
——, and field, 596; semantic, 619
——, and special meaning, 602
Urban, 10, 488, 616, 618, 623-36, 632, 676, 705
Use, 659-60, 662
——, and observer, 663
Utterance-Response, 425, 442
——, slots in, 148
Uttereme, 121, 133-44, 425; *see also* Sentence; Sentageme; Unit, beyond the sentence
——, within church service, 73-94
——, criteria for, 135-41
——, distribution classes of, 139
——, etic criteria of mode, 143
——, etic types, 136-38
——, feature mode of, high-layered, 424-30
——, minimum, 133
——, procedure of analysis, 141-43
——, sentence in slot, 148
——, beyond sentence, 404, 485; bibliography on, 145-48
——, segmentation of, 133-34
——, sermon as, 75
——, types of, 138-39
——, verse as, 146
Utteretics, 135-38; *see also* Etics

Vachek, 346, 357
Valence, 186-87, 283-84; *see also* Relationship

Vallancien, 544
Value, 677
Van Ginneken, 423
Van Schooneveld, 190, 541, 684
Variant, 85n *see also* Etic; Manifestation
——, alloclass, 332-35
——, breakfast, 124, 195-96
——, chart of types, 230
——, of class, 205-06, 461; of phonemes, 326-27; semantic, 206; in syntagmeme, 464; tagmemically-conditioned, 206; types of, 204-08
——, complementation, 511
——, completely free, 164
——, complex, 46
——, conditioned, 316; of class, 327; locally, 204; by meaning, 231; of syntagmeme, 463; of syntagmeme, table of, 463-64
——, dynamic, 550
——, expanded, 131, 234, 256; minimum, 153
——, of football team, 650
——, free, 46, 316; of class, 204, 327; of phoneme, 316; of stress group, 397; of syllable, 379; of syntagmeme, 463; of tagmeme, 229, 235
——, fused, 46; of class, 328; of hypermorpheme, 464; of phoneme, 317; of tagmeme, 235
——, in game, 104
——, and general semantics, 623
——, Heraclitus on, 656n
——, of hypermorpheme, 427-28
——, hyperphonemically conditioned, 312-13
——, intrusive, 314
——, irregular, 165
——, of John Doe, 177
——, local, 231; of tagmeme, 229; conditioned, 164-65; free, 164
——, of meaning, 631
——, minimum, of tagmeme, 234; *see also* Minimum
——, misplaced allophones, 314
——, of morpheme, 166; phonemically-conditioned, 166; phonological, 169; semantic, 166, 169; tagmemically-conditioned, 166, 212
——, of morpheme class, 204-08
——, morphemically-conditioned, 166
——, morphetically-complex, 166-67
——, of motif, 150
——, obligatory element, 131
——, overlapping, 299-300
——, patterned, 189-90
——, of pause, 403
——, of phoneme, 45-46, 306-17; grammatically-conditioned, 313-14; tagmemically-conditioned, 315
——, phonetically complex, of phoneme, 317
——, phonological, 206
——, positional, 46

——, regular, 165
——, relative to system, 297
——, of role, eme, 194-95
——, semantic, 231; of morpheme, 599-600
——, of slot occurrence, 461
——, by speed, 384
——, static, 550
——, of stress group, 397-99
——, of syllable, 377-83
——, of syntagmeme, 463
——, systemically-conditioned, of morpheme, 169; of tagmeme, 235
——, of tagmeme, 228-35; morphemically complex, 232-34; positional, 229
——, tagmemically-conditioned, 165, 206, 230
——, types of, in morpheme, 165
——, topologically-same, 312; of phoneme, 311-312; of syllable, 378; of system, 583; *see also* System, congruent
——, and universals, 623-24
Variation, range of, 299
Varon, 630, 682
Vector
——, in matrix, 548n
——, patterned, 163n
Vendreys, 149, 193, 418, 482
Verb
——, versus noun, 185
——, separate tagmemic charting of, 183
Vereecken, 411
Verhaar, 640
Verse; *see* Poetry
Vietnamese, 275, 489, 698, 709
Vigotsky, 486, 541, 640
Vinacke, 633-34, 639
Vocoid, 332-38, 346
——, versus vowel, 372
Voegelin, 33-34, 67, 72, 182, 273, 313-14, 347-48, 362, 411, 489, 493, 502, 561, 595, 704, 716, 723, 726
Voice Quality, 134, 136, 299, 323, 525-27, 529, 539, 582
——, bibliography on, 536-38
——, versus la langue, 536
——, morphemes of, 527
——, and psychiatry, 629
——, sound symbolism in, 629
——, as subsegmental, 526
Vogt, 144, 361, 414, 539
Von Laziczius, 540
Von Neumann, 94
Von Wiese, 669
Vos, 674
Vowel
——, absence of, 423
——, cluster, virtual, 361

——, glides, in English, 414
——, long, and chest pulse, 366; in relation to syllable, 367n, 369; sequence, 421, 423
——, in syllable, 372

Wagatsuma, 674, 688
Walker, 536
Wallace, 626
Wallis, 351, 541, 559
Walter, 58, 474, 675
Wang, 349, 723
Wangler, 544
Warkentin, 542, 715
Warner, 671, 673
Warren, 146, 531, 633, 727
Waterhouse, 148, 276, 470, 481, 483, 485-87, 489, 491, 593
Wave, 487, 508, 511
——, border of, 75
——, change by, 75
——, dialect in, 585
——, fusion in, 545-52
——, of grammar, 468
——, hierarchy of, 79, 393n
——, item-and-process in, 545-52
——, of meaning, 603n
——, nucleus of, 74-75, 307-08; of units in hierarchy, 575
——, phonological, 9, 307-09
——, segmentation of, 94, 349
——, stress group as, 393n; syllable in, 385
Weaver, 720
Weber, 33, 668, 673
Wedding, 21; *see also* Behavior
Weeks, 347
Weinreich, 65, 540-41, 593-95, 624
Weir, 148, 275, 607
Weismann, 499
Wellek, 146, 633
Wells, 59, 182, 279, 286, 359, 361, 407, 439, 478, 538-40, 559, 626
Welmers, 59, 65, 67, 315, 356, 359, 361, 542
West, 410, 542, 701
Whisper, 538
——, in tone language, 544
Whistle, 28
——, of consonants, 543
——, cf. humming, in Yiddish, 543
——, syllable in, 411
——, of tone, 543
White, 675, 717
Whitehall, 478
Whitehead, 56, 96, 557
Whitfield, 488
Whitney, 482
Whitteridge, 347, 366n, 370n, 393n, 417, 688, 703

Whorf, 360, 414, 625-26, 638-39, 676
Whyte, 670
Wiik, 357
Wilkins, 193
Williams, 144
Wimsatt, 632
Wise, 460, 481, 487
Wissler, 145, 669
Witoto, 414, 421
Wittgenstein, 285
Wolff, 347
Wonderly, 174n, 182, 184, 273, 280-81, 286, 321, 493, 549, 559, 563, 594, 631, 680
Woodworth, 638
Word, 321, 386, 421-22, 482; *see also* Morpheme; Syntagmeme
——, in Chinese, 481
——, classes of, 489
——, criteria for, 438
——, division, 67
——, function, 575-76
——, as a level, 437-38
——, loan, 594
——, part of speech, 488-90
——, phoneme distribution in, in English, 331-38
——, phonological, 418
——, search for, 639
——, segmentation of, 557; alternate, 173
——, and thought, 626
——, and tone, 542
——, as universal, 482
World View, 676; *see also* Whorf
Worth, 478, 500-01, 505
Wright, 95, 144, 667, 681

Xolodivič, 487

Yagua, 716
Yao, 542
Yegerlehner, 314, 347, 726
Yen, 147, 485
Yiddish, 543, 595, 727
Yngve, 192, 475, 478-79, 482, 495, 595
Yokuts, 416
Yoruba, 542, 718
Youtie, 554
Yuma, 693

Zapotec, 316, 467-68, 542, 703, 713
Zero, 297-98, 558
——, allomorph, 561
——, bibliography on, 561-64
——, phoneme, 561
——, phonological, 407
——, in tagmeme, 564

Zgusta, 57
Ziff, 628, 700
Žinkin, 541, 622
Zipf, 33, 96, 191, 344, 355
——, and unit, complex, 96
Zoque, 321, 385, 549, 692, 729
Zvelebil, 354, 487
Zwirner, 354

400
P63
1967